Organizational Behaviour

Concepts,

Controversies,

Applications

STEPHEN P. ROBBINS

San Diego University

NANCY LANGTON

University of British Columbia

Prentice Hall Canada Inc.
Scarborough, Ontario

In memory of my father, Peter X. Langton, 1922–1997

Canadian Cataloguing in Publication Data

Robbins, Stephen P., 1943-   .
    Organizational behaviour

ISBN 0-13-787011-6

1. Organizational behaviour. I. Langton, Nancy. II. Title.

HD58.7R62 1999   658.3   C98-932317-X

© 1999 Prentice-Hall Canada Inc., Scarborough, Ontario
A Division of Simon & Schuster/A Viacom Company

Original U.S. edition published by Prentice-Hall, Inc.
A Simon & Schuster Company, Upper Saddle River, New Jersey 07458
Copyright © 1998, 1996, 1993, 1991, 1989

Prentice-Hall, Inc., Upper Saddle River, New Jersey
Prentice-Hall International (UK) Limited, London
Prentice-Hall of Australia, Pty. Limited, Sydney
Prentice-Hall Hispanoamericana, S.A., Mexico City
Prentice-Hall of India Private Limited, New Delhi
Prentice-Hall of Japan, Inc., Tokyo
Simon & Schuster Southeast Asia Private Limited, Singapore
Editora Prentice-Hall do Brasil, Ltda., Rio de Janeiro

ISBN: 0-13-787011-6

Publisher: Patrick Ferrier
Acquisitions Editor: Mike Ryan
Senior Marketing Manager: Ann Byford
Senior Developmental Editor: Lesley Mann
Production Editor: Kelly Dickson
Copy Editor: Dianne Broad
Production Coordinator: Deborah Starks
Permissions/Photo Research: Karen Becker/Michaele Sinko/Susan Wallace-Cox
Art Direction: Julia Hall
Cover and Interior Design: Liz Harasymczuk
Cover Image: Peter Arnold, Inc./D. Bringard
Page Layout: Phyllis Seto
Stephen Robbins Photo: Laura F. Ospanik
Nancy Langton Photo: Gary Schwartz

1 2 3 4 5   03 02 01 00 99

Printed and bound in United States of America

Visit the Prentice Hall Canada Web site! Send us your comments, browse our catalogues, and more at
www.phcanada.com Or reach us through e-mail at phabinfo_pubcanada@prenhall.com

Every reasonable effort has been made to obtain permissions for all articles and data used in this edition.
If errors or omissions have occurred, they will be corrected in future editions provided written notification
has been received by the publisher.

BRIEF CONTENTS

CONTENTS

CBC

PART 2 STRIVING FOR PERFORMANCE   146

CBC

PART 4 THE UNEASY SIDES OF INTERACTION   446

CBC

PREFACE TO THE CANADIAN EDITION

This book is the first Canadian edition of Stephen P. Robbins' highly popular book *Organizational Behavior*. Since its fifth edition the American version of this book has continually been the number-one-selling organizational behaviour (OB) textbook in the United States and worldwide. Confirming the trend toward globalization of markets, this book actually sells more copies each year outside the U.S. than inside. For instance, the last edition (and its adaptations or translations) was the market leader in Australia, Hong Kong, Malaysia, the Philippines, India, Mexico, Brazil, Central America, and Scandinavia.

This first Canadian edition draws from all of the many positive aspects of its American cousin, at the same time providing the context for understanding organizational behaviour in the Canadian workplace. While we maintain the features of the previous edition that adopters continue to say they like, there is also a lot that is new. Therefore, let us highlight those features that that stand out from previous editions as well as what's new.

Retained from the Previous Edition

- *Three-level model of analysis*. This book continues to organize OB around three levels of analysis. We begin with individual behaviour and then move on to group behaviour. Finally, we add the organization system to capture the full complexity of organizational behaviour.

- *Writing style*. This text continues to present concepts in a clear and straightforward manner. Considerable effort is made to carefully explain complex topics and to illustrate application through extensive use of examples.

- *Comprehensive literature coverage*. This book is regularly singled out for its comprehensive and up-to-date coverage of OB-from both academic journals as well as business periodicals. For instance, this book had a chapter on conflict in 1979 and a chapter on organizational culture in 1983. Additionally, it was one of the first OB books to include the topics of diversity, globalization, power and politics, negotiation, socialization, the demise of bureaucracy, the virtual organization, the bi-modal workforce, and the importance of building trust.

- *Pedagogy*. The first Canadian edition continues the tradition of providing the most complete assortment of pedagogy available in any OB book. From Concepts to Skills and OB in the News boxes are placed within the body of each chapter. End-of-chapter materials include HR Implications; For Review and For Discussion questions; Learning About Yourself, Working with Others, and Ethical Dilemma Exercises; Case Incidents; CBC Video Cases; and Point/Counterpoint debates. An integrative Progressive Case is positioned at the end of each Part. The Canadian edition reinforces this pedagogical strength by providing cross-references in the text to every feature and exhibit, allowing students to read more effectively and make optimum use of exercises and cases.

- *Technology*. A text-specific Internet site is provided at **http://www.prenticehall.ca/robbins**. The site includes an interactive study guide, links

to sites of many of the organizations mentioned in the text, search tools, and a special section for instructors that includes a syllabus builder and other tools for effective teaching.

New to the First Canadian Edition

In order to create a Canadian edition of *Organizational Behaviour*, we have revised the entire research base from the 8th American edition. The scholarship reported is up to date and includes the research of Canadian scholars where possible. In addition, the examples have been updated, and many new ones have been added. While many of the new examples come from Canadian firms, we have included new examples from groundbreaking or controversial international organizations as well. Most of the chapters contain new opening vignettes, new "OB in the News" items, new Case Incidents, and entirely new video cases taken from the CBC's *Venture* series.

But these revisions, while important, are simply the enhancements one would expect to find in a Canadian edition of a textbook. Our history of leadership in the market continues through some important innovations that will be immediately apparent to users of previous American editions. This book reaches out beyond the scope of many OB texts that have been prepared for the Canadian marketplace. Rather than simply revealing the underlying theories of organizational behaviour (OB) and providing Canadian examples that illustrate those theories, we go a step further. Specifically, we ask, in many instances:

- Does this theory apply in the Canadian workplace of today?
- How is it likely to apply as the workplace undergoes transformations that have already started?
- What are the implications of the theory for managers and employees working in the 21st century?

For instance, we raise the following issues:

- Can organizations actually change values to create a workplace where diversity is truly respected?
- In what ways do women lead, negotiate, and communicate differently? (Comments by prominent Canadian businesswomen through the text and in our progressive case provide insights into these issues.)
- How do you manage change in a unionized environment?

The text emphasizes organizational behaviour as a field of interest of importance to everyone, from the bottom-rung employee to the CEO, as well as to any individual who has to interact with other people in the accomplishment of some task. Gone is the assumption that OB is strictly for managers. We remind you that OB is relevant far beyond your "9-to-5" job by concluding each chapter with a summary that outlines the implications for you not only in the workplace, but as an individual.

The text has been revamped and updated to emphasize to both teacher and student alike that we are moving into the 21st century and towards a way of working that may be considerably different from the past—more globally focused and competitive, with more part-time and contract jobs, and more demand for you as a worker to be entrepreneurial, either within the traditional workplace structure, as an individual seeking out an alternative job, or as the creator of your own new business. The text is meant to be

thought provoking. We want to get you to consider new and different options for the world of work, within the framework of OB.

The text is developed in a "story-line" format to remind you how all of the topics fit together. Each chapter opens with a "Roadmap", giving you a visual outline of your journey through the discipline of OB. Then at the end of each chapter you will find the "Roadmap Reminder" paragraph that encapsulates what you should have learned in the big picture sense, and where we're going in subsequent chapters.

The first four chapters, which comprise Part 1 of the text, place considerable emphasis on understanding the workplace in the Canadian context. These key chapters have been extensively rewritten. Chapters 1 and 2 resemble their counterparts in the 8th edition in only minor ways. In Chapter 4, the discussion of workplace diversity is framed within the discussion of values and attitudes in the workplace. Thus we discuss the difficulty of organizations simply announcing a value of diversity, without putting mechanisms into place to affect attitudes. We also consider the introduction of diversity initiatives in the workplace within this chapter.

There is a new chapter (Chapter 10) on Decision-Making, Creativity, and Ethics. Material that was spread across several chapters now comes together in a more integrated fashion. The more detailed discussion of creativity comes at a time when organizations are in need of dealing with increased competitiveness and globalization.

A new feature at the end of each chapter, HR Implications, builds upon the Chapter 15 human resources material in the 8th edition. However, we have integrated this content throughout the context of the relevant organizational behaviour theories. This is meant to serve as a reminder to students that human resource management is generally an application of organizational behaviour principles.

Weblinks in the margins give students access to Internet resources for companies and organizations discussed in the text, enhancing their understanding of real-world issues. To find a Weblink for a particular organization, look it up in the Name and Organization index, where the page on which the Weblink appears is printed in bold. The Destinations button of the book's Companion Website provides hyperlinks and regular updating of the URLs for all Weblinks (see **www.prenticehall.ca/robbins**).

Chapter-by-Chapter Highlights

Chapter 1: What is Organizational Behaviour? Completely rewritten to present an overview of the Canadian workplace as we move into the 21st century, this chapter considers how the effects of globalization, downsizing, and the need to be competitive have affected workplace relations. We consider why managing well makes a difference. Finally, the chapter introduces organizational behaviour as a field that everyone, and not just managers, needs to know about.

Chapter 2: Leading and Working in the 21st Century. Completely new for the Canadian edition, this chapter opens with a discussion of management for today and the future, underscoring the complex concerns that managers face. We develop an understanding of the role of managers through the use of the Competing Values Framework. After considering management and organizational needs, the chapter turns to learning, both at the individual and (new to this edition) at the organizational level. We emphasize the importance of becoming responsible for our own continuous learning while

at the same time organizations move toward becoming learning organizations.

Chapter 3: Perception and Personality. This entirely new chapter combines portions of chapters 2 and 3 from the 8th American edition. In it we learn about factors that affect our interpretation of others—that is, perception and personality. Thus we view perception as the lens through which we make judgments of others. At the same time we look at the role of personality to consider how our personality and the personalities of others affect how we get along in the workplace.

Chapter 4: Values, Attitudes, and Job Satisfaction. The chapter has been revised with special attention to the Canadian context of OB. Thus, there are discussions of Canadian values, including the notion of "generational values" as well as consideration of anglophone versus francophone values, aboriginal versus non-aboriginal values, and Canadian versus American values. The chapter retains its discussion of values in the international context, and also introduces "cultural self-presentation theory" to account for why some organizational behaviour concepts may not apply as readily in other cultures. We also consider the introduction of diversity initiatives into the workplace in light of our values for doing so. There is an expanded discussion of the effect of job satisfaction on employee performance.

Chapter 5: Basic Motivation Concepts. The various motivation theories have been grouped to make them more accessible. There is an expanded discussion of the notion that one can be "punished by rewards".

Chapter 6: Motivation: Aligning Incentives to Goals. This chapter has been reorganized to emphasize that rewards need to be tied to specific organizational goals in order to motivate effectively. We report numerous examples of how Canadian organizations motivate their employees. This chapter also considers whether more emphasis should be placed on designing more motivating workplaces, rather than concentrating simply on rewards. A new section on executive compensation also appears in this chapter, including information and questions about the compensation of Canadian executives.

Chapter 7: Foundations of Group Behaviour. An analysis of the factors that affect intergroup relations is now included in this chapter.

Chapter 8: Understanding Work Teams. The Canadian edition expands the discussion of the difficulties that sometimes occur when teams are used.

Chapter 9: Communication. Communication barriers between men and women are discussed in greater detail. We also look more closely at the use of e-mail in the workplace, with comments on its appropriate use and a look at privacy issues.

Chapter 10: Decision-Making, Creativity, and Ethics. This all-new chapter brings together material on decision-making that appeared in various chapters in the 8th edition. We've amalgamated this material to give more focused attention to the nuances of decision-making in the workplace. Next we look at creativity as an aspect of decision-making in organizations. Examples show how Canadian firms have introduced creativity training into the workplace, and Edward de Bono's work on creativity is discussed. Finally, we emphasize that taking an ethical stance comes out of a decision-making framework. There is an entirely new discussion of social responsibility, as well as an expanded discussion of making ethical decisions in an international context.

Chapter 11: Leadership. This chapter is considerably streamlined from the 8th American edition. We reduced the attention given to older theories of leadership, placing greater emphasis on leadership theories that have more empirical evidence to support them. The discussion of women's leader-

ship style is considerably expanded and includes statistics about women's positions in organizations and promotion rates. The chapter also includes quotations about leadership styles from a number of female executives in leading Canadian organizations. There is much more focus on Canadian researchers in this chapter, including Jane Howell at the University of Western Ontario's Richard Ivey School of Business, Peter Frost from the University of British Columbia, and Rabindra Kanungo from McGill University. New discussions cover topics such as dispersed leadership and leading from a distance, as well as using humour as part of a leadership style. The chapter also raises the difficulties of leading when you have a board of directors overseeing you.

Chapter 12: Power and Politics. This chapter contains an expanded discussion of empowerment, its use in the workplace, and what it means to truly empower employees. The discussion of sexual harassment has been expanded, and includes a look at difficulties that arise in an international context.

Chapter 13: Conflict and Negotiation. More examples of negotiating strategies have been developed for this chapter, including several examples of negotiation and conflict in a unionized environment.

Chapter 14: Foundations of Organization Structure. This chapter includes an enlarged discussion of new design options, rewritten to reflect the extent to which the design exceeds the internal boundaries of the organization.

Chapter 15: Work Design. A new section on job design in the context of labour unions has been added to this chapter.

Chapter 16: Organizational Culture. We have added to this chapter some additional material on the types of cultures organizations might have.

Chapter 17: Organizational Change and Stress Management. This chapter uses the topic of organizational change to help summarize the topics covered in the textbook. It presents a variety of organizational changes that worked, and then discusses the factors that helped accomplish the change.

Glossed Index: We've integrated the subject index and the glossary, providing a convenient one-stop location for finding and defining key terms and concepts. The text page on which a term is defined has been printed in bold, making it easy for readers to refer back to the original context for further information.

Supplements

One tradition that continues for the Canadian edition of *Organizational Behaviour* is the creation of an outstanding supplements package. The following materials are available:

Instructor's Resource Manual with CBC Video Guide: Prepared by Nancy Langton, the Canadian edition of the Instructor's Resource Manual includes learning objectives, chapter outlines and synopses, annotated lecture outlines, teaching guides for in-text exercises, a summary and analysis of the Point/Counterpoint features, and answers to questions found under For Review, For Discussion, Case Incidents, CBC Video Cases, and the Progressive Case. Available in both hard copy and disk formats. ISBN 0-13-010926-6 (hard copy) and 0-13-010928-2 (disk)

Test Item File: The Test Item File contains over 3000 items, including multiple choice, true/false, and discussion questions that relate not only to the body of the text but to the OB in the News, Point/Counterpoint, and case materials. For each question we've provided the correct answer, a page reference to the text, a difficulty rating (easy, moderate, or challenging), and

a classification (factual/application). Available in both hard copy and as a Word 6.0 disk, as well as in a Test Manager format (see below). ISBN 0-13-010929-0 (hard copy) and 0-13-010920-7 (disk)

WIN PH Test Manager: Utilizing our new Test Manager program, the Custom Test for this text offers a comprehensive suite of tools for testing and assessment. Test Manager allows educators to easily create and distribute tests for their courses, either by printing and distributing through traditional methods or by on-line delivery via a Local Area Network (LAN) server. Once you have opened Test Manager, you'll advance effortlessly through a series of folders allowing you to quickly access all available areas of the program. Test Manager has removed the guesswork from your next move by incorporating Screen Wizards that assist you with such tasks as managing question content, managing a portfolio of tests, testing students, and analyzing test results. In addition, this all-new testing package is backed with full technical support, telephone "request a test" service, comprehensive on-line help files, a guided tour, and complete written documentation. Available as a CD-ROM for Windows 95. ISBN 0-13-010931-2

Transparency Resource Package: Revised by Nancy Langton, the Canadian edition of the Transparency Resource Package includes over 350 slides of key figures from the text, prepared for electronic presentation in PowerPoint 7.0, plus black-and-white masters that can be duplicated for distribution in class. ISBN 0-13-010932-0

Colour Acetates: This package contains more than 120 full-colour transparencies, highlighting key concepts for classroom presentation. (Please contact your Prentice Hall sales representative for details.)

Prentice Hall/CBC Video Library: In an exclusive partnership, the CBC and Prentice Hall Canada have worked together to develop an exciting video package consisting of 18 segments from the prestigious series *Venture*. At an average of seven minutes in length, these segments show students issues of organizational behaviour as they affect real Canadian individuals and companies. Teaching notes are provided in Instructor's Resource Manual with CBC Video Guide. (Please contact your Prentice Hall sales representative for details. These videos are subject to availability and terms negotiated upon adoption of the text.)

Companion Website with Online Study Guide: Our exciting new Website includes a comprehensive online study guide that presents students with numerous review exercises and research tools. Practice tests with true/false and multiple choice questions offer instant feedback to students. Destinations (hyperlinks to the text's Weblinks) and search tools facilitate further research into key organizations and topics discussed in the text. A special section for instructors contains a syllabus builder and other materials. See **www.prenticehall.ca/robbins** and explore.

Acknowledgments

When John Fleming, President, Business and Science Publishing at Prentice Hall Canada, first approached me about Canadianizing Steve Robbins' *Organizational Behavior* text four years ago, I was both flattered and awed. Those of us teaching organizational behaviour at the University of British Columbia had already identified Steve's textbook as the best of those available in the field. To consider adapting that text for the Canadian market was indeed a challenging thought.

From that initial meeting has come this book. In making my acknowledgments, I would be remiss if I did not thank Steve Robbins for providing a truly excellent vehicle for adaptation. That said, my vision of a Canadian adaptation extended beyond the addition or substitution of a few Canadian examples, to producing a text that seriously addressed the issues of the Canadian workplace. In fact, it extended even beyond what you find we have created here, but time constraints in getting this edition to market have limited what we could accomplish our first time out. The process of producing this book has been rather like birthing a baby for the first time: not everything went as planned, and unexpected obstacles appeared here and there. There were also quite a number of joyous occasions.

My collaborators at Prentice Hall are regarded as the best in the business, and they would have to be in order to keep up with the production pace we set during this past year. We have taught each other a great deal in the process. Special thanks go to Lesley Mann and Mike Ryan. Lesley, as my developmental editor, devoted considerable effort to guiding me through the adaptation process, providing great insights, a wealth of material, and unflagging good humour at the bumpy parts in the road. Mike, the acquisitions editor, oversaw the project, and dealt with a variety of tricky issues while demonstrating a calm demeanor and good humour at various junctures. The two of them provided more support than I can ever acknowledge. I would also like to thank John Fleming and Pat Ferrier for their ongoing support of this project. There are a variety of others at Prentice Hall who also had their hand in turning my manuscript into the book that you see, most of whom had behind the scenes roles. Kelly Dickson, production editor, efficiently and calmly directed those efforts.

A special thank you is extended to Lee Simpson, Vice-President, Group Publisher at Maclean-Hunter, for agreeing to be the subject of the Progressive Case. Her openness and insights about her work experiences provided a wealth of material for this book's integrative case.

Finally, I want to acknowledge a number of people who provided personal support throughout the process of writing this book. My Industrial Relations Management Division colleagues at UBC brought various things to my attention, from newspaper articles to research reports, and engaged in various discussions with me about appropriate presentation of material. They also encouraged my writing efforts. I would like to thank them publicly for their support: Merle Ace, Brian Bemmels, Peter Frost, Dev Jennings, Tom Knight, Dave McPhillips, Craig Pinder, Sandra Robinson, Mark Thompson, and Skip Walter. Our divisional secretary, Irene Khoo, deserves special mention for helping to keep the project on track, managing the courier packages and faxes, and always being attentive to detail. I could not ask for a better, more dedicated, or more cheerful assistant.

A number of my friends worked hard to make sure that I would maintain my sanity under the pressure of deadlines, dragged me away from my writing from time to time just so I would have a break, and showed a lot of patience with me. These include Devon Knight, Rhona Steinberg, Chris O'Rourke and Vera Horiuchi. Margaret and Larry Moore provided several weekend diversions at critical times in the writing process. The members of the Carnavaron Quilt Guild provided Monday night breaks from grueling writing sessions, and always asked how things were going and encouraged me along the way. Last in this category of friends, but by no means least, Pat and Alan Carlson and their daughter Nicole provided a welcome refuge in California as I was trying to finish up the project and took care of a lot of

details to make things easier for me. Pat served as copyediting adviser, cheerleader, and nurturer during first and second pass of reviewing the manuscript. When it comes to friends, she is truly the best in the business.

Finally, I want to acknowledge the many reviewers of this textbook for their detailed and helpful comments:

Lewis Callahan,
Lethbridge Community College

Rob Cameron,
Lakehead University

Joan Condie,
Sheridan College

Lorraine Dyke,
Carleton University

Kristi Harrison,
Centennial College

Les Lewchuk,
Kwantlen University

Albert Mills,
Saint Mary's University

Laurie Milton,
Mount Royal College

Kim Morouney,
Wilfrid Laurier University

Barb Neil,
Northern Alberta Institute of
Technology

Siva Pal,
Carleton University

Linda Piper,
Canadore College and Nipissing
University

Judy Wahn,
University College of the Cariboo

Gerrie Waugh,
Capilano College

The beginning of this project marked the beginning of a final serious illness for my father, Peter X. Langton, who passed away on Boxing Day 1997. I regret that he did not live to see the completed book, though he certainly shared enthusiastically in its initial stages as I worked in his hospital room on early chapters. He was a man of many talents, and his understanding of organizational behaviour may have been greater than my own. It is to him that I have dedicated this book. And it is to my family that I give silent acknowledgment for everything else.

Nancy Langton

About the Authors

STEPHEN P. ROBBINS received his Ph.D. from the University of Arizona. He previously worked for the Shell Oil Company and Reynolds Metals Company. Since completing his graduate studies, Dr. Robbins has taught at the University of Nebraska at Omaha, Concordia University in Montreal, the University of Baltimore, Southern Illinois University at Edwardsville, and San Diego State University. Dr. Robbins' research interests have focused on conflict, power, and politics in organizations, as well as the development of effective interpersonal skills. His articles on these and other topics have appeared in such journals as *Business Horizons*, the *California Management Review*, *Business and Economic Perspectives*, *International Management*, *Management Review*, *Canadian Personnel and Industrial Relations*, and *The Journal of Management Education*. In recent years, Dr. Robbins has been spending most of his professional time writing textbooks. His other Prentice Hall books include *Managing Today!*, *Management*, 5th edition (with Mary Coulter); *Fun-*

damentals of Management, 2nd edition (with David DeCenzo); *Essentials of Organizational Behavior*, 5th edition; *Training in InterPersonal Skills*, 2nd edition (with Phillip Hunsaker); *Organization Theory*, 3rd edition; and *Supervision Today!*, 2nd edition (with David DeCenzo). These books are used at more than 1,000 U.S. colleges and universities, as well as hundreds of schools in Canada, Australia, New Zealand, Singapore, Hong Kong, Malaysia, China, the Philippine Islands, Mexico, the Netherlands, and Scandinavia.

In Dr. Robbins' "other life," he participates in masters' track competitions. In 1995 he reaffirmed his title of "the world's fastest human age-50-and-over" by winning the U.S. national indoor championships at 60 meters and 200 meters; winning the U.S. outdoor nationals at 100 meters and 200 meters; and capturing four gold medals (and setting three world records) at the XIth World Veteran Games. At the World Games, he won the 100-meter, 200-meter, and 400-meter dashes, and he anchored the victorious U.S. 4×1 relay team. Robbins was named the outstanding age-40-and-over male track and field athlete of 1995 by the Masters Track and Field Committee of USA Track & Field, the national governing body for athletics in the United States.

NANCY LANGTON received her Ph.D. from Stanford University. Since completing her graduate studies, Dr. Langton has taught at the University of Oklahoma and the University of British Columbia. She teaches at the undergraduate, MBA and Ph.D. level and conducts executive programs on women and management. Dr. Langton has received several major three-year research grants from the Social Sciences and Humanities Research Council of Canada, and her research interests have focused on human resource issues in the workplace, including pay equity, gender equity, and leadership and communication styles. She is currently conducting longitudinal research with entrepreneurs in the Greater Vancouver Region, trying to understand the relationship between their human resource practices and the success of their businesses. Her articles on these and other topics have appeared in such journals as *Administrative Science Quarterly*, *American Sociological Review*, *Sociological Quarterly*, *Journal of Management Education*, and *Gender, Work and Organizations*. She has won Best Paper commendations from both the Academy of Management and the Administrative Sciences Association of Canada.

Dr. Langton routinely wins high marks from her students for teaching. She has been nominated many times for the Commerce Undergraduate Society Awards, and has won several honourable mention plaques. In 1998 she won the University of British Columbia Faculty of Commerce's most prestigious award for teaching innovation, The Talking Stick. The award was given for Dr. Langton's redesign of the undergraduate organizational behaviour course as well as the many activities that were a spin-off of these efforts.

In Dr. Langton's "other life," she teaches the artistry of quiltmaking, and one day hopes to win first prize at *Visions*, the juried show for quilts as works of art. In the meantime she teaches art quilt courses on colour and design in her spare time. When she is not designing quilts, she is either reading mystery novels, or studying cookbooks for new ideas. All of her friends would say that she makes from scratch the best pizza in all of Vancouver.

The Prentice Hall Canada
companion Website...

Your Internet companion to the most exciting, state-of-the-art educational tools on the Web!

The Prentice Hall Canada Companion Website is easy to navigate and is organized to correspond to the chapters in this textbook. The Companion Website is comprised of four distinct, functional features:

1) Customized Online Resources

2) Online Study Guide

3) Reference Material

4) Communication

Explore the four areas in this Companion Website. Students and distance learners will discover resources for indepth study, research and communication, empowering them in their quest for greater knowledge and maximizing their potential for success in the course.

A NEW WAY TO DELIVER EDUCATIONAL CONTENT

1) Customized Online Resources

Our Companion Websites provide instructors and students with a range of options to access, view, and exchange content.

- **Syllabus Builder** provides *instructors* with the option to create online classes and construct an online syllabus linked to specific modules in the Companion Website.

- **Mailing lists** enable *instructors* and *students* to receive customized promotional literature.

- **Preferences** enable *students* to customize the sending of results to various recipients, and also to customize how the material is sent, e.g., as html, text, or as an attachment.

- **Help** includes an evaluation of the user's system and a tune-up area that makes updating browsers and plug-ins easier. This new feature will enhance the user's experience with Companion Websites.

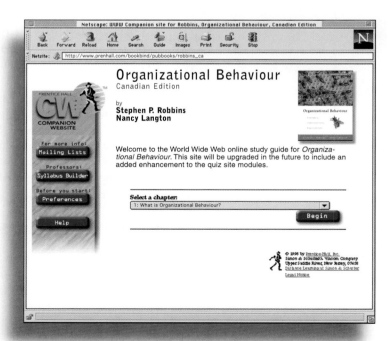

2) Online Study Guide

Interactive Study Guide modules form the core of the student learning experience in the Companion Website. These modules are categorized according to their functionality:

- True-False
- Multiple Choice
- Essay questions

The True-False and Multiple Choice modules provide students with the ability to send answers to our grader and receive instant feedback on their progress through our Results Reporter. Coaching comments and references back to the textbook ensure that students take advantage of all resources available to enhance their learning experience.

3) Reference Material

Reference material broadens text coverage with up-to-date resources for learning. **Web Destinations** provides a directory of Web sites relevant to the subject matter in each chapter. **NetNews (Internet Newsgroups)** are a fundamental source of information about a discipline, containing a wealth of brief, opinionated postings. **NetSearch** simplifies key term search using Internet search engines.

4) Communication

Companion Websites contain the communication tools necessary to deliver courses in a **Distance Learning** environment. **Message Board** allows users to post messages and check back periodically for responses. **Live Chat** allows users to discuss course topics in real time, and enables professors to host online classes.

Communication facilities of Companion Websites provide a key element for distributed learning environments. There are two types of communication facilities currently in use in Companion Websites:

- **Message Board** – this module takes advantage of browser technology providing the users of each Companion Website with a national newsgroup to post and reply to relevant course topics.

- **Live Chat** – enables instructor-led group activities in real time. Using our chat client, instructors can display Website content while students participate in the discussion.

Companion Websites are currently available for:

- Field: Human Behaviour in Organizations
- Dessler: Human Resources Management
- Robbins: Fundamentals of Management
- Starke: Contemporary Management in Canada
- Kotler: Principles of Marketing
- **Note:** CW '99 content will vary slightly from site to site depending on discipline requirements.

The Companion Websites can be found at:
www.prenticehall.ca/robbins

PRENTICE HALL CANADA

1870 Birchmount Road
Scarborough, Ontario M1P 2J7

To order:
Call: 1-800-567-3800
Fax: 1-800-263-7733

For samples:
Call: 1-800-850-5813
Fax: (416) 299-2539
E-mail: phcinfo_pubcanada@prenhall.com

Organizational Behaviour

CHAPTER 1

What Is Organizational Behaviour?

ROADMAP

LEARNING OBJECTIVES

After studying this chapter, you should be able to

- Define organizational behaviour (OB)

- List the major challenges and opportunities for managers

- Identify the contributions made by major behavioural science disciplines to OB

- Describe why individuals require a knowledge of OB

- Explain the value of the systematic study of OB

- Explain the need for a contingency approach to the study of OB

- Identify the three levels of analysis in this book's OB model

Meet Randy Powell, a 1982 graduate of Ontario's Sheridan College, with a marketing diploma. Recently appointed president of Toronto-based specialty coffee retailer Second Cup Limited, Randy is no stranger to presiding over companies. Just three years earlier, he was appointed president of Brantford, Ontario-based S.C. Johnson and Son Ltd. Randy's employees like working for him. While he was still at S.C. Johnson, 97 percent reported that they were proud and happy to work for the company. The secret to Randy's success? "I create teams that people want to be a part of. I realized early on that (to be successful) you move from managing projects to managing people." Randy believes that as a leader, he needs to "set a direction, give his people the freedom to do their work, provide the appropriate resources and remove any barriers to the team's success." He aims to instil pride in his employees by listening to them, and then acting on their input. His style clearly works. After just three years at the helm of S.C. Johnson, the company was enjoying record sales. Now at Second Cup, Randy's been hired "to transform the company from an entrepreneurial upstart to a recognized brand-name operator."[1]

Randy has learned what most good managers learn very quickly: much of the success in any management job involves developing good interpersonal or people skills. Lawrence Weinbach, chief executive at the accounting firm of Arthur Andersen & Co., puts it this way: "Pure technical knowledge is only going to get you to a point. Beyond that, interpersonal skills become critical."[2]

Recognition of the importance of developing managers' interpersonal skills is closely tied to the need for organizations to attract and keep high-performing employees. For instance, Robert Eaton, chief executive officer of Chrysler Corporation, views his workforce as an asset that provides his company with a sustainable competitive advantage. "The only way we can beat the competition is with people," says Eaton. "That's the only thing anybody has. Your culture and how you motivate and empower and educate your people is what makes the difference."[3] Howard Schultz, CEO of Starbucks, the rapidly growing Seattle-based coffee retailer that is establishing specialty coffee shops in cities across Canada, concurs: "Our only sustainable competitive advantage is the quality of our workforce."[4] ■

A study of 191 top executives at six Fortune 500 companies sought to answer the question: Why do managers fail? The single biggest reason for failure, according to these executives, is poor interpersonal skills.[5] The Center for Creative Leadership in Greensboro, North Carolina, estimates that half of all managers and 30 percent of all senior managers have some type of difficulty with people.[6] Consistent with these findings are surveys that have sought to determine what skills university recruiters consider most important for the job effectiveness of MBA graduates.[7] These surveys consistently identify interpersonal skills as most important.

We have come to understand that technical skills are necessary, but insufficient, for succeeding in management. In today's and tomorrow's increasingly competitive and demanding workplace, neither managers nor employees can succeed on their technical skills alone. They also must have good people skills. This book has been written to help managers, potential managers, and employees develop those people skills. It has also been written to help you think about business issues from an organizational behaviour perspective.

Enter Organizational Behaviour

We've noted the importance of acquiring and developing people skills, but neither this book nor the discipline upon which it is based is called People Skills. The term that is widely used to describe the discipline is *Organizational Behaviour*.

organizational behaviour
A field of study that investigates the impact that individuals, groups, and structure have on behaviour within organizations, for the purpose of applying such knowledge toward improving an organization's effectiveness.

Organizational behaviour (often abbreviated as OB) is a field of study that investigates the impact that individuals, groups, and structure have on behaviour within organizations. Organizational behaviour is a distinct area of expertise with a common body of knowledge. Organizational behaviour is concerned with the study of what people do in an organization and how that behaviour affects the performance of the organization. It emphasizes behaviour as related to jobs, work, absenteeism, employment turnover, productivity, human performance, working in groups, and management. Much of the material of organizational behaviour can even be generalized beyond the employment situation. The interactions among family members, the voluntary group that comes together to do something about reviving the downtown area, the parents who sit on the board of their child's day care centre, even the members of a lunchtime pick-up basketball team can be informed by the study of organizational behaviour. Researchers in OB often apply the knowledge gained from studying individuals, groups, and the effect of structure on behaviour to make organizations work more effectively.

There is increasing agreement as to the components or topics that constitute the subject area of OB. Although there is still considerable debate as to the relative importance of each, there appears to be general agreement that OB includes the core topics of motivation, leadership, power, interpersonal communication, group structure and processes, learning, attitude development and perception, change processes, conflict, and work design.[8]

The Challenges of the Canadian Workplace

Understanding organizational behaviour has never been more important for managers and employees as the Canadian workplace heads into the 21st century. Both the shape of the organization and employees' attitudes about

the organizations in which they work are changing in ways that require careful consideration. Organizations were once viewed as long-term employers, offering relatively stable employment over one's lifetime. Today's workforce, however, has been increasingly affected by downsizing, creating an environment where employees might well think of themselves as entrepreneurs, in terms of creating their own organizations, or as sellers of their most personal product: their labour. This new workplace, where fewer workers are hired for life, requires better career management by employees, and demands more commitment and involvement on the part of employees while they're actually employed.

Physical labour is increasingly a smaller requirement in the workplace, at the same time that decision-making abilities, the ability to work in teams, and the ability to respond flexibly to a changing environment have become assets for the organization. Organizations are realizing that their most important asset is their people, and the most important attribute that these employees bring to the workplace is their knowledge. Thus organizations are having to identify ways to manage that reflect that people are more valuable than capital assets in many instances.

The workplace that both employees and managers face today differs in some fairly fundamental ways from the workplace that we faced 20 years ago. With that comes a change in behavioural expectations for both employees and managers. The field of organizational behaviour is useful for addressing many of the challenges facing today's workplace. We'll review some of those challenges, including loss of respect, changing expectations, sharing power, managing in a changing and competitive environment, globalization, and workplace diversity.

Lack of Respect

Angus Reid
http://www.angusreid.com/

Bombardier Inc.
http://www.challenger.bombardier.com/

In a 1997 Angus Reid survey, Canadians were asked to name the company they most respect.[9] Forty percent either didn't know or would not state the name of a company they respected. Only one company, Montreal-based Bombardier Inc., received acknowledgment of more than 10 percent of those surveyed.[10] Moreover, while CEOs in the same survey reported that shareholders, managers, and employees had benefited from the recent economic

Canadian businesses are suffering from a lack of respect, according to a 1997 Angus Reid poll. Montreal-based Bombardier Inc., manufacturer of the Global Express shown here, was the company most frequently cited by respondents as commanding their respect.

upturn, 70 percent of non-CEO respondents cited managers and shareholders as the beneficiaries, not employees. One consultant claimed that these findings are "an explicit criticism of current Canadian management."[11]

What has caused this crisis in respect for corporate Canada? Canadian companies have undergone a long wave of downsizing in recent years, cutting employees and reducing costs to increase competitiveness. In many cases, fewer employees also resulted in less service for customers and clients. Canadians have expressed concern about the large number of layoffs that occurred during the 1990s. In the *Maclean's*/CBC News 1996 year-end poll, 58 percent of respondents said it was unacceptable for profitable corporations to lay off workers.[12] This chapter's OB in the News reveals further concerns expressed by Canadians about the workplace.

Has downsizing at least paid off to the corporate bottom line? A 1998 report by the American Management Association suggests not.[13] Only one-third of the companies surveyed realized long-term gains to shareholder value after downsizing. Many of the companies that reduced the number of employees were unable to maintain initial increases in productivity and op-

American Management Association
http://www.amanet.org/

OB IN THE NEWS

Canadians Expect More from Corporations

Many Canadians believe that corporations should show more responsibility to society. In a 1996 year-end poll conducted by *Maclean's* and the CBC, 58 percent of respondents said it was unacceptable for profitable corporations to lay off workers. Provinces that experienced the most layoffs were also the most likely to criticize companies for this practice (Quebec, 64 percent and the Atlantic provinces, 66 percent).

Canadians also believe that corporations should play a larger role in society, even as they express concerns about corporate responsibility. David Nitkin, president of consulting firm Ethic-Scan Canada, says Canadians view business as "badly fumbling the ball."

Len Brooks, executive director of the Clarkson Centre for Business Ethics at the University of Toronto, hopes businesses will become more aware of the need to be accountable to a number of different stakeholders, rather than just shareholders. He also hopes that businesses will evolve away from a "profit-at-any-cost environment." Brooks notes that a number of executives still don't recognize the need to become more active in the society around them. "Yes, I have run into executives who state their belief that the only thing that matters is the bottom line. I think we're going to have those for a long, long time."

However, many Canadians see change coming along more quickly. Despite their reservations about some current business practices, 87 percent of the poll respondents expect private enterprise to be playing a larger role in society by 2005. Moreover, 83 percent of respondents found it acceptable that business assume this bigger role. The results of this survey give us further evidence that the demands being placed on organizations of the 21st century are indeed increasing.

Source: "Haves & Have-Nots: Canadians Look For Corporate Conscience," *Maclean's*, December 30, 1996/January 6, 1997, pp. 26, 37.

Take It to the Net

We invite you to visit the Robbins page on the Prentice Hall Web site at:

http://www.prenticehall.ca/robbins

for this chapter's World Wide Web exercise.

Ontario Hydro
http://www.hydro.on.ca

erating costs.[14] Ontario Hydro's experience serves as a reminder of other negative effects companies face when productive employees are downsized.[15] A 1997 report found that problems with some of their nuclear reactors could be linked to poor management and a lack of staff stemming from the company's downsizing in 1993.

Changing Expectations About the Workplace

Financial Post
http://www.canoe.ca/FP/

Employees are increasingly demanding job satisfaction out of their jobs. In a recent *Financial Post* survey, 75 percent of the public deemed it extremely important for managers to make employees happy and satisfied. CEOs were not quite in sync, with only 55 percent of them responding similarly.[16] As Robert Gemmel, president and CEO of Toronto-based Salomon Brothers Canada Inc., notes: "Managing people has changed even over the past 10 years. Expectations for job satisfaction have grown. The main challenge is to ensure an environment to help meet expectations."[17] As we will discuss in Chapter 4, overall job satisfaction in the Canadian workplace is relatively high. However, individuals cite several factors that could be improved in the workplace. For instance, in a 1997 Angus Reid survey, 29 percent of employees did not consider their jobs to be mentally challenging.[18]

Dissatisfaction with the workplace is echoed by two twenty-somethings who successfully brought unions to their respective workplaces. Steven Emery worked at a Vancouver Starbucks outlet and did not appreciate Starbucks' Star Labor software, which created shift schedules that looked efficient on paper, but caused erratic work schedules. For example, Emery objected to a shift that began at 5 a.m., and ended at 9:30 a.m. "You're supposed to come in at that hour for such a tiny shift? It was crazy."[19]

Wynne Hartviksen started working at a Black Photo Corporation in Ontario while in high school, and then accepted a full-time position after graduating from university. When Black's purchased 103 photo shops owned by Astral Communications, Inc. in 1996, the workload at Black's skyrocketed, and the shifts became unpredictable, according to Hartviksen. When asked to explain her reasons for organizing a union for Black's employees, Hartviksen explained, "This really, ultimately, isn't about money. Sure we need money, but what we need more is to be able to tolerate our workplaces. It's about justice, which sounds kind of corny, but it's true. We don't want to get fired just because someone feels like it."[20]

The changing expectations about the workplace also reflect the fact that three different generational categories occupy the workplace at this time: the Elders, the Baby Boomers, and Generation X-ers. Chapter 4 will discuss the implications of having such diverse groups side by side.

Sharing Power

At the same time that managers are being held responsible for employee satisfaction and happiness, they are also being asked to share more of their power. If you read any popular business periodical nowadays, you'll find that managers are referred to as coaches, advisers, sponsors, or facilitators.[21]

Workers' responsibilities are similarly increasing. In many organizations, employees have become associates or teammates,[22] and the roles of managers and workers have blurred. Decision-making is being pushed down to the operating level, where workers are being given the freedom to make choices about schedules, procedures, and solving work-related problems. In the

1980s, managers were encouraged to involve their employees in work-related decisions.[23] Now, managers are going considerably further by providing employees with full control of their work. Self-managed teams, in which workers operate largely without bosses, have become the rage of the 1990s.[24] Organizations will likely continue this trend of teamwork and worker responsibility into the 21st century. To help you understand how to perform better as a team player we discuss the dynamics of teams in Chapter 8.

What's going on is that managers are **empowering** employees. They are putting employees in charge of what they do. In the process, managers are learning how to give up control, and employees are learning how to take responsibility for their work and make appropriate decisions. The roles for both managers and employees are changing, often without much guidance on how to perform these new roles. We will discuss the empowerment process further in Chapter 12.

Managing and Working in a Changing and Competitive Environment

In the past, the workplace could be characterized by long periods of stability, interrupted occasionally by short periods of change. Today's workplace would be more accurately described as long periods of ongoing change, interrupted occasionally by short periods of stability! The world that most managers and employees face today is one of "permanent temporariness."

In recent years, Canadian businesses have faced tough competition from the United States, Europe, Japan, and even China. To survive, they have had to cut fat, increase productivity, and improve quality. To do this, companies are implementing programs such as total quality management and re-engineering—programs that require extensive employee involvement. **Total quality management (TQM)**, for instance, is a philosophy of management that is driven by the constant attainment of customer satisfaction through the continuous improvement of all organizational processes.[25] **Re-engineering** asks managers and employees to reconsider how work would be done and their organization structured if they were starting over.[26] TQM and re-engineering have implications for OB because they require employees to rethink what they do and to become more involved in workplace decisions. We examine the implications of both of these movements in Chapter 15.

Changes in the workplace also mean that the actual jobs that workers perform are in a permanent state of flux, so workers need to continually update their knowledge and skills to perform new job requirements.[27] For example, production employees at companies such as the Vancouver Sun, Binney & Smith, and GM Canada now need to know how to operate computerized production equipment. This job skill was not part of their job description 15 years ago. Today's managers and employees must learn to cope with temporariness. They have to learn to live with flexibility, spontaneity, and unpredictability.

The changing and competitive environment means that not only do individuals have to become increasingly flexible, but organizations do too. They need to learn how to adjust to shifts in demand, technology, and the economy. For example, Burnaby, British Columbia-based George Third and Son, which fabricates and installs steel structures, was founded in 1909. Since then, George Third has undergone a number of changes, including moving into different manufacturing lines. The company owes its survival to the ability to shift with the times. "Corporate survival has depended on change,

empowerment
Putting employees in charge of what they do.

total quality management (TQM)
A philosophy of management that is driven by the constant attainment of customer satisfaction through the continuous improvement of all organizational processes.

re-engineering
Process that considers how work would be done and the organization structured if they were being created from scratch.

Vancouver Sun
http://www.vancouversun.com/

a feisty willingness to leap off a cliff," says Rob Third, grandson of the founder, and the individual responsible for production and purchasing. Adds brother Brett, who is in charge of marketing, sales, and administration, "We need to make changes to keep going in the business."[28]

In order to make the changes that need to be made, organizations and people must be committed to engaging in learning new skills, new ways to think, and new ways to do business. In Chapter 2 we will discuss learning, as a reminder of the importance of engaging in continuous learning over the lifetime of both the individual and the firm. This chapter's CBC Video Case on Patriot Computers illustrates the changing nature of the workplace, and the multiple roles of today's employees.

Patriot Computers
http://patriot.com/

Managing and Working in a Global Village

Twenty or 30 years ago, national borders acted to insulate most firms from foreign competitive pressures. Now organizations are no longer constrained by national borders. Trading blocks such as the North American Free Trade Agreement (NAFTA) and the European Union have significantly reduced tariffs and barriers to trade; capitalism is rapidly replacing government control in Eastern European companies; and North America and Europe no longer have a monopoly on highly skilled labour. The Internet has also enabled companies to become more globally connected, both through international sales, but also through increasing the opportunities to carry on business. For example, the Internet enables even small firms to bid on projects in different countries and compete with larger firms.

The world has truly become a global village. Burger King is owned by a British firm, and McDonald's Canada opened the first McDonald's restaurant in Moscow. Toyota and Honda produce cars here in Canada for export around the world. Hitachi Canadian Industries Ltd. in Saskatoon produces power-generating equipment components for their local market and supplies parts to the parent company in Japan. Oakville, Ontario-based Brew Store partners Gary Deathe and Dean Thrasher have launched brew-on-premise operations in the United States, Japan, and New Zealand. The message? As multinational corporations develop operations worldwide, as companies develop joint ventures with foreign partners, and as workers increasingly pursue

One of the challenges facing Canadian businesses is the increasing globalization of the workplace. McDonald's Canada opened the first McDonald's restaurant in Moscow. On opening day, shown here, hundreds lined up to taste their first Big Mac.

University of Western Ontario
http://www.uwo.ca/

job opportunities across national borders, managers and employees must become capable of working with people from different cultures. Managing people well and understanding the interpersonal dynamics of the workplace are not just issues for companies doing business in Canadian society.

Professor John Eggers, of the Richard Ivey School of Business at the University of Western Ontario, commenting on doing business in Asia, notes, "It is important to remember that business is conducted through relationships much more so than it is in western countries. It takes years to form and develop the relationships a company needs, and to build the trust necessary to do business....Business in Asia is conducted courteously and respectfully, and at a slower pace—foreign managers who do not act in a polite manner will not be well received."[29]

Managing and Working in a Culturally Diverse Workplace

One of the most important and broad-based challenges currently facing organizations is adapting to people who are different. The term we use for describing this challenge is *workforce diversity*. Whereas globalization focuses on differences among people from different countries, workforce diversity addresses differences among people within the same country, particularly as this is expressed in corporations.

workforce diversity
The heterogeneity of workers in organizations in terms of gender, race, ethnicity, disability, sexual preference, and age.

Workforce diversity arises because organizations are becoming more heterogeneous in terms of gender, race, and ethnicity. In addition to the more obvious groups—women, First Nations peoples, Asian Canadians, African Canadians, Indo-Canadians—the workplace also includes people with disabilities, gays and lesbians, and the elderly. Moreover, workforce diversity is an issue in the United States, Australia, South Africa, Japan, and Europe as well as Canada. For example, the "new" South Africa increasingly will be characterized by blacks' holding important technical and managerial jobs. Japan has experienced considerable change in its workplace as women, long confined to low-paying temporary jobs, are now employed in permanent careers and even moving into managerial positions. Immigration patterns and relatively open national borders in some countries have also led to changes in workforce diversity. For instance, managers and employees in Canada and Australia are having to learn to work side by side with Asian immigrants. Moreover, the creation of the European Union cooperative trade arrangement, which opened up borders throughout much of western Europe, has increased workforce diversity in organizations that operate in countries such as Germany, Portugal, Italy, and France.

Haven't organizations always included members of diverse groups? Yes, but they were a small percentage of the workforce and were, for the most part, ignored by large organizations. For instance, before the 1980s, the Canadian workforce was composed predominantly of male Caucasians working full-time to support a non-employed wife and school-aged children. Now such employees are the true minority! Between 1997 and 2010, white males will account for less of the new labour-force entrants, as the number of visible minorities increases their participation in the workplace.

We used to assume that people in organizations who were different from the stereotypical employee would somehow assimilate. We now recognize that employees don't set aside their cultural values and lifestyle preferences when they come to work. The challenge for organizations, therefore, is to accommodate diverse groups of people by addressing their different lifestyles, family needs, and work styles.[30] However, what motivates you

Psychologists at the Center for Creative Leadership systematically study the behaviour of managers in a controlled environment. Through one-way glass, they observe, videotape, and evaluate managers' leadership skills. They also gather data by surveying the managers and their co-workers, bosses, and subordinates. The goal of this scientific study: to teach managers how to lead others in their organizations effectively.

may not motivate them. Your style of communication may be straight-forward and open; they may find that style uncomfortable and threatening. To work effectively with different people, you'll need to understand their culture and how it has shaped them and to learn to adapt your management style.

Workforce diversity has important implications for management practice. Managers need to shift their philosophy from treating everyone alike to recognizing differences and responding to those differences in ways that will ensure employee retention and greater productivity while, at the same time, not discriminating. This shift includes, for instance, providing diversity training and revamping benefit programs to make them more "family-friendly." Diversity, if positively managed, can increase creativity and innovation in organizations as well as improve decision-making by providing different perspectives on problems.[31] When diversity is not managed properly, there is potential for higher turnover, more difficult communication, and more interpersonal conflicts. We will discuss further issues of workplace diversity in Chapter 4.

Does Managing Well Make a Difference?

Black Photo Corporation's president, Rod Smith, learned that not listening to employee demands can have undesirable consequences when he was confronted with a union drive at Black's. He's not pleased about working with a union. In fact, he argues that "one of the things that you lose when you get unionized is that ability to be compassionate, because the rules are the rules, and they catch people in ways we prefer not to catch them."[32]

Arlis Kaplanis, president and CEO of Toronto-based Teranet Land Information Services Inc., however, understands the importance of managing well. In an industry where turnover is typically 10 to 20 percent, Teranet's annual turnover rate is less than one percent. Kaplanis believes that his low turnover is the result of developing a corporate culture that is both humane and family-friendly. "My perspective is that the company has two assets—one is the customers, the other is our employees. Both of these assets have to be serviced."[33]

The evidence indicates that managing people well makes for better corporations overall. Exhibit 1-1 shows that many of the firms that made *Report on Business' 1998 Honour Roll of Most Respected Businesses* for

Exhibit 1-1
Firms that made *Report on Business'* 1998 Honour Roll of Most Respected Businesses for People Management

Rank on People Management	Rank on Innovation	Rank on Financial Performance	Rank on Corporate Responsibility	Rank on Investment Value
1. Royal Bank	n/a	1	1	1
2. Bank of Montreal	n/a	4	2	6
3. Magna International Inc.	4	5	10	7
4. Nortel (Northern Telecom)	1	6	7	4
5. Bombardier Inc.	2	2	n/a	2
6. Dofasco	n/a	n/a	n/a	n/a
7. BCE Inc.	n/a	7	3	3
8. Cascades Inc.	n/a	n/a	n/a	n/a
9. IBM Canada	7	n/a	n/a	n/a
10. Imperial Oil	n/a	n/a	5	n/a

Source: Vivian Smith, "Money Talks," *Report on Business,* April 1998, pp. 97–100.

people management also scored highly on innovation, financial performance, corporate responsibility, and investment value. The *Financial Post's 50 Best Managed Private Companies for 1997* also showed the importance of managing well. Two of the main characteristics of the Top 50 were firms that exhibited "a growing awareness of the need for a team approach, not just at the top, but throughout the organization" and "a growing investment in people using everything from advanced training to increased employee share ownership."[34]

Fortune magazine recently published a list of the 100 best companies to work for in the United States. They wanted to know what makes an employee love the organization where they work. *Fortune* identified three main traits of best-loved companies: (1) they are run by a powerful, visionary leader; (2) they offer a physical environment that employees like; and (3) they organize their workforces so that employees feel their jobs are important and have meaning.[35]

While the *Financial Post* results showed that managing well added to the bottom line, the *Fortune* study showed more directly the day-to-day return that managers receive from managing well. At *Fortune's* best companies to work for, turnover is low and employees want to stay with their firms, *even* when they are offered higher-paying jobs by other companies. When asked why they stayed with these companies, employees responded: "cutting-edge technology, exciting work, the chance to change careers within the same company, a shot at a challenging overseas assignment, the promise of promotion from within, flexible or reduced work hours that still keep you on the fast track, truly terrific benefits."[36] None of the employees mentioned money.

The message from each of these surveys: Managing people well pays off.

Fortune magazine
http://www.pathfinder.com/fortune/

OB: Making Sense of Behaviour in Organizations

Whether one wants to manage well, or guarantee satisfying and rewarding employment for one's self, an understanding of organizational behaviour pays off. OB is a systematic approach to the study of behaviour in organizations. Underlying this systematic approach is the belief that behaviour is not random. It stems from and is directed toward some end that the individual believes, rightly or wrongly, is in his or her best interest.

Certainly there are differences among individuals. Placed in similar situations, all people don't act exactly alike. However, there are certain fundamental consistencies underlying the behaviour of all individuals that can be identified and then modified to reflect individual differences.

These fundamental consistencies are very important because they allow predictability. When you get into your car, you make some definite and usually highly accurate predictions about how other people will behave. In North America, for instance, you would predict that other drivers will stop at stop signs and red lights, drive on the right side of the road, pass on your left, and not cross the solid double line on mountain roads. Notice that your predictions about the behaviour of people behind the wheels of their cars are almost always correct. Obviously, the rules of driving make predictions about driving behaviour fairly easy.

What may be less obvious is that there are rules (written and unwritten) in almost every setting. Therefore, it can be argued that it's possible to predict behaviour (undoubtedly, not always with 100 percent accuracy) in supermarkets, classrooms, doctors' offices, elevators, and in most structured situations. For instance, do you turn around and face the doors when you get into an elevator? Almost everyone does. Is there a sign inside the elevator that tells you to do this? Probably not! Just as we make predictions about drivers (where there are definite rules of the road), we can make predictions about the behaviour of people in elevators (where there are few written rules). In a class of 60 students, if you wanted to ask a question of the instructor, you would raise your hand. You don't clap, stand up, raise your leg, cough, or yell, "Hey, over here!" You have learned that raising your hand is appropriate behaviour in school. These examples support a major contention in this text: Behaviour is generally predictable, and the *systematic study* of behaviour is a means to making reasonably accurate predictions.

systematic study
The examination of behaviour in order to draw conclusions, based on scientific evidence, about causes and effects in relationships.

When we use the phrase **systematic study**, we mean looking at relationships, attempting to attribute causes and effects, and basing our conclusions on scientific evidence—that is, on data gathered under controlled conditions and measured and interpreted in a reasonably rigorous manner. A systematic approach does not mean that those things you have come to believe in an unsystematic way are necessarily incorrect. Some of the conclusions we make in this text, based on reasonably substantive research findings, will support what you always knew was true. You'll also be exposed to research evidence that runs counter to what you may have thought was common sense. In fact, one of the challenges to teaching a subject like organizational behaviour is to overcome the notion, held by many, that "it's all common sense."[37] You'll find that many of the so-called common-sense views you hold about human behaviour are, on closer examination, wrong. Moreover, what one person considers common sense frequently runs counter to another's version of common sense. Are leaders born or made? What is it that motivates people at work nowadays? You probably have answers to such questions, and individuals who have not reviewed the research are likely to differ on their answers. The point is that one of the objectives of this text is

to expose you to a systematic analysis of behaviour, in the belief that such analysis will improve your accuracy in explaining and predicting behaviour. If understanding behaviour was simply common sense, we wouldn't observe many of the problems that occur in the workplace, because managers and employees would know how to behave. Unfortunately, as you'll see from examples throughout the textbook, many individuals and managers exhibit less than desirable behaviour in the workplace.

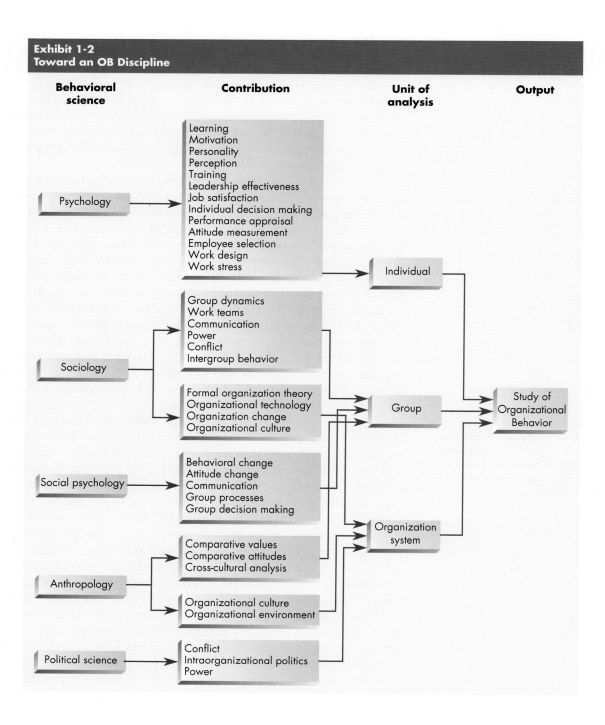

**Exhibit 1-2
Toward an OB Discipline**

Contributing Disciplines to the OB Field

Organizational behaviour is an applied behavioural science that is built upon contributions from a number of behavioural disciplines. The predominant areas are psychology, sociology, social psychology, anthropology, and political science.[38] As we will learn, psychology's contributions have been mainly at the individual or micro-level of analysis; the other four disciplines have contributed to our understanding of macro concepts such as group processes and organization. Exhibit 1-2 presents an overview of the major contributions to the study of organizational behaviour. To give you a simpler view of social science, Exhibit 1-3 shows a social scientist explaining his area of expertise.

Psychology

psychology
The science that seeks to measure, explain, and sometimes change the behaviour of humans and other animals.

sociology
The study of people in relation to other human beings.

social psychology
An area within psychology that blends concepts from psychology and sociology and that focuses on the influence of people on one another.

Psychology is the science that seeks to measure, explain, and sometimes change the behaviour of humans and other animals. Psychologists concern themselves with studying and attempting to understand individual behaviour. Those who have contributed and continue to add to the knowledge of OB are learning theorists, personality theorists, counselling psychologists, and, most important, industrial and organizational psychologists.

Early industrial and organizational psychologists concerned themselves with problems of fatigue, boredom, and other factors relevant to working conditions that could impede efficient work performance. More recently, their contributions have been expanded to include learning, perception, personality, training, leadership effectiveness, needs and motivational forces, job satisfaction, decision-making processes, performance appraisals, attitude measurement, employee selection techniques, work design, and job stress.

Sociology

Whereas psychologists focus on the individual, sociologists study the social system in which individuals fill their roles; that is, **sociology** studies people in relation to other human beings. Specifically, sociologists have made their greatest contribution to OB through their study of group behaviour in organizations, particularly in formal and complex organizations. Some of the areas within OB that have received valuable input from sociologists are group dynamics, design of work teams, organizational culture, formal organization theory and structure, organizational technology, communications, power, conflict, and intergroup behaviour.

Social Psychology

Social psychology is an area within psychology, but it blends concepts from psychology and sociology. It focuses on the influence of people on one another. One of the major areas receiving considerable investigation from social psychologists has

Exhibit 1-3

"I'm a social scientist, Michael. That means I can't explain electricity or anything like that, but if you ever want to know about people I'm your man."

Drawing by Handelsman in *The New Yorker*. Copyright © 1986 by The New Yorker Magazine. Reprinted by permission.

been change—how to implement it and how to reduce barriers to its acceptance. In addition, social psychologists are making significant contributions in the areas of measuring, understanding, and changing attitudes; communication patterns; the ways in which group activities can satisfy individual needs; and group decision-making processes.

Anthropology

anthropology
The study of societies to learn about human beings and their activities.

Anthropology is the study of societies to learn about human beings and their activities. Anthropologists' work on cultures and environments, for instance, has helped us understand differences in fundamental values, attitudes, and behaviour between people in different countries and within different organizations. Much of our current understanding of organizational culture, organizational environments, and differences between national cultures is the result of the work of anthropologists or researchers using their methodologies.[39]

Political Science

political science
The study of the behaviour of individuals and groups within a political environment.

Although frequently overlooked, the contributions of political scientists are significant to the understanding of behaviour in organizations. **Political science** studies the behaviour of individuals and groups within a political environment. Specific topics of concern include structuring of conflict, allocation of power, and the manipulation of power for individual self-interest.

Thirty years ago, little of what political scientists were studying was of interest to students of organizational behaviour. But times have changed. We have become increasingly aware that organizations are political entities; if we are to be able to accurately explain and predict the behaviour of people in organizations, we need to bring a political perspective to our analysis.

There Are Few Absolutes in OB

There are few, if any, simple and universal principles that explain organizational behaviour. There are laws in the physical sciences—chemistry, astronomy, physics—that are consistent and apply in a wide range of situations. They allow scientists to generalize about the pull of gravity or to confidently send astronauts into space to repair satellites. But as one noted behavioural researcher aptly concluded, "God gave all the easy problems to the physicists." Human beings are complex. Because they are not alike, our ability to make simple, accurate, and sweeping generalizations is limited. Two people often act very differently in the same situation, and the same person's behaviour changes in different situations. For instance, not everyone is motivated by money, and you behave differently at a religious service than you do at a party.

That doesn't mean, of course, that we can't offer reasonably accurate explanations of human behaviour or make valid predictions. It does mean, however, that OB concepts must reflect situational, or contingency, conditions. So, for example, OB scholars would avoid stating that effective leaders should always seek the ideas of their subordinates before making a decision. Rather, we may find that in some situations a participative style is clearly superior, but, in other situations, an autocratic decision style is more effective. In other words, the effectiveness of a particular leadership style depends upon the situation in which it is used, and therefore the OB scholar would try to describe the situations in which each style was suited.

As you proceed through this text, you'll encounter a wealth of research-based theories about how people behave in organizations. But don't expect to find a lot of straightforward cause-and-effect relationships. There aren't many! Organizational behaviour theories mirror the subject matter with which they deal. People are complex and complicated, and so too must be the theories developed to explain their actions.

Consistent with the contingency philosophy, point/counterpoint debates are provided at the conclusion of all chapters. These debates are included to reinforce the fact that within the OB field there are many issues over which there is significant disagreement. Directly addressing some of the more controversial issues using the point/counterpoint format gives you the opportunity to explore different points of view, discover how diverse perspectives complement and oppose each other, and gain insight into some of the debates currently taking place within the OB field.[40]

So at the end of one chapter, you'll find the argument that leadership plays an important role in an organization attaining its goals, followed by the argument that there is little evidence to support that claim. Similarly, at the end of other chapters, you'll read both sides of the debate on whether money is a motivator, clear communication is always desirable, and other controversial issues. These arguments are meant to demonstrate that OB, like many disciplines, has disagreements over specific findings, methods, and theories. Some of the point/counterpoint arguments are more provocative than others, but each makes some valid points that you should find thought-provoking. The key is to be able to decipher under what conditions each argument may be right or wrong.

Coming Attractions: Developing an OB Model

We conclude this chapter by presenting a general model that defines the field of OB, stakes out its parameters, and identifies its primary dependent and independent variables. The end result will be a "coming attraction" of the topics in the remainder of this book.

An Overview

model
An abstraction of reality; a simplified representation of some real-world phenomenon.

A **model** is an abstraction of reality, a simplified representation of some real-world phenomenon. A mannequin in a retail store is a model. So, too, is the accountant's formula: Assets = Liabilities + Owners' Equity. While Exhibit

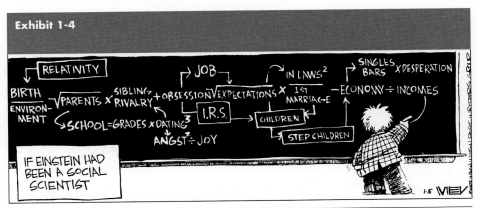

Exhibit 1-4

"Non-Sequitur" by Wiley in *The Washington Post*, January 5, 1993. Copyright © 1993, Washington Post Writers Group. Reprinted with permission.

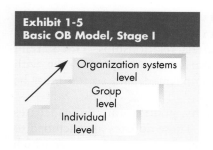

Exhibit 1-5
Basic OB Model, Stage I

Organization systems level
Group level
Individual level

1-4 shows how Einstein might have created a social science model, Exhibit 1-5 presents the skeleton on which we will construct our OB model. It proposes that there are three levels of analysis in OB, and that as we move from the individual level to the organization systems level, we add systematically to our understanding of behaviour in organizations. The three basic levels are analogous to building blocks: each level is constructed upon the previous level. Group concepts grow out of the foundation laid in the individual section; we overlay structural constraints on the individual and group in order to arrive at organizational behaviour.

The Dependent Variables

dependent variable
An outcome (or variable) that one is trying to explain or predict.

Dependent variables are the key factors that you want to explain or predict. What are the primary dependent variables in OB? Historically, scholars have tended to emphasize *productivity, absenteeism, turnover, job satisfaction,* and *organizational commitment.* Because of their wide acceptance, we will use those five as critical dependent variables in an organization's human resources effectiveness. Let's review those terms to ensure that we understand what they mean and why they have achieved the distinction of being OB's primary dependent variables.

productivity
A performance measure including effectiveness and efficiency.

effectiveness
Achievement of goals.

efficiency
The ratio of effective work output to the input required to produce the work.

PRODUCTIVITY An organization is productive if it achieves its goals and does so by transferring inputs to outputs at the lowest cost. As such, **productivity** implies a concern for both **effectiveness** and **efficiency**.

A hospital, for example, is *effective* when it successfully meets the needs of its clientele. It is *efficient* when it can do so at a low cost. If a hospital manages to achieve higher output from its present staff by reducing the average number of days a patient is confined to a bed or by increasing the number of staff-patient contacts per day, we say that the hospital has gained productive efficiency. A business firm is effective when it attains its sales or market-share goals, but its productivity also depends on achieving those goals efficiently. Measures of such efficiency may include return on investment, profit per dollar of sales, and output per hour of labour.

We can also look at productivity from the perspective of the individual employee. Take the cases of Mike and Sally, who are both long-distance truckers. If Mike is supposed to haul his fully loaded rig from Toronto to its destination in Vancouver in 75 hours or less, he is effective if he makes the 4600-kilometre trip within that period. But measures of productivity must take into account the costs incurred in reaching the goal. That's where efficiency comes in. Let's assume that Mike made the Toronto-to-Vancouver run in 68 hours and averaged three kilometres per litre. Sally, on the other hand, made the trip in 68 hours also but averaged four kilometres per litre (rigs and loads are identical). Both Mike and Sally were effective—they accomplished their goal—but Sally was more efficient than Mike because her rig consumed less gas and, therefore, she achieved her goal at a lower cost.

In summary, one of OB's major concerns is productivity. We want to know what factors will influence the effectiveness and efficiency of individuals, of groups, and of the overall organization.

absenteeism
Failure to report to work.

ABSENTEEISM The annual cost of **absenteeism** has been estimated at over $15 billion for Canadian firms in 1995 and $56 billion for U.S. organizations.[41] In Germany, absences cost industrial firms more than 60 billion Deutschmarks ($49.4 billion) each year.[42] At the job level, a one-day ab-

In getting a shave from a flight attendant, British Airways' CEO Robert Ayling signals his plan to boost the airline's efficiency by shaving $2.1 billion in operating costs. Ayling plans to create a stripped-down profit machine focused on delivering top-grade service on global routes by asking 5000 volunteers to leave the company, reducing costs in accounting and in baggage and cargo handling, and giving less profitable routes to smaller airlines to operate as franchises.

sence by a clerical worker can cost an employer up to $139 in reduced efficiency and increased supervisory workload.[43] These figures indicate the importance to an organization of reducing absenteeism.

It is obviously difficult for an organization to operate smoothly and to attain its objectives if employees fail to report to their jobs. The work flow is disrupted, and often important decisions must be delayed. In organizations that rely heavily upon assembly-line production, absenteeism can be considerably more than a disruption; it can result in a drastic reduction in quality of output, and in some cases, it can bring about a complete shutdown of the production facility. Levels of absenteeism beyond the normal range in any organization have a direct impact on that organization's effectiveness and efficiency.

Are *all* absences bad? Probably not! Although most absences have a negative impact on the organization, we can conceive of situations in which the organization may benefit by an employee's voluntarily choosing not to come to work. For instance, illness, fatigue, or excess stress can significantly decrease an employee's productivity, and a bad cold or case of the flu might spread, affecting co-workers' productivity as well. In jobs in which an employee needs to be alert—surgeons and airline pilots are obvious examples—it may well be better for the organization and for its clientele if the employee does not report to work rather than show up and perform poorly. The cost of an accident in such jobs could be prohibitive. Even in managerial jobs, where mistakes are less spectacular, performance may be improved when managers excuse themselves from work rather than make a poor decision under stress. However, these examples are clearly atypical. For the most part, we can assume that organizations benefit when employee absenteeism is low.

turnover
Voluntary and involuntary permanent withdrawal from the organization.

TURNOVER A high rate of **turnover** in an organization results in high recruiting, selection, and training costs. How high are those costs? A conservative estimate would be about $21000 per employee.[44] A high rate of turnover can also disrupt the efficient running of an organization when knowledgeable and experienced personnel leave and replacements must be found and prepared to assume positions of responsibility.

All organizations, of course, have some turnover. In fact, if the "right" people—the marginal and submarginal employees—are leaving the organization, turnover can be positive. It may create the opportunity to replace an underperforming individual with someone who has higher skills or motivation, open up increased opportunities for promotions, and bring individuals with new and fresh ideas to the organization.[45] In today's changing world of work, reasonable levels of employee-initiated turnover facilitate organizational flexibility and employee independence, and they can lessen the need for management-initiated layoffs.

But turnover often involves the loss of people the organization doesn't want to lose. For instance, one study covering 900 employees who had

resigned their jobs found that 92 percent earned performance ratings of "satisfactory" or better from their superiors.[46] So when turnover is excessive, or when it involves valuable performers, it can be a disruptive factor, hindering the organization's effectiveness.

job satisfaction
A general attitude toward one's job; the difference between the amount of rewards workers receive and the amount they believe they should receive.

JOB SATISFACTION   We define **job satisfaction** as the difference between the amount of rewards workers receive and the amount they believe they should receive. (We expand considerably on that definition in Chapter 4.) Unlike the previous three variables, job satisfaction represents an attitude rather than a behaviour. It has become a primary dependent variable for two reasons: its demonstrated relationship to performance factors and the value preferences held by many OB researchers.

The belief that satisfied employees are more productive than dissatisfied employees has been a basic tenet among managers for years. Although some evidence questions that assumed causal relationship, it can be argued that advanced societies should be concerned not only with the quantity of life—that is, concerns such as higher productivity and material acquisitions—but also with its quality. Those researchers with strong humanistic values argue that satisfaction is a legitimate objective of an organization. Not only is satisfaction negatively related to absenteeism and turnover, but, they argue, organizations also are responsible for providing employees with jobs that are challenging and intrinsically rewarding. Therefore, although job satisfaction represents an attitude rather than a behaviour, OB researchers typically consider it an important dependent variable. While we consider job satisfaction important, you may be interested in hearing an alternative viewpoint. This chapter's Point/Counterpoint feature looks at opposing views on the importance of job satisfaction. We revisit the issue of job satisfaction in Chapter 4.

organizational commitment
An employee's emotional attachment to the organization, resulting in identification and involvement with the organization.

ORGANIZATIONAL COMMITMENT   We use the term **organizational commitment** to refer to an employee's emotional attachment to the organization, resulting in identification and involvement with one's organization.[47] This type of commitment is often called *affective commitment* and represents the attitude of managers and employees who go beyond expected behaviours to provide extra service, extra insight, or whatever else is needed to get the job done. While there is some concern that organizational commitment carried to an extreme can have negative consequences, in that employees with strong organizational commitment may result in employees engaging in unethical behaviour to pro-

Autodesk
http://www.autodesk.com

Companies are coming up with creative ways to increase job satisfaction. One way that Autodesk, a California-based software developer, keeps its employees satisfied is by allowing them to bring their dogs to work. The practice helps Autodesk maintain a loyal and motivated workforce that rates high on job satisfaction and productivity and low on turnover. Autodesk's dog lovers are shown here with their pets during lunchtime.

tect the organization, this should not be a reason to avoid fostering commitment. For example, organizations can foster commitment through communication. When Siemens-Nixdorf Informationssysteme (SNI), the largest European supplier of information technology, needed to reduce the workforce from 52 000 to 35 000 in 1994, the CEO met with 11 000 employees to explain and ask for help in reducing costs. Employees showed a great deal of commitment to the organization, even in the face of downsizing—often working after hours to redesign the operations. Within a year, SNI was operating profitably, and employee satisfaction was almost doubled.

**Siemens-Nixdorf
Informations-systeme**
http://www.sni.de/public/
intro/ns_intro.htm

The Independent Variables

What are the major factors that affect productivity, absenteeism, turnover, job satisfaction, and organizational commitment? Our answer to that question brings us to the **independent variables**. Consistent with our belief that organizational behaviour can best be understood when viewed essentially as a set of increasingly complex building blocks, the base, or first level, of our model lies in understanding individual behaviour.

independent variable
The presumed cause of some change in the dependent variable.

INDIVIDUAL-LEVEL VARIABLES People enter organizations with certain characteristics that will influence their behaviour at work. The more obvious of these are personality characteristics, values, and attitudes. These characteristics are essentially intact when an individual enters the workforce, and for the most part, there is little management can do to alter them. Yet they have a very real impact on employee behaviour. Therefore, each of these factors will be discussed as independent variables in Chapters 3 and 4.

Three other individual-level variables have been shown to affect employee behaviour: learning, perception, and motivation. Chapter 2 discusses learning, while Chapter 3 examines the role of perception in our interactions and understandings. Chapter 5 discusses the importance of rewards for motivating employees, and Chapter 6 describes specific rewards that can be used in the workplace. You may find the discussion of motivation and rewards particularly interesting after realizing that a 1997 Angus Reid survey showed that 29 percent of employees do not feel they receive fair or reasonable rewards.[48]

GROUP-LEVEL VARIABLES The behaviour of people in groups is more than the sum total of all the individuals acting in their own way. The complexity of our model is increased when we acknowledge that people's behaviour when they are in groups is different from their behaviour when they are alone. Therefore, the next step in the development of an understanding of OB is the study of group behaviour.

Chapter 7 lays the foundation for an understanding of the dynamics of group behaviour. That chapter discusses how individuals in groups are influenced by the patterns of behaviour they are expected to exhibit, what the group considers to be acceptable standards of behaviour, and the degree to which group members are attracted to each other. Chapter 8 translates our understanding of groups to the design of effective work teams. You may be interested in these chapters because in a 1997 Angus Reid survey, only 50 percent of employees report having supportive colleagues.[49] Thus Chapters 7 and 8 discuss ways that individuals could learn to work together more effectively and be more supportive of one another.

Chapters 9, 10, and 11 demonstrate how communication patterns, decision-making, and leadership styles affect group behaviour, and help share the vision of the organization with its members. Again, these chapters may be of interest to you after realizing that a 1997 Angus Reid survey indicated that companies are not communicating enough information to their employees.[50] We discuss the specific topic of communication and how to do a better job at the individual, group, and organizational levels in Chapter 10.

Chapters 12 and 13 examine some of the more complex issues of interaction, including power and politics and conflict and negotiation. These chapters give you an opportunity to think about how communication processes sometimes become complicated because of office politicking and interpersonal and group conflict.

ORGANIZATION SYSTEMS-LEVEL VARIABLES Organizational behaviour reaches its highest level of sophistication when we add formal structure to our previous knowledge of individual and group behaviour. Just as groups are more than the sum of their individual members, so are organizations more than the sum of their member groups. The design of the formal organization, work processes, jobs, and the internal culture all have an impact on the dependent variables. These are discussed in detail in Chapters 14 through 16. Finally, in Chapter 17 we will discuss the cycle of organizational change and renewal, and ways to manage that change. As we have noted already, and as will become clear throughout the text, change is a key issue for organizations as they approach the 21st century.

Toward a Contingency OB Model

Our final model is shown in Exhibit 1-6. It shows the five key dependent variables and a large number of independent variables, organized by level of analysis, that research indicates have varying effects on the former. As complicated as this model is, it still does not do justice to the complexity of the OB subject matter, but it should help to explain the reasons for arranging the chapters in this book as they are and help you to explain and predict the behaviour of people at work.

For the most part, our model does not explicitly identify the vast number of contingency variables because of the tremendous complexity that would be involved in such a diagram. Rather, throughout this text we will introduce important contingency variables that will improve the explanatory linkage between the independent and dependent variables in our OB model.

Note that we have included the concepts of change and stress in Exhibit 1-6, acknowledging the dynamics of behaviour and the fact that work stress is an individual, group, and organizational issue. Also note that Exhibit 1-6 includes linkages between the three levels of analysis. For instance, organization structure is linked to leadership. This link is meant to convey that authority and leadership are related: management exerts its influence on group behaviour through leadership. Similarly, communication is the means by which individuals transmit information; thus, it is the link between individual and group behaviour.

Exhibit 1-6
Basic OB Model, Stage II

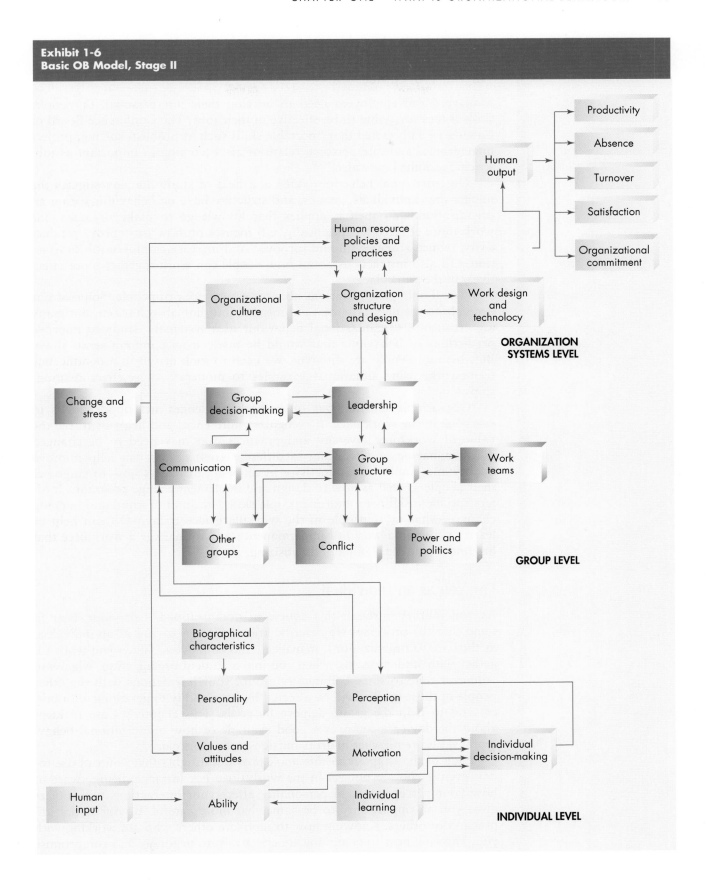

Summary and Implications

For the Workplace

Managers and employees need to develop their interpersonal, or people, skills if they are going to be effective in their jobs. The Conference Board of Canada recently noted that "portable skills such as problem-solving, project management and interpersonal relations are becoming as important as job-specific technical expertise."[51]

Organizational behaviour (OB) is a field of study that investigates the impact that individuals, groups, and structure have on behaviour within an organization, and then it applies that knowledge to make organizations work more effectively. Specifically, OB focuses on how to improve productivity, reduce absenteeism and turnover, and increase employee job satisfaction. OB also instructs us about how people can work together more effectively in the workplace.

We all hold generalizations about the behaviour of people. Some of our generalizations may provide valid insights into human behaviour, but many are erroneous. Organizational behaviour uses systematic study to improve predictions of behaviour that would be made from common sense alone. But, because people are different, we need to look at OB in a contingency framework, using situational variables to moderate cause-effect relationships.

Organizational behaviour offers both challenges and opportunities to everyone in the workplace. It recognizes differences and helps us to see the value of workforce diversity and practices that may need to be changed when managing and working in different countries. It can help improve quality and employee productivity by showing managers how to empower their people as well as how to design and implement change programs. It offers specific insights to improve people skills. In times of rapid and ongoing change—what most people in the workplace face today—OB can help us learn to cope in a world of impermanence and to manage a workforce that has undergone the trauma of downsizing.

For You as an Individual

As you journey through this course in organizational behaviour, bear in mind that the processes we describe are as relevant to you as an individual as they are to organizations, managers, and employees. When you work together with student teams, when you join a student organization, when you volunteer time to some community group, your interactions with the other people in those groups will be affected by your ability to get along with others and to help the group achieve its goals. This chapter's Case Incident about the day care centre is a good example of how organizational behavioural skills are relevant in areas outside of the workplace.

Each of the chapters in this book provides insights that you can use today, even if you are not yet in the workforce. For instance, being aware of how your perceptions and personality affect your interactions with others gives you an opportunity to be somewhat more careful in your initial impression of others. Knowing how to motivate others who are working with you, knowing how to communicate effectively, to negotiate and compromise where necessary are all elements of getting along in a variety of situations that are not necessarily work related. Finally, because we live in uncertain

times, and guaranteed jobs are no longer part of the Canadian workplace, you will find it helpful to keep yourself in a learning framework throughout your life, rather than confining learning to school. It may be the case that you decide to become an entrepreneur, as many people today are doing. In that case, having organizational behaviour skills becomes even more important to ensure that you can work effectively with your employees.

ROADMAP REMINDER

This chapter sets the context for why you might want to consider studying organizational behaviour. In the next chapter we will look at some of the specific challenges that managers face as organizations meet the demands of moving into the 21st century. We also consider some of the demands that you as an employee will face. Finally we encourage managers and employees to respond with a learning framework; that is, the willingness to continue the learning process throughout one's lifetime.

For Review

1. "Behaviour generally is predictable." Do you agree or disagree? Explain.
2. Define *organizational behaviour*.
3. What is an organization? Is the family unit an organization? Explain.
4. "Behaviour is generally predictable, so there is no need to formally study OB." Do you agree or disagree with this statement? Why?
5. What are some of the challenges and opportunities that managers face as we move into the 21st century?
6. What are the three levels of analysis in our OB model? Are they related? If so, how?
7. If job satisfaction is not a behaviour, why is it considered an important dependent variable?
8. What are effectiveness and efficiency, and how are they related to organizational behaviour?

For Discussion

1. "The best way to view OB is through a contingency approach." Build an argument to support that statement.
2. Why do you think the subject of OB might be criticized as being "only common sense," when one would rarely hear such a criticism of a course in physics or statistics?
3. Millions of workers have lost their jobs due to downsizing. At the same time, many organizations are complaining that they can't find people to fill vacancies. How do you explain this apparent contradiction?
4. On a scale of 1 to 10 measuring the sophistication of a scientific discipline in predicting phenomena, mathematical physics would probably be a 10. Where do you think OB would fall on the scale? Why?

C A S E
INCIDENT

I Thought These Problems Happened Only at Work

As the father of two young children, Marshall Rogers thought that serving on the board of Marysville Daycare would be a good way to stay informed with those who cared for his two children during the day. But he never dreamed that he would become involved in union-management negotiations with daycare centre workers.

Late one Sunday evening, in his ninth month as president of the daycare centre, Rogers received a phone call from Grace Ng, a union representative of the Provincial Government Employees' Union (PGEU). Ng informed Rogers that the daycare workers would be unionized the following week. Rogers was stunned to hear this news. Early the next morning, he had to present his new marketing plan to senior management at Techtronix Industries, where he was vice-president of marketing. Somehow he made it through the meeting, wondering why he hadn't been aware of the employees' unhappiness, and how this action would affect his children.

Following his presentation, Rogers received documentation from the Labour Relations Board indicating that the daycare employees had been working to unionize themselves for over a year. Rogers immediately contacted Xavier Breslin, the board's vice-president, and together they determined that no one on the board had been aware that the daycare workers were unhappy, let alone prepared to join a union.

Hoping that there was some sort of misunderstanding, Rogers called Emma Reynaud, Marysville's supervisor. Reynaud attended most of the board meetings, but she had never mentioned the union-organizing drive. Yet Reynaud now told Rogers she had actively encouraged the other daycare workers to consider joining the PGEU because the board had not been interested in the workers' concerns, had not increased their wages sufficiently over the last two years, and had not maintained communication channels between the board and the employees.

Each of the board members had a full-time job elsewhere, and many were upper- and middle-level managers in their own companies. They were used to dealing with unhappy employees in their own workplaces, although none had experienced a union-organizing drive. Like Rogers, they had chosen to serve on the board of Marysville to stay informed about the day-to-day events of the centre. They hadn't really thought of themselves as the centre's employer, although, as board members, they represented all the parents of children enrolled at Marysville. Their main tasks on the daycare centre board had been setting fees for the children and wages for the daycare workers. The board members usually saw the staff members several times a week, when they picked up their children, yet the unhappiness represented by the union-organizing drive was surprising to each of them. When they met at an emergency board meeting that evening, they tried to evaluate what had gone wrong at Marysville.

Questions

1. As either a board member or a parent, how would you know that the employees taking care of your children are unhappy with their jobs?

2. What might you do if you learned about their unhappiness?

3. What might Rogers have done differently as president of the board?

4. In what ways does this case illustrate that knowledge of organizational behaviour can be applied beyond your own workplace?

Source: © Nancy Langton and Joy Begley. The events described are based on an actual situation, although the participants, as well as the centre, have been disguised.

Stand Still, You Die

Markham, Ontario-based Patriot Computer, founded in 1991 by twin brothers Mark and John Durst and Rob Chernenko, illustrates the changing nature of organizations as we approach the 21st century. Patriot, calling itself "Canada's computer company," is a $50-million business—manufacturing everything from custom-designed personal computers to satellite television receivers.

Patriot thrives on a program of employee empowerment and mutual respect. As President and CEO Mark Durst notes, "If you treat your employees like dirt, you'll lose them." At Patriot, employees are encouraged to think and act like entrepreneurs, and "have fun," explains vice-president of sales, John Durst.

Patriot's employee purchase plan was developed by one of Patriot's employees, who informed the twins that they could make more sales if their customers could pre-qualify for loans to purchase computers. Though the twins were skeptical that a financial backer could be found for such a plan, the employee was encouraged to see his plan through. As Mark Durst notes, it was the employee's initiative that made this happen, not the work of the Durst twins.

Two other Patriot employees created Aegis Manufacturing in 1995 out of their idea to expand Patriot's assembly work to do the same for other firms. For the fiscal year ending in June 1997, Aegis had revenue of US$58 million, which was expected to double the following year. When the two employees approached the Durst twins about their idea, they were told that they could run the show if their idea worked. Patriot gave them 40 percent ownership in the new business.

Patriot's founders believe that employees must be involved if companies are to get ahead. John Durst notes, "Unless we're changing, we're going to be left behind. Innovate, and you survive." Employee ideas are what lead to change. Patriot's employees note that the founders are not afraid of ideas, and find it easy to support and encourage their employees when they bring new ideas to the table.

Questions

1. What does this case say about the changing workforce?

2. What kind of personal attributes do you think would be needed to work for a company such as Patriot?

3. How readily do you think most people will come up with new ideas and take them to their employer? Discuss.

Source: Based on "Patriot Computers," *Venture 585*; aired July 4, 1996.

POINT

The Importance of High Job Satisfaction

The importance of job satisfaction is obvious. Managers should be concerned with the level of job satisfaction in their organizations for at least four reasons: (1) There is clear evidence that dissatisfied employees skip work more often and are more likely to resign. (2) Dissatisfied workers are more likely to engage in destructive behaviours. (3) It has been demonstrated that satisfied employees have better health and live longer. (4) Satisfaction on the job carries over to the employee's life outside the job.

Satisfied employees have lower rates of both turnover and absenteeism. If we consider the two withdrawal behaviours separately, however, we can be more confident about the influence of satisfaction on turnover. Specifically, satisfaction is strongly and consistently negatively related to an employee's decision to leave the organization. Although satisfaction and absence are also negatively related, conclusions regarding the relationship should be more guarded.

Dissatisfaction is frequently associated with a high level of complaints and work grievances. Highly dissatisfied employees are more likely to resort to sabotage and passive aggression. For employees with limited alternative options, who would quit if they could, these forms of destructive actions act as extreme applications of neglect.

An often overlooked dimension of job satisfaction is its relationship to employee health. Several studies have shown that employees who are dissatisfied with their jobs are prone to health setbacks ranging from headaches to heart disease. Some research even indicates that job satisfaction is a better predictor of length of life than physical condition or tobacco use. These studies suggest that dissatisfaction is not solely a psychological phenomenon. The stress that results from dissatisfaction apparently increases one's susceptibility to heart attacks and the like. For managers, this means that even if satisfaction didn't lead to less voluntary turnover and absence, the goal of a satisfied workforce might be justifiable because it would reduce medical costs and the premature loss of valued employees by way of heart disease or strokes.

Our final point in support of job satisfaction's importance is the spin-off effect that job satisfaction has for society as a whole. When employees are happy with their jobs, it improves their lives off the job. In contrast, the dissatisfied employee carries that negative attitude home. In wealthy countries such as Canada, the United States, Great Britain, Australia, or Japan, doesn't management have a responsibility to provide jobs from which employees can receive high satisfaction? Some benefits of job satisfaction accrue to every citizen in society. Satisfied employees are more likely to be satisfied citizens. These people will hold a more positive attitude toward life in general and comprise a society of more psychologically healthy people.

The evidence is impressive. Job satisfaction is important. For management, a satisfied workforce translates into higher productivity due to fewer disruptions caused by absenteeism or good employees quitting, fewer incidences of destructive behaviour, as well as lower medical and life insurance costs. Additionally, there are benefits for society in general. Satisfaction on the job carries over to the employee's off-the-job hours. So the goal of high job satisfaction for employees can be defended in terms of both dollars and cents and social responsibility. ■

counterPOINT

Job Satisfaction Has Been Overemphasized

Few issues have been more blown out of proportion than the importance of job satisfaction.* Let's look closely at the evidence.

There is no consistent relationship indicating that satisfaction leads to productivity. And, after all, isn't productivity the name of the game? Organizations are not altruistic institutions. Management's obligation is to use efficiently the resources that it has available. It has no obligation to create a satisfied workforce if the costs exceed the benefits. As one executive put it, "I don't care if my people are happy or not! Do they produce?"

It would be naive to assume that satisfaction alone would have a major impact on employee behaviour. As a case in point, consider the issue of turnover. Certainly a number of other factors can have an equal or greater impact on whether an employee decides to remain with an organization or take a job somewhere else—length of time on the job, financial situation, and availability of other jobs, to name the most obvious. If I'm 55 years old, have been with my company 25 years, perceive few other opportunities in the job market, and have no other source of income besides my job, does my unhappiness have much impact on my decision to stay with the organization? No!

Did you ever notice who seems to be most concerned with improving employee job satisfaction? It's usually college professors and researchers! They've chosen careers that provide them with considerable freedom and opportunities for personal growth. They place a very high value on job satisfaction. The problem is that they impose their values on others. Because job satisfaction is important to them, they suppose that it's important to everyone. To a lot of people, a job is merely the means to get the money they need to do the things they desire during their nonworking hours. Assuming you work 40 hours a week and sleep eight hours a night, you still have 70 hours or more a week to achieve fulfilment and satisfaction in off-the-job activities. So the importance of job satisfaction may be oversold when you recognize that there are other sources—outside the job—where the dissatisfied employee can find satisfaction.

A final point against overemphasizing job satisfaction: Consider the issue in a contingency framework. Even if satisfaction were significantly related to performance, it's unlikely that the relationship would hold consistently across all segments of the workforce. In fact, evidence demonstrates that people differ in terms of the importance that work plays in their lives. To some, the job is their central life interest. But for most people, their primary interests are off the job. Non-job-oriented people tend not to be emotionally involved with their work. This relative indifference allows them to accept frustrating conditions at work more willingly. Importantly, most of the workforce probably falls into this non-job-oriented category. So while job satisfaction might be important to lawyers, surgeons, and other professionals, it may be irrelevant to the average worker because he or she is generally apathetic about the job's frustrating elements. ■

Source:
[1] See, for instance, G. Bassett, "The Case Against Job Satisfaction," *Business Horizons*, May–June 1994, pp. 61–68.

CHAPTER 2

Working in the Organization of the 21st Century

LEARNING OBJECTIVES

After studying this chapter, you should be able to

- Define organization and recognize the complex nature of organizations

- Identify critical skills for today's managers and managers of the 21st century

- Apply the competing values framework to managerial behaviour

- Summarize how learning theories provide insights into changing behaviour

- Distinguish among the four schedules of reinforcement

- Clarify the role of discipline in learning

- Summarize how organizations learn

- Understand the relevance and importance of lifelong learning for the individual

Maureen Kempston Darkes heads General Motors Canada—the first woman to rise to that level in the male-dominated auto industry.[1] Kempston Darkes knows the challenges she faces: General Motors has a history of labour conflict and one of the lowest productivity ratings in the industry. She wants to change those things around at GM, and states her ambition: "I want every employee to come to work at General Motors every day and say, 'I can make a difference. I can contribute to this business.'" Her colleagues view her as a team player who values communication. "When you work in a rigid, hierarchical structure, that limits opportunities for people to communicate," she explains. Consequently, she strives for less hierarchical ways to communicate.

Kempston Darkes faces the same balancing act that many managers do. She wants to satisfy her employees, while also focusing on issues beyond the workplace: customers, shareholders, suppliers, and so on. She believes in flexibility and communication, but also recognizes the need for control systems within the organization. In short, a variety of competing demands make her job, and the job of all managers, complex.

In this chapter we explore what organizations are, and what activities go on inside them, what managers do, and the responsibility of employees in a time of great change for workers and individuals alike. ∎

What Do We Mean by Organization?

organization
A consciously coordinated social unit, composed of two or more people, that functions on a relatively continuous basis to achieve a common goal or set of goals.

In our study of organizational behaviour it is important to understand what an organization is and the types of organizations in which individuals work. An **organization** is a consciously coordinated social unit, composed of two or more people, that functions on a relatively continuous basis to achieve a common goal or set of goals. Thus, manufacturing and service firms are organizations, and so are schools, hospitals, churches, military units, retail stores, police departments, and local, provincial, and federal government agencies. As students, you may tend to think that when we say "organization" we are referring to large manufacturing firms, to the exclusion of the variety of other forms of organization that exist, but this would be a very short-sighted thought. It is important to realize that only 14.2 percent of Canadians work in manufacturing organizations. Three-quarters of Canadians work in the service-producing sector of the economy, indicating that a large number of workers are engaged in people-related tasks for at least part of their jobs. Another 19 percent are engaged in wholesale and retail trade. To help you gain a clearer picture of where Canadians are employed, Exhibit 2-1 indicates the percentage of Canadians employed by each industry in 1996.

Besides being more service-oriented than manufacturing-oriented, the organizations in which Canadians work comprise a variety of types. When we think of organizations, we tend to think in terms of size, and often envision large organizations such as Chrysler Canada or MacMillan Bloedel. These large firms represent only three percent of the firms in Canada. Businesses with less than 50 employees accounted for 97 percent of the 928 000 firms in Canada in 1996. While big business employs more workers than small business, you might be surprised to learn that the share of jobs in big business is just over 40 percent, while small businesses account for about one-third of the jobs in Canada.[2] You also should be aware that in 1996, about 1.8 million individuals reported that they were self-employed, which represents 13 percent of the labour force. Between 1991 and 1996, there was an increase of 28 percent among individuals who were self-employed.[3] While self-employed individuals may not be acting as managers, they certainly interact with other individuals and organizations as part of their work, making the study of organizational behaviour equally important for them as for those who work in larger organizations.

Beyond the industry location and the size of the organization, other factors affect how organizations operate. Specifically, organizations can be located in the public or private sector; they can be unionized or not; they can be publicly traded or privately held. If they are publicly traded, senior managers typically are responsible to a board of directors, which may or may not take an active role in how the firm is run. The managers themselves may or may not own shares of the firm. If the firm is privately held, it may be run by the owners or the managers may report to the owners. Firms can also operate in the for-profit or non-profit sectors. All of these facts, taken as a whole, should suggest to you that when you think of an organization, the likelihood that you are thinking of a "typical" organization is small. It is difficult, given the variety of circumstances under which organizations operate, to indicate what a typical organization might be. The examples in this text try to present various organizations to help you reflect across the many types that exist. Though you might not have considered this before, the college or university you attend is every bit as much a "real" organization as is Eaton's or Canadian Airlines or The Globe and Mail. Therefore, the theories we

Chrysler Corporation
http://www2.chryslercorp.com/

MacMillan Bloedel
http://www.mb-mdf.com/

Canadian Airlines
http://www.cdnair.ca

Eaton's
http://www.eatons.com/home/

The Globe and Mail
http://www.globeandmail.com/

Exhibit 2-1
Percentage of Canadians Employed in Various Industries, 1996

Industry Category	Percentage employed [1]
Agricultural and related service industries	3.4
Fishing and trapping industries	.3
Logging and forestry industries	.7
Mining (including milling), quarrying and oil well industries	1.2
Manufacturing industries	14.2
Construction industries	5.7
Transportation and storage industries	4.2
Communication and other utility industries	3.1
Wholesale trade industries	5.0
Retail trade industries	12.4
Finance and insurance industries	3.6
Real estate operator and insurance agent industries	1.9
Business service industries	6.5
Government service industries	6.2
Educational service industries	7.0
Health and social service industries	9.8
Accommodation, food and beverage service industries	6.9
Other service industries	7.7
Goods-producing industries[2]	*27.0*
Service-producing industries[3]	*73.0*

(1) Numbers do not add to 100 percent, due to rounding.

(2) Goods Producing Industries include the following industry divisions: Agricultural and Related, Fishing and Trapping, Logging and Forestry Mining, Manufacturing and Construction; as well as the Other Utility Major Group from the Communications and Other Utility Industry Division.

(3) Service Producing Industries include the following industry divisions: Transportation and Storage, Wholesale Trade, Retail Trade, Finance and Insurance, Real Estate Operator and Insurance Agent, Business Service, Government Service, Educational Service, Health and Social Service, Accommodation, Food and Beverage Service, Other Services; as well as the Communication Major Group from the Communication and Other Utility Industry Division.

Source: *StatsCan Daily*, March 17, 1998.

cover should be considered in light of the variety of organizations you may encounter. We try to point out instances where the theory may be less applicable to a particular type of organization. In the absence of a caveat, however, you should expect that the discussions in this book apply across the broad spectrum of organizations.

The Complex Nature of Organizations

Successful organizations are continuously balancing a variety of concerns, from governmental regulations to shareholders, to environmental issues, to suppliers, to identifying their markets, to examining their production processes, to managing their employees. While an organization might be

operating reasonably well at a specific point in time, organizations often face new challenges. For instance, for many years the North American auto industry produced cars and then told consumers what was available for sale. In the mid-1970s, however, the price of gasoline started to rise, making it very expensive to drive large cars. Consequently, North Americans started buying smaller Japanese cars. Because of the North American auto industry's failure to recognize that this was indeed a consumer shift, it took them many years to recover from not having explored alternatives to producing large cars. This action illustrates how the North American automobile industry ignored environmental factors, or considered them to be short-term threats, failed to heed customer demand, and was slow to develop new products or the technology to make smaller cars.

Robert Quinn, Kim Cameron, and their colleagues have developed a model known as the "Competing Values Framework"[4] to categorize some of the issues organizations face. As Exhibit 2-2 indicates, the range of issues organizations face can be divided along two dimensions: an internal-external and a flexibility-control focus. The internal-external dimensions refer to the extent that organizations focus either inwardly toward employee needs and concerns and/or production processes and internal systems or outwardly, toward such factors as the marketplace, government regulations, and the changing social, environmental, and technological conditions of the future.

Exhibit 2-2
Competing Values Framework

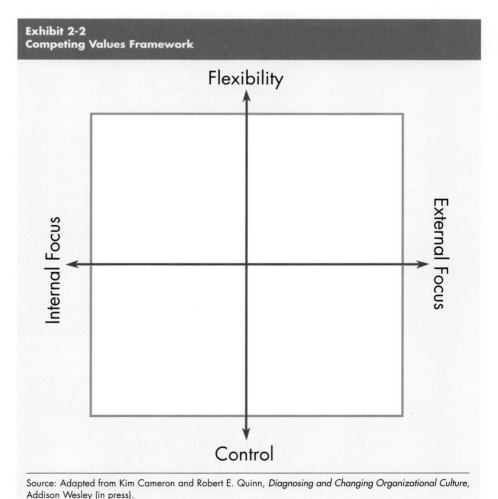

Source: Adapted from Kim Cameron and Robert E. Quinn, *Diagnosing and Changing Organizational Culture*, Addison Wesley (in press).

For example, prior to the oil crisis in the 1970s, North American auto manufacturers were more focused internally on maintaining their established systems of production and design, rather than looking outward toward the marketplace to anticipate what demands lay ahead.

The flexibility-control dimension refers to the competing demands of organizations to stay focused on doing what has been done in the past versus being more flexible in orientation and outlook. Some organizations are more controlling or stable, therefore maintaining the status quo and exhibiting less change. McDonald's, for instance, is an example of an organization that has successfully developed an assembly-line process to produce fast food. With respect to providing its product, McDonald's is an example of an organization that emphasizes stability. Other organizations are more flexible and dynamic, allowing more teamwork and participation from their employees as well as seeking new opportunities for products and services.

Because the grid of the competing values framework forms quadrants, it is easy to understand why some organizations might focus more on just one of the four quadrants. However, it is also fair to say that most organizations are faced with juggling the competing concerns that arise and consequently have at least some experience meeting the demands of each of the quadrants. Increasingly we see examples of organizations that look more stable at some periods in their history, and more flexible or changing at other times. For instance, for many years Canadian retailer Eaton's continued to operate much as it had in the past. However, in recent years, because of a need to reposition itself in the marketplace and to introduce new ideas into the organization, it has brought non-family members into crucial operating roles. Eaton's continues to look for ways to become more flexible in the ever-changing marketplace. This chapter's Case Incident examines Bata Shoes, which has been less flexible in adjusting to the competitive nature of the global marketplace.

Bata Shoes
http://www.bata.com/

Working in the Organization of the 21st Century

A simplistic view of work organizations would divide the participants into the following categories: owners, leaders and/or managers, and employees. These roles are probably the most well established for large, publicly held organizations, and become somewhat blurred as we discuss smaller, privately owned firms. For instance, the owners of a privately held company generally differ quite significantly from the owners of a large, publicly held corporation. Specifically, in a privately held company, ownership may be held by just one person or a small group of people. Sometimes it is held by a group of family members. Usually, though not always, these owners have a more hands-on approach to the running of the organization. In a publicly held corporation, however, the owners are the shareholders. The shares of a publicly held organization may be concentrated in the hands of relatively few owners, such as when a pension fund or a few shareholders hold a larger number of the shares, or the shares can be widely dispersed. Given the differences in what it means to be an owner, from one person owning the firm outright to many people having an interest mainly in the share prices of the corporation, the influence of the owners on the day-to-day operations of the firm will vary significantly.

When we talk about leadership in organizations, we typically mean the person or persons responsible for setting the overall vision of the organiza-

University of Manitoba
http://umanitoba.ca

**Conference Board
of Canada**
http://www.conferenceboard.
ca/

tion. We discuss leadership extensively in Chapter 11. Not all firms have leaders in the true sense of leadership. While there is an extensive literature comparing and contrasting leaders and managers, we do not feel it necessary to get into that debate here. As Professor John McCallum of the University of Manitoba notes, managers "organize, direct and motivate people, financial capital and hard assets with a specific goal in mind."[5]

At the same time that managers are organizing, directing, and motivating, however, employees are being asked to "move beyond their traditional role as inputs to the process of achieving organizational goals," explains Carolyn Farquhar of the Conference Board of Canada, who co-authored a 1996 study on "Creating High-Performance Organizations with People."[6] To some extent, then, the roles of individuals are becoming blurred in many organizations—particularly the roles between managers and employees. It is with that knowledge that we present information about the roles of managers below, while also encouraging you to realize that in many organizations today, employees are being asked to share in some of the decision processes of managers. In particular, in the high-performance organizations described in the Conference Board of Canada's 1996 report, "Employees are willing to be accountable for their own and the organization's success."[7] To be accountable will mean that employees "take charge of their own careers, decide what skills they need to acquire and determine where they wish to employ these skills."[8]

We discuss the types of skills needed in today's workplace below, and follow that with a more general discussion of learning, to help you understand the processes by which individuals and organizations acquire the knowledge and skills they need to be successful.

The Role of the Manager in Today's Organization

The people who oversee the activities of others and who are responsible for attaining goals in these organizations are managers (although they're sometimes called *administrators*, especially in not-for-profit organizations). Managers are responsible for helping organizations to balance and address the concerns raised above. The "competing values framework" mentioned above can also be used to inform managers about appropriate behaviours for managing organizations.

Because organizations face the competing demands illustrated in Exhibit 2-2, it becomes obvious that managers and even employees are better off with a variety of skills that help them to operate among the various quadrants at different points. For instance, the skills needed to maintain an efficient assembly-line process are not the same skills needed to scan the environment or to create opportunities in anticipation of changes in the environment. Because of rapid changes in technology, along with the influences of globalization, organizations and individuals are faced with becoming much more flexible in their outlook. As this chapter's CBC Video Case shows, in the aftermath of downsizing, many Canadian organizations are having to rebuild, and this involves providing creative opportunities for employees.

Becoming a Master Manager

Quinn and his colleagues use the term *master manager* to indicate that successful managers learn and apply skills that will help them manage across all four quadrants of organizational demands, at some times moving toward

Master managers need to develop a variety of skills, including the ability to achieve a balance between flexibility and control. Peggy Witte, chair, president and CEO of Royal Oak Mines had to learn to trust others more as part of learning to be more flexible.

flexibility, at others moving toward control, sometimes being more internally focused, sometimes being more externally driven.[9] While they note that most people have strengths in just some of the areas needed to be a master manager, they also suggest the importance of developing a broader repertoire of skills to be able to face all of the challenges that today's manager encounters. As organizations increasingly cut the number of layers in their organization, reducing the number of managers, while also relying more on the use of teams in the workplace, the skills of the master manager also apply to the skills of the master employee. In other words, extrapolating from the competing values framework, one can see that both managers and individual employees can learn new skills and new ways of interpreting their organizational contexts, rather than continuing to use traditional skills and practices that worked in the past.

At this point you may wonder whether it is possible for people to learn all of the skills necessary to become a master manager. More importantly, you may wonder whether one can change one's style, say from more controlling to more flexible. Here's what Peggy Witte, chairman, president, and CEO of Royal Oak Mines, says about how her managerial style changed from controlling to more flexible over time: "I started out being very dictatorial. Everybody in head office reported to me. I had to learn to trust other executives so we could work out problems together."[10] So, while it is probably true that each of us has preferred styles of operating, it is also the case that we can develop new skills, if that is something we choose to do.

Royal Oak Mines
http://www.royal-oak-mines.com/

Managerial Skills

The competing values framework helps us to identify the wide range of skills that are needed to be a successful manager in today's organization. On the flexibility side, organizations want to inspire their employees toward high-performance behaviour, which includes looking ahead to the future and

envisioning possible new directions for the organization. To do these things, managers need to think and act like mentors and facilitators. They also need to be innovators and brokers. On the control side, organizations need to set clear goals about productivity expectations, and they have to develop and implement systems to carry out the production process. To be effective on the production side, managers need to have the skills of monitors, coordinators, directors, and producers.

Using the competing values framework, Exhibit 2-3 outlines the many skills required of today's manager, giving you an indication of the complexities of the roles needed by managers and employees facing the changing workplace. The skills are organized in terms of those needed to maintain flexibility and discretion, those needed to maintain stability and control, those needed to maintain an external focus, and those needed to maintain an internal focus. By looking at your own strengths and weaknesses in these skill areas, you will have a better sense of how close you are to becoming a successful manager. In the Point/Counterpoint discussion you can read about the conflicting internal and external pressures that can lead to company bankruptcies.

Although the competing values framework organizes our thinking in terms of the skills needed by a successful manager, our discussion should not leave you with the impression that non-managers need not worry about acquiring such skills. For one thing, you may become a manager later in your career, and to do so you will have needed to acquire these skills. For another thing, as we point out in Chapter 12, organizations are relying on their em-

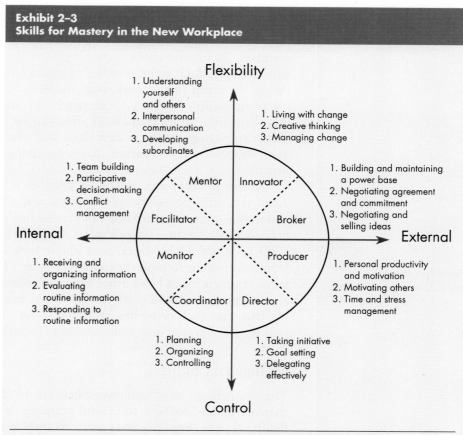

Exhibit 2-3
Skills for Mastery in the New Workplace

Source: R.E. Quinn, *Beyond Rational Management.* San Francisco: Jossey-Bass Inc., 1988, p. 86.

ployees to assume more decision-making responsibility, which means that employees are becoming more empowered and need the same kinds of skills as managers. Finally, as we noted above, self-employment provides a growing opportunity for individuals to create a work environment that can be designed to meet their own needs. However, running your own business, even if you have no additional employees, requires that you have all of the skills of a master manager.

Management Roles

The competing values framework gives one approach to understanding managerial roles. It is framed in terms of overall needs of organizations given competing demands. It is not, however, the only framework for looking at managerial roles. In the late 1960s, while still a graduate student, Henry Mintzberg, currently a management professor at McGill University in Montreal, undertook a careful study of five executives to determine what these managers did on their jobs. On the basis of his observations of these managers, Mintzberg concluded that managers perform 10 different, highly interrelated roles, or sets of behaviours attributable to their jobs.[11] As shown in Exhibit 2-4, these 10 roles can be grouped as being primarily concerned with interpersonal relationships, the transfer of information, and decision-making.

McGill University
http://www.mcgill.ca

INTERPERSONAL ROLES All managers are required to perform duties that are ceremonial and symbolic in nature. For example, when the president of a college or university hands out diplomas at commencement or a factory supervisor gives a group of high school students a tour of the plant, he or she is acting in a *figurehead* role. All managers also have a *leadership* role. This role includes hiring, training, motivating, and disciplining employees. The third role within the interpersonal grouping is the *liaison* role. Mintzberg described this activity as contacting outsiders who provide the manager with information. These may be individuals or groups inside or outside the organization. The sales manager who obtains information from the human resources manager in his or her own company has an internal liaison relationship. When that sales manager has contacts with other sales executives through a marketing trade association, he or she has an outside liaison relationship.

INFORMATION ROLES All managers, to some degree, collect information from organizations and institutions outside their own. Typically, they receive information by reading magazines and talking with other people to learn of changes in the public's tastes, what competitors may be planning, and the like. Mintzberg called this the *monitor* role. Managers also act as a conduit to transmit information to organizational members. This is the *disseminator* role. Managers additionally perform a *spokesperson* role when they represent the organization to outsiders.

DECISIONAL ROLES Finally, Mintzberg identified four roles that revolve around the making of choices. In the *entrepreneur* role, managers initiate and oversee new projects that will improve their organization's performance. As *disturbance handlers*, managers take corrective action in response to unforeseen problems. As *resource allocators*, managers are responsible for allocating human, physical, and monetary resources. Managers also perform a *negotiator* role, in which they discuss issues and bargain with other units to gain advantages for their own unit.

Exhibit 2-4
Mintzberg's Managerial Roles

Role	Description	Example
Interpersonal		
Figurehead	Symbolic head; required to perform a number of routine duties of a legal or social nature	Ceremonies, status requests, solicitations
Leader	Responsible for the motivation and direction of subordinates	Virtually all managerial activities involving subordinates
Liaison	Maintains a network of outside contacts who provide favours and information	Acknowledgment of mail, external board work
Informational		
Monitor	Receives wide variety of information; serves as nerve centre of internal and external information of the organization	Handling all mail and contacts categorized as concerned primarily with receiving information
Disseminator	Transmits information received from outsiders or from other subordinates to members of the organization	Forwarding mail into organization for informational purposes; verbal contacts involving information flow to subordinates such as review sessions
Spokesperson	Transmits information to outsiders on organization's plans, policies, actions, and results; serves as expert on organization's industry	Board meetings; handling contacts involving transmission of information to outsiders
Decisional		
Entrepreneur	Searches organization and its environment for opportunities and initiates projects to bring about change	Strategy and review sessions involving initiation or design of improvement projects
Disturbance handler	Responsible for corrective action when organization faces important, unexpected disturbances	Strategy and review sessions involving disturbances and crises
Resource allocator	Makes or approves significant organizational decisions	Scheduling; requests for authorization; budgeting; the programming of subordinates' work
Negotiator	Responsible for representing the organization at major negotiations	Contract negotiation

Source: Adapted from *The Nature of Managerial Work*, by H. Mintzberg. Copyright 1973 by H. Mintzberg. Reprinted by permission of Addison-Wesley Educational Publishers Inc.

Effective versus Successful Managerial Activities

Fred Luthans and his associates looked at the issue of what managers do from a somewhat different perspective.[12] They asked the question, Do managers who move up most quickly in an organization do the same activities and with the same emphasis as managers who do the best job? You would tend to think that the managers who were the most effective in their jobs would also be the ones who were promoted fastest. But that's not what appears to happen.

Luthans and his associates studied more than 450 managers. What they found was that these managers all engaged in four managerial activities:

- *Traditional management.* Decision-making, planning, and controlling
- *Communication.* Exchanging routine information and processing paperwork
- *Human resources management.* Motivating, disciplining, managing conflict, staffing, and training
- *Networking.* Socializing, politicking, and interacting with outsiders

The "average" manager in the study spent 32 percent of his or her time in traditional management activities, 29 percent communicating, 20 percent in human resource management activities, and 19 percent networking. However, the amount of time and effort that different managers spent on those four activities varied a great deal. Specifically, as shown in Exhibit 2-5, managers who were *successful* (defined in terms of the speed of promotion within their organization) had a very different emphasis than managers who were *effective* (defined in terms of the quantity and quality of their performance and the satisfaction and commitment of their subordinates). Among

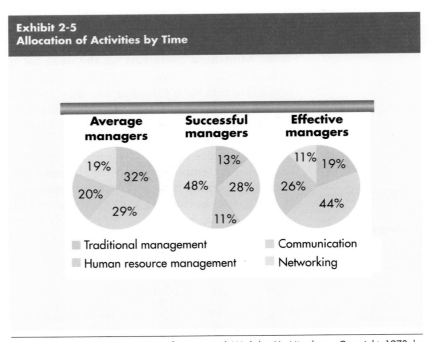

Exhibit 2-5
Allocation of Activities by Time

Average managers
19% 32% 20% 29%

Successful managers
13% 28% 48% 11%

Effective managers
11% 19% 26% 44%

Traditional management
Human resource management
Communication
Networking

Source: Adapted from *The Nature of Managerial Work* by H. Mintzberg. Copyright 1973 by H. Mintzberg. Reprinted by permission of Addison-Wesley Educational Publishers Inc.

successful managers, networking made the largest relative contribution to success, and human resource management activities made the least relative contribution. Among effective managers, communication made the largest relative contribution and networking the least.

This study adds important insights to our knowledge of what managers do. On average, managers spend approximately 20 to 30 percent of their time on each of the four activities: traditional management, communication, human resource management, and networking. However, successful managers don't give the same emphasis to each of those activities as do effective managers. In fact, their emphases are almost the opposite. This finding challenges the historical assumption that promotions are based on performance, vividly illustrating the importance that social and political skills play in getting ahead in organizations.

Developing Yourself as an Employee

Our discussion of managers suggests that they operate in very complex environments, juggle a variety of roles, and do so with differing degrees of effectiveness. Effective and successful managers were shown to need a variety of people skills. As mentioned above, you should not take our discussion of what managers do and what they need to learn as something that is not relevant to you if you do not plan to become a manager. The skills required of managers are also the skills that will make you an effective employee. Given the need to learn all of these new skills for the workplace of the 21st century, it is important to think of yourself as a lifelong learner—a person who is continually looking to acquire and develop new skills. Acquiring new skills means developing a learning mentality. Below we discuss how learning occurs, both for individuals and organizations. We consider learning an important process for both the successful individual and the successful organization of the 21st century.

Learning

Henry Mintzberg comments on the need for managers to learn: "I used to think that the brilliance of the U.S.'s management lay in its action orientation. Managers didn't think a lot; they just got things done. But now I find that the best managers are very thoughtful people…who are also highly action oriented. Unfortunately, too many others have stopped thinking. They want quick, easy answers."[13]

We introduce the topic of learning in this chapter to underscore the need for managers, employees and organizations to engage continuously in the process of learning if they expect to be successful in the 21st century. Almost all complex behaviour is learned. If we want to explain and predict behaviour, we need to understand how people learn. Learning is not confined to individuals, however. In fact, in today's organizational world, we talk about **the learning organization**.

A Definition of Learning

What is **learning**? A psychologist's definition is considerably broader than the layperson's view that "it's what we did when we went to school." In fact, each of us is continuously going "to school." Learning occurs all of the time. A generally accepted definition of learning is, therefore, any relatively

the learning organization
An organization that acquires, disseminates, and applies knowledge for continued success.

learning
Any relatively permanent change in behaviour that occurs as a result of experience.

permanent change in behaviour that occurs as a result of experience. Ironically, we can say that changes in behaviour indicate that learning has taken place and that learning is a change in behaviour.

Obviously, this definition suggests that we will never see someone "learning." We can see changes taking place, but not the learning itself. The concept is theoretical and, hence, not directly observable.

You have seen people in the process of learning, you have seen people who behave in a particular way as a result of learning, and some of you (in fact, probably most of you) have "learned" at some time in your life. In other words, we infer that learning has occurred if an individual behaves, reacts, responds as a result of experience in a manner different from the way he or she behaved formerly.[14]

Our definition has several components that deserve clarification. First, learning involves change. Change may be good or bad from an organizational perspective. People can learn unfavourable behaviours—to hold prejudices or to restrict their output, for example—as well as favourable behaviours—such as being responsible to monitor mistakes and make adjustments as necessary. Second, the change must be relatively permanent. Temporary changes may be only reflexive and fail to represent any learning. Therefore, the requirement that learning must be relatively permanent rules out behavioural changes caused by fatigue or temporary adaptations. Third, our definition is concerned with behaviour. Learning takes place when a change in actions occurs. Finally, some form of experience is necessary for learning. Experience may be acquired directly through observation or practice, or it may be acquired indirectly, as through reading. The crucial test still remains: Does this experience result in a relatively permanent change in behaviour? If the answer is yes, we can say that learning has occurred.

To indicate to you how important continuous learning can be, the OB in the News feature introduces you to Ron and Marie Jang, who have used learning to develop their company, Tanex, known in Western Canada as a key supplier of custom heritage woodwork.

Tanex
http://www.tanex.com/

Ron Jang, founder and co-owner of Tanex, a heritage supply business in British Columbia, relies heavily on continuous learning in order to keep his business thriving. Because he and his wife, co-owner Marie Jang, search out new information, Tanex is known as a key supplier of custom heritage woodwork in Western Canada.

OB IN THE NEWS

Learning Creates Tanex

When Ron and Marie Jang decided to renovate their heritage home, built in the 1800s in New Westminster, British Columbia, they had no idea that step would lead them to opening their own heritage supply business named Tanex. What started off as difficulty in finding mouldings and other finishing pieces that would match the character of their home, ended up creating a learning opportunity for both Ron and Marie.

Heritage homes are houses that were built in Canada in the 1800s and early 1900s and that reflect distinctive architectural styles. Cities such as Vancouver often encourage homeowners to preserve and restore these homes. As the Jangs underwent the remodelling, they started learning everything they could about 19th-century decorative wood mouldings so that they could preserve the character of their home. With their initial knowledge, they set up a booth and called themselves a "heritage resource centre." The orders started to flow almost immediately. Within a year, Ron quit his day job, even though he had no woodwork apprenticeship or training. To sum up his qualifications, Ron notes, "I had a grade 8 achievement award in woodwork!"

To improve their knowledge of wood finishing, the Jangs established a large reference library, and they still chat with and educate anyone who visits their business premises. "Today, someone can bring us a piece and we can tell them what decade the house was built and what style it's supposed to be and sometimes where the wood was milled," Marie says. Tanex has been in business now for 14 years, and has six full-time employees.

Even though annual sales have fluctuated between $300 000 and $500 000, in some years the business lost money. Neither Ron nor Marie had any formal business training before they started their business. Recently, Marie has turned to learning once again: this time she registered for courses and consulting help with the Business Development Bank. "As a result, Tanex has raised prices to meet market rates, started clocking production times and eliminated most of the unprofitable products."

The story of Tanex and the Jangs illustrates an important lesson of this chapter. Learning is a continuous process; it doesn't stop when we leave school, and it doesn't even stop when we start working. Because the Jangs continue to search out information on things they do not know, Tanex has made a name for itself in Western Canada "as a key supplier of custom heritage woodwork from the mid-1800s to the 1930s."

Source: Jenny Lee, "Tanex is Labour of Love for Jang Family," *Vancouver Sun*, March 4, 1998, p. D1.

Take It to the Net

We invite you to visit the Robbins page on the Prentice Hall Web site at:

http://www.prenticehall.ca/robbins

for this chapter's World Wide Web exercise.

Theories of Learning

How do we learn? Three theories have been offered to explain the process by which we acquire patterns of behaviour. These are classical conditioning (learning to react), operant conditioning (learning through feedback), and social learning (learning by observing). This chapter's Learning About Yourself exercise gives you an opportunity to evaluate your own learning style as well.

classical conditioning
A type of conditioning in which an individual responds to some stimulus that would not ordinarily produce such a response.

CLASSICAL CONDITIONING: LEARNING TO REACT   Classical conditioning grew out of experiments to teach dogs to salivate in response to the ringing of a bell, conducted at the turn of the century by a Russian physiologist, Ivan Pavlov.[15] A simple surgical procedure allowed Pavlov to measure accurately the amount of saliva secreted by a dog. When Pavlov presented the dog with a piece of meat, the dog exhibited a noticeable increase in salivation. When Pavlov withheld the presentation of meat and merely rang a bell, the dog did not salivate. Then Pavlov proceeded to link the meat and the ringing of the bell. After repeatedly hearing the bell before getting the food, the dog began to salivate as soon as the bell rang. After a while, the dog would salivate merely at the sound of the bell, even if no food was offered. In effect, the dog had learned to respond—that is, to salivate—to the bell. Let's review this experiment to introduce the key concepts in classical conditioning. (Exhibit 2-6 gives a humorous account of Pavlov's experiment with his dog.)

The meat was an *unconditioned stimulus*; it invariably caused the dog to react in a specific way. The reaction that took place whenever the unconditioned stimulus occurred was called the *unconditioned response* (or the noticeable increase in salivation, in this case). The bell was an artificial stimulus, or what we call the *conditioned stimulus*. Although it was originally

Exhibit 2-6

THE FAR SIDE   By GARY LARSON

Unbeknownst to most students of psychology, Pavlov's first experiment was to ring a bell and cause his dog to attack Freud's cat.

neutral, after the bell was paired with the meat (an unconditioned stimulus), it eventually produced a response when presented alone. The last key concept is the *conditioned response*. This describes the behaviour of the dog; it salivated in reaction to the bell alone.

Using these concepts, we can summarize classical conditioning. Essentially, learning a conditioned response involves building up an association between a conditioned stimulus and an unconditioned stimulus. When the stimuli, one compelling and the other one neutral, are paired, the neutral one becomes a conditioned stimulus and, hence, takes on the properties of the unconditioned stimulus.

Classical conditioning can be used to explain why comfort foods such as macaroni and cheese, chocolate pudding, or homemade chocolate-chip cookies often bring back pleasant memories of childhood to those who grew up in North America; the foods are associated with a quieter, perhaps more peaceful time of life. In an organizational setting, we can also see classical conditioning operating. For example, at one manufacturing plant, every time the top executives from the head office were scheduled to make a visit, the plant management would clean up the administrative offices and wash the windows. This behaviour continued for years. Eventually, employees would turn on their best behaviour whenever the windows were cleaned—even in those occasional instances when the cleaning was not paired with the visit from the top brass. People had learned to associate the window cleaning with a visit from head office.

Classical conditioning is passive. Something happens and we react in a specific way. It is elicited in response to a specific, identifiable event. As such, it can explain simple reflexive behaviours. But most behaviour—particularly the complex behaviour of individuals in organizations—is emitted rather than elicited. It is voluntary rather than reflexive. For example, employees choose to arrive at work on time, ask their boss for help with problems, or "goof off" when no one is watching. The learning of those behaviours is better understood by looking at operant conditioning.

OPERANT CONDITIONING: LEARNING THROUGH FEEDBACK **Operant conditioning** argues that behaviour is a function of its consequences. People learn to behave to get something they want or to avoid something they don't want. Operant behaviour means voluntary or learned behaviour in contrast to reflexive or unlearned behaviour. The tendency to repeat such behaviour is influenced by the reinforcement or lack of reinforcement brought about by the consequences of the behaviour. Reinforcement, therefore, strengthens a behaviour and increases the likelihood that it will be repeated.

What Pavlov did for classical conditioning, Harvard psychologist B.F. Skinner did for operant conditioning.[16] Building on earlier work in the field, Skinner's research extensively expanded our knowledge of operant conditioning. Even his staunchest critics, who represent a sizable group, admit that his operant concepts work.

Behaviour is assumed to be determined from without—that is, learned—rather than from within—reflexive or unlearned. Skinner argued that creating pleasing consequences to follow specific forms of behaviour would increase the frequency of that behaviour. People are most likely to engage in desired behaviours if they are positively reinforced for doing so. Rewards are most effective if they immediately follow the desired response. In addition, behaviour that is not rewarded, or is punished, is less likely to be repeated.

operant conditioning
A type of conditioning in which desired voluntary behaviour leads to a reward or prevents a punishment.

You see illustrations of operant conditioning everywhere. For example, any situation in which it is either explicitly stated or implicitly suggested that reinforcements are contingent on some action on your part involves the use of operant learning. For example, your instructor says that if you want a high grade in the course, you must supply correct answers on the test. A commissioned salesperson wanting to earn a sizable income finds that doing so depends on generating high sales in his or her territory. Of course, the linkage can also work to teach the individual to engage in behaviours that work against the best interests of the organization. Assume that your boss tells you that if you will work overtime during the next three-week busy season, you will be rewarded for it at the next performance appraisal. However, when performance appraisal time comes, you discover that you are given no positive reinforcement for your overtime work. The next time your boss asks you to work overtime, what will you do? You'll probably decline! Your behaviour can be explained by operant conditioning: If a behaviour fails to be positively reinforced, the probability that the behaviour will be repeated declines.

Methods of Reinforcement. There are four ways in which behaviours can be reinforced: through positive reinforcement, negative reinforcement, punishment, and extinction.

Following a response with something pleasant is called *positive reinforcement*. This would describe, for instance, the boss who praises an employee for a job well done. Following a response by the termination or withdrawal of something unpleasant is called *negative reinforcement*. When a manager stops criticizing an employee whose performance has improved, the manager is using negative reinforcement. The employee's improved behaviour leads to the termination of criticism. *Punishment* is causing an unpleasant condition in an attempt to eliminate an undesirable behaviour. Giving an employee a two-day suspension from work without pay for showing up drunk is an example of punishment. Eliminating any reinforcement that is maintaining a behaviour is called *extinction*. When the behaviour is not reinforced, it tends to be extinguished gradually. Instructors who wish to discourage students from asking questions in class can eliminate this behaviour in their students by ignoring those who raise their hands to ask questions. Hand raising will become extinct when it is invariably met with an absence of reinforcement.

Both positive and negative reinforcement result in learning. They strengthen a response and increase the probability of repetition. In the preceding illustrations, praise strengthens and increases the behaviour of doing a good job because praise is desired. The behaviour of "looking busy" is similarly strengthened and increased by its terminating the undesirable consequence of being called on by the teacher. Both punishment and extinction, however, weaken behaviour and tend to decrease its subsequent frequency. This chapter's Working With Others exercise gives you the opportunity to view how different forms of reinforcement affect behaviour.

Schedules of Reinforcement. The speed with which learning takes place and the permanence of its effects will be determined by the timing of reinforcement.[17] The two major types of reinforcement schedules are *continuous* and *intermittent*. A **continuous reinforcement** schedule reinforces the desired behaviour every time it is demonstrated. Take, for example, the case of someone who is typically late for work. Every time he or she is not tardy, the

continuous reinforcement
A desired behaviour is reinforced each and every time it is demonstrated.

manager might compliment the employee on the desirable behaviour. In an intermittent schedule, on the other hand, not every instance of the desirable behaviour is reinforced, but reinforcement is given often enough to make the behaviour worth repeating. This latter schedule can be compared to the workings of a slot machine, which people will continue to play even when they know that it is adjusted to give a considerable return to the casino. The intermittent payoffs occur just often enough to reinforce the behaviour of inserting coins and pulling the handle.

Continuous reinforcement schedules can lead to early satiation, and under this schedule behaviour tends to weaken rapidly when reinforcers are withheld. However, continuous reinforcers are appropriate for newly emitted, unstable, or low-frequency responses.

intermittent reinforcement
A desired behaviour is reinforced often enough to make the behaviour worth repeating but not every time it is demonstrated.

An **intermittent reinforcement** can be of a ratio or interval type. *Ratio schedules* depend upon how many responses the subject makes. The individual is reinforced after giving a certain number of specific types of behaviour. *Interval schedules* depend upon how much time has passed since the last reinforcement. With interval schedules, the individual is reinforced on the first appropriate behaviour after a particular time has elapsed. A reinforcement can also be classified as fixed or variable. Intermittent techniques for administering rewards can, therefore, be placed into four categories, as shown in Exhibit 2-7.

Evidence indicates that the intermittent, or varied, form of reinforcement tends to promote more resistance to extinction than does the continuous form.[18] Intermittent reinforcers preclude early satiation because they don't follow every response. They are appropriate for when either the desired behaviour has stabilized or when the behaviour occurs with high-frequency responses.

fixed-interval schedule
Rewards are spaced at uniform time intervals.

When rewards are spaced at uniform time intervals, the reinforcement schedule is of the **fixed-interval** type. The critical variable is time, and it is held constant. This is the predominant schedule for almost all salaried workers in North America. When you receive your paycheque on a weekly, semimonthly, monthly, or other predetermined time basis, you are rewarded on a fixed-interval reinforcement schedule.

variable-interval schedule
Rewards are distributed in time so that reinforcements are unpredictable.

If rewards are distributed in time so that reinforcements are unpredictable, the schedule is of the **variable-interval** type. When an instructor advises her class that pop quizzes will be given during the term (the exact number of which is unknown to the students) and the quizzes will account for 20 percent of the term grade, she is using a variable-interval schedule. Similarly, a series of randomly timed unannounced visits to a company office by the corporate audit staff is an example of a variable-interval schedule.

fixed-ratio schedule
Rewards are initiated after a fixed or constant number of responses.

In a **fixed-ratio** schedule, after a fixed or constant number of responses are given, a reward is initiated. For example, a piece-rate incentive plan is a fixed-ratio schedule; the employee receives a reward based on the number of work pieces generated. If the piece rate for a zipper installer in a dressmaking factory is $5.00 a dozen, the reinforcement (money in this case) is fixed to the number of zippers sewn into garments. After every dozen zippers are sewn in, the installer has earned another $5.00.

variable-ratio schedule
The reward varies relative to the behaviour of the individual.

When the reward varies relative to the behaviour of the individual, he or she is said to be reinforced on a **variable-ratio schedule**. Salespeople on commission are examples of individuals on such a reinforcement schedule. On some occasions, they may make a sale after only two calls on a potential customer.

Exhibit 2-7
Schedules of Reinforcement

	Interval	Ratio
Fixed	Fixed-interval	Fixed-ratio
Variable	Variable-interval	Variable-ratio

On other occasions, they might need to make 20 or more calls to secure a sale. The reward, then, is variable in relation to the number of successful calls the salesperson makes. Exhibit 2-8 depicts the four categories of intermittent schedules.

In general, variable schedules tend to lead to higher performance than fixed schedules. For example, as noted previously, most employees in organizations are paid on fixed-interval schedules. But such a schedule does not clearly link performance and rewards. The reward is given for time spent on the job rather than for a specific response (performance). In contrast, variable-interval schedules generate high rates of response and more stable and consistent behaviour because of a high correlation between performance and reward and because of the uncertainty involved—the employee tends to be more alert since there is a surprise factor.

Exhibit 2-8
Intermittent Schedules of Reinforcement

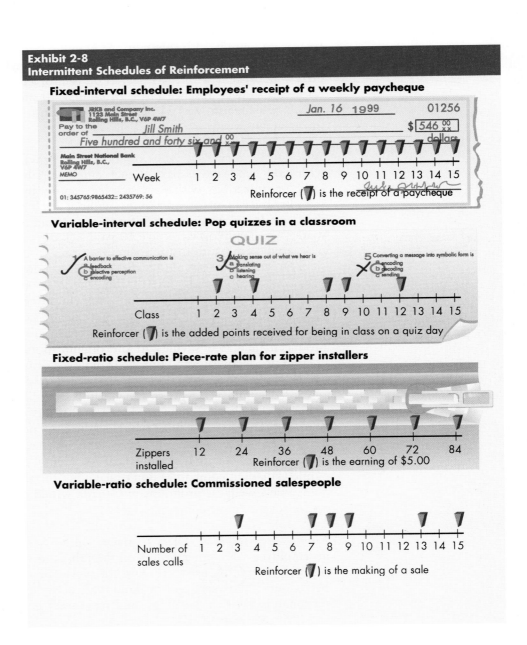

ORGANIZATIONAL APPLICATIONS OF REINFORCEMENT THEORY We have alluded to a number of situations in which reinforcement theory could be used to encourage change in the workplace. In this section, we will briefly look at three specific applications: using lotteries to reduce absenteeism, substituting well pay for sick pay, and disciplining problem employees.

Using Lotteries to Reduce Absenteeism. Management can use learning theory to design programs to reduce absenteeism. For example, New York Life Insurance Co. created a lottery that rewarded employees for attendance.[19] Each quarter, the names of all the head-office employees who had no absences are placed in a drum. In a typical quarter, about 4000 of the company's 7500 employees have their names placed in the drum. The first 10 names pulled earn a $280 bond, the next 20 earn a $140 bond, and 70 more receive a paid day off. At the end of the year, another lottery is held for those with 12 months of perfect attendance. Twelve prizes are awarded; two employees receive $1400 bonds, and 10 more earn five days off with pay. This lottery follows a variable-ratio schedule. A good attendance record increases an employee's probability of winning, yet having perfect attendance is no assurance that an employee will be rewarded by winning one of the prizes. Consistent with the research on reinforcement schedules, this lottery resulted in lower absence rates. In its first 10 months of operation, for instance, absenteeism was 21 percent lower than for the comparable period in the preceding year.

Well Pay Vs. Sick Pay. Most organizations provide their salaried employees with paid sick leave as part of each employee's benefits package. Yet, ironically, organizations with paid sick-leave programs experience almost twice the absenteeism of organizations without such programs.[20] The reality is that sick-leave programs reinforce the wrong behaviour—absence from work. When employees receive 10 paid sick days a year, it is the unusual employee who isn't sure to use them all up, regardless of whether he or she is sick. Organizations should reward attendance, not absence.

As a case in point, one North American organization implemented a well-pay program that paid a bonus to employees who had no absence for any given four-week period and then paid for sick leave only after the first eight hours of absence.[21] Evaluation of the well-pay program found that it produced increased savings to the organization, reduced absenteeism, increased productivity, and improved employee satisfaction.

Forbes magazine used the same approach to cut its health care costs.[22] It rewarded employees who stayed healthy and didn't file medical claims by paying them the difference between $700 and their medical claims, then doubling the amount. So if someone submitted no claims in a given year, he or she would receive $1400 ($700 × 2). By rewarding employees for good health, *Forbes* cut its major medical and dental claims by over 30 percent. While Canadian companies don't face quite the same medical claims as U.S. companies, wellness programs in Canada would reduce the high cost of absenteeism that most companies face.

Employee Discipline. Every manager will, at some time, have to deal with an employee who either drinks on the job, is insubordinate, steals company property, arrives consistently late for work, or engages in similar problem behaviours. Managers will respond with disciplinary actions such as verbal reprimands, written warnings, and temporary suspensions. But our knowl-

edge about punishment's effect on behaviour indicates that the use of discipline carries costs: It may provide only a short-term solution and could result in serious side effects.

Disciplining employees for undesirable behaviours only tells them what *not* to do. It doesn't tell them what alternative behaviours are preferred. The result is that this form of punishment frequently leads to only short-term suppression of the undesirable behaviour rather than its elimination. Continued use of punishment, rather than positive reinforcement, also tends to produce a fear of the manager. As the punishing agent, the employee begins to associate the employer with adverse consequences. Employees respond by "hiding" from their boss. Hence, the use of punishment can undermine manager-employee relations.

Discipline does have a place in organizations, however. In practice, it tends to be popular because of its ability to produce fast results in the short run. Moreover, managers are reinforced for using discipline because it produces an immediate change in the employee's behaviour. The suggestions offered in this chapter's From Concepts to Skills feature can help you to more effectively implement disciplinary action.

FROM CONCEPTS TO SKILLS

Effective Discipline Skills

The essence of effective disciplining can be summarized by the following eight behaviours.

1. *Respond immediately.* The more quickly a disciplinary action follows an offence, the more likely it is that the employee will associate the discipline with the offence rather than with you as the dispenser of the discipline. It's best to begin the disciplinary process as soon as possible after you notice a violation.

2. *Provide a warning.* You have an obligation to give warning before initiating disciplinary action. This means that the employee must be aware of the organization's rules and accept its standards of behaviour. Disciplinary action is more likely to be interpreted by employees as fair when they have received clear warning that a given violation will lead to discipline and when they know what that discipline will be.

3. *State the problem specifically.* Give the date, time, place, individuals involved, and any mitigating circumstances surrounding the violation. Be sure to define the violation in exact terms instead of just reciting com-

pany regulations or terms from a union contract. It's not the violation of the rules per se that you want to convey concern about. It's the effect that the rule violation has on the work unit's performance. Explain why the behaviour can't be continued by showing how it specifically affects the employee's job performance, the unit's effectiveness, and the employee's colleagues.

4. *Allow the employee to explain his or her position.* Regardless of what facts you have uncovered, due process demands that you give the employee the opportunity to explain his or her position. From the employee's perspective, what happened? Why did it happen? What was his or her perception of the rules, regulations, and circumstances?

5. *Keep discussion impersonal.* Penalties should be connected with a given violation, not with the personality of the individual violator. That is, discipline should be directed at what the employee has done, not at the employee.

6. *Be consistent.* Fair treatment of employees demands that disciplinary action be consistent. If you enforce rule violations in an inconsistent manner, the rules will lose their impact, morale will decline, and employees will likely question your competence. Consistency, however, need not result in treating everyone exactly alike; doing that would ignore mitigating circumstances. But the responsibility is yours to clearly justify disciplinary actions that might appear inconsistent to employees.

7. *Take progressive action.* Choose a punishment that's appropriate to the crime. Penalties should get progressively stronger if, or when, an offence is repeated. Typically, progressive disciplinary action begins with a verbal warning and then proceeds through a written reprimand, suspension, a demotion or pay cut, and finally, in the most serious cases, dismissal.

8. *Obtain agreement on change.* Disciplining should include guidance and direction for correcting the problem. Let the employee state what he or she plans to do in the future to ensure that the violation won't be repeated.

Sources: From A. Belohav, *The Art of Disciplining Your Employees* (Englewood Cliffs, NJ: Prentice Hall, 1985); and R.H. Lussier, "A Discipline Model for Increasing Performance," *Supervisory Management,* August 1990, pp.6–7.

SOCIAL LEARNING: LEARNING BY OBSERVING

Individuals can also learn by observing what happens to other people and just by being told about something, as well as by direct experiences. For example, much of what we have learned comes from watching models—parents, teachers, peers, motion picture and television performers, bosses, and so on. This view that we can learn through both observation and direct experience has been called **social-learning theory**.[23]

social-learning theory
People can learn through observation and direct experience.

Although social-learning theory is an extension of operant conditioning—that is, it assumes that behaviour is a function of consequences—it also acknowledges the existence of observational learning and the importance of perception in learning. People respond to how they perceive and define consequences, not to the objective consequences themselves.

Organizational Learning

Thus far we have discussed how individuals learn. In today's world, however, organizations are starting to focus more intently on organizational learning, i.e., the processes by which organizations acquire knowledge and change behaviour.

adaptive learning perspective
Organizations learn by feedback based on previous behaviour.

knowledge development perspective
Organizations collect, interpret, and then act upon information.

Theories about organizational learning can be classified into two major approaches: the **adaptive learning perspective** and the **knowledge development perspective**.[24] The adaptive learning perspective views organizations as learning by feedback, i.e., organizations repeat behaviours that have been successful in the past and avoid those behaviours that failed in the past.[25] The knowledge development perspective views organizations as collecting information, interpreting it, and then acting on the interpretations, possibly in entirely new ways.[26]

The adaptive learning approach views learning as a process of adjusting in response to one's experience. Thus it emphasizes experiential learning. "Organizational learning is assumed to be based on trial and error, where successful behaviour is repeated and unsuccessful behaviour is not."[27] The research indicates that adaptive learning works better in some situations

than others. For instance, adaptive learning makes sense when environmental and performance feedback signals are clear. Adaptive learning is less possible to implement in the presence of ambiguity about either the environment or how well performance is doing, because there is not enough information to know how to act. Organizations that learn from experience also have difficulty dealing with environmental change because they will not have experienced the new situation before. This is problematic because "environmental change makes adaptation essential, but it also makes learning from experience difficult."[28] (See Chapter 16's OB in the News, which discusses problems Maclean-Hunter had in making changes in its organization.)

The knowledge development perspective considers that organizations and organizational members share knowledge, impressions, beliefs, and thus transfer knowledge to one another. Organizations using this perspective to learn "allow valid information to be exposed, confrontations aired, viewpoints challenged, and choices informed and freely made."[29] These organizations are less likely to rely on traditional methods, and more apt to look for entirely new processes and procedures to carry out tasks. In our discussion of stretch targets in Chapter 6, you will encounter additional organizations that create opportunities to learn about new ways of doing business.

Organizations that try to learn simply through experience are less likely to be prepared to face new challenges for which they have no experience. To be a truly learning organization, then, it is important to take a knowledge development approach to learning, where one gathers new information and tries to use it in new ways.

Organizational Learning in Practice

Organizations are starting to develop processes that encourage their employees and managers to learn. Several Canadian and U.S. companies have established corporate universities, although they are much more predominant in the United States, where about 1200 U.S. companies now offer such facilities.[30] For example, the Bank of Montreal has an Institute of Learning in suburban Toronto, while the Canadian Imperial Bank of Commerce (CIBC) has a Leadership Centre in King City, located about an hour north of Toronto, where employees learn such skills as empowerment, entrepreneurship, and creativity. The banks are trying to turn employees from all levels into "continuous learners" who can both recognize and adapt to changes in customer demands, technology, economic conditions, and competitive threats. "A learning organization reacts much more quickly to dramatic change than a non-learning organization," says James Rush, senior vice-president and executive director of the Bank of Montreal's Institute of Learning. "If we can unleash the creativity and knowledge of our workers, we will be able to weather the storms."[31]

Hamilton, Ontario-based steel manufacturer Dofasco sends groups of employees on a three-day course at a ski resort located 165 kilometres north of the city. They participate in team building and other exercises intended to foster communication among employees. Not all teaching is done in such exotic settings, however, nor is all teaching done from a top-down position. For example, unionized workers at Chrysler Canada's minivan plant in Windsor, Ontario, teach quality awareness programs to managers. This chapter's HR Implications feature gives you further examples of how training occurs in the Canadian workplace.

Organizations are providing their employees with opportunities for continuous learning. At Second Cup Ltd., employees are sent to Coffee College to learn a variety of skills related to their employment.

Roadblocks to Organizational Learning

Holger Kluge, president of CIBC, notes that "Wealth, success and security will go to firms that can constantly adapt, firms where creativity and innovation belong to the many rather than the few, firms that are organized to exploit change, from whatever source, at a moment's notice—firms that recognize that just because something works today is no reason to assume it will work tomorrow."[32]

Unfortunately, organizations are not always so ready to give up on what works today to go out searching for something that might work tomorrow. Peter Senge, author of one of the landmark books on organizational learning, *The Fifth Discipline*, identifies a number of thought patterns that are roadblocks to learning, including:[33]

- *I am my position.* People often become so loyal to their jobs that they confuse their job with their identity. This becomes evident when a person is asked what they do, and they can describe their duties, but not the *purpose* of the greater enterprise. When people focus on their positions, they take little responsibility for the results that occur when all the positions interact together.

- *The enemy is out there.* When things go wrong in the organization, blame is always placed somewhere else in the organization. Individuals do not like to see that their actions may have contributed to the problem. For many Canadian companies the enemy might be viewed as foreign competition, labour unions, government regulations, or customers that chose to go elsewhere. This sort of thinking makes it more difficult to figure out how to turn challenges into opportunities.

- *The fixation of events.* We often see life as a series of events, and we try to attribute one obvious cause to each event. Consequently, we don't take time to find out the longer-term patterns of change related to those events. For instance, it is not uncommon to read a sentence like the following in the *Financial Post*: "The TSE average dropped

16 points today, because low fourth-quarter profits were announced yesterday." While those two events might be linked in a very real way, they tell us nothing about why fourth-quarter profits are low. The news also suggests that there was no way of knowing about the low profits until just yesterday, when in fact longer-term things are related to the drop in profits.

- *The parable of the boiled frog.* If you place a frog in boiling water, it will immediately jump out. However, if you place a frog in a pot of cold water on the stove and slowly bring it to boiling, the frog will eventually be boiled to death, without ever doing anything to react. The frog does this because it is geared to sense sudden changes in the environment, not slow, gradual changes. It is important to slow down enough to see the gradual processes that will eventually lead to threats, rather than waiting until the threats simply present themselves.

Knowledge of the roadblocks to learning is a step on the way to developing new insights and becoming open to learning.

Some Specific Applications of Organizational Learning

We have considered the move of organizations toward more of a focus on learning. In this section, we will briefly look at three specific applications of learning: developing effective employee training programs, creating mentoring programs for new employees, and applying learning theory to self-management.

DEVELOPING TRAINING PROGRAMS   Most U.S. organizations offer some type of systematic training program. More specifically, U.S. corporations with 100 or more employees spent $73 billion in one recent year on formal training for 47.3 million workers.[34] However, in Canada, less than one-third of firms do any training at all. The Conference Board of Canada surveyed 219 companies, schools, and hospitals to find out their 1995 training and

Mentoring programs help individuals learn the attitudes and behaviours that the organization wants to see developed in their employees. Mentoring can take many forms. Here an employee meets informally with her manager to share information about her job.

development budgets. The figures ranged from a high of $1142 on average to train employees in oil and gas firms to a low of $285 per worker in the education sector. Manufacturing firms averaged about $715 per worker.[35] Can these organizations draw from our discussion of learning in order to improve the effectiveness of their training programs? Certainly.

Social-learning theory offers such a guide. It tells us that training should offer a model to grab the trainee's attention; provide motivational properties; help the trainee to file away what he or she has learned for later use; provide opportunities to practise new behaviours; offer positive rewards for accomplishments; and, if the training has taken place off the job, allow the trainee some opportunity to transfer what he or she has learned to the job.

CREATING MENTORING PROGRAMS It's the unusual senior manager who, early in his or her career, didn't have an older, more experienced mentor higher up in the organization. This mentor took the protégé under his or her wing and provided advice and guidance on how to survive and get ahead in the organization. Mentoring, of course, is not limited to the managerial ranks. Union apprenticeship programs, for example, do the same thing by preparing individuals to move from unskilled apprentice status to that of skilled trade worker. A young electrician apprentice typically works under an experienced electrician for several years to develop the full range of skills necessary to execute his or her job effectively.

A successful mentoring program will be built on modelling concepts from social-learning theory. That is, a mentor's impact comes from more than merely what he or she explicitly tells a protégé. Mentors are role models. Protégés learn to convey the attitudes and behaviours that the organization wants by emulating the traits and actions of their mentors. They observe and then imitate. Top managers who are concerned with developing employees who will fit into the organization and with preparing young managerial talent for greater responsibilities should give careful attention to who takes on mentoring roles. The creating of formal mentoring programs—in which young individuals are officially assigned a mentor—allows senior ex-

3M uses learning theory in designing off-the job training programs. Employees at 3M's medical and surgical products plant visit the operating rooms of local hospitals to watch how doctors and nurses use the surgical tapes, prep solutions, and other products the employees make. From this interaction with customers, employees learn how important their jobs are in delivering high-quality products that completely satisfy customers.

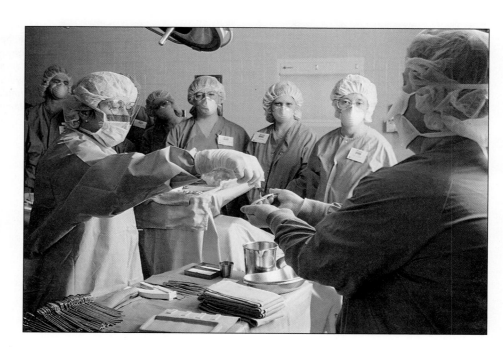

ecutives to manage the process and increases the likelihood that protégés will be moulded the way top management desires.

self-management
Learning techniques that allow individuals to manage their own behaviour so that less external management control is necessary.

SELF-MANAGEMENT   Organizational applications of learning concepts are not restricted to managing the behaviour of others. These concepts can also be used to allow individuals to manage their own behaviour and, in so doing, reduce the need for managerial control. This is called **self-management**.[36]

Self-management requires an individual to deliberately manipulate stimuli, internal processes, and responses to achieve personal behavioural outcomes. The basic processes involve observing one's own behaviour, comparing the behaviour with a standard, and rewarding oneself if the behaviour meets the standard.

So how might self-management be applied? Here's an illustration. A group of government-employed blue-collar employees received eight hours of training in which they were taught self-management skills.[37] They were then shown how the skills could be used for improving job attendance. They were instructed on how to set specific goals for job attendance, both short-term and intermediate-term. They learned how to write a behavioural contract with themselves and identify self-chosen reinforcers. Finally, they learned the importance of self-monitoring their attendance behaviour and administering incentives when they achieved their goals. The net result for these participants was a significant improvement in job attendance.

HR IMPLICATIONS

Training Programs

One of the responsibilities of the human resources department in many organizations is to develop training programs to assist employees with continuous learning. Below we identify some of the common methods of training and how to adapt these programs to employee learning styles.

Training Methods

Most training takes place on the job. This preference can be attributed to the simplicity and, usually, lower cost of on-the-job training methods. However, on-the-job training can disrupt the workplace and result in an increase in errors as learning proceeds. Also, some skill training is too complex to learn on the job. In such cases, it should take place outside the work setting.[1]

On-the-job training   Popular on-the-job training methods include job rotation and understudy assignments. *Job rotation* involves lateral transfers that enable employees to work at different jobs. Employees get to learn a wide variety of jobs and gain increased insight into the interdependency between jobs and a wider perspective on organizational activities. (We discuss job rotation in greater detail in Chapter 15.) New employees frequently learn their jobs by understudying a seasoned veteran. In the trades, this is usually called an *apprenticeship*. In white-collar jobs, it is called a *coaching*, or *mentor*, relationship. In each, the understudy works under the observation of an experienced worker, who acts as a model whom the understudy attempts to emulate.

Both job rotation and understudy assignments apply to the learning of technical skills. Interpersonal and problem-solving skills are acquired more effectively by training that takes place off the job.

Off-the-job training   There are a number of off-the-job training methods that managers may want to make available to employees. The more popular ones are classroom lectures, videos, and simulation exercises. *Classroom lectures* are well suited for conveying specific information. They can be used effectively for developing technical and problem-solving skills. *Videos* can also be used to explicitly demonstrate technical skills that are not easily presented by other methods. Interpersonal

and problem-solving skills may be best learned through *simulation exercises* such as case analyses, experiential exercises, role playing, and group interaction sessions. Complex computer models, such as those used by airlines in the training of pilots, are another kind of simulation exercise, which in this case is used to teach technical skills. So, too, is *vestibule training*, in which employees learn their jobs on the same equipment they will be using, only the training is conducted away from the actual work floor. Exhibit 2-9 describes the results from a survey of off-the-job instructional methods used for employee training.

Off-the-job training can rely on outside consultants, local community college or trade school faculty, or in-house personnel. Hongkong Bank of Canada began sending employees on five-day Outward Bound courses in 1989. Regina-based steel company Ipsco Inc. pays the tuition costs for some of its employees enrolled in MBA and other education programs.

Some firms create their own teaching facilities. Most of you are probably familiar with the fact that McDonald's has been training thousands of its managers and future managers since 1961 at its Hamburger University.[2] The heart of Hamburger U's curriculum is a two-week program that com-

bines operations enhancement, equipment management, and interpersonal skills training for restaurant managers and franchisees. Thousands of CIBC managers have been trained at CIBC's Leadership Centre in King City, north of Toronto. Managers attend week-long programs to talk about leadership and develop leadership skills.

Individualize Training to Fit the Employee's Learning Style

The way that you process, internalize, and remember new and difficult material isn't necessarily the same way that I do. This fact means that effective training should be individualized to reflect the learning style of the employee.[3]

Some examples of different learning styles include reading, watching, listening, and participating. Some people absorb information better when they read about it. They're the kind of people who can learn to use computers by sitting in their study and reading manuals. Some people learn best by observation. They watch others and then emulate the behaviours they've seen. Such people can watch someone use a computer for a while, then copy what they've seen. Listeners rely heavily on their auditory senses to absorb information. They would prefer to learn how to use a computer by lis-

---

Exhibit 2-9
Popularity Among Instructional Methods

Method	Percentage
Percentage of organizations using these methods for employee training	
Videotapes	95
Lectures	93
One-on-one instruction	76
Role plays	63
Games	58
Computer-based training	58
Audiotapes	54
Self-assessment/self-testing instruments	53
Case studies	52

Based on a national survey of U.S. companies with at least 100 employees.

tening to an audiotape. People who prefer a participating style learn by doing. They want to sit down, turn on the computer, and gain hands-on experience by practising.

You can translate these styles into different learning methods. To maximize learning, readers should be given books or other reading material to review; watchers should get the opportunity to observe individuals modelling the new skills either in person or on video; listeners will benefit from hearing lectures or audiotapes; and participants will benefit most from experiential opportunities where they can simulate and practise the new skills.

These different learning styles are obviously not mutually exclusive. In fact, good teachers recognize that their students learn differently and, therefore, provide multiple learning methods. They assign readings before class; give lectures; use visual aids to illustrate concepts; and have students participate in group projects, case analyses, role plays, and experiential learning exercises. If you know the preferred style of an employee, you can design his or her training program to optimize this preference. If you don't have that information, it's probably best to design the program to use a variety of learning styles. Overreliance on a single style places individuals who don't learn well from that style at a disadvantage.

Sources:

[1] For an extended discussion of on-the-job and off-the-job training methods, see D. DeCenzo and S.P. Robbins, *Human Resources Management*, 5th ed. (New York: Wiley 1996), pp. 243–45.

[2] D. Schaaf, "Inside Hamburger University," *Training*, December 1994, pp. 18–24.

[3] D.A. Kolb, "Management and the Learning Process," *California Management Review*, Spring 1976, pp. 21–31; and B. Kilipczak "Different Strokes: Learning Styles in the Classroom," *Training*, March 1995, pp. 43–48.

Summary and Implications

For the Workplace

As we enter the 21st century, the demands of technology and globalization require the development of new skills and new attitudes for the workplace. Managers and employees are asked to become partners in these new organizations, and to take responsibility for acquiring the skills and knowledge needed to get ahead.

Not only do individuals learn by themselves, but some organizations have also adapted themselves to become learning organizations. Learning organizations also encourage organizational members to look beyond today to prepare for the future, both for themselves and the organization. In the learning organization, both managers and learners become responsible for learning and working together to develop knowledge.

Some organizations have established their own corporate universities to reinforce the notion of continuous learning for employees at all levels. This sends a strong signal throughout the organization that learning is important. Positive reinforcement is a powerful tool for modifying behaviour. By identifying and rewarding performance-enhancing behaviours, management increases the likelihood that these behaviours will be repeated.

The demands of organizations in the future require that individuals develop a repertoire of skills that will ensure their competency in the workplace, and provide the opportunity to be more entrepreneurial. The chapter highlighted a variety of skills that one might wish to acquire.

For You as an Individual

Working in organizations that are undergoing the changes happening in today's society requires a flexibility that may not have been necessary for employees when they were hired 20 years ago. Today, employees are being

asked to work more in teams, and to learn more about technology, including computers.

The chapter outlines a variety of skills necessary to meet the challenges of the workplace of the future. One thing you might want to do is evaluate the skills you have and then work toward acquiring skills that you consider are lacking. The skills we presented work well both in someone else's company, and in your own, should you ever decide to become an entrepreneur.

We also discussed learning in this chapter. Some people mistakenly believe that learning is only supposed to happen when they're "in school." Or you might think that if something is unlikely to be on a test, then it is not necessary to learn it. This chapter encourages you to think about learning as an ongoing process, and even suggests that you think about learning things simply for the sake of learning. In this chapter's OB in the News feature, we saw the example of Ron and Marie Jang who learned about wood mouldings to restore their home, and in the process ended up starting their own business. This might suggest that we don't always know the direction in which learning will take us.

ROADMAP REMINDER

In the previous chapter we introduced you to the changes that are occurring on the Canadian workplace, and indicated why a knowledge of organizational behaviour might help you better understand those changes. In this chapter we developed the idea that managers and employees need a variety of skills in order to be more effective members of work organizations. We then discussed the importance of learning, for both the individual and the organization. In the next chapter, we introduce the concepts of perception and personality as a reminder that we work together with others, and what we bring as individuals to the workplace affects those around us.

For Review

1. What is the competing values framework?
2. What skills are required by individuals in order to be more flexible in the workplace?
3. Contrast classical conditioning, operant conditioning, and social learning.
4. Describe the four types of intermittent reinforcers.
5. If you had to take disciplinary action against an employee, how, specifically, would you do it?
6. What is the knowledge development process of organizational learning?
7. Describe the adaptive learning process for organizational learning.
8. What are the roadblocks to organizational learning?
9. How might employees actually learn unethical behaviour on their jobs?

For Discussion

1. Learning theory can be used to explain behaviour and to control behaviour. Can you distinguish between the two objectives? Can you give any ethical or moral arguments why managers should not seek

control over others' behaviour? How valid do you think these arguments are?

2. What have you learned about "learning" that could help you to explain the behaviour of students in a classroom if: (a) The instructor gives only one test—a final examination at the end of the course? (b) The instructor gives four exams during the term, all of which are announced on the first day of class? (c) The student's grade is based on the results of numerous exams, none of which is announced by the instructor in advance?

LEARNING ABOUT YOURSELF EXERCISE

What's Your Learning Style?

For each of the following, circle the number that is most true for you.

1. When I learn a subject, I like to learn the theory first and then work on concrete applications; or do you prefer to work on concrete applications first and then learn the theory behind what you have done?

1	2	3	4	5

Theory First   Applications First

2. When I learn a subject, I like to get the "big picture" first and then learn specific details; I like to see how what I am learning relates to what I have already learned; or do you prefer to learn the details first and then see how they are related to material you already know or have learned?

1	2	3	4	5

Big Picture First   Details First

3. I expect study group members to use group time to: (1) teach each other the "nitty-gritty" details and review problems; (2) ask each other questions to prepare for an exam; or (3) do everything that is necessary.

1	2	3

4. In drawing conclusions about a problem or case, I first seek facts and hard data before reaching a conclusion; or do you reach a conclusion and then seek facts that support your idea?

1	2	3	4	5

Data Then Conclusions   Conclusions Then Data

5. In drawing conclusions about a problem or case, I prefer to seek additional options and to postpone decision-making as long as possible; or do you prefer to seek closure early and make a decision?

1	2	3	4	5

Seek Additional Options   Seek Early Closure

6. When I learn a subject I am satisfied to know the *what* of the subject; or do you also want to know the *why* of things?

1	2	3	4	5

What Only   What and Why

7. When confronted with a difficult task, I am willing to spend whatever time it takes to comprehend it; or do you set time limits, and if you haven't mastered the material you go on to another subject?

1	2	3	4	5
Whatever Time it Takes				Set Time Limits

8. In order for me to know a subject I must have "hands-on" experience.

1	2	3	4	5
Must Have Hands On				Hands On Unnecessary

9. When I learn a subject, I prefer that the instructor lays out material in a logical fashion; or do you prefer not to be told everything so that you have the opportunity to discover the ideas for yourself?

1	2	3	4	5
Want It All Laid Out			Want Opportunity for Discovery	

10. When I work in a team, how important is group harmony to me? It is: (1) somewhat important; (2) important; or (3) very important.

1	2	3

11. How true of you is the following quotation: "I hear and I forget; I see and I remember; I do and then I learn"?

1	2	3	4	5
Very Accurate				Not Accurate At All

12. Who, or what, is your most important learning resource?

(1) The instructor   (2) The book   (3) Fellow students

13. Is learning primarily an intellectual or a social activity?

1	2	3
Intellectual		Social

Turn to page 697 for scoring directions and key.

Source: This exercise is adapted from W.A. Kahn, "An Exercise of Authority," *Organizational Behaviour Teaching Review*, vol. XIV, no. 2, 1989–90, pp. 28–42. Reprinted with permission.

WORKING WITH OTHERS EXERCISE

Positive and Negative Reinforcement

This 10-step exercise takes approximately 20 minutes.

Exercise Overview (Steps 1–4)

1. Two volunteers are selected to receive reinforcement from the class while performing a particular task. The volunteers leave the room.
2. The instructor identifies an object for the student volunteers to locate when they return to the room. (The object should be unobstructive but clearly visible to the class. Examples that have worked well include a small triangular piece of paper that was left behind when a notice was torn off a classroom bulletin board, a smudge on the chalkboard, and a chip in the plaster of a classroom wall.)
3. The instructor specifies the reinforcement contingencies that will be in effect when the volunteers return to the room. For negative reinforcement, students

should hiss and boo when the first volunteer is moving away from the object. For positive reinforcement, they should cheer and applaud when the second volunteer is getting closer to the object.

4. The instructor should assign a student to keep a record of the time it takes each of the volunteers to locate the object.

Volunteer 1 (Steps 5 and 6)

5. Volunteer 1 is brought back into the room and is told, "Your task is to locate and touch a particular object in the room and the class has agreed to help you. You can't use words or ask questions. Begin."

6. Volunteer 1 continues to look for the object until it is found, while the class assists by giving negative reinforcement.

Volunteer 2 (Steps 7 and 8)

7. Volunteer 2 is brought back into the room and is told, "Your task is to locate and touch a particular object in the room and the class has agreed to help you. You can't use words or ask questions. Begin."

8. Volunteer 2 continues to look for the object until it is found, while the class assists by giving positive reinforcement.

Class Review (Steps 9 and 10)

9. The timekeeper will present the results on how long it took each volunteer to find the object.

10. The class will discuss:

    a. What was the difference in behaviour of the two volunteers?

    b. What are the implications of this exercise to reinforcement schedules in organizations?

Source: Based on an exercise developed by Larry Michaelson of the University of Oklahoma. Used with permission.

CASE INCIDENT

The Troubles of Bata Shoes

In 1995, Don Mills, Ontario-based Bata Shoe Company seemed poised on the verge of rising from a recent history of poor performance.

Thomas Bata, co-owner of the firm, had appointed a non-family member as chief executive. The new CEO, Stan Heath, hired seven other outside executives. The belief was that the new leadership would turn the company around, bringing it back into a position of dominance. Within about 15 months, however, all but one of the outside senior executives were gone, including Heath, mainly because Tom Bata and his wife Sonja continued to maintain a strong hold over the company.

Moreover, Peter Legg, one of the outside managers brought in with Heath, filed a lawsuit against Bata in 1996, alleging that the Bata family "continually stymied efforts by the recently ousted management to move the company in a fresh direction." Legg also claims Tom Bata "was desirous and insistent on continuing to control and direct the day-to-day operations of Bata."

Bata Shoe Co., once dominant in Canada, is now fifth in shoe stores, just slightly ahead of Wal-Mart. So what happened? In terms of strategy, Bata does all of its own manufacturing, retailing and brand management on a large scale, unlike any other footwear company. It has continued to do what it has been doing for many years, without considering changes in both the marketplace and global forces.

Sonya and Tom Bata oversee most of the decisions made for the company, which is possible because the Bata family owns the company. Bata Shoes currently has an acting CEO and an "executive chairman" of global holdings, but no robust leadership. It seems to be resisting fundamental change. As *Report on Business* writer Kenneth Kidd notes, "Two opposing sets of values mingle uneasily—the aggressive, combative nature of the business world, versus the family's traditional nurturing role of protecting its weakest members."

Bata operates in an environment that is extremely competitive. Between 1987 and 1993, sales of shoes in Canada fell four percent, while the number of shoe shops fell to less than 2000 from 2600. Both Montreal-based Aldo Group Inc. and Toronto-based Roots have been successful under these conditions. Each has identified strategies that work in a competitive environment. Bata's leadership seems less able to make such a transition.

Questions

1. Given the facts of the case, does Bata appear to be acting as a learning organization?

2. What might be some of the major roadblocks to organizational learning for Bata?

3. How would you characterize Bata, using the competing values framework?

Source: K. Kidd, "Misfit: Why the Once-Dominant Bata Empire No Longer Measures Up Amid the Roots and Reeboks of Today," *Report on Business*, November, 1997, pp. 20–26; "Bata Hires Consultants to Undertake Sweeping Review," *Financial Post Daily*, August 21, 1996, p. 5.

Keeping Them

What kind of leadership is necessary in today's job market when unemployment is down and job creation is up? And when employees are starting to have their choice of jobs?

Management is finding that today's employees have no sense of loyalty and that they have more opportunities than in recent years. Employees feel cynical about the organizations in which they work, and, as a result, they are leaving their jobs.

Employees are leaving because they are being oversupervised; companies are not investing in training and development that would help employees acquire valuable skills; and they are not given enough flexibility in their jobs and hours. While the characteristics of the workplace are not new, employees are responding differently, and management must also respond differently.

Employees are looking for challenging work, and companies that provide such a work environment are more likely to keep their employees. At LGS Group Inc., for instance, four full-time career managers are employed to help workers stay on a learning curve about their careers. Employees discuss with the career managers the types of skills they need to learn to get ahead; they get a better understanding of the opportunities that are available; and they let their career managers know more about what they are looking for in their work. This helps LGS better understand how to allocate employees to their jobs.

Today's managers have an expanded set of roles to fulfil in dealing with the demands of today's employees. Employees want to be able to make some of their own decisions, and possibly determine their work hours. Managers are put in the position of needing to rethink their roles in today's changing workplace.

Questions

1. What does this case say about managing and leading in the 21st century?

2. What roles of management identified in the chapter might be important in addressing the problem of employee turnover?

3. How might creating a learning environment within the organization help reduce employee turnover?

Source: Based on "Keeping Them," *Venture 682*; aired March 24, 1998.

POINT

Managing Well Won't Overcome Economic Problems

Organizational behaviour researchers tell us that managing well can make a difference, but what's a manager to do in poor economic times? Business bankruptcies happen at higher rates when there are troubling economic times. For instance, in 1993, about 3700 incorporated businesses failed in Canada. And between 1980 and 1995 the incidence of bankruptcies increased from 10 failures per 1000 businesses to 14 failures per 1000 businesses.

Businesses in Canada go bankrupt because of external factors beyond their control. In a 1996 Statistics Canada study of bankrupt firms, the top three external causes of bankruptcy were economic downturn; increases in competition; and the loss of key customers. The study also showed that once a firm started to run into difficulties, there was little action management could take to turn the situation around. In other words, the economic climate created a serious impediment for managers of firms with financial difficulties.

Decreases in the bankruptcy rate in early 1998, a period of significant growth in the Canadian economy, give further evidence of how important the economic climate is in preventing bankruptcies. In January 1998, there were only 856 business failures from bankruptcy, down 20.2 percent from January 1997, when there were 1073 failures. Tim O'Neill, the Bank of Montreal's chief economist, identifies the strong link between the economy and bankruptcies: "Judging from our economic outlook for Canada, the incidence of consumer and business bankruptcies should decline in the coming years. Solid economic growth, low inflation and recent amendments to the *Bankruptcy and Insolvency Act* will all contribute to this trend."

Economic problems also cause bankruptcies in other countries besides Canada. Japan's bankruptcy rate increased 10.9 percent from 1996 to 1997, and even higher rates of bankruptcy were forecast for 1998. Given the current turmoil in Asian markets, this provides further evidence that the economy is a large factor in bankruptcy occurrences. And managers may not be able to do much about the economy. ■

Sources: "Business Bankruptcy in Canada, 1996," *Statistics Canada Daily*, December 11, 1997; A. Toulin, "January Bankruptcies Decline by 20%," *Financial Post*, March 28/30, 1998, p. 10; "Japan's Bankruptcy Liabilities Set Record in 1997," *Financial Post Daily*, January 20, 1998, p. 17.

counterPOINT

Managing Well Makes a Big Difference

Economic downturns might have some relationship to bankruptcy rates, but a 1997 study by Statistics Canada claims that "firms go bankrupt in Canada primarily because their managers lack the experience, know-how, or vision to run their businesses." In other words, firms falter not because of bad economic conditions, but because managers don't know how to manage their businesses.

According to the study, managers who face bankruptcy tend to have poor management skills overall, they don't have enough knowledge about how to manage their businesses, and they don't ask for help from outside advisors soon enough.

Brien Gray, vice-president of the Canadian Federation of Independent Business, believes that Statistics Canada's report is too quick to condemn managers, failing to take into account external factors. For example, he finds that banks are more likely to help the big companies (such as Eaton's) and less likely to help smaller companies in financial trouble. However, the Statistics Canada report does not support Gray's claim. In particular, while bankrupt firms did encounter roadblocks from financial institutions, usually this occurred because of internal management problems. Firms that couldn't get bank financing also could not raise enough equity through various other options.

The study found that small, young firms were most likely to be at financial risk. More than half of

the firms that fail in the first 10 years of life do so in the first two years. Often the managers of these younger firms have little outside managerial experience. Thus, these newer firms suffered more because the managers did not have the experience and knowledge needed to run a business.

The report identified the three most important internal factors related to business failure as shortcomings in (1) general management skills, (2) financial planning and management, and (3) marketing capabilities. These internal factors are so prevalent in young firms that most bankruptcies occurred because of them, according to the Statistics Canada study. Even when companies suffered bankruptcies due to external factors such as economic downturn, managerial shortcomings such as lack of vision, initiative, flexibility, and adaptability compounded the problem.

The Statistics Canada study illustrates what organizational behaviour researchers have known all along: managing well makes a difference. And in these changing times, having vision, initiative, flexibility, and adaptability are all important skills. These skills were also highlighted in the Competing Values Framework for leadership, presented in this chapter (see Exhibit 2-2). ■

Sources: "Business Bankruptcy in Canada, 1996," *Statistics Canada Daily*, December 11, 1997; T. Parvanova, "Managers to Blame for Business Bankruptcies," *Canadian Press Newswire*, December 11, 1997.

CHAPTER 3

Perception and Personality

LEARNING OBJECTIVES

After studying this chapter, you should be able to

- Explain how two people can see the same thing and interpret it differently

- List the three determinants of attribution

- Describe how shortcuts can assist in or distort our judgment of others

- Explain the factors that determine an individual's personality

- Describe the impact of job typology on the personality—job performance relationship

When people describe the personality of Magna International Chairman Frank Stronach, they typically use such words as "smart-alec," obnoxious, canny, crazy, and arrogant.[1] Stronach provides an excellent illustration of how an individual's personality shapes his or her behaviour.

Frank Stronach was born in Weiz, Austria in 1932, the son of a Communist factory worker. He moved to Canada at the age of 22, with $200 in his pocket, plus his expertise as a tool-and-die maker. Within two years he had scraped together enough money to start Multimatic Investments Ltd., a small automotive tool-and-die shop located in the east end of the Toronto. In the 45 years since then, he has built that shop into Magna—an auto-parts giant that employs 28 000 workers and has annual sales in excess of $6 billion dollars. In 1996, he was paid $26.5 million for running Magna.

Stronach personifies the driven executive in terms of his various business acquisitions over the years. He has also taken a number of risks, some of which have resulted in huge failure. In 1990, for example, Magna reported a loss of $224.2 million, incredible by almost any standard. But Stronach turned the company around, got back to its roots, and between 1990 and 1994 share prices rose from $2.25 to $66⅞. In October 1997, prices had risen to their highest yet, $101.50.

Recently Stronach has been concentrating more of his business in Austria. He feels he isn't appreciated in Canada. He likes Europe because "he enjoys being treated like royalty by city officials hungry for investment." In Canada, he says, "It doesn't matter what I did, I always got beaten up by the press. I've created a lot of jobs, but for some reason if you're successful here, everyone dumps on you." Stronach does receive a lot of criticism, partly because he's a risk-taker.

Frank Stronach's assertiveness and risk-seeking personality characteristics were in place long before he started Magna. But they play an important role in shaping his actions. His perception of how he's viewed in Canada has also affected his actions. *All* our behaviour is somewhat shaped by our perceptions, personalities, and experiences. In this chapter, we consider the role that perception plays in affecting the way we see the world and the people around us. We also consider how personality characteristics affect our attitudes toward people and situations. ■

What Is Perception, and Why Is It Important?

perception
A process by which individuals organize and interpret their sensory impressions in order to give meaning to their environment.

Perception can be defined as a process by which individuals organize and interpret their sensory impressions in order to give meaning to their environment. However, what one perceives can be substantially different from objective reality. It need not be, but there is often disagreement. For example, it is possible that all employees in a firm may view it as a great place to work—favourable working conditions, interesting job assignments, good pay, an understanding and responsible management—but, as most of us know, it is very unusual to find such agreement.

Why is perception important in the study of OB? Simply because people's behaviour is based on their perception of what reality is, not on reality itself. *The world as it is perceived is the world that is behaviourally important.*

Factors Influencing Perception

How do we explain that individuals may look at the same thing, yet perceive it differently? A number of factors operate to shape and sometimes distort perception. These factors can reside in the *perceiver*, in the object or *target* being perceived, or in the context of the *situation* in which the perception is made. This chapter's Working With Others exercise helps to give you an understanding of the role of perception in evaluating others.

The Perceiver

When an individual looks at a target and attempts to interpret what he or she sees, that interpretation is heavily influenced by personal characteristics of the individual perceiver. Have you ever bought a new car and then suddenly noticed a large number of cars like yours on the road? It's unlikely that the number of such cars suddenly increased. Rather, your own purchase has influenced your perception so that you are now more likely to notice them. This is an example of how factors related to the perceiver influence what he or she perceives.

A variety of factors affect our perception of an event. Our attitudes and motives, interests, and past experiences all shape the way we perceive an event. For instance, suppose you had a bad experience last term in a large class where students were not able to participate, and you would have preferred to interact more with the instructor and other students. This term, upon learning that you have been assigned to the largest section of a new course, you would be already dreading the experience because your perception is that you won't be able to participate enough in class. In this case, your attitude combined with your previous experience make it difficult to be open-minded about the new experience.

There are other ways that perceptions affect interpretations of the world around us. For example, bosses who like to see their employees do well will positively interpret employees' efforts to do outstanding work, but bosses who are insecure will feel threatened by such efforts and interpret them negatively. It is often the case that we interpret others' behaviours based on our knowledge of our own behaviour. Thus people who are devious are prone to view others as also devious.

Finally, *expectations* can distort your perceptions in that you will see what you expect to see. For example, if you expect police officers to be au-

Diversity advocate Ernest Drew, CEO of Hoechst Celanese, set a goal to have at least 34 percent representation of women and minorities at all levels of his company by 2001. To influence managers' perceptions of women and minorities, Drew requires that his top 26 officers join two organizations in which they are a minority. Drew put the policy in place to help managers break out of their comfort zones and experience what it's like to be a minority so they learn "that all people are similar." Drew is a board member of black Hampton University and of SER-Jobs for Progress, a Hispanic association. He's shown here visiting with Hampton students.

Hoechst Celanese
http://www.hcc.com

thoritarian, young people to be unambitious, human resources directors to "like people," or individuals holding public office to be unscrupulous, you may perceive them as such regardless of their actual traits.

The Target

Characteristics of the target that is being observed can affect what is perceived. Loud people are more likely to be noticed in a group than are quiet ones. So, too, are extremely attractive or unattractive individuals. Motion, sounds, size, and other attributes of a target shape the way we see it.

Because targets are not looked at in isolation, the relationship of a target to its background influences perception, as does our tendency to group close things and similar things together.

What we see is dependent on how we separate a figure from its general background. For instance, what you see as you read this sentence is black letters on a white page. You do not see funny-shaped patches of black and white because you recognize these shapes and organize the black shapes against the white background. Exhibit 3-1 dramatizes this effect. The object on the left may at first look like a yellow vase. However, if yellow is taken as the background, we see two purple profiles. At first observation, the group of objects on the right appears to be some purple modular figures against a yellow background. Closer inspection will reveal the word *FLY* once the background is defined as purple.

Objects that are close to each other will tend to be perceived together rather than separately. As a result of physical or time proximity, we often put together objects or events that are unrelated. Employees in a particular department are seen as a group. If two people in a four-member department suddenly resign, we tend to assume that their departures were related when, in fact, they may be totally unrelated. Timing may also imply dependence when, for example, a new sales manager is assigned to a territory and, soon after, sales in that territory skyrocket. The assignment of the new sales manager and the increase in sales may not be related—the increase may be due

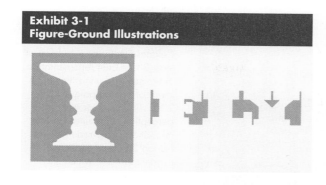

**Exhibit 3-1
Figure-Ground Illustrations**

to the introduction of a new product line or to one of many other reasons—but there is a tendency to perceive the two occurrences as related.

Persons, objects, or events that are similar to each other also tend to be grouped together. The greater the similarity, the greater the probability that we will tend to perceive them as a common group. People who are female, or black, or members of any other clearly distinguishable group, will tend to be perceived as similar not only in physical terms but in other, unrelated characteristics as well.

The Situation

The context in which we see objects or events is important. Elements in the surrounding environment influence our perceptions. You are more likely to notice your subordinates goofing off if your boss from the head office happens to be in town. Your subordinates may be acting quite "normally"; however, it is the situation that affects your perception. The time at which an object or event is seen can influence attention, as can location, light, heat, or any number of situational factors. Exhibit 3-2 summarizes the factors influencing perception.

Perception and Judgment: Attribution Theory

When we observe people, we attempt to develop explanations of why they behave in certain ways. Our perception and judgment of a person's actions, therefore, will be significantly influenced by the assumptions we make about that person's internal state.

attribution theory
When individuals observe behaviour, they attempt to determine whether it is internally or externally caused.

Attribution theory has been proposed to develop explanations of the ways in which we judge people differently, depending on what meaning we attribute to a given behaviour.[2] Basically, the theory suggests that when we observe an individual's behaviour, we attempt to determine whether it was internally or externally caused. That determination, however, depends largely on three factors: (1) distinctiveness, (2) consensus, and (3) consistency. First, let's clarify the differences between internal and external causation and then we will elaborate on each of the three determining factors.

Internally caused behaviours are those that are believed to be under the personal control of the individual. *Externally* caused behaviour is seen as resulting from outside causes; that is, the person is seen as having been forced into the behaviour by the situation. For example, if one of your employees is late for work, you might attribute his lateness to his partying into the wee hours of the morning and then oversleeping. This would be an internal attribution. But if you attribute his arriving late to a major automobile accident that tied up traffic on the road that this employee regularly uses, then you would be making an external attribution.

Distinctiveness refers to whether an individual displays different behaviours in different situations. Is the employee who arrives late today also the source of complaints by co-workers for "goofing off"? What we want to know is whether this behaviour is unusual. If it is, the observer is likely to give the behaviour an external attribution. If this action is not unusual, it will probably be judged as internal.

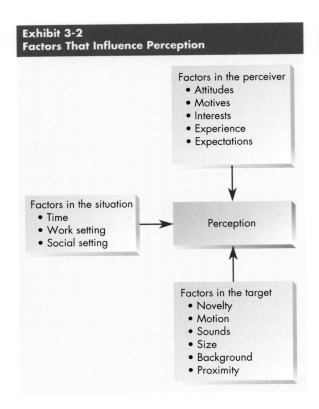

Exhibit 3-2
Factors That Influence Perception

Factors in the perceiver
• Attitudes
• Motives
• Interests
• Experience
• Expectations

Factors in the situation
• Time
• Work setting
• Social setting

Perception

Factors in the target
• Novelty
• Motion
• Sounds
• Size
• Background
• Proximity

If everyone who is faced with a similar situation responds in the same way, we can say the behaviour shows *consensus*. Our late employee's behaviour would meet this criterion if all employees who took the same route to work were also late. From an attribution perspective, if consensus is high, you would be expected to give an external attribution to the employee's tardiness, whereas if other employees who took the same route made it to work on time, your conclusion as to causation would be internal.

Finally, an observer looks for *consistency* in a person's actions. Does the person respond the same way over time? Arriving 10 minutes late for work is not perceived in the same way for the employee for whom it is an unusual case (she hasn't been late for several months) as it is for the employee for whom it is part of a routine pattern (he is regularly late two or three times a week). The more consistent the behaviour, the more likely the observer is to attribute it to internal causes.

Exhibit 3-3 summarizes the key elements in attribution theory. It would tell us, for instance, that if your employee—Kim Randolph—generally performs at about the same level on other related tasks as she does on her current task (low distinctiveness), if other employees frequently perform differently—better or worse—than Kim does on that current task (low consensus), and if Kim's performance on this current task is consistent over time (high consistency), you or anyone else who is judging Kim's work is likely to hold her primarily responsible for her task performance (internal attribution).

One of the more interesting findings from attribution theory is that there are errors or biases that distort attributions. For instance, there is substantial evidence that when we make judgments about the behaviour of other people, we tend to underestimate the influence of external factors and overestimate the influence of internal or personal factors.[3] This is called the **fundamental attribution error** and can explain why a sales manager is prone to attribute the poor performance of his or her sales agents to laziness rather than to the innovative product line introduced by a competitor. There is also a tendency for individuals to attribute their own successes to internal factors such as ability or effort while putting the blame for failure on external factors such as luck. This is called the **self-serving bias** and suggests that feedback provided to employees in performance reviews will be predictably distorted by recipients depending on whether it is positive or negative.

Are these errors or biases that distort attributions universal across different cultures? We can't answer that question definitively, but there is some preliminary evidence that indicates cultural differences. For instance, a study of Korean managers found that, contrary to the self-serving bias, they tended to accept responsibility for group failure "because I was not a capable leader" instead of attributing it to group members.[4] There have been enough suicides committed by Japanese executives who feel responsible for the problems of their companies to indicate that many Japanese executives also do not use the "self-serving" bias. In just the first half of 1998, high-profile suicides in Japan included a central banker, three top finance ministry

fundamental attribution error
The tendency to underestimate the influence of external factors and overestimate the influence of internal factors when making judgments about the behaviour of others.

self-serving bias
The tendency for individuals to attribute their own successes to internal factors while putting the blame for failures on external factors.

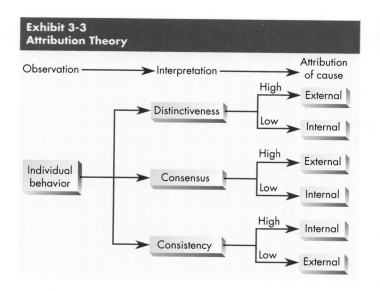

**Exhibit 3-3
Attribution Theory**

bureaucrats, a politician, and scores of executives. Toru Sekiya, who runs a psychiatric clinic in suburban Tokyo, explains these suicides as follows: "A lot of people used to die for the emperor. Now they die for the company." Professor Toyoma Fuse, from York University, notes that it is rarely the president of the company who commits suicide, however. Usually it is a subordinate; "caught in between the top brass and the workers, he really has to account for both."[5]

Attribution theory was developed largely in the United States on the basis of experiments with Americans, but there is no particular reason to believe it would not apply in Canada. However, the Korean study as well as evidence from Japan suggests caution in making attribution theory predictions outside the United States, especially in countries with strong collectivist traditions such as Spain, Portugal, and some of the eastern European countries.

Frequently Used Shortcuts in Judging Others

We use a number of shortcuts when we judge others. Perceiving and interpreting what others do is burdensome. As a result, individuals develop techniques for making the task more manageable. These techniques are frequently valuable—they allow us to make accurate perceptions rapidly and provide valid data for making predictions. However, they are not foolproof. They can and do get us into trouble. An understanding of these shortcuts can be helpful toward recognizing when they can result in significant distortions.

selective perception
People selectively interpret what they see based on their interests, background, experience, and attitudes.

SELECTIVE PERCEPTION Any characteristic that makes a person, object, or event stand out will increase the probability that it will be perceived. Why? Because it is impossible for us to assimilate everything we see—only certain stimuli can be taken in. This tendency explains why, as we noted earlier, you are more likely to notice cars like your own or why some people may be reprimanded by their boss for doing something that, when done by another employee, goes unnoticed. Since we can't observe everything going on about us, we engage in **selective perception**. A classic example shows how vested interests can significantly influence which problems we see.

Dearborn and Simon performed a perceptual study in which 23 business executives read a comprehensive case describing the organization and activities of a steel company.[6] Six of the 23 executives were in the sales function, five in production, four in accounting, and eight in miscellaneous functions. Each manager was asked to write down the most important problem he found in the case. Eighty-three percent of the sales executives rated sales important; only 29 percent of the others did so. This, along with other results of the study, led the researchers to conclude that the participants perceived aspects of a situation that were specifically related to the activities and goals of the unit to which they were attached. A group's perception of organizational activities is selectively altered to align with the vested interests they represent. In other words, when the stimuli are ambiguous, as in the steel

company case, perception tends to be influenced more by an individual's base of interpretation (that is, attitudes, interests, and background) than by the stimulus itself.

But how does selectivity work as a shortcut in judging other people? Since we cannot assimilate all that we observe, we take in bits and pieces. But those bits and pieces are not chosen randomly; rather, they are selectively chosen according to our interests, background, experience, and attitudes. Selective perception allows us to "speed-read" others, but not without the risk of drawing an inaccurate picture. Because we see what we want to see, we can draw unwarranted conclusions from an ambiguous situation. If there is a rumour going around the office that your company's sales are down and that large layoffs may be imminent, a routine visit by a senior executive from headquarters might be interpreted as the first step in management's identification of people to be fired, when in reality such an action may be the furthest thing from the mind of the senior executive.

HALO EFFECT When we draw a general impression about an individual on the basis of a single characteristic, such as intelligence, sociability, or appearance, a **halo effect** is operating. This phenomenon frequently occurs when students appraise their instructor. Students may give prominence to a single trait such as enthusiasm and allow their entire evaluation to be tainted by how they judge the instructor on that one trait. Thus, an instructor may be quiet, assured, knowledgeable, and highly qualified, but if his or her presentation style lacks enthusiasm, those students would probably give the instructor a low rating.

halo effect
Drawing a general impression about an individual based on a single characteristic.

The reality of the halo effect was confirmed in a classic study in which subjects were given a list of traits such as intelligent, skillful, practical, industrious, determined, and warm and were asked to evaluate the person to whom those traits applied.[7] When those traits were used, the person was judged to be wise, humorous, popular, and imaginative. When the same list was modified—cold was substituted for warm—a completely different set of perceptions was obtained. Clearly, the subjects were allowing a single trait to influence their overall impression of the person being judged.

The propensity for the halo effect to operate is not random. Research suggests that it is likely to be most extreme when the traits to be perceived are ambiguous in behavioural terms, when the traits have moral overtones, and when the perceiver is judging traits with which he or she has had limited experience.[8]

CONTRAST EFFECTS There's an old adage among entertainers who perform in variety shows: Never follow an act that has children or animals in it. Why? The common belief is that audiences love children and animals so much that you will look bad in comparison. In a similar vein, Stephen Robbins, your Seattle-based author, remembers when he was a first-year university student and had to give a presentation in a speech class. He was scheduled to speak third that morning. After both of the first two speakers stammered, stumbled, and forgot their lines, he suddenly got a rush of confidence because he figured that even though his talk might not go too well, he'd probably get a pretty good grade. He was counting on the instructor's raising his evaluation after contrasting his speech with those that immediately preceded it.

contrast effects
A person's evaluation is affected by comparisons with other individuals recently encountered.

These two examples demonstrate how **contrast effects** can distort perceptions. We don't evaluate a person in isolation. Our reaction to one person is often influenced by other persons we have recently encountered.

An illustration of how contrast effects operate is an interview situation in which one sees a pool of job applicants. Distortions in any given candidate's evaluation can occur as a result of his or her place in the interview schedule. The candidate is likely to receive a more favourable evaluation if preceded by mediocre applicants and a less favourable evaluation if preceded by strong applicants.

PROJECTION It is easy to judge others if we assume that they are similar to us. For instance, if you want challenge and responsibility in your job, you assume that others want the same. Or, you are honest and trustworthy, so you take it for granted that other people are equally honest and trustworthy. This tendency to attribute one's own characteristics to other people—which is called **projection**—can distort perceptions made about others.

projection
Attributing one's own characteristics to other people.

People who engage in projection tend to perceive others according to what they themselves are like rather than according to what the person being observed is really like. When observing others who actually are like them, these observers are quite accurate—not because they are perceptive but because they always judge people as being similar to themselves. So when they finally do find someone who is like them, they are naturally correct. When managers engage in projection, they compromise their ability to respond to individual differences. They tend to see people as more homogeneous than they really are.

STEREOTYPING When we judge someone on the basis of our perception of the group to which he or she belongs, we are using the shortcut called **stereotyping**. According to a popular literary anecdote, F. Scott Fitzgerald engaged in stereotyping when he told Ernest Hemingway, "The rich are very different from you and me," implying that the wealthy have values and behaviour unlike regular people. Hemingway's reply, "Yes, they have more money," indicated that he refused to generalize characteristics of people on the basis of their wealth. Generalization, of course, is not without advantages. It is a means of simplifying a complex world, and it permits us to maintain consistency. It is less difficult to deal with an unmanageable number of stimuli if we use stereotypes. As an example, assume you are a sales manager looking to fill a sales position in your territory. You want to hire someone who is ambitious and hardworking and who can deal well with adversity. You've had good success in the past by hiring individuals who participated in athletics while at university. So you focus your search by looking for candidates who participated in university athletics. In so doing, you have cut down considerably on your search time. Furthermore, to the extent that athletes *are* ambitious, hardworking, and able to deal with adversity, the use of this stereotype can improve your decision-making. The problem, of course, is when we inaccurately stereotype.[9] All university athletes are *not necessarily* ambitious, hardworking, or good at dealing with adversity, just as all accountants are *not necessarily* quiet and introspective. Moreover, when we stereotype like this, we run the risk of overlooking highly qualified people who do not meet our stereotypes.

stereotyping
Judging someone on the basis of one's perception of the group to which that person belongs.

In organizations, we frequently hear comments that represent stereotypes based on gender, age, race, ethnicity, and even weight[10]: "Women won't relocate for a promotion"; "men aren't interested in child care"; "older workers can't learn new skills"; "Asian immigrants are hardworking and conscientious"; "overweight people lack self-discipline." From a percep-

tual standpoint, if people expect to see these stereotypes, that is what they will perceive, whether or not they are accurate.

Obviously, one of the problems of stereotypes is that they are widespread, despite the fact that they may not contain a shred of truth or that they may be irrelevant. Their being widespread may mean only that many people are making the same inaccurate perception on the basis of a false premise about a group.

Specific Applications in Organizations

People in organizations are always judging each other. For instance, in order to become an organizational member, a person typically goes through an employment interview. Interviewers make perceptual judgments during the interview, which then affect whether the individual is hired. Studies show that if negative information is exposed early in the interview, it tends to be more heavily weighted than if that same information comes out later.[11] When multiple interviewers are present, agreement among interviewers is often poor; that is, different interviewers see different things in the same candidate and thus arrive at different conclusions about the applicant. If the employment interview is an important input into the hiring decision—and it usually is—you should recognize that perceptual factors influence who is hired and eventually the quality of an organization's labour force.

Although the impact of performance evaluations on behaviour will be discussed fully in the HR Implications in Chapter 6, it should be pointed out here that an employee's performance appraisal is another example of something in the workplace that is very much dependent on the perceptual process.[12] An employee's future is closely tied to his or her appraisal—promotions, pay raises, and continuation of employment are among the most obvious outcomes. The performance appraisal represents an assessment of an employee's work. Although the appraisal can be objective (for example, a salesperson is appraised on how many dollars of sales she generates in her territory), many jobs are evaluated in subjective terms. Subjective measures are easier to implement, they provide managers with greater discretion, and many jobs do not readily lend themselves to objective measures. Subjective measures are, by definition, judgmental. The evaluator forms a general impression of an employee's work. To the degree that managers use subjective measures in appraising employees, what the evaluator perceives to be good or bad employee characteristics or behaviours will significantly influence the outcome of the appraisal.

This chapter's Point/Counterpoint discussion presents another application of how perception can be applied in organizations. The discussion centres on whether individuals should be told only the positive aspects of their new jobs, or whether they should be told both negative and positive elements. The discussion highlights that the way that information is presented to us can affect our evaluation of the information.

Hiring and performance appraisals are not the only processes in organizations subject to perceptual bias. For instance, we evaluate how much effort our co-workers are putting into their jobs. When a new person joins a work team, he or she is immediately "sized up" by the other team members. As you can see, perception plays a large role in the way that day-to-day activities are carried out in an organization. Personality, which we review below, is another major factor affecting how people relate in the workplace.

Personality

Why are some people quiet and passive, while others are loud and aggressive? Are certain personality types better adapted for certain job types? What do we know from theories of personality that can help us explain and predict the behaviour of people like Frank Stronach of Magna International, whom we described at the opening of this chapter? How do we explain the risk-taking nature of Peggy Witte, CEO of Royal Oak Mines, who is featured in this chapter's CBC Video Case? In this section, we will attempt to answer such questions.

What Is Personality?

When we talk of personality, we don't mean that a person has charm, a positive attitude toward life, a smiling face, or is a finalist for "Happiest and Friendliest" in this year's Best Student contest. When psychologists talk of personality, they mean a dynamic concept describing the growth and development of a person's whole psychological system. Rather than looking at parts of the person, personality looks at some aggregate whole that is greater than the sum of the parts.

Gordon Allport produced the most frequently used definition of personality more than 60 years ago. He said personality is "the dynamic organization within the individual of those psychophysical systems that determine his unique adjustments to his environment."[13] For our purposes, you should think of **personality** as the sum total of ways in which an individual reacts to and interacts with others. It is most often described in terms of measurable traits that a person exhibits. For an interesting look at how personality can affect business dealings, you might want to read this chapter's OB in the News feature.

personality
The sum total of ways in which an individual reacts and interacts with others.

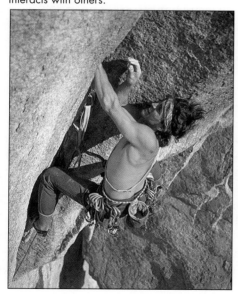

Body coordination, balance, stamina, strength and flexibility are physical abilities required for job performance at Black Diamond Equipment in Salt Lake City. But personality matters too. The rock-climbing equipment company ensures a high ability-job fit by hiring customers—sports enthusiasts who use its products and have a passion for climbing.

Personality Determinants

An early argument in personality research was whether an individual's personality was the result of heredity or of environment. Was the personality predetermined at birth, or was it the result of the individual's interaction with his or her environment? Clearly, there is no simple answer. Personality appears to be a result of both influences. In addition, today we recognize a third factor—the situation. Thus, an adult's personality is now generally considered to be made up of both hereditary and environmental factors, moderated by situational conditions.

HEREDITY Heredity refers to those factors that were determined at conception. Physical stature, facial attractiveness, gender, temperament, muscle composition and reflexes, energy level, and biological rhythms are characteristics that are generally considered to be either completely or substantially influenced by who your parents were: that is, by their biological, physiological, and inherent psychological makeup. The heredity approach argues that the ultimate explanation of an individual's personality is the molecular structure of the genes, located in the chromosomes.

Three different streams of research lend some credibility to the argument that heredity plays an important part in determin-

OB IN THE NEWS

Personality and the Lac Mineral Takeover

Did you ever wonder how much personality really mattered in the work-place? In mid-1994, Lac Minerals faced a hostile takeover, launched by Royal Oak Mines Inc. Finally, on July 22, Peter Allen, the chairman and chief executive officer of Lac, simply quit his job, before the takeover was even completed. He did not do so quietly. He resigned because "I am not prepared to let personalities define this takeover fight."

Who were the personalities involved? Peggy Witte, of Royal Oak, was characterized at the time as the "plucky, reliable, cost-conscious farm girl, short on glamour, long on sincerity." Peter Munk of American Barrick, which emerged as a rival to Royal Oak, was viewed as "the elegant interloper with a taste for lavish office furniture and a Midas touch in the mining sector."

Allen may not have liked dealing with personalities, but the fact is that companies are often defined as much by their leader as by their product or service. Just a few examples: Magna International's Frank Stronach, Hollinger Inc.'s Conrad Black, and Rogers Communications' Ted Rogers

serve as reminders that personality is an important piece of the business picture

When Allen walked out before the takeover was completed, he left Lac's shareholders with no human peg with which to identify the company. Jim Pitblado, a former investment dealer and a recent recruit to Lac's board, stepped in to take Allen's place, but the shareholders were trying to develop enthusiasm for an executive search while also facing a takeover bid. So, ultimately, the very absence of personality may have defined the fight Allen abandoned.

American Barrick, by the way, won its 1994 takeover bid. And in early 1998 the company sold off two of the largest mines it had acquired in the takeover, and was trading at $10 lower than its 52-week high. By mid-April 1998, Royal Oak had just been rescued from insolvency.

Sources: "The Personal Touch: However Strongly Executives May Deny It, Every Company Reflects an Individual's Vision and Preference," August 8, 1994, p. 32; Peter Kennedy, "Metals Firms Do Hard Time: Pegasus Gold Declares Bankruptcy, Royal Oak Has a Near Miss," *Financial Post*, January 17/19, 1998 pp. 1,2; David Thomas, "Barrick Sugar-Coats Some Bitter Medicine," *Financial Post*, September 13/15, 1997 p. 39.

Take It to the Net

We invite you to visit the Robbins page on the Prentice Hall Web site at:

http://www.prenticehall.ca/robbins

for this chapter's World Wide Web exercise.

ing an individual's personality. The first looks at the genetic underpinnings of human behaviour and temperament among young children. The second addresses the study of twins who were separated at birth. The third examines the consistency in job satisfaction over time and across situations.

Recent studies of young children lend strong support to the power of heredity.[14] Evidence demonstrates that traits such as shyness, fear, and distress are most likely caused by inherited genetic characteristics. This finding suggests that some personality traits may be built into the same genetic code that affects factors such as height and hair colour.

Researchers have studied more than 100 sets of identical twins who were separated at birth and raised separately.[15] If heredity played little or no part in determining personality, you would expect to find few similarities

between the separated twins. But the researchers found a lot in common. For almost every behavioural trait, a significant part of the variation between the twins turned out to be associated with genetic factors. For instance, one set of twins who had been separated for 39 years and raised 70 kilometres apart were found to drive the same model and colour car, chain-smoke the same brand of cigarette, own dogs with the same name, and regularly vacation within three blocks of each other in a beach community located 2000 kilometres away. Researchers have found that genetics accounts for about 50 percent of the personality differences and more than 30 percent of the variation in occupational and leisure interests.

Further support for the importance of heredity can be found in studies of individual job satisfaction. Research has uncovered an interesting phenomenon: individual job satisfaction is remarkably stable over time. Even when employers or occupations change, job satisfaction remains relatively stable during one's lifetime.[16] This result is consistent with what you would expect if satisfaction is determined by something inherent in the person rather than by external environmental factors.

If personality characteristics were *completely* dictated by heredity, they would be fixed at birth and no amount of experience could alter them. If you were relaxed and easygoing as a child, for example, that would be the result of your genes, and it would not be possible for you to change those characteristics. But personality characteristics are not completely dictated by heredity.

ENVIRONMENT   Among the factors that exert pressures on our personality formation are the culture in which we are raised, our early conditioning, the norms among our family, friends, and social groups, and other influences that we experience. The environment we are exposed to plays a substantial role in shaping our personalities.

For example, culture establishes the norms, attitudes, and values that are passed along from one generation to the next and create consistencies over time. An ideology that is intensely fostered in one culture may have only a moderate influence in another. For instance, North Americans have had the themes of industriousness, success, competition, independence, and the Protestant work ethic constantly instilled in them through books, the school system, family, and friends. North Americans, as a result, tend to be ambitious and aggressive relative to individuals raised in cultures that have emphasized getting along with others, cooperation, and the priority of family over work and career.

Careful consideration of the arguments favouring either heredity or environment as the primary determinant of personality forces the conclusion that both are important. Heredity sets the parameters or outer limits, but an individual's full potential will be determined by how well he or she adjusts to the demands and requirements of the environment.

SITUATION   A third factor, the situation, influences the effects of heredity and environment on personality. An individual's personality, although generally stable and consistent, does change in different situations. The different demands of different situations call forth different aspects of one's personality. We should not, therefore, look at personality patterns in isolation.[17]

It seems only logical to suppose that situations will influence an individual's personality, but a neat classification scheme that would tell us the impact of various types of situations has so far eluded us. "Apparently we are

The cultural environment in which people are raised plays a major role in shaping personality. In India, children learn from an early age the values of hard work, frugality, and family closeness. This photo of the Harilela family illustrates the importance placed on close family ties. Six Harilela brothers own real estate and hotels throughout Asia. Not only do the brothers work together, but their six families and that of a married sister also live together in a Hong Kong mansion.

not yet close to developing a system for clarifying situations so that they might be systematically studied."[18] However, we do know that certain situations are more relevant than others in influencing personality. We also know that situations seem to differ substantially in the constraints they impose on behaviour. Some situations, such as a religious service or an employment interview, constrain many behaviours; other situations, such as a picnic in a public park, constrain relatively few.[19]

Furthermore, although certain generalizations can be made about personality, there are significant individual differences. As we will see, the study of individual differences has come to receive greater emphasis in personality research, which originally sought out more general, universal patterns.

Personality Traits

The early work in the structure of personality revolved around attempts to identify and label enduring characteristics that describe an individual's behaviour. Popular characteristics include shy, aggressive, submissive, lazy, ambitious, loyal, and timid. Those characteristics, when they are exhibited in a large number of situations, are called **personality traits**.[20] The more consistent the characteristic and the more frequently it occurs in diverse situations, the more important that trait is in describing the individual.

Researchers have tried to identify the different personality traits, and one researcher identified 16 personality factors that he called the source, or primary, traits.[21] They are shown in Exhibit 3-4. These 16 traits have been found to be generally steady and constant sources of behaviour, allowing prediction of an individual's behaviour in specific situations by weighing the characteristics for their situational relevance.

Our personality traits, by the way, are evaluated differently by different people, which is partially a function of perception, which we discussed earlier in the chapter. In Exhibit 3-5, you will note that Lucy tells Charlie Brown a few things about his personality.

THE MYERS-BRIGGS TYPE INDICATOR One of the most widely used personality frameworks is called the **Myers-Briggs Type Indicator (MBTI)**.[22] It is

personality traits
Enduring characteristics that describe an individual's behaviour.

Myers-Briggs Type Indicator (MBTI)
A personality test that taps four characteristics and classifies people into one of 16 personality types.

Exhibit 3-4
Sixteen Primary Traits

1.	Reserved	vs.	Outgoing
2.	Less intelligent	vs.	More intelligent
3.	Affected by feelings	vs.	Emotionally stable
4.	Submissive	vs.	Dominant
5.	Serious	vs.	Happy-go-lucky
6.	Expedient	vs.	Conscientious
7.	Timid	vs.	Venturesome
8.	Tough-minded	vs.	Sensitive
9.	Trusting	vs.	Suspicious
10.	Practical	vs.	Imaginative
11.	Forthright	vs.	Shrewd
12.	Self-assured	vs.	Apprehensive
13.	Conservative	vs.	Experimenting
14.	Group-dependent	vs.	Self-sufficient
15.	Uncontrolled	vs.	Controlled
16.	Relaxed	vs.	Tense

essentially a 100-question personality test that asks people how they usually feel or act in particular situations.

On the basis of the answers individuals give to the test, they are classified as extroverted or introverted (E or I), sensing or intuitive (S or N), thinking or feeling (T or F), and perceiving or judging (P or J). These classifications are then combined into 16 personality types. (These types are different from the 16 primary traits in Exhibit 3-4.) To illustrate, let's take several examples. INTJs are visionaries. They usually have original minds and great drive for their own ideas and purposes. They are characterized as skeptical, critical, independent, determined, and often stubborn. ESTJs are organizers. They are realistic, logical, analytical, decisive and have a natural head for business or mechanics. They like to organize and run activities. The ENTP type is a conceptualizer. He or she is innovative, individualistic, versatile, and attracted to entrepreneurial ideas. This person tends to be resourceful in solving challenging problems but may neglect routine assignments. G.N. Landrum's *Profiles of Genius* profiled 13 contemporary business people who created super-successful firms including Apple Computer, Federal Express, Honda Motors, Microsoft, Price Club, and Sony. He found that all 13 are intuitive thinkers (NTs).[23] This result is particularly interesting because intuitive thinkers represent only about five percent of the population.

Apple Computer
http://www.apple.com/

Microsoft
http://www.microsoft.com

Price Club
http://www.pricecostco.com

Exhibit 3-5

Source: PEANUTS reprinted by permission of United Features Syndicate, Inc.

Though leaders have a variety of personality traits, one common characteristic of many who have founded their own companies is intuitiveness. Bill Gates, founder of Microsoft is one leader classified as an intuitive thinker (NT) on the Meyers-Briggs Type Indicator (MBTI).

Ironically, there is no hard evidence that the MBTI is a valid measure of personality. But lack of evidence doesn't seem to deter its use in a wide range of organizations. A number of popular books are available to help individuals identify both their own and their colleagues' "types." One of the benefits of thinking about individuals by type is that it will give you some insight into how a particular person might react in a situation. However, as we noted above in our discussion of stereotyping, relying solely on personality measures to judge people can have its problems.

The Big Five Model. The MBTI may lack for valid supporting evidence, but that can't be said for the five-factor model of personality—more typically called the "Big Five."[24] In recent years, an impressive body of research supports the notion that five basic personality dimensions underlie all others. The Big Five factors are:

Extroversion. This dimension captures one's comfort level with relationships. Extroverts (high in **extroversion**) tend to be friendly and outgoing and to spend much of their time maintaining and enjoying a large number of relationships. Introverts tend to be reserved and to have fewer relationships, and they are more comfortable with solitude than most people are.

Agreeableness. This dimension refers to an individual's propensity to defer to others. Highly agreeable people value harmony more than they value having their say or their way. They are cooperative and trusting of others. People who score low on **agreeableness** focus more on their own needs than on the needs of others.

extroversion
A personality dimension that describes someone who is sociable, talkative, and assertive.

agreeableness
A personality dimension that describes someone who is good-natured, cooperative, and trusting.

conscientiousness
A personality dimension that describes someone who is responsible, dependable, persistent, and achievement oriented.

emotional stability
A personality dimension that characterizes someone as calm, enthusiastic, secure (positive) versus tense, nervous, depressed, and insecure (negative).

openness to experience
A personality dimension that characterizes someone in terms of imaginativeness, artistic sensitivity, and intellectualism.

Conscientiousness. This dimension refers to the number of goals on which a person focuses. A highly **conscientious** person pursues fewer goals, in a purposeful way, and tends to be responsible, persistent, dependable, and achievement-oriented. Those who score low on this dimension tend to be more easily distracted, pursuing many goals, and more hedonistic.

Emotional stability. This dimension taps a person's ability to withstand stress. People with positive **emotional stability** tend to be characterized as calm, enthusiastic, and secure. Those with high negative scores tend to be nervous, depressed, and insecure.

Openness to experience. The final dimension addresses one's range of interests. Extremely open people are fascinated by novelty and innovation. They tend to be imaginative, artistically sensitive, and intellectual. Those at the other end of the **openness** category appear more conventional and find comfort in the familiar.

In addition to providing a unifying personality framework, research on the Big Five also has found important relationships between these personality dimensions and job performance.[25] A broad spectrum of occupations was examined: professionals (including engineers, architects, accountants, lawyers), police officers, managers, salespeople, and semiskilled and skilled employees. Job performance was defined in terms of performance ratings, training proficiency (performance during training programs), and personnel data such as salary level. The results showed that conscientiousness predicted job performance for all occupational groups. "The preponderance of evidence shows that individuals who are dependable, reliable, careful, thorough, able to plan, organized, hardworking, persistent, and achievement-oriented tend to have higher job performance in most if not all occupations."[26] For the other personality dimensions, predictability depended upon both the performance criterion and the occupational group. For instance, extroversion predicted performance in managerial and sales positions. This finding makes sense since those occupations involve high social interaction. Similarly, openness to experience was found to be important in predicting training proficiency, which also seems logical. What wasn't as clear was why positive emotional stability wasn't related to job performance. Intuitively, it would seem that people who are calm and secure would do better on almost all jobs than people who are anxious and insecure. The researchers suggested that the answer might be that only people who score fairly high on emotional stability retain their jobs. So the range among those people studied, all of whom were employed, would tend to be quite small.

The research that found the importance of conscientiousness in predicting performance examined studies conducted in North America. However, a similar analysis was performed in the European Community, and this work also supported the idea that conscientiousness is a critical predictor of performance across jobs.[27] Further work on conscientiousness has also shown that it is much more important for people whose jobs are more autonomous. For employees who are closely supervised or carefully monitored, conscientiousness is probably less critical.[28] Although conscientiousness is a good predictor of performance, it does not predict it perfectly. Conscientiousness has also been studied at the level of the individual; however, in today's organization, and certainly that of the 21st century, more people work or will work in teams. One researcher found that conscientiousness was related to

ability to perform well in teams.[29] However, another study found no significant relationship between conscientiousness and how teammates perceived an individual's contribution to group functioning or to team performance.[30] It is clear then, that more work remains to be done in evaluating the importance of conscientiousness to predicting performance, particularly performance on teams.

Major Personality Attributes Influencing OB

In this section, we want to more carefully evaluate specific personality attributes that have been found to be powerful predictors of behaviour in organizations. The first is related to where one perceives the locus of control in one's life. The others are Machiavellianism, self-esteem, self-monitoring, propensity for risk taking, and Type A personality. In this section, we shall briefly introduce these attributes and summarize what we know about their ability to explain and predict employee behaviour. If you want to know more about your own personal characteristics, this chapter's Increase Your Self-Awareness exercises present you with a variety of personality measures to explore. These exercises are described briefly in this chapter's From Concepts to Skills features.

internals
Individuals who believe that they control what happens to them.

externals
Individuals who believe that what happens to them is controlled by outside forces such as luck or chance.

locus of control
The degree to which people believe they are in control of their own fate

LOCUS OF CONTROL Some people believe that they are in control of their own destiny. Other people see themselves as pawns of fate, believing that what happens to them in their lives is due to luck or chance. The first type, those who believe that they control their destinies, have been labelled **internals**, whereas the latter, who see their lives as being controlled by outside forces, have been called **externals**.[31] A person's perception of the source of his or her fate is termed **locus of control**.

A large amount of research comparing internals with externals has con-

FROM CONCEPTS TO SKILLS

Self-Awareness: Do You Know Yourself?

A famous cartoonist once attended a cocktail party with some friends. Someone asked him to draw a caricature of everyone present, which he proceeded to do with a few skilled strokes of his pencil. When the sketches were passed around for the guests to identify, everyone recognized the other persons, but hardly anyone recognized his or her own caricature.

Many of us are like the people at that cocktail party. We really don't know ourselves. But you can expand your self-awareness. And when you do, you will better understand your personal strengths and weaknesses and how you are perceived by others. You will also gain insights into why others respond to you as they do.

A major component in gaining self-understanding is finding out how you rate on key personality characteristics. Later in our discussion of personality, we will review six major personality attributes: locus of control, Machiavellianism, self-esteem, self-monitoring, risk taking, and the Type A personality. Supplementing the review will be a series of self-awareness questionnaires that have been designed to measure these personality characteristics. Individually, the questionnaires will give you insights into how you rate on each attribute. In aggregate, they will help you to better understand who you are. (See the Increase Your Self-Awareness exercises at the end of this chapter.)

sistently shown that individuals who rate high in externality are less satisfied with their jobs, have higher absenteeism rates, are more alienated from the work setting, and are less involved on their jobs than are internals.[32]

Why are externals more dissatisfied? The answer is probably because they perceive themselves as having little control over those organizational outcomes that are important to them. Internals, facing the same situation, attribute organizational outcomes to their own actions. If the situation is unattractive, they believe that they have no one else to blame but themselves. Also, the dissatisfied internal is more likely to quit a dissatisfying job.

The impact of locus of control on absence is an interesting one. Internals believe that health is substantially under their own control through proper habits, so they take more responsibility for their health and have better health habits. Consequently, their incidences of sickness and, hence, of absenteeism, are lower.[33]

We shouldn't expect any clear relationship between locus of control and turnover, because there are opposing forces at work. "On the one hand, internals tend to take action and thus might be expected to quit jobs more readily. On the other hand, they tend to be more successful on the job and more satisfied, factors associated with less individual turnover."[34]

The overall evidence indicates that internals generally perform better on their jobs, but that conclusion should be moderated to reflect differences in jobs. Internals search more actively for information before making a decision, are more motivated to achieve, and make a greater attempt to control their environment. Externals, however, are more compliant and willing to follow directions. Therefore, internals do well on sophisticated tasks—which include most managerial and professional jobs—that require complex information processing and learning. In addition, internals are more suited to jobs that require initiative and independence of action. In contrast, externals should do well on jobs that are well structured and routine and in which success depends heavily on complying with the direction of others. If you are interested in determining your locus of control, you might want to complete Increase Your Self-Awareness Exercise #1, which can be found at the end of the chapter.

Machiavellianism
Degree to which an individual is pragmatic, maintains emotional distance, and believes that ends can justify means.

MACHIAVELLIANISM   The personality characteristic of **Machiavellianism** (Mach) is named after Niccolò Machiavelli, who wrote in the sixteenth century on how to gain and use power. An individual high in Machiavellianism is pragmatic, maintains emotional distance, and believes that ends can justify means. "If it works, use it" is consistent with a high-Mach perspective.

A considerable amount of research has been directed toward relating high- and low-Mach personalities to certain behavioural outcomes.[35] High Machs manipulate more, win more, are persuaded less, and persuade others more than do low Machs.[36] Yet these high-Mach outcomes are moderated by situational factors. It has been found that high Machs flourish (1) when they interact face to face with others rather than indirectly; (2) when the situation has a minimum number of rules and regulations, thus allowing latitude for improvisation; and (3) when emotional involvement with details irrelevant to winning distracts low Machs.[37]

Should we conclude that high Machs make good employees? That answer depends on the type of job and whether you consider ethical implications in evaluating performance. In jobs that require bargaining skills (such as labour negotiation) or that offer substantial rewards for winning (as in commissioned sales), high Machs will be productive. But if ends can't justify the means, if there are absolute standards of behaviour, or if the three situa-

tional factors noted in the preceding paragraph are not in evidence, our ability to predict a high Mach's performance will be severely curtailed. If you are interested in determining your level of Machiavellianism, you might want to complete Increase Your Self-Awareness Exercise #2, which can be found at the end of the chapter.

self-esteem

Individuals' degree of liking or disliking of themselves.

SELF-ESTEEM People differ in the degree to which they like or dislike themselves. This trait is called **self-esteem**.[38] The research on self-esteem (SE) offers some interesting insights into organizational behaviour. For example, self-esteem is directly related to expectations for success. High SEs believe that they possess the ability they need in order to succeed at work. Individuals with high self-esteem will take more risks in job selection and are more likely to choose unconventional jobs than are people with low self-esteem.

The most generalizable finding on self-esteem is that low SEs are more susceptible to external influence than are high SEs. Low SEs are dependent on the receipt of positive evaluations from others. As a result, they are more likely to seek approval from others and more prone to conform to the beliefs and behaviours of those they respect than are high SEs. In managerial positions, low SEs will tend to be concerned with pleasing others and, therefore, are less likely to take unpopular stands than are high SEs.

Not surprisingly, self-esteem has also been found to be related to job satisfaction. A number of studies confirm that high SEs are more satisfied with their jobs than are low SEs. If you are interested in determining your self-esteem score, you might want to complete Increase Your Self-Awareness Exercise #3, which can be found at the end of the chapter.

self-monitoring

A personality trait that measures an individual's ability to adjust his or her behaviour to external, situational factors.

SELF-MONITORING A personality trait that has recently received increased attention is called **self-monitoring**.[39] It refers to an individual's ability to adjust his or her behaviour to external, situational factors.

Individuals high in self-monitoring show considerable adaptability in adjusting their behaviour to external situational factors. They are highly sensitive to external cues and can behave differently in different situations. High self-monitors are capable of presenting striking contradictions between their public persona and their private self. Low self-monitors can't disguise themselves in that way. They tend to display their true dispositions and attitudes in every situation; hence, there is high behavioural consistency between who they are and what they do.

The research on self-monitoring is in its infancy, so predictions must be guarded. However, preliminary evidence suggests that high self-monitors tend to pay closer attention to the behaviour of others and are more capable of conforming than are low self-monitors.[40] In addition, high self-monitoring managers tend to be more mobile in their careers and receive more promotions (both internal and cross-organizational).[41] We might also hypothesize that high self-monitors will be more successful in managerial positions in which individuals are required to play multiple, and even contradicting, roles. The high self-monitor is capable of putting on different "faces" for different audiences. If you are interested in determining whether you are a high or low self-monitor, you might want to complete Increase Your Self-Awareness Exercise #4, which can be found at the end of the chapter.

RISK TAKING People differ in their willingness to take chances. Frank Stronach, the subject of this chapter's opening vignette and Case Incident, is a good example of a high risk-taker. This propensity to assume or avoid risk

has been shown to have an impact on how long it takes managers to make a decision and how much information they require before making their choice. For instance, 79 managers worked on simulated personnel exercises that required them to make hiring decisions.[42] High **risk-taking** managers made more rapid decisions and used less information in making their choices than did the low risk-taking managers. Interestingly, the decision accuracy was the same for both groups.

risk-taking
Refers to a person's willingness to take chances or risks.

While it is generally correct to conclude that managers in organizations are risk-aversive,[43] there are still individual differences on this dimension.[44] As a result, it makes sense to recognize these differences and even to consider aligning risk-taking propensity with specific job demands. For instance, a high risk-taking propensity may lead to more effective performance for a stock trader in a brokerage firm because that type of job demands rapid decision making. On the other hand, a willingness to take risks might prove a major obstacle to an accountant who performs auditing activities. The latter job might be better filled by someone with a low risk-taking propensity. If you are interested in determining where you stand on risk taking, you might want to complete Increase Your Self-Awareness Exercise #5, which can be found at the end of the chapter.

TYPE A PERSONALITY Do you know any people who are excessively competitive and always seem to be experiencing a chronic sense of time urgency? If you do, it's a good bet that those people have a Type A personality. A person with a **Type A personality** is "*aggressively* involved in a *chronic, incessant* struggle to achieve more and more in less and less time, and, if required to do so, against the opposing efforts of other things or other persons."[45] In the North American culture, such characteristics tend to be highly prized and positively associated with ambition and the successful acquisition of material goods.

Type A personality
A personality with aggressive involvement in a chronic, incessant struggle to achieve more and more in less and less time and, if necessary, against the opposing efforts of other things or other people.

Type A's

- are always moving, walking, and eating rapidly;
- feel impatient with the rate at which most events take place;
- strive to think or do two or more things at once;
- cannot cope with leisure time;
- are obsessed with numbers, measuring their success in terms of how many or how much of everything they acquire.

In contrast to the Type A personality is the Type B, who is exactly opposite. Type B's are "rarely harried by the desire to obtain a wildly increasing number of things or participate in an endless growing series of events in an ever-decreasing amount of time."[46]

Type B's

- never suffer from a sense of time urgency with its accompanying impatience;
- feel no need to display or discuss either their achievements or accomplishments unless such exposure is demanded by the situation;
- play for fun and relaxation, rather than to exhibit their superiority at any cost;
- can relax without guilt.

Type A's operate under moderate to high levels of stress. They subject themselves to more or less continuous time pressure, creating for themselves

a life of deadlines. These characteristics result in some rather specific behavioural outcomes. For example, Type A's are fast workers, because they emphasize quantity over quality. In managerial positions, Type A's demonstrate their competitiveness by working long hours and, not infrequently, making poor decisions because they make them too fast. Type A's are also rarely creative. Because of their concern with quantity and speed, they rely on past experiences when faced with problems. They will not allocate the time that is necessary to develop unique solutions to new problems. They rarely vary in their responses to specific challenges in their milieu; hence, their behaviour is easier to predict than that of Type B's.

Are Type A's or Type B's more successful in organizations? Despite the Type A's hard work, the Type B's are the ones who appear to make it to the top. Great salespersons are usually Type A's; senior executives are usually Type B's. Why? The answer lies in the tendency of Type A's to trade off quality of effort for quantity. Promotions in corporate and professional organizations "usually go to those who are wise rather than to those who are merely hasty, to those who are tactful rather than to those who are hostile, and to those who are creative rather than to those who are merely agile in competitive strife."[47] If you are interested in determining whether you have a Type A or Type B personality type, you might want to complete Increase Your Self-Awareness Exercise #6, which can be found at the end of the chapter.

Personality and National Culture

There are certainly no common personality types for a given country. You can, for instance, find high and low risk-takers in almost any culture. Yet a country's culture should influence the dominant personality characteristics of its population. Let's build this case by looking at two personality attributes—locus of control and the Type A personality.

There is evidence that cultures differ in terms of people's relationship to their environment.[48] In some cultures, such as those in North America, people believe that they can dominate their environment. People in other societies, such as Middle Eastern countries, believe that life is essentially preordained. Notice the close parallel to internal and external locus of control. We should expect a larger proportion of internals in the Canadian and American workforces than in the Saudi Arabian or Iranian workforces.

The prevalence of Type A personalities will be somewhat influenced by the culture in which a person grows up. There are Type A's in every country, but there will be more in capitalistic countries, where achievement and material success are highly valued. For instance, it is estimated that about 50 percent of the North American population is Type A.[49] This percentage shouldn't be too surprising. Canada and the United States both have a high emphasis on time management and efficiency. Both have cultures that stress accomplishments and the acquisition of money and material goods. In cultures such as Sweden and France, where materialism is less revered, we would predict a smaller proportion of Type A personalities.

Matching Personalities and Jobs

In the discussion of personality attributes, our conclusions were often qualified to recognize that the requirements of the job moderated the relationship between possession of the personality characteristic and job performance. This concern with matching the job requirements with personality character-

Southwest Airlines uses the personality-job fit theory in hiring employees. It hires social personality types—fun-loving, friendly people who enjoy helping and entertaining customers—as flight attendants. Antics like a flight attendant popping out of a luggage bin delight customers and increase employee job satisfaction, which helps make Southwest the most consistently profitable U.S. airline.

Exhibit 3-6
Holland's Typology of Personality and Congruent Occupations

Type	Personality Characteristics	Congruent Occupations
Realistic: Prefers physical activities that require skill, strength, and coordination	Shy, genuine, persistent, stable, conforming, practical	Mechanic, drill press operator, assembly-line worker, farmer
Investigative: Prefers activities that involve thinking, organizing, and understanding	Analytical, original, curious, independent	Biologist, economist, mathematician, news reporter
Social: Prefers activities that involve helping and developing others	Sociable, friendly, cooperative, understanding	Social worker, teacher, counsellor, clinical psychologist
Conventional: Prefers rule-regulated, orderly, and unambiguous activities	Conforming, efficient, practical, unimaginative, inflexible	Accountant, corporate manager, bank teller, file clerk
Enterprising: Prefers verbal activities where there are opportunities to influence others and attain power	Self-confident, ambitious, energetic, domineering	Lawyer, real estate agent, public relations specialist, small business manager
Artistic: Prefers ambiguous and unsystematic activities that allow creative expression	Imaginative, disorderly, idealistic, emotional, impractical	Painter, musician, writer, interior decorator

personality–job fit theory
Identifies six personality types and proposes that the fit between personality type and occupational environment determines satisfaction and turnover.

istics is best articulated in John Holland's **personality-job fit theory.**[50] The theory is based on the notion of fit between an individual's personality characteristics and his or her occupational environment. Holland presents six personality types and proposes that satisfaction and the propensity to leave a job depend on the degree to which individuals successfully match their personalities to an occupational environment.

Each one of the six personality types has a congruent occupational environment. Exhibit 3-6 describes the six types and their personality characteristics and gives examples of congruent occupations.

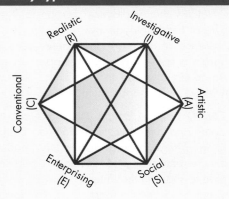

Exhibit 3-7
Relationships among Occupational Personality Types

Holland has developed a Vocational Preference Inventory questionnaire that contains 160 occupational titles. Respondents indicate which of these occupations they like or dislike, and their answers are used to form personality profiles. Using this procedure, research strongly supports the hexagonal diagram in Exhibit 3-7.[51] This figure shows that the closer two fields or orientations are in the hexagon, the more compatible they are. Adjacent categories are quite similar, whereas those diagonally opposite are highly dissimilar.

What does all this mean? The theory argues that satisfaction is highest and turnover lowest when personality and occupation are in agreement. Social individuals should be in social jobs, conventional people in conventional jobs, and so forth. A realistic person in a realistic job is in a more congruent situation than is a realistic person in an investigative job. A realistic person in a social job is in the most incongruent situation possible. The key points of this model are that (1) there appear to be intrinsic differences in personality among individuals, (2) there are different types of jobs, and (3) people in job environments congruent with their personality types should be more satisfied and less likely to voluntarily resign than should people in incongruent jobs. In this chapter's HR Implications we review aspects of career development to help you begin to think about how you will manage your career. This chapter has indicated that there is a link between personality and career choices that you might make.

HR IMPLICATIONS

Career Development

Our chapter has considered the roles that perception and personality play in judging and getting along with others. We have also examined the extent to which one should consider the match between personality and specific jobs. One thing that we have not discussed in our text to date is how you manage your career, however. We thought this would be an early opportunity, as you are starting to learn about the fundamentals of or-

ganizational behavior, to think about various career issues. Below we discuss both the role of the organization and your role in developing your career.

Few human resource issues have changed as much in the past couple of decades as the role of the organization in its employees' careers.[1] Twenty years ago, when a person was more likely to spend his or her entire work years with the same

employer, most medium-sized and large organizations engaged in extensive employee career planning. It focused exclusively on developing employees for opportunities within the specific organization. For instance, they would develop sophisticated replacement charts that would identify potential promotion candidates for key internal positions. They'd also offer a wide range of in-house career development programs to prepare employees for promotions.

Today, many more organizations are engaged in nearly continuous restructuring, through downsizing their operations, re-engineering processes, increasing flexibility. Bank and other mergers lead to layoffs when duplicate jobs are eliminated. New technologies make it possible to do more work with fewer people. And companies are increasingly taking their labour-intensive work to countries with lower labour costs, resulting in fewer jobs within the corporation at home. As a result of all of these changes, employees must take personal responsibility for planning their personal career track. They should not simply leave it to their manager or the company to define their future.

In spite of the need for employees to assume personal responsibility for their careers, there are benefits that accrue to organizations that offer career development programs.[2] These include ensuring the right people will be available for meeting changing staffing requirements, increasing workforce diversity, and providing employees with more realistic job expectations. Below, we describe both the organization's and employees' responsibilities for career development today.

First, however, let's define what we mean by the term *career*. A **career** is "the evolving sequence of a person's work experiences over time."[3] This definition does not imply advancement or success or failure. Any work, paid or unpaid, pursued over an extended period of time can constitute a career. In addition to formal job work, it may include schoolwork, homemaking, or volunteer work.[4]

The organization's responsibilities What, if any, responsibility does the organization have for career development under these new rules? Amoco Corp.'s career development program is a model for modern companies.[5] It's designed around employee self-reliance and to help employees reflect on their marketability both inside and outside the oil company. All workers are en-

couraged to participate in a half-day introduction to the program and full-day self-assessment and self-development sessions. The company supports its employees by providing information—a worldwide electronic job-posting system, a network of career advisers, and a worldwide directory of Amoco employees and their skills from which company managers can search for candidates for job openings. But the whole program is voluntary and assumes that it's the employees' responsibility to maintain his or her employability.

The essence of a progressive career development program is built on providing support for employees to continually add to their skills, abilities, and knowledge. This support includes:

1. *Clearly communicating the organization's goals and future strategies.* When people know where the organization is headed, they're better able to develop a personal plan to share in that future.
2. *Creating growth opportunities.* Employees should have the opportunity to get new, interesting, and professionally challenging work experiences.
3. *Offering financial assistance.* The organization should offer tuition reimbursement to help employees keep current.
4. *Providing the time for employees to learn.* Organizations should be generous in providing paid time off from work for off-the-job training. Additionally, workloads should not be so demanding that they preclude employees from having the time to develop new skills, abilities, and knowledge.

The employee's responsibilities Today's employees should manage their own careers like entrepreneurs managing a small business. They should think of themselves as self-employed, even if employed in a large organization.[6] In a world of "free agency," the successful career will be built on maintaining flexibility and keeping skills and knowledge up-to-date. The following suggestions are consistent with the view that you, and only you, hold primary responsibility for your career.[7]

1. *Know yourself.* Know your strengths and weaknesses. What talents can you bring to an employer? Personal career planning begins by being honest with yourself.

2. *Manage your reputation.* Without appearing as a braggart, let others both inside and outside your current organization know about your achievements. Make yourself and your accomplishments visible.

3. *Build and maintain network contacts.* In a world of high mobility, you need to develop contacts. Join national and local professional associations, attend conferences, and network at social gatherings.

4. *Keep current.* Develop those specific skills and abilities that are in high demand. Avoid learning organization-specific skills that can't be transferred quickly to other employers.

5. *Balance your specialist and generalist competencies.* You need to stay current within your technical specialty. But you also need to develop general competencies that give you the versatility to react to an ever-changing work environment. Overemphasis in a single functional area or even in a narrow industry can limit your mobility.

6. *Document your achievements.* Employers are increasingly looking to what you've accomplished rather than the titles you've held. Seek jobs and assignments that will provide increasing challenges and that will also offer objective evidence of your competencies.

7. *Keep your options open.* Always have contingency plans prepared that you can call on when needed. You never know when your group will be eliminated, your department downsized, your project cancelled, or your company acquired in a takeover. "Hope for the best but be prepared for the worst" may be cliché, but it's still not bad advice.

Sources:

[1] See H. Lancaster, "You and Only You, Must Stay in Charge of Your Employability," *Wall Street Journal*, November 15, 1994, p.B1; B. Filipczak, "You're On Your Own: Training, Employability, and the New Employment Contract," *Training*, January 1995, pp. 29–36; and M.B. Arthur, P.H. Claman, and R.J. DeFillippi, "Intelligent Enterprise, Intelligent Careers," *The Executive*, November 1995, pp. 7–20.

[2] See, for example, P.O. Benham, Jr., "Developing Organizational Talent: The Key to Performance and Productivity," *SAM Advanced Management Journal*, January 1993, pp. 34–39.

[3] M.B. Arthur, D.T. Hall, and B.S. Lawrence (eds.), *Handbook of Career Theory* (Cambridge: Cambridge University Press, 1989), p. 8.

[4] D.T. Hall, *Careers in Organizations* (Santa Monica, CA: Goodyear, 1976), pp. 3–4.

[5] M. Hequet, "Flat and Happy?" *Training*, April 1995, pp. 29–34.

[6] G. Johns, *Organizational Behavior: Understanding and Managing Life at Work*, 4th ed. (New York: HarperCollins, 1996), p. 622.

[7] See R.A. McGowan, "Career Deinstitutionalization." Working Paper 14–95. Faculty of Administrative Studies; York University; North York, Ontario, 1995.

Summary and Implications

For the Workplace

PERCEPTION. Individuals behave in a given manner based not on the way their external environment actually is but, rather, on what they see or believe it to be. An organization may spend millions of dollars to create a pleasant work environment for its employees. However, despite these expenditures, if an employee believes that his or her job is lousy, that employee will behave accordingly. It is the employee's perception of a situation that becomes the basis for his or her behaviour. The employee who perceives his or her supervisor as a hurdle reducer who helps him or her do a better job and the employee who sees the same supervisor as "big brother, closely monitoring every motion, to ensure that I keep working" will differ in their behavioural responses to their supervisor. The difference has nothing to do with the reality of the supervisor's actions; the difference in employee behaviour is due to different perceptions. Managers make similar perception judgments that may not be based in reality; therefore, the way they manage and the way they interact with top executives will be influenced by these perceptions.

The evidence suggests that what individuals perceive from their work situation will influence their productivity more than will the situation itself. Whether a job is actually interesting or challenging is irrelevant. Whether a

manager successfully plans and organizes the work of his or her subordinates and actually helps them to structure their work more efficiently and effectively is far less important than how subordinates perceive the manager's efforts. Similarly, issues such as fair pay for work performed, the validity of performance appraisals, and the adequacy of working conditions are not judged by employees in a way that assures common perceptions, nor can we be assured that individuals will interpret conditions about their jobs in a favourable light. Therefore, to be able to influence productivity, it is necessary to assess how workers *perceive* their jobs.

Absenteeism, turnover, job satisfaction, and organizational commitment are also reactions to the individual's perceptions. Dissatisfaction with working conditions or the belief that there is a lack of promotion opportunities in the organization are judgments based on attempts to make some meaning out of one's job. The employee's conclusion that a job is good or bad is an interpretation. Managers must spend time understanding how each individual interprets reality and, where there is a significant difference between what is seen and what exists, try to eliminate the distortions. Failure to deal with the differences when individuals perceive the job in negative terms will result in increased absenteeism and turnover and lower job satisfaction and commitment.

PERSONALITY   A review of the personality literature offers general guidelines that can lead to effective job performance. As such, it can improve hiring, transfer, and promotion decisions. Because personality characteristics create the parameters for people's behaviour, they give us a framework for predicting behaviour. For example, individuals who are shy, introverted, and uncomfortable in social situations would probably be ill-suited as salespeople. Individuals who are submissive and conforming might not be effective as advertising "idea" people.

Can we predict which people will be high performers in sales, research, or assembly-line work on the basis of their personality characteristics alone? The answer is "no." But a knowledge of an individual's personality can aid in reducing mismatches, which, in turn, can lead to reduced turnover and higher job satisfaction.

We can look at certain personality characteristics that tend to be related to job success, test for those traits, and use the data to make selection more effective. A person who accepts rules, conformity, and dependence and rates high on authoritarianism is likely to feel more comfortable in, say, a structured assembly-line job, as an admittance clerk in a hospital, or as an administrator in a large public agency than as a researcher or an employee whose job requires a high degree of creativity.

For You as an Individual

The summary above provides a number of ideas that are relevant to you as an individual, so we will focus on two issues here. First, the discussion of perception might be something to get you thinking about how you view the world. Sometimes when we perceive others as troublemakers, for instance, this is only a perception, and not a real characteristic of the other person. So, sometimes it is good to question your perception, just to be sure that you are not reading something into a situation that is not there.

Our discussion of personality illustrates that personality differences affect behaviour. One important thing to consider when looking for a job is

whether your personality will fit the organization to which you are applying. For instance, if it's a highly structured organization, but you, by nature, are much less formal, this might not be a good fit for you. The discussion of personalities might also help you understand that sometimes we have to identify ways to deal with the personality of others, so that we can get along. You may have noticed sometimes when working in groups that personalities get in the way. You might want to see if you can figure out ways to get personality differences working in favour of group goals.

ROADMAP REMINDER

Prior to this chapter we reviewed the changing nature of the Canadian workplace, and the importance of learning skills that would help us thrive in new and changing environments. In this chapter we considered the role of perception, to help you understand that what you perceive and what is "real" are not always the same. We also considered the role of personality in working with others. Both perception and personality are individual characteristics that affect our interactions with others. In the next chapter we consider values and attitudes, which also influence our behaviour. The focus on these individual characteristics is to give you some insight into understanding yourself and others with whom you work or carry out tasks.

For Review

1. Define perception.
2. What is attribution theory? What are its implications for explaining organizational behaviour?
3. What factors do you think might create the fundamental attribution error?
4. How does selectivity affect perception? Give an example of how selectivity can create perceptual distortion.
5. What is stereotyping? Give an example of how stereotyping can create perceptual distortion.
6. Give some positive results of using shortcuts when judging others.
7. What constrains the power of personality traits to precisely predict behaviour?
8. What behavioural predictions might you make if you knew that an employee had (a) an external locus of control? (b) a low-Mach score? (c) low self-esteem? (d) a Type A personality?
9. What is the Myers-Briggs Type Indicator?
10. What were the six personality types identified by Holland?

For Discussion

1. "That you and I agree on what we see suggests we have similar backgrounds and experiences." Do you agree or disagree? Discuss.
2. In what work-related situations do you think it is important to be able to determine whether others' behaviour stems primarily from internal or external causes?

3. "The type of job an employee does moderates the relationship between personality and job productivity." Do you agree or disagree with this statement? Discuss.

4. One day your boss comes in and he's nervous, edgy, and argumentative. The next day he is calm and relaxed. Does this behaviour suggest that personality traits aren't consistent from day to day?

INCREASE YOUR SELF-AWARENESS #1

Assess Your Locus of Control

Instructions: Read the following statements and indicate whether you agree more with choice A or choice B.

A	B
1. Making a lot of money is largely a matter of getting the right breaks.	1. Promotions are earned through hard work and persistence.
2. I have noticed that there is a direct connection between how hard I study and the grades I get.	2. Many times, the reactions of teachers seem haphazard to me.
3. The number of divorces indicates that more and more people are not trying to make their marriages work.	3. Marriage is largely a gamble.
4. It is silly to think that one can really change another person's basic attitudes.	4. When I am right I can convince others.
5. Getting promoted is really a matter of being a little luckier than the next person.	5. In our society, a person's future earning power is dependent upon his or her ability.
6. If one knows how to deal with people, they are really quite easily led.	6. I have little influence over the way other people behave.
7. The grades I make are the result of my own efforts; luck has little or nothing to do with it.	7. Sometimes I feel that I have little to do with the grades I get.
8. People like me can change the course of world affairs if we make ourselves heard.	8. It is only wishful thinking to believe that one can readily influence what happens in our society.
9. A great deal that happens to me is probably a matter of chance.	9. I am in control of my destiny.
10. Getting along with people is a skill that must be practised.	10. It is almost impossible to figure out how to please some people.

Source: Adapted from J.B. Rotter, "External Control and Internal Control," *Psychology Today,* June 1971, p. 42. Copyright 1971 by the American Psychological Association. Adapted with permission.

Scoring Key: Give yourself 1 point for each of the following selections: 1B, 2A, 3A, 4B, 5B, 6A, 7A, 8A, 9B, and 10A. Scores can be interpreted as follows:

8 — 10	=	High internal locus of control
6 — 7	=	Moderate internal locus of control
5	=	Mixed
3 — 4	=	Moderate external locus of control
1 — 2	=	High external locus of control

INCREASE YOUR SELF-AWARENESS #2

How Machiavellian Are You?

Instructions: For each statement, circle the number that most closely resembles your attitude.

Statement	Disagree			Agree	
	A Lot	**A Little**	**Neutral**	**A Little**	**A Lot**
1. The best way to handle people is to tell them what they want to hear.	1	2	3	4	5
2. When you ask someone to do something for you, it is best to give the real reason for wanting it rather than giving reasons that might carry more weight.	1	2	3	4	5
3. Anyone who completely trusts anyone else is asking for trouble.	1	2	3	4	5
4. It is hard to get ahead without cutting corners here and there.	1	2	3	4	5
5. It is safest to assume that all people have a vicious streak, and it will come out when they are given a chance.	1	2	3	4	5
6. One should take action only when it is morally right.	1	2	3	4	5
7. Most people are basically good and kind.	1	2	3	4	5
8. There is no excuse for lying to someone else.	1	2	3	4	5
9. Most people more easily forget the death of their father than the loss of their property.	1	2	3	4	5
10. Generally speaking, people won't work hard unless they're forced to do so.	1	2	3	4	5

Source: R. Christie and F.L. Geis, *Studies in Machiavellianism.* Academic Press 1970. Reprinted by permission.

Scoring Key: To obtain your Mach score, add the number you have checked on questions 1, 3, 4, 5, 9, and 10. For the other four questions, reverse the numbers you have checked: 5 becomes 1, 4 is 2, 2 is 4, and 1 is 5. Total your 10 numbers to find your score. The higher your score, the more Machiavellian you are. Among a random sample of American adults, the national average was 25.

INCREASE YOUR SELF-AWARENESS #3

How's Your Self-Esteem?

Instructions: Answer each of the following questions *honestly*. Next to each question write a 1, 2, 3, 4, or 5 depending on which answer best describes you.

1 = Very often

2 = Fairly often

3 = Sometimes

4 = Once in a great while

5 = Practically never

_____ 1. How often do you have the feeling that there is nothing that you can do well?

_____ 2. When you talk in front of a class or group of people your own age, how often do you feel worried or afraid?

_____ 3. How often do you feel that you have handled yourself well at social gatherings?

_____ 4. How often do you have the feeling that you can do everything well?

_____ 5. How often are you comfortable when starting a conversation with people you don't know?

_____ 6. How often do you feel self-conscious?

_____ 7. How often do you feel that you are a successful person?

_____ 8. How often are you troubled with shyness?

_____ 9. How often do you feel inferior to most people you know?

_____ 10. How often do you feel that you are a worthless individual?

_____ 11. How often do you feel confident that your success in your future job or career is assured?

_____ 12. How often do you feel sure of yourself when among strangers?

_____ 13. How often do you feel confident that some day people will look up to you and respect you?

_____ 14. In general, how often do you feel confident about your abilities?

_____ 15. How often do you worry about how well you get along with other people?

_____ 16. How often do you feel that you dislike yourself?

_____ 17. How often do you feel so discouraged with yourself that you wonder whether anything is worthwhile?

_____ 18. How often do you worry about whether other people like to be with you?

_____ 19. When you talk in front of a class or a group of people of your own age, how often are you pleased with your performance?

_____ 20. How often do you feel sure of yourself when you speak in a class discussion?

Source: Developed by A.H. Eagly and adapted from J.R. Robinson and P.R. Shaver, *Measures of Social Psychological Attitudes* (Ann Arbor, MI: Institute of Social Research, 1973), pp. 79–80. With permission.

Scoring Key: Add up your score from the left column for the following 10 items: 1, 2, 6, 8, 9, 10, 15, 16, 17, and 18. For the other 10 items, reverse your scoring (i.e., a 5 becomes a 1; a 4 becomes a 2). The higher your score, the higher your self-esteem.

INCREASE YOUR SELF-AWARENESS #4

Are You a High Self-Monitor?

Instructions: Indicate the degree to which you think the following statements are true or false by circling the appropriate number. For example, if a statement is always true, circle the 5 next to that statement.

5 = Certainly, always true

4 = Generally true

3 = Somewhat true, but with exceptions

2 = Somewhat false, but with exceptions

1 = Generally false

0 = Certainly, always false

1. In social situations, I have the ability to alter my behaviour if I feel that something else is called for.	5	4	3	2	1	0
2. I am often able to read people's true emotions correctly through their eyes.	5	4	3	2	1	0
3. I have the ability to control the way I come across to people, depending on the impression I wish to give them.	5	4	3	2	1	0
4. In conversations, I am sensitive to even the slightest change in the facial expression of the person I'm conversing with.	5	4	3	2	1	0
5. My powers of intuition are quite good when it comes to understanding others' emotions and motives.	5	4	3	2	1	0
6. I can usually tell when others consider a joke in bad taste, even though they may laugh convincingly.	5	4	3	2	1	0
7. When I feel that the image I am portraying isn't working, I can readily change it to something that does.	5	4	3	2	1	0
8. I can usually tell when I've said something inappropriate by reading the listener's eyes.	5	4	3	2	1	0
9. I have trouble changing my behaviour to suit different people and different situations.	5	4	3	2	1	0
10. I have found that I can adjust my behaviour to meet the requirements of any situation I find myself in.	5	4	3	2	1	0
11. If someone is lying to me, I usually know it at once from that person's manner of expression.	5	4	3	2	1	0
12. Even when it might be to my advantage, I have difficulty putting up a good front.	5	4	3	2	1	0
13. Once I know what the situation calls for, it's easy for me to regulate my actions accordingly.	5	4	3	2	1	0

Source: R.D. Lennox and R.N. Wolfe, "Revision of the Self-Monitoring Scale," *Journal of Personality and Social Psychology*, June 1984, p. 1361. Copyright 1984 by the American Psychological Association. Reprinted by permission.

Scoring Key: To obtain your score, add up the numbers circled, except reverse scores for questions 9 and 12. On those, a circled 5 becomes a 0, 4 becomes 1, and so forth. High self-monitors are defined as those with scores of 53 or higher.

INCREASE YOUR SELF-AWARENESS #5

Are You a Risk Taker?

Instructions: For each of the following situations, you will be asked to indicate the minimum odds of success you would demand before recommending that one alternative be chosen over another. Try to place yourself in the position of the adviser to the central person in each of the situations.

1. Mr. B, a 45-year-old accountant, has recently been informed by his physician that he has developed a severe heart ailment. The disease would be sufficiently serious to force Mr. B to change many of his strongest life habits—reducing his work load, drastically changing his diet, giving up favourite leisure-time pursuits. The physician suggests that a delicate medical operation could be attempted that, if successful, would completely relieve the heart condition. But its success could not be assured, and, in fact, the operation might prove fatal.

Imagine that you are advising Mr. B. Listed below are several probabilities or odds that the operation will prove successful. Check the *lowest probability* that you would consider acceptable for the operation to be performed.

_____ Place a check mark here if you think that Mr. B should *not* have the operation no matter what the probabilities.

_____ The chances are 9 in 10 that the operation will be a success.

_____ The chances are 7 in 10 that the operation will be a success.

_____ The chances are 5 in 10 that the operation will be a success.

_____ The chances are 3 in 10 that the operation will be a success.

_____ The chances are 1 in 10 that the operation will be a success.

2. Mr. D is the captain of University X's varsity football team. University X is playing its traditional rival, University Y, in the final game of the season. The game is in its final seconds, and Mr. D's team, University X, is behind in the score. University X has time to make one more play. Mr. D, the captain, must decide whether it would be best to try a play that would be almost certain to work and try to settle for a tie score, or, on the other hand, should he try a more complicated and risky play that would bring victory if it succeeded or defeat if it failed. Imagine that you are advising Mr. D. Listed below are several probabilities or odds that the risky play will work. Check the *lowest probability* that you would consider acceptable for the risky play to be attempted.

_____ Place a check mark here if you think that Mr. D should *not* attempt the risky play no matter what the probabilities.

_____ The chances are 9 in 10 that the risky play will work.

_____ The chances are 7 in 10 that the risky play will work.

_____ The chances are 5 in 10 that the risky play will work.

_____ The chances are 3 in 10 that the risky play will work.

_____ The chances are 1 in 10 that the risky play will work.

3. Ms. K is a successful businesswoman who has participated in a number of civic activities of considerable value to the community. Ms. K has been approached by the leaders of her political party as a possible candidate in the next provincial election. Ms. K's party is a minority party in the district, though the party has won occasional elections in the past. Ms. K would like to hold political office, but to do so would involve a serious financial sacrifice, since the party has insufficient campaign funds. She would also have to endure the attacks of her political opponents in a hot campaign.

Imagine that you are advising Ms. K. Listed below are several probabilities or odds of Ms. K's winning the election in her district. Check the *lowest probability* that you would consider acceptable to make it worthwhile for Ms. K to run for political office.

_____ Place a check here if you think that Ms. K should *not* run for political office no matter what the probabilities.

_____ The chances are 9 in 10 that Ms. K will win the election.

_____ The chances are 7 in 10 that Ms. K will win the election.

_____ The chances are 5 in 10 that Ms. K will win the election.

_____ The chances are 3 in 10 that Ms. K will win the election.

_____ The chances are 1 in 10 that Ms. K will win the election.

4. Ms. L, a 30-year-old research physicist, has been given a five-year appointment by a major university laboratory. As she contemplates the next five years, she realizes that she might work on a difficult, long-term problem that, if a solution could be found, would resolve basic scientific issues in the field and bring high scientific honours. If no solution were found, however, Ms. L would have little to show for her five years in the laboratory and it would be hard for her to get a good job afterward. On the other hand, she could, as most of her professional associates are doing, work on a series of short-term problems for which solutions would be easier to find but that are of lesser scientific importance.

Imagine that you are advising Ms. L. Listed below are several probabilities or odds that a solution will be found to the difficult, long-term problem that Ms. L has in mind. Check the _lowest probability_ that you would consider acceptable to make it worthwhile for Ms. L to work on the more difficult long-term problem.

_____ The chances are 1 in 10 that Ms. L will solve the long-term problem.

_____ The chances are 3 in 10 that Ms. L will solve the long-term problem.

_____ The chances are 5 in 10 that Ms. L will solve the long-term problem.

_____ The chances are 7 in 10 that Ms. L will solve the long-term problem.

_____ The chances are 9 in 10 that Ms. L will solve the long-term problem.

_____ Place a check mark here if you think Ms. L should _not_ choose the long-term, difficult problem, no matter what the probabilities.

Source: Adapted from N. Kogan and M.A. Wallach, _Risk Taking: A Study in Cognition and Personality_ (New York: Holt, Rinehart & Winston, 1964), pp. 256–61.

Scoring Key: These situations were based on a longer questionnaire. Your results are an indication of your general orientation toward risk rather than a precise measure. To calculate your risk-taking score, add up the chances you were willing to take and divide by four. For any of the situations in which you would not take the risk regardless of the probabilities, give yourself a 10. The lower your number, the more risk-taking you are.

INCREASE YOUR SELF-AWARENESS #6

Are You a Type A?

Instructions: Circle the number on the scale below that best characterizes your behaviour for each trait.

1. Casual about appointments	1	2	3	4	5	6	7	8	Never late
2. Not competitive	1	2	3	4	5	6	7	8	Very competitive
3. Never feel rushed	1	2	3	4	5	6	7	8	Always feel rushed
4. Take things one at a time	1	2	3	4	5	6	7	8	Try to do many things at once
5. Slow doing things	1	2	3	4	5	6	7	8	Fast (eating, walking, etc.)
6. Express feelings	1	2	3	4	5	6	7	8	"Sit on" feelings
7. Many interests	1	2	3	4	5	6	7	8	Few interests outside work

Source: Adapted from R.W. Bortner, "Short Rating Scale as a Potential Measure of Pattern A Behavior," _Journal of Chronic Diseases,_ June 1969, pp. 87–91. With permission.

Scoring Key: Total your score on the seven questions. Now multiply the total by three. A total of 120 or more indicates that you are a hard-core Type A. Scores below 90 indicate that you are a hard-core Type B. The following gives you more specifics:

Points	Personality Type
120 or more	A1
106—119	A
100—105	A2
90—99	B1
Less than 90	B

WORKING WITH OTHERS EXERCISE

Evaluating Your Interpersonal Perception

1. On a piece of paper, independently write down how you would describe *yourself* on the following dimensions:
   a. Friendliness
   b. Moodiness
   c. Sense of humour
   d. Career motivation
   e. Interpersonal skills
   f. Desire to be accepted by others
   g. Independence

2. Now form groups of three to five members. Evaluate each of the *other members* in your group (as best you can) on the same seven dimensions.

3. Going around the group so each member gets to participate, describe what each of you has written about Member A. After you have all provided your perceptions, Member A will share his or her own self-perceptions. Then do the same with Member B, and so forth, until all group members have received feedback and shared their own impressions.

4. The exercise concludes by each member analysing the similarities and differences between their perceptions of themselves on the seven dimensions and how they're perceived by the other members of their group.

CASE
INCIDENT

Frank Stronach, Risk Taker and Fair Enterprise Creator

Frank Stronach, Chairman of Toronto-based Magna International, believes in "fair enterprise," including a universal charter of rights, and a fairer distribution of wealth. He criticizes socialist systems ("they stifle individualism"), totalitarianism ("benefits the few"), and even free enterprise ("from time-to-time self-destroying"). This may seem like a paradox from someone who earned $26.5 million in 1996 for heading Magna. However, as Hugh Segal, former chief of staff to Brian Mulroney and contender for leadership of the Conservative Party in 1998, explains, "If Frank were the kind of person for whom conventional orthodoxy mattered, he'd probably still be running a one-man machine shop on Dupont (in Toronto)," where he first started out in the mid-1950s.

Stronach created Magna's corporate philosophy to foster a "strong sense of ownership and entrepreneurial energy" among his employees. Ten percent of pre-tax profit is allocated to employees in the form of cash and share purchase plans, thus giving all employees a share in the profits of the company. He insists that managers' salaries are to be pegged "below industry standards." At the same time, plant managers are given considerable autonomy over buying, selling, and hiring. Magna also tries to keep up with employee attitudes: plant managers are required to meet all their workers at least once a month, and employees return a comprehensive survey once a year.

Still, the Canadian Auto Workers Union (CAW) would like to unionize Magna employees. To date, they have carried out six campaigns, though none has been successful. They haven't given up, however. "I think one day we will organize Magna," says Maureen Kirincic, national director of organizing for the CAW. Jim Stanford, a CAW union economist, isn't quite so sure: "Relatively speaking, they treat employees better than most non-union employers. That's one of the reasons it has been hard to crack Magna."

Questions

1. Using the information in the case and the chapter opening vignette, to what extent would you say that Frank Stronach's personality is reflected in his corporate policy?

2. What might our study of perceptions tell us about CAW's attempts to organize Magna?

3. Are there people who might be unhappy working for Frank Stronach?

4. What are the pros and cons of being a manager under such a strong personality?

Sources: "Stronach's Pay Almost Matches Big 3 Combined," *Canadian Press Newswire*, October 31, 1997; B. Simon, "Work Ethic and the Magna Carta," *Financial Post Daily*, March 20, 1997, p. 14; "Magna In Overdrive: No Canadian Has Profited From Contracting Out as Much as Stronach," *Maclean's*, September 30, 1996, pp. 50–54; "Car and Striver (Will the World's Leading Auto-Parts Supplier Become the Globe's Newest Automaker?)," *Canadian Business*, September, 1996, pp 92–94; "Magna-Mania: Resurrecting His On-The-Brink Auto Parts Empire didn't Satisfy Frank Stronach who Plans Growth and Monuments with Equal Flair," *Financial Post*, August 12/14, 1995, pp. 12–13.

Peggy Witte

Peggy Witte, President and CEO of Royal Oak Mines, has real charisma. She can sweep people up in her enthusiasm, getting them to put high energy into helping her develop her projects. She also has a personality that isn't afraid of taking risks.

Over the past 10 years, Witte has been in charge of a number of controversial projects and decisions. In 1988, she had a bold plan to build a gold mine on a remote Northern Canadian site, but the site didn't work out. Next, she developed a strategy of trying to squeeze profits out of old high-cost mines, with mixed results. Then she took a defiant stance at Giant Mine in Yellowknife, refusing to settle with striking workers. That was followed by a failed billion-dollar takeover attempt of LAC Minerals. Then she gambled by buying Windy Craggy to mine its copper deposits, knowing that the B.C. government might declare the area a wilderness preserve. And it did. But Witte was able to force massive compensation from the government in exchange.

Witte takes one risk after another as she leads Royal Oak Mines. She is an aggressive player in the gold mining industry. She is known to be enthusiastic and optimistic when she starts new projects, only to produce less gold than projected. But that never dampens her enthusiasm for yet more projects. Witte's most recent risky project is the Kemess mine. She views this project as an opportunity to turn things around, transforming Royal Oak into a low-cost gold producer from its current position as the highest-cost producer in Canada. She's expecting that she can cut her costs from US $332 to US $205 per ounce of gold. But Witte isn't worried if her costs don't come in as low as she's estimated. She believes that she has room for a margin of error. And she has no doubt that she will succeed.

Questions

1. How would you describe Peggy Witte's personality?

2. To what extent would you say that personality plays a role in how Peggy Witte runs Royal Oak mines?

3. Do you think Witte's personality causes her to take bigger risks than someone else leading Royal Oak might take? Why?

Source: Based on "Peggy Witte," *Venture 677*; aired February 3, 1998.

"Be yourself"

is the worst advice

you can give some people.

– T. Masson

POINT

When Hiring Employees: Emphasize the Positive

Hiring new employees requires managers to become salespeople. They have to emphasize the positive, even if it means failing to mention the negative aspects in the job. While there is a real risk of setting unrealistic expectations about the organization and about the specific job, that's a risk managers have to take. As in dealing with any salesperson, it is the job applicant's responsibility to follow the dictum *caveat emptor*—let the buyer beware!

Why should managers emphasize the positive when discussing a job with a prospective candidate? They have no choice! First, there is a dwindling supply of qualified applicants for many job vacancies; and second, this approach is necessary to meet the competition.

The massive restructuring and downsizing of organizations that began in the late 1980s has drawn attention to corporate layoffs. What has often been overlooked in this process is the growing shortage of qualified applicants for literally millions of jobs. Through the foreseeable future, managers will find it increasingly difficult to get qualified people who can fill jobs such as legal secretary, nurse, accountant, salesperson, maintenance mechanic, computer-repair specialist, software programmer, social worker, physi-cal therapist, environmental engineer, telecommunications specialist, and airline pilot. But managers will also find it harder to get qualified people to fill entry-level, minimum-wage jobs. There may be no shortage of physical bodies, but finding individuals who can read, write, perform basic mathematical calculations, and have the proper work habits to effectively perform these jobs isn't so easy. There is a growing gap between the skills workers have and the skills employers require. So managers need to *sell* jobs to the limited pool of applicants. And this means presenting the job and the organization in the most favourable light possible.

Another reason management is forced to emphasize the positive with job candidates is that this is what the competition is doing. Other employers also face a limited applicant pool. As a result, to get people to join their organizations, they are forced to put a positive "spin" on their descriptions of their organizations and the jobs they seek to fill. In this competitive environment, any employer who presents jobs realistically to applicants—that is, openly provides the negative aspects of a job along with the positive—risks losing most or all of the most desirable candidates. ■

Y.H. Quek is president of Procter & Gamble Canada. He leads a company that values diversity in its workplace. Consider Procter & Gamble's statement on employee diversity:

Developing and managing a strong, diverse organization is essential to achieving our business purpose. We value the different perspectives that the diversity of Procter & Gamble people bring to the business. At Procter & Gamble, we operate on the fundamental belief that these diverse viewpoints are needed for organization creativity which produces genuine competitive advantage.[1]

We expect that an organization's values, like those of an individual, will be reflected in corresponding behaviour and attitudes. If a company stated that they value organizational diversity, and no behaviour flowed from that statement, we would question whether that value was really so important to the company. However, in Procter & Gamble's case, they back up their value statement with concrete policies and actions to show support for the value. For instance, they changed their recruiting practices to ensure diversity in their hiring. They broadened the number of universities from which they recruit, included French universities in Quebec, and targeted several campuses with high representation of visible minority students to ensure geographical, language, racial, and ethnic diversity. This resulted in a stronger and more diverse population at Procter & Gamble.

In this chapter, we look more carefully at how values influence an individual's behaviour and consider the relationship between values and attitudes. We then consider two specific issues that arise from our discussion of values and attitudes: workforce diversity and job satisfaction. ■

Values

Is capital punishment right or wrong? How about racial or gender quotas in hiring—are they right or wrong? If a person likes power, is that good or bad? The answers to these questions are value laden. Some might argue, for example, that capital punishment is right because it is an appropriate retribution for crimes such as murder. However, others might argue, just as strongly, that no government has the right to take anyone's life.

Values represent basic convictions that "a specific mode of conduct or end-state of existence is personally or socially preferable to an opposite or converse mode of conduct or end-state of existence."[2] They contain a judgmental element in that they carry an individual's ideas as to what is right, good, or desirable. Values have both content and intensity attributes. The content attribute says that a mode of conduct or end-state of existence is *important*. The intensity attribute specifies *how important* it is. When we rank an individual's values in terms of their intensity, we obtain that person's **value system**. All of us have a hierarchy of values that forms our value system. This system is identified by the relative importance we assign to such values as freedom, pleasure, self-respect, honesty, obedience, and equality.

Importance of Values

Values are important to the study of organizational behaviour because they lay the foundation for the understanding of attitudes and motivation and because they influence our perceptions. Individuals enter an organization with preconceived notions of what "ought" and what "ought not" to be. Of course, these notions are not value free. On the contrary, they contain interpretations of right and wrong. Furthermore, they imply that certain behaviours or outcomes are preferred over others. As a result, values cloud objectivity and rationality.

Values generally influence attitudes and behaviour.[3] Suppose that you enter an organization with the view that allocating pay on the basis of performance is right, whereas allocating pay on the basis of seniority is wrong or inferior. How will you react if you find that the organization you have just joined rewards seniority and not performance? You're likely to be disappointed—and this can lead to job dissatisfaction and the decision not to exert a high level of effort since "it's probably not going to lead to more money, anyway." Would your attitudes and behaviour be different if your values aligned with the organization's pay policies? Most likely. In this chapter's Learning About Yourself exercise, you are given the opportunity to examine some of the things that you value.

A Framework for Assessing Cultural Values

Before we look selectively at a variety of cultural value comparisons, it is helpful to know how cultures are examined. One of the most widely referenced approaches for analyzing variations among cultures has been done by Geert Hofstede.[4] He surveyed more than 116 000 IBM employees in 40 countries about their work-related values. He found that managers and employees vary on five value dimensions of national culture. They are listed and defined as follows:

> **Power distance.** The degree to which people in a country accept that power in institutions and organizations is distributed unequally.

---

values
Basic convictions that a specific mode of conduct or end-state of existence is personally or socially preferable to an opposite or converse mode of conduct or end-state of existence.

value system
A hierarchy based on a ranking of an individual's values in terms of their intensity.

IBM Corporation
http://www.ibm.com/

power distance
A national culture attribute describing the extent to which a society accepts that power in institutions and organizations is distributed unequally.

individualism
A national culture attribute describing a loosely knit social framework in which people emphasize only the care of themselves and their immediate family.

collectivism
A national culture attribute that describes a tight social framework in which people expect others in groups of which they are a part to look after them and protect them.

quantity of life
A national culture attribute describing the extent to which societal values are characterized by assertiveness and materialism.

quality of life
A national culture attribute that emphasizes relationships and concern for others.

uncertainty avoidance
A national culture attribute describing the extent to which a society feels threatened by uncertain and ambiguous situations and tries to avoid them.

long-term orientation
A national culture attribute that emphasizes the future, thrift, and persistence.

short-term orientation
A national culture attribute that emphasizes the past and present, respect for tradition, and fulfilling social obligation.

www.environics.net/

Ranges from relatively equal (low power distance) to extremely unequal (high power distance).

Individualism versus **collectivism.** Individualism is the degree to which people in a country prefer to act as individuals rather than as members of groups. Collectivism is the equivalent of low individualism.

Quantity of life versus **quality of life.** Quantity of life is the degree to which values like assertiveness, the acquisition of money and material goods, and competition prevail. Quality of life is the degree to which people value relationships, and show sensitivity and concern for the welfare of others.[5]

Uncertainty avoidance. The degree to which people in a country prefer structured over unstructured situations. In countries that score high on uncertainty avoidance, people have an increased level of anxiety, which manifests itself in greater nervousness, stress, and aggressiveness.

Long-term versus **short-term orientation.** People in cultures with long-term orientations look to the future and value thrift and persistence. A short-term orientation values the past and present, and emphasizes respect for tradition and fulfilling social obligations.

Canadian Social Values

In a recent book entitled *Sex in the Snow,* pollster Michael Adams attempted to identify the social values of today's Canadians.[6] He found that within three broad age groups of adult Canadians—those over 50 ("the elders"), baby boomers (born from the mid-1940s to the mid-1960s), and Generation X (born between the mid-1960s to the early 1980s)—there are at least 12 quite distinct "value tribes." We present some of the findings below. For further information and an opportunity to see where you might be classified in terms of your social values, visit the Environics web site.

THE ELDERS: These individuals are characterized as "playing by the rules," and their core values are belief in order, authority, discipline, the Judeo-Christian moral code, and the Golden Rule (do unto others as you would have others do unto you). About 80 percent of the elders resemble this description of traditional values, although there are variations within that 80 percent in the strength of fit.

THE BOOMERS: Although viewed as a somewhat spoiled, hedonistic, rebellious group, this belies the four categories of boomers: autonomous rebels (25%), anxious communitarians (20%), connected enthusiasts (14%), and disengaged Darwinists (41%). So, unlike the elders, boomers are a bit more fragmented in their views, although all but the disengaged Darwinists reflect to some extent the stereotypes of this generation: rejection of authority, skepticism regarding the motives of big business and government, a strong concern for the environment, and a strong desire for equality in the workplace and society. Of course, the disengaged Darwinists, the largest single group, do not fit this description as well. This group is characterized as being angry, intimidated by change, and anxious about their professional and financial futures.

GENERATION X: While this group is quite fragmented in its values, the research showed that the common values are experience-seeking, adaptability, and concern with personal image among peers. Despite these common values, Gen Xers can be divided into five tribes. Thrill-seeking materialists (25%) desire money and material possessions, as well as recognition, respect and admiration. Aimless dependents (27%) seek financial independence, security and stability. Social hedonists (15%) are experience-seeking, committed to their own pleasure and seek immediate gratification. New Aquarians (13%) are experience-seeking as well, and also egalitarian and ecologically minded. Finally, autonomous post-materialists (20%) seek personal autonomy and self-fulfilment, and are concerned about human rights.

Beyond the differences in the three generational groups, it is safe to say that overall the values of Canadians have changed a lot in the last 10 years. Air Canada recently studied the core values of Canadians as part of an effort to develop its brand strategy.[7] Their results show that Canadians have become more confident and less nationalistic. They are also human, caring, and humble, while also seeking respect. Finally, the Air Canada results indicate that while there is a strong social conscience among Canadians, there is currently more emphasis on the individual than the collective than there was in the past.

Air Canada
http://www.aircanada.ca/

The Application of Generational Values to the Workplace

An awareness of the overall value structure, as well as the very broad generalizations of the differing values among the generational groups identified above, helps us to understand better how to manage and interrelate in the workplace. Senior management is often led by the elders, although the boomers are now moving into head offices as well. Consequently, the "play-by-the-rules" leaders are being replaced by boomers who have a somewhat more egalitarian view of the workplace. Meanwhile, the Gen Xers enter the workplace, are comfortable in adapting, but also want more experiences. Managing the expectations of each of these very different groups is not an easy task.

Organizations more generally can consider moulding their workplace by hiring people with similar values, and/or aligning the jobs that people are given with their values. For instance, Toronto-based investment banking firm Griffiths McBurney & Partners Inc. hires people who are aggressive and risk-takers, because that is the kind of firm the partners have created. "Everyone starts the year with zero salary, zero draw, and no guarantees," and compensation is based on revenues.[8] Workplaces also try to change values through education or "propagandaistic interventions."[9] Later in the chapter, for instance, we discuss how workplaces have attempted to introduce the value of cultural diversity. Interestingly enough, however, there is little research that shows that values can be changed successfully.[10] Values tend to be relatively stable, and thus more interventions are aimed at changing attitudes. After our discussion of attitudes below, we note some of these specific interventions with respect to cultural diversity in the workplace.

Francophone and Anglophone Values

One of the larger issues that has confronted Canada in recent years is the question of Quebec separatism and anglophone-francophone differences. Consequently, it may be of interest to managers and employees in Canadian

Laurent Beaudoin, Chair of Bombardier Inc. (shown right) and Matthew Barrett, chair of the Bank of Montreal, were named the most admired chief executives in Canada in 1993. Many said the choice of the two reflected differences in anglophone and francophone Canada. Quebec executives are seen as more entrepreneurial, while those outside Quebec are seen as more managerial.

firms to be aware of some of the potential cultural differences when managing in various environments. A number of studies show that anglophones and francophones have distinctive value priorities. Francophones have been found to be more collectivist or group-oriented with a greater need for achievement, while anglophones were found to be more individualist or I-centred.[11] Francophones have also been shown to be more concerned about the interpersonal aspects of the workplace than at task competence.[12] Anglophones have been shown to take more risk.[13] Other studies have found that anglophone managers tended to value autonomy and intrinsic job values such as achievement and thus were more achievement oriented, while francophone managers tended to value affiliation and extrinsic job values such as technical supervision.[14]

A 1994 study conducted at the University of Ottawa and Laval University suggests that some of the differences reported in previous research may be decreasing.[15] For instance, that study reported that there were no significant differences in individualism and collectivism. While this is only one study, and thus needs further confirmation, the researchers suggest that some of the differences found in previous studies were a function of characteristics unrelated to whether a person was francophone or anglophone. Specifically, once the socioeconomic status of the individuals is controlled, there are no differences due to linguistic background. The researchers also concluded that both francophone and anglophone managers today would have been exposed to more of the same types of organizational theories during their training in post-secondary school, which might also influence their outlooks as managers. Thus we would not expect to find large differences in the way

that firms in francophone Canada are managed, compared to those in the rest of Canada. Throughout the textbook you will see a number of examples of Quebec-based businesses that support this conclusion.

Canadian Aboriginal Values

Entrepreneurial activity among Canada's aboriginal people has been increasing at the same time that there are more partnerships and alliances between aboriginal and non-aboriginal businesses. Because of these business interactions, it is important to examine the types of differences one might observe in how each culture manages its businesses. "Aboriginal values are usually perceived (by non-aboriginals) as an impediment to economic development and organizational effectiveness." These values include reluctance to compete, a time orientation different from Western time orientation, and an emphasis on consensus decision-making.[16] Aboriginals do not necessarily agree that these values are business impediments, however.

Specifically, while historically Canadian businesses and government have assumed that "non-Native people must teach Native people how to run their own organizations," the First Nations of Canada are not convinced.[17] They believe that traditional culture, values, and languages do not have to be compromised to build a self-sustaining economy. Moreover, they believe that their cultural values may actually be a positive force in conducting business.[18]

To use Hofstede's framework to understand aboriginal and non-aboriginal cultures, we can rely on the research of Lindsay Redpath of Athabasca University.[19] Aboriginal cultures are more collectivist in orientation than non-aboriginal cultures in either Canada or the United States. Aboriginal organizations are much more likely to reflect and advance the goals of the community. There is also a greater sense of family within the workplace, with greater affiliation and loyalty. Power distance in aboriginal cultures is

Prime Minister Jean Chrétien helped celebrate the opening of the Saskatoon head office of First Nations Bank of Canada. The Bank's opening ceremonies, as well as its operating procedures, emphasize a strong attachment to aboriginal values.

smaller than in non-aboriginal cultures of Canada and the United States, and there is an emphasis on consensual decision-making. Aboriginal cultures are lower on uncertainty avoidance than non-aboriginal cultures in either Canada or the United States. Aboriginal organizations and cultures tend to have fewer rules and regulations. Each of these differences suggests that organizations created by aboriginals will differ from non-aboriginal businesses, and both research and anecdotal evidence support this conjecture.[20]

Certainly the opening ceremony for the First Nations Bank of Canada's head office branch in Saskatoon in September 1997 was different from many openings of Western businesses. The ceremony was accompanied by the burning of sweetgrass. "This is a blessing," Blaine Favel, chief of the Federation of Saskatchewan Indian Nations, said to a large outdoor gathering. "We are celebrating a great accomplishment by our people."[21]

Saskatoon-based Adam's Active Autowrecking is owned by Sandra Bighead, a member of the Beardy's and Okemasis First Nation. Her philosophy about running her business exhibits the family-value orientation that is more likely to be found in aboriginal businesses. She believes in taking care of her staff: "For me, success is gaining personal satisfaction, self-confidence, and self-worth from the work I do," she said. "Part of that satisfaction comes from knowing that a lot of people and their families are depending on me."[22]

First Nations Bank of Canada
http://www.firstnationsbank.com/

Federation of Saskatchewan Indian Nations
http://www.fsin.com/

Values Across Cultures

In Chapter 1, we described the new global village and said "managers have to become capable of working with people from different cultures." Exhibit 4-1 provides a summary of how a number of countries rate on Hofstede's five dimensions (power distance; individualism versus collectivism; quantity of life versus quality of life; uncertainty avoidance; and long-term versus short-term orientation). Not surprisingly, most Asian countries are more collectivist than individualistic. On the other hand, the United States ranked highest among all countries surveyed on individualism.

Because values differ across cultures, an understanding of these differences should be helpful in explaining and predicting behaviour of employees from different countries. We will illustrate this point with a comparison of American culture with Canadian and Japanese cultures.[23] This is followed by a more general overview of some of the differences that researchers have found across other cultures. Additional insights are provided in this chapter's CBC Video Case.

Canadian and American Values

Pollster Michael Adams points out that "Americans have a greater faith in the family, the state (that is, 'America'), religion, and the market."[24] Americans are more comfortable with big business, probably because it means American big business, whereas in Canada big business means a foreign-owned, often American, business. The American business environment is characterized by intense competition, whereas Canada has historically had a more protectionist attitude in the market, as well as public-sector monopolies and private-sector oligopolies. While these "anti-market" forces are changing slowly, Canadian businesses are still adapting to the open markets that globalization has brought.

If we can talk about a national "personality," Canadians are more shy and deferential than Americans, as well as less violent and more courteous.

Exhibit 4-1
Examples of National Cultural Values

Country	Power Distance	Individualism*	Quantity of Life**	Uncertainty Avoidance	Long-term Orientation***
Canada	Moderate	High	High	Moderate	Low
China	High	Low	Moderate	Moderate	High
France	High	High	Moderate	High	Low
Germany****	Low	High	High	Moderate	Moderate
Hong Kong	High	Low	High	Low	High
Indonesia	High	Low	Moderate	Low	Low
Japan	Moderate	Moderate	High	Moderate	Moderate
Netherlands	Low	High	Low	Moderate	Moderate
Russia	High	Moderate	Low	High	Low
United States	Low	High	High	Low	Low
West Africa	High	Low	Moderate	Moderate	Low

*A low score is synonymous with collectivism. **A low score is synonymous with high quality of life. ***A low score is synonymous with a short-term orientation. ****Includes only former West Germany.

Source: Adapted from G. Hofstede, "Cultural Constraints in Management Theories," *Academy of Management Executive*, February 1993, p. 91; G. Hofstede, "The Cultural Relativity of Organizational Practices and Theories," *Journal of International Business Studies*, 14, 1983, pp. 75–89.

There is more emphasis on being polite and following the rules. Canadians are more pragmatic, and less ideological. Canadians value peace, order, and equality, whereas Americans value individuality and freedom.[25] Further discussion of differences between American and Canadian values comes from Donald Carty, a Canadian, and president of American Airlines. He notes that "there are a lot of values Canadians hold dear that Americans yearn for—diversity and fairness over divisiveness and racism, and the quality and consistency of our education."[26]

All of these differences in values suggest that Canadian and American workplaces will likely look and operate somewhat differently. Canadians may be more suited to the teams that many organizations are creating, and more willing to work together than to be individual stars. They may follow the directives of their managers more, even as the learning organization suggests that both employees and managers need to take more responsibility to learn and share information. An awareness of these values will help you understand some of the differences you might observe in Canadian and American businesses.

Japanese and American Values

American children are taught early the values of individuality and uniqueness. In contrast, Japanese children are socialized to be "team players," to work within the group, and to conform. A significant part of an American student's education is to learn to think, analyze, and question. Their Japanese counterparts are rewarded for recounting facts. These different socialization practices reflect different cultures and, not surprisingly, result in different types of employees. For example, the average U.S. worker is more

From their earliest years, Japanese children are taught the value of working together. This socialization practice extends into the workplace, where employees work well as a team. The team of workers shown here at Japan's Yokogawa Electric, maker of industrial testing and measuring equipment, is able to make decisions about redesigning products in short periods of time while meeting the company's cost-cutting goals.

competitive and self-focused than the Japanese worker. Predictions of employee behaviour, based on U.S. workers, are likely to be off-target when they are applied to a population of employees—such as the Japanese—who prefer and perform better in standardized tasks, as part of a work team, with group-based decisions and rewards.

Our discussion about differences in values cross-culturally might suggest to you that when Canadian firms develop overseas operations, or expand south of the Canadian border, the need to understand other cultures becomes important for employees transferred to foreign locations. Our Point/Counterpoint discussion investigates some of the pros and cons of cross-cultural training.

Implications for OB

While Canadian researchers have contributed to the body of knowledge we call *organizational behaviour,* much of the theory we use in Canada has been developed by Americans using American subjects within domestic contexts.[27] What this means is that (1) not all OB theories and concepts are universally applicable to managing people around the world, especially in countries where work values are considerably different from those in either the United States or Canada; and (2) you should take into consideration cultural values when trying to understand the behaviour of people in different countries.

In subsequent chapters we discuss such workplace practices as goal setting (Chapter 5), job enrichment (Chapter 15), quality circles (Chapter 15), and performance-based pay (Chapter 6). Researchers have noted that managerial interventions such as these have differed greatly in effectiveness among countries.[28] A recent theory—"cultural self-presentation theory"— suggests that workers' responses to these interventions are affected by the individual's interpretation of the dominant social values.[29] For instance, the introduction of pay-for-performance, which rewards individual behaviour, is less likely to be welcomed by workers in a more collectivist culture where the group is more important than any individual. Although more empirical

OB IN THE NEWS

Team Benefits of Workforce Diversity

Honeywell Limited in Scarborough, Ontario, believes in encouraging its diverse workforce to work together effectively. It wants to turn diversity into a competitive advantage.

Company chairman and CEO Dave Larkin and the plant's director of manufacturing, John MacMillan, are solidly committed to the "Learning for Life" program—Honeywell's name for an initiative that promotes education in the workplace.

The company's Human Resources specialist, Sujata Molyneux, explains how the program works:

"The diversity training programs…help people to solve conflicts, work in teams and become committed. Courses are given at the job site, some during, some after working hours, by community colleges, paid for by Honeywell. Employees receive a minimum of two hours of instruction every two weeks on problem solving, quality improvement, what input culture has on teams, and how issues can be resolved."

Honeywell has experienced valuable gains due to its learning programs. Five years after the programs were initiated, significant bottom-line results were obvious: productivity was up by 40 percent, inventory reduced by 60 percent, and employees' pride, dedication and self-esteem dramatically improved.

The Scarborough plant also sees benefits in the export market, which accounts for 80 percent of its production. Honeywell has employees who speak the languages and understand the cultures of their foreign clients. This makes products and services more marketable abroad.

With its diversity programs, the Canadian Honeywell operation is viewed as a role model. The U.S. divisions of the firm recognize the advantage of Scarborough's approach.

As Molyneux explains, "The process of teamwork for people from different cultures can cause great discomfort for some and, if left unaddressed, can increase conflict and ultimately deter commitment. It is therefore important to understand whether teams are culturally biased and what influence desire for harmony, social and family norms, and fatalism versus determinism have on people working together."

Source: Based on "People programs pay dividends," *Plant*, May 2, 1994 pp. 1,5 and K. Dorrell, "Breaking Down the Barriers: Work Teams and Partnership with Union Help Turn Honeywell Plant Around," *Plant*, November 24, 1997, pp. 12–13.

Take It to the Net

We invite you to visit the Robbins page on the Prentice Hall Web site at:

http://www.prenticehall.ca/robbins

for this chapter's World Wide Web exercise.

---

work needs to be done, the theory seems to be able to account for the differential effectiveness of some of the most common workplace interventions. To find out more about working with others from different cultures, you might want to examine this chapter's Case Incident.

Values and Workforce Diversity

Proctor & Gamble
http://www.pg.com

Many organizations have attempted to incorporate workforce diversity initiatives into their workplaces. For example, Procter & Gamble's explicit statement about employment diversity, presented in the chapter opening, is representative of the types of statements that organizations often include in their annual reports and employee information packets to signal the corpo-

rate values to both employees and other people who might do business with the company. Some corporations choose to signal the value of diversity because they think it is an important strategic goal. As an example of this, the OB in the News feature illustrates how diversity in the workplace can benefit teams.

When companies design and then publicize statements about the importance of diversity, essentially they are producing value statements. The desire, of course, is that the statements will then change the attitudes of the members of the organization. As noted above, values themselves do not often change. So the introduction of a company value statement is not likely, in and of itself, to change the values of organizational members. The organization can attempt to change attitudes, which requires intervention programs designed to encourage attitude change. Below we discuss the importance of attitudes in the workplace, and then more specifically discuss attitudes towards diversity in the workplace.

Attitudes

attitudes
Evaluative statements or judgments concerning objects, people, or events.

Attitudes are evaluative statements—either favourable or unfavourable—concerning objects, people, or events. They reflect how one feels about something. When I say "I like my job," I am expressing my attitude about work.

Attitudes are not the same as values, but the two are interrelated. In organizations, attitudes are important because they affect job behaviour. If workers believe, for example, that supervisors, auditors, bosses, and time-and-motion engineers are all in conspiracy to make employees work harder for the same or less money, then it makes sense to try to understand how these attitudes were formed, their relationship to actual job behaviour, and how they might be changed. In the From Concepts to Skills feature we discuss whether it is possible to change someone's attitude, and how that might happen in the workplace.

Types of Attitudes

A person can have thousands of attitudes, but OB focuses our attention on a very limited number of job-related attitudes. These job-related attitudes tap positive or negative evaluations that employees hold about aspects of their work environment. Most of the research in OB has been concerned with three attitudes: job satisfaction, job involvement, and organizational commitment.[30] We also consider attitudes towards diversity below, because, as we noted in Chapter 1, Canadian workplaces are increasingly becoming multicultural environments. In this chapter's Working With Others feature, you have the opportunity to examine the attitudes that you and others hold toward the Canadian workplace.

job satisfaction
An individual's general attitude toward his or her job.

JOB SATISFACTION The term **job satisfaction** refers to an individual's general attitude toward his or her job. A person with a high level of job satisfaction holds positive attitudes toward the job, while a person who is dissatisfied with his or her job holds negative attitudes about the job. When people speak of employee attitudes, more often than not they mean job satisfaction. In fact, the two are frequently used interchangeably. Because of the high importance OB researchers have given to job satisfaction, we'll review this attitude in considerable detail later in this chapter.

Changing Attitudes

Can you change unfavourable employee attitudes? Sometimes! It depends on who you are, the strength of the employee's attitude, the magnitude of the change, and the technique you choose to try to change the attitude.

People are most likely to respond to change efforts made by someone who is liked, credible, and convincing. If people like you, they're more apt to identify and adopt your message. Credibility implies trust, expertise, and objectivity. So you're more likely to change someone's attitude if that person views you as believable, knowledgeable about what you're talking about, and unbiased in your presentation. Finally, successful attitude change is enhanced when you present your arguments clearly and persuasively.

It's easier to change a person's attitude if he or she isn't strongly committed to it. Conversely, the stronger the belief about the attitude, the harder it is to change it. In addition, attitudes that have been expressed publicly are more difficult to change because it requires one to admit that he or she has made a mistake.

It's easier to change attitudes when that change isn't very significant. To get a person to accept a new attitude that varies greatly from his or her current position requires more effort. It may also threaten other deeply held attitudes and create increased dissonance.

All attitude-change techniques are not equally effective across situations. Oral persuasion techniques are most effective when you use a positive, tactful tone; present strong evidence to support your position; tailor your argument to the listener; use logic; and support your evidence by appealing to the person's fears, frustrations, and other emotions. But people are more likely to embrace change when they can experience it. The use of training sessions where employees share and personalize experiences, and practise new behaviours, can be powerful stimulants for change. Consistent with self-perception theory, changes in behaviour can lead to changes in attitudes.

job involvement
The degree to which a person identifies with his or her job, actively participates in it, and considers his or her performance important to self-worth.

JOB INVOLVEMENT The term **job involvement** is a more recent addition to the OB literature.[31] While there isn't complete agreement over what the term means, a workable definition states that job involvement measures the degree to which a person identifies psychologically with his or her job and considers his or her perceived performance level important to self-worth.[32] Employees with a high level of job involvement identify strongly with and really care about the kind of work they do.

High levels of job involvement have been found to be related to fewer absences and lower resignation rates.[33] However, it seems to predict turnover more consistently than absenteeism, accounting for as much as 16 percent of the variance in the former.[34]

organizational commitment
The degree to which an employee identifies with a particular organization and its goals, and wishes to maintain membership in the organization.

ORGANIZATIONAL COMMITMENT The third job attitude we shall discuss is **organizational commitment**, which is defined as a state in which an employee identifies with a particular organization and its goals, and wishes to maintain membership in the organization.[35] So, high *job involvement* means identifying with one's specific job, while high *organizational commitment* means identifying with one's employing organization.

As with job involvement, the research evidence demonstrates negative relationships between organizational commitment and both absenteeism and turnover.[36] In fact, studies demonstrate that an individual's level of organizational commitment is a better indicator of turnover than the far more frequently used job satisfaction predictor, explaining as much as 34 percent of

the variance.[37] Organizational commitment is probably a better predictor because it is a more global and enduring response to the organization as a whole than is job satisfaction.[38] An employee may be dissatisfied with his or her particular job and consider it a temporary condition, yet not be dissatisfied with the organization as a whole. But when dissatisfaction spreads to the organization itself, individuals are more likely to consider resigning. The HR Implications feature for this chapter indicates ways that organizations can determine employee attitudes.

Attitudes and Consistency

Did you ever notice how people change what they say so it doesn't contradict what they do? Perhaps a friend of yours has consistently argued that the quality of North American cars isn't up to that of the imports and that he'd never own anything but a foreign import. But his father gives him the used North American-made family car to drive to school, and suddenly they're not so bad. Or, when going to an interview for a new job, a graduating student believes that the company conducting the interview is really good and that working there would be important. If the student doesn't get the job, however, the response might be, "That company isn't all it's cracked up to be, anyway!"

Research has generally concluded that people seek consistency among their attitudes and between their attitudes and their behaviour. This means that individuals seek to reconcile divergent attitudes and align their attitudes and behaviour so they appear rational and consistent. When there is an inconsistency, forces are initiated to return the individual to an equilibrium state where attitudes and behaviour are again consistent. This can be done by altering either the attitudes or the behaviour, or by developing a rationalization for the discrepancy.

Cognitive Dissonance Theory

cognitive dissonance
Any incompatibility between two or more attitudes or between behaviour and attitudes.

Can we also assume from this consistency principle that an individual's behaviour can always be predicted if we know his or her attitude on a subject? Leon Festinger, in the late 1950s, proposed the theory of **cognitive dissonance**.[39] This theory sought to explain the linkage between attitudes and behaviour. Cognitive dissonance refers to any incompatibility that an individual might perceive between two or more of his or her attitudes, or between his or her behaviour and attitudes. Festinger argued that any form of inconsistency is uncomfortable and that individuals will attempt to reduce the dissonance and, hence, the discomfort. Therefore, individuals will seek a stable state where there is a minimum of dissonance.

Of course, no individual can completely avoid dissonance. You know that cheating on your income tax is wrong, but you "fudge" the numbers a bit every year, and hope you're not audited. Or you tell the members of your student team to get their work in on time, but *you* don't. So how do people cope? Festinger would propose that the desire to reduce dissonance would be determined by the *importance* of the elements creating the dissonance, the degree of *influence* the individual believes he or she has over the elements, and the *rewards* that may be involved in dissonance.

What are the organizational implications of the theory of cognitive dissonance? It can help to predict the propensity to engage in attitude and behavioural change. If individuals are required, for example, by the demands

of their job to say or do things that contradict their personal attitude, they will tend to modify their attitude in order to make it compatible with the cognition of what they have said or done. Additionally, the greater the dissonance—after it has been moderated by importance, choice, and reward factors—the greater the pressures to reduce it.

Attitudes and Workforce Diversity

Organizations are increasingly having to face diversity concerns, both as they espouse commitment to diversity and as Canada's workplaces become increasingly multicultural in nature. One of the intricacies of dealing with multicultural issues is trying to determine how to accommodate the needs of employees with diverse responsibilities and affiliations. This chapter's Case Incident gives an example of a situation where a workplace did not accommodate the needs of an employee.

Because of our multicultural workplace, managers are increasingly concerned with changing employee attitudes to reflect shifting perspectives on racial, gender, and other diversity issues. An ethnic joke or "flirtatious" remark that might have passed without comment 15 years ago can today become a career-limiting episode.[40] As such, organizations are investing in training to help reshape attitudes of employees. In our HR Implications, we present a variety of programs designed by organizations to change employee attitudes about diversity.

Michael Adams' *Sex in the Snow* provides some information to help us understand how diversity initiatives seeking to change attitudes might fare in the workplace in light of generational values. First, he notes that Gen Xers "eagerly embrace a number of egalitarian and pluralistic values."[41] This might suggest that as the Gen Xers move through the workplace, some of the tensions currently found with respect to the introduction of diversity initiatives may lessen. On the other hand, Snow also notes that there are 4.3 million boomers who belong to the disengaged Darwinist group, and many of these tend to be the younger boomers (i.e., closer to their mid-30s than their mid-50s). This group, together with the rational traditionalists of the elders group (representing 3.5 million Canadians), tends to be very conservative. As Snow notes, "Among the men in this group are a large number of

Diversity training at Harvard Pilgrim Health Care emphasizes practical conflict management. The managed care organization uses real-life case studies of situations employees face daily. The training includes role-playing workshops to teach employees how to respond to differences among people with sensitivity and respect. Harvard Pilgrim serves a growing number of racial and ethnic minority customers and a large gay and lesbian population. Its diversity training helps employees in providing care to diverse customers who demand that health care workers are not judgmental.

what have come to be known as 'angry white guys.'" They find that society has changed too much, too quickly, and for the worse. "They do not support the idea of women's equality or alternative family structures. They brand programs of affirmative action or employment equity for women or visible minorities as 'reverse discrimination'"[42] As a result of these generational differences, it is not inconceivable that tensions in the workplace over diversity initiatives will remain for some time to come.

The Attitude of Job Satisfaction

We noted above that there are a variety of attitudes of concern to those who study organizational behaviour, including job involvement, organizational commitment, and job satisfaction. While we discussed each of these attitudes briefly earlier in the chapter, we now examine job satisfaction at some length.

In 1997, the Angus Reid group surveyed Canadians nationwide to find out their attitudes toward their jobs and their workplaces.[43] Almost half of Canadian workers (47 percent) are very satisfied with their job and an additional 39 percent are somewhat satisfied. Closer analysis of the findings indicated that a large part of these positive findings could be explained by the fact that jobs were generally meeting the primary needs of workers. Forty-four percent strongly agreed that their work was challenging and interesting, and another 27 percent somewhat agreed. About 75 percent responded that they were treated fairly at work.

Not everyone is happy, however. Almost 40 percent of employees would not recommend their company as a good place to work. Forty percent also believe they never see any of the benefits of their company making money. Almost 40 percent reported that red tape and bureaucracy are among the biggest barriers to job satisfaction. A majority of the workforce (55 percent) reported that they felt the "pressure of having too much to do."

In this section, we want to dissect the concept of job satisfaction more carefully. How do we measure job satisfaction? What determines job satisfaction? What is its effect on employee productivity, absenteeism, and turnover rates? We answer each of these questions in this section.

Measuring Job Satisfaction

We've previously defined job satisfaction as an individual's general attitude toward his or her job. This definition is clearly a very broad one.[44] Yet this is inherent in the concept. Remember, a person's job is more than just the obvious activities of shuffling papers, waiting on customers, or driving a truck. Jobs require interaction with co-workers and bosses, following organizational rules and policies, meeting performance standards, living with working conditions that are often less than ideal, and the like.[45] This means that an employee's assessment of how satisfied or dissatisfied he or she is with his or her job is a complex summation of a number of discrete job elements. How, then, do we measure the concept?

The two most widely used approaches are a *single global rating* and a *summation score* made up of a number of job facets. The single global rating method is nothing more than asking individuals to respond to one question, such as "All things considered, how satisfied are you with your job?" Respondents then reply by circling a number between one and five that corresponds to answers from "highly satisfied" to "highly dissatisfied." It was

this approach that was used by the Angus Reid group in the findings reported above, which yielded the very high reports of job satisfaction.

The other approach—a summation of job facets—is more sophisticated. It identifies key elements in a job and asks for the employee's feelings about each. Typical factors that would be included are the nature of the work, supervision, present pay, promotion opportunities, and relations with co-workers.[46] These factors are rated on a standardized scale and then added up to create an overall job satisfaction score. This approach, though not done explicitly in the Angus Reid survey, is represented by the additional workplace attitude items reported above. You may recall that even though Canadians reported overall satisfaction, there were a number of individual items with which they were dissatisfied.

Is one of the foregoing measurement approaches superior to the other? Intuitively, it would seem that summing up responses to a number of job factors would achieve a more accurate evaluation of job satisfaction. The research, however, doesn't support this intuition.[47] This is one of those rare instances in which simplicity wins out over complexity. Comparisons of one-question global ratings with the more lengthy summation-of-job-factors method indicate that the former is more valid. The best explanation for this outcome is that the concept of job satisfaction is inherently so broad that the single question actually becomes a more inclusive measure.

What Determines Job Satisfaction?

We now turn to the question: What work-related variables determine job satisfaction? In Chapter 1 you read about the twenty-something employees who were organizing unions in their workplaces. They mentioned they were dissatisfied with their jobs because they didn't get respect from their employer. Their report is not inconsistent with our knowledge about job satisfaction. An extensive review of the literature indicates that the more important factors conducive to job satisfaction are mentally challenging work, equitable rewards, supportive working conditions, and supportive colleagues.[48] Keeping in mind the results of the Angus Reid survey, we'll review these factors and consider their implications for the Canadian workplace.

MENTALLY CHALLENGING WORK Employees tend to prefer jobs that give them opportunities to use their skills and abilities and offer a variety of tasks, freedom, and feedback on how well they are doing. These characteristics make work mentally challenging. Jobs that have too little challenge create boredom, but too much challenge creates frustration and feelings of failure. Under conditions of moderate challenge, most employees will experience pleasure and satisfaction.[49] As we noted above, 71 percent of Canadians do find their jobs challenging and rewarding. In Chapter 15, when we introduce job design, we will discuss factors that lead to more challenging jobs.

EQUITABLE REWARDS Employees want pay systems and promotion policies that they perceive as being just, unambiguous, and in line with their expectations. When pay is perceived as fair based on job demands, individual skill level, and community pay standards, satisfaction is likely to result. The Angus Reid study showed that 61 percent of workers feel their company offers fair or reasonable pay for the work done. In Chapter 5, we discuss further the need for equitable reward systems in the workplace.

Of course, not everyone seeks money. Many people willingly accept less money to work in a preferred location or in a less demanding job or to have greater discretion in the work they do and the hours they work. But the key in linking pay to satisfaction is not the absolute amount one is paid; rather, it is the perception of fairness. Similarly, employees seek fair promotion policies and practices. Promotions provide opportunities for personal growth, more responsibilities, and increased social status. Individuals who perceive that promotion decisions are made in a fair and just manner, therefore, are likely to experience satisfaction from their jobs.[50]

SUPPORTIVE WORKING CONDITIONS Employees are concerned with their work environment for both personal comfort and facilitating good job performance. Studies demonstrate that employees prefer physical surroundings that are not dangerous or uncomfortable. Temperature, light, noise, and other environmental factors should not be at either extreme—for example, workers should not have too much heat or too little light. Additionally, most employees prefer working relatively close to home, in clean and relatively modern facilities, and with adequate tools and equipment.

SUPPORTIVE COLLEAGUES People get more out of work than merely money or tangible achievements. For most employees, work also fills the need for social interaction. Not surprisingly, therefore, having friendly and supportive co-workers leads to increased job satisfaction. In the Angus Reid survey, 50 percent of the respondents reported that some of their good friends are their co-workers.

The behaviour of one's boss also is a major determinant of satisfaction. Studies generally find that employee satisfaction is increased when the immediate supervisor is understanding and friendly, offers praise for good performance, listens to employees' opinions, and shows a personal interest in them. This is a particular area where Canadian workplaces may not be doing enough for their employees. Only 44 percent said they received effective performance evaluations or feedback. In addition, only 44 percent of employees feel that they get any recognition for excelling at their jobs. At the organizational level, the feedback was not much better: only 45 percent of employees said their company communicates corporate changes effectively.

The state of the Canadian workplace is generally positive, particularly considering that over 75 percent of Canadians express overall satisfaction with their jobs. However, the survey results suggest quite a lot of room for improvement, and because this book is devoted to the study of organizational behaviour, we shall consider some of the factors that companies and managers might look at for improvement. Twenty-nine percent of employees did not find their jobs mentally challenging. Twenty-nine percent of employees did not feel they receive fair or reasonable rewards. Only 50 percent of the employees reported having supportive colleagues. Finally, the survey indicates that companies are not communicating enough information to their employees. All of these findings underscore the importance of understanding how the knowledge of organizational behaviour can be used in the workplace to improve conditions for employees, managers, and the company as a whole. Why is this important? The Angus Reid survey also found that employees who are more satisfied are more productive, less stressed, and more adaptable to the changing demands of the workplace. Despite all of the positive findings regarding job satisfaction, not everyone agrees on its importance in the workplace. You may want to review the Counterpoint in Chapter 1 to review this alternative position.

Do Individual Characteristics Affect Job Satisfaction?

Though the conditions in the workplace are a very important determinant of job satisfaction, it is critical to note the importance of a good personality–job fit and an individual's genetic disposition (some people are just inherently upbeat and positive about all things, including their job).

DON'T FORGET THE PERSONALITY–JOB FIT! In Chapter 3, we presented Holland's personality–job fit theory. As you remember, one of Holland's conclusions was that high agreement between an employee's personality and occupation results in a more satisfied individual. His logic was essentially this: People with personality types congruent with their chosen vocations should find that they have the right talents and abilities to meet the demands of their jobs. Thus, they are more likely to be successful on those jobs and, because of this success, have a greater probability of achieving high satisfaction from their work. Studies to replicate Holland's conclusions have been almost universally supportive.[51] It's important, therefore, to add this to our list of factors that determine job satisfaction.

IT'S IN THE GENES According to recent studies, as much as 30 percent of an individual's satisfaction can be explained by heredity.[52] Analysis of satisfaction data for a selected sample of individuals over a 50-year period found that individual results were consistently stable over time, even when these people changed employers and occupations. This and other research suggest that a significant portion of some people's satisfaction is genetically determined. That is, an individual's disposition toward life—positive or negative—is established by his or her genetic makeup, holds over time, and carries over into his or her disposition toward work. Given this evidence, it may well be that, at least for some employees, there isn't much managers

The Bulldog Group
http://www.bulldog.ca/bd/

Ellen Rubin (left) of Toronto-based The Bulldog Group interviews young employment applicants. Rubin's ideal employee is a "professional eclectic," a person who is creative, flexible, analytical, communicative, willing to learn, and thinks independently but can work with team members. Because the Toronto marketing firm specializes in interactive communications such as kiosks and CD-ROM publishing, candidates must have experience in graphic design or video production and demonstrate technical proficiency in at least four, but preferably nine, specialized software programs.

can do to influence employee satisfaction. Manipulating job characteristics, working conditions, rewards, and the job fit may have little effect. This suggests managers should focus attention on employee selection: If you want satisfied workers, make sure you screen out people who seem to be negative or who will derive little if any satisfaction from their jobs.[53]

The Effect of Job Satisfaction on Employee Performance

Managers' interest in job satisfaction tends to centre on its effect on employee performance. Researchers have recognized this interest, so we find a large number of studies that have been designed to assess the impact of job satisfaction on employee productivity, absenteeism, and turnover. Let's look at the current state of our knowledge.

SATISFACTION AND INDIVIDUAL PRODUCTIVITY The evidence suggests that the link between an individual's job satisfaction and his or her productivity is slightly positive.[54] It turns out the productivity can be affected as much by external conditions as it is by job satisfaction. For instance, a stockbroker's productivity is largely constrained by the general movement of the stock market. When the market is moving up and volume is high, both satisfied and dissatisfied brokers will ring up lots of commissions. Conversely, when the market is in the doldrums, the level of broker satisfaction is not likely to mean much. Job level also seems to be an important moderating variable.

The relationship between job satisfaction and productivity is stronger when the employee's behaviour is not constrained or controlled by outside factors. An employee's productivity on machine-paced jobs, for instance, will be much more influenced by the speed of the machine than by his or her level of satisfaction.

The evidence also shows that the satisfaction–performance correlations are stronger for higher-level employees. Thus, we might expect the relationship to be more relevant for individuals in professional, supervisory, and managerial positions.

There is another complication in the satisfaction-productivity link. Some studies have found that productivity leads to satisfaction rather than the other way around.[55] If you do a good job, you intrinsically feel good about it. Additionally, assuming that the organization rewards productivity, your higher productivity should increase verbal recognition, your pay level, and probabilities for promotion. These rewards, in turn, increase your level of satisfaction with the job.

SATISFACTION AND ORGANIZATIONAL PRODUCTIVITY The link between satisfaction and productivity is much stronger when we look not at individuals, but the organization as a whole.[56] When satisfaction and productivity data are gathered for the organization as a whole, rather than at the individual level, we find that organizations with more satisfied employees tended to be more effective than organizations with less satisfied employees.

Fortune magazine's 1998 list of the 100 Best Companies to Work For in America clearly shows a link between job satisfaction and productivity. "Of the 61 firms in the group that have been publicly traded for the past five years, 45 yielded higher returns to the shareholders than the Russell 3000, an index of large and small companies that mirrors our 100 Best. The 61 companies averaged annual returns of 27.5 percent, compared with 17.3 percent for the Russell 3000."[57] These companies exhibited the same supe-

rior performance when examined for the 10-year patterns in their returns: $1000 invested in a Russell 3000 firm would have yielded $3976 in a decade, while invested in the publicly traded 100 Best it would grow to $8188. That's a substantial difference in return, all for having happy workers. Happy workers don't guarantee financial gains, however. Both Southwest Airlines and Nordstrom had lower annual rates of return, but also faced very competitive economic climates.

The *Fortune* study identified four attitudes that, when taken together, correlated with higher profits: "workers feel they are given the opportunity to do what they do best every day; they believe their opinions count; they sense that other workers are committed to quality; and they've made a direct connection between their work and the company's mission."[58]

The *Fortune* study, coupled with previous research on organizational productivity, suggests that the reason we haven't received strong support for the *satisfaction causes productivity thesis* is that studies have focused on individuals rather than the organization and that individual-level measures of productivity don't take into consideration all the interactions and complexities in the work process.

SATISFACTION AND ABSENTEEISM We find a consistent negative relationship between satisfaction and absenteeism, but the correlation is moderate—usually less than +0.40.[59] While it certainly makes sense that dissatisfied employees are more likely to miss work, other factors have an impact on the relationship and reduce the correlation coefficient. For example, remember our discussion of sick pay versus well pay in Chapter 2. Organizations that provide liberal sick leave benefits are encouraging all their employees—including those who are highly satisfied—to take days off. Assuming that you have a reasonable number of varied interests, you can find work satisfying and yet still take off work to enjoy a three-day weekend, tan yourself on a warm summer day, or watch the World Series on television if those days come free with no penalties. Also, as with productivity, outside factors can act to reduce the correlation.

An excellent illustration of how satisfaction directly leads to attendance, where there is a minimum impact from other factors, is a study done at Sears, Roebuck.[60] Satisfaction data were available on employees at Sears' two headquarters in Chicago and New York. Additionally, it is important to note that Sears' policy was not to permit employees to be absent from work for avoidable reasons without penalty. The occurrence of a freak April 2 snowstorm in Chicago created the opportunity to compare employee attendance at the Chicago office with attendance in New York, where the weather was quite nice. The interesting dimension in this study is that the snowstorm gave the Chicago employees a built-in excuse not to come to work. The storm crippled the city's transportation, and individuals knew they could miss work this day with no penalty. This natural experiment permitted the comparison of attendance records for satisfied and dissatisfied employees at two locations—one where you were expected to be at work (with normal pressures for attendance) and the other where you were free to choose with no penalty involved. If satisfaction leads to attendance, where there is an absence of outside factors, the more satisfied employees should have come to work in Chicago, while dissatisfied employees should have stayed home. The study found that on this particular April 2, absenteeism rates in New York were just as high for satisfied groups of workers as for dissatisfied groups. But in Chicago, the workers with high satisfaction scores had much higher attendance than did those with lower satisfaction levels.

Nordstrom
http://www.nordstrom-pta.com/

These findings are exactly what we would have expected if satisfaction is negatively correlated with absenteeism.

SATISFACTION AND TURNOVER   Satisfaction is also negatively related to turnover, but the correlation is stronger than what we found for absenteeism.[61] Yet, again, other factors such as labour market conditions, expectations about alternative job opportunities, and length of tenure with the organization are important constraints on the actual decision to leave one's current job.[62]

Evidence indicates that an important moderator of the satisfaction–turnover relationship is the employee's level of performance.[63] Specifically, level of satisfaction is less important in predicting turnover for superior performers. Why? The organization typically makes considerable efforts to keep these people. They receive pay raises, praise, recognition, increased promotional opportunities, and so forth. Just the opposite tends to apply to poor performers. Few attempts are made by the organization to retain them. There may even be subtle pressures to encourage them to quit. We would expect, therefore, that job satisfaction is more important in influencing poor performers to stay than superior performers. Regardless of level of satisfaction, the latter are more likely to remain with the organization because the receipt of recognition, praise, and other rewards gives them more reasons for staying.

Consistent with our previous discussion, we shouldn't be surprised to find that a person's general disposition toward life also moderates the satisfaction–turnover relationship.[64] Specifically, some individuals generally gripe more than others and such individuals, when dissatisfied with their jobs, are less likely to quit than those who are more positively disposed toward life. So if two workers report the same level of job dissatisfaction, the one most likely to quit is the one with the highest predisposition to be happy or satisfied in general.

How Employees Can Express Dissatisfaction

One final point before we leave the issue of job satisfaction: Employee dissatisfaction can be expressed in a number of ways.[65] For example, rather than quit, employees can complain, be insubordinate, steal organizational property, or shirk a part of their work responsibilities. Exhibit 4-2 offers four responses that differ from one another along two dimensions: constructiveness/destructiveness and activity/passivity. They are defined as follows:[66]

exit
Dissatisfaction expressed through behaviour directed toward leaving the organization.

voice
Dissatisfaction expressed through active and constructive attempts to improve conditions.

loyalty
Dissatisfaction expressed by passively waiting for conditions to improve.

neglect
Dissatisfaction expressed through allowing conditions to worsen.

- **Exit:** Behaviour directed toward leaving the organization, including looking for a new position as well as resigning.

- **Voice:** Actively and constructively attempting to improve conditions, including suggesting improvements, discussing problems with superiors, and some forms of union activity.

- **Loyalty:** Passively but optimistically waiting for conditions to improve, including speaking up for the organization in the face of external criticism and trusting the organization and its management to "do the right thing."

- **Neglect:** Passively allowing conditions to worsen, including chronic absenteeism or lateness, reduced effort, and increased error rate.

Exit and neglect behaviours encompass our performance variables—productivity, absenteeism, and turnover. But this model expands employee response to include voice and loyalty—constructive behaviours that allow

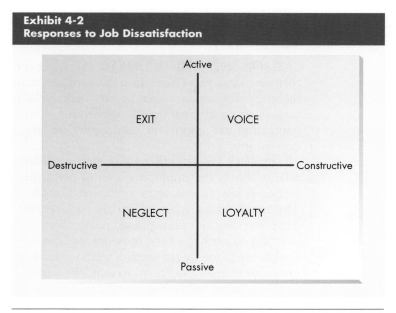

Exhibit 4-2
Responses to Job Dissatisfaction

Active

EXIT   VOICE

Destructive ————————————————— Constructive

NEGLECT   LOYALTY

Passive

Source: C. Rusbult and D. Lowery, "When Bureaucrats Get the Blues," *Journal of Applied Social Psychology,* Vol. 15, No. 1(1985), p. 83. With permission.

individuals to tolerate unpleasant situations or to revive satisfactory working conditions. It helps us to understand situations, such as those sometimes found among unionized workers, where low job satisfaction is coupled with low turnover.[67] Union members often express dissatisfaction through the grievance procedure or through formal contract negotiations. These voice mechanisms allow the union members to continue in their jobs while convincing themselves that they are acting to improve the situation.

HR IMPLICATIONS

Attitude Surveys and Diversity Training

Our HR Implications considers two key facets of this chapter.

First, it is important for organizations to find out about the attitudes of employees. To do this, organizations sometimes conduct attitude surveys. Second, sometimes organizations want to try to change the attitudes of their employees. A number of firms have made this attempt with respect to diversity issues, trying to encourage employees to see that meeting employment equity targets is not about imposed quotas, but rather an opportunity to increase the learning of the members of the organization by adding variation to the sources of information.

Determining Attitudes: Attitude Surveys

How does management get information about employee attitudes? The most popular method is through the use of **attitude surveys**.[1]

Exhibit 4-3 illustrates what an attitude survey might look like. Typically, attitude surveys present the employee with a set of statements or questions. Ideally, the items are tailored to obtain the specific information that management desires. An attitude score is achieved by summing up responses to individual questionnaire items. These scores can then be averaged for job groups, departments, divisions, or the organization as a whole.

Results from attitude surveys can frequently surprise management. For instance, Michael Gilliland

Exhibit 4-3
Sample Attitude Survey

Please answer each of the following statements using the following rating scale:

5 = Strongly agree

4 = Agree

3 = Undecided

2 = Disagree

1 = Strongly disagree

Statement	Rating
1. This company is a pretty good place to work.	——
2. I can get ahead in this company if I make the effort.	——
3. This company's wage rates are competitive with those of other companies.	——
4. Employee promotion decisions are handled fairly.	——
5. I understand the various fringe benefits the company offers.	——
6. My job makes the best use of my abilities.	——
7. My workload is challenging but not burdensome.	——
8. I have trust and confidence in my boss.	——
9. I feel free to tell my boss what I think.	——
10. I know what my boss expects of me.	——

owns and operates a chain of 12 food markets.[2] He and his management team developed a 10-item job-satisfaction questionnaire, which they administer to all employees twice a year. Recently Gilliland was surprised to find the worst complaints coming from employees at the store with the best working conditions and the most benefits. Careful analysis of the results uncovered that, although the manager at this store was well liked, employees were frustrated because he was behind on their performance reviews and had failed to fire a particularly unproductive employee. As one of Gilliland's associates put it, "We'd assumed it would be the happiest store, but it wasn't."

A corporatewide attitude survey at BP Exploration revealed that employees were unhappy with the way their direct superiors managed them.[3] In response, management introduced a formal upward-appraisal system that allows the company's 12 000 employees to evaluate their boss' managerial performance. Now managers pay a lot more attention to the needs of their employees because their employees' opinions play an important part in determining the manager's future in the organization.

Using attitude surveys on a regular basis provides managers with valuable feedback on how employees perceive their working conditions. Consistent with our discussion of perceptions in the previous chapter, the policies and practices that management views as objective and fair may be seen as inequitable by employees in general or by certain groups of employees. That these distorted perceptions have led to negative attitudes about the job and organization should be important to management. This is because employee behaviours are based on perceptions, not reality. Remember, the employee who quits because she believes she is underpaid—when, in fact, management has objective data to support that her salary is highly competitive—is just as gone as if she had actually been underpaid. The use of regular attitude surveys can alert management to potential problems and employees' intentions early so that action can be taken to prevent repercussions.[4]

Modifying Attitudes: Diversity Training

Diversity training programs are generally intended to provide a vehicle for increasing awareness and examining stereotypes. Participants learn to value

individual differences, increase their cross-cultural understanding, and confront stereotypes.[5]

Trevor Wilson, president of Toronto-based Omnibus Consulting, has presented employment equity programs to such clients as IBM Canada Ltd., Molson Co. Ltd. and National Grocers Co. Ltd. His approach has been popular because it supports a "no-guilt, no-blame, everybody's-not-the-same, business-friendly, all-inclusive" approach to equity, thus reducing the barriers that sometimes accompany equity training.[6] The core issues tackled in the actual training include the following: "that people tend to hire people like themselves; that we all harbour stereotypes; that cultural differences can lead you to misunderstand someone's qualifications; that continually talking to a colleague's breasts instead of her face is demeaning as well as illegal, and how would you like your wife or daughter to go through that?"[7]

Maureen Geddes, team facilitator/workplace diversity at Chatham, Ontario-based Union Gas, explains why the company sent all of its employees through diversity training, 25 employees at a time. "We certainly had some people who said we should be doing this because it's the right thing to do. Of course it's the right thing to do, but diversity training is a priority here today because it makes us more productive and competitive as an organization."[8]

What do these diversity programs look like and how do they address attitude change?[9] They almost all include a self-evaluation phase. People are pressed to examine themselves and to confront ethnic and cultural stereotypes they might hold. Then participants typically take part in group discussions or panels with representatives from diverse groups. So, for instance, a Hmong man might describe his family's life in Southeast Asia, and explain why they resettled in British Columbia; or a lesbian might describe how she discovered her sexual identity, and the reaction of her friends and family when she "came out."

Additional activities designed to change attitudes include arranging for people to do volunteer work in community or social service centers in order to meet face-to-face with individuals and groups from diverse backgrounds and using exercises that let participants feel what it's like to be different. For example, when participants see the film *Eye of the Beholder*, where people are segregated and stereotyped according to their eye colour, participants realize what it's like to be judged by something over which they have no control.

The typical program lasts from half a day to three days in length and includes role-playing exercises, lectures, discussions, and group experiences. For example, in the United States, Xerox has worked with Cornell University's theatre department to create a set of short plays that increases awareness of work-related racial and gender conflicts. The show has been presented to more than 1300 Xerox managers.[10] A training exercise at Hartford Insurance that sought to increase sensitivity to aging asked participants to respond to the following four questions:

(1) If you didn't know how old you are, how old would you guess you are? In other words, how old do you feel inside?

(2) When I was 18, I thought middle age began at age _____.

(3) Today, I think middle age begins at age _____.

(4) What would be your first reaction if someone called you an older worker?[11]

Answers to these questions were then used to analyse age-related stereotypes. In another program designed to raise awareness of the power of stereotypes, each participant was asked to write an anonymous paper detailing all groups—women, born-again Christians, blacks, gays, men, etc.—to which they had attached stereotypes.[12] They were also asked to explain why they'd had trouble working with certain groups in the past. Based on responses, guest speakers were brought into the class to shatter the stereotypes directed at each group. This was followed by extensive discussion.

Sources:

[1] See, for example, G.E. Lyne, "How to Measure Employee Attitudes," *Training and Development Journal*, December 1989, pp. 40–43; and P. Hise, "The Motivational Employee-Satisfaction Questionnaire," *INC.*, February 1994, pp. 73–75.

[2] P. Hise, "The Motivational Employee-Satisfaction Questionnaire," *INC.* February 1994, pp 73–75

[3] I. Barmash, "More Substance Than Show," *Across the Board*, May 1993, pp. 43–45.

[4] See G. Gallup, "Employee Research: From Nice to Know to Need to Know," *Personnel Journal*, August 1988, pp. 42–43; and T. Lammers, "The Essential Employee Survey," *INC.*, December 1992, pp. 159–61.

[5] See, for example, M. Galen, "Diversity: Beyond the Numbers Game," *Business Week*, August 14, 1995, pp. 60–61

[6] "Selling equity," *Financial Post Magazine*, September, 1994, pp. 20–25.

[7] "Selling equity," *Financial Post Magazine*, September, 1994, pp. 20–25.

[8] "Selling equity," *Financial Post Magazine*, September, 1994, pp. 20–25.

[9] This section is based on A. Rossett and T. Bickham, "Diversity Training: Hope, Faith and Cynicism," *Training*, January 1994, pp. 40–46. pp. 40–46.

[10] L.E. Wynter, "Theatre Program Tackles Issues of Diversity," *The Wall Street Journal*, April 18, 1991, p. B1.

[11] B. Hynes-Grace, "To Thrive, Not Merely Survive," in *Textbook Authors Conference Presentations* (Washington, DC: October 21, 1992), sponsored by the American Association of Retired Persons, p. 12.

[12] "Teaching Diversity: Business Schools Search for Model Approaches," *Newsline*, Fall 1992, p. 21.

Summary and Implications

For the Workplace

Why is it important to know an individual's values? Although they don't have a direct impact on behaviour, values strongly influence a person's attitudes. So knowledge of an individual's value system can provide insight into his or her attitudes.

An employee's performance and satisfaction are likely to be higher if his or her values fit well with the organization. For instance, the person who places high importance on imagination, independence, and freedom is likely to be poorly matched with an organization that seeks conformity from its employees. Managers are more likely to appreciate, evaluate positively, and allocate rewards to employees who "fit in," and employees are more likely to be satisfied if they perceive that they do fit. This argues for management to strive during the selection of new employees to find job candidates who not only have the ability, experience, and motivation to perform, but also a value system that is compatible with the organization's.

Managers should be interested in their employees' attitudes because attitudes give warnings of potential problems and because they influence behaviour. Satisfied and committed employees, for instance, have lower rates of turnover and absenteeism. Given that managers want to keep resignations and absences down—especially among their more productive employees—they will want to do those things that will generate positive job attitudes.

Managers should also be aware that employees will try to reduce cognitive dissonance. More important, dissonance can be managed. If employees are required to engage in activities that appear inconsistent to them or that are at odds with their attitudes, the pressures to reduce the resulting dissonance are lessened when the employee perceives that the dissonance is externally imposed and is beyond his or her control or if the rewards are significant enough to offset the dissonance.

For You as an Individual

Within the classroom, in various kinds of activities in which you participate, as well as in the workplace, you will encounter many people who have different values from you. We noted that values vary by both generation and culture, although they also vary within these groups. The chapter encourages you to try to understand value differences, and figure out ways to work positively with people who are different from you.

In our discussion of attitudes, we focused on the specific attitude of job satisfaction. We indicated that many Canadians were satisfied with their jobs, and mentioned the sources of some of the satisfactions. We also identified areas in which people were dissatisfied with their jobs. This information

may help you understand your own feelings about whether you're satisfied with your job. You might also be able to use some of the information on job satisfaction to help you when you're working on group projects, as some of the sources of satisfaction, such as challenging tasks, meaningful relationships with coworkers, and more open communication are things that help make groups function better as well.

ROADMAP REMINDER

With this chapter we conclude the first section of the text, which has examined the conditions within which organizations operate, the skills that managers and employees need to successfully navigate the transition to the 21st century workplace, and then looked at the perceptions, values, and attitudes that influence how people get along in the workplace. In moving to Part 2 of the text, we are making a transition from describing the workplace to thinking about how to actually get people to work together positively in terms of accomplishing tasks, and working in groups and teams. As a first step in understanding how to ensure that organizations are productive, we consider the subject of motivation. In the next two chapters, you will learn about motivating both yourself and others.

For Review

1. What are Hofstede's five value dimensions of national culture?
2. How might differences in generational values affect the workplace?
3. Compare aboriginal and non-aboriginal values.
4. How can managers get employees to more readily accept working with colleagues who are different from themselves?
5. Describe three job-related attitudes.
6. What role does genetics play in determining an individual's job satisfaction?
7. Are happy workers productive workers?
8. What is the relationship between job satisfaction and absenteeism? Turnover? Which is the stronger relationship?
9. Contrast exit, voice, loyalty, and neglect as employee responses to job dissatisfaction.

For Discussion

1. "Thirty-five years ago, young employees we hired were ambitious, conscientious, hardworking, and honest. Today's young workers don't have the same values." Do you agree or disagree with this manager's comments? Support your position.
2. Do you think there might be any positive and significant relationship between the possession of certain personal values and successful career progression in organizations such as Merrill Lynch, the Canadian Union of Postal Workers (CUPW), and the City of Regina's police department? Discuss.

3. "Managers should do everything they can to enhance the job satisfaction of their employees." Do you agree or disagree? Support your position.
4. Discuss the advantages and disadvantages of using regular attitude surveys to monitor employee job satisfaction.
5. When employees are asked whether they would again choose the same work or whether they would want their children to follow in their footsteps, typically less than half answer in the affirmative. What, if anything, do you think this implies about employee job satisfaction?

LEARNING ABOUT YOURSELF EXERCISE

What Do You Value?

Following are 16 items. Rate how important each one is to you on a scale of 0 (not important) to 100 (very important). Write the number 0 - 100 on the line to the left of each item.

Not important				Somewhat important				Very	important	
0	10	20	30	40	50	60	70	80	90	100

_____ 1. An enjoyable, satisfying job.

_____ 2. A high-paying job.

_____ 3. A good marriage.

_____ 4. Meeting new people; social events.

_____ 5. Involvement in community activities.

_____ 6. My religion.

_____ 7. Exercising, playing sports.

_____ 8. Intellectual development.

_____ 9. A career with challenging opportunities.

_____ 10. Nice cars, clothes, home, and so on.

_____ 11. Spending time with family.

_____ 12. Having several close friends.

_____ 13. Volunteer work for not-for-profit organizations, such as the Canadian Cancer Society.

_____ 14. Meditation, quiet time to think, pray, and so on.

_____ 15. A healthy, balanced diet.

_____ 16. Educational reading, television, self-improvement programs, and so on.

Turn to page 697 for scoring directions and key.

Source: R.N. Lussier, _Human Relations in Organizations: A Skill Building Approach_, 2nd ed. (Homewood, IL: Richard D. Irwin, 1993). Used with permission.

WORKING WITH OTHERS EXERCISE
Assessing Work Attitudes

Objective

To compare attitudes about the workforce.

Time

Approximately 30 minutes.

Procedure

Choose the best answers for the following five questions:

1. *Generally*, Canadian workers

   _____ **a.** are highly motivated and hardworking

   _____ **b.** try to give a fair day's effort

   _____ **c.** will put forth effort if you make it worthwhile

   _____ **d.** try to get by with a low level of effort

   _____ **e.** are lazy and/or poorly motivated

2. The people *I have worked with*

   _____ **a.** are highly motivated and hardworking

   _____ **b.** try to give a fair day's effort

   _____ **c.** will put forth effort if you make it worthwhile

   _____ **d.** try to get by with a low level of effort

   _____ **e.** are lazy and/or poorly motivated

3. *Compared to foreign workers*, Canadian workers are

   _____ **a.** more productive

   _____ **b.** equally productive

   _____ **c.** less productive

4. *Over the past 20 years*, Canadian workers have (pick one)

   _____ **a.** improved in overall quality of job performance

   _____ **b.** remained about the same in quality of job performance

   _____ **c.** deteriorated in overall quality of job performance

5. If you have a low opinion of the Canadian workforce, give the one step (or action) that could be taken that would lead to the most improvement.

GROUP DISCUSSION

a. Break into groups of three to five members each. Compare your answers to the five questions.

b. For each question where one or more members disagree, discuss *why* each member chose his or her answer.

c. After this discussion, members are free to change their original answer. Did any in your group do so?

d. Your instructor will lead the class in discussing the implications or accuracy of these attitudes.

Source: Based on D.R. Brown, "Dealing with Student Conceptions and Misconceptions About Worker Attitudes and Productivity," *Journal of Management Education*, May 1991, pp. 259–64.

"I Can't Work on Friday Nights"

CASE INCIDENT

Most Canadians understand that the Charter of Rights protects employees against discrimination based on gender or race bias. But most provincial Human Rights codes also prohibit discrimination on the basis of religion. Both the Canadian Union of Public Employees (CUPE) and the school board in the central Okanagan region of British Columbia didn't understand that they had a duty to accommodate an employee's need for a schedule change for religious reasons. As a result, a former employee brought a religious discrimination complaint against both of them.

The former employee, Larry S. Renaud, who is a Seventh-day Adventist, was terminated from his job at the Spring Valley Elementary School because the board and the union were unwilling to accommodate his request not to be scheduled to work on his church's sabbath, which is from sundown Friday until sundown Saturday. Renaud had used his seniority to move to Spring Valley to work as a custodian. Under the collective agreement, he was the only custodian scheduled for the 3:00 p.m. to 11:00 p.m. shift during the week, including Friday night. Immediately upon moving to the new job, he requested that the board accommodate a schedule change, so that he wouldn't have to work on his sabbath. The school board was willing to accommodate his request, but felt they needed the approval of his union. The union was unwilling to grant such an exception to the collective agreement as they felt it would seriously violate the terms of the collective agreement. When the school board and CUPE failed to reach an agreement, the school board fired Renaud because of his inability to work the Friday night shift.

After going through human rights tribunals and the lower courts, the case reached the Supreme Court of Canada, which ruled that both the school board and CUPE had a duty to accommodate Renaud's religious preferences, particularly when it would have been just as easy to allow him to clean the school on Sunday nights, rather than Friday nights. The school board was ordered to rehire Renaud, and CUPE and the school board were ordered to each pay Renaud $6250 for lost wages. Each was also responsible for paying him an additional $1000 for emotional distress.

This incident serves as a reminder to employers, especially in industries such as transportation, public safety, and retailing where weekend work is often an expected part of the job. The courts have ruled that employers must "reasonably accommodate" requests to observe religious days unless the request would cause "undue hardship" to the business. The employees' religious beliefs are assumed to be sincerely held unless proven otherwise.

Questions

1. Is there anything an employer could do at the time of hiring that could legally deter this problem from occurring?

2. Why do you think gender and race bias in Canada has received more attention than religious bias?

3. How could training to reduce religious discrimination fit in as part of diversity training?

4. What might a training program look like that seeks to eliminate discrimination on the basis of religion? Be specific.

Source: This case is based on Larry S. Renaud v. Board of School Trustees, School District No. 23 (Central Okanagan) and the Canadian Union of Public Employees, Local 523 [1992], S.C.J. No. 75.

Managing in a Cross-Cultural World

Canadian workplaces are multicultural, and many Canadian companies also work in international contexts, increasing the chances that people working side-by-side do not share all of the same values, expectations, and beliefs about behaviour.

Understanding differences among people begins with basic awareness about different cultures and societies. For instance, Asian countries such as China, Indonesia, and Japan are lower on individualism than Germany, the Netherlands, and the United States. Even within Canada there are differences in how strongly individualistic versus collectivist identities are shared when we consider how multicultural Canada has become.

Part of understanding others is avoiding assuming that everyone shares the same meanings about a situation. Sometimes "yes" does not mean "yes," but is a way of trying not to displease, rather than indicating strong agreement with a decision. People from some cultures are also much more low-key than in other cultures, but that does not mean that they are any less effective in doing a good job. For instance, in Dutch there is an expression that translates to "good wine doesn't need bragging."

The differences that we observe among individuals arise because of responses to one's environment, and each society and culture faces different environments. Sometimes this makes it harder to understand the differences observed in other people, because it is not part of our experience.

When working with people of different cultures, we may encounter situations that seem different from the way that we respond. For instance, in Canada, individuals are more likely to express support for the law rather than friendship if a friend has broken the law and we have been asked to testify about the event. In Korea, however, individuals would be more likely to support their friends rather than report that a friend had been driving 15 kilometres above the speed limit. These differences suggest that working with people of other cultures means trying to understand the norms of that culture.

Questions

1. To what extent might differences in values affect how individuals interact with one another?

2. How can organizations promote more understanding among workers from different cultures?

3. Should managers try to change the values of employees whose values differ from management?

Source: Based on "Cross-Culture," *Venture 552*; aired June 8, 1995.

When you prevent me

from doing anything I want to do,

that is persecution;

but when I prevent you

from doing anything you want to do,

that is law, order, and morals.

–G.B. Shaw

POINT

Cross-Cultural Training Doesn't Work

Academics seem to take it as a truism that the expanding global marketplace has serious implications for management practice. As a result, they have become strong advocates for the necessity of cross-cultural training. But most corporations don't provide cross-cultural training for employees. Studies indicate, for instance, that only 30 percent of managers who are sent on foreign assignments scheduled to last from one to five years receive any cross-cultural training before their departure.

Why don't most organizations provide their managers with cross-cultural training? We propose two possible explanations. One is that top managers believe that "managing is managing," so *where* it is done is irrelevant. The other explanation is that top management doesn't believe that cross-cultural training is effective.

Contrary to the evidence, many senior managers continue to believe that managerial skills are perfectly transferable across cultures. A good manager in Toronto or Vancouver, for instance, should be equally effective in Paris or Hong Kong. In organizations where this belief dominates, you won't find any concern with cross-cultural training. Moreover, there is likely to be little effort made to select candidates for foreign assignments based on their ability to fit into, or adapt to, a specific culture. Selection decisions for overseas postings in these organizations are primarily made using a single criterion: the person's domestic track record.

It's probably fair to say that most senior managers today recognize that cultural differences do affect managerial performance. But their organizations still don't provide cross-cultural training because these managers doubt the effectiveness of this training. They argue that people can't learn to manage in a foreign culture after only a few weeks or months of training. An understanding of a country's culture is

something one assimilates over many years based on input from many sources. It is not something that lends itself to short-term learning, no matter how intensive a training program might be.

Given the previous arguments, it would be surprising to find organizations offering cross-cultural training. We submit that top executives of organizations typically take one of three approaches in dealing with the selection of managerial personnel for staff foreign assignments. One approach is to ignore cultural differences. They don't worry about them, and make their selection decisions based solely on individuals' previous managerial records. Another approach is to hire nationals to manage foreign operations. Since cross-cultural training isn't effective, when a firm such as Xerox needs an executive to fill a key post in Italy, it might be best served by hiring an Italian. This solution has become even easier for North American firms in recent years as the number of foreigners in Canadian and American business schools has increased. For instance, there are now numbers of Italians, Arabs, Germans, Japanese, and other foreign nationals who have graduate business degrees from Canadian universities, understand Canadian business practices, and have returned to their homelands. The third solution to the problem is to either hire nationals or intensively train people to be expert advisors to management. AT&T, as a case in point, sent one executive and his family to Singapore for a lengthy stay to soak up the atmosphere and learn about the Singaporian way of doing business. He then returned to New York as the resident expert on Singapore. When problems involving that country arise, he is called upon to provide insight. ■

Sources: The evidence in this argument is drawn from J.S. Black and M. Mendenhall, "Cross-Cultural Training Effectiveness: A Review and a Theoretical Framework for Future Research," *Academy of Management Review,* January 1990, pp. 113–36; and A. Kupfer, "How to Be a Global Manager," *Fortune,* March 14, 1988, p. 52.

counterPOINT

Cross-Cultural Training
Is Effective

Yes, it's true that most corporations don't provide cross-cultural training. And that's a mistake! Clearly, the ability to adapt to the cultural differences in a foreign assignment is important to managerial success. Moreover, contrary to what many managers believe, cross-cultural training is very effective. Let's elaborate on this second point.

A comprehensive review of studies that specifically examined the effectiveness of cross-cultural training shows overwhelming evidence that this training fosters the development of cross-cultural skills and leads to higher performance. Training has been shown to improve an individual's relationships with host nationals, to allow that person to adjust more rapidly to a new culture, and to improve his or her work performance. In addition, training significantly reduces expatriate failure rates. For instance, in 1991 Mississauga, Ontario-based Northern Telecom (Nortel) discovered that some of its overseas employees were experiencing adjustment problems that affected their personal productivity and possibly the overall success of the business. In addition, the lack of preparation for being in a foreign country led to discontent that was manifested in incentive pay, better housing and perquisites, and in some cases, negative attitudes. After it introduced two training programs in 1993 and 1994, employees reported increased satisfaction with their overseas assignments.

Although these results are impressive, they don't say anything about the type of training the employee received. Does that make a difference?

There is a variety of training techniques available to prepare people for foreign work assignments. They range from documentary programs that merely expose people to a new culture through written materials on the country's sociopolitical history, geography, economics, and cultural institutions, to intense interpersonal experience training, where individuals participate in role-playing exercises, simulated social settings, and similar experiences to "feel" the differences in a new culture.

One research study looked at the effectiveness of these two approaches on a group of North American managers. These managers, who worked for an electronic products firm, were sent on assignment to Seoul, South Korea. Twenty of them received no training, 20 got only the documentary program, and 20 received only interpersonal experience training. The training activities were all completed in a three-day period. All participants, no matter which group they were in, received some language training, briefings covering company operations in South Korea, and a cursory three-page background description of the country. The results of this study confirmed the earlier evidence that cross-cultural training works. Specifically, the study found that managers who received either form of training were better performers and perceived less need to adjust to the new culture than those who received no such training. Additionally, neither method proved superior to the other.

In another study with civilian employees in a U.S. military agency, participants were grouped so they received either a documentary orientation, experiential training, some combination of the two, or no training at all. Findings from this study again confirmed the value of cross-cultural training. Either type of training proved to be more effective than no training in improving cross-cultural knowledge and behavioral performance, and the combination approach was found to be the most effective. The findings of both of these studies are consistent with what Nortel found after introducing its cross-cultural training programs, which include, among other topics, training in cultural self-awareness, sensitization to culture shock and the adaptation process and some basic language skills. ■

Sources: The evidence in this argument is drawn from J.S. Black and M. Mendenhall, "Cross-Cultural Training Effectiveness: A Review and a Theoretical Framework for Future Research," *Academy of Management Review,* January 1990, pp. 113–36; P.C. Earley, "Intercultural Training for Managers: A Comparison of Documentary and Interpersonal Methods," *Academy of Management Journal,* December 1987, pp. 685–98; S. Caudron, "Surviving Cross-Cultural Shock," *Industry Week,* July 6, 1992, pp. 35–38; J.S. Lublin, "Companies Use Cross-Cultural Training to Help Their Employees Adjust Abroad," *Wall Street Journal,* August 4, 1992, p. B1; J.K. Harrison, "Individual and Combined Effects of Behavior Modeling and the Cultural Assimilator in Cross-Cultural Management Training," *Journal of Applied Psychology,* December 1992, pp. 952–62; and S. R. Fishman, "Developing a Global Workforce: Assessment and Orientation Programs Help Employees Prepare For Successful International Assignments," *Canadian Business Review,* Spring, 1996, pp. 18–21.

PROGRESSIVE CASE • PART 1

Lee Simpson: Background and Reflections on New Organizational Challenges

Lee Simpson is Vice-President, Group Publisher at Maclean-Hunter. She was appointed to this position in July 1994, after serving as Publisher of *Chatelaine* for the previous 6 years. She's had extensive managerial experience and was kind enough to describe some of her experiences and share with us some of her insights related to OB.

You should find this progressive case (which appears at the end of each Part of the book) valuable for at least two reasons. First, it will help you integrate many of the OB concepts introduced in this book. Unfortunately, textbooks have to be linear—moving sequentially through an artificially created set of independent chapters. The real world, however, is

a juggling act of overlapping and highly interdependent activities. This case will make this interdependence clearer and help demonstrate how individual, group, and organization-system factors overlap. Second, this progressive case will show you the applicability of OB concepts to actual management practice. Most textbook examples or cases are short and designed to illustrate only one or two points. As an integrated and progressive story, the Lee Simpson case will show you how one real-life manager has dealt with dozens of OB issues.

In describing her previous job as publisher, Lee Simpson explains that "a publisher is like an orchestra leader. They have to know what all the instruments are supposed to sound like and bring them in on time, but they don't necessarily need to know how to play them. Therefore, what I did as publisher was lead an orchestra that consisted of an editor who was totally responsible for the editorial product of the magazine, an advertising director responsible for bringing in the advertising revenue from publications, a circulation director responsible for building up news stand readers and subscribers, a marketing director responsible for how the magazine is perceived, a production manager who took care of the physical details of producing the magazine, a research director, and a communications director." As publisher, Simpson reported to a vice-president who reported to the president.

While Simpson was appointed to her current position in 1994, in May 1998 her role responsibilities as Vice-President, Group Publisher shifted due to the appointment of two new publishers: the one for *Modern Woman* in 1997 and the one for *Chatelaine* in May 1998. These appointments have allowed Simpson to take on more of the day-to-day responsibilities of the Brand Development area for the Women's Group at Maclean-Hunter, which includes *Flare* as

* © Nancy Langton. Some facts, incidences, and quotes included in this progressive case have been slightly modified by the author to enhance student discussion and analysis.

Exhibit 1-1
Résumé

LEE SIMPSON
Vice-President
Group Publisher
Maclean-Hunter Publishing Limited

Education

Executive Program, University of Western Ontario, 1989
B.A., General Arts, University of Toronto, 1974
High School, Bishop's College, St. John's, Newfoundland, 1968

Professional Experience

1994-present	Maclean-Hunter Publishing Limited (Vice-President, Group Publisher, Publisher). Responsibilities: *Chatelaine, Modern Woman*
1988-1998	Maclean-Hunter Publishing Limited (Publisher). Responsibilities: *Chatelaine* (1988-1998), *Modern Woman* (1993-1997). *Modern Woman* was a new magazine launch.
1986-1988	Maclean-Hunter Publishing Limited (Associate Publisher). Responsibilities: *Chatelaine*
1984-1986	Maclean-Hunter Publishing Limited (Research Director). Responsibilities: *Chatelaine, City & Country, Home, Châtelaine*
1980-1984	Bristol Myers Canada (Media Marketing Manager)
1978-1980	Independent Media Analysis (Research Associate)
1975-1978	Maclaren Advertising (Media Estimator; Group Supervisor)

Personal

Marital Status: Married, one child

Hobbies and Interests: My husband and I are motorcycle enthusiasts. We now own a brand new Honda Shadow, a big cruising bike, and get out with friends whenever we can. I paint (watercolours) very badly but with great gusto. We love to cook together as a couple and are heavily into Indian cuisine. Our vast extended family (including parents, brothers, sisters, in-laws, cousins and more) is the centrepiece of our lives and just about every week contains some family event.

well as *Chatelaine* and *Modern Woman*. The publishers of *Chatelaine* and *Modern Woman* report to her. Simpson also oversees the revenue streams from subscriptions and advertising, and is expected to increase "third stream revenue," which comes from developing new services related to publishing the magazines. These new profit centres include separate new Brand extensions like the *Chatelaine* Car Confidence Club, a competitor to the Canadian Automobile Association, and a consulting service for other companies that want to know about marketing to women. "My job as vice-president is to ensure that not only are the magazines kept healthy and vital but also to guard this third stream revenue."

As Simpson moves into her new role at Maclean-Hunter, she emphasizes the need to continue learn-

ing. "I am looking forward to the opportunity to learn new things. I think 10 years of being in a publisher role has been a wonderfully creative learning process. It is only in the past two years that I have noticed any restlessness. I think that during the first eight years I really was learning something new every day. Now I will get to learn new things every day again, and yet I will still have the satisfaction of having somebody to teach. I think probably the crowning glory of anybody's career is when you get to teach the next person how to do it and then watch them take off and do it differently, more importantly, better than you did."

Simpson says she has no regrets about her career. "I think I have been fabulously lucky. I think so many times I have been in the right place at the right time and I had some incredible bosses." She does mention that she wishes she had learned the value of networking sooner. "I also wish I had recognized the power of the connective tissues that run between women executives." She spoke of Sheelagh Whittaker, president and CEO of EDS Canada Ltd., as one of her mentors, even though they are the same age.

Simpson notes the importance of interpersonal skills for managers. "I think that getting along well with others is the route to career success. I have rarely met a senior manager who advanced without the basic interpersonal skills to make other people want to be like him or just to do what he wanted them to do. How could you be a leader of other people if you don't have the interpersonal skills and charisma to make people want to be like you?" Simpson says her own strengths as a senior executive are in team building, in leadership, and in having a creative vision.

Simpson prefers to work with employees who take initiative. Rather than someone coming to her and saying "I am kind of bored with the job I have and I'd like a new challenge," she would prefer that they say "This is the challenge I would like." When Simpson hires employees, she looks for enthusiasm and a sense of humour. She also tends to appreciate people who are adept at using language and have a facility for words.

She is more careful not to hire people exactly like herself, however. "Early on, I was really most comfortable with people who exhibited the same sorts of skills that I did. I had to learn that it was necessary to go out and hire people who are your exact opposite if you want to make sure that the things that need to get done in the organization get done really well." Simpson also notes the importance of not hiring friends just because they are friends. She once hired a friend because she knew the person's record and knew what he could do. "I thought because I knew and liked him that he would change to be more what I needed him to be. I thought that he could take his facility with numbers and his understanding of the technical aspect of things and learn from me how to do the "sell." That was not right. I wrecked a friendship. I failed to recognize something I now know profoundly which is that people do not change very much."

Simpson observes that expectations of how employees work in organizations have changed thanks to recent improvements in the economic climate. "With downsizing and rightsizing very much evident, employees now are fairly visible in organizations, and this provides an opportunity for young people to rise more rapidly through being committed to what they do for a living."

What are the personal qualities that will help students succeed in the workplace they face upon graduation? "Well, I am going to put enthusiasm and optimism very high on this list," Simpson responds. "In this economic climate, it is not the time to be reserved. It is not the time to be cool. It is the time to impress your manager with your level of energy and your enthusiasm and commitment to the job. Fall in love with the job. Let yourself be a real company person. I see too many young people holding themselves back for fear of making themselves look overeager or foolish. That is a great shame because it is that enthusiasm and that tangible energy that will get you noticed and get rewarded to a far greater degree than any degree of sophistication will within an organization."

Questions

1. Do you agree with Simpson's observation that "people do not change very much"?

2. Simpson makes a case for managers needing interpersonal skills. To what extent do you agree with her?

3. What lessons might you learn from Simpson's observation that "hiring friends can be a mistake"?

4. What challenges might you face if you follow Simpson's advice "to be enthusiastic and optimistic" in today's economic climate?

CHAPTER 5

Basic Motivation Concepts

ROADMAP

LEARNING OBJECTIVES

After studying this chapter, you should be able to

- Outline the motivation process

- Contrast Theory X and Theory Y

- Describe Maslow's hierarchy of needs

- Differentiate motivators from hygiene factors

- List the characteristics that high achievers prefer in a job

- Summarize the types of goals that increase performance

- Clarify the key relationships in expectancy theory

- State the impact of underrewarding employees

- Explain how the theories of motivation complement each other

I NCENTIVE programs have long been part of the corporate land-scape in Canada, the United States, and Europe. With the exception of Japan, that hasn't been true in Asia. But things are changing.[1] Companies in countries such as Singapore, Hong Kong, China, Taiwan, and India are introducing incentive-based motivation programs to boost morale and employee productivity. Hong Kong's DHL Ltd. provides an illustrative example.

DHL was looking for a way to increase the productivity of its sales staff. It began, in September 1995, by setting specific goal targets for each salesperson. Then, to motivate people to achieve their goals, DHL's management created a cash and travel incentive program. "Travel [such as all-expense-paid holidays in Thailand] has all the ingredients to motivate and encourage," explains Michael Thibouville, DHL's regional human resources director. Each salesperson was given a model air-cargo container to fill up. Individuals who exceeded their monthly sales targets were given small blocks to fill their containers. These containers sit on the employees' desks as a visible reminder of how well they are doing. (The photo shows regional sales director Perry Lam holding his container.)

DHL's sales staff has a choice of redeeming the blocks for cash or choosing the travel prize. "The beauty of our incentive scheme is that it isn't competitive," says Thibouville. "We found that salespeople having problems with a particular deal would approach those who had filled up their [containers] for help. With the scheme, we're now able to share the best demonstrated sales practices while developing a consultant-style sales ability among staff."

Sales at DHL have exceeded targets since the incentive program's introduction. Within four months, 26 of its 36 sales staff beat their goals by 40 percent, two by 35 percent, and another two by 30 percent.

The management at DHL Ltd. is seeing some of the positive results that can accrue from a well-designed motivation system. Unfortunately, many managers still fail to understand the importance of motivation and creating a motivating work environment. In this chapter and the following chapter, we explain the basics of motivation and show you how to design effective motivation programs. ■

What Is Motivation?

motivation
The willingness to exert high levels of effort toward organizational goals to satisfy some individual need.

Because we are primarily concerned with one's motivation toward work, we'll define **motivation** as the willingness to exert effort toward achieving organizational goals to satisfy some individual need. The three key elements in our definition are effort, organizational goals, and needs.

The effort element is a measure of intensity. When someone is motivated, he or she tries hard. But high levels of effort are unlikely to lead to favourable job-performance outcomes unless the effort is channelled in a direction that benefits the organization.[2] Therefore we must consider the quality of the effort as well as its intensity. Effort that is directed toward, and is consistent with, the organization's goals is the kind of effort that we should be seeking. Finally, we will treat motivation as a process in which an individual is trying to get one or more needs met. A **need**, in our terminology, means some internal state that makes certain outcomes appear attractive.

need
Some internal state that makes certain outcomes appear attractive.

Therefore we can say that motivation is effort exerted to achieve a need. The more desirable the need to the person, the more effort exerted. Many people incorrectly view motivation as a personal trait—that is, some have it and others don't. Along these lines, Douglas McGregor proposed two distinct views of human beings: one basically negative, labelled **Theory X**, and the other basically positive, labelled **Theory Y**.[3] Theory X suggests that:

Theory X
The assumption that employees dislike work, are lazy, dislike responsibility, and must be coerced to perform.

- Employees inherently dislike work and, whenever possible, will attempt to avoid it.

- Since employees dislike work, they must be coerced, controlled, or threatened with punishment to achieve goals.

Theory Y
The assumption that employees like work, are creative, seek responsibility, and can exercise self-direction.

- Employees will avoid responsibilities and seek formal direction whenever possible.

- Most workers place security above all other factors associated with work and will display little ambition.

In contrast to these negative views about the nature of human beings, Theory Y suggests that:

- Employees can view work as being as natural as rest or play.

- People will exercise self-direction and self-control if they are committed to the objectives.

- The average person can learn to accept, even seek, responsibility.

- The ability to make innovative decisions is widely dispersed throughout the population and is not necessarily the sole province of those in management positions.

Theory X and Theory Y paint very different pictures of employees, and particularly about their motivation to do work. Our knowledge of motivation tells us that neither theory alone fully accounts for employee behaviour. What we know is that motivation is the result of the interaction of the individual and the situation. Certainly, individuals differ in their basic motivational drive. But the same employee who is quickly bored when pulling the lever on his or her drill press may pull the lever on a slot machine in Casino Windsor for hours on end without the slightest hint of boredom. You may read a complete novel at one sitting, yet find it difficult to concentrate on a textbook for more than 20 minutes. It's not necessarily you—it's the

situation. So as we analyze the concept of motivation, keep in mind that the level of motivation varies both between individuals and within individuals at different times.

Also, because we are focused here on organizational behaviour, we restrict our discussion of motivation to those activities compatible and consistent with the organization's goals. For example, some employees regularly spend a lot of time talking with friends at work in order to satisfy their social needs. While there is a high level of effort, it is unproductively directed toward personal rather than organizational objectives. However, other employees make good team leaders precisely because this meets their social needs, but at the same time direct their efforts to achieving organizational goals.

Theories of Motivation

There are a variety of theories of motivation, including needs theories (Maslow's hierarchy of needs, Herzberg's motivation-hygiene theory, Alderfer's ERG theory, and McClelland's theory of needs) and process theories (goal-setting theory, reinforcement theory, expectancy theory). Needs theories describe the types of needs that must be met in order to motivate individuals, while process theories help managers understand processes they might use to motivate employees. More recently, theorists have considered the issue of fairness as it relates to motivating behaviour. This has led us to consider equity theory and fair process, which present frameworks for understanding the comparisons that people make when thinking about rewards and treatment they receive in the workplace.

Needs Theories of Motivation

Hierarchy of Needs Theory

It's probably safe to say that the most well-known theory of motivation is Abraham Maslow's **hierarchy of needs**.[4] He hypothesized that within every human being there exists a hierarchy of five needs. These needs are:

hierarchy of needs theory
There is a hierarchy of five needs—physiological, safety, social, esteem, and self-actualization—and as each need is substantially satisfied, the next need becomes dominant.

1. *Physiological*: Includes hunger, thirst, shelter, sex, and other bodily needs.
2. *Safety*: Includes security and protection from physical and emotional harm.
3. *Social*: Includes affection, belongingness, acceptance, and friendship.
4. *Esteem*: Includes internal esteem factors such as self-respect, autonomy, and achievement; and external esteem factors such as status, recognition, and attention.
5. *Self-actualization*: The drive to become what one is capable of becoming is known as **self-actualization**; it includes growth, achieving one's potential, and self-fulfilment.

self-actualization
The drive to become what one is capable of becoming.

As each of these needs becomes substantially satisfied, the next need becomes dominant. In terms of Exhibit 5-1, the individual moves up the steps of the hierarchy. From the perspective of motivation, the theory would say that although no need is ever fully gratified, a substantially satisfied need no longer motivates. So if you want to motivate someone, according to

**Exhibit 5-1
Maslow's Hierarchy of Needs**

Self-actualization
Esteem
Social
Safety
Physiological

lower-order needs
Needs that are satisfied externally; physiological and safety needs.

higher-order needs
Needs that are satisfied internally; social, esteem, and self-actualization needs.

motivation-hygiene theory
Intrinsic factors are related to job satisfaction, while extrinsic factors are associated with dissatisfaction.

Maslow, you need to understand what level of the hierarchy that person is currently on and focus on satisfying those needs at or above that level.

Maslow separated the five needs into higher and lower orders. Physiological and safety needs were described as **lower-order,** and social, esteem, and self-actualization as **higher-order needs**. The differentiation between the two orders was made on the premise that higher-order needs are satisfied internally (within the person), whereas lower-order needs are predominantly satisfied externally (by such things as pay, union contracts, and tenure). In fact, the natural conclusion to be drawn from Maslow's classification is that in times of economic plenty, almost all permanently employed workers have their lower-order needs substantially met.

Maslow's need theory continues to receive wide recognition, particularly among practising managers. This can be attributed to the theory's intuitive logic and ease of understanding. Unfortunately, however, research does not generally validate the theory. Maslow himself provided no empirical substantiation, and several studies that sought to validate the theory found little support for the prediction that need structures are organized along the dimensions proposed by Maslow, that unsatisfied needs motivate, or that a satisfied need activates movement to a new need level.[5]

Motivation-Hygiene Theory

The **motivation-hygiene theory** was proposed by psychologist Frederick Herzberg.[6] In the belief that an individual's relation to his or her work is a basic one and that his or her attitude toward this work can very well determine the individual's success or failure, Herzberg investigated the question, "What do people want from their jobs?" He asked people to describe, in detail, situations when they felt exceptionally *good* and *bad* about their jobs. These responses were tabulated and categorized. Factors affecting job attitudes as reported in 12 investigations conducted by Herzberg are illustrated in Exhibit 5-2.

From the categorized responses, Herzberg concluded that the replies people gave when they felt good about their jobs were significantly different from the replies given when they felt bad. As seen in Exhibit 5-2, certain characteristics tend to be consistently related to job satisfaction (factors on the right side of the figure), and others to job dissatisfaction (the left side of the figure). Intrinsic factors, such as achievement, recognition, the work itself, responsibility, advancement, and growth, seem to be related to job satisfaction. When those questioned felt good about their work, they tended to attribute these characteristics to themselves. On the other hand, when they were dissatisfied, they tended to cite extrinsic factors, such as company policy and administration, supervision, interpersonal relations, and working conditions.

According to Herzberg, the data suggest that the opposite of satisfaction is not dissatisfaction, as was traditionally believed. Removing dissatisfying characteristics from a job does not necessarily make the job satisfying. As illustrated in Exhibit 5-3, Herzberg proposes that his findings indicate the existence of a dual continuum: the opposite of "Satisfaction" is "No Satisfaction," and the opposite of "Dissatisfaction" is "No Dissatisfaction."

Herzberg explained that the factors leading to job satisfaction are separate and distinct from those that lead to job dissatisfaction. Therefore, man-

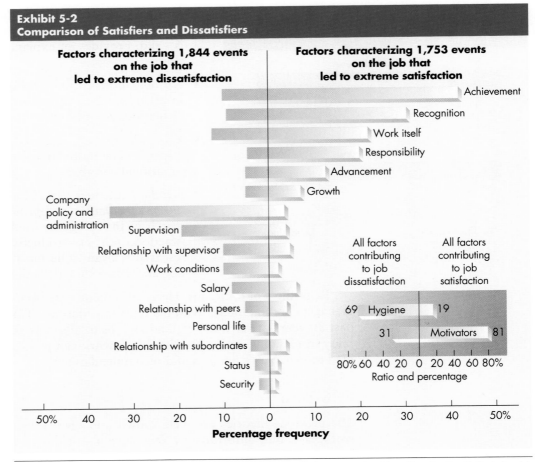

Exhibit 5-2
Comparison of Satisfiers and Dissatisfiers

Source: Reprinted by permission of *Harvard Business Review*. An exhibit from *One More Time: How Do You Motivate Employees?* by Frederick Herzberg, September/October 1987. Copyright ©1987 by the President and Fellows of Harvard College; all rights reserved.

agers who seek to eliminate factors that create job dissatisfaction can bring about peace, but not necessarily motivation. That is, they will be placating employees rather than motivating them. As a result, such characteristics as company policy and administration, supervision, interpersonal relations, working conditions, and salary have been characterized by Herzberg as **hygiene factors**. When they are adequate, people will not be dissatisfied; however, neither will they be satisfied. If we want to motivate people on their jobs, Herzberg suggests emphasizing achievement, recognition, the work itself, responsibility, and growth. These are the characteristics that people find intrinsically rewarding or motivating. In this chapter's Working With Others exercise you will have further opportunity to discover what motivates both you and others with respect to one's job.

The motivation-hygiene theory is not without its critics, who suggest the following:

- *The procedure that Herzberg used is limited by its methodology.* When things are going well, people tend to take credit themselves. Contrarily, they blame failure on the external environment.

- *The reliability of Herzberg's methodology is questioned.* Since raters have to make interpretations, it is possible that they may contaminate the findings by interpreting one response in one manner while treating another similar response differently.

hygiene factors
Those factors—such as company policy and administration, supervision, and salary—that, when adequate in a job, placate workers. When these factors are adequate, people will not be dissatisfied.

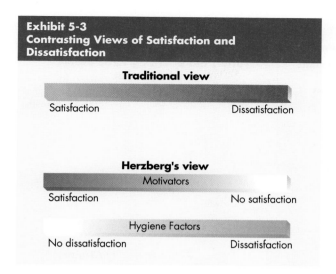

Exhibit 5-3
Contrasting Views of Satisfaction and Dissatisfaction

Traditional view

Satisfaction ——————— Dissatisfaction

Herzberg's view

Motivators

Satisfaction ——————— No satisfaction

Hygiene Factors

No dissatisfaction ——————— Dissatisfaction

- *Herzberg did not really produce a theory of motivation.* Instead, the theory, to the degree that it is valid, provides an explanation of job satisfaction.

- *No overall measure of satisfaction was utilized.* In other words, a person may dislike part of his or her job, yet still think the job is acceptable.

- *The theory is inconsistent with previous research.* The motivation-hygiene theory ignores situational variables.

- *Herzberg assumes that there is a relationship between satisfaction and productivity.* But the research methodology he used looked only at satisfaction, not at productivity. To make such research relevant, one must assume a high relationship between satisfaction and productivity.[7]

Regardless of criticisms, Herzberg's theory has been widely read and few managers are unfamiliar with his recommendations. The popularity over the past 30 years of vertically expanding jobs to allow workers greater responsibility in planning and controlling their work can probably be largely attributed to Herzberg's findings and recommendations.

ERG Theory

The previous theories are well known and often cited by managers in the workplace, but, unfortunately, they have not held up well under close examination. However, all is not lost.[8] Clayton Alderfer of Yale University has reworked Maslow's need hierarchy to align it more closely with the empirical research. His revised need hierarchy is labelled **ERG theory**.[9]

ERG theory
There are three groups of core needs: existence, relatedness, and growth.

Alderfer argues that there are three groups of core needs—existence, relatedness, and growth; hence the label ERG theory. The *existence* group is concerned with providing our basic material existence requirements. They include the items that Maslow considered to be physiological and safety needs. The second group of needs are those of *relatedness*—the desire we have for maintaining important interpersonal relationships. These social and status desires require interaction with others if they are to be satisfied, and they align with Maslow's social need and the external component of Maslow's esteem classification. Finally, Alderfer isolates *growth* needs—an intrinsic desire for personal development. These include the intrinsic component from Maslow's esteem category and the characteristics included under self-actualization.

Besides substituting three needs for five, how does Alderfer's ERG theory differ from Maslow's? In contrast to the hierarchy of needs theory, the ERG theory demonstrates that (1) more than one need may operate at the same time, and (2) if the gratification of a higher-level need is stifled, the desire to satisfy a lower-level need increases.

Maslow's need hierarchy follows a rigid, steplike progression. ERG theory does not assume that a rigid hierarchy exists in which a lower need must be substantially gratified before one can move on. A person can, for instance, be working on growth even though existence or relatedness needs are unsatisfied; or all three need categories could be operating simultaneously.

ERG theory also contains a frustration-regression dimension. Maslow, you'll remember, argued that an individual would stay at a certain need level

Employees of Honeywell have many opportunities to satisfy their relatedness needs. They can build important interpersonal relationships by participating in a number of diversity advisory councils that Honeywell has formed to accommodate its diverse global workforce, which represents 47 cultures and 90 ethnic backgrounds. Employees can interact with others by serving on councils such as the Work and Family Council, Women's Council, Older Workers League, and Council of Employees with Disabilities.

until that need was satisfied. ERG theory counters by noting that when a higher-order need level is frustrated, the individual's desire to increase a lower-level need takes place. Inability to satisfy a need for social interaction, for instance, might increase the desire for more money or better working conditions. So frustration can lead to a regression to a lower need.

In summary, ERG theory argues, like Maslow, that satisfied lower-order needs lead to the desire to satisfy higher-order needs; but, unlike Maslow, multiple needs can be operating as motivators at the same time, and frustration in attempting to satisfy a higher-level need can result in regression to a lower-level need.

ERG theory is more consistent with our knowledge of individual differences among people. Variables such as education, family background, and cultural environment can alter the importance or driving force that a group of needs holds for a particular individual. The evidence demonstrating that people in other cultures rank the need categories differently—for instance, natives of Spain and Japan place social needs before their physiological requirements[10]—would be consistent with ERG theory. Several studies have supported ERG theory,[11] but there is also evidence that it doesn't work in some organizations.[12] Overall, however, ERG theory represents a more valid version of the need hierarchy.

McClelland's Theory of Needs

McClelland's theory of needs was developed by David McClelland and his associates.[13] The theory focuses on three needs: achievement, power, and affiliation. They are defined as follows:

- **Need for achievement:** The drive to excel, to achieve in relation to a set of standards, to strive to succeed.
- **Need for power:** The need to make others behave in a way that they would not have behaved otherwise.
- **Need for affiliation:** The desire for friendly and close interpersonal relationships.

Some people have a compelling drive to succeed. They strive for personal achievement rather than the rewards of success per se. They have a de-

McClelland's theory of needs
Achievement, power, and affiliation are three important needs that help explain motivation.

achievement need
The drive to excel, to achieve in relation to a set of standards, to strive to succeed.

power need
The desire to make others behave in a way that they would not otherwise have behaved.

affiliation need
The desire for friendly and close interpersonal relationships.

sire to do something better or more efficiently than it has been done before. This drive is the achievement need (*nAch*). From research into the achievement need, McClelland found that high achievers differentiate themselves from others by their desire to do things better.[14] They seek situations where they can attain personal responsibility for finding solutions to problems, where they can receive rapid feedback on their performance so they can tell easily whether they are improving, and where they can set moderately challenging goals. High achievers are not gamblers; they dislike succeeding by chance. They prefer the challenge of working at a problem and accepting the personal responsibility for success or failure rather than leaving the outcome to chance or the actions of others. Importantly, they avoid what they perceive to be very easy or very difficult tasks. They want to overcome obstacles, but they want to feel that their success (or failure) is due to their own actions. This means they like tasks of intermediate difficulty.

High achievers perform best when they perceive their probability of success as being 0.5; that is, where they estimate that they have a 50-50 chance of success. They dislike gambling with high odds because they get no achievement satisfaction when success relies mainly on chance. Similarly, they dislike low odds (high probability of success) because then there is no challenge to their skills. They like to set goals that require stretching themselves a little. When there is an approximately equal chance of success or failure, there is the optimum opportunity to experience feelings of accomplishment and satisfaction from their efforts.

The need for power (*nPow*) is the desire to have impact, to be influential, and to control others. Individuals high in *nPow* enjoy being "in charge," strive for influence over others, prefer to be placed into competitive and status-oriented situations, and tend to be more concerned with prestige and gaining influence over others than with effective performance.

The third need isolated by McClelland is affiliation (*nAff*). This need has received the least attention from researchers. Affiliation is the desire to be liked and accepted by others. Individuals with a high affiliation motive strive for friendship, prefer cooperative situations rather than competitive ones,

Interplay Productions
http://www.interplay.com/

The performance of game testers in the quality assurance department of Interplay Productions, a producer of computer games, is evaluated on individual task outcomes, giving them the chance to meet achievement needs. The goal of game testers is to find "bugs" in the programming of the games. When they find a flaw, testers must be able to tell the programmers how they identified the flaw. They score extra points when they can also suggest how to fix the problem. Criteria for advancement in the company include the ability of game testers to explain a complex computer program in simple terms and to generate ideas for new games.

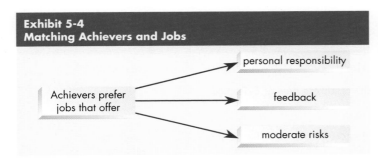

Exhibit 5-4
Matching Achievers and Jobs

Achievers prefer jobs that offer → personal responsibility

→ feedback

→ moderate risks

and desire relationships involving a high degree of mutual understanding.

How do you find out if someone is, for instance, a high achiever? There are questionnaires that tap this motive,[15] but most research uses a projective test in which subjects respond to pictures.[16] Each picture is shown briefly to the subject and then he or she writes a story based on the picture. As an example, the picture may show a male sitting at a desk in a pensive position, looking at a photograph of a woman and two children that sits at the corner of the desk. The subject will then be asked to write a story describing what is going on, what preceded this situation, what will happen in the future, and the like. The stories become, in effect, projective tests that measure unconscious motives. Each story is scored and a subject's ratings on each of the three motives is obtained.

Relying on an extensive amount of research, some reasonably well-supported predictions can be made based on the relationship between achievement need and job performance. Although less research has been done on power and affiliation needs, there are consistent findings here, too.

First, as shown in Exhibit 5-4, individuals with a high need to achieve prefer job situations with personal responsibility, feedback, and an intermediate degree of risk. When these characteristics are prevalent, high achievers will be strongly motivated. The evidence consistently demonstrates, for instance, that high achievers are successful in entrepreneurial activities such as running their own businesses and managing a self-contained unit within a large organization.[17]

Second, a high need to achieve does not necessarily lead to being a good manager, especially in large organizations. People with a high achievement need are interested in how well they do personally and not in influencing others to do well. High-*nAch* salespeople do not necessarily make good sales managers, and the good general manager in a large organization does not typically have a high need to achieve.[18]

Third, the needs for affiliation and power tend to be closely related to managerial success. The best managers are high in their need for power and low in their need for affiliation.[19] In fact, a high power motive may be a requirement for managerial effectiveness.[20] Of course, what the cause is and what the effect is are arguable. It has been suggested that a high power need may occur simply as a function of one's level in a hierarchical organization.[21] The latter argument proposes that the higher the level an individual rises to in the organization, the greater is the incumbent's power motive. As a result, powerful positions would be the stimulus to a high power motive.

Finally, employees have been successfully trained to stimulate their achievement need. Trainers have been effective in teaching individuals to think in terms of accomplishments, winning, and success, and then helping them to learn how to *act* in a high achievement way by preferring situations where they have personal responsibility, feedback, and moderate risks. So if the job calls for a high achiever, management can select a person with a high *nAch* or develop its own candidate through achievement training.[22]

Exhibit 5-5 illustrates the relationship of the various needs theories to each other. While the theories use different names for the needs, and also have different numbers of needs, we can see that they are somewhat consistent in the types of needs addressed. What can we conclude from the needs

Exhibit 5-5
Summarizing the Various Needs Theories

Theory	Maslow	Herzberg	Alderfer	McClelland
Needs	Physiological	Hygiene factors	Existence	
	Safety			
	Social	Motivators	Relatedness	Need for affiliation
	Esteem		Growth	Need for achievement
	Self-actualization			Need for power
View about hierarchy of needs	Argues that lower-order needs must be satisfied before one progresses to higher-order needs	Hygiene factors must be met if person is not to be dissatisfied. They will not lead to satisfaction, however. Motivators lead to satisfaction.	More than one need can be important at the same time. If a higher-order need is not being met, the desire to satisfy a lower-level need increases.	People vary in the types of needs they have. Their motivation and how well they perform in a work situation are related to whether they have a need for achievement, affiliation, or power.

theories? We can safely say that individuals do have needs, and that they can be highly motivated to achieve those needs. The importance of particular needs varies by individual, and probably varies over time for the same individual as well. When managers reward individuals, they should consider the needs of individuals, although obviously it would be difficult to design a reward structure that could completely take into account the specific needs of each employee. You might want to have a look at this chapter's Learning About Yourself exercise to get some ideas about the factors that might motivate you in the workplace.

Process Theories of Motivation

While needs theories address the different needs that individuals have that could be used for motivational purposes, process theories focus on the broader picture of how someone can set about motivating another individual. Within the process theories we will cover goal-setting theory, reinforcement theory, and expectancy theory.

Goal-Setting Theory

You've heard the phrase a number of times: "Just do your best. That's all anyone can ask for." But what does "do your best" mean? Do we ever know if we've achieved that vague goal? Might you have done better in your high school English class if your parents had said, "You should strive for 75 percent or higher on all your work in English" rather than telling you to "do your best"? The research on **goal-setting theory** addresses these issues, and

goal-setting theory
The theory that specific and difficult goals lead to higher performance.

General Mills uses goal-setting theory to motivate employees. When employees reach their goals, the company gives them a big reward. The team of Yoplait yogurt managers shown here each earned bonuses of up to $50 000 above their salaries for exceeding performance goals by 250 percent.

General Mills
http://www.generalmills.com/

the findings, as you will see, are impressive in terms of the effects of goal specificity, challenge, and feedback on performance.

In the late 1960s, Edwin Locke proposed that intentions to work toward a goal are a major source of work motivation.[23] That is, goals tell an employee what needs to be done and how much effort will need to be expended.[24] The evidence strongly supports the value of goals. More to the point, we can say that specific goals increase performance; that difficult goals, when accepted, result in higher performance than do easy goals; and that feedback leads to higher performance than does non-feedback.[25]

Specific hard goals produce a higher level of output than does the generalized goal of "do your best." The specificity of the goal itself acts as an internal stimulus. For instance, when a trucker commits to making 12 round-trip hauls between Toronto and Buffalo, New York, each week, this intention gives him or her a specific objective to try to attain. We can say that, all things being equal, the trucker with a specific goal will outperform his or her counterpart operating with no goals or the generalized goal of "do your best."

If factors such as ability and acceptance of the goals are held constant, we can also state that the more difficult the goal, the higher the level of performance. However, it's logical to assume that easier goals are more likely to be accepted. But once an employee accepts a hard task, he or she will exert a high level of effort until it is achieved, lowered, or abandoned.

People will do better when they receive feedback on how well they are progressing toward their goals because feedback helps to identify discrepancies between what they have done and what they want to do; that is, feedback acts to guide behaviour. But all feedback is not equally potent. Self-generated feedback—where the person is able to monitor his or her own progress—has been shown to be a more powerful motivator than externally generated feedback.[26]

If employees have the opportunity to participate in setting their own goals, will they try harder? The evidence is mixed regarding the superiority of participative over assigned goals.[27] In some cases, participatively set goals elicited superior performance, while in other cases, individuals performed best when assigned goals by their boss. But a major advantage of participa-

tion may be in increasing acceptance of the goal itself as a desirable one to work toward.[28] As we noted, resistance is greater when goals are difficult. If people participate in goal setting, they are more likely to accept even a difficult goal than if their boss arbitrarily assigns it. The reason is that individuals are more committed to choices in which they have a part. Thus, although participative goals may have no superiority over assigned goals when acceptance is taken as a given, participation does increase the probability that more difficult goals will be agreed to and acted upon.

Are there any contingencies in goal-setting theory or can we take it as a universal truth that difficult and specific goals will always lead to higher performance? In addition to feedback, three other factors have been found to influence the goals-performance relationship: goal commitment, adequate self-efficacy, and national culture. Goal-setting theory presupposes that an individual is *committed* to the goal; that is, he or she is determined not to lower or abandon the goal. This is most likely to occur when goals are made public, when the individual has an internal locus of control, and when the goals are self-set rather than assigned.[29] **Self-efficacy** refers to an individual's belief that he or she is capable of performing a task.[30] The higher your self-efficacy, the more confidence you have in your ability to succeed in a task. So, in difficult situations, we find that people with low self-efficacy are more likely to lessen their effort or give up altogether, while those with high self-efficacy will try harder to master the challenge.[31] In addition, individuals high in self-efficacy seem to respond to negative feedback with increased effort and motivation, whereas those low in self-efficacy are likely to lessen their effort when given negative feedback.[32] Finally, goal-setting theory is culture bound. It's well adapted to countries such as Canada and the United States because its key components align reasonably well with North American cultures. It assumes that subordinates will be reasonably independent (not too high a score on power distance), that managers and subordinates will seek challenging goals (low in uncertainty avoidance), and that performance is considered important by both (high in quantity of life). So don't expect goal setting to necessarily lead to higher employee performance in countries such as Portugal or Chile, where the opposite conditions exist.

Our overall conclusion is that intentions—as articulated in terms of hard and specific goals—are a potent motivating force. Under the proper conditions, they can lead to higher performance. However, there is no evidence that such goals are associated with increased job satisfaction.[33]

self-efficacy
The individual's belief that he or she is capable of performing a task.

Reinforcement Theory

reinforcement theory
Behaviour is a function of its consequences.

A counterpoint to goal-setting theory is **reinforcement theory**. The former is a cognitive approach, proposing that an individual's purposes direct his or her actions. In reinforcement theory, we have a behaviouristic approach, which argues that reinforcement conditions behaviour, and thus individuals respond to stimuli rather than act proactively. The two are clearly at odds philosophically. Reinforcement theorists view behaviour as being environmentally caused. You need not be concerned, they would argue, with internal cognitive events; what controls behaviour are reinforcers—any consequence that, when immediately following a response, increases the probability that the behaviour will be repeated.

Reinforcement theory ignores the inner state of the individual and concentrates solely on what happens to a person when he or she takes some action. Because it does not concern itself with what initiates behaviour, it is

not, strictly speaking, a theory of motivation. But it does provide a powerful means of analysis of what controls behaviour, and for this reason it is typically considered in discussions of motivation.[34] Reinforcement theory can also be used to inform us about how often one might want to give rewards (reinforcers) to individuals.

We discussed the reinforcement process in detail in Chapter 2. We showed how using reinforcers to condition behaviour gives us considerable insight into how people learn. Yet we cannot ignore the fact that reinforcement has a wide following as a motivational device. In its pure form, however, reinforcement theory ignores feelings, attitudes, expectations, and other cognitive variables that are known to affect behaviour. In fact, some researchers look at the same experiments that reinforcement theorists use to support their position and interpret the findings in a cognitive framework.[35]

Reinforcement is undoubtedly an important influence on behaviour, but few scholars are prepared to argue that it is the only influence. The behaviours you engage in at work and the amount of effort you allocate to each task are indeed affected by the consequences that follow from your behaviour. If you are consistently reprimanded for outproducing your colleagues, you will likely reduce your productivity. But your lower productivity may also be explained in terms of goals, inequity, or expectancies.

Expectancy Theory

Currently, one of the most widely accepted explanations of motivation is Victor Vroom's **expectancy theory**.[36] Although it has its critics,[37] most of the research evidence is supportive of the theory.[38]

expectancy theory
The strength of a tendency to act in a certain way depends on the strength of an expectation that the act will be followed by a given outcome and on the attractiveness of that outcome to the individual.

Golfers such as Prince Edward Island's Lorie Kane illustrate the effectiveness of the expectancy theory of motivation, where rewards are tied to effort and outcome. Players on the LPGA tour are paid strictly according to their performance, unlike members of professional team sports. Kane had her best season ever in 1997, earning over $425 964, with eight top-10 finishes.

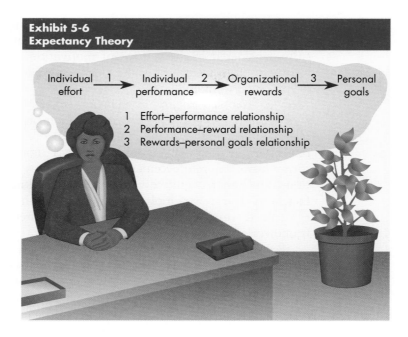

Exhibit 5-6
Expectancy Theory

Individual effort →1→ Individual performance →2→ Organizational rewards →3→ Personal goals

1 Effort–performance relationship
2 Performance–reward relationship
3 Rewards–personal goals relationship

Expectancy theory argues that the strength of a tendency to act in a certain way depends on the strength of an expectation that the act will be followed by a given outcome and on the attractiveness of that outcome to the individual. In more practical terms, expectancy theory says that an employee will be motivated to exert a high level of effort when he or she believes that effort will lead to a good performance appraisal; that a good appraisal will lead to organizational rewards such as a bonus, a salary increase, or a promotion; and that the rewards will satisfy the employee's personal goals. The theory, therefore, focuses on three relationships (see Exhibit 5-6):

- *Effort-performance relationship*: The probability perceived by the individual that exerting a given amount of effort will lead to performance.

- *Performance-reward relationship*: The degree to which the individual believes that performing at a particular level will lead to the attainment of a desired outcome.

- *Rewards-personal goals relationship*: The degree to which organizational rewards satisfy an individual's personal goals or needs and the attractiveness of those potential rewards for the individual.[39]

Expectancy theory can help to explain why some workers are motivated to work hard to accomplish their tasks. For instance, in this chapter's Case Incident, you will learn about the Lincoln Electric employees who are paid based on their performance. They understand that their performance matters and will be rewarded accordingly. Expectancy theory also helps to explain why many workers aren't motivated on their jobs and merely do the minimum necessary to get by. This is evident when we look at the theory's three relationships in a little more detail. We present them as questions that employees need to answer in the affirmative if their motivation is to be maximized.

First, *if I give maximum effort, will I be able to accomplish the task expected of me?* Employees are sometimes asked to do things for which they do not have the appropriate skills or training. When that is the case, they will be less motivated to try hard, because they already believe that they will not be

Lincoln Electric
http://www.lincolnelectric.com/

able to accomplish the task that is expected of them. This chapter's HR Implications discusses the importance of providing the proper training for employees to do their jobs so that effort will lead to task accomplishment.

Second, *if I give maximum effort, will it be recognized by my manager and/or in my performance appraisal?* For many employees, the answer is "no." Why? For one reason, their skill level may be deficient, which means that no matter how hard they try, they're unlikely to be a high performer. A second reason for not giving maximum effort is that an employee's manager might not be particularly observant. In a 1997 study by the Angus Reid group, only 44 percent of employees said that the workplace recognizes employees who excel at their job.[40] This suggests that many employees might conclude that giving maximum effort might not be worth their while. A third reason for not giving a great deal of effort is that the organization's performance appraisal system may be designed to assess non-performance factors such as loyalty, initiative, or courage, which means more effort on non-assessed behaviour won't necessarily result in a higher evaluation. Finally, the employee, rightly or wrongly, may perceive that he or she is disliked by the boss. As a result, the employee expects to receive a poor appraisal regardless of the level of effort. All of these examples suggest that one possible source of low employee motivation is the belief, by the employee, that no matter how hard he or she works, the likelihood of receiving a good performance appraisal is low.

Third, *if I receive a good performance appraisal, will it lead to organizational rewards?* Many employees view the performance-reward relationship in their job as weak. The reason, as we elaborate upon in the next chapter, is that organizations reward a lot of things besides just performance. For example, when pay is allocated to employees based on factors such as seniority, being cooperative, or for "kissing up" to the boss, employees are likely to view the performance-reward relationship as being weak and demotivating. If the employee knows that high levels of effort will lead to good performance, but that performance will not lead to organizational rewards, he or she will be less likely to exert effort for that particular activity. For instance, some organizations encourage employees to make suggestions for how to improve the workplace environment. However, in a 1997 study conducted by the Angus Reid Group, only 25 percent of employees agreed with the statement that "employees are rewarded for implementing ideas which save the company time or money."[41] If employees note that managers rarely act on these suggestions, and give no recognition to the employee for making them, then they are less likely to go out of their way to submit further suggestions.

Finally, *if I'm rewarded, are the rewards ones that I find personally attractive?* The employee works hard in hopes of getting a promotion but receives a pay raise instead. Or the employee wants a more interesting and challenging job but receives only a few words of praise. Or the employee puts in extra effort to be relocated to the company's Paris office but instead is transferred to Singapore. These examples illustrate the importance of the rewards being tailored to individual employee needs. Unfortunately, many managers are limited in the rewards they can distribute, which makes it difficult to individualize rewards. Moreover, some managers incorrectly assume that all employees want the same thing, thus overlooking the motivational effects of differentiating rewards. In either case, employee motivation is submaximized because the specific need they have is not being met through the reward structure. In our Point/Counterpoint feature we examine the extent to which money motivates

others. And in our CBC Video Case, we look at some of the types of material rewards that organizations can give to employees.

In summary, the key to expectancy theory is the understanding of an individual's goals and the linkage between effort and performance, between performance and rewards, and, finally, between the rewards and individual goal satisfaction. As a contingency model, expectancy theory recognizes that there is no universal principle for explaining everyone's motivations. Additionally, just because we understand what needs a person seeks to satisfy does not ensure that the individual perceives high performance as necessarily leading to the satisfaction of these needs.

Does expectancy theory work? Attempts to validate the theory have been complicated by methodological and measurement problems. As a result, many published studies that purport to support or negate the theory must be viewed with caution. Importantly, most studies have failed to replicate the methodology as it was originally proposed. For example, the theory proposes to explain different levels of effort from the same person under different circumstances, but almost all replication studies have looked at different people. Correcting for this flaw has greatly improved support for the validity of expectancy theory.[42] Some critics suggest that the theory has only limited use, arguing that it tends to be more valid in situations where effort-performance and performance-reward linkages are clearly perceived by the individual.[43] The results from the 1997 Angus Reid poll on workplace attitudes cited earlier suggest that many individuals do not perceive a high correlation between performance and rewards in their jobs.[44] Thus, the theory tends to be idealistic. If organizations actually rewarded individuals for performance rather than according to such criteria as seniority, effort, skill level, and job difficulty, then the theory's validity might be considerably greater. However, rather than invalidating expectancy theory, this criticism can be used in support of the theory, for it explains why a significant segment of the workforce exerts low levels of effort in carrying out job responsibilities.

Responses to the Reward System

To a large extent, motivation theory is about rewards, in that the theories suggest that individuals have needs, and they will exert effort in order to have those needs met. The needs theories specifically identify those needs. Goal setting, reinforcement, and expectancy all portray processes by which individuals act and then receive desirable rewards (intrinsic or extrinsic) for their behaviour. There are, however, additional factors to consider in the motivation process. Both equity theory and cognitive evaluation theory suggest that individuals not only respond to rewards, but also evaluate and interpret them, which further complicates the motivation process. Fair process goes one step further, suggesting that employees are sensitive to a variety of fairness issues in the workplace that extend beyond the reward system but also affect employee motivation.

Equity Theory

Jane Pearson graduated last year from university with a degree in accounting. After interviews with a number of organizations on campus, she accepted an articling position with one of the nation's largest public accounting firms and was assigned to their Edmonton office. Jane was very pleased

with the offer she received: challenging work with a prestigious firm, an excellent opportunity to gain valuable experience, and the highest salary any accounting major at her university was offered last year—$4150 a month. But Jane was the top student in her class; she was ambitious and articulate and fully expected to receive a commensurate salary.

Twelve months have passed since Jane joined her employer. The work has proved to be as challenging and satisfying as she had hoped. Her employer is extremely pleased with her performance; in fact, she recently received a $200-a-month raise. However, Jane's motivational level has dropped dramatically in the past few weeks. Why? Her employer has just hired a new graduate from Jane's university, who lacks the one-year experience Jane has gained, for $4400 a month—$50 more than Jane now makes! It would be an understatement to describe Jane as irate. Jane is even talking about looking for another job.

equity theory
Individuals compare their job inputs and outcomes with those of others and then respond so as to eliminate any inequities.

Jane's situation illustrates the role that equity plays in motivation. **Equity theory** suggests that employees make comparisons of their job inputs and outcomes relative to those of others. We perceive what we get from a job situation (outcomes) in relation to what we put into it (inputs), and then we compare our outcome-input ratio with the outcome-input ratio of relevant others. This is shown in Exhibit 5-7. If we perceive our ratio to be equal to that of the relevant others with whom we compare ourselves, a state of equity is said to exist. We perceive our situation as fair—that justice prevails. When we see the ratio as unequal, we experience this as inequity. For instance, consider you wrote a case analysis for your accounting professor, and spent 18 hours researching and writing it up. Your classmate spent six hours preparing the same analysis. Each of you received a mark of 75 percent. It is likely that you would perceive this as unfair, as you worked considerably harder (i.e., exerted more effort) than your classmate. J. Stacy Adams has proposed that those experiencing inequity are motivated to do something to correct it.[45] Thus, you might be inclined to spend considerably less time on your next assignment for your accounting professor.

In the case of the accounting assignment, the obvious referent is your classmate. However, in the workplace, the referent that an employee selects when making comparisons adds to the complexity of equity theory. Evidence indicates that the referent chosen is an important variable in equity theory.[46] There are four referent comparisons that an employee can use:

- *Self-inside*: An employee's experiences in a different position inside his or her current organization.

- *Self-outside*: An employee's experiences in a situation or position outside his or her current organization.

- *Other-inside*: Another individual or group of individuals inside the employee's organization.

Exhibit 5-7
Equity Theory

Ratio Comparisons*	Perception
$O/I_A < O/I_B$	Inequity due to being underrewarded
$O/I_A = O/I_B$	Equity
$O/I_A > O/I_B$	Inequity due to being overrewarded

*Where O/I_A represents the employee; and O/I_B represents relevant others.

- *Other-outside*: Another individual or group of individuals outside the employee's organization.

Employees might compare themselves to friends, neighbours, co-workers, colleagues in other organizations, or past jobs they have had. Which referent an employee chooses will be influenced by the information the employee holds about referents as well as by the attractiveness of the referent. This has led to focusing on four moderating variables—gender, length of tenure, level in the organization, and amount of education or professionalism.[47] Research shows that both men and women prefer same-sex comparisons. The research also demonstrates that women are typically paid less than men in comparable jobs and have lower pay expectations than men for the same work. For instance, Statistics Canada reports that in 1996 the gap between the full-time wages of men and women was the lowest ever, with women earning, on average, 73 cents for every dollar earned by men.[48] So a woman who uses another woman as a referent tends to have a lower comparative standard for pay than a woman who uses a man as the referent. If women are to be paid equally to men in comparable jobs, the standard of comparison—as used by both employees and employers—needs to be expanded to include both sexes. Employees with short tenure in their current organizations tend to have little information about others inside the organization, so they rely on their own personal experiences. On the other hand, employees with long tenure rely more heavily on co-workers for comparison. Upper-level employees, those in the professional ranks, and those with higher amounts of education, tend to be more cosmopolitan and have better information about people in other organizations. Therefore, these types of employees will make more other-outside comparisons.

Based on equity theory, when employees perceive an inequity, they can be predicted to make one of six choices:[49]

- *Change their inputs* (for example, don't exert as much effort)

- *Change their outcomes* (for example, individuals paid on a piece-rate basis can increase their pay by producing a higher quantity of units of lower quality)

- *Adjust perceptions of self* (for example, "I used to think I worked at a moderate pace but now I realize that I work a lot slower than everyone else.")

- *Adjust perceptions of others* (for example, "Mike's job isn't as desirable as I previously thought it was.")

- *Choose a different referent* (for example, "I may not make as much as my brother-in-law, but I'm doing a lot better than my Dad did when he was my age.")

- *Leave the field* (for example, quit the job)

Equity theory recognizes that individuals are concerned not only with the absolute amount of rewards they receive for their efforts, but also with the relationship of this amount to what others receive. They make judgments as to the relationship between their inputs and outcomes and the inputs and outcomes of others. Based on one's inputs, such as effort, experience, education, and competence, one compares outcomes such as salary levels, raises, recognition, and other factors. This suggests that individuals do not focus solely on a particular need being met (for instance, extra income), but also on whether the amount received appears fair compared to

Statistics Canada
http://www.statcan.ca/

what others received. Specifically, the theory establishes four propositions relating to inequitable pay:

- *Given payment by time, overrewarded employees will produce more than will equitably paid employees.* Hourly and salaried employees will generate high quantity or quality of production in order to increase the input side of the ratio and bring about equity.

- *Given payment by quantity of production, overrewarded employees will produce fewer, but higher-quality, units than will equitably paid employees.* Individuals paid on a piece-rate basis will increase their effort to achieve equity, which can result in greater quality or quantity. However, increases in quantity will only increase inequity, since every unit produced results in further overpayment. Therefore, effort is directed toward increasing quality rather than increasing quantity.

- *Given payment by time, underrewarded employees will produce less or poorer quality of output.* Effort will be decreased, which will bring about lower productivity or poorer-quality output than equitably paid subjects.

- *Given payment by quantity of production, underrewarded employees will produce a large number of low-quality units in comparison with equitably paid employees.* Employees on piece-rate pay plans can bring about equity because trading off quality of output for quantity will result in an increase in rewards with little or no increase in contributions.

These propositions have generally been supported, with a few minor qualifications.[50] First, inequities created by overpayment do not seem to have a very significant impact on behaviour in most work situations. Apparently, people have a great deal more tolerance of overpayment inequities than of underpayment inequities, or are better able to rationalize them. Second, not all people are equity sensitive. For example, there is a small part of the working population who simply do not worry about how their rewards compare to others. Predictions from equity theory are unlikely to be very accurate with these individuals.

These propositions also suggest that when organizations only reward senior managers after a year of increased profitability and performance, lower-level employees receive a powerful message. They learn that only shareholders and senior management matter. This can lead to employees withholding effort and initiative.

It's also important to note that while most research on equity theory has focused on pay, employees seem to look for equity in the distribution of other organizational rewards. For instance, it's been shown that the use of high-status job titles as well as large and lavishly furnished offices may function as outcomes for some employees in their equity equation.[51]

In conclusion, equity theory demonstrates that, for most employees, motivation is influenced significantly by relative rewards as well as by absolute rewards, but some key issues are still unclear.[52] For instance, how do employees handle conflicting equity signals, such as when unions point to other employee groups who are substantially *better off*, while management argues how much things have *improved*? How do employees define inputs and outcomes? How do they combine and weigh their inputs and outcomes to arrive at totals? When and how do the factors change over time? Yet, regardless of these problems, equity theory continues to offer some important insights into employee motivation.

Fair Process

distributive justice
Perceived fairness of the amount and allocation of rewards among individuals.

procedural justice
The perceived fairness of the process used to determine the distribution of rewards.

Recent research has been directed at expanding what is meant by equity or fairness.[53] Historically, equity theory focused on **distributive justice** or the perceived fairness of the *amount* and *allocation* of rewards among individuals. But equity should also consider **procedural justice**—the perceived fairness of the *process* used to determine the distribution of rewards. The evidence indicates that distributive justice has a greater influence on employee satisfaction than procedural justice, while procedural justice tends to affect an employee's organizational commitment, trust in his or her boss, and intention to quit.[54] Researchers have found that when managers and employees believe that the company's processes are fair, they are more likely to show a high level of trust and commitment to the organization. Employees engaged in negative behaviour when they felt the process was unfair.[55]

For example, employees at Volkswagen's Puebla, Mexico plant staged a lengthy walkout *after* being offered a 20 percent raise, because their union leaders had agreed to work-rule concessions without consulting them. The employees, even though happy about the raises, did not believe that the process that led to the change in the work rules was fair. By contrast, when Siemens-Nixdorf Informationssysteme (SNI), the largest European supplier of information technology, needed to reduce the workforce from 52 000 to 35 000 in 1994, the CEO met with 11 000 employees to explain the difficulties that SNI faced and ask for their help in reducing costs. Many employees did volunteer, often working after hours, and, within a year, SNI was operating profitably, and employee satisfaction was almost doubled. These examples are consistent with Princeton University economist Alan Blinder's findings that "Changing the way workers are *treated* may boost productivity more than changing the way they are *paid*."[56]

Managers should consider openly sharing information on how allocation decisions are made, following consistent and unbiased procedures, and engaging in similar practices to increase the perception of procedural justice. By increasing the perception of procedural fairness, employees are likely to view their bosses and the organization as positive even if they're dissatisfied with pay, promotions, and other personal outcomes.

Siemens-Nixdorf Informationssysteme (SNI)
http://www.siemensnixdorf.com/public/sni.htm

Volkswagen
http://www.vw.com

Interpersonal Differences and Motivation

Can we motivate all people the same way? The evidence presented in the chapter suggests the answers is "no" on at least two counts. First, needs theories suggest that people are either at different levels in the needs they want satisfied, or, more generally, that they have differing needs. The discussion of intrinsic and extrinsic motivation also suggests that people prefer different rewards, at least on occasion.

Several consultants have recently suggested that managers should provide recognition and rewards that fit an employee's personality.[57] According to this notion, people can be divided into four distinct temperaments: Preservers, Strategists, Mavericks, and Energizers. These temperaments can be related to the types identified by the Myers-Briggs Type Indicator (MBTI), which we discussed in Chapter 3.

Exhibit 5-8 summarizes the values and needs of these four types, and suggests the type of recognition each type prefers. Preservers, who like to see their loyalty to the organization acknowledged, are best rewarded with direct thanks, such as letters of praise, copies of which are also forwarded to

Exhibit 5-8
Linking Rewards to Temperament

Temperament	Values	Like to be recognized for	How they like to be recognized
Preservers	Dependability Responsibility Stability	Follow-through Adherence to rules and policies Dedication and loyalty	Tangible thanks for steady work
Strategists	Intelligence and innovation Competence Tireless effort	Ideas Knowledge Competence	Freedom to learn, or explore a challenge
Mavericks	Great skill Grace under pressure Risk-taking action	Responsiveness Cleverness Ingenuity	Unusual reward for successful and risky action
Energizers	Commitment and passion Independent thinking Sincerity and kindness	Ideas Uniqueness Championing change	Social recognition for synergizing a team

Source: B. Nelson, L. Good and T. Hill, "Motivate Employees According to Temperament," *HR Magazine*, March 1997, p. 52.

their managers and placed in the employee's file. They will also be motivated with such tangible awards as plaques or T-shirts acknowledging specific accomplishments. Strategists are the visionaries and change agents of the organization. They like autonomy, so giving them the opportunity to set their own work schedules and choose some of their assignments would motivate them. Also, providing opportunities to learn, through classes, journal subscriptions, and other activities will motivate strategists. Mavericks like to negotiate and troubleshoot for the organization. Situations where they are allowed to negotiate their own reward are almost as important as the reward itself. Energizers are the "big-picture" people in the organization, and they are concerned with fairness and people issues. Personal notes and rewards that acknowledge interpersonal skills are most motivating to them.

Linking rewards to personality types is an intriguing idea, though there is little concrete empirical evidence that backs it up. However, the basic idea, that not every individual or employee will be motivated by the same rewards, allows managers to consider a range of rewards that are more appropriate to different employees.

Don't Forget Ability and Opportunity

Robin and Chris both graduated from university a couple of years ago with their degrees in elementary education. They each took jobs as grade one teachers, but in different school districts. Robin immediately confronted a

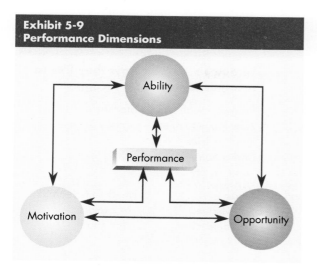

**Exhibit 5-9
Performance Dimensions**

Source: Adapted from M. Blumberg and C.D. Pringle, "The Missing Opportunity in Organizational Research: Some Implications for a Theory of Work Performance," *Academy of Management Review*, October 1982, p. 565.

opportunity to perform
High levels of performance are partially a function of an absence of obstacles that constrain the employee.

number of obstacles on the job: a large class (42 students), a small and dingy classroom, and inadequate supplies. Chris's situation couldn't have been more different, with only 15 students in the class, plus a teaching aide for 15 hours each week, a modern and well-lit room, a well-stocked supply cabinet, six Macintosh computers for students to use, and a highly supportive principal. Not surprisingly, at the end of their first school year, Chris had been considerably more effective as a teacher than had Robin.

The preceding episode illustrates an obvious but often overlooked fact. Success on a job is not simply related to an individual's actions. It is also facilitated or hindered by the existence or absence of support resources.

A popular, although arguably simplistic, way of thinking about employee performance is as a function of the interaction of ability and motivation; that is, performance = $f(A \times M)$. If either is inadequate, performance will be negatively affected. This helps to explain, for instance, the hardworking athlete or student with modest abilities who consistently outperforms his or her more gifted, but lazy, rival. So, as we noted in Chapter 3, a person's individual differences must be considered in addition to motivation if we are to be able to accurately explain and predict employee performance. But a piece of the puzzle is still missing. We need to add **opportunity to perform** to our equation—performance = $f(A \times M \times O)$.[58] Even though an individual may be willing and able, certain obstacles may constrain performance. This is shown in Exhibit 5-9.

When you attempt to assess why an employee may not be performing to the level that you believe he or she is capable of, take a look at the work environment to see if it's supportive. Does the employee have adequate tools, equipment, materials, and supplies? Does the employee have favourable working conditions, helpful co-workers, supportive work rules and procedures, sufficient information to make job-related decisions, adequate time to do a good job, and the like? If not, performance will suffer.

Integrating Contemporary Theories of Motivation

We've looked at a lot of motivation theories in this chapter. The fact that a number of these theories have been supported only complicates the matter. How simple it would have been if, after presenting several theories, only one was found valid. But these theories are not all in competition with one another! Because one is valid doesn't automatically make the others invalid. In fact, many of the theories presented in this chapter are complementary. The challenge is now to tie these theories together to help you understand their interrelationships.[59]

Exhibit 5-10 presents a model that integrates much of what we know about motivation. Its basic foundation is the expectancy model shown in Exhibit 5-8. Let's work through Exhibit 5-10.

We begin by explicitly recognizing that opportunities can aid or hinder individual effort. The individual effort box also has another arrow leading

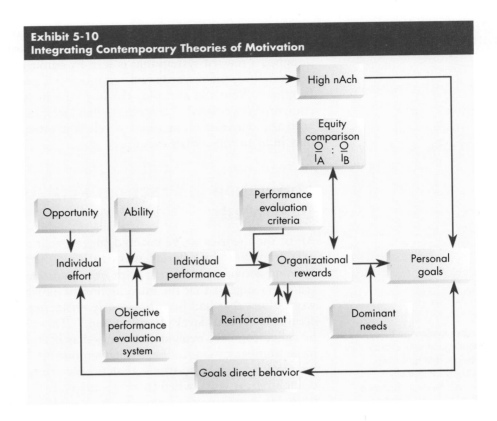

Exhibit 5-10
Integrating Contemporary Theories of Motivation

into it. This arrow flows out of the person's goals. Consistent with goal-setting theory, this goals-effort loop is meant to remind us that goals direct behaviour.

Expectancy theory predicts that an employee will exert a high level of effort if he or she perceives that there is a strong relationship between effort and performance, performance and rewards, and rewards and satisfaction of personal goals. Each of these relationships, in turn, is influenced by certain factors. For effort to lead to good performance, the individual must have the requisite ability to perform, and the performance appraisal system that measures the individual's performance must be perceived as being fair and objective. The performance-reward relationship will be strong if the individual perceives that it is performance (rather than seniority, being a personal favourite, or other criteria) that is rewarded. If cognitive evaluation theory were fully valid in the workplace, we would predict that basing rewards on performance should decrease the individual's intrinsic motivation. The final link in expectancy theory is the rewards-goals relationship. ERG theory would come into play at this point. Motivation would be high to the degree that the rewards an individual received for his or her high performance satisfied the dominant needs consistent with his or her individual goals.

A closer look at Exhibit 5-10 will also reveal that the model considers the achievement need and reinforcement and equity theories. The high achiever is not motivated by the organization's assessment of his or her performance or organizational rewards, hence, the jump from effort to personal goals for those with a high *nAch*. Remember, high achievers are internally driven as long as the jobs they are doing provide them with personal responsibility, feedback, and moderate risks. They are not concerned with the effort-performance, performance-rewards, or rewards-goal linkages.

Reinforcement theory enters our model by recognizing that the organization's rewards reinforce the individual's performance. If management has designed a reward system that is seen by employees as "paying off" for good performance, the rewards will reinforce and encourage continued good performance. Rewards also play the key part in equity theory. Individuals will compare the rewards (outcomes) they receive from the inputs they make with the outcome-input ratio of relevant others ($O/I_A:O/I_B$), and inequities may influence the effort expended.

Motivation in Practice: Perhaps Rewards are Overrated

All of the theories we've covered suggest that rewards can be used to motivate employees by offering ways to meet their needs in exchange for performing activities consistent with organizational goals. However, several researchers suggest that the introduction of extrinsic rewards, such as pay, for work effort that had been *previously rewarding intrinsically* will tend to decrease the overall level of motivation.[60] This proposal—which has come to be called **cognitive evaluation theory**—has been extensively researched, and a large number of studies have been supportive.[61] Alfie Kohn, often cited for his work on rewards, argues that people are actually punished by rewards, doing inferior work when they are enticed by money, grades, or other incentives. His extensive review of incentive studies concluded that "rewards usually improve performance only at extremely simple—indeed, mindless—tasks, and even then they improve only quantitative performance."[62]

Historically, motivation theorists have generally assumed that intrinsic motivations such as achievement, responsibility, and competence are independent of extrinsic motivators such as high pay, promotions, good supervisor relations, and pleasant working conditions. That is, the stimulation of one would not affect the other. But cognitive evaluation theory suggests otherwise. It argues that when extrinsic rewards are used by organizations as payoffs for superior performance, the intrinsic rewards, which are derived from individuals doing what they like, are reduced. In other words, when extrinsic rewards are given to someone for performing an interesting task, it causes intrinsic interest in the task itself to decline. For instance, while a taxi driver expects to be paid if he or she takes your best friend to the airport, you do not expect your friend to pay you if you volunteer to drive her to the airport. In fact, if offered pay, this may diminish your pleasure over doing a favour for your friend.

Why would such an outcome occur? The popular explanation is that the individual experiences a loss of control over his or her own behaviour when it is being rewarded by external sources. This causes the previous intrinsic motivation to diminish. Extrinsic rewards can produce a shift—from an internal to an external explanation—in an individual's perception of causation of why he or she works on a task. If you're reading a novel a week because your contemporary literature instructor requires you to, you can attribute your reading behaviour to an external source. If you stop reading novels the moment the course ends, this is more evidence that your behaviour was due to an external source. However, if you find yourself continuing to read a novel a week when the course ends, your natural inclination is to say, "I must enjoy reading novels because I'm still reading one a week!"

cognitive evaluation theory
Allocating extrinsic rewards for behaviour that had been previously intrinsically rewarded tends to decrease the overall level of motivation.

If cognitive evaluation theory is valid, it should have major implications for managerial practices. It has been a truism among compensation specialists for years that if pay or other extrinsic rewards are to be effective motivators, they should be made contingent on an individual's performance. But, cognitive evaluation theorists would argue, this will only tend to decrease the internal satisfaction that the individual receives from doing the job. We have substituted an external stimulus for an internal stimulus. In fact, if cognitive evaluation theory is correct, it would make sense to make an individual's pay non-contingent on performance in order to avoid decreasing intrinsic motivation. To help you think further about this issue, the OB in the News feature examines the idea of paying golfers a salary independent of the winnings from their tournaments.

OB IN THE NEWS

Paying for Showing Up, Rather Than Paying for Performance

When Fred Couples won the Players Championship in 1996, many people gasped that $882 000 was an obscene amount for winning one golf tournament. Many professional golfers did not, however. After all, Michael Jordan signed a $50-million deal for one season with the Chicago Bulls and Mark Messier signed a $28-million contract with the Vancouver Canucks.

"I think we're going to start making the money we should be making," Payne Stewart said while at the Bell Canadian Open in fall 1997. "I've maintained for a long time that professional golfers are probably the most underpaid athletes going. I think the top 30 [players] on the money list at the end of the year should all have a million dollars."

Sound out of line? Hockey journeyman Tie Domi made $1.8 million with the Toronto Maple Leafs in 1997. He gets paid even if he plays poorly, and the Maple Leafs pay all his expenses when the team's on the road. But PGA Tour players pay all their own expenses. If Stewart misses a cut, he loses money that week because of expenses, which include caddie fees.

Expectancy theory suggests that to motivate someone, rewards should be tied to effort and outcome. To date that has been true in golf. Unlike professional team sports, players on the PGA Tour are paid according to their performance. But many players say it's time they receive a minimum payment even if they miss a cut. "I'm a proponent [of the theory that] if you're good enough to get out here there's no reason you shouldn't be compensated for your expenses," Stewart says. "We play year-round. It's a grind out here. Everyone thinks it's a great way to make a living, but I'm away from my family a lot."

Will minimum payments to golfers improve their performance on the golf course? Or, will golfers feel less pressure to perform, knowing they have some guaranteed income? Only time will tell.

Source: Based on Tim O'Connor, "Tee Time: In Light of Other Astronomical Sports Salaries, are Larger Tournament Purses Too Much to Ask for?" *Financial Post Daily*, September 5, 1997, p. 45.

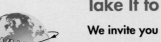

Take It to the Net

We invite you to visit the Robbins page on the Prentice Hall Web site at:

http://www.prenticehall.ca/robbins

for this chapter's World Wide Web exercise.

Although further research is needed to clarify some of the current ambiguity, the evidence does lead us to conclude that the interdependence of extrinsic and intrinsic rewards is a real phenomenon.[63] A large body of research shows that large external rewards can undermine the positive performance of employees.[64] When employees work for a large reward, they will explain their behaviour through that reward—"I did it for the money." However, in the absence of large rewards, employees are more likely to reflect on the interesting nature of the work or the positive benefits of being an organizational member to explain their behaviour. For example, when the University of British Columbia redesigned its MBA Core program several years ago, the five members of the original design team (Nancy Langton, your Vancouver-based author, was one of those members) met for many hours each week, far exceeding the course release time they were offered for the task. The explanation for this behaviour was that the team was charged with designing and implementing a new program, and that carried with it a great deal of responsibility *and* excitement. When organizations provide employees with intrinsically interesting work, they will often work longer and harder than one might predict from the actual external rewards.

In studies dating back to the 1940s, employees always have ranked other items, such as being shown appreciation for work done, feeling "in" on things and having interesting work as being more important to them than their salaries."[65] Employees at both Southwest Airlines and AES, an independent producer of electrical power, with offices in the United States, Argentina, China, Hungary, and other countries, indicated that they appreciated the positive working climates of these organizations more than the specific financial rewards they received.[66]

Southwest Airlines
http://iflyswa.com/

AES Corporation
http://www.aesc.

Jeffrey Pfeffer of Stanford University, one of the leaders in the field of organizational behaviour, in his 1998 book *The Human Equation* encourages organizations to examine the messages they are sending to employees through the rewards they offer. Pfeffer argues that relying exclusively on financial incentives in organizations does not work and notes that people will work hard if the atmosphere is fun. As he points out, "At Apple Computer in its early days, employees didn't work 80 or 90 hours a week to maximize the expected value of some discounted stream of future earnings or to maximize shareholder wealth; they did it because the work was fun and challenging and because they were changing how the world viewed personal computers."[67]

Apple Computer
http://www.apple.com/

Of course, organizations cannot simply ignore financial rewards. When people feel they are being treated unfairly in the workplace, pay often becomes a focal point of their concerns. If tasks are dull or unpleasant, extrinsic rewards will probably increase intrinsic motivation.[68] Even when a job is inherently interesting, there still exists a powerful norm for extrinsic payment.[69] But creating fun, challenging, and empowered workplaces may do more for motivation and performance than focusing simply on the compensation system. We will pursue this discussion further at the end of Chapter 6.

Caveat Emptor: Motivation Theories Are Culture Bound

In our discussion of goal setting, we said that care needs to be taken in applying this theory because it assumes cultural characteristics that are not universal. This is true for many of the theories presented in this chapter.

Most current motivation theories were developed in the United States by Americans and about Americans.[70] That may account for why Canada and the United States rely more heavily on extrinsic motivating factors than some other countries.[71] Japanese and German firms rarely make use of individual work incentives.[72]

Maybe the most blatant pro-American characteristic inherent in these theories is the strong emphasis on what we defined in Chapter 4 as individualism and quantity of life. For instance, both goal-setting and expectancy theories emphasize goal accomplishment as well as rational and individual thought. Many of the social psychological theories of motivation rely heavily on the notion of motivating the individual, through individual rewards. Therefore they emphasize, particularly in an organizational context, the meaning of pay, and give little attention to the informal rewards that come from group norms and prestige from peers.[73] In contrast, "large Japanese firms take a much more active role in shaping employee motivation...They do this in part by turning small work groups and company ideology into official reward mechanisms with powerful consequences for individual motivation."[74] In other words, Japanese organizations do not emphasize motivating each individual one at a time, but rely more heavily on group processes providing motivation to employees.

Let's take a look at whether an American bias has affected the motivation theories introduced in this chapter. Maslow's need hierarchy argues that people start at the physiological level and then move progressively up the hierarchy in this order: physiological, safety, social, esteem, and self-actualization. This hierarchy, if it has any application at all, aligns well with American culture and reasonably well with Canadian culture. However, in countries such as Japan, Greece, and Mexico, where uncertainty avoidance characteristics are strong, security needs would be on top of the need hierarchy. Countries that score high on quality-of-life characteristics—Denmark, Sweden, Norway, the Netherlands, and Finland—would have social needs on top.[75] We would predict, for instance, that group work will motivate employees more when the country's culture scores high on the quality-of-life criterion.

Nestlé
http://www.nestle.com/

While some cultural characteristics are not universal, it seems high achievers are in demand everywhere. Switzerland-based Nestlé, the world's largest branded food company, hires high achievers to sell its products in markets that span the globe. Cultural differences aside, Nestlé salespeople, such as the Red Hot Sales Force in Thailand shown here, are motivated by growth, achievement, responsibility, and recognition. These salespeople sell products to the North American-style supermarkets and superstores sprouting up in developing nations. Nestlé is counting on the Red Hot group to increase profits and market share as competition in Thailand increases.

Another motivation concept that clearly has an American bias is the achievement need. The view that a high achievement need acts as an internal motivator presupposes two cultural characteristics—a willingness to accept a moderate degree of risk (which excludes countries with strong uncertainty avoidance characteristics) and a concern with performance (which applies almost singularly to countries with strong quantity-of-life characteristics). This combination is found in anglophone cultures such as English-speaking Canada, the United States, and Great Britain.[76] The characteristics may apply to a lesser extent in Quebec. As we noted in Chapter 4 when we discussed differences in values between English- and French-speaking Canada, many previous studies suggest that, historically, francophones in Canada have valued the group and interpersonal relations more than anglophones in Canada. Thus, the achievement need likely would be lessened a bit in francophone Canada, although we also noted in Chapter 4 that there seems to be some convergence of anglophone and francophone values in a recent study. Achievement need characteristics are also relatively absent in countries such as Chile and Portugal.

But don't assume there aren't *any* cross-cultural consistencies. For instance, the desire for interesting work seems important to almost all workers, regardless of their national culture. In a study of seven countries, employees in Belgium, Britain, Israel, and the United States ranked "interesting work" number one among 11 work goals. And this factor was ranked either second or third in Japan, the Netherlands, and Germany.[77] Similarly, in a study comparing job-preference outcomes among graduate students in Canada, the United States, Australia, and Singapore, growth, achievement, and responsibility were rated the top three and had identical rankings.[78] Both of these studies suggest some universality to the importance of intrinsic factors in motivation-hygiene theory.

HR IMPLICATIONS

Improving Motivation in the Workplace through Training and Development Programs

One of the critical assumptions of many of the motivation theories presented in this chapter is that employees exert effort in order to satisfy needs.

This is implied in the needs theories, which discuss needs that individuals have. Expectancy theory explicitly discusses the effort-performance link. However, if an employee does not have the requisite skills to do an assigned task, one might conclude that motivation will be low, regardless of the reward offered. Organizations might do well to offer training and development programs to their employees so that they will continue to have the necessary skills to perform their jobs. Skills deteriorate and can become obsolete. Intensified competition, technological changes, and the search for improved productivity should motivate management to increase expenditures for training.

In support of training as part of the motivation process, Herzberg noted that:

Managers do not motivate employees by giving them higher wages, more benefits, or new status symbols. Rather, employees are motivated by their own inherent need to succeed at a challenging task. The manager's job, then, is not to motivate people to get them to achieve; instead, the manager should provide opportunities for people to achieve so they will become motivated.[1]

Not all Canadian organizations seem to be aware of the motivating potential of training, however. Canadians rate their workplaces worse than employees in 36 other nations for in-company training.[2] Less than one-third of Canadian firms do any training at all while about 74 percent of employees in Japan and 80 percent in Britain receive on-the-job training. The Conference Board of Canada surveyed 219 companies, schools and hospitals to find out their 1995 training and development budgets. The figures ranged from a high of $1142 on average to train employees in oil and gas firms to a low of $285 per worker in the education sector. Manufacturing firms averaged about $715 per worker.

Some firms do spend more on training, however. Hamilton, Ontario-based steel giant Dofasco Inc. spends about $2700 per worker, which comes to more than $20 million a year to train its 7200 workers.[3] Honeywell Limited in Scarborough, Ontario, is justifiably proud of its "Learning for Life" program—Honeywell's name for an initiative that promotes education in the workplace. Five years after the program was instituted productivity was up 40 percent, work-in-process inventory was reduced by 60 percent, and employees' pride, dedication and self-esteem rose dramatically.[4]

Canada spends far less than the U.S. on employee training. For instance, it was reported that U.S. corporations with 100 or more employees spent $52.2 billion (US$) in one recent year on formal training for 47.3 million workers, which averages to $1580 (CDN$) per employee.[5] Xerox alone spends over $300 million (US$) a year on training and retraining its employees.[6] Motorola, Federal Express, Andersen Consulting, Corning, and Singapore Airlines all spend at least three percent of their payroll costs on training.[7]

Through our focus on the human resources implications of motivation theory, we look at the type of skills that training can improve. We also examine mentoring programs as a way of helping employees develop skills. For more information about training that develops employee skills, take a look at HR Implications in Chapter 2.

Skill Categories

We can dissect skills into four general categories: basic literacy, technical, interpersonal, and problem solving. Most training activities seek to modify one or more of these skills.

Basic Literacy A recent Statistics Canada study reports that most Canadians aged 16 years and over can read to some extent. But about 22% have serious difficulty in dealing with printed material. Another 25% can only read material that is relatively simple.[8] These findings are consistent with a recent international adult-literacy survey, which found that about 42 per cent of Canadian adults between the ages of 16 and 65 don't have reading skills good enough for the demands of tomorrow's workplace.[9] Literacy problems are not confined to Canada. The American Management Association reports that one out of three applicants tested for jobs by its members in 1995 lacked sufficient reading or math skills to perform the jobs they were seeking.[10] Most workplace demands require a grade 10 or 11 reading level, but about 20 percent of Americans between the ages of 21 and 25 can't read at even a grade 3 level.[11] And in many Third World countries, few workers can read or have gone beyond the equivalent of grade 3.

Statistics Canada estimates that only two percent of company training involves literacy or basic skills training.[12] However, a recent Conference Board of Canada study found that enhancing general reading, writing, and numeracy skills can improve the bottom line for businesses. This includes lower costs and better quality work, as well as better team performance, and lower absenteeism. Literacy programs also resulted in improved labour-management relations in firms that had such programs.[13]

Some Canadian firms are showing leadership in promoting literacy training. Canada Post gives out "Flight for Freedom" awards to honour individual Canadians, companies and organizations that make a difference in the literacy movement. One recent winner of this award was Saint-Laurent, Quebec-based Kraft Canada for a highly successful project at its Mount-Royal plant involving trained volunteer employees helping other employees to improve their literacy skills.[14]

Technical Most training is directed at upgrading and improving an employee's technical skills. This applies as much to white-collar as to blue-collar jobs. Jobs change as a result of new technologies and improved methods. Today's employee working in an automated manufacturing plant needs a broad range of technical skills from math, science, and computers to advanced assembly techniques and quality management tools such

as statistical process control.[15] Few jobs go unaffected. For example, postal sorters have had to undergo technical training in order to learn to operate automatic sorting machines. Many auto repair personnel have had to undergo extensive training to fix and maintain recent models with front-wheel-drive trains, electronic ignitions, fuel injection, and other innovations. And millions of clerical personnel in the past decade have had to be trained to operate and interface with a computer terminal.

Interpersonal Almost all employees belong to a work unit. To some degree, their work performance depends on their ability to effectively interact with their co-workers and their boss. Some employees have excellent interpersonal skills, but others require training to improve theirs. This includes learning how to be a better listener, how to communicate ideas more clearly, and how to be a more effective team player.

One of the fastest-growing areas of interpersonal skill development is diversity training.[16] The two most popular types of this training focus on increasing awareness and building skills. *Awareness training* tries to create an understanding of the need for, and meaning of, managing and valuing diversity. *Skill-building training* educates employees about specific cultural differences in the workplace. Companies leading the way in diversity training include 3M Canada Co., Manitoba Hydro, and Procter & Gamble Inc. All three received 1996 Merit Awards for Initiatives in Employment Equity from the federal ministry of labour for their achievements in removing barriers to employment for women, aboriginal people, people with disabilities, and visible minorities.

Problem Solving Managers as well as many employees who perform nonroutine tasks have to solve problems on the job. When people require these skills but are deficient in them, they can participate in problem-solving training. This would include activities to sharpen their logic, reasoning, and problem-defining skills, as well as their abilities to assess causation, develop alternatives, analyse alternatives, and select solutions. Problem-solving training has become a basic part of almost every organizational effort to introduce self-managed teams or implement Total Quality Management.

Mentoring Programs

Another way that organizations can insure that employees develop the skills they need to maintain motivation is through mentoring programs. A **mentor** is a senior employee who sponsors and supports a less experienced employee (a protégé). The mentoring role includes coaching, counselling, and sponsorship.[17] As a coach, mentors help to develop their protégés' skills. As counsellors, mentors provide support and help bolster the protégés' self-confidence. As sponsors, mentors actively intervene on behalf of their protégés, lobby to get them visible assignments, and politick to get them rewards such as promotions and salary increases.

Is mentoring important? For those who want to get ahead, it seems to be. Business school graduates who have had mentors early in their career are promoted faster, make higher salaries, and are more satisfied with their career progress later in life.[18] And more than half the men who make it to executive positions report they had a mentor along the way.[19]

Formal mentoring programs are particularly important for members of minority groups and women. Why? Because the evidence indicates that individuals from these groups are less likely to be informally chosen as protégés than are white males and thus are less likely to accrue the benefits of mentorship.[20] Mentors tend to select protégés who are similar to themselves on criteria such as background, education, gender, race, ethnicity, and religion. "People naturally move to mentor and can more easily communicate with those with whom they most closely identify."[21] In Canada and the United States, for instance, upper-management positions in most organizations have been traditionally staffed by white males, so it's hard for minorities and women to be selected as protégés. In addition, in terms of cross-gender mentoring, senior male managers may select male protégés to minimize problems such as sexual attraction or gossip. So organizations have responded by replacing informal mentoring relationships with formal programs and providing training and coaching for potential mentors of special groups such as minorities and women.

In summary, employee training, development, and mentoring are all ways that companies can improve the motivation levels of employees, by helping them acquire the skills they need to perform well. These programs have bottom-line results that lead to improved productivity and satisfaction, and decreased absenteeism.

Sources:

[1] Frederick Herzberg, "Workers' Needs: The Same Around the World," *Industry Week*, 21, September 1987, p. 30.

[2] Information in this paragraph based on Peter Kuitenbrouwer, "Firms Underinvesting in Staff Training," *Financial Post Daily*, October 17, 1997, p.12.

[3] Peter Kuitenbrouwer, "Firms Underinvesting in Staff Training," *Financial Post Daily*, October 17, 1997, p.12.

[4] "People Programs Pay Dividends," *Plant*, v.53(7) May 2, 1994 p. 1,5.

[5] Cited in *Training*, October 1995, p. 38.

[6] Cited in J.C. Szabo, "Training Workers for Tomorrow," *Nation's Business*, March 1993, pp. 22–32.

[7] R. Henkoff, "Companies That Train Best," Fortune, March 22, 1993, p. 64; and "How SIA Nurtures High Fliers," *Asian Business*, December 1993, p. 44.

[8] Neville Nankivell, "Time for Canadian Firms to Invest in Programs to Upgrade Literacy Skills: Occupations in Demand Require Higher Skills, Report Shows," *Financial Post Daily*, September 17, 1996, p. 21.

[9] "Literacy Key in Changing Job Market, Group Told," *Canadian Press Newswire*, November 15, 1997.

[10] G. Koretz, "A Crash Course in the Three Rs?", *Business Week*, May 20, 1996, p. 26.

[11] Reported in *From School to Work* (Princeton, NJ: Educational Testing Service, 1990).

[12] Neville Nankivell, "Time for Canadian Firms to Invest in Programs to Upgrade Literacy Skills: Occupations in Demand Require Higher Skills, Report Shows," *Financial Post Daily*, September 17, 1996, p. 21.

[13] Neville Nankivell, "Literacy Spells Better Profitability: Raising Skills Can Improve Bottom Line, Study Says," *Financial Post Daily*, September 16, 1997, p. 21.

[14] Neville Nankivell, "Time for Canadian Firms to Invest in Programs to Upgrade Literacy Skills: Occupations in Demand Require Higher Skills, Report Shows," *Financial Post Daily*, September 17, 1996 , p. 21.

[15] M. Salter, "The New Blue Collar Elite," *Canadian Business*: Special Technology Issue, June 1995, pp. 55–57.

[16] See, for instance, S.E. Jackson (ed.), *Diversity in the Workplace* (New York: Guilford Press, 1992); M. Lee, "Diversity Training Grows at Small Firms," *Wall Street Journal*, September 2, 1993, p. B2; H.B. Karp, "Choices in Diversity Training," *Training*, August 1994, pp. 73–74; S. Rynes and B. Rosen, "What Makes Diversity Programs Work," *HR Magazine*, October 1994, pp. 67–73; and S. Nelton, "Nurturing Diversity," *Nation's Business*, June 1995, pp. 25–27.

[17] See, for example, K.E. Ram, *Mentoring at Work: Developing Relationships in Organizational Life* (Glenview, IL: Scott, Foresman, 1985).

[18] G. Dreher and R. Ash, "A Comparative Study of Mentoring Among Men and Women in Managerial, Professional, and Technical Positions," *Journal of Applied Psychology*, October 1990, pp. 539–46; and W. Whitely, T. Dougherty, and G. Dreher, "Relationship of Career Mentoring and Socioeconomic Origin to Managers' and Professionals' Early Career Progress," *Academy of Management Journal*, June 1991, pp. 331–51.

[19] Reported in G. Johns, *Organizational Behavior: Understanding and Managing Life at Work*, 4th ed. (New York: HarperCollins, 1996), p. 620.

[20] See, for example, B.R. Ragins, "Barriers to Mentoring: The Female Manager's Dilemma," *Human Relations*, January 1989, pp. 1–22; B.R. Ragins and D. McFarlin, "Perceptions of Mentor Roles in Cross-Gender Mentoring Relationships," *Journal of Vocational Behavior*, December 1990, pp. 321–39; and D.A. Thomas, "The Impact of Race on Managers' Experiences of Developmental Relationships: An Intra-Organizational Study," *Journal of Organizational Behavior*, November 1990, pp. 539–46.

[21] J.A. Wilson and N.S. Elman, "Organizational Benefits of Mentoring," *The Executive*, November 1990, p. 90.

Summary and Implications

For the Workplace

The theories we've discussed in this chapter do not all address our five dependent variables. Some, for instance, are directed at explaining turnover, while others emphasize productivity. The theories also differ in their predictive strength. In this section, we (1) review the key motivation theories to determine their relevance in explaining our dependent variables, and (2) assess the predictive power of each.[79]

NEED THEORIES We introduced four theories that focused on needs. These were Maslow's hierarchy, motivation-hygiene, ERG, and McClelland's needs theories. The strongest of these is probably the last, particularly regarding the relationship between achievement and productivity. If the other three have any value at all, that value relates to explaining and predicting job satisfaction.

GOAL-SETTING THEORY There is little dispute that clear and difficult goals lead to higher levels of employee productivity. This evidence leads us to conclude that goal-setting theory provides one of the more powerful explanations of this dependent variable. The theory, however, does not address absenteeism, turnover, satisfaction or organizational commitment.

REINFORCEMENT THEORY This theory has an impressive record for predicting factors such as quality and quantity of work, persistence of effort, absenteeism, tardiness, and accident rates. It does not offer much insight into employee satisfaction or the decision to quit.

EXPECTANCY THEORY Expectancy theory focuses on performance variables. It has proven to offer a relatively powerful explanation of employee productivity, absenteeism, and turnover. But expectancy theory assumes that employees have few constraints on their decision discretion. It makes many of the same assumptions that the rational model makes about individual decision-making (see Chapter 10). This acts to restrict its applicability.

For major decisions, such as accepting or resigning from a job, expectancy theory works well because people don't rush into decisions of this nature. They're more prone to take the time to carefully consider the costs and benefits of all the alternatives. However, expectancy theory is not a very good explanation for more typical types of work behaviour, especially for individuals in lower-level jobs, because such jobs come with considerable limitations imposed by work methods, supervisors, and company policies. We would conclude, therefore, that expectancy theory's power in explaining employee productivity increases where the jobs being performed are more complex and higher in the organization (where discretion is greater).

EQUITY THEORY Equity theory deals with all five dependent variables. However, it is strongest when predicting absence and turnover behaviours and weak when predicting differences in employee productivity. Equity theory suggests that there will be more organizational commitment when individuals find that reward allocations are fair.

A GUIDE THROUGH THE MAZE Exhibit 5-12 summarizes what we know about the power of the more well-known motivation theories to explain and predict our four dependent variables. While based on a wealth of research, it also includes some subjective judgments. However, it does provide a reasonable guide through the motivation theory maze.

For You as an Individual

With all of the theories presented in the chapter, it might be easy to conclude, particularly in the workplace, that motivation is something that someone (e.g., the manager) should be doing for you. This is not your best conclusion, however. Motivation is something that we can do for ourselves, for instance. Have you ever told yourself that when you finished reading a particularly long and dry chapter in a text that you would take a snack break? Or promised yourself a new CD once that major accounting assignment was finished? These are examples of how you motivate yourself.

You also have the ability to motivate others, even if you hadn't thought about this before. The people you interact with appreciate recognition. For example, Nancy Langton, your Vancouver-based author, is fortunate to work with a very good secretary. But because the author has absolutely no control over the reward structure at the University of British Columbia, she can't give her secretary a raise, merit pay, days off, or better benefits. Occasionally, however, she presents her secretary with brief notes on nice cards to mention a job well done and appreciated. Or she presents a basket of flowers. Sometimes just sending a pleasant thankful e-mail is enough to make the

Exhibit 5-12
Power of Motivation Theories

		THEORIES			
Variable	**Need**	**Goal Setting**	**Reinforce-ment**	**Equity**	**Expectancy**
Productivity	3[b]	5	3	3	4[c]
Absenteeism			4	4	4
Turnover				4	5
Satisfaction	2			2	
Organizational Commitment				4	

[a] Theories are rated on a scale of 1 to 5, 5 being highest.
[b] Applies to individuals with a high need to achieve.
[c] Limited value in jobs where employees have little discretionary choice.

Source: Based on F.J. Landy and W.S. Becker, "Motivation Theory Reconsidered," in L.L. Cummings and B.M. Staw (eds.), *Research in Organizational Behavior*, Vol. 9 (Greenwich, CT: JAI Press, 1987), p. 33.

person feel appreciated. All of these things are easy enough to do, and appreciated greatly by the recipient.

To take another example, if you're unhappy with the way a professor teaches, one of the challenges to yourself in learning about organizational behaviour is to think of ways that you might motivate the instructor to perform better. That is, you might consider giving positive, helpful feedback, and also participating more in class. This would convey interest in the course, which would be motivating to many instructors.

There are other small ways that you can engage in motivation practices yourself. In a new book, *The Psychology of Money*, authors Adrian Furnham and Michael Argyle report that waitresses receive bigger tips by drawing happy faces on the back of the bill (although this particular trick doesn't work for waiters, as it's viewed as gender inappropriate).[80] The researchers also found that the size of the first smile that came from the waitperson was directly proportional to the amount of the tip received. So, don't think of motivation as something that should be done for you. Think about motivating others, and yourself, as well.

ROADMAP REMINDER

This chapter marked the entry into Part 2 of the text, Striving Towards Performance. We have previously examined the context within which performance occurs in organizations: the changing face of Canada and the changing face of organizations. We explored how people's personality, perception, values, and attitudes influence their responses. Having done that, we now want to understand how we make it possible for people to work together. This chapter introduced the concept of motivation as part of the performance puzzle. The following chapter looks more closely at using specific rewards to achieve specific types of performance.

For Review

1. Does motivation come from within a person or is it a result of the situation? Explain.
2. What are the implications of Theories X and Y for motivation practices?
3. Compare and contrast Maslow's hierarchy of needs theory with (a) Herzberg's motivation-hygiene theory and (b) Alderfer's ERG theory.
4. Describe the three needs isolated by McClelland. How do they relate to worker behaviour?
5. What is the role of self-efficacy in goal setting?
6. Identify the variables in expectancy theory.
7. Contrast distributive and procedural justice.
8. Explain the formula: Performance = $f(A \times M \times O)$ and give an example.
9. Explain cognitive evaluation theory. How applicable is it to management practice?
10. What consistencies among motivation concepts, if any, apply cross-culturally?

For Discussion

1. "The cognitive evaluation theory is contradictory to reinforcement and expectancy theories." Do you agree or disagree? Explain.
2. "Goal setting is part of both reinforcement and expectancy theories." Do you agree or disagree? Explain.
3. Compare the application of Maslow's and Herzberg's theories in Newfoundland (where the unemployment rate has been about 19 percent in recent years) and British Columbia (where the unemployment rate has been closer to nine percent).
4. Can an individual be too motivated, so that his or her performance declines as a result of excessive effort? Discuss.
5. Identify three activities you really enjoy (for example, playing tennis, reading a novel, going shopping). Next, identify three activities you really dislike (for example, visiting the dentist, cleaning the house, following a low-fat diet). Using the expectancy model, analyze each of your answers to assess why some activities stimulate your effort while others don't.

What Motivates You?

Circle the number that most closely agrees with how you feel. Consider your answers in the context of your current job or past work experience.

		Strongly Disagree				Strongly Agree
1.	I try very hard to improve on my past performance at work.	1	2	3	4	5
2.	I enjoy competition and winning.	1	2	3	4	5
3.	I often find myself talking to those around me about non-work matters.	1	2	3	4	5
4.	I enjoy a difficult challenge.	1	2	3	4	5
5.	I enjoy being in charge.	1	2	3	4	5
6.	I want to be liked by others.	1	2	3	4	5
7.	I want to know how I am progressing as I complete tasks.	1	2	3	4	5
8.	I confront people who do things I disagree with.	1	2	3	4	5
9.	I tend to build close relationships with co-workers.	1	2	3	4	5
10.	I enjoy setting and achieving realistic goals.	1	2	3	4	5
11.	I enjoy influencing other people to get my way.	1	2	3	4	5
12.	I enjoy belonging to groups and organizations.	1	2	3	4	5
13.	I enjoy the satisfaction of completing a difficult task.	1	2	3	4	5
14.	I often work to gain more control over the events around me.	1	2	3	4	5
15.	I enjoy working with others more than working alone.	1	2	3	4	5

Turn to page 698 for scoring directions and key.

Source: Based on R. Steers and D. Braunstein, "A Behaviorally Based Measure of Manifest Needs in Work Settings," *Journal of Vocational Behavior*, October 1976, p. 254; and R.N. Lussier, *Human Relations in Organizations: A Skill Building Approach* (Homewood, IL: Richard D. Irwin, 1990), p. 120.

WORKING WITH OTHERS EXERCISE

What Do People Want from Their Jobs?

1. Each class member begins by completing the following questionnaire:

   Rate the following 12 job factors according to how important each is to you. Place a number on a scale of 1 to 5 on the line before each factor.

Very important		Somewhat important		Not important
5	4	3	2	1

   _____ 1. An interesting job

   _____ 2. A good boss

   _____ 3. Recognition and appreciation for the work I do

   _____ 4. The opportunity for advancement

   _____ 5. A satisfying personal life

   _____ 6. A prestigious or status job

   _____ 7. Job responsibility

   _____ 8. Good working conditions

   _____ 9. Sensible company rules, regulations, procedures, and policies

   _____ 10. The opportunity to grow through learning new things

   _____ 11. A job I can do well and succeed at

   _____ 12. Job security

2. This questionnaire taps the two dimensions in Herzberg's motivation hygiene theory. To determine if hygiene or motivating factors are important to you, place the numbers 1-5 that represent your answers below.

Hygiene factors score	Motivational factors score
2. _____	1. _____
6. _____	4. _____
8. _____	7. _____
9. _____	10. _____
12. _____	11. _____
Total points _____	Total points _____

   Add up each column. Did you select hygiene or motivating factors as being most important to you?

3. Now break into groups of five or six and compare your questionnaire results. (a) How similar are your scores? (b) How close did your group's results come to those found by Herzberg? (c) What motivational implications did your group arrive at based on your analysis?

This exercise is based on R.N. Lussier, *Human Relations in Organizations: A Skill Building Approach*, 2nd ed. Homewood, IL: Richard D. Irwin, 1993. With permission.

Lincoln Electric

Canadian companies are starting to modify their compensation practices to link pay to performance. This is probably more common today for middle and senior management positions than lower-level employees, however. In a 1994 survey of 84 Canadian firms including Canadian Imperial Bank of Commerce, IBM, Bell Canada, Eaton's, and SkyDome, 60 percent of companies include senior management positions in bonus plans and 90 percent of companies give bonuses to middle management positions.

By comparison, many companies in the United States have modified their compensation practices to link pay to performance. Many of these companies, in fact, had visited Cleveland-based Lincoln Electric Co. to look at its "model" pay-for-performance system. Lincoln Electric remains the classic example of a company that has successfully used pay-for-performance for many years and as such, has important relevance for the Canadian workplace.

Lincoln employs about 3400 people and generates 90 percent of its sales from manufacturing arc-welding equipment and supplies. Founded in 1895, the company's legendary profit-sharing incentive system and resultant productivity record have received much attention from people who design motivation programs.

Factory workers at Lincoln receive piece-rate wages with no guaranteed minimum hourly pay. After working for the firm for two years, employees begin to participate in the year-end bonus plan. Determined by a formula that considers the company's gross profits, the employees' base piece rate, and merit rating, it has been one of the most lucrative bonus systems for factory workers in North American manufacturing. The average size of the bonus over the past 55 years has been 95.5 percent of base wages!

The company has a guaranteed-employment policy, which it put in place in 1958. Since that time, it has not laid off a single worker. In return for job security, however, employees agree to several conditions. During slow times, they will accept reduced work periods. They also agree to accept work transfers, even to lower-paid jobs, if that is necessary to maintain a minimum of 30 hours of work per week.

You'd think the Lincoln Electric system would attract quality people, and it has. For instance, the company recently hired four Harvard MBAs to fill future management slots. But, consistent with company tradition, they started out, like everyone else, doing piecework on the assembly line.

Historically, Lincoln Electric's profit-sharing incentive system has provided positive benefits for the company as well as for its employees. In the early 1990s, one company executive estimated that Lincoln's overall productivity was about double that of its domestic competitors. To that point, the company had earned a profit every year since the depths of the 1930s Depression and had never missed a quarterly dividend. Lincoln also had one of the lowest employee turnover rates in U.S. industry.

But something interesting has recently happened at Lincoln Electric. The company is overhauling its pay system. Under pressure from institutional shareholders and independent board members, management has been looking for ways to improve earnings. The reason? Rapid growth and global competition resulted in the company losing money in 1992 and 1993, and employee bonuses have been dropping. In 1995, for instance, bonuses averaged 56 percent—the lowest in recent years. The result: Employees are disgruntled. Management decided it had to modify its pay system to make it more mainstream. One objective is to reduce the huge variations in worker pay—from roughly $32 000 to more than $100 000.

In early 1996, to revamp the pay scheme without stirring up resentment, management set up a committee to study the bonus program. It informed employees that

CASE INCIDENT

a new formula is in the works. It wants employees to provide input by focusing more on their overall earnings, not just the percentage bonus they receive. For instance, senior management wants to start raising base pay and, simultaneously, to start reducing annual bonuses.

Questions

1. Use expectancy theory to explain the past success of Lincoln's pay system.

2. Using two or more motivation theories, explain problems with the historical system.

3. What problems, if any, do you think management should expect as a result of its announced changes in the pay system?

4. What might be some obstacles you would see in trying to introduce pay-for-performance into a Canadian workplace for the first time?

Source: Based on S.J. Modic, "Fine-Tuning a Classic," *Industry Week*, March 6, 1989, pp. 15–18; C. Wiley, "Incentive Plan Pushes Production," *Personnel Journal*, August 1993, pp. 86–87; and Z. Schiller, "A Model Incentive Plan Gets Caught in a Vise," *Business Week*, January 22, 1996, pp. 89–92; Susan Yellin, "Top-to-Bottom Bonuses Wave of Incentive Future," *Vancouver Sun*, February 3, 1995.

Creating Incentives that Work

Organizations can use a variety of incentives to reward and motivate employees for good performance. They can certainly give out raises, but perhaps there are other tangible objects that can substitute for wages, from offering a wine-and-cheese party to a watch with the company's name on the band.

The Incentives Tradeshow tries to show employers various alternatives to wage hikes for employees. Each year, vendors display a variety of objects that companies can purchase to give to their employees for a job well done. Companies of all sizes have been known to attend the annual show, including Chrysler, Nabisco, Bell Canada, and Imperial Oil.

Organizations provide a number of different incentives for their employees. For example, both Campbell Soup and Kelloggs have given their employees a "Day in a Formula 2000," which cost the company $650 for each such prize awarded. Labatt, Teleglobe, and Bell Canada have rewarded their high-performing employees with pool tables. Bell Canada's employees also receive points when they do their jobs right, and these can be used toward such items as cordless drills or projection television sets.

Some of the rewards that can be given are more personalized, of course. Chrysler workers have received $150 watercolour prints with their names painted on them. And lapel pins are the main corporate award, and can be given for a variety of anniversaries, such as 10, 15, and more years of service.

These incentives are meant to reward employees for performance, and at the same time save companies money by not having to raise wages. When company representatives attend the Incentives Tradeshow, they need to consider how meaningful the rewards will be, and what it is they are trying to reward.

Questions

1. Which do you think is a better motivator: money or some of the items noted at the tradeshow? Why?

2. Which rewards might have the best incentive effects of the ones described at the tradeshow?

3. Did any of the possible rewards strike you as inappropriate to award good performance? Why?

Source: Based on "Incentives '94," *Venture 479*; aired March 13, 1994.

POINT

Money Motivates!

The importance of money as a motivator has been consistently downgraded by most behavioural scientists. They prefer to point out the value of challenging jobs, goals, participation in decision-making, feedback, cohesive work teams, and other non-monetary factors as stimulants to employee motivation. We argue otherwise here—that money is *the* crucial incentive to work motivation. As a medium of exchange, it is the vehicle by which employees can purchase the numerous need-satisfying things they desire. Furthermore, money also performs the function of a scorecard, by which employees assess the value that the organization places on their services and by which employees can compare their value to others.[1]

Money's value as a medium of exchange is obvious. People may not work only for money, but remove the money and how many people would come to work? A recent study of nearly 2500 employees found that while these people disagreed over what was their primary motivator, they unanimously ranked money as their number two.[2] This study reaffirms that for the vast majority of the workforce, a regular paycheque is absolutely necessary in order to meet their basic physiological and safety needs.

As equity theory suggests, money has symbolic value in addition to its exchange value. We use pay as the primary outcome against which we compare our inputs to determine if we are being treated equitably. That an organization pays one executive $80 000 a year and another $95 000 means more than the latter's earning $15 000 a year more. It is a message from the organization to both employees, of how much it values the contribution of each.

In addition to equity theory, both reinforcement and expectancy theories attest to the value of money as a motivator. In the former, if pay is contingent on performance, it will encourage workers to generate high levels of effort. Consistent with expectancy theory, money will motivate to the extent that it is seen as being able to satisfy an individual's personal goals and is perceived as being dependent upon performance criteria.

The best case for money as a motivator is a review of studies done by Ed Locke at the University of Maryland.[3] Locke looked at four methods of motivating employee performance: money, goal setting, participation in decision-making, and redesigning jobs to give workers more challenge and responsibility. He found that the average improvement from money was 30 percent; goal setting increased performance 16 percent; participation improved performance by less than one percent; and job redesign positively impacted performance by an average of 17 percent. Moreover, every study Locke reviewed that used money as a method of motivation resulted in some improvement in employee performance. Such evidence demonstrates that money may not be the *only* motivator, but it is difficult to argue that it *doesn't* motivate!

Sources:

[1] K.O. Doyle, "Introduction: Money and the Behavioral Sciences," *American Behavioral Scientist*, July 1992, pp. 641–57.

[2] S. Caudron, "Motivation? Money's Only No. 2," *Industry Week*, November 15, 1993, p. 33.

[3] E.A. Locke, et al., "The Relative Effectiveness of Four Methods of Motivating Employee Performance," in *Changes in Working Life*, eds. K.D. Duncan, M.M. Gruneberg, and D. Wallis (London: John Wiley, Ltd., 1980), pp. 363–83.

counterPOINT

Money Doesn't Motivate Most Employees Today!

Money can motivate *some* people under *some* conditions, so the issue isn't really whether money *can* motivate. The answer to that is: "It can!" The more relevant question is: Does money motivate most employees in the workforce today to higher performance? The answer to this question, we'll argue, is "no."

For money to motivate an individual's performance, certain conditions must be met. First, money must be important to the individual. Second, money must be perceived by the individual as being a direct reward for performance. Third, the marginal amount of money offered for the performance must be perceived by the individual as being significant. Finally, management must have the discretion to reward high performers with more money. Let's take a look at each of these conditions.

Money is not important to all employees. High achievers, for instance, are intrinsically motivated. Money should have little impact on these people. Similarly, money is relevant to those individuals with strong lower-order needs; but for most of the workforce, lower-order needs are substantially satisfied.

Money would motivate if employees perceived a strong linkage between performance and rewards in organizations. Unfortunately, pay increases are far more often determined by levels of skills and experience, community pay standards, the national cost-of-living index, and the organization's current and future financial prospects than by each employee's level of performance.

For money to motivate, the marginal difference in pay increases between a high performer and an average performer must be significant. In practice, it rarely is. For instance, a high-performing employee who currently is earning $50 000 a year is given a $335-a-month raise. After taxes, that amounts to about $42 a week. But this employee's co-worker, who is an average performer and earns $50 000, is rarely passed over at raise time. Instead of getting an eight percent raise, he is likely to get half of that. The net difference in their weekly paycheques is little more than $20. How much motivation is there in knowing that if you work really hard you're going to end up with $20 a week more than someone who is doing just enough to get by? For a large number of people, not much! Research indicates that merit raises must be at least seven percent of base pay for employees to perceive them as motivating. Unfortunately, recent surveys find non-managerial employees averaging merit increases of only 4.9 percent.[1]

Our last point relates to the degree of discretion that managers have in being able to reward high performers. Where unions exist, that discretion is almost zero. Pay is determined through collective bargaining and is allocated by job title and seniority, not level of performance. In non-unionized environments, the organization's compensation policies will constrain managerial discretion. Each job typically has a pay grade. Thus, a Systems Analyst III can earn between $5350 and $6350 a month. No matter how good a job that analyst does, her boss cannot pay her more than $6350 a month. Similarly, no matter how poorly someone does in that job, he will earn at least $5350 a month. In most organizations, managers have a very small area of discretion within which they can reward their higher-performing employees. So money might be theoretically capable of motivating employees to higher levels of performance, but most managers aren't given enough flexibility to do much about it. ■

Sources:

[1] See A. Mitra, N. Gupta, and G.D. Jenkins, Jr., "The Case of the Invisible Merit Raise: How People See Their Pay Raises," *Compensation & Benefits Review*, May–June 1995, pp. 71–76; B. Filipczak, "Can't Buy Me Love," *Training*, January 1996, pp. 29–34.

CHAPTER 6

Motivation: Aligning Incentives to Goals

ROADMAP

LEARNING OBJECTIVES

After studying this chapter, you should be able to

- Identify the four ingredients common to MBO programs

- Explain how employee stock ownership programs can increase employee motivation

- Contrast gainsharing and profit sharing

- Describe the link between skill-based pay plans and motivation theories

- Explain how flexible benefits turn benefits into motivators

- Explain how stretch targets operate

- Contrast the challenges of motivating professional employees versus low-skilled employees

- Contrast the challenges of motivating professional employees versus temporary workers

SHAMEE Samad and Jamie Sokalsky have struck gold. But that's appropriate since they work for Barrick Gold Corporation of Toronto. As the world's most profitable and third-largest gold mining operation, Barrick employees are enjoying the benefits from the company's generous stock-option program.[1]

In 1984, Barrick introduced the idea of supplementing employees' regular paycheques with stock. At the time, the company was strapped for cash so management decided to use stock options as a way to attract and motivate its employees. But in contrast to most stock option plans, Barrick's plan covers all 5000 employees, not just upper-level managers. So far, the program seems to be a winner for both employees and the company.

Ms. Samad, for example, has been an accounts payable clerk with the company for 10 years—she joined Barrick as a 19-year-old, fresh out of high school. In her first year with the company, she earned stock options worth $11 000, on top of her $24 000 salary. In the decade she's been with Barrick, Ms. Samad has cashed in $51 000 from options she's been granted and still holds another $64 000 worth. Mr. Sokalsky, meanwhile, has only been with the company for two years. As corporate treasurer, however, he's already racked up $320 000 worth of options. Not bad considering that his annual salary is just over $100 000.

Do stock options motivate? Ms. Samad thinks they do. "If I have to come in early or stay late, I do it. No questions asked." And the company has come a long way from the days when it was strapped for money. A share of Barrick stock bought in 1983 at an initial price of $1.75 was worth more than $32 in April 1998. The company has consistently outperformed other gold producers even during some very lean years in the gold business. ■

In this chapter, we focus on how to apply motivation concepts, linking theories to practice. For it's one thing to be able to regurgitate motivation theories. It's often another to see how, as a manager, you could use them.

In the following pages, we review a number of motivation techniques and programs that have gained varying degrees of acceptance in practice. For example, we discuss variable-pay plans such as the stock option program used by Barrick. We first present Management by Objectives (MBO), however, as a reminder of the need to link organizational goals, performance, and rewards. For each of the techniques and programs we review, we specifically address how they build on one or more of the motivation theories covered in the previous chapter.

Management by Objectives

Goal-setting theory, which we discussed in Chapter 5, has an impressive base of research support. But as a manager, how do you make goal setting operational? The best answer to that question is: Implement a management by objectives (MBO) program.

What Is MBO?

management by objectives (MBO)

A program that encompasses specific goals, participatively set, for an explicit time period, with feedback on goal progress.

Management by objectives (MBO) emphasizes participatively set goals that are tangible, verifiable, and measurable. It's not a new idea. In fact, more than 40 years ago Peter Drucker originally proposed it as a means of using goals to motivate people rather than to control them.[2] Today, no introduction to basic management concepts would be complete without a discussion of MBO.

MBO's appeal undoubtedly lies in its emphasis on converting overall organizational objectives into specific objectives for organizational units and individual members. MBO operationalizes the concept of objectives by devising a process by which objectives cascade down through the organization. As depicted in Exhibit 6-1, the organization's overall objectives are translated into specific objectives for each succeeding level (that is, divisional, departmental, individual) in the organization. But because lower-unit managers jointly participate in setting their own goals, MBO works from the "bottom up" as well as from the "top down." The result is a hierarchy of objectives that links objectives at one level to those at the next level. And for the individual employee, MBO provides specific personal performance objectives.

There are four ingredients common to MBO programs. These are goal specificity, participative decision-making, an explicit time period, and performance feedback.[3]

The objectives in MBO should be concise statements of specific accomplishments. It's not adequate, for example, to merely state a desire to cut costs, improve service, or increase quality. Such desires must be converted into tangible objectives that can be measured and evaluated. To cut departmental costs *by seven percent*, to improve service by ensuring that all telephone orders are processed *within 24 hours of receipt*, or to increase quality by keeping returns to *less than one percent of sales* are examples of specific objectives.

The objectives in MBO are not unilaterally set by the boss and then assigned to subordinates. MBO replaces imposed goals with participatively determined goals. The superior and subordinate jointly choose the goals and agree on how they will be measured.

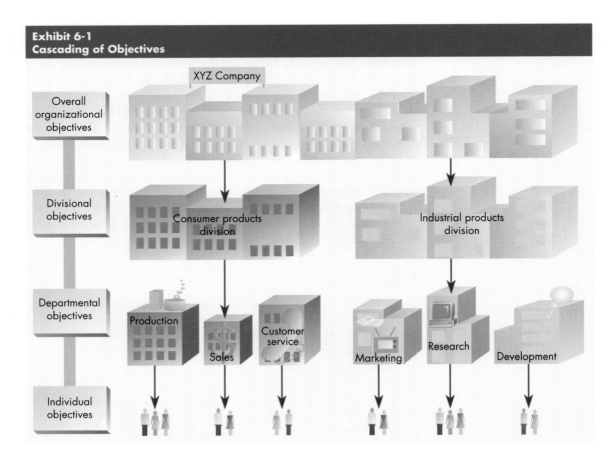

Exhibit 6-1
Cascading of Objectives

Each objective has a specific time period in which it is to be completed. Typically the time period is three months, six months, or a year. So managers and subordinates have specific objectives and stipulated time periods in which to accomplish them.

The final ingredient in an MBO program is feedback on performance. MBO seeks to give continuous feedback on progress toward goals. Ideally, this is accomplished by giving ongoing feedback to individuals so they can monitor and correct their own actions. This is supplemented by periodic managerial evaluations, when progress is reviewed. This applies at the top of the organization as well as at the bottom. The vice-president of sales, for instance, has objectives for overall sales and for each of his or her major products. He or she will monitor ongoing sales reports to determine progress toward the sales division's objectives. Similarly, district sales managers have objectives, as does each salesperson in the field. Feedback in terms of sales and performance data is provided to let these people know how they are doing. Formal appraisal meetings also take place at which superiors and subordinates can review progress toward goals and further feedback can be provided.

Linking MBO and Goal-Setting Theory

Goal-setting theory demonstrates that hard goals result in a higher level of individual performance than do easy goals, that specific hard goals result in higher levels of performance than do no goals at all or the generalized goal of "do your best," and that feedback on one's performance leads to higher performance. Compare these findings with MBO.

MBO directly advocates specific goals and feedback. MBO implies, rather than explicitly states, that goals must be perceived as feasible. Consistent with goal setting, MBO would be most effective when the goals are difficult enough to require the person to do some stretching.

The only area of possible disagreement between MBO and goal-setting theory relates to the issue of participation—MBO strongly advocates it, while goal-setting theory demonstrates that assigning goals to subordinates frequently works just as well. The major benefit to using participation, however, is that it appears to induce individuals to accomplish more difficult goals.[4] Allowing individuals to participate in goal setting also has the additional feature that the person is more likely to "buy in" to the goals, which may improve his or her overall commitment to the task. To learn more about goal setting and MBO, you might take a look at the Working With Others exercise at the end of the chapter.

MBO in Practice

How widely used is MBO? Reviews of studies that have sought to answer this question suggest that it's a popular technique. You'll find MBO programs in many business, health care, educational, government, and non-profit organizations.[5]

MBO's popularity should not be construed to mean that it always works. There are a number of documented cases where MBO has been implemented but failed to meet management's expectations.[6] A close look at these cases, however, indicates that the problems rarely lie with MBO's basic components. Rather, the culprits tend to be factors such as unrealistic expectations regarding results, lack of top-management commitment, and an inability or unwillingness by management to allocate rewards based on goal accomplishment. Nevertheless, MBO provides managers with the vehicle for implementing goal-setting theory.

Motivating for Specific Organizational Goals

Above we discussed goal setting as a way of helping employees identify what they need to accomplish. In determining the types of rewards to be used, organizations should also consider their own goals, ensuring that the incentives offered match the organizational goals desired. Below we discuss various reward programs in terms of the general outcomes they are trying to emphasize, such as employee recognition, improved productivity, learning, organizational commitment, and organizational change.

Motivating to Show People Matter

Laura Schendell only makes $7.50 an hour working at her fast-food job and the job isn't very challenging or interesting. Yet Laura talks enthusiastically about her job, her boss, and the company that employs her. "What I like is the fact that Guy (her supervisor) appreciates the effort I make. He compliments me regularly in front of the other people on my shift, and I've been chosen 'Employee of the Month' twice in the past six months. Did you see my picture on that plaque on the wall?"

Organizations are increasingly recognizing what Laura Schendell is acknowledging: Recognition can be a potent motivator.

Employee recognition programs send a signal to employees that good performance is appreciated. In 1998, the *Financial Post* recognized Theresa Butcher, its head librarian, as an Unsung Hero for all of her help to reporters and editors over many years.

What Are Employee Recognition Programs?

In today's highly competitive global economy, most organizations are under severe cost pressures. That makes recognition programs particularly attractive. Recognizing an employee's superior performance often costs little or no money. Maybe that's why a recent survey of 3000 employers found that two-thirds use or plan to use special recognition awards.[7]

Employee recognition programs can take numerous forms. For example, the *Financial Post* has an award called Unsung Hero. This award goes to someone who contributes mightily to the success of the newspaper, but gets little recognition. In 1998, the reward went to Theresa Butcher, head librarian, who has helped many of the reporters and editors verify facts and sources over the years.[8] *The Globe and Mail* gives the Stephen Godfrey Prize for Newsroom Citizenship. Virginia Galt won that award in 1998 for all of her work to improve relations among her colleagues. In addition to the prize, her accomplishments were printed in *The Globe and Mail*, giving her even more public recognition of her citizenship.[9]

The best recognition programs use multiple sources and recognize both individual and group accomplishments. Convex Computer Corporation, a supercomputer manufacturer based in Texas that employs 1200 people, provides an excellent illustration of a comprehensive recognition program.[10] On a quarterly basis, Convex's vice-president of operations recognizes individuals who have been nominated by their managers as having gone "above and beyond the call of duty." Annually, individuals may nominate their peers for the Customer Service Award, which recognizes such categories as risk taking, innovation, cost reduction, and overall customer service. And at the department level, recognition takes the form of team or department T-shirts,

Financial Post
http://www.canoe.ca/FP/

The Globe and Mail
http://www.globeandmail.com/

Stephanie Kwolek, a DuPont scientist, received the company's highest award, the Lavoisier Medal for Technical Achievement. Recognition programs reinforce positive employee behaviour, and provide information to all employees about which behaviours are important to the organization.

coffee mugs, banners, or pictures. Supervisors have used movie tickets, Friday afternoon bowling get-togethers, time off, and cash awards to acknowledge such achievements as three months of defect-free assembly, five years of perfect attendance, and completing a project early.

One of the most well-known and widely used recognition devices is the use of suggestion systems. Employees offer suggestions for improving processes or cutting costs and are recognized with small cash awards. At Toronto-based investment dealer Richardson Greenshields, employees are encouraged to find ways to do things "better, faster, cheaper" through their "Bright Ideas" program. The Japanese have been especially effective at making suggestion systems work. For instance, a typical high-performing Japanese plant in the auto-components business generates 47 suggestions per employee a year and pays the equivalent of $50 per suggestion. In contrast, a comparable Western factory generates about one suggestion per employee per year, but pays out $130 per suggestion.[11]

Beaverton, Oregon-based Tektronix Inc., an electronics maker, established the "You Done Good Award." Tektronix prints up notecards with that phrase on it in batches, and gives them to employees. Whenever an employee has praise for another, it is put in writing on one of those cards. "Even though people say nice things to you," said Joe Floren of Tektronix, "it means something more when people take the time to write their name on a piece of paper and say it. Employees usually post them next to their desks."[12]

Linking Recognition Programs and Reinforcement Theory

A few years ago, 1500 employees were surveyed in a variety of work settings to identify what they considered to be the most powerful workplace motivator. Their response? Recognition, recognition, and more recognition![13] Brent Trepel, CEO of Winnipeg-based Ben Moss Jewellers, Ltd., which has 31 stores across Canada, and employs more than 290 people, understands the importance of employee recognition. Every Monday afternoon he phones his top-performing employees.[14]

Ben Moss Jewellers
http://www.benmoss.com/

Consistent with reinforcement theory, rewarding a behaviour with recognition immediately following that behaviour is likely to encourage its repetition. Recognition can take many forms and both management and employees can give it. You can personally congratulate a colleague in private for a good job, just as management can. A manager can send a handwritten note or an e-mail message acknowledging something positive that the employee has done. For employees with a strong need for social acceptance, the company can publicly recognize accomplishments. And to enhance a group's cohesiveness and motivation, the company can encourage the team to celebrate team successes. Meetings can be used to recognize the contributions and achievements of successful work teams.

Employee recognition could reduce turnover in organizations, particularly that of good employees. When executives were asked the reasons why employees left for jobs with other companies, 34 percent said it was due to lack of recognition and praise, compared with 29 percent who mentioned low compensation, 13 percent who mentioned limited authority, and eight

percent who cited personality problems.[15] For a possible alternative view about recognition and reward, you should read over the Point/Counterpoint debate, which raises the issue of whether pay should be announced openly or kept secret.

Motivating for Improved Productivity

When organizations want to improve productivity, they can consider a variety of incentive schemes, some of which are more individually based, and others that rely on either team members or all of the organizational members to work together toward productivity goals. The rewards they use are all forms of **variable-pay programs**. What differentiates these forms of compensation from more traditional programs is that instead of paying a person only for time on the job or seniority, a portion of an employee's pay is based on some individual and/or organizational measure of performance. Unlike more traditional base-pay programs, variable pay is not an annuity. There is no guarantee that just because you made $60 000 last year that you'll make the same amount this year. With variable pay, earnings fluctuate up and down with the measure of performance.[16]

According to a 1996 Conference Board of Canada report, roughly two-thirds of non-management employees are affected by variable-pay plans, up from one-third in 1992. These programs are more predominant for non-unionized workers. As Conference Board's Prem Benimadhu notes, "Canadian unions have been very allergic to variable compensation."[17] Under variable-pay programs, individuals are not guaranteed specific annual wages, making their work experience a bit more risky. Union members, and others as well, may worry that they can't predict their wages ahead of time, thus leading to uncertainty. Union members are also concerned that there may be factors out of their control that might affect the extent to which bonuses are possible.

At Markham, Ontario-based Pillsbury Canada Limited, employees are eligible for the company's Value Incentive Plan, rewarding performance at three levels: corporate, team, and individual.[18] If the corporate financial target is met or exceeded, a percentage-of-pay bonus results. Employees can earn additional percentage-of-pay bonuses if teams meet their own goals, based on cost reduction, and quality and profit improvement are above the corporate plan. Finally, employees can earn an equivalent percentage-of-pay bonus if they meet two or three key individual objectives. While the theory behind individual, team, and company-wide incentive plans is similar, we review the programs separately, to underscore the importance of linking rewards to the appropriate level of performance. Not all organizations have such comprehensive three-level programs as Pillsbury Canada. This chapter's CBC Video Case gives some further examples of how firms motivate employees.

Individual-based Incentives

When salespeople are paid commissions based on sales, this is evidence of an individual performance award. Traders at Bayerische Vereinsbank, Germany's fourth-largest bank, earn 75 000 marks (about $80 000) a year in base pay. They also can earn as much as a 50 000-mark bonus if they meet their individual performance goals.[19]

variable-pay programs
A portion of an employee's pay is based on some individual and/or organizational measure of performance.

Pillsbury
http://www.pillsbury.com/

piece-rate pay plans
Workers are paid a fixed sum for each unit of production completed.

Piece-rate wages are one of the earliest forms of individual performance pay. Piece-rates have long been popular as a means for compensating production workers. In **piece-rate pay plans**, workers are paid a fixed sum for each unit of production completed. When an employee gets no base salary and is paid only for what he or she produces, this is a pure piece-rate plan. People who work at baseball parks selling peanuts and soft drinks frequently are paid this way. They might get to keep 25 cents for every bag of peanuts they sell. If they sell 200 bags during a game, they make $50. If they sell only 40 bags, their take is a mere $10. The harder they work and the more peanuts they sell, the more they earn. Many organizations use a modified piece-rate plan, where employees earn a base hourly wage plus a piece-rate differential. So a legal typist might be paid $8.50 an hour plus 30 cents per page. Such modified plans provide a floor under an employee's earnings, while still offering a productivity incentive.

Bonuses can be paid exclusively to executives or to all employees. For instance, annual bonuses in the millions of dollars are not uncommon in North American corporations. Robert A. Watson, for example, received a $14-million incentive bonus in 1993 for his success in dismantling Westinghouse's financial operation.[20] Increasingly, bonus plans are taking on a larger net within organizations to include lower-ranking employees. One of the most ambitious bonus systems has recently been put in place by Levi Strauss.[21] If the company reaches cumulative cash flow of $10.6 billion between 1996 and 2002, each of the company's 37 500 employees in 60 countries, regardless of position, will receive a full year's pay as a bonus. Levi Strauss estimates the potential cost of this bonus for the firm at about $1 billion. Variable-pay plans that use bonuses are becoming increasingly popular in Canada.[22] They are in use by such companies as Toronto-based Molson, Burnaby-based B.C. Tel, Ontario Hydro, and the Bank of Montreal. In 1992, typical senior executives in Canada could expect bonuses equal to 9.7 percent of their salaries. In 1996, that had almost doubled to 18.5 percent. And the growth rate in bonuses was even greater among hourly employees. The average bonus for an hourly worker during the same time period went from 1.1 percent of base pay to 5.8 percent.

Levi Strauss
http://www.levi.com/

Molson
http://www.molson.com

Despite this evidence, incentive-based pay is more common in the United States than in Canada, both in terms of the proportion of employees covered and the size of the rewards.[23] This occurs because Canada has a more unionized economy, a relative lack of competition, and a large public sector. In Ottawa, the only bonus for federal civil servants is $800 for those in bilingual jobs.

Group-based Incentives

The variable-pay program that has received the most attention in recent years is undoubtedly **gainsharing**.[24] This is a formula-based group incentive plan. Improvements in group productivity—from one period to another—determine the total amount of money that is to be allocated. The division of productivity savings can be divided between the company and employees in any number of ways, but 50-50 is fairly typical.

gainsharing
An incentive plan where improvements in group productivity determine the total amount of money that is allocated.

At British Columbia-based MacMillan Bloedel, gainsharing plans operate at the union local level as well as the corporate level. At the local level, the factors considered towards gainsharing include average competitor cost, safety, return-on-capital employed (ROCE), return-on-assets (ROA), machine up-time, and incremental improvement over last year's results.[25]

At MacMillan Bloedel unionized workers participate in a gainsharing program where they can earn bonuses of several thousand dollars. Gainsharing encourages employees to be more productive in their work.

Lumber grader Dan Derby, who works in a MacMillan Bloedel sawmill on Vancouver Island, recently took home $3500 in bonuses for helping make the mill one of the company's safest and most profitable.[26] Yet he was suspicious of the gainsharing program when it was first started four years ago. "One of the concerns was that it would force people to work harder and sweat more." Instead he and other employees are working smarter. "Everybody stays on top of what we're doing. You get suggestions from others. I don't think of it just from the point of view of how it's going to affect my monthly pay."

Gainsharing differs from profit-sharing, discussed below. Gainsharing focuses on productivity gains rather than profits, and so it rewards specific behaviours that are less influenced by external factors. Employees in a gainsharing plan can receive incentive awards even when the organization isn't profitable. At present, gainsharing's popularity seems to be narrowly focused among large, unionized manufacturing companies.[27] Both Molson Breweries and Hydro-Québec are other examples of companies that use gainsharing plans. It can be applied in other settings, however.

Organizational-based incentives

Workers at Allied-Signal's Forstoria, Ohio, sparkplug plant had their annual raise cut from three to two percent.[28] Employees were given the opportunity to earn more if they could increase productivity. Specifically, the plant's 1200 employees will receive their former three percent raise if they can raise productivity by six percent a year. If they push productivity up by nine percent, they will receive a six percent raise. With this sort of goal, it becomes obvious that individuals cannot work in isolation and hope that the company achieves its goal. Allied-Signal's plan, then, is an example of a company-wide performance-based pay plan.

Profit-sharing plans are organizationwide programs that distribute compensation based on some established formula designed around a company's profitability. These can be direct cash outlays or, particularly in the case of top managers, allocated as stock options. When you read about executives such as Michael Eisner, the CEO at Disney, earning over $280 million in one

Hydro-Québec
http://www.hydro.qc.ca/

Disney
http://www.disney.com/

profit-sharing plans
Organizationwide programs that distribute compensation based on some established formula designed around a company's profitability.

year, almost all of this comes from cashing in stock options previously granted based on company profit performance. Profit-sharing is not confined to top executives only, however. MacMillan Bloedel Ltd. has introduced a profit-sharing plan for unionized workers in 15 of 47 divisions. Workers whose divisions meet profit goals are eligible for bonuses of as much as 10 percent of annual pay. This will yield an average payout of about $3500.[29]

One thing to note about profit-sharing programs is that their focus is on past financial results. They don't necessarily focus employees on the future. They also tend to ignore factors such as customer service and employee development, which may not be seen as having a direct link to profits. In addition, some industries, such as the financial services industry, have a somewhat cyclical nature, and during slumping economic periods companies would offer few or no rewards. From an expectancy theory perspective, employees will be less motivated during these times because they know that the likelihood of receiving significant bonuses is low.

Peter Munk, CEO of Barrick Gold Corporation, uncovered a potential problem with stock options, if too many are given to employees without restrictions.[30] In 1986, one of his key employees notified him that he was quitting his job, and Munk was devastated. The employee told Munk that he had too much money to continue working. Much to Munk's surprise, the employee's stock options were worth $7 million. Munk realized that the very success of his company was causing his employees to quit. Munk made himself available for stock options shortly after this incident. At the end of 1995, Munk had unexercised options worth $55 million.

employee stock ownership plans (ESOPs)
Company-established benefit plans in which employees acquire stock as part of their benefits.

One of the ways to induce employees to have values more like top management is to make them owners of their firms. **Employee stock ownership plans (ESOPs)**[31] are company-established benefit plans in which employees acquire stock as part of their benefits. We encountered their use at Barrick in the chapter's opening case. Approximately 20 percent of Polaroid, for example, is owned by its employees. Employees own 71 percent of Avis Corporation. And Weirton Steel is 100 percent owned by its employees.[32]

Toronto-based Richardson Greenshields of Canada Ltd., an investment dealer to retail and institutional clients across Canada and around the world, introduced an ESOP plan after the Canadian investment industry had suffered a loss of 35 percent of its employees in just four years (between 1989 and 1994). In the face of those losses, Richardson Greenshields wanted to move its organizational climate from one of survival to one of customer-centred service.[33] Since the introduction of this and other incentive plans, Richardson Greenshields' return on capital over the past five years has consistently exceeded the industry average.

In the typical ESOP, an employee stock ownership trust is created. Companies contribute either stock or cash to buy stock for the trust and allocate the stock to employees. While employees hold stock in their company, they usually cannot take physical possession of their shares or sell them as long as they're still employed by the company.

The research on ESOPs indicates that they increase employee satisfaction.[34] Shamee Samad in our opening case agrees. In addition, ESOPs frequently result in higher performance. For instance, one study compared 45 ESOPs against 238 conventional companies.[35] The ESOPs outperformed the conventional firms both in terms of employment and sales growth.

ESOPs have the potential to increase employee job satisfaction and work motivation. But for this potential to be realized, employees need to psychologically experience ownership.[36] That is, in addition to merely having a fi-

nancial stake in the company, employees need to be kept regularly informed on the status of the business and also have the opportunity to exercise influence over the business. The evidence consistently indicates that it takes ownership *and* a participative style of management to achieve significant improvements in an organization's performance.[37]

Linking Productivity-Related Incentives to Motivation Theories

Variable pay is probably most compatible with expectancy theory predictions. Specifically, individuals should perceive a strong relationship between their performance and the rewards they receive if motivation is to be maximized. If rewards are allocated completely on non-performance factors—such as seniority or job title—then employees are likely to reduce their effort.

The evidence supports the importance of this linkage, especially for operative employees working under piece-rate systems. For example, one study of 400 manufacturing firms found that those companies with wage incentive plans achieved 43 to 64 percent greater productivity than those without such plans.[38]

Group and organizationwide incentives reinforce and encourage employees to sublimate personal goals for the best interests of their department or the organization. Group-based performance incentives are also a natural extension for those organizations that are trying to build a strong team ethic. By linking rewards to team performance, employees are encouraged to make extra efforts to help their team succeed.

Do variable-pay programs work? Do they increase motivation and productivity? The answer is a qualified "yes." Gainsharing, for example, has been found to improve productivity in a majority of cases and often has a positive impact on employee attitudes. An American Management Association study of 83 companies that used gainsharing also found, on average, that grievances dropped 83 percent, absences fell 84 percent, and lost-time accidents decreased by 69 percent.[39] The downside of variable pay, from an employee's perspective, is its unpredictability. With a straight base salary, employees know what they'll be earning. Adding in merit and cost-of-living increases, they can make fairly accurate predictions about what they'll be making next year and the year after. They can finance cars and homes based on reasonably solid assumptions. That's more difficult to do with variable pay. Your group's performance might slip this year or a recession might undermine your company's profits. Depending how your variable pay is determined, these can cut your income. Moreover, people begin to take repeated annual performance bonuses for granted. A 15 or 20 percent bonus, received three years in a row, begins to become expected in the fourth year. If it doesn't materialize, management will find itself with some disgruntled employees on its hands.

It is precisely the fluctuation in variable pay that has made these programs attractive to management. It turns part of an organization's fixed labour costs into a variable cost, thus reducing expenses when performance declines. Additionally, by linking pay to performance, earnings recognize contribution rather than being a form of entitlement. Low performers find over time that their pay stagnates, while high performers enjoy pay increases commensurate with their contribution. In a 1994 survey of 84 Canadian firms including the Canadian Imperial Bank of Commerce, IBM, Bell Canada, Eaton's, and SkyDome, 60 percent of companies include senior

management positions in bonus plans and 90 percent of companies give bonuses to middle-management positions.[40]

Among firms that haven't introduced performance-based compensation programs, common concerns tend to surface.[41] Managers worry over what should constitute performance and how it should be measured. They have to overcome the historical attachment to cost-of-living adjustments and the belief that they have an obligation to keep all employees' pay in step with inflation. Other barriers include salary scales keyed to what the competition is paying, traditional compensation systems that rely heavily on specific pay grades and relatively narrow pay ranges, and performance appraisal practices that produce inflated evaluations and expectations of full rewards. Of course, from the employees' perspective, the major concern is a potential drop in earnings. Pay for performance means employees must share in the risks as well as the rewards of their employer's business.

Incentive pay, especially when it is awarded to individuals, can have negative effects in terms of group cohesiveness and productivity, and in some cases may not offer significant benefits to a company.[42] For example, Montreal-based National Bank of Canada's $5 employee bonus for every time they referred clients for loans, mutual funds, or other bank products upset workers enough that the plan was abandoned after just three months.[43] The tellers complained that the bonus caused colleagues to compete against one another. Meanwhile, the bank could not determine whether the referrals actually generated new business. And organized labour is, in general, cool to the idea of pay-for-performance. Andrew Jackson, senior economist for the Canadian Labour Congress in Ottawa, explains that "it hurts co-operation in the workplace. It can lead to competition between workers, speeding up the pace of work. It's a bad thing if it creates a stressful work environment where older workers can't keep up."[44] Still, not all unions share that view, and the benefits and drawbacks on incentive plans must be carefully considered before implementation. In the HR Implications feature, we examine the process of performance evaluation to illustrate the procedures organizations take in order to be able to link pay with productivity.

National Bank of Canada
http://www.nbc.ca/

Canadian Labour Congress
http://www.clc-ctc.com/

Motivating to Encourage Learning

Organizations hire people for their skills, then typically put them in jobs and pay them based on their job title or rank. For example, the director of corporate sales earns $170 000 a year, the regional sales managers make $105 000, and the district sales managers get $85 000. But if organizations hire people because of their competencies or they want them to increase their competencies, why don't they pay them for those same competencies? Some organizations do.

At AT&T's Universal Card service centre in Jacksonville, Florida, the best-paid customer representatives have rotated through four to six troubleshooting assignments over two or three years, becoming adept at solving any billing, lost card, or any other problems a credit-card holder runs into. New employees at a Quaker Oats' pet-food plant in Topeka, Kansas, start at $8.75 an hour, but can reach a top rate of $14.50 when they master 10 to 12 skills such as operating lift trucks and factory computer controls. Salomon Brothers, a major brokerage firm, is using a skills-based pay system to turn narrowly trained and independent specialists into well-rounded product experts and to encourage them to be team players. Frito-Lay Corporation ties its compensation for managers to progress they make in develop-

Shell Canada
http://www.shell.ca/

ing their skills in leadership, group process facilitation, and communications.[45] At Edmonton's Shell Canada complex, skill acquisition by team members is encouraged. Each operational team is organized so that it has the necessary skill sets and information to do the job. Each operator on a team is responsible for learning and using technical skills, leadership skills (particularly self-managing), and at least one specialty skill (which may include environment, safety, maintenance, or training) as required by the team. Pay is based on the level of skill mastered, and employees are required to reach the top level of pay for each skill. Shell Canada holds teams responsible for developing and improving skills. Thus, the training system that helps employees acquire these skills was designed and is maintained by the operators and training specialists on each team.[46]

What Are Skill-Based Pay Plans?

skill-based pay
Pay levels are based on how many skills employees have or how many jobs they can do.

Skill-based pay is an alternative to job-based pay. Rather than having an individual's job title define his or her pay category, skill-based pay (also sometimes called competency-based pay) sets pay levels on the basis of how many skills employees have or how many jobs they can do.[47] For instance, at Polaroid Corporation, the highest pay a machine operator can earn is $14 an hour. However, because the company has a skill-based pay plan, if machine operators broaden their skills to include additional skills such as material accounting, maintenance of equipment, and quality inspection, they can earn up to a 10 percent premium. If they can learn some of their supervisor's skills, they can earn even more.[48]

What's the appeal of skill-based pay plans? From management's perspective: flexibility. Filling staffing needs is easier when employee skills are interchangeable. This is particularly true today, as many organizations cut the size of their workforce. Downsizing requires more generalists and fewer specialists. While skill-based pay encourages employees to acquire a broader range of skills, there are also other benefits. It facilitates communication across the organization because people gain a better understanding of others' jobs. It lessens dysfunctional "protection of territory" behaviour. Where skill-based pay exists, you're less likely to hear the phrase, "It's not my job!"

Skill-based pay additionally helps to meet the needs of ambitious employees who confront minimal advancement opportunities. These people can increase their earnings and knowledge without a promotion in job title. Finally, skill-based pay appears to lead to performance improvements. A broad-based survey of *Fortune 1000* firms found that 60 percent of those with skill-based pay plans rated their plans as successful or very successful in increasing organizational performance, while only six percent considered them unsuccessful or very unsuccessful.[49]

The increased use of skills as a basis for pay appears particularly strong among organizations facing aggressive foreign competition and those companies with shorter product life cycles and speed-to-market concerns.[50] Also, skill-based pay is moving from the shop floor to the white-collar workforce, and sometimes as far as the executive suite.[51]

A number of studies have investigated the use and effectiveness of skill-based pay. The overall conclusion, based on these studies, is that skill-based pay is expanding and that it generally leads to higher employee performance and satisfaction. For instance, between 1987 and 1993, the percentage of *Fortune 1000* firms using some form of skill-based pay increased from 40 to 60 percent.[52] A survey of 27 companies that pay employees for learning extra skills found that 70 to 88 percent reported higher job satisfaction,

product quality, or productivity. Some 70 to 75 percent cited lower operating costs or turnover.[53]

Skilled-based pay appears to be an idea whose time has come. As one expert noted, "Slowly, but surely, we're becoming a skill-based society where your market value is tied to what you can do and what your skill set is. In this new world where skills and knowledge are what really counts, it doesn't make sense to treat people as jobholders. It makes sense to treat them as people with specific skills and to pay them for those skills."[54]

But what about the down side of skill-based pay? People can "top out"—learning all the skills the program calls for them to learn. This can frustrate employees after they've become challenged by an environment of learning, growth, and continual pay raises. Skills can become obsolete. When this happens, management should consider rewarding employees who learn appropriate new skills. There is the problem, however, created by paying people for acquiring skills for which there may be no immediate need. This happened at IDS Financial Services.[55] The company found itself paying people more money even though there was little immediate use for their new skills. IDS eventually dropped its skill-based pay plan and replaced it with one that equally balances individual contribution and gains in work-team productivity. Finally, skill-based plans don't address level of performance. They deal only with the issue of whether someone can perform the skill. For some skills, such as checking quality or leading a team, level of performance may be equivocal. While it's possible to assess how well employees perform each of the skills and combine that with a skill-based plan, that is not an inherent part of skill-based pay.

Programs to Encourage New Learning

**Mainframe
Entertainment Inc.**
http://www.mainframe.bc.ca/

Not all rewards that are given to employees have to be monetary to be effective. At Vancouver-based Mainframe Entertainment Inc., young animators and designers get leadership opportunities, including the opportunity to direct shows. This is experience the employees would not get working at the bigger, higher paying animation studios in Los Angeles. CEO Chris Brough notes, "A number of our employees will leave and then come back. They may find themselves working for a bigger company, but it means they get stuck doing implosions for two years. Here you have a chance to grow."[56] His employees agree. Scott Speirs, age 29, has worked for Mainframe for five years. He reports that at his previous job, "I was constantly watching the clock. Here, I actually look forward to coming to work."[57] In this case, by giving leadership opportunities to its young employees, everyone benefits. The employees take the opportunity to acquire valuable new skills, and Mainframe has one of the lowest turnover rates in the animation business—less than two percent per year.

Linking Skill-Based Pay Plans to Motivation Theories

Skill-based pay plans are consistent with several motivation theories. Because they encourage employees to learn, expand their skills, and grow, they are consistent with ERG theory. Among employees whose lower-order needs are substantially satisfied, the opportunity to experience growth can be a motivator.

Paying people to expand their skill levels is also consistent with research on the achievement need. High achievers have a compelling drive to do

Animators at Vancouver-based Mainframe Entertainment get leadership opportunities that they would not get a higher paying studios in Los Angeles. Mainframe has one of the lowest turnover rates in the animation business because of its emphasis on giving its young employees the opportunity to acquire new skills.

things better or more efficiently. By learning new skills or improving the skills they already hold, high achievers will find their jobs more challenging.

There is also a link between reinforcement theory and skill-based pay. Skill-based pay encourages employees to develop their flexibility, to continue to learn, to cross-train, to be generalists rather than specialists, and to work cooperatively with others in the organization. To the degree that management wants employees to demonstrate such behaviours, skill-based pay should act as a reinforcer.

Skill-based pay may also have equity implications. When employees make their input-outcome comparisons, skills may provide a fairer input criterion for determining pay than factors such as seniority or education. To the degree that employees perceive skills as the critical variable in job performance, the use of skill-based pay may increase the perception of equity and help optimize employee motivation.

Motivating for Organizational Change

We noted in Chapter 2 that Canadian organizations as well as organizations throughout the world are facing increasing pressure to make changes to accommodate doing business in the global environment. **Stretch targets** are a relatively new technique for improving organizational effectiveness.[58] Stretch targets are virtually unachievable goals that force organizations to significantly alter their processes. "The purpose of stretch targets is not only to allow employees to stretch their abilities to new levels, but also to change the organization's competitive position by dynamically altering its business processes."[59]

stretch target
A virtually unachievable goal that forces an organization to significantly alter its processes.

The purpose of stretch targets is to encourage employees to think beyond ordinary solutions to extraordinary solutions. With hard but achiev-

able goals, employees tend to focus simply on working harder and longer. With stretch targets, employees have to look at ways to completely redesign the task. For example, Motorola used to take six weeks at the end of each year to close out its books. Using cross-divisional teams of employees, the time was reduced to four days. The team assigned to the task examined every part of the process, and then "made detailed process charts, developed strategies to speed processes, decided where to cut out unnecessary steps, and designed programs to standardize information flows."[60] Montreal-based Canadian National Railways' (CN) supply management department, GE, 3M Corporation, and Union Pacific Railroad are other examples of companies using stretch targets.

Canadian National Railways
http://www.cn.ca/

To some extent, stretch targets are inconsistent with what researchers in general have found about goal-setting, i.e., that when goals are perceived as too difficult, individuals will not try to attain the goals. However, in the case of Motorola described above, as well as other examples of stretch targets, the "virtually impossible" goals were accomplished. A recent study explains the conditions under which stretch targets can work: autonomy, empowerment, structural accommodation, and bureaucratic immunity.[61]

Teams that successfully handle stretch targets need to be autonomous and empowered. *Autonomy* refers to the ability of the group working on the goal to control the situation themselves. Teams that were successful were also *empowered*, which meant that they had power over resources and power to propose and implement changes as necessary. When teams feel that they have autonomy and are empowered, they are more willing to accept stretch targets.[62]

Successful stretch-target teams must also know that top management supports them. Successful teams experienced the *structural accommodation* of their organizations, meaning they had unlimited access to information and the power to change organizational procedures if necessary. For instance, the Motorola team working on reducing end-of-year reporting time was allowed to change the reporting forms the various departments used so that they could simplify procedures. In essence, when organizations make structural accommodations to their teams, they are telling the teams to do whatever it takes to accomplish their tasks.

Successful teams with stretch targets were also given *bureaucratic immunity*. This meant that they were not subject to the bureaucratic review process of other projects, and reported only to top management. Therefore the "stretch" team is not subject to the power politics of other groups during the time that they are trying to accomplish their targets. "At Motorola, for example, the words 'if it looks feasible' or 'if we can get groups to agree, we will make the change' were never spoken." Teams were told to do whatever it took, and they would be supported. This inspired their creativity and eliminated their fear of failure.

While any organization might be interested in achieving stretch targets, it must undergo important culture changes in order to provide the support that individuals need to achieve those targets. However, creating the environment that allows teams to work on stretch targets can result in significant changes in the way that processes within the organization are carried out. Teams that receive the structural support needed often do not require significant additional rewards because the actual process of working toward the goal is a major reward in itself.

Motivating While Accommodating Individual Differences

Not everyone is motivated by money. Not everyone wants a challenging job. The needs of women, singles, immigrants, the physically disabled, senior citizens, and others from diverse groups are not the same as the traditional worker of previous generations—a white Canadian male with a wife at home raising their three dependent children. A couple of examples can make this point clearer. Employees who are attending university typically place a high value on flexible work schedules. Such individuals may be attracted to organizations that offer flexible work hours, job sharing, or temporary assignments. A father may prefer to work the midnight to 8 a.m. shift in order to spend time with his children during the day while his wife is at work. The Case Incident at the end of the chapter illustrates how an individual's personal life can have an impact on work performance.

In order to maximize employees' motivation, employers must understand and respond to this workplace diversity. How? With flexibility. Employers must design work schedules, compensation plans, benefits, physical work settings, and the like to reflect employees' varied needs. For example, some employees are concerned with having an extended medical plan and enough life insurance to support a young family in the case of death. Other employees may not need extended medical and life insurance and might be more interested in extra vacation time and long-term financial benefits such as a tax-deferred savings plan. Or employees with family responsibilities might appreciate child and elder care, flexible work hours, and job sharing. New immigrants might prefer flexible leave policies to make an extended return trip to their homelands. Other employees who are going to school might like to vary their work schedules from semester to semester. In the Learning About Yourself exercise, you have the opportunity to consider how to apply flexible benefits in a variety of individual circumstances.

Some employees have also been willing to negotiate for job security in lieu of additional pay, particularly in the union sector. For Randy Somerville, a letter carrier in Saint John, New Brunswick, a reasonable assurance of stable employment is worth a lot more than a bigger paycheque. His contract provides only a one-per-cent pay increase per year, but it also contains a no-layoff clause and a guarantee that he will not be relocated outside a 40-kilometre radius. "The way most people look at it here," says Somerville, age 34, "we're just lucky to have a job."[63]

What Are Flexible Benefits?

flexible benefits

Employees tailor their benefit program to meet their personal needs by picking and choosing from a menu of benefit options.

Flexible benefits allow employees to choose among a menu of benefit options. The idea is to allow each employee to choose a benefit package that is individually tailored to his or her own needs and situation. It replaces the traditional "one-benefit-plan-fits-all" programs that have dominated organizations for more than 50 years.[64]

The average organization provides fringe benefits worth approximately 40 percent of an employee's salary. Traditional benefit programs were designed for the typical employee of the 1950s discussed above—a male with a wife and three children at home. Fewer employees now fit this stereotype. For instance, there are sizeable numbers of employees who are single or married without children. As such, these traditional programs don't tend to meet the needs of today's more diverse workforce. Flexible benefits, how-

ever, do meet these diverse needs. An organization sets up a flexible spending account for each employee, usually based on some percentage of his or her salary, and then a price tag is put on each benefit. Options might include extended medical plans with high deductibles; extended medical plans with low or no deductibles; hearing, dental, and eye coverage; vacation options; extended disability; a variety of savings and pension plans; life insurance; university tuition reimbursement plans; and extended vacation time. Employees then select benefit options until they have spent the dollar amount in their account.

At Richardson Greenshields, employees choose benefits that meet their needs. They can even transfer unused flex credits to a registered retirement savings plan (RRSP). This feature of the benefits program is particularly appealing to younger employees, who often have less need for more family-centred benefits, so can enjoy watching their retirement savings accumulate even quicker.

Flexible benefits offer both benefits and drawbacks for the employees and employers involved. For employees, flexibility is attractive because they can tailor their benefits and levels of coverage to their own needs. The major drawback, from the employee's perspective, is that the costs of individual benefits often go up, so fewer total benefits can be purchased.[65] For example, low-risk employees keep the cost of medical plans low for everyone. As they are allowed to drop out, the high-risk population occupies a larger segment and the costs of medical benefits go up. From the organization's perspective, the good news is that flexible benefits often produce savings. Many organizations use the introduction of flexible benefits to raise deductibles and premiums. Moreover, once in place, costly increases in dental insurance premiums, for example, often have to be substantially absorbed by the employee. The bad news for the organization is that these plans are more cumbersome for management to oversee and often more expensive to administer.

Linking Flexible Benefits and Expectancy Theory

Giving all employees the same benefits assumes that all employees have the same needs. Of course, we know this assumption is false. Thus, flexible benefits turn the benefits' expenditure into a motivator.

Consistent with expectancy theory's thesis that organizational rewards should be linked to each individual employee's goals, flexible benefits individualize rewards by allowing each employee to choose the compensation package that best satisfies his or her current needs. The fact that flexible benefits can turn the traditional homogeneous benefit program into a motivator was demonstrated at one company when 80 percent of the organization's employees changed their benefit packages when a flexible plan was put into effect.[66]

Special Issues in Motivation

Various groups provide specific challenges in terms of motivation. In this section we look at some of the unique problems faced in trying to motivate professional employees, contingent workers, low-skilled service workers, people doing highly repetitive tasks, and executives.

Motivating Professionals

In contrast to a generation ago, the typical employee today is more likely to be a highly trained professional with a college or university degree than a blue-collar factory worker. These professionals receive a great deal of intrinsic satisfaction from their work. They tend to be well paid. So what, if any, special concerns should you be aware of when trying to motivate a team of engineers at Corel, a software designer at Microsoft, or a group of accountants at Deloitte & Touche?

Stentor Resource Centre
http://www.stentor.ca/

Carol Stephenson, president and CEO of Ottawa-based Stentor Resource Centre, describes the challenge that managing professionals presents to her company: "I have very bright people in this company and I'm managing knowledge and intellectual capability. Knowledge workers like to be autonomous...they are more concerned with content of work rather than their place on the organization chart. If you manage by command and control, people will leave."[67]

Evidently, professionals are typically different from non-professionals.[68] They have a strong and long-term commitment to their field of expertise. Their loyalty is more often to their profession than to their employer. To keep current in their field, they need to regularly update their knowledge, and their commitment to their profession means they rarely define their workweek in terms of 8 to 5 and five days a week.

What motivates professionals? Money and promotions typically are low on their priority list. Why? Because they tend to be well paid and they enjoy what they do. In contrast, job challenge tends to be ranked high. They like to tackle problems and find solutions. Their chief reward in their job is the work itself. Professionals also value support. They want others to think what they're working on is important. Although this may be true for all employees, because professionals tend to be more focused on their work as their central life interest, non-professionals typically have other interests outside of work that can compensate for needs not met on the job.

This description implies a few guidelines to keep in mind if you're trying to motivate professionals. Provide them with ongoing challenging projects. Give them autonomy to follow their interests and allow them to structure their work in ways that they find productive. Reward them with educational opportunities—training, workshops, attending conferences—that allow them to keep current in their field. Also reward them with recognition, and ask questions and engage in other actions that demonstrate to them you're sincerely interested in what they're doing.

French computer services giant CAP Gemini Sogeti motivates its 17 000 software engineers and technicians by giving them the tools they need to tackle and solve challenging problems. The company's intranet, called Knowledge Galaxy, puts critical resources and expertise within every employee's reach, keeping the global workforce current on the latest technologies. CAP Gemini even installed an Internet café at its Paris headquarters, shown here, so employees can surf the Net during their breaks.

An increasing number of companies are creating alternative career paths for their professional/technical people, allowing employees to earn more money and status, without assuming managerial responsibilities. At Merck & Co., IBM, and AT&T, the best scientists, engineers, and researchers gain titles such as fellow and senior scientist. Their pay and prestige are comparable to those of managers but without the corresponding authority or responsibility.[69]

Motivating Contingent Workers

One of the more comprehensive changes taking place in organizations is the addition of temporary or contingent employees. As downsizing has eliminated millions of "permanent" jobs, an increasing number of new openings are for part-time, contract, and other forms of temporary workers. The number of Canadians relying on temporary jobs grew by 21 percent—from 799 000 to 970 000—between 1989 and 1994.[70] Because these contingent employees lack the security or stability that permanent employees have, they don't identify with the organization or display the commitment that other employees do. Temporary workers also are typically provided with no pension plans, and little or no extended healthcare benefits such as dental care, prescription plans, and vision care or similar benefits.[71]

There is no simple solution for motivating temporary employees. For that small set of temps who prefer the freedom of their temporary status so that they can also attend school, care for their children, or have the flexibility to travel or pursue other interests, the lack of stability may not be an issue. This status also might be preferred by those highly compensated doctors, engineers, accountants, and financial planners who don't want the demands of a full-time job. But these are the exceptions. For the most part, employees do not choose temporary jobs voluntarily.

What will motivate involuntarily temporary employees? An obvious answer is the opportunity for permanent status. In those cases where permanent employees are selected from the pool of temporaries, temporaries will often work hard in hopes of becoming permanent. A less obvious answer is the opportunity for training. The ability of a temporary employee to find a new job is largely dependent on his or her skills. If the employee sees that the job he or she is doing can help develop saleable skills, then motivation is increased. From an equity standpoint, there are repercussions of mixing permanent and temporary workers where pay differentials are significant. When temps work alongside permanent employees who earn more, and get benefits too, for doing the same job, the performance of temps is likely to suffer. Separating such employees or converting all employees to a variable-pay or skill-based pay plan might help to lessen this problem.

Motivating Low-Skilled Service Workers

Canada's economic recovery in the late 1990s has not led to the creation of many new jobs. At the same time, many young people are struggling to begin a career. Unemployment among 15- to 24-year-olds is around 17 percent across Canada, about twice the national average rate of unemployment. Service-sector jobs, which were once regarded as either a temporary after-school job or a stepping stone to a career, have become permanent positions for many young people. These jobs are often referred to as "McJobs." Pay levels are often little above minimum wage.

One of the most challenging motivation problems in industries such as retailing and fast food is: How do you motivate individuals who are making very low wages and who have little opportunity to significantly increase their pay in either their current jobs or through promotions?

Starbucks' outlets in Vancouver discovered what can happen when they don't pay attention to the concerns of these workers.[72] In the summer of 1996, the company introduced an unpopular computerized scheduling system. Then management rolled back a 50-cent increase to the starting wage, to match the new B.C. provincial minimum of $7 an hour. Finally, management cut "T-shirt Fridays," the only day each week when staff could wear Starbucks T-shirts, rather than the regulation dress shirts. For Steve Emery, a then-26-year-old employee of the coffee giant, that was the last straw. "The taboo on T-shirts triggered us," explains Emery. In July 1997, 110 workers at nine Starbucks outlets in the Vancouver area joined the Canadian Auto Workers Union, an action they took to protest Starbucks' policies towards its workers.

We noted in Chapter 1 that many employees working in these low-skilled service jobs feel that they don't get the respect they deserve from their employers. In response to similar employee concerns, Taco Bell, PepsiCo's Mexican fast-food chain, has tried to make some of its service jobs more interesting and challenging, but with limited results.[73] It has experimented with incentive pay and stock options for cashiers and cooks. These employees also have been given broader responsibility for inventory, scheduling, and hiring. But over a four-year period, this experiment has only reduced annual turnover from 223 percent to 160 percent.

What choices are left? Unless pay and benefits are significantly increased, high dissatisfaction is probably inevitable in these jobs. This can be somewhat offset by widening the recruiting net, making these jobs more appealing, and raising pay levels. Trying to understand the needs of these employees might help motivate them better. Non-traditional approaches may also be beneficial. To illustrate, Judy Wicks has found that celebrating employees' outside interests has dramatically reduced turnover among wait staff at her White Dog Café in Philadelphia.[74] For instance, to help create a close and family-like work climate, Wicks holds an annual event at which employees exhibit their art, read their poetry, explain their volunteer work, and introduce their new babies.

Motivating People Doing Highly Repetitive Tasks

Another category of employees who are difficult to motivate are those who do standardized and repetitive jobs. For instance, those working on an assembly line or transcribing court reports often find their jobs boring and even stressful.

Motivating individuals in these jobs can be made easier through careful selection. People vary in their tolerance for ambiguity. Many individuals prefer jobs that have a minimal amount of discretion and variety. Such individuals are obviously a better match to standardized jobs than are individuals with strong needs for growth and autonomy. Standardized jobs should also be the first considered for automation.

Many standardized jobs, especially in the manufacturing sector, pay well. This makes it relatively easy to fill vacancies. While high pay can ease recruitment problems and reduce turnover, it doesn't necessarily lead to highly motivated workers. And realistically, there are jobs that don't readily

lend themselves to being made more challenging and interesting or to being redesigned. Some tasks, for instance, are just far more efficiently done on assembly lines than in teams. This leaves limited options. Managers may not be able to do much more than try to make a bad situation tolerable by creating a pleasant work climate. This might include providing clean and attractive work surroundings, ample work breaks, the opportunity to socialize with colleagues during these breaks, and empathetic supervisors.

Executive Compensation

Throughout our discussion of motivation and compensation, we have tried consistently to demonstrate that academic theory argues that rewards should be consistent with performance. In theory, the relationship between the pay given to heads of organizations and organizational performance should also be linked. "Yet, for the most part, academic researchers have been stymied in their search for a meaningful association between executive pay and firm performance."[75]

Canadian Business
http://www.canbus.com/

Toronto Stock Exchange
http://www.TSE.com/

This lack of correspondence between executive compensation and firm performance applies as much to Canadian as to U.S. firms. For instance, *Canadian Business* recently compared the total cash compensation (salary plus long-term bonus) of 154 executives of companies on the TSE 300 and correlated that with the sum of annual shareholder returns covering the three-year period from 1994 to 1996.[76] In doing this, the survey uncovered a number of executives who were overpaid (stock prices were mediocre at best, while pay was high), as well as a group who were underpaid (stock prices soared, while pay was modest). Exhibit 6-2 identifies executives in both groups. In general, the underpaid executives worked at relatively young mining and high-tech companies, while the overpaid often headed the larger, more established companies of Canada. In the Ethical Dilemma exercise, you can examine your own feelings about the amount of compensation executives receive.

Determining how to reward executives has been an issue of concern for many companies, researchers, and even executives. When the annual executive compensation lists are published each year in both Canada and the United States, discussion focuses on those leaders who are compensated well but who head companies that have performed poorly. As a result, in recent years boards of directors have moved more towards giving their executives less fixed salary, and emphasizing more rewards linked to performance. Many argue, however, that financial measures (e.g., net earnings and return on investment) encourage short-term quick fixes rather than long-term strategic goals.[77] For instance, executives might forego risky strategic investment opportunities because these are more likely to have long-term payoffs, or they might reduce human resource expenditures aimed at developing a highly trained and productive workforce, concentrating instead on maximizing short-term profitability and shareholder wealth.[78]

Not everyone agrees, however, that the answer is to simply offer rewards based on non-financial measures. Some find that these measures, which might consider such factors as product quality and customer satisfaction, are far too subjective and can be easily manipulated by the CEO.

So which approach do companies prefer? In recent years, there has been a definite trend toward pay for performance, but not all companies pay that way. A recent study conducted in the United States assembled data from 317 large companies (annual sales ranging from $7.7 million to $32.1 billion). The researchers found that 36 percent of companies used non-financial mea-

Exhibit 6-2
Canada's Top 10 Overpaid Chief Executives (Part 1)

Rank	Executive	Company	Total Pay 1994–96	Share Increase (%)	Relative Index*
1	Donald Walker, president and CEO	Magna International Inc.	$7 918 000	22	0.46
2	Michael Brown, president	Thomson Corp.	$7 219 000	114	0.61
3.	Richard Thomson, chair and CEO (now chair)	Toronto-Dominion Bank	$6 161 000	65	0.62
4	Matthew Barrett, chair and CEO	Bank of Montreal	$6 200 000	73	0.63
5	Ted Rogers, president and CEO	Rogers Communications Inc.	$3 227 000	–53	0.63
6	Peter Munk, chair and CEO	Barrick Gold Corp.	$4 275 000	4.5	0.66
7	Peter Godsoe, chair, president and CEO	Bank of Nova Scotia	$5 615 000	66	0.67
8	Stephen Bachand, president and CEO	Canadian Tire Corp. Ltd.	$4 524 000	35	0.69
9	Paul Ivanier, president and CEO	Ivaco Inc.	$3 132 000	–42	0.71
10	Richard Currie, president	Loblaw Cos. Ltd.	$6 150 000	93	0.71

*Relative Index = the sum of the value of $100 invested after one year, two years and three years, divided by total pay, multiplied by 10,000.
Source: Adapted from David Berman, "Do They Deserve It?", *Canadian Business*, September 26, 1997, pp. 31–33.

sures. Those most likely to do so were companies pursuing strategies of innovation and new product development. Researchers have found that pay and performance are much more closely linked when firms have a dominant shareholder who can discipline top managers. Researchers have also discovered that executives of larger firms earn more than those working in smaller firms. This particular fact could provide the incentive for executives to diversify into areas that are not consistent with a firm's core competencies in order to increase the size of the firm.

In determining executive compensation, different firms will have different needs. For instance, a firm that values innovation should offer its executives incentives that reward investment in research and development. Exhibit 6-3 indicates some considerations for linking the strategy and performance of firms with executive compensation.

In looking at executive compensation, you might be interested to know that while stock options are commonly used in Canadian, U.S., and U.K. firms, these are not used worldwide to compensate executives. In fact, many European countries and Japan have had regulations that forbade offering stock options to executives. Consequently, executives in many other countries are paid on salary, with some very recent exceptions (changes in laws in Japan in 1997 and Germany in 1998 allowed some forms of stock options).

Exhibit 6-2
Canada's 10 Ten Underpaid Chief Executives (Part 2)

Rank	Executive	Company	Total Pay 1994–96	Share Increase (%)	Relative Index*
1	Michael McInnis, president (now chair)	International Curator Resources Ltd.	$258 000	3972	210.6
2	Eugene Melnyk, chair	Biovail Corp. International	$936 000	1801	42.8
3	Grenville Thomas, president	Aber Resources Ltd.	$285 000	401	36.9
4	Rubin Osten, president, CEO and chair	PC Docs Group International Inc.	$1 145 000	1151	17.8
5	Greg Noval, president and CEO	Canadian 88 Energy Corp.	$428 000	216	12.6
6	Terence Matthews, chair and CEO	Newbridge Networks Corp.	$439 000	125	11.7
7	Firoz Rasul, president and CEO	Ballard Power Systems Inc.	$717 000	295	10.3
8	Jean-Marc Eustache, president and chair	Transat AT Inc.	$1 198 000	800	9.6
9	Douglas Barber, president and CEO	Gennum Corp.	$853 000	409	9.5
10	Seymour Schulich, chair	Euro-Nevada Mining Corp.	$745 000	132	8.1

*Relative Index = the sum of the value of $100 invested after one year, two years and three years, divided by total pay, multiplied by 10,000.
Source: Adapted from David Berman, "Do They Deserve It?", *Canadian Business*, September 26, 1997, pp. 31–33.

European executives, and even Canadian executives, are often paid considerably less than their American counterparts. However, the perks in these other countries have often been higher: "European and Japanese companies have been very open-handed with executive perquisites—from $1-million golf-club memberships in Japan to chauffeured Rolls-Royces and lavish expense accounts in the U.K."[79] These perks do not necessarily compensate for the effect of stock options. For instance, Procter & Gamble's (U.S.) chief executive exercised $2.6 million in stock options in 1996. Similarly, as we discussed in Chapter 5, extensive stock options are available to Frank Stronach, Chairman of Magna International.

These changes in executive compensation packages for executives outside of North America will present an interesting research comparison as these international firms switch from salaries for executives to performance-based compensation.

Rewards for Teams

There are special considerations when trying to reward individuals who are members of a team. Specifically, if an organization wants a group of individ-

Exhibit 6-3
Strategies for Compensating Executives

- *Identify the firm's strategy and a decision-making horizon appropriate to it.* The appropriate decision-making horizon can be determined by identifying the key success factors necessary to achieve and sustain a competitive advantage. For example, high levels of current cash flow and operational efficiency are potentially key success factors for a cost leader. Long-term customer loyalty and innovation are probably key success factors for a firm pursuing a differentiation strategy.

- *Identify an appropriate measure of firm performance.* If current cash flow and operational efficiency are key success factors, then accounting performance is probably the best measure. If innovation is a key factor, then market-based measures are probably most appropriate.

- *Link CEO pay to the appropriate performance measure.* If short-term, accounting performance is the goal, then firms might adopt an annual bonus scheme. If longer-term market performance is the objective, then a firm might grant restricted shares or stock options.

- *Consider the timing of rewards.* A deferred compensation plan may be appropriate for companies pursuing intermediate- or long-term strategies.

Source: David Berman, "Do They Deserve It?", *Canadian Business*, September 26, 1997, pp. 31-33.

uals to function as a "team" (which will be defined in Chapter 8), emphasis needs to be on team-based rewards, rather than individual rewards. We will discuss the nature of team-based rewards in Chapter 8. OB in the News gives you an introduction to the trade-offs between individual- and team-based pay.

Reward Structures in an International Context

Reward strategies that have been used successfully in Canada and the United States do not always work successfully in other cultures. A study comparing sales reps at a large electronics company in the United States with one in Japan found that while Rolex watches, expensive dinners, and fancy vacations were appropriate rewards for star performers in the United States, taking the whole sales team bowling was more appreciated in Japan. The study's authors found that "being a member of a successful team with shared goals and values, rather than financial rewards, is what drives Japanese sales representatives to succeed."[80]

In the former Soviet Union, the effect of rewards was similar to North American findings, for the most part. At a cotton mill factory located 140 kilometres northwest of Moscow, a small group of employees were given either highly valued extrinsic rewards (North American T-shirts with logos, children's sweatpants, tapes of North American music, and a variety of other North American articles) or praise and recognition. Both types of rewards significantly increased worker productivity, with more top-grade fabric produced when rewards were delivered. Interestingly enough, however, the rewards did not increase the productivity very significantly for those who worked the Saturday shift. These findings illustrate that while rewards can

OB IN THE NEWS

Balancing Individual and Group Rewards

A number of companies award trips to their employees for achieving individual targets for the year. Trying to decide whether individual employees should travel alone, or whether the company should turn the incentive travel plan into a group travel effort is a delicate balancing act. Some employees view the reward as an opportunity for some personal time. As D.J. Connor notes, "the last thing [I need] to do is share [my] incentive vacation with familiar faces from around the office."

Judy Allen of Unionville, Ontario-based Judy Allen Productions presents a similar point of view. Allen co-ordinates special events and incentive programs worldwide for companies wanting to use travel-incentive reward programs. Allen notes that "In the winners' eyes, the prize is a holiday. People want private time to create personal memories with their spouse or significant other." This would suggest that companies would be better off sending their employees on travel rewards alone.

On the other hand, Allen notes, when groups of employees experience the travel reward together, "they relish the recognition from the company president and general manager. And they appreciate the chance to learn from each other and share ideas." Allen suggests that companies send their employees on group trips because "group incentives remind people why they are there." Companies should then alternate time between set programs and complete freedom.

Pat Pambianco, Petro-Canada's regional sales promotions manager, also supports the group approach to company travel rewards. "The idea is to get feedback for company members who set policy, and to help employees understand the company direction."

We have discussed in this chapter the importance of matching incentives to performance goals. However, as this article notes, sometimes employees would prefer slightly different incentives. Thus, it is a careful balancing act to match employee needs with appropriate incentives, particularly when trying to emphasize team behaviour.

Source: Based on "Losing the Pack", *The Financial Post*, February 28, 1998, p. R22.

Take It to the Net

We invite you to visit the Robbins page on the Prentice Hall Web site at:

http://www.prenticehall.ca/robbins

for this chapter's World Wide Web exercise.

be used to increase productivity in the former Soviet Union, the conditions of the work also affected productivity. Because the Soviet workers did not want to work the Saturday shift, the rewards had less impact on their productivity.[81] These findings about the importance of the job context itself are consistent with Herzberg's theory of motivation. We will also discuss further the effects of work context on motivation in Chapter 14.

In China, the reward structure is undergoing a fundamental shift. During the Cultural Revolution (1966-76), equal pay for everyone, regardless of productivity, was the rule. Since 1978, however, there has been more openness toward paying for productivity.[82] However, it is still the case that some companies pay everyone a bonus, regardless of individual productivity, and there is debate among Chinese workers about the standards set for performance.

One final study about rewards in the international context may be of particular interest due to the impact of the North American Free Trade

Agreement (NAFTA) on work arrangements in North America. In a study of a U.S.-owned manufacturing plant in Mexico, a researcher noted that Mexican workers prefer immediate feedback on their work, and thus a daily incentive system with automatic payouts for production exceeding quotas is preferable.[83] This is equivalent to piece-rate wages paid daily. Employers often add extra incentives that are meaningful to the workers including weekly food baskets, bonuses for quality, and free meals, bus service, and day care. The findings from these various countries support the need to examine the internal norms of a country in developing an incentive system, rather than simply importing one that is used effectively in Canada and the United States.

A Caveat Concerning Incentive Programs

For Joan Fleming, manager of a Royal Bank branch in Charlottetown, Prince Edward Island, 1995 was a disappointing year.[84] After her first full year in charge, the branch's ranking plunged from first to fifth position relative to other Royal Bank branches in PEI, even though the branch had maintained its market share. Fleming was quite pleased that her branch had kept its market share; however, she was disappointed that her branch wasn't rated well on service by its clients. As a result, Fleming and her employees experienced a 15 to 20 percent drop in the $1500 bonus they had taken home the previous Christmas. Can you imagine, for a moment, if Fleming and her employees had been given their bonus anyway, despite the complaints about customer service, on the grounds that the bank had retained market share? This approach brings us to the topic of management reward follies.

Perhaps more often than we'd like, organizations engage in what has been called "the folly of rewarding A, while hoping for B."[85] Organizations do this when they hope that employees will engage in one type of behaviour, but they reward for another type. Hoping for the behaviour you're not rewarding is not likely to make it get carried out to any great extent. In fact, as expectancy theory suggests, individuals will generally perform in ways to raise the probability of receiving the rewards offered. The story below illustrates this point.

When Peter Gorelkin worked as a tractor operator planting grain at a farm in Siberia in the former Soviet Union, he learned about how incentives can go awry.[86] His supervisor was paid by the number of hectares he was able to plant. While the grain was supposed to be planted at a depth of six centimetres to ensure it would germinate, his supervisor insisted that the grain be planted at a depth of only three centimetres. The supervisor knew that a tractor set to plant at six centimetres could only cover four hectares per day, whereas at a setting of three centimetres, 10 hectares could be planted. As Gorelkin reports, "The fact that we were able to plant more land meant nothing directly to us trainees, but not only did it mean more pay for our supervisor, it also meant the possibility of a bonus at the end of the job. The fact that most of the seeds might not survive the spring did not disturb him at all."

Exhibit 6-4 provides further examples of common management reward follies. A recent survey suggests that three themes seem to account for some of the biggest obstacles in dealing with the folly.[87] First, individuals are unable to break out of old ways of thinking about reward and recognition practices. This is demonstrated in such things as an emphasis on quantifiable

Exhibit 6-4
Management Reward Follies

We hope for...	But we reward...
Teamwork and collaboration	The best team members
Innovative thinking and risk taking	Proven methods and not making mistakes
Development of people skills	Technical achievements and accomplishments
Employee involvement and empowerment	Tight control over operations and resources
High achievement	Another year's effort
Long-term growth; environmental responsibility	Quarterly earnings
Commitment to total quality	Shipping on schedule, even with defects
Candor; surfacing bad news early	Reporting good news, whether it's true or not; agreeing with the boss, whether or not (s)he's right

Source: Constructed from Steven Kerr, "On the Folly of Rewarding A, While Hoping for B," *Academy of Management Executive*, vol. 9 no. 1, 1995, pp. 7–14; "More on the Folly," *Academy of Management Executive*, vol. 9 no. 1, 1995, pp. 15–16.

behaviours, to the exclusion of non-quantifiable behaviours; employees having an entitlement mentality (i.e., they don't support changing the reward system because they are comfortable with the current behaviours that are rewarded); and management being reluctant to change the existing performance system. A second factor is that organizations often don't look at the big picture of their performance system. Consequently, rewards are allocated at subunit levels, with the result that units often compete against each other. Finally, both management and shareholders often focus on short-term results, rather than rewarding employees for planning for longer ranges.

Organizations would do well to ensure that they do not send the wrong message when offering rewards. When organizations outline an organizational objective of "team performance," for example, but reward each individual according to individual productivity, this does not send a message that teams are valued. Or when a retailer tells commissioned employees that they are responsible for monitoring and replacing stock as necessary, employees are likely to concentrate, particularly in the short term, on making sales rather than stocking the floor. Employees motivated by the promise of rewards will do those things that earn them the rewards they value.

Our discussion of executive compensation illustrates two other examples of possible folly. In linking executive compensation to performance, two measures of performance have often been used for executives: accounting-based incentives and stock market-based incentives. Accounting-based incentives focus on the short term and many expenditures that might have long-term benefit are treated as expenses in determining current accounting earnings. To reduce expenses (and thus raise earnings, leading to greater compensation), executives may choose to reduce expenditures for "research and development that are necessary for product and process innovation,

those for advertising and promotion aimed at developing new markets, and those for continuing employee education and development."[88] Thus, rewarding executives on the basis of accounting measures may encourage executives to forego long-term strategies to minimize costs.[89]

On the other hand, stock market-based incentives for executives can also result in a similar folly with respect to rewarding A while hoping for B. Many institutional investors such as mutual funds, insurance companies, and pension plans are interested in high levels of current performance because of their own short-term reward schemes. But stock prices are affected by many external conditions that have little to do with the executive's performance on a day-to-day level. As a result, executives may decide to cut back on the risks they can control, hoping to keep share prices high. For instance, they may cut back on risky projects or diversify a firm's portfolio of business units, both of which may have long-term payoffs.[90]

These examples indicate that the way in which executive compensation is determined may lead to longer-term negative impacts if not monitored carefully. As mentioned above, it is probably important for the compensation of executives to include a mix of factors that account for both short-term performance and longer-term strategic decision-making.

Can We Just Eliminate Rewards?

To this point, the chapter has illustrated a variety of ways that organizations can provide incentives to motivate specific behaviours within the workplace. We conclude this chapter by raising a thought-provoking discussion about the possibility of eliminating rewards and concentrating more on the design of the workplace, to make the work experience itself more motivating. This discussion parallels the discussion we raised in Chapter 5 about the possibility that rewards could actually be punishing rather than motivating.

To understand how it might be possible to motivate without rewards, we start with the following story.[91] Morton, Illinois, is the Pumpkin Capital of the World, supplying 80 percent of the canned pumpkin in the United States. In 1996, several of the local residents got together to build an entry for the 11th Annual World Champion Punkin' Chunker contest, held in Lewes, Delaware. The idea behind the contest is to hurl four- to five-kilogram pumpkins through the air, and determine which pumpkin went farthest. Teams can build hurling devices of their choice, as long as they don't use explosives.

Matt Parker and several of the local Morton residents became inspired by the idea of building a better "punkin' chunker." As described in the *Wall Street Journal*:

> Soon (Parker) and some tinkering friends were swapping sketches on napkins in coffee shops. "It sounded kind of dumb at first," Parker says, "but pretty soon that's all we talked about."
>
> In a month's time, a group formed and built a machine largely from scrap parts, often working into the early morning at the shop of Rod Litwiller, a crew member. Friends and neighbors stopped in to help.

The team from Morton won the first time they entered the contest, setting a world distance record by "flinging a pumpkin 900 metres at a velocity of more than 950 kilometres per hour." The distance they achieved was 18 metres farther than the record.

Punkin' Chunkin
http://www.lewes-beach.com/
LS-PUNKINCHUNKIN.html

Wall Street Journal
http://www.wsj.com/

Fresh from success, the Morton team set itself a more difficult task for the 1997 contest: hurling a pumpkin into the air at Mach I—the speed of sound. They finished second with their Aludium Q-36 Pumpkin Modulator, but their previous year's win had a big impact on the contest. The 1997 winner went 1239 metres, more than 330 metres beyond the record set the previous year. Morton's team hurled their pumpkin 1180 metres, which represented a 30 percent increase for the team's performance over the previous year.

The reason that this story is interesting from an organizational behaviour perspective is that it represents a group of people who got together on their own to make something that in many ways had no real practical application (except to hurl pumpkins). It may have been a silly idea—the people who committed to the task didn't even know if they would win, and they certainly weren't motivated by the rewards. But the idea of building the machine captured their imagination, they pulled together the resources they needed (materials, support of friends and neighbours), worked long hours, and didn't require supervision.

This story illustrates a point made by Alfie Kohn in his book *Punished by Rewards*. He argues that "the desire to do something, much less to do it well, simply cannot be imposed; in this sense, it is a mistake to talk about motivating other people. All we can do is set up certain conditions that will maximize the probability of their developing an interest in what they are doing and remove the conditions that function as constraints."[92]

This story illustrates the type of commitment that would benefit many organizations, even though it's seldom found there. People will work hard if the job captures their passion and their imagination. And they will put in much more energy and devotion than they would if they were simply waiting to be rewarded every step of the way. And they generally do not require a lot of supervision in those situations.

Based on his research and consulting experience, Kohn proposes ways that organizations can create a motivating environment in their workplace:

- *Abolish incentives.* Pay people generously and fairly, make sure people don't feel exploited, and then make sure that pay is not on their minds. This way people will be more able to focus on the goals of the organization, rather than having as their main goal their paycheque.

- *Re-evaluate evaluation.* Rather than making performance appraisals look and feel like a punitive effort—who gets raises, who gets promoted, who is told they're performing poorly—the performance evaluation system might be structured more like a two-way conversation to trade ideas and questions, done continuously, not as a competition. And the discussion of performance should not be tied to compensation. "Providing feedback that employees can use to do a better job ought never to be confused or combined with controlling them by offering (or withholding) rewards."[93]

- *Create the conditions for authentic motivation.* A noted economist recently summarized the evidence about pay for productivity as follows: "Changing the way workers are *treated* may boost productivity more than changing the way they are *paid*."[94] There is some consensus about what these conditions might be: help employees rather than put them under surveillance; listen to their concerns and think about problems from their viewpoint; and provide plenty of informational feedback so they know what they've done right and what they need to improve.[95]

- *Collaboration.* People are more likely to perform better in well-functioning groups where they can get feedback and learn from each other.[96] Therefore, it is important to provide the necessary supports to create well-functioning teams.

- *Content.* People are generally the most motivated when their jobs give them an opportunity to learn new skills, provide variety in the tasks that are performed, and enable them to demonstrate competence. Some of this can be fostered by carefully matching people to their jobs, and giving them the opportunity to try new jobs. It is also possible to raise the meaningfulness of many jobs (which we will discuss in Chapter 15).

  But what about jobs that don't seem inherently interesting? One psychologist suggested that in cases where the jobs are fundamentally unappealing, the manager might acknowledge frankly that the task is not fun, give a meaningful rationale for why it must be done, and then give people as much choice as possible in how the task is completed.[97] One sociologist studying a group of garbage collectors in San Francisco discovered that they were quite satisfied with their work.[98] Their satisfaction came from the way the work and the company were organized: relationships among the crew were important, the tasks and routes were varied to provide interest, and the company was set up as a cooperative, so that each worker owned a share of the company, and thus felt "pride of ownership."

- *Choice.* "We are most likely to become enthusiastic about what we are doing—and all else being equal, to do it well—when we are free to make decisions about the way we carry out a task."[99] Extrinsic rewards (and punishments too) actually remove choice, because they focus us on rewards, rather than on tasks or goals. A variety of research suggests that burnout, dissatisfaction, absenteeism, stress, and coronary heart disease are related to situations where individuals did not have enough control over their work situations.[100] By choice we do not propose lack of management, but rather, involving people in the decisions that are to be made. For instance, in Chapter 5 we discussed how at Siemens-Nixdorf Informationssysteme (SNI) when the employees were asked to identify ways to turn the company around, many put in long hours helping out. This is an example of letting everyone in the organization participate in the solutions to the problems of the organization, often called **participative management**. We review participative management techniques in Chapter 8. You might want to know that a number of case studies indicate that participative management, when it includes full participation by everyone, is successful.[101]

participative management
A process where subordinates share a significant degree of decision-making power with their immediate superiors.

These steps represent an alternative to simply providing more and different kinds of incentives to try to induce people to work more effectively. They suggest that providing the proper environment may be more important than the reward structure. It would be difficult for many organizations to implement these ideas immediately and expect that they would work. It would require managers who are willing to relinquish control and instead take on the job of coaching. It would require employees who truly believed that their participation and input mattered, and that might require breaking down some of the suspicion that employees feel when managers give directives to employees, rather than seek collaborative input. Nevertheless, these steps, when implemented, can lead to quite a different workplace than what we of-

ten see. Moreover, these issues suggest that sometimes it is not the type or amount of rewards that makes a difference as much as whether the work itself is intrinsically interesting.

HR IMPLICATIONS

Performance Evaluation

This chapter has demonstrated that there are a variety of incentives to encourage employees to perform in accordance with the organization's goals. One of the roles of the HR specialist in an organization is to determine how to actually evaluate that performance. We remind you that the use of performance appraisals should be carefully considered, and care should also be used in ensuring that the purpose of performance appraisals is understood by employees. In some organizations they are used as coaching and learning devices, while in others they are strictly tied to the reward program.

Performance Evaluation and Motivation

In Chapter 5, considerable attention was given to the expectancy model of motivation. We argued that this model currently offers one of the best explanations of what conditions the amount of effort an individual will exert on his or her job. A vital component of this model is performance, specifically the effort-performance and performance-reward linkages.

But what defines *performance*? In the expectancy model, it's the individual's performance evaluation. To maximize motivation, people need to perceive that the effort they exert leads to a favourable performance evaluation and that the favourable evaluation will lead to the rewards that they value.

Following the expectancy model of motivation, if the objectives that employees are expected to achieve are unclear, if the criteria for measuring those objectives are vague, and if the employees lack confidence that their efforts will lead to a satisfactory appraisal of their performance or believe that there will be an unsatisfactory payoff by the organization when their performance objectives are achieved, we can expect individuals to work considerably below their potential.

What Do We Evaluate?

The criteria or criterion that management chooses to evaluate when appraising employee perfor-

mance will have a major influence on what employees do. Two examples illustrate this point.

In a public employment agency, which served workers seeking employment and employers seeking workers, employment interviewers were appraised by the number of interviews they conducted. Consistent with the thesis that the evaluating criteria influence behaviour, interviewers emphasized the *number* of interviews conducted rather than the *placements* of clients in jobs.[1]

A management consultant specializing in police research noticed that, in one community, officers would come on duty for their shift, proceed to get into their police cars, drive to the highway that cut through the town, and speed back and forth along this highway for their entire shift. Clearly this fast cruising had little to do with good police work, but this behaviour made considerably more sense once the consultant learned that the community's city council used kilometrage on police vehicles as an evaluative measure of police effectiveness.[2]

These examples demonstrate the importance of criteria in performance evaluation. This, of course, begs the question: What should management evaluate? The three most popular sets of criteria are individual task outcomes, behaviours, and traits.

Individual Task Outcomes If ends count, rather than means, then management should evaluate an employee's task outcomes. Using task outcomes, a plant manager could be judged on criteria such as quantity produced, scrap generated, and cost per unit of production. Similarly, a salesperson could be assessed on overall sales volume in his or her territory, dollar increase in sales, and number of new accounts established.

Behaviours In many cases, it's difficult to identify specific outcomes that can be directly attributable to an employee's actions. This is particularly true of personnel in staff positions and individuals whose work assignments are intrinsically part of a group effort. In the latter case, the group's perfor-

mance may be readily evaluated, but the contribution of each group member may be difficult or impossible to identify clearly. In such instances, it is not unusual for management to evaluate the employee's behaviour. Using the previous examples, behaviours of a plant manager that could be used for performance evaluation purposes might include promptness in submitting his or her monthly reports or the leadership style that the manager exhibits. Pertinent salesperson behaviours could be average number of contact calls made per day or sick days used per year.

Traits The weakest set of criteria, yet one that is still widely used by organizations, is individual traits.[3] We say they are weaker than either task outcomes or behaviours because they are farthest removed from the actual performance of the job itself. Traits such as having "a good attitude," showing "confidence," being "dependable" or "cooperative," "looking busy," or possessing "a wealth of experience" may or may not be highly correlated with positive task outcomes, but only the naive would ignore the reality that such traits are frequently used in organizations as criteria for assessing an employee's level of performance.

Who Should Do the Evaluating?

Who should evaluate an employee's performance? The obvious answer would seem to be his or her immediate boss! By tradition, a manager's authority typically has included appraising subordinates' performance. The logic behind this tradition seems to be that since managers are held responsible for their subordinates' performance, it only makes sense that these managers do the evaluating of that performance. But that logic may be flawed. Others may actually be able to do the job better.

Immediate superior As we implied, about 95 percent of all performance evaluations at the lower and middle levels of the organization are conducted by the employee's immediate boss.[4] Yet a number of organizations are recognizing the drawbacks to using this source of evaluation. For instance, many bosses feel unqualified to evaluate the unique contributions of each of their subordinates. Others resent being asked to "play God" with their employees' careers. Additionally, with many of today's organizations using self-managed teams, telecommuting, and other organizing devices that distance bosses from their employees, an employee's immediate superior may not be a reliable judge of that employee's performance.

Peers Peer evaluations are one of the most reliable sources of appraisal data. Why? First, peers are close to the action. Daily interactions provide them with a comprehensive view of an employee's job performance. Second, using peers as raters results in a number of independent judgments. A boss can offer only a single evaluation, but peers can provide multiple appraisals. And the average of several ratings is often more reliable than a single evaluation. On the downside, peer evaluations can suffer from co-workers' unwillingness to evaluate one another and from biases based on friendship or animosity.

Self-Evaluation Having employees evaluate their own performance is consistent with values such as self-management and empowerment. Self-evaluations get high marks from employees themselves; they tend to lessen employees' defensiveness about the appraisal process; and they make excellent vehicles for stimulating job performance discussions between employees and their superiors. However, as you might guess, they suffer from overinflated assessment and self-serving bias. Moreover, self-evaluations are often low in agreement with superiors' ratings.[5] Because of these serious drawbacks, self-evaluations are probably better suited to developmental uses than evaluative purposes. There is some evidence that women are more likely to underestimate their performance than men. In addition, with increasing diversity in the workplace, there are some cultural differences in how self-evaluation might be handled.

Immediate Subordinates A fourth judgment source is an employee's immediate subordinates. For instance, Datatec Industries, a maker of in-store computer systems, uses this form of appraisal.[6] The company's president says it's consistent with the firm's core values of honesty, openness, and employee empowerment.

Immediate subordinates' evaluations can provide accurate and detailed information about a manager's behaviour because the evaluators typically have frequent contact with the evaluatee. The obvious problem with this form of rating is fear of reprisal from bosses given unfavourable evaluations. Therefore, respondent anonymity is crucial if these evaluations are to be accurate.

The Comprehensive Approach: 360-degree Evaluations The latest approach to performance evaluation is the use of 360-degree evaluations.[7] They provide performance feedback from the full

Exhibit 6-5
360-Degree Evaluation

The primary objective of the 360-degree performance evaluation is to pool feedback from all of the employee's customers

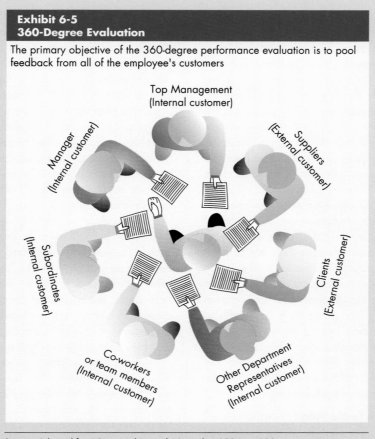

Top Management
(Internal customer)

Suppliers
(External customer)

Manager
(Internal customer)

Subordinates
(Internal customer)

Clients
(External customer)

Co-workers
or team members
(Internal customer)

Other Department
Representatives
(Internal customer)

Source: Adapted from *Personnel Journal*, November 1994, p. 100.

circle of daily contacts that an employee might have, ranging from mailroom personnel to customers to bosses to peers (see Exhibit 6-5). The number of appraisals can be as few as three or four evaluations or as many as 25; most organizations collect five to 10 per employee. Hudson's Bay Company has used 360-degree evaluations with their managers, who are sent to a three-week professional development course at the University of British Columbia.

What's the appeal of 360-degree evaluations? They fit well into organizations that have introduced teams, employee involvement, and TQM programs. By relying on feedback from co-workers, customers, and subordinates, these organizations are hoping to give everyone more of a sense of participation in the review process and gain more accurate readings on employee performance.

Methods of Performance Evaluation

The previous sections explained *what* we evaluate and *who* should do the evaluating. Now we ask:

How do we evaluate an employee's performance? That is, what are the specific techniques for evaluation? This section reviews the major performance evaluation methods.

Written Essays Probably the simplest method of evaluation is to write a narrative describing an employee's strengths, weaknesses, past performance, potential, and suggestions for improvement. The written essay requires no complex forms or extensive training to complete. But the results often reflect the ability of the writer. A good or bad appraisal may be determined as much by the evaluator's writing skill as by the employee's actual level of performance.

Critical Incidents Critical incidents focus the evaluator's attention on those behaviours that are key in making the difference between executing a job effectively and executing it ineffectively. That is, the appraiser writes down anecdotes that describe what the employee did that was especially effective or ineffective. The key here is that only specific behaviours, not vaguely defined personal-

ity traits, are cited. A list of critical incidents provides a rich set of examples from which the employee can be shown those behaviours that are desirable and those that call for improvement.

Graphic Rating Scales One of the oldest and most popular methods of evaluation is the use of graphic rating scales. In this method, a set of performance factors, such as quantity and quality of work, depth of knowledge, cooperation, loyalty, attendance, honesty, and initiative, is listed. The evaluator then goes down the list and rates each on incremental scales. The scales typically specify five points, so a factor like job knowledge might be rated 1 ("poorly informed about work duties") to 5 ("has complete mastery of all phases of the job").

Why are graphic ratings scales so popular? Though they don't provide the depth of information that essays or critical incidents do, they are less time consuming to develop and administer. They also allow for quantitative analysis and comparison.

Behaviourally Anchored Rating Scales Behaviourally anchored rating scales (BARS) combine major elements from the critical incident and graphic rating scale approaches: The appraiser rates the employees based on items along a continuum, but the points are examples of actual behaviour on the given job rather than general descriptions or traits.

BARS specify definite, observable, and measurable job behaviour. Examples of job-related behaviour and performance dimensions are found by asking participants to give specific illustrations of effective and ineffective behaviour regarding each performance dimension. These behavioural examples are then translated into a set of performance dimensions, each dimension having varying levels of performance. The results of this process are behavioural descriptions, such as *anticipates, plans, executes, solves immediate problems, carries out orders*, and *handles emergency situations*.

Multi-Person Comparisons Multi-person comparisons evaluate one individual's performance against the performance of one or more others. It is a relative rather than an absolute measuring device. The three most popular comparisons are group order ranking, individual ranking, and paired comparisons.

The **group order ranking** requires the evaluator to place employees into a particular classification, such as top one-fifth or second one-fifth. This method is often used in recommending students to

graduate schools. Evaluators are asked whether the student ranks in the top five percent of the class, the next five percent, the next 15 percent, and so forth. But when used by managers to appraise employees, managers deal with all their subordinates. Therefore, if a rater has 20 subordinates, only four can be in the top fifth and, of course, four must also be relegated to the bottom fifth.

The **individual ranking** approach rank-orders employees from best to worst. If the manager is required to appraise 30 subordinates, this approach assumes that the difference between the first and second employee is the same as that between the twenty-first and twenty-second. Even though some of the employees may be closely grouped, this approach allows for no ties. The result is a clear ordering of employees, from the highest performer down to the lowest.

The **paired comparison** approach compares each employee with every other employee and rates each as either the superior or the weaker member of the pair. After all paired comparisons are made, each employee is assigned a summary ranking based on the number of superior scores he or she achieved. This approach ensures that each employee is compared against every other, but it can obviously become unwieldy when many employees are being compared.

Multiperson comparisons can be combined with one of the other methods to blend the best from both absolute and relative standards. For example, in an effort to deal with grade inflation, Dartmouth College in the U.S recently changed its transcripts to include not only a letter grade but also class size and class average.[8] So a prospective employer or graduate school can now look at two students who each got a B in their physical geology courses and draw considerably different conclusions about each because next to one grade it says the average grade was a C, while next to the other it says the average grade was a B+. Obviously, the former student performed relatively better than did the latter.

Potential Problems

While organizations may seek to make the performance evaluation process free from personal biases, prejudices, and idiosyncrasies, a number of potential problems can creep into the process. To the degree that the following factors are prevalent, an employee's evaluation is likely to be distorted.

Single Criterion The typical employee's job is made up of a number of tasks. An airline flight attendant's job, for example, includes welcoming passengers, seeing to their comfort, serving meals, and offering safety advice. If performance on this job were assessed by a single criterion measure—say, the time it took to provide food and beverages to a hundred passengers—the result would be a limited evaluation of that job. More important, flight attendants whose performance evaluation included assessment on only this single criterion would be motivated to ignore the other tasks in their job. Similarly, if a football quarterback were appraised only on his percentage of completed passes, he would be likely to throw short passes and only in situations where he felt assured that they would be caught. Our point is that where employees are evaluated on a single job criterion, and where successful performance on that job requires good performance on a number of criteria, employees will emphasize the single criterion to the exclusion of other job-relevant factors.

Recency Effect A month before the annual performance appraisal, an employee has a spectacular sales success. Or an employee has the worst month of performance on record. Because these events happened shortly before the performance appraisal was due, some managers may give undue weight to these events. This is known as the recency effect, which means that undue weight is given to the most recent events that have occurred. While managers are supposed to give equal weight to the employee's performance during the entire year, it is often difficult for them to keep track of everything an employee does. Therefore, the manager may rely too heavily on recent events that may not even be representative of the employee's performance overall.

Leniency Error Every evaluator has his or her own value system that acts as a standard against which appraisals are made. Relative to the true or actual performance an individual exhibits, some evaluators mark high and others low. The former is referred to as positive leniency error, and the latter as negative leniency error. When evaluators are positively lenient in their appraisal, an individual's performance becomes overstated, that is, rated higher than it actually should be. This results in inflated evaluations, a problem widely acknowledged to exist in North American organizations.[9] A negative leniency error understates perfor-

mance, giving the individual a lower appraisal than deserved.

If all individuals in an organization were appraised by the same person, there would be no problem. Although there would be an error factor, it would be applied equally to everyone. The difficulty arises when we have different raters with different leniency errors making judgments. For example, assume that Jones and Smith are performing the same job for different supervisors, but they have absolutely identical job performance. If Jones's supervisor tends to err toward positive leniency, while Smith's supervisor errs toward negative leniency, we might be confronted with two dramatically different evaluations.

Halo Error The halo effect or error, as we noted in Chapter 3, is the tendency for an evaluator to let the assessment of an individual on one trait influence his or her evaluation of that person on other traits. For example, if an employee tends to be dependable, we might become biased toward that individual to the extent that we will rate him or her high on many desirable attributes.[10]

People who design teaching appraisal forms for college students to fill out to evaluate the effectiveness of their instructors each semester must confront the halo error. Students tend to rate a faculty member as outstanding on all criteria when they are particularly appreciative of a few things he or she does in the classroom. Similarly, habits like being slow in returning papers or assigning an extremely demanding reading requirement, might result in students' evaluating the instructor as "lousy" across the board.

Similarity Error When evaluators give special consideration to those qualities in other people that they perceive in themselves, they are making a similarity error. For example, evaluators who perceive themselves as aggressive may evaluate others by looking for aggressiveness. Those who demonstrate this characteristic tend to benefit, while others are penalized.[11]

Again, this error would tend to wash out if the same evaluator appraised all the people in the organization. However, interrater reliability obviously suffers when various evaluators are utilizing their own similarity criteria.

Low Differentiation It's possible that, regardless of whom the appraiser evaluates and what traits are used, the pattern of evaluation remains the same. It has been suggested that evaluators

may be classified as (1) high differentiators, who use all or most of the scale; or (2) low differentiators, who use a limited range of the scale.[12]

Low differentiators tend to ignore or suppress differences, perceiving the universe as being more uniform than it really is. High differentiators, on the other hand, tend to utilize all available information to the utmost extent and thus are better able to perceptually define anomalies and contradictions than are low differentiators.[13]

This finding tells us that evaluations made by low differentiators need to be carefully inspected and that the people working for a low differentiator have a high probability of being appraised as being significantly more homogeneous than they really are.

Forcing Information to Match Non-performance Criteria While rarely advocated, it is not an infrequent practice to find the formal evaluation taking place *following* the decision as to how the individual has been performing. This may sound illogical, but it merely recognizes that subjective, yet formal, decisions are often arrived at prior to the gathering of objective information to support those decisions.[14] For example, if the evaluator believes that the evaluation should not be based on performance, but rather on seniority, he or she may be unknowingly adjusting each "performance" evaluation so as to bring it into line with the employee's seniority rank. In this and other similar cases, the evaluator is increasing or decreasing performance appraisals to align with the nonperformance criteria actually being utilized.

Overcoming the Problems

Just because organizations can encounter problems with performance evaluations, managers should not give up on the process. Some things can be done to overcome most of the problems we have identified.[15] Below we outline some of the most useful approaches.

Use Multiple Criteria Since successful performance on most jobs requires doing a number of things well, all those "things" should be identified and evaluated. The more complex the job, the more criteria that will need to be identified and evaluated. But everything need not be assessed. The critical activities that lead to high or low performance are the ones that need to be evaluated.

Emphasize Behaviours Rather than Traits Many traits often considered to be related to good performance may, in fact, have little or no performance re-

lationship. For example, traits like loyalty, initiative, courage, reliability, and self-expression are intuitively appealing as desirable characteristics in employees. But the relevant question is: Are individuals who are evaluated as high on those traits higher performers than those who rate low? We can't answer this question easily. We know that there are employees who rate high on these characteristics and are poor performers. We can find others who are excellent performers but do not score well on traits such as these. Our conclusion is that traits like loyalty and initiative may be prized by managers, but there is no evidence to support that certain traits will be adequate synonyms for performance in a large cross-section of jobs.

Another weakness of trait evaluation is the judgment itself. What is "loyalty"? When is an employee "reliable"? What you consider "loyalty," I may not. So traits suffer from weak interrater agreement.

Document Performance Behaviours in a Diary By keeping a diary of specific critical incidents for each employee, evaluations tend to be more accurate.[16] Diaries, for instance, tend to reduce leniency and halo errors because they encourage the evaluator to focus on performance-related behaviours rather than traits.

Use Multiple Evaluators As the number of evaluators increases, the probability of attaining more accurate information increases. If rater error tends to follow a normal curve, an increase in the number of appraisers will tend to find the majority congregating about the middle. You see this approach being used in athletic competitions in such sports as diving and gymnastics. A set of evaluators judges a performance, the highest and lowest scores are dropped, and the final performance evaluation is made up from the cumulative scores of those remaining. The logic of multiple evaluators applies to organizations as well.

If an employee has had ten supervisors, nine having rated her excellent and one poor, we can discount the value of the one poor evaluation. Therefore, by moving employees about within the organization so as to gain a number of evaluations or by using multiple assessors (as provided in 360-degree appraisals), we increase the probability of achieving more valid and reliable evaluations.

Evaluate Selectively It has been suggested that appraisers should evaluate in only those areas in which they have some expertise.[17] If raters make

evaluations on only those dimensions on which they are in a good position to rate, we increase the interrater agreement and make the evaluation a more valid process. This approach also recognizes that different organizational levels often have different orientations toward ratees and observe them in different settings. In general, therefore, we would recommend that appraisers should be as close as possible, in terms of organizational level, to the individual being evaluated. Conversely, the more levels that separate the evaluator and evaluatee, the less opportunity the evaluator has to observe the individual's behaviour and, not surprisingly, the greater the possibility for inaccuracies.

The specific application of these concepts would result in having immediate supervisors, co-workers, subordinates, or some combination of these people provide the major input into the appraisal and having them evaluate those factors they are best qualified to judge. For example, it has been suggested that when professors are evaluating secretaries within a university, they use such criteria as judgment, technical competence, and conscientiousness, whereas peers (other secretaries) use such criteria as job knowledge, organization, cooperation with co-workers, and responsibility.[18] Using both professors and peers as appraisers is a logical and reliable approach, since it results in having people appraise only those dimensions on which they are in a good position to make judgments.

Train Evaluators If you can't find good evaluators, the alternative is to make good evaluators. There is substantial evidence that training evaluators can make them more accurate raters.[19]

Common errors such as halo and leniency have been minimized or eliminated in workshops where managers practise observing and rating behaviours. These workshops typically run from one to three days, but allocating many hours to training may not always be necessary. One case has been cited where both halo and leniency errors were decreased immediately after exposing evaluators to explanatory training sessions lasting only five minutes.[20] But the effects of training do appear to diminish over time.[21] This suggests the need for regular refresher sessions.

Provide Employees with Due Process The concept of due process can be applied to appraisals to increase the perception that employees are treated fairly.[22] Three features characterize due process systems: (1) Individuals are provided with adequate notice of what is expected of them; (2) all relevant evidence to a proposed violation is aired in a fair hearing so individuals affected can respond; and (3) the final decision is based on the evidence and free from bias.

There is considerable evidence that evaluation systems often violate employees' due process by providing them with infrequent and relatively general performance feedback, allowing them little input into the appraisal process, and knowingly introducing bias into performance ratings. However, where due process has been part of the evaluation system, employees report positive reactions to the appraisal process, perceive the evaluation results as more accurate, and express increased intent to remain with the organization.

Sources:

[1] P.M. Blau, *The Dynamics of Bureaucracy*, rev. ed. (Chicago: University of Chicago Press, 1963).

[2] "The Cop-Out Cops," *National Observer*, August 3, 1974.

[3] A.H. Locher and K.S. Teel, "Appraisal Trends," *Personnel Journal*, September 1988, pp. 139–45.

[4] G.P. Latham and K.N. Wexley, *Increasing Productivity Through Performance Appraisal* (Reading, MA: Addison-Wesley, 1981), p. 80.

[5] See Review in R.D. Bretz, Jr., G.T. Milkovich, and W. Read, "The Current State of Performance Appraisal Research and Practice: Concerns, Directions, and Implications," *Journal of Management*, June 1992, p. 326.

[6] "Appraisals: Reverse Reviews," *INC.*, October 1992, p. 33.

[7] See, for instance, J.F. Milliman, R.A. Zawacki, C. Norman, L. Powell, and J. Kirksey, "Companies Evaluate Employees From All Perspectives," *Personnel Journal*, November 1994, pp. 99–103; G. Yukl and R. Lepsinger, "How to Get the Most Out of 360-Degree Feedback," *Training*, December 1995, pp. 45–50; H. Lancaster, "Performance Reviews Are More Valuable When More Join In," *Wall Street Journal*, July 9, 1996, p. B1; and D. Antonioni, "Designing an Effective 360-Degree Appraisal Feedback Process," *Organizational Dynamics*, Autumn 1996, pp. 24–38.

[8] D. Goldin, "In a Change of Policy, and Heart, Colleges Join Fight Against Inflated Grades," *The New York Times*, July 4, 1996, p. Y-10.

[9] R.D. Bretz, G.T. Milkovich, and W. Read, "The Current State of Performance Appraisal Research and Practice," p. 333. See also J.S. Kanne, H.J. Bernardin, P. Villanova, and J. Peyrefitte, "Stability of Rater Leniency: Three Studies," *Academy of Management Journal*, August 1995, pp. 1036–51.

[10] For a review of the role of halo error in performance evaluation, see W.K. Balzer and L.M. Sulsky, "Halo and Performance Appraisal Research: A Critical Evaluation," *Journal of Applied Psychology*, December 1992, pp. 975–85.

[11] See T.A. Judge and G.R. Ferris, "Social Context of Performance Evaluation Decisions," *Academy of Management Journal*, February 1993, pp. 80–105.

[12] A. Pizam, "Social Differentiation—A New Psychological Barrier to Performance Appraisal," *Public Personnel Management*, July–August 1975, pp. 244–47.

[13] A. Pizam, "Social Differentiation—A New Psychological Barrier to Performance Appraisal," *Public Personnel Management*, July–August 1975, pp. 245–46.

14 See D.J. Woehr and J. Feldman, "Processing Objective and Question Order Effects on the Causal Relation Between Memory and Judgment in Performance Appraisal: The Tip of the Iceberg," *Journal of Applied Psychology*, April 1993, pp. 232–41.

15 See, for example, W.M. Fox, "Improving Performance Appraisal Systems," *National Productivity Review*, Winter 1987–88, pp. 20–27.

16 See J. Greenberg, "Determinants of Perceived Fairness of Performance Evaluations," *Journal of Applied Psychology*, May 1986, pp. 340–42; and B.P. Maroney and M.R. Buckely, "Does Research in Performance Appraisal Influence the Practice of Performance Appraisal? Regretfully Not!", *Public Personnel Management*, Summer 1992, pp. 185–96.

17 W.C. Borman, "The Rating of Individuals in Organizations: An Alternate Approach," *Organizational Behavior and Human Performance*, August 1974, pp. 105–24.

18 W.C. Borman, "The Rating of Individuals in Organizations: An Alternate Approach," *Organizational Behavior and Human Performance*, August 1974, pp. 105–24.

19 See, for instance, D.E. Smith, "Training Programs for Performance Appraisal: A Review," *Academy of Management Review*, January 1986, pp. 22–40; D.C. Martin and K. Bartol, "Training the Raters: A Key to Effective Performance Appraisal," *Public Personnel Management*, Summer 1986, pp. 101–09; and T.R. Athey and R.M. McIntyre, "Effect of Rater Training on Rater Accuracy: Levels-of-Processing Theory and Social Facilitation Theory Perspectives," *Journal of Applied Psychology*, November 1987, pp. 567–72.

20 H.J. Bernardin, "The Effects of Rater Training on Leniency and Halo Errors in Student Rating of Instructors," *Journal of Applied Psychology*, June 1978, pp. 301–08.

21 H.J. Bernardin, "The Effects of Rater Training on Leniency and Halo Errors in Student Rating of Instructors," *Journal of Applied Psychology*, June 1978, pp. 301–08; and J.M. Ivancevich, "Longitudinal Study of the Effects of Rater Training on Psychometric Error in Ratings," *Journal of Applied Psychology*, October 1979, pp. 502–08.

22 M.S. Taylor, K.B. Tracy, M.K. Renard, J.K. Harrison, and S.J. Carroll, "Due Process in Performance Appraisal: A Quasi-Experiment in Procedural Justice," *Administrative Science Quarterly*, September 1995, pp. 495–523.

Summary and Implications

For the Workplace

We've presented a number of motivation theories and applications in this and the previous chapter. While it's always dangerous to synthesize a large number of complex ideas into a few simple guidelines, the following suggestions summarize the essence of what we know about motivating employees in organizations.

RECOGNIZE INDIVIDUAL DIFFERENCES   Employees have different needs and shouldn't be treated alike. Managers should spend the time necessary to understand what's important to each employee and then align goals, level of involvement, and rewards with individual needs.

USE GOALS AND FEEDBACK   Employees should have hard, specific goals, as well as feedback on how well they are faring in pursuit of those goals.

ALLOW EMPLOYEES TO PARTICIPATE IN DECISIONS THAT AFFECT THEM
Employees can contribute to a number of decisions that affect them: setting work goals, choosing their own benefits packages, solving productivity and quality problems, and the like. This can increase employee productivity, commitment to work goals, motivation, and job satisfaction.

WHEN GIVING REWARDS, BE SURE THAT THEY REWARD DESIRED PERFORMANCE   Rewards should be linked to the type of performance expected. Importantly, employees must perceive a clear linkage. Regardless of how closely rewards are actually correlated to performance criteria, if individuals perceive this relationship to be low, the results will be low performance, a decrease in job satisfaction, and an increase in turnover and absenteeism.

CHECK THE SYSTEM FOR EQUITY   Rewards should be perceived by employees as equating with the inputs they bring to the job. At a simplistic level, this means that experience, skills, abilities, effort, and other obvious

inputs should explain differences in performance and, hence, pay, job assignments, and other obvious rewards.

For You as an Individual

This chapter concentrated heavily on illustrating the types of rewards that organizations might give to achieve specific types of outcomes such as productivity, learning, and organizational change. As an individual you might want to consider how you might use rewards to motivate the people on your student project team, or who work with you in a student or voluntary association. You might also consider how you could help create a more motivating environment in general in these different settings. When the individuals together create and share the goals of the group, that makes them more motivated.

ROADMAP REMINDER

In both this chapter and the preceding one, we've left you with some thoughts not only about how motivation is typically done in organizations, but also some possibilities of new ways of creating more motivating environments. In many ways our emphasis was on motivating individuals, even though, for the most part, people do not work alone in organizations. It is now time for us to consider the crucial role that groups and teams play in organizations. In the following two chapters we explore the issues concerning working with others.

For Review

1. Relate goal-setting theory to the MBO process. How are they similar? Different?
2. What is an ESOP? How might it positively influence employee motivation?
3. How do stretch targets differ from what goal setting theory suggests about goal difficulty?
4. What are the pluses of variable-pay programs from an employee's viewpoint? From management's viewpoint?
5. Contrast job-based and skill-based pay.
6. What is gainsharing? What explains its recent popularity?
7. What motivates professional employees?
8. What motivates contingent employees?
9. Is it possible to motivate low-skilled service workers? Discuss.
10. What can you do, as a manager, to increase the likelihood that your employees will exert a high level of effort?

For Discussion

1. Identify five different criteria by which organizations can compensate employees. Based on your knowledge and experience, do you think performance is the criterion most used in practice? Discuss.
2. "Recognition may be motivational for the moment but it doesn't have any staying power. It's an empty reinforcer. Why? Because they don't

take recognition at the Safeway or Sears!" Do you agree or disagree? Discuss.

3. "Performance can't be measured, so any effort to link pay with performance is a fantasy. Differences in performance are often caused by the system, which means the organization ends up rewarding the circumstances. It's the same thing as rewarding the weather forecaster for a pleasant day." Do you agree or disagree with this statement? Support your position.

4. What drawbacks, if any, do you see in implementing flexible benefits? (Consider this question from the perspective of both the organization and the employee.)

5. Your text argues for recognizing individual differences. It also suggests paying attention to members of diverse groups. Is this contradictory? Discuss.

LEARNING ABOUT YOURSELF EXERCISE

How Equity Sensitive Are You?

The following questions ask what you'd like your relationship to be with any organization for which you might work. For each question, divide 10 points between the two answers (a and b) by giving the most points to the answer that is most like you and the fewest points to the answer that is least like you. You can, if you'd like, give the same number of points to both answers. And you can use zeros if you'd like. Just be sure to use all 10 points on each question. Place your points in the blank next to each letter.

In any organization where I might work:

1. It would be more important for me to:
   _____ **a.** Get from the organization
   _____ **b.** Give to the organization

2. It would be more important for me to:
   _____ **a.** Help others
   _____ **b.** Watch out for my own good

3. I would be more concerned about:
   _____ **a.** What I receive from the organization
   _____ **b.** What I contribute to the organization

4. The hard work I would do should:
   _____ **a.** Benefit the organization
   _____ **b.** Benefit me

5. My personal philosophy in dealing with the organization would be:
   _____ **a.** If you don't look out for yourself, nobody else will
   _____ **b.** It's better to give than to receive

Turn to page 698 for scoring directions and key.

Source: Courtesy of Prof. Edward W. Miles, Georgia State University, and Dean Richard C. Huseman, University of Central Florida. With permission.

WORKING WITH OTHERS EXERCISE

Goal-Setting Task

Purpose This exercise will help you learn how to write tangible, verifiable, measurable, and relevant goals as might evolve from an MBO program.

Time Approximately 20 to 30 minutes.

Instructions 1. Break into groups of three to five.

2. Spend a few minutes discussing your class instructor's job. What does he or she do? What defines good performance? What behaviours will lead to good performance?

3. Each group is to develop a list of five goals that, although not established participatively with your instructor, you believe might be developed in an MBO program at your university. Try to select goals that seem most critical to the effective performance of your instructor's job.

4. Each group will select a leader who will share his or her group's goals with the entire class. For each group's goals, class discussion should focus on their: (a) specificity, (b) ease of measurement, (c) importance, and (d) motivational properties.

ETHICAL DILEMMA EXERCISE

Are Canadian CEOs Paid Too Much?

Critics have described the astronomical pay packages given to Canadian and American CEOs as "rampant greed." Take one example. Matthew Barrett, chair and CEO of Bank of Montreal, received a 54 percent pay increase in 1996, giving him a total compensation package of $3.9 million. That made his paycheque 66 times greater than the average salary of a Bank of Montreal employee. According to KPMG, Canadian executives saw an average 30 percent increase in their compensation—a combination of salaries and bonuses—between 1993 and 1995. When Toronto-based Canadian Tire Corp. Ltd. recruited its new CEO, Stephen Bachand, in 1993, they were willing to pay for someone who could lead it against growing competition from the United States. Consequently, Bachand's 1996 compensation package was $2.5 million. However, Bachand's compensation package looks like peanuts compared to Robert Gratton, CEO of Montreal-based Power Financial Corp. His total compensation in 1997 was $27.4 million, making him the highest-paid CEO in Canada.

How do you explain such large pay packages to CEOs? Some say this represents a classic economic response to a situation in which the demand is great for high-quality top-executive talent and the supply is low. Other arguments in favour of paying executives $1 million a year or more are the need to compensate people for the tremendous responsibilities and stress that go with such jobs; the motivating potential that seven- and eight-figure annual incomes provide to senior executives and

those who might aspire to be; and the influence of senior executives on the company's bottom line.

Critics of executive pay practices in the Canada and the United States argue that CEOs choose board members whom they can count on to support ever-increasing pay for top management. If board members fail to "play along," they risk losing their positions, their fees, and the prestige and power inherent in board membership.

In addition, it is not clear that executive compensation is tied to firm performance. For instance, KPMG found in one survey that for 40 percent of the respondents, there was no correlation between the size of the bonus and how poorly or well the company fared.

Is high compensation of chief executives a problem? If so, does the blame for the problem lie with CEOs or with the shareholders and boards that knowingly allow the practice? Are Canadian and American CEOs greedy? Are these CEOs acting unethically? Should their pay reflect more closely some multiple of their employees wages? What do you think?

Sources: David Berman, "A Bad Place to be Boss. Lesson #1 for Canadian CEOs: Learn to Live on a Lot Less Than Your International Peers," *Canadian Business*, July 1997, pp. 17–19; "Gimme Gimme: Greed, the Most Insidious of Sins, Has Once Again Embraced a Decade," *Financial Post*, September 28/30, 1996, pp 24–25; J.M. Pennings, "Executive Reward Systems: A Cross-National Comparison," *Journal of Management Studies*, March 1993, pp. 261–80; I. McGugan, "A Crapshoot Called Compensation," *Canadian Business*, July 1995, pp. 67–70; "50 Best-Paid CEOs," *Report on Business*, July 1998, pp. 87–88.

CASE INCIDENT

"What Am I Going to Do About Stella McCarthy?"

Jim Murray had worked as a cost accountant at Todd Brothers Chevrolet for nearly three years. When his boss retired in the spring of 1997, Ross Todd, the company's president, asked Jim to take over the accounting department. As the company controller, Jim supervises four people: Stella McCarthy, Judy Lawless, Tina Rothschild, and Mike Sohal.

Six months have passed since Jim took over his new job. As he expected, Judy, Tina, and Mike have been easy to work with. All have been in their jobs for at least four years. They know their jobs backward and forward, and require very little of Jim's time.

Stella McCarthy, unfortunately, is a completely different story. Stella was hired about three months before Jim got his promotion. Her age and education aren't significantly different from his other three employees—she's in her early 30s with an undergraduate degree in accounting. But in recent weeks she has become his number-one headache.

Stella's job is to handle general accounting records. She also acts as accounting's link to the service department. Stella provides advice and support to service on anything having to do with credit, cost control, the computer system, and the like.

The first sign of a problem began three weeks ago. Stella called in sick on both Monday and Tuesday. When she showed up for work on Wednesday morning, she looked like she hadn't slept in days. Jim called her into his office and, in an informal manner, began trying to find out what was going on. Stella was open. She admitted she hadn't been ill. She called in sick because she didn't have the emotional strength to come to work. She volunteered that her marriage was in trouble. Her husband had a serious drinking problem but wouldn't seek help. He had lost his third job in as many months on that last Friday. She was concerned about her children and her finances. Stella has a seven-year-old son from a previous marriage and twin daughters who are three years old. Jim tried to console Stella. He encouraged her to keep her spirits up and reminded her that the company's health plan provided six free counselling sessions. He suggested she consider using them.

Since that initial encounter, little seems to have changed with Stella. She's used up three more sick days. When she comes to the office, it's clear her mind is somewhere else. She is spending an inordinate amount of time on the telephone, and Jim suspects it's almost all related to personal matters. Twice in the past week, Jim has noticed Stella crying at her desk.

Yesterday was the third working day of the new month, and Stella should have completed the closing of last month's books. That is an important part of Stella's job. This morning, soon after Stella arrived, Jim asked her for the closing numbers. Stella got up and, with tears welling in her eyes, went to the washroom. Jim saw last month's books on Stella's desk. He opened them up. They were incomplete. Stella had missed her deadline, and Jim wasn't sure when he would have the final figures to give to Ross Todd.

Questions

1. Do any motivation techniques appear relevant to helping Jim deal with Stella? If so, what are they?

2. From an ethical perspective, how far do you think Jim should go in dealing with Stella's personal problems?

3. If you were Jim, what would you do?

Will You Get a Raise?

It's been a while since companies have given raises to their employees, but they're starting to again, now that Canada's recession is starting to ease. However, raises are minimal in the '90s—more likely to be around two percent—keeping workers even with the rate of inflation. This is quite a change from the five to eight percent raises awarded in the 1980s. Employers are trying to keep base wages down, so that they won't have a workforce of highly paid employees should another downturn in the economy occur.

Many more companies have started to introduce variable-based pay programs to their employees. In 1990, only 27 percent of companies had such programs, but in 1995, 45 percent reported using them. Companies using variable-based pay include AT&T Canada, Aetna Canada, Assurance vie Desjardins, B.C. Tel Mobility, CIBA Vision, Glaxo Canada, Imasco Ltd., Labatt, Quaker Oats, and Shoppers Drug Mart.

Variable-based pay means that employees have to meet targets in order to receive bonuses. These targets could include company goals, cost-cutting, or individual results. If the targets are made, a bonus is given, but if the target is missed, there is no bonus. At Royal York Hotel in Toronto, each department's performance is evaluated, and if the department meets its goals, all members of the department receive a bonus. For instance, in the housekeeping department, savings in housekeeping costs per occupied room and savings in the costs of laundry are placed into a bonus pool. If the housekeeping department meets its annual cost-cutting goals, bonuses are awarded from the bonus pool of savings.

Variable pay is not a completely new idea. Commissioned sales agents and top management have experienced this program for years. But now it's trickling down to lower-level employees, sometimes all the way down to the receptionist. And it means that employees can't depend on pay increases coming at regular intervals. Instead, increases are based on employee performance. Variable pay can change the dynamics in the workplace as well, as there is generally more scrutiny and measurement to determine whether goals are being met. It does mean that slackers need to look out, as they may not receive wage increases ever again.

Questions

1. How does variable pay motivate employees?

2. Can you see any problems with using variable pay as a motivator?

3. How would you react if variable pay were introduced into your workplace, replacing the annual cost-of-living increases you had come to expect?

Source: Based on "Will You Get a Raise?", *Venture 534*; aired February 4, 1995.

POINT

The Case for Pay Secrecy

"Oh, and one last point," said the director of human resources to the new employee. "We treat salary information as a private matter around here. What you make is your business and no one else's. We consider it grounds for termination if you tell anyone what you make."

This policy of pay secrecy is the norm in most organizations, though in most cases, it's communicated informally. The message trickles down and new employees quickly learn from their boss and peers not to inquire about what other people make or to openly volunteer their own salary. For those raised in democratic societies, it may be tempting to surmise that there is something inherently wrong with pay secrecy. On the other hand, if it's wrong, why do the vast majority of successful corporations in democracies follow the practice? There are a number of logical reasons why organizations practise pay secrecy and why they are likely to continue to do so.

First, pay is privileged information to both the organization and the individual employee. Organizations hold many things privileged—manufacturing processes, product formulas, new-product research, marketing strategies—and courts have generally supported the argument that pay rightly belongs in this category. Salary information has been held to be confidential and the property of management. Employees who release such data can be discharged for willful misconduct. Moreover, most employees want their pay kept secret. Many people's egos are tied to their paycheque. They are as comfortable discussing their specific pay as they are providing details of their sex life to strangers. Employees have a right to privacy, and this includes ensuring that their pay is kept secret.

Second, pay secrecy lessens the opportunity for comparisons among employees and the exposure of perceived inequities. No pay system will ever be perceived as fair by everyone. One person's "merit" is another person's "favouritism." Knowledge of what other employees are making only highlights perceived inequities and causes disruptions.

Third, pay differences are often perfectly justified, yet only for subtle, complicated, or difficult-to-explain reasons. For instance, people doing similar jobs were hired under different market conditions. Or two managers have similar titles, although one supervises 10 people while the other supervises 20. Or one person earns more today than a co-worker because of responsibilities held or contributions made to the organization in a different job several years earlier.

Fourth, pay secrecy saves embarrassing underpaid and underperforming employees. By definition, half of an organization's workforce will be below average. What kind of organization would be so cold and insensitive as to publicly expose those in the lower half of the performance distribution?

Finally, pay secrecy gives managers more freedom in administering pay because every pay differential doesn't have to be explained. A policy of openness encourages managers to minimize differences and allocate pay more evenly. Since employee performance in an organization tends to follow a normal distribution, only through pay secrecy can managers feel comfortable in giving large rewards to high performers and few or no rewards to low performers. ■

Sources: Based on J. Solomon, "Hush Money," *The Wall Street Journal*, April 18, 1990, pp. R22–R24; and K. Tracy, M. Renard, and G. Young, "Pay Secrecy: The Effects of Open and Secret Pay Policies on Satisfaction and Performance," in A. Head and W.P. Ferris (eds.), *Proceedings of the 28th Annual Meeting of the Eastern Academy of Management*, Hartford, CT, May 1991, pp. 248–51.

counterPOINT

Let's Make Pay Information Open to All!

Open pay policies make good sense. They already exist for employees of most public institutions and for top executives in all publicly held corporations. A few private-sector companies have also seen the benefits that can accrue from making the pay of all employees public knowledge. For instance, the software maker NeXT Inc. (recently purchased by Apple Computer) used to hang lists of all its employees' salaries in company offices for anyone to consult.

Why do open pay policies make good sense? We can articulate at least five reasons.

First, such pay policies open communication and build trust. As one executive stated, "Anything less than openness doesn't establish the same level of trust." If the organization can be open about such a sensitive issue as pay, it makes employees believe that management can be trusted about other concerns that are not so sensitive. In addition, if an organization's pay system is fair and equitable, employees report greater satisfaction with pay and with pay differentials where pay is open.

Second, an employee's right to privacy needs to be balanced against his or her right to know. Laws to protect an employee's right to know have become more popular in recent years, especially in the area of hazardous working conditions. The case can be made that the right to a free flow of information includes the right to know what others in one's organization earn.

Third, pay secrecy is often supported by organizations not to prevent embarrassment of employees but to prevent embarrassment of management. Pay openness threatens exposing system inequities caused by a poorly developed and administered pay system. An open pay system not only says to employees that management believes its pay policies are fair, but is itself a mechanism for increasing fairness. When true inequities creep into an open pay system,

they are much more likely to be quickly identified and corrected than when they occur in pay-secrecy systems. Employees will provide the checks and balances on management.

Fourth, what management calls "freedom" in administering pay is really a euphemism for "control." Pay secrecy allows management to substitute favoritism for performance criteria in pay allocations. To the degree that we believe that organizations should reward good performance rather than good political skills, open pay policies take power and control away from managers. When pay levels and changes are public knowledge, organizational politics is less likely to surface.

Finally, and maybe most importantly, pay secrecy obscures the connection between pay and performance. Both equity and expectancy theories emphasize the desirability of linking rewards to performance. To maximize motivation, employees should know how the organization defines and measures performance, and the rewards attached to differing levels of performance. Unfortunately, when pay information is kept secret, employees make inaccurate perceptions. Even more unfortunately, those inaccuracies tend to work against increasing motivation. Specifically, research has found that people overestimate the pay of their peers and their subordinates and underestimate the pay of their superiors. So where pay is kept secret, actual differences tend to be discounted, which reduces the motivational benefits of linking pay to performance. ■

Sources: Based on E.E. Lawler III, "Secrecy About Management Compensation: Are There Hidden Costs?", *Organizational Behaviour and Human Performance*, May 1967, pp. 182–89; J. Solomon, "Hush Money," *The Wall Street Journal*, April 18, 1990, pp. R22–R24; and K. Tracy, M. Renard, and G. Young, "Pay Secrecy: The Effects of Open and Secret Pay Policies on Satisfaction and Performance," in A. Head and W.P. Ferris (eds.), *Proceedings of the 28th Annual Meeting of the Eastern Academy of Management*, Hartford, CT, May 1991, pp. 248–51.

CHAPTER 7

Foundations of Group Behaviour

ROADMAP

LEARNING OBJECTIVES

After studying this chapter, you should be able to

- Differentiate between formal and informal groups

- Compare two models of group development

- Explain how group interaction can be analysed

- Identify the key factors in explaining group behaviour

- Explain how role requirements change in different situations

- Describe how norms exert influence on an individual's behaviour

- Define social loafing and its effect on group performance

- Identify the benefits and disadvantages of cohesive groups

- Explain the factors that affect intergroup relations

- Identify methods for managing intergroup relations

The pulp and paper products industry in Canada has been under cost pressures for more than a decade. One particular player in this industry, MacMillan Bloedel Ltd. (MacBlo), has responded by closing mills, shutting down machines, and cutting its workforce from 25 000 to 13 500 during the 1990s. These efforts at downsizing have helped MacBlo, but the company still continues to post annual losses. As a result, MacBlo recently announced that it will trim its labour force to 10 800.[1]

If you think these cutbacks at MacBlo haven't sat well with the company's unions, you'd be right. In fact, the company and its unions have a long history of antagonism. Garry Worth, president of the Pulp, Paper and Woodworkers of Canada, said he "was shocked by the ludicrous job cuts" most recently proposed. MacBlo's CEO Tom Stephens (pictured right) countered that "union changes are inevitable," and he "remains confident concessions will be reached."

MacBlo has been trying to change its labour relations climate by getting workers more involved in company decision-making. Its woodlands and mill managers now share detailed financial data and production plans in regular meetings with workers. Joint union-management committees have been created to solicit suggestions for improving productivity. Some division managers are even taking union representatives along on sales trips so they can see, firsthand, the industry's competitive conditions.

Management's efforts to improve relations with its union members haven't met with a great deal of success. Union leaders openly question management's motives. They claim that joint committees just dupe union members into making suggestions that increase productivity at the cost of jobs. Worth wonders whether the mills can operate efficiently or safely with even further reductions. ■

The labour-management problems at MacMillan Bloedel illustrate the importance of understanding groups in the workplace. The behaviour of individuals in groups is something more than the sum total of each person acting in his or her own way. In other words, when individuals are in groups, they act differently than they do when they're alone. For instance, the employee who would individually accept change and cooperate with management might become belligerent and try to hinder that change if he or she is a union member and the union seeks to maintain the status quo.

Union members are just one example of a work group. As we show in this chapter, organizations are composed of a number of formal and informal groups, and understanding these groups is critical to explaining organizational behaviour.

Defining Groups

group
Two or more individuals, interacting and interdependent, who have come together to achieve particular objectives.

A **group** is defined as two or more individuals, interacting and interdependent, who have come together to achieve particular objectives. The reasons for coming together can be quite varied, from serving on a committee or task force at work, to serving on the board of a day care centre, to working together on a class project. Sometimes a group of people also get together to do something socially as well, so groups don't have to have work-related objectives.

There is no single reason why individuals join groups. Because most people belong to a number of groups, it's obvious that different groups provide different benefits to their members. Exhibit 7-1 summarizes the most popular reasons people have for joining groups. Because you will be a member of groups throughout your life, both within and outside the work organization, we review in this chapter the ways that groups function, how they can be made better, and what causes problems. Because most of you will work in student groups during your college and university days, you might want to think about applying the topics in this chapter to your own student groups. For some, the issue of working in groups is controversial. You may want to review the Point/Counterpoint discussion to learn more of this controversy.

Stages of Group Development

When people get together for the first time with the purpose of achieving some objective, they may not realize that acting as a group is not something simple, easy, or genetically programmed. Working in a group is often difficult, particularly in the initial stages, when people don't necessarily know each other. As it turns out, groups go through various stages over time, although the stages are not necessarily exactly the same for each group. In this section, we review the better-known five-stage model of group development, and then the more recently discovered punctuated-equilibrium model.

The Five-Stage Model

From the mid-1960s, it was believed that groups passed through a standard sequence of five stages.[2] As shown in Exhibit 7-2, these five stages have been labelled forming, storming, norming, performing, and adjourning. Although we now know that not all groups pass through these stages in a linear fash-

Exhibit 7-1
Why Do People Join Groups?

Security

By joining a group, individuals can reduce the insecurity of "standing alone." People feel stronger, have fewer self-doubts, and are more resistant to threats when they are part of a group.

Status

Inclusion in a group that is viewed as important by others provides recognition and status for its members.

Self-Esteem

Groups can provide people with feelings of self-worth. That is, in addition to conveying status to those outside the group, membership can also give increased feelings of worth to the group members themselves.

Affiliation

Groups can fulfil social needs. People enjoy the regular interaction that comes with group membership. For many people, these interactions are their primary way of satisfying their needs for affiliation.

Power

What cannot be achieved individually often becomes possible through group action. There is power in numbers.

Goal Achievement

There are times when it takes more than one person to accomplish a particular task: there is a need to pool talents, knowledge, or power in order to complete a job.

ion, the stages are helpful in addressing your anxieties about working in groups.

Think about the first time you met with a new group that has been put together to accomplish some task. Do you remember how some people seemed silent and others felt confused about the task? Those feelings arise during the first stage of group development, know as **forming**. Forming is characterized by a great deal of uncertainty about the group's purpose, structure, and leadership. Members are "testing the waters" to determine what types of behaviour are acceptable. This stage is complete when members have begun to think of themselves as part of a group.

Do you remember how some people in your group just didn't seem to get along, and sometimes even power struggles emerged? These reactions are

forming
The first stage in group development, characterized by much uncertainty.

Exhibit 7-2
Stages of Group Development

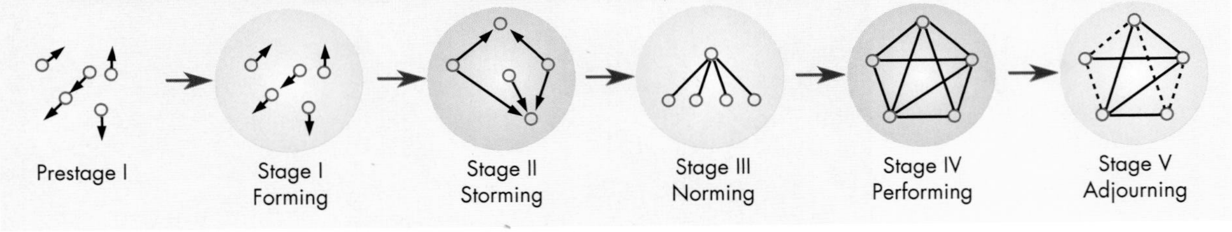

| Prestage I | Stage I Forming | Stage II Storming | Stage III Norming | Stage IV Performing | Stage V Adjourning |

storming
The second stage in group development, characterized by intragroup conflict.

typical of the **storming** stage, which is one of intragroup conflict. Members accept the existence of the group, but resist the constraints that the group imposes on individuality. Furthermore, there is conflict over who will control the group. When this stage is complete, a relatively clear hierarchy of leadership will emerge within the group.

Some groups never really emerge from the storming stage, or they move back and forth through storming and the other stages. A group that remains forever planted in the storming stage may have less ability to complete the task because of all the interpersonal problems.

Many groups resolve the interpersonal conflict and reach the third stage, in which close relationships develop and the group demonstrates cohesiveness. There is now a strong sense of group identity and camaraderie. This **norming** stage is complete when the group structure solidifies, and the group has assimilated a common set of expectations of what defines correct member behaviour.

norming
The third stage in group development, characterized by close relationships and cohesiveness.

Finally, and you may have noticed this in some of your own group interactions, some groups seem to just come together well, and start to do their work. This fourth stage, when significant task progress is being made, is called **performing**. The structure at this point is fully functional and accepted. Group energy has moved from getting to know and understand each other to performing the task at hand.

performing
The fourth stage in group development, when the group is fully functional.

For permanent work groups, performing is the last stage in their development. However, for temporary committees, teams, task forces, and similar groups that have a limited task to perform, there is an **adjourning** stage. In this stage, the group prepares for its disbandment. High task performance is no longer the group's top priority. Instead, attention is directed toward wrapping up activities. Group members' responses vary in this stage. Some are upbeat, basking in the group's accomplishments. Others may be depressed over the loss of camaraderie and friendships gained during the work group's life.

adjourning
The final stage in group development for temporary groups, characterized by concern with wrapping up activities rather than task performance.

Many interpreters of the five-stage model have assumed that a group becomes more effective as it progresses through the first four stages. While this assumption may be generally true, what makes a group effective is more complex than this model acknowledges. Under some conditions, high levels

Because speed and flexibility are important to the success of MagneTek in supplying electrical products to the growing worldwide market, the company has formed task groups to complete customer orders. The task groups shown here work as teams that adapt quickly to changes in the size, schedule, and complexity of customer orders.

of conflict are conducive to high group performance, as long as the conflict is directed towards the task and not toward group members. So we might expect to find situations where groups in Stage II outperform those in Stages III or IV. Similarly, groups do not always proceed clearly from one stage to the next. Sometimes, in fact, several stages go on simultaneously, as when groups are storming and performing at the same time. Groups even occasionally regress to previous stages. Therefore, even the strongest proponents of this model do not assume that all groups follow the five-stage process precisely or that Stage IV is always the most preferable.

Another problem with the five-stage model, in terms of understanding work-related behaviour, is that it ignores organizational context.[3] For instance, a study of a cockpit crew in an airliner found that, within 10 minutes, three strangers assigned to fly together for the first time had become a high-performing group. What allowed for this speedy group development was the strong organizational context surrounding the tasks of the cockpit crew. This context provided the rules, task definitions, information, and resources needed for the group to perform. They didn't need to develop plans, assign roles, determine and allocate resources, resolve conflicts, and set norms the way the five-stage model predicts. Within the workplace, some group behaviour takes place within a strong organizational context, and it would appear that the five-stage development model may have limited applicability for those groups. However, there are a variety of situations in the workplace where groups are assigned to tasks, and the individuals do not know each other, and therefore must work out interpersonal differences at the same time as they work through the assigned task.

The Punctuated-Equilibrium Model

Studies of more than a dozen field and laboratory task force groups confirmed that while groups don't develop in a universal sequence of stages,[4] the timing of when groups form and change the way they work is highly consistent. Specifically, it has been found that (1) the first meeting sets the group's direction; (2) the first phase of group activity is one of inertia; (3) a transition takes place at the end of the first phase, which occurs exactly when the group has used up half its allotted time; (4) the transition initiates major changes; (5) a second phase of inertia follows the transition; and (6) the group's last meeting is characterized by markedly accelerated activity. These findings are shown in Exhibit 7-3. It is important for you to under-

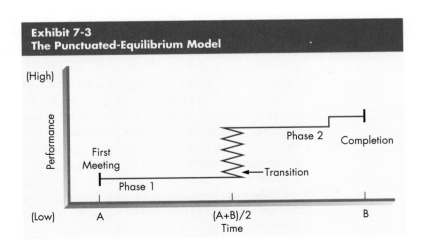

Exhibit 7-3
The Punctuated-Equilibrium Model

stand the shifts in group behaviour, if for no other reason than when you're in a group that is not working well, you can start to think of ways to help the group move to a more productive phase.

As both a group member and possibly a group leader, it is important that you recognize that the first meeting sets the group's direction. A framework of behavioural patterns and assumptions through which the group will approach its project emerges in this first meeting. These lasting patterns can appear as early as the first few seconds of the group's life.

Once set, the group's direction becomes "written in stone" and is unlikely to be re-examined throughout the first half of the group's life. This is a period of inertia—that is, the group tends to stand still or become locked into a fixed course of action. Even if it gains new insights that challenge initial patterns and assumptions, the group is incapable of acting on these new insights in Phase 1. You may recognize that in some groups during the early period of trying to get things accomplished, no one really did their tasks. You may also recognize this phase as one where everyone carries out their tasks, but not in a very coordinated fashion.

At some point, however, the group moves out of the inertia stage and recognizes that work needs to get completed. One of the more interesting discoveries made in these studies was that each group experienced its transition at the same point in its calendar—precisely halfway between its first meeting and its official deadline—despite the fact that some groups spent as little as an hour on their project while others spent six months. It was as if the groups universally experienced a midlife crisis at this point. The midpoint appears to work like an alarm clock, heightening members' awareness that their time is limited and that they need to "get moving." When you work on your next group project, you might want to examine when your group starts to "get moving."

This transition ends Phase 1 and is characterized by a concentrated burst of changes, dropping of old patterns, and adoption of new perspectives. The transition sets a revised direction for Phase 2, which is a new equilibrium or period of inertia. In this phase, the group executes plans created during the transition period. The group's last meeting is characterized by a final burst of activity to finish its work.

We can use this model to describe some of your experiences with student teams created for doing group term projects. At the first meeting, a basic timetable is established. Members size up one another. They agree they have nine weeks to do their project. The instructor's requirements are discussed and debated. From that point, the group meets regularly to carry out its activities. About four or five weeks into the project, however, problems are confronted. Criticism begins to be taken seriously. Discussion becomes more open. The group reassesses where it has been and aggressively moves to make necessary changes. If the right changes are made, the next four or five weeks find the group developing a first-rate project. The group's last meeting, which will probably occur just before the project is due, lasts longer than the others. In it, all final issues are discussed and details resolved.

In summary, the punctuated-equilibrium model characterizes groups as exhibiting long periods of inertia interspersed with brief revolutionary changes triggered primarily by their members' awareness of time and deadlines. To use the terminology of the five-stage group development model, the group begins by combining the forming and norming stages, then goes through a period of low performing, followed by storming, then a period of high performing, and, finally, adjourning.

What Makes Groups Work (or Not Work)?

Why are some group efforts more successful than others? The answer to that question is complex, but it includes variables such as the ability of the group's members, the size of the group, the level of conflict, and the internal pressures on members to conform to the group's norms. Exhibit 7-4 presents the major components that determine group performance and satisfaction.[5] It can help you sort out the key variables and their interrelationships. You might want to read OB in the News to see how the City of Vancouver's planning department has moved to a group structure rather than have one person administer the unit. The news feature may raise some questions as you start to study how groups can be made to operate more effectively.

Perhaps the most important factor to consider is that work groups don't exist in isolation. They are part of a larger organization. A research team in Vancouver-based MacMillan Bloedel's forestry division, for instance, must live within the rules and policies dictated from the division's headquarters and MacBlo's corporate offices. So every work group is influenced by both internal *and* external conditions.

Internally, the work group has a distinct set of resources determined by its membership. This includes such things as intelligence and motivation of members. It also has an internal structure that defines member roles and norms. These factors—group member resources and structure—determine interaction patterns and other processes within the group.

Finally, whether the group is able to perform, and also its degree of satisfaction, are moderated by the type of task that the group is working on. In the following pages, we'll elaborate on each of the basic boxes identified in Exhibit 7-4.

The Effects of the Workplace on the Group

When you work in an organization as part of different groups, you will notice that sometimes groups function well, and other times they don't function as well. Some of this is related to interpersonal issues. However, sometimes groups have more or less difficulty depending on what organizational conditions exist, and what resources are provided. For example, when the University of British Columbia (UBC) redesigned its MBA program several years ago, the faculty members who worked on the design teams were given some release time from their teaching responsibilities for their efforts,

City of Vancouver
http://www.city.vancouver.bc.ca/

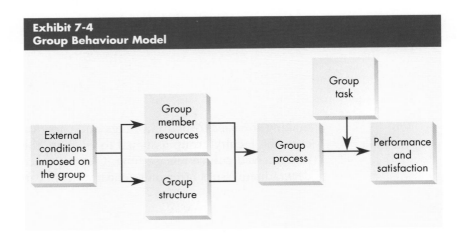

Exhibit 7-4
Group Behaviour Model

OB IN THE NEWS

Five-Person Group Runs Department

In 1994, the City of Vancouver, one of the fastest-growing cities in North America, decided to try an experiment. Tom Fletcher had just left his position as director of city planning to assume the same post in Delta, British Columbia. Instead of hiring a new director of city planning, the city decided to operate the city planning department with a five-person team.

This decision was met with a variety of responses. Planning departments from across Canada watched with great interest to see whether this was something they might consider. Architects and developers were less happy, with the situation causing them anxiety and some consternation.

John Sewell, a former mayor of Toronto, and someone who is active in writing and consulting on planning and development issues, summarized much of the concern about this group-headed approach to city planning: "A good director is a marvellous thing for a city. That person can clarify murky issues and give clear direction to council. I don't know of any other city that has no director. You usually put people in charge so everyone knows who's in charge."

So, did the city of Vancouver make a mistake with their approach? The five associate directors at the top don't think so. They see plenty of advantages, and they're saving the city the $150 000 for a director's salary and benefits.

The city manager of corporate services further explains why a group approach might be best: "The whole concept that we've got to have one person who's more intelligent than anyone else, more visionary than anyone else to drive these things, I'm not sure is necessarily accurate."

Larry Beasley, associate director responsible for the downtown, explains how the group operates: "We don't make contradictory decisions, and [we] make sure that no one says 'I don't know who makes the decision.' And all associate directors get out in public, articulating a vision for the future of the city." Beasley says the consequences of the new arrangement have all been positive. "Staff morale is high. Departments that used to work in isolation and often at cross-purposes are now more coordinated."

As former visionary planning director for Vancouver, Ray Spaxman notes that it will take some time to know whether this sort of group structure is appropriate for the task of city planning. "The impact of the city planning department can only be measured after five, seven, 10 years, so you don't know until that period is over."

What we do know for now, however, is that the experiment was only slated to last two years. However, in mid-1998, the planning department was still run by a group of associate directors.

Source: Frances Bula, "Team Approach to Planning Builds Dispute," *Vancouver Sun*, November 1, 1995, pp. A1, A2.

Take It to the Net

We invite you to visit the Robbins page on the Prentice Hall Web site at:

http://www.prenticehall.ca/robbins

for this chapter's World Wide Web exercise.

making it easier to plan meetings and carry out tasks. More recently, however, the faculty group assigned to evaluate the undergraduate program has not received course release time. Clearly the committee working on the undergraduate issues faces more constraints in carrying out their tasks.

To begin understanding the behaviour of a work group, you need to view it as a subsystem embedded in a larger system.[6] That is, when we realize that groups are a subset of a larger organization system, we can extract part of the explanation of the group's behaviour from an explanation of the organization to which it belongs.

ORGANIZATIONAL STRATEGY Many members of organizations observe that some groups within the organization get more attention than others. This treatment relates to organizational strategy. An organization's overall strategy, typically put in place by top management, outlines the organization's goals and the means for attaining these goals. It might, for example, direct the organization toward reducing costs, improving quality, expanding market share, or shrinking the size of its overall operations. The strategy that an organization is pursuing, at any given time, will influence the power of various work groups, which, in turn, will determine the resources that the organization's top management is willing to allocate to it for performing its tasks.

To illustrate, an organization that is retrenching through selling off or closing down major parts of its business will have work groups with a shrinking resource base, increased member anxiety, and the potential for heightened intragroup conflict.[7] Even in that situation, however, some groups will be allocated more resources to do their task than others. For instance, the group designated the task of determining how to carry out the downsizing effectively would likely receive more resources than the group assigned to a project likely to be cut in the downsizing.

ORGANIZATIONAL INFRASTRUCTURE Groups are constrained to work within the framework of an organization. Some organizations are more flexible than others, and this will affect the ability of the group to carry out its tasks. Below we consider several elements of the organization's infrastructure that can affect group behaviour.

Leadership. When organizations create groups, they often designate some sort of hierarchy within the team. The person assigned the leadership role generally reports to management on behalf of the team and has authority that other group members don't have. This can sometimes cause problems, however, if a work group ends up being led by someone who emerges informally from within the group.

McDonald's
http://www.mcdonalds.com/

Rules. All organizations have rules, although some have far fewer than others. The rules (or lack thereof) in the organization affect the ability of the group to function. For instance, because McDonald's has standard operating procedures for taking orders, cooking hamburgers, and filling soft-drink containers, the discretion of work-group members to set independent standards of behaviour is severely limited. The more formal regulations that the organization imposes on all its employees, the more the behaviour of work-group members will be consistent and predictable. The less formal the regulations, the more flexible and adaptable the group can be in responding to various situations.

Resources. Some organizations are large and profitable, with an abundance of resources. Their employees, for instance, will have modern, high-quality tools and equipment to do their jobs. Other organizations aren't as fortunate. When organizations have limited resources, so do their work groups. What a group actually accomplishes is, to a large degree, determined by what it is capable of accomplishing. The presence or absence of resources such as money, time, raw materials, and equipment—which are allocated to the group by the organization—have a large bearing on the group's behaviour.

Evaluation and Rewards. Another organization-wide variable that affects how groups perform is the performance evaluation and reward system.[8] Does the organization reward the accomplishment of individual or group objectives? Group members' behaviour will be influenced by how the organization evaluates performance and what behaviours are rewarded. You might have noticed that the behaviour of some members of student groups working on class assignments is different, depending on whether every member of the group will receive the same mark on an assignment or whether the group, together with the professor, will allocate marks on the basis of individual participation to the group project. Because the assignment of marks (or rewards) has some impact on individual behaviour, this is an important factor for organizations (and instructors) to think about.

ORGANIZATIONAL CULTURE Beyond the ordinary infrastructure of the organization, every organization has an unwritten culture that defines standards of acceptable and unacceptable behaviour for employees. Within a few months, most employees understand their organization's culture. They know how to dress for work, whether rules are rigidly enforced, what kinds of questionable behaviours will get them into trouble and which ones are likely to be overlooked, the importance of honesty and integrity, and the like. Members of work groups must accept the standards implied in the organization's dominant culture if they are to remain in good standing. Because of an organization's culture, organizational members often know whether they have been assigned to a committee that is of importance to the organization. If they recognize that they have been assigned to one of the "unimportant" committees, they may not exert as much effort. In some universities, for instance, research activity is more highly valued than teaching activities. Consequently, members assigned to the research development committee recognize the importance of being asked to serve, while those asked to serve on the teaching development committee might feel that their activities will not be valued.

The Effects of Group Members

While various organizational factors affect a group's performance, the group also depends on the resources that its members individually bring to the group. In this section, we will examine two resources that have received the greatest amount of attention: abilities and personality characteristics. As you learn more about the effects of group members on group performance in this section, you may want to examine the Learning About Yourself exercise, which helps you to assess how attracted you are to group work.

ABILITIES Part of a group's performance can be predicted by assessing the task-relevant and intellectual abilities of its individual members. It's true that

we occasionally read about the athletic team composed of mediocre players who, because of excellent coaching, determination, and precision teamwork, beat a far more talented group of players. But such cases make the news precisely because they represent an aberration. As the old saying goes, "The race doesn't always go to the swiftest nor the battle to the strongest, but that's the way to bet." A group's performance is not merely the summation of its individual members' abilities. However, these abilities set parameters for what members can do and how effectively they will perform in a group.

What predictions can we make regarding ability and group performance? First, evidence indicates that individuals who hold crucial abilities for attaining the group's task tend to be more involved in group activity, generally contribute more, are more likely to emerge as the group leaders, and are more satisfied if their talents are effectively utilized by the group.[9] Second, intellectual ability and task-relevant ability have both been found to be related to overall group performance.[10] However, the correlation is not particularly high, suggesting that other factors, such as the size of the group, the type of tasks being performed, the actions of its leader, and level of conflict within the group, also influence performance.

PERSONALITY CHARACTERISTICS You may remember that we discussed personality as it relates to individual performance extensively in Chapter 3. There has also been a great deal of research on the relationship between personality traits and group attitudes and behaviour. The general conclusion is that attributes that tend to have a positive connotation in our culture tend to be positively related to group productivity, morale, and cohesiveness. These include traits such as sociability, self-reliance, and independence. In contrast, negatively evaluated characteristics such as authoritarianism, dominance, and unconventionality tend to be negatively related to the dependent variables.[11] These personality traits affect group performance by strongly influencing how the individual will interact with other group members.

Is any one personality characteristic a good predictor of group behaviour? The answer to that question is "no." The magnitude of the effect of any *single* characteristic is small, but taking personality characteristics *together*, the consequences for group behaviour are of major significance. This chapter's HR Implications discusses some of the selection procedures that organizations use in order to hire employees. Selection is a key factor in having employees who will be able to work in groups, if that is what is important to the organization.

The Effects of Group Structure

Work groups are not unorganized mobs. They have a structure that shapes the behaviour of members and makes it possible to explain and predict a large portion of individual behaviour within the group as well as the performance of the group itself. What are some of these structural variables? They include formal leadership, roles, norms, group status, group size, composition of the group, and the degree of group cohesiveness.

FORMAL LEADERSHIP Almost every work group has a formal leader. He or she is typically identified by titles such as unit or department manager, supervisor, foreperson, project leader, task force head, or committee chair. This leader can play an important part in the group's success—so much so, in fact, that we have devoted an entire chapter to the topic of leadership. In

Chapter 11, we will review the research on leadership and the effect that leaders have on individual and group performance variables.

ROLES Shakespeare said, "All the world's a stage, and all the men and women merely players." Using the same metaphor, all group members are actors, each playing a **role**. By this term, we mean a set of expected behaviour patterns attributed to someone occupying a given position in a social unit. The understanding of role behaviour would be dramatically simplified if each of us chose one role and "played it out" regularly and consistently. Unfortunately, we are required to play a number of diverse roles, both on and off our jobs. As we will see, one of the tasks in understanding behaviour is grasping the role that a person is currently playing.

For example, Bill Patterson is a plant manager with a large electrical equipment manufacturer in Saskatchewan. He has a number of roles that he fulfils on that job—for instance, employee, member of middle management, electrical engineer, and the primary company spokesperson in the community. Off the job, Bill Patterson finds himself in still more roles: husband, father, Catholic, tennis player, foodbank volunteer, and coach of his son's softball team. Many of these roles are compatible; some create conflicts. For instance, how does his religious involvement influence his managerial decisions regarding layoffs, expense account padding, and providing accurate information to government agencies? A recent offer of promotion requires Bill to relocate, yet his family very much wants to stay in Saskatoon. Can the role demands of his job be reconciled with the demands of his husband and father roles?

The issue should be clear: Like Bill Patterson, we all are required to play a number of roles, and our behaviour varies with the role we are playing. Bill's behaviour when he attends church on Sunday morning is different from his behaviour on the tennis court later that same day. Different groups impose different role requirements on individuals.

Role Identity. There are certain attitudes and actual behaviours consistent with a role, and they create the **role identity**. People have the ability to shift roles rapidly when they recognize that the situation and its demands clearly require major changes. For instance, when union stewards were promoted to supervisory positions, it was found that their attitudes changed from pro-union to pro-management within a few months of their promotion. When these promotions had to be rescinded later because of economic difficulties in the firm, it was found that the demoted supervisors had once again adopted their pro-union attitudes.[12]

Role Perception. One's view of how one is supposed to act in a given situation is a **role perception**. Based on an interpretation of how we believe we are supposed to behave, we engage in certain types of behaviour.

Where do we get these perceptions? We get them from stimuli all around us—friends, books, movies, television. The primary reason that apprenticeship programs exist in many trades and professions is to allow beginners to watch an "expert," so that they can learn to act as they are supposed to.

Role Expectations. **Role expectations** are defined as how others believe you should act in a given situation. How you behave is determined to a large extent by the role defined in the context in which you are acting. The role of a Supreme Court judge is viewed as having propriety and dignity, whereas a hockey coach is seen as aggressive, dynamic, and inspiring to his players. In

role
A set of expected behaviour patterns attributed to someone occupying a given position in a social unit.

role identity
Certain attitudes and behaviours consistent with a role.

role perception
An individual's view of how he or she is supposed to act in a given situation.

role expectations
How others believe a person should act in a given situation.

the same context, we might be surprised to learn that the neighbourhood priest moonlights during the week as a bartender because our role expectations of priests and bartenders tend to be considerably different. When role expectations are concentrated into generalized categories, we have role stereotypes.

In the workplace, it can be helpful to look at the topic of role expectations through the perspective of the **psychological contract**. There is an unwritten agreement that exists between employees and their employer. As researcher Sandra Robinson from the University of British Columbia and her colleagues note, this psychological contract sets out mutual expectations— what management expects from workers, and vice versa.[13] In effect, this contract defines the behavioural expectations that go with every role. Management is expected to treat employees justly, provide acceptable working conditions, clearly communicate what is a fair day's work, and give feedback on how well the employee is doing. Employees are expected to respond by demonstrating a good attitude, following directions, and showing loyalty to the organization.

What happens when role expectations as implied in the psychological contract are not met? If management is negligent in holding up its part of the bargain, we can expect negative repercussions on employee performance and satisfaction. When employees fail to live up to expectations, the result is usually some form of disciplinary action up to and including firing.

The psychological contract should be recognized as a "powerful determiner of behaviour in organizations."[14] It points out the importance of accurately communicating role expectations. In Chapter 16, we discuss how organizations socialize employees in order to get them to play out their roles in the way management desires.

Role Conflict. When an individual is confronted by divergent role expectations, the result is **role conflict**. It exists when an individual finds that compliance with one role requirement may make more difficult compliance with another.[15] At the extreme, it would include situations in which two or more role expectations are mutually contradictory.

Our previous discussion of the many roles Bill Patterson had to deal with included several role conflicts—for instance, Bill's attempt to reconcile the expectations placed on him as a husband and father with those placed on him as an executive with his firm. The former, as you will remember, emphasizes stability and concern for the desire of his wife and children to remain in Saskatoon. His company, on the other hand, expects its employees to be responsive to its needs and requirements. Although it might be in Bill's financial and career interests to accept a relocation, the conflict comes down to choosing between family and career role expectations.

All of us have faced and will continue to face role conflicts. The critical issue, from our standpoint, is how conflicts imposed by divergent expectations within the organization impact behaviour. Certainly, they increase internal tension and frustration. There are a number of behavioural responses one may engage in. For example, one can give a formalized bureaucratic response. The conflict is then resolved by relying on the rules, regulations, and procedures that govern organizational activities. For example, a worker faced with the conflicting requirements imposed by the corporate controller's office and his own plant manager decides in favour of his immediate boss—the plant manager. Other behavioural responses may include withdrawal, stalling, negotiation, or, as we found in our discussion of dissonance in Chapter 4, redefining the facts or the situation to make them appear congruent.

psychological contract
An unwritten agreement that sets out what management expects from the employee, and vice versa.

role conflict
A situation in which an individual is confronted by divergent role expectations.

task-oriented roles
Roles performed by group members to ensure that the tasks of the group are accomplished.

maintenance roles
Roles performed by group members to maintain good relations within the group.

individual roles
Roles performed by group members that are not productive for keeping the group on task.

norms
Acceptable standards of behaviour within a group that are shared by the group's members.

Roles Within Groups. The practical implication of our lengthy discussion on roles is to consider whether roles contribute to an understanding of group development and functioning. Within almost any group, two sets of role relationships need to be considered: **task-oriented roles** and **maintenance roles**. The task-oriented roles are performed by group members to ensure that the tasks of the group are accomplished. The maintenance roles are carried out to ensure that group members maintain good relations. Effective groups maintain some balance between task orientation and maintenance of relations. Occasionally within groups, you will see people take on **individual roles** that are not productive for keeping the group on task. When this happens, the individual is demonstrating more concern for himself or herself than the group as a whole. Exhibit 7-5 identifies a number of task-oriented, maintenance, and individual roles that you might find in a group.

NORMS Did you ever notice that golfers don't speak while their partners are putting on the green or that employees don't criticize their bosses in public? Why? The answer is: "Norms!"

All groups have established **norms**, that is, acceptable standards of behaviour that are shared by the group's members. Norms tell members what they ought and ought not to do under certain circumstances. From an individual's perspective, they tell what is expected of you in certain situations. When agreed to and accepted by the group, norms act as a means of influencing the behaviour of group members with a minimum of external controls. Norms differ among groups, communities, and societies, but they all have them.[16]

Formalized norms are written up in organizational manuals setting out rules and procedures for employees to follow. By far, most norms in organizations are informal. You don't need someone to tell you that throwing paper airplanes or engaging in prolonged gossip sessions at the water cooler are unacceptable behaviours when the "big boss from Toronto" is touring the office. Similarly, we all know that when we're in an employment interview discussing what we didn't like about our previous job, there are certain things we shouldn't talk about (difficulty in getting along with co-workers or our supervisor), while it's very appropriate to talk about other things (inadequate opportunities for advancement or unimportant and meaningless work). Evidence suggests that even high school students recognize that in such interviews certain answers are more socially desirable than others.[17]

Norms for both work groups and organizations cover a wide variety of circumstances. Some of the most common norms have to do with performance (such as how hard to work, what kind of quality, levels of tardiness), appearance (personal dress, as well as norms about when to look busy, when to goof off, how to show loyalty), social arrangement (how the informal groups interact), and allocation of resources (pay, assignments, allocation of tools and equipment).

The "How" and "Why" of Norms. How do norms develop? *Why* are they enforced? A review of the research allows us to answer these questions.[18]

Norms typically develop gradually as group members learn what behaviours are necessary for the group to function effectively. Of course, critical events in the group might short-circuit the process and act quickly to solidify new norms. Most norms develop in one or more of the following four ways:

Exhibit 7-5
Roles Required for Effective Group Functioning

	Function	Description	Example
Roles that build task accomplishment	Initiating	Stating the goal or problem, making proposals about how to work on it, setting time limits.	"Let's set up an agenda for discussing each of the problems we have to consider."
	Seeking Information and Opinions	Asking group members for specific factual information related to the task or problem or for their opinions about it.	"What do you think would be the best approach to this, Jack?"
	Providing Information and Opinions	Sharing information or opinions related to the task or problems.	"I worked on a similar problem last year and found...."
	Clarifying	Helping one another understand ideas and suggestions that come up in the group.	"What you mean, Sue, is that we could...?"
	Elaborating	Building on one another's ideas and suggestions.	"Building on Don's idea, I think we could...."
	Summarizing	Reviewing the points covered by the group and the different ideas stated so that decisions can be based on full information.	Appointing a recorder to take notes on a blackboard.
	Consensus Testing	Periodic testing about whether the group is nearing a decision or needs to continue discussion.	"Is the group ready to decide about this?"
Roles that build and maintain a group	Harmonizing	Mediating conflict among other members, reconciling disagreements, relieving tensions.	"Don, I don't think you and Sue really see the question that differently."
	Compromising	Admitting error at times of group conflict.	"Well, I'd be willing to change if you provided some help on...."
	Gatekeeping	Making sure all members have a chance to express their ideas and feelings and preventing members from being interrupted.	"Sue, we haven't heard from you on this issue."
	Encouraging	Helping a group member make his or her point. Establishing a climate of acceptance in the group.	"I think what you started to say is important, Jack. Please continue."

Source: "Team Processes," in D. Ancona, T. Kochan, M. Scully, J. Van Maanen, D. E. Westney, *Managing for the Future*, Cincinnati, Ohio: South-Western College Publishing, 1996, p. 9.

(1) *Explicit statements made by a group member*—often the group's supervisor or a powerful member. The group leader might, for instance, specifically say that no personal phone calls are allowed during working hours or that coffee breaks must be no longer than 10 minutes. (2) *Critical events in the group's history.* These set important precedents. A bystander is injured while standing too close to a machine and, from that point on, members of the work group regularly monitor each other to ensure that no one other than the operator gets within two metres of any machine. (3) *Primacy.* The first behaviour pattern that emerges in a group frequently sets group expectations. Groups of students who are friends often stake out seats near each other on the first day of class and become upset if an outsider takes "their" seats in a later class. (4) *Carry-over behaviours from past situations.* Group members bring expectations with them from other groups of which they have been members. This can explain why work groups typically prefer to add new members who are similar to current ones in background and experience. This is likely to increase the probability that the expectations they bring are consistent with those already held by the group.

But groups don't establish or enforce norms for every conceivable situation. The norms that the group will enforce tend to be those that are important to it. What makes a norm important? (1) *It facilitates the group's survival.* Groups don't like to fail, so they seek to enforce those norms that increase their chances for success. This means that they'll try to protect themselves from interference from other groups or individuals. (2) *It increases the predictability of group members' behaviours.* Norms that increase predictability enable group members to anticipate each other's actions and to prepare appropriate responses. (3) *It reduces embarrassing interpersonal problems for group members.* Norms are important if they ensure the satisfaction of their members and prevent as much interpersonal discomfort as possible. (4) *It allows members to express the central values of the group and clarify what is distinctive about the group's identity.* Norms that encourage expression of the group's values and distinctive identity help to solidify and maintain the group.

Conformity.   As a group member, you desire acceptance by the group. Because of your desire for acceptance, you are susceptible to conforming to the group's norms. Considerable evidence shows that groups can place strong pressures on individual members to change their attitudes and behaviours to conform to the group's standard.[19]

Do individuals conform to the pressures of all the groups to which they belong? Obviously not, because people belong to many groups and their norms vary. In some cases, they may even have contradictory norms. So what do people do? They conform to the important groups to which they belong or hope to belong. The important groups have been referred to as **reference groups** and are characterized as ones where the person is aware of the others in the group; the person defines himself or herself as a member, or would like to be a member; and the person feels that the group members are significant to him or her.[20] The implication, then, is that all groups do not impose equal conformity pressures on their members.

The impact that group pressures for **conformity** can have on an individual member's judgment and attitudes was demonstrated in the now classic studies by Solomon Asch.[21] Asch organized groups of seven or eight people, who sat in a classroom and were asked to compare two cards held by the experimenter. One card had one line, the other had three lines of varying

reference groups
Important groups to which individuals belong or hope to belong and with whose norms individuals are likely to conform.

conformity
Adjusting one's behaviour to align with the norms of the group.

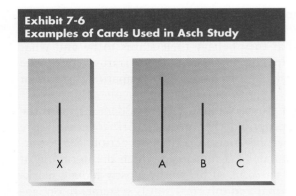

Exhibit 7-6
Examples of Cards Used in Asch Study

length. As shown in Exhibit 7-6, one of the lines on the three-line card was identical to the line on the one-line card. Also as shown in Exhibit 7-6, the difference in line length was quite obvious; under ordinary conditions, subjects made errors less than one percent of the time. Each subject was to announce aloud which of the three lines matched the single line. But what happens if the members in the group begin to give incorrect answers? Will the pressures to conform result in an unsuspecting subject (USS) altering his or her answer to align with the others? That was what Asch wanted to know. So he arranged the group so that only the USS was unaware that the experiment was "fixed." The seating was prearranged: the USS was placed so as to be the last to announce his or her decision.

The experiment began with several sets of matching exercises. All the subjects gave the right answers. On the third set, however, the first subject gave an obviously wrong answer—for example, saying "C" in Exhibit 7-6. The next subject gave the same wrong answer, and so did the others until it got to the unknowing subject. He knew "B" was the same as "X," yet everyone had said "C." The decision confronting the USS was this: Do you publicly state a perception that differs from the preannounced position of the others in your group? Or do you give an answer that you strongly believe is incorrect in order to have your response agree with that of the other group members?

The results obtained by Asch demonstrated that over many experiments and many trials, subjects conformed in about 35 percent of the trials; that is, the subjects gave answers that they knew were wrong but that were consistent with the replies of other group members.

What can we conclude from this study? The results suggest that certain group norms pressure us toward conformity. We desire to be one of the group and avoid being visibly different. We can generalize further to say that when an individual's opinion of objective data differs significantly from that of others in the group, he or she is likely to feel extensive pressure to align his or her opinions to conform with those of the others.

STATUS While teaching a university course on adolescence, the instructor asked the class to list things that contributed to status when they were in grade 12. The list was long and included being an athlete or a cheerleader and being able to cut class without getting caught. Then the instructor asked the students to list things that didn't contribute to status. Again, it was easy for the students to create a long list: getting straight A's, having your mother drive you to school, and so forth. Finally, the students were asked to develop a third list—those things that didn't matter one way or the other. There was a long silence. At last one student in the back row volunteered, "In grade 12, nothing didn't matter."[22]

status
A socially defined position or rank given to groups or group members by others.

Status—that is, a socially defined position or rank given to groups or group members by others—permeates society far beyond the walls of high school. It would not be extravagant to rephrase the preceding quotation to read, "In the status hierarchy of life, nothing doesn't matter." We live in a class-structured society. Despite all attempts to make it more egalitarian, we have made little progress toward a classless society. Even the smallest group will develop roles, rights, and rituals to differentiate its members. Status is

an important factor in understanding human behaviour because it is a significant motivator and has major behavioural consequences when individuals perceive a disparity between what they believe their status to be and what others perceive it to be. To help you understand how status works, the Working With Others exercise asks you to assess the occupational status of various positions.

In his classic 1954 restaurant study, William F. Whyte demonstrated the importance of status.[23] Whyte proposed that people work together more smoothly if high-status personnel customarily originate action for lower-status personnel. He found a number of instances in which the initiating of action by lower-status people (at the time of his study, mostly female workers) created a conflict between formal and informal status systems. In one instance he cited, waitresses were passing their customers' orders directly on to countermen—which meant that low-status servers were initiating action for high-status cooks. By the simple addition of an aluminum spindle to which the order could be hooked, a buffer was created between the lower-status waitresses and the higher-status countermen, allowing the latter to initiate action on orders when they felt ready.

Whyte also noted that in the kitchen, supply men secured food supplies from the chefs. This was, in effect, a case of low-skilled employees initiating action to be taken by high-skilled employees. Conflict was stimulated when supply men, either explicitly or implicitly, urged the chefs to "get a move on." However, Whyte observed that one supply man had little trouble with the chefs because he gave the order and asked that the chef call him when it was ready, thus reversing the initiating process. In his analysis, Whyte suggested several changes in procedures that aligned interactions more closely with the accepted status hierarchy and resulted in substantial improvements in worker relations and effectiveness.

Status and Norms. Status has been shown to have some interesting effects on the power of norms and pressures to conform. For instance, high-status members of groups often are given more freedom to deviate from norms than are other group members.[24] High-status people also are better able to resist conformity pressures than their lower-status peers. An individual who is highly valued by a group but who doesn't much need or care about the social rewards the group provides is particularly able to pay minimal attention to conformity norms.[25]

The previous findings explain why many star athletes, famous actors, top-performing salespeople, and outstanding academics seem oblivious to appearance or social norms that constrain their peers. As high-status individuals, they're given a wider range of discretion. But this is true only as long as the high-status person's activities aren't severely detrimental to group goal achievement.[26]

Status Equity. It is important for group members to believe that the status hierarchy is equitable. When inequity is perceived, it creates disequilibrium that results in various types of corrective behaviour.[27]

The concept of equity presented in Chapter 5 applies to status. People expect rewards to be proportionate to costs incurred. If Isaac and Anne are the two finalists for the head-nurse position in a hospital, and it is clear that Isaac has more seniority and better preparation for assuming the promotion, Anne will view the selection of Isaac to be equitable. However, if Anne is chosen because she is the daughter-in-law of the hospital director, Isaac will

believe that an injustice has been committed. The trappings that go with formal positions are also important elements in maintaining equity. When we believe there is an inequity between the perceived ranking of an individual and the status accoutrements that the person is given by the organization, we are experiencing status incongruence. Examples of this kind of incongruence are the more desirable office location being held by a lower-ranking individual and paid country-club memberships being provided by the company for division managers but not for vice-presidents. Pay incongruence has long been a problem in the insurance industry, where top sales agents often earn two to five times more than senior corporate executives. The result is that insurance companies find it difficult to entice successful agents into management positions. Our point is that employees expect the things an individual has and receives to be congruent with his or her status.

Groups generally agree within themselves on status criteria, and hence, there is usually high concurrence in group rankings of individuals. However, individuals can find themselves in conflict when they move between groups whose status criteria are different or when they join groups whose members have heterogeneous backgrounds. For instance, business executives may use personal income or the growth rate of their companies as determinants of status. Government bureaucrats may use the size of their budgets. Professional employees and entrepreneurs may use the degree of autonomy that comes with their job assignment. Blue-collar workers may use years of seniority. In groups composed of heterogeneous individuals or when heterogeneous groups are forced to be interdependent, status differences may initiate conflict as the group attempts to reconcile and align the differing hierarchies. As we'll see in the next chapter, this can be a particular problem when management creates teams composed of employees from across varied functions within the organization.

SIZE Does the size of a group affect the group's overall behaviour? The answer to this question is a definite "yes," but the effect depends on what dependent variables you look at.[28]

The evidence indicates, for instance, that smaller groups are faster at completing tasks than are larger ones. However, if the group is engaged in problem solving, large groups consistently get better marks than their smaller counterparts. Translating these results into specific numbers is a bit more hazardous, but we can offer some parameters. Large groups—with a dozen or more members—are good for gaining diverse input. So if the goal of the group is fact finding, larger groups should be more effective. On the other hand, smaller groups are better at doing something productive with that input. Groups of approximately seven members, therefore, tend to be more effective for taking action.

One of the most important findings related to the size of a group has been labelled **social loafing**. Social loafing is the tendency for individuals to expend less effort when working collectively than when working individually.[29] It directly challenges the logic that the productivity of the group as a whole should at least equal the sum of the productivity of each individual in that group.

A common stereotype about groups is that the sense of team spirit spurs individual effort and enhances the group's overall productivity. In the late 1920s, a German psychologist named Ringelmann compared the results of individual and group performance on a rope-pulling task.[30] He expected that the group's effort would be equal to the sum of the efforts of individu-

social loafing
The tendency for individuals to expend less effort when working collectively than when working individually.

als within the group. That is, three people pulling together should exert three times as much pull on the rope as one person, and eight people should exert eight times as much pull. Ringelmann's results, however, did not confirm his expectations. Groups of three people exerted a force only 2.5 times the average individual performance. Groups of eight collectively achieved less than four times the solo rate.

Replications of Ringelmann's research with similar tasks have generally supported his findings.[31] Increases in group size are inversely related to individual performance. More may be better in the sense that the total productivity of a group of four is greater than that of one or two people, but the individual productivity of each group member declines.

What causes this social loafing effect? It may be due to a belief that others in the group are not carrying their fair share. If you view others as lazy or inept, you can re-establish equity by reducing your effort. Another explanation is the dispersion of responsibility. Because the results of the group cannot be attributed to any single person, the relationship between an individual's input and the group's output is clouded. In such situations, individuals may be tempted to become "free riders" and coast on the group's efforts. In other words, there will be a reduction in efficiency where individuals believe that their contribution cannot be measured.

The implications for OB of this effect on work groups are significant. Where managers utilize collective work situations to enhance morale and teamwork, they must also provide means by which individual efforts can be identified. If this is not done, management must weigh the potential losses in productivity from using groups against any possible gains in worker satisfaction.[32] However, this conclusion has a Western bias. It's consistent with individualistic cultures, such as Canada and the United States, that are dominated by self-interest. It is not consistent with collective societies where individuals are motivated by in-group goals. For instance, in studies comparing employees from the United States with employees from the People's Republic of China and Israel (both collectivist societies), the Chinese and Israelis showed no propensity to engage in social loafing. In fact, the Chinese and Israelis actually performed better in a group than when working alone.[33]

The research on group size leads us to two additional conclusions: (1) groups with an odd number of members tend to be preferable to those with an even number; and (2) groups composed of five or seven members do a fairly good job of exercising the best elements of both small and large groups.[34] Having an odd number of members eliminates the possibility of ties when votes are taken. And groups composed of five or seven members are large enough to form a majority and allow for diverse input, yet small enough to avoid the negative outcomes often associated with large groups, such as domination by a few members, development of subgroups, inhibited participation by some members, and excessive time taken to reach a decision.

COMPOSITION Most group activities require a variety of skills and knowledge. Given this requirement, it would be reasonable to conclude that heterogeneous groups—those composed of dissimilar individuals—would be more likely to have diverse abilities and information and should be more effective. Research studies generally substantiate this conclusion.[35]

When a group is heterogeneous in terms of gender, personalities, opinions, abilities, skills, and perspectives, there is an increased probability that

the group will possess the needed characteristics to complete its tasks effectively.[36] The group may be more conflict laden and less expedient as diverse positions are introduced and assimilated, but the evidence generally supports the conclusion that heterogeneous groups perform more effectively than do those that are homogeneous. But what about diversity created by racial or national differences? The evidence indicates that these elements of diversity interfere with group processes, at least in the short term.[37] Cultural diversity seems to be an asset on tasks that call for a variety of viewpoints. But culturally heterogeneous groups have more difficulty in learning to work with each other and solving problems. The good news is that these difficulties seem to dissipate over time. While newly formed culturally diverse groups underperform newly formed culturally homogeneous groups, the differences disappear after about three months. The reason is that it takes diverse groups a while to learn how to work through disagreements and different approaches to solving problems. In the Case Incident you are asked to consider some of the interpersonal issues that arise when groups confront diversity considerations.

An offshoot of the composition issue has recently received a great deal of attention by group researchers. This is the degree to which members of a group share a common demographic attribute, such as age, sex, race, educational level, or length of service in the organization, and the impact of this attribute on turnover. We call this variable **group demography**. Let's work through the logic of group demography, review the evidence, and then consider the implications.

Groups and organizations are composed of **cohorts**, which we define as individuals who hold a common attribute. For instance, everyone born in 1960 is the same age. This means they also have shared common experiences. People born in 1980 have experienced the information revolution, but not the Vietnam War. People born in 1945 shared Trudeaumania, Quebec's Quiet Revolution, and the national euphoria of Expo 67, but not the Great Depression. Women in Canadian organizations today who were born before 1945 matured prior to the women's movement and have had substantially different experiences than women born after 1960. Group demography, therefore, suggests that such attributes as age or the date that someone joins a specific work group or organization should help us to predict turnover. Es-

group demography
The degree to which members of a group share a common demographic attribute, such as age, sex, race, educational level, or length of service in the organization, and the impact of this attribute on turnover.

cohorts
Individuals who, as part of a group, hold a common attribute.

Pepsi-Cola International's marketing team members in Great Britain share a common demographic attribute—they're all young. To execute its plan of increasing international soft drink sales, Pepsi is banking on youthful cohorts who have a passion for change, can embrace risk, act quickly, innovate constantly, and aren't afraid to break the rules of soft drink marketing.

PepsiCo
http://www.pepsiworld.com/
index2.html

sentially, the logic goes like this: Turnover will be greater among those with dissimilar experiences because communication is more difficult. Conflict and power struggles are more likely, and more severe when they occur. The increased conflict makes group membership less attractive, so employees are more likely to quit. Similarly, the losers in a power struggle are more apt to leave voluntarily or be forced out.

Several studies have sought to test this thesis, and the evidence is quite encouraging.[38] For example, in departments or separate work groups where a large portion of members entered at the same time, there is considerably more turnover among those outside this cohort. Also, where there are large gaps between cohorts, turnover is higher. People who enter a group or an organization together, or at approximately the same time, are more likely to associate with one another, have a similar perspective on the group or organization, and thus be more likely to stay. On the other hand, discontinuities or bulges in the group's date-of-entry distribution are likely to result in a higher turnover rate within that group.

The implication of this line of inquiry is that the composition of a group may be an important predictor of turnover. Differences per se may not predict turnover. But large differences within a single group will lead to turnover. If everyone is only moderately dissimilar from everyone else in a group, the feelings of being an outsider are reduced. So, it's the degree of dispersion on an attribute, rather than the level, that matters most. We can speculate that variance within a group with respect to attributes other than date of entry, such as social background, gender differences, and levels of education, might similarly create discontinuities or bulges in the distribution that will encourage some members to leave. To extend this idea further, the fact that a group member is a female may, in itself, mean little in predicting turnover. In fact, if the work group is composed of nine women and one man, we'd be more likely to predict that the lone male would leave. In the executive ranks of organizations, however, where females are in the minority, we would predict that this minority status would increase the likelihood that female managers would quit.

cohesiveness
Degree to which group members are attracted to each other and are motivated to stay in the group.

COHESIVENESS Groups differ in their **cohesiveness**; that is, the degree to which members are attracted to each other and are motivated to stay in the group.[39] For instance, some work groups are cohesive because the members have spent a great deal of time together, the group's small size facilitates high interaction, or the group has experienced external threats that have brought members close together. Cohesiveness is important because it has been found to be related to the group's productivity.[40]

Studies consistently show that the relationship of cohesiveness and productivity depends on the performance-related norms established by the group. If performance-related norms are high (for example, high output, quality work, cooperation with individuals outside the group), a cohesive group will be more productive than will a less cohesive group. If cohesiveness is high and performance norms are low, productivity will be low. If cohesiveness is low and performance norms are high, productivity increases but less than in the high cohesiveness-high norms situation. Where cohesiveness and performance-related norms are both low, productivity will tend to fall into the low-to-moderate range. These conclusions are summarized in Exhibit 7-7.

We consider how to increase group cohesion later in the chapter.

Exhibit 7-7
Relationship Between Group Cohesiveness, Performance Norms, and Productivity

	Cohesiveness	
	High	Low
Performance norms — High	High productivity	Moderate productivity
Performance norms — Low	Low productivity	Moderate to low productivity

Group Processes

The next component of our group behaviour model considers the processes that go on within a work group—the communication patterns used by members for information exchanges, group decision processes, leader behaviour, power dynamics, conflict interactions, and the like. Chapters 9 through 13 elaborate on many of these processes.

Why are processes important to understanding work group behaviour? One way to answer this question is to return to the topic of social loafing. We found that 1+1+1 doesn't necessarily add up to three. In group tasks where each member's contribution is not clearly visible, individuals tend to decrease their effort. Social loafing, in other words, illustrates a process loss as a result of using groups. But group processes can also produce positive results. That is, groups can create outputs greater than the sum of their inputs. Exhibit 7-8 illustrates how group processes can impact a group's actual effectiveness.[41]

Synergy is a term used in biology that refers to an action of two or more substances that results in an effect that is different from the individual summation of the substances. We can use the concept to better understand group processes.

Social loafing, for instance, represents negative synergy. The whole is less than the sum of its parts. On the other hand, research teams are often used in research laboratories because they can draw on the diverse skills of various individuals to produce more meaningful research as a group than could be generated by all of the researchers working independently. That is, they produce positive synergy. Their process gains exceed their process losses.

Another line of research that helps us to better understand group processes is the social facilitation effect.[42] Have you ever noticed that performing a task in front of others can have a positive or negative effect on your performance? For instance, you privately practise a complex springboard dive at your home pool for weeks. Then you do the dive in front of a group of friends and you do it better than ever. Or you practise a speech in private and finally get it down perfectly, but you "bomb" when you have to give the speech in public.

The **social facilitation effect** refers to this tendency for performance to improve or decline in response to the presence of others. While this effect is not entirely a group phenomenon—people can work in the presence of others and not be members of a group—the group situation is more likely to provide the conditions for social facilitation to occur. The research on social facilitation tells us that the performance of simple, routine tasks tends to be speeded up and made more accurate by the presence of others. Where the work is more complex, requiring closer attention, the presence of others is likely to have a negative effect on performance.[43] So what are the implications of this research in terms of managing process gains and losses? The implications relate to learning and training. People seem to perform better on a task in the presence of others if that task is very well learned, but poorly if it is not well learned. So process gains will be maximized by training people for simple tasks in groups, while training people for complex tasks in individual private practice sessions.

synergy
An action of two or more substances that results in an effect that is different from the individual summation of the substances.

social facilitation effect
The tendency for performance to improve or decline in response to the presence of others.

Exhibit 7-8
Effects of Group Processes

| Potential group effectiveness | + | Process gains | − | Process losses | = | Actual group effectiveness |

Group Tasks

Imagine, for a moment, that there are two groups at a major oil company. The job of the first is to consider possible location sites for a new refinery. The decision is going to affect people in many areas of the company—production, engineering, marketing, distribution, purchasing, real estate development, and the like—so key people from each of these areas will need to provide input into the decision. The job of the second group is to coordinate the building of the refinery after the site has been selected, the design finalized, and the financial arrangements completed. Research on group effectiveness tells us that management would be well advised to use a larger group for the first task than for the second.[44] The reason is that large groups facilitate pooling of information. The addition of a diverse perspective to a problem-solving committee typically results in a process gain. But when a group's task is coordinating and implementing a decision, the process loss created by each additional member's presence is likely to be greater than the process gain he or she makes. So the size-performance relationship is moderated by the group's task requirements.

The preceding conclusions can be extended: The impact of group processes on the group's performance and member satisfaction is also moderated by the tasks that the group is doing. The evidence indicates that the complexity and interdependence of tasks influence the group's effectiveness.[45]

Tasks can be generalized as either simple or complex. Complex tasks are ones that tend to be novel or nonroutine. Simple ones are routine and standardized. We would hypothesize that the more complex the task, the more the group will benefit from discussion among members on alternative work methods. If the task is simple, group members don't need to discuss such alternatives. They can rely on standardized operating procedures for doing the job. Similarly, if there is a high degree of interdependence among the tasks that group members must perform, they'll need to interact more. Effective communication and minimal levels of conflict, therefore, should be more relevant to group performance when tasks are interdependent.

These conclusions are consistent with what we know about information-processing capacity and uncertainty.[46] Tasks that have higher uncertainty—those that are complex and interdependent—require more information processing. This, in turn, puts more importance on group processes. So just because a group is characterized by poor communication, weak leadership, high levels of conflict, and the like, it doesn't necessarily mean that it will be low performing. If the group's tasks are simple and require little interdependence among members, the group still may be effective.

Can We Build a Better Working Group?

Working in groups is probably an inevitable life experience, even for people who prefer to work alone. There are always student groups, task forces, and neighbourhood associations in addition to all of the workplace demands for working in a group. Therefore, it might be helpful to think a little about how to improve group performance and interaction. The From Concepts to Skills feature for this chapter gives guidelines for conducting a group meeting. These will help in many instances to keep discussions on track.

Beyond meetings, however, there are factors for both organizations and individuals to consider with respect to creating conditions that will lead

FROM CONCEPTS TO SKILLS

Conducting a Group Meeting

Group meetings have a reputation for inefficiency. For instance, noted Canadian-born economist John Kenneth Galbraith has said, "Meetings are indispensable when you don't want to do anything."

When you're responsible for conducting a meeting, what can you do to make it more efficient and effective? Follow these 12 steps:

1. *Prepare a meeting agenda.* An agenda defines what you hope to accomplish at the meeting. It should state the meeting's purpose; who will be in attendance; what, if any, preparation is required of each participant; a detailed list of items to be covered; the specific time and location of the meeting; and a specific finishing time.

2. *Distribute the agenda in advance.* Participants should have the agenda sufficiently in advance so they can adequately prepare for the meeting.

3. *Consult with participants before the meeting.* An unprepared participant can't contribute to his or her full potential. It is your responsibility to ensure that members are prepared, so check with them ahead of time.

4. *Get participants to go over the agenda.* The first thing to do at the meeting is to have participants review the agenda, make any changes, then approve the final agenda.

5. *Establish specific time parameters.* Meetings should begin on time and have a specific time for completion. It is your responsibility to specify these time parameters and to hold to them.

6. *Maintain focused discussion.* It is your responsibility to give direction to the discussion; to keep it focused on the issues; and to minimize interruptions, disruptions, and irrelevant comments.

7. *Encourage and support participation of all members.* To maximize the effectiveness of problem-oriented meetings, each participant must be encouraged to contribute. Quiet or reserved personalities need to be drawn out so their ideas can be heard.

8. *Maintain a balanced style.* The effective group leader pushes when necessary and is passive when need be.

9. *Encourage the clash of ideas.* You need to encourage different points of view, critical thinking, and constructive disagreement.

10. *Discourage the clash of personalities.* An effective meeting is characterized by the critical assessment of ideas, not attacks on people. When running a meeting, you must quickly intercede to stop personal attacks or other forms of verbal insult.

11. *Be an effective listener.* You need to listen with intensity, empathy, objectivity, and do whatever is necessary to get the full intended meaning from each participant's comments.

12. *Bring proper closure.* You should close a meeting by summarizing the group's accomplishments; clarifying what actions, if any, need to follow the meeting; and allocating follow-up assignments. If any decisions are made, you also need to determine who will be responsible for communicating and implementing them.

Source: S.P. Robbins and P.L. Hunsaker, *Training in Interpersonal Skills*, 2nd ed. (Upper Saddle River, NJ: Prentice Hall, 1996), pp. 168–84.

groups to engage in higher productivity. These include the type of tasks assigned to a group, specific organizational supports, and ways that groups can increase their cohesiveness.

Assigning Appropriate Tasks

Perhaps the first consideration for group effectiveness is the type of task that the group is asked to perform. Some tasks are simply more inspiring to

groups than others, and therefore will result in a better work product. Richard Hackman (whose Hackman-Oldham model we will consider in Chapter 15) has outlined the following conditions under which we would expect groups to work "especially hard":[47]

- The group task requires members to use a variety of relatively high-level skills.
- The group task is a whole and meaningful piece of work with a visible outcome.
- The outcomes of the group's work on the task have significant consequences for other people (e.g., other organization members or external clients).
- The task provides group members with substantial autonomy for deciding about how they do the work—in effect, the group "owns" the task and is responsible for the work outcomes.
- Work on the task generates regular, trustworthy feedback about how well the group is performing.

This chapter's CBC Video Case illustrates ways that groups can figure out the necessary tasks, and then assign them.

Providing Organizational Support

Organizations can do a variety of things to provide support for groups to work together. These include the following:[48]

- *Assign appropriate people to the group.* Members of effective teams have the technical and interpersonal skills to function well together. It is often thought that having technical skills is enough, but for groups to work together they also need to trust each other. This trust leads to open and supportive relationships and a "we" feeling.
- *Provide appropriate group training.* Individuals do not necessarily know how to function well in a group. Therefore organizations should provide programs for all members to improve technical and interpersonal skills. This should be part of the learning process we discussed in Chapter 2.
- *Provide adequate and timely information.* Managers should ensure that employees have the information they need to carry out their group tasks. When information is not available or forthcoming, managers should also explain this to the employees.
- *Give challenging, specific performance objectives.* We noted when discussing goal setting that individuals do well when faced with moderately difficult goals. The same is true for groups. Groups respond to the challenge of meeting deadlines, knowing what quality needs to be achieved, and so on. However, it is also important that the task be interesting and meaningful, as we noted above.
- *Give rewards for excellent performance.* We noted in Chapters 5 and 6 that people tend to engage in activities that are rewarded. The same is true for groups. The nature of the rewards can vary, from recognition to more specific tangible items. It is also the case, as we discussed in Chapter 6, that a motivating task is often a reward in itself.
- *Direct rewards and objectives to the group level.* If an organization wants a set of individuals to function as a group, then the activities and the rewards must be group-based. Organizational reward systems

often focus on individuals, which creates an incentive for individuals to focus on their own needs, rather than those of the group.

Building Group Cohesiveness

When teams function well, everyone is energized and works toward the task. While organizations can provide tasks that groups find challenging and motivating, and can provide some of the structural support needed to do the task appropriately, the group itself must create an internal climate that makes participating in the group worthwhile both from an organizational and a personal perspective. Parker identifies 12 characteristics that he believes differentiate between effective and ineffective teams:[49]

- *Clear purpose.* The group has clear and jointly agreed-upon goals.

- *Participation.* Group members share information, and all contributions are respected and valued.

- *Civilized disagreement.* Conflict will naturally occur in most groups. Effective groups learn to manage the conflict and develop mechanisms to resolve it.

- *Open communications.* Group members communicate openly with each other, helping to build trust among group members. Group members use both formal and informal opportunities to communicate.

- *Listening.* Group members listen effectively—not only to understand the information presented, but also to achieve interpersonal understanding and empathy.

- *Informal climate.* The group operates in a comfortable and relaxed atmosphere. This leads to more open communication as well as flexibility.

- *Consensus decisions.* The group allows people to express opinions, reservations, disagreements, and then comes together for a solution that the entire group can support. Everyone does not necessarily have to agree on the solution itself, but they do need to agree that the solution is supported by the group as a whole. In other words, "A consensus is reached when all members can say they either agree with the decision or have had their 'day in court' and were unable to convince the others of their viewpoint. In the final analysis, everyone agrees to support the outcome."[50]

- *Clear roles and work assignments.* For the group to function there must be clear agreement about the roles, responsibilities, and assignments of group members. When these are unclear, conflict often occurs.

- *Shared leadership.* Members of the group work together, not burdening one person with all of the responsibility for how the team functions.

- *Style diversity.* Groups accept that there are differences in their members, and learn to use these differences in advantageous ways.

- *External relationships.* The group collects information from a variety of sources, rather than simply relying on its own resources.

- *Self-assessment.* Groups need to do periodic self-assessments to examine how well they are doing. This gives team members the opportunity to ask, "How well are we doing?", "What are we doing right?",

"How can we improve our performance?", "Are there any interpersonal problems?", and "Is everyone contributing adequately to the group's performance?"

By going through a checklist such as the above, groups have an opportunity to examine themselves as they work toward their goals. You might consider, when working in your next student group, working on the items above, so that you could improve your group's performance.

Intergroup Relations

So far we have dealt with intragroup activities, but we need to understand relationships between groups as well as within groups.[51] In this section, we'll focus on intergroup relationships. These are the coordinated bridges that link two distinct organizational groups.[52] As we'll show, the efficiency and quality of these relationships can have a significant bearing on either or both of the groups' performances and their members' satisfaction.

Factors Affecting Intergroup Relations

Successful intergroup performance is a function of several factors. The umbrella concept that overrides these factors is *coordination*. In Exhibit 7-9, Cathy describes the difficulties accounting is having in obtaining the expense reports from the media department. Conflicts such as these arise because of coordination difficulties. Each of the following can affect efforts at coordination.

INTERDEPENDENCE The first overriding question we need to ask is: Do the groups really need coordination? The answer lies in determining the degree of interdependence that exists between the groups. That is, do the groups

Exhibit 7-9

**Exhibit 7-10
Types of Interdependence**

Pooled

Sequential

Reciprocal

pooled interdependence
Relationship between two groups that function with relative independence but their combined output contributes to the organization's overall goals.

sequential interdependence
Relationship where one group depends on another for its input, but the dependency is only one way.

reciprocal interdependence
Relationship among groups that exchange inputs and outputs.

Corel Corporation
http://www.corel.com

In any organization, departments have to interact with each other in order to get work done. The extent of those interactions, and the dependencies they create, varies however. At Ottawa-based Corel Corporation the product development department and the shipping department face pooled interdependence.

depend on each other, and if so, how much? The three most frequently identified types of interdependence are pooled, sequential, and reciprocal.[53] Each requires an increasing degree of group interaction (see Exhibit 7-10).

When two groups function with relative independence but their combined output contributes to the organization's overall goals, **pooled interdependence** exists. At a firm such as Ottawa-based Corel Corporation, for instance, this would describe the relationship between the product development department and the shipping department. Both are necessary if Corel is to develop new products and get those products into consumers' hands, but each is essentially separate and distinct from the other. All other things being equal, coordination requirements between groups linked by pooled interdependence are less than with sequential or reciprocal interdependence.

The purchasing and parts assembly departments at Corel are **sequentially interdependent**. One group—software developers—depends on another—purchasing—for its inputs, but the dependency is only one way. Purchasing is not directly dependent on software development for its inputs. In sequential interdependence, if the group that provides the input doesn't perform its job properly, the group that is dependent on the first will be significantly affected. In our Corel example, if purchasing fails to order new computers when the developers need them, then the software development department may have to slow down or temporarily close its development operations.

The most complex form of interdependence is **reciprocal**. In these instances, groups exchange inputs and outputs. For example, sales and product development groups at Corel Corporation are reciprocally interdependent. Salespeople, who are in contact with customers, acquire information about their future needs. Sales then relays this information to product development so they can create new computer products. The long-term implications are that if product development doesn't develop new products that potential customers find desirable, sales personnel will not get orders. So there is high interdependence—product development needs sales for information on customer needs so it can create successful new products, and sales de-

pends on the product development group to create products that it can successfully sell. This high degree of dependency translates into greater interaction and increased coordination demands.

TASK UNCERTAINTY The next coordination question is: What type of tasks are the groups involved in? For simplicity's sake, we can think of a group's tasks as ranging from highly routine to highly nonroutine.[54] (See Exhibit 7-11.)

Highly routine tasks have little variation. Problems that group members face tend to contain few exceptions and are easy to analyze. Such group activities lend themselves to standardized operating procedures. For example, manufacturing tasks in a tire factory are made up of highly routine tasks. At the other extreme are nonroutine tasks. These are activities that are unstructured, with many exceptions and problems that are hard to analyze. Many of the tasks undertaken by marketing research and product development groups are of this variety. Of course, many group tasks fall somewhere in the middle or combine both routine and nonroutine tasks.

The key to **task uncertainty** is that nonroutine tasks require considerably more processing of information. Tasks with low uncertainty tend to be standardized. Further, groups that do standardized tasks do not have to interact much with other groups. In contrast, groups that undertake tasks that are high in uncertainty face problems that require custom responses. This, in turn, leads to a need for more and better information. We would expect the people in the marketing research department at Bombardier's to interact much more with other departments and constituencies—marketing, sales, product design, tire dealers, advertising agencies, and the like—than would people in Bombardier's manufacturing group.

TIME AND GOAL ORIENTATION How different are the groups in terms of their members' background and thinking? This is the third question relevant to the degree of coordination necessary between groups. Research demonstrates that a work group's perceptions of what is important may differ on the basis of the time frame that governs their work and their goal orientation.[55] This can make it difficult for groups with different perceptions to work together.

Why might work groups have different time and goal orientations? Top management historically divided work up by putting common tasks into common functional groups and assigning these groups specific goals. Then people were hired with the appropriate background and skills to complete the tasks and help the group achieve its goals. This differentiation of tasks and hiring of specialists made it easier to coordinate intragroup activities, but made it increasingly difficult to coordinate interaction between groups.

To illustrate how orientations differ between work groups, manufacturing personnel have a short-term time focus. They worry about today's pro-

task uncertainty
The greater the uncertainty in a task, the more customized the response. Conversely, low uncertainty encompasses routine tasks with standardized activities.

Bombardier Inc.
http://www.challenger.
bombardier.com/

Exhibit 7-11 **Task Continuum**		
High	**Degree of routinization**	**Low**
Low ⟵——————— Task uncertainty ———————⟶		High
High ⟵——————— Standardization ———————⟶		Low
Low ⟵——————— Information requirements ———————⟶		High

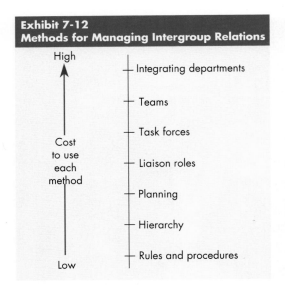

Exhibit 7-12
Methods for Managing Intergroup Relations

High

Cost
to use
each
method

Low

— Integrating departments

— Teams

— Task forces

— Liaison roles

— Planning

— Hierarchy

— Rules and procedures

duction schedule and this week's productivity. In contrast, people in research and development focus on the long run. They're concerned about developing new products that may not be produced for several years. Similarly, work groups often have different goal orientations. As we noted earlier in the chapter, sales typically want to sell anything and everything. Goals centre on sales volume and increasing revenue and market share. Although customers' ability to pay for the sales made by the sales group is not its concern, the people in the credit department want to ensure that sales are made only to creditworthy customers. These differences in goals often make it difficult for sales and credit to communicate. It also makes it harder to coordinate their interactions.

Methods for Managing Intergroup Relations

What coordination methods are available for managing intergroup relations? There are a number of options; the seven most frequently used are identified in Exhibit 7-12. These seven are listed on a continuum, in order of increasing cost.[56] They also are cumulative in the sense that succeeding methods higher on the continuum add to, rather than are substituted for, lower methods. In most organizations, the simpler methods listed at the lower end of the continuum are used in conjunction with the more complex methods listed at the upper end. For instance, if a manager is using teams to coordinate intergroup relations, that manager is also likely to be using rules and procedures.

RULES AND PROCEDURES The most simple and least costly method for managing intergroup relations is to establish, in advance, a set of formalized rules and procedures that will specify how group members are to interact with each other. In large organizations, for example, standard operating procedures are likely to specify that when additional permanent staff are needed in any department, a "request for new staff" form is to be filed with the human resources department. Upon receipt of this form, human resources begins a standardized process to fill the request. Notice that such rules and procedures minimize the need for interaction and information flow between the departments or work groups. The major drawback to this method is that it works well only when intergroup activities can be anticipated in advance and when they recur often enough to justify establishing rules and procedures for handling them. Under conditions of high uncertainty and change, rules and procedures alone may be inadequate to guarantee effective coordination of intergroup relations.

HIERARCHY If rules and procedures are inadequate, the use of the organization's hierarchy becomes the primary method for managing intergroup relations. This means that coordination is achieved by referring problems to a common superior higher in the organization. In a university, if the chairpersons for the English and speech communication departments can't agree on where the new courses in debate will be taught, they can take the issue to the dean for a resolution. The major limitation to this method is that it increases demands on the common superior's time. If all differences were resolved by this means, the organization's chief executive would be overwhelmed with resolving intergroup problems, leaving little time for other matters.

Pharmaceutical giant Merck & Co. created a human resources task force after it acquired Medco Containment Services, a pharmacy benefits management firm. Task force members, including Katherine Harrison of Merck (left) and Cynthia Gilhooly of Medco, worked on many issues related to the firms' cultural, managerial, and business integration. Members of the temporary team shared information about compensation and benefits, employee relations, employee development, management approaches, and work environments.

PLANNING The next step up the continuum is the use of planning to facilitate coordination. If each work group has specific goals for which it is responsible, then each knows what it is supposed to do. Intergroup tasks that create problems are resolved in terms of the goals and contributions of each group. In a provincial motor-vehicle office, each of the various work groups—testing and examinations, driving licences, vehicle registration, cashiering, and the like—has a set of goals that defines its area of responsibility and acts to reduce intergroup conflicts. Planning tends to break down as a coordination device where work groups don't have clearly defined goals or where the volume of contacts between groups is high.

LIAISON ROLES Liaison roles are specialized roles designed to facilitate communication between two interdependent work units. In one organization, where accountants and engineers had a long history of conflict, management hired an engineer with an MBA degree and several years of experience in public accounting. This person could speak the language of both groups and understood their problems. After this new liaison role was established, conflicts that had previously made it difficult for the accounting and engineering departments to coordinate their activities were significantly reduced. The major drawback to this coordination device is that there are limits to any liaison person's ability to handle information flow between interacting groups, especially where the groups are large and interactions are frequent.

TASK FORCES A task force is a temporary group composed of representatives from a number of departments. It exists only long enough to solve the problem it was created to handle. After a solution is reached, task-force participants return to their normal duties.

Task forces are an excellent device for coordinating activities when the number of interacting groups is more than two or three. For example, when Audi began receiving numerous customer complaints about its cars accelerating when the transmission was put in reverse, the company created a task force to assess the problem and develop a solution. Representatives from de-

sign, production, legal, and engineering departments were brought together. After a solution was determined, the task force was disbanded.

TEAMS As tasks become more complex, additional problems arise during the act of execution. Previous coordination devices are no longer adequate. If the delays in decisions become long, lines of communication become extended, and top managers are forced to spend more time on day-to-day operations, the next response is to use permanent teams. They are typically formed around frequently occurring problems—with team members maintaining a responsibility to both their primary functional department and to the team. When the team has accomplished its task, each member returns full time to his or her functional assignment.

Seattle-based Boeing uses a cross-functional team to coordinate investigations of air crashes. When a Boeing aircraft is involved in an accident, the company immediately dispatches a team comprising members from various departments—including design, production, legal, and public relations. Whenever an accident occurs, designated members of the team immediately drop their current departmental tasks, go directly to the accident site, and join the other team members to begin their investigation.

Boeing
http://www.boeing.com/

INTEGRATING DEPARTMENTS When intergroup relations become too complex to be coordinated through plans, task forces, teams, and the like, organizations may create integrating departments. These are permanent departments with members formally assigned to the task of integration between two or more groups. While they're permanent and expensive to maintain, they tend to be used when an organization has a number of groups with conflicting goals, nonroutine problems, and intergroup decisions that have a significant impact on the organization's total operations. They are also excellent devices to manage intergroup conflicts for organizations facing long-term retrenchments. When organizations are forced to shrink in size—as has recently occurred in a wide range of industries—conflicts over how cuts are to be distributed and how the smaller resource pie is to be allocated become major and ongoing dilemmas. The use of integrating departments in such cases can be an effective means for managing these intergroup relations.

Effectively Managing Intergroup Relations

It may help to put this discussion in perspective to consider methods for managing intergroup relations in terms of effectiveness.

Researchers state that the effectiveness of intergroup relations can be evaluated in terms of efficiency and quality.[57] Efficiency considers the costs to the organization of transforming an intergroup conflict into actions agreed to by the groups. Quality refers to the degree to which the outcome results in a well-defined and enduring exchange agreement. Using these definitions, the seven methods introduced in this section were presented, in order, from most efficient to least efficient. That is, ignoring outcomes for a moment, rules and procedures are less costly to implement than hierarchy, hierarchy is less costly than planning, and so forth. But, of course, keeping costs down is only one consideration. The other element of effectiveness is quality, or how well the coordination device works in facilitating interaction and reducing dysfunctional conflicts. As we've shown, the least costly alternative may not be adequate. So managers have a number of options at their disposal for managing intergroup relations. But since they tend to be cumulative, with costs rising as you move up the continuum in Exhibit 7-12, the

most effective coordination device will be the one lowest on the continuum that facilitates an enduring integrative exchange.

HR IMPLICATIONS

Selecting Organizational Members

This chapter focused on people working in groups and the problems they encounter. It also noted some of the pros and cons of diversity in organizations. One of the tasks of the HR manager is selecting (or hiring) the people who will work for the organization. While fit with groups already in the organization may not be the sole criterion used to hire a new employee, it is certainly one of the considerations. Below we describe the process of selection in the organization.

Selection Practices

The objective of effective selection is to match individual characteristics (ability, experience, and so on) with the requirements of the job.[1] If the job also requires that the individual work closely as part of a team, then interpersonal characteristics may also become important. When management fails to get a proper match, both employee performance and satisfaction suffer.

Selection Devices

Organizations can use application forms, interviews, employment tests, background checks, and reference letters to obtain information about a job applicant. This information can help the organization determine whether the applicant's skills, knowledge, and abilities are appropriate for the job in question. In this section, we review the more important of these selection devices—interviews, written tests, and performance simulation tests.

Interviews Do you know anyone who has received a job without at least one interview? You may have an acquaintance who got a part-time or summer job through a close friend or relative without having to go through an interview, but such instances are rare. Of all the selection devices that organizations use to differentiate candidates, the interview continues to be the one most frequently used.[2]

The interview also seems to carry a great deal of weight. That is, not only is it widely used, but its results also tend to have a disproportionate amount of influence on the selection decision. The candidate who performs poorly in the employment interview is likely to be cut from the applicant pool, regardless of his or her experience, test scores, or reference letters. Conversely, "all too often, the person most polished in job-seeking techniques, particularly those used in the interview process, is the one hired, even though he or she may not be the best candidate for the position."[3]

These findings are important because of the unstructured manner in which the selection interview is frequently conducted. The unstructured interview—short in duration, casual, and made up of random questions—has been proven to be an ineffective selection device.[4] The data gathered from such interviews are typically biased and often unrelated to future job performance. Without structure, a number of biases can distort results. These biases include interviewers tending to favour applicants who share their attitudes, giving unduly high weight to negative information, and allowing the order in which applicants are interviewed to influence evaluations.[5] By having interviewers use a standardized set of questions, providing interviewers with a uniform method of recording information, and standardizing the rating of the applicant's qualifications, the variability in results across applicants is reduced and the validity of the interview as a selection device is greatly enhanced.

The evidence indicates that interviews are most valuable for assessing an applicant's intelligence, level of motivation, and interpersonal skills.[6] When these qualities are related to job performance, the validity of the interview as a selection device is increased. For example, these qualities have demonstrated relevance for performance in upper managerial positions. This may explain why applicants for senior management positions typically undergo dozens of interviews with executive recruiters, board members, and other company executives before a final decision is made. It

can also explain why organizations that design work around teams may similarly put applicants through an unusually large number of interviews.

Written Tests Typical written tests are tests of intelligence, aptitude, ability, interest, and integrity. Long popular as selection devices, they have generally declined in use since the late 1960s. The reason is that such tests have frequently been characterized as discriminatory, and many organizations have not validated, or cannot validate, such tests as being job related.

Tests in intellectual ability, spatial and mechanical ability, perceptual accuracy, and motor ability have shown to be moderately valid predictors for many semi-skilled and unskilled operative jobs in industrial organizations.[7] Intelligence tests have proven to be particularly good predictors for jobs that require cognitive complexity.[8] Japanese auto makers, when staffing plants in the United States, have relied heavily on written tests to predict candidates that will be high performers.[9] Getting a job with Toyota Canada, for instance, can take up to three days of testing and interviewing. Written tests typically focus on skills such as reading, mathematics, mechanical dexterity, and ability to work with others.

As ethical problems have increased in organizations, integrity tests have gained popularity. These are paper-and-pencil tests that measure factors such as dependability, carefulness, responsibility, and honesty. The evidence is impressive that these tests are powerful in predicting supervisory ratings of job performance and counterproductive employee behaviour on the job such as theft, discipline problems, and excessive absenteeism.[10]

Performance Simulation Tests What better way is there to find out if an applicant can do a job successfully than by having him or her do it? That's precisely the logic of performance simulation tests.

Performance simulation tests have increased in popularity during the past two decades. Undoubtedly the enthusiasm for these tests comes from the fact that they are based on job analysis data, and therefore, they more easily meet the requirement of job relatedness than do most written tests. Performance simulation tests are made up of actual job behaviours rather than surrogates, as are written tests.

The two best-known performance simulation tests are work sampling and assessment centres. The former is suited to routine jobs, whereas the latter is relevant for the selection of managerial personnel.

Work sampling is an effort to create a miniature replica of a job. Applicants demonstrate that they possess the necessary talents by actually doing the tasks. By carefully devising work samples based on job analysis data, the knowledge, skills, and abilities needed for each job are determined. Then each work sample element is matched with a corresponding job performance element. For instance, a work sample for a job where the employee has to use computer spreadsheet software would require the applicant to actually solve a problem using a spreadsheet.

The results from work sample experiments are impressive. Studies almost consistently demonstrate that work samples yield validities superior to written aptitude and personality tests.[11]

A more elaborate set of performance simulation tests, specifically designed to evaluate a candidate's managerial potential, is administered in **assessment centres**. In assessment centres, line executives, supervisors, and/or trained psychologists evaluate candidates as they undergo two to four days of exercises that simulate real problems that they would confront on the job. Based on a list of descriptive dimensions that the actual job incumbent has to meet, activities might include interviews, in-basket problem-solving exercises, group discussions, and business decision games. For instance, a candidate might be required to play the role of a manager who must decide how to respond to 10 memos in his or her in-basket within a two-hour period.

How valid is the assessment centre as a selection device? The evidence on the effectiveness of assessment centres is extremely impressive. They have consistently demonstrated results that predict later job performance in managerial positions.[12]

Sources:

1. See, for instance, C.T. Dortch, "Job-Person Match," *Personnel Journal*, June 1989, pp. 49–75; and S. Rynes and B. Gerhart, "Interviewer Assessments of Applicant 'Fit': An Exploratory Investigation," *Personnel Psychology*, Spring 1990, pp. 13–34.

2. R.L. Dipboye, *Selection Interviews: Process Perspectives* (Cincinnati: South-Western Publishing, 1992), p. 6; and J.E. Rigdon, "Talk Isn't Cheap," *Wall Street Journal*, February 27, 1995, p. R13.

3. T.J. Hanson and J.C. Balestreri-Spero, "An Alternative to Interviews," *Personnel Journal*, June 1985, p. 114.

4. See A.J. Huffcutt and W. Arthur Jr., "Hunter and Hunter (1984) Revisited: Interview Validity for Entry-Level Jobs," *Journal of Applied Psychology*, April 1994, pp. 184–90; M.A. McDaniel, D.L. Whetzel, F.L. Schmidt, and S.D. Maurer, "The Validity of Employment Interviews: A Comprehensive Review and Meta-Analysis," *Journal of Applied Psychology*, August 1994, pp. 599–616; and J.M. Conway,

R.A. Jako, and D.F. Goodman, "A Meta-Analysis of Interrater and Internal Consistency Reliability of Selection Interviews," *Journal of Applied Psychology*, October 1995, pp. 565–79.

5. R.L. Dipboye, *Selection Interviews: Process Perspectives* (Cincinnati: South-Western Publishing, 1992), pp. 42–44.

6. W.F. Cascio, *Applied Psychology in Personnel Management*, 4th ed. (Englewood Cliff, NJ: Prentice-Hall, 1991), p. 271.

7. E.E. Ghiselli, "The Validity of Aptitude Tests in Personnel Selection," *Personnel Psychology*, Winter 1973, p. 475.

8. R.J. Herrnstein and C. Murray, *The Bell Curve: Intelligence and Class Structure in American Life* (New York: Free Press, 1994); and M.J. Ree, J.A. Earles, and M.S. Teachout, "Predicting Job Performance: Not Much More Than g," *Journal of Applied Psychology*, August 1994, pp. 518–24.

9. J.Flint, "Can You Tell Applesauce From Pickles?" *Forbes*, October 9, 1995, pp. 106–08.

10. D.S. Ones, C. Viswesvaran, and F.L. Schmidt, "Comprehensive Meta-Analysis of Integrity Test Validities: Findings and Implications for Personnel Selection and Theories of Job Performance," *Journal of Applied Psychology*, August 1993, pp. 679–703.

11. J.J. Asher and J.A. Sciarrino, "Realistic Work Sample Tests: A Review," *Personnel Psychology*, Winter 1974, pp. 519–33; and I.T. Robertson and R.S. Kandola, "Work Sample Tests: Validity, Adverse Impact and Application Reaction," *Journal of Occupational Psychology*, Spring 1982, pp. 171–82.

12. G.C. Thornton, *Assessment Centers in Human Resource Management* (Reading, MA: Addison-Wesley, 1992).

Summary and Implications

For the Workplace

We've covered a lot of territory in this chapter. Since we essentially organized our discussion around the group behaviour model in Exhibit 7-4, let's use this model to summarize our findings regarding performance and satisfaction. Then we'll look at the impact of group relations.

PERFORMANCE Any predictions about a group's performance must begin by recognizing that work groups are part of a larger organization and that factors such as the organization's strategy, authority structure, selection procedures, and reward system can provide a favourable or unfavourable climate for the group to operate within. For example, if an organization is characterized by distrust between management and workers, it is more likely that work groups in that organization will develop norms to restrict effort and output than will work groups in an organization where trust is high. So managers shouldn't look at any group in isolation. Rather, they should begin by assessing the degree of support external conditions provide the group. It is obviously a lot easier for any work group to be productive when the overall organization of which it is a part is growing and it has both top management's support and abundant resources. Similarly, a group is more likely to be productive when its members have the requisite skills to do the group's tasks and the personality characteristics that facilitate working well together.

A number of structural factors show a relationship to performance. Among the more prominent are role perception, norms, status inequities, size of the group, its demographic composition, the group's task, and cohesiveness.

There is a positive relationship between role perception and an employee's performance evaluation.[58] The degree of congruence that exists between an employee and his or her boss in the perception of the employee's job influences the degree to which that employee will be judged as an effective performer by the boss. To the extent that the employee's role perception fulfils the boss's role expectations, the employee will receive a higher performance evaluation.

Norms control group-member behaviour by establishing standards of right and wrong. If managers know the norms of a given group, it can help to explain the behaviours of its members. Where norms support high out-

put, managers can expect individual performance to be markedly higher than where group norms aim to restrict output. Similarly, acceptable standards of absenteeism will be dictated by the group norms.

Status inequities create frustration and can adversely influence productivity and the willingness to remain with an organization. Among those individuals who are equity sensitive, incongruence is likely to lead to reduced motivation and an increased search for ways to bring about fairness (i.e., taking another job).

The impact of size on a group's performance depends upon the type of task in which the group is engaged. Larger groups are more effective at fact-finding activities. Smaller groups are more effective at action-taking tasks. Our knowledge of social loafing suggests that if management uses larger groups, efforts should be made to provide measures of individual performance within the group.

We found the group's demographic composition to be a key determinant of individual turnover. Specifically, the evidence indicates that group members who share a common age or date of entry into the work group are less prone to resign.

We also found that cohesiveness can play an important function in influencing a group's level of productivity. Whether or not it does depends on the group's performance-related norms.

The primary contingency variable moderating the relationship between group processes and performance is the group's task. The more complex and interdependent the tasks, the more that inefficient processes will lead to reduced group performance.

Intergroup conflicts can also affect an organization's performance. Where organizational performance depends on effective group relations and where there is high interdependence between groups, management needs to ensure that the proper integrative device is put in place. However, there is no reason to believe that all intergroup conflicts lead to problems. As you will see in Chapter 13, some minimal levels of conflict can facilitate critical thinking among group members, make a group more responsive to the need for change, and provide similar benefits that can enhance group and organizational performance.

SATISFACTION As with the role of the perception-performance relationship, high congruence between a boss and employee as to the perception of the employee's job shows a significant association with high employee satisfaction.[59] Similarly, role conflict is associated with job-induced tension and job dissatisfaction.[60]

Most people prefer to communicate with others at their own status level or a higher one rather than with those below them.[61] As a result, we should expect satisfaction to be greater among employees whose job minimizes interaction with individuals who are lower in status than themselves.

The group size-satisfaction relationship is what one would intuitively expect: Larger groups are associated with lower satisfaction.[62] As size increases, opportunities for participation and social interaction decrease, as does the ability of members to identify with the group's accomplishments. At the same time, having more members also prompts dissension, conflict, and the formation of subgroups, which all act to make the group a less pleasant entity of which to be a part.

For You as an Individual

Many commerce and business courses require students to work in groups, so one of the first ways that you might use the lessons in this chapter is to think about how they might apply to either a group you are in now, or one you have participated in previously. In many groups, the task often gets in the way of building the foundation of group relationships that would make the group function more easily and more cohesively. Because students can be very goal oriented (with good reason, since that's how higher grades are achieved), it becomes easy to focus on the group product rather than group relationships.

You may notice, however, that in poorly functioning groups, at the end, when the group is trying to finish their project and the deadline is looming, the conflict among group members becomes stronger, and major difficulties arise in getting everyone to work together toward a shared goal. To try to avoid this situation, it is helpful if the group works out the shared goals and norms in the early stages of group development, even if it seems like a waste of time at the beginning. The successful student groups agree to go out to dinner or otherwise celebrate after the team project is presented. The least successful groups don't want to speak with each other after the project is over. As instructors, we have observed many examples of both kinds of groups. Managing the relationships during the development of the group project is something that might make your next group experience more positive. The chapter gives you several ideas about doing this. Two that might be especially helpful are Exhibit 7-5, to remind you of the kinds of roles you need within the group for both tasks and relationship success, and the section on group cohesiveness on page 263, which reminds you of effective behaviours by groups.

ROADMAP REMINDER

We arrived at our discussion of groups through the path of motivation. Much of our discussion of motivation was at the individual level, but the fact of the matter is that working in an organization is generally not an isolating experience. In general, within organizations are many shared activities that need to be done. In this chapter we've explored the functioning of groups, and how to build a better group. In the next chapter we move on to teams. Teams and groups are not synonymous, as you'll soon see. A team is meant to be a much higher-performing category than a group.

For Review

1. What might motivate you to join a group?
2. What is the relationship between a work group and the organization of which it is a part?
3. What is the difference between task oriented roles and maintenance roles?
4. Explain the implications from the Asch experiments.
5. What are the implications of Whyte's restaurant study for OB?
6. How can a group's demography help you to predict turnover?
7. What can organizations do to provide support for groups?

8. How do you build group cohesiveness?
9. How do you assess the effectiveness of intergroup relations?

For Discussion

1. How could you use the punctuated-equilibrium model to better understand group behaviour?
2. Identify five roles you play. What behaviours do they require? Are any of these roles in conflict? If so, in what way? How do you resolve these conflicts?
3. "High cohesiveness in a group leads to higher group productivity." Do you agree or disagree? Explain.
4. What effect, if any, do you expect that workforce diversity has on a group's performance and satisfaction?

LEARNING ABOUT YOURSELF EXERCISE

Are You Attracted to the Group?

Most of us have written a term paper. Some of these papers have been individual assignments. That is, the instructor expected each student to hand in a separate paper and your grade was determined solely by your own effort and contribution. But sometimes instructors assign group term papers, where students must work together on the project and share in the grade.

Think back to a recent experience in doing a group term paper. Now envision yourself at about the halfway point in the completion of that group assignment. Using your mind-set at this halfway point, answer the following 20 questions. This questionnaire measures your feelings about that work group.*

	Agree	Disagree
1. I want to remain a member of this group.	1 2 3 4 5	6 7 8 9
2. I like my group.	1 2 3 4 5	6 7 8 9
3. I look forward to coming to the group.	1 2 3 4 5	6 7 8 9
4. I don't care what happens in this group.	1 2 3 4 5	6 7 8 9
5. I feel involved in what is happening in my group.	1 2 3 4 5	6 7 8 9
6. If I could drop out of the group now, I would.	1 2 3 4 5	6 7 8 9
7. I dread coming to this group.	1 2 3 4 5	6 7 8 9
8. I wish it were possible for the group to end now.	1 2 3 4 5	6 7 8 9
9. I am dissatisfied with the group.	1 2 3 4 5	6 7 8 9
10. If it were possible to move to another group at this time, I would.	1 2 3 4 5	6 7 8 9
11. I feel included in the group.	1 2 3 4 5	6 7 8 9
12. In spite of individual differences, a feeling of unity exists in my group.	1 2 3 4 5	6 7 8 9
13. Compared to other groups, I feel my group is better than most.	1 2 3 4 5	6 7 8 9
14. I do not feel a part of the group's activities.	1 2 3 4 5	6 7 8 9
15. I feel it would make a difference to the group if I were not here.	1 2 3 4 5	6 7 8 9
16. If I were told my group would not meet today, I would feel bad.	1 2 3 4 5	6 7 8 9

17. I feel distant from the group.   1 2 3 4 5 6 7 8 9
18. It makes a difference to me how this group turns out.   1 2 3 4 5 6 7 8 9
19. I feel my absence would not matter to the group.   1 2 3 4 5 6 7 8 9
20. I would not feel bad if I had to miss a meeting of this group.   1 2 3 4 5 6 7 8 9

Turn to page 699 for scoring directions and key.

*Reproduced from N.J. Evans and P.A. Jarvis, "The Group Attitude Scale: A Measure of Attraction to Group," *Small Group Behavior*, May 1986, pp. 203–16. Reprinted by permission of Sage Publications, Inc.

WORKING WITH OTHERS EXERCISE
Assessing Occupational Status

Rank the following 20 occupations from most prestigious (1) to least prestigious (20):

_____ Accountant	_____ Coach of a women's basketball team
_____ Air traffic controller	_____ Electrical engineer
_____ Coach of a pro hockey team	_____ Environmental scientist
_____ Freelance financial consultant	_____ Physician
_____ Lawyer	_____ Plumber
_____ Manager of a clothing manufacturer	_____ Real estate salesperson
_____ Manager of an automobile plant	_____ Sports agent
_____ Mayor of a large city	_____ Teacher in a primary school
_____ Minister	_____ Armed forces colonel
_____ Pharmacist	_____ Used-car salesperson

Now form into groups of three to five students each. Answer the following questions:

a. How closely did your top five choices (1-5) match?
b. How closely did your bottom five choices (16-20) match?
c. What occupations were generally easiest to rate? Which were most difficult? Why?
d. What does this exercise tell you about criteria for assessing status?
e. What does this exercise tell you about stereotypes?

CASE INCIDENT

The Law Offices of Dickinson, Stilwell, and Gardner (DSG)

James Dickinson and Richard Stilwell opened their Richmond, British Columbia, law office in 1963. It has since grown to employ 25 people. Dickinson is now deceased and Stilwell is semi-retired. The firm's senior managing partner is now Charles Gardner. Gardner has been with the firm for more than 20 years.

Today, the law office of DSG has five partners and 12 full-time associates. Additionally, the firm employs an administrative manager (Linda Chan) and an assistant administrative manager, a receptionist, four secretaries, and two legal interns who work 20 hours a week doing research.

Richmond has a large Chinese community. For various reasons, DSG has historically not done a very effective job of hiring and keeping Chinese-Canadian employees. Until very recently, none of the partners was Chinese-Canadian and only two of the associates were. Five months ago, the firm lured a prominent Chinese lawyer, Richard Lee, away from a competitor. Lee was brought in as a partner, at a base salary higher than any other DSG employee, with the exception of Charles Gardner.

The hiring of Lee has created a number of interpersonal issues at DSG. Many of the associates are unhappy. They feel the company hired Lee solely because he was one of the few big-name Chinese lawyers in Richmond and could open doors for the firm into the Chinese community. The associates were also concerned that the hiring of a new partner from the outside would lower the likelihood that they would become partners in the firm.

It was also clear that a clique was forming within the firm. This clique was made up of Lee, Ms. Chan, the two Chinese associates, and one of the secretaries (all of whom are Chinese by background). Morale has suffered in recent months. Privately, several employees have made complaints to Gardner such as "Linda gives favoured treatment to Richard and the Chinese associates," "the Chinese associates are suddenly working on the most visible and important cases within the firm," and "there's no future around here if you're not Chinese."

Questions

1. What do you think you can learn from this case about diversity and group behaviour?

2. What should Gardner do to deal with this dilemma?

3. In what ways might group cohesiveness be increased at DSG?

Planning for Action

One of the most difficult tasks groups face is trying to come up with an action plan so that everyone contributes to the overall success of the project. Consultant David Talbott developed the "Business Huddle," a computer-augmented business meeting, to show clients how to work more effectively in groups. He developed his idea based on athletes huddled with their coach or manager, making plans together. He believes that people in business should also come together to plan, because planning makes a big difference.

Talbott is helping Home Products to launch a new product, Merlin, a motion sensor for garden lights, which has to get to market in six weeks. He meets with the people responsible for getting the product to market. The steps he takes in helping the group formulate its plans would be useful to any group trying to complete a project.

The management of Home Products comes together to build the plan. They start by looking ahead to a critical date in the future, and then determining what needs to be done by that date to achieve success. The group states its objectives, visualizing the big picture.

Next, all of the team members get to see all of the information presented in the discussion of goals and objectives because Talbott displays this information through a computer and video monitor. This helps everyone to pay attention to the task at hand. Group members are also provided with minutes of the meetings.

Once the group members identify these objectives, they are asked to outline all of the obstacles they face. This gives everyone the opportunity to speak up and express concerns. All of these concerns will also be addressed during the ensuing discussion.

The group then develops an action plan that includes all of the tasks needing to be completed, the date by which completion is expected, and the name of the person who will be responsible for the task. The purpose of this step is to get everyone in the group to accept responsibility for some part of the project, to agree to the milestone dates, and to commit to actually meeting the dates. To help with this commitment, each person is given a detailed action plan in writing so that everyone's responsibilities are clear.

Questions

1. What are the benefits of the "Business Huddle" for group members trying to make a deadline?

2. How might you apply the lessons of the "Business Huddle" to a project group of your own?

3. What role do you think the action plan plays in ensuring that people get jobs done? How would you use this in a group of your own?

Source: Based on "Business Huddle," *Venture* 589; aired May 5, 1996.

http://www.tv.cbc.ca/venture/archives/business_huddle_960505/two.html

One of the truly remarkable things

about work groups

is that they can make 2+2=5.

Of course,

they also have the capability

of making 2+2=3.

–Stephen P. Robbins

POINT

Designing Jobs Around Groups

It's time to take small groups seriously; that is, to use groups, rather than individuals, as the basic building blocks for an organization. We should design organizations from scratch around small groups rather than the way we have traditionally done it—around individuals.

Why would management want to do such a thing? At least seven reasons can be identified. First, small groups seem to be good for people. They can satisfy important membership needs. They can provide a moderately wide range of activities for individual members. They can provide support in times of stress and crisis. They are settings in which people can learn not only cognitively but also empirically to be reasonably trusting and helpful to one another. Second, groups seem to be good problem-finding tools. They seem to be useful in promoting innovation and creativity. Third, in a wide variety of decision situations, groups make better decisions than individuals do. Fourth, they are great tools for implementation. Groups gain commitment from their members so that group decisions are likely to be willingly carried out. Fifth, they can control and discipline individual members in ways that are often extremely difficult through impersonal quasi-legal disciplinary systems. Sixth, as organizations grow large, small groups appear to be useful mechanisms for fending off many of the negative effects of large size. They help to prevent communication lines from growing too long, the hierarchy from growing too steep, and the individual from getting lost in the crowd. There is also a seventh,

but altogether different, kind of argument for taking groups seriously. Groups are natural phenomena and facts of organizational life. They can be created, but their spontaneous development cannot be prevented.

Operationally, how would an organization that was truly designed around groups function? One answer to this question is merely to take the things that organizations do with individuals and apply them to groups. The idea would be to raise the level from the atom to the molecule and select groups rather than individuals, train groups rather than individuals, pay groups rather than individuals, promote groups rather than individuals, fire groups rather than individuals, and so on down the list of activities that organizations have traditionally carried on in order to use human beings in their organizations.

In the past, the human group has been primarily used for patching and mending organizations that were built around the individual. The time has come for management to discard the notion that individuals are the basic building blocks of organizations and to redesign organizations around groups. Importantly, a number of organizations seem to be moving in this direction. Hundreds of major companies, including Honeywell, Toyota Canada, and Microsoft, have essentially designed their current operations around small groups.[1] ■

Source:

[1] Based on H.J. Leavitt, "Suppose We Took Groups Seriously," in E.L. Cass and F.G. Zimmer (eds.), *Man and Work in Society* (New York: Van Nostrand Reinhold, 1975), pp. 67–77.

counterPOINT

Jobs Should Be Designed Around Individuals

The argument that organizations can and should be designed around groups might hold in a socialistic society but not in capitalistic countries such as Canada, the United States, Australia, Germany, and the United Kingdom. Even though Canadians have a stronger orientation toward society as a whole than do Americans, many people strongly value individual achievement here, just as people in the United States and other capitalist countries do. They praise competition. Even in team sports, they want to identify individuals for recognition. Sure, they enjoy group interaction. They like being part of a team, especially a winning team. But it is one thing to be a member of a work group while maintaining a strong individual identity and another to sublimate one's identity to that of the group.

Many workers like a clear link between individual effort and a visible outcome. They are frustrated in job situations where their contribution is commingled and homogenized with the contributions of others.

Individuals want to be hired based on their individual talents. They want to be evaluated on their individual efforts. They also want to be rewarded with pay raises and promotions based on their individual performances. As we noted in Chapter 4 when we discussed values, Canadians believe in an authority and status hierarchy even more than Americans do. They accept a system where there are bosses and subordinates. They are not completely comfortable accepting a group's decision on such issues as their job assignments and wage increases. It's harder to imagine that they would be comfortable in a system where the sole basis for their promotion or termination would be the performance of their group.

One of the best examples of how fully the individual ethic has permeated the Canadian psyche is the general lack of enthusiasm that university students display toward group term papers. When students are offered the option to write term papers individually or as members of a small group, and the class must decide as a whole on a binding decision, the class almost always chooses individual term papers. This is really not all that surprising. It's consistent with someone who wants to rise or fall based on his or her own work performance. However, given this preference to do individual work, one might ask the question: Are the students examples of future full-time employees who would be satisfied and reach their full productive capacities in a group-centred organization? Probably not! ■

CHAPTER 8

Understanding Work Teams

LEARNING OBJECTIVES

After studying this chapter, you should be able to

- Explain the growing popularity of teams in organizations

- Contrast teams with groups

- Identify three types of teams

- Demonstrate the linkage between group concepts and high-performing teams

- Identify ways managers can build trust among team members

- Explain how organizations can create team players

- Describe the advantages and disadvantages of diversity to work teams

- Explain how management can keep teams from becoming stagnant and rigid

Anyone who followed the saga of the 1997-98 Vancouver Canucks or Vancouver Grizzlies teams might readily conclude that a group can call themselves a team, but that does not actually make them function like a team. Throughout the season, both "teams" exhibited plenty of evidence that there was little or no team spirit among the players and that team members were performing as individuals only. Both teams ended their seasons with very poor records.

Early in the season, the Canucks had hoped that they might be able to turn their early season record around. The team hired Mike Keenan as head coach in mid-November. After some early wins under his coaching, the team returned to the lacklustre performance that had resulted in Pat Quinn, the previous coach, being fired. Within a month of Keenan's arrival, the lack of team spirit became obvious, not just in performance, but also in the considerable public bickering among team members.

The Canucks' inability to function as a team did not escape Keenan. As *Vancouver Sun* sports writer Iain MacIntyre noted, "Keenan came with the mandate to shake the Canucks from their stupor of mediocrity, and he said early on in his reign that he needed to change the culture of the team." Although the team ended its season with an 18-game win and 63-game loss record, Keenan may well be on his way to building a better team. As MacIntyre pointed out in March 1998, "The team is now bigger, tougher, younger, and more economical than when Keenan took over."[1] Only three players remain from the team that lost game seven of the Stanley Cup in 1994.

Bret Hedican, one of those players, notes that this turnover was probably good for the team, even though some of his friends are gone. "I was thinking the other day about how the group of players we had here, that core, had stayed together. But maybe that was part of the reason we didn't play that well the last few years. Maybe there was a comfort zone. Change is hard, but if you want to win you have to change....That energy is coming back now."[2] ■

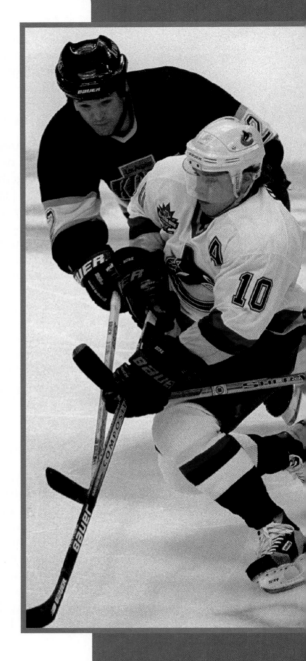

Coaches of athletic teams have long understood the importance of building teamwork. They also realize that sometimes you have to change the mix, in order to ensure "chemistry." However, that hasn't necessarily been true for business firms. One reason, of course, is that business organizations have traditionally been organized around individuals. That's no longer true. Teams have increasingly become the primary means for organizing work in contemporary business firms.

Teams versus Groups: What's the Difference?

work group
A group that interacts primarily to share information and to make decisions to help each other perform within his or her area of responsibility.

Groups and teams are not the same thing.[3] In the last chapter, we defined a *group* as two or more individuals, interacting and interdependent, who have come together to achieve particular objectives. A **work group** is a group that interacts primarily to share information and to make decisions to help each member perform within his or her area of responsibility.

Work groups have no need or opportunity to engage in collective work that requires joint effort. So their performance is merely the summation of each group member's individual contribution. There is no positive synergy that would create an overall level of performance that is greater than the sum of the inputs. You may remember, for example, that at the end of Chapter 7 we discussed several types of groups that could be set up to manage intergroup relations, such as liaison groups or task forces. These are examples of groups, not teams.

work team
A group whose individual efforts result in a performance that is greater than the sum of those individual inputs.

A **work team** generates positive synergy through coordinated effort. Their individual efforts result in a level of performance that is greater than the sum of those individual inputs. Exhibit 8-1 highlights the differences between a group and a team.

Why Have Teams Become So Popular?

Zellers
http://www.hbc.com/zellers/

Sears Canada
http://www.sears.ca/

San Diego Zoo
http://www.sandiegozoo.org/

Twenty years ago, when companies such as Volvo, Toyota, and General Foods introduced teams into their production processes, it made news because no other company was doing it. Today, it's just the opposite. It's the organization that *doesn't* use teams that has become newsworthy. Pick up almost any business periodical today and you'll read how teams have become an essential part of the way business is being done in companies such as Zellers, Xerox, Sears Canada, General Electric, AT&T, Hewlett-Packard, Motorola, Apple Computer, Shiseido, Federal Express, Chrysler, Saab, 3M Co., John Deere, Texas Instruments, Australian Airlines, Johnson & Johnson, and London Life. Even the world-famous San Diego Zoo has restructured its native habitat zones around cross-departmental teams. A 1994 Conference Board of Canada Report found that over 80 percent of its 109 respondents used teams in the workplace.[4] This compares with 78 percent of U.S. organizations.[5]

The reason that so many organizations have recently restructured work processes around teams is that management is looking for the positive synergy coming from teams that will allow their organization to increase performance. The extensive use of teams creates the *potential* for an organization to generate greater outputs with no increase in inputs. Notice, however, we said "potential." There is nothing inherently magical in the creation of teams that ensures the achievement of this positive synergy. Merely calling a

Exhibit 8-1
Not All Groups Are Teams: How To Tell the Difference

Work Group	**Team**
• Strong, clearly focused leader	• Shared leadership roles
• Individual accountability	• Individual and mutual accountability
• The group's purpose is the same as the broader organizational mission	• Specific team purpose that the team itself delivers
• Individual work-products	• Collective work-products
• Runs efficient meetings	• Encourages open-ended discussion and active problem-solving meetings
• Measures its effectiveness indirectly by its influence on others (e.g., financial performance of the business)	• Measures performance directly by assessing collective work-products
• Discusses, decides, and delegates	• Discusses, decides, and does real work together

Source: Jon R. Katzenback and Douglas K. Smith, "The Discipline of Teams," *Harvard Business Review,* March-April, 1993, p. 10.

group a *team* doesn't automatically increase its performance. As we will show later in this chapter, successful or high-performing teams have certain common characteristics. If management hopes to gain increases in organizational performance through the use of teams, it must ensure that its teams possess these characteristics.

Do teams work? The evidence suggests that teams typically outperform individuals when the tasks being done require multiple skills, judgment, and experience.[6] As organizations have restructured themselves to compete more effectively and efficiently, they have turned to teams as a way to better utilize employee talents. Management has found that teams are more flexible and responsive to changing events than are traditional departments or other forms of permanent groupings. Teams have the capability to quickly assemble, deploy, refocus, and disband.

According to Ian Tostenson, president of B.C.-based Calona Vineyards, the introduction of its Chilean Vineyards line was attributed entirely to his change to the use of teams at the winery. While much of the earlier product development came from strategic brainstorming by the management elite who then announced new product lines, the Chilean Vineyards line came from within the Calona sales force. Concludes Tostenson, "More minds solving the issues—that's better for me, better for the company, and less risky to boot."[7] Teams are not necessarily appropriate in every situation, however. Read this chapter's Point/Counterpoint to see a debate on the positives and negatives of teams.

Calona Vineyards
http://www.discoverywines.com/calona/

Employee Involvement: The Precursor to Teams

Before we review how teams are used in the workplace, let's examine employee involvement at a more general level. Employee participation and involvement refers to involving workers in those decisions that affect them. The idea is that by increasing their autonomy and control over their work lives, employees will become more motivated, more committed to the organization, more productive, and more satisfied with their jobs.[8]

Examples of Employee Involvement Programs

The extent to which employees are actually empowered to participate in their workplaces varies considerably. In some workplaces, employees are asked to participate in discussion groups, but have no formal decision-making authority. At the other end of the spectrum, in high-performance teams, employees are given free rein to develop and manage their tasks. In this section we review two forms of employee involvement (participative management and representative participation) that require little autonomy by the employees. These programs serve as a reminder that allowing employees more say in the workplace does not mean that they are working on teams, using the definition of work teams presented at the beginning of the chapter. However, employee participation can be a precursor to teamwork at a later stage.

participative management
A process where subordinates share a significant degree of decision-making power with their immediate superiors.

PARTICIPATIVE MANAGEMENT The distinct characteristic common to all **participative management** programs is the use of joint decision-making. That is, subordinates actually share a significant degree of decision-making power with their immediate superiors.

Participative management has, at times, been promoted as a panacea for poor morale and low productivity. One author has even argued that participative management is an ethical imperative.[9] But participative management is not appropriate for every organization or every work unit. For it to work, there must be adequate time to participate, the issues in which employees get involved must be relevant to their interests, employees must have the ability (intelligence, technical knowledge, communication skills) to participate, and the organization's culture must support employee involvement.[10]

Why would management want to share its decision-making power with subordinates? For a number of good reasons. As jobs have become more complex, managers often don't know everything their employees do. Thus, participation allows those who know the most to contribute. The result can be better decisions. The interdependence in tasks that employees often do today also requires consultation with people in other departments and work units. This increases the need for teams, committees, and group meetings to resolve issues that affect them jointly. Participation additionally increases commitment to decisions. People are less likely to undermine a decision at the time of its implementation if they shared in making that decision. Finally, participation provides intrinsic rewards for employees; it can make their jobs more interesting and meaningful.

representative participation
Workers participate in organizational decision-making through a small group of representative employees.

REPRESENTATIVE PARTICIPATION Although less common in Canada and the United States, almost every country in Western Europe has some type of legislation requiring companies to practise **representative participation**. That is, rather than participate directly in decisions, workers are represented by a small group of employees who actually participate. Representative participa-

tion has been called "the most widely legislated form of employee involvement around the world."[11]

The goal of representative participation is to redistribute power within an organization, putting labour on a more equal footing with the interests of management and stockholders.

The two most common forms of representative participation are works councils and board representatives.[12] **Works councils** link employees with management. They are groups of nominated or elected employees who must be consulted when management makes decisions involving personnel. For example, in the Netherlands, if a Dutch company is being taken over by another firm, the former's works council must be informed at an early stage, and if the council objects, it has 30 days to seek a court injunction to halt the takeover.[13] **Board representatives** are employees who sit on a company's board of directors and represent the interests of the firm's employees. In some countries, large companies may be legally required to ensure that employee representatives have the same number of board seats as stockholder representatives.

The overall influence of representative participation on employees seems to be minimal.[14] For instance, the evidence suggests that works councils are dominated by management and have little impact on employees or the organization. And while this form of employee involvement might increase the motivation and satisfaction of those individuals who are doing the representing, there is little evidence that this trickles down to the operating employees whom they represent. Overall, "the greatest value of representative participation is symbolic. If one is interested in changing employee attitudes or in improving organizational performance, representative participation would be a poor choice."[15]

The Effects of Participation on Performance

There is considerable evidence that participative management programs are successful on several different measures, both in North America and in countries such as Japan and Sweden.[16] Several economists, in looking at profit-sharing programs (which we discussed in Chapter 6), unexpectedly found that "worker participation both enhances the success of such programs and 'also has beneficial effects of its own.'"[17] Another study, reviewing 47 studies, found that participation in decision-making positively affected both productivity and job satisfaction, regardless of the types of occupations held by employees. Moreover, the effect was stronger in "real-world" research than in laboratory-simulation studies.[18]

Participation programs do not always work, however. The evidence suggests that they are less likely to work when employees are not given enough participation; "too few employees were included; the program didn't last long enough to do any good; the decisions workers were permitted to make were relatively inconsequential; or upper management essentially ignored employees' recommendations."[19] The limitations to participation by employees may well be common in both Canadian and U.S. firms.[20] For instance, the Conference Board of Canada estimates that less than 25 percent of employees' work was participatory, even when the Canadian organizations surveyed reported widespread use of teams.[21] Employees can often be skeptical of participation as well, and thus refrain from participating in the program.[22] Their skepticism is more likely to increase when they are encouraged to participate in joint decision-making activities, but then feel that their suggestions were not heard or acted upon.

works councils
Groups of nominated or elected employees who must be consulted when management makes decisions involving personnel.

board representatives
A form of representative participation; employees sit on a company's board of directors and represent the interests of the firm's employees.

This discussion of employee participation and involvement might serve as a reminder that to be truly participatory, individuals must believe that their contributions matter. Otherwise they will often choose not to participate. Teams, by their nature, are intended to increase the level of participation much more than the participative management and representative participation. Below we will discuss the types of teams used in organizations, followed by a discussion of both the problems teams face in operating in the workplace, and how they can be used more effectively. In general, the level of participation granted to team members will have a strong effect on the success of the teams.

Types of Teams

Teams can be classified based on their objective. The three most common forms of teams you're likely to find in an organization are problem-solving (or process-improvement) teams, self-managed (or self-directed) teams, and cross-functional teams (see Exhibit 8-2).

Problem-Solving Teams

If we look back 15 years or so, teams were just beginning to grow in popularity, and most of these teams took a similar form. These were typically composed of five to 12 hourly employees from the same department who met for a few hours each week to discuss ways of improving quality, efficiency, and the work environment.[23] We call these **problem-solving** or **process-improvement teams**.

In problem-solving teams, members share ideas or offer suggestions on how to improve work processes and methods. Rarely, however, are these teams given the authority to unilaterally implement any of their suggested actions. Clairol Canada Inc., however, headquartered in Montreal, gives employees more problem-solving ability. When a Clairol employee identifies a problem, he or she has the authority to call together an ad hoc group to investigate and then define and implement solutions. Clairol presents GOC Awards (Group Operating Committee) to teams for their efforts.

One of the most widely practised applications of problem-solving teams is the quality circle, which became quite popular in North America and Europe during the 1980s.[24] The quality circle concept is often mentioned as one of the techniques that Japanese firms use that has allowed them to make high-quality products at low costs. However, they originated in the United States and were exported to Japan in the 1950s.[25]

A **quality circle** is a work group of eight to 10 employees and supervisors who share an area of responsibility. They meet regularly—typically once a week, on company time and on company premises—to discuss their quality

problem-solving teams
Groups of five to 12 employees from the same department who meet for a few hours each week to discuss ways of improving quality, efficiency, and the work environment.

quality circle
A work group of employees who meet regularly to discuss their quality problems, investigate causes, recommend solutions, and take corrective actions.

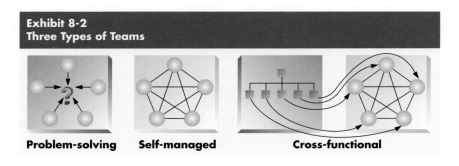

Exhibit 8-2
Three Types of Teams

Problem-solving   Self-managed   Cross-functional

Many employees are asked to work in teams in order to accomplish their tasks. In a self-managed work team, members make decisions about how to manage and schedule production, and also monitor the quality of their output.

problems, investigate causes of the problems, recommend solutions, and take corrective actions. They assume responsibility for solving quality problems, and generate and evaluate their own feedback. But management typically retains control over the final decision regarding implementation of recommended solutions. Of course, it is not presumed that employees inherently have the ability to analyze and solve quality problems. Therefore, part of the quality circle concept includes teaching participating employees group communication skills, various quality strategies, and measurement and problem analysis techniques. Exhibit 8-3 describes a typical quality-circle process.

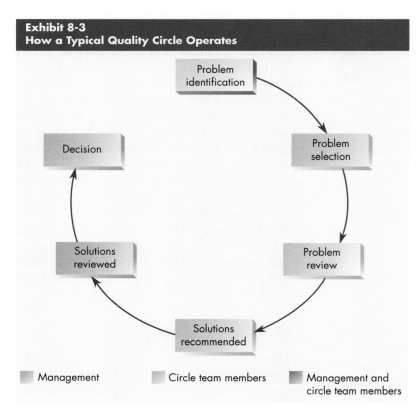

Exhibit 8-3
How a Typical Quality Circle Operates

Problem identification

Problem selection

Problem review

Solutions recommended

Solutions reviewed

Decision

Management   Circle team members   Management and circle team members

Do quality circles improve employee productivity and satisfaction? A review of the evidence indicates that they are much more likely to positively affect productivity. They tend to show little or no effect on employee satisfaction, and while many studies report positive results from quality circles on productivity, these results are by no means guaranteed.[26] The failure of many quality-circle programs to produce measurable benefits has also led to the discontinuation of a large number of them.

Canadian Auto Workers Union
http://www.caw.ca/

The Canadian Auto Workers Union (CAW) has not been entirely pleased with changes introduced at Chrysler plants, where workers have been asked to assume more responsibility for work through quality circles. Ken Lewenza, president of a Windsor-area CAW local, explains, "A key change has been to transfer responsibility for monitoring and resolving quality problems at the minivan and truck plants from management employees to teams of unionized workers."[27] But he adds that the union "is resisting company efforts to establish Japanese-style cells of assembly workers because of concerns that the concept could lead to job losses through increased efficiency."

One author has even gone as far as to say that while quality circles were the management fad of the 1980s, they've "become a flop."[28] He offers two possible explanations for their disappointing results. First is the little bit of time that actually deals with employee involvement. "At most, these programs operate for one hour per week, with the remaining 39 hours unchanged. Why should changes in 2.5 percent of a person's job have a major impact?"[29] Second, the ease of implementing quality circles often worked against them. They were viewed as a simple device that could be added on to the organization with few changes required outside the program itself. In many cases, the only significant involvement by management was funding the program. So quality circles became an easy way for management to get on the employee involvement bandwagon. And, unfortunately, the lack of planning and top-management commitment often contributed to quality-circle failures.

CAE Electronics
http://www.cae.ca/

However, failure does not have to be inevitable for quality circles. A case in point involves Montreal-based CAE Electronics Ltd., which showed that a company can overcome some of the failures associated with quality circles. CAE struggled through two failed quality-circle attempts before making its third attempt in 1990.[30] Managers believed that previous quality-circle attempts had not addressed the "right" problems, and the problems took too long to solve. In its third attempt, CAE modified the quality-circle process to reduce the problem-solving time, assigned workers to specific teams, and selected the problems for the team. These modifications proved successful. Between 1990 and 1995, 43 of the 44 major projects presented to management were accepted. The projects saved over $650 000, based on an 18-month payback period. CAE's success with quality circles indicates that they can work even where they have previously failed, if management introduces the proper supports. White Rock, British Columbia-based Toyota Captin, a wheel-manufacturing plant, has also used quality circles for a number of years, with good effect.

Self-Managed Work Teams

Problem-solving teams were on the right track but they didn't go far enough in involving employees in work-related decisions and processes. This led to experiments with truly autonomous teams that could not only solve problems but also implement solutions and assume responsibility for outcomes.

self-managed work teams
Groups of 10 to 15 people who take on responsibilities of their former supervisors.

Self-managed or **self-directed work teams** are groups of employees (typically 10 to 15 in number) who assume the responsibilities of their former supervisors.[31] Typically, this includes planning and scheduling of work, collectively controlling the pace of work, making operating decisions, and taking action on problems. Fully self-managed work teams even select their own members and have the members evaluate each other's performance. As a result, supervisory positions take on decreased importance and may even be eliminated.

Toyota Canada's Toronto parts distribution centre reorganized its workforce into work teams in 1995. Workers have a team-focused mission statement, and employees are divided into six work teams, each with its own leader. Teams rotate through shift and work assignment schedules, making their own adjustments as necessary. At the Honeywell Ltd. plant in Scarborough, Ontario, unionized workers have been known to shut down the production line, not for more money, but to correct a production line defect. Team member Karen Orr explains, "When you manage your own team, you learn all the jobs, not just one. You become more aware of what's going on and you notice immediately if anything's wrong."[32] According to the Conference Board of Canada, self-directed work teams are found in a variety of manufacturing (such as auto industry, chemicals, equipment repair) and service environments (such as banks and airlines).[33] Xerox Canada, Honeywell, General Motors, Coors Brewing, PepsiCo, and Hewlett-Packard are just a few familiar names that have implemented self-managed work teams. The Case Incident for this chapter gives you the opportunity to determine some of the opportunities and challenges of introducing self-managed teams in the workplace.

Business periodicals have been chock-full of articles describing successful applications of self-managed teams. Texas Instruments' defence group gives self-directed teams credit for helping it win the Malcolm Baldrige National Quality Award and for allowing it to achieve the same level of sales with 25 percent fewer employees.[34] Shell Canada has implemented a number of self-directed work teams, with many of the teams being completely responsible for decisions about the work process. Self-directed teams don't have to be used only in manufacturing either. The housekeeping staff at Banff Springs Hotel are organized into self-managed teams that are responsible for supervision, checking their own work, and writing their own work orders.

Banff Springs Hotel
http://www.resort2fitness.com/banff2.htm

Syncrude Canada
http://www.syncrude.com/

In the late 1980s, after struggling because of the oil-price drops of the mid-1980s and a devastating fire in the early 1980s, Alberta-based oil producer Syncrude Canada had to cut costs.[35] To gain employee support, Syncrude organized semi-autonomous self-managing work teams, with team members responsible for day-to-day decisions. Workers did become involved, finding ways to keep equipment running themselves, rather than depending on maintenance crews to fix it faster. The workers found they could minimize additional downtime by doing quick, frequent clean-ups while the reactor was running. They made a number of other improvements as well, so that whereas seven years ago machinery worked about 73 percent of available hours, the same plant ran 83 percent of the time after their improvements. Involving workers in management at Syncrude led to cuts in the workplace—especially supervisors, and at least some of the workers approve, even if it means taking more responsibility in the workplace. "I don't need anyone telling me what to do," says dragline operator Dave Plews, age 29, a five-year veteran on the huge diggers. "Productivity's gone up because you don't have anyone hounding you," he says. "It should have been implemented years ago."

In spite of these impressive stories, a word of caution needs to be offered here. Some organizations have been disappointed with the results from self-managed teams and the overall research on the effectiveness of self-managed work teams has not been uniformly positive.[36] For example, individuals on these teams tend to report higher levels of job satisfaction. However, counter to conventional wisdom, employees on self-managed work teams seem to have higher absenteeism and turnover rates than do employees working in traditional work structures. The specific reasons for these findings are unclear, which implies a need for additional research.

In some cases, the introduction of these teams is viewed negatively by workers. For instance, employees at Douglas Aircraft Co. (part of McDonnell Douglas), which has been undergoing large layoffs, have revolted against self-managed teams. They've come to view cooperating with the team concept as an exercise in assisting one's own executioner.[37] Their concerns may be well founded. At Honeywell's Scarborough plant, one-third of the 75 salaried positions were eliminated between 1991 and 1994 as a result of the shift to self-managed teams. The plant now runs with 40 percent fewer workers, with no drop in production.

Cross-Functional Teams

cross-functional teams
Employees from about the same hierarchical level, but from different work areas, who come together to accomplish a task.

The Boeing Company used the latest application of the team concept to develop its 777 jet. This application is called **cross-functional** or **project teams**. These teams are made up of employees from about the same hierarchical level, but from different work areas, who come together to accomplish a task.[38]

task force
A temporary cross-functional team.

committee
Group composed of members from across departmental lines.

Many organizations have used horizontal, boundary-spanning groups for years. For example, IBM created a large task force in the 1960s—made up of employees from across departments in the company—to develop the highly successful System 360. And a **task force** is really nothing other than a temporary cross-functional team. Similarly, **committees** composed of members from across departmental lines are another example of cross-functional teams.

But the popularity of cross-discipline work teams exploded in the late 1980s. All the major automobile manufacturers—including Toyota, Honda, Nissan, BMW, GM, Ford, and Chrysler—have turned to this form of team to coordinate complex projects. The 1998 Chrysler Intrepid and its elegant cousin, the Concorde, both produced at Chrysler's Bramalea, Ontario assembly plant, were developed in record time through the teamwork of staff from design, engineering, manufacturing, marketing, and finance. Chrysler budgeted 31 months and $3.9 billion to produce five 1998 cars: the Intrepid, Concorde, Eagle Vision, Chrysler LHS, and Chrysler 300. This compares to Ford spending six years and $11 billion to develop the Ford Contour and Mercury Mystique. The new teams are not always comprised solely of the employees of a single organization. Markham, Ontario-based AMP of Canada Ltd., manufacturer of electrical connectors and interconnection systems, puts together teams who may or may not be employees to bring a project to completion. Motorola's Iridium Project includes diverse expertise from people in dozens of other companies as well, such as McDonnell Douglas, Raytheon, Russia's Khrunichev Enterprise, Lockheed Martin, Scientific-Atlanta, and General Electric.[39]

In summary, cross-functional teams are an effective means for allowing people from diverse areas within an organization (or even between organiza-

tions) to exchange information, develop new ideas and solve problems, and coordinate complex projects. Of course, cross-functional teams are no picnic to manage.[40] Their early stages of development are often very time consuming as members learn to work with diversity and complexity. It takes time to build trust and teamwork, especially among people from different backgrounds, with different experiences and perspectives. Later in this chapter, we'll discuss ways managers can help facilitate and build trust among team members. In our HR Implications feature we discuss further things that organizations can do to turn individuals into team players.

Linking Teams and Group Concepts: Toward Creating High-Performance Teams

In order for teams to function successfully, organizations need to build appropriate infrastructure to support team goals, and then allow the team to develop its own working style. To build an effective team, management should consider the skill needs of the team, and be aware of appropriate size considerations. The organization also needs to develop performance evaluation systems that are team-related, and provide rewards that are team-based.

OB IN THE NEWS

Introducing Teamwork

How do organizations introduce teams into a previously non-team-oriented workplace? The experience of Delta Lloyd Insurance, based in Amsterdam, provides some insight. In the early 1990s Delta Lloyd found that paperwork for insurance cases was moving much too slowly. To address this problem, the company introduced teamwork to its 2300 employees. They created teams that ranged in size from 4 to 15.

Although each team is led by a player-coach, the team as a whole is responsible for carrying out the task (issuing policies, adjusting claims, making payments), identifying and reaching targets (revenue, profit, customer satisfaction, team innovation, task accomplishment, speed of service deliv-

ery), and scheduling (overtime, vacations, resource requests).

To ensure success, Delta Lloyd looked for the right people to implement teamwork. All 268 of the managers were asked to reapply for their jobs, and 58 percent of them won jobs in the new organization. Delta Lloyd also started a massive training program, including simulations on working in teams. The team process worked—files that had been taking two to three weeks for completion are now finished the same day in 70 to 80 percent of the cases.

Source: Based on D. Brian Harrison, "Shaping the Organization of the Future," *Canadian Business Review*, v. 22(4) Winter, 1995, pp. 13–16.

Take It to the Net

We invite you to visit the Robbins page on the Prentice Hall Web site at:

http://www.prenticehall.ca/robbins

for this chapter's World Wide Web exercise.

FROM CONCEPTS TO SKILLS

Building Trust

Team leaders have a significant impact on a team's trust climate. As a result, team leaders need to build trust between themselves and team members. The following summarizes ways to build team trust.

Demonstrate that you're working for others' interests as well as your own. All of us are concerned with our own self-interest, but if others see you using them, your job, or the organization for your personal goals to the exclusion of your team, department, and organization's interests, your credibility will be undermined.

Be a team player. Support your work team both through words and actions. Defend the team and team members when they're attacked by outsiders. This will demonstrate your loyalty to your work group.

Practise openness. Mistrust comes as much from what people don't know as from what they do know. Openness leads to confidence and trust. So keep people informed, explain your decisions, be candid about problems, and fully disclose relevant information.

Be fair. Before making decisions or taking actions, consider how others will perceive them in terms of objectivity and fairness. Give credit where it's due, be objective and impartial in performance evaluations, and pay attention to equity perceptions in reward distributions.

Speak your feelings. Managers and leaders who convey only hard facts come across as cold and distant. By sharing your feelings, others will view you as real and human. They will know who you are and will increase their respect for you.

Show consistency in the basic values that guide your decision-making. Mistrust comes from not knowing what to expect. Take the time to think about your values and beliefs. Then let them consistently guide your decisions. When you know your central purpose, your actions will follow accordingly, and you'll project a consistency that earns trust.

Maintain confidences. You trust those you can confide in and rely on. So if people tell you something in confidence, they need to feel assured that you won't discuss it with others or betray that confidence. If people perceive you as someone who "leaks" personal confidences or someone who can't be depended upon, you won't be perceived as trustworthy.

Demonstrate competence. Develop the admiration and respect of others by demonstrating technical and professional ability and good business sense. Pay particular attention to developing and displaying your communication, team building, and other interpersonal skills.

Teams should approach their own development as part of a search for continuous improvement.

Sources: Based on F. Bartolome, "Nobody Trusts the Boss Completely—Now What?" *Harvard Business Review*, March–April 1989, pp. 135–42; and P. Pascarella, "15 Ways to Win People's Trust," *Industry Week*, February 1, 1993, pp. 47–51.

Once the team has been formally constituted, the team itself has to carry out work that may at first seem unrelated to the task, but contributes to the overall effectiveness of the team. The main things that teams must consider early on in their development are leadership, commitment to common purpose, specific goals, accountability, and trust. These organizational and internal factors are discussed below. This chapter's OB in the News illustrates some of the organizational supports that Delta Lloyd Insurance introduced when it moved to teamwork for the entire firm.

Organizational Supports

TEAM SIZE AND COMPOSITION   The best work teams tend to be small. When they have more than about 10 to 12 members, it becomes difficult to

get much done. Group members have trouble interacting constructively and agreeing on much. Large numbers of people usually can't develop the cohesiveness, commitment, and mutual accountability necessary to achieve high performance. So in designing effective teams, managers should keep them to under a dozen people. If a natural working unit is larger and you want a team effort, consider breaking the group into subteams.

The individuals selected for the team should be chosen on the basis of their personalities and preferences. High-performing teams properly match people to various roles. For example, the hockey coaches who continually win over the long term have learned how to size up prospective players, identify their strengths and weaknesses, and then assign them to positions that best fit with their skills and allow them to contribute most to the overall team's performance. Coaches recognize that winning teams need a variety of skills—for example, goaltenders, power scorers, and defensive specialists.

To perform effectively, a team requires three different types of skills. First, it needs people with *technical expertise*. Second, it needs people with the *problem-solving* and *decision-making skills* to be able to identify problems, generate alternatives, evaluate those alternatives, and make competent choices. Finally, teams need people with good listening, feedback, conflict resolution, and other *interpersonal skills*.[41] This chapter's From Concepts to Skills discusses the importance of building trust as part of team building activities.

No team can achieve its performance potential without developing all three types of skills. The right mix is crucial. Too much of one at the expense of others will result in lower team performance. But teams don't need to have all the complementary skills in place at their beginning. It's not uncommon for one or more members to take responsibility to learn the skills in which the group is deficient, thereby allowing the team to reach its full potential.

We can identify nine potential team roles that successful teams need filled (see Exhibit 8-4).[42] On many teams, individuals will play multiple roles. Managers need to understand the individual strengths that each person can bring to a team, select members with their strengths in mind, and allocate work assignments that fit with members' preferred styles. By matching individual preferences with team role demands, managers increase the likelihood that the team members will work well together. This chapter's Working With Others exercise examines the issue of team building by encouraging you to apply the concepts of this chapter to building one of your own teams.

APPROPRIATE PERFORMANCE EVALUATION How do you get team members to be both individually and jointly accountable? The traditional, individually oriented evaluation must be modified to reflect team performance.[43] At Imperial Oil, team members provide feedback to each other in three critical areas: team results, team functioning/effectiveness, and personal effectiveness. Exhibit 8-5 illustrates the behaviours expected of team members at Imperial Oil. This type of appraisal reminds members of their responsibilities to their team. Teams should not rely solely on the formal performance appraisal process, however. To manage the team process more effectively, they might encourage presentations of work in progress to get feedback from other members and/or outsiders on quality and completeness of work. Sitting down together informally and reviewing both individual and team behaviour helps keep the team on track.

Exhibit 8-4
Key Roles on Teams

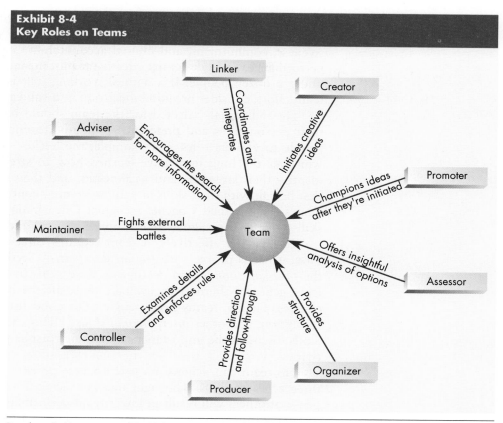

Based on C. Margerison and D. McCann, *Team Management: Practical New Approaches* (London: Mercury Books, 1990).

REWARD SYSTEMS THAT ACKNOWLEDGE TEAM EFFORT Fixed hourly wages, individual incentives, and the like are not consistent with the development of high-performance teams. So in addition to evaluating and rewarding employees for their individual contributions, management must consider group-based appraisals, profit sharing, gainsharing, small-group incentives, and other system modifications that will reinforce team effort and commitment. A Conference Board of Canada study of teams in the workplace found that the most commonly used incentive to acknowledge teamwork was recognition, including "small financial rewards, plaques, ceremonies, publicity in company newspapers, and celebrations of success at company gatherings," used by well over half of the companies surveyed.[44] Other forms of team reward were found less often, with the most common of those being the use of team cash bonus plans by 25 percent of the surveyed companies and gainsharing by 17 percent of the companies.[45]

Companies across Canada are using team rewards. For example, Canadian Tire offers team incentives to employees of its gas bars. "Secret" retail shoppers visit the outlets on a regular basis, and score them on such factors as cleanliness, manner in which the transaction was processed, and the type of products offered, using a 100-point scoring system. Scores above a particular threshold provide additional compensation that is shared by the team. Xerox Canada has its XTRA program, which rewards districts for achieving profit and customer satisfaction targets. Everyone in the district shares equally in the bonuses.

Exhibit 8-5
Team Behaviour at Imperial Oil

Individuals are asked to assess team members in three major areas. Behaviours related to these areas are indicated.

Team Results

Effort
Achieving individual
    role requirements
Collaborating with
    others toward
    achieving common
    goals
Smoothing
    relationships with
    customers/suppliers
Adhering to standards
Realizing tactical plans

Team Functioning

Sustaining morale and
    team spirit
Recognizing others'
    contributions and
    opinions
Listening
Solving problems
    without taking total
    ownership
Resolving conflict but
    maintaining
    everyone's dignity
Helping the team carry
    out strategic, long-term
    thinking and planning
Living up to company
    principles, values and
    ethics
Building trust by
    meeting commitments
    and keeping
    agreements

Personal Effectiveness

Giving personal support
Giving recognition
Giving clear and useful feedback
Enthusiasm
Understanding or priorities
Skill expansion
Understanding of roles and
    behaviours
Growth and development
Mentoring
Understanding interpersonal
    relationships
Pointing out opportunities and
    risks regarding career
    development

Source: Extracted from P. Booth, *Challenge and Change: Embracing the Team Concept*, Report 123–94, Conference Board of Canada.

Internal Team Needs

LEADERSHIP AND STRUCTURE   Goals define the team's end targets. But high-performance teams also need leadership and structure to provide focus and direction. Defining and agreeing upon a common approach, for example, ensure that the team is unified on the means for achieving its goals.

Team members must agree on who is to do what and ensure that all members contribute equally in sharing the workload. Additionally, the team needs to determine how schedules will be set, what skills need to be developed, how the group will resolve conflicts, and how the group will make and modify decisions. Agreeing on the specifics of work and how they fit together to integrate individual skills requires team leadership and structure. This, incidentally, can be provided directly by management or by the team members themselves as they fulfil promoter, organizer, producer, maintainer, and linker roles (refer back to Exhibit 8-4).

HAVING A COMMITMENT TO A COMMON PURPOSE   Does the team have a meaningful purpose to which all members aspire? This purpose is a vision. It's broader than specific goals. Effective teams have a common and mean-

ingful purpose that provides direction, momentum, and commitment for members.

The New Brunswick government's Department of Economic Development and Tourism illustrates how a common purpose can empower employees. The Department's vision statement, which includes the mandates "Help create jobs for our fellow New Brunswickers" and "Do things well or not at all," inspired some of its employees to develop strategies to attract telemarketing firms to New Brunswick. When the provincial government agreed to provide them with only half of the anticipated $100 000 needed to implement their strategy, the employees didn't give up. Instead, they successfully approached NB Tel for the other $50 000. Less than a year later, telemarketing and call centres became the fastest-growing sector in New Brunswick.[46]

Members of successful teams put a tremendous amount of time and effort into discussing, shaping, and agreeing upon a purpose that belongs to them both collectively and individually. This common purpose, when accepted by the team, becomes the equivalent of what celestial navigation is to a ship captain—it provides direction and guidance under any and all conditions.

NB Tel
http://www.nbtel.nb.ca/

ESTABLISHING SPECIFIC GOALS Successful teams translate their common purpose into specific, measurable, and realistic performance goals. Just as we demonstrated in Chapter 5 how goals lead individuals to higher performance, goals also energize teams. These specific goals facilitate clear communication. They also help teams maintain their focus on achieving results. At Harrisburg, Pennsylvania-based AMP, a leading global supplier of electronic interconnect equipment, customer satisfaction is a primary goal. Every team determines how it contributes to that goal and then determines how to measure that contribution. Progress toward team objectives is posted in a company-wide Excellence Index.

Along with goals, teams should be encouraged to develop milestones—tangible steps toward completion of the project. This allows teams to focus on their goal, and evaluate progress toward the goal. The milestones should be sufficiently important and readily accomplished so that teams can celebrate some of their accomplishments along the way.

ACCOUNTABILITY We learned in the previous chapter that individuals can hide inside a group. They can engage in social loafing and coast on the group's effort because their individual contributions can't be identified. High-performing teams undermine this tendency by holding themselves accountable at both the individual and team level.

Successful teams make members individually and jointly accountable for the team's purpose, goals, and approach. They clearly define what they are individually responsible for and what they are jointly responsible for. For example, joint responsibility led the New Brunswick government's Department of Economic Development and Tourism to gamble their jobs on a new tourism strategy. In 1992, the department developed a $750 000, three-year tourism strategy. Realizing the provincial government might be reluctant to approve such a request, the department guaranteed cabinet that if their strategy didn't result in a 10 percent increase in tourism to the province, they would return the money and pay a matching penalty. Before presenting this high-risk measure to cabinet, the tourism group polled the team to confirm each individual's commitment to this possibly risky strategy. After all, failure to achieve their goal would certainly involve loss of jobs for many of the employees. However, so confident were the team members of the unit

Performance goals energized this team of Mattel toy designers. It had just five months to design and develop a new car for the Hot Wheels line so it could be shown at the New York Toy Fair. While most toy cars take 18 months to perfect, this team of artists, designers, and computer experts developed the new Top Speed model in time to unveil it to the 20 000 buyers who attended the toy show.

who had done the research, that they gave unanimous approval to the proposal to return the money and pay the penalty if their strategy failed. Within only one year, the program had realized 60 percent of its goal.[47] Tourism has continued to increase in New Brunswick since then.

Developing High Mutual Trust

trust
A characteristic of high-performance teams where members believe in the integrity, character, and ability of each other.

High-performance teams are characterized by high mutual **trust** among members. That is, members believe in the integrity, character, and ability of each other. But as you know from personal relationships, trust is fragile. It takes a long time to build, can be easily destroyed, and is hard to regain.[48] Also, since trust begets trust and distrust begets distrust, maintaining trust requires careful attention by management. As trust is one issue in accountability, you may want to look at the Learning About Yourself exercise to gain a sense of whether others would view you as trustworthy.

Recent research has identified five dimensions that underlie the concept of trust (see Exhibit 8-6)[49]:

- *Integrity*: Honesty and truthfulness.
- *Competence*: Technical and interpersonal knowledge and skills.
- *Consistency*: Reliability, predictability, and good judgment in handling situations.
- *Loyalty*: Willingness to protect and save face for a person.
- *Openness*: Willingness to share ideas and information freely.

Exhibit 8-6
Dimensions of Trust

In terms of trust among team members, it's been found that the importance of these five dimensions is relatively constant: integrity > competence > loyalty > consistency > openness.[50] Moreover, integrity and competence are the most critical characteristics that an individual looks for in determining another's trustworthiness. Integrity seems to be rated highest because "without a perception of the other's 'moral character' and 'basic honesty,' other dimensions of trust were meaningless."[51] The high ranking

of competence is probably due to the need for peer interaction by team members in order to successfully complete their job responsibilities. This chapter's CBC Video Case shows a team brought together to learn how to interact in more productive ways

Contemporary Issues in Managing Teams

In this section, we address two issues related to managing teams: (1) What are the implications of workforce diversity on team performance? and (2) How does management re-energize stagnant teams?

Teams and Workforce Diversity

Managing diversity on teams is a balancing act (see Exhibit 8-7). Diversity typically provides fresh perspectives on issues but it makes it more difficult to unify the team and reach agreements.

The strongest case for diversity on work teams is when these teams are engaged in problem-solving and decision-making tasks.[52] Heterogeneous teams bring multiple perspectives to the discussion, thus increasing the likelihood that the team will identify creative or unique solutions. Additionally, the lack of a common perspective usually means diverse teams spend more time discussing issues, which decreases the possibility that a weak alternative will be chosen. As we pointed out in the previous chapter, diverse groups have more difficulty working together and solving problems, *but this dissipates with time* as the members come to know each other. Expect the value-added component of diverse teams to increase as members become more familiar with each other and the team becomes more cohesive.

Studies tell us that members of cohesive teams have greater satisfaction, lower absenteeism, and lower attrition from the group.[53] Yet cohesiveness is likely to be lower on diverse teams.[54] So here is a potential negative of diversity: it is detrimental to group cohesiveness. But again, referring to the last chapter, we found that the relationship between cohesiveness and group productivity was moderated by performance-related norms. We suggest that if the norms of the team are supportive of diversity, then a team can maximize

Wainwright Industries is a team-oriented company, and its teams played a critical role in the company winning a Malcolm Baldrige National Quality Award. Wainwright's teams are small (about six members plus a team leader), so members can easily share ideas and implement improvements. The company's owners believe that teams help create an environment in which employees take more ownership in each other and in the company.

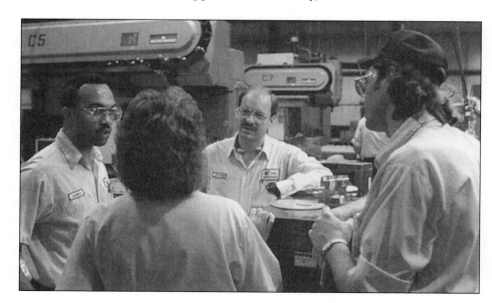

Exhibit 8-7
Advantages and Disadvantages of Diversity

Advantages	Disadvantages
Multiple perspectives	Ambiguity
Greater openness to new ideas	Complexity
Multiple interpretations	Confusion
Increased creativity	Miscommunication
Increased flexibility	Difficulty in reaching a single agreement
Increased problem-solving skills	Difficulty in agreeing on specific actions

Source: From *International Dimensions of Organizational Behavior*, 2nd ed., by Nancy J. Adler. Copyright © 1991. By permission of South-Western College publishing, a division of International Thomson Publishing, Inc., Cincinnati, OH 45227.

Honeywell Ltd.
http://www.honeywell.ca

the value of heterogeneity while also achieving the benefits of high cohesiveness.[55] This makes a strong case for team members to participate in diversity training.

Honeywell Ltd. in Scarborough, Ontario, which has a large number of employees for whom English is a second language, uses a "Learning for Life" program to help employees cope in a diverse workforce. Employees take courses at the workplace during and after hours to learn about empowerment, conflict resolution, and working in teams. Honeywell's training program looks for practical solutions to address conflicts arising from differences in race, age, gender, religion, values, and cultural norms. The company also tries to help employees understand that conflict resolution varies by culture.[56]

Reinvigorating Mature Teams

Just because a team is performing well at a given point in time is no assurance that it will continue to do so.[57] Effective teams can become stagnant. Initial enthusiasm can give way to apathy. Time can diminish the positive value from diverse perspectives as cohesiveness increases.

In terms of the five-stage development model introduced in the previous chapter, teams don't automatically stay at the "performing stage." Familiarity breeds apathy. Success can lead to complacency. And maturity brings less openness to novel ideas and innovation.

groupthink
Phenomenon in which the norm for consensus overrides the realistic appraisal of alternative courses of action.

Mature teams are particularly prone to suffer from **groupthink**. Members begin to believe they can read everyone's mind so they assume they know what others are thinking. As a result, team members become reluctant to express their thoughts and less likely to challenge each other.

Another source of problems for mature teams is that their early successes are often due to having taken on easy tasks. It's normal for new teams to begin by taking on those issues and problems that they can handle most easily. But as time passes, the easy problems are resolved and the team must confront more difficult issues. At this point, the team has typically developed entrenched processes and routines, and members are reluctant to change the "perfect" system they've already developed. The results can often be disastrous. Internal team processes no longer work smoothly. Communication bogs down. Conflicts increase because problems are less likely to have obvious solutions. And team performance can drop dramatically.

Playfair, Inc. of Berkeley, California, is a training firm that specializes in developing exercises that help employees enjoy the satisfaction that teamwork can provide. In this photo, Playfair's founder Matt Weinstein (right) and staff members have fun doing an exercise they developed. It involves using craft materials to design a sculpture that represents a company's vision.

How can mature teams be reinvigorated? We can offer four suggestions: (1) *Prepare members to deal with the problems of maturity*. Remind team members that they're not unique—all successful teams must confront maturity issues. They shouldn't feel defeated or lose their confidence in the team concept when the initial euphoria subsides and conflicts surface. (2) *Offer refresher training*. When teams get into ruts, it may help to provide them with refresher training in communication, conflict resolution, team processes, and similar skills. This can help members regain confidence and trust in one another. (3) *Offer advanced training*. The skills that worked with easy problems may be insufficient for more difficult ones. So mature teams can often benefit from advanced training to help members develop stronger problem-solving, interpersonal, and technical skills. (4) *Encourage teams to treat their development as a constant learning experience*. Teams should approach their own development as part of a search for continuous improvement. Teams should look for ways to improve, to confront member fears and frustrations, and to use conflict as a learning opportunity.

HR IMPLICATIONS

Turning Individuals into Team Players

In this chapter we've made a strong case for the value and growing popularity of teams. But many people are not inherently team players. Instead, they're loners or people who want to be recognized for their individual achievements. There are also many organizations that have historically nurtured individual accomplishments. These companies have created competitive work environments where only the strong survive. If these organizations now introduce a team-based structure, what do they do about the selfish, "I-got-to-look-out-for-me" employees that they've created? Finally, as we discussed in Chapter 4, countries differ in terms of how they rate on individualism and collectivism. Teams fit well with countries that score high on collectivism.

But what if an organization wants to introduce teams into a work population that is composed largely of individuals born and raised in a highly individualistic society, such as Canada, the United States, Great Britain, or Australia? James Mitchell, president of Steelcase Canada Ltd., sums up the difficulties of introducing teams to the workplace: "People talk about teams, but very few operate in a pure team sense. They tend to think that if they get cross-functional groups together—a person out

of marketing, one out of sales, one out of product development, another out of engineering—somehow they've got a team-based organization. But they haven't. They have a committee."[1]

The Challenge

The previous points are meant to highlight two substantial barriers to using work teams: individual resistance and management resistance.

When an employee is assigned to a team, his or her success is no longer defined in terms of individual performance. To perform well as team members, individuals must be able to communicate openly and honestly, to confront differences and resolve conflicts, and to sublimate personal goals for the good of the team. For many employees, this is a difficult, if not impossible, task. The challenge of creating team players will be greatest where (1) the national culture is highly individualistic and (2) the teams are being introduced into an established organization that has historically valued individual achievement. This describes, for instance, what faced managers at AT&T, Ford, Motorola, and other large Canadian and U.S.-based companies. These firms prospered by hiring and rewarding corporate stars, and they bred a competitive climate that encouraged individual achievement and recognition. Employees in these types of firms can be jolted by this sudden shift to the importance of team play.[2] A veteran employee of a large company, who had done well working alone, described the experience of joining a team: "I'm learning my lesson. I just had my first negative performance appraisal in 20 years."[3]

On the other hand, the challenge for management is less demanding when teams are introduced where employees have strong collectivist values—such as in Japan or Mexico—or in new organizations that use teams as their initial form for structuring work. For example, when Toyota opened plants in Canada, the working environment was designed around teams from their inception. Employees were hired with the knowledge that they would be working in teams. The ability to be a good team player was a basic hiring qualification that all new employees had to meet.

While it might seem easy enough to blame individual resistance as the cause of team failure, in many organizations there is no genuine infrastructure created to build teams. When organizations focus their rewards at the individual level, employees have no incentive to operate within a team

structure. In some situations, managers are quite reluctant to give up their power and, in fact, share power with the other team members. This also makes it difficult for a real team to develop. As we mentioned in our extensive discussion of incentive programs in Chapter 6, organizations must align their incentives with their goals. If team behaviour is important to the organization, the incentive system must reflect this objective.

Below we discuss some individual and organizational factors that can be carried out through the human resources function of the organization to improve team performance.

NASA knows that turning individuals into team players takes time and training. Astronauts (such as Canadian Roberta Bondar) are high-achieving indviduals who undergo an extremely competitive selection process to become astronauts. But when they become part of a shuttle crew, they must work harmoniously with other crew members to achieve their mission's goal. NASA shapes astronauts into team players by training them to work together—including brushing their teeth together—every day for a year or two before their shuttle mission. By stressing that the mission's success depends on teamwork, NASA teaches astronauts to compromise and make decisions that benefit the entire team.

Shaping Team Players

The following summarizes the primary options managers have for trying to turn individuals into team players.

Selection Some people already possess the interpersonal skills to be effective team players. When hiring team members, in addition to the technical skills required to fill the job, care should be taken to ensure that candidates can fulfil their team roles as well as technical requirements.

Many job candidates don't have team skills. This is especially true for those socialized around individual contributions. When faced with such candidates, managers have three options. The candidates can undergo training to "make them into team players." If this isn't possible or doesn't work, the other two options are to transfer the individual to another unit within the organization, without teams (if this possibility exists); or don't hire the candidate. In established organizations that decide to redesign jobs around teams, it should be expected that some employees will resist being team players and may be untrainable.

As part of her training to become an astronaut, Roberta Bondar worked with other NASA astronauts to become a team player. Members of shuttle crews have to work harmoniously with other crew members to achieve the mission's goals. By stressing that the mission's success depends on teamwork, NASA teaches astronauts how to compromise and make decisions that benefit the entire team.

Unfortunately, such people typically become casualties of the team approach.

Training On a more optimistic note, a large proportion of people raised on the importance of individual accomplishment can be trained to become team players. To develop team-related skills, Markham, Ontario-based AMP of Canada Ltd. put all 40 of its management people through a one-year team and project management training program of about 500 hours in 1991. They were taught how to manage commitments to each other, make specific promises and requests, and manage projects together. During 1994, the 260 people in the company underwent an intensive six-week team and project management training program called People in Action.[4]

In other companies, training specialists conduct exercises that allow employees to experience the satisfaction that teamwork can provide. They typically offer workshops to help employees improve their problem-solving, communication, negotiation, conflict-management, and coaching skills. Employees also learn the five-stage group development model described in Chapter 7. At Bell At-

lantic, for example, trainers focus on how a team goes through various stages before it finally gels. And employees are reminded of the importance of patience—because teams take longer to make decisions than if employees were acting alone.[5]

Performance evaluation Performance evaluation concepts have been almost exclusively developed with only individual employees in mind. This reflects the historic belief that individuals are the core building block around which organizations are built. But as we've described throughout this book, more and more organizations are restructuring themselves around teams. In those organizations using teams, how should they evaluate performance? Four suggestions have been offered for designing a system that supports and improves the performance of teams.[6]

1. *Tie the team's results to the organization's goals.* It's important to find measurements that apply to important goals that the team is supposed to accomplish.

2. *Begin with the team's customers and the work process that the team follows to satisfy customers' needs.* The final product the customer re-

ceives can be evaluated in terms of the customer's requirements. The transactions between teams can be evaluated based on delivery and quality. And the process steps can be evaluated based on waste and cycle time.

3. *Measure both team and individual performance.* Define the roles of each team member in terms of accomplishments that support the team's work process. Then assess each member's contribution and the team's overall performance.

4. *Train the team to create its own measures.* Having the team define its objectives and those of each member ensures everyone understands their role on the team and helps the team develop into a more cohesive unit.

Rewards The reward system should be reworked to encourage cooperative efforts rather than competitive ones. For instance, Hallmark Cards, Inc. added an annual bonus based on achievement of team goals to its basic individual-incentive system. Imperial Oil adjusted its system to reward both individual goals and team behaviours.

If companies value teamwork, then promotions, pay raises, and other forms of recognition should be given to individuals for how effective they work as a collaborative team member. This doesn't mean individual contribution is ignored; rather, it is balanced with selfless contributions to the team. Examples of behaviours that should be rewarded include training new colleagues, sharing information with teammates, helping to resolve team conflicts, and mastering new skills that the team needs but in which it is deficient.

However, Canadian organizations that use teams have been slow to link team performance to rewards in a clear way. The Conference Board of Canada reported that only 10 percent of respondents assessed contribution to team performance as part of the regular performance appraisal. Of the 45 companies that evaluated contributions to team performance as part of an employees performance appraisal, only 19 included peer review as part of the appraisal system, with 10 more reporting that they were considering implementing it.[7]

Although explicit links between team performance and extrinsic rewards are important, don't forget the intrinsic rewards that employees can receive from teamwork. Teams provide camaraderie. It's exciting and satisfying to be an integral part of a successful team. The opportunity to engage in personal development and to help teammates grow can be a very satisfying and rewarding experience for employees. For instance, at Steelcase Canada teams are invited to conferences to present their successes to delegates and top company management. Teams are encouraged to celebrate when they reach their goals, including designing the celebration themselves.

Sources:

[1] D.B. Harrison and H.P. Conn, "Mobilizing Abilities Through Teamwork," *Canadian Business Review*, Autumn 1994, p. 21.

[2] T.D. Schellhardt, "To Be a Star Among Equals, Be a Team Player," *Wall Street Journal*, April 20, 1994, p. B1.

[3] T.D. Schellhardt, "To Be a Star Among Equals, Be a Team Player," *Wall Street Journal*, April 20, 1994, p. B1.

[4] D.B. Harrison and H.P. Conn, "Mobilizing Abilities Through Teamwork," *Canadian Business Review*, Autumn 1994, p. 21.

[5] T.D. Schellhardt, "To Be a Star Among Equals, Be a Team Player," *Wall Street Journal*, April 20, 1994, p. B1.

[6] J. Zigon, "Making Performance Appraisal Work for Teams," *Training*, June 1994, pp. 58–63.

[7] P. Booth, Challenge and Change: Embracing the Team Conflict. Report 123–94, Conference Board of Canada, 1994, p. 7.

Summary and Implications

For the Workplace

Few trends have influenced employee jobs as much as the massive movement to introduce teams into the workplace. The shift from working alone to working on teams requires employees to cooperate with others, share information, confront differences, and sublimate personal interests for the greater good of the team.

High-performing teams have been found to have common characteristics. They tend to be small. They contain people with three different types of skills: technical, problem-solving and decision-making, and interpersonal. They properly match people to various roles. These teams have a commit-

ment to a common purpose, establish specific goals, and have the leadership and structure to provide focus and direction. They also hold themselves accountable at both the individual and team levels by having well-designed evaluation and reward systems. Finally, high-performing teams are characterized by high mutual trust among members.

Because individualistic organizations and societies attract and reward individual accomplishment, it is more difficult to create team players in these environments. To make the conversion, management should try to select individuals with the interpersonal skills to be effective team players, provide training to develop teamwork skills, and reward individuals for cooperative efforts.

Once teams are mature and performing effectively, management's job isn't over. This is because mature teams can become stagnant and complacent. Managers must support mature teams with advice, guidance, and training if these teams are to continue to improve.

For You as an Individual

You will be asked to work on teams and groups both during your undergraduate years and later on in life. A team experience is often a more intense experience than working in a group, because team experiences require more interdependent work. This chapter gave a number of ideas about how to get teams to perform better. Many of those examples related ways that the team itself had to pull together, develop trust, and build cohesion. You might want to use some of those suggestions as you are working to build a team. You might also want to refer to some of those suggestions when a team on which you are working seems to be suffering difficulties.

ROADMAP REMINDER

In the previous chapter we discussed the concept of groups and explained how groups developed and formed norms. In this chapter we moved to a discussion of teams, indicating that many collections of individuals form groups, not teams, and that a requirement of teams was higher participation levels. We indicated a variety of ways that teams could improve their performance. In the next chapter we move to the topic of communication. Now that we have discussed how to motivate individuals and have them work together, we want to consider how to improve communication among individuals in the workplace. The chapter on communication also opens Part 3, Sharing the Organizational Vision.

For Review

1. How can teams increase employee motivation?
2. Contrast *self-managed* and *cross-functional* teams.
3. List and describe nine team roles.
4. How do high-performing teams minimize social loafing?
5. How do high-performing teams minimize groupthink?
6. What are the five dimensions that underlie the concept of trust?
7. Under what conditions will the challenge of creating team players be greatest?

8. Contrast the pros and cons of having diverse teams.
9. How can management reinvigorate mature teams?

For Discussion

1. Don't teams create conflict? Isn't conflict bad? Why, then, would management support the concept of teams?
2. Are there factors in the Japanese society that make teams more acceptable in the workplace than in Canada or the United States? Explain.
3. What problems might surface in teams at each stage in the five-stage group development model?
4. How do you think member expectation might affect team performance?
5. Would you prefer to work alone or as part of a team? Why? How do you think your answer compares with others in your class?

LEARNING ABOUT YOURSELF EXERCISE

Do Others See Me as Trustworthy?

To get some insight into how others may view your trustworthiness, complete this questionnaire. First, however, identify the person that will be evaluating you (i.e., a colleague, friend, supervisor, team leader).

Use the following scale to score each question:

Strongly Disagree   1   2   3   4   5   6   7   8   9   10   Strongly Agree

Score

1. I can be expected to play fair. _____

2. You can confide in me and know I will keep what's told to me in confidence. _____

3. I can be counted on to tell the truth. _____

4. I would never intentionally misrepresent my point of view to others. _____

5. If I promise to do a favour, I can be counted on to carry out that promise. _____

6. If I have an appointment with someone, I can be counted on to show up promptly. _____

7. If I'm lent money, I can be counted on to pay it back as soon as possible. _____

Turn to page 699 for scoring directions and key.

Source: Based on C. Johnson-George and W.C. Swap, "Measurement of Specific Interpersonal Trust: Construction and Validation of a Scale to Assess Trust in a Specific Other," *Journal of Personality and Social Psychology*, December 1982, pp. 1306–17.

WORKING WITH OTHERS EXERCISE

Building Effective Work Teams

Objective

This exercise is designed to allow class members to (a) experience working together as a team on a specific task and (b) analyse this experience.

Time

Teams will have 90 minutes to engage in steps 2 and 3 that follow. Another 45-60 minutes will be used in class to critique and evaluate the exercise.

Procedure

1. Class members are assigned to teams of about six people.
2. Each team is required to:
    a. Determine a team name   b. Compose a team song
3. Each team is to try to find the following items on its scavenger hunt:
    a. A picture of a team
    b. A newspaper article about a group or team
    c. A piece of apparel with the university name or logo
    d. A set of chopsticks
    e. A ball of cotton
    f. A piece of stationery from a university or college department
    g. A bottle of Liquid Paper
    h. A CD-ROM
    i. A cup from McDonald's
    j. A dog leash
    k. A utility bill
    l. A calendar from last year
    m. A book by Robertson Davies
    n. An ad brochure for a Chrysler product
    o. A test tube
    p. A pack of gum
    q. An ear of corn
    r. An Alanis Morissette tape or CD
4. After 90 minutes, all teams must be back in the classroom. (A penalty, determined by the instructor, will be imposed on late teams.) The team with the most items on the list will be declared the winner. The class and instructor will determine whether the items meet the requirements of the exercise.
5. Debriefing of the exercise will begin by having each team engage in self-evaluation. Specifically, it should answer the following:
    a. What was the team's strategy?
    b. What roles did individual members perform?
    c. How effective was the team?
    d. What could the team have done to be more effective?
6. Full class discussion will focus on issues such as:
    a. What differentiated the more effective teams from the less effective teams?
    b. What did you learn from this experience that is relevant to the design of effective teams?

Source: Adapted from M.R. Manning and P.J. Schmidt, "Building Effective Work Teams: A Quick Exercise Based on a Scavenger Hunt," *Journal of Management Education*, August 1995, pp. 392-98. With permission.

CASE INCIDENT

XEL Communications

XEL Communications is a small fish in a big pond. The company employs 180 people and manufactures custom circuit boards. It competes against the likes of Nortel and AT&T.

Bill Sanko and his partners bought the company from GTE Corp. GTE is its major customer, but Bill wants to reduce its dependence on GTE. He needs to sell more to the Baby Bells and to big industrial customers that operate their own phone systems.

Bill's problem is that to compete successfully for new business he has to improve XEL's agility dramatically. He wants lightning turnaround of orders, more quickly than any big company could manage. He wants speedy response to customer needs. And he wants all of this done with close attention to cost. Unfortunately, XEL is not designed for speed or flexibility. Its costs are also too high to give the firm a competitive advantage.

For example, on the shop floor, it takes XEL eight weeks to get a product through the production cycle—from start-up to finished product. This ties up a lot of money in inventory and frustrates customers who want quick delivery. Sanko believes that high-performing teams could cut this down to four days or less. The company's structure is also burdensome. Line workers report to supervisors, who report to unit or departmental managers, who report on up the ladder to Sanko and a crew of top executives. This high vertical structure delays decision-making and increases expenses. "If a hardware engineer needs some software help, he goes to his manager," Sanko says. "The manager says, 'Go write it up.' Then the hardware manager takes the software manager to lunch and they talk about it."

Sanko has decided to reorganize his company around self-managed teams. He believes that a well-designed team structure can help him better satisfy his customers by cutting cycle time from eight weeks to four days, significantly improve quality, cut assembly costs by 25 percent, and reduce inventory costs by 50 percent. Ambitious goals? You bet! But Sanko thinks it's possible. Moreover, achieving these goals might be necessary if his company is to survive.

Questions

1. Describe, in detail, the steps you think Sanko should take in planning and implementing self-managed teams.

2. What problems should Sanko watch for?

Source: Based on J. Case, "What the Experts Forgot to Mention," *INC.*, September 1993, pp. 66–78.

Improv(e)ing Team Performance

Improv. You may have seen Second City, famed for their comedy skits, and laughed at the antics of actors engaged in improv. But improvisation is now becoming a business technique—a way of teaching employees in an organization how to form better teams. In fact, corporations are sending their employees to improv seminars to help them gain a sense of how to relate to one another, see things from another's perspective, and communicate with one another.

One such company is Saatchi and Saatchi, the large advertising agency, who sent a group of its "suits" and "creative types" to experts at Second City for some teamwork tips. Although the suits and the creatives have different working styles, in the end, they must work together in order to please the client. The lessons in improv were meant to help them reach a meeting of the minds.

During the training session, Saatchi and Saatchi employees learned about intuition, body language, sharing and accepting ideas, freedom in thinking, and courage in contributing. They did this through a variety of improv techniques including completing sentences, telling stories, and acting out scenes. One of the most important activities when working improvisationally is to accept the ideas of another, and work with those ideas. Not change the idea, but advance with the idea offered.

Not everyone understands the notion of offers and acceptance, however. One of Saatchi and Saatchi's employees did not like the story his teammates were telling, and proceeded to introduce Arnold Schwarzennegger into the story. The story immediately fell flat, as the team member went further and further away from the initial story. His team members refused to continue after his interruption. Thus, he had affected how the group was able to perform.

When asked later, the offending team member realized how distant he felt from his team after he had tried to change his story, and indicated regret.

Questions

1. Why might improv be an effective way of learning how to work together as a team?

2. Discuss the impact of the team member who refused to accept the group's story, and introduced his own instead.

3. What lessons about improv can you use in trying to do team building with a group with whom you are working?

Source: Based on "Improv," *Venture 464*; aired November 28, 1993.

Is it true that

everyone's responsibility is,

in reality,

nobody's responsibility?

–Anonymous

POINT

Teams: The Way to Go

The value of teams is now well known. Let's summarize the primary benefits that experts agree can result from the introduction of work teams.

Increased employee motivation. Work teams enhance employee involvement. They typically make jobs more interesting. They help employees meet their social needs. They also create social pressures on slackers to exert higher levels of effort in order to remain in the team's good graces.

Higher levels of productivity. Teams have the potential to create positive synergy. In recent years, the introduction of teams in most organizations has been associated with cuts in staff. What management has done is to use the positive synergy to get the same or greater output from fewer people.

Increased employee satisfaction. Employees have a need for affiliation. Working in teams can help meet this need by increasing worker interactions and creating camaraderie among team members.

Common commitment to goals. Teams encourage individuals to sublimate their individual goals for those of the group. The process of developing a common purpose, of committing to that purpose, and of agreeing upon specific goals—combined with the social pressures exerted by the team—results in a high unity of commitment to team goals.

Improved communication. Self-managed teams create interpersonal dependencies that require members to interact considerably more than when they work on jobs alone.

Expanded job skills. The implementation of teams almost always comes with expanded training building employees' technical and interpersonal skills.

Organizational flexibility. Teams focus on processes rather than functions. They encourage cross-training, so members can do each other's jobs, and expansion of skills. It's not unusual for compensation on teams to be based on the number of skills a member has acquired. This expansion of skills increases organizational flexibility.

Does the introduction of teams *always* achieve these benefits? No! For instance, a study by Ernst & Young found that forming teams to investigate and improve products and processes led to measurable improvement only in organizations that were performing poorly in their markets in terms of profit, productivity, and quality.[1] In medium-performing companies, the study found, bottom-line results were unaffected by team activities. In high-performing companies, the introduction of new team-based work systems actually lowered performance.

There are obviously contingency factors that influence the acceptance and success of teams. Some examples might be tasks that benefit from combining multiple skills; when the market will pay a premium for improved quality or innovation; with employees who value continual learning and enjoy complex tasks; and where management-employee relations already have a strong basis of mutual trust. Nevertheless, the team movement currently has tremendous momentum and reflects management's belief that teams can be successful in a wide range of settings.

Source:

[1] Cited in R. Zemke, "Rethinking the Rush to Team Up," *Training*, November 1993, p. 56.

counterPOINT

Teams Are Not Always the Answer

Beliefs about the benefits of teams have achieved an unquestioned place in the study of organizations. But teams are no panacea. Let's take a critical look at four of the assumptions that seem to underlie this team ideology.

Mature teams are task oriented and have successfully minimized the negative influences of other group forces. Task-oriented teams still experience anti-task behaviour, and indeed have much in common with other types of groups. For instance, they often suffer from infighting over assignments and decision outcomes, low participation rates, and member apathy.

Individual, group, and organizational goals can all be integrated into common team goals. Contrary to what team advocates assume, people are not so simply motivated by the sociability and self-actualization supposedly offered by work teams. These teams suffer from competitiveness, conflict, and hostility. Additionally, contrary to the notion that teams increase job satisfaction, the evidence suggests that individuals experience substantial and continuing stress as team members. Rarely is the team experience satisfying. Moreover, certain types of workers and certain types of work are better suited to solitary work situations. For the hard-driving, competitive person who thrives on individual achievement, the cult of the team player is likely to produce only frustration and stress.

Participative or shared leadership is always effective. The team ideology oversimplifies the requirement for leadership. It downplays the importance of leadership by suggesting that high-performing teams can dispense with, or ignore, leadership concerns. Group process theorists are unanimous that all groups will experience phases of identifying with, rejecting, and working through relations with authority.

This process cannot be eliminated simply by eliminating leaders from groups. The abdication of leadership can, in effect, paralyse teams.

The team environment drives out the subversive forces of politics, power, and conflict that divert groups from doing their work efficiently. Recipes for effective teams rate them on the quality of decision-making, communication, cohesion, clarity and acceptance of goals, acceptance of minority views, and other criteria. Such recipes betray the fact that teams are composed of people with self-interests who are prepared to make deals, reward favourites, punish enemies, and engage in similar behaviours to further those self-interests. Neither training nor organizational actions will alter the intrinsically political nature of teams.

The argument here has been that the team ideology, under the banner of benefits for all, ignores that teams are frequently used to camouflage coercion under the pretence of maintaining cohesion; conceal conflict under the guise of consensus; convert conformity into a semblance of creativity; delay action in the supposed interests of consultation; legitimize lack of leadership; and disguise expedient arguments and personal agendas. Teams do not necessarily provide fulfilment of individual needs, nor do they necessarily contribute to individual satisfaction and performance or organizational effectiveness. On the contrary, it's likely that the infatuation with teams and making every employee part of a team results in organizations not getting the best performance from many of their members.

Source: Based on A. Sinclair, "The Tyranny of a Team Ideology," *Organization Studies*, Vol. 13, No. 4 (1992), pp. 611–26.

PROGRESSIVE CASE • PART 2

Lee Simpson: Managing and Inspiring Individuals and Teams

"I believe the greatest motivation you can give an employee is pride in work well done. This is done by encouraging them to feel their own pride in what they have accomplished, rather than simply telling them that you feel proud of them." Lee Simpson feels that she learned a lot about motivation from being a mother. "I am a much better manager today because I have had the experience of being a mother. Now this does not mean that you can only be a good manager if you are a mother. I don't mean that. But I do believe that parenting skills and the things that you learn through reading books about parenting could serve as excellent guidelines to managers."

Simpson notes that what motivates employees to perform well individually is not necessarily the same as what motivates the organization as a whole. For instance, Maclean-Hunter values advertising revenue and increases in subscription renewal rates. Simpson explains, "The firm values these because it has an obligation to the shareholders to ensure that those items give the appropriate returns on investment. Employees have a very hard time feeling good about what the shareholders care about. So despite the fact that we motivate employees through salaries and commissions, you also have to find the things that will make them smile."

Maclean-Hunter conducts formal performance appraisals separately from salary reviews and at a different time of the year. This means that performance appraisals focus on helping employees understand how they are doing, not on their compensation. Simpson does the performance appraisals of those who report to her. She acknowledges that the Rogers and Maclean-Hunter joint salary appraisal program has restrictions that limit her ability to reward people extraordinarily, i.e., above and beyond the industry average.

While performance appraisals give formal feedback, Simpson says she is a great believer in memos as a way of communicating informally about effective performance to her employees. "I write very good memos and people like to receive them. I learned this

very early when somebody shyly, very shyly showed me a memo I'd written to them two years before, remarking on a job they had done, and they kept it in their file. And I thought, 'Wow, I had no idea my words had so much meaning to them.' People really care about hearing positive feedback and it takes no money to write a memo." The memos serve as intrinsic rewards for good performance.

Simpson explained that extrinsic rewards in the form of bonuses are given for either qualitative or quantitative results. For instance, those assigned to raising advertising revenue might be given a bonus for bringing in extra revenue. A department manager might be given a bonus for carrying out a successful department reorganization. The food editor might be rewarded for increases in reader satisfaction based on recipes and their presentation. For each employee, goals for the year are set by the employee and the manager together. An employee might propose to do X amount of work next year, while the manager might say, "You know, I think you can do X plus three percent." With other employees, the manager might say, "It's best to do X minus five percent. You are over-reaching and failing to service existing clients properly."

Simpson is considering encouraging her editors to develop projects that may lead to bonuses. She notes, "I would be quite heartened if an editor came to me and said, 'You know, three of my associate editors say they would really like the opportunity to receive a cash bonus built in for a specific objective.'" Simpson believes that employees should show initiative in the workplace, and she is willing to encourage initiative-taking behaviour. For instance, if employees in Brand Development bring forward new ideas that are implemented, they will get a percentage of eventual proceeds from the new project or occasionally get a cash bonus on the spot.

Though Simpson emphasises the positive benefits of rewards, she also says that it is important to let people know when their performance or attitude is not satisfactory or if their particular job is not suitable

for them. She thinks this should be done early enough that employees can make their own decisions and live with their ego intact.

While many of the rewards Simpson has mentioned are for individual effort, she notes that a lot of the work at Maclean-Hunter is done through teams. For instance, in the editorial group, "You have a number of people working on an article, including the art director, the copyeditor, the managing editor, the supervising editor, and the freelance writer. All of these people have to work together to produce an article and the photographs that go with it." To develop better team relationships, team-building exercises and activities are often included at conferences for both the editorial and sales groups.

Team members don't evaluate each other in a formal sense, but Simpson is confident that at the end of most meetings, team members have a good sense of whether ideas they have proposed will be pursued by other team members. Many employees have the opportunity, if they want, to serve on other cross-functional teams as well, including Physical Planning, Strategic Planning, or the United Way Campaign. "Anyone who wants to be a lone wolf should find a career other than publishing. Publishing really is more dependent on this kind of teamwork than most other jobs."

Questions

1. To what extent do you think Simpson should feel responsible for her employees' performance?

2. What theories could help explain Simpson's motivation techniques?

3. What do you think about encouraging employees (such as the editors, in this case) to come up with their own initiatives for bonuses?

4. What do you think of the reward structure at Maclean-Hunter as it relates to teams?

CHAPTER 9

Communication

ROADMAP

LEARNING OBJECTIVES

After studying this chapter, you should be able to

- Define communication

- Identify factors affecting the use of the informal network or grapevine

- List common barriers to effective communication

- Describe an effective communication program in an organization undergoing dramatic changes

- Outline the behaviours related to effective active listening

- Contrast the meaning of talk for men versus women

- Describe potential problems in cross-cultural communication

- Discuss how technology is changing organizational communication

Can the misunderstanding of a few words literally mean the difference between life and death? They can in the airline business. A number of aviation disasters have been largely attributed to problems in communication.[1] Consider the following:

History's worst aviation disaster occurred in 1977 at foggy Tenerife in the Canary Islands. The captain of a KLM flight thought the air traffic controller had cleared him to take off. But the controller intended only to give departure instructions. Although the language spoken between the Dutch KLM captain and the Spanish controller was English, confusion was created by heavy accents and improper terminology. The KLM Boeing 747 hit a Pan Am 747 at full throttle on the runway, killing 583 people.

In 1990, Colombian Avianca pilots, after several holding patterns caused by bad weather, told controllers as they neared New York Kennedy Airport that their Boeing 707 was "running low on fuel." Controllers hear those words all the time, so they took no special action. While the pilots knew there was a serious problem, they failed to use a key phrase—"fuel emergency"—which would have obligated controllers to direct the Avianca flight ahead of all others and clear it to land as soon as possible. The people at Kennedy never understood the true nature of the pilots' problem. The jet ran out of fuel and crashed 25 kilometres from Kennedy. Seventy-three people died.

In 1997, a Garuda Airlines Airbus crashed into a highland jungle in Indonesia, killing all 234 passengers and crew aboard. The control tower had first instructed the pilot to turn right, and then requested a confirmation of a left turn. When the pilot, a bit confused, replied, "Confirm turning left? We are starting turning right now," the controller replied, "OK. Continue turning right." Immediately thereafter the plane smashed into trees and exploded. ■

The preceding examples tragically illustrate how miscommunication can have deadly consequences. In this chapter, we'll show (obviously not in as dramatic a fashion) that good communication is essential to any group's or organization's effectiveness.

Research indicates that poor communication is probably the most frequently cited source of interpersonal conflict.[2] Individuals spend nearly 70 percent of their waking hours communicating—writing, reading, speaking, listening—which means that they have many opportunities in which to engage in poor communication. It is also likely that one of the most inhibiting forces to successful group performance is a lack of effective communication. In 1997, a WorkCanada survey of 2039 Canadians in six industrial and service categories explored the state of communication in Canadian businesses.[3] The survey found that 61 percent of senior executives believe that they do a good job of communicating with employees. However, those who work below the senior executives fail to share this feeling; only 33 percent of the managers and department heads believe that senior executives were effective communicators. The report of communication was even lower for those in non-managerial positions: only 22 percent of hourly workers, 27 percent of clerical employees, and 22 percent of professional staff reported that senior executives did a good job of communicating with them.

The examples from our opening vignette and the survey of communication practices in the Canadian workplace both highlight that communication is an important problem and consideration for both organizations and individuals. In this chapter we explore the topic of communication, illustrating what it takes to communicate effectively, and also underscoring the barriers to effective communication.

communication
The transference and understanding of meaning.

No group can exist without **communication**: the transference of meaning among its members. After all, it is only through transmitting meaning from one person to another that information and ideas can be conveyed. Communication, however, is more than merely imparting meaning; it must also be understood. For example, in a group where one member speaks only German and the others do not know German, the German-speaking individual will not be fully understood. Therefore, communication must include both the *transference* and the *understanding* of meaning.

An idea, no matter how great, is useless until it is transmitted and understood by others. Perfect communication, if there were such a thing, would exist when a thought or an idea was transmitted so that the mental picture perceived by the receiver was exactly the same as that envisioned by the sender. Although elementary in theory, perfect communication is never achieved in practice, for reasons we will expand upon later.

Before making too many generalizations concerning communication and problems in communicating effectively, we need to review briefly the functions that communication performs and describe the communication process.

Functions of Communication

Communication serves four major functions within a group or organization: motivation, emotional expression, information, and control.[4]

Communication fosters *motivation* by clarifying to employees what is to be done, how well they are doing, and how to improve performance if it's subpar. We saw this operating in our review of goal-setting and reinforce-

ment theories in Chapter 5. The formation of specific goals, feedback on progress toward the goals, and reinforcement of desired behaviour all stimulate motivation and require communication.

For many employees, their work group is a primary source for social interaction. The communication that takes place within the group is a fundamental mechanism by which members show their frustrations and feelings of satisfaction. Communication, therefore, provides a release for the *emotional expression* of feelings and for fulfilment of social needs.

Communication also provides the *information* that individuals and groups need to make decisions by transmitting the data to identify and evaluate alternative choices. The quality of the communication, in the form of information, will have a direct effect on the quality of the decision made.

Finally, communication acts to *control* member behaviour in several ways. Organizations have authority hierarchies and formal guidelines that employees are required to follow. When employees, for instance, are required to first communicate any job-related grievance to their immediate boss, to follow their job description, or to comply with company policies, communication is performing a control function. But informal communication also controls behaviour. For example, when work groups tease or harass a member who produces too much (and makes the rest of the group look bad), they are informally communicating with, and controlling, the member's behaviour.

None of these four functions should be viewed as being more important than the others. For groups to perform effectively, they need to stimulate members to perform, provide a means for emotional expression, make decision choices, and maintain some form of control over members. You can assume that almost every communication interaction that takes place in a group or organization performs one or more of these four functions.

The Communication Process

Home Depot
www.homedepot.com/

Communication can be thought of as a process or flow. Communication problems occur when deviations or blockages occur in that flow. In this section, we describe the process in terms of a communication model and consider how distortions can disrupt the process.

Communication at Home Depot is designed to give employees information, build their morale, and provide a release for the emotional expression of their feelings. Company founders Bernard Marcus and Arthur Blank spend about 40 percent of their time in stores talking with employees, who are encouraged to express their opinions without fear of being fired or demoted. During a closed-circuit television program called "Breakfast with Bernie and Art," Marcus (shown here) and Blank speak to employees from one of their stores, updating them on corporate news, sharing sales and profits results, and answering their questions.

A Communication Model

Before communication can take place, a purpose, expressed as a message to be conveyed, is needed. It passes between a source (the sender) and a receiver. The message is encoded (converted to symbolic form) and is passed by way of some medium (channel) to the receiver, who retranslates (decodes) the message initiated by the sender. The result is a transference of meaning from one person to another.[5]

Exhibit 9-1 depicts the **communication process**. This model is composed of seven parts: (1) the communication source, (2) encoding, (3) the message, (4) the channel, (5) decoding, (6) the receiver, and (7) feedback.

The source initiates a message by **encoding** a thought. Four conditions have been described that affect the encoded message: skill, attitudes, knowledge, and the social-cultural system.

Our success in communicating to you depends upon our writing skills; if the authors of textbooks lack the requisite writing skills, their messages will not reach students in the form desired. One's total communicative success also includes speaking, reading, listening, and reasoning skills. As we discussed in Chapter 4, our attitudes influence our behaviour. We hold predisposed ideas on numerous topics, and our communications are affected by these attitudes. Furthermore, we are restricted in our communicative activity by the extent of our knowledge of the particular topic. We cannot communicate what we don't know, and should our knowledge be too extensive, it's possible that our receiver will not understand our message. Clearly, the amount of knowledge the source holds about his or her subject will affect the message that he or she seeks to transfer. And, finally, just as attitudes influence our behaviour, so does our position in the social-cultural system in which we exist. Your beliefs and values, which are all part of your culture, act to influence you as a communicative source.

The **message** is the actual physical product from the source encoding. "When we speak, the speech is the message. When we write, the writing is the message. When we paint, the picture is the message. When we gesture, the movements of our arms, the expressions on our face are the message."[6] Our message is affected by the code or group of symbols we use to transfer meaning, the content of the message itself, and the decisions that we make in selecting and arranging both codes and content.

The **channel** is the medium through which the message travels. It is selected by the source, who must determine which channel is formal and which one is informal. Formal channels are established by the organization and transmit messages that pertain to the job-related activities of members. They traditionally follow the authority network within the organization. Other forms of messages, such as personal or social, follow the informal channels in the organization. Examples of channels are formal memos, voice mail, e-mail, meetings, and so on.

communication process
The steps between a source and a receiver that result in the transference and understanding of meaning.

encoding
Converting a communication message to symbolic form.

message
What is communicated.

channel
The medium through which a communication message travels.

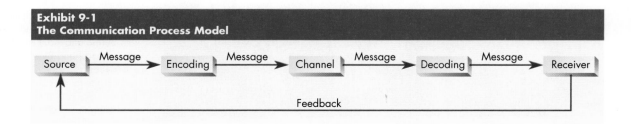

Exhibit 9-1
The Communication Process Model

Source → Message → Encoding → Message → Channel → Message → Decoding → Message → Receiver

Feedback

decoding
Retranslating a sender's communication message.

The receiver is the object to whom the message is directed. But before the message can be received, the symbols in it must be translated into a form that can be understood by the receiver. This is the **decoding** of the message. Just as the encoder was limited by his or her skills, attitudes, knowledge, and social-cultural system, the receiver is equally restricted. Just as the source must be skilled in writing or speaking, the receiver must also be skilled in reading or listening, and both must be able to reason. To find out more about your listening abilities, see the Learning About Yourself exercise at the end of this chapter.

feedback loop
The final link in the communication process; puts the message back into the system as a check against misunderstandings.

The final link in the communication process is a **feedback loop**. "If a communication source decodes the message that he encodes, if the message is put back into his system, we have feedback."[7] Feedback is the check on how successful we have been in transferring our messages as originally intended. It determines whether understanding has been achieved.

Sources of Distortion

Unfortunately, most of the seven components in the process model have the potential to create distortion and, therefore, impinge upon the goal of communicating perfectly. These sources of distortion explain why the message that is decoded by the receiver is rarely the exact message that the sender intended.

If the encoding is done carelessly, the message will be distorted. The poor choice of symbols and confusion in the content of the message can cause problems. Of course, the channel can distort a communication if a poor one is selected or if the noise level is high. The receiver represents the final potential source for distortion. His or her prejudices, knowledge, perceptual skills, attention span, and care in decoding are all factors that can result in interpreting the message somewhat differently than envisioned by the sender. (See Exhibit 9-2.)

Exhibit 9-2
Empty Words That Create Distortions

Many people today use a vocabulary of "filler words" that contribute to imprecise language. The following are examples of words and phrases that distort communication because they're confusing, ambiguous, or offer no additional information to many listeners. They can be eliminated (indicated by X) or written in a shorter form (shown in parentheses):

OK (X)

basically (X)

it will be necessary to (I, you, or we must)

involve the necessity of (demand, require)

is a person who (X)

all things being equal (X)

needless to say (X)

for the reason that, for this reason (because)

Source: Some of these examples were taken from Ron S. Blicq, *Communicating at Work*, (Scarborough, ON: Prentice Hall Canada Inc., 1997).

Communication Fundamentals

A working knowledge of communication requires a basic understanding of some fundamental concepts. In this section, we review those concepts. Specifically, we look at the flow patterns of communication, compare formal and informal communication networks, describe the importance of nonverbal communication, consider how individuals select communication channels, and summarize the major barriers to effective communication.

Direction of Communication

Communication can flow vertically or laterally. The vertical dimension can be further divided into downward and upward directions.[8]

DOWNWARD   Communication that flows from one level of a group or organization to a lower level is a downward communication.

   When we think of managers communicating with subordinates, the downward pattern is the one we usually think of. Group leaders and managers use this approach to assign goals, provide job instructions, inform subordinates of policies and procedures, identify problems that need attention, and offer feedback about performance. The complex issues associated with performance feedback are discussed in more detail in our HR Implications feature at the end of this chapter. But downward communication doesn't have to involve verbal or face-to-face contact. For example, when management sends letters to employees' homes to advise them of the organization's new sick-leave policy, it is using downward communication.

UPWARD   Upward communication flows to a higher level in the group or organization. It is used to provide feedback to one's supervisor or others higher in the organization to inform them of progress toward goals, and communicate current problems. Upward communication informs managers of how employees feel about their jobs, co-workers, and the organization in general. Managers also rely on upward communication for ideas on areas of improvement.

Lee Kun Hee, chairman of the South Korean conglomerate Samsung, uses downward communication to deliver what he calls "shock therapy" to his 180 000 employees. To correct customer complaints about defective products, unappealing designs, and poor after-sales service, Lee prepared 300 hours of videotapes and 750 hours of audiotapes that tell employees what they must do to improve the quality of Samsung products. Lee, shown here on video, told employees to "change everything but your wives and children."

Some organizational examples of upward communication are performance reports prepared by lower management for review by middle and top management, suggestion boxes, employee attitude surveys, grievance procedures, superior-subordinate discussions, and informal sessions where employees have the opportunity to identify and discuss problems with their boss or representatives of higher management. For example, at Vancouver-based heavy-equipment dealer Finning International, employees complete climate surveys and reviews of management. Finning notes that the attention management gives to these surveys has led to improved employee satisfaction and safety. At British Columbia-based A&W Food Services of Canada, management encourages employee feedback through regular open and honest discussions. And when Tom Stephens' became CEO of Vancouver-based MacMillan Bloedel, his first goal was to change the culture. He started by becoming more accessible, and urging employees to express their concerns on his voice-mail. He found that many of the messages complained of poor communication in the company, something he's worked hard to change during his first year as CEO.[9] Similarly, at Xerox Canada, the annual employee attitude survey includes a section on management practices and behaviour, to elicit feedback on management performance separate from the objective numbers of production. And if managers want additional feedback on their management styles, they may also conduct a "management practices" survey at any time during the year.[10] Dianne McGarry, president and CEO of Xerox Canada, has deliberately attempted "to foster an open, honest environment that gets issues out on the table, that gets people to talk about what's on their minds."[11]

Despite these examples, however, in general few Canadian firms rely on upward communication. In their study of 375 Canadian organizations, David Saunders of McGill University and Joanne Leck of École des Hautes Études Commerciales found that unionized organizations were more likely to use upward communication. Seventy percent of unionized firms had grievance procedures, compared to six percent of non-unionized firms. Committees and meetings were the next most frequent upward communication technique (33 percent for non-unionized, 44 percent for unionized). Less than 15 percent of either type of firm used suggestion programs.[12] It is important to note that simply collecting information from employees, but then not acting on it, even if it's just to inform the employees that their concerns are being considered, will have a negative effect on employees overall. Most workers do not appreciate solicitation of information if it will not be used for some purpose.

LATERAL When communication occurs among members of the same work group, among members of work groups at the same level, among managers at the same level, or among any horizontally equivalent personnel, we describe it as lateral communication.

Why would there be a need for horizontal communications if a group or organization's vertical communications are effective? The answer is that horizontal communications are often necessary to save time and facilitate coordination. In some cases, these lateral relationships are formally sanctioned. Often, they are informally created to short-circuit the vertical hierarchy and expedite action. So lateral communications can, from management's perspective, be good or bad. Since strict adherence to the formal vertical structure for all communications can impede the efficient and accurate transfer of information, lateral communications can be beneficial. In such cases, they

occur with the knowledge and support of superiors. But they can create dysfunctional conflicts when the formal vertical channels are breached, when members go above or around their superiors to get things done, or when bosses find out that actions have been taken or decisions made without their knowledge.

Formal versus Informal Networks

communication networks
Channels by which information flows.

formal networks
Task-related communications that follow the authority chain.

informal network
The communication grapevine.

Communication networks define the channels by which information flows. These channels are one of two varieties—either formal or informal. **Formal networks** are typically vertical, follow the authority chain, and are limited to task-related communications. In contrast, the **informal network**—usually better known as the grapevine—is free to move in any direction, skip authority levels, and is as likely to satisfy group members' social needs as it is to facilitate task accomplishments.

FORMAL SMALL-GROUP NETWORKS Exhibit 9-3 illustrates three common small-group networks. These are the chain, wheel, and all-channel. The chain rigidly follows the formal chain of command. The wheel relies on the leader to act as the central conduit for all the group's communication. The all-channel network permits all group members to communicate actively with each other.

As Exhibit 9-4 demonstrates, the effectiveness of each network depends on the dependent variable you are concerned about. For instance, the structure of the wheel facilitates the emergence of a leader, the all-channel network is best if you are concerned with having high member satisfaction, and the chain is best if accuracy is most important. Exhibit 9-4 leads us to the conclusion that no single network will be best for all occasions.

THE INFORMAL NETWORK The previous discussion of networks emphasized formal communication patterns, but the formal system is not the only communication system in a group or between groups. Now let's turn our attention to the informal system, where information flows along the well-known grapevine and rumours can flourish.

The grapevine has three main characteristics.[13] First, it is not controlled by management. Second, it is perceived by most employees as being more believable and reliable than formal communiqués issued by top management. Third, it is largely used to serve the self-interests of those people within it.

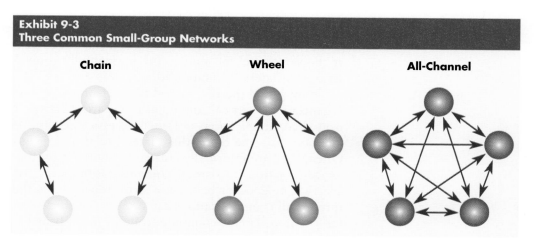

Exhibit 9-3
Three Common Small-Group Networks

Chain   **Wheel**   **All-Channel**

Exhibit 9-4
Small-Group Networks and Effectiveness Channels

Criteria	Networks		
	Chain	**Wheel**	**All-Channel**
Speed	Moderate	Fast	Fast
Accuracy	High	High	Moderate
Emergence of a leader	Moderate	High	None
Member satisfaction	Moderate	Low	High

liaison
Person who passes information on to others.

One of the most famous studies of the grapevine investigated the communication pattern among 67 managerial personnel in a small manufacturing firm.[14] The basic approach used was to learn from each communication recipient how he or she first received a given piece of information and then trace it back to its source. It was found that, while the grapevine was an important source of information, only 10 percent of the executives acted as **liaison** individuals, that is, passed the information on to more than one other person. For example, when one executive decided to resign, 81 percent of the executives knew about it, but only 11 percent transmitted this information on to others.

Two other conclusions from this study are also worth noting. Information on events of general interest tended to flow between the major functional groups (for example, between production and sales) rather than within them. Also, no evidence surfaced to suggest that members of any one group consistently acted as liaisons; rather, different types of information passed through different liaison persons.

An attempt to replicate this study among employees in a small government office also found that only a small percentage (10 percent) acted as liaison individuals.[15] This is interesting, since the replication contained a wider spectrum of employees including rank-and-file as well as managerial personnel. However, the flow of information in the government office took place within, rather than between, functional groups. It was proposed that this discrepancy might be due to comparing an executive-only sample against one that also included rank-and-file workers. Managers, for example, might feel greater pressure to stay informed and thus cultivate others outside their immediate functional group. Also, in contrast to the findings of the original study, the replication found that a consistent group of individuals acted as liaisons by transmitting information in the government office.

Is the information that flows along the grapevine accurate? The evidence indicates that about 75 percent of what is carried is accurate.[16] But what conditions foster an active grapevine? What gets the rumour mill rolling?

It is frequently assumed that rumours start because they make titillating gossip. However, this is rarely the case. Rumours have at least four purposes: (1) to structure and reduce anxiety; (2) to make sense of limited or fragmented information; (3) to serve as a vehicle to organize group members, and possibly outsiders, into coalitions; and (4) to signal a sender's status ("I'm an insider and, with respect to this rumour, you're an outsider") or power ("I have the power to make you into an insider").[17] Research indicates that rumours emerge as a response to situations that are important to us, where there is ambiguity, and under conditions that arouse anxiety.[18]

Work situations frequently contain these three elements, which explains why rumours flourish in organizations. The secrecy and competition that typically prevail in large organizations around such issues as the appointment of new bosses, the relocation of offices, and the realignment of work assignments create conditions that encourage and sustain rumours on the grapevine. A rumour will persist either until the wants and expectations creating the uncertainty underlying the rumour are fulfilled or until the anxiety is reduced.

What can we conclude from this discussion? Certainly the grapevine is an important part of any group or organization's communication network and well worth understanding.[19] It identifies for managers those confusing issues that employees consider important and anxiety provoking. It acts, therefore, as both a filter and a feedback mechanism, picking up the issues that employees consider relevant. Perhaps more important, again from a managerial perspective, it seems possible to analyse grapevine information and to predict its flow, given that only a small set of individuals (around 10 percent) actively passes on information to more than one other person. By assessing which liaison individuals will consider a given piece of information to be relevant, we can improve our ability to explain and predict the pattern of the grapevine.

Can management entirely eliminate rumours? No! What management should do, however, is minimize the negative consequences of rumours by limiting their range and impact. Exhibit 9-5 offers a few suggestions for minimizing those negative consequences.

Creating Effective Mechanisms for Communication

How many of us have been told "If you have any problems, just let us know?" Or been told by a professor "Class participation is important in this course, so please speak up in class"? In both of these instances, the person giving us the message may genuinely want information or participation, but often this does not inspire a person to act on that request. For instance, the request for feedback about problems does not really inform the person about how to let the person know about the problems. And the request for more class participation does not necessarily convey how to participate.

mechanisms
Practices designed to reinforce your message and enable people to carry it out.

Jim Collins, co-author of the bestselling management book *Built to Last*,[20] notes the importance of creating effective **mechanisms**, "the practices that bring what you stand for to life and stimulate change."[21] Mechanisms can be used to support the messages that managers and organizations are

---

Exhibit 9-5
Suggestions for Reducing the Negative Consequences of Rumours

1. Announce timetables for making important decisions.
2. Explain decisions and behaviours that may appear inconsistent or secretive.
3. Emphasize the downside, as well as the upside, of current decisions and future plans.
4. Openly discuss worst-case possibilities — it is almost never as anxiety provoking as the unspoken fantasy.

Source: Adapted from L. Hirschhorn, "Managing Rumors," in L. Hirschhorn (ed.), *Cutting Back* (San Francisco: Jossey-Bass, 1983), pp. 54–56. With permission.

trying to convey. For instance, Collins cites the example of Granite Rock Co., which wanted to signal to customers its commitment to quality and customer service. To make this clear to customers, each Granite Rock invoice contains the guarantee: "If you're not satisfied with something, don't pay us for it. Simply scratch out the related line item and send your cheque for the remaining balance." By doing this, Granite Rock is not simply claiming a strategy of good customer service, but it is also putting in place a mechanism so that if a customer is dissatisfied, he or she knows what to do. And the company clearly receives the message that there's a problem when a line item is crossed off the invoice by the customer and less money is received than expected.

When Collins was a professor at the Stanford Graduate School of Business, he wanted to ensure that if students had an important insight to share with the class, that they had the opportunity to be heard. He also knew, however, that with 66 students in his class, some very important insights might go unnoticed. So, he created a mechanism to guarantee students that when they had something really important to say, they would have the opportunity to speak up. At the beginning of the term he gave each student a sheet of bright red paper and told them "This is your red flag. You get to raise it only one time in a quarter, but when you do—no matter what's going on—the world will stop for you. So when you have your best contribution to make, your key insight or challenge or story, that's your red-flag point. You're the only screen. Raise the flag, and the floor is yours."

In the workplace, Collins notes that most executives try to solve problems with initiatives and memos, rather than creating mechanisms that signal how people are to act. He suggests that an executive facing the problem of getting people to share their important ideas might have come into Collins' classroom and addressed the students by saying, "It's come to my attention that people may not be getting their comments in...I really want to emphasize again that if you have something important to say, make sure you get heard." However, this would not have conveyed how students could ensure that they were heard. So the next step is to create the mechanism to ensure that happens. Organizations and managers could improve communication by providing mechanisms to employees, customers, and clients so that they know specifically the action they are to take.

Organizations may also help employees improve communication through evaluation of their communication styles. The Johari Window, one model used by training specialists for this purpose, is discussed in more detail in this chapter's Point/Counterpoint feature, along with a counterargument proposing that ambiguity in communication is often more effective and desirable than openness.

Nonverbal Communication

Anyone who has ever paid a visit to a singles bar or a nightclub is aware that communication need not be verbal in order to convey a message. A glance, a stare, a smile, a frown, a provocative body movement—they all convey meaning. This example illustrates that no discussion of communication would be complete without a discussion of **nonverbal communications**. This includes body movements, facial expressions, and the physical distance between the sender and receiver. To understand more about the implications of the absence of nonverbal communication, turn to the Working With Others exercise at the end of the chapter.

Granite Rock Inc.
www.graniterock.com/

nonverbal communications
Messages conveyed through body movements, facial expressions, and the physical distance between the sender and receiver.

kinesics
The study of body motions, such as gestures, facial configurations, and other movements of the body.

The academic study of body motions has been labelled **kinesics**. It refers to gestures, facial configurations, and other movements of the body. It is a relatively new field, and it has been subject to far more conjecture and popularizing than the research findings support. Hence, while we acknowledge that body movement is an important segment of the study of communication and behaviour, conclusions must be guarded. Recognizing this qualification, let us briefly consider the ways in which body motions convey meaning.

It has been argued that every body movement has a meaning and that no movement is accidental.[22] For example, through body language, we can say such things as, "Help me, I'm confused," or "Leave me alone, I'm really angry." And rarely do we send our messages consciously. We act out our state of being with nonverbal body language. We lift one eyebrow for disbelief. We rub our noses for puzzlement. We clasp our arms to isolate ourselves or to protect ourselves. We shrug our shoulders for indifference, wink one eye for intimacy, tap our fingers for impatience, slap our forehead for forgetfulness.[23] Babies and young children provide another good illustration of effective use of nonverbal communication. Although they lack developed language skills, they often use fairly sophisticated body language to communicate their physical and emotional needs. Such a use of body language underscores its importance in communicating needs throughout life.

While we may disagree with the specific meaning of these movements, body language adds to and often complicates verbal communication. A body position or movement does not by itself have a precise or universal meaning, but when it is linked with spoken language, it gives fuller meaning to a sender's message.

If you read the verbatim minutes of a meeting, you could not grasp the impact of what was said in the same way you could if you had been there or saw the meeting on video. Why? There is no record of nonverbal communication. The *intonations* or emphasis given to words or phrases is missing.

The *facial expression* of the instructor will also convey meaning. A snarling face says something different from a smile. Facial expressions, along with intonations, can show arrogance, aggressiveness, fear, shyness, and other characteristics that would never be communicated if you read a transcript of the meeting.

The way individuals space themselves in terms of *physical distance* also has meaning. What is considered proper spacing is largely dependent on cultural norms. For example, what is considered to be businesslike distance in some European countries would be viewed as intimate in many parts of North America. If someone stands closer to you than expected according to your cultural norms, you may interpret the action as an expression of aggressiveness or sexual interest. However, if the person stands farther away than you expect, you might think he or she is displeased with you or uninterested. Someone whose cultural norms differ from yours might be very surprised by your interpretation.

It is important for the receiver to be alert to these nonverbal aspects of communication. You should look for nonverbal cues as well as listen to the literal meaning of a sender's words. You should particularly be aware of contradictions between the messages. The boss may say that she is free to talk to you about that raise you have been seeking, but you may see non-

Words are not the only source of meaning for the receiver. Body language adds shades of meaning to verbal communication.

verbal signals that suggest that this is not the time to discuss the subject. Regardless of what is being said, an individual who frequently glances at her watch is giving the message that she would prefer to end the conversation. We misinform others when we express one emotion verbally, such as trust, but nonverbally communicate a contradictory message that reads, "I don't have confidence in you." These contradictions often suggest that "actions speak louder (and more accurately) than words."

Choice of Communication Channel

communication apprehension
Undue tension and anxiety about oral communication, written communication, or both.

Why do people choose one channel of communication over another; for instance, a phone call instead of a face-to-face talk? One answer might be: Anxiety! An estimated 5 to 20 percent of the population[24] suffer from debilitating **communication apprehension** or anxiety. We all know people who dread speaking in front of a group, but some people may find it extremely difficult to talk with others face-to-face or become extremely anxious when they have to use the telephone. As a result, they may rely on memos, letters, or e-mail to convey messages when a phone call would not only be faster but also more appropriate.

But what about the 80 to 95 percent of the population who don't suffer from this problem? Is there any general insight we might be able to provide regarding choice of communication channel? The answer is a qualified "yes." A model of media richness has been developed to explain channel selection among managers.[25]

channel richness
The amount of information that can be transmitted during a communication episode.

Recent research has found that channels differ in their capacity to convey information. Some are rich in that they have the ability to (1) handle multiple cues simultaneously, (2) facilitate rapid feedback, and (3) be very personal. Others are lean in that they score low on these three factors. As Exhibit 9-6 illustrates, face-to-face talk scores highest in terms of **channel richness** because it provides for the maximum amount of information to be

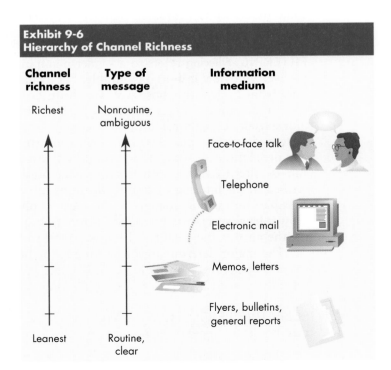

Exhibit 9-6
Hierarchy of Channel Richness

Channel richness	Type of message	Information medium
Richest	Nonroutine, ambiguous	Face-to-face talk
		Telephone
		Electronic mail
		Memos, letters
Leanest	Routine, clear	Flyers, bulletins, general reports

transmitted during a communication episode. That is, it offers multiple information cues (words, postures, facial expressions, gestures, intonations), immediate feedback (both verbal and nonverbal), and the personal touch of "being there." Impersonal written media such as bulletins and general reports rate lowest in richness.

The choice of one channel over another depends on whether the message is routine or nonroutine. The former types of messages tend to be straightforward and have a minimum of ambiguity. The latter are likely to be complicated and have the potential for misunderstanding. Managers can communicate routine messages efficiently through channels that are lower in richness. However, they can communicate nonroutine messages effectively only by selecting rich channels. Evidence indicates that high-performing managers tend to be more media sensitive than low-performing managers.[26] That is, they're better able to match appropriate media richness with the ambiguity involved in the communication.

The media richness model is consistent with organizational trends and practices during the past decade. It is not just coincidence that more and more senior managers have been using meetings to facilitate communication and are regularly leaving the isolated sanctuary of their executive offices to manage by walking around. These executives are relying on richer channels of communication to transmit the more ambiguous messages they need to convey. The past decade has been characterized by organizations closing facilities, imposing large layoffs, restructuring, merging, consolidating, and introducing new products and services at an accelerated pace—all nonroutine messages high in ambiguity and requiring the use of channels that can convey a large amount of information. It is not surprising, therefore, to see the most effective managers expanding their use of rich channels.

Barriers to Effective Communication

We conclude our discussion of communication fundamentals by reviewing some of the more prominent barriers to effective communication of which you should be aware.

filtering
A sender's manipulation of information so that it will be seen more favourably by the receiver.

General Motors Canada
www.gmcanada.com

FILTERING **Filtering** refers to a sender manipulating information so that the receiver will view it more favourably. For example, when a manager tells his boss what he feels his boss wants to hear, he is filtering information. Does this happen much in organizations? Sure! As information is passed up to senior executives, subordinates must condense and synthesize it so that those on top don't become overloaded with information. The personal interests and perceptions of what is important by those doing the synthesizing will result in filtering. As a former group vice-president of General Motors described it, the filtering of communications through levels at GM made it impossible for senior managers to receive objective information because "lower-level specialists provided information in such a way that they would get the answer they wanted. I know. I used to be down below and do it."[27]

The major determinant of filtering is the number of levels in an organization's structure. The more vertical levels in the organization's hierarchy, the more opportunities there are for filtering.

SELECTIVE PERCEPTION We have mentioned selective perception before in this book. It appears again because the receivers in the communication

process selectively see and hear based on their needs, motivations, experience, background, and other personal characteristics. Receivers also project their interests and expectations into communications as they decode them. For example, the employment interviewer who believes that young people are more interested in spending time on leisure and social activities than working extra hours to further their careers is likely to apply that stereotype to all young job applicants. As we discussed in Chapter 3, we don't see reality; rather, we interpret what we see and call it reality.

DEFENSIVENESS When people feel that they're being threatened, they tend to react in ways that reduce their ability to achieve mutual understanding. That is, they become defensive—engaging in behaviours such as verbally attacking others, making sarcastic remarks, being overly judgmental, and questioning others' motives. So when individuals interpret another's message as threatening, they often respond in ways that hinder effective communication.

LANGUAGE Words mean different things to different people. "The meanings of words are not in the words; they are in us."[28] Age, education, and cultural background are three of the more obvious variables that influence the language a person uses and the definitions he or she gives to words. For instance, when Alanis Morissette sang "Isn't It Ironic?", middle-aged English professors complained that she completely misunderstood the meaning of "irony"—but the millions who bought her CD understood what she meant.

In an organization, employees usually come from diverse backgrounds and, therefore, have different patterns of speech. Additionally, the grouping of employees into departments creates specialists who develop their own jargon or technical language. In large organizations, members are also frequently widely dispersed geographically—even operating in different countries—and individuals in each locale will use terms and phrases that are unique to their area. The existence of vertical levels can also cause language problems. The language of senior executives, for instance, can be mystifying to operative employees who are unfamiliar with management jargon.

The point is that while you and I speak a common language, English, our usage of that language is far from uniform. If we knew how each of us modified the language, communication difficulties would be minimized. The problem is that members in an organization usually don't know how others with whom they interact have modified the language. Senders tend to assume that the words and terms they use mean the same to the receiver as they do to them. This, of course, is often incorrect, thus creating communication difficulties. For more about effective listening skills, refer to the From Concepts to Skills feature below.

Thus far, we have pointed out that even when the communicating parties speak English, and have done so since birth, there can be confusions in the use of words, as well as their intent. The multicultural environment of many of today's workplaces makes communication issues even more complex. Many of us interact, or will interact, with colleagues for whom English is a second language. This means that even more opportunities arise for confusion about meaning. It is therefore important to be aware that your understanding of the particular meaning of a word or phrase may not be shared similarly.

FROM CONCEPTS TO SKILLS

Effective Listening

Too many people take listening skills for granted. They confuse hearing with listening.

What's the difference? Hearing is merely picking up sound vibrations. Listening is making sense out of what we hear. That is, listening requires paying attention, interpreting, and remembering sound stimuli.

The average person normally speaks at a rate of 125 to 200 words per minute. However, the average listener can comprehend up to 400 words per minute. This leaves a lot of time for idle mind-wandering while listening. For most people, it also means they've acquired a number of bad listening habits to fill in the "idle time."

The following eight behaviours are associated with effective listening skills. If you want to improve your listening skills, look to these behaviours as guides:

1. *Make eye contact.* How do you feel when somebody doesn't look at you when you're speaking? If you're like most people, you're likely to interpret this behaviour as aloofness or lack of interest. We may listen with our ears, but others tend to judge whether we're really listening by looking at our eyes.

2. *Exhibit affirmative head nods and appropriate facial expressions.* The effective listener shows interest in what is being said. How? Through nonverbal signals. Affirmative head nods and appropriate facial expressions, when added to good eye contact, convey to the speaker that you're listening.

3. *Avoid distracting actions or gestures.* The other side of showing interest is avoiding actions that suggest your mind is somewhere else. When listening, don't look at your watch, shuffle papers, play with your pencil, or engage in similar distractions. They make the speaker feel you're bored or uninterested. Maybe more importantly, they indicate that you aren't fully attentive and may be missing part of the message that the speaker wants to convey.

4. *Ask questions.* The critical listener analyses what he or she hears and asks questions.

This behaviour provides clarification, ensures understanding, and assures the speaker that you're listening.

5. *Paraphrase.* Paraphrasing means restating what the speaker has said in your own words. The effective listener uses phrases like: "What I hear you saying is. . ." or "Do you mean . . . ?" Why rephrase what's already been said? Two reasons! First, it's an excellent control device to check on whether you're listening carefully. You can't paraphrase accurately if your mind is wandering or if you're thinking about what you're going to say next. Second, it's a control for accuracy. By rephrasing what the speaker has said in your own words and feeding it back to the speaker, you verify the accuracy of your understanding.

6. *Avoid interrupting the speaker.* Let the speaker complete his or her thought before you try to respond. Don't try to second-guess where the speaker's thoughts are going. When the speaker is finished, you'll know it!

7. *Don't overtalk.* Most of us would rather speak our own ideas than listen to what someone else says. Too many of us listen only because it's the price we have to pay to get people to let us talk. While talking may be more fun and silence may be uncomfortable, you can't talk and listen at the same time. The good listener recognizes this fact and doesn't overtalk.

8. *Make smooth transitions between the roles of speaker and listener.* When you're a student sitting in a lecture hall, you find it relatively easy to get into an effective listening frame of mind. Why? Because communication is essentially one-way: The teacher talks and you listen. But the teacher-student dyad is atypical. In most work situations, you're continually shifting back and forth between the roles of speaker and listener. The effective listener, therefore, makes transitions smoothly from speaker to listener and back to speaker. From a listening perspective,

this means concentrating on what a speaker has to say and practising not thinking about what you're going to say as soon as you get an opportunity.

Sources: Based on S.P. Robbins and P.L. Hunsaker, *Training in Interpersonal Skills; TIPs for Managing People at Work*, 2nd ed. (Upper Saddle River, NJ: Prentice Hall, 1996), Chapter 3; and data in R.C. Huseman, J.M. Lahiff, and J.M. Penrose, *Business Communication: Strategies and Skills* (Chicago: Dryden Press, 1988), pp. 380 and 425.

Employee Communications When Undergoing Changes

As we've noted throughout this book, organizations around the world are restructuring in order to reduce costs and improve competitiveness. Almost all *Fortune 100* companies, for instance, have scaled back the size of their labour force in the last five years or so through attrition and layoffs. Many Canadian companies have done the same.

A recent study examined employee communications programs in 10 leading companies that had successfully undertaken major restructuring programs.[29] The companies in the study were chosen because they had developed reputations for having excellent internal communication programs. The authors were interested in seeing whether common factors determined the effectiveness of these firms' employee communications. The authors specifically chose companies that had undergone restructuring and reorganizations because they believed that the true test of a firm's communication effectiveness was how well it worked in times of major organizational change. While we discuss many more issues having to do with organizational change in Chapter 17, it might be helpful for you to understand how communication affects the process of change.

The authors identified eight factors that were related to the effectiveness of employee communications during times of organizational change in these 10 firms: (1) CEO commitment to communication; (2) matching actions and words; (3) commitment to two-way communication; (4) emphasis on face-to-face communication; (5) shared responsibility for employee communication; (6) positive ways of dealing with bad news; (7) shaping messages for intended audience; and (8) treating communication as an ongoing process. Since the companies studied came from a variety of industries and organizational settings, the authors propose that these eight characteristics should apply to many types of organizations.

Let's look at these eight factors because they provide some research-based guidance to managers in helping decide how best to communicate with employees.

The CEO Must Be Committed to the Importance of Communication

The most significant factor to a successful employee-communications program is the chief executive's leadership. That is, he or she must be philosophically and behaviourally committed to the notion that communicating with employees is essential to the achievement of the organization's goals. If the organization's senior executive is committed to communication through his or her words and actions, it "trickles down" to the rest of the organization.

In addition to espousing a philosophical commitment to employee communications, the CEO must be a skilled and visible communications role model and be willing to personally deliver key messages. The CEOs in this study spent a significant amount of their time talking with employees, responding to questions, listening to their concerns, and conveying their vision of the company. Importantly, they tended to do this "in person" and didn't delegate the task to other managers. By personally championing the cause of good communication, they lessen employee fears about changes that are being implemented and set the precedent for other managers to follow.

Managers Match Actions and Words

Closely related to CEO support and involvement is managerial action. As we've noted previously, actions speak louder than words. When the implicit messages that managers send contradict the official messages as conveyed in formal communications, the managers lose credibility with employees. Employees will listen to what management has to say regarding changes being made and where the company is going, but these words must be supported with matching actions.

Commitment to Two-Way Communication

Ineffective programs are dominated by downward communication. Successful programs balance downward and upward communication.

How does a firm promote upward communication and stimulate employee dialogue? The company that displayed the highest commitment to two-way communication used interactive television broadcasts that allowed employees to call in questions and get responses directly from top management. Company publications offered question-and-answer columns and employees were encouraged to submit questions. The company developed a grievance procedure that processed complaints quickly. Managers were trained in feedback techniques and then were rewarded for using them.

General Electric and Hallmark are two companies that have perfected two-way communication. General Electric, for instance, launched a company-wide town meeting effort in the late 1980s. Managers credit these meetings for "uncovering all kinds of crazy stuff we were doing."[30] And Hallmark regularly selects 50 to 100 non-management employees at random for a 90-minute face-to-face discussion with the company's CEO.[31]

General Electric
www.ge.com/

Hallmark
www.hallmark.com/

Ed Clark, president and CEO of Canada Trust (CT), shows his commitment to communication by personally visiting CT's 400 branch locations. His philosophy is that you can't sit in an office and tell people what to do. He frequently holds pizza-and-pop sessions with employees. Clark's approachable style and ability to explain complex issues without talking down to listeners has earned him the loyalty of employees.

Emphasis on Face-to-Face Communication

In times of uncertainty and change—which characterize major restructuring efforts—employees have many fears and concerns. Is their job in jeopardy? Will they have to learn new skills? Will their work group be disbanded? Consistent with our previous discussion of channel richness, these messages are nonroutine and ambiguous. The maximum amount of information can be transmitted through face-to-face conversation. Because the firms in this study were all undergoing significant changes, their senior executives personally carried their messages to operating employees. Candid, open, face-to-face communication with employees presents executives as living, breathing people who understand workers' needs and concerns.

Shared Responsibility for Employee Communications

Top management provides the "big picture" of where the company is going. Supervisors link the big picture to their work group and to individual employees. Every manager has some responsibility in ensuring that employees are well informed, with the implications for changes becoming more specific as they flow down the organization hierarchy.

People prefer to hear about the changes that might affect them from their boss, not from their peers or through the grapevine. This requires top management to keep middle and lower managers fully apprised of planned changes. And it means that middle- and lower-level managers must quickly share information with their work group to minimize ambiguity.

Dealing with Bad News

Organizations with effective employee communications aren't afraid to confront bad news. In fact, they typically have a high bad-news to good-news ratio. This doesn't mean that these firms have more problems; rather that they don't penalize the "bearer of bad news."

Increasingly, many corporations are using their company publications to keep employees current on setbacks as well as upbeat news. Allied-Signal's *Horizons* magazine, for instance, carried a recent article by the company's president on the loss of a major bid from Northrop.[32]

All organizations will, at times, experience product failures, delivery delays, customer complaints, or similar problems. The issue is how comfortable people feel in communicating those problems. When bad news is candidly reported, a climate is created in which people aren't afraid to be truthful and good news gains increased credibility.

The Message Is Shaped for Its Intended Audience

Different people in the organization have different information needs. What is important to supervisors may not be so to middle managers. Similarly, what is interesting information to someone in product planning may be irrelevant to someone in accounting.

What information do individuals and groups want to know? When do they need to know it? In what form (at home, newsletter, e-mail, team meeting) is the best way for them to receive it? Employees vary in the type of information they need and the most effective way for them to receive it. Managers must recognize this distinction and design their communication program accordingly.

Treat Communication as an Ongoing Process

These leading companies viewed employee communications as a critical management process. This is illustrated by five common activities in which these firms engaged.

MANAGERS CONVEY THE RATIONALE UNDERLYING DECISIONS As change occurs more frequently, and their future becomes less certain, employees increasingly want to know the rationale underlying the decisions and changes that are being made. Why is this occurring? How will it affect me?

As the historical social contract that traded employee loyalty for job security has eroded, employees have new expectations from management. In times of permanent employment, comprehensive explanations of management decisions weren't as critical for employees because no matter what the changes, their jobs were relatively secure. But under the new covenant, with workers assuming much greater responsibility for their own careers, employees feel a need for more information so they can make intelligent career decisions. Employees are looking for something from management to make up the difference between what they used to have guaranteed and what they have now. One of those things is information. Even confidential financial information, generally off-limits to employees, is now made accessible to workers in companies that practise open-book management. See our OB in the News feature for a discussion of this new trend in communications.

TIMELINESS IS VITAL It's important for managers to communicate what they know, when they know it. Employees don't want to be treated as children, parcelled out bits of information piece by piece or kept from information for fear that it might be misconstrued. They want the facts as soon as they become available. This lessens the power of the grapevine and increases management's credibility. The cost of not communicating in a timely manner is disaffection, anger, and loss of trust.

New technologies make speedy communications possible. Federal Express, as a case in point, has built a $10-million internal television network so it can communicate quickly with employees. For example, when FedEx purchased Flying Tigers in 1989, the company's chief executive was on the air with the announcement just minutes after the news hit the financial wires.[33]

COMMUNICATE CONTINUOUSLY Communication should be continuous, particularly during periods of change or crisis. When employees need information and it's not forthcoming, they'll fall back on informal channels to fill the void, even if those channels provide only unsubstantiated rumours. In those organizations where management strives to keep the information continuously flowing, employees are also more forgiving of the occasional error or omission.

Irving Paper
www.ifdn.com/paper/paper.
htm

Communication, Energy and Paperworkers Union (CEP)
http://207.216.64.40/index.
html

LINK THE "BIG PICTURE" WITH THE "LITTLE PICTURE" Truly effective communication does not occur until employees understand how the "big picture" affects them and their jobs. Changes in the economy, among competitors in the industry, or in the organization as a whole must be translated into implications for each location, department, and employee. This responsibility falls most directly on employees' direct supervisors. In 1997, Saint John, New Brunswick-based Irving Paper was able to sign a six-year contract with its two locals of the Communication, Energy and Paperworkers

OB IN THE NEWS

Empowering Employees by Opening Up Communication

Dave Loney wants every one of his 72 employees to feel they play a direct role in making his company a success.

That's why all staff at Guelph, Ontario-based Eagle's Flight Creative Training Excellence Inc. know what financial targets they need to reach to keep Eagle's Flight growing and profitable. "We have no secrets," says co-president Loney of his company, which conducts corporate training programs. "People can ask any questions about what's going on in terms of profit or how the business is run."

Eagle's Flight practises open-book management, a growing business philosophy that lets employees know about financial information that is typically kept confidential. Employees better understand how they relate to the bottom line and are more committed to helping the company meet its financial goals.

"In open-book management, everyone shares the challenges and rewards," says Pam Robertson of Langdon Associates, a management consulting firm in Toronto. "Open-book is steadily growing across North America, in small and big businesses," says Robertson, although it's more prevalent in the United States. But, she says, the philosophy is being received positively in Canada, albeit somewhat more slowly. Eagle's Flight experience with the concept shows that it works. In 1995, the company had sales of nearly $5 million, up 1164 percent from 1990, which won it a position on the PROFIT 100 in 1996.

Open-book management is also practised at Mississauga, Ontario-based IntelaTech Inc., a 1997 PROFIT 100 company. "All information on the company is shared," says president Michael Ruscigno, including sales and profitability numbers. "We reveal all key company performance statistics to each employee on a weekly, monthly, quarterly, and annual basis. With a better understanding of all that's going on at the firm," says Ruscigno, "each person in the company is aware of all major opportunities, as well as major threats."

Sources: Based on Michela Pasquali, "Opening the Books to Better Biz: Letting Everyone in on Your Financial Game Plan Can Increase Trust, Accountability and Perhaps Profits," *Profit: The Magazine for Canadian Entrepreneurs*, September 1997, p. 69; Rick Spence, "Secrets of the Growth Gurus," *Profit: The Magazine for Canadian Entrepreneurs*, June 1997, pp. 84–85; and "Growing Your Business in Four Easy Lessons," *Profit: The Magazine for Canadian Entrepreneurs*, June, 1996, pp. 42–44.

Take It to the Net

We invite you to visit the Robbins page on the Prentice Hall Web site at:

http://www.prenticehall.ca/robbins

for this chapter's World Wide Web exercise.

Pollard Banknote Ltd.
www.pollardusa.com/

Union (CEP) in part because it chose to share more information with its employees about its financial status. Instead of simply giving the information to union leaders, management erected information bulletin boards and production boards to ensure that all employees know how much money the company is making and whether productivity quotas are being met. Management also took union members to visit other mills to show them what change might look like, and to make them more comfortable with engaging in the change process at Irving.[34] Similarly, Winnipeg-based Pollard Bank-note Ltd., a lottery ticket printing company with plants in Kamloops,

British Columbia, and Barrhead, Alberta, as well as Winnipeg, set up a joint planning committee of management and employees to ensure that employees have access to the company's information.[35] The committee meets regularly, and critical numbers such as sales and profits are open to scrutiny.

DON'T DICTATE THE WAY PEOPLE SHOULD FEEL ABOUT THE NEWS Employees don't want to be told how they should interpret and feel about change. Trust and openness are not enhanced by claims such as "These new changes are really exciting!" or "You're going to like the way that the department is being restructured!" More often than not, these attempts to sway opinion only provoke antagonistic responses.

It's more effective to communicate "who, what, when, where, why, and how" and then let employees draw their own conclusions. Although this study looked at companies undergoing change, the recommendations for effective communication apply to organizations at any time, and not just during the change process.

Current Issues in Communication

We close this chapter by addressing three current issues: Why do men and women often have difficulty communicating with each other? How can individuals improve their cross-cultural communications? And how is electronics changing the way people communicate with each other in organizations?

Communication Barriers between Women and Men

Research by Deborah Tannen provides us with some important insights into the differences between men and women in terms of their conversational styles.[36] In particular, she has been able to explain why gender often creates oral communication barriers.

The essence of Tannen's research is that men use talk to emphasize status, while women use it to create connection. Tannen states that communication is a continual balancing act, juggling the conflicting needs for intimacy and independence. Intimacy emphasizes closeness and commonalities. Independence emphasizes separateness and differences. Consequently, women speak and hear a language of connection and intimacy; men speak and hear a language of status and independence. So, for many men, conversations are primarily a means to preserve independence and maintain status in a hierarchical social order. For many women, however, conversations are negotiations for closeness in which people try to seek and give confirmation and support. The following examples will illustrate Tannen's thesis.

Men frequently complain that women talk on and on about their problems. Women criticize men for not listening. What's happening is that when men hear a problem, they frequently assert their desire for independence and control by offering solutions. Many women, on the other hand, view telling a problem as a means to promote closeness. The women present the problem to gain support and connection, not to get the male's advice. Mutual understanding, as sought by women, is symmetrical. But giving advice is asymmetrical—it sets the (male) advice giver up as more knowledgeable, more reasonable, and more in control. This contributes to distancing men and women in their efforts to communicate.

In conversation, women and men tend to approach points of conflict in different ways. A woman might say, "Have you looked at the marketing de-

partment's research on that point?" (the implication being that the report will show the error). Rather than simply relying on her own knowledge or beliefs, she presents the supporting evidence. A man might say, "I think you're wrong on that point," and may not even provide documented evidence. These lead to gendered interpretations of the communication. Men frequently view female indirectness as "covert" or "sneaky," and they also interpret weakness when women won't take definitive stands, whereas women interpret male directness as an assertion of status and one-upmanship. Neither position is correct. It is helpful, though, to begin to understand the ways that females and males sometimes interpret the same dialogue differently.

Finally, men often criticize women for seeming to apologize all the time. Men tend to see the phrase "I'm sorry" as a weakness because they interpret the phrase to mean the woman is accepting blame. However, women typically use "I'm sorry" to express empathy: "I know you must feel bad about this; I probably would too in the same position." This chapter's CBC Video Case shows employees of the CIBC participating in the bank's training program, developed to improve communication gaps between men and women.

Cross-Cultural Communication

Effective communication is difficult under the best of conditions. Cross-cultural factors clearly create the potential for increased communication problems. This is illustrated in Exhibit 9-7. A gesture that is well understood and acceptable in one culture can be meaningless or lewd in another.[37]

One author has identified some specific problems related to language difficulties in cross-cultural communications.[38] First, there are *barriers caused by semantics*. As we've noted previously, words mean different things to different people. This is particularly true for people from different national cultures. Some words, for instance, don't translate between cultures.

Exhibit 9-7
Hand Gestures Mean Different Things in Different Countries

The A-OK Sign	**"V" for Victory Sign**	**Finger-Beckoning Sign**

In the United States and Canada, this is just a friendly sign for "All right!" or "Good going." In Australia and Islamic countries, it is equivalent to what generations of high school students know as "flipping the bird."	In many parts of the world, this means "victory" or "peace." In England, if the palm and fingers face inward, it means "Up yours!" especially if executed with an upward jerk of the fingers.	This sign means "come here" in the United States and Canada. In Malaysia, it is used only for calling animals. In Indonesia and Australia, it is used for beckoning "ladies of the night."

Source: "What's A-O.K. in the U.S.A. Is Lewd and Worthless Beyond," *New York Times*, August 18, 1996, p. E7. From Roger E. Axtell, *Gestures: The Do's and Taboos of Body Language Around the World*. Copyright © 1991. This material is used by permission of John Wiley & Sons, Inc.

Understanding the word *sisu* will help you in communicating with people from Finland, but this word is untranslatable into English. It means something akin to "guts" or "dogged persistence." Similarly, the new capitalists in Russia may have difficulty communicating with their Canadian or British counterparts because English terms such as *efficiency*, *free market*, and *regulation* cannot be directly translated into Russian.

Second, there are *barriers caused by word connotations*. Words imply different things in different languages. The Japanese word *hai* translates as "yes," but its connotation may be "yes, I'm listening," rather than "yes, I agree." Western executives, particularly male managers who as we've discussed tend to use language to emphasize status, may be hampered in their negotiations if they don't understand this connotation.

Third are *barriers caused by tone differences*. In some cultures, language is formal, in others it's informal. In some cultures, the tone changes depending on the context: people speak differently at home, in social situations, and at work. Using a personal, informal style in a situation where a more formal style is expected can be embarrassing and off-putting.

When communicating with people from a different culture, what can you do to reduce misperceptions, misinterpretations, and misevaluations? Following these four rules can be helpful:[39]

- *Assume differences until similarity is proven.* Most of us assume that others are more similar to us than they actually are. But people from different countries often are very different from us. So you are far less likely to make an error if you assume others are different from you rather than assuming similarity until difference is proven.

- *Emphasize description rather than interpretation or evaluation.* Interpreting or evaluating what someone has said or done, in contrast to description, is based more on the observer's culture and background than on the observed situation. As a result, delay judgment until you've had sufficient time to observe and interpret the situation from the differing perspectives of all the cultures involved.

- *Practise empathy.* Before sending a message, put yourself in the recipient's shoes. What are his or her values, experiences, and frames of reference? What do you know about his or her education, upbringing, and background that can give you added insight? Try to see the other person as he or she really is.

- *Treat your interpretations as a working hypothesis.* Once you've developed an explanation for a new situation or think you empathize with someone from a foreign culture, treat your interpretation as a hypothesis that needs further testing rather than as a certainty. Carefully assess the feedback provided by recipients to see if it confirms your hypothesis. For important decisions or communiqués, you can also check with other foreign and home-country colleagues to ensure that your interpretations are on target.

For further information about communication problems based on cultural differences, see this chapter's Case Incident.

Electronic Communications

Until the last 15 or to 20 years, very few technological breakthroughs had significantly affected organizational communications. Early in this century, the telephone dramatically reduced personal, face-to-face communication.

The popularization of the photocopy machine in the late 1960s was the death knell for carbon paper and made the copying of documents faster and easier. But beginning in the early 1980s, we've been subjected to an onslaught of new electronic technologies that are largely reshaping the way we communicate in organizations.[40] These include pagers, fax machines, video conferencing, electronic meetings, e-mail, cellular phones, voice messaging, and palm-sized personal communicators.

Electronic communications no longer make it necessary for you to be at your work station or desk to be "available." Pagers, cellular phones, and personal communicators allow you to be reached when you're in a meeting, during your lunch break, while visiting in a customer's office across town, in the middle of watching a movie in a crowded theatre, or during a golf game on Saturday morning. The line between an employee's work and non-work life is no longer distinct. In the electronic age, all employees can theoretically be "on call" 24 hours a day.

Organizational boundaries become less relevant as a result of electronic communications. Why? Because networked computers—that is, computers that are interlinked to communicate with each other—allow employees to jump vertical levels within the organization, work full time at home or someplace other than an organizationally operated facility, and carry ongoing communications with people in other organizations. For example, the market researcher who wants to discuss an issue with the vice-president of marketing (who is three levels up in the hierarchy), can bypass the people in between and send an e-mail message directly. And in so doing, the traditional status hierarchy, largely determined by level and access, becomes essentially negated. Or that same market researcher may choose to live in the Cayman Islands and work at home via telecommuting rather than do his or her job in the company's Halifax office. And when an employee's computer is linked to suppliers' and customers' computers, the boundaries separating organizations become further blurred. Hundreds of suppliers, for instance, are linked into Wal-Mart's computers. This allows people at companies such as Levi Strauss to be able to monitor Wal-Mart's inventory of Levi jeans and to replace merchandise as needed, clouding the distinction between Levi and Wal-Mart employees.

Although the telephone allows people to transmit verbal messages instantly, it's only been very recently that this same speed has become available for the written word. In the mid-1960s, organizations were almost completely dependent on interoffice memos for internal, on-site messages, and on wire services and the post office for external messages. Then came overnight express delivery and fax machines. Today, with almost all organizations having introduced e-mail and an increasing number providing their employees with access to the Internet, written communications can be transmitted with all the speed of the telephone.

Electronic communications have revolutionized both the ability to access other people and to reach them almost instantaneously. Unfortunately, this access and speed have come with some costs. Electronic mail, for instance, doesn't provide the nonverbal communication component that the face-to-face meeting does. Nor does e-mail convey the emotions and nuances that come through from verbal intonations in telephone conversations. Similarly, it's been noted that meetings have historically served two distinct purposes: fulfilling a need for group affiliation and serving as a forum for completing task work.[41] Videoconferences and electronic meetings do a good job at supporting tasks but don't address affiliation needs. For people with a high

need for social contact, a heavy reliance on electronic communications is likely to lead to lower job satisfaction.

A number of companies are setting up intranets for their employees as a way of increasing the communication flow within an organization. These are the equivalent of an internal Internet, accessible only by employees of the firm. Although intranets are not currently used to their full capacity, they can be used to store information centrally and exchange ideas among employees easily. Intranets can also bring together teams of people to discuss ideas through on-line forums. They can be used to provide quicker problem-solving mechanisms, and give greater access to those who have the expertise to solve a particular problem. Employees can also be encouraged to share ideas about how to do work more efficiently on the intranet.

As electronic interaction becomes more widespread and more accepted, it will no doubt have a profound impact on how communication is conducted. For example, Nancy Langton, your Vancouver-based author, interacted with numerous people from Prentice Hall Canada while working on this textbook, many of whom she never met face-to-face or talked to on the telephone, and most of whom worked across the country in Toronto. In fact, contract negotiations for the book were done almost exclusively by e-mail and fax. Additionally, it has been her experience that one can conduct entire friendships via e-mail.

Despite many advantages to e-mail, it is important to realize that it is virtually indestructible once it gets backed up on your company's server. And its very speed and accessibility often lend themselves to miscommunication and misdirected messages. With these issues in mind, consider the following tips for writing and sending e-mail:[42] (1) don't write anything that you don't want anyone other than the intended receiver to see; (2) be careful in addressing your e-mail—a simple typo can send your e-mail to the wrong person; (3) think about the e-mail you're sending, and perhaps wait an hour before you do send it off; and (4) be careful when forwarding e-mail that you are not circulating something that is untrue. You should also consider whether the originator of the message would approve of your copying it to others, especially co-workers and superiors. Employees should also be aware that e-mail is not necessarily private, and companies often take the position that they have the right to scrutinize your e-mail. For example, the Canadian

Morgan Stanley
www.ms.com/

Investment bank Morgan Stanley distributes data and information to employees at its 37 offices around the world on the company's intranet, an internal corporate web. For example, the global network allows traders in Japan to receive up-to-the-minute information on securities transactions from colleagues in New York. Morgan Stanley has also connected its "hoot-and-holler" worldwide voice-messaging system to its intranet, allowing salespeople to receive messages from their workstation speakers on the trading floor.

Auto Workers Union (CAW) expressed outrage in early 1998 when they discovered that Montreal-based Canadian National Railway Co. (CN) was reading employees' e-mail messages.[43] "Our people feel violated. You're given an e-mail address and you have a password, and it's yours. It's personal," is the view of Abe Rosner, a national CAW representative. Canadian National Railway, however, disagrees. "E-mail is to be used for CN business-approved activities only. Flowing from this is that any communication exchanged on the system is viewed as company property," explains Mark Hallman, a CN spokesperson.

Ann Cavoukian, head of the Information and Privacy Commission of Ontario, notes that "employees deserve to be treated like adults and companies should limit surveillance to rare instances, such as when there is suspicion of criminal activity or harassment."[44] She suggests that employers use respect and courtesy when dealing with employees' e-mail, and likens e-mail to office phone calls, which generally are not monitored by the employer. It is clearly important, in any event, that employees be aware of their company's policy on e-mail. For further discussion of e-mail privacy, see the Ethical Dilemma Exercise "Employee Monitoring: How Far Is Too Far?" in Chapter 14.

HR IMPLICATIONS

Providing Performance Feedback

For many managers, few activities are more unpleasant than providing performance feedback to employees.[1] In fact, unless pressured by organizational policies and controls, managers are likely to ignore this responsibility.[2]

Why the reluctance to give performance feedback? There seem to be at least three reasons. First, managers are often uncomfortable discussing performance weaknesses directly with employees. Given that almost every employee could undoubtedly improve in some areas, managers fear a confrontation when presenting negative feedback. This apparently even applies when people give negative feedback to a computer! Bill Gates reports that Microsoft recently conducted a project that required users to rate their experience with a computer. "When we had the computer the users had worked with ask for an evaluation of its performance, the responses tended to be positive. But when we had a second computer ask the same people to evaluate their encounters with the first machine, the people were significantly more critical. Their reluctance to criticize the first computer 'to its face' suggested that they didn't want to hurt

its feelings, even though they knew it was only a machine."[3] Second, many employees tend to become defensive when their weaknesses are pointed out. Instead of accepting the feedback as constructive and a basis for improving performance, some employees challenge the evaluation by criticizing the manager or redirecting blame to someone else. Finally, employees tend to have an inflated assessment of their own performance. Statistically speaking, half of all employees must be below-average performers. But the evidence indicates that the average employee's estimate of his or her own performance level generally falls around the 75th percentile.[4] So even when managers are providing good news, employees are likely to perceive it as not good enough!

The solution to the performance feedback problem is not to ignore it, but to train managers in how to conduct constructive feedback sessions. An effective review in which the employee perceives the appraisal as fair, the manager as sincere, and the climate as constructive can result in the employee leaving the interview in an upbeat mood, informed about the performance areas in which he

or she needs to improve, and determined to correct the deficiencies.[5] In addition, the performance review should be designed more as a counselling activity than a judgmental process. This can best be accomplished by allowing the review to evolve out of the employee's own self-evaluation. (To practise assessing performance and observing performance feedback, please see the HR Exercise "Evaluating Performance and Providing Feedback" on page 359).

Performance reviews can also include feedback from sources other than just one's manager. For example, the Toronto-Dominion Bank uses a Customer Service Index to measure service and quality, in addition to sales. The results are posted for each branch monthly, so that they can compare themselves with other branches. The results are also linked directly to TD's performance appraisal system.[6]

Toronto-based Consumers Gas has gone one step further with its performance appraisal feedback, using one of the newest management trends—360-degree feedback assessment.[7] In this system, not just your boss, but also your colleagues, subordinates, customers, and other people with whom you deal regularly are part of the evaluation process. Millar Western Industries, a family-owned forestry company based in Edmonton, introduced 360-degree feedback for its 250 supervisory and managerial staff in 1995, and has been working toward using it for all of its employees.

The 360-degree feedback can cause anxiety in employees at first, as they learn perhaps more than they ever wanted to know about what others think of them. However, Millar's human resources manager found that employees actually liked knowing where they stood and how they were doing. A variety of companies, including Ciba-Geigy Canada, Hudson's Bay, Maclean-Hunter, IBM, Disney, and Federal Express use 360-degree feedback. This feedback system emphasizes the importance of communication to all levels of employees, not just the manager. It also shows customers and suppliers that they have a voice in the company. (See page 228 for more details about 360-degree feedback.)

Sources:

[1] J.S. Lublin, "It's Shape-up Time for Performance Reviews," *Wall Street Journal*, October 3, 1994, p. B1.

[2] Much of this section is based on H.H. Meyer, "A Solution to the Performance Appraisal Feedback Enigma," *Academy of Management Executive*, February 1991, pp. 68–76.

[3] B. Gates, *The Road Ahead*, (New York: Viking, 1995), p. 86.

[4] R.J. Burke, "Why Performance Appraisal Systems Fail," *Personnel Administration*, June 1972, pp. 32–40.

[5] B.R. Nathan, A.M. Mohrman, Jr., and J. Milliman, "Interpersonal Relations as a Context for the Effects of Appraisal Interviews on Performance and Satisfaction: A Longitudinal Study," *Academy of Management Journal*, June 1991, pp. 352–69.

[6] Material in this paragraph based on "A Jury System For Jobs," *Maclean's*, August 5, 1996, p. 45.

[7] P. Booth, *Challenge and Change: Embracing the Team Concept.* Report 123-94, Conference Board of Canada, 1994, p. 10.

Summary and Implications

For the Workplace

A careful review of this chapter finds a common theme regarding the relationship between communication and employee satisfaction: the less the uncertainty, the greater the satisfaction. Distortions, ambiguities, and incongruities all increase uncertainty and hence, they have a negative impact on satisfaction.[45]

The less distortion that occurs in communication, the more that goals, feedback, and other management messages to employees will be received as they were intended.[46] This, in turn, should reduce ambiguities and clarify the group's task. Extensive use of vertical, lateral, and informal channels will increase communication flow, reduce uncertainty, and improve group performance and satisfaction. We should also expect incongruities between verbal and nonverbal communiqués to increase uncertainty and to reduce satisfaction.

Findings in the chapter further suggest that the goal of perfect communication is unattainable. Yet there is evidence that demonstrates a positive relationship between effective communication (which includes factors such as perceived trust, perceived accuracy, desire for interaction, top-management receptiveness, and upward information requirements) and worker productivity.[47] Choosing the correct channel, being an effective listener, and utilizing feedback may, therefore, make for more effective communication. But the human factor generates distortions that can never be fully eliminated. The communication process represents an exchange of messages, but the outcome is meanings that may or may not approximate those that the sender intended. Whatever the sender's expectations, the decoded message in the mind of the receiver represents his or her reality. And this "reality" will determine performance, along with the individual's level of motivation and his or her degree of satisfaction. The issue of motivation is critical, so we should briefly review how communication is central in determining an individual's degree of motivation.

You will remember from expectancy theory that the degree of effort an individual exerts depends on his or her perception of the effort-performance, performance-reward, and reward-goal satisfaction linkages. If individuals are not given the data necessary to make the perceived probability of these linkages high, motivation will suffer. If rewards are not made clear, if the criteria for determining and measuring performance are ambiguous, or if individuals are not relatively certain that their effort will lead to satisfactory performance, then effort will be reduced. So communication plays a significant role in determining the level of employee motivation.

A final implication from the communication literature relates to predicting turnover. The use of realistic job previews acts as a communication device for clarifying role expectations (see "Counterpoint" in Chapter 3). Employees who have been exposed to a realistic job preview have more accurate information about that job. Comparisons of turnover rates between organizations that use the realistic job preview versus either no preview or only presentation of positive job information show that those not using the realistic preview have, on average, almost 29 percent higher turnover.[48] This makes a strong case for managers to convey honest and accurate information about a job to applicants during the recruiting and selection process.

For You as an Individual

Communication difficulties occur as often outside the workplace as they do inside. As a result, it may be helpful to think about interactions you have had where the communication did not work, and try to assess your contribution to the breakdown. In general, when two people are having difficulty communicating, each of them is contributing something to that breakdown, even if you are inclined to believe that the other person is the more responsible party.

The chapter identifies a number of barriers to communication of which you might want to be aware. Often either selective perception or defensiveness get in the way of communication. As you work in your groups on student projects you may want to observe communication flows more critically to help you understand ways that communication can be improved.

ROADMAP REMINDER

In the two previous chapters we examined group and team behaviour, and how to get people to work together on important goals. In this chapter we focused on communication, which is a large factor in determining how well people will get along. We want you to be aware of the factors that lead to both better and worse communication. In the next chapter we consider decision making. Both communication and decision making are elements of sharing the vision of an organization to an employee.

For Review

1. Describe the functions that communication provides within a group or organization. Give an example of each.
2. Contrast encoding and decoding.
3. Describe the communication process and identify its key components. Give an example of how this process operates with both oral and written messages.
4. Identify three common small-group networks and give the advantages of each.
5. What is *kinesics*? Why is it important?
6. What characterizes a communication that is rich in capacity to convey information?
7. What conditions stimulate the emergence of rumours?
8. List three specific problems related to language difficulties in cross-cultural communication.
9. What are the managerial implications from the research contrasting male and female communication styles?
10. What are some of the factors that lead to effective communication in organizations?

For Discussion

1. "Ineffective communication is the fault of the sender." Do you agree or disagree? Discuss.
2. What can you do to improve the likelihood that your communiqués will be received and understood as you intend?
3. How might managers use the grapevine for their benefit?
4. Using the concept of channel richness, give examples of messages best conveyed by e-mail, by face-to-face communication, and on the company bulletin board.
5. Why do you think so many people are poor listeners?

LEARNING ABOUT YOURSELF EXERCISE

Listening Self-Inventory

Go through this 15-item questionnaire twice. The first time, mark the yes or no box next to each question. Mark as truthfully as you can in light of your behaviour in recent meetings or gatherings you attended. The second time, mark a plus (+) next to your answer if you are satisfied with that answer, or a minus (–) next to the answer if you wish you could have answered that question differently.

	Yes	No	+ or −
1. I frequently attempt to listen to several conversations at the same time.	_____	_____	_____
2. I like people to give me only the facts and then let me make my own interpretations.	_____	_____	_____
3. I sometimes pretend to pay attention to people.	_____	_____	_____
4. I consider myself a good judge of nonverbal communications.	_____	_____	_____
5. I usually know what another person is going to say before he or she says it.	_____	_____	_____
6. I usually end conversations that don't interest me by diverting my attention from the speaker.	_____	_____	_____
7. I frequently nod, frown, or whatever to let the speaker know how I feel about what he or she is saying.	_____	_____	_____
8. I usually respond immediately when someone has finished talking.	_____	_____	_____
9. I evaluate what is being said while it is being said.	_____	_____	_____
10. I usually formulate a response while the other person is still talking.	_____	_____	_____
11. The speaker's delivery style frequently keeps me from listening to content.	_____	_____	_____
12. I usually ask people to clarify what they have said rather than guess at the meaning.	_____	_____	_____
13. I make a concerted effort to understand other people's point of view.	_____	_____	_____
14. I frequently hear what I expect to hear rather than what is said.	_____	_____	_____
15. Most people feel that I have understood their point of view when we disagree.	_____	_____	_____

Turn to page 699 for scoring directions and key.

Source: E.C. Glenn and E.A. Pood, "Listening Self-Inventory," *Supervisory Management*, January 1989, pp. 12–15. With permission.

WORKING WITH OTHERS EXERCISE

An Absence of Nonverbal Communication

This exercise will help you to see the value of nonverbal communication to interpersonal relations.

1. The class is to divide into pairs (Party A and Party B).
2. Party A is to select a topic from the following list:
   a. Managing in the Middle East is significantly different from managing in North America.
   b. Employee turnover in an organization can be functional.
   c. Some conflict in an organization is good.
   d. Whistleblowers do more harm than good for an organization.
   e. Bureaucracies are frustrating to work in.
   f. An employer has a responsibility to provide every employee with an interesting and challenging job.
   g. Everyone should vote.
   h. Organizations should require all employees to undergo regular tests for AIDS.
   i. Organizations should require all employees to undergo regular drug tests.
   j. Individuals who have majored in business or economics make better employees than those who have majored in history or English.
   k. The place where you get your university degree is more important in determining career success than what you learn while you're there.
   l. Effective managers often have to lie as part of their job.
   m. It's unethical for a manager to purposely distort communications to get a favourable outcome.
3. Party B is to choose his or her position on this topic (for example, arguing *against* the view that "some conflict in an organization is good). Party A now must automatically take the opposite position.
4. The two parties have 10 minutes in which to debate their topic. The catch is that individuals can only communicate verbally. They may *not* use gestures, facial movements, body movements, or any other non-verbal communication. It may help for each party to maintain an expressionless look and to sit on his or her hands to remind them of their restrictions.
5. After the debate is over, the class should discuss the following:
   a. How effective was communication during these debates?
   b. What barriers to communication existed?
   c. What purposes does nonverbal communication serve?
   d. Relate the lessons learned in this exercise to problems that might occur when communicating on the telephone or through e-mail.

HR EXERCISE

Evaluating Performance and Providing Feedback

Objective   To experience the assessment of performance and observe the providing of performance feedback.

Time   Approximately 30 minutes.

Procedure   A class leader is to be selected. He or she may be either a volunteer or someone chosen by your instructor. The class leader will preside over the class discussion and perform the role of manager in the evaluation review.

Your instructor will leave the room. The class leader is then to spend up to 15 minutes helping the class to evaluate your instructor. Your instructor understands that this is only a class exercise and is prepared to accept criticism (and, of course, any praise you may want to convey). Your instructor also recognizes that the leader's evaluation is actually a composite of many students' input. So be open and honest in your evaluation and have confidence that your instructor will not be vindictive.

Research has identified seven performance dimensions to the college instructor's job: (1) instructor knowledge, (2) testing procedures, (3) student-teacher relations, (4) organizational skills, (5) communication skills, (6) subject relevance, and (7) utility of assignments. The discussion of your instructor's performance should focus on these seven dimensions. The leader may want to take notes for personal use but will not be required to give your instructor any written documentation.

When the 15-minute class discussion is complete, the leader will invite the instructor back into the room. The performance review will begin as soon as the instructor walks through the door, with the class leader becoming the manager and the instructor playing himself or herself.

When completed, class discussion will focus on performance evaluation criteria and how well your class leader did in providing performance feedback.

Have We Got a Communication Problem Here?

"I don't want to hear your excuses. Just get those planes in the air," Jim Tuchman was screaming at his gate manager. As head of American Airlines' operations at the Mexico City airport, Tuchman has been consistently frustrated by the attitude displayed by his Mexican employees. Transferred from Dallas to Mexico City only three months ago, Tuchman was having difficulty adjusting to the Mexican style of work. "Am I critical of these people? You bet I am! They don't listen when I talk. They think things are just fine and fight every change I suggest. And they have no appreciation for the importance of keeping on schedule."

If Tuchman is critical of his Mexico City staff, it's mutual. They universally dislike him. Here's a few anonymous comments made about their boss: "He's totally insensitive to our needs." "He thinks if he yells and screams, that things will improve. We don't see it that way." "I've been working here for four years. Before he came here, this was a good place to work. Not anymore. I'm constantly in fear of being chewed out. I feel stress all the time, even at home. My husband has started commenting on it a lot."

Tuchman was brought in specifically to tighten up the Mexico City operation. High on his list of goals is improving American's on-time record in Mexico City, increasing productivity, and improving customer service. When Tuchman was asked if he thought he had any problems with his staff, he replied, "Yep. We just can't seem to communicate."

Questions

1. Does Jim Tuchman have a communication problem? Explain.

2. What suggestions would you make to Jim to help him improve his managerial effectiveness?

He Says/She Says

Canadian Imperial Bank of Commerce president Holger Kluge explains why he believes it's important for men and women to learn more about communicating with each other: "I hope it hasn't suddenly become politically incorrect to say this, but men and women are different. They approach problems differently. They resolve conflict differently. They communicate differently."

He illustrates his comment with the following example: "I remember the time my wife told me she had a splitting headache. I suggested she take some Tylenol. And she got upset with me! She wasn't looking for a solution to her problem. She knew how to get rid of a headache. She was looking for sympathy, empathy, and understanding. But being a man, I had only seen a problem that needed fixing. No wonder the book *Men Are From Mars, Women Are From Venus* is a bestseller."

In 1993, CIBC developed a program to bridge communication gender gaps in the workplace. The program attempts to help employees better understand the different ways men and women approach problems, make decisions, and convey information.

CIBC sends groups of employees to weekend retreats where they learn that there are differences in the ways men and women communicate. They learn that "yes" does not always mean "yes"—at least when spoken by a woman. And they learn some of the frustrations that each gender faces in communicating with the other. Not all of what they learn is easy, and in some situations it seems like men and women are crossing through fields covered with land mines while trying to talk to one another. However, after spending time listening to one another, they achieve a better understanding of differences in how each gender communicates.

Kluge believes that the gender communication program is a success for the CIBC workplace. He explains: "We wanted to ensure that (we) were not weakened by misunderstanding between the sexes. The fact that more women are moving into our management and leadership ranks—and are interacting with their male colleagues at a very high level—makes this program even more valuable."

Questions

1. Do you think adults can unlearn specific gender-related communication styles? Defend your position.

2. What suggestions would you make so women can communicate more effectively at work?

3. What suggestions would you make for men?

Sources: Based on "Men/Women," *Venture 480*, aired March 20, 1994; and Holger Kluge, "Reflections on Workplace Diversity," *Canadian Speeches*, March 1997, pp. 53–59.

POINT

The Case for Mutual Understanding: The Johari Window

The Johari Window (named after its creators, Joseph Luft and Harry Ingram) is a popular model used by training specialists to evaluate communication styles. The essence of the model is the belief that mutual understanding improves perceptual accuracy and communication.

The model classifies an individual's tendencies to facilitate or hinder interpersonal communication along two dimensions: exposure and feedback. Exposure is defined as the extent to which an individual openly and candidly divulges feelings, experiences, and information when trying to communicate. Feedback is the extent to which an individual successfully elicits exposure from others. As shown in Exhibit 9-A, these dimensions translate into four "windows": open, blind, hidden, and unknown. The *open* window is information known to you as well as others. The *blind* window encompasses certain things about you that are apparent to others but not to yourself. This is the result of no one ever telling you or because you're defensively blocking them out. The *hidden* window is information known by you and unknown by others. It encompasses those feelings that we're aware of but don't share with others for fear they'll think less of us or possibly use the information against us. The *un-*

known window includes feelings, experience, and information of which you and others are unaware.

Although there is no substantive body of research to support the following conclusion, the Johari Window model argues for more open communication on the assumption that people understand each other better when the amount of information in the open area increases. If you accept this conclusion, how would you increase the open area? According to Luft and Ingram, you do this through disclosure and feedback. By increasing self-disclosure, you reveal your inner feelings and experiences. In addition, the evidence suggests that self-disclosure encourages others to be similarly forthcoming and open. So disclosure breeds more disclosure. When others provide feedback on their insights into your behaviour, you reduce your blind window.

Although advocates of the Johari Window encourage a climate of openness, where individuals self-disclose freely with each other, they recognize that there are conditions where guarded communication may be appropriate. These include transitory relationships, where one party has violated trust in the past, in competitive situations, or where the culture of the organization doesn't support openness. Although critics might argue that one or more of those conditions just about covers almost all communication situations in organizations, proponents of the Johari Window are more optimistic. They view openness, authenticity, and honesty to be valued qualities in interpersonal relationships. Although they don't say so directly, they imply that it is in the individual's self-interest to expand the size of the open window by increasing self-disclosure and by being willing to listen to feedback from others even if it is unflattering. ■

Sources: Based on J. Luft, *Group Processes*, 3rd ed. (Palo Alto, CA: Mayfield Publishing, 1984), pp. 11–20; and J. Hall, "Communication Revisited," *California Management Review*, Fall 1973, pp. 56–67.

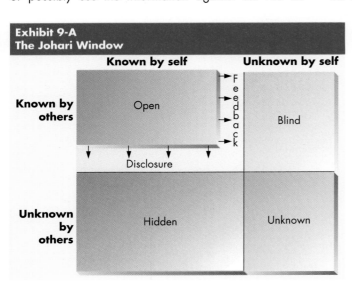

**Exhibit 9-A
The Johari Window**

counterPOINT

The Case for Ambiguous Communication

The argument for mutual understanding and openness, while honourable, is incredibly naive. It assumes that communicators actually want to achieve mutual understanding and that openness is the preferred means toward that end. Unfortunately, that argument overlooks a very basic fact: It's often in the sender's and/or receiver's best interest to keep communication ambiguous.

"Lack of communication" has become the explanation for every problem in an organization. If the newly "empowered" workforce is unmotivated, it's a communication problem. If the quality-improvement program fails to garner the promised benefits, it's a communication problem. If employees ignore or abuse customers despite training that instructs them otherwise, it's a communication problem. We're continually hearing that problems would go away if we could "just communicate better." Some of the basic assumptions underlying this view need to be looked at carefully.

One assumption is that better communication will necessarily reduce strife and conflict. But each individual's definition of better communication, like his or her definition of virtuous conduct, becomes that of having the other party accept his or her views, which would reduce conflict at that party's expense. A better understanding of the situation might serve only to underline the differences rather than to resolve them. Indeed, many of the techniques thought of as poor communication were apparently developed with the aim of bypassing or avoiding confrontation.

Another assumption that grows from this view is that when a conflict has existed for a long time and shows every sign of continuing, lack of communication must be one of the basic problems. Usually, if the situation is examined more carefully, plenty of communication will be found; the problem is, again, one of equating communication with agreement.

Still a third assumption is that it is always in the interest of at least one of the parties to an interaction, and often of both, to attain maximum clarity as measured by some more or less objective standard. Aside from the difficulty of setting up this standard—whose standard? And doesn't this give him or her control of the situation? There are some sequences, and perhaps many of them, in which it is in the interests of both parties to leave the situation as fuzzy and undefined as possible. This is notably true in culturally or personally sensitive and taboo areas involving prejudices, preconceptions, and so on, but it can also be true when the area is merely a new one that could be seriously distorted by using old definitions and old solutions.

Too often we forget that keeping communications fuzzy cuts down on questions, permits faster decision making, minimizes objections, reduces opposition, makes it easier to deny one's earlier statements, preserves freedom to change one's mind, helps to preserve mystique and hide insecurities, allows one to say several things at the same time, permits one to say "No" diplomatically, and helps to avoid confrontation and anxiety.

If you want to see the fine art of ambiguous communication up close, all you have to do is watch a television interview with a politician who is running for office. The interviewer attempts to get specific information, while the politician tries to retain multiple possible interpretations. Such ambiguous communications allow the politician to approach his or her ideal image of being "all things to all people." ◼

Sources: Based on C.O. Kursh, "The Benefits of Poor Communication," *The Psychoanalytic Review,* Summer-Fall 1971, pp. 189–208; E.M. Eisenberg and M.G. Witten, "Reconsidering Openness in Organizational Communication," *Academy of Management Review,* July 1987, pp. 418–26; and B. Filipczak, "Obfuscation Resounding," *Training,* July 1995, pp. 29–36.

CHAPTER 10

Decision-Making, Creativity, and Ethics

LEARNING OBJECTIVES

After studying this chapter, you should be able to

- List the strengths and weaknesses of group decision-making

- Explain how perception affects the decision-making process

- Outline the six steps in the rational decision-making model

- Describe how bounded rationality affects the actions of decision-makers

- Identify the conditions in which individuals are most likely to use intuition in decision-making

- Describe how shortcuts can assist in or distort our judgment of others

- Define heuristics and explain how they bias decisions

- Describe four styles of decision-making

- Contrast the effectiveness of interacting, brainstorming, nominal, and electronic meeting groups

- Explain the factors that influence ethical decision-making

Should corporations take an active role and try to change the societies in which they operate? One corporation that has taken a stand on social and enviromental issues is The Body Shop Canada, a Don Mills, Ontario-based franchise of The Body Shop International PLC of Littlehampton, England. The Body Shop has been operating in Canada since 1980.[1]

In its spring 1997 campaign to STOP Violence Against Women, The Body Shop held Make-over Marathon Days across Canada to raise funds for violence prevention and recovery programs. "With this year's campaign, we want to encourage Canadians to understand that they really can make a positive difference," said Margot Franssen, president and partner, The Body Shop Canada.

Also in 1997, The Body Shop focused their efforts on raising awareness about the issue of global warming. The company pledged to donate $1.50 from every purchase of a special $12 fluorescent lightbulb to the David Suzuki Foundation and Sierra Club of Canada. The retailer also invited customers to sign and send a prepaid postcard to Prime Minister Jean Chrétien, demanding the federal government sign a legally binding treaty at the December 1997 Global Climate Summit in Kyoto, Japan, pledging a 20 percent reduction in greenhouse gas emissions by the year 2005.

In spring 1998, The Body Shop, in cooperation with Amnesty International, participated in an international campaign called "Make Your Mark for Human Rights" to raise awareness of human rights violations around the world and mark the 50th Anniversary of the Universal Declaration of Human Rights (UDHR).

The campaign encouraged customers to stop by The Body Shop to participate in a unique thumbprint petition; to pick up a fundraising candle to support the continuing efforts of Amnesty International; and to sign a protest postcard, which will be forwarded to the president of the Tibet Autonomous Region.

The activities of The Body Shop reflect decisions that the organization has made with respect to their core values—animal protection, environmental protection, and protecting and promoting human rights.

The Body shop is not alone in making these kinds of decisions. Courtney Pratt, former chief executive of resources giant Noranda Inc., has urged business leaders to pitch in and fill the void caused by shrinking government spending. As chair of the Imagine campaign, a national non-profit organization that promotes giving, he planned to convene a forum of business leaders in 1998" to forge a consensus on the role business should play" in that area.[2] ■

In this chapter, we'll describe how decisions in organizations are made, as well as how creativity is linked to decision making. We'll also look at the ethical and socially responsible aspects of decision making as part of our discussion. But first, we discuss perceptual processes and show how they are linked to individual decision making.

The Link Between Perception and Individual Decision-Making

decisions
The choices made from among two or more alternatives.

The Body Shop
www.the-body-shop.com/

Noranda
www.noranda.com/

problem
A discrepancy between some current state of affairs and some desired state.

Individuals in organizations make **decisions**. That is, they make choices from among two or more alternatives. Top managers such as Margot Franssen at The Body Shop and Courtney Pratt (formerly at Noranda, now President of Caldwell Partners International Inc.), for instance, determine their organization's goals, what products or services to offer, how best to finance operations, or where to locate a new high-tech research and development facility. Middle- and lower-level managers determine production schedules, select new employees, and decide how pay raises are to be allocated. Of course, making decisions is not the sole province of managers. Nonmanagerial employees also make decisions that affect their jobs and the organizations they work for. The more obvious of these decisions might include whether to come to work on any given day, how much effort to put forward once at work, and whether to comply with a request made by the boss. In addition, an increasing number of organizations in recent years have been empowering their nonmanagerial employees with job-related decision-making authority that historically was reserved for managers alone. Individual decision-making, therefore, is an important part of organizational behaviour. But how individuals in organizations make decisions and the quality of their final choices are largely influenced by their perceptions.

Decision-making occurs as a reaction to a **problem**. That is, there is a discrepancy between some *current* state of affairs and some *desired* state, requiring consideration of alternative courses of action. So if your car breaks down and you rely on it to get to school, you have a problem that requires a decision on your part. Unfortunately, most problems don't come neatly packaged with a label "problem" clearly displayed on them. One person's *problem* is another person's *satisfactory state of affairs*. One manager may view her division's two percent decline in quarterly sales to be a serious problem requiring immediate action on her part. In contrast, her counterpart in another division of the same company, who also had a two percent sales decrease, may consider that percentage quite satisfactory. So the awareness that a problem exists and that a decision must be made is a perceptual issue.

Moreover, every decision requires interpretation and evaluation of information. Data are typically received from multiple sources, and they need to be screened, processed, and interpreted. Which data, for instance, are relevant to the decision and which are not? The perceptions of the decision-maker will answer that question. Alternatives will be developed, and the strengths and weaknesses of each will need to be evaluated. Again, because alternatives don't come with "red flags" identifying them as such or with their strengths and weaknesses clearly marked, the individual decision-maker's perceptual process will have a large bearing on the final outcome.

How Should Decisions Be Made?

Let's begin by describing how individuals should behave in order to maximize or optimize a certain outcome. We call this the *rational decision-making process.*

The Rational Decision-Making Process

rational
Refers to choices that are consistent and value maximizing.

rational decision-making
A decision-making model that describes how individuals should behave in order to maximize some outcome.

The optimizing decision-maker is **rational**. That is, he or she makes consistent, value-maximizing choices within specified constraints.[3] These choices are made following a six-step **rational decision-making model**.[4] Moreover, specific assumptions underlie this model.

THE RATIONAL MODEL The six steps in the rational decision-making model are listed in Exhibit 10-1.

The model begins by *defining the problem.* As noted previously, a problem exists when a discrepancy occurs between an existing and a desired state of affairs.[5] If you calculate your monthly expenses and find you're spending $50 more than you allocated in your budget, you have defined a problem. Many poor decisions can be traced to the decision-maker overlooking a problem or defining the wrong problem.

Once a decision-maker has defined the problem, he or she needs to *identify the decision criteria* that will be important in solving the problem. In this step, the decision-maker determines what is relevant in making the decision. This step brings the decision-maker's interests, values, and similar personal preferences into the process. Identifying criteria is important because what one person thinks is relevant another person may not. Also keep in mind that any factors not identified in this step are considered irrelevant to the decision-maker.

The criteria identified are rarely all equal in importance. So the third step requires the decision-maker to *weight the previously identified criteria* in order to give them the correct priority in the decision.

The fourth step requires the decision-maker to *generate possible alternatives* that could succeed in resolving the problem. No attempt is made in this step to appraise these alternatives, only to list them.

Once the alternatives have been generated, the decision-maker must critically analyse and evaluate each one. This is done by *rating each alternative on each criterion.* The strengths and weaknesses of each alternative become evident as they are compared with the criteria and weights established in the second and third steps.

The final step in this model requires *computing the optimal decision.* This is done by evaluating each alternative against the weighted criteria and selecting the alternative with the highest total score.

**Exhibit 10-1
Steps in the Rational Decision-Making Model**

1. Define the problem.
2. Identify the decision criteria.
3. Allocate weights to the criteria.
4. Develop the alternatives.
5. Evaluate the alternatives.
6. Select the best alternative.

ASSUMPTIONS OF THE MODEL   The rational decision-making model we just described contains a number of assumptions.[6] Let's briefly outline those assumptions.

- *Problem clarity.* The problem is clear and unambiguous. The decision-maker is assumed to have complete information regarding the decision situation.

- *Known options.* It is assumed the decision-maker can identify all the relevant criteria and can list all the viable alternatives. Furthermore, the decision-maker is aware of all the possible consequences of each alternative.

- *Clear preferences.* Rationality assumes that the criteria and alternatives can be ranked and weighted to reflect their importance.

- *Constant preferences.* It's assumed that the specific decision criteria are constant and that the weights assigned to them are stable over time.

- *No time or cost constraints.* The rational decision-maker can obtain full information about criteria and alternatives because it is assumed that there are no time or cost constraints.

- *Maximum payoff.* The rational decision-maker will choose the alternative that yields the highest perceived value.

How Are Decisions Actually Made in Organizations?

But are decision-makers in organizations rational? Do they carefully assess problems, identify all relevant criteria, use their creativity to identify all viable alternatives, and painstakingly evaluate every alternative to find an optimizing choice? When decision-makers are faced with a simple problem having few alternative courses of action, and when the cost of searching out and evaluating alternatives is low, the rational model provides a fairly accurate description of the decision process.[7] However, such situations are the exception. Most decisions in the real world don't follow the rational model. For instance, people are usually content to find an acceptable or reasonable solution to their problem rather than an optimizing one. As such, decision-makers generally make limited use of their creativity. Choices tend to be confined to the neighbourhood of the problem symptom and to the neighbourhood of the current alternative. As one expert in decision-making recently concluded: "Most significant decisions are made by judgment, rather than by a defined prescriptive model."[8]

The following reviews a large body of evidence to provide you with a more accurate description of how most decisions in organizations are actually made.

Bounded Rationality

When you considered which university or college to attend, did you look at *every* viable alternative? Did you carefully identify all the criteria that were important in your decision? Did you evaluate each alternative against the criteria in order to find the optimum school? The answer to these questions is probably "no," but don't feel bad. Few people selected their educational institution this way. Instead of optimizing, you probably "satisfied."

satisfice
A decision model that relies on solutions that are both satisfactory and sufficient.

bounded rationality
Individuals make decisions by constructing simplified models that extract the essential features from problems without capturing all their complexity.

When faced with a complex problem, most people respond by reducing the problem to a level at which it can be readily understood. This is because the limited information processing capability of human beings makes it impossible to assimilate and understand all the information necessary to optimize. So people **satisfice**; that is, they seek solutions that are both satisfactory and sufficient.

Since the capacity of the human mind for formulating and solving complex problems is far too small to meet the requirements for full rationality, individuals operate within the confines of **bounded rationality**. That is, they construct simplified models that extract the essential features from problems without capturing all their complexity.[9] Individuals can then behave rationally within the limits of the simple model.

How does bounded rationality work for the typical individual? Once a problem is identified, the search for criteria and alternatives begins, but the list of criteria is likely to be far from exhaustive. The decision-maker will identify a limited list of the more conspicuous choices. These are the choices that are easy to find and that tend to be highly visible. In most cases, they will represent familiar criteria and previously tried-and-true solutions. Once this limited set of alternatives is identified, the decision-maker will review it. But this review will not be comprehensive—not all the alternatives will be carefully evaluated. Instead, the decision-maker will begin with alternatives that differ only in a relatively small degree from the choice currently in effect. Following along familiar and well-worn paths, the decision-maker proceeds to review alternatives only until he or she identifies an alternative that is "good enough"—one that meets an acceptable level of performance. The first alternative that meets the "good enough" criterion ends the search. So the final solution represents a satisficing choice rather than an optimum one.

One of the more interesting aspects of bounded rationality is that the order in which alternatives are considered is critical in determining which alternative is selected. Remember, in the fully rational decision-making model, all alternatives are eventually listed in a hierarchy of preferred order. Because all alternatives are considered, the initial order in which they are evaluated is irrelevant. Every potential solution would receive a full and complete evaluation. But this isn't the case with bounded rationality. Assuming that a problem has more than one potential solution, the satisficing choice will be the first *acceptable* one the decision-maker encounters. Since decision-makers use simple and limited models, they typically begin by identifying alternatives that are obvious, ones with which they are familiar, and those not too far from the status quo. Those solutions that depart least from the status quo and meet the decision criteria are most likely to be selected. A unique and creative alternative may present an optimizing solution to the problem; however, it is unlikely to be chosen because an acceptable solution will be identified well before the decision-maker is required to search very far beyond the status quo.

Intuition

Jessie Lam has just committed her corporation to spend in excess of $40 million to build a new plant in New Westminster, British Columbia, to manufacture electronic components for satellite communication equipment. A vice-president of operations for her firm, Jessie had before her a comprehensive analysis of five possible plant locations developed by a site-location consulting firm she had hired. This report ranked the New Westminster location third among the five alternatives. After carefully reading the report and its

conclusions, Jessie decided against the consultant's recommendation. When asked to explain her decision, Jessie said, "I looked the report over very carefully. But in spite of its recommendation, I felt that the numbers didn't tell the whole story. Intuitively, I just sensed that New Westminster would prove to be the best bet over the long run."

Intuitive decision-making, like that used by Jessie Lam, has recently come out of the closet and gained some respectability. Experts no longer automatically assume that using intuition to make decisions is irrational or ineffective.[10] There is growing recognition that rational analysis has been overemphasized and that, in certain instances, relying on intuition can improve decision-making.

What do we mean by intuitive decision-making? There are a number of ways to conceptualize intuition.[11] For instance, some consider it a form of extrasensory power or sixth sense, and some believe it is a personality trait that a limited number of people are born with. For our purposes, we define **intuitive decision-making** as a subconscious process created out of distilled experience. It doesn't necessarily operate independently of rational analysis; rather, the two complement each other.

intuitive decision-making
A subconscious process created out of distilled experience.

Research on chess playing provides an excellent example of how intuition works.[12] Novice chess players and grandmasters were shown an actual, but unfamiliar, chess game with about 25 pieces on the board. After five or 10 seconds, the pieces were removed and each was asked to reconstruct the pieces by position. On average, the grandmaster could put 23 or 24 pieces in their correct squares, while the novice was able to replace only six. Then the exercise was changed. This time the pieces were placed randomly on the board. Again, the novice placed only about six correctly, but so did the grandmaster! The second exercise demonstrated that the grandmaster didn't have any better memory than the novice. What he or she did have, however, was the ability, based on the experience of having played thousands of chess games, to recognize patterns and clusters of pieces that occur on chessboards in the course of games. Studies further show that chess professionals can play 50 or more games simultaneously, where decisions often must be made in only seconds, and they can exhibit only a moderately lower level of skill than when playing one game under tournament conditions, where decisions take half an hour or longer. The expert's experience allows him or her to recognize a situation and draw upon previously learned information associated with that situation to arrive quickly at a decision choice. The result is that the intuitive decision-maker can decide rapidly with what appears to be very limited information.

When are people most likely to use intuitive decision-making? Eight conditions have been identified: (1) when a high level of uncertainty exists; (2) when there is little precedent to draw on; (3) when variables are less scientifically predictable; (4) when "facts" are limited; (5) when facts don't clearly point the way to go; (6) when analytical data are of little use; (7) when there are several plausible alternative solutions to choose from, with good arguments for each; and (8) when time is limited and there is pressure to come up with the right decision.[13]

Although intuitive decision-making has gained respectability since the early 1980s, don't expect people—especially in North America, Great Britain, and other cultures where rational analysis is the approved way of making decisions—to acknowledge they are using it. People with strong intuitive abilities don't usually tell their colleagues how they reached their conclusions. Since rational analysis is considered more socially desirable, intuitive ability is often disguised or hidden. As one top executive com-

mented, "Sometimes one must dress up a gut decision in 'data clothes' to make it acceptable or palatable, but this fine-tuning is usually after the fact of the decision."[14]

Problem Identification

Problems don't come with flashing neon lights to identify themselves. And one person's *problem* is another person's *acceptable status quo*. So how do decision-makers identify and select problems?

Problems that are visible tend to have a higher probability of being selected than ones that are important.[15] Why? We can offer at least two reasons. First, it's easier to recognize visible problems. They are more likely to catch a decision-maker's attention. This explains why politicians are more likely to talk about the "crime problem" than the "illiteracy problem." Second, remember we're concerned with decision-making in organizations. Decision-makers want to appear competent and "on top of problems." This motivates them to focus attention on problems that are visible to others.

Don't ignore the decision-maker's self-interest. If a decision-maker faces a conflict between selecting a problem that is important to the organization and one that is important to the decision-maker, self-interest tends to win out.[16] This also ties in with the issue of visibility. It's usually in a decision-maker's best interest to attack high-profile problems. It conveys to others that things are under control. Moreover, when the decision-maker's performance is later reviewed, the evaluator is more likely to give a high rating to someone who has been aggressively attacking visible problems than to someone whose actions have been less obvious.

Alternative Development

Since decision-makers rarely seek an optimum solution, but rather a satisficing one, we should expect to find a minimal use of creativity in the search for alternatives. That expectation is generally on target.

Efforts will be made to try to keep the search process simple. It will tend to be confined to the neighbourhood of the current alternative. More complex search behaviour, which includes the development of creative alternatives, will be resorted to only when a simple search fails to uncover a satisfactory alternative.

Rather than formulating new and unique problem definitions and alternatives, with frequent journeys into unfamiliar territory, the evidence indicates that decision-making is incremental rather than comprehensive.[17] This means decision-makers avoid the difficult task of considering all the important factors, weighing their relative merits and drawbacks, and calculating the value for each alternative. Instead, they make successive limited comparisons. This branch approach simplifies decision choices by comparing only those alternatives that differ in relatively small degrees from the choice currently in effect. This approach also makes it unnecessary for the decision-maker to thoroughly examine an alternative and its consequences; one need investigate only those aspects in which the proposed alternative and its consequences differ from the status quo.

What emerges is a decision-maker who takes small steps toward his or her objective. Acknowledging the non-comprehensive nature of choice selection, decision-makers make successive comparisons because decisions are never made forever and written in stone, but rather decisions are made and remade endlessly in small comparisons between narrow choices.

Constraints Affecting the Decision Choice

When a person finally reaches the point of making a decision, various internal and external factors affect how the final decision is made. We review a few of the common constraints and influences, including judgment shortcuts, individual decision-making styles, and organizational barriers.

Judgment Shortcuts

Two eminent psychologists, Daniel Kahneman and Amos Tversky, discovered that even when people are trying to be coldly logical, they give radically different answers to the same question when posed in different ways.[18] For instance, consider choices A and B in scenario 1 in Exhibit 10-2. Most people come to opposite conclusions when faced with these two problems, even though they're identical. The only difference is that the first states the problem in terms of lives saved, while the second states it in terms of lives lost. On the basis of his research in decision-making, Kahneman concluded that "we can't assume our judgments are good building blocks for decisions because the judgments themselves may be flawed."[19]

The judgment error described above is referred to as **framing**, and refers to how the selective use of perspective alters the way one might view a situation in formulating a decision. In examining the ways that people make decisions, the two psychologists discovered that individuals often rely on additional **heuristics** or judgmental shortcuts to simplify the decision process, rather than going through all of the steps of the rational decision-making model.[20]

Framing is one of the errors people make, but others are also made. For instance, sometimes people make judgments using **statistical regression to the mean**. This heuristic may be of particular interest to those trying to decide

framing
Error in judgment arising from the selective use of perspective (that is, the way in which a set of ideas, facts, or information is presented) that alters the way one views a situation in forming a decision.

heuristics
Judgmental shortcuts in decision-making.

statistical regression to the mean
The statistical observation that either very good performances or very poor performances are followed by their opposite, resulting in a record of average performance over time.

Exhibit 10-2
Examples of Decision Biases

Scenario 1: Answer part A *before* reading part B.
A: Threatened by a superior enemy force, the general faces a dilemma. His intelligence officers say his soldiers will be caught in an ambush in which 600 of them will die unless he leads them to safety by one of two available routes. If he takes the first route, 200 soldiers will be saved. If he takes the second, there's a one-third chance that 600 soldiers will be saved and a two-thirds chance that none will be saved. Which route should he take?

B: The general again has to choose between two escape routes. But this time his aides tell him that if he takes the first, 400 soldiers will die. If he takes the second, there's a one-third chance that no soldiers will die, and a two-thirds chance that 600 soldiers will die. Which route should he take?

Scenario 2:
Linda is 31, single, outspoken, and very bright. She majored in philosophy in university. As a student, she was deeply concerned with discrimination and other social issues and participated in anti-nuclear demonstrations. Which statement is more likely:

a. Linda is a bank teller.
b. Linda is a bank teller and active in the feminist movement.

Source: Kevin McKean, "Decisions, Decisions," *Discover*, June, 1985, pp. 22–31.

whether rewards or punishments work better with employees, colleagues, children, and even friends. Although many studies indicate that rewards are a more effective teaching tool than punishment, Kahneman was once faced with a student who begged to differ on this point. "I've often praised people warmly for beautifully executed manoeuvres, and the next time they almost always do worse. And I've screamed at people for badly executed manoeuvres, and by and large the next time they improve." What the student failed to recognize is that generally an exceptional performance is followed by a lesser performance, while a poorer performance is more likely followed by a better performance. This happens because each person has an average performance level, so the highs and the lows balance out. The rewards and punishments had little effect on the short-term performance being observed. Rather, improvements happen over the long term. Thus, in this example, it would be helpful to realize that screaming is less likely to result in long-term improvements in behaviour and also tends to damage the relationship between the two parties.

Consider another example of a judgmental shortcut. Many more people suffer from fear of flying than from fear of driving in a car. The reason is that many people think flying is more dangerous. It isn't, of course. With apologies in advance for this graphic example, if flying on a commercial airline were as dangerous as driving, the equivalent of two 747s filled to capacity would have to crash every week, killing all aboard, to match the risk of being killed in a car accident. Because the media give a lot more attention to air accidents, we tend to overstate the risk in flying and understate the risk in driving.

availability heuristic
The tendency for people to base their judgments on information that is readily available to them.

This illustrates an example of the **availability heuristic**, which is the tendency for people to base their judgments on information that is readily available to them. Events that evoke emotions, that are particularly vivid, or that have occurred more recently tend to be more available in our memory. As a result, we tend to be prone to overestimating unlikely events like an airplane crash. The availability heuristic can also explain why managers, when doing annual performance appraisals, tend to give more weight to recent behaviours of an employee than to those behaviours of six or nine months ago.

representative heuristic
Assessing the likelihood of an occurrence by drawing analogies and seeing identical situations where they don't exist.

Many youngsters in Canada dream of playing hockey in the National Hockey League (NHL) when they grow up. In reality, they have a better chance of becoming medical doctors than they do of playing in the NHL, but these kids are suffering from a **representative heuristic**. They tend to assess the likelihood of an occurrence by trying to match it with a pre-existing category. They hear about a boy from their neighbourhood 10 years ago who went on to play professional hockey, or they watch NHL games on television and think that those players are like them. We all are guilty of using this heuristic at times. Managers, for example, frequently predict the performance of a new product by relating it to a previous product's success. Or if three graduates from the same university were hired and turned out to be poor performers, managers may predict that a current job applicant from the same university will not be a good employee. Scenario 2 in Exhibit 10-2 gives an additional example of representativeness. In that case, Linda is assumed to be a bank teller and a feminist, given her concerns about social issues, even though the probability of both situations being true is much less than the probability of just being a bank teller.

ignoring the base rate
Error in judgment that occurs when someone ignores the statistical likelihood of an event when making a decision.

Yet another biasing error that people make is **ignoring the base rate**. For instance, if you were planning to become an entrepreneur, and we were to ask you whether your business would succeed, you would almost undoubt-

edly respond with a resounding "yes." This is no different from venture capitalists funding new ventures even when the failure rate of new businesses is quite high. Each individual believes that he or she will beat the odds, even when, in the case of founding a business, the failure rate is close to 90 percent.

Finally, the last bias we will discuss is the common tendency by decision-makers to escalate commitment to a failing course of action.[21] **Escalation of commitment** is an increased commitment to a previous decision in spite of negative information. For example, a friend had been dating a man for about four years. Although she admitted that things weren't going too well in the relationship, she was determined to marry the man. When asked to explain this seemingly nonrational choice of action, she responded: "I have a lot invested in the relationship!" Similarly, another friend was explaining why she was working on a doctorate in education, although she disliked teaching and didn't want to continue her career in education. In fact, she really wanted to be a software programmer, but she offered her escalation of commitment explanation: "I already have a master's in education and I'd have to go back and complete some deficiencies if I changed to work on a degree in software programming now."

It has been well documented that individuals escalate commitment to a failing course of action when they view themselves as responsible for the failure. That is, they "throw good money after bad" to demonstrate that their initial decision wasn't wrong and to avoid having to admit they made a mistake. Escalation of commitment is also congruent with evidence that people try to appear consistent in what they say and do. Increasing commitment to previous actions conveys consistency. You may note that escalation of commitment has some related properties to cognitive dissonance, which we previously discussed in Chapter 4. In both cases, the individual tries to provide a rational explanation for behaviour that is not entirely rational on its face.

Escalation of commitment has obvious implications for managerial decisions. Many organizations have suffered large losses because a manager was determined to prove his or her original decision was right by continuing to commit resources to what was a lost cause from the beginning. Additionally, consistency is a characteristic often associated with effective leaders. As a result, many managers, in an effort to appear effective, may be motivated to

escalation of commitment
An increased commitment to a previous decision despite negative information.

After buying Snapple Beverage Corporation in 1994 for a hefty $1.7 billion, Quaker Oats CEO William Smithburg's self-interest in boosting Snapple sales was enormous. Smithburg adopted a completely new, but ultimately unsuccessful, advertising campaign and even personally promoted new diet Snapple, leading the handout of more than $40 million worth of free samples, as shown in this photo. Despite this escalation of commitment, Snapple lost $100 million in 1996 alone. In 1997 Quaker Oats sold Snapple for $300 million to New York-based Triarc—at a loss of $1.4 billion.

be consistent when, in fact, it may be more appropriate to adopt a new course of action. In actuality, effective managers are those who are able to differentiate between situations in which persistence will pay off and situations in which it will not.

Individual Differences: Decision-Making Styles

Put Chad and Marie-Therese into the same decision situation and Chad almost always seems to take longer to reach a solution. Chad's final choices aren't necessarily always better than Marie-Therese's, he's just slower in processing information. Additionally, if there's an obvious risk dimension in the decision, Marie-Therese seems to consistently prefer a riskier option than does Chad. This example illustrates that all of us bring our individual style to the decisions we make. To learn more about your style of decision-making, refer to the Learning About Yourself exercise later in the chapter.

Research on decision styles has identified four different individual approaches to making decisions.[22] This model was designed to be used by managers and aspiring managers, but its general framework can be used with any individual decision-maker.

The basic foundation of the model is the recognition that people differ along two dimensions. The first is their way of *thinking*. Some people are logical and rational. They process information serially. In contrast, some people are intuitive and creative. They perceive things as a whole. Note that these differences are above and beyond general human limitations such as we described regarding bounded rationality. The other dimension addresses a person's *tolerance for ambiguity*. Some people have a high need to structure information in ways that minimize ambiguity, while others are able to process many thoughts at the same time. When these two dimensions are diagrammed, they form four styles of decision-making (see Exhibit 10-3). These are directive, analytic, conceptual, and behavioural.

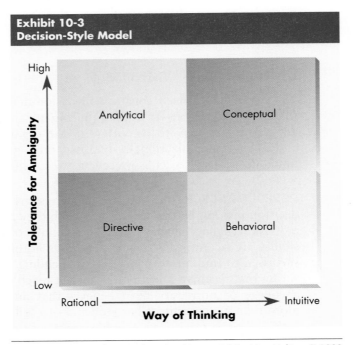

**Exhibit 10-3
Decision-Style Model**

Source: A.J. Rowe and J.D. Boulgarides, *Managerial Decision Making*, © 1992 Prentice Hall, Upper Saddle River, NJ, p. 29.

People using the *directive* style have low tolerance for ambiguity and seek rationality. They are efficient and logical, but their efficiency concerns result in decisions made with minimal information and with few alternatives assessed. Directive types make decisions fast and they focus on the short run.

The *analytic* type has a much greater tolerance for ambiguity than do directive decision-makers. This leads to the desire for more information and consideration of more alternatives than is true for directives. Analytic managers would be best characterized as careful decision-makers with the ability to adapt to or cope with new situations.

Individuals with a *conceptual* style tend to be very broad in their outlook and consider many alternatives. Their focus is long range and they are adept at finding creative solutions to problems.

The final category—the *behavioural* style—characterizes decision-makers who work well with others. They're concerned with the achievement of peers and subordinates and are receptive to suggestions from others, relying heavily on meetings for communicating. This type of manager avoids conflict and seeks acceptance.

Although these four categories are distinct, most managers have characteristics that fall into more than one. It's probably best to think in terms of a manager's dominant style and his or her back-up styles. Some managers rely almost exclusively on their dominant style; more flexible managers can make shifts depending on the situation.

Business students, lower-level managers, and top executives tend to score highest in the analytic style. That's not surprising given the emphasis that formal education, particularly business education, gives to developing rational thinking. For instance, courses in accounting, statistics, and finance all stress rational analysis.

In addition to providing a framework for looking at individual differences, focusing on decision styles can be useful for helping you to understand how two equally intelligent people, with access to the same information, can differ in the ways they approach decisions and the final choices they make.

Organizational Constraints

The organization itself constrains decision-makers. Managers, for instance, shape their decisions to reflect the organization's performance evaluation and reward system, to comply with the organization's formal regulations, and to meet organizationally imposed time constraints. Previous organizational decisions also act as precedents to constrain current decisions.

PERFORMANCE EVALUATION   Managers are strongly influenced in their decision-making by the criteria by which they are evaluated. For example, if a division manager believes that the manufacturing plants under his responsibility are operating best when he hears nothing negative, we shouldn't be surprised to find his plant managers spending a good part of their time ensuring that negative information doesn't reach the division boss. Similarly, if a college or university dean believes that an instructor should never fail more than 10 percent of her students—to fail more reflects on the instructor's ability to teach—we should expect that new instructors, who want to receive favourable evaluations, will decide not to fail too many students.

REWARD SYSTEMS The organization's reward system influences decision-makers by suggesting to them what choices are preferable in terms of personal payoff. For example, if the organization rewards risk aversion, managers are more likely to make conservative decisions. For example, from the 1930s through the mid-1980s, General Motors consistently awarded promotions and bonuses to those managers who kept a low profile, avoided controversy, and were good team players. The result was that GM managers became very adept at dodging tough issues and passing controversial decisions on to committees.

GM Canada
www.gmcanada.com

PROGRAMMED ROUTINES Amir Jadeep, a shift manager at a McDonald's restaurant in the Maritimes, describes the constraints he faces on his job: "I've got rules and regulations covering almost every decision I make—from how long to cook the french fries to how often I need to clean the washrooms. My job doesn't come with much freedom of choice."

Jadeep's situation is not unique. All but the smallest of organizations create rules, policies, procedures, and other formalized regulations in order to standardize the behaviour of their members. By programming decisions, organizations are able to get individuals to achieve high levels of performance without paying for the years of experience that would be necessary in the absence of regulations. Amir Jadeep, for instance, earns about $29 000 a year, but he's only 20 years old and has no university exposure. To get the same quality of decisions from someone in Jadeep's job without providing him or her with extensive operations manuals to follow, McDonald's would need to hire managers with considerably more work experience and training—and probably have to pay them $40 000 or more per year.

SYSTEM-IMPOSED TIME CONSTRAINTS Organizations impose deadlines on decisions. For instance, department budgets need to be completed by next Friday; or the report on new-product development must be ready for the executive committee to review by the first of the month. A host of decisions must be made quickly to stay ahead of the competition and keep customers satisfied. And almost all important decisions come with explicit deadlines. These conditions create time pressures on decision-makers and often make it difficult, if not impossible, to gather all the information they might like to have before making a final choice. The rational model ignores the reality that, in organizations, decisions come with time constraints.

HISTORICAL PRECEDENTS Rational decision-making takes an unrealistic and insulated perspective. It views decisions as independent and discrete events, but that isn't the way it is in the real world! Decisions aren't made in a vacuum. They have a context. In fact, as noted at the beginning of this chapter, individual decisions are more accurately characterized as points in a stream of decisions.

Decisions made in the past are ghosts that continually haunt current choices. For instance, past commitments may constrain current options. To use a social situation as an example, the decision you might make after meeting "Mr. or Ms. Right" is more complicated if you're married than if you're single. Prior commitments—in this case, having chosen to get married—constrain your options. In a business context, Eastman Kodak is a good example of a firm that has had to live with its past mistakes.[23] Starting in the early 1970s, Kodak's management concluded that the days of silver halide photography were numbered. They predicted that other technologies,

such as electronic photography, would soon replace it. But instead of approaching the problem deliberately, Kodak management panicked. They took off in all directions, and today virtually all of Kodak's problems can be traced to the decisions made and not made since then. Throughout the 1990s, Kodak has had trouble focusing its business objectives and has tried to maintain efforts in various fronts, rather than focusing on what it could do well. This has resulted in declining share prices and loss of profits for much of the decade, as well as hefty layoffs that have not yet resulted in substantial turnaround of the business. Government budget decisions also offer an illustration of our point. It is common knowledge that the largest determining factor of the size of any given year's budget is last year's budget.[24] Choices made today, therefore, are largely a result of choices made over the years.

Cultural Differences

The rational model makes no acknowledgment of cultural differences. However, Canadians don't necessarily make decisions the same way that people from other backgrounds do. Therefore, we need to recognize that the cultural background of the decision-maker can have significant influence on his or her selection of problems, depth of analysis, the importance placed on logic and rationality, or whether organizational decisions should be made autocratically by an individual manager or collectively in groups.[25]

Cultures, for example, differ in terms of time orientation, the importance of rationality, and preference for collective decision-making. Differences in time orientation help us understand why managers in Egypt will make decisions at a much slower and more deliberate pace than their North American counterparts. While rationality is valued in North America, that's not the case everywhere in the world. As discussed earlier in the chapter, a North American manager might make an important decision intuitively, but he or she knows that it is important to appear to proceed in a rational fashion. In countries where intuition, tradition, deference to authority, or other values play a greater role in decision-making, strictly and exclusively logical justifications for decisions may not be as important. Finally, decision-making by Japanese managers is much more group oriented than in Canada and the United States. The Japanese value conformity and cooperation. Before Japanese CEOs make an important decision, they collect a large amount of information, which they then use in consensus-forming group decisions.

Group Decision-Making

While a variety of decisions in both life and organizations are made at the individual level, the belief—characterized by juries—that two heads are better than one has long been accepted as a basic component of North American and many other countries' legal systems. This belief has expanded to the point that, today, many decisions in organizations are made by groups, teams, or committees. In this section, we will review group decision-making and compare it to individual decision-making.

Groups versus the Individual

Decision-making groups may be widely used in organizations, but does that imply that group decisions are preferable to those made by an individual

alone? The answer to this question depends on a number of factors. Let's begin by looking at the strengths and weaknesses of group decision-making.[26]

STRENGTHS OF GROUP DECISION-MAKING Groups generate *more complete information and knowledge*. By aggregating the resources of several individuals, groups bring more input into the decision process. In addition to more input, groups can bring heterogeneity to the decision process. They offer *increased diversity of views*. This offers the opportunity to consider more approaches and alternatives. The evidence indicates that a group will almost always outperform even the best individual. So groups generate *higher-quality decisions*. Finally, groups lead to *increased acceptance of a solution*. Many decisions fail after the final choice is made because people don't accept the solution. Group members who participated in making a decision are likely to enthusiastically support the decision and encourage others to accept it.

WEAKNESSES OF GROUP DECISION-MAKING In spite of the advantages noted, group decisions involve certain drawbacks. First, they're *time consuming*. They typically take more time to reach a solution than would be the case if an individual were making the decision alone. Second, there are *conformity pressures* in groups. The desire by group members to be accepted and considered an asset to the group can result in squashing any overt disagreement. Third, group discussion can be *dominated by one or a few members*. If this dominant coalition is composed of low- and medium-ability members, the group's overall effectiveness will suffer. Finally, group decisions suffer from *ambiguous responsibility*. In an individual decision, it's clear who is accountable for the final outcome. In a group decision, the responsibility of any single member is watered down.

EFFECTIVENESS AND EFFICIENCY Whether groups are more effective than individuals depends on the criteria you use for defining effectiveness. In terms of *accuracy*, group decisions will tend to be more accurate. The evidence indicates that, on the average, groups make better-quality decisions than individuals.[27] However, if decision effectiveness is defined in terms of *speed*, individuals are superior. If *creativity* is important, groups tend to be more effective than individuals. And if effectiveness means the degree of *acceptance* the final solution achieves, the nod again goes to the group.[28]

Effectiveness, however, cannot be considered without also assessing efficiency. In terms of efficiency, groups almost always stack up as a poor second to the individual decision-maker. With few exceptions, group decision-making consumes more work hours than an individual who is tackling the same problem alone. The exceptions tend to be those instances where, to achieve comparable quantities of diverse input, the single decision-maker must spend a great deal of time reviewing files and talking to people. Because groups can include members from diverse areas, the time spent searching for information can be reduced. However, as we noted, these advantages in efficiency tend to be the exception. Groups are generally less efficient than individuals. In deciding whether to use groups, then, consideration should be given to assessing whether increases in effectiveness are sufficient to offset the losses in efficiency.

In summary, groups offer an excellent vehicle for performing many of the steps in the decision-making process. They are a source of both breadth and depth of input for information gathering. If the group is composed of individuals with diverse backgrounds, the alternatives generated should be more extensive and the analysis more critical. When the final solution is

agreed upon, there are more people in a group decision to support and implement it. These advantages, however, can be more than offset by the time consumed by group decisions, the internal conflicts they create, and the pressures they generate toward conformity.

Groupthink and Groupshift

groupthink
Phenomenon in which the norm for consensus overrides the realistic appraisal of alternative courses of action.

groupshift
The phenomenon in which the initial positions of individual members of a group are exaggerated toward a more extreme position.

Two byproducts of group decision-making have received a considerable amount of attention by researchers in OB. As we'll show, these two phenomena have the potential to affect the group's ability to appraise alternatives objectively and arrive at quality decision solutions.

The first phenomenon, called **groupthink**, is related to norms. It describes situations in which group pressures for conformity deter the group from critically appraising unusual, minority, or unpopular views. Groupthink is a disease that attacks many groups and can dramatically hinder their performance. The second phenomenon is called **groupshift**. It indicates that in discussing a given set of alternatives and arriving at a solution, group members tend to exaggerate the initial positions that they hold. In some situations, caution dominates, and there is a conservative shift. More often, however, the evidence indicates that groups tend toward a risky shift. Let's look at each phenomenon in more detail.

GROUPTHINK A number of years ago, Stephen Robbins, your Seattle-based author, had a peculiar experience while attending a faculty meeting. During the meeting, a motion was placed on the floor stipulating each faculty member's responsibilities with respect to counselling students. The motion received a second, and the floor was opened for questions. There were none. After about 15 seconds of silence, the chairperson asked if he could "call for the question" (fancy terminology for permission to take the vote). No objections were voiced. When the chair asked for those in favour, a vast majority of the 32 faculty members in attendance raised their hands. The motion was passed, and the chair proceeded to the next item on the agenda.

Nothing in the process seemed unusual, but the story is not over. About 20 minutes after the meeting ended, a professor burst into Robbins' office with a petition. The petition said that the motion on counselling students had been rammed through and requested the chairperson to replace the motion on the next month's agenda for discussion and a vote. When Robbins asked this professor why he had not spoken up less than an hour earlier, he gave a frustrated look. He then proceeded to explain that in talking with people after the meeting, he realized there actually had been considerable opposition to the motion. He conceded that he didn't speak up because he thought he was the only one opposed. Conclusion: The faculty meeting had been attacked by the deadly groupthink "disease." Have you ever felt like speaking up in a meeting, classroom, or informal group, but decided against it? One reason may have been shyness. On the other hand, you may have been a victim of groupthink, the phenomenon that occurs when group members become so enamoured with seeking concurrence that the norm for consensus overrides the realistic appraisal of alternative courses of action and the full expression of deviant, minority, or unpopular views. It describes a deterioration in an individual's mental efficiency, reality testing, and moral judgment as a result of group pressures.[29]

We have all seen the symptoms of the groupthink phenomenon:

- *Rationalized resistance*. Group members rationalize any resistance to the assumptions they have made. No matter how strongly the evidence may contradict their basic assumptions, members behave so as to reinforce those assumptions continually.
- *Peer pressure*. Members apply direct pressures on those who momentarily express doubts about any of the group's shared views or who question the validity of arguments supporting the alternative favoured by the majority.
- *Minimized doubts*. Those members who have doubts or hold differing points of view seek to avoid deviating from what appears to be group consensus by keeping silent about misgivings and even minimizing to themselves the importance of their doubts.
- *Illusion of unanimity*. If someone doesn't speak, it's assumed that he or she is in full accord. In other words, abstention becomes viewed as a "Yes" vote.[30]

As the Bre-X scandal was unfolding in early 1997, many people who possibly should have known better refused to accept the initial evidence that there might not be any gold at Busang. Because investors and the companies involved had convinced themselves that they were sitting on the gold find of the century, they were reluctant to challenge their beliefs when the first evidence of tampered core samples was produced.

Groupthink appears to be closely aligned with the conclusions Solomon Asch drew in his experiments with a lone dissenter. (You'll remember the discussion on pages 252–253 in Chapter 7 of the studies in which unsuspecting subjects were tested on their willingness to dissent from patently incorrect answers offered by others in a group, and were found to conform with the group's incorrect answers in about 35 percent of the trials.) Individuals who hold a position that is different from that of the dominant majority are under pressure to suppress, withhold, or modify their true feelings and beliefs. As members of a group, we find it more pleasant to be in agreement—to be a positive part of the group—than to be a disruptive force, even if disruption is necessary to improve the effectiveness of the group's decisions.

David Walsh convinced friends and a stock brokerage firm to invest in his company, Bre-X, so that it could explore for gold at the Busang Mine in Indonesia. As rumours started to circulate in early 1997 that the initial gold samples may have been tampered with, a number of investors engaged in groupthink, refusing to believe that collectively they could have invested in a fraudulent deal.

Are all groups equally vulnerable to groupthink? The evidence suggests not. Researchers have focused on three moderating variables—the group's cohesiveness, its leader's behaviour, and its insulation from outsiders—but the findings have not been consistent.[31] At this point, the most valid conclusions we can make are: (1) highly cohesive groups have more discussion and bring out more information, but it's unclear whether such groups discourage dissent; (2) groups with impartial leaders who encourage member input generate and discuss more alternative solutions; (3) leaders should avoid expressing a preferred solution early in the group's discussion because this tends to limit critical analysis and significantly increases the likelihood that the group will adopt this solution as the final choice; and (4) insulation of the group leads to fewer alternatives being generated and evaluated.

One might also consider that overcoming groupthink can have positive outcomes. You may remember Randy Powell, from Second Cup, who appeared in Chapter 1. About a previous experience working for Campbell Soup Co., he says "Groupthink can happen, and what the senior person says tends to rule. I have always believed I should speak for what I believe to be true."[32] Randy's first test with overcoming groupthink happened just one month after he'd been hired by Campbell's. At a presentation to senior executives, Campbell's CEO David Clark told the group that Prego's spaghetti sauce was a poor performer and outlined the reasons why. Randy believed he knew the product better than the CEO. After some hesitation, he pointed this out: "It took every ounce of courage I had but I said, 'David, I beg to differ.'" After the meeting, Powell's immediate supervisor approached him and admitted, "I wanted to say that, but I just didn't have the courage to step in front of David." Powell was congratulated for speaking up, and in his own words says, "That established my reputation at Campbell's, without a doubt." In this case, speaking up really did make a difference.

GROUPSHIFT In comparing group decisions with the individual decisions of members within the group, evidence suggests that there are differences.[33] In some cases, the group decisions are more conservative than the individual decisions. More often, the shift is toward greater risk.[34]

What appears to happen in groups is that the discussion leads to a significant shift in the positions of members toward a more extreme position in the direction in which they were already leaning before the discussion. So conservative types become more cautious and the more aggressive types assume more risk. The group discussion tends to exaggerate the initial position of the group.

Groupshift can be viewed as a special case of groupthink. The group's decision reflects the dominant decision-making norm that develops during the group's discussion. Whether the shift in the group's decision is toward greater caution or more risk depends on the dominant pre-discussion norm.

The greater occurrence of the shift toward risk has generated several explanations for the phenomenon.[35] It's been argued, for instance, that the discussion creates familiarization among the members. As they become more comfortable with each other, they also become more bold and daring. Another argument is that our society values risk, that we admire individuals who are willing to take risks, and that group discussion motivates members to show that they are at least as willing as their peers to take risks. The most plausible explanation of the shift toward risk, however, seems to be that the group diffuses responsibility. Group decisions free any single member from

Second Cup
www.northbayliving.com/
second/index.html

accountability for the group's final choice. Greater risk can be taken because even if the decision fails, no one member can be held wholly responsible.

How should you use the findings on groupshift? You should recognize that group decisions exaggerate the initial position of the individual members, that the shift has been shown more often to be toward greater risk, and that whether a group will shift toward greater risk or caution is a function of the members' prediscussion inclinations.

Group Decision-Making Techniques

interacting groups
Typical groups, where members interact with each other face-to-face.

The most common form of group decision-making takes place in **interacting groups.** In these groups, members meet face-to-face and rely on both verbal and nonverbal interaction to communicate with each other. But as our discussion of groupthink demonstrated, interacting groups often censor themselves and pressure individual members toward conformity of opinion. Brainstorming, the nominal group technique, and electronic meetings have been proposed as ways to reduce many of the problems inherent in the traditional interacting group.

brainstorming
An idea-generation process that specifically encourages any and all alternatives, while withholding any criticism of those alternatives.

Brainstorming is meant to overcome pressures for conformity in the interacting group that retard the development of creative alternatives.[36] It achieves this by utilizing an idea-generation process that specifically encourages any and all alternatives, while withholding any criticism of those alternatives.

In a typical brainstorming session, a half-dozen to a dozen people sit around a table. The group leader states the problem in a clear manner so that all participants understand it. Members then "free-wheel" as many alternatives as they can in a given period of time. No criticism is allowed, and all the alternatives are recorded for later discussion and analysis. With one idea stimulating others and judgments of even the most bizarre suggestions withheld until later, group members are encouraged to "think the unusual."

How successful can a brainstorming session be? You may have noticed in one of your recent visits to a fast-food restaurant something called a "wrap."[37] *Food in Canada* rated wraps as the hot trend for 1997-98. What you might not know is that the wrap was the result of a brainstorming session by four twenty-something Californians—Will Weisman, Matthew Blair, Keith Cox, and Eduardo Rallo-Verdugo—who developed the concept while vacationing in Mexico in 1993. Weisman, who at the time was a 25-year-old programmer with Intuit and is now executive director of marketing with World Wrapp Inc., explains how the wrap came about: "The four of us started doing a lot of brainstorming about what was going on in the restaurant industry with food trends, and we wanted to do something with the burrito concept." Their brainstorming session has also reached Canada. Both Mr. Submarine, a Canadian franchise, and the Red Robin restaurant, which has locations in British Columbia and Alberta, now sell wraps. A number of wrap outlets have opened across Canada, including That's A Wrap in downtown Calgary and Bad Ass Jack's Subs and Wraps in Edmonton. In downtown Vancouver there is Wrap City Burritos and Wrap Zone. And on Bloor Street in Toronto you'll find Wrap N Roll and Wraptors.

A more recent variant of brainstorming is electronic brainstorming, which is done by people interacting on computers to generate ideas. For example, Calgary-based Jerilyn Wright and Associates uses electronic brainstorming to help clients design their workspaces through software that has been adapted for office-space design. Calgary-based Tarragon Oil and Gas

World Wrapp Inc.
www.wraps.com/

Jerilyn Wright and Associates
www.jwadesign.com/

Vancouver's Wrap Zone is one of the many examples of a brainstorming session to do something new with the burrito concept.

was the first company to use Wright's services to help plan its move from a 6900-square-metre space to an 11 000-square-metre space in a renovated downtown building. Of the electronic brainstorming for this purpose, Ray Chan, senior vice-president and chief financial officer of Tarragon, says, "There are both tangible and intangible benefits. Firstly, we would not know all the daily needs of the company. Through group participation, we got new ideas that might work better. The process also gives our employees the impression that we value their opinions, and we do. Sometimes a pat on the back isn't enough."[38]

However, brainstorming isn't always the right strategy to use. For example, President and CEO Terry Graham of Scarborough, Ontario-based Image Processing Systems Inc., which won Canada's 1997 Export Award given to leading exporting firms, notes that brainstorming can backfire. He learned this from his business dealings in China. He says that meetings with Chinese business people "are definitely not for brainstorming. We learned this lesson the hard way. Our team thought we could show our creativity by placing fresh alternatives in front of an important manager. It was two years before the company would talk to us again."[39]

Brainstorming, we should also note, is merely a process for generating ideas. The following two techniques go further by offering methods of actually arriving at a preferred solution.[40]

nominal group technique
A group decision-making method in which individual members meet face-to-face to pool their judgments in a systematic but independent fashion.

The **nominal group technique** restricts discussion or interpersonal communication during the decision-making process, hence, the term *nominal*. Group members are all physically present, as in a traditional committee meeting, but members operate independently. Specifically, a problem is presented and then the following steps take place:

- Members meet as a group, but before any discussion takes place, each member independently writes down his or her ideas on the problem.
- After this silent period, each member presents one idea to the group. Each member takes his or her turn, presenting a single idea until all ideas have been presented and recorded. No discussion takes place until all ideas have been recorded.
- The group then discusses the ideas for clarity and evaluates them.
- Each group member silently and independently ranks the ideas. The idea with the highest aggregate ranking determines the final decision.

The chief advantage of the nominal group technique is that it permits the group to meet formally but does not restrict independent thinking, as does the interacting group.

electronic meeting
A meeting where members interact on computers, allowing for anonymity of comments and aggregating of votes.

The most recent approach to group decision-making blends the nominal group technique with sophisticated computer technology.[41] It's called the **electronic meeting**. Once the technology is in place, the concept is simple. Up to 50 people sit around a horseshoe-shaped table, which is empty except for a series of computer terminals. Issues are presented to participants and they type their responses onto their computer screen. Individual comments, as well as aggregate votes, are displayed on a projection screen in the room.

The major advantages of electronic meetings are anonymity, honesty, and speed. Participants can anonymously type any message they want and it flashes on the screen for all to see at the push of a participant's board key. It also allows people to be brutally honest without penalty. And it's fast because chitchat is eliminated, discussions don't digress, and many participants can "talk" at once without stepping on one another's toes. The future of group meetings undoubtedly will include extensive use of this technology.

Each of these four group decision techniques offers its own strengths and weaknesses. The choice of one technique over another will depend on what criteria you want to emphasize and the cost-benefit trade-off. For instance, as Exhibit 10-4 indicates, the interacting group is effective for building group cohesiveness; brainstorming keeps social pressures to a minimum; the nominal group technique is an inexpensive means for generating a large number of ideas; and electronic meetings process ideas quickly.

The Influence of the Leader on Group Decision-Making

You're the head of your own business, or you're the manager of your division at work, and you're trying to decide whether you should make a decision yourself, or involve the members of your team in the decision. Is there anything that informs you about whether it is better for the leader to make the decision, or to get everyone involved in the decision-making process?

Exhibit 10-4
Evaluating Group Effectiveness

Effectiveness Criteria	Type of Group			
	Interacting	**Brainstorming**	**Nominal**	**Electronic**
Number of ideas	Low	Moderate	High	High
Quality of ideas	Low	Moderate	High	High
Social pressure	High	Low	Moderate	Low
Money costs	Low	Low	Low	High
Speed	Moderate	Moderate	Moderate	High
Task orientation	Low	High	High	High
Potential for interpersonal conflict	High	Low	Moderate	Low
Feelings of accomplishment	High to low	High	High	High
Commitment to solution	High	Not applicable	Moderate	Moderate
Develops group cohesiveness	High	High	Moderate	Low

Source: Based on J.K. Murnighan, "Group Decision Making: What Strategies Should You Use?", *Management Review*, February 1981, p. 61.

leader-participation model
A leadership theory that provides a set of rules to determine the form and amount of participative decision-making in different situations.

Back in 1973, Victor Vroom and Phillip Yetton developed a **leader-participation model** to account for various actions the leader might take with respect to the decision-making processes of the group he or she led.[42] Vroom and Yetton's model was normative—it provided a sequential set of rules that should be followed for determining the form and amount of participation desirable by the group leader or manager in decision-making, as dictated by different types of situations. The model was a complex decision tree incorporating seven contingencies (whose relevance could be identified by making "Yes" or "No" choices) and five alternative leadership styles.

More recent work by Vroom and Arthur Jago has resulted in a revision of this model.[43] The new model retains the same five alternative leadership styles but expands the contingency variables to 12, 10 of which are answered along a five-point scale. Exhibit 10-5 lists the 12 variables.

The model assumes that any of five possible behaviours that leaders could use may be feasible in a given situation—Autocratic I (AI), Autocratic II (AII), Consultative I (CI), Consultative II (CII), and Group II (GII). Thus the group leader or manager has the following alternatives from which to choose when deciding how involved he or she should be with decisions that affect a work group.

AI: You solve the problem or make a decision yourself using whatever facts you have at hand.

AII: You obtain the necessary information from subordinates and then decide on the solution to the problem yourself. You may or may not tell them about the nature of the situation you face. You seek only relevant facts from them, not their advice or counsel.

CI: You share the problem with relevant subordinates one-on-one, getting their ideas and suggestions. However, the final decision is yours alone.

CII: You share the problem with your subordinates as a group, collectively obtaining their ideas and suggestions. Then you make the decision that may or may not reflect your subordinates' influence.

GII: You share the problem with your subordinates as a group. Your goal is to help the group concur on a decision. Your ideas are not given any greater weight than those of others.

Vroom and Jago have developed a computer program that cuts through the complexity of the new model. But managers can still use decision trees to select their leader style if there are no shades of grey (that is, when the status of a variable is clear-cut so that a "Yes" or "No" response will be accurate), there are no critically severe time constraints, and subordinates are not geographically dispersed. Exhibit 10-6 illustrates one of these decision trees. To help you become more familiar with using one of these decision trees, the Working With Others exercise presents several cases for you to analyse.

Research testing of the original leader-participation model was very encouraging.[44] Because the revised model is new, its validity still needs to be assessed. But the new model is a direct extension of the 1973 version and it is also consistent with our current knowledge of the benefits and costs of participation. So, at this time, we have every reason to believe that the revised model provides an excellent guide to help managers choose the most appropriate leadership style in different situations.

One last point before we move on. The revised leader-participation model is very sophisticated and complex, which makes it impossible to

Exhibit 10-5
Contingency Variables in the Revised Leader-Participation Model

QR: Quality Requirement
How important is the technical quality of this decision?

1	2	3	4	5
No Importance	Low Importance	Average Importance	High Importance	Critical Importance

CR: Commitment Requirement
How important is subordinate commitment to the decision?

1	2	3	4	5
No Importance	Low Importance	Average Importance	High Importance	Critical Importance

LI: Leader Information
Do you have sufficient information to make a high-quality decision?

1	2	3	4	5
No	Probably No	Maybe	Probably Yes	Yes

ST: Problem Structure
Is the problem well structured?

1	2	3	4	5
No	Probably No	Maybe	Probably Yes	Yes

CP: Commitment Probability
If you were to make the decision by yourself, is it reasonably certain that your subordinates would be committed to the decision?

1	2	3	4	5
No	Probably No	Maybe	Probably Yes	Yes

GC: Goal Congruence
Do subordinates share the organizational goals to be attained in solving this problem?

1	2	3	4	5
No	Probably No	Maybe	Probably Yes	Yes

CO: Subordinate Conflict
Is conflict among subordinates over preferred solutions likely?

1	2	3	4	5
No	Probably No	Maybe	Probably Yes	Yes

SI: Subordinate Information
Do subordinates have sufficient information to make a high-quality decision?

1	2	3	4	5
No	Probably No	Maybe	Probably Yes	Yes

TC: Time Constraint
Does a critically severe time constraint limit your ability to involve subordinates?

1	5
No	Yes

GD: Geographical Dispersion
Are the costs involved in bringing together geographically dispersed subordinates prohibitive?

1	5
No	Yes

MT: Motivation — Time
How important is it to you to minimize the time it takes to make the decision?

1	2	3	4	5
No Importance	Low Importance	Average Importance	High Importance	Critical Importance

MD: Motivation — Development
How important is it to you to maximize the opportunities for subordinate development?

1	2	3	4	5
No Importance	Low Importance	Average Importance	High Importance	Critical Importance

Source: V.H. Vroom and A.G. Jago, (eds.), *The New Leadership: Managing Participation in Organizations*, ©1988. Reprinted with permission of Prentice Hall, Inc., Upper Saddle River, NJ.

Exhibit 10-6
The Revised Leadership-Participation Model
(Time-Driven Decision Tree Group Problems)

QR	Quality requirement:	How important is the technical quality of this decision?
CR	Commitment requirement:	How important is subordinate commitment to the decision?
LI	Leader's information:	Do you have sufficient information to make a high-quality decision?
ST	Problem structure:	Is the problem well structured?
CP	Commitment probability:	If you were to make the decision by yourself, is it reasonably certain that your subordinate(s) would be committed to the decision?
GC	Goal congruence:	Do subordinates share the organizational goals to be attained in solving this problem?
CO	Subordinate conflict:	Is conflict among subordinates over preferred solutions likely?
SI	Subordinate information:	Do subordinates have sufficient information to make a high-quality decision?

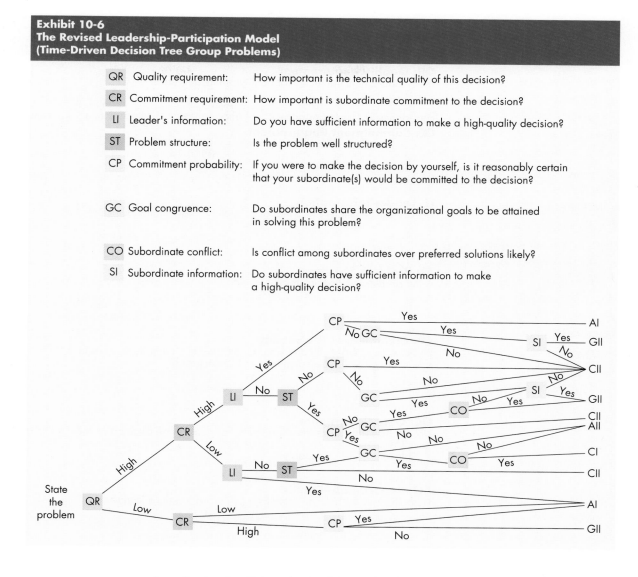

describe in detail in a basic OB textbook. However, the variables identified in Exhibit 10-5 provide you with some solid insights about when you as a leader should participate in a group decision, make the decision yourself, or delegate to someone else.

Creativity in Organizational Decision-Making

Creativity is another important aspect of decision-making in organizations. A survey conducted in the mid-1990s by the Toronto- and Montreal-based law firm Goodman Phillips and Vineberg found that large public companies and entrepreneurs both recognize a link between creative thinking within the organization and having a competitive edge.[45] "It [creative thinking] will not necessarily spell the difference between success and failure. But it is one of those tangential issues that can add a few cents per share profit," noted the head of an Ontario agriproducts company, who was not identified by the survey.

The study interviewed 100 CEOs of public companies and 100 entrepreneurs across Canada. Of those surveyed, 58 percent believe that the results

Monsanto
www.monsanto.com/

creativity
The process of creating products, ideas, or procedures that are novel or original, and are potentially relevant or useful to an organization.

of a creative thinking process are important to their company's overall success. Many *Fortune 500* companies, such as DuPont, Monsanto, Royal Bank, Disney, Thomson Corporation, Bell, Hewlett-Packard, Bank of Montreal, and CIBA Vision are training their employees specifically to "think outside the box"; that is, to think creatively.[46] To do this, the companies either bring in creativity experts to train their people or they attempt to guide thinking along more creative routes during planning sessions.

Before we discuss decision-making issues, let's consider what we mean by creativity in organizations. A variety of definitions exist for the concept of creativity, with some viewing it as a characteristic of a person, while others view it as a process.[47] Most contemporary researchers and theorists use a definition that addresses either the product or the outcome of the product development process.[48] In our discussion below, we consider **creativity** as the process of creating products, ideas, or procedures that are novel or original, and are potentially relevant or useful to an organization.[49]

Factors that Affect Individual Creativity

A large body of literature has examined the personal attributes associated with creative achievement.[50] In general, "these studies have demonstrated that a stable set of core personal characteristics, including broad interests, attraction to complexity, intuition, aesthetic sensitivity, toleration of ambiguity, and self-confidence, relate positively and consistently to measures of creative performance across a variety of domains."[51]

One study explicitly examined some of the work conditions that might affect a person's degree of creativity on the job.[52] The results indicate that on balance, people who score higher on creativity-relevant personality characteristics are more creative. Thus, people are not equal in their ability to be creative. Highly creative individuals will fare better in terms of creativity in jobs that are complex and enriched (we will discuss enriched jobs in more detail in Chapter 15) and managed in a supportive, non-controlling fashion. In other words, creative people need some freedom in order to function well. This study also found that people who are less creative may well exhibit more creativity in a more structured environment.

Improving Creativity in Decision-Making

The rational decision-maker needs creativity; that is, the ability to combine ideas in a unique way or to make unusual associations between ideas.[53] Why? Creativity allows the decision-maker to more fully appraise and understand the problem, including recognizing problems that others can't see. However, creativity's most obvious value is in helping the decision-maker identify all viable alternatives. This chapter's CBC Video Case features Eureka Ranch, where companies go for help with developing creative ideas.

CREATIVE POTENTIAL Most people have creative potential that they can use when confronted with a decision-making problem. To unleash that potential, they have to get out of the psychological ruts most of us get into and learn how to think about a problem in divergent ways.

We can start with the obvious. People differ in their inherent creativity. Einstein, Edison, Picasso, and Mozart were individuals of exceptional creativity. Not surprisingly, exceptional creativity is scarce. For example, a study of lifetime creativity of 461 men and women found that less than one percent were exceptionally creative.[54] But 10 percent were highly creative

and about 60 percent were somewhat creative. This suggests that most of us have creative potential, if we can learn to unleash it.

There is some evidence that the brain is set up to think linearly, rather than laterally, and yet lateral thinking is needed for creative thinking. Edward de Bono, a leading authority on creative and conceptual thinking for over 25 years, has written a number of books on this topic, including *Six Thinking Hats* and *The Mechanism of Mind*.[55] He has identified various tools for helping one use more lateral thinking. One such tool is called provocation, where people create a crazy idea and then transform it into a workable new concept. Toronto-based real estate firm Cambridge Shopping Centres used provocation to identify ways to build more cost-efficient office towers.[56] The provocation exercise of the cross-functional planning team was to imagine that there was no air conditioning in the towers. This led the team to the idea "that in multi-towered projects, excess air conditioning capacity from existing buildings could be used to cool adjoining towers," which was a radical new concept.

De Bono's "six thinking hats" concept is a simple yet powerful tool that is intended to change the way people think. He suggests that innovative and creative problem solving can develop from working through decisions using each of the frameworks represented by one of the hats. The hats are metaphors to represent different kinds of thinking.[57]

Cambridge Shopping Centres
www.cambridgemalls.com/

- The *white hat* represents impartial thinking, focusing strictly on the facts.
- The *red hat* represents expression of feelings, passions, intuitions, emotions.
- The *black hat* stands for a critical, deliberate, evaluating outlook.
- The *yellow hat* represents an optimistic, upbeat, positive outlook.
- The *green hat* represents creativity, inspiration, imagination, and the free flow of new concepts.
- The *blue hat* represents control, an overall "managerial" perspective of the process.

Each hat has its own place in the decision-making process. De Bono suggests that we use all six in order to fully develop our capacity to think more creatively. Toronto-based Royal Trust used this framework to collect ideas from employees across Canada on how to generate revenue and reduce costs.[58] The company received numerous ideas and discovered that the creativity process helped to remove barriers between senior management and front-line employees.

ADDITIONAL METHODS FOR STIMULATING INDIVIDUAL CREATIVITY

Sometimes the most simple action can be very powerful. That seems to be true with stimulating creativity. Evidence indicates that the mere action of instructing someone to "be creative" and to avoid obvious approaches to a problem results in more unique ideas.[59] This *direct-instruction* method is based on evidence that people tend to accept obvious solutions, which prevents them from performing up to their capabilities. So the mere statement that unique and creative alternatives are sought acts to encourage such ideas. Or overtly telling yourself that you are going to seek out creative options should lead to an increase in unique alternatives.

Another technique is *attribute listing*.[60] In attribute listing, the decision-maker isolates the major characteristics of traditional alternatives. Each major attribute of the alternative is then considered in turn and is changed in every conceivable way. No ideas are rejected, no matter how ridiculous they may seem. Once this extensive list is completed, the constraints of the problem are imposed in order to eliminate all but the viable alternatives.

Creativity can also be stimulated by practising zig-zag or *lateral thinking*.[61] This is a replacement for the more traditional vertical thinking, where each step in the process follows the previous step in an unbroken sequence. Vertical thinking is often viewed as rational thinking because it must be correct at every step and it deals only with what is relevant. With lateral thinking, individuals emphasize thinking sideways: not developing a pattern but restructuring a pattern. It is not sequential. For example, you could tackle a problem from the solution end rather than the starting end, and back into various beginning states. Lateral thinking doesn't have to be correct at each step. In fact, in some cases it may be necessary to pass through a "wrong" area in order to reach a position from which a correct path may be visible. Finally, lateral thinking is not restricted to relevant information. It deliberately uses random or irrelevant information to bring about a new way of looking at the problem.

A final suggestion: *synectics* uses analogies and inverted rationale to make the strange familiar and the familiar strange.[62] It operates on the assumption that most problems aren't new. The challenge is to view the problem in a new way, trying to abandon the familiar or routine ways that you look at things. For instance, most of us think of hens laying eggs, but how many of us have considered that a hen is only an egg's way of making another egg? One of the most famous examples in which analogy resulted in a creative breakthrough was Alexander Graham Bell's observation that it might be possible to take concepts that operate in the ear and apply them to his "talking box." He noticed that the bones in the ear are operated by a delicate, thin membrane. He wondered why, then, a thicker and stronger piece of membrane shouldn't be able to move a piece of steel. Out of that analogy, the telephone was conceived.

CREATIVITY BLOCKS Teresa Amabile, who has spent 20 years researching and consulting on creativity in business organizations, has found that "the social environment that people are working in can have an impact on their creativity and whether they will realize whatever potential they have for doing creative work."[63]

Amabile has identified five factors that act to block a manager's or employee's creativity:

- *Expected evaluation.* Focusing on how your work will be evaluated rather than focusing on the purpose of your work.

- *Surveillance.* Being watched while you are working.

- *External motivators.* Emphasizing external, tangible rewards rather than intrinsic rewards.

- *Competition.* Facing a win-lose situation with other people rather than being able to simply do your best.

- *Constrained choice.* Being given limits on how you can do your work rather than being encouraged to do your very best work.

All of these points highlight the need to be able to focus on doing one's best in a less constrained environment if one is to be able to produce in a creative manner.

What About Ethics in Decision-Making?

No contemporary discussion of decision-making would be complete without the inclusion of ethics because ethical considerations should be an important criterion in organizational decision-making. In this final section, we present three ways to ethically frame decisions and examine the factors that shape an individual's ethical decision-making behaviour. We also examine organizational responses to the demand for ethical behaviour as well as consideration of ethical decisions when doing business in other cultures. To learn more about your ethical decision-making approach, see the Ethical Dilemma exercise at the end of the chapter.

Three Ethical Decision Criteria

An individual can use three different criteria in making ethical choices.[64] The first is the *utilitarian* criterion, in which decisions are made solely on the basis of their outcomes or consequences. The goal of **utilitarianism** is to provide the greatest good for the greatest number. This view tends to dominate business decision-making. It is consistent with goals such as efficiency, productivity, and high profits. By maximizing profits, for instance, a business executive can argue that he or she is securing the greatest good for the greatest number—as he or she hands out dismissal notices to 15 percent of employees.

Another ethical criterion is to focus on *rights*. This calls on individuals to make decisions consistent with fundamental liberties and privileges as set forth in documents such as the Canadian Charter of Rights and Freedoms. An emphasis on rights in decision-making means respecting and protecting the basic rights of individuals, such as the right to privacy, to free speech, and to due process. For instance, use of this criterion would protect whistleblowers when they report unethical or illegal practices by their organization to the media or to government agencies on the grounds of their right to free speech.

A third criterion is to focus on *justice*. This requires individuals to impose and enforce rules fairly and impartially so there is an equitable distribution of benefits and costs. Union members typically favour this view. It justifies paying people the same wage for a given job, regardless of performance differences, and using seniority as the primary determination in making layoff decisions.

Each of these three criteria has advantages and liabilities. A focus on utilitarianism promotes efficiency and productivity, but it can result in ignoring the rights of some individuals, particularly those with minority representation in the organization. The use of rights as a criterion protects individuals from injury and is consistent with freedom and privacy, but it can create an overly legalistic work environment that hinders productivity and efficiency. A focus on justice protects the interests of the underrepresented and less powerful, but it can encourage a sense of entitlement that reduces risk taking, innovation, and productivity.

Decision-makers, particularly in for-profit organizations, tend to feel safe and comfortable when they use utilitarianism. Many questionable actions can be justified when framed as being in the best interests of "the organization" and stockholders. But many critics of business decision-makers ar-

utilitarianism
Decisions are made so as to provide the greatest good for the greatest number.

Robert Holland, the former CEO of Ben & Jerry's Homemade Inc., made decisions based on the company's founding principle of balancing profits and social responsibility. When a Japanese firm offered to distribute Ben & Jerry's ice cream in Japan, Holland turned down the lucrative offer because the firm did not have a reputation for backing social causes. Holland said the only reason to take the opportunity was to make money, a decision that could be justified in utilitarian terms but would not have been compatible with the company's concern for social justice.

Ben & Jerry's
www.benjerry.com/

gue that this perspective should change.[65] Increased concern in society about individual rights and social justice suggests the need for managers to develop ethical standards based on nonutilitarian criteria. This presents a solid challenge to today's managers because making decisions using criteria such as individual rights and social justice involves far more ambiguities than using utilitarian criteria such as effects on efficiency and profits. This helps to explain why managers are increasingly criticized for their actions. Raising prices, selling products with questionable effects on consumer health, closing down plants, laying off large numbers of employees, moving production to other countries to cut costs, and similar decisions can be justified in utilitarian terms. However, that may no longer be the single criterion by which good decisions should be judged.

Factors Influencing Ethical Decision-Making Behaviour

What accounts for unethical behaviour in organizations? Is it immoral individuals or work environments that promote unethical activity? The answer is *both*! The evidence indicates that ethical or unethical actions are largely a function of both the individual's characteristics and the environment in which he or she works.[66]

Exhibit 10-7 presents a model for explaining ethical or unethical behaviour. **Stages of moral development** assess a person's capacity to judge what is morally right.[67] The higher one's moral development, the less dependent he or she is on outside influences and, hence, the more he or she will be predisposed to behave ethically. For instance, most adults are at a midlevel of moral development—they're strongly influenced by peers and will follow an organization's rules and procedures. Those individuals who have progressed to the higher stages place increased value on the rights of others, regardless of the majority's opinion, and are likely to challenge organizational practices they personally believe are wrong.

We discussed *locus of control* in Chapter 3. It's a personality characteristic that taps the extent to which people believe they are responsible for the events in their lives. Research indicates that people with an external locus of

stages of moral development
An assessment of a person's capacity to judge what is morally right.

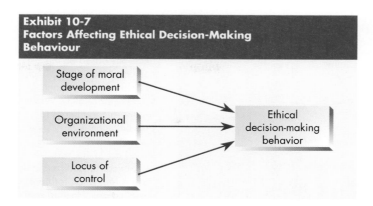

Exhibit 10-7
Factors Affecting Ethical Decision-Making Behaviour

control (i.e., what happens to them in life is due to luck or chance) are less likely to take responsibility for the consequences of their behaviour and are more likely to rely on external influences. Internals, on the other hand, are more likely to rely on their own internal standards of right or wrong to guide their behaviour.

The *organizational environment* refers to an employee's perception of organizational expectations. Does the organization encourage and support ethical behaviour by rewarding it or discourage unethical behaviour by punishing it? Written codes of ethics, high moral behaviour by senior management, realistic performance expectations, performance appraisals that evaluate means as well as ends, visible recognition and promotions for individuals who display high moral behaviour, and visible punishment for those who act unethically are some examples of an organizational environment that is likely to foster high ethical decision-making.

In summary, people who lack a strong moral sense are much less likely to make unethical decisions if they are constrained by an organizational environment that frowns on such behaviours. Conversely, very righteous individuals can be corrupted by an organizational environment that permits or encourages unethical practices.

Organizational Response to Demands for Ethical Behaviour and Social Responsibility

As the demand for ethical behaviour has increased in recent years, Canadian organizations have responded in a variety of ways to signal their concern for members of the organization acting ethically, as well as for the organization itself acting socially responsible. Below we consider organizational developments along both of these fronts. In addition, there is further information about the types of ethical policies that organizations implement in this chapter's HR Implications feature.

ETHICS During the 1990s, one could say an ethics explosion has occurred in Canada and the United States. In Canada, more than 120 ethics specialists now offer services as in-house moral arbitrators, mediators, watchdogs, and listening posts. Some work at Canada's largest corporations, including the Canadian Imperial Bank of Commerce, Canada Post, Magna International, the Royal Bank of Canada, Northern Telecom, and McDonald's Restaurants of Canada. These corporate ethics officers hear about issues such as colleagues making phone calls on company time, managers yelling at their subordinates, product researchers being asked to fake data to meet a

deadline, or a company wanting to terminate a contract because the costs are higher than anticipated. University of British Columbia ethics professor Wayne Norman believes that ethics officers are a positive trend, noting, "All sorts of studies show the companies that take ethics seriously tend to be more successful."[68]

Many corporations are also developing ethics codes. For example, about 60 percent of Canada's top 300 corporations have them, while about 90 percent of the companies on the *Fortune 500* index have them. Twenty percent of the top 300 Canadian organizations employ ethics specialists, compared with 30 percent of the *Fortune 500* companies in the United States. Unlike the United States, however, Canada does not legally require companies to create an ethical culture. In the United States, when a company is sued for illegal practices, financial damages may be reduced considerably if the company has a fully functioning ethics program in place.

Saint Laurent, Quebec-based telecommunications producer Nortel (Northern Telecom) is one company that has developed a code of business conduct. Because Nortel wanted its employees to feel committed to the code, Nortel involved them in the process of revising the code through participation in 36 focus groups around the world. They gave all employees opportunities to comment on early drafts which were available on Nortel's intranet. A copy of Nortel's business conduct code is also available on the Internet.

Vancouver-based VanCity Savings is "far and away the leader" in championing an ethical culture, according to Larry Colero, an ethics specialist with Vancouver-based Crossroads Group.[69] The 38-branch, $5-billion-asset credit union emphasizes a full range of proactive, educational ethical programs. The company also does not have an ethics officer, although it has considered the possibility of hiring one. Mark Lee, VanCity's manager of corporate responsibility, explains that there are "worries that the existence of an ethics officer might offload the responsibility that the 1400-employee credit union feels to build ethics into every aspect of operations."[70]

SOCIAL RESPONSIBILITY A number of Canadian corporations are beginning to acknowledge the need to accept responsibilities beyond those of the shareholder. The Imagine Campaign, for instance, is an effort by the Canadian Centre for Philanthropy to promote charitable giving by Canadian corporations. As a result of a campaign designed in 1997 by Allan Taylor, retired chair of the Royal Bank of Canada, 436 firms pledged to donate one percent of their pretax profits to charity. Courtney Pratt, former CEO of Noranda Inc. and current chair of the Imagine Campaign, wants companies to do even more. He suggests that companies encourage employees to volunteer their time and skills to voluntary and charitable organizations. He also suggests that companies create family-friendly workplaces and help workers upgrade their skills, so they will be employable, even if they are laid off.[71]

Not everyone agrees with this position of organizations assuming social responsibility, however. For example, economist Milton Friedman remarked in *Capitalism and Freedom* that "few trends could so thoroughly undermine the very foundations of our free society as the acceptance by corporate officials of a social responsibility other than to make as much money for their stockholders as possible."[72] Not all Canadian companies agree with Friedman, however. Both Vancouver-based VanCity Savings Credit Union and Bolton, Ontario-based Husky Injection Molding Systems Ltd. have "taken comprehensive steps to include customer, employee, community and environmental concerns in both long-term planning and day-to-day decision-making."[73] Furthermore, Al Flood, chairman of the Canadian Imperial Bank

KPMG
www.kpmg.ethics

Nortel
www.nortel.com/cool/ethics/

Canadian Centre for Philanthropy
www.ccp.ca/

HOW TO BE A LOCAL HERO

BE PICKY Do you ever feel overwhelmed by all the good causes that ask for donations? You'd like to help every one, but it's just not possible. Local Heroes know that the answer is to be picky. ❦ Review the causes you already support and be sure that your experience with each of them is rewarding. ❦ Then think about other issues you feel are critical to you and your community. ❦ Now look for the organizations that work in these areas. Call them up, visit their offices, or write for their brochures and find out all you can about what they do. The more involved you get, the more satisfaction you'll get back. ❦ Nobody expects you to say yes all the time, but you can be a Local Hero by making some causes, "Your Causes". So be picky. And be a Local Hero.

IMAGINE
A New Spirit of Giving

A national program to encourage giving and volunteering.

Being a local hero is part of Courtney Pratt's strategy to encourage Canadian companies and employees to volunteer more time to local charities. Pratt is the former CEO of Noranda Inc., is now President of Caldwell Partners International Inc. and 1998 Chair of the Imagine Campaign.

Xerox
www.xerox.com/

Tembec Inc.
www.tembec.ca/

of Commerce, notes that "good corporate ethics have to be the foundation of our business."[74] For more on the debate about social responsibility versus concentrating on the bottom line, see this chapter's Point/Counterpoint feature.

In recognition of the changes occurring in the Canadian workforce, the *Financial Post* singled out several firms for corporate social responsibility in 1997.[75] Vancouver-based Viceroy Resource Corp., a gold mining firm, was chosen for its environmental responsibility. The firm follows the most rigorous environmental and reclamation standards in its Castle Mountain Mine in California. Viceroy has been praised by both environmentalists and regulators alike and has won numerous environmental awards in the 1990s, including being designated as a model mine in 1995 by the U.S. Bureau of Land Management. Similarly, Winnipeg-based The North West Co., Inc., a clothing, food, and general merchandise retailer with 160 stores in Northern Canada, was cited for its commitment to aboriginal people. The company is the largest private-sector employer of aboriginal people in Canada, and much of its donation budget goes towards the northern communities and national aboriginal and northern issues. Montreal-based Tembec Inc. was cited for its community contribution. Tembec is a forest-products company that, among other things, gives its employees five paid days off per year to volunteer for the non-profit group of their choice. And Xerox Canada was cited for its women-friendly policies.

All of the companies noted above are not only contributing to the well-being of Canada, but are also contributing to the well-being of their shareholders—illustrating that being profitable while acting in a socially responsible manner is possible. Exhibit 10-8 identifies additional companies that are committed to social responsibility in Canada. The Case Incident in this chapter examines the practice of ethical investing. And OB in the News highlights Toronto-based Imperial Oil's programs for being a social responsible corporate citizen.

What About National Culture?

We have already shown that there are differences in the legal treatment of ethics violations and the creation of an ethical corporate culture between Canada and the United States. However, it is important to note that what is considered unethical in one country may not be viewed similarly in another country. The reason is that there are no global ethical standards. Contrasts between Asia and the West provide an illustration.[76] In Japan, people doing business together often exchange gifts, even expensive ones. This is part of Japanese tradition. When North American and European companies started doing business in Japan, most North American executives weren't aware of the Japanese tradition of exchanging gifts and wondered whether this was a

Exhibit 10-8
Corporate Responsibility, 1997: The Financial Post's Top 50 Canadian Corporations[1]

Alcan Aluminum Ltd.	National Bank of Canada
Archer Resources Ltd.	NewTel Enterprises Ltd.
Ault Foods Ltd.	Noranda Inc.
Bank of Montreal	PanCanadian Petroleum Ltd.
BCE Inc.	Petro-Canada
BCE Mobile Comm's Inc.	Petromet Resources Ltd.
BC TELECOM Inc.	Phoenix Int'l Life Sciences Inc.
Bruncor Inc.	Renaissance Energy Ltd.
Canadian Airlines Corp.	Royal Bank of Canada
Canadian Tire Corp., Ltd.	Shaw Communications Inc.
Chieftain International, Inc.	Stampeder Exploration Ltd.
CIBC	Summit Resources Ltd.
Dominion Textile Inc.	Talisman Energy Inc.
DuPont Canada Inc.	TELUS Corp.
Emco Ltd.	Tembec Inc.
Geac Computer Corp. Ltd.	The Bank of Nova Scotia
Great-West Lifeco Inc.	The North West Co. Inc.
G.T.C. Transcontinental Group Ltd.	The Toronto-Dominion Bank
Hudson's Bay Co.	Torstar Corp.
Investors Group Inc.	TransAlta Corp.
Le Groupe Vidéotron Ltée	TransCanada PipeLines Ltd.
London Insurance Group Inc.	Transwest Energy Inc.
Maritime Tel. and Tel. Co. Ltd.	Viceroy Resources Corp.
Merfin International Inc.	Wascana Energy Inc.
Moore Corp.	Xerox Canada Inc.

[1] List arranged in alphabetical, not ranked, order. Companies for the analysis were limited to those on the TSE in late November 1996.

Source: R. Walker and S. Flanagan, "The ethical imperative: if you don't talk about a wider range of values, you may not have a bottom line," *Financial Post 500*, 1997, p. 31.

form of bribery. Most have come to accept this tradition now and have even set different limits on gift giving in Japan than in other countries.[77]

In another instance illustrating the differences between Asia and North America, professor Thomas Donaldson, an international ethics expert at the Wharton School of Business, reports the story of a manager of a large U.S. company that operates in China. The manager caught an employee stealing, and following company policy, she fired him. She also turned him over to the local authorities for his act. Later she discovered, much to her horror, that the former employee had been executed for his deed.[78] Both the gift-giving illustration for Japan and the execution story of China indicate that standards for ethical behaviour and the consequences of particular acts are not universally similar. This presents a variety of problems for those doing business in other countries.

OB IN THE NEWS

Corporate Responsibility at Imperial Oil

Toronto-based Imperial Oil Ltd. is seen as an exemplar of corporate responsibility by both CEOs across Canada as well as the average Canadian citizen. Imperial's budget for charitable donations in 1995 was $6 million, based on one percent of average pretax earnings for 1991-1994. Between 1980 and 1994, Imperial has donated $107 million to various charities.

CEO Bob Peterson says that Imperial is committed to social responsibility in both good times and bad. For example, when Imperial underwent a major downsizing between 1989 and 1994, reducing the number of employees from 15 000 to 8250, and the number of service stations from 4300 to 3220, the company continued programs to promote health, safety, environmental protection, and employee involvement in community volunteer activities. The firm's environmental initiatives include enhanced oil-spill clean-up capabilities, reduced plant emissions, and the development of less-polluting gasoline formulas.

One of Imperial's major objectives in its charitable donations and volunteer activity is education and youth. The firm sponsors "everything from a summer camp for children with cancer to funding for university expansion projects to a work-placement program for teens still in school called KAPOW (Kids and the Power of Work)." Peterson believes that education is an important foundation of Canadian society: "Canada's future depends on education: We need to give young people a zest for lifelong learning."

Imperial also encourages ethical behaviour among its employees, and each year all employees must sign a statement acknowledging the companies ethics policy. The policy is contained in a booklet entitled *Is it Legal? Is It Responsible? Can I Justify It?*

Beyond charity and ethics, Imperial is now placing greater emphasis on "operations integrity." This includes designing, building, and operating facilities so that "we don't screw up and we don't harm anyone," Peterson explains. Imperial's approach to running the business reflects long-term economic interests, and Peterson notes that it is not difficult to enforce. "You create the right culture because people like to do good work and to be perceived as doing good work."

Sources: Based on Robert Bott, "Everyday Ethics," *Report on Business*, April 1995, pp. 74, 76.

Take It to the Net

We invite you to visit the Robbins page on the Prentice Hall Web site at:

http://www.prenticehall.ca/robbins

for this chapter's World Wide Web exercise.

Companies operating branches in foreign countries are faced with tough decisions about how to conduct business under different ethical standards from those in Canada. For instance, Canadian companies must decide whether they want to operate in countries such as China, Burma, and Nigeria, which abuse human rights. Although the Canadian government permits investing in these countries, it also encourages companies to act ethically. Along the same lines, several Canadian companies are involved in the controversial Three Gorges dam project in China, although Ontario Hydro recently withdrew because of its concerns about China. Toronto-based shoe manufacturer Bata, on the other hand, has decided not to manufacture its products in China because of issues such as safety and child labour, although it will open stores there.

Because bribery is commonplace in countries such as Nigeria, Bolivia, Russia, and Mexico, a Canadian working in these countries might face the dilemma: Should I pay a bribe to secure business if it is an accepted part of that country's culture? The Bata shoe empire decided in October 1997 to sell their business holdings in Nigeria because of corruption by officials there. Sonja Bata, president of Bata Ltd., explained this decision: "The corruption killed us. Telephone lines were cut, power was cut, products couldn't get through customs. We decided not to play along and finally moved out. It's heartbreaking."[79] Facing the dilemma of bribery is a common feature of doing business for many organizations. A 1997 World Bank survey of 3600 businesses found that 40 percent of them were paying bribes in 69 countries.[80] Some have estimated that bribery accounts for 10 to 20 percent of contract amounts worldwide, which means that bribery is costing companies billions of dollars.

While ethical standards may seem ambiguous in the West, criteria defining right and wrong are actually much clearer in the West than in Asia. Few issues are black-and-white there; most are grey. John B. McWilliams, senior vice-president and general counsel for Calgary-based Canadian Occidental Petroleum Ltd., notes that requests for bribes are not necessarily direct: "Usually, they don't say, 'Give me X thousands of dollars and you've got the deal.' It's a lot more subtle than that."[81] Michael Davies, vice-president and general counsel for Toronto-based General Electric Canada Inc., describes it as "a payment made to an administrative official to do the job that he's supposed to do. In other words, you pay a fellow over the counter $10 when you're in the airport in Saudi Arabia to get on the flight you're supposed to get on, because, otherwise, he's going to keep you there for two days."[82]

The need for global organizations to establish ethical principles for decision-makers in countries such as India and China may be critical if high standards are to be upheld and if consistent practices are to be achieved. In December 1997, "all 29 members of the OECD signed an anticorruption convention that commits them to criminalizing the bribing of foreign officials."[83] Prior to that, only the United States had taken that step. The World Bank has ordered random audits of projects, barred corrupt firms from bidding on contracts, and requested no-bribery pledges from companies that bid on public-sector contracts. Other organizations that have adopted declarations, reports, and conventions against bribery include the United Nations, the International Chamber of Commerce, the Organization of American States, and the European Union. The Canadian government might introduce an anti-bribery law in 1999. There is a section of the Criminal Code that addresses conspiracies to bribe foreign officials, but it has not been used for this purpose.[84] Moreover, Canada has a much greater propensity for paying bribes, according to Transparency International, an international agency that investigates and tries to stop bribery. It ranks Canada eleventh on a scale of 12 countries most disposed to offering bribes. Belgium/Luxembourg scored in first place, France second, and Japan ranked twelfth.[85] The United States did not appear on the list. It also has the most stringent anti-bribery law in the world: the U.S. Foreign Corrupt Practices Act (FCPA).

It's clear that despite Canada's domestic record of ethical concern, when it comes to international dealings we have a long way to go.

HR IMPLICATIONS

Developing Corporate Ethics Policies

Canadian corporations have chosen a variety of ways to implement ethics programs. These include developing training sessions, writing out explicit codes, making more general principles, or developing a culture of ethics. In the examples below, we indicate companies that have chosen one or more of these ways of developing their ethics approach.[1]

Northern Telecom hired a senior ethics advisor to help the company get its 68 000 employees around the world to agree on a definition of right and wrong. Megan Barry, who is based in Nashville, Tennessee, started interviewing employees in 1994, and the process was still going on in late 1997. Her job is to understand how Nortel employees think about ethical issues at the same time that she also trains them about Nortel's policy. Nortel developed its codes of ethics in 1994 and believes that it has resulted in improved employee morale and better relations with customers and suppliers.

To introduce its code, Northern Telecom distributed copies to its employees globally and also placed the code on its intranet and Internet sites.[2] Placing it on the Internet has alerted those outside Nortel to how important the company views corporate ethics. Nortel includes ethics training modules as part of its new employee training, and newly promoted managers receive ethics modules. Nortel produces the modules locally, so that the relevant business examples are provided in the proper cultural context.

In 1995, the Department of Defence appointed a team headed by Rosalie Bernier to develop a statement of ethics that would apply across all ranks and divisions of the department, both military and bureaucratic. Bernier, who now serves as manager of the defence ethics program at the Department of Defence, noted that the team tried to take a positive approach by establishing a set of values rather than rules. The core values are loyalty, honesty, courage, diligence, fairness, and responsibility. There are also three principles to frame the values: "to respect the dignity of all persons; to serve Canada before self; and to obey and support lawful authority."

At the Bank of Montreal, Glenn Higginbotham, vice-president, corporate compliance, has chosen to avoid the "corporate-cop" approach to ethical behaviour, and instead rely on people to be guided by their conscience. "If you have a good ethical culture, people will be making the right decisions," he says. The Bank of Montreal has chosen to encourage a strong ethical culture among its employees, and so far, that approach has worked well for the bank.

Glaxo Wellcome Inc. used to leave ethical issues to the judgment of its employees. However, following the 1995 takeover of Burroughs Wellcome, the company decided to rebuild its corporate culture due to the merging of employees from the two different companies. The company is still working on a comprehensive document covering a range of moral issues. It will also include specific examples for situations where there often is no right or wrong answer.

John Zych, ethics officer for Imperial Oil, believes he must work hard just to keep his company's code of ethics current. The company's original document was written 30 years ago, and it has been revised four times in the last 10 years. Imperial Oil's code of ethics has been in place longer than most Canadian companies. Imperial takes its ethics responsibilities seriously and in 1997 was ranked by EthicScan Canada near the top of a recent survey of ethical corporations.

It should be obvious from these examples that there is no one right way to introduce ethics to employees, and that it also takes some realistic planning to do so.

Sources:

[1] Information about these companies is based, except where noted below, on John Greenwood, "The Guardians: Six Portraits in the Emerging Discipline of Playing Watchdog Over a Company's Code of Conduct," *Financial Post 500*, 1997, pp. 40–50.

[2] Information in this paragraph based on N. Richardson and M. Barry, "Minding Your Ps and Qs at Nortel," *CMA Management Accounting Magazine*, May, 1997, p. 20–22.

Summary and Implications

For the Workplace

We described the rational decision-making process and then discussed how it is often difficult to implement because of time and information constraints. Yet organizations could improve the decisions made by employees by ensuring, where possible, that people have the information they need to make the decision.

Organizations that use teams face additional problems and synergies with respect to decision-making. We described instances where teams make better decisions than individuals, including when problems are sufficiently complex that no one person has all of the relevant information. The leader participation model can also be used to determine the extent to which managers should be involved in team decision-making.

We examined the process of creativity in organizations and noted that when organizations reward for not making mistakes, employees are less likely to feel free to look for creative solutions that might include better ways of getting something done. We also indicated conditions under which creativity is more likely to occur.

What can we conclude regarding ethics? Managers should seek to convey high ethical standards to employees through the actions taken. By what managers say, do, reward, punish, and overlook, they set the ethical tone for their employees. When hiring new employees, managers have an opportunity to weed out ethically undesirable applicants. The selection process—for instance, interviews, tests, and background checks—should be viewed as an opportunity to learn about an individual's level of moral development and locus of control. This can then be used to identify individuals whose ethical standards might be in conflict with those of the organization or who are particularly vulnerable to negative external influences.

We also noted that organizations are trying to become more socially responsible. One outlet for this is the Imagine Campaign's idea to contribute one percent of pretax corporate earnings to social causes.

For You as an Individual

Individuals think and reason before they act. It is because of this that an understanding of how people make decisions can be helpful for explaining and predicting their behaviour.

In some decision situations, you might follow the rational decision-making model. But in many cases, this is probably more the exception than the rule. Given the evidence we've described on how decisions are actually made, what can be done to improve decision-making? We offer four suggestions.

First, analyse the situation. Make sure you understand the complexities of the decision to be made.

Second, be aware of biases. We all bring biases to the decisions we make. If you understand the biases influencing your judgment, you can begin to change the way you make decisions to reduce those biases.

Third, combine rational analysis with intuition. These are not conflicting approaches to decision-making. By using both, you can actually improve your decision-making effectiveness. As you gain experience, you should feel

increasingly confident in imposing your intuitive processes on top of your rational analysis.

Finally, use creativity-stimulation techniques. You can improve your overall decision-making effectiveness by searching for innovative solutions to problems. This can be as basic as telling yourself to think creatively and to look specifically for unique alternatives. Additionally, you can practise the attribute listing and lateral thinking techniques described in this chapter.

We also considered ethics in this chapter and provided an overview of ways to decide whether a decision was ethical. We noted the complexity of making ethical decisions when working in other countries. Individuals would do well first to understand their own ethical limits, and then seek to understand how these match with one's employer's ethical demands.

ROADMAP REMINDER

In the previous chapter we considered communication, how firms can let employees know what is important, and how individuals can improve their communication. Decision-making relates to communication in that one formulates decisions and then needs to convey them. In this chapter we considered how one makes decisions and then explored creativity and ethics in decision-making. In the next chapter we will examine leadership as a way of addressing the role of individuals responsible for carrying out decisions.

For Review

1. What is the rational decision-making model? Under what conditions is it applicable?
2. Describe organizational factors that might constrain decision-makers.
3. What role does intuition play in effective decision-making?
4. Describe the three criteria individuals can use in making ethical decisions.
5. What is *groupthink*? What is its effect on decision-making quality?
6. What is *groupshift*? What is its effect on decision-making quality?
7. Identify factors that block creativity.
8. What factors influence ethical (or unethical) decision-making?

For Discussion

1. "For the most part, individual decision-making in organizations is an irrational process." Do you agree or disagree? Discuss.
2. What factors do you think differentiate good decision-makers from poor ones? Relate your answer to the six-step rational decision-making model.
3. Have you ever increased your commitment to a failed course of action? If so, analyse the follow-up decision to increase your commitment and explain why you behaved as you did.
4. If group decisions consistently achieve better-quality outcomes than those achieved by individuals, how did the phrase "a camel is a horse designed by a committee" become so popular and ingrained in our culture?

ETHICAL DILEMMA EXERCISE

Five Ethical Decisions: What Would You Do?

Assume you're a middle manager in a company with about 1000 employees. How would you respond to each of the following situations?

1. You're negotiating a contract with a potentially very large customer whose representative has hinted that you could almost certainly be assured of getting his business if you gave him and his wife an all-expense-paid cruise to the Caribbean. You know the representative's employer wouldn't approve of such a "payoff," but you have the discretion to authorize such an expenditure. What would you do?

2. You have the opportunity to steal $100 000 from your company with absolute certainty that you would not be detected or caught. Would you do it?

3. Your company policy on reimbursement for meals while travelling on company business is that you will be repaid for your out-of-pocket costs, which are not to exceed $50 a day. You don't need receipts for these expenses—the company will take your word. When travelling, you tend to eat at fast-food places and rarely spend in excess of $15 a day. Most of your colleagues submit reimbursement requests in the range of $40 to $45 a day regardless of what their actual expenses are. How much would you request for your meal reimbursements?

4. You want to get feedback from people who are using one of your competitor's products. You believe you'll get much more honest responses from these people if you disguise the identity of your company. Your boss suggests you contact possible participants by using the fictitious name of the Consumer Marketing Research Corporation. What would you do?

5. You've discovered that one of your closest friends at work has stolen a large sum of money from the company. Would you: Do nothing? Go directly to an executive to report the incident before talking about it with the offender? Confront the individual before taking action? Make contact with the individual with the goal of persuading that person to return the money?

Sources: Several of these scenarios are based on D.R. Altany, "Torn between Halo and Horns," *Industry Week*, March 15, 1993, pp. 15–20.

CASE INCIDENT

Ethical Investing and Profit Making

Ethical Funds, Canada's largest family of "green" mutual funds, has a dilemma. How does it decide whether a company is one "good enough" in which to invest?

Ethical Funds invests only in companies that can pass its ethical screens. The mutual-fund company gives high marks for harmonious labour relations and generous charitable contributions. Firms that manufacture tobacco products and nuclear power are not considered. Even with these rules, however, deciding which companies to invest in is not an easy task.

Michael Jantzi, who heads MJRA, a firm that tracks the ethical records of publicly traded companies, admits that sometimes these ethical mutual funds must "settle for the least-bad actors." For instance, ethical funds typically favour stocks in the financial services industry, because companies in this industry are nonpolluting. However, it is the rare bank that has never made a loan to a natural-resource firm or a defence contractor. Natural-resource firms are often off limits for ethical investors, particularly in the United States. However, this screen is not applied so vigorously in Canada where resource companies comprise more than 40 percent of the Toronto Stock Exchange. If these companies are eliminated from investment consideration, it would considerably reduce the ability of the funds to be diversified.

Another area that poses a dilemma is tobacco. Ethical funds generally avoid tobacco companies. However, what about a firm that manufactures packaging for tobacco companies? David Shuttleworth, vice-president, marketing and sales for Ethical Funds, says he would invest in the packaging company "if less than 20 percent of its business is making tobacco packaging." And how does he arrive at the 20 percent figure? "Well, that's just the cutoff point we set."

Some of the information gathered by the analysts for ethical funds may also be questionable. In particular, not all of the information gathered comes from independent or neutral sources. The analysts also send questionnaires to companies, and review the annual reports and other published information about each company. This can lead to problems, however. For instance, The Body Shop International has come under scrutiny for having stated goals and achievements in their public documents that were not always consistent with their practices.

Do ethical funds make a difference to society? Jantzi argues that companies respond to the negative publicity of not being considered for these ethical mutual fund so he believes that the funds can, over time, affect corporate behaviour. But John Bishop, a professor at Trent University, believes that with ethical investing accounting "for less than one percent of the market, the impact is negligible, like taking a bucket of water out of the shallow end of a swimming pool and emptying it into the deep end."

Moreover, the funds overall must produce decent returns, or even investors who want to support ethical considerations may be unwilling to invest. "The bottom line is still money," Shuttleworth says. "We have to make a profit for our investors."

Questions

1. What dilemmas do ethical fund companies face in choosing firms in which to invest?

2. Are these funds striking a compromise with their ethics?

3. Is it possible to reconcile making a profit with ethical decisions?

4. Analyse this case in terms of decision-making styles.

Source: Based on P.C. Judge, "In Search of Saintly Stock Picks," *Report on Business*, October 1995, p. 45.

Eureka Ranch

What does a company do when it wants to develop new products? Molson, Lipton Canada, Nike, Disney, and Procter & Gamble turn to Doug Hale, President of Eureka Ranch, in Cincinnati, Ohio. At Eureka, Hale conducts product-storming sessions, helping companies to create new ideas. Clients come to the ranch to think and have their creativity flow.

Tyson Foods is one of Eureka's clients. Tyson is the world's largest chicken producer and the company wants to develop new chicken ideas. Hale has created a "chicken for lunch" three-day session for them, so that they can develop at least a dozen new food concepts to take back to head office. During their brainstorming session some of the ideas include chicken pudding, chicken drinks, and crunchy chicken feet.

At Eureka, brainstorming is key. And no idea is to be killed. As Hale says, "Newborn ideas are sacred. It takes no courage to kill an idea. It takes courage to take an idea that's absolutely ridiculous and do something with it." Hale teaches his clients to get the killing feeling for new ideas out of their system by having them engage in a mini-war. Here, they can expend their "killing energies" and have fun at the same time. Then they can get down to the business at hand: loving everyone's ideas as they're presented, so that every idea has a chance.

Hale notes that at the ranch, executives have to think creatively, something they're not used to doing. Usually they spend about three percent of their time thinking and creating. He hopes to expand this to 30 percent of their time while they're at the ranch.

Not all of the brainstorming session is "work," however. Play is very much a part of thinking creatively. Clients take play breaks so that they can get away from the work for a bit, refocus, and then go back to work ready to brainstorm some more.

Creativity can bring out tensions as well. Not everyone gets along all the time, and not everyone remembers to love every idea that comes out. Hale keeps the group on track, however. Even with a passionate discussion of ideas, people are encouraged to be respectful of each other's ideas. Hale views his work as simply helping people to get a vision. The company can develop the product once the vision is there. But getting that vision can be difficult—which is the reason for Doug Hale and Eureka Ranch.

Questions

1. Describe the brainstorming process at Eureka Ranch.

2. Why would play help brainstorming develop more effectively?

3. What ways might you use brainstorming in a group in which you are a member?

Source: Based on "Eureka Ranch," *Venture 679*; aired March 3, 1998.

POINT

Organizations Should Just Stick to the Bottom Line

The major goals of organizations are and should be efficiency, productivity, and high profits. By maximizing profits, businesses ensure that they will survive and thus make it possible to provide employment. Doing so is in the best interests of the organization, employees, and stockholders. Moreover, it is up to individuals to show that they are concerned about the environment through their investment and purchasing activities, not for corporations to lead the way. Let's examine some of the reasons why it is not economically feasible to place all of the burden of protecting the environment on the shoulders of big business.

Shareholder demands necessitate avoiding environmental regulations if possible. For instance, Toronto-based Noranda Inc., Canada's largest resource conglomerate, announced in 1997 that it was selling off its forestry, oil, and gas subsidiaries to focus on the more profitable metals and mining sector. Craig Campbell, the partner in charge of the forest industry group at Price Waterhouse in Montreal, notes, "It's all being driven by shareholders (who are) ...demanding higher share value. The cost of logging is increasing rapidly because of environmental pressures. Companies now have to completely clean up a site when they've finished logging.... These kind of expenditures didn't have to be paid before."[1]

Studies show that environmental regulations are too costly. The Conference Board of Canada suggested that environmental regulations cost Canadian companies $580 to $600 million a year.[2] Finally, the Fraser Institute in Vancouver reported that all regulations, including those designed to protect the environment, cost Canadian industry $85 billion a year.[3]

Environmental regulations can also be harmful to jobs. Consider the case of MacMillan Bloedel (MacBlo), British Columbia's largest forest firm, whose president and CEO, Thomas Stephens, announced January 21,1998 that he would fire 2700 of the firm's 13 000 employees by the end of the year. Stephens criticized B.C.'s Forest Practices Code as part of the problem MacBlo experienced in recent years. The two-year-old Forest Practices Code is said to have added $1 billion a year to harvesting costs in British Columbia. Stumpage fees are three times higher than in Ontario and Quebec.

While businesses are concerned with the high cost that results from environmental regulations, the general public is not completely supportive of protecting the environment either, particularly if it will inconvenience them.[4]

Companies would be better off sticking to the bottom line, and governments should stay away from imposing costly environmental regulations on business. Stringent environmental standards cause trade distortions, and governments rarely consider the cost of complying with regulations. Companies should be allowed to take their lead from shareholders and customers. If these constituencies want businesses to pay for environmental protection, they will indicate this by investing in firms that do so. Until they do, the cost of environmental legislation is simply too high. ■

Sources:

[1] Michael MacDonald, "Noranda to Restructure Operations," *Canadian Press Newswire*, November 18, 1997.

[2] Allan Howatson, *Lean Green: Benefits From a Streamlined Canadian Environmental Regulatory System* (Ottawa: The Conference Board of Canada, April 1996).

[3] Fazil Mihlar, *Regulatory Overkill: The Cost of Regulation in Canada* (Vancouver: The Fraser Institute, September 1996).

[4] Robin Brunet, "To Survive and Thrive: Bled Dry by the NDP, BC Business Plots a New Course for the 21st Century," *British Columbia Report*, February 9, 1998, pp. 18–22.

counterPOINT

Environmental Responsibility is Part of the Bottom Line

Going green makes good economic sense. The studies reported in the *Point* argument tend to overstate the cost of environmental regulations.[1] They do not consider the benefits to society of those regulations.

Companies are starting to see the value of protecting the environment on their bottom line. During the last five years, a number of companies have conducted environmental audits, including Ottawa-based E.B. Eddy; Toronto-based Noranda; Scarborough, Ontario-based Consumers' Gas; Hamilton, Ontario-based Dofasco; Montreal-based Avenor; and Calgary-based Shell. At least some private-sector firms are finding that focusing on the environment saves costs, is a competitive strategy, and has social benefits.

A closer look at a few companies that have devoted efforts to being more environmentally friendly will illustrate the benefits of this approach. John Grant, CEO of Quaker Oats Canada from 1967 to 1994, reports that Quaker Oats started working towards a "greener" work environment in 1987. One of the plants, located in Peterborough, Ontario, saved over $1 million in three years through various environmental initiatives. Grant reports that employees responded with pride to the environmental culture and the best university graduates wanted to work at a company that had strong environmental values. Grant also believes that shareholders receive a value in their shares that goes beyond the quarterly earnings and annual reports when a company commits itself to improving the environment. Moreover, suppliers and customers, the public, and consumers also respond favourably to products designed and produced in an environmentally friendly manner. Grant summarizes his views on why business should be concerned with the environment: "Environmental stewardship goes hand-in-hand with improved efficiency, productivity, profitability, and world competitiveness.... To achieve a healthy economy requires environmental stewardship. The two are mutually interdependent and it is not a choice of one or the other."[2]

Inco Ltd., for example, has worked to repair the environmental abuse of past generations at its Sudbury, Ontario, operations. Inco spent $600 million to change the way it produces nickel in order to be less devastating to the local environment. Their new smelting process is the most energy efficient and environmentally friendly process in the world. At the same time, Inco continues to work to restore the appearance of Sudbury. Trees have grown back, the wildlife has returned, and the air is clean. Sudbury has even been listed as one of the 10 most desirable places to live in Canada. While Inco invested a lot of money to change its production process, Doug Hamilton, controller at Inco's Ontario division in Sudbury, says, "Our Sulphur Dioxide Abatement Program was an awesome undertaking. Not only did this investment allow us to capture 90 percent of the sulphur in the ore we mine, but the new processes save the company $90 million a year in production costs. That strikes me as a pretty smart investment."[3]

London, Ontario-based 3M Canada Inc. started a Pollution Prevention Pays (3P) program over 20 years ago. The program emphasizes stopping pollution at the source to avoid the expense and effort of cleaning it up or treating it after the fact. The recycling program at 3M Canada's tape plant in Perth, Ontario, reduced their waste by 96 percent and saved the company about $650 000 annually. The capital cost for the program was only $30 000.

The examples of Quaker Oats, Inco, and 3M show that companies that are environmentally friendly have an advantage over their competitors. If organizations control their pollution costs better than their competitors, they will use their resources more efficiently and therefore increase profitability. ■

Sources:

[1] Gary Gallon, "Bunk Behind the Backlash: Highly Publicized Reports Exaggerate the Costs of Environmental Regulation, *Alternatives*, Fall 1997, pp. 14–15.

[2] Jon K. Grant, "Whatever Happened to Our Concern About the Environment?" *Canadian Speeches*, April 1997, pp. 37–42.

[3] "The Business of Being Green," Advertising Supplement, *Canadian Business*, January 1996, pp. 41–56.

CHAPTER 11

Leadership

LEARNING OBJECTIVES

After studying this chapter, you should be able to

- Describe the nature of leadership

- Summarize the path-goal theory

- Explain why no one leadership style is ideal in all situations

- Describe charismatic leadership

- Differentiate between transactional, transformational, and laissez-faire leaders

- Understand differences between male and female leadership styles

- Explain how leadership needs are changing for the 21st century

Can one person make a difference in an organization's performance? Apple Computer thinks so. After years of underperforming under the leadership of both Michael Spindler and Gil Amelio, Apple Computer is once again headed by Steve Jobs, its legendary co-founder who was ousted from his original leadership position in 1985.[1]

Despite undergoing two massive restructurings, firing thousands of employees, replacing entire groups of senior executives, and discontinuing several unprofitable products under Amelio, Apple faced red ink every quarter except one in the 18 months of Amelio's leadership. In December 1996, Apple brought Jobs back in an advisory role and expanded his role further when Amelio was dismissed in July 1997. Despite speculation about who would become the next CEO at Apple throughout the fall and winter of 1997-98, and Jobs' denials that he would assume the CEO role, Jobs holds the title of "interim CEO" for now. And even though that might seem like a temporary role for a leader, Jobs has led a remarkable turnaround at Apple since July 1997. No one sees him acting as an "interim" leader.

In October 1997, Jobs reported at the Seybold Publishing conference that Apple is "getting exciting again. Apple has had some tough times. It's not out of it completely but we are going to turn this thing around." He noted that "employees are again working long hours and cars are in the parking lots past 6 o'clock at night and on weekends." ■

Steve Jobs is what is known as a charismatic leader. He can inspire those around him to do more than they might have considered doing on their own. He is not without his critics, however. A 1998 book about him (*Apple: The Inside Story of Intrigue, Egomania & Business Blunders* by Jim Carlton) describes Jobs as mercurial, arrogant, and having a rather large ego.[2]

Despite these possible flaws, those who have watched Jobs perform his turnaround note that he is different from his predecessors in an important way: he's not afraid to make tough decisions quickly. "He's not afraid to make a call," says analyst Louis Mazzuchelli of Gerard Klauer Mattison and Co. In January 1998, Apple Computer Inc. reported its first profitable quarter in several years, and by March 1998 its stock price had nearly reached the 52-week high, moving from $17 in December 1997 to almost $38 in mid-March 1998. Apple was also expected to post a profit in its second quarter of 1998.

As Steve Jobs is demonstrating once again at Apple, leaders can make a difference. In this chapter, we examine the various studies on leadership to determine what makes an effective leader and what differentiates leaders from nonleaders. Understanding leadership is important because as the 21st century approaches, workplace changes will continue to place greater emphasis on individuals learning to lead themselves. Thus learning about leadership helps you relate better to leaders and to take on the role of leader if necessary. So let's clarify what we mean by the term leadership.

What Is Leadership?

Few terms in OB inspire less agreement on definition than *leadership*. As one expert put it, "there are almost as many definitions of leadership as there are persons who have attempted to define the concept."[3]

Although almost everyone seems to agree that leadership involves an influence process, differences tend to centre around whether leadership must be noncoercive (as opposed to using authority, rewards, and punishments to exert influence over followers) and whether it is distinct from management.[4] The latter issue has been a particularly heated topic of debate in recent years, with most experts arguing that leadership and management are different.

For instance, Abraham Zaleznik of the Harvard Business School argues that leaders and managers differ in motivation, personal history, and how they think and act.[5] Zaleznik says that managers tend to adopt impersonal, if not passive, attitudes toward goals, whereas leaders take a personal and active attitude toward goals. Managers tend to view work as an enabling process involving some combination of people and ideas interacting to establish strategies and make decisions. Leaders work from high-risk positions—indeed, they are often temperamentally disposed to seek out risk and danger, especially when opportunity and reward appear high. Managers prefer to work with people; they avoid solitary activity because it makes them anxious. They relate to people according to the role they play in a sequence of events or in a decision-making process. Leaders, who are concerned with ideas, relate to people in more intuitive and empathic ways.

John Kotter, a colleague of Zaleznik at Harvard, also argues that leadership is different from management, but for other reasons.[6] Management, he proposes, is about coping with complexity. Good management brings about order and consistency by drawing up formal plans, designing rigid organization structures, and monitoring results against the plans. Leadership, by

contrast, is about coping with change. Leaders establish direction by developing a vision of the future; then they align people by communicating this vision and inspiring them to overcome hurdles. Kotter views both strong leadership and strong management as necessary for optimum organizational effectiveness. But he believes that most organizations are underled and overmanaged. He claims we need to focus more on developing leadership in organizations because the managers in charge today are too concerned with keeping things on time and on budget and with doing what was done yesterday, only doing it five percent better.

So where do we stand? We will use a broad definition of leadership—one that can encompass all the current approaches to the subject. Thus, we define **leadership** as the ability to influence a group toward the achievement of goals. The source of this influence may be formal, such as that provided by the possession of managerial rank in an organization. Since management positions come with some degree of formally designated authority, a person may assume a leadership role simply because of the position he or she holds in the organization. But not all leaders are managers; nor, for that matter, are all managers leaders.

It is important to note that just because an organization provides its managers with certain formal rights is no assurance that they will be able to lead effectively. We find that non-sanctioned leadership—that is, the ability to influence that arises outside the formal structure of the organization—is often as important or more important than formal influence. For instance, Steve Jobs' second chance at leadership at Apple was not heralded with a formal title when Gil Amelio was dismissed in July 1997. But almost immediately he started acting as temporary advisor to Apple's management and board. And by August 1997, Jobs was involved in day-to-day as well as strategic decisions at Apple, including making changes in policy such as sabbatical leave and severance pay. Although Jobs was not formally given the title of interim CEO until October 1997, everyone in the organization had been acting as if he were CEO for several months before then.

A Brief History of Leadership Theories

The leadership literature is voluminous, and much of it is confusing and contradictory. In order to make our way through this "forest," we'll point out a few conclusions that can be drawn from leadership theories developed during the 20th century, and then consider in greater detail the ways that leadership is considered as we move into the 21st century.

Trait Theories of Leadership

The dominant research on leadership up until the 1940s was the trait approach, where researchers looked to find universal personality traits that leaders had to some greater degree than nonleaders.[7] Trait theory was also revisited for a time in the late 1980s.[8] Trait theory emerged in the hope that by being able to identify the traits of leaders, it would be easier to select people to fill leadership roles.

The media have long been believers in **trait theories of leadership**. They identify people such as Margaret Thatcher, Pierre Trudeau, Ronald Reagan, and Nelson Mandela as leaders, and then describe them in terms such as *charismatic, enthusiastic, decisive,* and *courageous*. Well, the media aren't

leadership
The ability to influence a group toward the achievement of goals.

trait theories of leadership
Theories that sought personality, social, physical, or intellectual traits that differentiated leaders from non-leaders.

alone. The search for personality, social, physical, or intellectual attributes that would describe leaders and differentiate them from nonleaders goes back to the 1930s and research done by psychologists.

Research efforts at isolating leadership traits resulted in a number of dead ends.[9] The bulk of the studies considered one of three main categories of traits: "physical traits, such as physique, height, and appearance; abilities, such as intelligence and fluency of speech; and personality characteristics, such as conservatism, introversion-extroversion, and self-confidence."[10] Researchers have not found a set of traits that would always differentiate leaders from followers and effective from ineffective leaders. However, six traits have been identified that were consistently associated with leadership: ambition and energy; the desire to lead; honesty and integrity; self-confidence; intelligence; and job-relevant knowledge.[11] Additionally, recent research provides strong evidence that people who are high self-monitors—that is, are highly flexible in adjusting their behaviour in different situations—are much more likely to emerge as leaders in groups than low self-monitors.[12] Overall, the cumulative findings from more than half a century of research lead us to conclude that some traits increase the likelihood of success as a leader, but none of the traits *guarantees* success.[13]

ATTRIBUTION THEORY OF LEADERSHIP One recent advance in trait research is the argument that "traits influence how people are perceived so that being a leader or a follower is inferred by people from evidence about traits that they exhibit."[14] This idea relates to attribution theory, which we discussed in Chapter 3 in relation to perception.

Attribution theory, as you remember, deals with people trying to make sense out of cause-effect relationships. When something happens, they want to attribute it to something. In the context of leadership, attribution theory says that leadership is merely an attribution that people make about other individuals.[15] Using the attribution framework, researchers have found that people characterize leaders as having such traits as intelligence, outgoing personality, strong verbal skills, aggressiveness, understanding, and industriousness.[16]

At the organizational level, the attribution framework accounts for the conditions under which people use leadership to explain organizational outcomes. Those conditions are extremes in organizational performance. When an organization has either extremely negative or extremely positive performance, people are prone to make leadership attributions to explain the performance.[17] This helps to account for the vulnerability of CEOs when their organizations suffer a major financial setback, regardless of whether they had much to do with it. It also accounts for why these CEOs tend to receive credit for extremely positive financial results—again, regardless of how much or how little they contributed.

attribution theory of leadership
Theory that proposes that leadership is merely an attribution that people make about other individuals.

One of the more interesting themes in the **attribution theory of leadership** literature is the perception that effective leaders are generally considered consistent or unwavering in their decisions.[18] That is, one explanation for why Pierre Trudeau and Brian Mulroney were perceived as strong leaders is that they were fully committed to the goals they set and undeterred by criticism. On the other hand, John Turner's flip-flopping on patronage issues cost him the 1984 election. More recently, when Sheila Copps broke her promise to resign if the GST was not repealed, she lost the confidence of the public and was demoted from deputy Prime Minister.

Randy Jones ranks high in the traits associated with leadership. His ambition, energy, desire to lead, self-confidence, intelligence, and knowledge of publishing increase the likelihood of his success as the leader in establishing *Worth* as a new financial management magazine. Jones is also a high self-monitor, taking the lead in promoting his new product, whether it's participating in event marketing (shown here), dining with influential political and media people, or working with his sales reps in making presentations to win advertisers.

Behavioural Theories of Leadership

The inability to strike "gold" in the trait "mines" led researchers to look at the behaviours that specific leaders exhibited. They wondered if there was something unique in the way that effective leaders behave. If the behavioural approach to leadership were successful, it would have implications quite different from those of the trait approach. If trait research had been successful, it would have provided a basis for *selecting* the "right" persons to assume formal positions in groups and organizations requiring leadership. In contrast, if behavioural studies were to identify critical behavioural determinants of leadership, we could *train* people to be leaders.

The three most well-known **behavioural theories of leadership** are the Ohio State University studies conducted beginning in the late 1940s,[19] the University of Michigan studies conducted at about the same time, and Blake and Mouton's Managerial Grid, which reflects the behavioural definitions of both the Ohio and Michigan studies. All three approaches consider two main dimensions by which managers can be characterized: attention to production and attention to people.

In the Ohio State studies, these two dimensions are known as *initiating structure* and *consideration*. **Initiating structure** refers to the extent to which a leader is likely to define and structure his or her role and those of subordinates in the search for goal attainment and includes behaviour that attempts to organize work, work relationships, and goals. **Consideration** is described as the extent to which a person is likely to have job relationships that are characterized by mutual trust, respect for subordinates' ideas, and regard for their feelings. He or she shows concern for followers' comfort, well-being, status, and satisfaction.

The Michigan group also developed two dimensions of leadership behaviour that they labelled **employee oriented** and **production oriented**.[20] Leaders who were employee oriented were described as emphasizing interpersonal

behavioural theories of leadership
Theories proposing that specific behaviours differentiate leaders from nonleaders.

initiating structure
The extent to which a leader is likely to define and structure his or her role and those of subordinates in the search for goal attainment.

consideration
The extent to which a leader is likely to have job relationships characterized by mutual trust, respect for subordinates' ideas, and regard for their feelings.

employee-oriented leader
A leader who emphasizes interpersonal relations.

production-oriented leader
A leader who emphasizes technical or task aspects of the job.

relations; they took a personal interest in the needs of their subordinates and accepted individual differences among members. The production-oriented leaders, in contrast, tended to emphasize the technical or task aspects of the job—their main concern was in accomplishing their group's tasks, and the group members were a means to that end.

A graphic portrayal of a two-dimensional view of leadership style was developed by Blake and Mouton.[21] They proposed a **Managerial Grid** based on the styles of "concern for people" and "concern for production," which essentially represent the Ohio State dimensions of consideration and initiating structure or the Michigan dimensions of employee oriented and production oriented.

The grid depicted in Exhibit 11-1 has nine possible positions along each axis, creating 81 different positions in which the leader's style may fall. The grid does not show results produced but, rather, the dominating factors in a leader's thinking with respect to getting results.

Each of the three approaches received some empirical support for the idea that being people oriented was an important behaviour of leaders,

Managerial Grid
A nine-by-nine matrix outlining 81 different leadership styles.

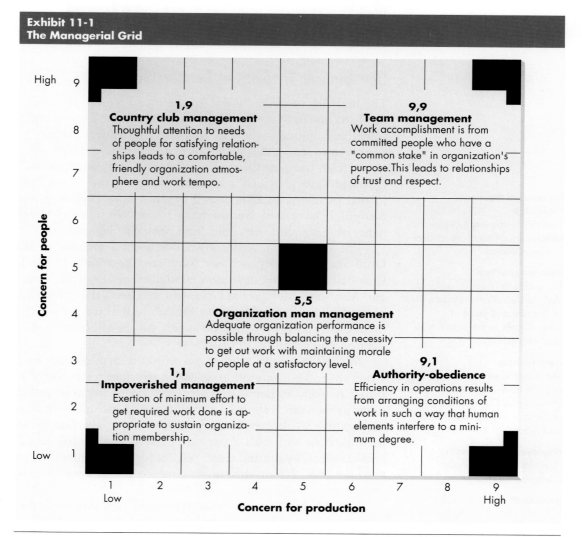

Exhibit 11-1
The Managerial Grid

Concern for people

1,9
Country club management
Thoughtful attention to needs of people for satisfying relationships leads to a comfortable, friendly organization atmosphere and work tempo.

9,9
Team management
Work accomplishment is from committed people who have a "common stake" in organization's purpose. This leads to relationships of trust and respect.

5,5
Organization man management
Adequate organization performance is possible through balancing the necessity to get out work with maintaining morale of people at a satisfactory level.

1,1
Impoverished management
Exertion of minimum effort to get required work done is appropriate to sustain organization membership.

9,1
Authority-obedience
Efficiency in operations results from arranging conditions of work in such a way that human elements interfere to a minimum degree.

Concern for production

although there were also exceptions in each case. In the Ohio studies, leaders who were production oriented (i.e., high on initiating structure) experienced greater rates of grievances, absenteeism, and turnover, and lower levels of job satisfaction from workers performing routine tasks. In the Michigan studies, employee-oriented leaders were associated with higher group productivity and higher job satisfaction. Production-oriented leaders tended to be associated with low group productivity and lower job satisfaction.

The results based on the findings of Blake and Mouton are consistent with those of the Ohio and Michigan studies. Managers were found to perform best under a 9,9 (team management style), as contrasted, for example, with a 9,1 (authority-obedience) or 1,9 (country club) style.[22] However, there is little substantive evidence to support the conclusion that a 9,9 style is most effective in all situations.[23]

Early on in the development of the Ohio studies, inconsistent results were noted. Similar problems arose with both the Michigan studies and the Managerial Grid. Thus, starting in the 1960s, leadership theories started to examine the situational factors that affect the leader's ability to act. To understand the role of situation, consider changes that have occurred at Eaton's in the last few years. For the first 127 years of Eaton's existence, members of the Eaton family provided the leadership. However, the family leadership involvement ended in 1997 when the company realized that it needed to bring in outsiders to help lead the company out of bankruptcy. In other words, the situation for Eaton's had changed and the once-successful leadership no longer worked. Unfortunately, the behavioural approaches don't recognize the impact of changes in situations.

Situational or Contingency Theories

It became increasingly clear to those who were studying the leadership phenomenon that predicting leadership success was more complex than simply isolating a few traits or preferable behaviours. The failure to obtain consistent results led to a focus on situational influences. The relationship between leadership style and effectiveness suggested that under condition a, style x would be appropriate, while style y would be more suitable for condition b, and style z for condition c. But what were the conditions a, b, c, and so forth? It was one thing to say that leadership effectiveness was dependent on the situation and another to be able to isolate those situational conditions.

There has been no shortage of studies attempting to isolate critical situational factors that affect leadership effectiveness. For instance, popular moderating variables used in the development of **situational or contingency theories** include the degree of structure in the task being performed, the quality of leader–member relations, the leader's position power, subordinates' role clarity, group norms, information availability, subordinate acceptance of leader's decisions, and subordinate maturity.[24]

We will consider one model to illustrate what situational theories add to pure behavioural models of leadership: the path-goal model. Three other theories—the Fiedler model, Hersey and Blanchard's situational theory, and leader-member exchange theory—have either received less empirical support for their approaches, were the subject of controversy and debate, or are difficult to apply in the work situation.[25]

PATH-GOAL THEORY   Currently, one of the most respected approaches to leadership is the path-goal theory. Developed by Robert House (formerly at

situational or contingency theories
Theories that note the importance of considering the context within which leadership occurs.

the University of Toronto, but now at the Wharton School of Business), path-goal theory is a contingency model of leadership that extracts key elements from the Ohio State leadership research on initiating structure and consideration and the expectancy theory of motivation.[26]

The essence of the theory is that it is the leader's job to assist followers in attaining their goals and to provide the necessary direction and/or support to ensure that their goals are compatible with the overall objectives of the group or organization. The term *path-goal* derives from the belief that effective leaders clarify the path to help their followers get from where they are to the achievement of their work goals, and to make the journey along the path easier by reducing roadblocks and pitfalls.

According to **path-goal theory**, a leader's behaviour is *acceptable* to subordinates to the degree that it is viewed by them as an immediate source of satisfaction or as a means of future satisfaction. A leader's behaviour is *motivational* to the degree that it (1) makes subordinate need satisfaction contingent on effective performance and (2) provides the coaching, guidance, support, and rewards that are necessary for effective performance. To test these statements, House identified four leadership behaviours. The *directive leader* lets subordinates know what is expected of them, schedules work to be done, and gives specific guidance as to how to accomplish tasks. This closely parallels the Ohio State dimension of initiating structure. The *supportive leader* is friendly and shows concern for the needs of subordinates. This is essentially synonymous with the Ohio State dimension of consideration. The *participative leader* consults with subordinates and uses their suggestions before making a decision. The *achievement-oriented leader* sets challenging goals and expects subordinates to perform at their highest level. House assumes that leaders are flexible and can display any or all of these behaviours depending on the situation.

As Exhibit 11-2 illustrates, path-goal theory proposes two classes of situational or contingency variables that moderate the leadership behaviour–outcome relationship: those in the environment that are outside the control of the subordinate (task structure, the formal authority system, and the work group) and those that are part of the personal characteristics of the subordi-

path-goal theory
The theory that a leader's behaviour is acceptable to subordinates insofar as they view it as a source of either immediate or future satisfaction.

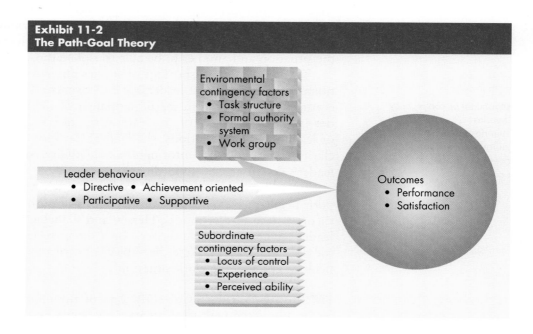

Exhibit 11-2
The Path-Goal Theory

Environmental contingency factors
• Task structure
• Formal authority system
• Work group

Leader behaviour
• Directive • Achievement oriented
• Participative • Supportive

Outcomes
• Performance
• Satisfaction

Subordinate contingency factors
• Locus of control
• Experience
• Perceived ability

nate (locus of control, experience, and perceived ability). Environmental factors determine the type of leader behaviour required as a complement if subordinate outcomes are to be maximized, while personal characteristics of the subordinate determine how the environment and leader behaviour are interpreted. So the theory proposes that leader behaviour will be ineffective when it is redundant with sources of environmental structure or incongruent with subordinate characteristics.

The following are some examples of hypotheses that have evolved out of path-goal theory:

- Directive leadership leads to greater satisfaction when tasks are ambiguous or stressful than when they are highly structured and well laid out.
- Supportive leadership results in high employee performance and satisfaction when subordinates are performing structured tasks.
- Directive leadership is likely to be perceived as redundant among subordinates with high perceived ability or with considerable experience.
- The more clear and bureaucratic the formal authority relationships, the more leaders should exhibit supportive behaviour and de-emphasize directive behaviour.
- Directive leadership will lead to higher employee satisfaction when there is substantive conflict within a work group.
- Subordinates with an internal locus of control (those who believe they control their own destiny) will be more satisfied with a participative style.
- Subordinates with an external locus of control will be more satisfied with a directive style.
- Achievement-oriented leadership will increase subordinates' expectancies that effort will lead to high performance when tasks are ambiguously structured.

Research to validate hypotheses such as these is generally encouraging.[27] The evidence supports the logic underlying the theory. That is, employee performance and satisfaction are likely to be positively influenced when the leader compensates for things lacking in either the employee or the work setting. However, the leader who spends time explaining tasks when those tasks are already clear or when the employee has the ability and experience to handle them without interference is likely to be ineffective because the employee will see such directive behaviour as redundant or even insulting.

What does the future hold for path-goal theory? Its framework has been tested and appears to have moderate to high empirical support. We can, however, expect to see more research focused on refining and extending the theory by incorporating additional moderating variables.[28]

The situational theories suggest that there is an interaction between the situation and the appropriate leadership style. One question that arises is whether leaders can actually adjust their behaviour to various situations. The cartoon in Exhibit 11-3 proposes adjusting the individual to the coat, rather than vice versa. In terms of leadership, we can think of "coat" as analogous to "situation." If an individual's leadership style range is very narrow and thus can't be adjusted, that individual needs to be placed into the appropriately sized situation if he or she is to lead successfully. If House is right and people can adjust their styles, the individual leader has to assess

Exhibit 11-3

Source: B. Parker and J. Hart, *Let There Be Reign* (Greenwich, CT: Fawcett Books, 1972). By permission of Johnny Hart and Creators Syndicate, Inc.

the situation that is available and adjust his or her style accordingly. Whether we should adjust the situation to fit the person or fix the person to fit the situation is an important issue. As we know, individuals differ in their behavioural flexibility. Some people show considerable ability to adjust their behaviour to external, situational factors; they are adaptable. Others, however, exhibit high levels of consistency regardless of the situation. High self-monitors are generally able to adjust their leadership style to suit changing situations better than low self-monitors.[29] To find out more about your style of leadership, see the Learning About Yourself exercise at the end of the chapter.

LEADERS WHO REPORT TO BOARDS OF DIRECTORS The situational or contingency theories focus more on how leaders might adjust to their subordinates. However, not all leaders have only subordinates to face. For instance, in publicly traded organizations, leaders answer to a board of governors or a board of directors. So, just as there is pressure from below to adjust leadership style, there can be pressure from above. The recent example of Rowland Fleming, president and CEO of the Toronto Stock Exchange (TSE), illustrates the effect of boards on leadership ability.[30] After an April 20, 1998 board meeting, Fleming was reminded by board chair Barbara Stymiest and vice-chair Daniel Sullivan just who was in charge. Critics say that Fleming "has failed to grasp that he runs Canada's premier exchange on behalf of the brokerage firms that own it. 'He doesn't own the country club. He's been hired to manage it.'"

The board has asked Fleming to work with it more closely. But sources say he does not have the temperament or the background to lead by consensus. This may be a partial answer to our question above about whether leaders can change their style. In the case of Fleming, the answer appears to be that he might not be able to. Corporate boards usually set strategies by responding to the CEO's vision, and this is what Fleming's career experience has been. However, at the TSE, Fleming is being asked to do the opposite—respond to strategy set by the board and TSE committees. Moreover, Fleming quit a 23-year career with Scotiabank in 1994 because of problems with the company's autocratic manage-

Roland Fleming, president and CEO of the Toronto Stock Exchange has learned that being a leader is not always easy. His actions as leader are scrutinized by his board of directors.

ment, and then left Dominion of Canada General Insurance Co. Ltd. and National Trust Co. after short terms as CEO with each. Each of these experiences suggests a person unwilling to work with superiors who don't share his vision.[31] The case of Fleming and the TSE is a reminder that when we discuss situations for leaders, this includes a variety of events, including the types of subordinates, the environment of the organization, as well as the demands of the board when a company is publicly traded. Each of these alone, and certainly several factors working together, can seriously affect a leader's ability to lead.

Sometimes Leadership Is Irrelevant!

In keeping with the contingency spirit, we want to conclude this section by offering this notion: leadership may not always be important. Data from numerous studies collectively demonstrate that, in many situations, whatever behaviours leaders exhibit are irrelevant. Certain individual, job, and organizational variables can act as *substitutes* for leadership or *neutralize* the leader's effect to influence his or her subordinates.[32]

Neutralizers make it impossible for leader behaviour to make any difference to subordinate outcomes. They negate the leader's influence. Substitutes, on the other hand, make a leader's influence not only impossible but also unnecessary. They act as a replacement for the leader's influence. For instance, characteristics of subordinates such as their experience, training, "professional" orientation, or indifference toward organizational rewards can substitute for, or neutralize the effect of, leadership. Experience and training, for instance, can replace the need for a leader's support or ability to create structure and reduce task ambiguity. Jobs that are inherently unambiguous and routine or that are intrinsically satisfying may place fewer demands on the leadership variable. Organizational characteristics such as explicit formalized goals, rigid rules and procedures, and cohesive work groups can replace formal leadership (see Exhibit 11-4).

Exhibit 11-4
Substitutes and Neutralizers for Leadership

Defining Characteristics	Relationship-Oriented Leadership	Task-Oriented Leadership
Individual		
Experience/training	No effect on	Substitutes for
Professionalism	Substitutes for	Substitutes for
Indifference to rewards	Neutralizes	Neutralizes
Job		
Highly structured task	No effect on	Substitutes for
Provides its own feedback	No effect on	Substitutes for
Intrinsically satisfying	Substitutes for	No effect on
Organization		
Explicit formalized goals	No effect on	Substitutes for
Rigid rules and procedures	No effect on	Substitutes for
Cohesive work groups	Substitutes for	Substitutes for

Source: Based on S. Kerr and J.M. Jermier, "Substitutes for Leadership: Their Meaning and Measurement," *Organizational Behavior and Human Performance,* December 1978, p. 378.

This recent recognition that leaders don't always have an impact on subordinate outcomes should not be that surprising. After all, we have introduced a number of variables—attitudes, personality, ability, and group norms, to name but a few—that have been documented as having an effect on employee performance and satisfaction. Yet supporters of the leadership concept have tended to place an undue burden on this variable for explaining and predicting behaviour. It is too simplistic to consider subordinates as guided to goal accomplishments solely by the behaviour of their leader. It is important, therefore, to recognize explicitly that leadership is merely another independent variable in our overall OB model. In some situations it may contribute a lot to explaining employee productivity, absence, turnover, and satisfaction, but in other situations it may contribute little toward that end. For more discussion of when leadership is necessary and when it is less important, you might want to examine this chapter's Point/Counterpoint feature.

Looking for Common Ground: What Can We Learn From This Historical Overview?

The topic of leadership certainly doesn't lack for theories, but from an overview perspective, what does it all mean? Let's try to identify commonalities among the leadership theories developed through the early 1980s and attempt to determine what, if any, practical value the theories hold for application to organizations.

Careful examination discloses that the concepts of "task" and "people"—often expressed in more elaborate terms that hold substantially the same meaning—permeate most of the theories.[33] The task dimension goes by such names as "initiating structure," "directive leadership," "production orientation," and "concern for production." The people dimension gets similar treatment, going under such aliases as "consideration," "employee-oriented," "supportive," or "relationship-oriented" leadership. Leadership behaviour tends to be reduced to two dimensions—task and people—but researchers continue to differ as to whether the orientations are two ends of a single continuum (you could be high on one or the other but not both) or two independent dimensions (you could be high or low on both).

Leadership theorists don't agree on the issue of whether a leader's style is fixed or flexible. As previously noted, our position is that it depends on the leader's personality. High self-monitors are most likely to adjust their leadership style to changing situations than are low self-monitors.[34] So the need to adjust the situation to the leader in order to improve the leader–situation match seems to be necessary only with low self-monitoring individuals.

How should we interpret the findings presented so far in this chapter? Some traits have proved, over time, to be modest predictors of leadership effectiveness. But knowing that a manager possesses intelligence, ambition, self-confidence, or the like would by no means assure us that his or her subordinates would be productive and satisfied employees. The ability of these traits to predict leadership success is just not that strong.

The early task–people approaches (such as the Ohio State, Michigan, and Managerial Grid theories) also offer us little substance. The strongest statement one can make based on these theories is that leaders who rate high in people orientation should end up with satisfied employees. The research is too mixed to make predictions regarding employee productivity or the effect of a task orientation on productivity and satisfaction.

Rhonda Fryman is a team leader at Toyota Motor Manufacturing's plant in Georgetown, Kentucky. She exemplifies Toyota's philosophy of striving to create a warm, caring atmosphere with a high degree of respect for employees, which leads to their high levels of motivation and productivity. Consistent with the contingency models, Fryman is an effective leader because she assists her team in meeting their daily production goals and provides direction and support in achieving Toyota's quality goals.

The path-goal model provides a framework for explaining and predicting leadership effectiveness that has developed a solid, empirical foundation. It recognizes that a leader's success depends on adjusting his or her style to the environment the leader is placed in, as well as to the individual characteristics of followers. In a limited way, path-goal theory also validates contingency variables in other situational leadership theories.

The Most Recent Approaches to Leadership

We conclude our review of leadership theories by presenting three more recent approaches to the subject. These are charismatic leadership; transactional, transformational leadership and laissez-faire leadership; and visionary leadership. If there is one theme to the approaches in this section, it is that they all de-emphasize theoretical complexity and look at leadership more the way the average "person on the street" views the subject. More importantly, these theories move away from considering leadership as influencing group goals, to leadership as a process of identifying for subordinates a sense of what is important, and then giving a sense of direction and purpose to the employees so that they will work toward a common vision.[35]

Charismatic Leadership Theory

charismatic leadership
Followers make attributions of heroic or extraordinary leadership abilities when they observe certain behaviours.

Charismatic leadership theory is an extension of attribution theory. It says that followers make attributions of heroic or extraordinary leadership abilities when they observe certain behaviours.[36] Studies on charismatic leadership have been directed at identifying those behaviours that differentiate charismatic leaders from their non-charismatic counterparts. Some examples of individuals frequently cited as being charismatic leaders include René Lévesque, Jean Charest, Lucien Bouchard, Bobbie Gaunt (Ford Canada), Walt Disney, Steve Jobs (co-founder of Apple Computer), Mary Kay Ash (founder of Mary Kay Cosmetics), Lee Iacocca (former chairman of Chrysler), and Craig Kielburger (the Canadian teenager who founded Free the Children to promote children's rights and combat exploitation of child labour). Richard Branson, founder and CEO of Virgin Group Limited, is another charismatic leader. He is featured in this chapter's CBC Video Case.

Free the Children
www.freethechildren.org/

Virgin Group Ltd.
www.virgin.com/

One of the most often cited studies of the effects of charismatic leadership was done at the University of British Columbia in the early 1980s by Jane Howell (now at the Richard Ivey School of Business at the University of Western Ontario) and Peter Frost (at the University of British Columbia).[37] Their study compared the charismatic leadership style to structuring (i.e., task-oriented) and considerate (i.e., employee-oriented) styles, and found that those who worked under a charismatic leader generated more ideas and reported higher job satisfaction than those working under structuring leaders. Charismatic leaders also produced better results than considerate leaders, with subordinates performing at a higher level. Those working under charismatic leaders also showed higher job satisfaction and stronger bonds of loyalty. Howell, in summarizing these results says, "While it is true that considerate leaders make people feel good, that doesn't necessarily translate into increased productivity. In contrast, charismatic leaders know how to inspire people to think in new directions."[38]

Several authors have attempted to identify personal characteristics of the charismatic leader. Robert House (of path-goal fame) identified three: extremely high confidence, dominance, and strong convictions in his or her beliefs.[39] He further notes that such leaders motivate subordinates by sharing a vision of an exciting, challenging future. They do this by describing what kind of organization they want the company to become, setting high performance standards, and expressing confidence that their subordinates can achieve that vision.[40] House also notes that charismatic leaders demonstrate a high level of integrity and place the company goals above their own personal goals.

Warren Bennis, after studying 90 of the most effective and successful leaders in the United States, found that they had four common competencies: they had a compelling vision or sense of purpose; they could communicate that vision in clear terms that their followers could readily identify with; they demonstrated consistency and focus in the pursuit of their vision; and they knew their own strengths and capitalized on them.[41]

The most comprehensive analysis of charismatic leadership, however, has been completed by Jay Conger and Rabindra Kanungo (of McGill University).[42] After considerable research investigating the dimensions of charismatic leadership, including validating their measures with managers from Canada, the United States, and India, they have proposed five dimensions that characterize charismatic leadership. Among their conclusions, they propose that charismatic leaders articulate a strategic vision, are sensitive to the environment, are sensitive to member needs, engage in personal risk in carrying out their vision, and are perceived as unconventional in their behaviour. Exhibit 11-5 summarizes their findings on the key characteristics that appear to differentiate charismatic leaders from noncharismatic ones.

Attention has recently been focused on trying to determine how charismatic leaders actually influence followers. The process begins by the leader articulating an appealing vision. This vision provides a sense of continuity for followers by linking the present with a better future for the organization. The leader then communicates high performance expectations and expresses confidence that followers can attain them. This enhances follower self-esteem and self-confidence. Next, the leader conveys through words and actions, a new set of values and, by his or her behaviour, sets an example for followers to imitate. Finally, the charismatic leader makes self-sacrifices and engages in unconventional behaviour to demonstrate courage and convictions about the vision.[43]

What can we say about the charismatic leader's effect on his or her followers? There is an increasing body of research that shows impressive

Exhibit 11-5
Key Characteristics of Charismatic Leaders

1. *Self-confidence.* They have complete confidence in their judgment and ability.

2. *A vision.* This is an idealized goal that proposes a future better than the status quo. The greater the disparity between this idealized goal and the status quo, the more likely that followers will attribute extraordinary vision to the leader.

3. *Ability to articulate the vision.* They are able to clarify and state the vision in terms that are understandable to others. This articulation demonstrates an understanding of the followers' needs and, hence, acts as a motivating force.

4. *Strong convictions about the vision.* Charismatic leaders are perceived as being strongly committed and willing to take on high personal risk, incur high costs, and engage in self-sacrifice to achieve their vision.

5. *Behaviour that is out of the ordinary.* Those with charisma engage in behaviour that is perceived as being novel, unconventional, and counter to norms. When successful, these behaviours evoke surprise and admiration in followers.

6. *Perceived as being a change agent.* Charismatic leaders are perceived as agents of radical change rather than as caretakers of the status quo.

7. *Environment sensitivity.* These leaders are able to make realistic assessments of the environmental constraints and resources needed to bring about change.

Source: Based on J.A. Conger and R.N. Kanungo, "Behavioral Dimensions of Charismatic Leadership," in J.A. Conger and R.N. Kanungo, *Charismatic Leadership* (San Francisco: Jossey-Bass, 1988), p. 91.

correlations between charismatic leadership and high performance and satisfaction among followers.[44] People working for charismatic leaders are motivated to exert extra work effort and, because they like their leader, express greater satisfaction. An unpublished study by Robert House and some colleagues of 63 U.S. and 49 Canadian companies (including Nortel, Molson, Gulf Canada, and Manulife) found that "between 15 and 25 percent of the variation in profitability among the companies was accounted for by the leadership qualities of their CEO."[45] That is, charismatic leaders led more profitable companies. To learn more about charisma and profitability, you might look at this chapter's OB in the News feature, which reports on Mogen Smeds of Calgary-based furniture manufacturer SMED International Inc.

SMED International Inc.
www.smednet.com/

If charisma is desirable, can people learn to be charismatic leaders? Or are charismatic leaders born with their qualities? While a small minority still think charisma cannot be learned, most experts believe that individuals can be trained to exhibit charismatic behaviours and can thus enjoy the benefits that accrue to being labelled "a charismatic leader."[46] For instance, one set of authors proposes that a person can learn to become charismatic by following a three-step process.[47] First, an individual needs to develop the aura of charisma by maintaining an optimistic view; using passion as a catalyst for generating enthusiasm; and communicating with the whole body, not just with words. Second, an individual draws others in by creating a bond that inspires others to follow. And third, the individual brings out the potential in followers by tapping into their emotions. This approach seems to work, as evidenced by researchers who have succeeded in actually scripting undergraduate business students to "play" charismatic leaders.[48] The students were taught to articulate an overarching goal, communicate high

OB IN THE NEWS

Mogens Smed: Charismatic Leader of SMED International

Mogens Smed is the 49-year-old president and CEO of Calgary-based SMED International, an upscale office-furniture maker. He has a reputation as an outstanding salesperson and a charismatic leader.

SMED's competitors include American giants such as Herman Miller, Steelcase, and Knoll, all of which are larger than SMED. SMED is really only a small player in the office-furniture industry, with about one percent of market share. Herman Miller has 10 percent and Steelcase has 25 percent of market share.

Smed's charismatic leadership style doesn't cause him to fret about his small market share, however. SMED's motto is: "Our only competition is conventional thinking." Smed explains that SMED is different from the competition: "We do not play by the rules. There are no rules. We offer something completely different from them. We don't just make products and offer them to the customer. We ask the customer what they want and then make it for them."

SMED's vision is that the customer is always first. To remind everyone of this, brochures, magazines, and books supporting this philosophy are evident in both the foyer and other parts of the organization, including *Culture Shift* and *The Employee Handbook of New Work Habits for a Radically Changing World* by Price Pritchett and *The Customer-Driven Company* by Richard Whiteley.

Like all charismatic leaders, Smed has truly inspired his employees. In fact, industry analysts have commented on the nearly messianic fervour of the company. "In some ways, SMED is like a cult," says James David, an analyst at HSBC James Capel Canada Inc. in Montreal. "Mogens Smed displays a great deal of charisma and enthusiasm, and that carries down through the ranks. The people around him are so much on the same page, it's scary."

Characteristic of charismatic leaders, Smed interacts personally with both employees and clients. He is willing to go anywhere, any time, if he thinks it will clinch a sale. He can do this because, like many charismatic leaders, he makes all the major decisions, but leaves the day-to-day operations to his executive vice-presidents.

Smed's vision and charisma are paying off. SMED, founded in 1982, has showrooms in over 30 major markets on three continents and has clients in over 40 countries. Some of his most well-known clients include Steven Spielberg's Dream-Works in Los Angeles, the NFL Players' Union in New York City, the Royal Bank, the Toronto-Dominion Bank, the Canadian Imperial Bank of Commerce, Fox Television, and Calvin Klein.

Sources: Based on Mel Duvall, "New plant provides impetus for SMED's growth," *Financial Post Daily*, October 3, 1997, p. 19; and Curtis Gillespie, "Selling Smed: Mogens Smed is passionate about making SMED International a global player in office furniture," *Financial Post Magazine*, October 1997, pp. 70–81.

Take It to the Net

We invite you to visit the Robbins page on the Prentice Hall Web site at:

http://www.prenticehall.ca/robbins

for this chapter's World Wide Web exercise.

Mogen Smeds, president and CEO of Calgary-based SMED International, has a reputation as a charismatic leader. He believes his upscale office-furniture making company differs from the competitors because "We do not play by the rules. There are no rules."

Royal Trust
www.royalbank.com/english/
gss/rtnews.html

United Way
www.clark.net/pub/pwalker/
United_Ways_on_the_Internet/

performance expectations, exhibit confidence in the ability of subordinates to meet these expectations, and empathize with the needs of their subordinates. They learned to project a powerful, confident, and dynamic presence, and they practised using a captivating and engaging voice tone. To further capture the dynamics and energy of charisma, the leaders were trained to evoke charismatic nonverbal characteristics: they alternated between pacing and sitting on the edges of their desks, leaned toward the subordinate, maintained direct eye contact, and had relaxed postures and animated facial expressions. These researchers found that these students could learn how to project charisma. Moreover, subordinates of these leaders had higher task performance, task adjustment, and adjustment to the leader and to the group than did subordinates who worked under groups led by noncharismatic leaders. To learn more about how to be charismatic, see the Working With Others exercise at the end of the chapter.

One last word on this topic: charismatic leadership may not always be needed to achieve high levels of employee performance. It may be most appropriate when the follower's task has an ideological component.[49] This may explain why, when charismatic leaders surface, it is more likely to be in politics, religion, wartime, or when a business firm is introducing a radically new product or facing a life-threatening crisis. Thus when Canada Post and Royal Trustco faced major turnaround opportunities in the 1980s, charismatic leaders emerged to take on the task. Don Lander, president and CEO of Canada Post from 1986 to 1993, is credited with transforming the corporation from an inefficient government department to a sleeker, profitable Crown corporation. His success with Canada Post is viewed as a classic case of corporate culture change.[50]

Michael Cornelissen, another example of a charismatic leader, was appointed CEO of ailing Royal Trustco in 1983 to turn things around at the organization. "Beginning in the fall of 1984, fear and respect for the tall, imposing taskmaster were galvanized into a religious zeal by Vision 1990, a week-long, residential training seminar that was mandatory for everyone from branch managers up to the most senior executive."[51] Dennis Nixon, a former Trustco executive who is now with the Bank of Montreal, explains how employees responded to the charismatic leadership of Cornelissen. "(He) had a very strong personality. So if Mike was exercising, people would jump on board and go off exercising because it seemed like the next thing to do. When the United Way campaign would take place in Royal Trust, it was very clear there was this added dimension of 'We can't let Mike down.'" Not all charismatic leaders have happy endings, however. Cornelissen departed Royal Trustco in 1992, and the company collapsed in 1993.[52]

Charismatic leaders, in fact, may become a liability to an organization once the crisis and need for dramatic change subside.[53] Why? Because then

Apple Computer
www.apple.com/

the charismatic leader's overwhelming self-confidence often becomes a liability. He or she is unable to listen to others, becomes uncomfortable when challenged by aggressive subordinates, and begins to hold an unjustifiable belief in his or her "rightness" on issues. Steve Jobs is a good example of how charismatic leadership can sometimes become a liability. Jobs achieved unwavering loyalty and commitment from the technical staff he oversaw at Apple Computer during the late 1970s and early 1980s by articulating a vision of personal computers that would dramatically change the way people lived. By 1985 he was forced out of Apple when the board of directors felt that Apple needed a leadership change. However, as the chapter-opening case shows, Jobs has been brought back to Apple because of his vision and charisma, in the hopes of restoring Apple to some of its former glory.

Transactional, Transformational, and Laissez-Faire Leadership

The final stream of research we'll address is the recent interest in differentiating transformational leaders from transactional and laissez-faire leaders.[54] As you'll see, because transformational leaders are also charismatic, there is some overlap between this topic and our previous discussion of charismatic leadership.

transactional leaders
Leaders who guide or motivate their followers in the direction of established goals by clarifying role and task requirements.

Most of the leadership theories presented in this chapter have concerned **transactional leaders**. These kinds of leaders guide or motivate their followers in the direction of established goals by clarifying role and task requirements. These managers typically use a management-by-objectives approach (which we discussed in Chapter 6). In some styles of transactional leadership, the leader uses rewarding and recognizing behaviour, and this results in performance that meets expectations, though rarely does one see results that exceed performance in those led by transactional leaders.[55] In other styles of transactional leadership, the leader emphasizes correction and possibly punishment rather than rewards and recognition. "The style of the boss who plays 'bad cop,' waiting and watching for mistakes to correct, backfires. It results in performance below expectations, and discourages innovation and initiative in the workplace."[56] It should be noted that leaders should not ignore poor performance, but effective leaders emphasize how to achieve expectations, rather than dwell on mistakes.

transformational leaders
Leaders who provide individualized consideration and intellectual stimulation, and who possess charisma.

There is also another type of leader who inspires followers to transcend their own self-interests for the good of the organization, and who is capable of having a profound and extraordinary effect on his or her followers. These are **transformational leaders** such as Ross Fitzpatrick of Vancouver-based Viceroy Resource Group, Leslie Wexner of The Limited retail chain, and Jack Welch at General Electric. They pay attention to the concerns and developmental needs of individual followers; they change followers' awareness of issues by helping them to look at old problems in new ways; and they are able to excite, arouse, and inspire followers to exert extra effort to achieve group goals. Jane Howell and her colleagues note that humour is also a characteristic more likely to be found in transformational than transactional or laissez-faire leaders.[57] Exhibit 11-6 identifies humour strategies commonly used by transformational leaders.

laissez-faire leaders
Leaders who give up responsibility for leading. They are indecisive and indifferent and often inaccessible.

Finally, there are also **laissez-faire leaders** who believe that they are empowering the employees, and then give up responsibility for leading. Employees of laissez-faire leaders find them indecisive and indifferent, as well as often inaccessible. This type of leadership results in poor performance and

Exhibit 11-6
Humour Strategies of Transformational Leaders

1. They used humour to take the edge off stressful situations.

2. They told a funny story to turn an argument in their favour.

3. They used amusing stories to defuse conflicts.

4. They used humour to laugh at themselves when they were being too serious.

5. They used wit to make friends of the opposition.

Source: J. Howell, B. Avolio and J. Sosik, "A Funny Thing Happened on the Way to the Bottom Line," in *Leadership: Achieving Exceptional Performance*, A Special Supplement Prepared by the Richard Ivey School of Business, *The Globe and Mail*, May 15, 1998, p. C2.

low morale. It also tends to stifle initiative, creativity, and responsibility. Exhibit 11-7 identifies and defines characteristics that differentiate transactional, transformational, and laissez-faire leaders.

Transactional and transformational leadership should not, however, be viewed as opposing approaches to getting things done.[58] Transformational leadership is built *on top of* transactional leadership—it produces levels of subordinate effort and performance that go beyond what would occur with a transactional approach alone. Moreover, transformational leadership is more than charisma. "The purely charismatic [leader] may want followers to adopt the charismatic's world view and go no further; the transformational leader will attempt to instill in followers the ability to question not only established views but eventually those established by the leader."[59]

The evidence supporting the superiority of transformational leadership over the transactional variety is overwhelmingly impressive. For instance, a number of studies with U.S., Canadian, and German military officers found, at every level, that transformational leaders were evaluated as more effective than their transactional counterparts.[60] And managers at Federal Express who were rated by their followers as exhibiting more transformational leadership were evaluated by their immediate supervisors as higher performers and more promotable.[61] Jane Howell and her colleagues found in a study of 250 executives and managers at a major financial-services company that "transformational leaders had 34 percent higher business unit performance results than other types of leaders."[62]

In summary, the overall evidence indicates that transformational leadership is more strongly correlated than transactional leadership with lower turnover rates, higher productivity, and higher employee satisfaction.[63] For those who want to move toward a more transformational style, Howell and her colleagues recommend that leaders develop an awareness of how often they use the five key behaviours of visioning, inspiring, stimulating, coaching, and team-building noted in Exhibit 11-7.[64] Leaders could then set goals for themselves for working on areas where they need improvement. It is important to note, however, that organizations themselves must be encouraging and supporting of transformational leadership in order for leaders to be able to work toward the goal of becoming a more transformational leader. Performance appraisals that measure and reward transformational behaviours are one element crucial to

> **Exhibit 11-7**
> **Characteristics of Transactional, Transformational, and Laissez-Faire Leaders**
>
> **Transactional Leader**
>
> *Contingent Reward:* Contracts exchange of rewards for effort, promises rewards for good performance, recognizes accomplishments.
>
> *Management by Exception* (active): Watches and searches for deviations from rules and standards, takes corrective action.
>
> *Management by Exception* (passive): Intervenes only if standards are not met.
>
> **Laissez-Faire**
>
> Abdicates responsibilities, avoids making decisions.
>
> **Transformational Leader**
>
> *Charisma:* Provides vision and sense of mission, instills pride, gains respect and trust.
>
> *Inspiration:* Communicates high expectations, uses symbols to focus efforts, expresses important purposes in simple ways.
>
> *Intellectual Stimulation:* Promotes intelligence, rationality, and careful problem solving.
>
> *Individualized Consideration:* Gives personal attention, treats each employee individually, coaches, advises.
>
> Source: B.M. Bass, "From Transactional to Transformational Leadership: Learning to Share the Vision," *Organizational Dynamics*, Winter 1990, p. 22. Reprinted by permission of the publisher. *American Management Association*, New York. All rights reserved.

changing behaviour. Cultures that encourage creative ideas, risk-taking and change are also more supportive of transformational leadership.

Visionary Leadership

The term *vision* recurred throughout our discussion of charismatic leadership, but visionary leadership goes beyond charisma. In this section, we review recent revelations about the importance of visionary leadership.

Visionary leadership is the ability to create and articulate a realistic, credible, attractive vision of the future for an organization or organizational unit that grows out of and improves upon the present.[65] This vision, if properly selected and implemented, is so energizing that it "in effect jump-starts the future by calling forth the skills, talents, and resources to make it happen."[66]

A review of various definitions finds that a vision differs from other forms of direction setting in several ways: "A vision has clear and compelling imagery that offers an innovative way to improve, which recognizes and draws on traditions, and connects to actions that people can take to realize change. Vision taps people's emotions and energy. Properly articulated, a vision creates the enthusiasm that people have for sporting events and other leisure time activities, bringing the energy and commitment to the workplace."[67]

The case in favour of visionary leadership has been made by many writers. For instance: "the 21st-century organization virtually demands visionary leadership. It cannot function without it, for an organization driven by accelerating technological change, staffed by a diverse, multicultural mix of highly intelligent knowledge workers, facing global complexity, a vast kalei-

visionary leadership
The ability to create and articulate a realistic, credible, attractive vision of the future for an organization or organizational unit that grows out of and improves upon the present.

doscope of individual customer needs, and the incessant demands of multiple constituencies would simply self-destruct without a common sense of direction."[68] Another argues that vision is "the glue that binds individuals into a group with a common goal. . . . When shared by employees, [it] can keep an entire company moving forward in face of difficulties, enabling and inspiring leaders and employees alike."[69]

A survey of 1500 senior leaders, 870 of them CEOs from 20 different countries, additionally attests to the growing importance of visionary leadership.[70] The leaders were asked to describe the key traits or talents desirable for a CEO in the year 2000. The dominant characteristic most frequently mentioned was that the CEO must convey a "strong sense of vision." Ninety-eight percent rated this trait as "most important." Another study contrasted 18 visionary companies with 18 comparable non-visionary firms over a 65-year period.[71] The visionary companies were found to have outperformed the comparison group by six times on standard financial criteria and their stocks outperformed the general market by 15 times.

The key properties of a vision seem to be inspirational possibilities that are value centred, realizable, with superior imagery and articulation.[72] Visions should be able to create possibilities that are inspirational, unique, and offer a new order that can produce organizational distinction. A vision is likely to fail if it doesn't offer a view of the future that is clearly and demonstrably better for the organization and its members. Desirable visions fit the times and circumstances and reflect the uniqueness of the organization. People in the organization must also believe that the vision is attainable. The vision should be perceived as challenging yet doable. Visions that have clear articulation and powerful imagery are more easily grasped and accepted.

What do visions look like? They're typically easier to talk about than to actually create, but here are some examples. Toronto-based Sony Music Entertainment Canada's Vision 1997 statement, developed in 1994, begins with two key phrases, "Our passion is music. Our commitment is to our artists."[73] While Vision 1997 primarily addressed Sony Music's role in Canada, for Vision 2000 "the company's vision will include acknowledgment as one of the top three Sony Music International affiliates in the world for its artists and repertoire." Vancouver-based Finning Ltd.'s vision statement is: "We provide best solutions by building relationships based on an intimate understanding of each customer's problem."[74] This statement is actually a shortened version of two statements that Finning developed while working toward its mission statement: "To consistently provide the best solutions to people who move, harvest and transform goods or materials so they can meet the needs of their customers," and, "Our (distinctive excellence is our) ability to create a climate in which people, when serving a Finning customer, have the competence and freedom to form and deliver on a relationship base."

Here are some additional organization-specific examples.[75] Walt Disney single-handedly reinvented the idea of an amusement park when he described his vision of Disneyland in the early 1950s. Mary Kay Ash's vision of women as entrepreneurs selling products that improved their self-image gave impetus to her cosmetics company. Scandinavian Airlines CEO Jan Carlzon used the notion of "50 000 daily moments of truth" to depict the emphasis to be placed on customer service. Carlzon wanted every employee to ensure that each "moment of truth"—those instances where customers come into contact with employees—would be a positive experience for all customers. Steve Jobs created a vision for Apple Computer that energized

Sony Music Entertainment Canada
www.sonymusic.com/world/

employees around the idea of not just building computers but also dramatically changing the world.

What skills do visionary leaders exhibit? Once the vision is identified, these leaders appear to have three qualities that are related to effectiveness in their visionary roles.[76]

First is the ability to explain the vision to others. The leader needs to make the vision clear in terms of required actions and aims through clear oral and written communication. The best vision is likely to be ineffective if the leader isn't a strong communicator. Ronald Reagan—the so-called "great communicator"—used his years of acting experience to help him articulate a simple vision for his presidency: a return to happier and more prosperous times through less government, lower taxes, and a strong military.

The second skill needed is to be able to express the vision not just verbally but also through the leader's behaviour. This requires behaving in ways that continually convey and reinforce the vision. Herb Kelleher at Southwest Airlines lives and breathes his commitment to customer service. He's famous within the company for jumping in, when needed, to help check in passengers, load baggage, fill in for flight attendants, or do anything else to make the customer's experience more pleasant.

The third skill is being able to extend the vision to different leadership contexts. This is the ability to sequence activities so the vision can be applied in a variety of situations. For instance, the vision has to be as meaningful to the people in accounting as to those in marketing, and to employees in Tokyo as well as in Toronto. Of course, not everyone agrees that vision is always needed, or even always appropriate. This chapter's Case Incident, "The Case Against Vision," raises some intriguing ideas about the use of vision in organizations.

Southwest Airlines
www.iflyswa.com/

Contemporary Issues in Leadership

Can followers lead themselves? What unique demands do teams place on leaders? How is the current popularity of *empowerment* affecting the way managers lead? Since leaders aren't leaders unless they have followers, what can managers do to make employees more effective followers? Do men and women rely on different leadership styles? If so, is one style inherently superior to the other? How does one lead in a workplace now characterized by telecommuting, contracting out, and globalization where workers and leaders may not even occupy the same physical location? How does national culture affect the choice of leadership style? Is there a moral dimension to leadership?

In this section, we briefly address these contemporary issues in leadership.

Dispersed Leadership

The theories presented above (charismatic, transactional/transformational/laissez-faire, and visionary) can be characterized as part of the New Leadership Approach.[77] While these approaches have proved fruitful in a number of ways, they are also subject to criticism because they focus on heroic leaders, leaders at the top echelons of the organization, and also on individuals rather than teams. To address these failings, a number of new approaches have been introduced in the late 1980s and the 1990s that are referred to as

Dispersed Leadership. These theories aim to explain how one can get individuals and teams to be more responsible for themselves, and in effect, lead themselves. We examine these new approaches below.

TURNING CONSTITUENTS INTO LEADERS   Several researchers have developed the idea that good leaders develop the leadership skills of their subordinates.[78] One set of researchers actually refers to this as SuperLeadership, which they view as the leadership design of the future.[79] A major feature of SuperLeadership is the emphasis on "leading others to lead themselves," so that the followers also become leaders.[80] This view is not inconsistent with the transformational view of leadership, although the emphasis is placed much more heavily on how leaders can get followers to lead themselves. This is done by leaders developing leadership capacity in others and nurturing subordinates so that they do not feel the need to depend on formal leaders. It is also done by leaders liberating subordinates so that they will use their own abilities to lead themselves.

PROVIDING TEAM LEADERSHIP   Leadership is increasingly taking place within a team context. As teams grow in popularity, the role of the leader in guiding team members takes on heightened importance.[81] Here the role of team leader is different from the traditional leadership role performed by first-line supervisors.

Many leaders are not equipped to handle the change to teams. As one prominent consultant noted, "Even the most capable managers have trouble making the transition because all the command-and-control type things they were encouraged to do before are no longer appropriate. There's no reason to have any skill or sense of this."[82] This same consultant estimated that "probably 15 percent of managers are natural team leaders; another 15 percent could never lead a team because it runs counter to their personality. (They're unable to sublimate their dominating style for the good of the team.) Then there's that huge group in the middle: team leadership doesn't come naturally to them, but they can learn it."[83]

The challenge for most managers, then, is to learn how to become an effective team leader who can build commitment and confidence, remove obstacles, create opportunities, and be part of the team.[84] They have to learn skills such as the patience to share information, to trust others, to give up authority, and to understand when to intervene. Effective leaders have mastered the difficult balancing act of knowing when to leave their teams alone and when to intercede. New team leaders may try to retain too much control at a time when team members need more autonomy, or they may abandon their teams at times when the teams need support and help.[85]

A recent study of 20 organizations that had reorganized themselves around teams found certain common responsibilities that all leaders had to assume. These included coaching, facilitating, handling disciplinary problems, reviewing team/individual performance, training, and communication.[86] Many of these responsibilities apply to managers in general. A more meaningful way to describe the team leader's job is to focus on two priorities: managing the team's external boundary and facilitating the team process.[87] We've divided these priorities into four specific roles.

First, team leaders are *liaisons with external constituencies*. These include upper management, other internal teams, customers, and suppliers. The leader represents the team to other constituencies, secures needed resources, clarifies others' expectations of the team, gathers information from the outside, and shares this information with team members.

Second, team leaders are *troubleshooters*. When the team has problems and asks for assistance, team leaders sit in on meetings and try to help resolve the problems. This rarely relates to technical or operation issues because the team members typically know more about the tasks being done than does the team leader. The leader is most likely to contribute by asking penetrating questions, by helping the team discuss problems, and by getting needed resources from external constituencies. For instance, when a team in an aerospace firm found itself short-handed, its team leader took responsibility for getting more staff. He presented the team's case to upper management and got the approval through the company's human resources department.

Third, team leaders are *conflict managers*. When disagreements surface, they help process the conflict. What's the source of the conflict? Who is involved? What are the issues? What resolution options are available? What are the advantages and disadvantages of each? By getting team members to address questions such as these, the leader minimizes the disruptive aspects of intrateam conflicts.

Finally, team leaders are *coaches*. They clarify expectations and roles, teach, offer support, cheerlead, and whatever else is necessary to help team members improve their work performance. In this chapter's From Concepts to Skills feature, we give you tips on how to become a more effective coach.

empowerment
Giving employees responsibility for what they do.

LEADING THROUGH EMPOWERMENT   An important trend has developed over the past decade that has immense implications for leadership. That trend is for managers to embrace **empowerment**. More specifically, managers are being advised that effective leaders share power and responsibility with their employees.[88] The empowering leader's role is to show trust, provide vision, remove performance-blocking barriers, offer encouragement, motivate, and coach employees. The list of companies that have jumped on the "empowerment bandwagon" includes such world-famous corporations as General Electric, Intel, Ford, Saturn, Scandinavian Airline Systems, Harley-Davidson, Goodyear, and Conrail. They also include smaller Canadian corporations such as Vancouver-based Dominion Directory and Langley, British Columbia-based Redwood Plastics. The empowerment strategies of both Dominion Directory and Redwood Plastics are discussed further in Chapter 12. Many other organizations have introduced empowerment as part of their corporatewide efforts in implementing total quality management.[89] Because of factors such as downsizing, higher employee skills, commitment of organizations to continuous training, implementation of total quality management programs, and introduction of self-managed teams, there seems to be no doubt that an increasing number of situations call for a more empowering approach to leadership. But it might not work in *all* situations! Blanket acceptance of empowerment, or *any* universal approach to leadership, is inconsistent with the best and most current evidence we have on the subject.[90]

Gender: Do Males and Females Lead Differently?

HOW MANY WOMEN MAKE IT TO THE TOP?   In October 1997, 10 of the top 500 publicly traded companies in Canada were run by women.[91] The United States, by comparison, had just two women in comparable positions. With the exception of the Canadian branches of large American corporations, however, Canada's biggest, most profitable companies do not have women running them. Regardless of the industry, a woman may be senior vice-

FROM CONCEPTS TO SKILLS

Coaching

Effective managers are increasingly being described as *coaches* rather than *bosses*. They are expected to provide instruction, guidance, advice, and encouragement to help employees improve their job performance. If a manager wants to transform him- or herself into a coach, what needs to be done? More specifically, what actions characterize effective coaching?

There are three general skills that managers should exhibit if they are to help their employees generate breakthroughs in performance. The following reviews these general skills and the specific behaviours associated with each.

1. *Ability to analyse ways to improve an employee's performance and capabilities.* A coach looks for opportunities for an employee to expand his or her capabilities and improve performance.

   a. Observe your employee's behaviour on a day-to-day basis.

   b. Ask questions of the employee: Why do you do a task this way? Can it be improved? What other approaches might be used?

   c. Show genuine interest in the person as an individual, not merely as an employee. Respect his or her individuality. More important than any technical expertise you can provide about improving job performance is the insight you have into the employee's uniqueness.

   d. Listen to the employee. You can't understand the world from an employee's perspective unless you listen.

2. *Ability to create a supportive climate.* It is the coach's responsibility to reduce barriers to development and to facilitate a climate that encourages performance improvement.

   a. Create a climate that contributes to a free and open exchange of ideas.

   b. Offer help and assistance. Give guidance and advice when asked.

   c. Encourage your employees. Be positive and upbeat. Don't use threats.

   d. Focus on mistakes as learning opportunities. Change implies risk and employ-

ees must not feel that mistakes will be punished. When failure occurs, ask: "What did we learn that can help us in the future?"

   e. Reduce obstacles. What factors do you control that, if eliminated, would help the employee to improve his or her job performance?

   f. Express to the employee the value of his or her contribution to the unit's goals.

   g. Take personal responsibility for the outcome, but don't rob employees of their full responsibility. Validate the employees' efforts when they succeed, and point to what was missing when they fail. Never blame the employees for poor results.

3. *Ability to influence employees to change their behaviour.* The ultimate test of coaching effectiveness is whether an employee's performance improves. However, this is not a static concept. We are concerned with ongoing growth and development.

   a. Encourage continual improvement. Recognize and reward small improvements and, consistent with TQM, treat coaching as helping employees to continually work toward improvement. There are no absolute upper limits to an employee's job performance.

   b. Use a collaborative style. Employees will be more responsive to accepting change if they participate in identifying and choosing among improvement ideas.

   c. Break difficult tasks down into simpler ones. By breaking down more complex jobs into a series of tasks of increasing difficulty, discouraged employees are more likely to experience success. Achieving success on simpler tasks encourages them to take on more difficult ones.

   d. Model the qualities that you expect from your employees. If you want

openness, dedication, commitment, and responsibility from your employees, you must demonstrate these qualities yourself. Your employees will look to you as a role model, so make sure your deeds match your words.

Source: C.D. Orth, H.E. Wilkinson, and R.C. Benfari, "The Manager's Role as Coach and Mentor," *Organizational Dynamics*, Spring 1987, p. 67.

president of human resources or corporate communications, but she is usually not the president or CEO. In addition, just nine percent of all directors in Canada's top corporations are women, according to a study released by Spencer Stuart, a Toronto-based consulting firm. Women have greatest representation among the entrepreneurial ranks, where women are starting businesses at three to four times the rate of men. To put these numbers in perspective, women make up 34 percent of managers and administrators, 45 percent of the labour force, 57 percent of graduate degree holders, and 51 percent of the Canadian population.

Environics Communications recently surveyed more than 650 affluent Canadian women (i.e., those in households with more than $137 000 in annual income), most of whom had careers.[92] Sixty-nine percent said the opportunities offered to women are more limited than those offered men. Marti Smye, president of Toronto-based PeopleTech Consulting Inc., explains how women get left out of decision-making in organizations. "In a lot of these organizations, the senior decisions are talked about on a one-on-one basis," she says. "So people pick the people to talk to. Women get left out of

Bobbi Gaunt, president of Ford Motor Co. of Canada, believes that women who run businesses view them more holistically and are more willing to make long-term investments in the company.

that loop. They aren't the ones you run into in the hall or they aren't the ones who are specifically sought out."[93]

A study by the Center for Creative Leadership found that there were some differences, as well as many similarities, in the promotion processes of men and women.[94] By examining the promotions of 16 men and 13 women to middle and upper management through discussions with the person promoted, that person's promoting supervisor, the promoting supervisor's supervisor, and an HR representative, the researchers discovered that for both men and women, "credentials, experience, track record, skills, work ethic, ability to work on a team, interpersonal skills, and growth potential" were important. The differences for promotion were more subtle. The men's supervisors mentioned in 75 percent of the cases that they felt comfortable with the candidate at an interpersonal level, and that's what led to their promotions. This was cited in only 23 percent of the women's cases. For women, it was more important that they exhibit personal strength and a willingness to take risks and accept responsibility. For women's promotions, continuity with the job (i.e., moving up along the same career track) was cited in 38 percent of the promotions, whereas this was cited in only six percent of the men's cases. This suggests that men are more likely to be promoted into new opportunities, whereas women are more likely to be promoted in areas where they can continue using their existing knowledge. To illustrate the significance of this point, in one case a supervisor waited to promote a woman until an opportunity appeared in the plant where she worked. The supervisor "thought it would be easier for the woman to succeed in a new job in a location where she already had credibility." The woman would have preferred to take a similar opportunity elsewhere sooner and "felt restricted by having to wait for the right opportunity to open up" in her own plant.

While it is heartening to note that on many dimensions men and women are evaluated similarly with respect to promotion opportunities, the study above also indicates that more work needs to be done to ensure that women and men have the same promotion opportunities. Part of the problem is that men and women do not even agree on what is happening in today's workplace. In 1997, Linda Duxbury, of the Centre for Research and Education on Women and Work at Carleton University, produced a study looking at differences in perceptions of men and women at work.[95] She found that 86 percent of men surveyed said organizations actively communicate with employees, but only 65 percent of women agreed. Women were also less likely to state that their companies had established a policy of inclusion, with 44 percent of the women and 73 percent of the men agreeing with this statement.

Lorna Rosenstein, general manager of Lotus Development Canada Ltd., accounts for some of the difficulties women face in reaching the top: "Women have to be smarter, more creative, more focused, more bottom-line oriented, simply better than men overall if they want to rise as far. And they still get just 70 cents on the dollar in earnings compared with their male counterparts."[96]

It has become common to refer to women "hitting the glass ceiling," meaning that they reach a point beyond which they don't seem able to be promoted. Canada has women at the top of some large organizations, including GM Canada, Ford Canada, Xerox Canada, EDS, Stentor Resource Centre, Kraft Canada, Pillsbury Canada, General Mills Canada, and Home Depot Canada. However, this does not mean that women are making it to

the top as easily as men. Sheelagh Whittaker, president and CEO of EDS Canada Ltd., notes: "I've always said that we'll have true equality when we have as many incompetent women in positions as we have incompetent men."[97] And Diane McGarry, chair, CEO, and president of Xerox Canada, refers not to the glass ceiling, but rather the "plastic ceiling" in corporations "because plastic is even harder to break than glass."[98]

SIMILARITIES AND DIFFERENCES IN WOMEN'S AND MEN'S LEADERSHIP STYLES   With respect to whether men and women lead differently, an extensive review of the literature suggests two conclusions.[99] First, the similarities between men and women tend to outweigh the differences. Second, what differences there are seem to be that women fall back on a more democratic leadership style, while men feel more comfortable with a directive style.

The similarities among men and women leaders shouldn't be completely surprising. Almost all the studies looking at this issue have used managerial positions as being synonymous with leadership. As such, gender differences apparent in the general population don't tend to be as evident because of career self-selection and organization selection. Just as people who choose careers in law enforcement or civil engineering have a lot in common, individuals who choose managerial careers also tend to have commonalities. People with traits associated with leadership—such as intelligence, confidence, and sociability—are more likely to be perceived as leaders and encouraged to pursue careers where they can exert leadership. This is true regardless of gender. Similarly, organizations tend to recruit and promote people into leadership positions who project leadership attributes. The result is that, regardless of gender, those who achieve formal leadership positions in organizations tend to be more alike than different.

Despite the previous conclusion, studies indicate some differences in the inherent leadership styles between women and men. Women tend to adopt a style of shared leadership. They encourage participation, share power and information, and attempt to enhance followers' self-worth. They prefer to lead through inclusion and rely on their charisma, expertise, contacts, and interpersonal skills to influence others. Men, on the other hand, are more likely to use a directive command-and-control style. They rely on the formal authority of their position for their influence base. Exhibit 11-8 summarizes the views of several women heading major corporations in Canada on whether gender makes a difference for leadership. Their views are consistent with the research evidence we've noted here.

Given that men have historically held the great majority of leadership positions in organizations, it's tempting to assume that the existence of the noted differences between men and women would automatically work to favour men. It doesn't. In today's organizations, flexibility, teamwork, trust, and information sharing are replacing rigid structures, competitive individualism, control, and secrecy. The best managers listen, motivate, and provide support to their people. And many women seem to do those things better than men. As a specific example, the expanded use of cross-functional teams in organizations means that effective managers must become skilled negotiators. The leadership styles women typically use can make them better at negotiating, as they are less likely to focus on wins, losses, and competition, as do men. They tend to treat negotiations in the context of a continuing relationship—trying hard to make the other party a winner in its own and other's eyes. Chapter 13 discusses differences between men's and women's

> ### Exhibit 11-8
> ### Do Men and Women Lead Differently? What Women at the Top Say
>
> **Sheelagh Whittaker,** president and CEO of EDS Canada Ltd., one of the country's leading providers of information technology services: "Women in business are less preoccupied with status, if only because they have been granted so little in corporate life."
>
> **Peggy Witte,** founder, president and CEO of Royal Oak Mines Inc.: While she might be more inclined than a man to consider the social effects of her actions, "at the end of the day, the hard decisions are probably exactly the same."
>
> **Carol Stephenson,** president and CEO of Stentor Resource Centre Inc.: "Women by nature tend to possess better interpersonal skills and are more suited than men to the task of consensus-building."
>
> **Bobbi Gaunt,** president and CEO of Ford Motor Co. of Canada: "Women tend to view their businesses holistically: not only are they more mindful of employees, but they are more aware of their company's image in the eyes of customers and investors—and willing to make long-term investments to improve it."
>
> **Maureen Kempston Darkes,** president and general manager of General Motors of Canada Ltd. may be the dissenting voice in the group: "The challenges that confront chief executives are the same whether they are men or women. Once you get to the CEO spot, you're focused on the same kinds of issues that men would focus on."
>
> Source: Dianne Maley, "Canada's Top Women CEOs," *Maclean's*, October 20, 1997.

Stentor Resource Centre
www.stentor.ca/

negotiating styles in greater detail. In this chapter's HR Implications feature, in addition to discussing how to improve the leadership skills of all employees, we also consider some specific ways for organizations to prepare women for more leadership opportunities.

Leading From a Distance

As organizations are facing more telecommuting by workers (which we discuss in Chapter 15), more contracting out, and globalization, it is becoming more common that the person doing the leading is not necessarily in the same building, let alone the same organization or country as the person being led. Leaders must develop ways to carry out "long-distance" leading that does not involve face-to-face contact.

Jane Howell and one of her students at the Richard Ivey School of Business, Kate Hall-Merenda, have considered the issues of leading from a distance.[100] They note that physical distance can create many potential problems, with employees feeling isolated, forgotten, and perhaps not cared about. This may result in lowered productivity. Their study of 109 business leaders and 371 followers in a large financial institution found that physical distance makes it more difficult for managers and employees to develop high-quality relationships. However, they also discovered that it is possible to be an effective leader at a distance when employees and managers have good relations.

Howell and Hall-Merenda suggest that some of the same characteristics of transformational leaders are appropriate for long-distance managing. In particular, they emphasize the need to articulate a compelling vision to em-

ployees and to communicate that vision in an inspiring way. Encouraging employees to think about ways to strive toward that vision is another important task of the leader. Their research also indicates that communication does not have to be done face-to-face, as long as the vision is communicated clearly in some fashion.

What About Followership?

When someone was once asked what it took to be a great leader, he responded: Great followers! While the response may have seemed sarcastic, it has some truth. We have long known that many managers can't lead a horse to water. But, then again, many subordinates can't follow a parade. Only recently have we begun to recognize that in addition to having leaders who can lead, successful organizations need followers who can follow.[101] In fact, it's probably fair to say that all organizations have far more followers than leaders, so ineffective followers may be more of a handicap to an organization than ineffective leaders. The *Far Side* cartoon shown in Exhibit 11-9 gives you some indication of what can happen when someone finally realizes that they're "a follower, too."

What qualities do effective followers have? One writer focuses on four.[102]

- *They manage themselves well.* They are able to think for themselves. They can work independently and without close supervision.

Exhibit 11-9

THE FAR SIDE   By GARY LARSON

"Well, what d'ya know! . . . *I'm* a follower, too!"

- *They are committed to a purpose outside themselves.* Effective followers are committed to something—a cause, a product, a work team, an organization, an idea—in addition to the care of their own lives. Most people like working with colleagues who are emotionally, as well as physically, committed to their work.

- *They build their competence and focus their efforts for maximum impact.* Effective followers master skills that will be useful to their organizations, and they hold higher performance standards than their job or work group requires.

- *They are courageous, honest, and credible.* Effective followers establish themselves as independent, critical thinkers whose knowledge and judgment can be trusted. They hold high ethical standards, give credit where credit is due, and aren't afraid to own up to their mistakes.

National Culture as an Added Contingency Variable

One general conclusion that surfaces from our discussion of leadership is that effective leaders don't use any single style. They adjust their style to the situation. While not mentioned explicitly in any of the theories we presented, certainly national culture is an important situational factor determining which leadership style will be most effective.[103] We propose that you consider it as another contingency variable. It can help explain, for instance, why executives at the highly successful Asia Department Store in central China blatantly brag about practising "heartless" management, require new employees to undergo two to four weeks of military training with units of the People's Liberation Army in order to increase their obedience, and conduct the store's in-house training sessions in a public place where employees can openly suffer embarrassment from their mistakes.[104]

One way that national culture affects leadership style is by cultural expectations and norms of subordinates. Leaders, particularly when they are working in international situations, are constrained by the cultural conditions that their subordinates have come to expect. For example, a manipulative or autocratic style is compatible with high power distance, and we find high power distance scores in Arab, Far Eastern, and Latin countries. Power distance rankings should also be good indicators of employee willingness to accept participative leadership. Participation is likely to be most effective in such low power distance cultures as exist in Norway, Finland, Denmark, and Sweden. Not incidentally, this may explain (a) why a number of leadership theories (for example the University of Michigan behavioural studies) implicitly favour the use of a participative or people-oriented style; (b) the emergence of development-oriented leader behaviour found by Scandinavian researchers; and (c) the recent enthusiasm in North America with empowerment. Remember that most leadership theories were developed by North Americans, using North American subjects; and the United States, Canada, and Scandinavian countries all rate below average on power distance.

In 1997, Joseph Di Stefano and one of his students, Nick Bontis, both of the Richard Ivey School of Business at the University of Western Ontario, studied differences in leadership styles across cultures.[105] They were particularly interested in the behaviours that were used to generate exceptional performance by employees. In general, they reported that there were quite a lot of similarities in looking at managers from the United States, Northern Eu-

rope, Southern Europe, Latin America, the Far East, and Commonwealth countries, including Canada. In order to achieve exceptional performance from employees, leaders from all of these countries used visioning, coaching, and stimulating (encouraging new ideas) behaviours similarly, and as their chief strategies. U.S. leaders reported they were more likely to correct employees' behaviour than did Far Eastern or Latin managers. Americans also used team building more often than did Asian managers. Far Eastern managers were less likely to include recognition as part of how they encouraged their employees' exceptional performance than were Southern European leaders. These findings suggest that there are some minor differences in how leaders throughout the world achieve exceptional performance from their employees. However, they also suggest a great degree of similarity in what it takes to get high-performing employees.

Is There a Moral Dimension to Leadership?

The topic of leadership and ethics has surprisingly received little attention. Only very recently have ethicists and leadership researchers begun to consider the ethical implications in leadership.[106] Why now? One reason may be the growing general interest in ethics throughout the field of management. Another reason may be the discovery by probing biographers that some of our past leaders suffered from ethical shortcomings. Regardless, no contemporary discussion of leadership is complete without addressing its ethical dimension.

Ethics touches on leadership at a number of junctures. Transformational leaders, for instance, have been described by one authority as fostering moral virtue when they try to change the attitudes and behaviours of followers.[107] Charisma, too, has an ethical component. Unethical leaders are more likely to use their charisma to enhance power over followers, directed toward self-serving ends. Ethical leaders are considered to use their charisma in a socially constructive way to serve others.[108] There is also the issue of abuse of power by leaders, for example, when they give themselves large salaries and bonuses while also seeking to cut costs by laying off longtime employees. And, of course, the topic of trust explicitly deals with honesty and integrity in leadership.

Leadership effectiveness needs to address the *means* that a leader uses in trying to achieve goals as well as the content of those goals. GE's Jack Welch, for instance, is consistently described as a highly effective leader because he has succeeded in achieving outstanding returns for shareholders. But Welch is also widely regarded as one of the world's toughest managers. He is regularly listed high on *Fortune*'s annual list of the most hated and reviled executives. Similarly, Bill Gates' success in leading Microsoft to domination of the world's software business has been achieved by means of an extremely demanding work culture. Microsoft's culture demands long work hours by employees and is intolerant of individuals who want to balance work and their personal life. Additionally, ethical leadership must address the content of a leader's goals. Are the changes that the leader seeks for the organization morally acceptable? Is a business leader effective if he or she builds an organization's success by selling products that damage the health of its users? This question might be asked of tobacco executives. Or is a military leader successful by winning a war that should not have been fought in the first place?

Microsoft
www.microsoft.com

Leadership is not value free. Before we judge any leader to be effective, we should consider both the means used by the leader to achieve his or her goals and the moral content of those goals.

HR IMPLICATIONS

Developing Leadership Potential

One of the challenges of the human resources function in organizations is to identify the skill and learning needs of employees, and help employees get appropriate training. We have previously discussed in Chapter 2 the importance of learning and training with respect to developing employee skills. It is also important to ensure that those in management and leadership positions are considered for educational opportunities. This is especially important now as many executives are looking for better ways to lead their companies as they face challenges such as continual change, flatter corporate structures that have removed the familiar hierarchical leadership, and the demands of globalization. As a consequence, many executives are returning to the classroom. Below we discuss general management training, and then we follow that with some specific examples of what has been done to promote women's leadership skills and abilities.

General Management Training

There are a variety of programs that executives can take. Some opt to go for their master of business administration degrees. "The executive MBA is the ultimate in self-improvement," says Don Nightingale, executive director of the executive MBA programs at Queen's University's School of Business.[1]

An MBA isn't the only educational option executives have, however. Senior and middle managers are taking everything from four- or five-day programs on specific topics to five- to six-week executive programs. They study such issues as managing change, strategic decision-making, leadership, global management, and teamwork.

While management development courses traditionally have been almost exclusively in budgeting, planning, and managing, increasingly there is an emphasis on "personal development" courses, where those who attend are encouraged to learn more about themselves to help them become a better person. As an example of this new trend, Vancouver-based Fletcher Challenge Canada has sent some of its employees to a course called "The Seven Habits of Highly Effective People" offered by the Covey Leadership Centre, headquartered in Utah. Lois Nahirney, one of Fletcher Challenge's employees, found the course extremely useful, partly because it gave her time to reflect on her own goals in life: "It's very much about personal vision, personal mastery," she says. Fletcher Challenge believes programs such as these benefit both the individual and the company, and over 600 employees have been through such courses as leadership, communication, and facilitation.

The Hongkong Bank of Canada sends two or three executives a year to external courses, often university-based. BCTV has sent senior managers to the Covey course. BC Hydro, Coast Hotels, and A&W have also sent managers to various programs. Vancouver-based A&B Sound has sent more than a dozen people to Seattle's Pacific Institute "affirmation" program.

All of these companies believe that courses help their managers. For example, BC Hydro's Gary Rodford says course participants come back to work "better managers and better people." Lois Nahirny at Fletcher Challenge agrees: "The better you understand who you are and who you want to be, the better you can approach your job and the people you do it with. A company which helps its people do that is going to be more successful."[2]

Efforts to Develop Women's Leadership Capabilities

Some corporations have become increasingly aware that women do not seem to be making it into higher management positions. As a result, some have started tying compensation directly to senior executives' identification and promotion of "high potential" women. Burnaby-based B.C. Tel has been doing this since 1994.[3] "We're not

simply encouraging people to ensure we have the appropriate representation of women within the organization, we're requiring that by putting their variable compensation at risk," says Paul Smith, the company's senior vice-president of human resources. To accomplish this objective, 20 percent of a manager's variable compensation is tied to the "people issues" on the manager's performance appraisal. For 1998, every senior executive at B.C. Tel will be required to have a career-development strategy in place for women. "Everyone is going to have to participate in that in order to maximize their variable pay," says Smith. B.C. Tel also identified managers who were not prepared to support the new women-friendly environment and they have been encouraged to look for jobs elsewhere.

When Tony Comper became president of the Bank of Montreal (BMO) in 1990, he was determined to find out why 75 percent of the bank's employees were women, but only nine percent of women had made it into the executive ranks. He created a task force to investigate the problems and develop action plans for change. The task force's report, submitted in November 1991, found that women were held back by stereotypical attitudes, myths, and "conventional wisdoms." The following fictions and facts, highlighted in the report, illustrate some of those conventional wisdoms:[4]

Fiction: women were less committed to their work, less educated than men, and tended to turn in weaker job performances.

Fact: women in the bank turned out to be at least as fully qualified as men in every respect — just as educated and just as dedicated.

Fiction: women had not been in the pipeline long enough.

Fact: women had put in longer service than men at every level, except senior management, where their presence was a recent development.

Fiction: child-rearing women tend to quit, and ergo, are not committed to their careers.

Fact: 98 percent of women returned to the company after giving birth.

Fiction: time will take care of gender imbalances.

Fact: if the bank relied on time solving the problem, women's representation at executive and senior management levels would rise to only 18 percent and 22 percent respectively by the year 2000.

The task force also determined that more direct involvement to promote women was necessary. The bank's women employees were well educated, had received better performance appraisals than men at all levels, and wanted advancement as much as the men did, but they weren't making it. Comper recognized that simply waiting for things to right themselves wouldn't work. In light of that fact, the task force concluded that the bank needed to act aggressively to move women up the ranks. In order to do that, they tied performance appraisals and compensation of managers to the promotion of women. The bank also created a more family-friendly environment to help their employees manage the stress of work and home and introduced such things as flex work arrangements and people-care days to the workplace. By late 1998, women held 25 percent of all executive positions at BMO. Comper would still like to see 50 percent of the top offices held by women by the year 2007.

It is clear from the examples of both B.C. Tel and the Bank of Montreal that senior management needs to be involved in the training and development of women to ensure that they have the same access as men to leadership positions in organizations.

Sources:

[1] Johanna Powell, "Forging Fearless Leaders," *Financial Post Daily*, March 13, 1997, pp. 14,16.

[2] "Camp Overhaul: Where BC Companies Send Their Best and Brightest for Management Development," *B.C. Business Magazine*, February, 1995, pp. 27–30.

[3] Information on B.C. Tel and Bank of Montreal based on Jennifer Wells, "Stuck on the Ladder: Not Only Is the Glass Ceiling Still in Place, But Men and Women Have Very Different Views of the Problem," *Maclean's*, October 20, 1997, p. 60.

[4] Jennifer Wells, "Stuck on the Ladder; Not only is the Glass Ceiling Still in Place, But Men and Women Have Very Different Views of the Problem," *Maclean's*, October 20, 1997, p. 60; and Matthew Barrett, "Workplace Equality: Pursuing a Goal That Makes the Best of Business Sense," *CMA Management Accounting Magazine*, September, 1993, p. 11.

Summary and Implications

For the Workplace

Leadership plays a central part in understanding group behaviour, for it's the leader who usually provides the direction toward goal attainment. Therefore, a more accurate predictive capability should be valuable in improving group performance.

In this chapter, we described a transition in approaches to the study of leadership—from the simple trait orientation to increasingly complex and sophisticated transactional models such as the path-goal model. With the increase in complexity has also come an increase in our ability to explain and predict behaviour.

A major breakthrough in our understanding of leadership came when we recognized the need to include situational factors. Recent efforts have moved beyond mere recognition toward specific attempts to isolate these situational variables. We can expect further progress to be made with leadership models, but in the last decade, we have taken several large steps—large enough that we now can make moderately effective predictions as to who can best lead a group, and we can explain under what conditions a given approach (such as task oriented or people oriented) is likely to lead to high employee performance and satisfaction.

In addition, the study of leadership has expanded to include more heroic and visionary approaches to leadership. As we learn more about the personal characteristics that followers attribute to charismatic and transformational leaders, and about the conditions that facilitate their emergence, we should be better able to predict when followers will exhibit extraordinary commitment and loyalty to their leaders and to those leaders' goals.

Finally, we addressed a number of contemporary issues in leadership. We learned, for instance, that male and female leadership styles have some similarities, but that women's propensity to rely on shared leadership is more in line with organizational needs in the 1990s and beyond than the directive style often preferred by men. Effective team leaders were found to perform four roles: they act as liaisons with external constituencies; they are troubleshooters; they manage conflict; and they coach team members. Empowered leadership was shown to be increasingly popular, but managers should not assume that empowering employees is the ideal leadership style for all occasions. Also, consistent with the contingency approach, managers should be sure to consider national culture as an important variable in choosing a leadership style. Finally, we propose that leadership is not value free. We should look at the moral content of a leader's goals and the means he or she uses to achieve those goals.

For You as an Individual

It is easy to imagine that theories of leadership are more important to those who are leaders or who plan in the near future to become leaders. However, this attitude would be a mistake. As the chapter suggests in outlining the new approaches to leadership, more emphasis is being placed on individuals either to learn to lead themselves or to be good followers. In other words, you are being asked to contribute more to the organization.

Understanding leadership is important beyond the workplace, however. Most of you will work on teams doing school projects over the next few years. In addition, you may serve on committees, student groups, or even neighbourhood or volunteer groups. In all of these instances, you will need to know enough about leadership to understand how to relate to the leader, to take on the role of leader if necessary, and to be an effective team player.

ROADMAP REMINDER

In the previous two chapters we considered ways that the organization shares the vision of the organization with its members through communication and decision-making. In this chapter we consider the role of leadership in sharing the vision, and note that the most recent theories of leadership have increased the emphasis on communicating vision. In the next chapter we consider the role of power and politics as it affects both leaders and subordinates. The distribution of power in the organization is a crucial factor affecting a person's ability to lead.

For Review

1. Trace the development of leadership research.
2. Describe the strengths and weaknesses in the trait approach to leadership.
3. What is the Managerial Grid?.
4. When might leaders be irrelevant?
5. Describe the strengths and weaknesses of a charismatic leader.
6. What are the differences among transactional, transformational and laissez-faire leaders?
7. What is dispered leadership? What are some examples of dispersed leadership?
8. Why do you think effective female and male managers often exhibit similar traits and behaviours?
9. What characteristics define an effective follower?
10. What is moral leadership?

For Discussion

1. Develop an example where you operationalize path-goal theory.
2. Reconcile path-goal theory and substitutes for leadership.
3. What kind of activities could a full-time college or university student pursue that might lead to the perception that he or she is a charismatic leader? In pursuing those activities, what might the student do to enhance this perception of being charismatic?
4. Based on the low representation of women in upper management, to what extent do you think that organizations should actively promote women into the senior ranks of management?

LEARNING ABOUT YOURSELF EXERCISE

Are You a Charismatic Leader?

Instructions: The following statements refer to the possible ways in which you might behave toward others when you are in a leadership role. Please read each statement carefully and decide to what extent it applies to you. Then circle the appropriate number.

To a very great extent	1
To a considerable extent	2
To a moderate extent	3
To a slight extent	4
To little or no extent	5

You ...

Pay close attention to what others say when they are talking	1 2 3 4 5
Communicate clearly	1 2 3 4 5
Are trustworthy	1 2 3 4 5
Care about other people	1 2 3 4 5
Do not put excessive energy into avoiding failure	1 2 3 4 5
Make the work of others more meaningful	1 2 3 4 5
Seem to focus on the key issues in a situation	1 2 3 4 5
Get across your meaning effectively, often in unusual ways	1 2 3 4 5
Can be relied on to follow through on commitments	1 2 3 4 5
Have a great deal of self-respect	1 2 3 4 5
Enjoy taking carefully calculated risks	1 2 3 4 5
Help others feel more competent in what they do	1 2 3 4 5
Have a clear set of priorities	1 2 3 4 5
Are in touch with how others feel	1 2 3 4 5
Rarely change once you have taken a clear position	1 2 3 4 5
Focus on strengths, of yourself and others	1 2 3 4 5
Seem most alive when deeply involved in some project	1 2 3 4 5
Show others that they are all part of the same group	1 2 3 4 5
Get others to focus on the issues you see as important	1 2 3 4 5
Communicate feelings as well as ideas	1 2 3 4 5
Let others know where you stand	1 2 3 4 5
Seem to know just how you "fit" into a group	1 2 3 4 5
Learn from mistakes, do not treat errors as disasters, but as learning	1 2 3 4 5
Are fun to be around	1 2 3 4 5

Turn to page 700 for scoring directions and key.

Source: Marshall Sashkin and William C. Morris, *Experiencing Management*, © 1987 by Addison-Wesley Publishing Company, Inc.

WORKING WITH OTHERS EXERCISE

Practising to Be Charismatic

People who are charismatic engage in the following behaviours:

1. *Project a powerful, confident, and dynamic presence.* This has both verbal and nonverbal components. They use a captivating and engaging voice tone. They convey confidence. They also talk directly to people, maintaining direct eye contact, and holding their body posture in a way that says they're sure of themselves. They speak clearly, avoid stammering, and avoid sprinkling their sentences with non-content phrases such as "ahhh" and "you know."

2. *Articulate an overarching goal.* They have a vision for the future, unconventional ways of achieving the vision, and the ability to communicate the vision to others.

   The vision is a clear statement of where they want to go and how they're going to get there. They are able to persuade others how the achievement of this vision is in the others' self-interest.

   They look for fresh and radically different approaches to problems. The road to achieving their vision is novel but also appropriate to the context.

   They not only have a vision but they're able to get others to buy into it. The real power of Martin Luther King, Jr., was not that he had a dream, but that he could articulate it in terms that made it accessible to millions.

3. *Communicate high-performance expectations and confidence in others' ability to meet these expectations.* They demonstrate their confidence in people by stating ambitious goals for them individually and as a group. They convey absolute belief that they will achieve their expectations.

4. *Are sensitive to the needs of followers.* Charismatic leaders get to know their followers individually. They understand their individual needs and are able to develop intensely personal relationships with each. They do this through encouraging followers to express their points of view, being approachable, genuinely listening to and caring about their followers' concerns, and by asking questions so they can learn what is really important to them.

Now that you know what charismatic leaders do, you get the opportunity to practise projecting charisma.

   a. The class should break into pairs.

   b. Student A's task is to "lead" Student B through a new-student orientation to your college. The orientation should last about 10 to 15 minutes. Assume Student B is new to your college and is unfamiliar with the campus. Remember, Student A should attempt to project himself or herself as charismatic.

   c. Roles now reverse and Student B's task is to "lead" Student A in a 10- to 15-minute program on how to study more effectively for college exams. Take a few minutes to think about what has worked well for you and assume that Student B is a new student interested in improving his or her study habits. Again remember that Student B should attempt to project himself or herself as charismatic.

   d. When both role plays are complete, each pair should assess how well they did in projecting charisma and how they might improve.

Source: This exercise is based on J.M. Howell and P.J. Frost, "A Laboratory Study of Charismatic Leadership," *Organizational Behavior and Human Decision Processes*, April 1989, pp. 243–69.

The Case Against Vision

When Robert J. Eaton took over the post of CEO at Chrysler Corp. in 1992, he had big shoes to fill. The position had been held previously by "Mr. Charisma," Lee Iacocca. Iacocca had assumed the top position at Chrysler in 1980, when the company was on the verge of bankruptcy. In only a few short years, Iacocca had turned Chrysler into a money-making machine. Iacocca's style was bold and visionary. He developed several grand strategies for Chrysler. To make the company immediately profitable, he created a basic compact model—the K car—and used its platform to create a host of new cars including the incredibly successful minivan. To fill the need for subcompacts, he began importing cars from Japan and putting Chrysler Corp. nameplates on them.

But that was then and this is now. Robert Eaton has joined an impressive group of chief executives who no longer accept the notion that leaders need to provide grand visions or long-term strategies for their companies. Instead, they are emphasizing the short-term bottom line.

"Internally, we don't use the word *vision*," says Eaton. "I believe in quantifiable short-term results—things we can all relate to—as opposed to some esoteric thing no one can quantify."

That view is also being articulated by CEOs at IBM, Aetna Life & Casualty, and General Motors. When asked for his recipe for an IBM comeback, the recently appointed chairman, Louis V. Gerstner, said, "The last thing IBM needs right now is a vision." Apple Computer's former CEOs John Sculley and Gil Amelio also did not believe in articulating a vision for the company when they each headed it.

It appears that, at least among some leaders, grand visions are out of fashion. Instead, they're concentrating on the nuts and bolts of running their businesses.

Questions

1. Isn't this short-term focus likely to hurt companies in the longer term?

2. What's the purpose of a grand vision? What takes its place if a company's leader doesn't provide it?

3. Don't organizations need radical new ideas to win in the marketplace?

4. Eaton says his goal for Chrysler is "getting a little bit better every single day." Is that a viable goal for a real "leader"?

Source: Based on D. Lavin, "Robert Eaton Thinks 'Vision' Is Overrated and He's Not Alone," *The Wall Street Journal*, October 4, 1993, p. A1.

Richard Branson

Richard Branson, CEO of Virgin Group Ltd., Britain's largest private company, leads a conglomerate that encompasses more than 120 companies, including Virgin Airlines, Virgin Records, and Virgin Cola. He's even created a beachhead in Canada, establishing Virgin Records in Vancouver in December 1996. How does he maintain responsibility for so many companies? By delegating.

Branson is free-spirited, innovative, and irreverent, and his company is just like him. He relishes the opportunity to be different, and he enjoys a challenge. He has repeatedly gone after the industry giants and believes he sees how to do things better than them.

Branson doesn't believe in micromanaging organizations. He has only a thin corporate structure beneath him, no bureaucracy, and no corporate headquarters. Each of his small companies (none has more than 20 percent of market share in an area) is headed by managing directors that run them. The directors have lots of freedom to make decisions. They also have a stake in the company, so they can run the company as if it were their own.

Branson says, "My job is empowering people and helping them to get up and go, and then leave them to do it." This is evidence of his charismatic leadership—he can trust those he's empowered to run the Virgin companies in successful ways. Branson's style of management ensures also that he will not be spread too thin, as those running each of the companies are responsible for making decisions.

Branson's charisma is demonstrated outside of the workplace as well. He has enormous personal popularity in Britain. In a 1997 survey asking Londoners to name their choice for mayor, he was the hands-down winner. An impressive approval rating indeed for a free spirit in a country known for its conformity.

Questions

1. How does charisma make it possible for Richard Branson to run the 120 or so businesses of Virgin Group Ltd.?

2. Why is it possible for Branson to have almost no bureaucracy in his company?

3. What kinds of limitations might be associated with Branson's charismatic style?

Source: Based on "Richard Branson," *Venture 613*; aired October 20, 1996.

Lead, follow, or

get out of the

way!

– Anonymous

POINT

Leaders Make a Real Difference!

There can be little question that the success of an organization, or any group within an organization, depends largely on the quality of its leadership. Whether in business, government, education, medicine, or religion, the quality of an organization's leadership determines the quality of the organization itself. Successful leaders anticipate change, vigorously exploit opportunities, motivate their followers to higher levels of productivity, correct poor performance, and lead the organization toward its objectives.

The importance relegated to the leadership function is well known. Rarely does a week go by that we don't hear or read about some leadership concern: "President Fails to Provide the Leadership America Needs!" "The Conservative Party Searches for New Leadership!" "Is Steve Jobs Taking the CEO Position at Apple?" A review of the leadership literature led two academics to conclude that the research shows "a consistent effect for leadership explaining 20 to 45 percent of the variance on relevant organizational outcomes."[1]

Why is leadership so important to an organization's success? The answer lies in the need for coordination and control. Organizations exist to achieve objectives that are either impossible or extremely inefficient to achieve if done by individuals acting alone. The organization itself is a coordination and control mechanism. Rules, policies, job descriptions, and authority hierarchies are illustrations of devices created to facilitate coordination and control. But leadership, too, contributes toward integrating various job activities, coordinating communication between organizational subunits, monitoring activities, and controlling deviations from standard. No amount of rules and regulations can replace the experienced leader who can make rapid and firm decisions.

The importance of leadership is not lost on those who staff organizations. Corporations, government agencies, school systems, and institutions of all shapes and sizes cumulatively spend billions of dollars every year to recruit, select, evaluate, and train individuals for leadership positions. The best evidence, however, of the importance that organizations place on leadership roles is exhibited in salary schedules. Leaders are routinely paid ten, twenty, or more times the salary of those in nonleadership positions. For example, the head of General Motors earns more than $1.5 million annually. The highest skilled auto worker, in contrast, earns under $50 000 a year. The president of this auto worker's union makes better than $100 000 a year. Police officers typically earn $30 000 to $45 000 a year. Their boss probably earns 25 percent more, and his or her boss another 25 percent. The pattern is well established. The more responsibility a leader has, as evidenced by his or her level in the organization, the more he or she earns. Would organizations voluntarily pay their leaders so much more than their nonleaders if they didn't strongly believe that leaders make a real difference? ■

Source:
[1] D.V. Day and R.G. Lord, "Executive Leadership and Organizational Performance: Suggestions for a New Theory and Methodology," *Journal of Management*, Fall 1988, pp. 453–64.

counterPOINT

Leaders Don't Make a Difference!

Given the resources that have been spent on studying, selecting, and training leaders, you'd expect there would be overwhelming evidence supporting the positive effect of leadership on organizational performance, but that's not the case!

Currently, the two most popular approaches to leadership are contingency models and the study of charisma. For the most part, both operate under the naive assumption that through selection and/or training, leaders can learn to exhibit certain behaviours that, when properly matched to the situation, will result in improved employee and organizational performance. There are a number of flaws in this assumption.

First, leaders exist in a social system that constrains their behaviour. They have to live with role expectations that define behaviours that are acceptable and unacceptable. Pressures to conform to the expectations of peers, subordinates, and superiors all limit the range of behaviours that a leader can exhibit.

Second, organizational rules, procedures, policies, and historical precedents all act to limit a leader's unilateral control over decisions and resources. Hiring decisions, for instance, must be made according to procedures. And budget allocations are typically heavily influenced by previous budget precedents.

Third, there are factors outside the organization that leaders can't control but which have a large bearing on organizational performance. For example, consider the executive in a home-construction firm. Costs are largely determined by the operations of the commodities and labour markets, and demand is largely dependent on interest rates, availability of mortgage money, and economic conditions that are affected by governmental policies over which the executive has little control. Or consider the case of school superintendents. They have little control over

birth rates and community economic development, both of which profoundly affect school system budgets. While a leader may react to problems as they arise or attempt to forecast and anticipate external changes, he or she has little influence over the environment. On the contrary, the environment typically puts significant limits and constraints on the leader.

Finally, the trend in recent years is toward leaders playing a smaller and smaller role in organizational activities. Important decisions are increasingly made by committees, not individuals. Additionally, the widespread popularity of employee involvement programs, the empowerment movement, and self-managed work teams has contributed to reducing any specific leader's influence.

There is a basic myth associated with leadership. We believe in attribution—when something happens, we believe something has *caused* it. Leaders play that role in organizations, and the fact that leaders earn higher pay than nonleaders is a symbolic gesture that organizations have created to further add to the impression that leaders make a difference. So while leaders may not really matter, the *belief* in leadership does. Although leaders take the credit for successes and the blame for failures, a more realistic conclusion would probably be that, except in times of rapid growth, change, or crisis, leaders don't make much of a difference in an organization's actual performance. However, people want to believe that leadership is the cause of performance changes, particularly at the extremes. ■

Sources: Ideas in this argument came from J. Pfeffer, "The Ambiguity of Leadership," *Academy of Management Review*, January 1977, pp. 104–11; A.B. Thomas, "Does Leadership Make a Difference to Organizational Performance?" *Administrative Science Quarterly*, September 1988, pp. 388–400; C.C. Manz and H.P. Sims, Jr., "SuperLeadership: Beyond the Myth of Heroic Leadership," *Organizational Dynamics*, Spring 1991, pp. 18–35; and G. Gemmill and J. Oakley, "Leadership: An Alienating Social Myth?" *Human Relations*, February 1992, pp. 113–29.

PROGRESSIVE CASE • PART 3

Lee Simpson: Leading and Making Decisions

"I think my strength as a leader is in allowing people to see that there is a clear path to follow and that we are making progress towards that goal or along that path. I think that I have a knack for working with a group of people and helping them feel part of something good, interesting, sound, and sometimes fun," says Lee Simpson. She describes her leadership style as flexible, and sees that as a requirement for being a good leader.

Simpson notes that she can be both authoritative and consultative, depending upon the situation. "I believe there is a time for consultation and getting everybody to work together because it is the right thing to do and I believe there is time to simply state 'Here is the problem, and this is how we are going to fix it'." She does not think that leaders should shy away from being authoritative just because it seems the politically correct thing to do. Sometimes leaders have to take on the mantle of responsibility.

Simpson encourages a more consultative environment by providing clear communication with her employees. She writes out a goal board each quarter, with target dates accompanying each goal for her division. One copy of the goal board hangs right outside Simpson's door, so that everyone readily knows what the goals are. It has everything on it, from 'Here's how we are doing on our profit target versus where we thought we were going' to 'We will have the carpet in the reception area fixed by July 12th'."

Simpson notes that being a leader is not as simple as choosing between either the authoritative style or the consultative style. Instead, leaders need to use a variety of styles, depending on situations. She notes that one of her styles is to take on the role of learner, such as when she's had to learn the production process in publishing. "My leadership style, when I need to know something, is to make sure that I have the best possible resources for our team to be guided through new experiences. Sometimes it's extremely important that you recognize you are not the leader and find somebody who can be."

Simpson says that her decision-making style is swift and decisive. She tends to take both an intuitive and a rational approach to her decision-making. Even if she feels from her gut that a decision is an appropriate one, she writes down all of the pros and cons of a decision and then evaluates her intuitive decision against the weight of the evidence. "I am very disciplined about this because I do make decisions very quickly. I have to make sure I am making them for the right reasons and sometimes I have to reverse myself. Sometimes I simply cannot find the right number of pros for making the decision that my gut tells me to make. So I have to rethink it, but by and large, I make decisions quickly." While she notes that delaying making a decision can be an effective tactic, she argues that delays should not occur simply because a person can't figure out how to make a decision.

Simpson acknowledges that making decisions is not always easy. She recommends that we examine our decision-making process for clues as to whether we are making the right decisions. For instance, she describes a difficult decision she made about running a specific advertisement in *Chatelaine*. The ad, worth over $50 000 in revenue, featured a rather erotic image of a male and a female. Simpson says that when she was first approached with the ad copy, "I looked at it and thought 'Oh, this is beautiful,' and my gut said, 'No problem—run this'." But she also knew that nudity might possibly upset *Chatelaine*'s readership. To test her own positive reaction to the ad against concerns about possible readership reaction, Simpson put together an informal focus group. The group gave mixed reactions to the ad and with no clear outcome she decided that *Chatelaine* would run it—only to have 300 readers protest her decision, including 100 who cancelled their subscriptions, all saying they were shocked and appalled at the material. A complaint was even made to Advertising Standards Canada, which ruled that *Chatelaine* is an adult women's magazine and that there was nothing wrong with the ad. As Simpson notes, the ruling meant that *Chatelaine* had the right to run the ad again. "But this time, I did the right thing and picked up the phone and said to the advertiser, 'I can't run

your ad again'." In this instance Simpson says she made the "right" decision too late. "I knew right from the start, by the amount of time I was taking to think it through, that I shouldn't run it, but I wanted it because I liked it. I thought it was beautiful. I still do." But her own reactions to the ad did not necessarily reflect the will of the *Chatelaine* readers.

Simpson says that the other difficulty in decision-making that crops up is that occasionally she finds it difficult to disengage after a decision has been made. She will start to wonder whether there might have been a better way to handle the situation. While this doesn't happen very often to her, she thinks it's best to simply make decisions and move forward, rather than trying to second guess herself later. In the fast-paced and complex environment of organizations today, that is probably good advice for all of us.

Questions

1. Simpson describes a contingency model of leadership, moving from authoritative to consultative as needed. What influence might this style have on employees?

2. What do you think Simpson means when she says that leaders must also be learners?

3. What role would you say intuition plays when Simpson makes decisions?

4. Does supplementing intuition with a rational approach to decision-making suggest that intuition is not a valuable means for making decisions?

Power and Politics

ROADMAP

LEARNING OBJECTIVES

After studying this chapter, you should be able to

- Contrast leadership and power

- Define the five bases of power

- Clarify what creates dependency in power relationships

- List seven power tactics and their contingencies

- Explain how sexual harassment is about the abuse of power

- Describe the importance of a political perspective

- List those individual and organizational factors that stimulate political behaviour

- Identify seven techniques for managing the impression one makes on others

- Explain how defensive behaviours can protect an individual's self-interest

- List the three questions that can help determine whether a political action is ethical

The Canadian industrial environment is characterized very much by power and politics. As an example, on November 19, 1997, the Canadian Union of Postal Workers (CUPW) went on strike after Canada Post's management and CUPW failed to reach an agreement on their many differences.[1] Negotiations had started four months prior to the strike, but two government-appointed conciliators and a mediator were unsuccessful in getting both sides to reach an agreement. After the strike began, the federal government waited nine days, hoping that mediation would bring the two sides together. When this did not happen, Ottawa legislated CUPW's strikers back to work, 15 days after they had gone out on strike. Union officials were upset by the wage settlement the government chose to impose. The imposed settlement is far from what CUPW wanted and is somewhat less than the offer Canada Post had on the bargaining table when talks finally collapsed. CUPW director of research Geoff Bickerton said this about the imposed settlement: "I can think of only one reason the government acted as it did—pure vindictiveness, payback time for the workers."

Political comments were not limited to CUPW, however. The Liberal government, through both Labour Minister Lawrence MacAulay and Public Works Minister Alfonso Gagliano, continually described the settlement as "fair." However, both the Reform and NDP labour critics claimed that the government had mismanaged the affair. ■

Power has been described as the last dirty word. Politics is considered an equally negative word. It is easier for most of us to discuss money than it is to talk about power. People who have it deny it, people who want it try not to appear to be seeking it, and those who are good at getting it are secretive about how they got it or about the politics of obtaining it.[2] Organizational behaviour researchers have learned a lot in recent years about how people gain and use power in organizations. Part of using power in organizations is engaging in organizational politics.

A major theme throughout this chapter is that power is a natural process in any group or organization. As such, you need to know how it is acquired and exercised if you're going to fully understand organizational behaviour. As part of our discussion on power, we inform you about empowerment to remind you that in the workplace of the 21st century, managers are often expected to share their power, which means that employees are having to learn how to accept and use power appropriately. Although you may have heard the phrase "power corrupts, and absolute power corrupts absolutely," power is not always bad. As one author has noted, most medicines can kill if taken in the wrong amount, and thousands die each year in automobile accidents, but we don't abandon chemicals or cars because of the dangers associated with them. Rather, we consider danger an incentive to get training and information that will help us to use these forces productively.[3] The same applies to *power*. It's a reality of organizational life, and it's not going to go away. It is increasingly shared by managers and employees. By learning how power works in organizations, you'll be able to use your political knowledge to help you be a more effective manager.

A Definition of Power

power
A capacity that A has to influence the behaviour of B so that B acts in accordance with A's wishes.

Power refers to a capacity that A has to influence the behaviour of B, so that B acts in accordance with A's wishes.[4] This definition implies a *potential* that need not be actualized to be effective and a *dependency* relationship. In addition, power may exist but not be used. It is, therefore, a capacity or potential. One can have power but not impose it.

dependency
B's relationship to A when A possesses something that B requires.

Probably the most important aspect of power is that it is a function of **dependency**. The greater B's dependence on A, the greater is A's power in the relationship. Dependence, in turn, is based on alternatives that B perceives and the importance that B places on the alternative(s) that A controls. A person can have power over you only if he or she controls something you desire. For example, if you want a post-secondary degree and have to pass a certain course to get it, and your current instructor is the only faculty member who teaches that course, he or she has power over you. Your alternatives are highly limited, and you place a high degree of importance on obtaining a passing grade. Similarly, if you're attending college or university on funds totally provided by your parents, you probably recognize the power that they hold over you. You're dependent on them for financial support. But once you're out of school, have a job, and are making a solid income, your parents' power is reduced significantly. Who among us, though, has not known or heard of the rich relative who is able to control a large number of family members merely through the implicit or explicit threat of "writing them out of the will"?

Contrasting Leadership and Power

A careful comparison of our description of power with our description of leadership in Chapter 11 reveals that the two concepts are closely intertwined. Leaders use power as a means of attaining group goals. Leaders achieve goals, and power is a means of facilitating their achievement.

What differences are there between the two terms? One difference relates to goal compatibility. Power does not require goal compatibility, merely dependence. Leadership, on the other hand, requires some congruence between the goals of the leader and those being led. A second difference relates to the direction of influence. Leadership focuses on the downward influence on one's subordinates. It minimizes the importance of lateral and upward influence patterns. Power does not. Still another difference deals with research emphasis. Leadership research, for the most part, emphasizes style. It seeks answers to such questions as: How supportive should a leader be? How much decision-making should be shared with subordinates? In contrast, the research on power has tended to encompass a broader area and focus on tactics for gaining compliance. It has gone beyond the individual as exerciser because power can be used by groups as well as by individuals to control other individuals or groups.

Bases of Power

Where does power come from? What is it that gives an individual or a group influence over others? The answer to these questions is a five-category classification scheme identified by French and Raven.[5] They proposed that there were five bases or sources of power: coercive, reward, legitimate, expert, and referent (see Exhibit 12-1).

Coercive Power

coercive power
Power that is based on fear.

The **coercive power** base is defined by French and Raven as being dependent on fear. One reacts to this power out of fear of the negative results that

---

Exhibit 12-1
Measuring Bases of Power

Does a person have one or more of the five bases of power? Affirmative responses to the following questions can answer this question:

- The person can make things difficult for people, and you want to avoid getting him or her angry. [coercive power]

- The person is able to give special benefits or rewards to people, and you find it advantageous to trade favours with him or her. [reward power]

- The person has the right, considering his or her position and your job responsibilities, to expect you to comply with legitimate requests. [legitimate power]

- The person has the experience and knowledge to earn your respect, and you defer to his or her judgment in some matters. [expert power]

- You like the person and enjoy doing things for him or her. [referent power]

Source: G. Yukl and C.M. Falbe, "Importance of Different Power Sources in Downward and Lateral Relations," *Journal of Applied Psychology*, June 1991, p. 417. With permission.

might occur if one failed to comply. It rests on the application, or the threat of application, of physical sanctions such as the infliction of pain, the generation of frustration through restriction of movement, or the controlling by force of basic physiological or safety needs.

Of all the bases of power available, the power to hurt others is possibly most often used, most often condemned, and most difficult to control: the state relies on its military and legal resources to intimidate nations, or even its own citizens. Businesses rely upon the control of economic resources. Schools and universities rely upon their rights to deny students formal education, while religious institutions threaten individuals of dire consequences in the afterlife if they do not conduct themselves properly in this life. At the personal level, individuals exercise coercive power through a reliance upon physical strength, verbal facility, or the ability to grant or withhold emotional support from others. These bases provide the individual with the means to physically harm, bully, humiliate, or deny love to others.[6]

At the organizational level, A has coercive power over B if A can dismiss, suspend, or demote B, assuming that B values his or her job. Similarly, if A can assign B work activities that B finds unpleasant or treat B in a manner that B finds embarrassing, A possesses coercive power over B.

Reward Power

reward power
Power that achieves compliance based on the ability to distribute rewards that others view as valuable.

The opposite of coercive power is **reward power**. People comply with the wishes or directives of another because doing so produces positive benefits; therefore, one who can distribute rewards that others view as valuable will have power over those others. These rewards can be anything that another person values. In an organizational context, we think of money, favourable performance appraisals, promotions, interesting work assignments, friendly colleagues, important information, and preferred work shifts or sales territories. Coercive power and reward power are actually counterparts of each other. If you can remove something of positive value from another or inflict something of negative value upon him or her, you have coercive power over that person. If you can give someone something of positive value or remove something of negative value, you have reward power over that person. Again, as with coercive power, you don't have to be a manager to be able to exert influence through rewards. Rewards such as friendliness, acceptance, and praise are available to everyone in an organization. To the degree that an individual seeks such rewards, your ability to give or withhold them gives you power over that individual.

Legitimate Power

legitimate power
The power a person receives as a result of his or her position in the formal hierarchy of an organization.

In formal groups and organizations, probably the most frequent access to one or more of the power bases is one's structural position. This is called **legitimate power**. It represents the power a person receives as a result of his or her position in the formal hierarchy of an organization.

Positions of authority include coercive and reward powers. Legitimate power, however, is broader than the power to coerce and reward. Specifically, it includes acceptance by members of an organization of the authority of a position. When school principals, bank presidents, or army captains speak (assuming that their directives are viewed to be within the authority of their positions), teachers, tellers, and lieutenants listen and usually comply. You will note in Exhibit 12-2 that one of the men in the meeting identifies himself as the rule maker, which means that he has legitimate power.

Exhibit 12-2

"I was just going to say 'Well, I don't make the rules.' But, of course, I _do_ make the rules."

Source: Drawing by Leo Cullum in *The New Yorker*. Copyright © 1986 *The New Yorker Magazine*. Reprinted by permission.

Expert Power

expert power
Influence based on special skills or knowledge.

Expert power is influence wielded as a result of expertise, special skill, or knowledge. Expertise has become one of the most powerful sources of influence as the world has become more technologically oriented. As jobs become more specialized, we become increasingly dependent on experts to achieve goals. So, while it is generally acknowledged that physicians have expertise and hence expert power—most of us follow the advice that our doctor gives us—you should also recognize that computer specialists, tax accountants, solar engineers, industrial psychologists, and other specialists are able to wield power as a result of their expertise.

Referent Power

referent power
Influence based on possession by an individual of desirable resources or personal traits.

The last category of influence that French and Raven identified was **referent power**. Its base is identification with a person who has desirable resources or personal traits. If I admire and identify with you, you can exercise power over me because I want to please you.

Referent power develops out of admiration of another and a desire to be like that person. In a sense, then, it is a lot like charisma. If you admire someone to the point of modelling your behaviour and attitudes after him or her, this person possesses referent power over you. Referent power explains why celebrities are paid millions of dollars to endorse products in commercials.

Microsoft Chairman Bill Gates has *legitimate power* as co-founder and chairman of Microsoft. His expert power is based on his software development expertise. Gates also has *referent power*, because his employees look up to him and admire his incredible accomplishments.

Roots
www.roots.com/home.html

Marketing research shows that people such as Elvis Stojko can influence your choice of breakfast drinks or your choice of computer printers, and some advertisers (such as Toronto-based Roots Canada Ltd., for example) are hoping to use the "bad boy" image of Olympic gold-medallist and snowboarder Ross Rebagliati to convince people to buy products. With a little practice, you and I could probably deliver as smooth a sales pitch as these celebrities, but the buying public doesn't identify with you and me. In organizations, if you are articulate, domineering, physically imposing, or charismatic, you hold personal characteristics that may be used to get others to do what you want.

Dependency: The Key to Power

Earlier in this chapter it was said that probably the most important aspect of power is that it is a function of dependence. In this section, we show how an understanding of dependency is central to furthering your understanding of power itself.

The General Dependency Postulate

Let's begin with a general postulate: *The greater B's dependency on A, the greater the power A has over B.* When you possess anything that others require but that you alone control, you make them dependent upon you and, therefore, you gain power over them.[7] Dependency, then, is inversely proportional to the alternative sources of supply. If something is plentiful, possession of it will not increase your power. If everyone is intelligent, intelligence gives no special advantage. Similarly, among the superrich, money is no longer power. But, as the old saying goes, "In the land of the blind, the one-eyed man is king!" If you can create a monopoly by controlling information, prestige, or anything that others crave, they become dependent on you. Conversely, the more that you can expand your options, the less power you place in the hands of others. This explains, for example, why most organizations develop multiple suppliers rather than give their business to only one. It also explains why so many of us aspire to financial independence. Fi-

Roots hired Ross Rebagliati as a spokesperson after his controversial Gold medal performance in the 1998 Winter Olympics. The Toronto-based company was relying on Rebagliati's *referent* power with teens and twenty-somethings to increase sales.

nancial independence reduces the power that others can have over us.

In our discussion of leadership in Chapter 11, we noted that Rowland Fleming, president and CEO of the Toronto Stock Exchange (TSE), was having a difficult time with the board of the TSE. The board reminded Fleming of his dependency on them when they told him that they, not he, were in charge, and that his job was to carry out the strategy set by the board and TSE committees. However, Steve Jobs of Apple Computer, also featured in Chapter 11, is an example where the board is dependent on the leader. Jobs refused to accept the position of CEO while leading Apple through a difficult period in the summer and fall of 1997. The board was unable to find someone who would assume that role, given Jobs' strong leadership. So, for the moment, the Apple board is dependent on Jobs to lead Apple through to profitability.

Apple Computer
www.apple.com/

What Creates Dependency?

Dependency is increased when the resource you control is important, scarce, and non-substitutable.[8]

IMPORTANCE If nobody wants what you've got, there is no dependency. To create dependency, the thing(s) you control must be perceived as being important. It's been found, for instance, that organizations actively seek to avoid uncertainty.[9] We should therefore expect that those individuals or groups who can absorb an organization's uncertainty will be perceived as controlling an important resource. For instance, a study of industrial organizations found that the marketing departments in these firms were consistently rated as the most powerful.[10] The researcher concluded that the most critical uncertainty facing these firms was selling their products. This might suggest that during a labour strike, the organization's negotiating representatives have increased power, or that engineers, as a group, would be more powerful at Intel than at Procter & Gamble. These inferences appear to be generally valid. Labour negotiators do become more powerful within the

personnel area and the organization as a whole during periods of labour strife. At organizations such as Intel, which are heavily technologically oriented and highly dependent on its engineers to maintain its products' technical advantages and quality, engineers are clearly a powerful group. At Procter & Gamble, marketing is the name of the game, and marketers are the most powerful occupational group. These examples support not only the view that the ability to reduce uncertainty increases a group's importance, and hence its power, but also that what's important is situational. It varies between organizations and undoubtedly also varies over time within any given organization.

SCARCITY   As noted previously, if something is plentiful, possession of it will not increase your power. A resource must be perceived as scarce to create dependency.

This can help to explain how low-ranking members in an organization who have important knowledge not available to high-ranking members gain power over the high-ranking members. Possession of a scarce resource—in this case, important knowledge—makes the high-ranking member dependent on the low-ranking member. This also helps to make sense out of behaviours of low-ranking members that otherwise might seem illogical, such as destroying the procedure manuals that describe how a job is done, refusing to train people in their jobs or even to show others exactly what they do, creating specialized language and terminology that inhibit others from understanding their jobs, or operating in secrecy so an activity will appear more complex and difficult than it really is. The use of knowledge and the power it brings is something that will be increasingly important in organizations of the 21st century. As we previously mentioned in Chapter 2, one of the major tasks of organizations is to figure out ways to handle the volume of information that is available. Individuals who acquire excellent information handling abilities will have more power in their organizations.

The scarcity–dependency relationship can further be seen in the power of occupational categories. Individuals in occupations in which the supply of personnel is low relative to demand can negotiate compensation and benefit packages that are far more attractive than can those in occupations where there is an abundance of candidates. For example, college and university administrators have no problem today finding English instructors. There are more individuals who have degrees enabling them to work as English instructors than there are positions available in Canada. The market for corporate finance professors, by contrast, is extremely tight, with the demand high and the supply limited. The result is that the bargaining power of finance faculty allows them to negotiate higher salaries, lighter teaching loads, and other benefits.

NON-SUBSTITUTABILITY   The more that a resource has no viable substitutes, the more power that control over that resource provides. In the case of Apple Computer, most observers as well as the board believe that no one other than Steve Jobs can turn the company around. Higher education again provides another excellent example of non-substitutability. In universities where there are strong pressures for the faculty to publish books and journal articles, we can say that a department head's power over a faculty member is inversely related to that member's publication record. The more recognition the faculty member receives through publication, the more mobile he or she is. That is, since other universities want faculty members who are highly published and visible, there is an increased demand for his or her services. Although the concept of tenure can act to alter this relationship by restrict-

ing the department head's alternatives, those faculty members with little or no publications have the least mobility and are subject to the greatest influence from their superiors.

Identifying Where the Power Is

How do you determine where the power is in an organization at any given point in time? We can answer this question from both the departmental and individual manager levels.

At the department level, answers to the following questions will give you a good idea of how powerful that department is: What proportion of the organization's top-level managers came up through the department? Is the department represented on important interdepartmental teams and committees? How does the salary of the senior manager in the department compare with others at his or her level? Is the department located in the headquarters building? What's the average size of offices for people working in the department compared to offices in other departments? Has the department grown in number of employees relative to other departments? How does the promotion rate for people in the department compare to other units? Has the department's budget allocation been increasing relative to other departments?[11]

At the level of the individual manager, there are certain symbols you should be on the lookout for that suggest that a manager has power.[12] These include the ability to intercede favourably on behalf of someone in trouble in the organization, to get approval for expenditures beyond the budget, to get items on the agenda at major meetings, and to get fast access to top decision-makers in the organization.

Power Tactics

power tactics
Ways in which individuals translate power bases into specific actions.

This section is a logical extension of our previous discussions. We've reviewed where power comes from. Now we move to the topic of **power tactics** to learn how employees translate their power bases into specific actions. Recent research indicates that there are standardized ways by which powerholders attempt to get what they want.[13]

When 165 managers were asked to write essays describing an incident in which they influenced their bosses, co-workers, or subordinates, 370 power tactics grouped into 14 categories were identified. These answers were condensed, rewritten into a 58-item questionnaire, and given to over 750 employees. These respondents were asked not only how they went about influencing others at work but also for the possible reasons for influencing the target person. The results, which are summarized here, give us considerable insight into power tactics—how managerial employees influence others and the conditions under which one tactic is chosen over another.[14]

The findings identified seven tactical dimensions or strategies:

- *Reason*: Using facts and data to make a logical or rational presentation of ideas;

- *Friendliness*: Using flattery, creating goodwill, acting humble, and being friendly prior to making a request;

- *Coalition*: Getting the support of other people in the organization to back up the request;

- *Bargaining*: Using negotiation through the exchange of benefits or favours;

- *Assertiveness*: Using a direct and forceful approach such as demanding compliance with requests, repeating reminders, ordering individuals to do what is asked, and pointing out that rules require compliance;

- *Higher authority*: Gaining the support of higher levels in the organization to back up requests;

- *Sanctions*: Using organizationally derived rewards and punishments such as preventing or promising a salary increase, threatening to give an unsatisfactory performance evaluation, or withholding a promotion.

The researchers found that employees do not rely on the seven tactics equally. However, as shown in Exhibit 12-3, the most popular strategy was the use of reason, regardless of whether the influence was directed upward or downward. Additionally, the researchers uncovered four contingency variables that affect the selection of a power tactic: the manager's relative power; the manager's objectives for wanting to influence; the manager's expectation of the target person's willingness to comply; and the organization's culture.

A manager's relative power affects the selection of tactics in two ways. First, managers who control resources that are valued by others or who are perceived to be in positions of dominance use a greater variety of tactics than do those with less power. Second, managers with power use assertiveness with greater frequency than do those with less power. Initially, we can expect that most managers will attempt to use simple requests and reason. Assertiveness is a back-up strategy, used when the target of influence refuses

---

**Exhibit 12-3
Popularity of Power Tactics**

	When Managers Influenced Superiors*	When Managers Influenced Subordinates
Most Popular	Reason	Reason
	Coalition	Assertiveness
	Friendliness	Friendliness
	Bargaining	Coalition
	Assertiveness	Bargaining
	Higher authority	Higher authority
Least Popular		Sanctions

*The dimension of sanctions is omitted in the scale that measures upward influence

Source: Reprinted, by permission of the publisher, from "Patterns of Managerial Influence: Shotgun Managers, Tacticians, and Bystanders," by D. Kipnis et al., *Organizational Dynamics*, Winter 1984, p. 62. © 1984 Periodicals Division, American Management Association, New York. All rights reserved.

or appears reluctant to comply with the request. Resistance leads to managers using more directive strategies. Typically, they shift from using simple requests to insisting that their demands be met. The manager with relatively little power is more likely to stop trying to influence others when he or she encounters resistance because he or she perceives the costs associated with assertiveness as unacceptable.

Managers vary their power tactics in relation to their objectives. When managers seek benefits from a superior, they tend to rely on kind words and the promotion of pleasant relationships; that is, they use friendliness. In comparison, managers attempting to persuade their superiors to accept new ideas usually rely on reason. This matching of tactics to objectives also holds true for downward influence. For example, managers use reason to sell ideas to subordinates and friendliness to obtain favours.

The manager's expectations of success guide his or her choice of tactics. When past experience indicates a high probability of success, managers use simple requests to gain compliance. Where success is less predictable, managers are more tempted to use assertiveness and sanctions to achieve their objectives.

Finally, we know that organizational cultures differ markedly. For example, some are warm, relaxed, and supportive; others are formal and conservative. The organizational culture in which a manager works, therefore, will have a significant bearing on defining which tactics are considered appropriate. Some cultures encourage the use of friendliness; some encourage reason; and still others rely on sanctions and assertiveness. The organization itself will influence which subset of power tactics managers will view as acceptable for use. The Working With Others Exercise gives you the opportunity to explore how power is used differently, depending on where in the organization one is located.

Empowerment: Giving Power to Employees

Thus far our discussion has implied, at least to some extent, that power is something that is more likely to reside in the hands of management to be used as part of their interaction with employees. However, in today's workplace, there is a movement toward sharing more power with employees by putting them in teams and also by making them responsible for some of the decisions regarding their jobs. Organizational specialists refer to this increasing responsibility as **empowerment**. We briefly mentioned in Chapter 11 that one of the current trends in leadership is empowering workers.

empowerment
Giving employees responsibility for what they do.

Although many organizations talk about empowering their employees, not all organizations achieve this goal. Some organizations tell employees that they have decision-making responsibility, but they do not give them the authority to carry out their decisions. In order for an employee to be fully empowered, he or she needs access to the information required to make decisions, rewards for acting in appropriate, responsible ways, and authority to make the necessary decisions. Empowerment means that the employee understands how his or her job fits into the organization and is able to make decisions regarding job action in light of the organization's purpose and mission.

The concept of empowerment has caused much cynicism in many workplaces. Employees are told that they are empowered, and yet they do not feel that they have the authority to act, or they feel that their manager still

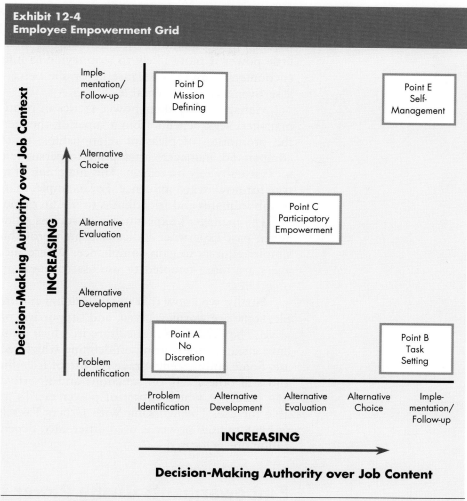

Exhibit 12-4
Employee Empowerment Grid

Source: R.C. Ford and M.D. Fottler, "Empowerment: A Mattter of Degree", *Academy of Management Executive*, August 1995, p. 24.

micro-manages their performance. Some managers are reluctant to empower their employees, because this means sharing or even relinquishing their own power. Other managers worry that empowered workers may decide to work on goals and jobs that are not as closely aligned to the organizational goals.

One study that helps us to understand the degrees of empowerment looks at jobs in terms of both their context and their content.[15] The **content** of a job represents the tasks and procedures necessary for carrying out a particular job. The **context** of a job is the reason for the job being done and reflects the organizational mission, objectives, and setting. The context of the job would also include the organization's structure, culture, and reward systems.

When employees are empowered, as we noted above, they are given decision-making authority over some aspect of their job. In Chapter 10 we described the steps of the decision-making model as identifying the problem, discovering alternative solutions, evaluating the alternatives, making a choice, and then carrying out the choice. We can use this same decision-making model to understand the degree of empowerment an employee has. Exhibit 12-4 links the steps of the decision-making model to job-content and job-context decisions.

job content
The tasks and procedures necessary for carrying out a particular job.

job context
The reason for the job and the setting in which it is done.

As shown on the horizontal grid of Exhibit 12-4, an employee's (or team's) decision-making authority over job content increases as he or she is permitted to complete more of the steps. At the very left the employee has little power, and at the very right, the employee has a great deal of power. On the vertical axis, an employee's (or team's) decision-making authority over job context increases similarly. On the very bottom an employee has very little power, while at the very top the employee has a great deal of power.

Exhibit 12-4 indicates five particular points on the grid, representing stages of employee power, including no discretion, task setting, participatory empowerment, mission defining, and self-management. The five types of power and their effects on employees are:[16]

- *No Discretion* (Point A) is the typical assembly-line job—highly routine and repetitive. The worker is assigned the task, given no discretion, and most likely monitored by a supervisor. When employees have no power, they are less likely to be satisfied with their jobs. They can also be less productive because the lack of discretion may cause a "rule mentality" where the employee chooses to operate strictly by the rules, rather than showing initiative.

- *Task Setting* (Point B) is typical of most workers who have been empowered today. The worker can determine how the job gets done but has no discretion in determining what jobs get done. Management defines the general tasks, giving the employee discretion over the timing and procedures for completing the task. Employees who are granted task-setting power may become more energized about their work, as they look to find new ways to do the work, and they may develop new skills to help them do the work in a better fashion. Consequently, many workers will feel more motivated and satisfied when they have task-setting power, leading them to do higher-quality work.

- *Participatory Empowerment* (Point C) represents the situation of autonomous work groups that are given some decision-making authority over both job content and job context. There is some evidence of higher job satisfaction and productivity in such groups.[17] One of the best-known success stories of autonomous work groups is the Saturn plant of General Motors in Spring Hill, Tennessee. This plant is described in this chapter's OB in the News feature.

- *Mission Defining* (Point D) represents a more unusual situation in the workplace, although not an impossible one. It is not unusual for a design team, for instance, to set out the broad goals of a project, but not be responsible for carrying out the tasks of that project. For instance, in a number of business schools in recent years, design teams have tried to restructure MBA programs. Often the design team set out the broad goals of what a new program would look like, but the actual implementation was left to a set of instructors who found it more difficult to implement the design.

- *Self-Management* (Point E) represents employees who have total decision-making power for both job content and job context. Granting an employee this much power requires considerable faith on the part of management that the employee will carry out the goals and mission of the organization in an effective manner. Generally this sort of power is reserved for those in top management, although it is also sometimes granted to high-level salespeople. Obviously this kind of power can be very rewarding to those who hold it.

General Motors Canada
www.gmcanada.com

OB IN THE NEWS

Saturn Workers Vote for Continued Empowerment

Alternative work schedules, which not too long ago were viewed as disruptions to the office workplace and as a "mothers only" perk, have become an important strategic tool as organizations try to offer the flexibility their employees need in a changing society.

General Motors' Saturn car plant faced some uncertainty about whether their employees, members of the United Auto Workers, would vote in March 1998 to keep their current contract. Workers were asked to choose between the current "innovative contract, which encourages worker-management co-operation," and a traditional-style contract "that includes job and pay protection and more workplace rules."

Although the union members might not have thought about it this way, they were voting about the extent to which they wanted to continue being empowered. Empowerment is what they overwhelmingly chose: two-thirds of the almost 6200 workers voting approved retaining the innovative contract.

Saturn's workers have more freedom than many autoworkers. They work in teams and are given more responsibility for quality and costs. This freedom does come at a price, however. Pay is tied to performance, and recently Saturn sales have slumped, shrinking worker bonuses. The bonuses are tied to profit, quality, productivity, training and other benchmarks. Production at the plant was cut in 1997 after sales fell 10 percent last year.

General Motors Corp.'s Saturn division wanted the workers to support their innovative contract, even though it initially meant that more than 6000 workers would have received no bonuses in 1998 unless the factory built and sold 310 000 vehicles. Prior to the contract vote, GM agreed to pay bonuses if the plant builds 280 000 cars, which is a more realistic assessment. From the workers' perspective, producing the cars is not a problem. Rather, small-car sales are falling, and they don't want to be penalized for this, as they have little control over market forces. GM also agreed to pay bonuses of up to $7000.

The strong supporting vote to continue the contract that reflects empowered workers was important to Saturn, which advertises itself as "a different kind of car company" that gives workers a major role in making decisions and protecting quality.

Sources: Based on "Saturn workers retain old contract," *Financial Post Daily*, March 12, 1998, p. 14; and "Saturn to pay bonus to appease workers," *Financial Post Daily*, February 27, 1998, p. 12.

Take It to the Net

We invite you to visit the Robbins page on the Prentice Hall Web site at:

http://www.prenticehall.ca/robbins

for this chapter's World Wide Web exercise.

When employees are empowered, it means that they are expected to act, at least in a small way, as owners of the company, rather than just employees. Ownership is not necessary in the financial sense, but in terms of identifying with the goals and mission of the organization. For employees to be empowered, however, and have an ownership mentality, managers must be willing to share power and reward employees for taking responsibility for their actions.

Two British Columbia firms have discovered the bottom-line rewards of empowering their employees.[18] Vancouver-based Dominion Directory, which

Workers at Redwood Plastics in Langley, British Columbia have been cross-trained so that they know the jobs that other employees do. This training is part of Redwood Plastics' aim to empower its workers and reach 100 percent on-time delivery.

publishes *The Yellow Pages*, cut customer complaints by 40 percent in three years. They also reduced the time it takes to fix complaints from 27 days down to 48 hours. Not ready to rest on this accomplishment, however, they are aiming for same-day complaint resolution. Dominion reports that their employee-empowerment efforts also led to revenues that have grown 40 percent during the past six years and an annual employee turnover that is the lowest in the business at 5.27 percent.

Similarly, Langley-based Redwood Plastics has increased its on-time deliveries to 92 percent of the time, from 60 percent. The company is hoping to reach 100 percent on-time delivery. To improve their procedures, Redwood's vice-president Dan Pearce said they "asked people on the line what we could do to eliminate problems and we did a lot of cross-training. Salespeople would make some parts and floor people would watch the people in the office. All of that caused a huge coming-together of the business and it has increased our quality exponentially."

Doug Martin, executive director of the Quality Council of British Columbia, summarizes what he believes is the importance of empowering employees: "You really need to involve anybody who is in a position where they can influence how the business works. If people aren't relying on a hierarchy to fix problems, they can take action right where it counts." He points out that this has a bottom-line positive outcome.

Power in Groups: Coalitions

Those "out of power" and seeking to be "in" will first try to increase their power individually. Why share the spoils if one doesn't have to? If this proves ineffective, the alternative is to form a **coalition**. There is strength in numbers.

The natural way to gain influence is to become a powerholder. Therefore, those who want power will attempt to build a personal power base, but in many instances this may be difficult, risky, costly, or impossible. In such cases, efforts will be made to form a coalition of two or more "outs" who, by joining together, can combine their resources to increase rewards for themselves.[19]

Redwood Plastics
www.redwood-plastics.com/

coalition
Two or more individuals who combine their power to push for or support their demands.

Ellen Wessel (right) is founder and president of Moving Comfort, a manufacturer of women's athletic wear. She has created a corporate culture that encourages the use of kind words and friendliness. The environment at Moving Comfort is warm and relaxed because Wessel is supportive in empowering employees to make decisions. She views employees as goodwill ambassadors for her company and attributes the company's rapid growth to giving employees the freedom to make things happen.

Historically, blue-collar workers in organizations who were unsuccessful in bargaining on their own behalf with management resorted to labour unions to bargain for them. In recent years, white-collar employees and professionals have increasingly turned to unions after finding it difficult to exert power individually to attain higher wages and greater job security.

What predictions can we make about coalition formation?[20] First, coalitions in organizations often seek to maximize their size. In political science theory, coalitions move the other way—they try to minimize their size. They tend to be just large enough to exert the power necessary to achieve their objectives. But legislatures are different from organizations. Specifically, decision-making in organizations does not end just with selection from among a set of alternatives. The decision must also be implemented. In organizations, the implementation of and commitment to the decision is at least as important as the decision itself. It's necessary, therefore, for coalitions in organizations to seek a broad constituency to support the coalition's objectives. This means expanding the coalition to encompass as many interests as possible. This coalition expansion to facilitate consensus building, of course, is more likely to occur in organizational cultures where cooperation, commitment, and shared decision-making are highly valued. In autocratic and hierarchically controlled organizations, however, this search for maximizing the coalition's size is less likely to be sought.

Another prediction about coalitions relates to the degree of interdependence within the organization. More coalitions will likely be created where there is a great deal of task and resource interdependence. In contrast, there will be less interdependence among subunits and less coalition formation activity where subunits are largely self-contained or resources are abundant.

Finally, coalition formation will be influenced by the actual tasks that workers do. The more routine the task of a group, the greater the likelihood that coalitions will form. The more that the work that people do is routine, the greater their substitutability for each other, and thus the greater their dependence. To offset this dependence, they can be expected to resort to a coalition. We see, therefore, that unions appeal more to low-skill and non-professional workers than to skilled and professional types. Of course, where the supply of skilled and professional employees is high relative to their demand or where organizations have standardized traditionally nonroutine jobs, we would expect these incumbents to find unionization attractive.

The Abuse of Power: Sexual Harassment in the Workplace

People who engage in sexual harassment in the workplace are typically abusing their power position. The issue of sexual harassment has received

increasing attention by corporations and the media in the 1990s because of the growing ranks of female employees, especially in nontraditional work environments, and because of a number of high-profile cases. For example, the Canadian Armed Forces has been subject to intense media scrutiny during 1998 for alleged cover-ups of sexual harassment. Similarly, Sears Canada had a notorious incident that led to the death of two employees. (This case is discussed in more detail in the HR Implications at the end of the chapter.) Sexual harassment has also generated much discussion at several universities in recent years, including the University of British Columbia and Simon Fraser University. Moreover, the continuing debate about what happened between U.S. President Bill Clinton and White House intern Monica Lewinsky has kept sexual harassment in the spotlight in both Canada and the United States.

sexual harassment
Unwelcome behaviour of a sexual nature in the workplace that negatively affects the work environment or leads to adverse job-related consequences for the employee.

The Supreme Court of Canada defines **sexual harassment** as unwelcome behaviour of a sexual nature in the workplace that negatively affects the work environment or leads to adverse job-related consequences for the employee. Despite the legal framework for defining sexual harassment, there continues to be disagreement as to what *specifically* constitutes sexual harassment. Sexual harassment includes unwanted physical touching, recurring requests for dates when it is made clear the person isn't interested, and coercive threats that a person will lose her or his job if she or he refuses a sexual proposition. The problems of interpreting sexual harassment often surface around some of its more subtle forms—unwanted looks or comments, off-colour jokes, sexual artifacts such as nude calendars in the workplace, sexual innuendo, or misinterpretations of where the line between "being friendly" ends and "harassment" begins. The Case Incident, "Damned If You Do, Dammed If You Don't," illustrates how these problems can make people feel uncomfortable in the workplace. Most studies confirm that the concept of power is central to understanding sexual harassment.[21] This seems to be true whether the harassment comes from a supervisor, a co-worker, or even a subordinate.

The supervisor–employee relationship best characterizes an unequal power relationship, where position power gives the supervisor the capacity to reward and coerce. Supervisors give subordinates their assignments, evaluate their performance, make recommendations for salary adjustments and promotions, and even decide whether an employee retains his or her job. These decisions give a supervisor power. Since subordinates want favourable performance reviews, salary increases, and the like, it's clear that supervisors control the resources that most subordinates consider important and scarce. It's also worth noting that individuals who occupy high-status roles (such as management positions) sometimes believe that sexually harassing female subordinates is merely an extension of their right to make demands on lower-status individuals. Because of power inequities, sexual harassment by one's boss typically creates the greatest difficulty for those who are being harassed. If there are no witnesses, it is her word against his. Are there others whom this boss has harassed, and if so, will they come forward? Because of the supervisor's control over resources, many of those who are harassed are afraid of speaking out for fear of retaliation by the supervisor.

Although co-workers don't have position power, they can have influence and use it to sexually harass peers. In fact, although co-workers appear to engage in somewhat less severe forms of harassment than do supervisors, co-workers are the most frequent perpetrators of sexual harassment in organizations. How do co-workers exercise power? Most often it's by providing or

withholding information, cooperation, and support. For example, the effective performance of most jobs requires interaction and support from co-workers. This is especially true nowadays as work is assigned to teams. By threatening to withhold or delay providing information that's necessary for the successful achievement of your work goals, co-workers can exert power over you.

Although it doesn't receive nearly the attention that harassment by a supervisor does, women in positions of power can be subjected to sexual harassment from males who occupy less powerful positions within the organization. This is usually achieved by the subordinate devaluing the woman through such actions as making belittling remarks about her lack of career commitment if she leaves work at regular hours to meet family commitments; refusing to take directives from female superiors by indicating that their authority is not respected; or defining a woman as weak or incompetent because she is unable to perform physical actions that go beyond the strength limitations of her smaller size. All of these responses are designed to reflect negatively on the woman in power. A subordinate may engage in such practices to attempt to gain some power over the higher-ranking female or to minimize power differentials.

One of the places where there has been a dramatic increase in the number of sexual harassment complaints is at university campuses across Canada, according to Paddy Stamp, sexual harassment officer at the University of Toronto.[22] However, agreement on what constitutes sexual harassment, and how it should be investigated, is no clearer for universities than for industry. The University of British Columbia, Simon Fraser University, University of Victoria, University of Western Ontario, and University of New Brunswick have all been involved in high-profile cases during the 1990s where either the definition of harassment or how it was investigated was under scrutiny. The University of Alberta and the University of Calgary have also faced debate about their harassment policy.

While non-consensual sex between professors and students is rape and subject to criminal charges, it is harder to evaluate apparently consensual relationships that occur outside the classroom. There is some argument over whether truly consensual sex is ever possible between students and professors. In an effort to underscore the power discrepancy and potential for abuse of it by professors, Yale University recently decided that there could be no sexual relations between students and professors. Most universities have been unwilling to adopt such an extreme stance. However, this issue is certainly one of concern, as the power distance between professors and students is considerable. Similar issues have been raised with the alleged consensual sexual relationship between U.S. President Bill Clinton and White House intern Monica Lewinsky. The main question asked by some is whether an unpaid intern should be considered an equal to the president in agreeing to "consensual" sex. The issue of defining consensual sex when there are power differences among the participants is not confined to the university or the White House, however. It also arises in the factory and the office.

In concluding this discussion, we would like to point out that the topic of sexual harassment is about power. It's about an individual controlling or threatening another individual. It's wrong. Moreover, it's illegal. You can understand how sexual harassment surfaces in organizations if you analyse it in power terms. This chapter's HR Implications explores further issues of sexual harassment in the workplace.

Sexual Harassment in an International Context

Policies governing sexual harassment are not uniformly agreed upon around the world. While Canada and the United States have relatively similar policies, significant differences arise in other countries. For example, though the North American automobile industry is still predominantly male (as we note in the HR Implications feature at the end of the chapter), a North American firm would not print and distribute a calendar of nude women to its clients, as is done by tiremaker Pirelli SpA of Italy.[23]

Italy is not alone in its differences from North America in this regard. Japan, for instance, does not have laws regarding sexual harassment. Mayumi Makita, an editor of Femin, a Japanese magazine published by the rights group Women's Democratic Club, says that "Japanese companies do not treat women as proper workers and they do not care about sexual harassment."[24] This has led to problems when Japanese companies have set up business in North America. For instance, Mitsubishi Motors Corp. of America settled one lawsuit with 27 women in August 1997. A second well-publicized sexual harassment suit filed in April 1996 involving about 300 women was settled in June 1998 for US $34 million, more than three times the amount of any other harassment case ever settled in the U.S. The women who are part of the claim will receive payments according to the extent of the harassment suffered. Those who suffered the most extensive harassment could receive up to US $300 000.

It is notable that the Equal Employment Opportunity Commission has labelled the Mitsubishi case as one "of a new and more disturbing order of magnitude" compared with other sexual harassment cases in the United States.[25] The women at Mitsubishi's Normal, Illinois, plant complained that "workers and supervisors demeaned women, demanded sex, fondled women, or called them foul names. They also complained about a work environment where sexual material was displayed and Japanese management took male workers to strip clubs."

One of the difficulties that Mitsubishi faced may have been in not understanding the climate in the United States regarding sexual harassment. As stated above, many manufacturing and financial companies in Japan do not have internal rules governing sexual harassment, nor do they provide training in this area. Even Honda, which operates internationally, states, "We leave it to each person's common sense."[26]

Closer to home, a report in *Canadian Business* suggested that Calgary-based Husky Oil company's problems with sexual harassment stem from the mixed cultures of being based in Canada with a more progressive and relatively democratic culture, but being run by CEO John Chin-Sung Lau, a Hong Kong native who governs with a more "Chinese, paternalistic, and strictly authoritarian" style.[27] Consequently, when women from Husky first complained of sexual harassment in the workplace, Lau ignored them, as sexual harassment does not receive the same legal sanctions in Hong Kong. Lower management simply followed his cue and also ignored the complaints. Eventually, after more complaints of sexual harassment arose in the mid-1990s, the management structure was changed, says CEO Lau. "All the previous difficulties are gone, Husky is different now. We have to treat humans right. World standards are changing. If we don't do it, we'll be out of style."[28] Both the Husky and Mitsubishi examples illustrate the problems of doing business in other countries, where values may be different from one's own.

Politics: Power in Action

When people get together in groups, power will be exerted. People want to carve out a niche from which to exert influence, to earn awards, and to advance their careers.[29] When employees in organizations convert their power into action, we describe them as being engaged in politics. Those with good political skills have the ability to use their bases of power effectively.[30]

Definition

political behaviour
Those activities that are not required as part of one's formal role in the organization, but that influence, or attempt to influence, the distribution of advantages and disadvantages within the organization.

There has been no shortage of definitions for organizational politics. Essentially, however, they have focused on the use of power to affect decision-making in the organization or on behaviours by members that are self-serving and organizationally nonsanctioned.[31] For our purposes, we will define **political behaviour** in organizations as those activities that are not required as part of one's formal role in the organization, but that influence, or attempt to influence, the distribution of advantages and disadvantages within the organization.[32]

This definition encompasses key elements from what most people mean when they talk about organizational politics. Political behaviour is *outside* one's specified job requirements. The behaviour requires some attempt to use one's *power* bases. Additionally, our definition encompasses efforts to influence the goals, criteria, or processes used for *decision-making* when we state that politics is concerned with "the distribution of advantages and disadvantages within the organization." Our definition is broad enough to include such varied political behaviours as withholding key information from decision-makers, whistleblowing, spreading rumours, leaking confidential information about organizational activities to the media, exchanging favours with others in the organization for mutual benefit, and lobbying on behalf of or against a particular individual or decision alternative. Exhibit 12-5 provides a quick measure to help you assess how political your workplace is.

legitimate political behaviour
Normal everyday politics.

A final comment relates to what has been referred to as the "legitimate–illegitimate" dimension in political behaviour.[33] **Legitimate political behaviour** refers to normal everyday politics—complaining to your supervisor, bypassing the chain of command, forming coalitions, obstructing organizational policies or decisions through inaction or excessive adherence to rules, and developing contacts outside the organization through one's professional activities. On the other hand, there are also **illegitimate political behaviours** that violate the implied rules of the game. Those who pursue such extreme activities are often described as individuals who "play hardball." Illegitimate activities include sabotage, whistleblowing, and symbolic protests such as wearing unconventional clothes or protest buttons, and groups of employees simultaneously calling in sick.

illegitimate political behaviour
Extreme political behaviour that violates the implied rules of the game.

The vast majority of all organizational political actions are of the legitimate variety. The reasons are pragmatic: The extreme illegitimate forms of political behaviour pose a very real risk of loss of organizational membership or extreme sanctions against those who use them and then fall short in having enough power to ensure that they work. Now that you have learned a bit about political behaviour, you may want to assess your own political behaviour in our Learning About Yourself exercise.

The Reality of Politics

Politics is a fact of life in organizations. People who ignore this fact of life do so at their own peril. Why, you may wonder, must politics exist? Isn't it

Exhibit 12-5
A Quick Measure of How Political Your Workplace Is

How political is your workplace? Answer the 12 questions using the following scale:

SD = Strongly disagree
D   Disagree
U   Uncertain
A   Agree
SA   Strongly agree

1. Managers often use the selection system to hire only people who can help them in their future. _____

2. The rules and policies concerning promotion and pay are fair; it is how supervisors carry out the policies that is unfair and self-serving. _____

3. The performance ratings people receive from their supervisors reflect more of the supervisors' "own agenda" than the actual performance of the employee. _____

4. Although a lot of what my supervisor does around here appears to be directed at helping employees, it is actually intended to protect my supervisor. _____

5. There are cliques or "in-groups" that hinder effectiveness around here. _____

6. My co-workers help themselves, not others. _____

7. I have seen people deliberately distort information requested by others for purposes of personal gain, either by withholding it or by selectively reporting it. _____

8. If co-workers offer to lend some assistance, it is because they expect to get something out of it. _____

9. Favouritism rather than merit determines who gets ahead around here. _____

10. You can usually get what you want around here if you know the right person to ask. _____

11. Overall, the rules and policies concerning promotion and pay are specific and well defined. _____

12. Pay and promotion policies are generally clearly communicated in this organization. _____

This questionnaire taps the three salient dimensions that have been found to be related to perceptions of politics: supervisor behaviour; co-worker behaviour; and organizational policies and practices. To calculate your score for items 1–10, give yourself 1 point for Strongly disagree; 2 points for Disagree; and so forth (through 5 points for Strongly agree). For items 11 and 12, reverse the score (i.e., 1 point for Strongly agree, etc.). Sum up the total: the higher the total score, the greater degree of perceived organizational politics.

Source: G.R. Ferris, D.D. Frink, D.P.S. Bhawuk, J. Zhou, and D.C. Gilmore, "Reactions of Diverse Groups to Politics in the Workplace," *Journal of Management,* vol. 22, no. 1, 1996, pp. 32–33.

possible for an organization to be politics free? It's *possible,* but most unlikely. Organizations are made up of individuals and groups with different values, goals, and interests.[34] This sets up the potential for conflict over resources. Departmental budgets, space allocations, project responsibilities, and salary adjustments are just a few examples of the resources about whose allocation organizational members will disagree.

Resources in organizations are also limited, which often turns potential conflict into real conflict. If resources were abundant, then all the various constituencies within the organization could satisfy their goals. Because they are limited, not everyone's interests can be provided for. Furthermore, whether true or not, gains by one individual or group are often *perceived* as being at the expense of others within the organization. These forces create a competition among members for the organization's limited resources.

Maybe the most important factor leading to politics within organizations is the realization that most of the "facts" that are used to allocate the limited resources are open to interpretation. What, for instance, is *good* performance? What's an *adequate* improvement? What constitutes an *unsatisfactory* job? One person's view that an act is a "selfless effort to benefit the organization" is seen by another as a "blatant attempt to further one's interest."[35] The manager of any major law firm knows that a legal secretary who types 100 words a minute is a high performer and one who types 35 words a minute is a poor performer. You don't need to be a genius to know you should hire the better typist. But what if you have to choose between a legal secretary who types 100 words a minute and one who types 90 words a minute? Then other factors—less objective ones—come into play: attitude, potential, ability to perform under pressure, loyalty to the firm, and so on. More managerial decisions resemble choosing between a 90-word and a 100-word typist than deciding between a 35-word and a 100-word typist. It is in this large and ambiguous middle ground of organizational life—where the facts *don't* speak for themselves—that politics flourish (see Exhibit 12-6).

Exhibit 12-6
Politics Is in the Eye of the Beholder

A behaviour that one person labels as "organizational politics" is very likely to be characterized as an instance of "effective management" by another. The fact is not that effective management is necessarily political, although in some cases it might be. Rather, a person's reference point determines what he or she classifies as organizational politics. Take a look at the following labels used to describe the same phenomenon. These suggest that politics, like beauty, is in the eye of the beholder.

"Political" label	**"Effective management" label**
1. Blaming others	1. Fixing responsibility
2. "Kissing up"	2. Developing working relationships
3. Apple polishing	3. Demonstrating loyalty
4. Passing the buck	4. Delegating authority
5. Covering your rear	5. Documenting decisions
6. Creating conflict	6. Encouraging change and innovation
7. Forming coalitions	7. Facilitating teamwork
8. Whistleblowing	8. Improving efficiency
9. Scheming	9. Planning ahead
10. Overachieving	10. Competent and capable
11. Ambitious	11. Career minded
12. Opportunistic	12. Astute
13. Cunning	13. Practical minded
14. Arrogant	14. Confident
15. Perfectionist	15. Attentive to detail

Source: This exhibit is based on T.C. Krell, M.E. Mendenhall, and J. Sendry, "Doing Research in the Conceptual Morass of Organizational Politics," paper presented at the Western Academy of Management Conference, Hollywood, CA, April 1987.

Finally, because most decisions must be made in a climate of ambiguity—where facts are rarely fully objective, and thus are open to interpretation—people within organizations will use whatever influence they can to taint the facts to support their goals and interests. That, of course, creates the activities we call *politicking*. For more about how one engages in politicking, see the From Concepts to Skills feature.

FROM CONCEPTS TO SKILLS

Politicking

Forget, for a moment, the ethics of politicking and any negative impressions you may have of people who engage in organizational politics. If you wanted to be more politically adept in your organization, what could you do? The following eight suggestions are likely to improve your political effectiveness.

1. *Frame arguments in terms of organizational goals.* Effective politicking requires camouflaging your self-interest. No matter that your objective is self-serving; all the arguments you marshal in support of it must be framed in terms of the benefits that will accrue to the organization. People whose actions appear to blatantly further their own interests at the expense of the organization's are almost universally denounced, are likely to lose influence, and often suffer the ultimate penalty of being expelled from the organization.

2. *Develop the right image.* If you know your organization's culture, you understand what the organization wants and values from its employees—in terms of dress; associates to cultivate, and those to avoid; whether to appear risk taking or risk aversive; the preferred leadership style; the importance placed on getting along well with others, and so forth. Then you are equipped to project the appropriate image. Because the assessment of your performance is not a fully objective process, both style and substance must be addressed.

3. *Gain control of organizational resources.* The control of organizational resources that are scarce and important is a source of power. Knowledge and expertise are particularly effective resources to control. They make you more valuable to the organization and, therefore, more likely to gain se-

curity, advancement, and a receptive audience for your ideas.

4. *Make yourself appear indispensable.* Because we're dealing with appearances rather than objective facts, you can enhance your power by appearing to be indispensable. That is, you don't have to really be indispensable as long as key people in the organization believe that you are. If the organization's prime decision-makers believe there is no ready substitute for what you are giving the organization, they are likely to go to great lengths to ensure that your desires are satisfied.

5. *Be visible.* Because performance evaluation has a substantial subjective component, it's important that your boss and those in power in the organization be made aware of your contribution. If you are fortunate enough to have a job that brings your accomplishments to the attention of others, it may not be necessary to take direct measures to increase your visibility. But your job may require you to handle activities that are low in visibility, or your specific contribution may be indistinguishable because you're part of a team endeavor. In such cases—*without appearing to be tooting your own horn or creating the image of a braggart*—you'll want to call attention to yourself by highlighting your successes in routine reports, having satisfied customers relay their appreciation to senior executives in your organization, being seen at social functions, being active in your professional associations, developing powerful allies who speak positively about your accomplishments, and similar tactics. Of course, the skilled politician actively and successfully lobbies to get those projects that will increase his or her visibility.

6. *Develop powerful allies*. It helps to have powerful people in your camp. Cultivate contacts with potentially influential people above you, at your own level, and in the lower ranks. They can provide you with important information that may not be available through normal channels. Additionally, there will be times when decisions will be made in favour of those with the greatest support. Having powerful allies can provide you with a coalition of support if and when you need it.

7. *Avoid "tainted" members*. In almost every organization, there are fringe members whose status is questionable. Their performance and/or loyalty is suspect. Keep your distance from such individuals. Given the reality that effectiveness has a large subjective component, your own effectiveness might be called into question if you're perceived as being too closely associated with tainted members.

8. *Support your boss*. Your immediate future is in the hands of your current boss. Since he or she evaluates your performance, you will typically want to do whatever is necessary to have your boss on your side. You should make every effort to help your boss succeed, make her look good, support her if she is under siege, and spend the time to find out what criteria she will be using to assess your effectiveness. Don't undermine your boss, and don't speak negatively of her to others.

Source: S.P. Robbins and P.L. Hunsaker, *Training in Interpersonal Skills: Tips for Managing People at Work*, 2nd. ed. (Upper Saddle River, NJ: Prentice Hall, 1996), pp. 131–34.

Therefore, to answer the earlier question of whether it is possible for an organization to be politics free, we can say "yes," if all members of that organization hold the same goals and interests, if organizational resources are not scarce, and if performance outcomes are completely clear and objective. However, that doesn't describe the organizational world that most of us live in! The debate about the importance of politics continues in this chapter's Point/Counterpoint feature. Politics can also cross organizational boundaries. This chapter's Video Case shows Oberto Oberti trying to convince various groups of the wisdom of developing a new ski resort in British Columbia.

Factors Contributing to Political Behaviour

Not all groups or organizations are equally political. In some organizations, for instance, politicking is overt and rampant, while in others, politics plays a small role in influencing outcomes. Why is there this variation? Recent research and observation have identified a number of factors that appear to encourage political behaviour. Some are individual characteristics, derived from the unique qualities of the people the organization employs; others are a result of the organization's culture or internal environment. Exhibit 12-7 illustrates how both individual and organizational factors can increase political behaviour and provide favourable outcomes (increased rewards and averted punishments) for both individuals and groups in the organization.

INDIVIDUAL FACTORS   At the individual level, researchers have identified certain personality traits, needs, and other factors that are likely to be related to political behaviour. In terms of traits, we find that employees who are high self-monitors, who possess an internal locus of control and who have a high need for power are more likely to engage in political behaviour.[36]

The high self-monitor is more sensitive to social cues, exhibits higher levels of social conformity, and is more likely to be skilled in political behav-

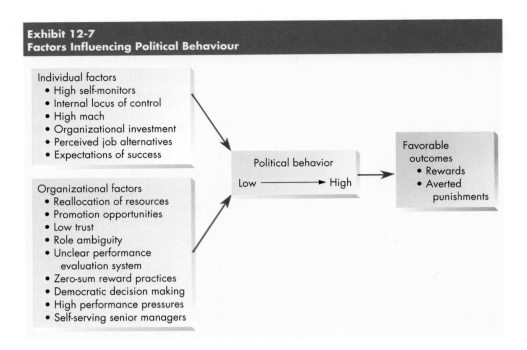

Exhibit 12-7
Factors Influencing Political Behaviour

Individual factors
- High self-monitors
- Internal locus of control
- High mach
- Organizational investment
- Perceived job alternatives
- Expectations of success

Organizational factors
- Reallocation of resources
- Promotion opportunities
- Low trust
- Role ambiguity
- Unclear performance evaluation system
- Zero-sum reward practices
- Democratic decision making
- High performance pressures
- Self-serving senior managers

Political behavior
Low ————→ High

Favorable outcomes
- Rewards
- Averted punishments

iour than the low self-monitor. Individuals with an internal locus of control, because they believe they can control their environment, are more prone to take a proactive stance and attempt to manipulate situations in their favour. You may remember our discussion of Machiavellianism in Chapter 3. Not surprisingly, the Machiavellian personality—which is characterized by the will to manipulate and the desire for power—is comfortable using politics as a means to further his or her self-interest.

Additionally, an individual's investment in the organization, perceived alternatives, and expectations of success will influence the degree to which he or she will pursue illegitimate means of political action.[37] The more that a person has invested in the organization in terms of expectations of increased future benefits, the more a person has to lose if forced out and the less likely he or she is to use illegitimate means. The more alternative job opportunities an individual has—due to a favourable job market or the possession of scarce skills or knowledge, a prominent reputation, or influential contacts outside the organization—the more likely he or she is to risk illegitimate political actions. Finally, if an individual has a low expectation of success in using illegitimate means, it is unlikely that he or she will attempt to do so. High expectations of success in the use of illegitimate means are most likely to be the province of both experienced and powerful individuals with polished political skills and inexperienced and naive employees who misjudge their chances.

ORGANIZATIONAL FACTORS Political activity is probably more a function of the organization's characteristics than of individual difference variables. Why? Many organizations have a large number of employees with the individual characteristics we listed, yet the extent of political behaviour varies widely.

Although we acknowledge the role that individual differences can play in fostering politicking, the evidence more strongly supports that certain situations and cultures promote politics. More specifically, when an organization's resources are declining, when the existing pattern of resources is changing, and when there is opportunity for promotions, politics is more

likely to surface.[38] In addition, cultures characterized by low trust, role ambiguity, unclear performance evaluation systems, zero-sum reward allocation practices, democratic decision-making, high pressures for performance, and self-serving senior managers will create breeding grounds for politicking.[39]

When organizations downsize to improve efficiency, such as happened throughout the early 1990s, reductions in resources have to be made. Threatened with the loss of resources, people may engage in political actions to safeguard what they have. Any changes, especially those that imply significant reallocation of resources within the organization, are likely to stimulate conflict and increase politicking.

Promotion decisions have consistently been found to be one of the most political in organizations. The opportunity for promotions or advancement encourages people to compete for a limited resource and to try to positively influence the decision outcome.

The less trust there is within the organization, the higher the level of political behaviour and the more likely that the political behaviour will be of the illegitimate kind. High trust should suppress the level of political behaviour in general and inhibit illegitimate actions in particular.

Role ambiguity means that the prescribed behaviours of the employee are unclear. There are fewer limits, therefore, to the scope and functions of the employee's political actions. Since political activities are defined as those not required as part of one's formal role, the greater the role ambiguity, the more one can engage in political activity with little chance of it being visible.

The practice of performance evaluation is far from a perfected science. The more that organizations use subjective criteria in the appraisal, emphasize a single outcome measure, or allow significant time to pass between the time of an action and its appraisal, the greater the likelihood that an employee can get away with politicking. Subjective performance criteria create ambiguity. The use of a single outcome measure encourages individuals to do whatever is necessary to "look good" on that measure, but often at the expense of performing well on other important parts of the job that are not being appraised. The amount of time that elapses between an action and its appraisal is also a relevant factor. The longer the time period, the more unlikely that the employee will be held accountable for his or her political behaviours.

The more that an organization's culture emphasizes the zero-sum or win-lose approach to reward allocations, the more employees will be motivated to engage in politicking. The zero-sum approach treats the reward "pie" as fixed so that any gain one person or group achieves has to come at the expense of another person or group. If I win, you must lose! If $10 000 in annual raises is to be distributed among five employees, then any employee who receives more than $2000 takes money away from one or more of the others. Such a practice encourages making others look bad and increasing the visibility of what you do.

In the last 25 years, there has been a general move in North America and among most developed nations toward making organizations less autocratic. Managers in these organizations are being asked to behave more democratically. They're told that they should allow subordinates to advise them on decisions and that they should rely more on group input into the decision process. Such moves toward democracy, however, are not necessarily embraced by all individual managers. Many managers sought their positions in order to have legitimate power so as to be able to make unilateral decisions. They fought hard and often paid high personal costs to achieve their influential positions. Sharing their power with others runs directly against their desires. The result

is that managers, especially those who began their careers in the 1950s and 1960s, may use the required committees, conferences, and group meetings in a superficial way, as arenas for manoeuvring and manipulating.

The more pressure that employees feel to perform well, the more likely they are to engage in politicking. When people are held strictly accountable for outcomes, this puts great pressure on them to "look good." If a person perceives that his or her entire career is riding on next quarter's sales figures or next month's plant productivity report, there is motivation to do whatever is necessary to ensure that the numbers come out favourably.

Finally, when employees see the people on top engaging in political behaviour, especially when they do so successfully and are rewarded for it, a climate is created that supports politicking. Politicking by top management, in a sense, gives permission to those lower in the organization to play politics by implying that such behaviour is acceptable.

Making Office Politics Work

The reason that office politics occurs is that people with different interests are each trying to get their interests heard, in the hopes that their view will win. We discuss different negotiation strategies in Chapter 13, including a "win-lose" strategy, which means if I win, you lose, and a "win-win" strategy, which means creating situations where both of us can win. Suppose you have something that you would like to see carried out in your organization. Is there an effective way to engage in office politics that is less likely to be disruptive or negative? *Fast Company*, an online business magazine, identifies several rules that may help to improve the climate of the organization, while negotiating through the office politics maze:[40]

Fast Company
www.fastcompany.com/home.
html

- *Nobody wins unless everybody wins.* The most successful proposals look for ways to acknowledge, if not include, the interests of others. This requires building support for your ideas across the organization. "Real political skill isn't about campaign tactics," says Lou Di Natale, a veteran political consultant at the University of Massachusetts. "It's about pulling people toward your ideas and then pushing those ideas through to other people." When ideas are packaged to look like they're best for the organization as a whole and will help others, it is harder for others to counteract your proposal.

- *Don't just ask for opinions—change them.* It is helpful to find out what people think and then, if necessary, set out to change their opinions so that they can see what you want to do. It is also important to seek out the opinions of those you don't know well, or who are less likely to agree with you. Gathering together people who always support you is often not enough to build an effective coalition.

- *Everyone expects to be paid back.* In organizations, as in life, we develop personal relationships with those around us. And it is those personal relationships that affect much of the behaviour in organizations. By building good relationships with colleagues, supporting them in their endeavours, and showing appreciation for what they accomplish, you are building a foundation of support for your own ideas.

- *Success can create opposition.* As part of the office politics, success can be viewed as a "win-lose" strategy, which we identified above. Some people may feel that your success either gets you a higher profile, or that it means a project of theirs will be received less favourably. You have to be prepared to deal with this opposition.

General Electric wants its managers to share their power with employees. GE is breaking down autocratic barriers between labour and management that "cramp people, inhibit creativity, waste time, restrict visions, smother dreams, and above all, slow things down." GE expects managers to behave more democratically by fostering teamwork and rewarding employees who suggest ideas for improvement. This photo illustrates GE's move toward democracy, as a manager at the company's plant in Louisville, Kentucky, and an employee work together to improve the plant's profitability.

Impression Management

General Electric
www.ge.com/

impression management
The process by which individuals attempt to control the impression others form of them.

We know that people have an ongoing interest in how others perceive and evaluate them. For example, North Americans spend billions of dollars on diets, health-club memberships, cosmetics, and plastic surgery—all intended to make them more attractive to others.[41] Being perceived positively by others should have benefits for people in organizations. It might, for instance, help them initially to get the jobs they want in an organization and, once hired, to get favourable evaluations, superior salary increases, and more rapid promotions. In a political context, it might help sway the distribution of advantages in their favour.

The process by which individuals attempt to control the impression others form of them is called **impression management**.[42] It is a subject that only quite recently has gained the attention of OB researchers.[43]

Is everyone concerned with impression management (IM)? No! Who, then, might we predict to engage in IM? No surprise here! It's our old friend, the high self-monitor.[44] Low self-monitors tend to present images of themselves that are consistent with their personalities, regardless of the beneficial or detrimental effects for them. In contrast, high self-monitors are skilled at reading situations and moulding their appearances and behaviour to fit each situation.

Given that you want to control the impression others form of you, what techniques could you use? Exhibit 12-8 summarizes some of the more popular IM techniques and provides an example of each.

Keep in mind that IM does not imply that the impressions people convey are necessarily false (although, of course, they sometimes are).[45] Excuses and

Exhibit 12-8
Impression Management (IM) Techniques

Conformity

Agreeing with someone else's opinion in order to gain his or her approval.

Example: A manager tells his boss, "You're absolutely right on your reorganization plan for the western regional office. I couldn't agree with you more."

Excuses

Explanations of a predicament-creating event aimed at minimizing the apparent severity of the predicament.

Example: Sales manager to boss, "We failed to get the ad in the paper on time, but no one responds to those ads anyway."

Apologies

Admitting responsibility for an undesirable event and simultaneously seeking to get a pardon for the action.

Example: Employee to boss, "I'm sorry I made a mistake on the report. Please forgive me."

Acclamations

Explanation of favourable events to maximize the desirable implications for oneself.

Example: A salesperson informs a peer, "The sales in our division have nearly tripled since I was hired."

Flattery

Complimenting others about their virtues in an effort to make oneself appear perceptive and likable.

Example: New sales trainee to peer, "You handled that client's complaint so tactfully! I could never have handled that as well as you did."

Favours

Doing something nice for someone to gain that person's approval.

Example: Salesperson to prospective client, "I've got two tickets to the theatre tonight that I can't use. Take them. Consider it a thank-you for taking the time to talk with me."

Association

Enhancing or protecting one's image by managing information about people and things with which one is associated.

Example: A job applicant says to an interviewer, "What a coincidence. Your boss and I were roommates in university."

Sources: Based on B.R. Schlenker, *Impression Management* (Monterey, CA: Brooks/Cole, 1980); W.L. Gardner and M.J. Martinko, "Impression Management in Organizations," *Journal of Management,* June 1988, p. 332; and R.B. Cialdini, "Indirect Tactics of Image Management: Beyond Basking," in R.A. Giacalone and P. Rosenfeld (eds.), *Impression Management in the Organization* (Hillsdale, NJ: Lawrence Erlbaum Associates, 1989), pp. 45–71.

acclamations, for instance, may be offered with sincerity. Referring to the examples used in Exhibit 12-8, you can *actually* believe that ads contribute little to sales in your region or that you are the key to the tripling of your division's sales. But misrepresentation can have a high cost. If the image claimed is false, you may be discredited.[46] If you "cry wolf" once too often, no one is likely to believe you when the wolf really comes. The impression manager must be cautious not to be perceived as insincere or manipulative.[47]

Are there *situations* where individuals are more likely to misrepresent themselves or more likely to get away with it? Yes—situations that are characterized by high uncertainty or ambiguity.[48] These situations provide rela-

tively little information for challenging a fraudulent claim and reduce the risks associated with misrepresentation.

Only a limited number of studies have been undertaken to test the effectiveness of IM techniques, and these have been essentially limited to determining whether IM behaviour is related to job-interview success. This makes a particularly relevant area of study since applicants are clearly attempting to present positive images of themselves and there are relatively objective outcome measures (written assessments and typically a "hire–don't hire" recommendation).

The evidence is that IM behaviour works.[49] In one study, for instance, interviewers believed that those applicants for a position as a customer-service representative who used IM techniques performed better in the interview, and they seemed somewhat more likely to hire these people.[50] Moreover, when the researchers considered applicants' credentials, they concluded that it was the IM techniques alone that influenced the interviewers. That is, it didn't seem to matter whether applicants were well or poorly qualified. If they used IM techniques, they did better in the interview.

Another employment interview study examined whether certain IM techniques work better than others.[51] The researchers compared applicants who used IM techniques that focused the conversation on themselves (called a *controlling style*) to applicants who used techniques that focused on the interviewer (referred to as a *submissive style*). The researchers hypothesized that applicants who used the controlling style would be more effective because of the implicit expectations inherent in employment interviews. We tend to expect job applicants to use self-enhancement, self-promotion, and other active controlling techniques in an interview because they reflect self-confidence and initiative. The researchers predicted that these active controlling techniques would work better for applicants than submissive tactics such as conforming their opinions to those of the interviewer and offering favours to the interviewer. The results confirmed the researchers' predictions. Those applicants who used the controlling style were rated higher by interviewers on factors such as motivation, enthusiasm, and even technical skills—and they received more job offers.

A 1995 study confirmed the value of a controlling style over a submissive one.[52] Specifically, recent university graduates who used more self-promotion tactics got higher evaluations by interviewers and more follow-up job-site visits, even after adjusting for grade point average, gender, and job type.

Defensive Behaviours

Organizational politics includes protection of self-interest as well as promotion. Individuals often engage in reactive and protective "defensive" behaviours to avoid action, blame, or change.[53] This section discusses common varieties of **defensive behaviours**, classified by their objective.

defensive behaviours
Reactive and protective behaviours to avoid action, blame, or change.

AVOIDING ACTION Sometimes the best political strategy is to avoid action. That is, the best action is no action! However, role expectations typically dictate that one at least give the impression of doing something. Here are six popular ways to avoid action:

- *Overconforming.* You strictly interpret your responsibility by saying things like, "The rules clearly state . . . " or "This is the way we've always done it." Rigid adherence to rules, policies, and precedents avoids the need to consider the nuances of a particular case.

- *Passing the buck*. You transfer responsibility for the execution of a task or decision to someone else.

- *Playing dumb*. This is a form of strategic helplessness. You avoid an unwanted task by falsely pleading ignorance or inability.

- *Depersonalization*. You treat other people as objects or numbers, distancing yourself from problems and avoiding having to consider the idiosyncrasies of particular people or the impact of events on them. For example, hospital physicians often refer to patients by their room number or disease to avoid becoming too personally involved with them.

- *Stretching and smoothing*. Stretching refers to prolonging a task so that you appear to be occupied—for example, you turn a two-week task into a four-month job. Smoothing refers to covering up fluctuations in effort or output. Both practices are designed to make you appear continually busy and productive.

- *Stalling*. This "foot-dragging" tactic requires you to appear more or less supportive publicly while doing little or nothing privately.

AVOIDING BLAME How can you avoid blame for actual or anticipated negative outcomes? You can try one of the following six tactics:

- *Buffing*. This is a nice way to refer to "covering your bum." It describes the practice of rigorously documenting activity to project an image of competence, efficiency, and thoroughness. "I can't provide that information unless I get a formal written requisition from you," is an example.

- *Playing safe*. This encompasses tactics designed to evade situations that may reflect unfavourably on you. It includes taking on only projects with a high probability of success, having risky decisions approved by superiors, qualifying expressions of judgment, and taking neutral positions in conflicts.

- *Justifying*. This tactic includes developing explanations that lessen your responsibility for a negative outcome and/or apologizing to demonstrate remorse.

- *Scapegoating*. This is the classic effort to place the blame for a negative outcome on external factors that are not entirely blameworthy. "I would have submitted the paper on time but my computer went down—and I lost everything—the day before the deadline."

- *Misrepresenting*. This tactic involves the manipulation of information by distortion, embellishment, deception, selective presentation, or obfuscation.

- *Escalation of commitment*. One way to vindicate an initially poor decision and a failing course of action is to escalate support for the decision. By further increasing the commitment of resources to a previous course of action, you indicate that the previous decision was not wrong. When you "throw good money after bad," you demonstrate confidence in past actions and consistency over time.

AVOIDING CHANGE Finally, there are two forms of defensiveness frequently used by people who feel personally threatened by change:

- *Resisting change.* This is a catch-all name for a variety of behaviours, including some forms of overconforming, stalling, playing safe, and misrepresenting.

- *Protecting turf.* This is defending your territory from encroachment by others. As one purchasing executive commented, "Tell the people in production that it's our job to talk with vendors, not theirs."

EFFECTS OF DEFENSIVE BEHAVIOUR In the short run, extensive use of defensiveness may well promote an individual's self-interest. In the long run, it more often than not becomes a liability. This is because defensive behaviour frequently becomes chronic or even pathological over time. People who constantly rely on defensiveness find that, eventually, it is the only way they know how to behave. At that point, they lose the trust and support of their peers, bosses, subordinates, and clients. In moderation, however, defensive behaviour can be an effective device for surviving and flourishing in an organization because management often deliberately or unwittingly encourages it.

In terms of the organization, defensive behaviour tends to reduce effectiveness. In the short run, defensiveness delays decisions, increases interpersonal and intergroup tensions, reduces risk taking, makes attributions and evaluations unreliable, and restricts change efforts. In the long term, defensiveness leads to organizational rigidity and stagnation, detachment from the organization's environment, an organizational culture that is highly politicized, and low employee morale.

The Ethics of Behaving Politically

We conclude our discussion of politics by providing some ethical guidelines for political behaviour. While there are no clear-cut ways to differentiate ethical from unethical politicking, there are some questions you should consider.

Exhibit 12-9 illustrates a decision tree to guide ethical actions.[54] The first question you need to answer addresses self-interest versus organizational goals. Ethical actions are consistent with the organization's goals. Spreading untrue rumours about the safety of a new product introduced by your company in order to make that product's design team look bad is unethical.

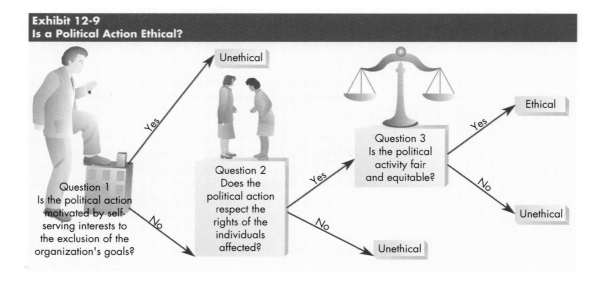

Exhibit 12-9
Is a Political Action Ethical?

Question 1
Is the political action motivated by self-serving interests to the exclusion of the organization's goals?

Question 2
Does the political action respect the rights of the individuals affected?

Question 3
Is the political activity fair and equitable?

Unethical / Ethical

However, there may be nothing unethical if a department head exchanges favours (for instance, offering to help with a report) with the division's purchasing manager in order to get a critical contract processed quickly.

The second question concerns the rights of other parties. If the department head described in the previous paragraph went down to the mail room at lunch and read through the mail directed to the purchasing manager—with the intent of "getting something" that would force the purchasing manager to expedite the contract—the department head would be acting unethically, having violated the purchasing manager's right to privacy.

The final question that needs to be addressed relates to whether the political activity conforms to standards of equity and justice. The department head that inflates the performance evaluation of a favoured employee and deflates the evaluation of a disfavoured employee—then uses these evaluations to justify giving the former a big raise and nothing to the latter—has treated the disfavoured employee unfairly.

Unfortunately, the answers to the questions in Exhibit 12-9 are often argued in ways to make unethical practices seem ethical. Powerful people, for example, can become very adept at explaining self-serving behaviours in terms of the organization's best interests. Similarly, they can persuasively argue that unfair actions are really fair and just. Our point is that immoral people can justify almost any behaviour. Those who are powerful, articulate, and persuasive are most vulnerable because they are likely to be able to get away with unethical practices successfully. When faced with an ethical dilemma regarding organizational politics, try to answer the questions in Exhibit 12-9 truthfully. If you have a strong power base, recognize the ability of power to corrupt. Remember, it's a lot easier for the powerless to act ethically, if for no other reason than they typically have very little political discretion to exploit.

HR IMPLICATIONS

Dealing with Sexual Harassment in the Workplace

The Ontario Human Rights Commission reported in March 1998 that sexual harassment complaints have more than doubled over the past 10 years, from 106 complaints to 225.[1] In a poll conducted in British Columbia in April 1998, 39 percent of 400 women and 14 percent of 400 men said they'd experienced sexual harassment at work.[2] Below we review the legal aspects of sexual harassment, and then discuss how organizations are dealing with it in their workplaces.

Sexual Harassment and Canadian Law

The Supreme Court of Canada defines **sexual harassment** as unwelcome behaviour of a sexual nature in the workplace that negatively affects the work environment or leads to adverse job-related consequences for the employee. In 1987, the Court ruled that employers will be held responsible for harassment by their employees. The Court also said the employer is in the best position to stop harassment and should promote a workplace that is free of it. The court recommended that employers have clear guidelines to prevent harassment, which included procedures to investigate complaints.

Protection from sexual harassment is governed by human-rights legislation, which prohibits discrimination on the basis of sex (and age, ethnic origin, race, disability, religion and sexual orientation, among other things). At both the provincial/territorial and federal levels these laws

have been widely interpreted to mean both quid pro quo harassment involving exchange of sexual acts for job-related benefits, and a range of behaviours that create a hostile work environment for the person to whom the attention is directed. The Canadian Human Rights Act is set for review in 1998, and one of the issues it will consider is overhauling the way it deals with these complaints, given that sexual harassment is still so prevalent in the workplace.[3] Typically sexual harassment complaints that are not resolved in the workplace are heard by a provincial or territorial human rights tribunal. However, in an effort to provide more venues for hearing sexual harassment complaints, the Ontario Labour Relations Board conceded in August 1997 that sexual harassment is a health and safety issue, and thus could be addressed by that board.[4] This may lead to a movement in other provinces to make similar moves.

Dealing with Sexual Harassment in the Workplace

Examples of several recent cases in sexual harassment can be used to illustrate procedures that organizations can use to lessen its prevalence in the workplace. For instance, researchers representing Women in Trades and Technology interviewed a number of women who worked on the Hibernia offshore-oil project based in Bull Arm, Newfoundland, in 1995. The women interviewed expressed concerns ranging from "not being allowed to do the heavy work they were trained and hired to do" to "degrading and sexual remarks made by male co-workers." The women reported being uncomfortable bringing the problems to their unions or management, and they received little support or help when they did. The researchers made a number of recommendations for both the Hibernia project, which has since been completed, as well as for future projects such as the Terra Nova offshore oil development and the Voisey Bay nickel discovery in Labrador. These recommendations include:[5]

a) developing formal avenues to consult with women about integrating into non-traditional jobs;

b) planning work camps with the needs of women in mind;

c) providing better on-site education about sexual harassment;

d) creating an employment equity plan covering recruitment, training, and promotion.

In another example, Markham, Ontario-based Magna International Inc. is facing a sexual harassment suit in the United States brought by a former saleswoman in the parts maker's Detroit sales office. The woman alleges that she faced harassment in the office, and her male co-workers regularly entertained customers at area strip clubs. One of the allegations in the complaint is that one of the Magna sales managers spent $23 000 in 1996 entertaining customers at strip joints and other bars and restaurants. Magna denies the charges and has issued a memo to customers and employees in the Detroit area that the company "does not tolerate any form of sexual discrimination or harassment." However, auto industry executives and observers agree that the auto business remains male-dominated, and that some purchasing executives are entertained at strip clubs. Scott Upham, president of Providata Inc., an analyst firm located in Southgate, Michigan, said that entertaining this way "is less prevalent than it used to be. I used to work at suppliers where this sort of conduct was commonplace. There are certain customers who want to be entertained that way, just like some like to go to the ball game."

The Magna example raises questions for both employers and employees about appropriate client and customer relationships, particularly with both more women in the workplace and more women in the roles of clients and customers. Behaviour that may have once been tolerated because it was restricted to interactions between males is less tolerated in today's working environment.

Sears Canada faced a sexual harassment issue that turned into a murder-suicide at a Sears store in Windsor, Ontario. Theresa Vince, a human resources supervisor, was killed by her store manager, Russell Davis, on June 2, 1996. Davis, who'd been sexually harassing her, then turned the gun on himself. Davis was infatuated with Vince and continuously gave her praise and compliments. Vince complained to her regional human resources manager and confronted Davis with her objections. Though he apologized, the situation persisted. Even co-workers noticed the abnormal attention Davis paid to Vince. However, Vince rejected Sears Canada's recommendation that Davis be transferred, instead requesting that Sears Canada not pursue Davis further. Sears honoured Vince's wishes. However, the harassment did not stop, and Vince decided to retire. She was killed on her last day on the job. This example raises the question of when and how an employer should become involved in a sexual harassment complaint.

A coroner's inquest into the murder-suicide released recommendations in December 1997 to various groups involved in dealing with sexual harassment in Ontario. These recommendations could equally apply to the other provinces and territories in Canada:[6]

Employers: Should have effective workplace harassment and discrimination policies and procedures in place. Confidential sources of help should be offered.

Ontario Human Rights Commission: Should develop an advertising campaign, encouraging victims to come forward with their complaints. The commission's services should be periodically reviewed by an outside audit.

Ontario Ministry of Labour: Should make a priority of the ongoing study of sexual harassment as a health and safety issue, so an informed decision about including it under labour legislation can be made.

Province: Should make funds available to the human rights commission, allowing it to increase its investigation capabilities and "prevent cases from falling through the cracks."

Though sexual harassment is defined by the law, and there are procedures for dealing with it through human rights tribunals, organizations are still trying to define their own policies and procedures. Vancouver-based lawyer Heather MacKenzie notes that: "Companies have a direct financial interest in ensuring they have a comprehensive policy in place. The courts have said you also have to educate all members of the organization about how the policy works."[7]

Sources:

[1] J. Goddu, "Sexual Harassment Complaints Rise Dramatically," *Canadian Press Newswire*, March 6, 1998.

[2] M. Jimenez, "Sexual Harassment at Work Prevalent in B.C., Poll Shows," *Vancouver Sun*, May 4, 1998, pp. A1, A2.

[3] J. Tibbets, "Human Rights Agency Says Protection Laws at Standstill," *Canadian Press Newswire*, March 24, 1998.

[4] P. Arab, "Sexual Harassment Ruled a Workplace Safety Hazard," *Canadian Press Newswire*, August 22, 1997.

[5] "Female Workers Mistreated at Hibernia, Study Says," *Plant*, September 2, 1996, p. 4.

[6] "Harassment Inquest Doesn't Go Far Enough, Say Critics," *Canadian Press Newswire*, December 2, 1997.

[7] Marina Jiminez, "Sexual Harassment at Work Prevalent in B.C., Poll Shows, "*Vancouver Sun*, May 4, 1998, pp.A1, A2.

Summary and Implications

For the Workplace

If you want to get things done in a group or organization, it helps to have power. To maximize your power, you will want to increase others' dependence on you. You can, for instance, increase your power in relation to your boss by developing knowledge or a skill that he or she needs and for which there is no ready substitute. However, power is a two-way street. You will not be alone in attempting to build your power bases. Others, particularly subordinates, will be seeking to make you dependent on them. The result is a continual battle. While you seek to maximize others' dependence on you, you will be seeking to minimize your dependence on others. And, of course, others you work with will be trying to do the same.

Few employees relish being powerless in their job and organization. It has been argued, for instance, that when people in organizations are difficult, argumentative, and temperamental, it may be because they are in positions of powerlessness where the performance expectations placed on them exceed their resources and capabilities.[55]

There is evidence that people respond differently to the various power bases.[56] Expert and referent power are derived from an individual's personal qualities. In contrast, coercion, reward, and legitimate power are essentially organizationally derived. Since people are more likely to enthusiastically accept and commit to an individual whom they admire or whose knowledge they respect (rather than someone who relies on his or her position to reward or coerce them), the effective use of expert and referent power should

lead to higher employee performance, commitment, and satisfaction. Evidence indicates, for instance, that employees working under managers who use coercive power are unlikely to be committed to the organization and more likely to resist the managers' influence attempts.[57] In contrast, expert power has been found to be the most strongly and consistently related to effective employee performance.[58] For example, in a study of five organizations, knowledge was the most effective base for getting others to perform as desired.[59] Competence appears to offer wide appeal, and its use as a power base results in high performance by group members. The message here for managers seems to be: Develop and use your expert power base!

The power of your boss may also play a role in determining your job satisfaction. "One of the reasons many of us like to work for and with people who are powerful is that they are generally more pleasant—not because it is their native disposition, but because the reputation and reality of being powerful permits them more discretion and more ability to delegate to others."[60]

The effective manager accepts the political nature of organizations. By assessing behaviour in a political framework, you can better predict the actions of others and use this information to formulate political strategies that will gain advantages for you and your work unit.

In terms of office politics, we can report that the more political employees perceive an organization to be, the lower their satisfaction.[61] However, this conclusion must be moderated to reflect the employees' level in the organization.[62] Lower-ranking employees, who lack the power base and the means of influence needed to benefit from the political game, perceive organizational politics as a source of frustration and indicate lower satisfaction. But higher-ranking employees, who are in a better position to handle political behaviour and benefit from it, don't tend to exhibit this negative attitude.

A final thought on organizational politics: Regardless of level in the organization, some people are just significantly more "politically astute" than are others. Although there is little evidence to support or negate the following conclusion, it seems reasonable that the politically naive or inept are likely to exhibit lower job satisfaction than their politically astute counterparts. The politically naive and inept tend to feel continually powerless to influence those decisions that most affect them. They look at actions around them and are perplexed at why they are regularly "shafted" by colleagues, bosses, and "the system."

For You as an Individual

Power and politics reveal themselves in a variety of ways, and not just in the workplace. Within volunteer organizations, and even in informal groups, some people seem to have more power than others. We identified some of the factors that lead to differences in power, including the amount of information one has, the kind of role one plays, and the scarcity of resources. In other words, there are ways to increase your power. In particular, you could acquire more knowledge about a situation and then use that information to help your group perform better on one of its projects.

We also discussed politicking, which involves getting others to understand and appreciate your ideas. We presented positive ways of doing this that may make you a more effective team member. In particular, building coalitions where everyone feels that decisions will be "win-win" creates a more productive environment than one where some people become upset at the thought that they have lost something.

ROADMAP REMINDER

In the previous chapter we considered leadership and how leaders can inspire organizational members to perform. In this chapter we looked at the notion of power. Leaders have power, but they are not the only people in the organization who hold power. The secretary to the president also wields considerable power, as he or she determines who will actually get to speak or meet with the boss. We also considered office politics. In the next chapter we consider the topic of conflict and negotiation. Conflict is often the result of power struggles, and negotiation is part of the process of politics.

For Review

1. What is power? How do you get it?
2. Contrast power tactics with power bases. What are some of the key contingency variables that determine which tactic a powerholder is likely to use?
3. Which of the five power bases lie with the individual? Which are derived from the organization?
4. State the general dependency postulate. What does it mean?
5. What creates dependency? Give an applied example.
6. What is a coalition? When is it likely to develop?
7. How are power and politics related?
8. Define political behaviour. Why is politics a fact of life in organizations?
9. What factors contribute to political activity?
10. Define sexual harassment. Who is most likely to harass a female employee: her boss, co-worker, or subordinate?

For Discussion

1. Based on the information presented in this chapter, what would you do as a recent university graduate entering a new job to maximize your power and accelerate your career progress?
2. "More powerful managers are good for an organization. It is the powerless, not the powerful, who are the ineffective managers." Do you agree or disagree with this statement? Discuss.
3. You're a sales representative for an international software company. After four excellent years, sales in your territory are off 30 percent this year. Describe three defensive responses you might use to reduce the potential negative consequences of this decline in sales.
4. "Sexual harassment should not be tolerated at the workplace." "Workplace romances are a natural occurrence in organizations." Are both of these statements true? Can they be reconciled?
5. Which impression management techniques have you used? What ethical implications are there in using impression management?

LEARNING ABOUT YOURSELF EXERCISE

How Political Are You?

To determine your political tendencies, please answer the following questions. Check the answer that best represents your behaviour or belief, even if that particular behaviour or belief is not present all the time.

	True	False
1. You should make others feel important through an open appreciation of their ideas and work.	_____	_____
2. Because people tend to judge you when they first meet you, always try to make a good first impression.	_____	_____
3. Try to let others do most of the talking, be sympathetic to their problems, and resist telling people that they are totally wrong.	_____	_____
4. Praise the good traits of the people you meet and always give people an opportunity to save face if they are wrong or make a mistake.	_____	_____
5. Spreading false rumours, planting misleading information, and backstabbing are necessary, if somewhat unpleasant, methods to deal with your enemies.	_____	_____
6. Sometimes it is necessary to make promises that you know you will not or cannot keep.	_____	_____
7. It is important to get along with everybody, even with those who are generally recognized as windbags, abrasive, or constant complainers.	_____	_____
8. It is vital to do favours for others so that you can call in these IOUs at times when they will do you the most good.	_____	_____
9. Be willing to compromise, particularly on issues that are minor to you but major to others.	_____	_____
10. On controversial issues, it is important to delay or avoid your involvement if possible.	_____	_____

Turn to page 701 for scoring directions and key.

Source: J.F. Byrnes, "The Political Behavior Inventory." With permission.

WORKING WITH OTHERS EXERCISE

Understanding Power Dynamics

1. **Creation of groups**

   Students are to turn in a loonie (or similar value of currency) to the instructor and are divided into three groups based on criteria given by the instructor, assigned to their workplaces, and instructed to read the following rules and tasks. The money is divided into thirds, giving two-thirds of it to the top group, one-third to the middle group, and none to the bottom group.

2. **Conduct exercise**

   Groups go to their assigned work places and have 30 minutes to complete their tasks.

   Rules

   a. Members of the top group are free to enter the space of either of the other groups and to communicate whatever they wish, whenever they wish. Members of the middle group may enter the space of the lower group when they wish but must request permission to enter the top group's space (which the top group can refuse). Members of the lower group may not disturb the top group in any way unless specifically invited by the top. The lower group does have the right to knock on the door of the middle group and request permission to communicate with them (which can also be refused).

   b. The members of the top group have the authority to make any change in the rules that they wish, at any time, with or without notice.

   Tasks

   a. Top Group: To be responsible for the overall effectiveness and learning from the exercise, and to decide how to use its money.

   b. Middle Group: To assist the top group in providing for the overall welfare of the organization, and to decide how to use its money.

   c. Bottom Group: To identify its resources and to decide how best to provide for learning and the overall effectiveness of the organization.

3. **Debriefing**

   Each of the three groups chooses two representatives to go to the front of the class and discuss the following questions:

   a. Summarize what occurred within and among the three groups.

   b. What are some of the differences between being in the top group versus being in the bottom group?

   c. What can we learn about power from this experience?

   d. How accurate do you think this exercise is to the reality of resource allocation decisions in large organizations?

Source: This exercise is adapted from L. Bolman and T.E. Deal, *Exchange*, vol. 3, no. 4, 1979, pp. 38–42. Reprinted by permission of Sage Publications, Inc.

CASE INCIDENT

Damned If You Do; Damned If You Don't

Fran Gilson has spent 15 years with the Thompson Grocery Company, starting out as a part-time cashier and rising up through the ranks of the grocery store chain.* Today, at 34, she is a regional manager, overseeing seven stores and earning nearly $110 000 a year. About five weeks ago, she was contacted by an executive-search firm inquiring about her interest in the position of vice-president and regional manager for a national drugstore chain. The position would be responsible for more than 100 stores in five provinces. After two meetings with top executives at the drugstore chain, she was notified two days ago that she was one of two finalists for the job.

The only person at Thompson who knows this news is Fran's good friend and colleague, Ken Hamilton. Ken is director of finance for the grocery chain. "It's a dream job, with a lot more responsibility," Fran told Ken. "The pay is almost double what I earn here and I'd be their only female vice-president. The job would allow me to be a more visible role model for young women and give me a bigger voice in opening up doors for women and ethnic minorities in retailing management."

Since Fran wanted to keep the fact that she was looking at another job secret, she asked Ken, whom she trusted completely, to be one of her references. He promised to write a great recommendation for her. Fran made it very clear to the recruiter that Ken was the only person at Thompson who knew she was considering another job. She knew that if anyone heard she was talking to another company, it might seriously jeopardize her chances for promotion. It's against this backdrop that this morning's incident became more than just a question of sexual harassment. It became a full-blown ethical and political dilemma for Fran.

Jennifer Chung has been a financial analyst in Ken's department for five months. Fran met Jennifer through Ken and her impression of Jennifer is quite positive. In many ways, Jennifer strikes Fran as a lot like she was 10 years ago. This morning, Jennifer came into Fran's office. It was immediately evident that something was wrong. Jennifer was very nervous and uncomfortable, which was most unlike her. Jennifer said that about a month after she joined Thompson, Ken began making off-colour comments to her when they were alone. And from there the behaviour escalated further. Ken would leer at her, put his arm over her shoulder when they were reviewing reports, even pat her bum. Every time one of these occurrences happened, Jennifer would ask him to stop and not do it again, but it fell on deaf ears. Yesterday, Ken reminded Jennifer that her six-month probationary review was coming up. "He told me that if I didn't sleep with him that I couldn't expect a very favourable evaluation."

Jennifer said that she had come to Fran because she didn't know what to do or to whom to turn. "I came to you, Fran, because you're a friend of Ken's and the highest-ranking woman here. Will you help me?" Fran had never heard anything like this about Ken before, but had no reason to suspect that Jennifer was lying either.

Questions

1. Analyse Fran's situation in a purely legal sense.
2. Analyse Fran's dilemma in political terms.
3. Analyse Fran's situation in an ethical sense. What is the ethically right thing for her to do? Is that also the politically right thing to do?
4. If you were Fran, what would you do?

* The identity of this organization and the people described are disguised for obvious reasons.

Jumbo Glacier

The Jumbo Glacier Alpine Resort, proposed by Vancouver-based Pheidias Project Management Corp., has been buried by the B.C. government's environmental-approval process since 1991. The proposed resort, located in the Purcell Mountains of East Kootenays, British Columbia, would be the highest, longest, wildest ski hill in North America. However, the project is opposed by environmentalists. They believe the resort will harm B.C.'s grizzly-bear population. There's also concern about the number of people who will venture to the resort area, which currently is the largest undisturbed wilderness remaining in the region.

Oberto Oberti, Pheidias' president, on the other hand, sees the site as perfect for skiing, because the climate and glacier would allow for year-round skiing, which is currently only available in Europe. To try to convince some of his opposition, he had a meeting with British Columbia's Government Review Committee in December 1995. The politics of the decision showed in those meetings. At his practice debate at the local school, students seemed cool to his ideas. The representative for the local residents stressed that they don't want their area turned into another Banff or Whistler. An American ski guide, brought to show another side of the story, argued that Oberti's idea is innovative, and that there is no known comparable ski resort in North America. And Oberti claims he's not trying to make money so much as develop the ideal ski resort.

Oberti recognizes the politics of the situation, however. As he notes, "You can have clients who get upset, and they'll kill your project in one day." He still believes he can manage the politics, however. And he doesn't intend to give up on his dream of a European-like ski resort in North America.

The fate of the development will be decided by British Columbia's Minister of Environment, Lands and Parks, and the Minister of Employment and Investment in late 1998.

Questions

1. Describe how power and politics affect the decision to develop Jumbo Glacier.

2. Describe the bases of power in use by the environmental group and the local residents.

3. What political strategies might Oberto Oberti use to possibly persuade the residents and environmentalists to be more supportive of the Jumbo Glacier Alpine Resort?

Sources: Based on "Jumbo Glacier," *Venture 570;* aired December 17, 1995; and E. Shilts, "Resort retort," *Canadian Geographic,* November/December 1997, p. 20.

POINT

It's a Political Jungle Out There!

Nick is a talented television camera operator. He has worked on a number of popular television shows over a 10-year period, but he has had trouble keeping those jobs. While most other camera operators and production employees are rehired from one season to the next, Nick seems never to be called back for a second year. It isn't that Nick isn't competent. Quite the contrary, his technical knowledge and formal education are typically more impressive than the directors he works for. Nick's problem is that he frequently disagrees with the camera angles that directors want him to set up, and he has no qualms about expressing his displeasure to those directors. He also feels some need to offer unsolicited suggestions to directors and producers on how to improve camera placements and shots.

Ellen is also a camera operator. Like Nick, Ellen sees directors and producers regularly making decisions that she doesn't agree with. But Ellen holds her tongue and does what she's told. She recently finished her third straight year as the lead camera operator on one of Canada's most successful comedies.

Ellen gets it. Nick doesn't. Nick has failed to recognize the reality that organizations are political systems. While Ellen is secure in her job, Nick's career continues to suffer because of his political naiveté.

It would be nice if all organizations or formal groups within organizations could be described as supportive, harmonious, objective, trusting, collaborative, or cooperative. A nonpolitical perspective can lead one to believe that employees will always behave in ways consistent with the interests of the organization, and that competence and high performance will always be rewarded. In contrast, a political view can explain much of what may seem to be irrational behaviour in organizations. It can help to explain, for instance, why employees withhold information, restrict output, attempt to "build empires," publicize their successes, hide their failures, distort performance figures to make themselves look better, and en-

gage in similar activities that appear to be at odds with the organization's desire for effectiveness and efficiency.

For those who want tangible evidence that "it's a political jungle out there" in the real world, let's look at two studies. The first analyzed what it takes to get promoted fast in organizations. The second addressed the performance appraisal process.

Fred Luthans and his associates[1] studied more than 450 managers. They found that these managers engaged in four managerial activities: traditional management (decision-making, planning, and controlling), communication (exchanging routine information and processing paperwork), human resource management (motivating, disciplining, managing conflict, staffing, and training), and networking (socializing, politicking, and interacting with outsiders). Those managers who were promoted fastest spent 48 percent of their time networking. The average managers spent most of their efforts on traditional management and communication activities and only 19 percent of their time networking. We suggest that this provides strong evidence of the importance that social and political skills play in getting ahead in organizations.

Longenecker and his associates[2] held in-depth interviews with 60 upper-level executives to find out what went into performance ratings. What they found was that executives frankly admitted to deliberately manipulating formal appraisals for political purposes. Accuracy was not a primary concern of these executives. Rather, they manipulated the appraisal results in an intentional and systematic manner to get the outcomes they wanted. ■

Sources

[1] F. Luthans, R.M. Hodgetts, and S.A. Rosenkrantz, *Real Managers* (Cambridge, MA: Ballinger, 1988).

[2] C.O. Longenecker, D.A. Gioia, and H.P. Sims, Jr., "Behind the Mask: The Politics of Employee Appraisal," *Academy of Management Executive*, August 1987, pp. 183–94.

counterPOINT

Corporate Politics: What You See Is What You Get!

Organizational behaviour currently appears to be undergoing a period of fascination with workplace politics. Proponents argue that politics is inevitable in organizations—that power struggles, alliance formations, strategic manoeuvrings, and cutthroat actions are as endemic to organizational life as work schedules and meetings. But is organizational politics inevitable? Maybe not. The existence of politics may be a perceptual interpretation.[1]

A recent study suggests that politics are more myth and interpretation than reality.[2] In this study of 180 experienced managers, 92 men and 88 women completed questionnaires. They analysed a series of decisions and indicated the degree to which they thought the decisions were influenced by politics. They also completed a measure that assessed political inevitability. This included items such as: "Politics is a normal part of any decision-making process," and "Politics can have as many helpful outcomes for the organizations as harmful ones." Additionally, the questionnaire asked respondents their beliefs about power and control in the world at large. Finally, respondents provided data on their income, job responsibilities, and years of managerial experience.

The study found that beliefs about politics affected how respondents perceived organizational events. Those managers who held strong beliefs in the inevitability of politics tended to see their own organization and the decision situations in the questionnaire in highly political terms. Moreover, there was evidence suggesting that these beliefs encompass not only beliefs about politics but also about power and control in the world at large. Managers who viewed the world as posing difficult and complex problems and ruled by luck also tended to perceive events as highly politicized. That is, they perceived organizations as part of a disorderly and unpredictable world where politics is inevitable.

Interestingly, not *all* managers viewed organizations as political jungles. It was typically the inexperienced managers, with lower incomes and more limited responsibilities, who held this view. The researchers concluded that because junior managers often lack clear understandings of how organizations really work, they tend to interpret events as irrational. It's through their attempts to make sense of their situations that these junior managers may come to make political attributions.

This study attempted to determine whether the corporate political jungle is myth, reality, or a matter of interpretation. The popular press often presents the political jungle as the dominant corporate reality where gamesmanship and manipulation are key to survival. However, the findings of this study suggest that a manager's political reality is somewhat mythical in nature, partially constructed through his or her beliefs about politics' inevitability and about power and control in the world. More specifically, it's the inexperienced managers—those who are likely to hold the fewest and least accurate interpretations of organizational events—who perceive the extent of organizational politics to be greatest.

So if there is a corporate political jungle, it appears to be mostly in the eyes of the young and inexperienced. Because they tend to have less understanding of organizational processes and less power to influence outcomes, they are more likely to see organizations through a political lens. More experienced and higher-ranking managers, on the other hand, are more likely to see the corporate political jungle as a myth. ■

Sources:

[1] See, for instance, C.P. Parker, R.L. Dipboye, and S.L. Jackson, "Perceptions of Organizational Politics: An Investigation of Antecedents and Consequences," *Journal of Management*, vol. 21, no. 5, 1995, pp. 891–912; and G.R. Ferris, D.D. Frink, M.C. Galang, J. Zhou, K.M. Kacmar, and J.L. Howard, "Perceptions of Organizational Politics: Prediction, Stress-Related Implications, and Outcomes," *Human Relations*, February 1996, pp. 233–66.

[2] Cited in C. Kirchmeyer, "The Corporate Political Jungle: Myth, Reality, or a Matter of Interpretation," in C. Harris and C.C. Lundberg (eds.), *Proceedings of the 29th Annual Eastern Academy of Management* (Baltimore, 1992), pp. 161–64.

CHAPTER 13

Conflict and Negotiation

ROADMAP

LEARNING OBJECTIVES

After studying this chapter, you should be able to

- Define conflict

- Differentiate between functional and dysfunctional conflict

- Outline the conflict process

- Describe the five conflict-handling intentions

- Contrast distributive and integrative bargaining

- Describe the five steps in the negotiation process

For 37 years, Wallace McCain and his older brother Harrison shared command of McCain Foods Ltd., the New Brunswick-based french-fry empire they had built together.[1] In August 1993, however, that partnership came to an end, after the *Financial Post* profiled Wallace's son Michael, referring to him as "the leading candidate to become the potato king." Apparently, it was that reference to Michael (shown in the photo at right) as successor that started what the newspapers called "the feud of the century."

The public display of animosity came as somewhat of a surprise. The brothers started McCain Foods in 1956 and "one brother never made a decision without consulting the other." Their offices in Florenceville, New Brunswick were linked by an unlocked door. They seemed suited to working together. Harrison was the outgoing salesman. Wallace was quieter, the number-cruncher who managed the books. The partnership worked. In the first year, sales were $152 678. And sales of McCain Foods products are expected to top $5 billion in 1998. While the core of the business remains french fries, non-food subsidiaries include a large trucking division and a national courier company.

What brought these two brothers down was a conflict, which had simmered quietly for 20 years, over who would succeed the brothers to run the family business. Harrison convinced other family members that Wallace and his sons would not share the business with the other McCains. The dispute ended up in a New Brunswick arbitration court where Wallace McCain was ousted as co-CEO. Eighteen months after the *Financial Post* article appeared, Wallace left McCain Foods and moved to Toronto to become chairman of Maple Leaf Foods Ltd. Meanwhile, Harrison fired his nephew Michael, and ordered the locks changed on his office door. Michael joined his father at Maple Leaf, where he is now President and CEO. Ultimately the brothers could not resolve their conflict, and more than four years after the feud went public, Harrison acknowledged, "There are still strained relations in our family holding company. I wish I could say the bitterness is all gone, but that would be an overstatement." ■

For a closer look at the conflict in the McCain family business, see the first of this chapter's two CBC video cases. Conflict can be a serious problem in *any* organization. It might not lead to co-CEOs going after each other in court—as happened at McCains—but it certainly can hurt an organization's performance as well as lead to the loss of many good employees. However, as we show in this chapter, all conflicts aren't bad. Conflict has a positive side and a negative side. We explain the differences in this chapter and provide a guide to help you understand how conflicts develop. We also present the topic of negotiation in this chapter, to give you further information about how conflicts between parties can be resolved. But let's begin by clarifying what we mean by conflict.

A Definition of Conflict

There has been no shortage of definitions of conflict.[2] Despite the divergent meanings the term has acquired, several common themes underlie most definitions. Conflict must be *perceived* by the parties to it; whether conflict exists is a perception issue. If no one is aware of a conflict, then it is generally agreed that no conflict exists. Additional commonalities in the definitions are opposition or incompatibility and some form of interaction.[3] These factors set the conditions that determine the beginning point of the conflict process.

conflict
A process that begins when one party perceives that another party has negatively affected, or is about to negatively affect, something that the first party cares about.

We can define **conflict**, then, as a process that begins when one party perceives that another party has negatively affected, or is about to negatively affect, something that the first party cares about.[4]

This definition is deliberately broad. It describes that point in any ongoing activity when an interaction "crosses over" to become an interparty conflict. It encompasses the wide range of conflicts that people experience in organizations—incompatibility of goals, differences over interpretations of facts, disagreements based on behavioural expectations, and the like. Finally, our definition is flexible enough to cover the full range of conflict levels—from overt and violent acts to subtle forms of disagreement.

Functional versus Dysfunctional Conflict

The board of Sunbeam-Oster fired the company's chairman, Paul Kazarian, in 1993.[5] Three years earlier, Kazarian took over the company when it was in bankruptcy. He sold off losing businesses, restructured the remaining appliance operation, and turned a $56-million loss in 1990 into a $66-million profit in 1991. A few days before he was fired, the company reported a 40 percent jump in quarterly profits. But Kazarian's "crime" was that he rubbed a lot of people in the company the wrong way. He aggressively confronted managers, employees, and suppliers. People complained that his style was abrasive. Kazarian, however, defended his actions as necessary: "You don't change a company in bankruptcy without making a few waves. I wasn't there to be a polite manager. I was there to create value for stockholders."

Sunbeam-Oster
http://www.oster.com/

In the Sunbeam-Oster example, the board clearly felt that conflict was bad for the organization, and they fired Kazarian to get rid of the conflict. Kazarian, by contrast, could argue that the quick turnaround in profits was a direct result of the conflicts he created. These opposing viewpoints suggests that one should not label all conflict as either good *or* bad. Rather,

functional conflict
Conflict that supports the goals of the group and improves its performance.

dysfunctional conflict
Conflict that hinders group performance.

some conflicts support the goals of the group and improve its performance; these are **functional**, constructive forms of conflict. Additionally, there are conflicts that hinder group performance; these are **dysfunctional** or destructive forms of conflict. The conflict among brothers Harrison and Wallace McCain reported in the chapter opening was clearly in the dysfunctional category.

Of course, it is one thing to argue that conflict can be valuable for the group, and another to be able to tell whether a conflict is functional or dysfunctional.[6] The demarcation between functional and dysfunctional is neither clear nor precise. No one level of conflict can be regarded as acceptable or unacceptable under all conditions. The type and level of conflict that creates healthy and positive involvement toward one group's goals today may, in another group or in the same group at another time, be highly dysfunctional.

The criterion that differentiates functional from dysfunctional conflict is group performance. Since groups exist to attain a goal or goals, it is the impact that the conflict has on the group, rather than on any individual member, that determines functionality. Of course, the impact of conflict on the individual and its impact on the group are rarely mutually exclusive, so the ways that individuals perceive a conflict may have an important influence on its effect on the group. However, this need not always be the case. For instance, while many people at Sunbeam-Oster thought the conflicts created by Paul Kazarian were dysfunctional, Kazarian was convinced they were functional because they improved Sunbeam's performance. So the conflicts created problems for individuals at Sunbeam-Oster at the same time that they appear to have increased performance for the company as a whole. For more on the debate about whether conflict is positive or dysfuntional, see this chapter's Point/Counterpoint debate.

ME International
http://www.cam.org/~meitcon
/page6.html

These employees of ME International, a manufacturer of metal grinding balls, illustrate the positive view of conflict. The president of ME challenged his workers to develop a statement of corporate values. He hired consultant Rob Lebow (standing, centre) to maintain an ongoing minimum level of conflict during the process by encouraging employees to express personal beliefs and opinions and openly question and disagree with each others' ideas. Such conflict kept employees self-critical and creative, improving their performance in determining a set of shared values and in choosing the words that best reflect those values.

The Conflict Process

The conflict process can be seen as comprising five stages: potential opposition or incompatibility, cognition and personalization, intentions, behaviour, and outcomes. The process is diagrammed in Exhibit 13-1.

Stage I: Potential Opposition or Incompatibility

The first step in the conflict process is the presence of conditions that create opportunities for conflict to arise. They *need not* lead directly to conflict, but one of these conditions is necessary if conflict is to arise. For simplicity's sake, these conditions (which also may be looked at as causes or sources of conflict) have been condensed into three general categories: communication, structure, and personal variables.[7]

COMMUNICATION Susan Namura had worked in purchasing at a large pharmaceutical company for three years. She enjoyed her work in large part because her boss, Tim McGuire, was a great guy to work for. Then Tim got promoted six months ago and Chuck Benson took his place. Susan says her job is a lot more frustrating now. "Tim and I were on the same wavelength. It's not that way with Chuck. He tells me something and I do it. Then he tells me I did it wrong. I think he means one thing but says something else. It's been like this since the day he arrived. I don't think a day goes by when he isn't yelling at me for something. You know, there are some people you just find it easy to communicate with. Well, Chuck isn't one of those!"

Susan's comments illustrate that communication can be a source of conflict. It represents those opposing forces that arise from semantic difficulties, misunderstandings, and "noise" in the communication channels. Much of this discussion can be related back to our comments on communication in Chapter 9.

One of the major myths that most of us carry around with us is that poor communication is the reason for conflicts—"if we could just communicate with each other, we could eliminate our differences." Such a conclusion is not unreasonable, given the amount of time each of us spends communicating. But, of course, poor communication is certainly not the source of all conflicts, though there is considerable evidence to suggest that problems in the communication process act to retard collaboration and stimulate misunderstanding.

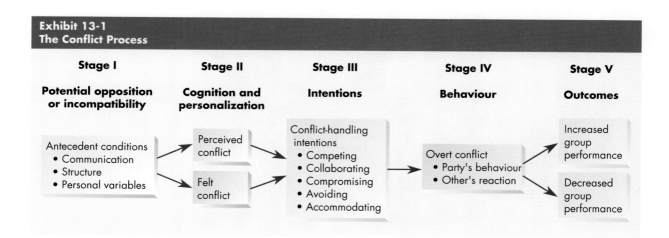

Exhibit 13-1
The Conflict Process

As we saw in Chapter 9, semantic difficulties, insufficient exchange of information, and noise in the communication channel are all barriers to communication. Therefore these are potential antecedent conditions to conflict. Specifically, evidence demonstrates that semantic difficulties arise as a result of differences in training, selective perception, and inadequate information about others. Research has further demonstrated a surprising finding: the potential for conflict increases when either too little or too much communication takes place. Apparently, an increase in communication is functional up to a point, whereupon it is possible to overcommunicate, with a resultant increase in the potential for conflict. Too much information as well as too little can lay the foundation for conflict. Furthermore, the channel chosen for communicating can have an influence on stimulating opposition. The filtering process that occurs as information is passed between members and the divergence of communications from formal or previously established channels offer potential opportunities for conflict to arise.

STRUCTURE Charlotte and Teri both work at a large discount-furniture retailer. Charlotte is a salesperson on the floor; Teri is the company credit manager. The two women have known each other for years and have much in common—they live within two blocks of each other, and their oldest daughters attend the same junior high school and are best friends. In reality, if Charlotte and Teri had different jobs they might be best friends themselves, but these two women are consistently fighting battles with each other. Charlotte's job is to sell furniture and she does a great job. But most of her sales are made on credit. Because Teri's job is to ensure that the company minimizes credit losses, she regularly has to turn down the credit application of a customer to whom Charlotte has just closed a sale. It's nothing personal between Charlotte and Teri—the requirements of their jobs just bring them into conflict.

The conflicts between Charlotte and Teri are structural in nature. The term *structure* is used, in this context, to include variables such as size, degree of specialization in the tasks assigned to group members, jurisdictional clarity, member-goal compatibility, leadership styles, reward systems, and the degree of dependence between groups.

Research indicates that size and specialization act as forces to stimulate conflict. The larger the group and the more specialized its activities, the greater the likelihood of conflict. Tenure and conflict have been found to be inversely related. The potential for conflict tends to be greatest where group members are younger and where turnover is high.

The greater the ambiguity in precisely defining where responsibility for actions lies, the greater the potential for conflict to emerge. Such jurisdictional ambiguities increase intergroup fighting for control of resources and territory.

Groups within organizations have diverse goals. For instance, research and development's goals are to identify new niches and develop innovative products, purchasing is concerned with the timely acquisition of inputs at low prices, marketing's goals concentrate on disposing of outputs and increasing revenues, quality control's attention is focused on improving quality and ensuring that the organization's products meet standards, and production units seek efficiency of operations by maintaining a steady production flow. This diversity of goals among groups is a major source of conflict. When groups within an organization seek diverse ends, some of which—such as sales and credit at the discount-furniture retailer—are inherently at odds, there are increased opportunities for conflict.

There is some indication that a close style of leadership—tight and continuous observation with general control of others' behaviours—increases conflict potential, but the evidence is not particularly strong. Too much reliance on participation may also stimulate conflict. Research tends to confirm that participation and conflict are highly correlated, apparently because participation encourages the promotion of differences. Reward systems, too, are found to create conflict when one member's gain is at another's expense. Finally, if a group is dependent on another group (in contrast to the two being mutually independent) or if interdependence allows one group to gain at another's expense, opposing forces are stimulated.

PERSONAL VARIABLES Did you ever meet someone to whom you took an immediate dislike? Most of the opinions they expressed, you disagreed with. Even insignificant characteristics—the sound of their voice, the smirk when they smiled, their personality—annoyed you. We've all met people like that. When you have to work with such individuals, there is often the potential for conflict.

Our last category of potential sources of conflict is personal variables. As indicated, they include the individual value systems that each person has and the personality characteristics that account for individual idiosyncrasies and differences.

The evidence indicates that certain personality types—for example, individuals who are highly authoritarian and dogmatic, and who demonstrate low esteem—lead to potential conflict. Most important, and probably the most overlooked variable in the study of social conflict, is differing value systems. Value differences, for example, are the best explanation of such diverse issues as prejudice, disagreements over one's contribution to the group and the rewards one deserves, and assessments of whether this particular book is any good. That John dislikes Indo-Canadians and Dana believes John's position indicates his ignorance, that an employee thinks he is worth $60 000 a year but his boss believes him to be worth $55 000, and that Ann thinks this book is interesting to read while Jennifer views it as garbage are all value judgments. And differences in value systems are important sources for creating the potential for conflict.

Stage II: Cognition and Personalization

If the conditions cited in Stage I negatively affect something that one party cares about, then the potential for opposition or incompatibility becomes actualized in the second stage. The antecedent conditions can only lead to conflict when one or more of the parties are affected by, and aware of, the conflict.

As we noted in our definition of conflict, perception is required. Therefore, one or more of the parties must be aware of the existence of the antecedent conditions. However, because a conflict is **perceived** does not mean that it is personalized. In other words, "A may be aware that B and A are in serious disagreement . . . but it may not make A tense or anxious, and it may have no effect whatsoever on A's affection toward B."[8] It is at the **felt** level, when individuals become emotionally involved, that parties experience anxiety, tension, frustration, or hostility.

Keep in mind two points. First, Stage II is important because it's where conflict issues tend to be defined. This is the place in the process where the parties decide what the conflict is about.[9] And, in turn, this "sense making"

perceived conflict
Awareness by one or more parties of the existence of conditions that create opportunities for conflict to arise.

felt conflict
Emotional involvement in a conflict creating anxiety, tenseness, frustration, or hostility.

Positive emotions played a key role in shaping perceptions when a new member joined the world-famous Tokyo String Quartet. The chemistry among the original members, all Japanese musicians, was incredibly strong, as they had practised and performed together for decades. When one of the original artists left the group, remaining members Kazukide Isomura, Sadao Harada, and Kikuei Ikeda asked Canadian violinist Peter Oundjian to take his place. With an outsider's perspective, Oundjian began questioning everything the ensemble did, from musical selections to tour destinations. Rather than perceiving the new violinist's ideas in a negative way, the other members framed the conflict as a potential win-win situation. They took a positive approach, viewing the situation as an opportunity to make the group more creative and innovative.

is critical because the way a conflict is defined goes a long way toward establishing the sort of outcomes that might settle it. For instance, if I define our salary disagreement as a zero-sum situation—that is, if you receive the increase in pay you want, there will be just that amount less for me—I will be far less willing to compromise than if I frame the conflict as a potential win-win situation (i.e., the dollars in the salary pool might be increased so that both of us could get the added pay we want). So the definition of a conflict is important, for it typically delineates the set of possible settlements. Our second point is that emotions play a major role in shaping perceptions.[10] For example, negative emotions have been found to produce oversimplification of issues, reductions in trust, and negative interpretations of the other party's behaviour.[11] In contrast, positive feelings have been found to increase the tendency to see potential relationships among the elements of a problem, to take a broader view of the situation, and to develop more innovative solutions.[12]

Stage III: Intentions

intentions
Decisions to act in a given way in a conflict episode.

Intentions intervene between people's perceptions and emotions and their overt behaviour. These intentions are decisions to act in a given way.[13]

Why are intentions separated out as a distinct stage? You have to infer the other's intent in order to know how to respond to that other's behaviour. Many conflicts are escalated merely by one party attributing the wrong intentions to the other party. Additionally, there is typically a great deal of slippage between intentions and behaviour, so that behaviour does not always accurately reflect a person's intentions.

Exhibit 13-2 represents one author's effort to identify the primary conflict-handling intentions. Using two dimensions—*cooperativeness* (the degree to which one party attempts to satisfy the other party's concerns) and *assertiveness* (the degree to which one party attempts to satisfy his or her own concerns)—five conflict-handling intentions can be identified: *competing* (assertive and uncooperative), *collaborating* (assertive and cooperative), *avoiding* (unassertive and uncooperative), *accommodating* (unassertive and cooperative), and *compromising* (mid-range on both assertiveness and cooperativeness).[14]

competing

A desire to satisfy one's interests, regardless of the impact on the other party to the conflict.

COMPETING When one person seeks to satisfy his or her own interests, regardless of the impact on the other parties to the conflict, he or she is **competing**. Examples include intending to achieve your goal at the sacrifice of the other's goal, attempting to convince another that your conclusion is correct and his or hers is mistaken, and trying to make someone else accept blame for a problem.

Competition at any level can cause problems in an organization, but when it occurs in the upper echelons there may be very serious consequences. For years, Montreal-based Birks & Sons Ltd. was known as one of Canada's oldest family-owned jewellery stores. However, the conflicts between the three Birks brothers, Thomas, Barrie, and Jonathan, great-great-grandsons of the founder, over the image and direction of the company proved to be too difficult to resolve.[15] Each brother wanted to lead the organization. In 1990, unable to resolve the conflicts among the brothers, Jonathan bought the other two out for a highly leveraged $87 million and tried to remake the company in his own image. Unfortunately, his attempt was unsuccessful, and after three difficult years of trying to run the company himself, Birks was sold to Borgosesia SpA, an Italian giftware maker. That sale, and the inability to resolve the conflicts of the three brothers, ended more than a century of family tradition.

COLLABORATING When the parties to conflict each desire to fully satisfy the concerns of all parties, we have cooperation and the search for a mutually

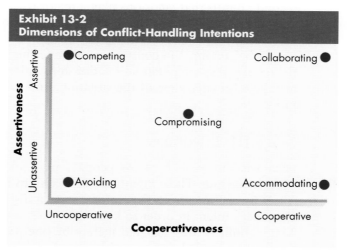

Exhibit 13-2
Dimensions of Conflict-Handling Intentions

Source: K. Thomas, "Conflict and Negotiation Processes in Organizations," in M.D. Dunnette and L.M. Hough (eds.), *Handbook of Industrial and Organizational Psychology*, 2nd ed., vol. 3 (Palo Alto, CA: Consulting Psychologists Press, 1992), p. 668. With permission.

collaborating
A situation where the parties to a conflict each desire to satisfy fully the concerns of all parties.

beneficial outcome. In **collaborating**, the intention of the parties is to solve the problem by clarifying differences rather than by accommodating various points of view. Examples include attempting to find a win-win solution that allows both parties' goals to be completely achieved and seeking a conclusion that incorporates the valid insights of both parties.

AVOIDING A person may recognize that a conflict exists and want to withdraw from it or suppress it. Examples of **avoiding** include trying to just ignore a conflict and avoiding others with whom you disagree.

avoiding
The desire to withdraw from or suppress a conflict.

ACCOMMODATING When one party seeks to appease an opponent, that party may be willing to place the opponent's interests above his or her own. In other words, in order for the relationship to be maintained, one party is willing to be self-sacrificing. We refer to this intention as **accommodating**. Examples are a willingness to sacrifice your goal so the other party's goal can be attained, supporting someone else's opinion despite your reservations about it, and forgiving someone for an infraction and allowing subsequent ones.

accommodating
The willingness of one party in a conflict to place the opponent's interests above his or her own.

COMPROMISING When each party to the conflict seeks to give up something, sharing occurs, resulting in a compromised outcome. In **compromising**, there is no clear winner or loser. Rather, there is a willingness to ration the object of the conflict and accept a solution that provides incomplete satisfaction of both parties' concerns. The distinguishing characteristic of compromising, therefore, is that each party intends to give up something. Examples might be willingness to accept a raise of $1.50 an hour rather than the $2 desired and the $1 initially offered by the employer; to acknowledge partial agreement with a specific viewpoint; and to take partial blame for an infraction.

compromising
A situation in which each party to a conflict is willing to give up something.

Intentions provide general guidelines for parties in a conflict situation. They define each party's purpose. Yet, people's intentions are not fixed. During the course of a conflict, they might change because of reconceptualization or because of an emotional reaction to the behaviour of the other party. However, research indicates that people have an underlying disposition to handle conflicts in certain ways.[16] Specifically, individuals have preferences among the five conflict-handling intentions just described; these preferences tend to be relied upon quite consistently, and a person's intentions can be predicted rather well from a combination of intellectual and personality characteristics. So it may be more appropriate to view the five conflict-handling intentions as relatively fixed rather than as a set of options from which individuals choose to fit an appropriate situation. That is, when confronting a conflict situation, some people want to win it all at any cost, some want to find an optimum solution, some want to run away, others want to be obliging, and still others want to "split the difference." This chapter's Learning About Yourself exercise gives you the opportunity to discover your own conflict-handling style. The chapter summary outlines specific contingencies that might affect conflict-handling style as well.

Stage IV: Behaviour

When most people think of conflict situations, they tend to focus on Stage IV. Why? Because this is where conflicts become visible. The behaviour stage includes the statements, actions, and reactions made by the conflicting parties.

These conflict behaviours are usually overt attempts to implement each party's intentions. But these behaviours have a stimulus quality that is separate from intentions. As a result of miscalculations or unskilled enactments, overt behaviours sometimes deviate from original intentions.[17]

It helps to think of Stage IV as a dynamic process of interaction. For example, you make a demand on me; I respond by arguing; you threaten me; I threaten you back; and so on. Exhibit 13-3 provides a way of visualizing conflict behaviour. All conflicts exist somewhere along this continuum. At the lower part of the continuum, we have conflicts characterized by subtle, indirect, and highly controlled forms of tension. An illustration might be a student questioning in class a point the instructor has just made. Conflict intensities escalate as they move upward along the continuum until they become highly destructive. Strikes and lockouts, riots, and wars clearly fall in this upper range. For the most part, you should assume that conflicts that reach the upper ranges of the continuum are almost always dysfunctional. Functional conflicts are typically confined to the lower range of the continuum.

If a conflict is dysfunctional, what can the parties do to de-escalate it? Or, conversely, what options exist if conflict is too low and needs to be increased? This brings us to **conflict management** techniques. Exhibit 13-4 lists the major resolution and stimulation techniques that allow managers to control conflict levels. Notice that several of the resolution techniques were earlier described as conflict-handling intentions. This, of course, shouldn't be surprising. Under ideal conditions, a person's intentions should translate into comparable behaviours.

Stage V: Outcomes

The action-reaction interplay between the conflicting parties results in consequences. As our model (see Exhibit 13-1) demonstrates, these outcomes may

conflict management
The use of resolution and stimulation techniques to achieve the desired level of conflict.

Exhibit 13-3
Conflict Intensity Continuum

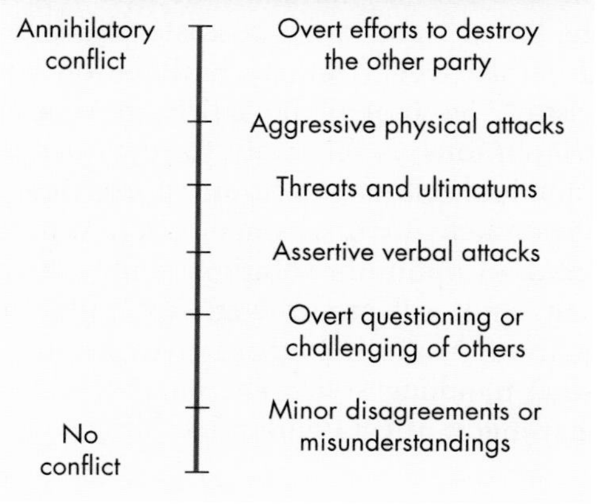

Annihilatory conflict — Overt efforts to destroy the other party

Aggressive physical attacks

Threats and ultimatums

Assertive verbal attacks

Overt questioning or challenging of others

Minor disagreements or misunderstandings

No conflict

Source: Based on S.P. Robbins, *Managing Organizational Conflict: A Nontraditional Approach* (Upper Saddle River, NJ: Prentice Hall, 1974), pp. 93–97; and F. Glasl, "The Process of Conflict Escalation and the Roles of Third Parties," in G.B.J. Bomers and R. Peterson (eds.), *Conflict Management and Industrial Relations* (Boston: Kluwer-Nijhoff, 1982), pp. 119–40.

Exhibit 13-4
Conflict Management Techniques

Conflict Resolution Techniques

Problem solving	Face-to-face meeting of the conflicting parties for the purpose of identifying the problem and resolving it through open discussion.
Superordinate goals	Creating a shared goal that cannot be attained without the cooperation of each of the conflicting parties.
Expansion of resources	When a conflict is caused by the scarcity of a resource—say, money, promotion opportunities, office space—expansion of the resource can create a win-win solution.
Avoidance	Withdrawal from, or suppression of, the conflict.
Smoothing	Playing down differences while emphasizing common interests between the conflicting parties.
Compromise	Each party to the conflict gives up something of value.
Authoritative command	Management uses its formal authority to resolve the conflict and then communicates its desires to the parties involved.
Altering the human variable	Using behavioural change techniques such as human relations training to alter attitudes and behaviours that cause conflict.
Altering the structural variables	Changing the formal organization structure and the interaction patterns of conflicting parties through job redesign, transfers, creation of coordinating positions, and the like.

Conflict Stimulation Techniques

Communication	Using ambiguous or threatening messages to increase conflict levels.
Bringing in outsiders	Adding employees to a group whose backgrounds, values, attitudes, or managerial styles differ from those of present members.
Restructuring the organization	Realigning work groups, altering rules and regulations, increasing interdependence, and making similar structural changes to disrupt the status quo.
Appointing a devil's advocate	Designating a critic to purposely argue against the majority positions held by the group.

Source: Based on S.P. Robbins, *Managing Organizational Conflict: A Nontraditional Approach* (Upper Saddle River, NJ: Prentice Hall, 1974), pp. 59–89.

be functional in that the conflict results in an improvement in the group's performance, or dysfunctional in that it hinders group performance.

FUNCTIONAL OUTCOMES   How might conflict act as a force to increase group performance? It is hard to visualize a situation where open or violent

aggression could be functional. But there are a number of instances where it is possible to envision how low or moderate levels of conflict could improve the effectiveness of a group. Because people often find it difficult to think of instances where conflict can be constructive, let's consider some examples and then review the research evidence.

Conflict is constructive when it improves the quality of decisions, stimulates creativity and innovation, encourages interest and curiosity among group members, provides the medium through which problems can be aired and tensions released, and fosters an environment of self-evaluation and change. The evidence suggests that conflict can improve the quality of decision-making by allowing all points, particularly the ones that are unusual or held by a minority, to be weighed in important decisions.[18] Conflict is an antidote for groupthink. It doesn't allow the group passively to "rubber-stamp" decisions that may be based on weak assumptions, inadequate consideration of relevant alternatives, or other debilities. Conflict challenges the status quo and therefore supports the creation of new ideas, promotes reassessment of group goals and activities, and increases the probability that the group will respond to change.

Eaton's
www.eatons.com/home/

For examples of companies that have suffered because they had too little functional conflict, you don't have to look further than Eaton's and IBM Canada prior to the 1990s. Many of the problems that faced both of these companies as they entered the 1990s can be traced to a lack of functional conflict. They hired and promoted individuals who were loyal to the organization to the point of never questioning company actions. Managers for the most part resisted change—they preferred looking back to past successes rather than forward to new challenges. Moreover, both firms kept their senior executives sheltered in headquarters' offices, protected from hearing anything they didn't want to hear, and a world away from the changes that were dramatically altering the retailing and computer industries. Eaton's, for instance, ignored signs of trouble such as losses endured by its in-store drug sections in competition with Shoppers Drug Mart and the drain on profits of small-town stores.[19]

Research studies in diverse settings confirm the functionality of conflict, particularly as it relates to productivity. For instance, it was demonstrated that among established groups, performance tended to improve more when conflict occurred among members than when there was fairly close agreement. The investigators observed that when groups analysed decisions that had been made by the individual members of that group, the average improvement among the high-conflict groups was 73 percent greater than was that of those groups characterized by low-conflict conditions.[20] Others have found similar results: groups composed of members with different interests tend to produce higher-quality solutions to a variety of problems than do homogeneous groups.[21]

George Eaton resigned as president and CEO of Eaton's in May 1997, leading the way for the first non-family member ever to head the business when George Kosich was appointed to replace him the next month. After years of avoiding conflict and change, the company had been on the verge of financial ruin in recent years.

The preceding leads us to predict that the increasing cultural diversity of the workforce should provide benefits to organizations. And that's what the evidence indicates. Research demonstrates that heterogeneity among group and organization members can increase creativity, improve the quality of decisions, and facilitate change by

enhancing member flexibility.[22] For example, U.S. researchers compared decision-making groups composed of all-Anglo individuals with groups that also contained members from Asian, Hispanic, and African-American ethnic groups. The ethnically diverse groups produced more effective and more feasible ideas, and the unique ideas they generated tended to be of higher quality than the unique ideas produced by the all-Anglo group.

Similarly, studies of professionals—systems analysts and research and development scientists—support the constructive value of conflict. An investigation of 22 teams of systems analysts found that the more incompatible groups were likely to be more productive.[23] Research and development scientists have been found to be most productive where a certain amount of intellectual conflict exists.[24] These findings might suggest that conflict within a group indicates strength rather than weakness.

DYSFUNCTIONAL OUTCOMES   The destructive consequences of conflict upon a group or organization's performance are generally well known. A reasonable summary might state: Uncontrolled opposition breeds discontent, which acts to dissolve common ties, and eventually leads to the destruction of the group. And, of course, there is a substantial body of literature to document how conflict—the dysfunctional varieties—can reduce group effectiveness.[25] Among the more undesirable consequences are a retarding of communication, reductions in group cohesiveness, and subordination of group goals to the primacy of infighting between members. At the extreme, conflict can bring group functioning to a halt and potentially threaten the group's survival.

Canada Post is a classic example of a company facing dysfunctional conflict. Canada experienced a 15-day postal strike just before the Christmas 1997 holiday season because of the labour conflict at the Crown corporation. As federal government Public Works Minister Alphonso Gagliano commented after the strike ended, "Labour-management relations are not the

Canada Post
www.canadapost.ca/

Raymond Floyd (far right), site manager at Exxon Chemical Company's plant in Baytown, Texas, believes that cultural diversity creates a more energized and productive workforce. Floyd builds high-performance work teams by training employees to recognize and understand the inherent differences in cultures that influence what individuals believe and how they behave. The training helps employees value differences and appreciate the special contributions of diverse cultural perspectives in improving business processes. The plant, honoured as one of America's best, benefits by receiving some 24 000 improvement ideas from employees each year.

cognitive conflict
Conflict related to differences in perspectives and judgments.

affective conflict
Emotional conflict aimed at a person rather than an issue.

way you and I would like them to be. There is a historical mistrust here," he added. "Management is the enemy. Worker is the enemy."[26]

This discussion returns us to the issue of what is functional and what is dysfunctional. Research on conflict has yet to clearly identify those situations where conflict is more likely to be constructive than destructive. However, there is growing evidence that the source of the conflict is a significant factor determining functionality.[27] **Cognitive conflict**, which occurs because of differences in perspectives and judgments, can often result in identifying potential solutions to problems. Thus it would be regarded as functional conflict. **Affective conflict**, which is emotional, and aimed at a person rather than an issue, tends to be dysfunctional conflict. One study of 53 teams found that cognitive conflict led to better decisions, more acceptance of the decision, and ownership of the decision. Teams experiencing affective conflict had poorer decisions and lower levels of acceptance of the decision.[28] Because conflict can involve our emotions in a variety of ways, it can also lead to stress. You may want to refer to Chapter 17's discussion on stress to give you some ideas of how to manage the stress that might arise from conflicts you experience.

CREATING FUNCTIONAL CONFLICT We briefly mentioned conflict stimulation as part of Stage IV of the conflict process. Since the topic of conflict stimulation is relatively new and somewhat controversial, you might be wondering: If managers accept the view that conflict can have positive value, what can they do to encourage functional conflict in their organizations?[29]

There seems to be general agreement that creating functional conflict is a tough job, particularly in large corporations. As one consultant put it, "A high proportion of people who get to the top are conflict avoiders. They don't like hearing negatives, they don't like saying or thinking negative things. They frequently make it up the ladder in part because they don't irritate people on the way up." Another suggests that at least 7 out of 10 people in business hush up when their opinions are at odds with those of their superiors, allowing bosses to make mistakes even when they know better.

Such anti-conflict cultures may have been tolerable in the past but not in today's fiercely competitive global economy. Those organizations that don't encourage and support dissent may not survive into the 21st century. Let's look at some of the approaches organizations are taking to encourage their people to challenge the system and develop fresh ideas.

Hewlett-Packard
www.hp.com/

Herman Miller Inc.
http://www.hermanmiller.com/

IBM Corporation
www.ibm.com/

Hewlett-Packard rewards dissenters by recognizing go-against-the-grain types, or people who stay with the ideas they believe in even when those ideas are rejected by management. Herman Miller Inc., an office-furniture manufacturer, has a formal system in which employees evaluate and criticize their bosses. IBM also has a formal system that encourages dissension. Employees can question their boss with impunity. If the disagreement can't be resolved, the system provides a third party for counsel. The OB in the News feature describes Spectrum Associates, another organization that deliberately creates functional conflict.

One common ingredient in organizations that successfully create functional conflict is that they reward dissent and punish conflict avoiders. The president of Innovis Interactive Technologies, for instance, fired a top executive who refused to dissent. His explanation: "He was the ultimate yes-man. In this organization, I can't afford to pay someone to hear my own opinion." But the real challenge for managers is when they hear news that they don't want to hear. The news may make their blood boil or their hopes col-

lapse, but they can't show it. They have to learn to take the bad news without flinching. No tirades, no tight-lipped sarcasm, no eyes rolling upward, no gritting of teeth. Rather, managers should ask calm, even-tempered questions: "Can you tell me more about what happened?" "What do you think we ought to do?" A sincere "Thank you for bringing this to my attention" will probably reduce the likelihood that managers will be cut off from similar communications in the future.

OB IN THE NEWS

Spectrum Associates Deliberately Builds Conflict Into Its Structure

Spectrum Associates is a small but rapidly growing software company. In 1988, the company's first year of operations, revenues were only $565 000. Five years later, revenues were $35 million. Spectrum's founders attribute a large part of the company's success to the way it's structured. The firm is designed to create conflict. All product teams and support groups compete against each other for internal resources and outside markets.

"We've kept the company growing by making sure nobody gets comfortable," says one of the founders. The company simulates internally what all companies face externally. By setting internal groups against each other, the company simulates "the pricing pressure, the delivery pressure, and the growth pressure that we encounter in the marketplace." The result is a workforce in a perpetual state of readiness. "It keeps us healthy. A little insecurity can be very healthy."

The company only hires self-starters. New employees are told that "the company is not your parent. It's just a facility where you can come and lower your risks significantly because you have benefits, you have a base salary. But you're on your own." Recruits are encouraged to "grow your own business" within Spectrum. If it succeeds, they share in the wealth. If it fails, they are urged to try again.

Spectrum's competitive culture is a shock for some. One employee, for example, said she was not prepared to have her own colleagues blocking her shots. "It took me a while to realize that meant convincing the salespeople to flip work to me instead of to someone else in the organization—that it meant bidding more aggressively to get a job."

But "it's not a free-for-all" says one co-founder. "Yeah, people compete, but they do it in groups. One individual is not out there trying to do in another person." The two owners referee squabbles as they arise, but they refuse to formalize boundaries or set rules. "Behind it all there's a very healthy thing going on, which is a struggle to do what's right for the customer," argues one of the founders. "When I talk to customers, I can say, 'Look, what do you want? The best quality, the best price, and the best delivery. It so happens that we're organized in such a way that we can guarantee all that.'"

Spectrum has created a bunch of different businesses competing for the organization's limited resources. In contrast to the typical firm whose competition is with outside companies, Spectrum's people have to compete against products created by its own internal groups.

Source: Based on A. Murphy, "The Enemy Within," *INC.*, March 1994, pp. 58–69. Note: The Company's Name Was Changed to Pivotpoint Associates in April 1996.

Take It to the Net

We invite you to visit the Robbins page on the Prentice Hall Web site at:

http://www.prenticehall.ca/robbins

for this chapter's World Wide Web exercise.

Conflict Management in the Workplace

Kathleen Eisenhardt of the Stanford Graduate School of Business and her colleagues studied top management teams to understand how they manage conflict.[30] They observed the interactions of 12 teams in technology-based companies. Each team consisted of five to nine executives. Four teams had little conflict to observe. Four teams experienced considerable conflict, but reported their interactions as "open," "fun," and "productive." As one member of one of these teams noted: "We scream a lot, then laugh, and then resolve the issue." Four other teams had a lot of conflict, which included interpersonal conflict. They were more likely to describe each other as "manipulative," "secretive," and "political."

Before we examine the findings regarding the teams that successfully negotiated conflict, you might want to think about group situations you have been in that were characterized by conflict. In which cases did the conflict spill over into interpersonal relationships? Were there other situations where you felt the conflict was resolved without harming the relationships of the people involved in the conflict?

Eisenhardt and her colleagues' research identified six tactics that helped teams successfully manage the interpersonal conflict that can accompany group interactions. By handling the interpersonal conflict well, these groups were able to achieve their goals without letting conflict get in the way. The six tactics that helped reduce conflict were:[31]

- team members worked with more, rather than less, information and debated on the basis of facts;
- team members developed multiple alternatives to enrich the level of debate;
- team members shared commonly agreed-upon goals;
- team members injected humour into the decision process;
- team members maintained a balanced power structure;
- team members resolved issues without forcing consensus.

Whenever people work together on important strategic issues, or even if the task is completing a class project, it is not surprising, or even necessarily bad, that conflict occurs. What is important, however, is that the group have mechanisms by which they can manage the conflict. From the research reported above, one could conclude that sharing information and goals, and striving to be open and get along are helpful strategies for negotiating one's way through the maze of conflict. A sense of humour and a willingness to understand the points of others without insisting that everyone agree on all points are also important. Group members should also try to focus on the issues, rather than on personalities, and strive to achieve fairness and equity in the group process.

Groups should not try to avoid conflict, although many individuals prefer to avoid conflict whenever possible. Eisenhardt and her colleagues found that groups that didn't have conflict were generally less effective, with the members becoming withdrawn and only superficially harmonious. Often, if there was no conflict, the alternative was not agreement, but apathy and disengagement. Conflict also has an effect on performance. Those teams that avoided conflict tended to have lower performance levels, forgot to consider key issues, or were unaware of important aspects of their situation. They also did not take the opportunity to question assumptions or consider

enough alternatives. You might want to review the Case Incident to help you determine situations where conflict needs to be reduced or increased.

Negotiation

Negotiation permeates the interactions of almost everyone in groups and organizations. There's the obvious: labour bargains with management. There's the not so obvious: managers negotiate with subordinates, peers, and bosses; salespeople negotiate with customers; purchasing agents negotiate with suppliers. And there's the subtle: a worker agrees to answer a colleague's phone for a few minutes in exchange for some past or future benefit. In today's team-based organizations, where members are increasingly finding themselves having to work with colleagues over whom they have no direct authority and with whom they may not even share a common boss, negotiation skills become critical.

We'll define **negotiation** as a process in which two or more parties exchange goods or services and attempt to agree upon the exchange rate for them.[32] Note that we use the terms *negotiation* and *bargaining* interchangeably.

In this section, we'll contrast two bargaining strategies, provide a model of the negotiation process, ascertain the role of personality traits on bargaining, review cultural differences in negotiation, and take a brief look at third-party negotiations. To learn more about your negotiating skills, see the Working With Others exercise at the end of the chapter.

Bargaining Strategies

There are two general approaches to negotiation—*distributive bargaining* and *integrative bargaining*.[33] These are compared in Exhibit 13-5.

DISTRIBUTIVE BARGAINING You see a used car advertised for sale in the newspaper. It appears to be just what you've been looking for. You go out to see the car. It's great and you want it. The owner tells you the asking price. You don't want to pay that much. The two of you then negotiate over the price. The negotiating strategy you're engaging in is called **distributive bargaining**. Its most identifying feature is that it operates under zero-sum

negotiation
A process in which two or more parties exchange goods or services and attempt to agree upon the exchange rate for them.

distributive bargaining
Negotiation that seeks to divide up a fixed amount of resources; a win-lose situation.

Exhibit 13-5
Distributive versus Integrative Bargaining

Bargaining Characteristic	Distributive Bargaining	Integrative Bargaining
Available resources	Fixed amount of resources to be divided	Variable amount of resources to be divided
Primary motivations	I win, you lose	I win, you win
Primary interests	Opposed to each other	Convergent or congruent with each other
Focus of relationships	Short term	Long term

Source: Based on R.J. Lewicki and J.A. Litterer, *Negotiation* (Homewood, IL: Irwin, 1985), p. 280.

conditions. That is, any gain I make is at your expense, and vice versa. Referring back to the used-car example, every dollar you can get the seller to cut from the car's price is a dollar you save. Conversely, every dollar more the seller can get from you comes at your expense. So the essence of distributive bargaining is negotiating over who gets what share of a fixed pie.

Probably the most widely cited example of distributive bargaining is in labour-management negotiations over wages. Typically, labour representatives come to the bargaining table determined to get as much money as possible out of management. Since every cent more that labour negotiates increases management's costs, each party bargains aggressively and treats the other as an opponent who must be defeated. The essence of distributive bargaining is depicted in Exhibit 13-6. Parties A and B represent two negotiators. Each has a *target point* that defines what he or she would like to achieve. Each also has a *resistance point*, which marks the lowest outcome that is acceptable—the point below which they would break off negotiations rather than accept a less favourable settlement. The area between these two points makes up each one's aspiration range. As long as there is some overlap between A and B's aspiration ranges, there exists a settlement range where each one's aspirations can be met.

When engaged in distributive bargaining, one's tactics focus on trying to get one's opponent to agree to one's specific target point or to get as close to it as possible. Examples of such tactics are persuading your opponent of the impossibility of reaching his or her target point and the advisability of accepting a settlement near yours; arguing that your target is fair, while your opponent's isn't; and attempting to get your opponent to feel emotionally generous toward you and thus accept an outcome close to your target point.

INTEGRATIVE BARGAINING A sales representative for a women's sportswear manufacturer has just closed a $20 000 order from a small clothing retailer. The sales rep calls in the order to her firm's credit department. She is told that the firm can't approve credit to this customer because of a past slow-pay record. The next day, the sales rep and the firm's credit manager meet to discuss the problem. The sales rep doesn't want to lose the business. Neither does the credit manager, but she also doesn't want to get stuck with an uncollectable debt. The two openly review their options. After considerable discussion, they agree on a solution that meets both their needs: the credit manager will approve the sale, but the clothing store's owner will provide a bank guarantee that will ensure payment if the bill isn't paid within 60 days.

integrative bargaining
Negotiation that seeks one or more settlements that can create a win-win solution.

This sales-credit negotiation is an example of **integrative bargaining**. In contrast to distributive bargaining, integrative bargaining operates under the assumption that there exists one or more settlements that can create a win-win solution.

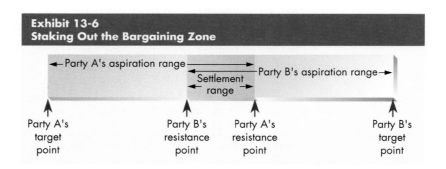

Exhibit 13-6
Staking Out the Bargaining Zone

←—Party A's aspiration range—————→ ←—Party B's aspiration range—→

Settlement range

Party A's target point   Party B's resistance point   Party A's resistance point   Party B's target point

In terms of intraorganizational behaviour, all things being equal, integrative bargaining is preferable to distributive bargaining. Why? Because the former builds long-term relationships and facilitates working together in the future. It bonds negotiators and allows each to leave the bargaining table feeling that he or she has achieved a victory. Distributive bargaining, on the other hand, leaves one party a loser. It tends to build animosities and deepen divisions when people must work together on an ongoing basis.

Why, then, don't we see more integrative bargaining in organizations? The answer lies in the conditions necessary for this type of negotiation to succeed. These include parties who are open with information and candid about their concerns, a sensitivity by both parties to the other's needs, the ability to trust one another, and a willingness by both parties to maintain flexibility.[34] Since these conditions often don't exist in organizations, it isn't surprising that negotiations often take on a win-at-any-cost dynamic. For examples of effective approaches to conflict resolution through negotiation in Canadian businesses, see this chapter's HR Implications feature.

The Negotiation Process

Exhibit 13-7 provides a simplified model of the negotiation process. It views negotiation as made up of five steps: (1) preparation and planning; (2) definition of ground rules; (3) clarification and justification; (4) bargaining and problem solving; and (5) closure and implementation.[35]

PREPARATION AND PLANNING Before you start negotiating, you need to do your homework. What's the nature of the conflict? What's the history leading up to this negotiation? Who's involved and what are their perceptions of the conflict?

What do you want from the negotiation? What are *your* goals? If you're a purchasing manager at Dell Computer, for instance, and your goal is to get a significant cost reduction from your supplier of keyboards, make sure that this goal stays paramount in your discussions and doesn't become overshadowed by other issues. It often helps to put your goals in writing and develop a range of outcomes—from "most hopeful" to "minimally acceptable"—to keep your attention focused.

You also want to prepare an assessment of what you think the other party to your negotiation's goals are. What are they likely to ask for? How entrenched are they likely to be in their position? What intangible or hidden interests may be important to them? What might they be willing to settle on? When you can anticipate your opponent's position, you are better equipped to counter his or her arguments with the facts and figures that support your position.

Use the information you've gathered to develop a strategy. Like a chess match, expert chess players have a strategy. They know in advance how they will respond to any given situation. As part of your strategy, you should determine your and the other side's *Best Alternative To a Negotiated Agreement* (**BATNA**).[36] Your BATNA determines the lowest value acceptable to you for a negotiated agreement. Any offer you receive that is higher than your BATNA is better than an impasse. Conversely, you shouldn't expect success in your negotiation effort unless you're able to make the other side an offer they find more attractive than their BATNA. If you go into your negotiation having a good idea of what the other party's BATNA is, even if you're not able to meet theirs, you might be able to get them to change it.

**Exhibit 13-7
The Negotiation Process**

Preparation and planning

↓

Definition of ground rules

↓

Clarification and justification

↓

Bargaining and problem solving

↓

Closure and implementation

BATNA
The best alternative to a negotiated agreement; the lowest acceptable value to an individual for a negotiated agreement.

DEFINITION OF GROUND RULES Once you've done your planning and developed a strategy, you're ready to begin defining the ground rules and procedures with the other party over the negotiation itself. Who will do the negotiating? Where will it take place? What time constraints, if any, will apply? To what issues will negotiation be limited? Will there be a specific procedure to follow if an impasse is reached? During this phase, the parties will also exchange their initial proposals or demands.

CLARIFICATION AND JUSTIFICATION When initial positions have been exchanged, both you and the other party will explain, amplify, clarify, bolster, and justify your original demands. This needn't be confrontational. Rather, it is an opportunity for educating and informing each other on the issues, why they are important, and how each arrived at their initial demands. This is the point where you might want to provide the other party with any documentation that helps support your position.

BARGAINING AND PROBLEM SOLVING The essence of the negotiation process is the actual give-and-take in trying to hash out an agreement. Concessions will undoubtedly need to be made by both parties. The From Concepts to Skills feature on negotiating directly addresses some of the actions you should take to improve the likelihood that you can achieve a good agreement.

CLOSURE AND IMPLEMENTATION The final step in the negotiation process is formalizing the agreement that has been worked out and developing any procedures that are necessary for implementation and monitoring. For major negotiations—which would include everything from labour-management negotiations, to bargaining over lease terms, to buying a piece of real estate, to negotiating a job offer for a senior management position—this will require hammering out the specifics in a formal contract. For most cases, however, closure of the negotiation process is nothing more formal than a handshake. This chapter's second CBC video case, "How to Get a Raise," gives you an overview of the complete negotiation process for when you next need to negotiate your own raise.

Issues in Negotiation

We conclude our discussion of negotiation by reviewing four contemporary issues in negotiation: the role of personality traits, gender differences in negotiating, the effect of cultural differences on negotiating styles, and the use of third parties to help resolve differences.

THE ROLE OF PERSONALITY TRAITS IN NEGOTIATION Can you predict an opponent's negotiating tactics if you know something about his or her personality? It's tempting to answer "Yes" to this question. For instance, you might assume that high risk takers would be more aggressive bargainers who make fewer concessions. Surprisingly, the evidence doesn't support this intuition.[37]

Overall assessments of the personality-negotiation relationship finds that personality traits have no significant direct effect on either the bargaining process or negotiation outcomes. This conclusion is important. It suggests that you should concentrate on the issues and the situational factors in each bargaining episode and not on your opponent's personality.

FROM CONCEPTS TO SKILLS

Negotiating

Once you've taken the time to assess your own goals, considered the other party's goals and interests, and developed a strategy, you're ready to begin actual negotiations. The following suggestions should improve your negotiating skills.

Begin with a positive overture. Studies on negotiation show that concessions tend to be reciprocated and lead to agreements. As a result, begin bargaining with a positive overture—perhaps a small concession—and then reciprocate your opponent's concessions.

Address problems, not personalities. Concentrate on the negotiation issues, not on the personal characteristics of your opponent. When negotiations get tough, avoid the tendency to attack your opponent. It's your opponent's ideas or position that you disagree with, not him or her personally. Separate the people from the problem, and don't personalize differences.

Pay little attention to initial offers. Treat an initial offer as merely a point of departure. Everyone has to have an initial position. These initial offers tend to be extreme and idealistic. Treat them as such.

Emphasize win-win solutions. Inexperienced negotiators often assume that their gain must come at the expense of the other party. As noted with integrative bargaining, that needn't be the case. There are often win-win solutions. But assuming a zero-sum game means missed opportunities for trade-offs that could benefit both sides. So if conditions are supportive, look for an integrative solution. Frame options in terms of your opponent's interests and look for solutions that can allow your opponent, as well as yourself, to declare a victory.

Create an open and trusting climate. Skilled negotiators are better listeners, ask more questions, focus their arguments more directly, are less defensive, and have learned to avoid words and phrases that can irritate an opponent (i.e., "generous offer," "fair price," "reasonable arrangement"). In other words, they are better at creating the open and trusting climate necessary for reaching an integrative settlement.

Source: These suggestions are based on J.A. Wall, Jr. and M.W. Blum, "Negotiations," *Journal of Management*, June 1991, pp. 278–82.

GENDER DIFFERENCES IN NEGOTIATIONS Do men and women negotiate differently? The answer appears to be "It depends."[38] It is difficult to generalize about gender differences in negotiating styles, because the research yields many opinions, but few reliable conclusions. Some researchers have documented interesting and relevant differences, however.

Kolb and Coolidge found four basic areas of difference.[39] The first difference was that women are more inclined to be concerned with feelings and perceptions, and thus take a longer-term view. Men are more inclined to focus on resolving the matter at hand. Bill Forbes, president of Edmonton-based career management firm CDR Associates, observes that women assume they're not going to earn as much as men. They focus "on getting a position that utilizes their skills and gives them some challenge. When presented with the compensation range for their job classification, women generally aren't worried if they end up in the bottom half, whereas males might often be concerned if they're not in the top."[40] Unfortunately, employers may take advantage of these differing expectations to offer women lower wages when they first negotiate salary. This may be changing in more recent times, however. For example, University of Waterloo psychology professor Serge Desmarais found that the narrowest pay gap between men and women

existed with those who had graduated from university since 1992. The difference in wages for those men and women was only six percent.[41]

A second gender difference in bargaining that Kolb and Coolidge identified is that men view the bargaining session as a separate event, whereas women view it as part of the overall relationship with the individual. A third finding was that women tend to want all parties in the negotiation to be empowered, whereas men are more likely to use power as part of the bargaining strategy. Finally, the researchers reported differences in dialogue. Men more often used dialogue to persuade other parties in the negotiation, whereas women were more likely to use dialogue to achieve understanding. Desmarais, whose work we noted above, suggests that men are socialized to be more aggressive negotiators, which would then result in some of the observed differences in men's and women's styles.[42] One important thing to note is that even if a difference in style of negotiation exists, one style may not always be preferable to the other. The best style may, in fact, depend on the situation. For instance, in situations where trust, openness, and long-term relationships are critical, a women's style may be more useful. However, when conflict, competition, and self-interest are an important part of the agenda, a man's style may be more effective.[43]

Another thing to note is that the belief that women are nicer than men in negotiations may well be the result not of gender, but the lack of power typically held by women in most large organizations. The research indicates that low-power managers, regardless of gender, attempt to placate their opponents and tend to use softly persuasive tactics rather than direct confrontation and threats. Where women and men have similar power bases, there may be less significant differences in their negotiation styles.

Women's attitudes toward negotiation and toward themselves as negotiators also appear to be quite different from men's. Managerial women demonstrate less confidence in anticipation of negotiating and are less satisfied with their performance after the process is complete, despite the fact that their performance and the outcomes they achieve are similar to men. This latter conclusion suggests that women may unduly penalize themselves by failing to engage in negotiations when such action would be in their best interests.

The outcomes of negotiations for women and men also seem to differ. One researcher found that when women negotiated to buy a car, the opening offer by the salesperson was higher than it was for men.[44] In a study of salary offers, researchers found that men were offered higher starting salaries in a negotiating process than were women.[45] While in each of these instances the opening offers were just that, offers to be negotiated, women fared less well than men at the end of the negotiating process, even when they used the same negotiating tactics as men.

CULTURAL DIFFERENCES IN NEGOTIATIONS Although there appears to be no significant direct relationship between an individual's personality and negotiation style, cultural background does seem to be relevant. Negotiating styles clearly vary across national cultures.[46]

The French like conflict. They frequently gain recognition and develop their reputations by thinking and acting against others. As a result, the French tend to take a long time in negotiating agreements and they aren't overly concerned about whether their opponents like or dislike them.[47] The Chinese also draw out negotiations but that's because they believe negotiations never end. Just when you think you've pinned down every detail and

reached a final solution with a Chinese executive, that executive might smile and start the process all over again. Like the Japanese, the Chinese negotiate to develop a relationship and a commitment to work together rather than to tie up every loose end.[48] Americans are known around the world for their impatience and their desire to be liked. Astute negotiators from other countries often turn these characteristics to their advantage by dragging out negotiations and making friendship conditional on the final settlement.

The cultural context of the negotiation significantly influences the amount and type of preparation for bargaining, the relative emphasis on task versus interpersonal relationships, the tactics used, and even where the negotiation should be conducted. Chris Brough, CEO of Vancouver-based Mainframe Entertainment Inc., the animation company that produces the cartoons *ReBoot* and *Beasties*, speaks about negotiating differences based on his experiences working in both Los Angeles and Vancouver: "There is a wonderful softness and self-deprecation about Canadians that I have come to enjoy. When you do a deal in Canada, very often you can extend a handshake and there is a firm belief the deal is solid. In Los Angeles, on the other hand, you can have a signed contract and it is still based on the idea of 'Okay, you're not happy, sue me.'"[49]

To further illustrate some of these differences, let's look at two studies comparing the influence of culture on business negotiations. The first study compared North Americans, Arabs, and Russians.[50] Among the factors that were looked at were their negotiating style, how they responded to an opponent's arguments, their approach to making concessions, and how they handled negotiating deadlines. North Americans tried to persuade by relying on facts and appealing to logic. They countered opponents' arguments with objective facts. They made small concessions early in the negotiation to establish a relationship, and usually reciprocated opponents' concessions. North Americans treated deadlines as very important. The Arabs, however, tried to persuade by appealing to emotion. They countered opponent's arguments with subjective feelings. They made concessions throughout the bargaining process and almost always reciprocated opponents' concessions. The Arabs also approached deadlines very casually. The Russians based their arguments on asserted ideals. They made few, if any, concessions. Any concession offered by an opponent was viewed as a weakness and almost never reciprocated. Finally, the Russians tended to ignore deadlines.

The second study looked at verbal and nonverbal negotiation tactics exhibited by North Americans, Japanese, and Brazilians during half-hour bargaining sessions.[51] Some of the differences were particularly interesting. For instance, the Brazilians on average said "no" 83 times, compared to five times for the Japanese and nine times for the North Americans. The Japanese displayed more than five periods of silence lasting longer than 10 seconds during the 30-minute sessions. North Americans averaged 3.5 such periods; the Brazilians had none. The Japanese and North Americans interrupted their opponent about the same number of times, but the Brazilians interrupted 2.5 to 3

Mainframe Entertainment Inc.
http://www.mainframe.bc.ca/

Chris Brough, CEO of Mainframe Entertainment in Vancouver, finds the negotiating styles of Canadians much more pleasant than that of Americans. He particularly appreciates their softness and self-deprecation.

times more often than the North Americans and the Japanese. Finally, while the Japanese and the North Americans had no physical contact with their opponents during negotiations except for handshaking, the Brazilians touched each other almost five times every half-hour.

THIRD-PARTY NEGOTIATIONS To this point, we've discussed bargaining in terms of direct negotiations. Occasionally, however, individuals or group representatives reach a stalemate and are unable to resolve their differences through direct negotiations. In such cases, they may turn to a third party to help them find a solution. There are four basic third-party roles: mediator, arbitrator, conciliator, and consultant.[52]

A **mediator** is a neutral third party who facilitates a negotiated solution by using reasoning and persuasion, suggesting alternatives, and the like. Mediators are widely used in labour-management negotiations and in civil-court disputes.

The mediated decision of Alberta-based Syncrude Canada Ltd.'s case against its maintenance company for a fire at the Fort McMurray, Alberta, oil-sands plant in August 1984 indicates the savings that a mediated decision can yield. The case did not reach the court until 1992, and by then tens of millions of dollars in legal fees had been spent. While the court case was under way, Syncrude and the maintenance company met on the side with mediator Yves Fortier, a lawyer with Ogilvy Renault of Montreal. Two years later, the two sides achieved a mediated solution, while the court had only heard just one side of the case. The total cost of mediation was less than $200 000.[53]

The overall effectiveness of mediated negotiations is fairly impressive. The settlement rate is approximately 60 percent, with negotiator satisfaction at about 75 percent. But the situation is the key to whether mediation will succeed; the conflicting parties must be motivated to bargain and resolve their conflict. Additionally, conflict intensity cannot be too high; mediation is most effective under moderate levels of conflict. Finally, perceptions of the mediator are important; to be effective, the mediator must be perceived as neutral and non-coercive.

An **arbitrator** is a third party with the authority to dictate an agreement. Arbitration can be voluntary (requested) or compulsory (forced on the parties by law or contract).

The authority of the arbitrator varies according to the rules set by the negotiators. For instance, the arbitrator might be limited to choosing one of the negotiator's last offers or to suggesting an agreement point that is non-binding, or free to choose and make any judgment that he or she wishes.

The big advantage of arbitration over mediation is that it always results in a settlement. Whether or not there is a negative side depends on how "heavy-handed" the arbitrator appears. If one party is left feeling overwhelmingly defeated, that party is certain to be dissatisfied and unlikely to accept the arbitrator's decision graciously. Therefore, the conflict may resurface at a later time.

In an effort to prevent the negative consequences of arbitration outlined above, the federal government appointed New Brunswick judge Guy Richard as a *mediator-arbitrator* in January 1998 to help Canada Post and the 45 000-member Canadian Union of Postal Workers (CUPW) settle their differences over job security, changes to letter carriers' routes, and overhauling the mail-delivery system. Richard and the two parties were given 90 days to negotiate a deal, with an extension possible if both sides agreed. How-

mediator
A neutral third party who facilitates a negotiated solution by using reasoning, persuasion, and suggestions for alternatives.

arbitrator
A third party to a negotiation who has the authority to dictate an agreement.

Canadian Union of Postal Workers (CUPW)
http://www.cupw-sttp.org/

ever, if a deal could not be reached, Richard was to act as an arbitrator and render his own settlement. As of June 1998, a mediated settlement was still a possibility.

A **conciliator** is a trusted third party who provides an informal communication link between the negotiator and the opponent. Conciliation is used extensively in international, labour, family, and community disputes. Comparing its effectiveness to mediation has proven difficult because the two overlap a great deal. In practice, conciliators typically act as more than mere communication conduits. They also engage in fact finding, interpreting messages, and persuading disputants to develop agreements.

In February 1998, talks between Canadian National Railway Co. (CN) and the Canadian Auto Workers, as well as talks between Canadian Pacific Railway Co. (CP) and the Brotherhood of Maintenance of Way Employees, used the services of federal conciliators. In both cases the unions were hoping to resolve outstanding issues with the railway companies. The Brotherhood of Maintenance of Way Employees signed an agreement with both CN and CP, although agreement had not yet been reached with the Canadian Autoworkers as of spring 1998.

A **consultant** is a skilled and impartial third party who attempts to facilitate problem solving through communication and analysis, aided by his or her knowledge of conflict management. In contrast to the previous roles, the consultant's role is not to settle the issues but, rather, to improve relations between the conflicting parties so that they can reach a settlement themselves. Instead of putting forward specific solutions, the consultant tries to help the parties learn to understand and work with each other. Therefore, this approach has a longer-term focus: to build new and positive perceptions and attitudes between the conflicting parties.

conciliator
A trusted third party who provides an informal communication link between the negotiator and the opponent.

Brotherhood of Maintenance of Way Employees
http://www.bmwe.org/

consultant as negotiator
An impartial third party, skilled in conflict management, who attempts to facilitate creative problem solving through communication and analysis.

HR IMPLICATIONS

Resolving Union-Management Conflict

Conflict in the workplace arises for a variety of reasons, but one major conflict that occurs in many of Canada's businesses is conflict between labour and management. A number of unions and businesses are trying to figure out ways to resolve that conflict so that both sides work together more effectively. We present several examples below, to give you some indications of ways that management and unions can work together.

Ville d'Anjou-based Transport Provost Inc. and the Communications, Energy and Paperworkers Union of Canada (CEP) decided to form a partnership in 1992 to try to resolve some of the many conflicts that had arisen between them. Transport Provost introduced a two-year conflict prevention program costing $276 000 to teach communication skills, problem solving, and effective conflict management. Representatives of both management

and the union attended the workshops. At first union members were somewhat suspicious of the introduction of this program, worrying that it was a way of co-opting the union. However, after some experience with the program, Joel Nerome, former president of the local union, noted that "most of the employees see more positives in it than negatives."[1]

The workers and management at Leaside, Ontario-based Alcatel Canada Wire Inc. were facing the prospect of plant closure in the late 1980s, partly due to severe management-union conflict. In 1990, they started to realize that the world was changing and the company was going to have to become more profitable to survive. Kevin Corrigan, then president of the local union, decided that perhaps the union should extend an olive branch to management. An independent facilitator was

brought in to help the two sides discover the common goals that would allow them to work together. Corrigan reports that the facilitator "got us feeling positive about the process and what might need to be done. After the first two-day session, a joint communiqué of common goals and objectives was drafted." Not everything has been perfect among union and management at Alcatel, but relations have been better as a result of both sides working together to understand and help determine the company goals.[2]

At Alberta-based AGT, the union asked managers to attend a two-day training seminar on mutual gains bargaining (MGB) in 1990. Management agreed, as they recognized the need to foster better relations. Before the training sessions, management and the union generally engaged in win-lose bargaining. Under the new process, both sides look to see the mutual gains in bargaining. Thus, each side shifts their focus to finding things that will work for the other side. Former business manager of the local, Tom Panelli notes that MGB has resulted in "less stressful negotiations, less concurrent turmoil at work sites and faster, more cost-effective use of management and union time."[3] Engaging in mutual gains bargaining has not resolved all of the problems of union and management at AGT, but it has helped their bargaining process considerably.

These examples are just a few of the ways that groups that might naturally have conflicting interests can choose to work towards a more positive environment. In some cases the union extended the olive branch; in others, it was management. The mechanisms for addressing conflict ranged from formal programs such as a conflict prevention program and consultation through an independent facilitator to a short-term training seminar on MGB. In all of the instances described, the relationships did not become perfect after agreement was made to work together. But each side agreed that the relationship was considerably better.

These examples, which come from the union-management perspective, do not have to be isolated to that sector. In any conflict situation, it is helpful if at least one of the sides takes the opportunity to try to resolve the conflict by making an offer to work together.

Sources:

[1] "An Industrial Transportation Company Counts on Conflict Prevention to Deal with a Changing Market," in *Labour Management Innovation in Canada*, Ottawa: Minister of Supply and Services, 1994, pp. 38–41.

[2] "Plugging In: Dialogue at a Wire and Cable Plant," in *Labour Management Innovation in Canada*, Ottawa: Minister of Supply and Services, 1994, pp. 42—45.

[3] "Mutual Gains Bargaining Means Less Strain and More Gain," in *Labour Management Innovation in Canada*, Ottawa: Minister of Supply and Services, 1994, pp. 96–99.

Summary and Implications

For the Workplace

Many people automatically assume that conflict is related to lower group and organizational performance. This chapter has demonstrated that this assumption is frequently incorrect. Conflict can be either constructive or destructive to the functioning of a group or unit. As shown in Exhibit 13-8, levels of conflict can be either too high or too low. Either extreme hinders performance. An optimal level is where there is enough conflict to prevent stagnation, stimulate creativity, allow tensions to be released, and initiate the seeds for change, yet not so much as to be disruptive or deter coordination of activities.

Inadequate or excessive levels of conflict can hinder the effectiveness of a group or an organization, resulting in reduced satisfaction of group members, increased absence and turnover rates, and, eventually, lower productivity. On the other hand, when conflict is at an optimal level, complacency and apathy should be minimized, motivation should be enhanced through the creation of a challenging and questioning environment with a vitality that makes work interesting, and there should be the amount of turnover needed to rid the organization of misfits and poor performers.

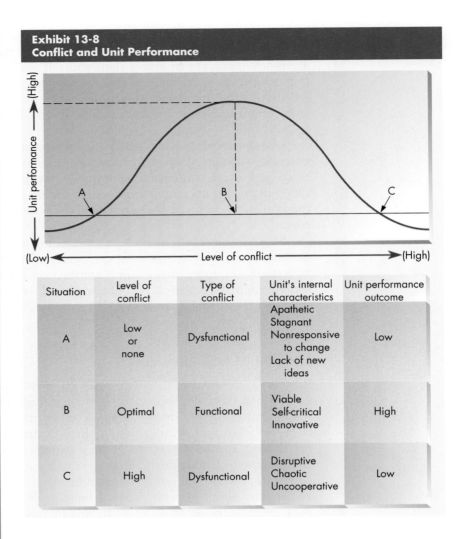

Exhibit 13-8
Conflict and Unit Performance

Situation	Level of conflict	Type of conflict	Unit's internal characteristics	Unit performance outcome
A	Low or none	Dysfunctional	Apathetic Stagnant Nonresponsive to change Lack of new ideas	Low
B	Optimal	Functional	Viable Self-critical Innovative	High
C	High	Dysfunctional	Disruptive Chaotic Uncooperative	Low

What advice can we give managers faced with excessive conflict and the need to reduce it? Don't assume that one conflict-handling intention will always be best! You should select an intention appropriate for the situation. The following provides some guidelines:[54]

Use *competition* when quick, decisive action is vital (in emergencies); on important issues, where unpopular actions need implementing (in cost cutting, enforcing unpopular rules, discipline); on issues vital to the organization's welfare when you know you're right; and against people who take advantage of noncompetitive behaviour.

Use *collaboration* to find an integrative solution when both sets of concerns are too important to be compromised; when your objective is to learn; to merge insights from people with different perspectives; to gain commitment by incorporating concerns into a consensus; and to work through feelings that have interfered with a relationship.

Use *avoidance* when an issue is trivial, or more important issues are pressing; when you perceive no chance of satisfying your concerns; when potential disruption outweighs the benefits of resolution; to let people cool down and regain perspective; when gathering information supersedes immediate decision; when others can resolve the conflict more effectively; and when issues seem tangential or symptomatic of other issues.

Use *accommodation* when you find you're wrong and to allow a better position to be heard, to learn, and to show your reasonableness; when issues are more important to others than yourself and to satisfy others and maintain cooperation; to build social credits for later issues; to minimize loss when you are outmatched and losing; when harmony and stability are especially important; and to allow subordinates to develop by learning from mistakes.

Use *compromise* when goals are important but not worth the effort of potential disruption of more assertive approaches; when opponents with equal power are committed to mutually exclusive goals; to achieve temporary settlements to complex issues; to arrive at expedient solutions under time pressure; and as a backup when collaboration or competition is unsuccessful.

Negotiation was shown to be an ongoing activity in groups and organizations. Distributive bargaining can resolve disputes but it often negatively affects one or more negotiators' satisfaction because it is focused on the short term and because it is confrontational. Integrative bargaining, in contrast, tends to provide outcomes that satisfy all parties and that build lasting relationships.

For You as an Individual

Conflict is something that you will experience in a variety of situations throughout your life. Some people like to avoid conflict, feeling that it is an unpleasant process. However, we pointed out that avoiding conflict does not necessarily have a positive outcome (for instance, it caused major problems for Eaton's and IBM Canada as they struggled to turn around their once-complacent organizations). When you work in your student groups to accomplish tasks, it will not be unusual for conflict to arise. You may have disagreements about how to proceed on a project, or there may be conflicts over meeting times, as different people in your group have different needs they are trying to accommodate. The chapter gives you a variety of ideas about how to resolve these conflicts, including ways to negotiate differences so that each of the people involved in the conflict can learn to accommodate the needs of the other.

ROADMAP REMINDER

In both the previous chapter on power and politics and this one on conflict and negotiation we have stressed that a variety of issues arise in organizations about which there is no general agreement on how to settle the disagreement. In the previous chapter we noted that people often engage in politics as a way to advance their position. This can lead to conflict. This chapter discusses the positives and negatives of conflicts, and offers some ways of resolving more serious conflicts. In the next chapter we move away from our discussions of how interactions in the organization work, and consider the design of organizations.

For Review

1. What are the disadvantages to conflict? What are its advantages?
2. What is the difference between functional and dysfunctional conflict? What determines functionality?
3. Under what conditions might conflict be beneficial to a group?
4. What are the components in the conflict-process model? From your own experiences, give an example of how a conflict proceeded through the five stages.
5. How could a manager stimulate conflict in his or her department?
6. What defines the settlement range in distributive bargaining?
7. Why isn't integrative bargaining more widely practised in organizations?
8. How do men and women differ, if at all, in their approaches to negotiation?
9. How can you improve your negotiating effectiveness?
10. What are the different strategies managers can use to reduce conflict in the workplace?

For Discussion

1. Do you think competition and conflict are different? Explain.
2. "Participation is an excellent method for identifying differences and resolving conflicts." Do you agree or disagree? Discuss.
3. Assume your immediate subordinate had to negotiate a contract with someone from China. What problems might he or she face? What suggestions would you make to help facilitate a settlement?
4. From your own experience, describe a situation you were involved in where the conflict was dysfunctional. Describe another example, from your experience, where the conflict was functional. Now analyse how other parties in both conflicts might have interpreted the situation in terms of whether the conflicts were functional or dysfunctional.
5. Is it possible to stimulate functional conflict without increasing emotional conflict in the process? Discuss the steps you could take to limit emotional conflict.

LEARNING ABOUT YOURSELF EXERCISE

What Is Your Primary Conflict-Handling Intention?

Indicate how often you rely on each of the following tactics by circling the number that you feel is most appropriate.

		Rarely				Always
1.	I argue my case with my co-workers to show the merits of my position.	1	2	3	4	5
2.	I negotiate with my co-workers so that a compromise can be reached.	1	2	3	4	5
3.	I try to satisfy the expectations of my co-workers.	1	2	3	4	5
4.	I try to investigate an issue with my co-workers to find a solution acceptable to us.	1	2	3	4	5
5.	I am firm in pursuing my side of the issue.	1	2	3	4	5
6.	I attempt to avoid being put on the spot and try to keep my conflict with my co-workers to myself.	1	2	3	4	5
7.	I hold on to my solution to a problem.	1	2	3	4	5
8.	I use give-and-take so that a compromise can be made.	1	2	3	4	5
9.	I exchange accurate information with my co-workers to solve a problem together.	1	2	3	4	5
10.	I avoid open discussion of my differences with my co-workers.	1	2	3	4	5
11.	I accommodate the wishes of my co-workers.	1	2	3	4	5
12.	I try to bring all our concerns out in the open so that the issues can be resolved in the best possible way.	1	2	3	4	5
13.	I propose a middle ground for breaking deadlocks.	1	2	3	4	5
14.	I go along with the suggestions of my co-workers.	1	2	3	4	5
15.	I try to keep my disagreements with my co-workers to myself in order to avoid hard feelings.	1	2	3	4	5

Turn to page 700 for scoring directions and key.

Source: This is an abbreviated version of a 35-item instrument described in M.A. Rahim, "A Measure of Styles of Handling Interpersonal Conflict," *Academy of Management Journal*, June 1983, pp. 368–76.

WORKING WITH OTHERS EXERCISE

A Negotiation Role-Play

This role play is designed to help you develop your negotiating skills. The class is to break into pairs. One person will play the role of Terry, the department supervisor. The other person will play Dale, Terry's boss.

The Situation: Terry and Dale work for Bauer. Terry supervises a research laboratory. Dale is the manager of research and development. Terry and Dale are former skaters who have worked for Bauer for more than six years. Dale has been Terry's boss for two years.

One of Terry's employees has greatly impressed Terry. This employee is Lisa Roland. Lisa was hired 11 months ago. She is 24 years old and holds a master's degree in mechanical engineering. Her entry-level salary was $52 500 a year. She was told by Terry that, in accordance with corporation policy, she would receive an initial performance evaluation at six months and a comprehensive review after one year. Based on her performance record, Lisa was told she could expect a salary adjustment at the time of the one-year evaluation.

Terry's evaluation of Lisa after six months was very positive. Terry commented on the long hours Lisa was working, her cooperative spirit, the fact that others in the lab enjoyed working with her, and that she was making an immediate positive impact on the project she had been assigned. Now that Lisa's first anniversary is coming up, Terry has again reviewed Lisa's performance. Terry thinks Lisa may be the best new person the R&D group has ever hired. After only a year, Terry has ranked Lisa as the number-three performer in a department of 11.

Salaries in the department vary greatly. Terry, for instance, has a basic salary of $67 000, plus eligibility for a bonus that might add another $5000 to $8000 a year. The salary range of the 11 department members is $30 400 to $56 350. The lowest salary is a recent hire with a bachelor's degree in physics. The two people that Terry has rated above Lisa earn base salaries of $52 700 and $56 350. They're both 27 years old and have been at Bauer for three and four years, respectively. The median salary in Terry's department is $46 660.

Terry's Role: You want to give Lisa a big raise. While she's young, she has proven to be an excellent addition to the department. You don't want to lose her. More importantly, she knows in general what other people in the department are earning and she thinks she's underpaid. The company typically gives one-year raises of five percent, although 10 percent is not unusual and 20 to 30 percent increases have been approved on occasion. You'd like to get Terry as large an increase as Dale will approve.

Dale's Role: All your supervisors typically try to squeeze you for as much money as they can for their people. You understand this because you did the same thing when you were a supervisor, but your boss wants to keep a lid on costs. He wants you to keep raises

for recent hires generally in the range of five to eight percent. In fact, he's sent a memo to all managers and supervisors stating this objective. However, your boss is also very concerned with equity and paying people what they're worth. You feel assured that he will support any salary recommendation you make, as long as it can be justified. Your goal, consistent with cost reduction, is to keep salary increases as low as possible.

The Negotiation: Terry has a meeting scheduled with Dale to discuss Lisa's performance review and salary adjustment. Take a couple of minutes to think through the facts in this exercise and to prepare a strategy. Then you have up to 15 minutes to conduct your negotiation. When your negotiation is complete, the class will compare the various strategies used and pair outcomes.

Not Your Dream Team

Mallory Murray hadn't had much experience working as part of a team. A recent graduate of the University of Saskatchewan, her business program had focused primarily on individual projects and accomplishments. What little exposure she had had to teams was in her organizational behaviour, marketing research, and strategy formulation courses. When she interviewed with ThinkLink, an educational software firm, she didn't give much concern to the fact that ThinkLink made extensive use of cross-functional teams. During on-site interviews, she told interviewers and managers alike that she had limited experience on teams. But she did tell them she worked well with people and thought that she could be an effective team player. Unfortunately, Mallory Murray didn't realize that working on a team is generally more complicated than simply working one-on-one with other people.

Mallory joined ThinkLink as an assistant marketing manager for the company's high school core programs. These are essentially software programs designed to help students learn algebra and geometry. Mallory's boss is Lin Chen (marketing manager). Other members of her team include Todd Schlotsky (senior programmer); Laura Willow (advertising); Sean Traynor (vice-president for strategic marketing); Joyce Rothman (co-founder of ThinkLink, who now only works part-time in the company; formerly a high-school math teacher; the formal leader of this project); and Harlow Gray (educational consultant).

After her first week on the job, Mallory was seriously considering quitting. "I never imagined how difficult it would be working with people who are so opinionated and competitive. Every decision seems to be a power contest. Sean, Joyce, and Harlow are particularly troublesome. Sean thinks his rank entitles him to the last word. Joyce thinks her opinions should carry more weight because she was instrumental in creating the company. And Harlow views everyone as less knowledgeable than he is. Because he consults with a number of software firms and school districts, Harlow's a 'know-it-all.' To make things worse, Lin is passive and quiet. He rarely speaks up in meetings and appears to want to avoid any conflicts."

"What makes my job particularly difficult," Mallory continued, "is that I don't have any specific job responsibilities. It seems that someone else is always interfering with what I'm doing or telling me how to do it. Our team has seven members—six chiefs and me!"

The project team that Mallory is working on has a deadline to meet that is only six weeks away. Currently the team is at least two weeks behind schedule. Everyone is aware that there's a problem but no one seems able to solve it. What is especially frustrating to Mallory is that neither Lin Chen nor Joyce Rothman is showing any leadership. Lin is preoccupied with a number of other projects, and Joyce can't seem to control Sean and Harlow's strong personalities.

Questions

1. Discuss cross-functional teams in terms of their propensity to create conflict.

2. What techniques or procedures might help reduce conflict on cross-functional teams?

3. If you were Mallory, is there anything you could do to lessen the conflict on the core project? Elaborate.

Family Business

Family businesses are important to the future of Canada, as they provide a large number of new jobs. And there are some notable families in business, such as the Bronfmans, the Irvings, the Southams, and the McCains. But family businesses face a great deal of difficulty when the second generation of family members stands ready to take over the business. For example, Wallace and Harrison McCain had a very public fight when it was time for the two brothers to step aside to let their children run their business. In the end, after spending millions on lawyers, shrinks, and consultants, they could not come to an agreement, and Wallace and Harrison went their separate ways.

Succession in the family business is one of the most difficult issues a family business owner faces. It requires the ability to deal with conflict and effectively engage in negotiation. And yet, most family businesses do not manage the process with much success. Almost 70 percent of family businesses do not survive a transition to the second generation. And 90 percent of businesses don't make it to the third generation.

Much of the reason that succession in family business is difficult is that family members have not learned the negotiation skills and conflict resolution skills necessary to manage the process of change. Family members forget to remain objective when they're working through transition issues. It's sometimes helpful to get outsiders involved as well, but many don't do this. The McCains, for instance, refused to consider appointing outside members to their board. When dealing with family members, people's judgment becomes clouded. Outsiders help family members understand how to manage their relationships with each other.

Questions

1. Describe how conflict intentions (such as competing, collaborating, and so on) may be related to succession issues in family businesses.

2. Describe how the successful conflict negotiation strategies that Eisenhardt identified in her research might be used by those in family business to handle a succession problem.

3. Describe how the negotiation model can be applied to a succession issue in a firm.

Source: Based on "Family Business," *Venture 553*; aired August 13, 1995.

Negotiating a Raise

You've decided you want a raise, and now you have to face your boss. Is there an appropriate strategy for getting that raise?

Asking for a raise is a negotiation process, and understanding that may make it easier for you to be successful at this often uncomfortable task. Your boss needs to know what value you add to the company. Having the courage to ask for what you believe you deserve makes it more likely you'll be able to move ahead in your career.

When negotiating for a raise, you might consider emphasizing the following points:

- what do you have to offer to the company?
- how has your performance affected the company's bottom line?

You should not personalize your request for a raise, for instance, by mentioning your children, bills, or other considerations. You should also consider possible alternatives to a raise, such as a car allowance, conferences, or even Internet access, which may give you more information to help you get ahead with your job.

And finally, in your negotiations, consider the value of silence. If you stop talking, it puts the responsibility on the other person to respond.

Questions

1. How could BATNA be applied to the negotiation process for a raise?
2. In what ways might you improve your own negotiation skills?

Source: Based on "How to Get a Raise," *Venture 534*; aired February 4, 1995.

POINT

Conflict Is Good for an Organization

We've made considerable progress in the last 25 years toward overcoming the negative stereotype given to conflict. Most behavioural scientists and an increasing number of practising managers now accept that the goal of effective management is not to eliminate conflict. Rather, it's to create the right intensity of conflict so as to reap its functional benefits.

Since conflict can be good for an organization, it is only logical to acknowledge that there may be times when managers will purposely want to increase its intensity. Let's briefly review how stimulating conflict can provide benefits to the organization.

- *Conflict is a means by which to bring about radical change.* It's an effective device by which management can drastically change the existing power structure, current interaction patterns, and entrenched attitudes.

- *Conflict facilitates group cohesiveness.* While conflict increases hostility between groups, external threats tend to cause a group to pull together as a unit. Intergroup conflicts raise the extent to which members identify with their own group and increase feelings of solidarity, while, at the same time, internal differences and irritations dissolve.

- *Conflict improves group and organizational effectiveness.* The stimulation of conflict initiates the search for new means and goals and clears the way for innovation. The successful solution of a conflict leads to greater effectiveness, to more trust and openness, to greater attraction of members for each other, and to

depersonalization of future conflicts. In fact, it has been found that as the number of minor disagreements increases, the number of major clashes decreases.

- *Conflict brings about a slightly higher, more constructive level of tension.* This enhances the chances of solving the conflicts in a way satisfactory to all parties concerned. When the level of tension is very low, the parties are not sufficiently motivated to do something about a conflict.

These points are clearly not comprehensive. As noted in the chapter, conflict provides a number of benefits to an organization. However, groups or organizations devoid of conflict are likely to suffer from apathy, stagnation, groupthink, and other debilitating diseases. In fact, more organizations probably fail because they have *too little* conflict, not because they have too much. Take a look at a list of large organizations that have failed or suffered serious financial setbacks over the past decade or two. You see names like Olympia and York Developments, Consumers Distributing, Eaton's, and General Motors. The common thread through these companies is that they stagnated. Their management became complacent and unable or unwilling to facilitate change. These organizations could have benefited by having had more conflict—the functional kind. ■

Source: The points presented here were influenced by E. Van de Vliert, "Escalative Intervention in Small-Group Conflicts," *Journal of Applied Behavioral Science*, Winter 1985, pp. 19–36.

counterPOINT

All Conflicts Are Dysfunctional!

It may be true that conflict is an inherent part of any group or organization. It may not be possible to eliminate it completely. However, just because conflicts exist is no reason to deify them. All conflicts are dysfunctional, and it is one of management's major responsibilities to keep conflict intensity as low as humanly possible. A few points will support this case.

- *The negative consequences from conflict can be devastating.* The list of negatives associated with conflict is awesome. The most obvious are increased turnover, decreased employee satisfaction, inefficiencies between work units, sabotage, labour grievances and strikes, and physical aggression.

- *Effective managers build teamwork.* A good manager builds a coordinated team. Conflict works against such an objective. A successful work group is like a successful sports team; each member knows his or her role and supports his or her teammates. When a team works well, the whole becomes greater than the sum of the parts. Management creates teamwork by minimizing internal conflicts and facilitating internal coordination.

- *Competition is good for an organization, but not conflict.* Competition and conflict should not be confused with each other. Conflict is behaviour directed against another party, whereas competition is behaviour aimed at obtaining a goal without interference from another party. Competition is healthy; it's the source of organizational vitality. Conflict, on the other hand, is destructive.

- *Managers who accept and stimulate conflict don't survive in organizations.* The whole argument on the value of conflict may be moot as long as most senior executives in organizations view conflict traditionally. In the traditional view, any conflict will be seen as bad. Since the evaluation of a manager's performance is made by higher-level executives, those managers who do not succeed in eliminating conflicts are likely to be appraised negatively. This, in turn, will reduce opportunities for advancement. Any manager who aspires to move up in such an environment will be wise to follow the traditional view and eliminate any outward signs of conflict. Failure to follow this advice might result in the premature departure of the manager. ■

PROGRESSIVE CASE • PART 4

Lee Simpson: Managing Politics and Conflict

"Anyone who says they don't engage in politicking is either lying or not paying attention. Throughout the organization, from work teams through the management board of the organization, forming coalitions is a very important part of getting what you want to happen." Lee Simpson explains that she has seen all kinds of politicking in organizations, from ingratiating behaviour and blatant flattery to very impressive and effective coalition building.

Simpson believes that men and women politick differently. Women build coalitions through persuasion, reason, and logic for whatever they want to see happen, from board decisions to organizational change. Men, by contrast, do coalition by obligation. "They call in their markers and they recognize that as their right." She describes a specific situation when she and a male colleague were working on a board together and sided with each other on a particular issue, but against the other members of the board. When they discussed how they would persuade the other 30 members of the board to change their minds, Simpson realized that they would need to talk individually to each board member. Her plan was to divide up the list of board members alphabetically, and she and her colleague would each call 15 of them, using persuasion, reason, logic, and even emotion to communicate their position. Her male colleague had a slightly different idea. He would call 15 of the members of the board, but he wanted to select those that owed him a favour and with whom he already had special connections.

Simpson notes that she so believed in her idea, she hadn't thought to use any politicking method beyond logic and persuasion. She envisioned phoning board members and saying, "Here are the great reasons why we should be doing this." Her male colleague, though equally firm in his belief about the idea, saw that persuasion would work better if he could couch it in terms of board members "owing him one", rather than simply relying on the merits of his position. His phone conversation, she says, would be something like "Hey Harry, you know, that meeting is coming up on the 15th. I am really looking to you to side with me on that vote." Simpson reports that they did split the list between them, and she used logic and persuasion, while he used his references to obligation. "And you know what? He got what he wanted and I got what I wanted. We both stayed comfortable doing it our own different ways." Nevertheless, she suggests that woman might benefit from expanding their repertoire of politicking. "I am not sure women have the knack of calling in markers. I don't think we are really good at coalition by obligation."

Has Simpson done particular things to build her own power bases as she moved up the organization? Her response is: "Rarely deliberately and probably not as effectively as I might." She notes that she has really solid people she knows she can depend on, both within her own group at work and as colleagues throughout the organization. She also feels that some of the relationships she's developed might not be as helpful as she would like. "Unfortunately, or otherwise, I am one of those people who wants everybody to be happy all the time. It is very draining to keep everybody happy all the time, and it took me a long time to recognize that it's okay if not everyone likes you. But that is a real tough one for women to get over."

When asked to comment specifically on sexual harassment in the workplace, she observes that while there have been a couple of incidents of sexual harassment at Maclean-Hunter, they were dealt with early and seriously, and that issue does not characterize the work environment there in any way. "I think the publishing environment might have a tendency to be more enlightened than some other workplaces because it was never an exclusively male preserve. Magazine publishing was always an environment where there were a lot of women." She suggests that environments that were more exclusively male in the past, such as the military, and law, medical, and engineering schools, may have experienced more sexual harassment because there were fewer women in those early environments to help define a more appropriate culture.

While Simpson limits the definition of workplace harassment to linking sex with job-related actions such as promotions, she does note that when a person is being offensive to another employee, such as making unwanted passes, the workplace needs to provide a place where the person can go and feel their complaint will be legitimately received. She believes that Maclean-Hunter has been responsible in this area. She also feels that this type of complaint should be linked to a climate of proper respect for one another in the workplace. For instance, she cites examples of women speaking to women they perceived to be lower on the office pecking order in tones that were totally inappropriate and men speaking to male shipping room clerks rudely and dismissively. Both of these behaviours are also inappropriate, she declares, even though they are not sexual harassment.

Simpson says that she deals with conflict directly and swiftly. "I am not afraid of it. I will even admit there are times when I relish confrontation." When in a situation that causes conflict, Simpson says that she likes to decide upon her strategies in advance and then get it over with. For instance, if she heard someone treating a receptionist rudely, she would speak to that person on the spot: "You know, a few minutes ago, I heard you speak to the receptionist in a tone that I thought was rather odd. Did she aggravate you in some way, or did you kind of forget your manners for a couple of minutes?" She believes that it is important for managers to remind people of appropriate behaviour in instances such as this. If it is not stopped early, inappropriate behaviour can create problems for the whole organization.

Questions

1. Evaluate Simpson's analysis of gender differences in politicking styles.

2. In what ways might men and women effectively learn from each other regarding styles of politicking?

3. To what extent do you agree with Simpson's observation that environments that are more male-dominated might have more instances of sexual harassment?

4. What do you think of Simpson's conflict-handling style?

Foundations of Organizational Structure

LEARNING OBJECTIVES

After studying this chapter, you should be able to

- Identify the six key elements that define an organization's structure

- Explain the characteristics of a bureaucracy

- Describe a matrix organization

- Explain the characteristics of a "virtual" organization

- Summarize why managers want to create boundaryless organizations

- Contrast mechanistic and organic structural models

- List the factors that favour different organizational structures

- Explain the behavioural implications of different organizational designs

WORKPLACE

Lisette (Lee) McDonald won the 1997 Canadian Woman Entrepreneur of the Year Award for International Competitiveness for her business, Southmedic Inc. The Barrie, Ontario-based organization, founded in 1982, manufactures and distributes surgical instruments for hospital operating rooms. The company has a staff of 41, and McDonald says her growth rate has been in excess of 50 percent a year, mainly because of her custom manufacturing division. "We are one of the few companies in North America able to take a prototype from design to packaging in the short time of six weeks. The big companies can do it but not at my speed."[1]

What makes Southmedic run so effectively? It may be the company's organizational structure. McDonald believes she's succeeded in the all-male world of medical supply because she listens to people and does not believe in hierarchy. "I believe in a horizontal management team. There are no pyramids here. I couldn't structure the company as if the world depended on me. My managers have a lot of autonomy." McDonald chose this flattened, more participative structure for Southmedic to accommodate her own needs. Because of the business, she has a heavy travel schedule. More importantly, she has three young children at home. "I have to be able to come and go without this place falling apart," she says.

Deciding how to organize the people who work in a company into positions is the task of those who design the organization's structure. The structure can represent a tall pyramid or it can be relatively flat. For instance, Exhibit 14-1 shows a pyramidal organization with five layers (and some organizations can have even more), while Exhibit 14-2 shows a flatter organization, with only three layers. The organizational structure also can be something intermediate between pyramid and flat. Among other things, the structure determines the reporting relationships of people. Thus, in a flat organization, if you have a problem, you can talk to the person at the top of the organization. In a pyramidal structure, you would talk to your manager, who might talk to his or her manager, who talks to the manager above, until finally, if the message finally reaches the top of the organization, it might be very different from the original message you told your manager. ■

The actual structure of an organization is chosen for a variety of reasons. In the case of Lee McDonald and Southmedic, she wanted a structure that would suit her travelling and family needs. Consequently, she gives her managers a lot of freedom to make decisions, and by positioning them horizontally, the managers share power in the organizational decisions. McDonald does not place herself ahead of the others in the organization; rather, to some extent, she shares power with her managers.

Not all organizations are flat like Southmedic. When Paul Tellier became president and CEO of Montreal-based Canadian National Railway (CN), he eliminated five vice-presidents and reduced the number of layers of management. When he arrived at CN, in some cases there were 10 layers of authority between the president and any line employee. Now there are no more

Canadian National Railways
www.cn.ca/

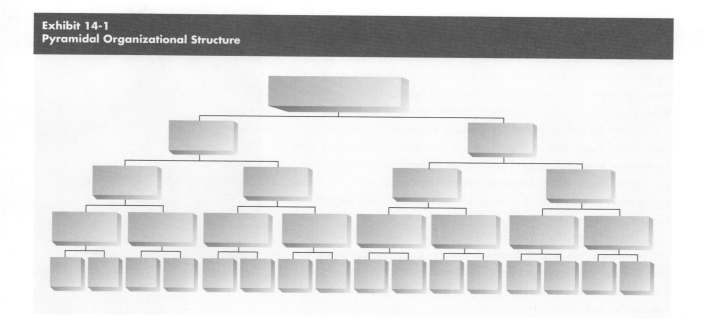

Exhibit 14-1
Pyramidal Organizational Structure

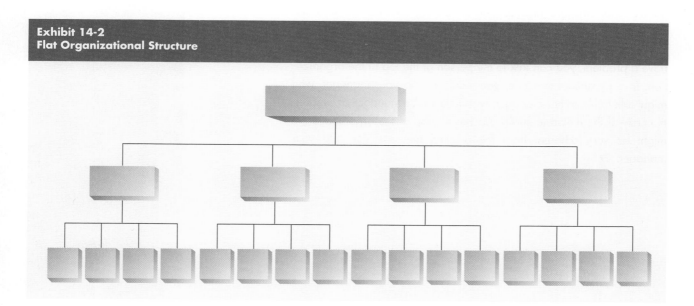

Exhibit 14-2
Flat Organizational Structure

than five. Even though five layers are flatter than 10, it comprises a lot more layers than Southmedic's structure, which is closer to just two layers, given the autonomy she offers her managers. CN is a much larger organization than Southmedic, however, which means that it would be much more difficult to operate it with the same organizational structure.

The theme of this chapter is that organizations have different structures and that these structures have a bearing on employee attitudes and behaviour. Moreover, as we noted in Chapter 1, as companies move into the 21st century they are becoming more team oriented. Workers are becoming more empowered because managers are being asked to share power, and organizations are becoming more globally focused. All of these factors cause organizations to think more carefully about the best way to organize the ways that people in the organization are connected to each other. These connections form the basis for organizational structure.

In the following pages, we define the key components that comprise an organization's structure, present six structural design options from which managers can choose, identify the contingency factors that make certain structural designs preferable in varying situations, and conclude by considering the different effects that various organizational designs have on employee behaviour. Because this is a textbook on organizational behaviour, we are particularly interested in how structure affects behaviour. Some organizational structures that allow only limited freedom in choosing how to do your job, such as an assembly-line process, might cause you extreme dissatisfaction. On the other hand, a very flat structure, such as Southmedic's, might make you feel as though you could contribute more to the organization. Bear in mind, however, that individuals differ in their reactions to organizational structure, so you should not assume that everyone will respond the same way you might respond.

What Is Organizational Structure?

organizational structure
How job tasks are formally divided, grouped, and coordinated.

An **organizational structure** defines how job tasks are formally divided, grouped, and coordinated. There are six key elements that managers need to address when they design their organization's structure. These are work specialization, departmentalization, chain of command, span of control, centralization and decentralization, and formalization.[2] Exhibit 14-3 presents each of these elements as answers to an important structural question. The following sections describe these six elements of structure.

Work Specialization

Early in this century, Henry Ford became rich and famous by building automobiles on an assembly line. Every Ford worker was assigned a specific, repetitive task. For instance, one person would just put on the right-front wheel, and someone else would install the right-front door. By breaking jobs up into small standardized tasks which could be performed over and over again, Ford was able to produce cars at the rate of one every 10 seconds, while using employees who had relatively limited skills. Ford's changes modelled those that happened during the Industrial Revolution, which encouraged economies of scale through the specialization of work.

work specialization
The degree to which tasks in the organization are subdivided into separate jobs.

Ford demonstrated that work can be performed more efficiently if employees are allowed to specialize. Today we use the term **work specialization**

Exhibit 14-3
Six Key Questions That Managers Need to Answer in Designing the Proper Organizational Structure

The Key Question	The Answer Is Provided By
1. To what degree are tasks subdivided into separate jobs?	Work specialization
2. On what basis will jobs be grouped together?	Departmentalization
3. To whom do individuals and groups report?	Chain of command
4. How many individuals can a manager efficiently and effectively direct?	Span of control
5. Where does decision-making authority lie?	Centralization and decentralization
6. To what degree will there be rules and regulations to direct employees and managers?	Formalization

Bombardier Inc.
www.challenger.bombardier.com/

or *division of labour* to describe the degree to which tasks in the organization are subdivided into separate jobs.

The essence of work specialization is that, rather than an entire job being completed by one individual, it is broken down into a number of steps, with each step being completed by a separate individual. In essence, individuals specialize in doing part of an activity rather than the entire activity.

By the late 1940s, most manufacturing jobs in industrialized countries were being done with high work specialization. Management viewed this as a means to make the most efficient use of its employees' skills. In most organizations, some tasks require highly developed skills; others can be performed by the untrained. If all workers were engaged in each step of, say, an organization's manufacturing process, all would have to have the skills necessary to perform both the most demanding and least demanding jobs. The result would be that, except when performing the most skilled or highly complex tasks, employees would be working below their skill levels. And since skilled workers are paid more than unskilled workers and their wages tend to reflect their highest level of skill, it represents an inefficient usage of organizational resources to pay highly skilled workers to do easy tasks.

Managers also looked for other efficiencies that could be achieved through work specialization. Employee skills at performing a task successfully increase through repetition. Less time is spent in changing tasks, in putting away one's tools and equipment from a prior step in the work process, and in preparing for another. Equally important, training for specialization is more efficient from the organization's perspective. It is easier and less costly to find and train workers to do specific and repetitive tasks. This is especially true of highly sophisticated and complex operations. For example, could Montreal-based Bombardier produce even one CRJ plane a year if one person had to build the entire plane alone? Not likely! Finally, work specialization increases efficiency and productivity by encouraging the creation of special inventions and machinery.

For much of the first half of this century, managers viewed work specialization as an unending source of increased productivity. And they were probably right. Because specialization was not widely practised, its introduc-

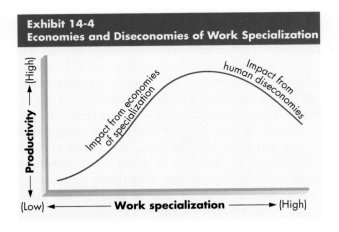

Exhibit 14-4
Economies and Diseconomies of Work Specialization

Productivity → (High) / (Low)

Impact from economies of specialization

Impact from human diseconomies

(Low) ◄— **Work specialization** —► (High)

tion almost always generated higher productivity. But by the 1960s, there became increasing evidence that a good thing can be carried too far. The point had been reached in some jobs where the human diseconomies from specialization—which surfaced as boredom, fatigue, stress, low productivity, poor quality, increased absenteeism, and high turnover—more than offset the economic advantages (see Exhibit 14-4). In such cases, productivity could be increased by enlarging, rather than narrowing, the scope of job activities. Additionally, a number of companies found that by giving employees a variety of activities to do, allowing them to do a whole and complete job, and by putting them into teams with interchangeable skills, they often achieved significantly higher output with increased employee satisfaction.

Most managers today view work specialization as neither obsolete nor as an unending source of increased productivity. Rather, they recognize the economies it provides in certain types of jobs and the problems it creates when it's carried too far. You'll find, for example, high work specialization being used by McDonald's to make and sell hamburgers and fries efficiently, and by medical specialists in hospitals. On the other hand, companies such as Saturn Corporation have had success by broadening the scope of jobs and reducing specialization.

INDIVIDUAL RESPONSES TO WORK SPECIALIZATION The evidence generally indicates that *work specialization* contributes to higher employee productivity but at the price of reduced job satisfaction. However, this statement ignores individual differences and the type of job tasks people do.

As we noted previously, work specialization is not an unending source of higher productivity. Problems start to surface and productivity begins to suffer, when the human diseconomies of doing repetitive and narrow tasks overtake the economies of specialization. As the workforce has become more highly educated and desirous of jobs that are intrinsically rewarding, the point where productivity begins to decline seems to be reached more quickly than in decades past.

While more people today are undoubtedly turned off by overly specialized jobs than were their parents or grandparents, it would be naive to ignore the reality that there is still a segment of the workforce that prefers the routine and repetitiveness of highly specialized jobs. Some individuals want work that makes minimal intellectual demands and provides the security of routine. For these people, high work specialization is a source of job satisfaction. The empirical question, of course, is whether this represents two percent or 52 percent of the workforce. Given that there is some self-selection operating in the choice of careers, we might conclude that a high degree of specialization will produce the most dissatisfaction in professional jobs occupied by individuals with high needs for personal growth and diversity.

Departmentalization

departmentalization
The basis by which jobs are grouped together.

Once you've divided up jobs through work specialization, you need to group together these jobs so that common tasks can be coordinated. The basis by which jobs are grouped together is called **departmentalization**.

One of the most popular ways to group activities is by *functions* performed. For example, a manufacturing manager might organize his or her plant by separating engineering, accounting, manufacturing, human resources, and purchasing specialists into common departments. Of course, departmentalization by function can be used in all types of organizations. Only the functions change to reflect the organization's objectives and activities. Similarly, a hospital might have departments devoted to research, patient care, accounting, and so forth. A professional hockey franchise might have departments entitled player personnel, ticket sales, and travel and accommodations. The major advantage to this type of grouping is obtaining efficiencies from putting together similar specialists. Functional departmentalization seeks to achieve economies of scale by placing people with common skills and orientations into common units. Exhibit 14-5 illustrates how Composites Atlantic of Nova Scotia, which designs and manufactures advanced composites for aerospace, space, and defence, organizes its departments by function.

Tasks can also be departmentalized by the type of *product* the organization produces. Estée Lauder, which produces the Clinique, Prescriptives, and Origins lines in addition to Canadian-created MAC cosmetics and its own original line of Estée Lauder products, operates each of these products as a distinct company. The major advantage to this type of grouping is increased accountability for product performance, since all activities related to a specific product are under the direction of a single manager. If an organization's activities are service rather than product related, each service would be grouped autonomously. For instance, many of the big accounting firms, such as KPMG, now call themselves "professional services firms" to reflect the

Estée Lauder
http://www.prnewswire.com/
gh/cnoc/comp/251850.html

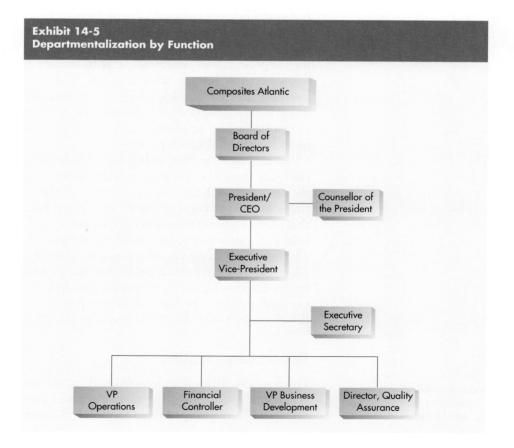

Exhibit 14-5
Departmentalization by Function

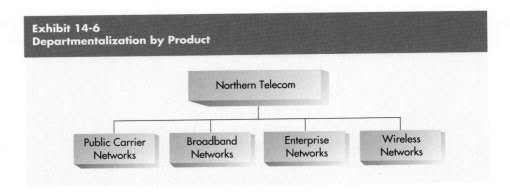

Exhibit 14-6
Departmentalization by Product

Northern Telecom

Public Carrier Networks | Broadband Networks | Enterprise Networks | Wireless Networks

variety of services that they now offer, including tax, management consulting, auditing, and the like. Each of the different services is under the direction of a product or service manager. Exhibit 14-6 illustrates Northern Telecom's (Nortel) four separate businesses, which are organized by product lines to make it easier to service customers.

Another way to departmentalize is on the basis of *geography* or territory. The sales function, for instance, may be divided regionally with departments for British Columbia, the Prairies, Central Canada, and Atlantic Canada. Each of these regions is, in effect, a department organized around geography. If an organization's customers are scattered over a large geographic area and have similar needs based on their location, then this form of departmentalization can be valuable. Exhibit 14-7 illustrates how Royal Bank organizes itself by regional units (not all of its regional units are included in the exhibit, however).

At a Reynolds Metals aluminum-tubing plant in upstate New York, production is organized into five departments: casting; press; tubing; finishing; and inspecting, packing, and shipping. This is an example of *process* departmentalization because each department specializes in one specific phase in the production of aluminum tubing. The metal is cast in huge furnaces; sent to the press department, where it is extruded into aluminum pipe; transferred to the tube mill, where it is stretched into various sizes and shapes of tubing; moved to finishing, where it is cut and cleaned; and finally arrives in the inspecting, packing, and shipping department. Since each process requires different skills, this method offers a basis for the homogeneous categorizing of activities.

Process departmentalization can be used for processing customers as well as products. For example, in some provinces, to get a driver's licence, you may go through a series of steps handled by several departments before

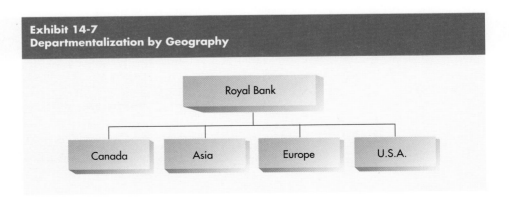

Exhibit 14-7
Departmentalization by Geography

Royal Bank

Canada | Asia | Europe | U.S.A.

receiving your licence: (1) validation by motor-vehicles division; (2) processing by the licensing department; and (3) payment collection by the treasury department.

A final category of departmentalization is to use the particular type of *customer* the organization seeks to reach. The sales activities in an office supply firm, for instance, can be broken down into three departments to service retail, wholesale, and government customers. A large law office can segment its staff on the basis of whether they service corporate or individual clients. The assumption underlying customer departmentalization is that customers in each department have a common set of problems and needs that can best be met by having specialists for each. Exhibit 14-8 illustrates how Dell Canada is divided into sales marketing units, according to the type of customer serviced.

Large organizations may use all of the forms of departmentalization that we've described. A major Japanese electronics firm, for instance, organizes each of its divisions along functional lines and its manufacturing units around processes; it departmentalizes sales around seven geographic regions, and divides each sales region into four customer groupings. Two general trends, however, seem to be gaining momentum in the 1990s. First, customer departmentalization is growing in popularity. In order to better monitor the needs of customers and to be better able to respond to changes in those needs, many organizations have given greater emphasis to customer departmentalization. Xerox, for example, has eliminated its corporate marketing staff and placed marketing specialists out in the field.[3] This allows the company to better understand who their customers are and to respond faster to their requirements. The second trend is that rigid, functional departmentalization is being complemented by teams that cross over traditional departmental lines. As we described in Chapter 8, as tasks have become more complex, and more diverse skills are needed to accomplish those tasks, management has turned to cross-functional teams.

Organizations may choose to go a step further than departmentalization and actually turn departments into divisions that are separate profit centres. For instance, within Estée Lauder's product-based departmentalization (discussed earlier), the Clinique, Prescriptive, and MAC lines are each separate profit centres, responsible for setting their own strategic goals.

Chain of Command

Twenty years ago, the chain-of-command concept was a basic cornerstone in the design of organizations. As you'll see, it has far less importance today.

Dell Canada
www.dell.com

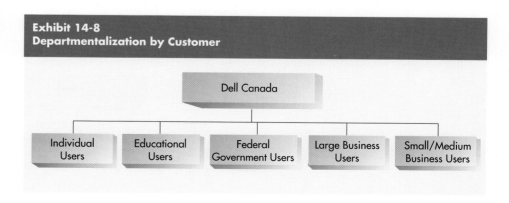

Exhibit 14-8
Departmentalization by Customer

Dell Canada

Individual Users | Educational Users | Federal Government Users | Large Business Users | Small/Medium Business Users

But contemporary managers should still consider its implications when they decide how best to structure their organizations.

The **chain of command** is an unbroken line of authority that extends from the top of the organization to the lowest echelon and clarifies who reports to whom. It answers questions for employees such as, "To whom do I go if I have a problem?" and "To whom do I report?"

You can't discuss the chain of command without discussing two complementary concepts: *authority* and *unity of command*. **Authority** refers to the rights inherent in a managerial position to give orders and expect the orders to be obeyed. To facilitate coordination, each managerial position is given a place in the chain of command, and each manager is given a degree of authority in order to meet his or her responsibilities. This chapter's Working With Others exercise helps you examine your reaction to authority.

The **unity-of-command** principle helps preserve the concept of an unbroken line of authority. It states that a person should have one and only one superior to whom he or she directly reports. If the unity of command is broken, a subordinate might have to cope with conflicting demands or priorities from several superiors. Times change and so do the basic tenets of organizational design. The concepts of chain of command, authority, and unity of command have substantially less relevance today because of advancements in computer technology and the trend toward empowering employees. Just how different things are today is illustrated in the following excerpt from an article in *Business Week*.

chain of command
The unbroken line of authority that extends from the top of the organization to the lowest echelon and clarifies who reports to whom.

authority
The rights inherent in a managerial position to give orders and to expect the orders to be obeyed.

unity of command
A subordinate should have only one superior to whom he or she directly reports.

Having control over the production line does not occur only in non-union environments. At the Honeywell Ltd. plant in Scarborough, Ontario, unionized workers have the authority to shut down the production line to correct production defects.

Puzzled, Charles Chaser scanned the inventory reports from his company's distribution centers one Wednesday morning in mid-March. According to the computer printouts, stocks of Rose Awakening Cutex nail polish were down to three days' supply, well below the three-and-a-half week stock Chesebrough-Pond's Inc. tries to keep on hand. But Chaser knew his Jefferson City (Missouri) plant had shipped 346 dozen bottles of the polish just two days before. Rose Awakening must be flying off store shelves, he thought. So Chaser turned to his terminal next to the production line and typed in instructions to produce 400 dozen more bottles on Thursday morning.

All in a day's work for a scheduling manager, right? Except for one detail: Chaser isn't management. He's a line worker—officially a "line coordinator"—one of hundreds who routinely tap the plant's computer network to track shipments, schedule their own workloads, and generally perform functions that used to be the province of management.[4]

One of the changes in today's workplace is that in many instances, low-level employees can access information in seconds that 20 years ago was avail-

able only to top managers. Similarly, computer technology increasingly allows employees anywhere in an organization to communicate with anyone else without going through formal channels. Moreover, the concepts of authority and maintaining the chain of command are increasingly less relevant as operating employees are being empowered to make decisions that previously were reserved for management. This chapter's From Concepts to Skills feature presents strategies that management can use to effectively delegate authority. Add to this the popularity of self-managed and cross-functional teams and the creation of new structural designs that include multiple bosses, and the unity-of-command concept takes on less relevance. There are, of course, still many organizations that find they can be most productive by enforcing the chain of command. There just seem to be fewer of them nowadays.

Span of Control

span of control
The number of subordinates a manager can efficiently and effectively direct.

How many subordinates can a manager efficiently and effectively direct? This question of **span of control** is important because, to a large degree, it determines the number of levels and managers an organization has. All things being equal, the wider or larger the span, the more efficient the organization. An example can illustrate the validity of this statement.

Assume that we have two organizations, both of which have approximately 4100 operative-level employees. As Exhibit 14-9 illustrates, if one has a uniform span of four and the other a span of eight, the wider span would have two fewer levels and approximately 800 fewer managers. If the average manager earned $56 000 a year, the wider span would save $45 million a year in management salaries! Obviously, wider spans are more efficient in terms of cost. However, at some point wider spans reduce effectiveness. That is, when the span becomes too large, employee performance suffers because supervisors no longer have the time to provide the necessary leadership and support.

Small spans have their advocates. By keeping the span of control to five or six employees, a manager can maintain close control.[5] For instance, the Ethical Dilemma exercise illustrates several instances of close employee

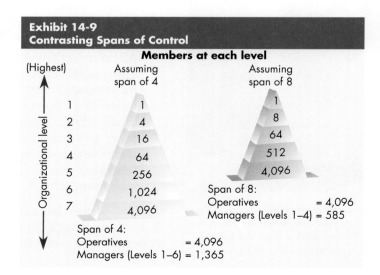

Exhibit 14-9
Contrasting Spans of Control

Members at each level

Assuming span of 4:

Organizational level	Members
1	1
2	4
3	16
4	64
5	256
6	1,024
7	4,096

Span of 4:
Operatives = 4,096
Managers (Levels 1–6) = 1,365

Assuming span of 8:

Members
1
8
64
512
4,096

Span of 8:
Operatives = 4,096
Managers (Levels 1–4) = 585

FROM CONCEPTS TO SKILLS

Delegating Authority

If you're a manager and want to delegate some of your authority to someone else, how do you go about it? The following summarizes the primary steps you need to take.

1. *Clarify the assignment.* The place to begin is to determine what is to be delegated and to whom. You need to identify the person most capable of doing the task, then determine if he or she has the time and motivation to do the job.

   Assuming you have a willing and able subordinate, it is your responsibility to provide clear information on what is being delegated, the results you expect, and any time or performance expectations you hold.

   Unless there is an overriding need to adhere to specific methods, you should delegate only the end results. That is, get agreement on what is to be done and the end results expected, but let the subordinate decide on the means.

2. *Specify the subordinate's range of discretion.* Every act of delegation comes with constraints. You're delegating authority to act, but not *unlimited* authority. What you're delegating is authority to act on certain issues and, on those issues, within certain parameters. You need to specify what those parameters are so subordinates know, in no uncertain terms, the range of their discretion.

3. *Allow the subordinate to participate.* One of the best sources for determining how much authority will be necessary to accomplish a task is the subordinate who will be held accountable for that task. If you allow employees to participate in determining what is delegated, how much authority is needed to get the job done, and the standards by which they'll be judged, you increase employee motivation, satisfaction, and accountability for performance.

4. *Inform others that delegation has occurred.* Delegation should not occur in a vacuum. Not only do you and the subordinate need to know specifically what has been delegated and how much authority has been granted, but anyone else who may be affected by the delegation act also needs to be informed.

5. *Establish feedback controls.* The establishment of controls to monitor the subordinate's progress increases the likelihood that important problems will be identified early and that the task will be completed on time and to the desired specifications. For instance, agree on a specific time for completion of the task, and then set progress dates when the subordinate will report back on how well he or she is doing and any major problems that have surfaced. This can be supplemented with periodic spot checks to ensure that authority guidelines are not being abused, organization policies are being followed, and proper procedures are being met.

monitoring. But small spans pose three major drawbacks. First, as already described, they're expensive because they add levels of management. Second, they make vertical communication in the organization more complex. The added levels of hierarchy slow down decision-making and tend to isolate upper management. Third, small spans of control encourage overly tight supervision and discourage employee autonomy.

The trend in recent years has been toward larger spans of control. For example, at Vancouver-based MacMillan Bloedel's (MB's) Powell River pulp and paper mill in British Columbia, supervisors have seen the size of their work crews increase from 8 to 16 as the result of downsizing.[6] The span for managers at companies such as General Electric and Reynolds Metals has

Computer technology is increasing sales managers' span of control at Owens-Corning, a building-supply manufacturer and retailer. The company has equipped its salespeople with computers loaded with software that provides up-to-date information about products, customers, and marketplace trends. The information empowers salespeople to manage their territory by making on-the-spot decisions on their own. Regional sales manager Charles Causey (left) expects the computer system to increase his span of control from nine salespeople to 15.

Owens-Corning
http://www.owenscorning.
com/

centralization
The degree to which decision-making is concentrated at a single point in the organization.

decentralization
Decision discretion is pushed down to lower-level employees.

expanded to 10 or 12 subordinates—twice the number of 20 years ago.[7]

Two recent trends have contributed to wider spans of control: downsizing and the move to teamwork in some organizations. Wide spans of control are also consistent with recent efforts by companies to reduce costs, cut overhead, speed up decision-making, increase flexibility, get closer to customers, and empower employees. However, to ensure that performance doesn't suffer because of these wider spans, organizations have been investing heavily in employee training. Managers recognize that they can handle a wider span when employees know their jobs inside and out or can turn to their co-workers when they have questions.

INDIVIDUAL RESPONSES TO SPAN OF CONTROL A review of the research indicates that it is probably safe to say that there is no evidence to support a relationship between *span of control* and employee performance. While it is intuitively attractive to argue that large spans might lead to higher employee performance because they provide more distant supervision and more opportunity for personal initiative, the research fails to support this notion. At this point it is impossible to state that any particular span of control is best for producing high performance or high satisfaction among subordinates. The reason is, again, probably individual differences. That is, some people like to be left alone, while others prefer the security of a boss who is quickly available at all times. Consistent with several of the contingency theories of leadership discussed in Chapter 11, we would expect factors such as employees' experiences and abilities and the degree of structure in their tasks to explain when wide or narrow spans of control are likely to contribute to their performance and job satisfaction. However, there is some evidence to indicate that a *manager's* job satisfaction increases as the number of subordinates he or she supervises increases.

Centralization and Decentralization

In some organizations, top managers make all the decisions. Lower-level managers merely carry out top management's directives. At the other extreme, there are organizations where decision-making is pushed down to those managers who are closest to the action. The former organizations are highly centralized; the latter are decentralized.

The term **centralization** refers to the degree to which decision-making is concentrated at a single point in the organization. The concept includes only formal authority, that is, the rights inherent in one's position. Typically, it's said that if top management makes the organization's key decisions with little or no input from lower-level personnel, then the organization is centralized. In contrast, the more that lower-level personnel provide input or are actually given the discretion to make decisions, the more **decentralization** there is. As Dilbert points out in Exhibit 14-10, however, some organizations do not seem able to decide upon an appropriate level of decentralization.

Exhibit 14-10

Source: S. Adams, *Dogbert's Big Book of Business,* DILBERT reprinted by permission of United Feature Syndicate, Inc.

An organization characterized by centralization is an inherently different structural animal from one that is decentralized. In a decentralized organization, action can be taken more quickly to solve problems, more people provide input into decisions, and employees are less likely to feel alienated from those who make the decisions that affect their work lives. Decentralized departments make it easier to address customer concerns as well. Toronto-based Rogers Cantel's CEO Charles Hoffman began decentralizing Cantel's business a month after he assumed the top post in January 1998. One of his first moves was to eliminate the top executive floor at Toronto headquarters, and move the bosses to offices on the same floor as their departments. He believes that "wireless companies have to build their markets locally, and so centralized processes and procedures rarely make sense—especially when competition is intense."[8] For another example of a company that decentralized its structure in an effort to improve its performance, see this chapter's OB in the News feature discussion of Rogers Cantel Mobile Communications.

Consistent with recent management efforts to make organizations more flexible and responsive, there has been a marked trend toward decentralizing decision-making. A survey of 100 international corporations found that 36 percent of them are centrally structured today, compared with 53 percent in

OB IN THE NEWS

Restructuring at Rogers Cantel Mobile Communications

Rogers Cantel Mobile Communications Inc. posted one of its worst quarters in history at the end of 1997, following a year where analysts said that "Cantel's management has done a poor job running the wireless carrier in the past 12 months." That set the scene for the transfer of presidential and CEO duties from Stanley Kabala to Charles Hoffman in January 1998. Within a month, Hoffman was changing the organizational structure of Toronto-based Cantel and giving regional operations more freedom.

Not everyone agrees that all aspects of Hoffman's change in structure will be effective, however. Cantel is criticized for having too many managers, and even with the change in structure, there will be 32 people at the vice-president level or higher, which is the same as before the restructuring. Thirteen of these executives will report directly to Hoffman.

One of Hoffman's plans is to get the people at Cantel closer to their customers. "We can't treat a customer in B.C. like we would a customer in Ontario because they are different," notes Heather Armstrong, a Cantel spokeswoman. Cantel's new structure will have three regional operations: Western Canada, Ontario, and Eastern Canada. Each division will do its own sales, advertising, and public relations. Previously, the Toronto headquarters made decisions not only for Ontario, but also for Western and Eastern Canada.

Cantel's restructuring illustrates two key points from this chapter. One can restructure without changing the number of managers, although it is questionable whether others would view this as a restructuring. Also, a company can decentralize its decision process, as Cantel did, by creating new divisions that deal more directly with the customer, rather than allowing head office to make all of the decisions.

Source: Philip DeMong, "Cantel's CEO Decentralizes Management," *Financial Post*, March 21/23, 1998, p. 6, and Philip DeMont, "Analysts Say Floundering Cantel Has Hit Rock Bottom," *Financial Post Daily*, February 24, 1998, p. 29.

Take It to the Net

We invite you to visit the Robbins page on the Prentice Hall Web site at:

http://www.prenticehall.ca/robbins

for this chapter's World Wide Web exercise.

1990.[9] The reason for decentralization in large companies is that lower-level managers are closer to "the action" and typically have more detailed knowledge about problems than do top managers. Big retailers such as The Bay and Sears have given their store managers considerably more discretion in choosing what merchandise to stock. This allows those stores to compete more effectively against local merchants. Similarly, the Bank of Montreal grouped its 1164 branches into 236 "communities," or groups of branches within limited geographical areas.[10] Each community is led by a community area manager, who typically works within a 20-minute drive of the other branches. These area managers can respond more quickly and more intelligently to problems in their communities than could some senior executive located in Montreal. IBM Europe's chairperson Renato Riverso has similarly sliced the continent into some 200 autonomous business units, each with its own profit plan, employee incentives, and customer focus. "We used to man-

age from the top, like an army," said Riverso. "Now we're trying to create entities that drive themselves."[11]

INDIVIDUAL RESPONSES TO CENTRALIZATION   We find fairly strong evidence linking *centralization* and job satisfaction. In general, organizations that are less centralized have a greater amount of participative decision-making. And the evidence suggests that participative decision-making is positively related to job satisfaction. But, again, individual differences surface. The decentralization–satisfaction relationship is strongest with employees who have low self-esteem. Because individuals with low self-esteem have less confidence in their abilities, they place a higher value on shared decision-making, which means that they're not held solely responsible for decision outcomes.

Formalization

formalization
The degree to which jobs within the organization are standardized.

Formalization refers to the degree to which jobs within the organization are standardized. If a job is highly formalized, then the job incumbent has a minimum amount of discretion over what is to be done, when it is to be done, and how he or she should do it. Employees can be expected always to handle the same input in exactly the same way, resulting in a consistent and uniform output. There are explicit job descriptions, lots of organizational rules, and clearly defined procedures covering work processes in organizations where there is high formalization. Where formalization is low, job behaviours are relatively nonprogrammed, and employees have a great deal of freedom to exercise discretion in their work. Since an individual's discretion on the job is inversely related to the amount of behaviour in that job that is preprogrammed by the organization, the greater the standardization, the less input the employee has into how his or her work is to be done. Standardization not only eliminates the possibility of employees engaging in alternative behaviours, but it even removes the need for employees to consider alternatives.

Employees' jobs at McDonald's restaurants are highly formalized. To provide customers with consistent product quality and fast service, workers are expected to follow defined food-preparation procedures. Learning these procedures is an important part of employee training at McDonald's Hamburger University training centre, shown here.

The degree of formalization can vary widely between organizations and within organizations. Certain jobs, for instance, are well known to have little formalization. University textbook sellers—the representatives of publishers who call on professors to inform them of their company's new publications—have a great deal of freedom in their jobs. They have no standard sales "spiel," and the extent of rules and procedures governing their behaviour may be little more than the requirement that they submit a weekly sales report and some suggestions on what to emphasize for the various new titles. At the other extreme, there are clerical and editorial positions in the same publishing houses where employees are required to "clock in" at their workstations by 8:00 a.m. or be docked a half-hour's pay and, once at that workstation, to follow a set of precise procedures dictated by management.

McDonald's is an example of a company where employee routines are highly formalized.

Employees are instructed in such things as how to greet the customer (smile, be sincere, make eye contact), ask and receive payment (state amount of order clearly and loudly, announce the amount of money customer gives to the employee, count change out loud and efficiently), and thank the customer (give a sincere thank-you, make eye contact, ask customer to come again). McDonald's includes this information in training and employee handbooks, and managers are given a checklist of these behaviours so that they can observe their employees to ensure that the proper procedures are followed.[12]

Common Organizational Designs

In the previous section, we described six elements of organizational structure. If you think of these as design decisions that an owner or CEO makes about his or her organization, you begin to realize that a variety of organizational forms might emerge based on individual responses to each of the structural questions. Management in some firms may choose a highly formalized and centralized structure, while others might choose a structure that is more loose and amorphous. A variety of other designs exists somewhere between these two extremes.

Exhibit 14-11 presents two extreme models of organizational design. One extreme we'll call the **mechanistic model**. It has extensive departmentalization, high formalization, a limited information network (mostly downward communication), and little participation by low-level members in decision-making. Historically, government bureaucracies have tended to operate at a more mechanistic level. At the other extreme is the **organic model**. This model is flat, uses cross-hierarchical and cross-functional teams, has low formalization, possesses a comprehensive information network (utilizing lateral and upward communication as well as downward), and it involves high participation in decision-making.[13] High-tech firms, particularly those in their early years, operate in a more organic fashion, with individuals collaborating on many of the tasks.

mechanistic model
A structure characterized by extensive departmentalization, high formalization, a limited information network, and centralization.

organic model
A structure that is flat, uses cross-hierarchical and cross-functional teams, has low formalization, possesses a comprehensive information network, and relies on participative decision-making.

Exhibit 14-11
Mechanistic versus Organic Models

The mechanistic model

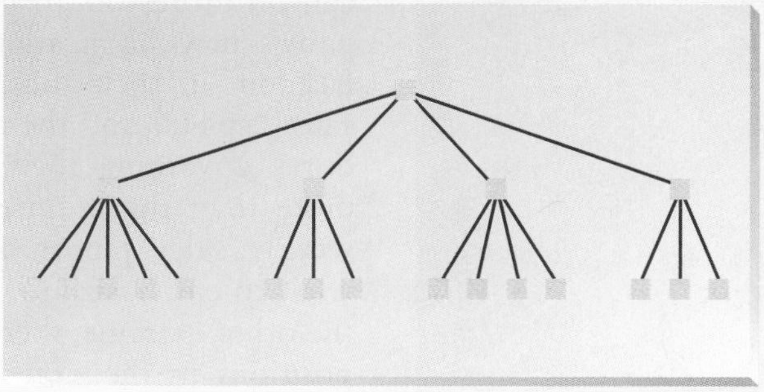

- High specialization
- Rigid departmentalization
- Clear chain of command
- Narrow spans of control
- Centralization
- High formalization

The organic model

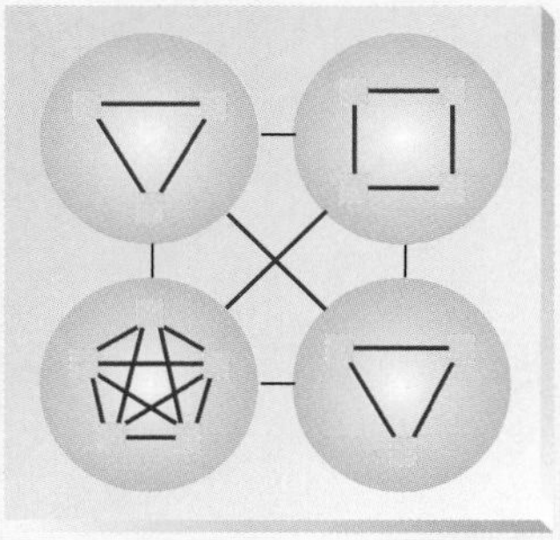

- Cross-functional teams
- Cross-hierarchical teams
- Free flow of information
- Wide spans of control
- Decentralization
- Low formalization

INDIVIDUAL RESPONSES TO ORGANIZATIONAL STRUCTURE As we review the different design possibilities of organization, you might want to think about how organizational design would affect you. Your response to organizational design will be affected by factors such as your experience, personality, and the work task. For simplicity's sake, it might help to keep in mind that individuals with a high degree of bureaucratic orientation (see the Learning about Yourself exercise at the end of this chapter) tend to place a heavy reliance on higher authority, prefer formalized and specific rules, and prefer formal relationships with others on the job. These people seem better suited to mechanistic structures. Individuals with a low degree of bureaucratic orientation would probably fit better in organic structures. Additionally, cultural background influences preference for structure. Thus, employees from high power distance cultures, such as found in Greece, France, and most of Latin America, will be much more accepting of mechanistic structures than will employees who come from low power distance countries. So you need to consider cultural differences along with individual differences when making predictions on how structure will affect employee performance and satisfaction. These same factors should be considered if you are ever in the position to design a new organization, for instance, if you would choose to become an entrepreneur.

Traditional Designs

With the extremes of mechanistic and organic models in mind, we now turn to describing some of the more common organizational designs found in use: the *simple structure*, the *bureaucracy*, and the *matrix structure*. We follow this with a discussion of some of the newer design options in use: the *team structure*, the *virtual organization*, and the *boundaryless organization*.

The Simple Structure

What do a small retail store, a start-up electronics firm run by a hard-driving entrepreneur, a new Planned Parenthood office, and an airline in the midst of a companywide pilot's strike have in common? They probably all utilize the **simple structure**.

simple structure
A structure characterized by a low degree of departmentalization, wide spans of control, authority centralized in a single person, and little formalization.

The simple structure is said to be characterized most by what it is not rather than what it is. The simple structure is not elaborated.[14] It has a low degree of departmentalization, wide spans of control, authority centralized in a single person, and little formalization. The simple structure is a "flat" organization; it usually has only two or three vertical levels, a loose body of employees, and one individual in whom the decision-making authority is centralized.

The simple structure is most widely practised in small businesses in which the manager and the owner are one and the same. This, for example, is illustrated in Exhibit 14-12, an organization chart for a retail men's store. Jack Gold owns and manages this store. Although Jack Gold employs five full-time salespeople, a cashier, and extra staff for weekends and holidays, he "runs the show." Langley, British-Columbia-based Sepp's Gourmet Foods Ltd. represents an example of a simple structure for head office. There is no secretary or reception area there, and CEO Tom Poole, CFO James Pratt, and John Wallace, director of corporate development, each take turns answering the phone.[15]

Exhibit 14-12
A Simple Structure (Jack Gold's Men's Store)

The strength of the simple structure lies in its simplicity. It's fast, flexible, inexpensive to maintain, and accountability is clear. One major weakness is that it's difficult to maintain in anything other than small organizations. It becomes increasingly inadequate as an organization grows because its low formalization and high centralization tend to create information overload at the top. As size increases, decision-making typically becomes slower and can eventually come to a standstill as the single executive tries to continue making all the decisions. This often proves to be the undoing of many small businesses. When an organization begins to employ 50 or 100 people, it's very difficult for the owner-manager to make all the choices. If the structure isn't changed and made more elaborate, the firm often loses momentum and can eventually fail. This chapter's CBC Video Case gives you the opportunity to see how a simple organizational structure may not be sufficient as a business starts to grow more rapidly. The simple structure's other weakness is that it's risky—everything depends on one person. One serious illness can literally destroy the organization's information and decision-making centre.

The simple structure isn't strictly limited to small organizations, it's just harder to make it work effectively in larger firms. One large company that seems to have succeeded with the simple structure is Nucor Corp., a $3.2-billion steel company that operates minimills in Indiana and Arkansas.[16] Its headquarters in Charlotte, North Carolina, employs just 24 people. And there are only three levels between the company's president and mill workers. This lean structure has helped Nucor to become one of the most profitable steelmakers in the United States.

The Bureaucracy

Standardization! That's the key concept that underlies all bureaucracies. Take a look at the bank where you keep your chequing account, the department store where you buy your clothes, or the government offices that collect your taxes, enforce health regulations, or provide local fire protection. They all rely on standardized work processes for coordination and control.

The **bureaucracy** is characterized by highly routine operating tasks achieved through specialization, very formalized rules and regulations, tasks

bureaucracy
A structure with highly routine operating tasks achieved through specialization, very formalized rules and regulations, tasks that are grouped into functional departments, centralized authority, narrow spans of control, and decision-making that follows the chain of command.

that are grouped into functional departments, centralized authority, narrow spans of control, and decision-making that follows the chain of command.

The primary strength of the bureaucracy lies in its ability to perform standardized activities in a highly efficient manner. Putting together similar specialties in functional departments results in economies of scale, minimum duplication of staff and equipment, and employees who have the opportunity to talk "the same language" with their peers. Furthermore, bureaucracies can get by nicely with less talented—and, hence, less costly—middle- and lower-level managers. The pervasiveness of rules and regulations substitutes for managerial discretion. Standardized operations, coupled with high formalization, allow decision-making to be centralized. There is little need, therefore, for innovative and experienced decision-makers below the level of senior executives.

One of the major weaknesses of a bureaucracy, however, is that it can create subunit conflict. For instance, the production department believes that it has the most important role in the organization because nothing happens until something is produced. Meanwhile, the research and development department may believe that designing something is far more essential than producing it. At the same time, the marketing department views its role as selling the product, and believes that is the most important task in the organization. Finally, the accounting department sees itself in the central role of tallying up the results. Thus each department focuses more on what it perceives as its own value and contribution to the organization, and fails to understand how the departments are really interdependent on each other, with each having to perform well for the company as a whole to survive. The conflict that can happen among functional units means that sometimes functional unit goals can override the overall goals of the organization.

In thinking about the possible conflicts that can arise in a bureaucracy, you might want to refer to Chapter 12, which discussed the relationship of dependency to power. That chapter pointed out that importance, scarcity, and non-substitutability will all affect the degree of power an individual or unit has. We also noted that the amount of power that an engineering department has, for instance, will vary, depending upon the specific organization and its overall goals.

The other major weakness of a bureaucracy is something we've all experienced at one time or another when dealing with people who work in these organizations: obsessive concern with following the rules. When cases arise that don't precisely fit the rules, there is no room for modification. The bureaucracy is efficient only as long as employees confront problems that they have previously encountered and for which programmed decision rules have already been established.

Bureaucracy's popularity peaked during in the 1950s and 1960s. At that time, for instance, just about every major corporation in the world—firms such as IBM, General Electric, Volkswagen, Matsushita, and Royal Dutch Shell—was organized as a bureaucracy. Although the bureaucracy is currently out of fashion—critics argue that it can't respond rapidly to change and hinders employee initiative[17]—most large organizations still take on basic bureaucratic characteristics, particularly specialization and high formalization. However, spans of control have generally been widened, authority has become more decentralized, and functional departments have been supplemented with an increased use of teams. Another trend is toward dividing bureaucracies into smaller, though fully functioning, mini-bureaucracies.[18] These smaller versions, with 150 to 250 people, each have their own mission and profit goals.

matrix structure
A structure that creates dual lines of authority; combines functional and product departmentalization.

It's been estimated that about 15 percent of large corporations have taken this direction.[19] For instance, Eastman Kodak has transformed over 100 production units into separate businesses. ABB Asea Brown Boveri, a $32-billion corporation with 210 000 employees, has broken itself into 1300 companies divided into almost 5000 profit centres that are located in 140 countries.

The Matrix Structure

Another popular organizational design option is the **matrix structure**. You'll find it being used in advertising agencies, aerospace firms, research and development laboratories, construction companies, hospitals, government agencies, universities, management consulting firms, and entertainment companies.[20] Essentially, the matrix combines two forms of departmentalization: functional and product.

The strength of functional departmentalization lies in putting together similar specialists, which minimizes the number necessary, while it allows the pooling and sharing of specialized resources across products. Its major disadvantage is the difficulty of coordinating the tasks of diverse functional specialists so that their activities are completed on time and within budget. Product departmentalization, on the other hand, has exactly the opposite benefits and disadvantages. It facilitates coordination among specialties to achieve on-time completion and meet budget targets. Furthermore, it provides clear responsibility for all activities related to a product, but with duplication of activities and costs. The matrix attempts to gain the strengths of each, while avoiding their weaknesses.

The most obvious structural characteristic of the matrix is that it breaks the unity-of-command concept. Employees in the matrix have two bosses—their functional department managers and their product managers. Therefore, the matrix has a dual chain of command.

Exhibit 14-13 shows the matrix form as used in a faculty of business administration. The academic departments of accounting, economics, marketing, and so forth are functional units. Additionally, specific programs (that is, products) are overlaid on the functions. In this way, members in a matrix

---

Exhibit 14-13
Matrix Structure for a Faculty of Business Administration

Programs / Academic departments	Undergraduate	Master's	Ph. D.	Research	Executive development	Community service
Accounting						
Administrative studies						
Finance						
Information and decision sciences						
Marketing						
Organizational behaviour						
Quantitative methods						

structure have a dual assignment—to their functional department, and to their product groups. For instance, a professor of accounting who is teaching an undergraduate course reports to the director of undergraduate programs as well as to the chairperson of the accounting department.

The strength of the matrix lies in its ability to facilitate coordination when the organization has a multiplicity of complex and interdependent activities. As an organization becomes larger, its information-processing capacity can become overloaded. In a bureaucracy, complexity results in increased formalization. The direct and frequent contact between different specialties in the matrix can result in improved communication and more flexibility. Information permeates the organization and more quickly reaches those people who need to take account of it. Furthermore, the matrix reduces "bureaupathologies." The dual lines of authority reduce tendencies of departmental members to become so busy protecting their little worlds that the organization's overall goals become secondary.

The matrix offers another fundamental advantage: it facilitates the efficient allocation of specialists. When individuals with highly specialized skills are lodged in one functional department or product group, their talents are monopolized and underutilized. The matrix achieves the advantages of economies of scale by providing the organization with both the best resources and an effective way of ensuring their efficient deployment.

The major disadvantages of the matrix lie in the confusion it creates, its propensity to foster power struggles, and the stress it places on individuals.[21] When you dispense with the unity-of-command concept, ambiguity is significantly increased and ambiguity often leads to conflict. For example, it's frequently unclear who reports to whom, and it is not unusual for product managers to fight over getting the best specialists assigned to their products. Confusion and ambiguity also create the seeds of power struggles. Bureaucracy reduces the potential for power grabs by defining the rules of the game. When those rules are "up for grabs," power struggles between functional and product managers result. For individuals who desire security and absence from ambiguity, this work climate can produce stress. Reporting to more than one boss introduces role conflict, and unclear expectations introduce role ambiguity. The comfort of bureaucracy's predictability is absent, replaced by insecurity and stress.

Toronto Hydro has tried to solve some of the problems of a matrix organization by adopting a "soft matrix" structure to help it go through an organizational change process. The soft matrix retains the functional structure of one-employee, one-boss while introducing flexibility through temporary, time-sensitive project or task teams with people drawn from a variety of functions. The teams do not have the authority to make sweeping cross-departmental decisions or changes, only to develop recommendations to present to higher management. For Toronto Hydro, the advantage is that the day-to-day delivery of product occurs with minimal disruption, while the project teams make recommendations for change.[22] This chapter's Case Incident allows you to examine additional considerations related to the matrix structure of an organization.

New Design Options

Since the early 1980s, senior managers in a number of organizations have been working to develop new structural options that can better help their

firms compete effectively. All of these options involve breaking down the boundaries of the organization in some fashion, either internally, externally, or a combination of the two. In this section, we'll describe four such structural designs: the *team structure*, which modifies internal boundaries; the *modular* and *virtual organizations*, which modify external organizational boundaries; and the *boundaryless organization*, which attempts to break down both internal and external boundaries.[23]

Breaking the Boundaries Internally

THE TEAM STRUCTURE As described in Chapter 8, teams have become an extremely popular means around which to organize work activities. Forty-two percent of 109 Canadian companies surveyed reported widespread team-based activity and an almost equal number indicated that teams operated among certain employee groupings or in specific areas.[24] When management uses teams as its central coordination device, you have a **team structure**. The primary characteristics of the team structure are that it breaks down departmental barriers and decentralizes decision-making to the level of the work team. Team structures also require employees to be generalists as well as specialists.[25]

In smaller companies, the team structure can define the entire organization. For instance, Toyota Canada's parts distribution centre in Toronto reorganized its workforce into work teams in 1995. Workers have a team-focused mission statement, and the staff is split into six work teams, each with its own leader. Among larger organizations such as Xerox Canada and GM Canada, the team structure often complements what is typically a bureaucratic structure. This allows the organization to achieve the efficiency of bureaucracy's standardization, while gaining the flexibility that teams provide. A team-structured organization does not have to be a small organization, however. As described in Chapter 8, Delta Lloyd Insurance based in the Netherlands transformed its 2300 employees into a team-based organization.

Teams generally consist of 3 to 20 persons who work together for a common purpose on either a short-term or permanent basis. Project teams usually work on a functional or cross-functional project with an explicit set of goals and objectives. For instance, when companies such as Boeing or Hewlett-Packard need to design new products or coordinate major projects, they'll structure activities around cross-functional teams. Projects can be short-term or longer-term in duration, and the team disbands once the project is completed. Quality-oriented, problem-solving, and process-improvement teams generally operate parallel to the organizational structure. To improve productivity at the operating level, for instance, companies such as Chrysler, Saturn, Motorola, and Xerox have made extensive use of self-managed teams.

Breaking the Boundaries Externally

THE MODULAR ORGANIZATION Why do it all when sometimes someone else can do it better? That question captures the essence of the **modular organization**, which is typically a small, core organization that outsources major business functions.[26]

Vancouver-based Palmer Jarvis Communications represents the modular structure at its best, able to flexibly meet the needs of clients. Traditional, large advertising agencies of the past were huge, vertically integrated, full-service corporations. Committed to full service, they would often refuse to

team structure
The use of teams as the central device to coordinate work activities.

modular organization
A small, core organization that outsources major business functions.

do a single brochure, an annual report, or a public relations program. Palmer Jarvis set out to deliver advertising differently, however, building a strong network of people and resources that successfully serves clients regionally, nationally, and internationally. The modular corporation concept allows Palmer Jarvis to use its various strengths independently or in concert. The agency's primary responsibility is seamlessly integrating all of the elements of advertising, design, strategic planning, public relations, promotions, direct marketing, media, or research. This structural form allows each project to be staffed with the talent most suited to its demands, rather than just choosing from among those people whom the studio employs. It minimizes bureaucratic overhead since fewer functions are done in-house. And it lessens long-term risks and their costs because often there is no "long term" —a team is assembled for a finite period and then disbanded. Finally, as in Palmer Jarvis' case, the modular corporation allows the company to respond to clients as individuals, devising solutions that are imaginative, appealing to both consumers and clients.[27]

Benetton
http://www.benetton.com/
index.cgi

Companies such as Nike, Reebok, Liz Claiborne, Emerson Radio, and Dell Computer are just a few of the thousands of companies that have found that they can do hundreds of millions of dollars in business without owning manufacturing facilities. Dell Computer, for instance, owns no plants and merely assembles computers from outsourced parts. Benetton, based in Italy, subcontracts almost 95 percent of its manufacturing, distribution, and sales activities, keeping only raw material purchases and cutting and dyeing in-house. These activities are retained in-house to provide a measure of central control.[28] Both Nike and Reebok succeed by concentrating on designing and marketing high-tech fashionable footwear. The two companies contract out almost all of their production to suppliers in Taiwan, South Korea, and other low-cost-labour countries.

What's going on here? A quest for maximum flexibility. These organizations have created networks of relationships that allow them to contract out manufacturing, distribution, marketing, or any other business function where management believes that others can do it better or more cheaply. The modular organization stands in sharp contrast to the typical bureaucracy that has many vertical levels of management and where control is sought through ownership. In such organizations, research and development are done in-house, production occurs in company-owned plants, and sales and marketing are performed by the company's own employees. To support all this, management must employ extra staff, including accountants, human resource specialists, and lawyers. The modular organization, however, outsources many of these functions and concentrates on what it does best. For many Canadian firms, that means focusing on design or marketing. Montreal-based Bauer Inc., designer and manufacturer of hockey and performance skates, announced plans to close its 400-person skate manufacturing plant in Cambridge, Ontario, at the end of 1998. Pierre Boivin, the company's CEO and president, says Bauer wants to outsource the manufacture of certain products to maintain competitiveness and flexibility, but will continue to work on design and marketing.[29] Making the decision to contract out, however, does not necessarily come without other costs particularly when the decision is made to manufacture overseas. Nike and several other companies have come under attack for relying on low-paid, exploited labourers, many of whom are children. These organizations are having to make decisions about the trade-offs between low-cost production strategies and criticisms from potential customers who are concerned about human rights.

Exhibit 14-14 shows a modular organization in which management outsources the marketing, sales and service functions of the business. Top management oversees directly the activities that are done in-house and coordinates relationships with the other organizations that perform the sales, marketing, and service functions for the modular organization. Managers in modular structures spend some of their time coordinating and controlling external relations, typically by way of computer network links.

There are several advantages to modular organizations. Organizations can devote their technical and managerial talent to their most critical activities. They can respond more quickly to environmental changes, and there is increased focus on customers and markets. The primary drawback to this structure is that it reduces management's control over key parts of its business. The organization is forced to rely on outsiders, which decreases operational control.

virtual organization
A continually evolving network of independent companies—suppliers, customers, even competitors—linked together to share skills, costs, and access to one another's markets.

THE VIRTUAL ORGANIZATION   The **virtual organization** "is a continually evolving network of independent companies—suppliers, customers, even competitors—linked together to share skills, costs, and access to one another's markets."[30] In a virtual organization, units of different firms join together in an alliance to pursue common strategic objectives. While control in the modular structure remains with the core organization (such as Nike, Dell Computer, and Bauer), in the virtual organization participants relinquish some of their control and act more interdependently. Virtual organizations may not have a central office, an organizational chart, or a hierarchy. Typically, the organizations come together to exploit specific opportunities or attain specific strategic objectives. In May 1997, Air Canada founded Star Alliance with UAL Corp.'s United Airlines, Lufthansa AG, Scandinavian Airlines Systems, and Thai Airways International Co. Varig Brazilian Airlines came on board later, bringing the alliance's combined revenues to about $63 billion. Airlines code-share so that travellers can buy a single ticket for a trip although it may involve boarding several different airlines' planes to reach a destination. En route, travellers will collect frequent-flyer points redeemable for flights on the home airline and even relax in the partners' lounges on a "seamless" journey. Airlines are also integrating their services and opera-

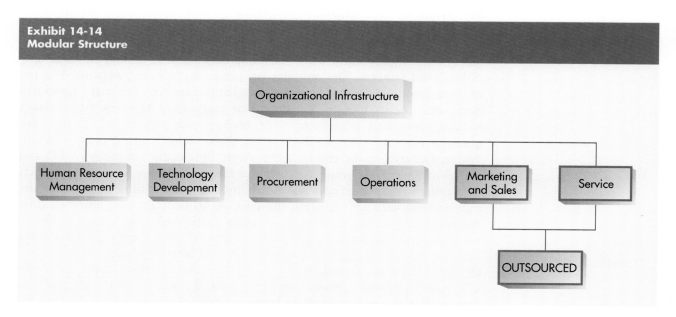

Exhibit 14-14
Modular Structure

Organizational Infrastructure

Human Resource Management | Technology Development | Procurement | Operations | Marketing and Sales | Service

OUTSOURCED

tions. The airlines say the alliances can increase consumer choice. For instance, Air Canada and United were able to launch a Montreal-Chicago route, which neither airline believed that it could launch alone, offering airline travellers an alternative to American Airlines.

Canadian firms are actively seeking domestic and foreign alliance partners and are taking part in various forms of interfirm cooperative agreements. About one in nine Canadian companies has some sort of arrangement of this type. These alliances take many forms, ranging from precompetitive consortia to coproduction, cross-equity arrangements, and equity joint ventures with separate legal entities.[31] Exhibit 14-15 illustrates a possible virtual structure where the reference firm is responsible for technology development, and then works together with the alliance partners to complete the other functions. Another example of a virtual structure is ING Direct, a Dutch-owned "virtual" bank. Canadian Tire joined forces with ING Direct in the spring of 1998, installing ATMs in five of its stores in London, Ontario.

There are several advantages to virtual organizations. They allow organizations to share costs and skills, provide access to global markets, and increase market responsiveness. However, there are also distinct disadvantages. The boundaries between companies become blurred due to interdependence. In order to work together, companies must relinquish operational and strategic control. This form of organization also requires new managerial skills. Managers must build relations with other companies, negotiate "win-win" deals, find compatible partners in terms of values and goals, and then develop appropriate communication systems to keep everyone informed.[32]

Breaking the Boundaries Externally and Internally

THE BOUNDARYLESS ORGANIZATION Both the modular organization and the virtual organization break down external boundaries of the organization without generally affecting the internal workings of each of the cooperating organizations. Some organizations, however, strive to break down *both* the internal and external boundaries. General Electric chairman Jack Welch

ING Direct
http://www.ingdirect.ca/

Canadian Tire Corp. Ltd.
www.canadiantire.com/

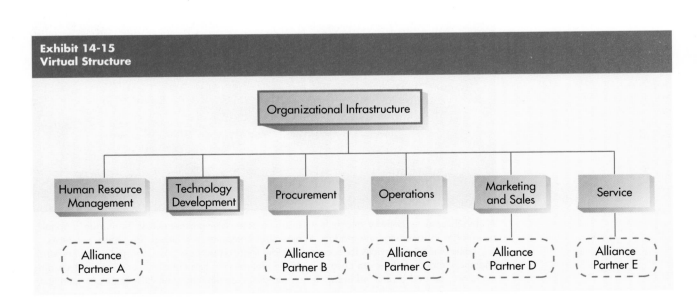

**Exhibit 14-15
Virtual Structure**

boundaryless organization
An organization that seeks to eliminate the chain of command, have limitless spans of control, and replace departments with empowered teams.

coined the term **boundaryless organization** to describe his idea of what he wanted GE to become. Welch wanted to turn his company into a "$60 billion family grocery store."[33] That is, in spite of its monstrous size, he wanted to eliminate *vertical* and *horizontal* boundaries within GE and break down *external* barriers between the company and its customers and suppliers. The boundaryless organization seeks to eliminate the chain of command, have limitless spans of control, and replace departments with empowered teams.

Although GE hasn't yet achieved this boundaryless state—and probably never will—it has made significant progress toward this end. So have other companies such as Hewlett-Packard, AT&T, and Motorola. Let's take a look at what a boundaryless organization would look like and what some firms are doing to make it a reality.[34]

By removing *vertical* boundaries, management flattens the hierarchy. Status and rank are minimized. And the organization looks more like a silo than a pyramid, where the grain at the top is no different than the grain at the bottom. Cross-hierarchical teams (which include top executives, middle managers, supervisors, and operative employees), participative decision-making practices, and the use of 360-degree performance appraisals (where peers and others above and below the employee evaluate his or her performance) are examples of how GE is breaking down vertical boundaries.

Functional departments create *horizontal* boundaries. The way to reduce these barriers is to replace functional departments with cross-functional teams and to organize activities around processes. For instance, Xerox now develops new products through multidisciplinary teams that work in a single process instead of around narrow functional tasks. Similarly, some AT&T units are now completing annual budgets based not on functions or departments, but on processes such as the maintenance of a worldwide telecommunications network. Another way that management can cut through horizontal barriers is to use lateral transfers and rotate people into and out of different functional areas. This turns specialists into generalists.

Texas Instruments
www.ti.com/

A global computer network allows Texas Instruments to communicate across intraorganizational boundaries in speeding new products to market. A company unit named Tiris, which produces tiny communications devices for security and identification purposes, is managed out of Bedford, England. Product designs are developed in the Netherlands and Germany, and the products are manufactured and assembled in Japan and Malaysia. Employees at all these locations send text, diagrams, and designs to each other using TI's networked computers. Shown here are assembly employees in Malaysia.

The boundaryless organization also breaks down barriers to external constituencies and barriers created by geography. Globalization, strategic alliances, supplier–organization and customer–organization linkages, and telecommuting are all examples of practices that reduce external boundaries. Many organizations are blurring the line between themselves and their suppliers. For instance, the CEO of Merix Corp., a 750-employee electronics firm, said, "We have people who work here that I thought were Merix employees. They have our badges, and I see them every day, but it turns out that they really work for our suppliers." Companies such as AT&T and Northwest Airlines are allowing customers to perform functions that previously were done by management. For instance, some AT&T units are receiving bonuses based on customer evaluations of the teams that serve them. Northwest gives its frequent flyers ten $50 award certificates each year and asks these customers to distribute these awards to Northwest employees when they see them do something good. This practice, in essence, allows Northwest's customers to participate in employee appraisals. Finally, telecommuting is blurring organizational boundaries. The security analyst with Merrill Lynch who performs his job from his ranch in Montana, or the software designer who works for a Vancouver company but does her job in Calgary are just two examples of the millions of workers who are now doing their jobs outside the physical boundaries of their employers' premises.

Chrysler's Neon Project is a recent example of how a boundaryless organization might work. While Lee Iacocca was seeking an automotive partner to help build the next generation subcompact, Robert P. Marcella, head of Chrysler's small car engineering team, convinced Iacocca that no partner was needed. Instead, the Neon team pulled together Chrysler workers from engineering, marketing, purchasing, finance, and production, as well as suppliers and consumers to work together on the project.[35]

The one common technological thread that makes the boundaryless organization possible is networked computers. They allow people to communicate across intraorganizational and interorganizational boundaries.[36] Electronic mail, for instance, enables hundreds of employees to share information simultaneously and allows rank-and-file workers to communicate directly with senior executives. And interorganizational networks now make it possible for Wal-Mart suppliers such as Procter & Gamble and Levi Strauss to monitor inventory levels of laundry soap and jeans, respectively, because both companies' computer systems are networked to Wal-Mart's system.

One of the drawbacks is that boundaryless organizations are difficult to manage. It is difficult to overcome the political and authority boundaries inherent in many organizations. It can also be time-consuming and difficult to manage the coordination necessary with so many different stakeholders. That said, the well-managed boundaryless organization offers the best talents of employees across several different organizations; enhances cooperation across functions, divisions, and external groups; and potentially offers much quicker response time to the environment.

Why Do Structures Differ?

With an understanding of the various structures possible, we are now prepared to address the question: What are the forces that influence the design that is chosen? Why are some organizations structured along more mechanistic lines while others follow organic characteristics? In the following

pages, we present the major forces that have been identified as causes or de-terminants of an organization's structure.[37]

Strategy

An organization's structure is a means to help management achieve its objec-tives. Since objectives are derived from the organization's overall strategy, it is only logical that strategy and structure should be closely linked. More specifically, structure should follow strategy. If management makes a signifi-cant change in its organization's strategy, the structure will need to be modi-fied to accommodate and support this change.[38]

Most current strategy frameworks focus on three strategy dimensions—innovation, cost minimization, and imitation—and the structural design that works best with each.[39]

To what degree does an organization introduce major new products or services? An **innovation strategy** does not mean a strategy merely for simple or cosmetic changes from previous offerings, but rather one for meaningful and unique innovations. Obviously, not all firms pursue innovation. This strategy may appropriately characterize 3M Co., but it certainly is not a strategy pursued by Reader's Digest.

An organization that is pursuing a **cost-minimization strategy** tightly con-trols costs, refrains from incurring unnecessary innovation or marketing ex-penses, and cuts prices in selling a basic product. This would describe the strategy pursued by Wal-Mart or the sellers of generic grocery products.

Organizations following an **imitation strategy** try to capitalize on the best of both of the previous strategies. They seek to minimize risk and maximize opportunity for profit. Their strategy is to move into new products or new markets only after viability has been proven by innovators. They take the successful ideas of innovators and copy them. Manufacturers of mass-marketed fashion goods that are "rip-offs" of designer styles follow the imi-tation strategy. This label also probably characterizes such well-known firms as IBM and Caterpillar. They essentially follow their smaller and more inno-vative competitors with superior products, but only after their competitors have demonstrated that the market is there.

Exhibit 14-16 describes the structural option that best matches each strategy. Innovators need the flexibility of the organic structure, while cost minimizers seek the efficiency and stability of the mechanistic structure. Imi-tators combine the two structures. They use a mechanistic structure in order

innovation strategy
A strategy that emphasizes the introduction of major new products and services.

cost-minimization strategy
A strategy that emphasizes tight cost controls, avoidance of unnecessary innovation or marketing expenses, and price cutting.

imitation strategy
A strategy that seeks to move into new products or new markets only after their viability has already been proven.

IBM Corporation
www.ibm.com/

Caterpillar
http://www.cat.com/

Exhibit 14-16
The Strategy-Structure Thesis

Strategy	Structural Option
Innovation	**Organic:** A loose structure; low specialization, low formalization, decentralized
Cost-minimization	**Mechanistic:** Tight control; extensive work specialization, high formalization, high centralization
Imitation	**Mechanistic and organic:** Mix of loose with tight properties; tight controls over current activities and looser controls for new undertakings

to maintain tight controls and low costs in their current activities, while at the same time they create organic subunits in which to pursue new undertakings.

Organization Size

A quick glance at the organizations we deal with regularly in our lives would lead most of us to conclude that size would have some bearing on an organization's structure. The more than 45 000 Canada Post postal workers, for example, do not neatly fit into one building, or into several departments supervised by a couple of managers. It's pretty hard to envision 45 000 people being organized in any manner other than one that contains a great deal of specialization and departmentalization; uses a large number of procedures and regulations to ensure uniform practices; and follows a high degree of decentralized decision-making. On the other hand, a local courier service that employs 10 people and generates less than $400 000 a year in service fees is unlikely to need decentralized decision-making or formalized procedures and regulations.

There is considerable evidence to support the idea that an organization's size significantly affects its structure.[40] For instance, large organizations—those typically employing 2000 or more people—tend to have more specialization, more departmentalization, more vertical levels, and more rules and regulations than do small organizations. However, the relationship isn't linear. Rather, size affects structure at a decreasing rate. The impact of size becomes less important as an organization expands. Why is this? Essentially, once an organization has around 2000 employees, it's already fairly mechanistic. An additional 500 employees will not have much impact. On the other hand, adding 500 employees to an organization that has only 300 members is likely to result in a shift toward a more mechanistic structure.

As an illustration of the effects of size, Greater Vancouver Area's Richmond Credit Union, which is small compared to the national banks, claims that its size enables it to be far more responsive to consumer needs than the big banks such as Bank of Montreal and the Canadian Imperial Bank of Commerce. Consumers have responded particularly well to Richmond Credit Union's "humungous bank" ads, which take a jab at the large banks. The chapter's Point/Counterpoint discussion gives further illustrations of the positives and negatives of large organizational size.

Technology

technology
The way in which an organization transfers its inputs into outputs.

The term **technology** refers to the way in which an organization transfers its inputs into outputs. Every organization has at least one technology for converting financial, human, and physical resources into products or services. The Ford Motor Co., for instance, predominantly uses an assembly-line process to make its products. On the other hand, universities may use a number of instruction technologies—the ever-popular formal lecture method, the case-analysis method, the experiential exercise method, the programmed learning method, and so forth. In this section we want to show that organizational structures adapt to their technology.

Numerous studies have been carried out on the technology–structure relationship.[41] The details of those studies are quite complex, so we'll go straight to "the bottom line" and attempt to summarize what we know.

The common theme that differentiates technologies is their *degree of routineness*. By this we mean that technologies tend toward either routine or

Richmond Credit Union, based in British Columbia, wants customers to know that smaller is better. They criticize the large "Humungous Bank" for being impersonal and inflexible.

Humungous Bank
www.humungous.com

nonroutine activities. The former are characterized by automated and standardized operations, such as an assembly line, where one might affix a car door to a car at set intervals. Nonroutine activities are customized. They include such varied operations as furniture restoring, custom shoemaking, and genetic research.

What relationships have been found between technology and structure? Although the relationship is not overwhelmingly strong, we find that routine tasks are associated with taller and more departmentalized structures. The relationship between technology and formalization, however, is stronger. Studies consistently show routineness to be associated with the presence of rule manuals, job descriptions, and other formalized documentation. Finally, an interesting relationship has been found between technology and centralization. It seems logical that routine technologies would be associated with a centralized structure, whereas nonroutine technologies, which rely more heavily on the knowledge of specialists, would be characterized by delegated decision authority. This position has met with some support. However, a more generalizable conclusion is that the technology–centralization relationship is moderated by the degree of formalization. Both formal regulations and centralized decision-making are control mechanisms, and management can substitute one for the other. Routine technologies should be associated with centralized control if there is a minimum of rules and regulations. However, if formalization is high, routine technology can be accompanied by decentralization. So, we would predict that routine technology would lead to centralization, but only if formalization is low.

Environment

environment
Those institutions or forces outside the organization that potentially affect the organization's performance.

An organization's **environment** is composed of those institutions or forces outside the organization that potentially affect the organization's performance. These typically include suppliers, customers, competitors, government regulatory agencies, public pressure groups, and the like.

Why should an organization's structure be affected by its environment? The answer is environmental uncertainty. Some organizations face relatively static environments—few forces in their environment are changing. There are, for example, no new competitors, no new technological breakthroughs by current competitors, or little activity by public pressure groups to influence the organization. Other organizations face very dynamic environments—rapidly changing government regulations affecting their business, new competitors, difficulties in acquiring raw materials, continually changing product preferences by customers, and so on. Static environments create significantly less uncertainty for managers than do dynamic ones. And since uncertainty is a threat to an organization's effectiveness, management will try to minimize it. One way to reduce environmental uncertainty is through adjustments in the organization's structure.[42]

Recent research has helped clarify what is meant by environmental uncertainty. It's been found that there are three key dimensions to any organization's environment: capacity, volatility, and complexity.[43]

The *capacity* of an environment refers to the degree to which it can support growth. Rich and growing environments generate excess resources, which can buffer the organization in times of relative scarcity. Abundant capacity, for example, leaves room for an organization to make mistakes, while scarce capacity does not. In 1997, firms operating in the multimedia software business had relatively abundant environments, whereas those in the full-service brokerage business faced relative scarcity.

The degree of instability in an environment is captured in the *volatility* dimension. Where there is a high degree of unpredictable change, the environment is dynamic. This makes it difficult for management to predict accurately the probabilities associated with various decision alternatives. At the other extreme is a stable environment. The recent turmoil in Asian financial markets caught many by surprise and has created a lot of instability in 1998, particularly in resource industries. It is expected that Canada's resource exports will suffer as demand shrinks in Asia. This has led to widespread layoffs in the B.C. lumber industry, and Japan's steel producers are now demanding a cut in the price they pay for Canadian coal. The instability is not limited to the resource sector, however. Small manufacturers have also been hit. In summer 1996, Viceroy Homes Ltd. of Toronto opened a plant in Vancouver to produce prefabricated houses for the Asian market. Initially, Japan accounted for as much as 62 percent of Viceroy's sales until the yen fell, the market collapsed, and profits fell 30 percent in the first six months of 1997.[44]

More turmoil for various industries is likely to appear. Until the Asian crisis, economists were predicting that Canada's gross domestic product would increase by about 3.2 percent in 1998, creating 275 000 new jobs. After the crisis, analysts were scrambling to adjust those figures downward. If Japan enters into a full-blown recession, it could slice a full percentage point from Canada's GDP and push the unemployment rate back over 10 percent.[45] The experience of the recent Asian crisis is a valuable reminder to all organizations that they are operating in a global environment.

Finally, the environment needs to be assessed in terms of *complexity*; that is, the degree of heterogeneity and concentration among environmental elements. Simple environments are homogeneous and concentrated. This might describe the tobacco industry, since there are relatively few players. It's easy for firms in this industry to keep a close eye on the competition. In contrast, environments characterized by heterogeneity and dispersion are called complex. This sums up the current environment for firms competing in the Internet connection business. Every day, there seems to be another

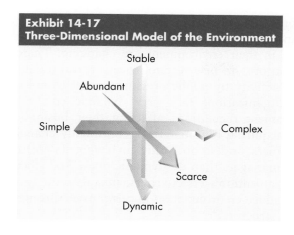

Exhibit 14-17
Three-Dimensional Model of the Environment

"new kid on the block" with whom current Internet service providers must deal.

Exhibit 14-17 summarizes our definition of the environment along its three dimensions. The arrows in this figure are meant to indicate movement toward higher uncertainty. Organizations that operate in environments characterized as scarce, dynamic, and complex face the greatest degree of uncertainty. Why? They have little room for error, high unpredictability, and a diverse set of elements in the environment to monitor constantly.

Given this three-dimensional definition of environment, we can offer some general conclusions. There is evidence that relates the degrees of environmental uncertainty to different structural arrangements. Specifically, the more scarce, dynamic, and complex the environment, the more organic a structure should be. The more abundant, stable, and simple the environment, the more the mechanistic structure will be preferred.

Structural Changes Over Time

We've shown that four variables—strategy, size, technology, and environment—are the primary forces that determine whether an organization is mechanistic or organic. Now let's use our previous analysis to explain the evolution of structural designs throughout this century.

The Industrial Revolution encouraged economies of scale and the rise of the modern, large corporation. As companies grew from their original simple structures, they took on mechanistic characteristics and became bureaucracies. The rise of bureaucracy to become the dominant structure in industrialized nations from the 1920s through the 1970s can be largely explained by three facts. First, the environment was relatively stable and certain over this period. The monopoly power of the large corporations, coupled with little international competition, kept environmental uncertainty to a minimum. Second, economies of scale and minimal competition allowed these corporations to introduce highly routine technologies. And third, most of these large corporations chose to pursue cost minimization or imitation strategies—leaving innovation to the smaller operators. Combine these strategies with large size, routine technologies, and relatively abundant, stable, and simple environments, and you have a reasonably clear explanation for the rise and domination of the bureaucracy.

Things began to change in the late 1970s, when the environment became significantly more uncertain. Interest rates soared in 1979 and then again in 1981. Advances in computer technology—especially the availability of increasingly powerful systems at dramatically falling prices—began to lessen the advantage that accrued to large size. And, of course, competition moved to the global arena. To compete effectively, top management responded by restructuring their organizations. Some went to the matrix to give their companies increased flexibility. Some added team structures so they could respond more rapidly to change. Today, senior managers in most large corporations are "debureaucratizing" their organizations—making them more organic by reducing staff, cutting vertical levels, decentralizing authority, and the like—primarily because the environment continues to be uncertain. Despite the profound impact restructuring has on employees (discussed in detail below in this chapter's HR Implications feature), managers realize that in a dynamic and changing environment, inflexible organizations end up as bankruptcy statistics.

HR IMPLICATIONS

The Effects of Restructuring on Employees

In this chapter we noted that organizational structures are changing as companies face globalization and other pressures as they approach the 21st century. More organizations are opting for flatter structures, which has led to widespread corporate restructuring. For instance, in December 1996, Canadian Broadcasting Corp. eliminated close to 1000 jobs from its payroll in its own attempt at restructuring. Restructuring often goes by various names, including downsizing, rightsizing, and delayering, but all of these terms are really euphemisms for layoffs.

Restructuring happens in a variety of ways. Sometimes whole divisions or business units are combined, or disaggregated, or even spun off. Sometimes business functions, such as engineering, operations, and distribution, might be joined together. Or some of these functions might be contracted out. Delayering is another restructuring technique, which means that the organization reduces the number of layers, or hierarchical levels. Finally, restructuring can also involve downsizing, or layoffs.

Generally the intent behind layoffs is not some planned approach to a new organizational structure, but rather it serves as an attempt to increase shareholder well-being.[1] Consider, for instance, the case of AT&T Corp. In December 1995, AT&T announced that it would cut 40 000 employees from its rolls. Several months later, chairman Robert Allen said the job cuts would be closer to 10 000. However, the impact of announcing that 40 000 jobs would be lost was that AT&T's stock price jumped $9.[2]

AT&T is not unique in the relationship of layoffs to increased earnings. The statistics for 1995 show that General Motors of Canada reported a record profit for any Canadian company in 1995 ($1.39 billion) and fired 2500 of its workers. Canada's largest banks—Royal Bank, Toronto-Dominion, Bank of Montreal, Nova Scotia, and CIBC—announced record collective profits in 1995 ($4.9 billion) and laid off 2800 people. Bell Canada enjoyed a healthy profit in 1995 and dismissed 3200 of its employees. Similar stories happened at Inco, Imperial Oil, Petro-Canada, Maritime Telephone and Telegraph, CP Rail, and Shell Canada, among others.

Industry Minister John Manley worries about the impact of these cuts for society: "I think it's part of my job to push the corporate sector and urge them to take into account the enormous damage it does when you cast people aside instead of retraining them."[3] Canadian citizens are also concerned about the impact of layoffs and the responsibilities of corporations. When the *Maclean's*/CBC News 1996 year-end poll asked respondents about the acceptability of profitable corporations laying off workers, 58 percent did not find this acceptable.[4] Negative reactions to downsizing are even higher in the regions experiencing the most difficult economic times, with Quebec (64 percent) and the Atlantic provinces (66 percent) giving the most unfavourable views. In Alberta, where the economy has been booming, fewer people were reluctant to criticize companies for layoffs (49 percent).

Len Brooks, executive director of the Clarkson Centre for Business Ethics at the University of Toronto, says laying off employees to maximize profit and improve cash flow "is really a dumb idea. Only a third of its practitioners achieve their financial objectives while paying a huge price as employee morale craters."[5]

Brooks' views are supported by a study conducted by the American Management Association (AMA) in 1995. The AMA surveyed 700 companies that had downsized between 1989 and 1994 and found that these actions do not necessarily pay off over the long term, even if there are short-term gains.[6] For instance, productivity fell in 30 percent of the cases, while rising in 34 percent of the cases. Profits fell 30 percent of the time, and rose 51 percent of the time. Employee morale fell in 83 percent of the companies, so the biggest gain in downsizing is an increase in employee ill will, which may not be good for the company overall.

Lloyd Cooper, in charge of career management at Watson Wyatt Worldwide, explains some of the reasons for low morale after downsizing. He notes that many companies have been cutting jobs to cut payroll costs. "But they haven't been downsizing the workload. They just went on with more, faster, quicker but without thinking: 'What are we actually doing?'"[7]

If there is any consolation to the downsizing/shareholder dilemma, it may be that

the emphasis on shareholder value is less in Canada than in the United States. A survey in 1994 found that 69 percent of executives in the United States consider shareholder value a "critical" issue.[8] In Canada, the figure was 43 percent, while in Europe it was only 25 percent.

There are several options that the human resources department can recommend to senior executives as alternatives to downsizing.[9] A number of Canadian corporations have developed options such as job sharing, voluntarily reduced work time, and phased-in retirement as ways to avoid downsizing. These companies have chosen this option as a way of preserving employee morale.

For instance, Bell Canada, began a three-year program to cut about 10 000 of its 45 900 employees in 1995. Among other things, it has set up five counselling centres to provide workshops and financial and retirement counselling to its employees. As a result, 12 000 employees have applied for buyouts and 4000 others are on reserve.[10] These options make it easier for employees to deal with layoffs, although employee morale at Bell Canada remains a problem. A *Financial Post* article noted that "Employee morale, the *sine qua non* of a service business, has fallen so low that one articulate union member made a failed public bid to get elected to the board of directors of BCE Inc. at its May 7 (1996) annual meeting."[11]

The reports of declines of employee morale after downsizing are an indication that companies need to consider the tradeoffs of short-term profits and long-term employee productivity issues more closely.

Sources:

[1] Robert W. Keidel, "Rethinking Organizational Design," *Academy of Management Executive*, 8, 1994, pp. 12–30.

[2] "Haves & Have-nots: Canadians Look for Corporate Conscience," *Maclean's*, December 30, 1996/January 6, 1997, pp. 26, 37.

[3] "Haves & Have-nots": Canadians Look for Corporate Conscience," *Maclean's*, December 30, 1996/January 6, 1997, pp. 26, 37.

[4] "Haves & Have-nots": Canadians Look for Corporate Conscience," *Maclean's*, December 30, 1996/January 6, 1997, pp. 26, 37.

[5] "Haves & Have-nots": Canadians Look for Corporate Conscience," *Maclean's*, December 30, 1996/January 6, 1997, pp. 26, 37.

[6] "Shareholders versus Job Holders. Do Corporations Have an Obligation to Provide Work? Or, Are They Solely Economic Units That Have No Social Function?" *Canada and the World Backgrounder*, October, 1996, pp. 11–13.

[7] "Mistake to Downsize Just for Profit, Experts Say," *Canadian Press Newswire*, May 9, 1996.

[8] "Shareholders Versus Job Holders": Do Corporations Have an Obligation to Provide Work? Or, Are They Solely Economic Units That Have No Social Function?" *Canada and the World Backgrounder*, October, 1996, pp. 11–13.

[9] "Work Option Plans Can Soften Blows of Layoffs," *Financial Post*, May 4/6, 1996, p. 37.

[10] "Mistake to Downsize Just for Profit, Experts Say." *Canadian Press Newswire*, May 9, 1996.

[11] "Bell's New Attitude: Long-Distance Competition Showed the Giant Phone Company that It's Wise to be Lean and Customer Friendly," *Financial Post*, May 25/27, 1996, p. 14.

Summary and Implications

For the Workplace

The theme of this chapter has been that an organization's internal structure contributes to explaining and predicting behaviour. That is, in addition to individual and group factors, the structural relationships in which people work have an important bearing on employee attitudes and behaviour.

What's the basis for the argument that structure has an impact on both attitudes and behaviour? To the degree that an organization's structure reduces ambiguity for employees and clarifies such concerns as: "What am I supposed to do?" "How am I supposed to do it?" "To whom do I report?" and "To whom do I go if I have a problem?" That structure shapes their attitudes and facilitates and motivates them to higher levels of performance.

Of course, structure also constrains employees to the extent that it limits and controls what they do. For example, organizations structured around high levels of formalization and specialization, strict adherence to the chain of command, limited delegation of authority, and narrow spans of control give employees little autonomy. Controls in such organizations are tight, and behaviour will tend to vary within a narrow range. In contrast, organiza-

tions that are structured around limited specialization, low formalization, wide spans of control, and the like provide employees with greater freedom and, thus, will be characterized by greater behavioural diversity.

Exhibit 14-18 visually summarizes what we've discussed in this chapter. Strategy, size, technology, and environment determine the type of structure an organization will have. For simplicity's sake, we can classify structural designs around one of two models: mechanistic or organic. The specific effect of structural designs on performance and satisfaction is moderated by employees' individual preferences and cultural norms.

One last point: managers need to be reminded that structural variables such as work specialization, span of control, formalization, and centralization are objective characteristics that can be measured by organizational researchers. The findings and conclusions we've offered in this chapter, in fact, are directly a result of the work of these researchers. But employees don't objectively measure these structural characteristics! They observe things around them in an unscientific fashion and then form their own implicit models of what the organization's structure is like. How many people did they have to interview with before they were offered their jobs? How many people work in their departments and buildings? Does an organization policy manual exist? If so, is it readily available and do employees follow it closely? How are the organization and its top management described in newspapers and periodicals? Answers to questions such as these, when combined with an employee's past experiences and comments made by peers, lead members to form an overall subjective image of what their organization's structure is like. This image, though, may in no way resemble the organization's actual objective structural characteristics.

The importance of these implicit models of organizational structure should not be overlooked. As we noted in Chapter 3, people respond to their perceptions rather than objective reality. The research, for instance, on the relationship between many structural variables and subsequent levels of performance or job satisfaction is far from consistent. We explained some of this as being attributable to individual differences. However, an additional contributing cause to these inconsistent findings might be diverse perceptions of the objective characteristics. Researchers typically focus on actual levels of the various structural components, but these may be irrelevant if people interpret similar components differently. The bottom line, therefore, is to understand how employees interpret their organization's structure. That should prove a more meaningful predictor of their behaviour than the objective characteristics themselves.

Exhibit 14-18
Organization Structure: Its Determinants and Outcomes

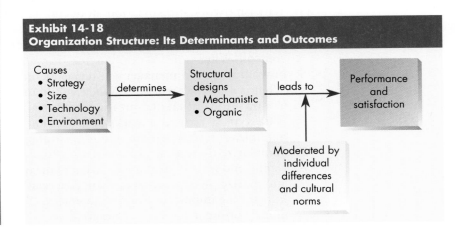

For You as an Individual

Our discussion of structure was meant to get you to think about two things. The first is to consider the type of organization in which you might like to work, trying to determine for yourself whether you're a person who prefers a more formalized mechanistic structure or a highly organic organizational structure. Each of us differs in our reactions to these two types, and of course some organizations fall in between these extremes. Part of choosing a job that is a good fit for you is to understand how the structure of the organization will affect you.

Another thing that you might be considering is becoming an entrepreneur. If you start your own company, you will need to determine, among other things, how much responsibility you want to take for yourself compared with how much you are willing to share with other managers or employees. We saw in the case of Lee McDonald of Southmedic that she preferred to share more of the responsibility of running the organization with her managers. This suited both her travel schedule and her personal needs. A knowledge of the different organizational considerations can help you create an organization that meets your needs as both a business person and a person with additional interests.

ROADMAP REMINDER

In arriving at this chapter, we moved away from some of the internal dynamics of the organization, such as power and politics, to consider how employees and managers are grouped into units that relate to the various tasks, responsibilities, and goals of the organization. We noted that some designs may have more conflict embedded in them than others. This would happen, for example, if each functional unit viewed itself as "the most important" in the organization. As mentioned previously, structure relates to organizing the major units of the organization. It is also necessary to organize the major tasks that need to be done within the organization. Therefore, in the next chapter we will consider job design, which informs us about how to group the various tasks of a job into different configurations.

For Review

1. Why isn't work specialization an unending source of increased productivity?
2. All things being equal, which is more efficient, a wide or narrow span of control? Why?
3. In what ways can management departmentalize?
4. What is a matrix structure? When would management use it?
5. Contrast the virtual organization with the boundaryless organization.
6. What type of structure works best with an innovation strategy? A cost-minimization strategy? An imitation strategy?
7. Summarize the size–structure relationship.
8. Define and give an example of what is meant by the term *technology*.
9. Summarize the environment–structure relationship.
10. Explain the importance of the statement: "Employees form implicit models of organizational structure."

For Discussion

1. How is the typical large corporation of today organized in contrast to how that same organization was probably organized in the 1960s?
2. Do you think most employees prefer high formalization? Support your position.
3. If you were an employee in a matrix structure, what pluses do you think the structure would provide? What about minuses?
4. What could management do to make a bureaucracy more like a boundaryless organization?
5. What behavioural predictions would you make about people who worked in a "pure" boundaryless organization (if such a structure were ever to exist)?

LEARNING ABOUT YOURSELF EXERCISE

Bureaucratic Orientation Test

Instructions: For each statement, check the response (either mostly agree or mostly disagree) that best represents your feelings.

	Mostly Agree	Mostly Disagree
1. I value stability in my job.	_____	_____
2. I like a predictable organization.	_____	_____
3. The best job for me would be one in which the future is uncertain.	_____	_____
4. The federal government would be a nice place to work.	_____	_____
5. Rules, policies, and procedures tend to frustrate me.	_____	_____
6. I would enjoy working for a company that employed 85 000 people worldwide.	_____	_____
7. Being self-employed would involve more risk than I'm willing to take.	_____	_____
8. Before accepting a job, I would like to see an exact job description.	_____	_____
9. I would prefer a job as a freelance house painter to one as a clerk for the Department of Motor Vehicles.	_____	_____
10. Seniority should be as important as performance in determining pay increases and promotion.	_____	_____
11. It would give me a feeling of pride to work for the largest and most successful company in its field.	_____	_____
12. Given a choice, I would prefer to make $70 000 per year as a vice-president in a small company to $85 000 as a staff specialist in a large company.	_____	_____
13. I would regard wearing an employee badge with a number on it as a degrading experience.	_____	_____
14. Parking spaces in a company lot should be assigned on the basis of job level.	_____	_____

15. If an accountant works for a large organization, he or she cannot be a true professional. _____ _____

16. Before accepting a job (given a choice), I would want to make sure that the company had a very fine program of employee benefits. _____ _____

17. A company will probably not be successful unless it establishes a clear set of rules and procedures. _____ _____

18. Regular working hours and vacations are more important to me than finding thrills on the job. _____ _____

19. You should respect people according to their rank. _____ _____

20. Rules are meant to be broken. _____ _____

Turn to page 700 for scoring directions and key.

Source: Adapted from A.J. DuBrin, *Human Relations: A Job Oriented Approach,* 5th edition, © 1992. Reprinted with permission of Prentice Hall, Inc., Upper Saddle River, NJ.

WORKING WITH OTHERS EXERCISE

Authority Figures

Purpose: To learn about one's experiences with and feelings about authority.

Time: Approximately 75 minutes. (Note: The time for this exercise can be reduced in several ways. The first is to allocate only 20 minutes for discussion to groups. The second is to divide the groups in half, so that some perform Step 2, while others perform Step 3. Then the groups can share their discussions during the debriefing.)

Procedure:

1. Your instructor will separate class members into groups based on their birth order. Groups are formed consisting of "only children," "eldest," "middle," and "youngest," according to placement in families. Larger groups will be broken into smaller ones, with four or five members, to allow for freer conversation.

2. Each group member should talk about how he or she "typically reacts to the authority of others." Focus should be on specific situations that offer general information about how individuals deal with authority figures (for example, bosses, teachers, parents, or coaches). The group has 25 minutes to develop a written list of how the group generally deals with others' authority. Be sure to separate tendencies that group members share and those they do not.

3. Repeat Step 2, except this time discuss how group members "typically function as authority figures." Again make a list of shared characteristics.

4. Each group will share its general conclusions with the entire class.

5. Class discussion will focus on questions such as:
   a. What patterned differences have surfaced between the groups?
   b. What may account for these differences?
   c. What hypotheses might explain the connection between how individuals react to the authority of others and how they are as authority figures?

Source: This exercise is adapted from W.A. Kahn, "An Exercise of Authority," *Organizational Behavior Teaching Review,* vol. XIV, Issue 2, 1989–90, pp. 28–42. Reprinted with permission.

ETHICAL DILEMMA EXERCISE

Employee Monitoring: How Far Is Too Far?

When does management's effort to control the actions of others become an invasion of privacy? Consider three cases.[1]

At call centres in New Brunswick, managers monitor almost all aspects of their employees' work, from taping calls and analysing them with the employee, to calculating the length of calls and determining why some employees are on the phone longer than others.

In December 1996, a physicist working for Canada's Department of National Defence was arrested and charged with possessing and distributing child pornography. The evidence was contained in his office computer, with files downloaded from the World Wide Web.

The law firm of Fasken Campbell Godfrey in Toronto periodically monitors employee e-mails. Employees are notified that this may happen occasionally.

Are any of these cases—monitoring calls, computer activities, or e-mail—an invasion of privacy? When does management overstep the bounds of decency and privacy by silently (even covertly) scrutinizing the behaviour of its employees or associates?

Managers defend these practices in terms of ensuring quality, productivity, and proper employee behaviour. For instance, silent surveillance of telephone calls can be used to help employees perform their jobs better. Surveillance can also prevent employees from taking unauthorized looks at the tax returns of friends, neighbours, or celebrities, or examining their health or financial records.

In banking, insurance, telecommunications, and travel, as many as 80 percent of employees may be subject to some level of monitoring.[2] While it is an offence under the Criminal Code in Canada to intercept private communications, the law is less clear about how privacy may be applied in the workplace. Unionized employees may have a bit more security. The Canada Labour Code requires employers operating under a collective agreement to disclose information about plans for technological change. This might provide unions an opportunity to bargain over electronic surveillance.

When does management's need for information about employee performance cross over the line and interfere with a worker's right to privacy? For example, must employees be notified in advance that they will be monitored? Does management's right to protect its interests extend to electronic monitoring of every place a worker might be—washrooms and locker rooms?

Sources:

[1] J. Markoff, "The Snooping Mayor," *New York Times*, May 4, 1990, p. B1; G. Bylinsky, "How Companies Spy on Employees," *Fortune*, November 4, 1991, pp. 131–40; D. Warner, "The Move to Curb Worker Monitoring," *Nations's Business*, December 1993, pp. 37–38; and M. Picard, "Working Under an Electronic Thumb," *Training*, February 1994, pp. 47–51.

[2] A. Gahtan, "Title: Big Brother or Good Business?", *WebWorld*, March 1997, p. 24.

CASE INCIDENT

The ABB Way

If you ask Benny Karl-Erik Olsson today where he is from, he'll tell you Mexico. But nine months ago he was Venezuelan. Before that he was from Madrid, and before that, the 44-year-old executive was from Barcelona. In fact, Olsson is of Swedish descent but was born in South Africa.

Olsson's multiple ancestry is merely the result of having spent 20 years with Zurich-based ABB Asea Brown Boveri AG. Currently he's ABB's country manager in Mexico, one of 500 corporate missionaries that the worldwide builder of power plants, industrial factories, and infrastructure projects believes are essential to its survival against the likes of Siemens, General Electric, and Alcatel-Alsthom. These people—always multilingual—relocate from operation to operation, moving among the company's 5000 profit centres in 140 countries. Their job is to cut costs, improve efficiency, and get local businesses in line with the ABB world view.

Few organizations have been as successful as ABB in creating a class of managers that gets global strategies to work with local operations. "Our strength comes from pulling together," says Percy Barnevik, the company's chairman and the person who masterminded the 1988 merger of a Swedish and Swiss firm that created ABB. He says, "If you can make this work real well, then you get a competitive edge out of the organization which is very, very difficult to copy."

Barnevik is trying to create a company with no geographic base—one that has many "home" markets and that can draw on expertise from around the globe. To glue the company together, he has created a set of managers like Olsson who can adapt to local cultures while executing ABB's global strategies.

Olsson's experience in Mexico illustrates some of the difficulties in trying to execute this unusual structural arrangement. ABB requires local business units, such as Mexico's motor factory, to report to Olsson and to a business area manager who sets motor strategy for ABB worldwide. The goals of the local factory can clash with worldwide priorities. It is up to managers like Olsson to sort out constant conflicts.

Olsson says his predecessor in Mexico too often made decisions that favoured Mexican operations at the expense of ABB's worldwide businesses. For example, he had solicited bids from more than one ABB factory making equipment for power generators. That violated ABB's "allocation" rules, which dictate which ABB factories can supply other operations with components. Olsson's goal is to better balance the needs of the Mexican operations with the needs of the overall corporation.

Questions

1. How would you classify the ABB structure? Defend your choice.

2. What are the advantages to this structure?

3. What are its disadvantages?

4. What kind of skills, abilities, and characteristics do you think are required to successfully do the type of job Olsson has?

Source: This case is based on J. Guyon, "ABB Fuses Units with One Set of Values," *The Wall Street Journal*, October 2, 1996, p. A12.

Growing Big Can Be Hard To Do

DCB Productions, headed by Deb Belinsky and Cheryl Benson have hit it big with their business of sport entertainment. The "two girls from Winnipeg" produce shows and entertainment for audiences of the Calgary Flames as well as for a number of U.S. organizations, including the Disney Sports organization, the Mighty Ducks hockey team, and the L.A. Clippers.

The two women started their business almost on a shoe-string. After producing one game for the Winnipeg Jets, they borrowed $6000 from their parents and approached the Disney Corporation about doing the entertainment for the Mighty Ducks. How could these women market a successful proposal to Disney, home of entertainment in the U.S.? The Disney entertainers didn't know hockey, and their Mighty Duck productions weren't working with the fans. They were happy to hire someone who knew how to reach hockey fans.

The business has grown fairly rapidly, but Cheryl is based in Anaheim, California, while Deb is based in Calgary, so getting together for business meetings is full of complications. They are starting to feel some of the pains of expanding rapidly, a situation many entrepreneurs face as their businesses grow. Whereas at one time they used to be able to put out their business fires, now they're having more difficulty doing so. Moreover, their clients only want either Deb or Cheryl to run the show, but the two women know they can't be everywhere all the time. They've already acknowledged that they need to hire a business manager to manage the organizational affairs. So the challenge these two women from Winnipeg face is: how do they get away from the daily grind of the business so that they can grow as fast as the sports entertainment business is growing?

Questions

1. Describe the organizational structure of DCB Productions.

2. In what ways might this structure have helped the organization grow successfully in a short period of time?

3. In what ways does the organizational structure need to be changed to meet the growing demands placed on Deb and Cheryl by their clients?

Source: Based on "Duck Ladies," *Venture* 593; aired June 2,1996.

POINT

Small Is Beautiful

The Davids are beating up on the Goliaths. Big corporations are going the way of the dinosaurs because they're overly rigid, technologically obsolete, and too bureaucratic. They're being replaced by small, agile companies. These small organizations are the technology innovators, able to respond quickly to changing market opportunities, and have become the primary job generators in almost all developed countries.

In almost every major industry, the smaller and more agile firms are outperforming their larger competitors. Among steel producers, Regina-based IPSCO is outperforming Ontario-based Dofasco and Stelco. CanWest's Global Television Network has taken on CBC and CTV with impressive results, winning a large pile of awards at the 1998 Geminis, and sharing top honours with the CBC in several instances. Greater Vancouver Area's VanCity Credit Union and Richmond Credit Union have been far more responsive to consumers than big banks such as the Bank of Montreal and Canadian Imperial Bank of Commerce. Consumers have particularly responded well to Richmond Credit Union's "humungous bank" ads, which take a jab at the large banks. Winnipeg-based McNally Robinson Booksellers Ltd. made plans to open the first Canadian mega-bookstore while Canada's two largest booksellers, SmithBooks and Coles Book Stores, were too busy negotiating the merger that eventually led to the creation of their own superstore, Chapters. In a cross-Canada bookstore study conducted in March 1997, the Winnipeg superstore outshone Chapters in terms of customer service and product selection, illustrating that a small, independent retailer can beat a bigger player at its own game.

What's going on? The law of economies of scale is being repealed! The law of economies of scale argued that larger operations drove out smaller ones because with large size came greater efficiency. Fixed costs, for instance, could be spread over more units. Large companies could use standardization and mass production to produce the lowest-cost products. But that no longer applies because of market fragmentation, strategic alliances, and technology.

Niche markets have removed the advantages of large size. Southwest can compete successfully against American and United because it doesn't try to match the larger airlines' full-service strategy. It doesn't use hubs, it doesn't transfer baggage, it doesn't compete in every market, it doesn't offer meals, and it provides no reserved seats.

Strategic alliances offer small firms the opportunity to share others' expertise and development costs, allowing little companies to compete with big ones. For example, many small North American book publishers don't have the money to develop marketing operations and sales staffs in Australia or Asia. By joining forces with publishers in those countries to market their books, they can behave like the "big guys."

Technology is also taking away a lot of the advantage that used to go to size. Computer and satellite linkage and flexible manufacturing systems are examples of such technology. Quick & Reilly can execute orders as efficiently as Merrill Lynch through computer links to exchanges, even though it's a fraction of Merrill's size.

In today's increasingly dynamic environment, large size has become a serious handicap. It restricts the creativity to develop new products and services. It also limits job growth. More specifically, it's the small organizations that innovate and create jobs. For instance, Statistics Canada reports that between 1979 and 1995, small business (i.e., those under 50 employees) created 755 000 new jobs; medium companies (those between 50 and 499 employees) created 515 000 new jobs; and large companies (those with more than 500 employees) created 227 000 jobs.

Big companies are getting the message. They're laying off tens of thousands of employees. They're selling businesses that don't fit with their core competencies. And they're restructuring themselves to be more agile and responsive. ■

Sources: This argument is based on J. Case, "The Disciples of David Birch," *INC.*, January 1989, pp. 39–45; T. Peters, "Rethinking Scale," *California Management Review*, Fall 1992, pp. 7–28; G. Gendron, "Small Is Beautiful! Big Is Best!" *INC.*, May 1995, pp. 39–49; G.G. Dess, M.A.R. Abdul, K.J. McLaughlin, and R. Priem, "The New Corporate Architecture," *Academy of Management Executive*, August 1995, pp. 7–18; C. Harris, "Prime Numbers: A Statistical Look at the Trends and Issues That Will Dominate Our Future," *Financial Post*, November 15/17 1997, p. P13; D. Saunders, "Global the Big Surprise at the Geminis," *The Globe and Mail*, March 2, 1998, p. A1.

counterPOINT

"Small Is Beautiful" Is a Myth!

It's now become the "conventional wisdom" to acknowledge that large organizations are at a disadvantage in today's dynamic environment. Their large size limits their agility. Additionally, competitive and technological forces have ganged up to take away the economies that derived from scale. Well, the conventional wisdom is wrong! The hard evidence shows that the importance of small businesses as job generators and as engines of technological dynamism has been greatly exaggerated. Moreover, large organizations have discovered how to become less rigid, more entrepreneurial, and less hierarchical while still maintaining the advantages that accrue to large size. Moreover, small businesses may not be the best place to work. While they win high marks for providing a pleasant work environment and effective decision-making, they get low marks for job opportunities and financial rewards.

The research showing that small companies have been the prime job generators in recent years is flawed. The early data that were used exaggerated the incidence of startups and covered too short a period. It failed to recategorize companies once they grew or shrunk, which systematically inflated the relative importance of small firms. While it is the case that businesses with less than 50 employees accounted for 97 percent of the 928 000 firms in Canada in 1996, less than five percent of these firms accounted for 45 percent of the job growth. Many of the remaining firms were really individuals creating jobs for themselves because of losing a job to downsizing. These firms were not creating jobs for others. The vast majority of job creation over time is contributed by a tiny fraction of new firms. The job creation statistics also fail to consider that many new small businesses fail, and the failure rate is largely dependent on the economy. For instance, from 1990 through 1994, there were 706 000 small business births and 686 000 deaths, for a net gain of 20 000 firms over the period. This contrasts to a net gain of 110 000 firms during the 1986 through 1990 period when 763 000 firms were started. So, many of the firms creating jobs at one period in time are responsible for lost jobs when the firms fail. Overall, small business accounts for only about one-third of the jobs in Canada, while big business' share is over 40 percent. The same arguments about employment levels holds internationally: In Germany, Japan, and the United States, large businesses have been the big net-job producers.

It's true that the typical organization is becoming smaller. The average Canadian and American business establishment has shrunk dramatically during the last 25 years. But what these numbers don't reveal is that these smaller establishments are increasingly part of a large, multi-location firm with the financial and technological resources to compete in a global marketplace. In other words, these smaller organizations are de facto part of the large enterprise, and this practice is going on throughout the world.

Technology favours the big guys. Studies demonstrate that small firms turn out to be systematically backward when it comes to technology. For example, on every continent, the big companies are far more likely than the small ones to invest in computer-controlled factory automation.

Everyone agrees with the fact that large organizations are improving their flexibility by increasing their use of strategic alliances, interorganizational networks, and similar devices. This worldwide trend, coupled with efforts to widen spans of control, decentralize decision-making, cut vertical levels, and sell off or close operations that don't fit with the organization's primary purpose have made large firms increasingly agile and responsive. ∎

Source: This argument is based on B. Harrison, *Lean and Mean: The Changing Landscape of Corporate Power in the Age of Flexibility* (New York: BasicBooks, 1994). See also M.J. Mandel, "Land of the Giants," *Business Week*, September 11, 1995, pp. 34–35; Catherine Harris, "Prime Numbers: A Statistical Look at the Trends and Issues that Will Dominate our Future," *Financial Post*, November 15/17, 1997, p. P13; C. Winn, "FP/COMPAS Poll: An Exclusive Survey of CEOs and Canadians At Large. This Week: Small is Beautiful, Sort Of," *Financial Post*, November 15/17, 1997, p. P17.

CHAPTER 15

Work Design

LEARNING OBJECTIVES

After studying this chapter, you should be
able to

- Explain the job characteristics model

- Contrast the social information processing
  model to the job characteristics model

- Describe how a job can be enriched

- Describe the role of the PDCA cycle in
  continuous improvement

- Explain the current popularity of
  re-engineering

- Contrast re-engineering and TQM

- Describe the implications of flexible
  manufacturing systems for people who
  work within them

- Contrast the benefits and drawbacks (from
  the employee's point of view) to
  alternatives to traditional workplace
  arrangements, such as telecommuting, the
  compressed workweek, job sharing, and
  flextime

- Describe some of the reasons why
  management and labour unions might
  resist job redesigns

For many years the Lindsay, Ontario, plant of Binney & Smith manufactured Crayola Crayons in an assembly-line fashion.[1] Tasks were divided up into relatively small segments; for instance, hand-pouring wax into crayon moulds, gluing labels onto crayon sticks, running the packing machine that assembled crayons into boxes. Employees were assigned to just one of these tasks, and they might perform the same task for many years. In 1989, Binney & Smith decided that it was time to make their three crayon production plants more productive (the other two were located in Easton, Pennsylvania, and Winfield, Kansas). Binney & Smith wanted to reduce excess inventory, make crayons as they were needed by retailers, and have the flexibility to move quickly out of colours such as Purple Pizzazz and into Radical Red. By the time the transformation was completed, Gloria Golloher, who had run the glue-labelling machine for 43 years (attaching 172 labels per minute!), was not just running the labelling machine, but also logging on to the computer to study production quotas and running the packing machine. After this switch, Gloria still liked the labelling machine best, but she was willing to do the other tasks.

Gloria Golloher's story illustrates two points about the changing workplace of today: many workers are facing changes in the types of jobs they do, and not everyone is completely comfortable with the changes that they face. As Gloria noted, her original job was still her favourite. ■

In this chapter we explore how organizations arrange work tasks into jobs. Jobs can be limited in activity, such as running a glue-labelling machine or they can include a large variety of tasks. Organizations try to identify optimum levels of variety in employee's jobs, because jobs themselves can cause people to be either motivated or unmotivated. When companies arrange tasks into jobs, they are engaging in job design. To understand the complexities of job design, we begin this chapter by considering the factors that affect how people view their jobs. We then discuss the various ways that organizations arrange jobs, as well as the new ways of arranging jobs that have been occurring in the workplace. This chapter's CBC Video Case features telemarketing, giving you the opportunity to think about job design for a high turnover position.

Conceptual Frameworks for Analyzing How People Respond to Their Work Tasks

Gloria Golloher, you may recall, was actually satisfied running the labelling machine. She'd done this job for 43 years without complaint. Over the years, some of the other labellers had either applied for transfers to different jobs, or left Binney & Smith altogether. These different actions by people doing the same job acknowledge basic facts we all know: (1) people's preferences for jobs are different; (2) jobs themselves are different; and (3) some jobs are more interesting and challenging than others. These facts have not gone unnoticed by OB researchers. They have responded by developing a number of **task characteristics theories** that seek to identify task characteristics of jobs, how these characteristics are combined to form different jobs, and the relationship of these task characteristics to employee motivation, satisfaction, and performance.

There are at least seven task characteristics theories that explain why some people like some jobs better than others.[2] Below, we review the three most important task characteristics theories—requisite task attributes theory, the job characteristics model, and the social information processing model.

Requisite Task Attributes Theory

The task characteristics approach began with the pioneering work of Turner and Lawrence in the mid-1960s.[3] They developed a research study to assess the effect of different kinds of jobs on employee satisfaction and absenteeism. They predicted that employees would prefer jobs that were complex and challenging; that is, such jobs would increase satisfaction and result in lower absence rates. They defined job complexity in terms of six task characteristics: (1) variety; (2) autonomy; (3) responsibility; (4) knowledge and skill; (5) required social interaction; and (6) optional social interaction. The higher a job scored on these characteristics, according to Turner and Lawrence, the more complex it was.

Their findings confirmed their absenteeism prediction. Employees in high-complexity tasks had better attendance records. But they found no general correlation between task complexity and satisfaction—until they broke down their data according to the background of employees. When individual differences in the form of urban versus rural background were taken into account, employees from urban settings were shown to be more satisfied with low-complexity jobs. Employees with rural backgrounds reported

task characteristic theories
Seek to identify task characteristics of jobs, how these characteristics are combined to form different jobs, and their relationship to employee motivation, satisfaction, and performance.

higher satisfaction in high-complexity jobs. Turner and Lawrence concluded that workers in larger communities had a variety of nonwork interests and thus were less involved and motivated by their work. In contrast, workers from smaller towns had fewer nonwork interests and were more receptive to the complex tasks of their jobs.

Turner and Lawrence's requisite task attributes theory was important for at least three reasons. First, they demonstrated that employees did respond differently to different types of jobs. Second, they provided a preliminary set of task attributes by which jobs could be assessed. And third, they focused on the need to consider the influence of individual differences on employees' reaction to jobs.

The Job Characteristics Model

job characteristics model (JCM)
Identifies five job characteristics and their relationship to personal and work outcomes.

skill variety
The degree to which the job requires a variety of different activities.

task identity
The degree to which the job requires completion of a whole and identifiable piece of work.

task significance
The degree to which the job has a substantial impact on the lives or work of other people.

autonomy
The degree to which the job provides substantial freedom and discretion to the individual in scheduling the work and in determining the procedures to be used in carrying it out.

feedback
The degree to which carrying out the work activities required by a job results in the individual obtaining direct and clear information about the effectiveness of his or her performance.

Turner and Lawrence's requisite task attributes theory laid the foundation for what is today the dominant framework for defining task characteristics and understanding their relationship to employee motivation, performance, and satisfaction. That is Hackman and Oldham's **job characteristics model** (JCM).[4]

According to the JCM, any job can be described in terms of five core job dimensions, defined as follows:

Skill variety: The degree to which the job requires a variety of different activities so the worker can use a number of different skills and talent.

Task identity: The degree to which the job requires completion of a whole and identifiable piece of work.

Task significance: The degree to which the job has a substantial impact on the lives or work of other people.

Autonomy: The degree to which the job provides substantial freedom, independence, and discretion to the individual in scheduling the work and in determining the procedures to be used in carrying it out.

Feedback: The degree to which carrying out the work activities required by the job results in the individual obtaining direct and clear information about the effectiveness of his or her performance.

Exhibit 15-1 offers examples of job activities that rate high and low for each characteristic.

Exhibit 15-2 presents the job characteristics model. Notice how the first three dimensions—skill variety, task identity, and task significance—combine to create meaningful work. That is, if these three characteristics exist in a job, we can predict that the incumbent will view the job as being important, valuable, and worthwhile. Notice, too, that jobs that possess autonomy give job incumbents a feeling of personal responsibility for the results and that, if a job provides feedback, employees will know how effectively they are performing. From a motivational perspective, the model says that internal rewards are obtained by individuals when they *learn* (knowledge of results) that they *personally* (experienced responsibility) have performed well on a task that they *care* about (experienced meaningfulness).[5] The more that these three psychological states are present, the greater will be employees' motivation, performance, and satisfaction, and the lower their absenteeism and likelihood of leaving the organization. As Exhibit 15-2 shows, the links between the job dimensions and the outcomes are moderated or adjusted by the strength of the individual's growth need; that is, by the employee's desire

Exhibit 15-1
Examples of High and Low Job Characteristics

Skill Variety

High variety	The owner-operator of a garage who does electrical repair, rebuilds engines, does body work, and interacts with customers
Low variety	A body shop worker who sprays paint eight hours a day

Task Identity

High identity	A cabinet maker who designs a piece of furniture, selects the wood, builds the object, and finishes it to perfection
Low identity	A worker in a furniture factory who operates a lathe solely to make table legs

Task Significance

High significance	Nursing the sick in a hospital intensive care unit
Low significance	Sweeping hospital floors

Autonomy

High autonomy	A telephone installer who schedules his or her own work for the day, makes visits without supervision, and decides on the most effective techniques for a particular installation
Low autonomy	A telephone operator who must handle calls as they come according to a routine, highly specified procedure

Feedback

High feedback	An electronics factory worker who assembles a radio and then tests it to determine if it operates properly
Low feedback	An electronics factory worker who assembles a radio and then routes it to a quality control inspector who tests it for proper operation and makes needed adjustments

Source: Adapted from G. Johns, *Organizational Behavior: Understanding and Managing Life at Work*, 4th ed. Copyright © 1981 by HarperCollins College Publishers. Reprinted by permission of Addison-Wesley Educational Publishers, Inc.

motivating potential score (MPS)
A predictive index suggesting the motivation potential in a job.

for self-esteem and self-actualization. This means that individuals with a high growth need are more likely to experience the critical psychological states when their jobs are enriched than are their counterparts with a low growth need. Moreover, they will respond more positively to the psychological states when they are present than will individuals with a low growth need.

The job characteristics model can be viewed as a model of how to create jobs in the workplace that will motivate employees. The core job dimensions can be combined into a single predictive index, called the **motivating potential score** (MPS). Its computation is shown in Exhibit 15-3.

Jobs that are high on motivating potential must be high on at least one of the three factors that lead to experienced meaningfulness, and they must be high on both autonomy and feedback. If jobs score high on motivating potential, the model predicts that motivation, performance, and satisfaction will be positively affected, while the likelihood of absence and turnover will be lessened.

The job characteristics model has been well researched. Most of the evidence supports the general framework of the theory—that is, there is a mul-

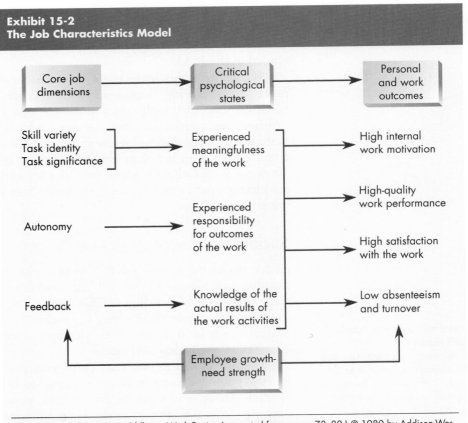

Exhibit 15-2
The Job Characteristics Model

Source: J.R. Hackman, G.R. Oldham, *Work Design* (excerpted from pages 78–80.) © 1980 by Addison-Wesley Publishing Co., Inc. Reprinted by permission of Addison-Wesley Longman Inc.

tiple set of job characteristics and these characteristics impact behavioural outcomes.[6] But there is still considerable debate around the five specific core dimensions in the JCM, the multiplicative properties of the MPS, and the validity of growth-need strength as a moderating variable.

There is some question as to whether task identity adds to the model's predictive ability,[7] and there is evidence suggesting that skill variety may be redundant with autonomy.[8] Furthermore, a number of studies have found that by adding all the variables in the MPS, rather than adding some and multiplying by others, the MPS becomes a better predictor of work outcomes.[9] Finally, the strength of an individual's growth needs as a meaningful moderating variable has recently been called into question.[10] Other variables, such as the presence or absence of social cues, perceived equity with comparison groups, and propensity to assimilate work experience,[11] may be

Exhibit 15-3
Computing a Motivating Potential Score

$$
\text{Motivating Potential Score (MPS)} = \left[\frac{\text{Skill variety} + \text{Task identity} + \text{Task significance}}{3} \right] \times \text{Autonomy} \times \text{Feedback}
$$

more valid in moderating the job characteristics–outcome relationship. Given the current state of research on moderating variables, one should be cautious in unequivocally accepting growth-need strength as originally included in the JCM.

Where does this leave us? Given the current state of evidence, we can make the following statements with relative confidence: (1) People who work on jobs with high core job dimensions are generally more motivated, satisfied, and productive than are those who do not. (2) Job dimensions operate through the psychological states in influencing personal and work outcome variables rather than influencing them directly.[12] The first part of the Working With Others exercise provides an opportunity for you to apply the job characteristics model to a chosen job. You will also calculate its motivating potential score.

Social Information Processing Model

At the beginning of this section on task characteristics theories, do you remember that Gloria Golloher liked working on the labelling machine, but some other employees didn't? This suggests to us that people don't respond to the *objective* jobs themselves, but rather as *they perceive them*. This is the central thesis in our third task characteristics theory. It's called the **social information processing (SIP) model**.[13]

The SIP model argues that employees may adopt attitudes and behaviours in response to the social cues provided by others with whom they have contact. These others can be co-workers, supervisors, friends, family members, or customers. For instance, Gary Ling got a summer job working in a B.C. sawmill. Since jobs were scarce and this one paid particularly well, Gary arrived on his first day of work highly motivated. Two weeks later, however, his motivation was quite low. What happened was that his co-workers consistently bad-mouthed their jobs. They said the work was boring, that having to clock in and out proved management didn't trust them, and that supervisors never listened to their opinions. The objective characteristics of Gary's job had not changed in the two-week period; rather, Gary had reconstructed reality based on messages he had received from others.

A number of studies generally confirm the validity of the SIP model.[14] For instance, it has been shown that employee motivation and satisfaction can be manipulated by such subtle actions as a co-worker or boss commenting on the existence or absence of job features such as difficulty, challenge, and autonomy. At the Dartmouth, Nova Scotia, Imperial Oil refinery, a former employee observed that before the Joint Industrial Council (which for decades had governed relations between management and wage earners in Dartmouth's non-union shop) was disbanded, "You had guys with [a] high school [education] earning $65 000 a year, who did nothing but complain about being asked to work."[15]

This tells us that managers should give as much (or more) attention to employees' attitudes about and perceptions of their jobs as to the actual characteristics of those jobs. They might spend more time telling employees how interesting and important their jobs are. And managers should also not be surprised that newly hired employees and people transferred or promoted to a new position are more likely to be receptive to social information than are those with greater seniority.

Work Redesign Options

Why might a manager want to redesign jobs, and what are some of the options that managers have at their disposal if they want to redesign or change the composition of employees' jobs? Consider the organization at Canada Post's South Central Toronto letter-processing plant. The work is divided into such specific jobs that one employee's entire daily job is to take bag after bag of unopened mail from a conveyor belt, and just place it into a shallow moving bucket. John Wozney, a manager at the plant, notes that under these circumstances, "if a couple of key people call in sick, you're behind the eight ball." The South Central management is currently examining how to redesign both the plant and jobs.[16]

Several factors affect the decision to redesign jobs. From a simple human resources perspective, the manager may note that employees seem less motivated, they are absent more, satisfaction is low, and/or turnover is high. These factors suggest that employees are having negative reactions to their jobs. From a strategic level, managers may need to redesign jobs because technology in the industry is changing or head office has requested increased and/or more efficient production by employees. To understand how to address these workplace issues, we begin with the simplest case of job redesign, where the concern is with an individual worker or group of workers. We identify four options for redesign: job rotation, job enlargement, job enrichment, and team-based designs. Later in the chapter we will discuss redesigns that result from technology or productivity improvements. In these cases the jobs of the whole organization are redesigned, incorporating a variety of elements from job rotation, job enlargement, job enrichment, and teams.

Job Rotation

job rotation
The periodic shifting of a worker from one task to another.

If employees suffer from overroutinization of their work, one alternative is to use **job rotation** (or what many now call *cross-training*). When an activity is no longer challenging, the employee is rotated to another job at the same level that has similar skill requirements.[17] At the Crayola factory discussed in the chapter opening, it might have been possible for employees simply to rotate between the labelling machine and the packing machine, for instance.

G.S.I. Transcomm Data Systems Inc. in Pittsburgh uses job rotation to keep its staff of 110 people from becoming bored.[18] Over one two-year period, nearly 20 percent of Transcomm's employees made lateral job switches. Management believes that the job rotation program has been a major contributor to cutting employee turnover from 25 percent to less than seven percent a year. Brazil's Semco SA makes extensive use of job rotation. "Practically no one," says Semco's president, "stays in the same position for more than two or three years. We try to motivate people to move their areas completely from time to time so they don't get stuck to the technical solutions, to ways of doing things in which they have become entrenched."[19]

The strengths of job rotation are that it reduces boredom and increases motivation through diversifying the employee's activities. Of course, it can also have indirect benefits for the organization since employees with a wider range of skills give management more flexibility in scheduling work, adapting to changes, and filling vacancies. On the other hand, job rotation is not without its drawbacks. Training costs are increased, and productivity is

reduced by moving a worker into a new position just when his or her efficiency at the prior job was creating organizational economies. Job rotation also creates disruptions. Members of the work group must adjust to the new employee. The supervisor may also have to spend more time answering questions and monitoring the work of the recently rotated employee. Finally, job rotation can demotivate intelligent and ambitious trainees who seek specific responsibilities in their chosen specialty.

Job Enlargement

job enlargement
The horizontal expansion of jobs.

More than 35 years ago, the idea of expanding jobs horizontally, or what we call **job enlargement**, grew in popularity. Increasing the number and variety of tasks that an individual performed resulted in jobs with more diversity. Instead of only sorting the incoming mail by department, for instance, a mail sorter's job could be enlarged to include delivering the mail to the various departments or running outgoing letters through the postage meter.

Efforts at job enlargement have sometimes met with less than enthusiastic results.[20] As one employee who experienced such a redesign on his job remarked, "Before I had one lousy job. Now, through enlargement, I have three!" However, there have been some successful applications of job enlargement. For example, GM Canada's Synchronous Administration through Managerial Excellence (SAME) system ensures that all of the employees in a work unit can perform each of the tasks of any of the individuals in the unit. The system significantly reduces the need for meetings, halves the cost of office equipment, and allows job continuity when workers leave the company or go on holiday.[21] The Candour unit of Montreal-based Bombardier's aerospace group moved to job enlargement to get away from having a large number of highly specialized manufacturing jobs.[22] Serge Perron, vice-president and general manager of operations, notes that the move gave Bombardier more flexibility, with workers installing several types of parts instead of just one, and also led to productivity improvements.

While job enlargement attacked the lack of diversity in overspecialized jobs, it did little to add challenge or meaningfulness to a worker's activities. Job enrichment was introduced to deal with the shortcomings of enlargement.

Bombardier Inc.
www.challenger.bombardier.com/

Marriott
http://www.marriott.com/

A red jacket worn by an employee at a Marriott hotel used to identify the employee as a doorman. But red jacket wearers at the Marriott Hotel in Schaumberg, Illinois, are now known as "guest service associates." To increase employee job satisfaction, the hotel has enlarged the doorman's job to include the tasks of bellman, front-desk clerk, and concierge. Job enlargement is also part of Marriott's strategy to improve service quality through programs such as First 10, which focuses on giving customers excellent service during their first 10 minutes at the hotel.

Job Enrichment

job enrichment
The vertical expansion of jobs.

Job enrichment refers to the vertical expansion of jobs. It increases the degree to which the worker controls the planning, execution, and evaluation of his or her work. An enriched job organizes tasks so as to allow the worker to do a complete activity, increases the employee's freedom and independence, increases responsibility, and provides feedback, so an individual will be able to assess and correct his or her own performance.[23] You might want to complete the Learning About Yourself exercise to find out your preferences with respect to job characteristics.

Remember Gloria Goloher at Lindsay's Crayola plant? When her job was enriched, she began logging on to the computer to study production quotas. This gave her the opportunity *and* the responsibility to determine how to allocate some of her time among the various production tasks of making crayons. Job enrichment raises the responsibility level of employees by encouraging and/or requiring employees to make some of the decisions about their work.

Lawrence Buettner enriched the jobs of employees in his international trade banking department at First Chicago Corporation.[24] His department's chief product is commercial letters of credit—essentially a bank guarantee to stand behind huge import and export transactions. When he took over the department of 300 employees, he found paperwork crawling along a document "assembly line," with errors creeping in at each handoff. And employees did little to hide the boredom they were experiencing in their jobs. Buettner replaced the narrow, specialized tasks that employees were doing with enriched jobs. Each clerk is now a trade expert who can handle a customer from start to finish. After 200 hours of training in finance and law, the clerks became full-service advisors who could turn around documents in a day while advising clients on such arcane matters as bank procedures in Turkey and U.S. munitions' export controls. And the results? Productivity has more than tripled, employee satisfaction has soared, and transaction volume has risen more than 10 percent a year. Additionally, increased skills have translated into higher pay for the employees who are performing the enriched jobs. These trade service representatives, some of whom had come to the bank directly out of high school, now earn from $35 000 to $70 000 a year.

The First Chicago example shouldn't be taken as a blanket endorsement of job enrichment, however. The overall evidence generally shows that job enrichment reduces absenteeism and turnover costs and increases satisfaction, but on the critical issue of productivity, the evidence is inconclusive.[25] In some situations, such as at First Chicago, job enrichment increases productivity; in others, it decreases it. However, even when productivity goes down, there does seem to be consistently more conscientious use of resources and a higher quality of product or service. This chapter's From Concepts to Skills feature provides specific guidelines on the kinds of changes that help increase the motivating potential of jobs.

Team-Based Work Designs Revisited

Increasingly, people are doing work in groups and teams. What, if anything, can we say about the design of group-based work to try to improve employee performance in those groups? We know a lot more about individual-based work design than we do about design at the group level,[26] mostly because the wide popularity of teams—specifically assigning tasks to a group

FROM CONCEPTS TO SKILLS

Designing Enriched Jobs

How does management enrich an employee's job? The following suggestions, based on the job characteristics model, specify the types of changes in jobs that are most likely to lead to improving their motivating potential.

1. *Combine tasks.* Managers should seek to take existing and fractionalized tasks and put them back together to form a new and larger module of work. This increases skill variety and task identity.

2. *Create natural work units.* The creation of natural work units means that the tasks an employee does form an identifiable and meaningful whole. This increases employee "ownership" of the work and improves the likelihood that employees will view their work as meaningful and important rather than as irrelevant and boring.

3. *Establish client relationships.* The client is the user of the product or service that the employee works on (and may be an "internal customer" as well as someone outside the organization). Wherever possible, man-

agers should try to establish direct relationships between workers and their clients. This increases skill variety, autonomy, and feedback for the employee.

4. *Expand jobs vertically.* Vertical expansion gives employees responsibilities and control that were formerly reserved to management. It seeks to partially close the gap between the "doing" and the "controlling" aspects of the job, and it increases employee autonomy.

5. *Open feedback channels.* By increasing feedback, employees not only learn how well they are performing their jobs, but also whether their performance is improving, deteriorating, or remaining at a constant level. Ideally, this feedback about performance should be received directly as the employee does the job, rather than from management on an occasional basis.

Source: J.R. Hackman, "Work Design," in J.R. Hackman and J.L. Suttle (eds.), *Improving Life at Work* (Santa Monica, CA: Goodyear, 1977), pp. 132–33.

of individuals instead of to a single person—is a relatively recent phenomenon. That said, the best work in this area offers two sets of suggestions.[27]

First, the JCM recommendations seem to be as valid at the group level as they are at the individual level. Managers should expect a group to perform at a high level when (1) the group task requires members to use a variety of relatively high-level skills; (2) the group task is a whole and meaningful piece of work, with a visible outcome; (3) the outcomes of the group's work on the task have significant consequences for other people; (4) the task provides group members with substantial autonomy for deciding how they do the work; and (5) work on the task generates regular, trustworthy feedback about how well the group is performing.

Second, group composition is critical to the success of the work group. Consistent with findings described in Chapter 8, managers should try to ensure that the following four conditions are met: (1) individual members have the necessary task-relevant expertise to do their work; (2) the group is large enough to perform the work; (3) members possess interpersonal as well as task skills; and (4) membership is moderately diverse in terms of talents and perspectives. In the second part of the Working With Others exercise, you can determine different ways to redesign jobs to show how you might increase their motivation potential.

Technology and New Work Designs

We introduced the term *technology* in the previous chapter's discussion of why structures differ. We said it was how an organization transfers its inputs into outputs. In recent years, the term has become widely used by economists, managers, consultants, and business analysts to describe machinery and equipment that utilizes sophisticated electronics and computers to produce those outputs.

The common theme among new technologies in the workplace is that they substitute machinery for human labour in transforming inputs into outputs. This substitution of capital for labour has been going on essentially non-stop since the Industrial Revolution began in the mid-1800s. For instance, the introduction of electricity allowed textile factories to introduce mechanical looms that could produce cloth far faster and more cheaply than was previously possible when the looms were powered by individuals. But it's been the computerization of equipment and machinery in the last 25 years that has been the prime mover in reshaping the twentieth-century workplace. Automated teller machines, for example, have replaced tens of thousands of human tellers in banks. Auto-guided vehicles at Pacific Press (publisher of *The Vancouver Sun* and *The Province*) pick up and deliver 1500-kg rolls of newsprint, replacing the fork-lift operators who used to do this task. IBM has built a plant in Austin, Texas, that can produce laptop computers without the help of a single worker. Everything—from the time parts arrive at the IBM plant to the final packing of finished products—is completely automated. And an increasing number of companies, small and large alike, are turning to multimedia and interactive technology for employee training. Exhibit 15-4 gives a humorous perspective on just how extensive some of the technological changes have been during the 20th century.

This book is concerned with the behaviour of people at work. No coverage of this topic today would be complete without discussing how recent advances in technology are changing the workplace and affecting the work lives of employees. In this section, we'll look at three ways that organizations are redesigning their entire operation (or large parts of it) by using TQM and continuous improvement processes, re-engineering, and flexible manufacturing systems. Each of these processes builds from the original job design methods of job rotation, job enlargement, job enrichment, and work production in teams.

Continuous Improvement Processes

Total quality management (TQM) is a philosophy of management that's driven by the constant attainment of customer satisfaction through the continuous improvement of all organizational processes.[28] Managers in many organizations, especially in North America, have been criticized for accepting a level of performance that is below perfection. TQM, however, argues that *good*

Pacific Press
http://www.pacific-press.com/

total quality management (TQM)
A philosophy of management that is driven by the constant attainment of customer satisfaction through the continuous improvement of all

Exhibit 15-4

THE WALL STREET JOURNAL

COCHRAN!

"Cool! A keyboard that writes without a printer."

Source: *Wall Street Journal*, October 11, 1995. With permission from Cartoon Features Syndicate.

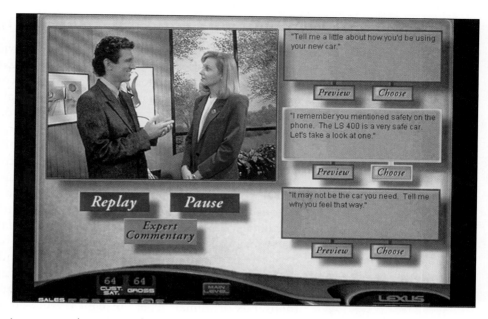

Luxury car maker Lexus, a division of Toyota Motor Sales, has turned to technology for training its salespeople. Computerized simulation exercises help salespeople develop their interpersonal skills through buyer/seller role-playing simulations. Trainees learn how to conduct honest negotiations with buyers, how to treat customers with respect and courtesy, and how to tailor a presentation to a customer's specific interest, as shown in this photo. The company's Fact Lab provides product information about Lexus and competing models, equipping salespeople with the knowledge necessary to achieve the Lexus goal of "complete customer satisfaction."

isn't *good enough*! To dramatize this point, it's easy to assume that 99.9 percent error-free performance represents the highest standards of excellence. Yet it doesn't look so impressive when you recognize that this standard would result in Canada Post's South Central Toronto letter processing plant losing 6000 pieces of mail per day, or U.S. doctors performing 500 incorrect surgical operations per week, or two plane crashes occurring each day at O'Hare Airport in Chicago![29]

TQM programs seek to achieve continuous process improvements so that variability in the quality of the output is constantly reduced. When you eliminate variations, you increase the uniformity of the product or service. This, in turn, results in lower costs and higher quality. For instance, when Winnipeg-based Reimer Express Lines wanted to improve its delivery rates, it adopted a TQM approach. The movement of freight can be divided into eight major steps, from city pickup through transfer to a highway unit to delivery. Workers at Reimer were led through seminars on each of the eight steps, so that they learned about the entire process, how their jobs fit into the process, and how to do the other steps. At a minimum, the changes at Reimer involved job rotation, in that individuals learned how to perform each step. However, at Reimer, employees did more than just rotate through the tasks. Their jobs were enriched because they had to make decisions about the best way to route things through the freight-movement steps.

Continuous improvement runs counter to the more historical North American management approach of seeing work projects as being linear—with a beginning and an end. For example, Canadian and U.S. managers traditionally viewed cost cutting as a short-term project. They set a goal of cutting costs by 20 percent, achieved it, and then said: "Whew! Our cost cutting is over." The Japanese, on the other hand, have regarded cost control

Reimer Express Lines
http://www.roadway.com/
rexnex6.htm

kaizen
Japanese techniques of continuous improvements in manufacturing.

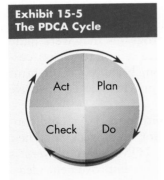

**Exhibit 15-5
The PDCA Cycle**

Schneider Corporation
http://www.theschneidercorp.com/

as an ongoing endeavour. The search for continual improvement creates a race without a finish line. This chapter's Case Incident describes how one Canadian company introduced **kaizen**—that is, Japanese techniques of continuous improvements in manufacturing. The quest for never-ending improvement requires a circular rather than a linear approach. This is illustrated in the Plan-Do-Check-Act (PDCA) cycle shown in Exhibit 15-5.[30] Management plans a change, does it, checks the results, and, depending on the outcome, acts to standardize the change or begin the cycle of improvement again with new information. This cycle treats all organizational processes as being in a constant state of improvement.

Kitchener, Ontario-based Schneider Corporation used the PDCA cycle in 1991 to improve production in its meat-packing plant. Management encouraged employees to take steps to incrementally improve the products they make and the processes used to make them. For instance, workers noted that there was wasted time and motion when half-finished meat products were moved from one floor to another, or parked in coolers waiting for the next step. They were involved in suggesting and implementing changes that reduced the down time. For example, when an old sausage steamer broke down, workers in the smoke room were able to take over the task and the steamer wasn't replaced—saving the company $250 000. Workers had been steaming sausages in the smoke room for years, but management hadn't known about it because they'd never asked. Continuous improvement helped Schneider improve profits, reduce production cuts substantially, and even decrease absenteeism.

Outcomes from TQM can be impressive, at least in the short run. At Schneider, earnings from operations in 1990 were $6 million on sales of $628 million, for a net loss of $1.7 million. After TQM was under way, earnings and profits improved. In 1991, revenues increased just 2.3 percent, but earnings soared to $16 million for a net profit of $5.1 million. In 1993, again, there was a substantial profit. However, by 1996, Schneider was laying off many of its workers, and in late 1997 Schneider was up for sale. Total quality management has been successfully introduced not only in the private sector, but also in the public sector. A commitment to TQM brought the province of New Brunswick a balanced budget in 1994. University of Alberta Hospitals and North York, Ontario's school board also successfully introduced total quality management programs.[31]

Overall, the results of TQM have been mixed. There have been a number of successful implementations, but there have also been notable failures. When accounting for some of the failures of TQM, authors have suggested that sometimes firms were not actually performing TQM, they were just calling it that.[32] Other researchers have suggested that managers had unrealistic expectations of what could be accomplished with TQM, with managers "expecting to do in a year or two what it took some of the leading Japanese companies 30 years to achieve."[33] Other failures occurred because the programs did not assure employees' job security, did not provide adequate training,[34] or did not appreciate the complexity of changes involved.[35]

A 1997 study looking at successful and unsuccessful implementations of TQM among U.S. suppliers of components to automobile manufacturers found that the managerial attitude toward TQM explained much of the success or lack thereof of TQM initiatives.[36] In particular, managers who viewed TQM as a tool for increasing the firm's business introduced the most widespread and successful implementations of TQM. Managers who introduced TQM because customers requested it, and who focused on the importance of customer needs, initiated less extensive TQM programs. These firms

were more likely to introduce TQM in a piecemeal fashion and to seek the publicity that accompanied having a TQM program, rather than being fully committed to TQM as an overall business strategy. Workers in these firms were also less likely to see the value of TQM or to find that it was not introduced as a coherent strategy.

The researchers also identified a group of managers who were reluctant to introduce TQM and therefore only did it under great pressure from customers. These firms had the least successful implementation of TQM. The researchers concluded that those firms that introduced TQM as a tool for expanding the business were more likely to have programs that were quite successful. They noted that the decision to introduce it just to please customers was not necessarily a wise strategic decision, because "if all firms conform to customers' specifications, conformance provides no competitive advantage."[37]

As literally tens of thousands of organizations introduce TQM and continuous process improvement, what does it mean for employees and their jobs? Probably the most significant implication of TQM for employees is that management looks to them as the prime source for improvement ideas. The essence of TQM is process improvement, and employee involvement is the linchpin of process improvement. In other words, TQM requires management to encourage employees to share ideas and act on what they suggest. It means they're no longer able to rest on their previous accomplishments and successes. Some people are likely to lose their jobs. Therefore, employees may experience increased stress from a work climate that no longer accepts complacency with the status quo. A race with no finish line means a race that's never over, which creates constant tension. While this tension may be positive for the organization (remember *functional conflict* from Chapter 13), the pressures from an unrelenting search for process improvements can create anxiety and stress in some employees. Therefore it is important for companies that introduce TQM programs to examine the impact of those programs on their employees. In this chapter's HR Implications, we discuss the performance appraisal implications of TQM.

TEAMS AND TOTAL QUALITY MANAGEMENT In his book *Developing Superior Work Teams*, Kinlaw noted that "none of the various TQM processes and techniques will catch on and be applied except in work teams. All such techniques and processes require high levels of communication and contact, response and adaptation, and coordination and sequencing. They require, in short, the environment that can be supplied only by superior work teams."[38]

Teams provide the natural vehicle for employees to share ideas and to implement improvements. As stated by Gil Mosard, a TQM specialist at McDonnell Douglas: "When your measurement system tells you your process is out of control, you need teamwork for structured problem solving. Not everyone needs to know how to do all kinds of fancy control charts for performance tracking, but everybody does need to know where their process stands so they can judge if it is improving."[39] Examples from Cartier Group Ltd. and Ford Motor Co. illustrate how teams are being used in TQM programs.[40]

To understand how teams are being used in TQM programs, let's consider two examples. Montreal-based Cartier Group Ltd., an engineering firm, adopted its TQM program in 1989. Members of project teams are expected to assume full responsibility for quality and to be proactive rather than reactive. Team members seek out the information they need to complete assignments and, when needed, suggest changes.

Ford Motor Co. began its TQM efforts in the early 1980s with teams as the primary organizing mechanism. "Because this business is so complex, you can't make an impact on it without a team approach," noted one Ford manager. In designing its quality problem-solving teams, Ford's management identified five goals. The teams should (1) be small enough to be efficient and effective; (2) be properly trained in the skills their members will need; (3) be allocated enough time to work on the problems they plan to address; (4) be given the authority to resolve the problems and implement corrective action; and (5) each have a designated "champion" whose job it is to help the team get around roadblocks that arise.

Successful TQM requires not just the formation of teams, but also training and development to help team members learn how to work together. Successful Canadian implementation of TQM has been achieved at Pratt and Whitney, AMP, Steelcase, and Cargill, all of which provide teams with clear goals and recognition for achieving those goals. Pratt and Whitney, for instance, uses a portion of savings resulting from improvements to reward team, rather than individual, efforts.[41]

Re-engineering Work Processes

re-engineering
Reconsiders how work would be done and the organization structured if they were being created from scratch.

In times of rapid and dramatic change, it's sometimes necessary to approach improving quality and productivity from the perspective of "How would we do things around here if we were starting over from scratch?" That, in essence, is the approach of **re-engineering**. It asks managers to reconsider how work would be done and their organization structured if they were starting over.[42] To illustrate the concept of re-engineering, consider a manufacturer of roller skates. The product is essentially a shoe with wheels beneath it. The typical roller skate was a leather boot with shoelaces, attached to a steel platform that held four wooden wheels. If our manufacturer took a continuous improvement approach to change, he or she would look for small incremental improvements to be introduced in the product. For instance, he or she might consider adding hooks to the upper part of the boot for speed lacing; or changing the weight of leather used for improved comfort; or using different ballbearings to make the wheels spin more smoothly. Now most of us are familiar with in-line skates. They represent a re-engineering approach to roller skates. The goal was to develop a skating device that could improve skating speed, mobility, and control. In-line skates fulfilled those goals in a completely different type of shoe. The upper was made of injected plastic, which was made popular in skiing. Laces were replaced by easy-close clamps. And the four wooden wheels, set in pairs of two, were replaced by four to six in-line plastic wheels. The re-engineered result, which didn't look much like the traditional roller skate, proved universally superior. The rest, of course, is history. In-line skates have revolutionized the roller-skate business.

The term *re-engineering* comes from the historical process of taking apart an electronics product and designing a better version. Michael Hammer coined the term for organizations. When he found that companies were using computers simply to automate outdated processes, rather than finding fundamentally better ways of doing things, he realized the same re-engineering principles could be applied to business. So, as applied to organizations, re-engineering means management should start with a clean slate—rethinking and redesigning those processes by which the organization creates value and does work, ridding itself of operations that have become antiquated in the computer age.[43]

Top management at Union Carbide's industrial chemicals division led the drive to re-engineer work processes in plant and equipment maintenance, which accounted for 30 percent of costs. Directed to work in teams and to set ambitious cost-cutting goals, employees (shown here) worked out the details of their new work process by developing new repair and maintenance procedures. The re-engineering effort saved Union Carbide $38 million, 50 percent more than management's target. Companywide, Union Carbide has used re-engineering to cut $560 million out of fixed costs over a recent three-year period.

KEY ELEMENTS OF RE-ENGINEERING Three key elements of re-engineering are identifying an organization's distinctive competencies, assessing core processes, and reorganizing horizontally by process.

An organization's **distinctive competencies** define what it is that the organization is more superior at delivering than its competition. Examples might include superior store locations, a more efficient distribution system, higher-quality products, more knowledgeable sales personnel, or superior technical support. Dell Computer, for instance, differentiates itself from its competitors by emphasizing high-quality hardware, comprehensive service and technical support, and low prices. Why is identifying distinctive competencies so important? Because it guides decisions regarding which activities are crucial to the organization's success.

distinctive competencies
Defines what it is that the organization is more superior at delivering than its competition.

Management also needs to assess the core processes that clearly add value to the organization's distinctive competencies. These are the processes that transform materials, capital, information, and labour into products and services that the customer values. When the organization is viewed as a series of processes, ranging from strategic planning to after-sales customer support, management can determine to what degree each adds value. Not surprisingly, this **process value analysis** typically uncovers many activities that add little or nothing of value and whose only justification is "we've always done it this way."

process value analysis
Determination to what degree each organizational process adds value to the organization's distinctive competencies.

Re-engineering requires management to reorganize around horizontal processes. This means cross-functional and self-managed teams. It means focusing on processes rather than functions. So, for instance, the vice-president of marketing might become the "process owner of finding and keeping customers."[44] And it also means eliminating levels of middle management. As Hammer pointed out, "Managers are not value-added. A customer never buys a product because of the calibre of management. Management is, by definition, indirect. So if possible, less is better. One of the goals of re-engineering is to minimize the necessary amount of management."[45]

The story of Imperial Oil's Dartmouth, Nova Scotia, refinery illustrates how successful process re-engineering can be. In July 1991, Dartmouth refinery manager Ken Ball received a report card showing that his refinery placed in the bottom quartile of 116 other North American refineries. With

that news, Ball knew that the refinery was in danger of being closed. In an effort to prevent his refinery from being sold or closed, in January 1992 Ball presented his plan to turn things around at Dartmouth to head office in Toronto. On February 4, 1992, Imperial Oil gave him until year-end to go from among the worst-performing refineries to among the best.

Ball had less than a year to turn things around, and faced a workforce "where people were interested more in their job descriptions than the refinery's margin on a barrel of crude. A culture in which a mechanic who found a way to help an electrician would have to convince up to four supervisors the idea was worthwhile."[46]

Ball faced a difficult task, one made easier only because the employees realized that remaining with the status quo would certainly mean plant closure. Facing that, Ball's unilateral moves to improve processes were adopted. Almost immediately, Ball disbanded the Joint Industrial Council (JIC) that had governed employee-management relations for years, eliminated seniority rights, emphasized individual performance, and instituted a team approach to work. Each of the four main work teams, composed of 40 to 50 workers per team, now took responsibility for an entire chunk of the plant's operation. By the early 1993, costs had fallen 30 percent in the plant, and most believed the refinery would remain open. In fact, in February 1998, Dartmouth was still operating, with about 240 employees, the same number as in 1993.

WHY RE-ENGINEERING NOW? Isn't re-engineering something management should have been doing all along? Why has it become such a hot topic in the 1990s? The answers, according to Michael Hammer, are a changing global environment and organizational structures that had become top heavy.

Traditional mechanistic organizations worked fine in times of stable growth. Activities could be fragmented and specialized to gain economic efficiencies. This described the environment faced by most North American organizations in the 1950s, 1960s, and much of the 1970s. But most organizations today operate in global conditions of overcapacity. Customers are much more informed and sophisticated than they were 30 years ago. Moreover, markets, production, and capital are all globally mobile. Investors in Australia, for example, can invest their money in opportunities in Canada, Japan, or anywhere else in the world if they see better returns than they can receive at home. Global customers now demand quality, service, and low cost. If *you* can't provide it, they'll get it from someone else.

Work specialization, functional departments, narrow spans of control, and the like drove down direct labour costs, but the bureaucracies they created had massive overhead costs. That is, to coordinate all the fragmentation and specialization, the organization had to create numerous levels of middle management to glue together the fragmented pieces. So while bureaucracies drove down costs at the operating level, they required increasingly expensive coordinating systems. Those organizations that introduced teams, decentralized decisions, widened spans of control, and flattened structures became more efficient and challenged the traditional ways of doing things.

RE-ENGINEERING VERSUS TQM Is re-engineering just another term for TQM? No! They do have some common characteristics, though.[47] They both, for instance, emphasize processes and satisfying the customer. After that, they diverge radically. This is evident in their goals and the means they use for achieving their goals.

TQM seeks incremental improvements, while re-engineering looks for quantum leaps in performance. That is, the former is essentially about improving something that is basically okay; the latter is about taking something that is irrelevant, discarding it, and starting over. And the means that the two approaches use are totally different. TQM relies on bottom-up, participative decision-making in both the planning of a TQM program and its execution. Re-engineering, on the other hand, is initially driven by top management. When re-engineering is complete, the workplace is largely self-managed. But getting there is a very autocratic, non-democratic process. Re-engineering's supporters argue that it must be this way because the level of change that the process demands is highly threatening to people and they aren't likely to accept it voluntarily. When top management commits to re-engineering, employees have no choice. As Hammer is fond of saying, "You either get on the train, or we'll run over you with the train."[48] Of course, autocratically imposed change is likely to face employee resistance. While there is no easy solution to the resistance that top-down change creates, some of the techniques presented in Chapter 17 in our discussion of overcoming resistance to change can be helpful. A study of Canadian companies suggests that the most significant factor leading to a positive re-engineering experience is top management support (78%), followed by keeping lines of communication open (44%), a strong project management team (41%), and appropriate leadership (41%).[49]

DOES RE-ENGINEERING WORK? University of Waterloo researcher Neil Chandler and his graduate student Howard Armitage studied 324 Canadian organizations with 1995 net sales over $100 million and found that Canadian companies reported higher success rates of completed projects than those reported by American firms. Ninety-four percent of Canadian firms were at least moderately successful, compared to Ernst & Young's survey of U.S. companies, which reported a success rate of only 54 percent.[50] However, in terms of measurable success, the Canadian findings raise some interesting questions. Of the companies that had completed a project, 32 percent experienced increased competitive advantage, 17 percent experienced increased profits, and 18 percent experienced an increase in the quality of their products and/or services. The value of a company's stock increased for only four percent of the respondents.[51] Based on this Canadian study, the re-engineering efforts do not appear to improve shareholder value. And there have been some notable failures in re-engineering. In 1995, after several years and an investment of several million dollars, SaskTel wound down its re-engineering project due to widespread negative reactions from management and employees alike. Almost half of the 20 employees involved in the re-engineering team ended up on stress leave.[52]

IMPLICATIONS FOR EMPLOYEES Re-engineering is rapidly gaining momentum in business and industry.[53] In a 1995 survey by Ernst & Young and *CFO Magazine* conducted among top financial officers at 80 major North American corporations, including eight from Canada, the survey found that 50 percent of respondents were conducting re-engineering projects and 88 percent had them in the works.[54]

Some of the companies that have implemented re-engineering in at least some of their divisions include Petro-Canada, Abitibi-Price, Eaton's, Canadian Tire, Sears, Volkswagen Canada, Amex Canada, Banca di America e di Italia, Siemens, and KPMG Peat Marwick. Re-engineering's popularity isn't surprising. In today's highly competitive global marketplace, companies are

SaskTel
http://www.sasktel-international.com/

finding that they're forced to re-engineer their work processes if they're going to survive. And employees will "have to get on the train."

Many people will lose their jobs as a direct result of re-engineering efforts. Just how many depends on the pace at which organizations adopt the new techniques. Some experts say that re-engineering will eliminate from 1 million to 2.5 million jobs each year for the foreseeable future.[55] Undoubtedly much of the downsizing movement can be directly traced to re-engineering efforts. But regardless of the number, the impact won't be uniform across the organization. Staff support jobs, especially middle managers, will be most vulnerable. So, too, will clerical jobs in service industries. For instance, one knowledgeable observer predicts that re-engineering will reduce employment in commercial banks and thrift institutions by 30 to 40 percent during the 1990s.[56]

Remember Carol Golloher and the improvements at Lindsay's Crayola Crayon factory? Initially those changes led to substantial improvements in production. From its inception, the Lindsay plant had been the exclusive producer of Crayola Crayons for the Canadian market. In 1992, however, after it had revamped its production process and trained its employees to work in teams, the plant received its first-ever crayon order for the American market. The improvements had allowed the Lindsay plant to double its productions in just several months, and it met the American order on time and with perfect quality. By 1992, the Lindsay plant was producing a fabric paint product for the Sears Wish Book. By 1994, it was producing UPC/Item/Article number stickers for Costco and Price Club's membership customers. All success stories were linked to the re-engineering of the Lindsay plant. Then, in February 1997, Binney & Smith announced that it was moving Lindsay's crayon, paint and modelling-compound operations to Easton, Pennsylvania. This resulted in a loss of almost 50 jobs at the Lindsay plant, although the marker, activity kit, and plastic moulding operations for the Canadian market were to remain at Lindsay.[57] However, just one month later, Binney & Smith Canada launched a new product, Crayola IQ, a new line of crayons, pencils, and markers for the tween market (eight- to 12-year-olds). This line was so successful that the company's U.S. parent was considering bringing out its own tween product line sometime in 1998.[58] Once again, Binney & Smith Canada had turned itself around, in part due to its overall re-engineering efforts.

Those employees that keep their jobs after re-engineering will find that they aren't the same jobs any longer. These new jobs will typically require a wider range of skills, include more interaction with customers and suppliers, offer greater challenge, contain increased responsibilities, and provide higher pay. However, the three- to five-year period involved in implementing re-engineering is usually tough on employees. They suffer from uncertainty and anxiety associated with taking on new tasks and having to discard long-established work practices and formal social networks.

Flexible Manufacturing Systems

They look like something out of a science-fiction movie in which remote-controlled carts deliver a basic casting to a computerized machining centre. With robots positioning and repositioning the casting, the machining centre calls upon its hundreds of tools to perform varying operations that turn the casting into a finished part. Completed parts, each a bit different from the others, are finished at a rate of one every 90 seconds. Neither skilled

flexible manufacturing system
Integration of computer-aided design, engineering, and manufacturing to produce low-volume products at mass-production costs.

Pratt & Whitney Canada
http://www.pwc.ca/

machinists nor conventional machine tools are used. Nor are there any costly delays for changing dies or tools in this factory. A single machine can make dozens or even hundreds of different parts in any order management wants. Welcome to the world of **flexible manufacturing systems**.[59]

In a global economy, those manufacturing organizations that can respond rapidly to change have a competitive advantage. They can, for instance, better meet the diverse needs of customers and deliver products faster than their competitors. When customers were willing to accept standardized products, fixed assembly lines made sense. But nowadays, flexible technologies are increasingly necessary to compete effectively.

The unique characteristic of flexible manufacturing systems is that by integrating computer-aided design, engineering, and manufacturing, they can produce low-volume products for customers at a cost comparable to what had been previously possible only through mass production. Flexible manufacturing systems are, in effect, repealing the laws of economies of scale. Management no longer must mass-produce thousands of identical products to achieve low per-unit production costs. With flexible manufacturing, when management wants to produce a new part, it doesn't change machines—it just changes the computer program.

Some automated plants can build a wide variety of flawless products and switch from one product to another on cue from a central computer. Pratt & Whitney Canada Inc.'s Halifax facility, for instance, produces 1600 engines a year across 127 models without plant shutdowns for retooling. Before the onset of flexible manufacturing, it was producing 3000 engines a year but only 20 different models. While the automated technology of the Halifax facility attracts a lot of attention, plant manager Peter Wressel believes the true key to the plant's success lies in its motivated workforce. There are only six managers, including Wressell, for close to 450 workers. Employees work in teams and are involved in all aspects of plant administration including pay, benefits, job rotation, and community relations. They have even established a work schedule of five days on and five days off.[60] Similarly, National Bicycle Industrial Co., which sells its bikes under the Panasonic brand, uses flexible manufacturing to produce any of 11 231 862 variations on 18 models of racing, road, and mountain bikes in 199 colour

A flexible manufacturing system at IBM's plant in Charlotte, North Carolina, can produce 27 different computer products at the same time. The automated assembly lines are controlled by computer instructions that vary based on diverse customer needs. The computers also give employees assembly instructions. This flexible system brings efficiency to IBM's manufacturing process and helps the company deliver products to customers more quickly than competitors.

patterns and an almost unlimited number of sizes. This allows Panasonic to provide almost customized bikes at mass-produced prices.[61]

What do flexible manufacturing systems mean for the people who work within them?[62] They require a different breed of industrial employee. At Halifax's Pratt & Whitney operation, employees are hired for their high-tech skills, initiative, and ability to thrive in a self-managing environment. In addition to greater skills, workers in flexible manufacturing plants also need more training. This is because there are fewer employees, so each must be able to do a greater variety of tasks. For instance, at a flexible Carrier plant in Arkansas, an organization that makes compressors for air conditioners, all employees undergo six weeks of training before they start their jobs. This training includes learning to read blueprints, computing math such as fractions and metric calculations, understanding statistical process-control methods, upgrading some computer skills, and solving the problems involved in dealing with other workers. In addition to higher skills, employees in flexible plants are typically organized into teams and given considerable decision-making discretion. Consistent with the objective of high flexibility, these plants tend to have organic structures. They decentralize authority into the hands of the operating teams.

Job Redesign in the Canadian Context: The Role of Unions

Until recently, labour unions have been largely resistant to participating in discussions with management over job-design issues. As noted above, these redesigns often result in loss of jobs, and labour unions try to protect workers' jobs. Union head offices, however, can sometimes be at odds with their membership on the acceptance of job redesign. Some members value the opportunity for skill development and more interesting work. During the 1990s, at least some of the larger unions are becoming more open to discussions about job redesign. This is reflected, for instance, in the position taken by the Communications, Energy and Paperworkers Union of Canada (CEP).[63] The CEP asserts that unions should be involved in the decisions and share in the benefits of work redesign. It calls for negotiated workplace changes, with greater union input into the conception, development, and implementation of work reorganization initiatives. The union also believes that basic wages, negotiated through a collective agreement, must remain the primary form of compensation, although they are open to other forms of compensation as long as they do not detract from basic wages determined through collective bargaining. While managers may regard job redesign as more difficult under a collective agreement, the reality is that for change to be effective in the workplace, management must gain employees' acceptance of the plan whether or not they are unionized.

As a case in point, in 1990 Lac-Megantic, Quebec-based Bestar Inc., a furniture maker, joined with its union, the National Brotherhood of Carpenters, Joiners, Foresters and Industrial Workers, to try to save the plant from serious financial difficulties.[64] Bestar wanted to introduce some quality programs, and it required convincing both management and union members that it was in everyone's best interest to work together. Not all of the managers supported employee participation, however. Sylvain Roy, then-president of the union at Bestar, recalled that "the least adaptable managers, who did not want to accept worker involvement, either left the company of their own accord or were let go." This signalled to both management and

union members that everyone needed to work together on quality initiatives. Roy also noted that once the workers were encouraged to become more involved, they were "more conscious of losses and mistakes" and realized that their job survival depended on focusing on quality. The Lac-Megantic plant has continued to thrive. In December 1997, it announced a three-year, $10-million expansion at the plant. And in April 1998, it announced record profits and sales for the first quarter of 1998.

Although there are union-management success stories in gaining changes in the workplace, there have been a number of difficulties as well. The Case Incident in Chapter 16 highlights evidence of the difficulties that Canada Post and the Canadian Union of Postal Workers (CUPW) have had in working together for workplace change. While CUPW has resisted most attempts at change, the Bestar example indicates that management can also be resistant to change.

Flexible Work Arrangements

Statistics Canada
www.statcan.ca/

Historically, most people worked an eight-hour day, five days a week. They started at a fixed time and left at a fixed time. However, a 1995 Statistics Canada survey of work arrangements found that only 39 percent of employed Canadians had "normal" schedules in which they worked Monday to Friday at regular starting times.[65] A number of organizations have introduced flexible work schedule options, including job-sharing, telecommuting, compressed workweeks, and flextime as a way to improve employee motivation, productivity, and satisfaction. Statistics Canada reported that 24 percent of employees had some sort of flexible work arrangement in 1995.

These arrangements also help employees ease the stress of juggling family needs alongside work demands. Gay Bank, vice-president of human resources at the Royal Bank of Canada, notes that "it is estimated that as many as three in four working Canadians have responsibility for caring for children or aging parents."[66] Helping workers to juggle the demands of work and career has important benefits to companies, according to James Bond, vice-president of New York-based Families and Work Institute, which conducted a national survey of workers in the United States in 1997. He reports that "the more support employees receive on the job—the more flexible their work arrangements and supportive their supervisors—the higher their productivity, the more willing they are to go the extra mile."[67]

A 1998 survey of Royal Bank and Royal Trust employees supports Bond's points. That survey found the following:[68]

- 94 percent of flex workers are very satisfied with their work arrangements;
- 70 percent of flex workers reported less stress;
- 81 percent of flex workers said they were more effective at balancing work and their outside lives;
- 63 percent of managers would highly recommend flex work arrangements. (Notable about this is that a similar survey conducted in 1994 found that only 34 percent of managers would have highly recommended flex work in 1994);
- 37 percent of managers reported that flex work led to an increase in employee efficiency;

- 48 percent of employees use flex work to deal with family responsibilities and child and/or elder care;
- 36 percent of employees said they would leave the company if flex work were not available;
- 78 percent of employees on flexwork said their opportunities for advancement were the same or better than when they worked a traditional schedule.

Compressed Workweek

compressed workweek
A four-day week, with employees working 10 hours a day.

There are two common forms of **compressed workweek:** the four 10-hour days per week plan (known as the 4-40 program) and the nine days over two weeks plan, where workers get either a Friday or Monday off once every two weeks in exchange for working slightly longer hours the other days. These compressed workweek programs were conceived to allow workers more leisure time and shopping time, and to permit them to travel to and from work during non-rush-hour times. Supporters suggest that such a program can increase employee enthusiasm, morale, and commitment to the organization; increase productivity and reduce costs; reduce machine downtime in manufacturing; reduce overtime, turnover, and absenteeism; and make it easier for the organization to recruit employees.

These programs can also have a positive impact on the environment, with fewer cars involved in rush-hour gridlock, as well as providing additional support for managing work and family conflicts. For instance, Burnaby-based B.C. Tel pilot-tested compressed workweeks in 1998 as a way to provide service and remain competitive without increasing staff or overtime. Calgary-based Amoco offered compressed workweeks to all employees in head office two years ago, with the result that 85 percent take off every second Friday and work slightly longer hours on the other days. Other Canadian companies that offer flexible workweeks include B.C. Hydro, Air Canada, Revenue Canada, Hewlett-Packard, IBM, Xerox, Johnson and Johnson, and Coca-Cola. Companies vary in their way of determining an appropriate flexible workweek schedule, however. For instance, while the Royal Bank also has a compressed workweek, because of concerns about possible reduced customer service, very few employees are offered a four-day week as an option.

Amoco Corp.
www.amoco.com/

Proponents argue that the compressed workweek may positively affect productivity in situations in which the work process requires significant start-up and shutdown periods.[69] When start-up and shutdown times are a major factor, productivity standards take these periods into consideration in determining the time required to generate a given output. Consequently, in such cases, the compressed workweek will increase productivity even though worker performance is not affected, simply because the improved work scheduling reduces nonproductive time. Not all employers agree that a compressed week is beneficial to performance, however. In this chapter's OB in the News, you can read about the City of Vancouver's controversial decision to abolish the four-day workweek.

The evidence on the impact of compressed workweek schedules on employees is generally positive.[70] In one study, for instance, when employees were asked whether they wanted to continue their 4–40 program, which had been in place for six months, or go back to a traditional five-day week, 78 percent wanted to keep the compressed workweek.[71] However, some employees complain of fatigue near the end of the day, and about the diffi-

OB IN THE NEWS

Vancouver Takes Back Four-Day Workweeks

In late April 1998, the City of Vancouver announced a plan to abolish its 22-year program of four-day workweeks, effective September 1, 1998. The program had been very popular with the staff, but received many complaints from resentful users of city services.

When the new policy was first announced, City Manager Ken Dobell acknowledged that the City would probably lose some employees as a result of the change, and suffer a decline in employee morale as well. So why would the City take this action? Dobell's report on the situation concluded that the four-day workweek "was creating a situation where effectively business could only be done three days a week, since so many employees were absent on Mondays or Fridays." The City was also receiving a number of complaints from those who were having difficulty reaching City workers, and who had to work five-day weeks themselves.

City employees were immediately upset about the planned changes. Benny Mah, a plan-checker with the city for six years whose wife also works for the City, noted that because of the shortened workweek, he and his wife only needed day care for their three young children three days a week. It also gave them the opportunity to arrange appointments so that they would not have to take days off.

Within two weeks of the announcement, a backlash occurred among city workers. Managers resigned from the staff-appreciation committee, withdrew voluntary services, and wrote anguished letters to councillors "about the emotional and financial impact it would have on them, city hall and the community if the city returns to more traditional work schedules." Dobell's response was that "the rest of the world is on a five-day workweek and the city is out of step."

Not everyone agreed with Dobell on this, however. Jane Boyd, president of B.C.-based Work, Family, and Life Consulting Services, noted that "this is to my knowledge the first time I've ever seen a case where a company is talking about taking it (compressed workweek) away." Most companies, in fact, see flexible work arrangements as both a recruiting benefit for companies, and a way to build staff morale.

A month after the city had announced its plan, it was back "in the shop for repair, after it stirred up a never-before-seen tornado of staff opposition." In July 1998, however, the City decided that abolishing the four-day workweek was indeed the right way to go.

Sources: Frances Bula, "City Staff Face Losing Four-Day Work Week," *Vancouver Sun*, 28 April, 1998, pp. B2, B3; Frances Bula, "City's Plan to End 4-day Week Sparks Backlash," *Vancouver Sun*, 15 May, 1998, pp. B1, B3; Frances Bula, "Bid to Alter Work Week In City Shop for Repairs," *Vancouver Sun*, 26 May, 1998, pp. B1, B3.

Take It to the Net

We invite you to visit the Robbins page on the Prentice Hall Web site at:

http://www.prenticehall.ca/robbins

for this chapter's World Wide Web exercise.

culty of coordinating their jobs with their personal lives—the latter posing a problem especially for working mothers. A 1996 Statistics Canada study reported more stress for women working a compressed week than those working a traditional week (30 percent compared to 21 percent).[72] However, these findings may not indicate that the compressed workweek itself causes stress. Rather, those who opt to take the compressed workweek option are more likely to be doing so to balance out work and family conflicts, and thus these employees have more stress in their lives in general.

Shorter Workweek

How does a reduced four-day, 32-hour workweek sound? What if it included a 20 percent cut in pay? A number of Western European countries are considering the former as a solution to high unemployment. But if unions have their way, it won't be with any pay cut.[73] Western Europe has 20 million unemployed workers. In an effort to deal with this problem, countries such as Germany, France, Spain, and Belgium are seriously considering spreading the available work among more people by cutting the workweek by 20 percent. With the jobless rate nearly 12 percent and rising in France and Germany, political pressures are building for this proposal. Volkswagen, for instance, has given an ultimatum to the union that represents its 103 000 workers: accept a four-day workweek with a 20 percent drop in pay, or nearly every third job will be cut.

French Premier Lionel Jospin announced in October 1997 that by January 1, 2000, his goal was to make 35 hours the standard workweek for companies with more than 10 employees.[74] It's not clear at this point whether the 35-hour workweek will become the new standard in Western Europe. Moreover, even if it does, it isn't certain that employees will have to take a commensurate cut in pay. Proposals currently being considered at the federal level include having employers absorb the full cost—paying workers for 40 hours, even if they work only 35; having the government pick up the tab; or some combination of cost sharing among workers, employers, and government. The impact on employees of a shorter workweek can only be speculative at this time. While the program would create more jobs, employees are likely to focus on how it affects them individually rather than the positive effect on their country's employment rate. A 20 percent cut in hours, with no cut in pay, should have generally positive effects on employee satisfaction and negative effects on productivity. If the cut in hours is matched with a 20 percent reduction in pay, satisfaction is likely to drop.

Flextime

flextime
Employees work during a common core time period each day but have discretion in forming their total workday from a flexible set of hours outside the core.

Flextime is short for flexible work hours. It allows employees some discretion over when they arrive at and leave work. Employees must work a specific number of hours a week, but they are free to vary the hours of work within certain limits. As shown in Exhibit 15-6, each day consists of a common core, usually six hours, with a flexibility band surrounding the core. For example, exclusive of a one-hour lunch break, the core may be 9 a.m. to 3 p.m., with the office actually opening at 6 a.m. and closing at 6 p.m. All employees are required to be at their jobs during the common core period, but they are allowed to accumulate their other two hours before and/or after the core time. Some flextime programs allow extra hours to be accumulated and turned into a free day off each month.

Exhibit 15-6
Example of a Flextime Schedule

Flexible hours	Common core	Lunch	Common core	Flexible hours
6 A.M. 9 A.M.		12 noon 1 P.M.		3 P.M. 6 P.M.

Time during the day

Flextime has become an extremely popular scheduling option, although in Canada women are less likely than men to have flexible work schedules. In 1992, 30 percent of women had flexible work schedules, compared with 40 percent of men.[75] Flextime in the United States is more common. For instance, a recent study of firms with more than 1000 employees found that 53 percent offered employees the option of flextime.[76] Levi Strauss & Co. Canada, the Bank of Montreal, and Toronto-based legal publishers CCH Canadian Ltd. are examples of companies that offer flextime to their workers.

The benefits claimed for flextime are numerous. They include reduced absenteeism, increased productivity, reduced overtime expenses, a lessening in hostility toward management, reduced traffic congestion around work sites, elimination of tardiness, and increased autonomy, and responsibility for employees that may increase employee job satisfaction.[77] But beyond the claims, what's flextime's record?

Most of the performance evidence stacks up favourably. Flextime tends to reduce absenteeism and frequently improves worker productivity,[78] probably for several reasons. Employees can schedule their work hours to align with personal demands, thus reducing tardiness and absences, and employees can adjust their work activities to those hours in which they are individually more productive.

Flextime's major drawback is that it's not applicable to every job. It works well with clerical tasks where an employee's interaction with people outside his or her department is limited. It is not a viable option for receptionists, sales personnel in retail stores, or similar jobs where comprehensive service demands that people be at their work stations at predetermined times.

Job Sharing

job sharing
The practice of having two or more people split a 40-hour-a-week job.

A recent work scheduling innovation is **job sharing**. It allows two or more individuals to split a traditional 40-hour-a-week job. So, for example, one person might perform the job from 8 a.m. to noon, while another performs the same job from 1 p.m. to 5 p.m.; or the two could work full, but alternate, days. In 1995, about 171 000 individuals, or eight percent of all part-time paid workers in Canada, shared a job with someone.[79] Only about 30 percent of large organizations offer this option.[80]

The Royal Bank is one organization that offers job sharing.[81] Kim Bietel handles loans and mortgages in a downtown Regina branch of the bank. She shares her job with another employee. Each employee works one week on, one week off. The two leave notes for each other about the status of loan applications so that each will know what has happened during the week off. Neither employee knew the other when they started the job sharing, but Beitel reports that the arrangement is working well. Calgary-based Phillips Petroleum Resources and Gulf Canada Resources also offer job-sharing arrangements for some of their employees.

From management's standpoint, job sharing allows the organization to draw upon the talents of more than one individual in a given job. A bank manager who oversees two job sharers describes it as an opportunity to get two heads, but "pay for one."[82] It also opens up the opportunity to acquire skilled workers—for instance, women with young children and retirees—who might not be available on a full-time basis. From the employee's perspective, job sharing increases flexibility. As such, it can increase motivation and satisfaction for those for whom a 40-hour-a-week job is just not practical.

Telecommuting

It might be close to the ideal job for many people. No commuting, flexible hours, freedom to dress as you please, and little or no interruptions from colleagues. It's called **telecommuting** and refers to employees who do their work at home or outside the corporate office on a computer that is linked to their office.[83] Telecommuting is on the rise in Canada. In 1988-89, 11 percent of organizations surveyed indicated they offered a work-at-home or telecommuting arrangement with employees. At the end of 1995, that number had increased to 28 percent of companies reporting work-at-home or telecommuting arrangements with employees.[84] Estimates suggest that the number of employees engaging in telecommuting is almost 1.5 million.[85] One projection for the United States predicts that by the year 2000, more than 60 million American workers—about half the workforce—will do some kind of work at home.[86] Employers have been enthusiastic about the concept, claiming it enhances worker productivity, improves the organization's ability to retain valuable employees, and increases employee loyalty.

Brampton, Ontario-based Northern Telecom (Nortel) operates one of the biggest telecommuting programs in Canada.[87] Nearly 30 percent of its workforce telecommutes to some extent. Some, including 60 percent of those in the Ottawa office who telecommute, do so part time, maintaining offices both at home and work. The rest work entirely from home, showing up at the office occasionally for mail. About two-thirds of the telecommuters are male, mostly thirty-somethings. Nortel sets up home offices with regulation office furniture and equipment, makes sure there is a secure computer line connecting the home to the office, and requires telecommuters to attend some meetings and lunches in the office, so that employees can maintain contact. Nortel's telecommuters reported in a recent survey that they were "overwhelmingly happier, less stressed out and more productive than when they used to come to the office."

IBM Canada is another organization whose experience with telecommuting has been very positive.[88] IBM introduced Flexiplace, a program to move employees out of expensive corporate offices and into suburban satellite centres, offices in their own homes, and to customer sites in 1992. When it started, there were 150 trial workers. Less than a year later, that number had grown to 700, of whom 450 worked out of offices in their homes. In some regions, managers are aiming eventually to have 30 percent of sales and marketing staff working from home. IBM is projecting $5.7 million in real estate savings over six years by having their employees work elsewhere. Stentor's 2000-plus employees are spread out across Canada, often based in other companies. A manager located in Vancouver may report to an executive in Montreal, and his or her direct reports may work in Calgary and Toronto. B.C. Tel and Bank of Montreal also have well-developed telecommuting policies. Telecommuters do not always work from home, however. In one B.C. Tel program, for example, workers avoid up to three hours a day commuting to and from downtown Vancouver by reporting for work at a specially established satellite office in suburban Langley nearer their homes. Telecommuting does, however, typically mean that employees are remote from their supervisors.

Telecommuting employees can be very productive. One B.C. Tel employee stationed in the Langley centre found he could handle 25 percent more service calls in a day simply because he was no longer arriving at work tired and stressed from a long rush-hour commute. Furthermore, two order-entry clerks found they could achieve in 3.5 days what they had been doing in five at a

At the Mississauga, Ontario office of Revenue Canada auditors do not have designated work spaces. Instead, they compete for desks on a first-come, first-served basis every day. Revenue Canada's arrangement with its auditors represents *hotelling*.

downtown office because there were fewer interruptions in the Langley office.[89] Telecommuting agents at American Express Travel Services have been equally productive, handling 26 percent more calls at home than at the office.[90] Why? One agent thinks it's due to an absence of distractions: "I don't feel like I'm working any harder. It's just that I don't have Suzy next to me telling me her husband is a jerk. I'm not worried about who's going into the boss's office, or noticing who's heading to the bathroom for the tenth time today."

Not all employees embrace the idea of telecommuting, however. After the massive Los Angeles earthquake in January 1994, many L.A. firms began offering telecommuting for their workers as the city infrastructure underwent repairs.[91] It was popular for a week or two, but the novelty soon faded. Many workers complained they were missing out on important meetings and informal interactions that led to new policies and ideas. The vast majority of employees were willing to put up with two- and three-hour commutes, while bridges and highways were being rebuilt, in order to maintain their social contacts at work.

The long-term future of telecommuting depends on some questions for which we don't yet have definitive answers. For instance, will employees who do their work at home be at a disadvantage in office politics? Might they be less likely to be considered for salary increases and promotions? Is being out of sight equivalent to being out of mind? Will non-work-related distractions such as children, neighbours, and the close proximity of the television and refrigerator significantly reduce productivity for those without superior willpower and discipline? We also do not know the effects on individuals working in somewhat isolated circumstances day after day, if they do most of their work away from the office. Experts agree that home telecommuters in particular should come into the central office at least once a week. At IBM, Flexiplace employees come in on average once or twice a week for group meetings and to pick up mail and faxes.

Hotelling

hotelling
Shared office space, with no individual offices or desks.

One of the latest trends in reducing office space is **hotelling**, where no one "owns" a workspace anymore. Instead, desks, offices and conference rooms are booked for the time required.[92] Most of the employees at the Toronto office of the Deloitte & Touche Consulting Group were stripped of their offices in early 1995. The employees were also told to shred their files, locate them in the central filing system, or take them home. Each employee was then given one or two personal file drawers (depending on rank) for a limited number of files.

In fact, the concept of hotelling is so new to Canada that no statistics are available on its use to date. It is more common in the United States, where it is used in the management-consulting, financial, and high-tech sectors. Often, organizations have extra space in these industries because employees work from home or are on the road. To save building costs, they have moved to hotelling. In Canada, it is frequently used among the smaller and newer boutique advertising agencies, and it is being considered for the federal public service.

Larry Haiven, of the College of Commerce at the University of Saskatchewan, suggests that hotelling, like re-engineering, rightsizing, and

other restructuring techniques "ends up damaging organizations." It also changes the way work is done. For example, at the Mississauga, Ontario, office of Revenue Canada, which has no reservation system in place, 250 auditors compete for desks on a first-come, first-served basis. The results, according to a *Report on Business* article, are "a bullpen of tension, frayed nerves—even fistfights—in a profession not known for excitability." Seventy-five percent of the auditors have filed grievances against Revenue Canada through the collective bargaining process. The resulting tensions and grievances suggest that the auditors may have difficulty performing their jobs effectively. Ralph Herman, a spokesperson for the union that represents the auditors (Professional Institute of the Public Service of Canada), says that hotelling "hurts productivity because it eliminates the informal socializing and learning among employees sitting next to each other."

Michael Brill, a professor of architecture at the University of Buffalo and a leading advocate of hotelling, was advising a hotelling project at the Toronto-North York office of Revenue Canada in late 1997. He claims that "there are no drops in job performance or job satisfaction; there are no increases either. But then, it is not designed to increase job performance or job satisfaction." Actually, its main savings are in overhead costs to firms.

The strategies for work redesign that we've described have already had a profound impact on the ways Canadian perform and think about their jobs. Some even argue that "jobs" as we know them are becoming obsolete—that demands by employers and workers alike for greater flexibility and autonomy will result in the development of a contingent workforce with very little resemblance to jobholders of the past. A critical debate about the future of jobs is set out in this chapter's Point/CountPoint feature.

Professional Institute of the Public Service of Canada
http://www.pipsc.ca/

HR IMPLICATIONS

Performance Appraisals Under Total Quality Management

The effective implementation of TQM requires that employees work together, and develop, with management, systems that help to increase productivity. As a result, the performance of any particular individual is tied more heavily to how the system operates, including other members of the team, as well as whatever processes are installed to aid the quality programs. In fact, W.E. Deming, one of the major writers on TQM, argues that in a TQM system, 85 percent of performance variance across individuals is actually due to the system, and only 15 percent is due to person factors.[1] Ordinary performance evaluation programs that consider the role of the individual as the primary source of performance are not adequate for evaluating individuals working in a more team-based environment.

Deming suggests the elimination of performance appraisal, or at least a reduction in it. How-

ever, many organizations might find that an extreme approach. Because the TQM system that is implemented is largely responsible for differences in outcome, one approach to performance appraisal would be to use it to detect large differences among individuals (i.e., those meeting expectations, those exceeding expectations, and those underperforming).[2] Those who are exceeding expectations could be groomed for promotion and those who were underperforming could receive remedial training or be reassigned. If a company was interested in developing more of its employees, then a finer grading of categories could be used.

When those who work in TQM systems are evaluated, what gets evaluated may well be different from areas covered in the more usual performance appraisal system. (We reviewed regular performance appraisal systems in HR Implications

in Chapter 6.) Team-orientation, flexibility, continuous learning, and organizational citizenship are important characteristics for TQM. It may be especially useful to use self-rating mechanisms under TQM, as the individual in these systems is expected to be more aware of how the system could be improved, and his or her role in that improvement. Rating team effort is similarly important.

Sources:
[1] W.E. Deming, *Out of the Crisis* (Cambridge: MIT Institute for Advanced Engineering Study, 1986).
[2] R. L. Cardy, G. H. Dobbins, and K. P. Carson, "TQM and HRM: Improving Performance Appraisal Research, Theory and Practice," *Canadian Journal of Administrative Sciences*, 12, pp. 106–115.

Summary and Implications

For the Workplace

An understanding of work design can help managers design jobs that positively affect employee motivation. For instance, jobs that score high in motivating potential increase an employee's control over key elements in his or her work. Therefore, jobs that offer autonomy, feedback, and similar complex task characteristics help to satisfy the individual goals of those employees who desire greater control over their work. Of course, consistent with the social information processing model, the perception that task characteristics are complex is probably more important in influencing an employee's motivation than the objective task characteristics themselves. The key, then, is to provide employees with cues that suggest that their jobs score high on factors such as skill variety, task identity, autonomy, and feedback.

Technology is changing people's jobs and their work behaviour. TQM and its emphasis on continuous process improvement can increase employee stress as individuals find that performance expectations are constantly being increased. Re-engineering is eliminating millions of jobs and completely reshaping the jobs of those that remain. Flexible manufacturing systems require employees to learn new skills and accept increased responsibilities. And technology is making many job skills obsolete and shortening the life span of almost all skills—technical, administrative, and managerial.

Alternative work schedule options such as the compressed workweek, shorter workweeks, flextime, job sharing, and telecommuting have grown in popularity in recent years. They have become an important strategic tool as organizations try to increase the flexibility their employees need in a changing workplace.

For You as an Individual

Our discussion on job design gives you some insight into how jobs are arranged in the workplace, both in terms of the tasks done (from very specialized, to being responsible for a variety of tasks) and the arrangement of workplace hours. These are factors that you may want to consider when you begin your job search, as the studies reviewed indicate that job satisfaction is related to types of jobs, as well as the ability to have a flexible schedule.

Should you ever decide to become an entrepreneur, you will have to make decisions about how to allocate tasks to people, and the job characteristics model should give you some indication of the motivation potential of various arrangements. As an entrepreneur, you might also want to consider

what kinds of hours your employees will be assigned if you want to help them manage their jobs and families.

ROADMAP REMINDER

In the previous chapter we examined the structure of organizations: that is, how the different individuals who are employed by the organization are arranged into work units. In this chapter we considered work arrangement at the individual level: what are the tasks that are assigned to each individual employee. Both the structural arrangement and the job design in an organization affect employees' motivation and job satisfaction. In the next chapter we consider the role of organizational culture, which we view as the glue that holds organizations together.

For Review

1. Describe three jobs that score high on the JCM. Describe three jobs that score low.
2. What are the implications of the social information processing model for predicting employee behaviour?
3. What are the implications for employees of a continuous improvement program?
4. What are the implications for employees of a re-engineering program?
5. What are flexible manufacturing systems?
6. What can you do through work design to improve employee performance on teams?
7. What are the advantages of flextime from an employee's perspective? From management's perspective?
8. What are the advantages of job sharing from an employee's perspective? From management's perspective?
9. From an employee's perspective, what are the pros and cons of telecommuting?

For Discussion

1. Re-engineering needs to be autocratically imposed in order to overcome employee resistance. This runs directly counter to the model of a contemporary manager who is a good listener, a coach, motivates through employee involvement, and who possesses strong team support skills. Can these two positions be reconciled?
2. How has technology changed the manager's job over the past 20 years?
3. Would you want a full-time job telecommuting? How do you think most of your friends would feel about such a job? Do you think telecommuting has a future?
4. What can management do to improve employees' perceptions that their jobs are interesting and challenging?
5. What do you expect the effects of telecommuting, job sharing and other work arrangements where employees are less often in the workplace might be on communication in the organization?

LEARNING ABOUT YOURSELF EXERCISE

Is an Enriched Job for You?

INSTRUCTIONS People differ in what they like and dislike in their jobs. Listed below are 12 pairs of jobs. For each pair, indicate which job you would prefer. Assume that everything else about the jobs is the same—pay attention only to the characteristics actually listed for each pair of jobs. If you would prefer the job in Column A, indicate how much you prefer it by putting a checkmark in a blank to the left of the Neutral point. If you prefer the job in Column B, check one of the blanks to the right of Neutral. Check the Neutral blank only if you find the two jobs equally attractive or unattractive. Try to use the Neutral blank rarely.

Column A

Column B

1. A job that offers little or no challenge.

Strongly prefer A   Neutral   Strongly prefer B

A job that requires you to be completely isolated from co-workers.

2. A job that pays well.

Strongly prefer A   Neutral   Strongly prefer B

A job that allows considerable opportunity to be creative and innovative.

3. A job that often requires you to make important decisions.

Strongly prefer A   Neutral   Strongly prefer B

A job in which there are many pleasant people to work with.

4. A job with little security in a somewhat unstable organization.

Strongly prefer A   Neutral   Strongly prefer B

A job in which you have little or no opportunity to participate in decisions that affect your work.

5. A job in which greater responsibility is given to those who do the best work.

Strongly prefer A   Neutral   Strongly prefer B

A job in which greater responsibility is given to loyal employees who have the most *seniority*.

6. A job with a supervisor who sometimes is highly critical.

Strongly prefer A   Neutral   Strongly prefer B

A job that does not require you to use much of your talent.

7. A very routine job.

Strongly prefer A   Neutral   Strongly prefer B

A job in which your co-workers are not very friendly.

8. A job with a supervisor who respects you and treats you fairly.

Strongly prefer A   Neutral   Strongly prefer B

A job that provides constant opportunities for you to learn new and interesting things.

9. A job that gives you a real chance to develop yourself personally.

Strongly prefer A   Neutral   Strongly prefer B

A job with excellent vacation and fringe benefits.

10. A job in which there is a real chance you could be laid off.

Strongly prefer A   Neutral   Strongly prefer B

A job with very little chance to do challenging work.

11. A job with little freedom and independence to do your work in the way you think best.

Strongly prefer A   Neutral   Strongly prefer B

A job with poor working conditions.

12. A job with very satisfying teamwork.

Strongly prefer A   Neutral   Strongly prefer B

A job that allows you to use your skills and abilities to the fullest extent.

Turn to page 701 for scoring directions and key.

Source: J.R. Hackman and G.R. Oldham, *The Job Diagnostic Survey: An Instrument for the Diagnosis of Jobs and the Evaluation of Job Redesign Projects.* Technical Report No. 4 (New Haven, Conn.: Yale University, Department of Administrative Sciences, 1974). Reprinted with permission.

WORKING WITH OTHERS EXERCISE

Analysing and Redesigning Jobs

Break into groups of five to seven members each. Each student should describe the worst job he or she has ever had. Use any criteria you want to select one of these jobs for analysis by the group.

Members of the group will analyse the job selected by determining how well it scores on the job characteristics model. Use the following scale for your analysis of each job dimension:

> 7 = Very high
>
> 6 = High
>
> 5 = Somewhat high
>
> 4 = Moderate
>
> 3 = Somewhat low
>
> 2 = Low
>
> 1 = Very low

Following are sample questions that can guide the group in its analysis of the job in question:

- *Skill variety*: Describe the different identifiable skills required to do this job. What is the nature of the oral, written, and/or quantitative skills needed? Physical skills? Does the jobholder get the opportunity to use all of his or her skills?

- *Task identity*: What is the product that the jobholder creates? Is he or she involved in its production from beginning to end? If not, is he or she involved in a particular phase of its production from beginning to end?

- *Task significance*: How important is the product? How important is the jobholder's role in producing it? How important is the jobholder's contribution to the people he or she works with? If the jobholder's job were eliminated, how inferior would the product be?

- *Autonomy*: How much independence does the jobholder have? Does he or she have to follow a strict schedule? How closely is he or she supervised?

- *Feedback*: Does the jobholder get regular feedback from his or her supervisor? From peers? From subordinates? From customers? How about intrinsic performance feedback when doing the job?

Using the formula in Exhibit 15-3, calculate the job's motivating potential. Then using the suggestions offered in the chapter for redesigning jobs, describe specific actions management could take to increase this job's motivating potential.

Calculate the costs to management of redesigning the job in question. Do the benefits exceed the costs?

Conclude the exercise by having a representative of each group share his or her group's analysis and redesign suggestions with the entire class. Possible topics for class discussion might include: similarities in the jobs chosen, problems in rating job dimensions, and the cost-benefit assessment of design changes.

Source: This exercise is based on W.P. Ferris, "Enlivening the Job Characteristics Model," in C. Harris and C.C. Lundberg, *Proceedings of the 29th Annual Eastern Academy of Management Meeting*; Baltimore, MD; May 1992, pp. 125–28.

CASE INCIDENT

Continuous Improvement through *Kaizen* at Ventra Group

Kaizen is the Japanese term for the techniques of continuous manufacturing improvements. It can include such things as tagging unproductive equipment for removal, colour-coding the shop floor to represent different parts of the manufacturing process, altering routine maintenance on a production line, or moving to just-in-time delivery of parts. In Canadian assembly plants for such Japanese automakers as Honda Motor Co. Ltd., Toyota Motor Corp., and Suzuki Motor Corp., there are clear incentives to adopt *kaizen* techniques.

Cambridge, Ontario-based auto-parts company Ventra Group Inc. has been using *kaizen* techniques since 1988. When it acquired Seeburn, a leading maker of car jacks, there was talk of developing a third plant, because Seeburn was at overcapacity. However, through *kaizen*, the need for a third plant was eliminated. In 1993, Seeburn had $45 million in annual sales, but *kaizen* allowed it to move to $70 million in 1995, with room for another $30 million, without having to build a new plant.

Former president Frank Legate brought more *kaizen* culture to Ventra's Chatham, Ontario plastics plant after the plant lost a big contract to supply Ford's Mustang with taillight lenses in spring 1995. The contract had accounted for about 25 percent of the plant's output. Significant layoffs resulted when the contract was lost. "The loss of the Mustang contract is an incentive to make change to the organization. It highlights to people if we don't do things right, this is what the customer is going to do to us. Our jobs are at risk," noted Legate at the time. One major *kaizen* improvement was freeing up 900 square metres of space and reducing the need for a costly warehouse. To do this, hourly workers attached a red tag to every piece of equipment they felt was not needed. Management then took action, based on the red tags.

The next *kaizen* activity is to improve the Chatham plant's layout. Gary Nettleton, the plant's manufacturing manager, believes this will increase productivity significantly. He estimates that his hourly workers waste about 75 percent of their work time on such things as "getting presses ready for production runs, moving tools between presses and double handling of material." In other words, workers are preparing to work, rather than working.

The adjustment to kaizen procedures is not completely smooth, however. Plant manager Steve Hackney notes that "the problem is that the plant is 60 percent different on Thursday than Monday. The rate of change is schizophrenic here. There are just too many things to do in a day." Hackney at least tries to adjust to the changes. He reports that some of the hourly workers resist change at all costs, calling them hardliners. Legate, however, doesn't view the hardliners as a problem.

"The hardliners are the most valuable. On the face of it, they're the most negative, but their bitches are really suggestions. The trick is to harness those suggestions."

Questions

1. Identify the *kaizen* activities at Ventra. Would you have expected them to be as successful as they appear to have been?

2. What do you think it would be like to work in a plant that was engaged in "a continuous improvement process"?

3. Why might some of the "hardliners" be resistant to the changes going on at Ventra?

Source: "The Kaizen Advantage: Japanese Term for the Unglamorous Techniques You Use to Get Continuous Manufacturing Improvements," *Financial Post*, October 21/23, 1995, pp. 10–11; "Performance 500 Top 10," *Canadian Business 500*, June 1997, pp. 137–146.

Hold Those Phones

Dread that telemarketing call that interrupts your dinner? Imagine working for a telemarketing firm, sitting in a room all evening with a large number of people who are all making the same phone calls across the country.

Telemarketing is the new assembly-line job—highly routinized, very little worker flexibility, specific expectations for hourly production. It is also a growing business in Canada, where there are more than 6000 of these centres. Provincial governments often view them as key job creators rather than places for low-skilled labour. For instance, New Brunswick has had 43 calling centres open there since 1992, creating 6000 new jobs in a province with a workforce of 315 000.

Sitel Corporation's telemarketing campaign for Tracker Corporation shows just what a telemarketer does. The job starts with learning the script for the product. Telephone service representatives (TSRs) undergo rigorous training to get the script right, practising with each other possible responses to a contact's refusals to listen to the sales pitch. During the three-hour calling session, managers try to motivate the TSRs through encouragement, back rubs, and even little contests where they can earn $10 bonuses for making the first sale of the time period.

The training can be demoralizing, however. One TSR shows fatigue and dismay at not being able to field all of the negative responses given by her role-playing partner. The TSRs are also carefully monitored. A computer tracks the number of calls they've made, the number of sales, and both the client and managers have ready access to this information. TSRs are told their sales goals, and those of Sitel were expected to make three sales per hour. After three days, however, they were averaging closer to one sale per hour. On the fourth day of the Tracker project, four of six TSRs called in sick.

So, the next time you pick up the phone and hear a sales pitch, imagine the telemarketer and his or her job conditions.

Questions

1. Describe the job design of telemarketing work.

2. How might you improve the working conditions of the telemarketer without doing a complete job redesign?

3. How would you use the Hackman-Oldham model to propose a possible redesign of the telemarketer's job? How might your proposed design affect sales?

Source: Based on "Telemarketing," *Venture 584*; aired March 31, 1996; see **http://www.tv.cbc.ca/venture/ archives/telemarketing_960331/two.html** for a CBC case presentation.

POINT

The Notion of Jobs Is Becoming Obsolete

Prior to 1800, very few people had a job. People worked hard raising food or making things at home. They had no regular hours, no job descriptions, no bosses, and no employee benefits. Instead, they put in long hours on shifting clusters of tasks, in a variety of locations, on a schedule set by the sun and the weather and the needs of the day. It was the industrial revolution and the creation of large manufacturing companies that brought about the concept of what we have come to think of as *jobs*. But the conditions that created "the job" are disappearing. Customized production is pushing out mass production; most workers now handle information, not physical products; and competitive conditions are demanding rapid response to changing markets. Although economists and social analysts continue to talk about the disappearance of jobs in certain countries or industries, they're missing a more relevant point: What's actually disappearing is *the job itself*.

In a fast-moving economy, jobs are rigid solutions to an elastic problem. We can rewrite a person's job description occasionally, but not every week. When the work that needs doing changes constantly—which increasingly describes today's world—organizations can't afford the inflexibility that traditional jobs bring with it.

In the near future, very few people will have jobs as we have come to know them. In place of jobs, there will be part-time and temporary work situations. Organizations will be transformed from a structure built out of jobs into a field of work needing to be done. These organizations will be essentially made up of "hired guns"—contingent employees (temporaries, part-timers, consultants, and contract workers) who join project teams created to complete a specific task. When that task is finished, the team disbands. People will work on more than one team at a time, keeping irregular hours, and maybe never meeting their co-workers face-to-face. Computers, pagers, cellular phones, modems, and the like will allow people to work for multiple employers, at the same time, in locations throughout the world. Few of these employees will be working nine to five at specific work spots, and they'll have little of the security that their grandfathers had, who worked for IBM Canada, MacMillan Bloedel, General Motors, Sears, Bank of Montreal, or similar large bureaucracies. In place of security and predictability, they'll have flexibility and autonomy. They'll be able to put together their own place-time combinations to support their diverse work, family, lifestyle, and financial needs. ■

Source: This argument is based on W. Bridges, *JobShift* (Reading, MA: Addison-Wesley, 1994).

counterPOINT

Jobs Are the Essence of Organizational Life

The central core to any discussion of work or organizational behaviour is the concept of a job. It is the aggregation of tasks that defines an individual's duties and responsibilities.

When an organization is created, managers have to determine what tasks need to be accomplished for the organization to achieve its goals and who will perform those tasks. These decisions precede the hiring of a workforce. Remember, it's the tasks that determine the need for people, not the other way around. Job analysis is the formal process managers use to define the jobs within the organization and the behaviours that are necessary to perform those jobs. For instance, what are the duties of a purchasing specialist, grade 3, who works for International Paper? What minimal knowledge, skills, and abilities are necessary for adequate performance of a grade 3 purchasing specialist's job? How do the requirements for a purchasing specialist, grade 3, compare with those for a purchasing specialist, grade 2, or a purchasing analyst? These are questions that job analysis can answer.

Can you conceive of an organization without jobs? No more than you can conceive of a car without an engine. There are no doubt changes taking place in organizations that are requiring managers to redefine what a job is. For instance, today's jobs often include extensive customer interaction as well as team responsibilities. In many cases, organizations are having to make job descriptions more flexible to reflect the more dynamic nature of work today. Because it's inefficient to rewrite job descriptions on a weekly basis, managers are rethinking what makes up a job and defining jobs in more fluid terms. But the concept of jobs continues to be at the core of any work design effort and a fundamental cornerstone to understanding formal work behaviour in organizations.

For those who believe that the concept of jobs is on the wane, all they need to do is look to the trade union movement and its determination to maintain clear job delineations. Labour unions have a vested interest in the status quo and will fight hard to protect the security and predictability that traditional jobs provide. Moreover, if it looked like the jobless society was to become a widespread reality, politicians would be under strong pressure to create legislation to outlaw it. A world of part-time and temporary employment is a threat to the stability of our society. Working people want stability and predictability, and they will look to their elected representatives to protect that. Those politicians who ignore this desire face the wrath of the electorate. ■

CHAPTER 16

Organizational Culture

ROADMAP

LEARNING OBJECTIVES

After studying this chapter, you should be able to

- Describe institutionalization and its relationship to organizational culture

- Define the common characteristics making up organizational culture

- Contrast strong and weak cultures

- Identify the functional and dysfunctional effects of organizational culture on people and the organization

- Explain the factors determining an organization's culture

- List the factors that maintain an organization's culture

- Clarify how culture is transmitted to employees

- Outline the various socialization alternatives available to management

From Mazda Motor Corp.'s Hiroshima headquarters, its president is trying to change his company's corporate culture.[1] Henry Wallace (see photo) has his work cut out for him. Mazda's internal culture closely mirrors Japan's national culture. The company values indirect communication, loyalty, obedience, and relationships. Wallace believes that these cultural values, which worked in the company's favour in the postwar years, are outdated in the current, highly competitive, global economy. He was brought in by Ford Motor Co., which owns a controlling interest in Mazda, in the spring of 1996 to turn around declining sales and return Mazda to profitability. In 1995, Mazda made only 771 000 cars, half the number it made in 1990.

Wallace, a gangly Scot, stands out like a sore thumb in Japan. As the only foreigner running a Japanese company of any size, he is both a celebrity and a curiosity. His outsider status provides him both advantages and disadvantages. Since foreigners are always expected to act differently, he is given more leeway in introducing non-Japanese practices at Mazda. However, he lacks fluency in Japanese, and many Mazda employees believe Wallace just doesn't understand the unique culture of Mazda.

Wallace faces an organizational culture where people are afraid to speak up in meetings and where employees and parts suppliers are set for life. Wallace wants to change this. He has transformed carefully staged meetings into freewheeling brainstorming sessions. He expects people to ask questions and to challenge ideas. He has forced Mazda staff members to use more marketing data to back up new product proposals. He's injecting more English, the international business language, into the company. Although he hasn't laid off any employees yet, he talks about it as a possibility, and that's raising concerns throughout the company. But one of his biggest challenges is breaking up Japan's traditional system of long-time, family-like relationships with suppliers. Hundreds of suppliers receive blueprints from Mazda and build parts to company specifications. Wallace wants to reduce the number of suppliers that Mazda works with and increase competition among those remaining. ■

Mazda Motor Corp.
http://www.mazda.com/

Mazda has what we could call a strong organizational culture. The culture provides employees with a clear understanding of "the way things are done around here." It provides stability to an organization, but, as evidenced at Mazda, it can also be a major barrier to change. Culture sets the tone for how organizations operate and how individuals within the organization interact. You may have noticed in stopping at the main reception desk at a large organization that in some places you are told "Ms. Dettweiler" will be with you in a moment, while at another organization, the receptionist will tell you that "Emma" will be available as soon as she gets off the phone. These two ways of referring to individuals convey different meanings to you—in one organization the rules are more formal than the other.

Because culture sets the tone for how people interact within the organization, it also has an impact on the employees who work for the firm. Thus, as you start to think about different organizations where you might work, you will want to think about their cultures. An organization that has a culture where employees are expected to work 15 hours a day may not be one in which you would like to work. For instance, Steve Jobs recently reported that Apple is now back to its "old self," with cars in the parking lot late at night and on weekends. An understanding of culture might help you discover that before you accept a job.

In this chapter we show that every organization has a culture. We examine how that culture is manifested and the impact it has on the attitudes and behaviours of members of organizations. To help you think more about culture and its impact on you, you may want to complete the Learning About Yourself exercise for this chapter, which assesses the extent to which you would be more comfortable in either a formal, rule-oriented culture or a more informal, flexible culture.

Institutionalization: A Forerunner of Culture

The idea of viewing organizations as cultures—where there is a system of shared meaning among members—is a relatively recent phenomenon. Until the mid-1980s, organizations were, for the most part, simply thought of as rational means by which to coordinate and control a group of people. They had vertical levels, departments, authority relationships, and so forth, but organizations are more than this. They have personalities too, just like individuals. They can be rigid or flexible, unfriendly or supportive, innovative or conservative. For example, Bombardier's offices and people *are* different from the offices and people at MacMillan Bloedel. The University of Western Ontario's Richard Ivey School of Business and the University of British Columbia's Faculty of Commerce are in the same business—education—but each has a unique feeling and character beyond its structural characteristics. Organizational theorists now acknowledge this by recognizing the important role that culture plays in the lives of organization members. Interestingly, though, the origin of culture as an independent variable affecting an employee's attitudes and behaviour can be traced back 50 years ago to the notion of **institutionalization**.[2]

institutionalization
The process whereby an organization takes on a life of its own, apart from any of its members, and acquires immortality.

When an organization becomes institutionalized, it takes on a life of its own, apart from its founders or any of its members. For example, Disney Corporation founder Walt Disney died in 1966, but the company has continued to thrive despite his death. Birks, the Hudson's Bay Corporation, and Sony Canada are examples of organizations that have existed beyond the life of any one member. Additionally, when an organization becomes institution-

alized, it becomes valued for itself, not merely for the goods or services it produces. It acquires immortality. If its original goals are no longer relevant, it doesn't go out of business. Rather, it redefines itself. For example, when the demand for Timex's watches declined, the company merely redirected itself into the consumer electronics business—making, in addition to watches, clocks, computers, and health-care products such as digital thermometers and blood-pressure testing devices. Timex took on an existence that went beyond its original mission to manufacture low-cost mechanical watches.

Institutionalization operates to produce common understandings among members about what is appropriate and fundamentally meaningful behaviour.[3] So when an organization takes on institutional permanence, acceptable modes of behaviour become largely self-evident to its members. As we'll see, this is essentially the same thing that organizational culture does. An understanding of what makes up an organization's culture and how it is created, sustained, and learned will enhance our ability to explain and predict the behaviour of people at work.

Timex
http://www.timex.com/

What Is Organizational Culture?

When Henry Mintzberg, professor at McGill University, was asked to compare organizational structure and corporate culture, he said: "Culture is the soul of the organization—the beliefs and values, and how they are manifested. I think of the structure as the skeleton, and as the flesh and blood. And culture is the soul that holds the thing together and gives it life force."[4] Mintzberg's culture metaphor provides a clear image of how to think about culture. We will add a basic definition to help us better understand the phenomenon. In this section, we propose a specific definition and review several peripheral issues that revolve around this definition.

A Definition

organizational culture
A system of shared meaning and common perception held by members of an organization that distinguishes it from other organizations.

There seems to be wide agreement that **organizational culture** refers to a system of shared meaning held by members that distinguishes the organization from other organizations.[5] This system of shared meaning is, on closer examination, a set of key characteristics that the organization values. The most recent research suggests that seven primary characteristics, in aggregate, capture the essence of an organization's culture.[6]

- *Innovation and risk taking*: The degree to which employees are encouraged to be innovative and take risks.
- *Attention to detail*: The degree to which employees are expected to exhibit precision, analysis, and attention to detail.
- *Outcome orientation*: The degree to which management focuses on results or outcomes rather than on the techniques and processes used to achieve these outcomes.
- *People orientation*: The degree to which management decisions take into consideration the effect of outcomes on people within the organization.
- *Team orientation*: The degree to which work activities are organized around teams rather than individuals.
- *Aggressiveness*: The degree to which people are aggressive and competitive rather than easygoing.

A people orientation is a key characteristic that captures the essence of Birkenstock Footwear's organizational culture. Birkenstock's management supports employees' desires to participate in causes they believe in. When employees wanted to heighten the company's environmental consciousness, management responded by allowing them to spend an hour each week working on environmental projects and gave them the resources to develop an in-house environmental library, compile a guide to non-toxic resources, and organize monthly meetings with other businesses to share ideas on conservation products and issues.

- *Stability*: The degree to which organizational activities emphasize maintaining the status quo in contrast to growth.

Each of these characteristics exists on a continuum from low to high. Appraising the organization on these seven characteristics, then, gives a composite picture of the organization's culture. This picture becomes the basis for feelings of shared understanding that members have about the organization, how things are done in it, and the way members are supposed to behave. Exhibit 16-1 demonstrates how these characteristics can be mixed to create highly diverse organizations. To help you understand some of the characteristics of culture, you may want to look at the Working With Others exercise, which asks you to rate your classroom culture. This chapter's From Concepts to Skills feature gives you additional information about how to read an organization's culture.

Culture Is a Descriptive Term

Organizational culture is concerned with how employees perceive the characteristics of an organization's culture, not with whether they like them. That is, it is a descriptive term. This is important because it differentiates this concept from that of job satisfaction.

Research on organizational culture has sought to measure how employees view their organization: Does it encourage teamwork? Does it reward innovation? Does it stifle initiative?

In contrast, job satisfaction seeks to measure affective responses to the work environment. It is concerned with how employees feel about the organization's expectations, reward practices, and the like. Although the two terms undoubtedly have overlapping characteristics, keep in mind that the term *organizational culture* is descriptive, while *job satisfaction* is evaluative.

Do Organizations Have Uniform Cultures?

Organizational culture represents a common perception held by the organization's members. This was made explicit when we defined culture as a system of *shared* meaning. We should expect, therefore, that individuals with different backgrounds or at different levels in the organization will tend to describe the organization's culture in similar terms.[7]

Acknowledgment that organizational culture has common properties does not mean, however, that there cannot be subcultures within any given culture. Most large organizations have a dominant culture and numerous sets of subcultures.[8]

A **dominant culture** expresses the core values that are shared by a majority of the organization's members. When we talk about an *organization's* culture, we are referring to its dominant culture. It is this macro view of culture that gives an organization its distinct personality.[9] **Subcultures** tend to develop in large organizations to reflect common problems, situations, or

dominant culture
A system of shared meaning that expresses the core values shared by a majority of the organization's members.

subcultures
Minicultures within an organization, typically defined by department designations and geographical separation.

FROM CONCEPTS TO SKILLS

How to "Read" an Organization's Culture

The ability to read and assess an organization's culture can be a valuable skill. If you're looking for a job, you'll want to choose an employer whose culture is compatible with your values and in which you'll feel comfortable. If you can accurately assess a prospective employer's culture before you make your decision, you may be able to save yourself a lot of grief and reduce the likelihood of making a poor choice. Similarly, you'll undoubtedly have business transactions with numerous organizations during your professional career. You'll be trying to sell a product or service, negotiate a contract, arrange a joint venture, or merely be seeking out which individual in an organization controls certain decisions. The ability to assess another organization's culture can be a definite plus in successfully completing these pursuits.

For the sake of simplicity, we'll approach the problem of reading an organization's culture from that of a job applicant. We'll assume you're interviewing for a job. Here's a list of things you can do to help learn about a potential employer's culture:

- Observe the physical surroundings. Pay attention to signs, pictures, style of dress, length of hair, degree of openness between offices, and office furnishings and arrangements.
- With whom did you meet? Just the person who would be your immediate supervisor? Or potential colleagues, managers from other departments, or senior executives? And based on what they revealed, to what degree do people other than the immediate supervisor have input to the hiring decision?
- How would you characterize the style of the people you met? Formal? Casual? Serious? Jovial?
- Does the organization have formal rules and regulations printed in a personnel policy manual? If so, how detailed are these policies?
- Ask questions of the people with whom you meet. The most valid and reliable information tends to come from asking the same

questions of many people (to see how closely their responses align) and by talking with boundary spanners. Boundary spanners are employees whose work links them to the external environment and includes jobs such as human resources interviewer, salesperson, purchasing agent, labour negotiator, public relations specialist, and company lawyer. Questions that will give you insights into organizational processes and practices might include:

- What is the background of the founders?
- What is the background of current senior managers? What are their functional specializations? Were they promoted from within or hired from outside?
- How does the organization integrate new employees? Is there an orientation program? Training? If so, could you describe these features?
- How does your boss define his or her job success? (Amount of profit? Serving customers? Meeting deadlines? Acquiring budget increases?)
- How would you define fairness in terms of reward allocations?
- Can you identify some people here who are on the "fast track"? What do you think has put them on the fast track?
- Can you identify someone who seems to be considered a deviant in the organization? How has the organization responded to this person?
- Can you describe a decision that someone made here that was well received?
- Can you describe a decision that didn't work out well? What were the consequences for the decision-maker?
- Could you describe a crisis or critical event that has occurred recently in the organization? How did top management respond? What was learned from this experience?

Source: See N.J. Adler, *International Dimensions of Organizational Behaviour*, 2nd ed. (Boston: PWS–Kent Publishing, 1991), pp. 58–60.

Exhibit 16-1
Contrasting Organizational Cultures

Organization A

This organization is a manufacturing firm. Managers are expected to fully document all decisions; and "good managers" are those who can provide detailed data to support their recommendations. Creative decisions that incur significant change or risk are not encouraged. Because managers of failed projects are openly criticized and penalized, they try not to implement ideas that deviate much from the status quo. One lower-level manager quoted an often used phrase in the company: "If it ain't broke, don't fix it."

There are extensive rules and regulations in this firm that employees are required to follow. Managers supervise employees closely to ensure there are no deviations. Management is concerned with high productivity, regardless of the impact on employee morale or turnover.

Work activities are designed around individuals. There are distinct departments and lines of authority, and employees are expected to minimize formal contact with other employees outside their functional area or line of command. Performance evaluations and rewards emphasize individual effort, although seniority tends to be the primary factor in the determination of pay raises and promotions.

Organization B

This organization is also a manufacturing firm. Here, however, management encourages and rewards risk taking and change. Decisions based on intuition are valued as much as those that are well rationalized. Management prides itself on its history of experimenting with new technologies and its success in regularly introducing innovative products. Managers or employees who have a good idea are encouraged to "run with it," and failures are treated as "learning experiences." The company prides itself on being market driven and rapidly responsive to the changing needs of its customers.

There are few rules and regulations for employees to follow, and supervision is loose because management believes that its employees are hardworking and trust-worthy. Management is concerned with high productivity, but believes that this comes through treating its people right. The company is proud of its reputation as being a good place to work.

Job activities are designed around work teams and team members are encouraged to interact with people across functions and authority levels. Employees talk positively about the competition between teams. Individuals and teams have goals, and bonuses are based on achievement of these outcomes. Employees are given considerable autonomy in choosing the means by which the goals are attained.

---

core values
The primary or dominant values that are accepted throughout the organization.

experiences that members face. These subcultures are likely to be defined by department designations and geographical separation. The purchasing department, for example, can have a subculture that is uniquely shared by members of that department. It will include the **core values** of the dominant culture plus additional values unique to members of the purchasing department. Similarly, an office or unit of the organization that is physically separated from the organization's main operations may take on a different personality. Again, the core values are essentially retained but modified to reflect the separated unit's distinct situation. If organizations had no dominant culture and were composed only of numerous subcultures, the value of organizational culture as an independent variable would be significantly less-

ened because there would be no uniform interpretation of what represented appropriate and inappropriate behaviour. It is the "shared meaning" aspect of culture that makes it such a potent device for guiding and shaping behaviour. But we cannot ignore the reality that many organizations also have subcultures that can influence the behaviour of members.

Strong versus Weak Cultures

It has become increasingly popular to differentiate between strong and weak cultures.[10] The argument here is that strong cultures have a greater impact on employee behaviour and are more directly related to reduced turnover.

strong cultures
Cultures where the core values are intensely held and widely shared.

In a **strong culture**, the organization's core values are both intensely held and widely shared.[11] The more members who accept the core values and the greater their commitment to those values is, the stronger the culture is. Consistent with this definition, a strong culture will have a great influence on the behaviour of its members because the high degree of sharedness and intensity creates an internal climate of high behavioural control. For example, Seattle-based retailer Nordstrom has developed one of the strongest service cultures in the retailing industry. Nordstrom employees know what is expected of them and these expectations go a long way in shaping their behaviour.

Nordstrom
www.nordstrom-pta.com/

St. Joseph's Printing, located in Concord, Ontario, and one of the fastest-growing printing companies in Canada, illustrates some benefits of strong culture. St. Joseph's culture is strongly family-oriented (it's been owned by the Gagliano family for 40 years), and also emphasizes learning by encouraging employees to "play" with the new equipment. These aspects of the culture translate into employee enthusiasm. For example, when the company introduced its new press in 1997 (only the second of its type installed in Canada at that time), employees had it up to speed three months ahead of what management had expected.[12]

One specific result of a strong culture should be lower employee turnover. A strong culture demonstrates high agreement among members about what the organization stands for. Such unanimity of purpose builds cohesiveness, loyalty, and organizational commitment. These qualities, in turn, lessen employees' propensity to leave the organization.[13] This chapter's HR Implications feature illustrates specific types of strong cultures, including a family-friendly culture, a culture of diversity, and a culture of innovation.

Culture versus Formalization

A strong organizational culture increases behavioural consistency. In this sense, we should recognize that a strong culture can act as a substitute for formalization.

In Chapter 14, we discussed how formalization's rules and regulations act to regulate employee behaviour. High formalization in an organization creates predictability, orderliness, and consistency. Our point is that a strong culture achieves the same end without the need for written documentation. Therefore, we should view formalization and culture as two different roads to a common destination. The stronger an organization's culture, the less management need be concerned with developing formal rules and regulations to guide employee behaviour. Those guides will be internalized in employees when they accept the organization's culture. MGI Packers Inc. in

Japan's electronic giant Matsushita Electric Company recognizes that national culture has a greater impact on employees than does organizational culture. Matsushita tries to accommodate national cultural values in managing its 150 plants in 38 countries throughout Southeast Asia, North America, Europe, the Middle East, Latin America, and Africa. At its plants in Malaysia, the company offers special ethnic food in its cafeterias for Muslim Malays, Chinese, and Indian employees and accommodates Muslim religious customs by providing special prayer rooms at each plant and allowing two prayer sessions per shift.

Islamic Society of North America
http://www.isna.net/

Matsushita Electric Company
http://www.panasonic.co.jp/

Kitchener, Ontario, illustrates how a strong organizational culture can be used to communicate the internal values of a firm to the external world. MGI, which is owned by four non-Muslims, exports *halal* (food prepared according to the rules of the Koran) beef to the Muslim world from Egypt to Indonesia. To prepare *halal* meat, MGI must ensure that animals are killed according to Islamic law, which means it must be done without anger or violence, and showing compassion for the life that is ending. The Islamic Society of North America is responsible for certifying meat as *halal*. When the society's director for Canadian operations, Mohammad Ashraf, was asked if he ever conducts surprise inspections of MGI's plant to ensure compliance with Islamic slaughtering rules, Ashraf replied that the non-Muslim owners seemed like honest people, and he believed he could rely on MGI's Muslim employees to alert him to problems at the plant. Ashraf's confidence arises from MGI's strong cultural norms for providing a quality product to the Muslim community.[14]

Organizational Culture versus National Culture

We opened this chapter by describing the challenges facing Mazda's new president as he tries to change Mazda's organizational culture. But we also saw how Japan's national culture was closely intertwined with Mazda's corporate culture. Throughout this book we've argued that national differences—that is, national cultures—must be taken into account if accurate predictions are to be made about organizational behaviour in different countries. It seems appropriate at this point, then, to ask the question: Does national culture override an organization's culture? Is an IBM facility in Germany, for example, more likely to reflect German ethnic culture or IBM's corporate culture?

The research indicates that national culture has a greater impact on employees than does their organization's culture.[15] German employees at an IBM facility in Munich, therefore, will be influenced more by German culture than by IBM's culture. These findings, incidentally, are consistent with what the new president at Mazda found—that Japan's national culture has strongly shaped this company's organizational culture, and that Japanese employees resist Ford-type cultural values. Our conclusion: as influential as organizational culture is to understanding the behaviour of people at work, national culture is even more so.

The preceding conclusion must be further qualified to reflect the self-selection that goes on at the hiring stage. IBM, for example, may be less concerned with hiring the "typical Italian" for its Italian operations than in hiring an Italian who fits within the IBM way of doing things.[16] Historically, Italians who have a high need for autonomy are more likely to go to Olivetti than IBM. Why? Olivetti's organizational culture is informal and nonstructured. It has tended to allow employees considerably more freedom than IBM does.[17] In fact, Olivetti seeks to hire individuals who are impatient, risk taking, and innovative—qualities in job candidates that IBM's Italian operations historically sought to exclude in new hires.

Some organizations do try to import organizational cultures from other countries, however. A number of elements of Japanese organizational culture, including *keiretsu* (where companies form partnerships with one another, rather than strictly hierarchical relationships) and *kaizen*, have been introduced in North America. In mainland China, Zhang Ruimin, president and chair of Haier Group, the state-owned maker of white goods such as towels and sheets, stands out as one of the few managers to receive star status in a country that tends to celebrate the proletariat rather than management. He has been importing culture. "From the Japanese, we have learned about teamwork and the Americans have shown how to encourage innovation, creativity."[18]

Haier Group
http://www.haier.com/

What Does Culture Do?

We've alluded to organizational culture's impact on behaviour. We've also explicitly argued that a strong culture should be associated with reduced turnover. In this section, we will more carefully review the functions that culture performs and assess whether culture can be a liability for an organization.

Culture's Functions

Culture performs a number of functions within an organization. First, it has a boundary-defining role; that is, it creates distinctions between one organization and others. Second, it conveys a sense of identity for organization members. Third, culture facilitates the generation of commitment to something larger than one's individual self-interest. Fourth, it enhances social-system stability. Culture is the social glue that helps to hold the organization together by providing appropriate standards for what employees should say and do. Finally, culture serves as a sense-making and control mechanism that guides and shapes the attitudes and behaviour of employees. It is this last function that is of particular interest to us.[19] As the following quotation makes clear, culture defines the rules of the game:

> Culture by definition is elusive, intangible, implicit, and taken for granted. But every organization develops a core set of assumptions, understandings, and implicit rules that govern day-to-day behaviour in the workplace. . . . Until newcomers learn the rules, they are not accepted as full-fledged members of the organization. Transgressions of the rules on the part of high-level executives or front-line employees result in universal disapproval and powerful penalties. Conformity to the rules becomes the primary basis for reward and upward mobility.[20]

The role of culture in influencing employee behaviour appears to be increasingly important in the 1990s.[21] As organizations have widened spans of control, flattened structures, introduced teams, reduced formalization, and empowered employees, the *shared meaning* provided by a strong culture ensures that everyone is pointed in the same direction. Geoffrey Relph, IBM's director of services marketing compared the culture of his previous company (G.E. Appliances in Louisville, Kentucky) with IBM Canada: "The priorities in G.E. are: 'Make the financial commitments. Make the financial commitments. Make the financial commitments.' At IBM, the company's attention is divided among customer satisfaction, employee morale, and positive financial results."[22] These two cultures give employees and managers different messages about where they should direct their attention.

Culture can also influence people's ethical behaviour. When lower-level employees see their managers padding expense reports, this sends a signal that the firm tolerates this dishonest behaviour. As another example, firms that emphasize individual sales records may encourage unhealthy competition among sales staff, including "misplacing" phone messages, and not being helpful to someone else's client. Toronto-based Griffiths McBurney & Partners, on the other hand, emphasizes a teamwork culture. Founding partner Brad Griffith notes that "the corporate culture is to make an environment where everybody feels they're involved. We want to be successful, but not at the expense of the individual."[23] (For further discussion of the effect of culture on ethical behaviour, see this chapter's Ethical Dilemma exercise, "Cultural Factors and Unethical Behaviour.")

As we show later in this chapter, who receives a job offer to join the organization, who is appraised as a high performer, and who gets the promotion are strongly influenced by the individual–organization "fit"—that is, whether the applicant or employee's attitudes and behaviour are compatible with the culture.

Culture as a Liability

We are treating culture in a nonjudgmental manner. We haven't said that it's good or bad, only that it exists. Many of its functions, as outlined, are valuable for both the organization and the employee. Culture enhances organizational commitment and increases the consistency of employee behaviour. These are clearly benefits to an organization. From an employee's standpoint, culture is valuable because it reduces ambiguity. It tells employees how things are done and what's important. However, we shouldn't ignore the potentially dysfunctional aspects of culture, especially a strong one, on an organization's effectiveness.

BARRIER TO CHANGE Culture is a liability when the shared values are not in agreement with those that will further the organization's effectiveness. This is most likely to occur when the organization's environment is dynamic. When the environment is undergoing rapid change, the organization's entrenched culture may no longer be appropriate. Consistency of behaviour is an asset to an organization when it faces a stable environment. However, it may burden the organization and make it difficult to respond to changes in the environment. For many organizations with strong cultures, practices that led to previous successes can lead to failure when those practices no longer match up well with environmental needs.[24] The difficulties of cultural change at Canada Post are discussed in detail in this chapter's Case Incident.

In the examples below we look at how cultural change has been implemented at Ontario Hydro and MacMillan Bloedel.

Former Hydro president Allan Kupcis described how Ontario Hydro's nuclear division went from one of the best nuclear divisions in the world in the 1970s and 1980s to being declared as operating at a minimally acceptable level in 1997.[25] "The problems in Ontario Hydro's nuclear division began when nuclear-plant workers started believing they were the best in the world and became complacent. Back in the 1970s and 1980s, our CANDU system was unique in the world and Hydro was continually setting records for nuclear efficiency. But when people stop looking outside to see what others are doing in terms of getting better, you tend to forget that the target is raised every time someone sets a record."

When Tom Stephens arrived to take over as CEO of troubled MacMillan Bloedel in late 1997, he was faced with a company that hadn't generated a free cash flow in 10 years and whose stock had underperformed in the market for 20 years.[26] The firm was clearly in need of a culture change. Stephens was appalled by the opulence of the company's Vancouver headquarters. In his own office, there is a glass-topped cathedral ceiling that rises for three storeys over his head. To him, this was symbolic of the company not facing the reality of hard times. He received further confirmation of this as he met with various managers to find out what they were doing and why. Repeatedly he ended up telling them, "That hasn't worked for 10 years, so why do you believe that?" Stephens has a tough job of culture change ahead of him: "In the past 30 years, MacMillan Bloedel has beaten every CEO who has tried to tame it." Stephens may have had some early success in his attempt to change the culture, however. In June 1998, MacBlo announced a plan to phase out clearcutting. The company will also restrict harvesting in old-growth forests.

BARRIER TO DIVERSITY Hiring new employees who, because of race, gender, ethnic, or other differences, are not like the majority of the organization's members creates a paradox.[27] Management wants new employees to accept the organization's core cultural values. Otherwise, these employees are unlikely to fit in or be accepted. But at the same time, management wants to openly acknowledge and demonstrate support for the differences that these employees bring to the workplace.

Strong cultures put considerable pressure on employees to conform. They limit the range of values and styles that are acceptable. It's not a coincidence that employees at Disney theme parks appear to be almost universally attractive, clean, and wholesome looking, with bright smiles. That's the image Disney seeks. The company selects employees who will maintain that image. And once on the job, a strong culture, supported by formal rules and regulations, ensures that Disney theme-park employees will act in a relatively uniform and predictable way.

A strong culture that condones prejudice can even undermine formal corporate diversity policies. A recent example is the Texaco case in the United States, where senior managers made disparaging remarks about minorities and, as a result of legal action on behalf of 1400 employees, paid a settlement of $246 million.[28] Organizations seek out and hire diverse individuals because of the alternative strengths that these people bring to the workplace. Yet these diverse behaviours and strengths are likely to diminish in strong cultures as people attempt to fit in. Strong cultures, therefore, can be liabilities when they effectively eliminate those unique strengths that

people of different backgrounds bring to the organization. Moreover, strong cultures can also be liabilities when they support institutional bias or become insensitive to people who are different.

BARRIER TO MERGERS AND ACQUISITIONS Historically, the key factors that management looked at in making merger or acquisition decisions were related to financial advantages or product synergy. In recent years, cultural compatibility has become the primary concern.[29] While a favourable financial statement or product line may be the initial attraction of an acquisition candidate, whether the acquisition actually works seems to have more to do with how well the two organizations' cultures match up.

A number of mergers consummated in the 1990s already have failed or show signs of failing. And the primary cause is conflicting organizational cultures.[30] For instance, many Canadian banks are dealing with culture problems these days. After deregulation in 1987, most of the chartered banks bought large brokerage firms: Royal Bank of Canada acquired Dominion Securities Inc.; Bank of Montreal has Nesbitt Burns; and Scotiabank bought McLeod Young Weir. Banks and investment houses historically have had two different cultures. Banks are hierarchical, with fixed reporting relationships and career paths; investment bankers can be prima donnas, with much more flamboyant styles. The Canadian Imperial Bank of Commerce's (CIBC) problems are representative of what happens when a company tries to merge two cultures after an acquisition. In the first six months of 1996, more than 25 top-ranked individuals left Toronto-based CIBC Wood Gundy to move to more entrepreneurial brokerage firms. Many of the brokers did not like the new compensation scheme, where bonuses above $50 000 are paid over three years, rather than all at once. Richard Dufresne, who worked at Gundy for four years, recently left for Nesbitt Burns Inc. in Montreal. "You're marrying two cultures, so you can expect it's not going to work well for everybody."

In early 1998, the Royal Bank of Canada and the Bank of Montreal announced their plans to merge. Shortly thereafter, the Toronto-Dominion Bank and CIBC announced similar plans. Although it is still too early to know whether the Canadian government will permit either of these mergers, it is safe to say that if the mergers do occur, bringing together the cultures of two organizations into one bank will pose some challenging issues. For starters, the CEOs have very different styles. Bank of Montreal's CEO Matthew Barrett is widely viewed as flamboyant, travelling in limousines and corporate jets, whereas Royal Bank's chair and CEO, John Cleghorn, drives a more modest car or takes public transit to work. With this much difference in the styles of the CEOs, one could easily anticipate difficulties in merging the cultures. Royal Bank's Cleghorn is aware of some of the difficulties the merger might cause. "Bringing a bank together with a securities firm, a trust business or an insurance company involves a wedding of several different cultures. And it is no small challenge to get the mechanics of integration right," he says.[31] Rod McQueen, a writer for the *Financial Post*, predicts that the Royal Bank's culture will come out on top because of Cleghorn's strong leadership characteristics.[32]

Creating and Sustaining Culture

An organization's culture doesn't pop out of thin air. Once established, it rarely fades away. What forces influence the creation of a culture? What re-

inforces and sustains these forces once they are in place? We answer both of these questions in this section.

How a Culture Begins

An organization's current customs, traditions, and general way of doing things are largely due to what it has done before and the degree of success it has had with those endeavours. This leads us to the ultimate source of an organization's culture: its founders.[33]

The founders of an organization traditionally have a major impact on that organization's early culture. They have a vision of what the organization should be. They are unconstrained by previous customs or ideologies. The small size that typically characterizes new organizations further facilitates the founders' imposition of their vision on all organizational members.

Microsoft's culture is largely a reflection of co-founder and current CEO, Bill Gates. Gates is personally aggressive, competitive, and highly disciplined. Those are the same characteristics often used to describe the software giant he heads. Other contemporary examples of founders who have had an immeasurable impact on their organization's culture are Akio Morita at Sony, Ted Rogers at Rogers Communications, Murray Pezim at Prime Equities International Corp., Mary Kay at Mary Kay Cosmetics, and Richard Branson at the Virgin Group.

Keeping a Culture Alive

Once a culture is in place, there are human resource practices within the organization that act to maintain it by giving employees a set of similar experiences.[34] For example, the selection process, performance evaluation criteria, training and career development activities, and promotion procedures ensure that those hired fit in with the culture, reward those who support it, and penalize (and even expel) those who challenge it. Three forces play a particularly important part in sustaining a culture: selection practices, the actions of top management, and socialization methods. Let's take a closer look at each.

SELECTION The explicit goal of the selection process is to identify and hire individuals who have the knowledge, skills, and abilities to perform the jobs within the organization successfully. Typically, more than one candidate will

Microsoft
www.microsoft.com

Virgin Group
http://www.virgin.com/

Nike
http://www.nike.com/

The core value of enhancing people's lives through sports and fitness is intensely held and widely shared by Nike employees. Nike founder Philip Knight has created a strong sports-oriented culture and promotes it through company practices such as paying employees extra for biking to work instead of driving. Nike is recognized worldwide as an athlete's company that hires former varsity, professional, and Olympic athletes to design and market its shoes and clothing for sports enthusiasts. Nike headquarters in Beaverton, Oregon, is a large campus with walking and jogging trails and buildings named for sports heroes such as the Joan Benoit Samuelson Center, the Bo Jackson Fitness Center, and the Joe Paterno Day Care Center.

be identified who meets any given job's requirements. When that point is reached, it would be naive to ignore that the final decision as to who is hired will be significantly influenced by the decision-maker's judgment of how well the candidates will fit into the organization. This attempt to ensure a proper match, either deliberately or inadvertently, results in the hiring of people who have values essentially consistent with those of the organization, or at least a good portion of those values.[35]

Additionally, the selection process provides information to applicants about the organization. Candidates learn about the organization, and if they perceive a conflict between their values and those of the organization, they can self-select themselves out of the applicant pool. Selection, therefore, becomes a two-way street, allowing the employer or applicant to abrogate a marriage if there appears to be a mismatch. In this way, the selection process sustains an organization's culture by selecting out those individuals who might attack or undermine its core values.

Applicants for entry-level positions in brand management at Procter & Gamble (P&G) experience an exhaustive application and screening process. Their interviewers are part of an elite cadre who have been selected and trained extensively via lectures, videotapes, films, practice interviews, and role-plays to identify applicants who will successfully fit in at P&G. Applicants are interviewed in depth for such qualities as their ability to "turn out high volumes of excellent work," "identify and understand problems," and "reach thoroughly substantiated and well-reasoned conclusions that lead to action." P&G values rationality and seeks applicants who think that way. University and college applicants receive two interviews and a general-knowledge test on campus before being flown back to head office for three more one-on-one interviews and a group interview at lunch. Each encounter seeks corroborating evidence of the traits that the firm believes correlate highly with "what counts" for success at P&G.[36]

Similarly, applicants for positions at Compaq Computer are carefully chosen for their ability to fit into the company's teamwork-oriented culture. As one executive put it, "We can find lots of people who are competent. . . . The No. 1 issue is whether they fit into the way we do business."[37] At Compaq, that means job candidates who are easy to get along with and who feel comfortable with the company's consensus management style. To increase the likelihood that loners and those with big egos get screened out, it's not unusual for an applicant to be interviewed by 15 people, who represent all departments of the company and a variety of seniority levels.[38]

TOP MANAGEMENT The actions of top management also have a major impact on the organization's culture.[39] Through what they say and how they behave, senior executives establish norms that filter down through the organization as to whether risk taking is desirable; how much freedom managers should give their subordinates; what is appropriate dress; what actions will pay off in terms of pay raises, promotions, and other rewards; and the like. This chapter's OB in the News feature discusses how Maclean-Hunter Ltd.'s adherence for 106 years to the values of its Presbyterian founders made it unable to take the risks it needed to resist a takeover by Ted Rogers.

New management can also try to change the culture of an organization, although this is not an easy task. When John Cruickshank took over as editor-in-chief for the *Vancouver Sun* in September 1995, he wanted to demonstrate quickly and definitively that the old culture of the newspaper

OB IN THE NEWS

Culture Causes a Takeover: Maclean-Hunter Ltd.

When Ted Rogers staged his takeover of media conglomerate Maclean-Hunter Ltd. in 1994, the cultures of the two organizations couldn't have been more different. Rogers was everything Maclean-Hunter wasn't, including having heavy debt loads, not paying out common share dividends in more than a decade, and rarely posting a profitable year.

At the time of its takeover, Maclean-Hunter represented the tale "of a company that for 106 years has continued to reflect the values of its Presbyterian founders—men with sober minds and sharp pencils who assembled their assets with prudence and care. It is about subsequent generations of managers who dutifully sat at the edge of the pool for the prescribed period of time, digesting each additional acquisition before plunging back into the water."

"Ultimately, however, it was Maclean-Hunter's entrenched corporate culture of restraint and moderation that made it so vulnerable—and so utterly unfashionable—in a market where current tastes favour lean, focused companies that offer the potential for rapid growth. The company's cumbersome size and diverse holdings also made it difficult for Maclean-Hunter to react swiftly in self-defence against a determined and experienced hunter. Even when it became painfully obvious that they were following outdated guidelines, Maclean-Hunter management stayed their steady course. And when Ted Rogers finally cornered his prey last week, company executives conceded his victory with gracious stoicism. They didn't win, but Col. John Maclean and Horace Hunter would probably have been proud of how they played the game."

Source: Based on "The Rules of the Game: Maclean-Hunter Takeover by Rogers Communications," *Maclean's*, March 21, 1994, p. 45.

Take It to the Net

We invite you to visit the Robbins page on the Prentice Hall Web site at:

http://www.prenticehall.ca/robbins

for this chapter's World Wide Web exercise.

Newspaper Guild
http://www.tng.org/

was being replaced.[40] Three quick moves signalled his intent. He met with representatives of the Newspaper Guild, the union that represents Sun staffers; instituted a daily post-mortem of the paper; and rejected the large corner suite with a built-in boardroom in favour of an office with a wall of windows that overlooks the newsroom. Cruickshank, in replacing previous editor-in-chief Ian Hayson, who was widely viewed as remote, was signalling that he would be working hands-on with his reporters to improve the newspaper's quality. "In much the same way that a new chief executive seeks to shape a corporate culture when taking the helm, new editors put their mark on a newspaper, and Cruickshank lost no time in remaking the *Vancouver Sun*.... By week two of his tenure, the newspaper had a new look." While the jury is still out on how successful these changes have been, one small indicator is improved circulation. Only four of the country's largest newspapers increased their circulation in 1997: the *Vancouver Sun* was one of them.[41] We would not want to leave you with the impression that changing culture is easy, however. In fact, it is a difficult process. We discuss the process of changing culture in greater detail in Chapter 17.

When John Cruickshank took over as editor-in-chief of the *Vancouver Sun*, he planned a new era for the newspaper. Cruickshank's goal is to change the culture at the *Sun*, improving both the reporting and the circulation figures.

socialization

The process that adapts employees to the organization's culture.

SOCIALIZATION No matter how effectively the organization recruits and selects new employees, they are not fully indoctrinated in the organization's culture when they start their job. Maybe most important, because they are unfamiliar with the organization's culture, new employees are potentially likely to disturb the beliefs and customs that are in place. The organization will, therefore, want to help new employees adapt to its culture. This adaptation process is called **socialization**.[42] Sometimes employees are not fully socialized. For instance, you will note in Exhibit 16-2 that the employees of that organization had learned they were supposed to wear checkerboard caps to work, but they clearly hadn't been told why.

Xerox Canada shares its corporate vision to be the leader in the global document market with its American parent. It's up to Diane McGarry, president and CEO of Xerox Canada since November 1993, to ensure that the vision gets carried out in Canada. To accomplish this, "New employees must take a week-long course where, among other things, they are taught the customer must come first; and how to operate as part of a team, with McGarry as coach."[43]

Starbucks
www.starbucks.com/

Similarly, new Sanyo employees undergo an intensive five-month training program (trainees eat and sleep together in company-subsidized dorms and are required to vacation together at company-owned resorts) where they learn the Sanyo way of doing everything—from how to speak to superiors to proper grooming and dress.[44] The company considers this program essential for transforming young employees, fresh out of school, into dedicated *kaisha senshi*, or corporate warriors. Starbucks, the rapidly growing gourmet-coffee chain, doesn't go to the extreme that Sanyo does, but it seeks the same outcome.[45] All new employees go through 24 hours of training. Just for an entry-level job in a retail store making coffee? Yes! Classes cover everything necessary to transform new employees into brewing consultants. They learn the Starbucks philosophy, the company jargon (including phrases such as "half-decaf double tall almond skim mocha"), and even how to help customers make decisions about beans, grind, and espresso machines. The result is employees who understand Starbucks' culture and who project an enthusiastic and knowledgeable interface with customers.

Exhibit 16-2

"*I don't know how it started, either. All I know is that it's part of our corporate culture.*"

Drawing by Mick Stevens in *The New Yorker*, October 3, 1994. Copyright © 1994 by The New Yorker Magazine, Inc. Reprinted by permission.

As we discuss socialization, keep in mind that the most critical socialization stage occurs at the time of entry into the organization. This is when the organization seeks to mould the outsider into an employee "in good standing." Those employees who fail to learn the essential or pivotal role behaviours risk being labelled "non-conformists" or "rebels," which often leads to expulsion. Moreover, the organization will be socializing every employee, though maybe not as explicitly, throughout his or her career in the organization. This further contributes to sustaining the culture.

Socialization can be conceptualized as a process composed of three stages: prearrival, encounter, and metamorphosis.[46] The first stage encompasses all the learning that occurs before a new member joins the organization. In the second stage, the new employee sees what the organization is really like and confronts the possibility that expectations and reality may diverge. In the third stage, the relatively long-lasting changes take place. The new employee masters the skills required for his or her job, successfully performs his or her new roles, and makes the adjustments to his or her work group's values and norms.[47] This three-stage process has an impact on the new employee's work productivity, commitment to the organization's objectives, and eventual decision to stay with the organization. Exhibit 16-3 depicts this process.

prearrival stage
The period of learning in the socialization process that occurs before a new employee joins the organization.

The **prearrival stage** explicitly recognizes that each individual arrives with a set of values, attitudes, and expectations. These cover both the work to be done and the organization. For instance, in many jobs, particularly professional work, new members will have undergone a considerable degree of prior socialization in training and in school. One major purpose of a business school, for example, is to socialize business students to the attitudes and behaviours that business firms want. If business executives believe that successful employees value the profit ethic, are loyal, will work hard, and desire to achieve, they can hire individuals out of business schools who have been premoulded in this pattern. But prearrival socialization goes beyond the specific job. The selection process is used in most organizations to inform prospective employees about the organization as a whole. In addition, as noted previously, the selection process also acts to ensure the inclusion of

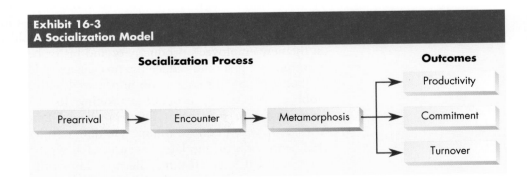

Exhibit 16-3
A Socialization Model

Socialization Process   Outcomes

Prearrival → Encounter → Metamorphosis

Productivity

Commitment

Turnover

the "right type"—those who will fit in. "Indeed, the ability of the individual to present the appropriate face during the selection process determines his or her ability to move into the organization in the first place. Thus, success depends on the degree to which the aspiring member has correctly anticipated the expectations and desires of those in the organization in charge of selection."[48]

encounter stage
The stage in the socialization process in which a new employee sees what the organization is really like and confronts the possibility that expectations and reality may diverge.

Upon entry into the organization, the new member enters the **encounter stage**. Here the individual confronts the possible dichotomy between her expectations—about her job, her co-workers, her boss, and the organization in general—and reality. If expectations prove to have been more or less accurate, the encounter stage merely provides a reaffirmation of the perceptions gained earlier. However, this is often not the case. Where expectations and reality differ, the socialization period for the new employee should be designed to help him or her detach from previous assumptions and replace them with another set that the organization deems desirable. Of course, not all organizations actively socialize their members such that the adoption of a new set of assumptions is perfectly completed. At the extreme, new members may become totally disillusioned with the realities of their job and resign. Proper selection should significantly reduce the probability of the latter occurrence.

metamorphosis stage
The stage in the socialization process in which a new employee adjusts to his or her work group's values and norms.

Finally, the new member must work out any problems discovered during the encounter stage. This may mean going through changes—hence, we call this the **metamorphosis stage**. The options presented in Exhibit 16-4 are alternatives designed to bring about the desired metamorphosis. Note, for example, that the more management relies on socialization programs that are formal, collective, fixed, serial, and emphasize divestiture, the greater the likelihood that newcomers' differences and perspectives will be stripped away and replaced by standardized and predictable behaviours. Careful selection by management of newcomers' socialization experiences can—at the extreme—create conformists who maintain traditions and customs, or inventive and creative individualists who consider no organizational practice sacred.

We can say that metamorphosis and the entry socialization process is complete when the new member has become comfortable with the organization and his or her job. The new employee has internalized the norms of the organization and the work group and understands and accepts these norms. The new member feels accepted by his or her peers as a trusted and valued individual, is self-confident that he or she has the competence to complete the job successfully, and understands the system—not only his or her own tasks, but also the rules, procedures, and informally accepted practices. Finally, the new employee understands how he or she will be evaluated, that is, what criteria will be used to measure and appraise his or her work. He or she knows what is expected and what constitutes a job "well done." As Exhibit 16-3 shows, successful metamorphosis should have a positive impact on the new employee's productivity and his or her commitment to the organization, and it should reduce the propensity to leave the organization.

Some people, of course, do not fit well with the company culture. Doug Hobbes, director of product marketing for Globe Information Services, lasted just four months at Ontario-based GlobeStar Systems Inc.[49] In his words, "It was a culture thing." He didn't enjoy going out for hamburgers after work or working late, "even though the organization's key people often stayed till 9 or 10 p.m." Because his work habits were different from theirs, his co-workers viewed him as unenterprising and aloof. His story

Exhibit 16-4
Entry Socialization Options

Formal vs. Informal The more a new employee is segregated from the ongoing work setting and differentiated in some way to make explicit his or her newcomer's role, the more formal socialization is. Specific orientation and training programs are examples. Informal socialization puts the new employee directly into his or her job, with little or no special attention.

Individual vs. Collective New members can be socialized individually. This describes how it's done in many professional offices. They can also be grouped together and processed through an identical set of experiences, as in military boot camp.

Fixed vs. Variable This refers to the time schedule in which newcomers make the transition from outsider to insider. A fixed schedule establishes standardized stages of transition. This characterizes rotational training programs. It also includes probationary periods, such as the eight- to ten-year "associate" status used by accounting and law firms before deciding on whether or not a candidate is made a partner. Variable schedules give no advanced notice of their transition timetable. Variable schedules describe the typical promotion system, where one is not advanced to the next stage until he or she is "ready."

Serial vs. Random Serial socialization is characterized by the use of role models who train and encourage the newcomer. Apprenticeship and mentoring programs are examples. In random socialization, role models are deliberately withheld. The new employee is left on his or her own to figure things out.

Investiture vs. Divestiture Investiture socialization assumes that the newcomer's qualities and qualifications are the necessary ingredients for job success, so these qualities and qualifications are confirmed and supported. Divestiture socialization tries to strip away certain characteristics of the recruit. Fraternity and sorority "pledges" go through divestiture socialization to shape them into the proper role.

Source: Based on J. Van Maanen, "People Processing: Strategies of Organizational Socialization," *Organizational Dynamics,* Summer 1978, pp. 19–36; and E.H. Schein, "Organizational Culture," *American Psychologist,* February 1990, p. 116.

serves as a reminder to make sure that you fit with the organization's culture when you accept a job.

How Cultures Form

Exhibit 16-5 summarizes how an organization's culture is established and sustained. The original culture is derived from the founder's philosophy. This, in turn, strongly influences the criteria used in hiring. The actions of the current top management set the general climate of what is acceptable behaviour and what is not. How employees are to be socialized will depend both on the degree of success achieved in matching new employees' values to those of the organization's in the selection process and on top management's preference for socialization methods.

Bolton, Ontario-based Husky Injection Molding Systems Ltd. illustrates how a company forms and maintains its culture. Robert Schad, the company's 68-year-old founder, believes in a competitive, ecologically friendly, healthy, and humane workplace.[50] Through employee councils, workers at head office meet with Schad monthly and are able to voice any concerns they have, which has led to better lighting in the parking lot, speed bumps

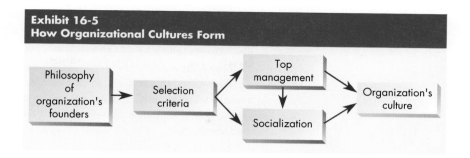

Exhibit 16-5
How Organizational Cultures Form

on access roads, tightened security, a fitness centre on-site, and a performance-review process that has received no complaints since 1995. Husky's cafeteria serves hot organic vegetarian meals, which are subsidized by the company. There are free herbal teas, but no candy, doughnuts, or vending machines on the premises. The firm believes in egalitarianism, and thus executives and employees share the parking lot, dining room, and washrooms. Employees receive an annual report and monthly newsletter that provide them with financial information about the company. They also receive salaries at the high end of the industry scale. The salaries, together with Husky's benefits package, allows the company to attract and retain the very brightest technical people, according to Husky's former director of human resources, David Alcock. Employees serve on the hiring committee as well, to evaluate and recommend potential employees. When the committee is divided over a candidate, the person often is not hired, because it is not clear that he or she fits in with Husky's culture.

How Employees Learn Culture

Culture is transmitted to employees in a number of forms, the most potent being stories, rituals, material symbols, and language. You can observe some of the ways Wal-Mart brought its culture to Canada in this chapter's CBC Video Case.

Stories

During the days when Henry Ford II was chairman of the Ford Motor Co., one would have been hard-pressed to find a manager who hadn't heard the story about Mr. Ford reminding his executives, when they became too arrogant, that "it's my name that's on the building." The message was clear: Henry Ford II ran the company!

For many years, Ford Motor Co. has paid attention to women car buyers. One company anecdote about senior designer Mimi Vandermolen, a Canadian who headed the interior-design team of the Taurus, reminds employees of the extent to which they should go to consider all of their customers' needs. "Vandermolen decreed that every member of her team, both male and female, would wear their fingernails long in order to better understand the needs of women drivers."[51] Her team obliged, and the car became one of the best-selling sedans in North America.

Nordstrom employees are fond of the following story. It strongly conveys the company's policy toward customer returns: When this specialty retail chain was in its infancy, a customer came in and wanted to return a set of automobile tires. The sales clerk was a bit uncertain how to handle the problem. As the customer and sales clerk spoke, Mr. Nordstrom walked by and overheard the conversation. He immediately interceded, asking the cus-

tomer how much he had paid for the tires. Mr. Nordstrom then instructed the clerk to take the tires back and provide a full cash refund. After the customer had received his refund and left, the perplexed clerk looked at the boss. "But, Mr. Nordstrom, we don't sell tires!" "I know," replied the boss, "but we do whatever we need to do to make the customer happy. I mean it when I say we have a no-questions-asked return policy." Nordstrom then picked up the telephone and called a friend in the auto-parts business to see how much he could get for the tires.

Stories such as these circulate through many organizations. They typically contain a narrative of events about the organization's founders, rule breaking, rags-to-riches successes, reductions in the workforce, relocation of employees, reactions to past mistakes, and organizational coping.[52] These stories anchor the present in the past and provide explanations and legitimacy for current practices.[53]

Rituals

rituals

Repetitive sequences of activities that express and reinforce the key values of the organization, what goals are most important, which people are important, and which are expendable.

Rituals are repetitive sequences of activities that express and reinforce the key values of the organization, what goals are most important, which people are important, and which ones are expendable.[54] College and university faculty members undergo a lengthy ritual in their quest for permanent employment—tenure. Typically, the faculty member is on probation for six years. At the end of that period, the member's colleagues must make one of two choices: extend a tenured appointment or issue a one-year terminal contract. What does it take to obtain tenure? It usually requires satisfactory teaching performance, service to the department and university, and scholarly activity. Of course, what satisfies the requirements for tenure in one department at one university may be appraised as inadequate in another. The key is that the tenure decision, in essence, asks those who are tenured to assess whether the candidate has demonstrated, based on six years of performance, whether he or she fits in. Colleagues who have been socialized properly will have proved themselves worthy of being granted tenure. Every year, hundreds of faculty members at colleges and universities are denied tenure. In some cases, this action is a result of poor performance across the board. More often, however, the decision can be traced to the faculty member's not doing well in those areas that the tenured faculty believe are important. The instructor who spends dozens of hours each week preparing for class and achieves outstanding evaluations by students but neglects research and publication activities may be passed over for tenure. What has happened, simply, is that the instructor has failed to adapt to the norms set by the department. The astute faculty member will assess early on in the probationary period what attitudes and behaviours his or her colleagues want and will then proceed to give them what they want. By demanding certain attitudes and behaviours, the tenured faculty have made significant strides toward standardizing tenure candidates.

One of the best-known corporate rituals is Mary Kay Cosmetics' annual award meeting.[55] Looking like a cross between a circus and a Miss America pageant, the meeting takes place over two days in a large auditorium, on a stage in front of a large, cheering audience, with all the participants dressed in glamorous evening clothes. Saleswomen are rewarded with an array of flashy gifts—gold and diamond pins, fur stoles, pink Cadillacs—based on success in achieving sales quota. This "show" acts as a motivator by publicly recognizing outstanding sales performance. In addition, the ritual

A ritual at Mary Kay Cosmetics is the annual sales meeting. Recognizing high achievements is an important part of the company's culture, which values hard work and determination. The ritual of praise and recognition honours the beauty consultants' accomplishments in meeting their sales quotas, which contribute to the success of the company.

Mary Kay Cosmetics
www.marykaycosmetics.com

aspect reinforces Mary Kay's personal determination and optimism, which enabled her to overcome personal hardships, found her own company, and achieve material success. It conveys to her salespeople that reaching their sales quota is important and that through hard work and encouragement they too can achieve success.

Material Symbols

The layout of corporate headquarters, the types of automobiles top executives are given, and the presence or absence of corporate aircraft are a few examples of material symbols. Others include the size of offices, the elegance of furnishings, executive perks, and dress attire.[56] These material symbols convey to employees who is important, the degree of egalitarianism desired by top management, and the kinds of behaviour (for example, risk taking, conservative, authoritarian, participative, individualistic, social) that are appropriate. For instance, Sony Music Canada's ending statement to its mission statement—"our success is in our attitude"—is reflected in its Toronto head office layout. Rick Camilleri, Sony's CEO, spent $60 million to create a "state-of-the-art, one-stop, funky playhouse for adults, replete with writing, editing, and recording studios,... a Main Street thoroughfare, gourmet cafeteria,... and floor-to-ceiling murals." Camilleri describes both head office and Sony Canada as follows: "We want to be irreverent, to be renegades, to be different. Successful companies are not followers."[57]

The design of General Motors Canada's corporate office in Oshawa reflects the values of Maureen Kempston Darkes, president and general manager of General Motors of Canada since 1994. The office is functional, modest, and almost spartan; she doesn't even have her own formal office—just a desk at the end of a row of desks. Not surprisingly, her friends describe her as "direct, solid, rooted and without airs—the antithesis of flash."[58] Her headquarters conveys to employees that Kempston Darkes values openness, equality, creativity, and flexibility.

Ford Canada's new president and chief executive officer, Bobbie Gaunt, has the same huge desk in her office in Toronto as does Ford Motor Co. CEO Alex Trotman and every other Ford divisional head. The design of the

office buildings for each of these heads is also the same (although the size may differ). This corporate decision reflects the continuing influence of Henry Ford, who believed it was more efficient that way.[59] Similarly, Ontario-based St. Joseph's Printing uses its office layout to encourage an atmosphere of friendliness among its employees. The building has a large atrium, an art gallery displaying local artists' work, and a gym with lunchtime aerobics classes.[60]

Corporations differ in how much separation they want to make between their executives and employees, and this plays out in how material benefits are distributed to executives. Some corporations provide their top executives with chauffeur-driven limousines and, when they travel by air, unlimited use of the corporate jet. Others may not get to ride in limousines or private jets, but they might still get a car and air transportation paid for by the company (only the car is a Chevrolet with no driver, and the jet seat is in the economy section of a commercial airliner). At Bolton, Ontario-based Husky Injection Molding Systems, a more egalitarian culture is favoured. Employees and management share the parking lot, dining room, and even washrooms.

Language

Many organizations and units within organizations use language as a way to identify members of a culture or subculture. By learning this language, members attest to their acceptance of the culture and, in so doing, help to preserve it.

At the Saint John headquarters of New Brunswick Telephone Co. Ltd., "Gerryisms," named for Gerry Pond, president and CEO, abound. The Gerryisms serve as mantras for NBTel and staffers, who refer to the company's vision with such catchphrases as "electronic service integration," "LivingLAB," or "NB First."[61] At St. Joseph's Printing, a large poster hangs in the plant, declaring, "Let's all make learning a process that never ends."[62] When Louis Gerstner left RJR Nabisco to head up IBM, he had to learn a whole new vocabulary that included *the Orchard* (IBM's Armonk, New York corporate headquarters, which was once an apple orchard); *big iron* (mainframe computers); *hypo* (a high-potential employee); *a one performer* (an employee with IBM's top performance rating); and *PROFS* (Professional Office Systems, IBM's internal electronic mail system).[63]

Over time, organizations often develop unique terms to describe equipment, offices, key personnel, suppliers, customers, or products that relate to its business. New employees are frequently overwhelmed with acronyms and jargon that, after six months on the job, have become fully part of their language. Once assimilated, this terminology acts as a common denominator that unites members of a given culture or subculture.

Changing Organizational Culture

The intent of this chapter was to acquaint you with the ideas of culture, and to show you how culture is transmitted to new employees and to the world outside of the organization. As a result, our presentation of culture has been limited to a discussion of cultures that already exist within an organization. We have not discussed the difficulty of changing the culture of an organization. Chapter 17, which is about organizational change, specifically addresses the topic of culture change. To help you begin to think about these

ideas, you might want to consult the Point/Counterpoint discussion, which gives you two views on the ease with which culture can be changed. For a specific example of the difficulties of culture change, you should read this chapter's Case Incident, which examines culture change attempts at Canada Post.

HR IMPLICATIONS

Examples of Organizational Cultures

Organizations can introduce specific cultures that represent important values to the organization. For instance, culture can be used to signal that a company values families through its family-friendly policy, values diversity through an emphasis on diversity throughout the firm, or values innovation through a culture of innovation. We examine these three examples of cultures in turn.

Family-Friendly Workplaces

In today's diverse workforce, more and more employees are females, single parents, stepparents, individuals responsible for aging relatives, or members of two-career households. These employees have different needs than the traditional stereotype of a working dad, with a stay-at-home wife and two kids. An increasing number of organizations are responding to their diverse workforce by creating family-friendly workplaces.

So what's a **family-friendly workplace?** The term refers to an umbrella of work/family programs such as on-site day-care, child-care and elder-care referrals, flexible hours, compressed workweeks, job sharing, telecommuting, temporary part-time employment, and relocation assistance for employees' family members.[1]

Creating a family-friendly work climate was initially motivated by management's concern to improve employee morale and productivity and to reduce absenteeism. At Quaker Oats, for instance, 60 percent of employees admitted being absent at least three days a year because of children's illnesses, and 56 percent said they were unable to attend company-related functions or work overtime because of child-care problems.[2] However, the overall evidence indicates that the major benefit to creating a family-friendly workplace is that it makes it easier for employers to recruit and retain first-class workers.[3]

For many parents, the ultimate determinant of whether they are able to work is the availability of child care. Ontarians faced a crisis in the fall of 1997 when teachers went out on strike. Some large employers, such as Toronto-based law firm McMillan Binch and several branches of the Royal Bank of Canada, set up temporary day-care facilities for younger children.[4] Ottawa-based Mitel did even more. They established resources for their employees' children to continue studying at Mitel. The parents referred to this as "Mitel High," and it made it easier for parents to cope with the strike. Mitel also kept about 65 high-school students busy each day, offering them résumé-writing and job-hunting seminars.

Husky Injection Molding Systems, the world's third-largest firm in the plastics industry, is a model of what a company can do for the children of its employees.[5] Husky built Copper House, a 1600-square-metre child-care centre that cost $5 million to develop. According to Valerie Nease, director of Copper House, "no expense was spared to build and equip" the centre. Staff have at least a diploma, though many have degrees in early childhood education. The child-staff ratio is well below legal requirements. Nease says: "There are other companies that have implemented child-care centres. But in 20 years of working, I've never seen anything done to this degree."

As the population ages, an increasing number of employees find themselves responsible for caring for parents or grandparents.[6] Employees who spend time worrying about elder care have less time for, and are less focused on, work-related issues. Therefore many organizations are widening child-care concerns to cover all dependants, including elderly family members.

One of the more interesting findings related to family-friendly workplaces is its appeal to both

sexes. The common assumption is that family-friendly programs are used mostly by women. The evidence suggests that this is not the case. Workers of both sexes make trade-offs for family; and men are as likely as women to seek these programs.[7] Similarly, men are increasingly rejecting relocation, overnight travel, and overtime to spend more time with their families. For instance, at Du Pont, 41 percent of men in management or professional jobs told their supervisors they weren't available for relocation; and 19 percent told their bosses they would not accept a job that required extensive travel. Among those in manufacturing jobs at Du Pont, 39 percent of men refused to work overtime in order to spend more time with family.[8]

Organizations that Value Diversity

Some organizations have been more proactive than others in indicating the need to promote more inclusive environments where employees from various cultures and races could work easily side by side. We noted in Chapter 4 that Procter & Gamble Canada explicitly values diversity in the workplace. Another example to consider is GM Canada. Maureen Kempston Darkes (president and general manager of General Motors Canada) believes in emphasizing the importance of promoting ethnic, gender, and racial diversity for GM. "Unless we can create a culture where everyone can contribute," she says, "we'll never be very successful." Long before she arrived at her post in Canada, she had been promoting diversity initiatives at GM. In the early 1980s, she spearheaded the creation of GM's women's advisory council to deal with such issues as employment equity and networking opportunities. She's also worked to make improvements to GMs flextime hours and telecommuting programs, to make them more family friendly. At GM Canada she has initiated a Diversity Strategy Team with a goal "to create a workforce that mirrors the multinational character of customers in the showrooms."[9]

The Culture of Innovation

What does it take to be an innovative company? Several of Canada's most well-known companies fit the bill. Montreal-based Bank of Montreal, Bombardier, and forestry giant Avenor Inc., Brampton, Ontario-based Northern Telecom, Vancouver-based zinc producer Cominco Ltd., Ottawa-based software developer Corel Corp., and Calgary-based ABB Vetco Gray Inc., (a company that invented a spill-free system to retrieve oil from the ocean floor) have all been cited for their innovative actions.[10]

Jean Monty, CEO of Northern Telecom Ltd. (Nortel) from 1992 to 1997, took a company with demoralized employees and stagnant revenue and built it into one of Canada's few high-tech multinationals, creating an innovative organization at the same time. Monty replaced Paul Stern, who had "chopped R&D spending, alienated customers and obliterated employee morale" according to a *Report on Business* story.[11] Monty's vision was to have world-class research and development happening at Nortel, because the rapid pace in technology required that Nortel stay ahead. Therefore, he says, "We invested massively, particularly in R&D, and we didn't try to shrink ourselves to greatness."[12] He also wanted to improve both employee morale and customer relations. To do this, he spent many hours communicating his vision directly to his employees and tying customer satisfaction levels to managers' pay. "He's an outstanding field commander who inspires his troops with strong leadership," says Lynton "Red" Wilson, chairman and chief executive of BCE Inc., which owns 51.6 percent of Nortel.[13]

While Monty managed to return Nortel to innovative status after the company suffered under Paul Stern, many companies are still trying to do this. Typically an organization stimulates organizational innovation through its culture. How does it do this? The standard toward which many organizations strive is that achieved by the 3M Co.[14] It has developed a reputation for being able to stimulate innovation over a long period of time. 3M has a stated objective that 30 percent of its sales are to come from products less than four years old. In 1995, the figure was 32 percent. In one recent year alone, 3M launched more than 200 new products.

Innovative organizations tend to have similar cultures. They encourage experimentation. They reward both successes and failures. They celebrate mistakes. At Hewlett-Packard, for instance, CEO Lewis Platt has successfully built a corporate culture that supports people who try something that doesn't work out.[15] Platt himself protects people who stick their neck out, fearful that to do otherwise would stifle the risk-taking culture he encourages among his managers. Unfortunately, in too many organizations, people are rewarded for the

absence of failures rather than for the presence of successes. Such cultures extinguish risk taking and innovation. People will suggest and try new ideas only where they feel such behaviours exact no penalties. Managers in innovative organizations recognize that failures are a natural by-product of venturing into the unknown. When Babe Ruth set his record for home runs in one season, he also led the league in strikeouts. He is remembered for the former, not the latter!

Companies that believe in creating the future for themselves are also likely to be more innovative. That certainly describes Nortel's moves under Monty, with its increased budget for research and development. The Bank of Montreal's introduction of mbanx in October 1996 came about when CEO Matthew Barrett and his senior team sat down and asked, "What about those people who are too busy to go to the bank?" according to Bryan Smith of Toronto-based Innovation Associates.[16] Mbanx is a virtual banking division of the Bank of Montreal and is viewed as a new form of banking.

Within the human resources category, innovative organizations actively promote the training and development of their members so that they keep current; offer high job security so employees don't fear getting fired for making mistakes; and encourage individuals to become champions of change. Once a new idea is developed, idea champions actively and enthusiastically promote the idea, build support, overcome resistance, and ensure that the innovation is implemented.[17] The evidence indicates that champions have common personality characteristics: extremely high self-confidence, persistence, energy, and a tendency to take risks. Idea champions also display characteristics associated with transformational leadership. They inspire and energize others with their vision of the potential of an innovation and through their strong personal conviction in their mission. They are also good at gaining the commitment of others to support their mission. In addition, idea champions have jobs that provide considerable decision-making discretion. This autonomy helps them introduce and implement innovations in organizations.[18]

Given the status of 3M as a premier product innovator, we would expect it to have most of the properties we've identified. And it does. The company is so highly decentralized that it has many of the characteristics of small, organic organizations.

The structure relies on extensive redundancy. For instance, every division, department, and product group has its own labs—many of which are deliberately duplicating the work of others. Consistent with the need for cross-fertilization of ideas, the company holds internal trade shows where divisions will show their technologies to employees of other divisions. All of 3M's scientists and managers are challenged to "keep current." Idea champions are created and encouraged by allowing scientists and engineers to spend up to 15 percent of their time on projects of their own choosing. And if a 3M scientist comes up with a new idea but finds resistance within the researcher's own division, he or she can apply for a $70 000 grant from an internal venture-capital fund to further develop the idea. The company encourages its employees to take risks—and rewards the failures as well as the successes. And 3M's management has the patience to see ideas through to successful products. It invests nearly seven percent of company sales revenue (more than $1.4 billion a year) in research and development, yet management tells its R&D people that *not everything will work*. It also fosters a culture that allows people to defy their supervisors. For instance, each new employee and his or her supervisor take a one-day orientation class where, among other things, stories are told of victories won by employees despite the opposition of their boss. Finally, while 3M incurred its first layoffs in decades during 1995, the company still continues to be a model of corporate stability. The average tenure for company officers is 31 years, and the overall annual turnover rate within the company is a minuscule three percent.

Sources:

[1] See, for instance, A. Saltzman, "Family Friendliness," U.S. *News & World Report*, February 22, 1993, pp. 59–66; M. Galen, "Work & Family," *Business Week*, June 28, 1993, pp. 80-88; S. Hand and R.A. Zawacki, "Family-Friendly Benefits: More Than a Frill, *HR Magazine*, October 1994, pp. 79–84; S. Nelton, "Adjusting Benefits for Family Needs," *Nation's Business*, August 1995, pp. 27–28; L.T. Thomas and D.C. Ganster, "Impact of Family-Supportive Work Variables on Work-Family Conflict and Strain: A Control Perspective," *Journal of Applied Psychology*, Feburary 1995, pp. 6–15; and K.H. Hammonds, "Balancing Work and Family," *Business Week*, September 16, 1996, pp. 74–80.

[2] Cited in M.A. Verespej, "People-First Policies," *Industry Week*, June 21, 1993, p. 20.

[3] S. Shellenbarger, "Data Gap," *Wall Street Journal*, June 21, 1993, p. R6.

[4] D. Jenish, "Going to the Wall: A Power Struggle Hits Two Million Ontario Children," *Maclean's*, November 10, 1997, p. 18.

5 Information on Husky based on B. Livesey, "Provide and Conquer," Report on *Business Magazine*, March 1997, pp. 34–44.

6 S. Shellenbarger, "The Aging of America Is Making 'Elder Care' a Big Workplace Issue," *Wall Street Journal*, February 16, 1994, p. A1.

7 See S.J. Lambert, An Investigation of Workers' Use and Appreciation of Supportive Workplace Policies, in D.P. Moore (ed.), *Academy of Management Best Paper Proceedings* (Vancouver, BC, 1995), pp. 136–40; and T. Lewin, "Workers of Both Sexes Make Trade-offs for Family, Study Shows," The *New York Times*, October 29, 1995, p. Y14.

8 Cited in T. Lewin, "Workers of Both Sexes Make Trade-offs for Family, Study Shows." The *New York Times*, October 29, 1995, p. Y14.

9 M. Posner, "The 28 Billion Dollar Woman." *Chatelaine*, December 1997, pp. 70–75.

10 A. Walmsley, "Smart Company," *Report on Business Magazine*, April 1997, pp. 24–29.

11 B. Livesey, "Tag Team," *Report on Business Magazine*, July 1997, pp. 39–46.

12 B. Livesey, "Tag Team," *Report on Business Magazine*, July 1997, p. 40.

13 "Northern Exposure: For His Outstanding Turnaround at Northern Telecom, Jean Monty is Canada's CEO of the Year," *Financial Post*, June 28/30, 1997, p. 8.

14 Discussion of the 3M Co. are based on K. Labich, "The Innovators," *Fortune*, June 6, 1988, p. 49; R. Mitchell, "Masters of Innovation," *Business Week*, April 10, 1989, p. 58; K. Kelly, "The Drought Is Over at 3M," *Business Week*, November 7, 1994, pp. 140–41; T.A. Stewart, "3M Fights Back," *Fortune*, February 5, 1996, pp. 94–99; and T.D. Schellhardt, "David in Goliath," *Wall Street Journal*, May 23, 1996, p. R14.

15 J.H. Sheridan, "Lew Platt: Creating a Culture for Innovation," *Industry Week*, December 19, 1994, pp. 26–30.

16 A. Walmsley, "Smart Company," *Report on Business Magazine*, April 1997, p. 26.

17 J.M. Howell and C.A. Higgins, "Champions of Change," *Business Quarterly*, Spring 1990, pp. 31–32; and D.L. Day, "Raising Radicals: Different Processes for Championing Innovative Corporate Ventures," *Organization Science*, May 1994, pp. 148–72.

18 J.M. Howell and C.A. Higgins, "Champions of Change," *Business Quarterly*, Spring 1990, pp. 31–32.

Summary and Implications

For the Workplace

Exhibit 16-6 depicts organizational culture as an intervening variable. Employees form an overall subjective perception of the organization based on such factors as degree of risk tolerance, team emphasis, and support of people. This overall perception becomes, in effect, the organization's culture or personality. These favourable or unfavourable perceptions then affect employee performance and satisfaction, with the impact being greater for stronger cultures.

Just as people's personalities tend to be stable over time, so too do strong cultures. This makes strong cultures difficult for managers to change. When a culture becomes mismatched to its environment, management will want to change it. But as the Point/Counterpoint debate demonstrates, changing an organization's culture is a long and difficult process. The result, at least in the short term, is that managers should treat their organization's culture as relatively fixed.

One of the more important managerial implications of organizational culture relates to selection decisions. Hiring individuals whose values don't

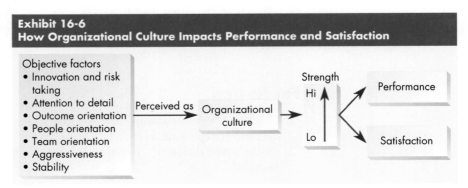

Exhibit 16-6
How Organizational Culture Impacts Performance and Satisfaction

Objective factors
• Innovation and risk taking
• Attention to detail
• Outcome orientation
• People orientation
• Team orientation
• Aggressiveness
• Stability

Perceived as → Organizational culture → Strength Hi / Lo → Performance / Satisfaction

align with those of the organization are likely to lead to employees who lack motivation and commitment and who are dissatisfied with their jobs and the organization.[64] Not surprisingly, employee "misfits" have considerably higher turnover rates than do individuals who perceive a good fit.[65]

We should also not overlook the influence socialization has on employee performance. An employee's performance depends to a considerable degree on knowing what he should or should not do. Understanding the right way to do a job indicates proper socialization. Furthermore, the appraisal of an individual's performance includes how well the person fits into the organization. Can he or she get along with co-workers? Does he or she have acceptable work habits and demonstrate the right attitude? These qualities differ between jobs and organizations. For instance, on some jobs employees will be evaluated more favourably if they are aggressive and outwardly indicate that they are ambitious. On another job, or on the same job in another organization, such an approach may be evaluated negatively. As a result, proper socialization becomes a significant factor in influencing both actual job performance and how others perceive it.

For You as an Individual

The culture of an organization has a strong impact on how you will feel about working for that organization. The same is true for how the culture of your college or university might affect you. In both cases, the organization offers particular expectations about behaviours, and you, as the employee or student, are expected to follow the norms. You will feel more comfortable in cultures that share your values and expectations. This may be as simple as being in classes where participation is valued, and you enjoy participating. If the classroom culture is one of participation and you like to remain passive, however, that class might make you feel less comfortable.

When you work in groups on student projects, the groups create mini-cultures of their own. You will probably observe this if you pay attention to the other groups in the class. Some will be quite cohesive, and others will look as if the members hardly know each other. These outcomes occur, in part, because of the cultures that the groups create.

ROADMAP REMINDER

In the two previous chapters, we examined the structure of the organization and how tasks for jobs were put together. Both structure and job design reflect elements of the overall culture of an organization. In this chapter we addressed more specifically what culture was and how it formed. In the next, and final, chapter we consider how organizational change occurs, looking specifically at how cultural change can be enacted.

For Review

1. What is the relationship between institutionalization, formalization, and organizational culture?
2. What is the difference between job satisfaction and organizational culture?

3. Can an employee survive in an organization if he or she rejects its core values? Explain.
4. How can an outsider assess an organization's culture?
5. What defines an organization's subcultures?
6. Contrast organizational culture with national culture.
7. How can culture be a liability to an organization?
8. How does a strong culture affect an organization's efforts to improve diversity?
9. What benefits can socialization provide for the organization? For the new employee?
10. How is language related to organizational culture?

For Discussion

1. Contrast individual personality and organizational culture. How are they similar? How are they different?
2. Is socialization brainwashing? Explain.
3. If management sought a culture characterized as innovative and autonomous, what might its socialization program look like?
4. Can you identify a set of characteristics that describes your college's or university's culture? Compare them with several of your peers. How closely do they agree?
5. "We should be opposed to the manipulation of individuals for organizational purposes, but a degree of social uniformity enables organizations to work better." Do you agree or disagree with this statement? Discuss.

LEARNING ABOUT YOURSELF EXERCISE

What Kind of Organizational Culture Fits You Best?

For each of the following statements, circle the level of agreement or disagreement that you personally feel:

SA = Strongly Agree
A = Agree
U = Uncertain
D = Disagree
SD = Strongly disagree

1. I like being part of a team and having my performance assessed in terms of my contribution to the team.   SA   A   U   D   SD
2. No person's needs should be compromised in order for a department to achieve its goals.   SA   A   U   D   SD
3. I like the thrill and excitement from taking risks.   SA   A   U   D   SD
4. If a person's job performance is inadequate, it's irrelevant how much effort he or she made.   SA   A   U   D   SD

5. I like things to be stable and predictable.   SA   A   U   D   SD

6. I prefer managers who provide detailed and rational
   explanations for their decisions.   SA   A   U   D   SD

7. I like to work where there isn't a great deal of
   pressure and where people are essentially easygoing.   SA   A   U   D   SD

Turn to page 701 for scoring direction and key

WORKING WITH OTHERS EXERCISE

Rate Your Classroom Culture

Listed here are 10 statements. Score each statement by indicating the degree to which you agree with it. If you strongly agree, give it a five. If you strongly disagree, give it a 1.

1. My classmates are friendly and supportive.   _____

2. My instructor is friendly and supportive.   _____

3. My instructor encourages me to question and challenge him
   or her as well as other classmates.   _____

4. My instructor clearly expresses his or her expectations to the class.   _____

5. I think the grading system used by my instructor is based on clear
   standards of performance.   _____

6. My instructor's behaviour during examinations demonstrates his
   or her belief that students are honest and trustworthy.   _____

7. My instructor provides regular and rapid feedback on my
   performance.   _____

8. My instructor uses a strict bell curve to allocate grades.   _____

9. My instructor is open to suggestions on how the course might
   be improved.   _____

10. My instructor makes me want to learn.   _____

Add up your score for all the statements except number eight. For number eight, reverse the score (strongly agree=1; strongly disagree=5) and add it to your total. Your score will fall between 10 and 50.

A high score (37 or above) describes an open, warm, human, trusting, and supportive culture. A low score (25 or below) describes a closed, cold, task-oriented, autocratic, and tense culture.

Form groups of five to seven members each. Compare your scores. How close do they align? Discuss and resolve discrepancies.

ETHICAL DILEMMA EXERCISE

Cultural Factors and Unethical Behaviour

An organization's culture socializes people. It subtly conveys to members that certain actions are acceptable, even though they are illegal. For instance, when executives at General Electric, Westinghouse, and other manufacturers of heavy electrical equipment illegally conspired to set prices in the early 1960s, the defendants invariably testified that they came new to their jobs, found price fixing to be an established way of life, and simply entered into it as they did into other aspects of their job. One GE manager noted that every one of his bosses had directed him to meet with the competition: "It had become so common and gone on for so many years that I think we lost sight of the fact that it was illegal."[1]

The strength of an organization's culture has an influence on the ethical behaviour of its managers. A strong culture will exert more influence on managers than a weak one. If the culture is strong and supports high ethical standards, it should have a very powerful positive influence on a manager's ethical behaviour. However, in a weak culture, managers are more likely to rely on subculture norms to guide their behaviour. Work groups and departmental standards will more strongly influence ethical behaviour in organizations that have weak overall cultures.

It is also generally acknowledged that the content of a culture affects ethical behaviour. Assuming this is true, what would a culture look like that would shape high ethical standards? What could top management do to strengthen that culture? Do you think it's possible for a manager with high ethical standards to uphold those standards in an organizational culture that tolerates, or even encourages, unethical practices?

Source:

[1] As described in P.C. Yeager, "Analyzing Corporate Offenses: Progress and Prospects," in W.C. Frederick and L.E. Preston (eds.), *Business Ethics: Research Issues and Empirical Studies* (Greenwich, CT: JAI Press, 1990), p. 174.

CASE INCIDENT

The Difficulty of Culture Change at Canada Post

Canada's postal service has been faced with labour troubles for much of the past 50 years. Many trace the problems back to extensive hiring of returning veterans after the Second World War. This created a garrison culture. "The paramilitary environment [created at Canada Post at that time] spawned some of the most aggressive and self-centred unions in Canadian history," says Michael Warren, who served as president of Canada Post in the early 1980s. That culture has been difficult to change.

Canada Post needs to change its culture because it is under pressure from the federal government to cut about $200 million from its operating costs. Critics contend that the Crown corporation refuses to implement cost-cutting efficiencies that a truly private enterprise would be forced to undertake. In the private sector, when companies have to cut costs, they downsize and/or make changes in the labour process. However, the Canadian Union of Postal Workers' (CUPW) collective agreement makes it difficult for Canada Post to impose cost-saving work rules. They rarely want to go along with the proposals by management for changing work procedures.

One example of a cost-saving measure that Canada Post is trying to introduce is to shave 10 minutes off every route in the country. The company plans to examine how many steps a letter carrier should be taking to deliver the mail. In the private sector this would be done as part of a re-engineering process. "What we're doing is looking at their whole day and how we can make productive time out of unproductive time," Canada Post spokesperson John Caines said. "No one will be working any longer than they are now and nobody will be losing any salary." He also said that Canada Post can save $2 million for every minute cut from the routes.

But CUPW's Tingley notes, "Basically every minute cut from the routes means 32 jobs lost. If they are successful in getting 10 minutes out, it equates to between 300 and 400 jobs." Tingley believes that Canada Post is just trying to give already-overworked postal workers an even heavier load. "I don't know how much you can get from a stone, but postal workers already work hard and they're just trying to squeeze a lot of orange from the juice."

Canada Post's Caines characterizes the dispute between the two parties as "boiling down to the fundamental issue of who is going to control the workplace—management or the union." The clearer issue, however, is, how do you change a culture that is so entrenched, with each of the parties unwilling to see what the other side wants?

Questions

1. Describe Canada Post's current culture.

2. How might cultural change efforts be different in public-sector organizations than in for-profit business firms?

3. What suggestions would you have for top management that could help it enlist the unions in their cultural change efforts?

4. Discuss the specific suggestions you would make to top management that could help it succeed in changing Canada Post's culture into one that was more friendly.

Sources: Based on B. Came, "Handle With Care: Canada Post Tries to Avert a Nationwide Postal Strike," *Maclean's*, November 17, 1997, p. 86; J. Ditchburn, "Canada Post, Union Return to Bargaining Table," *Canadian Press Newswire*, August 19, 1997; G. McIntosh, "Canada Post Says Carriers Should do the Quick Step," *Canadian Press Newswire*, April 4, 1997.

Wal-Mart's Culture Comes to Canada

In early 1994, Wal-Mart started its move into Canada, transforming Woolco stores and turning Woolco employees into Wal-Mart associates. Wal-Mart faced resistance, however, as Canadians were aware that the giant retailer had often caused local businesses to be eliminated, had refused to buy any of Woolco's unionized stores, and had even sent English-only flyers to potential customers in Quebec.

So, how has Wal-Mart managed its move into Canada? By bringing its corporate culture with it. Wal-Mart has a strong culture, replete with slogans, posters, and socialization practices. The company even introduced its culture using cheerleading techniques more readily identified with Americans than Canadians, with workers and trainers shouting "We are family!" and "Who's number one? The customer, always."

Wal-Mart's office space is covered with posters, including "Eight Steps to Building your Business," "Corporate Beliefs," and "The Top 10 Principles of Success." The Wal-Mart operation is fuelled by slogans such as "Pride Through Performance." Employees also understand the importance of these slogans. As one employee reports, after mentioning some of the slogans ("respect for individual", "meet the needs of the customer", "be the best in all we do"), "The slogans are what we do."

As Wal-Mart moved in to Canada, it understood the importance of introducing its corporate culture to Canadian workers. The company wanted to ensure that Woolco employees would adopt the mindset of Wal-Mart Associates. It even hired a "morning kicker" to help employees get into the spirit. Wal-Mart does seem successful at making its northern move. Although there have been some rumblings about unionization, these have not resulted in successful campaigns. In the fall of 1997, the second unionization attempt it faced was turned down by Nelson, British Columbia, workers. The first unionization attempt, in Windsor, Ontario, was also rebuffed, although the Ontario Labor Relations Board certified the union anyway. However, in the late spring of 1998, the Windsor workers appealed the Ontario Board's ruling, indicating that they preferred to be decertified. And, in April 1998, Wal-Mart announced the opening of four more stores.

Questions

1. Describe how Wal-Mart's slogans reinforce its culture.

2. What difficulties might you anticipate in bringing Wal-Mart's "American culture" into Canada?

3. Do you think everyone would be interested in a strong culture such as Wal-Mart? Why or why not?

Source: Based on "Wal-Martization of Canada," *Venture 508*; aired February 10, 1994.

POINT

Organizational Cultural Doesn't Change

That an organization's culture is made up of relatively stable characteristics would imply that culture is very difficult for management to change. Such a conclusion would be correct.

An organization's culture develops over many years and is rooted in deeply held values to which employees are strongly committed. In addition, there are a number of forces continually operating to maintain a given culture. These would include written statements about the organization's mission and philosophy, the design of physical spaces and buildings, the dominant leadership style, hiring criteria, past promotion practices, entrenched rituals, popular stories about key people and events, the organization's historic performance evaluation criteria, and the organization's formal structure.

Selection and promotion policies are particularly important devices that work against cultural change. Employees chose the organization because they perceived their values to be a "good fit" with the organization. They become comfortable with that fit and will strongly resist efforts to disturb the equilibrium. The terrific difficulties that organizations such as General Motors, MacMillan Bloedel, and Canada Post have had in trying to reshape their cultures attest to this dilemma. These organizations historically tended to attract individuals who desired and flourished in situations that were stable and highly structured. Those in control in organizations will also select senior managers who will continue the current culture. Even attempts to change a culture by going outside the orga-

nization to hire a new chief executive are unlikely to be effective. The evidence indicates that the culture is more likely to change the executive than the other way around. Why? It's too entrenched, and change becomes a potential threat to member self-interest. In fact, a more pragmatic view of the relationship between an organization's culture and its chief executive would be to note that the practice of filling senior-level management positions from current managerial employees ensures that those who run the organization have been fully indoctrinated in the organization's culture. Promoting from within provides stability and lessens uncertainty. When Exxon's board of directors selects as a new chief executive officer an individual who has spent 30 years in the company, it virtually guarantees that the culture will continue unchanged.

Our argument, however, should not be viewed as saying that culture can never be changed. In the unusual case when an organization confronts a survival-threatening crisis—a crisis that is universally acknowledged as a true life-or-death situation—members of the organization will be responsive to efforts at cultural change. For instance, it was only when IBM Canada and General Motors' executives were able to successfully convey to employees the crises faced from competitors that these organizations' cultures began to show signs of adaptation. However, anything less than a crisis is unlikely to be effective in bringing about cultural change. ■

counterPOINT

How to Change an Organization's Culture

Changing an organization's culture is extremely difficult, but cultures *can* be changed. For example, Lee Iacocca came to Chrysler Corp. in 1978, when the company appeared to be only weeks away from bankruptcy. It took him about five years, but in what is now a well-worn story, he took Chrysler's conservative, inward-looking, and engineering-oriented culture and changed it into an action-oriented, market-responsive culture.

The evidence suggests that cultural change is most likely to occur when most or all of the following conditions exist:

A dramatic crisis. This is the shock that undermines the status quo and calls into question the relevance of the current culture. Examples of these crises might be a surprising financial setback, the loss of a major customer, or a dramatic technological breakthrough by a competitor. Calgary-based Suncor hired Richard George as president and CEO in 1992 to take it from a downsizing to a growth culture, and experienced a dramatic turnaround in three years. The results have continued. Profits reached a record high in 1997, following five years of reporting profits. Executives at Pepsi-Cola and Ameritech even admit to creating crises in order to stimulate cultural change in their organizations.[1]

Turnover in leadership. New top leadership, which can provide an alternative set of key values, may be perceived as more capable of responding to the crisis. This would definitely be the organization's chief executive but also might need to include all senior management positions. The hiring of outside CEOs at MacMillan Bloedel (Tom Stephens) and IBM (Louis Gerstner) illustrate attempts to introduce new leadership.

Young and small organization. The younger the organization is, the less entrenched its culture will be. Similarly, it's easier for management to communicate its new values when the organization is small. This again helps to explain the difficulty that multibillion-dollar corporations have in changing their cultures.

Weak culture. The more widely held a culture is and the higher the agreement among members on its values, the more difficult it will be to change. Conversely, weak cultures are more amenable to change than strong ones.

If conditions support cultural change, you should consider the following suggestions:

1. Have top-management people become positive role models, setting the tone through their behaviour.
2. Create new stories, symbols, and rituals to replace those currently in vogue.
3. Select, promote, and support employees who espouse the new values that are sought.
4. Redesign socialization processes to align with the new values.
5. Change the reward system to encourage acceptance of a new set of values.
6. Replace unwritten norms with formal rules and regulations that are tightly enforced.
7. Shake up current subcultures through transfers, job rotation, and/or terminations.
8. Work to get peer group consensus through utilization of employee participation and creation of a climate with a high level of trust.

Implementing most or all of these suggestions will not result in an immediate or dramatic shift in the organization's culture. For, in the final analysis, cultural change is a lengthy process—measured in years rather than months. But if the question is, "Can culture be changed?" the answer is "Yes!" ■

Source:
[1] B. Dumaine, "Times Are Good? Create a Crisis," *Fortune,* June 28, 1993, pp. 123–30.

Organizational Change and Stress Management

ROADMAP

CHAPTER 17: OUTLINE

LEARNING OBJECTIVES

After studying this chapter, you should be able to

- Describe forces that act as stimulants to change

- Contrast first-order and second-order change

- Summarize the types of changes that organizations make

- Summarize sources of individual and organizational resistance to change

- Describe potential sources of stress

- Explain individual difference variables that moderate the stress–outcome relationship

In 1997, when John Wetmore took over as the new head of Markham, Ontario-based IBM Canada Inc., it was a good time to be leading an IBM subsidiary.[1] Profits were up and no layoffs were in sight. This was not the case five years earlier, when IBM worldwide was facing eroding profits, questionable product directions, and numerous layoffs. IBM Canada first realized it had a problem in the spring of 1991, when the company discovered that it would not reach the revenue and profit plans for that year. Gaye Emery, vice-president and general manager of marketing for IBM Canada, attributes the problems at IBM Canada to maintaining the status quo due to four solid decades of unparalleled growth. Specifically, she notes that IBM Canada had stopped listening to the customer and neglected to watch the competition.

IBM Canada recognized immediately that it needed a culture change. As Emery reports, "What we found was a culture that included many wonderful traits: confidence, loyalty, perseverance, and an admirable work ethic. But we also found a degree of arrogance, a sense of entitlement, and an entrenched aversion to risk." Over the next several years, IBM Canada set out to change that culture and, among other things, trained its managers and professionals in leadership skills, teamwork, empowerment, and risk taking. This encouraged managers to function more as coaches and employees to work better as team members.

What are the conditions that organizations undergoing change are likely to experience? What factors will contribute to successful change in the workplace of the 21st century? Changing the culture of an organization—in fact, engaging in any kind of change in an organization—is not easy. Below we examine the forces of change and consider how organizational change comes about. ■

Forces for Change

In Chapter 1 we outlined a series of changes affecting the Canadian workplace, indicating that all of these represented forces for change in today's organization. There are demands on employers to make the workplace more responsive to employees. There are pressures on employees and managers to be more team oriented and to upgrade their skills, including technological skills. Due to globalization, there are pressures on organizations to become leaner, more productive, and more quality oriented. We also noted that both the increasingly diverse Canadian society and more opportunities to work abroad led to pressures to understand how to work with people different from ourselves. Finally, we noted that employees need to learn to live with flexibility, spontaneity, and unpredictability. In other words, they face an environment of continual change.

While Chapter 1 outlined the major sources of pressures for change, as we proceeded through the textbook we developed a further appreciation of the internal demands of the workplace that placed pressures on individuals to change and adapt. For instance, in Part 1 we noted that it was important for individuals to continue the process of learning and indicated factors that might affect how people get along in the workplace. In Part 2 we noted the importance of motivating employees and discussed a variety of programs that could be used to motivate individuals for specific outcomes. We also talked about the increasing emphasis on working on teams in organizations. In Part 3 of the text we noted the importance of sharing the vision with employees, gave examples of how to communicate more effectively, and suggested that organizations are moving toward more ethically and socially responsible positions. We also discussed the new leadership challenges of sharing power with employees, as well as the need for employees to be good followers in some instances. In Part 4 we looked at some of the uneasy sides of interaction, including power and politics. We noted that power could be used in negative ways in organizations, including using power to engage in sexual harassment. We discussed conflict, and we indicated some of the more positive ways to engage in negotiation. Finally, in Part 5 of the text to this point we have discussed reorganizing the workplace, noting how recent changes in organizational structure have, in some instances, led to more flattened organizations, as well as more interconnections with other organizations. We described job redesign as a way of motivating employees and indicated that increasing factors such as autonomy and feedback generally increased satisfaction. We also noted that the culture of the organization was like the glue that held the organization together, and that sometimes, the entire culture of the organization needed to be changed in order to effect change.

Throughout these discussions, to some extent we may have implied that change happened easily, perhaps overnight, and did not require careful thought or planning. This implication occurred because we did not discuss how these changes actually occurred in the workplace, what one needed to do in order to effect change, and how difficult change actually was. We wanted you to understand what changes were possible before we actually discussed how to carry out that change.

In this chapter we consider the process of organizational change, of actually examining organizations whose processes and structures may have worked in the 1980s and early 1990s but needed to make changes for the late 1990s and beyond. We discuss what it takes to become more productive

in an era of globalization, changing technology, and demands for efficiency. In exploring change we also consider resistance to change, as well as one specific consequence of change that may affect most workers at one stage or another of their careers: employee stress.

In covering stress in this chapter we do not mean to imply that stress only occurs when organizations are undergoing change. In fact, some organizations create stressful environments for their employees even without undergoing a process of change. Our HR Implications presents a discussion of how organizations can help employees to better manage stress levels.

Types of Organizational Change

When we discuss change in this chapter, we're concerned with activities that are proactive and purposeful; that is, change as an intentional, goal-oriented activity. We refer to this as **planned change**.

What are the goals of planned change? Essentially there are two. First, it seeks to improve the ability of the organization to adapt to new factors in its environment. Second, it seeks to modify employee behaviour.

You might find it helpful to think of planned change in terms of order of magnitude.[2] **First-order change** is linear and continuous. It implies no fundamental shifts in the assumptions that organizational members hold about the world or how the organization can improve its functioning. In contrast, **second-order change** is a multidimensional, multilevel, discontinuous, radical change involving reframing of assumptions about the organization and the world in which it operates. Mikio Kitano, director of all production engineering at Toyota, is introducing first-order change in his company.[3] He's pursuing slow, subtle, incremental changes in production processes to improve the efficiency of Toyota's plants. On the other hand, Boeing's top executives have recently committed themselves to radically reinventing their company.[4] Responding to a massive airline slump, aggressive competition from Airbus, and the threat of Japanese competitors, this second-order change process at Boeing includes slashing costs by up to 30 percent, reducing the time it takes to make a 737 from 13 months to six months, dramatically cutting inventories, putting the company's entire workforce through a four-day course in "competitiveness," and bringing customers and suppliers into the once-secret process of designing new planes.

If an organization is to survive, it must respond to changes in its environment. When competitors introduce new products or services, government agencies enact new laws, important sources of supply go out of business, or similar environmental changes take place, the organization must adapt. Efforts to stimulate innovation, empower employees, and introduce work teams are examples of second-order planned change activities directed at responding to changes in the environment. Organizations have also had to change where they manufacture goods in response to public criticism, as happened to Nike when some criticized its use of exploited labour in the Third World.

Since an organization's success or failure is essentially due to the things that its employees or managers may do or fail to do, planned change also is concerned with changing the behaviour of individuals and groups within the organization. In this chapter we review techniques that organizations can use to get people to behave differently in the tasks they perform and in their interactions with others.

planned change
Change as an intentional and goal-oriented activity.

first-order change
Change that is linear and continuous.

second-order change
Change that is multidimensional, multilevel, discontinuous, and radical.

Boeing Company
www.boeing.com/

What Do Organizations Change?

Organizational change affects five aspects of a company: its culture, structure, technology, physical setting, and people.[5] (See Exhibit 17-1.) Changing *culture* may well be the most profound of the changes an organization makes because it requires changing the underlying values and goals of the organization. We referred earlier to culture as the glue that holds the organization together, which is why culture change is the most dramatic, as the opening vignette on IBM Canada suggests. Changing *structure* involves altering authority relations, coordination mechanisms, job redesign, or similar structural variables. Changing *technology* encompasses modifications in the way work is processed and in the methods and equipment used. Changing the *physical setting* covers altering the space and layout arrangements in the workplace. Changing *people* refers to changes in employee skills, expectations, and/or behaviour. Below we examine each of these changes in turn, reserving our discussion of culture change to the end because of its complex and wide-ranging impact.

Changing Structure

In Chapter 14 we discussed structural issues such as work specialization, span of control, and various organizational designs. However, organizational structures are not set in concrete. Changing conditions demand structural changes. As a result, organizations sometimes modify the organization's structure.

An organization's structure is defined by how tasks are formally divided, grouped, and coordinated. Organizations can alter one or more of the key elements in an organization's design. For instance, departmental responsibilities can be combined, vertical layers removed, and spans of control widened to make the organization flatter and less bureaucratic. More rules and procedures can be implemented to increase standardization. An increase in decentralization can be made to speed up the decision-making process.

Organizations can also introduce major modifications in the actual structural design. This might include a shift from a simple structure to a team-based structure or the creation of a matrix design. Organizations

**Exhibit 17-1
Change Options**

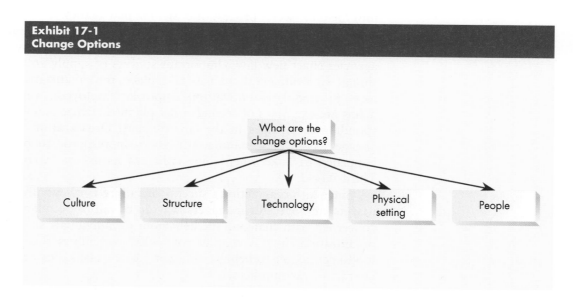

might consider redesigning jobs or work schedules. Job descriptions can be redefined, jobs enriched, or flexible work hours introduced. Still another option is to modify the organization's compensation system. Motivation could be increased by, for example, introducing performance bonuses or profit sharing.

Paul Tellier, President and CEO of Montreal-based Canadian National Railway (CN), had to make major changes to the railway after taking the helm. In order to transform CN into a profitable company that would be responsive to customer needs, Tellier "reduced the number of layers of management and abolished five vice-president posts, so that where formerly there were sometimes 10 layers of authority between the president and any line employee, there are now no more than five."[6] Managers were given more breadth of command, and communication became clearer as there were fewer communication channels through which messages had to travel. While these are not the only changes CN undertook, they do illustrate the types of structural changes organizations might make. The changes that CN started in the early 1990s and continued through the decade have been very successful. By March 1998, CN was two years ahead of schedule in efficiency improvements, as measured by its operating ratio (the percentage of each dollar of revenue needed to run the railway).[7]

You may remember from Chapter 8's OB in the News feature that Amsterdam-based Delta Lloyd decided to implement team work to speed up its insurance processing. To ensure that teamwork would be implemented, Delta Lloyd asked all 268 of its managers to reapply for their jobs, and only 58 percent of them won jobs in the new organization. In this instance Delta Lloyd was signalling to managers and employees alike that teamwork was an important component of the new work process, and if you couldn't function in a team, you might not have a job with the company. As we reported in Chapter 8, the team process worked, and files that were taking two to three weeks to complete are now finished the same day in 70 to 80 percent of the cases.

Canadian National Railways
www.cn.ca/

When Paul Tellier took over as President and CEO of Montreal-based Canadian National Railways, his major focus was to turn it into a profitable company. Among the changes Tellier undertook was structural change, reducing the number of management layers and increasing the ease of communication.

Changing Technology

Most of the early studies in management and organizational behaviour dealt with efforts aimed at technological change. At the turn of the century, for example, scientific management sought to implement changes based on time-and-motion studies that would increase production efficiency. Today, major technological changes usually involve the introduction of new equipment, tools, methods, automation, or computerization.

Competitive factors or innovations within an industry often require organizations to introduce new equipment, tools, or operating methods. For example, many aluminum companies have significantly modernized their plants in recent years to compete more effectively. More efficient handling equipment, furnaces, and presses have been installed to reduce the cost of manufacturing a ton of aluminum.

Automation is a technological change that replaces people with machines. It began in the Industrial Revolution and continues as a change option today. Examples of automation are the introduction of automatic mail sorters by Canada Post and robots on automobile assembly lines.

As noted in previous chapters, the most visible technological change in recent years has been expanding computerization. Many organizations now have sophisticated management information systems. Large supermarkets have converted their cash registers into input terminals and linked them to computers to provide instant inventory data. The office of 1999 is dramatically different from its counterpart of 1979, predominantly because of computerization. This is typified by desktop microcomputers that can run hundreds of business software packages and network systems that allow these computers to communicate with one another.

In 1996, executives at West Coast Energy's Chatham, Ontario-based Union Gas Ltd. and Willowdale, Ontario-based Centra Gas units requested that their regional managers install a new computerized financial system project by an ambitious January 1, 1997 deadline. The response from the regional managers was, "Forget it, buster."[8] The executives were planning to have the computers shipped in the fall, but what they had failed to realize is that September to December is the "light-up" season, "when customer service departments are pushed to their limits serving customers who want their furnaces started, checked, and repaired."[9]

While employees are often resistant to change, the above story illustrates a failure on the part of senior management to plan for a major change to be introduced at an appropriate time. Senior management was surprised by the resistance and hired change management specialists from Price Waterhouse to talk to the financial system project team and employees who would be using the system. The change specialists discovered that there was not a lot of support for the introduction of the new technology. How did Union and Centra deal with the resistance? They hired Price Waterhouse to join the project team and help with the transition. "Plans were explained to the staff, training plans were put in place, and employees from all over the field who were informal champions of the new technology were recruited to help turn the situation around."[10] One of the critical changes made to the schedule was to install all of the computers in a six-week period during the summer. Training was also done during summer months, so that when light-up season started, the whole system was up and running.

Union's and Centra's experiences with introducing change are not unique. However, they did a number of things correctly to ensure that

change occurred in as smooth a manner as possible. First, they listened to their employees about the causes of their resistance. Second, they hired a consulting agency to further identify sources of resistance. Third, they brought together a team that could help inspire the change, including bringing Price Waterhouse onto the team, and also recruiting supportive employees who would help encourage their peers. Finally, they scheduled the change for a time that would be less likely to induce stress for the employees. Ken Kawall, director of information technology for Union Gas and Centra Gas, also offers a piece of advice: "Make sure people issues are included as a major part of the planning exercise."[11]

Changing the Physical Setting

Workplace layout should not be set up piecemeal or at random. Typically, management thoughtfully considers work demands, formal interaction requirements, and social needs when making decisions about space configurations, interior design, equipment placement, and the like. For example, by eliminating walls and partitions and opening up an office design, it becomes easier for employees to communicate with each other. Similarly, management can change the quantity and types of lights, the level of heat or cold, the levels and types of noise, and the cleanliness of the work area, as well as interior design aspects such as furniture, decorations, and colour schemes.

Cobourg, Ontario-based Rusco Canada Ltd., a manufacturer of vinyl windows, steel entrance doors, and steel security screens, redesigned their plant in 1996 after their largest client told them to "deliver on time or lose our orders."[12] Rusco had been struggling with getting orders out on time because no one seemed to have all the information to know when an order would be completed or where it was once it was shipped. Faced with losing their biggest client, they engaged in a variety of changes. One such change involved the physical layout of the plant. They "moved all the machines and production equipment into a new layout during the peak business period...expanding and redesigning production into a progressive, straight-line configuration over a few weekends and after shifts." Among other things, this configuration made it possible for line workers to see the progress of products along the line and into shipping, which helped everyone have a better sense of when products would be ready for shipping.

Rusco's redesign of its plant was done in a way to minimize the disruption on production. Much of the move was done during a few weekends and after shifts. The redesign paid off. Within six weeks, the company was having trouble keeping up with new orders. In early 1997, CEO Bob Young reported, "We have gone up to 369 windows a period with 8 workers from 200 with 14 people, and now we are vertically integrating."

Changing People

Organizations can also help individuals and groups within the organization to work more effectively together. This category typically involves changing the attitudes and behaviors of organizational members through processes of communication, decision-making, and problem solving.

When Gilles Pansera purchased Lac-Megantic, Quebec-based Industries Manufacturières Mégantic Inc. (IMMI) in 1990 and became its president, the operation had been losing money for the previous 10 years.[13] Pansera believed, however, that it could be profitable, if the company retargeted the

market and upgraded machinery. Pansera decided to concentrate on "doorskin" plywood, which requires a much more labour-intensive production process, needing the careful involvement of employees. Pansera realized that to improve productivity, he would have to modify employees' habits. He quickly discovered that this was "a much harder proposal than expected." While the employees were generally good, they had not been offered responsibility under the previous owners, and therefore there were employees who had worked for the company for 20 years yet knew nothing about the other end of the plant.

Pansera shut down the plant for two hours after he bought it, discussing the situation with the employees, and showing the books to them. He discussed the problems with the company and outlined what he intended to do about it. He repeats these sessions every quarter, because he believes that employees should know everything about the company. IMMI is unionized, and the employees appreciated his openness. After their first meeting, they agreed to renegotiate their collective agreement in return for ending the private deals that the previous owners had made with favoured employees.

Dealing with the union turned out to be one of Pansera's easier problems, as it turned out. In 1992, he wanted to establish a total quality management program and produced an employee manual describing the changes and procedures. That was when he discovered that 30 percent of his employees did not know how to read. He scrapped the manual and, with the support of the local school board, started a program to teach literacy and basic mathematics to workers. IMMI spends $200 000 a year on staff training, and Pansera believes that it is a worthwhile investment. He notes, "Everybody has what it takes to learn more complex tasks, and above all to assimilate the programs" he wanted to implement.

In the case of IMMI, change worked for two main reasons. First, Pansera communicated openly with employees. Second, when he discovered that they lacked the skills to implement the changes he had in mind, he helped them to acquire those skills. This made it less likely they would resist the change, because they had the skills to confront new demands.

This chapter's OB in the News feature describes how John Gilbank changed the decision-making authority of managers at Calgary-based CE Franklin Ltd., modified the reward structure to match the new decision-making structure, and saw Franklin turn around from a failing company to a highly successful one in just five years.

CE Franklin Ltd.
http://www.cefranklin.com/

Changing the Culture of the Organization

Culture sets the tone for how employees interact with each other, what things are valued by the organization, and what the expectations for managers and employees are. Often, changing just the structure, or the technology, or the people may not be enough to achieve fundamental change in the organization. That is because culture often represents the mindset of the employees and managers. In this section we consider several examples of culture change and how they were accomplished in Canadian organizations.

When Brian Groff bought Waterloo, Ontario-based Sutherland Schultz Inc., a construction company, in 1996, he had on his hands a company that had lost money for the previous four years.[14] Moreover, it was characterized by infighting among the 400 workers spread across 13 divisions. The divisions represented such things as electrical and mechanical contracting as well as pipefitting, and thus traditional trade rivalries plagued the company.

OB IN THE NEWS

CE Franklin Ltd.'s Remarkable Turnaround

When John Gilbank assumed control of Calgary-based Franklin Supply, an oilfield parts distributor, the bank had given 90 days' notice for repayment of Franklin's $13 million loan. Franklin had once been one of the leading businesses in its field.

Gilbert has since set the company, now named CE Franklin Ltd., on a new course, introducing a sophisticated inventory control system, turning its 42 service outlets into independently run profit centres, becoming a client-focused reseller, and acquiring other firms.

Gilbank was named chairman and CEO a few months after his arrival. He felt that Franklin needed "a little bit of delicate surgery followed by a great deal more of nurturing new growth. The external environment had changed drastically, while inside, everything was on cruise. It was time to take it off auto-pilot and start flying it in a new direction."

One of the problems Gilbank faced was a disagreement among the employees about whether Franklin should return to being an enterprising family-style business, or working at being larger and benefit from economies of scale. Gilbank could see the pros and cons of both, and decided on a "big/small strategy." The firm continued its volume buying and centralized back-office functions but also had a radical decentralization. Thus the public face of CE Franklin is a family-run store, and employees know all their clients by name.

Gilbank turned all the firm's outlets into independent profit centres that pay an internal "tax" for warehousing and administrative services. To help his managers run these profit centres he wrote an employee manual on the principles of operating a successful enterprise. He also gave evening lectures on small-business management. Store managers are responsible for making their own inventory, service and pricing decisions. Managers' compensation is tied to store performance. Gilbank also encouraged Franklin staff to actively look for ways to help oil and gas companies "reduce their costs and improve their quality."

Franklin currently distributes 10 percent of its net income to its staff. The staff also hold stock options. Gilbank explains his philosophy for doing this: "The people who generate good things should share in good things, and they'll generate more good things."

Today, Franklin is again a leader in its industry. Gilbank was named the Prairie region's Turnaround winner in the 1997 Entrepreneur of the Year awards. Sales earned the firm profits of $6.7 million in 1996 on sales of $259 million. Net income has grown by 1,056% over the past five years. This increase in income also means an increase in the rewards to Franklin employees.

Source: Based on George Koch, Michela Pasquali, Donna Green, "A Change For the Bettor," *Profit: The Magazine for Canadian Entrepreneurs*, December 1997/January 1998, pp. 58–61.

Take It to the Net

We invite you to visit the Robbins page on the Prentice Hall Web site at:

http://www.prenticehall.ca/robbins

for this chapter's World Wide Web exercise.

The divisions were unwilling to work together, and Groff characterized the company as a war zone. "Even worse, long-time customers doing business with one division didn't realize there were other divisions they might use. Relations had so deteriorated that, given the chance, staff would often recommend competitors."

Groff recognized that in order to resolve this kind of infighting, an organization needed more than just a simple structural change—it needed a cul-

tural change as well. Two months after taking over, he closed two small divisions and fired five key division managers. He then replaced these managers with five experienced individuals from outside the company. This gave Groff an aggressive, knowledgeable, team-oriented management group to help him turn the culture around. Groff believed that his employees needed more knowledge about each other, how each division operated, and how to work as a team. To do this, he set up a training program aimed at management and field supervisors that would cover everything from teamwork to problem-solving skills. Employees were initially quite resistant about devoting time to learning, although gradually they came to understand the value of the training. An added benefit was that by bringing together the managers from all the divisions in one room for training, they came to know more about each other's problems and could learn to work together. Eventually employees came to realize that there were major advantages to acting as a multi-trade organization, rather than trying to protect the turf of individual trades, as they had done in the past. After just one year under Groff's culture change program, Sutherland-Schultz doubled its sales to $105 million and produced its first profitable year since 1992.

Groff's success at turning around the culture of Sutherland-Schultz occurred in part because of the extensive training provided for employees. This gave them the opportunity to learn about the other divisions and how they could work together, rather than referring business outside the company. Had Groff simply replaced the five division managers he fired and not engaged in extensive training, the change may not have occurred as successfully, because he would have had difficulty getting the other employees to understand the changes that needed to be made.

Suncor Energy Inc.
http://www.suncor.com/

As the 1990s began, Calgary-based Suncor Energy, Inc. underwent major downsizing, suffered a major fire at one of its plants, had operating groups that did not communicate with each other, and experienced a decline in profits.[15] In facing these problems, Suncor recognized that it needed to change its culture and did so. By 1996, Suncor had turned itself around, moving its oil sands business into a success story, seeing its Resources Group breaking all of its production and reserve replacement records, and developing efficient refinery and retail businesses.

To change its culture, Suncor started with a vision statement. They determined that their core purpose is to "consistently deliver outstanding achievements in Canadian petroleum and related businesses." To achieve this core purpose, they outlined a number of related activities, which are identified in Exhibit 17-2. Suncor also moved from a command-and-control system "to a more flexible, more innovative environment that is open to ideas and focuses on individual initiative." In making the changes, Suncor strove to inform employees that they were a valuable part of the organization, because the change required enormous commitment on the part of the employees. Suncor also kept employees informed of changes, even in one case stopping trading on their stock for an hour so that they could inform employees directly of imminent downsizing, rather than having their employees find out about it in the news. Peter Spelliscy, former senior vice-president, human resources and communication at Suncor, states that this action "earned (Suncor) a level of trust and commitment that made the turnaround happen quickly and professionally."

Are there appropriate ways to carry out change in organizations? One researcher has identified 17 key elements to successful change, which are discussed in this chapter's From Concepts to Skills feature. At Suncor, Spelliscy

> **Exhibit 17-2**
> **Elements of Suncor's Vision Statement**
>
> - Seize opportunities that we identify or create in the rapidly changing business environment.
> - Capitalize on the existing core assets and businesses.
> - Ensure excellence in execution in all aspects of our business.
> - Earn exceptional loyalty in relationships with our customers by consistently providing quality, cost-effective products and services.
> - Set and attain progressive standards in health, safety, environment, workforce diversity, business ethics, and community involvement.
> - Encourage individual and collective contribution to these achievements to create the opportunity for personal growth, reward, and satisfaction.
>
> Source: P. Spelliscy, "Changing the Corporate Culture from Downsizing to Growth," *Canadian Speeches*, June 1996, pp. 45–50.

developed ABCs of change that would be relevant to any organization undergoing a major change in its workplace:

> "A is to achieve awareness that things must change. You have to create a compelling case for change and convince people the need is real. Too often we fail to share information and involve people in the business issues. If people don't feel a sense of personal involvement and ownership, they just don't care.
>
> B is to build belief among employees that they are part of the change. There's nothing more frustrating than realizing you are being changed. It is necessary for individuals to contribute to and control their destiny.
>
> Once people know change needs to happen, and they understand that it is possible, then and only then can you expect to achieve C, a commitment to change. If you don't get everyone involved in the changes, they either won't happen or they won't be effective."

Managing Organizational Change

A General Overview of the Process: Lewin's Three-Step Model

Kurt Lewin argued that successful change in organizations should follow three steps: **unfreezing** the status quo, **moving** to a new state, and **refreezing** the new change to make it permanent.[16] (See Exhibit 17-3.) The value of this model can be seen in the following example where the management of a large oil company decided to reorganize its marketing function in

unfreezing
Change efforts to overcome the pressures of both individual resistance and group conformity.

moving
Efforts to get employees involved in the change process.

refreezing
Stabilizing a change intervention by balancing driving and restraining forces.

> **Exhibit 17-3**
> **Lewin's Three-Step Change Model**

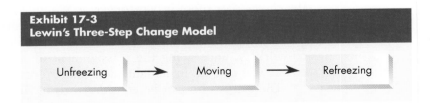

Unfreezing → Moving → Refreezing

FROM CONCEPTS TO SKILLS

Assessing the Climate for Change

Why do some change programs succeed and others fail? One major factor is change readiness. Research by Symmetrix, a Massachusetts consulting firm, identified 17 key elements to successful change. The more affirmative answers you get to the following questions, the greater the likelihood that change efforts will succeed.

1. Is the sponsor of change high up enough to have power to effectively deal with resistance?
2. Is day-to-day leadership supportive of the change and committed to it?
3. Is there a strong sense of urgency from senior management about the need for change, and is it shared by the rest of the organization?
4. Does management have a clear vision of how the future will look different from the present?
5. Are there objective measures in place to evaluate the change effort, and are reward systems explicitly designed to reinforce them?
6. Is the specific change effort consistent with other changes occurring within the organization?
7. Are functional managers willing to sacrifice their personal self-interest for the good of the organization as a whole?

8. Does management pride itself on closely monitoring changes and actions taken by competitors?
9. Is the importance of the customer and a knowledge of customer needs well accepted by everyone in the workforce?
10. Are managers and employees rewarded for taking risks, being innovative, and looking for new solutions?
11. Is the organizational structure flexible?
12. Are communication channels open both downward and upward?
13. Is the organization's hierarchy relatively flat?
14. Has the organization successfully implemented major changes in the recent past?
15. Is employee satisfaction and trust in management high?
16. Is there a high degree of cross-boundary interactions and cooperation between units in the organization?
17. Are decisions made quickly, taking into account a wide variety of suggestions?

Source: Based on T.A. Stewart, "Rate Your Readiness to Change," *Fortune*, February 7, 1994, pp. 106–10.

Western Canada. The oil company had three divisional offices in the West, located in Winnipeg, Calgary, and Vancouver. The decision was made to consolidate the divisions into a single regional office to be located in Calgary. The reorganization meant transferring over 150 employees, eliminating some duplicate managerial positions, and instituting a new hierarchy of command. As you might guess, a move of this magnitude was difficult to keep secret. The rumour of its occurrence preceded the announcement by several months. The decision itself was made unilaterally. It came from the executive offices in Toronto. Those people affected had no say whatsoever in the choice. For those in Vancouver or Winnipeg, who may have disliked the decision and its consequences—the problems inherent in transferring to another city, pulling youngsters out of school, making new friends, having new co-workers, undergoing the reassignment of responsibilities—their only recourse was to quit. In actuality, less than 10 percent did.

The status quo can be considered to be an equilibrium state. To move from this equilibrium—to overcome the pressures of both individual resis-

driving forces
Forces that direct behaviour away from the status quo.

restraining forces
Forces that hinder movement away from the status quo.

tance and group conformity—unfreezing is necessary. It can be achieved in one of three ways. (See Exhibit 17-4.) The **driving forces**, which direct behaviour away from the status quo, can be increased. The **restraining forces**, which hinder movement from the existing equilibrium, can be decreased. A third alternative is to *combine the first two approaches*.

The oil company's management could expect employee resistance to the consolidation. To deal with that resistance, management could use positive incentives to encourage employees to accept the change. For instance, increases in pay can be offered to those who accept the transfer. Very liberal moving expenses can be paid by the company. Management might offer low-cost mortgage funds to allow employees to buy new homes in Calgary. Of course, management might also consider unfreezing acceptance of the status quo by removing restraining forces. Employees could be counselled individually. Each employee's concerns and apprehensions could be heard and specifically clarified. Assuming that most of the fears are unjustified, the counsellor could assure the employees that there was nothing to fear and then demonstrate, through tangible evidence, that restraining forces are unwarranted. If resistance is extremely high, management may have to resort to both reducing resistance and increasing the attractiveness of the alternative if the unfreezing is to be successful.

Once the consolidation change has been implemented, if it is to be successful, the new situation must be refrozen so that it can be sustained over time. Unless this last step is taken, there is a very high chance that the change will be short-lived and that employees will attempt to revert to the previous equilibrium state. The objective of refreezing, then, is to stabilize the new situation by balancing the driving and restraining forces.

How could the oil company's management refreeze its consolidation change? It could systematically replace temporary forces with permanent ones. For instance, management might impose a permanent upward adjustment of salaries or permanently remove time clocks to reinforce a climate of trust and confidence in employees. The formal rules and regulations governing behaviour of those affected by the change should also be revised to reinforce the new situation. Over time, of course, the work group's own norms will evolve to sustain the new equilibrium. But until that point is reached, management will have to rely on more formal mechanisms. The Working With Others exercise gives you the opportunity to identify driving and restraining forces for another company experiencing problems with change, and to make some recommendations for change.

A key feature of Lewin's three-step model is its conception of change as an episodic activity. For a debate about whether change can continue to be implemented as an activity with a beginning, a middle, and an end, or whether the structure of the 21st century workplace will require change to occur as an ongoing if not chaotic process, see this chapter's Point/Counterpoint feature.

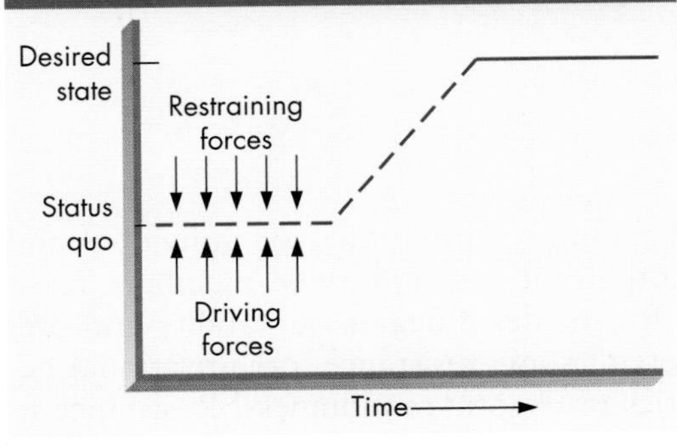

Carrying Out Organizational Change

In their 1997 review of three U.S. organizations that have effectively undergone major changes recently (Sears, Roebuck & Company; Royal Dutch Shell; and the U.S. Army) three organizational change consultants used the U.S. Army's *After Action Review* to summarize how an effective

Exhibit 17-4
Unfreezing the Status Quo

change process can be carried out in both business and the military. The After Action Review is a non-hierarchical team debriefing to help participants understand performance. The consultants identified seven disciplines embedded in the After Action Review:[17]

- *Build an intricate understanding of the business.* Organizational members need to have the big picture revealed to them so they know why change is needed and what is happening in the industry. Let organizational members know what is expected of them as the change proceeds.

- *Encourage uncompromising straight talk.* Communication cannot be based on hierarchy, but must allow everyone to contribute freely to the discussion.

- *Manage from the future.* Rather than setting goals that are directed toward a specific future point in time (and thus encouraging everyone to stop when the goal is achieved), manage from the perspective of always looking toward the future and future needs.

- *Harness setbacks.* When things do not go as planned, and there are setbacks, it is natural to blame one's self, others, or bad luck. Instead, teach everyone to view setbacks as learning opportunities and opportunities for improvement.

- *Promote inventive accountability.* While employees know what the specific targets and goals are, they should also be encouraged in the change process to look to being inventive and taking initiative when new opportunities arise.

- *Understand the quid pro quo.* When organizations undergo change processes, this puts a lot of stress and strain on employees. Organizations must ensure that employees are rewarded for their efforts. To build appropriate commitment, organizations must develop four levels of incentives:
  a) reward and recognition for effort;
  b) training and skill development that will make the employee marketable;
  c) meaningful work that provides intrinsic satisfaction;
  d) communication about where the organization is going and some say in the process for employees.

- *Create relentless discomfort with the status quo.* People are more willing to change when the current situation looks less attractive than the new situation.

  These points indicate that effective change is a comprehensive process, requiring a lot of commitment from both the organization's leaders and its members. This chapter's CBC Video Case reviews CP Railway's recent move to Alberta, and indicates a variety of problems managers and employees faced.

Resistance to Change

One of the most well-documented findings from studies of individual and organizational behaviour is that organizations and their members resist change. In a sense, this is positive. It provides a degree of stability and predictability to behaviour. If there weren't some resistance, organizational behaviour would take on characteristics of chaotic randomness. Resistance to change can also be a source of functional conflict. For example, resistance to

a reorganization plan or a change in a product line can stimulate a healthy debate over the merits of the idea and result in a better decision. However, there is a definite downside to resistance to change: it hinders adaptation and progress.

Resistance to change doesn't necessarily surface in standardized ways. Resistance can be overt, implicit, immediate, or deferred. It is easiest for management to deal with resistance when it is overt and immediate. For instance, a change is proposed, and employees respond immediately by voicing complaints, engaging in a work slowdown, threatening to go on strike, or the like. The greater challenge is managing resistance that is implicit or deferred. Implicit resistance efforts are more subtle—loss of loyalty to the organization, loss of motivation to work, increased errors or mistakes, increased absenteeism due to "sickness"—and hence more difficult to recognize. Similarly, deferred actions cloud the link between the source of the resistance and the reaction to it. A change may produce what appears to be only a minimal reaction at the time it is initiated, but then resistance surfaces weeks, months, or even years later. Or a single change that in and of itself might have little impact becomes the straw that breaks the camel's back. Reactions to change can build up and then explode in some response that seems totally out of proportion to the change action it follows. The resistance, of course, has merely been deferred and stockpiled. What surfaces is a response to an accumulation of previous changes.

Let's look at the sources of resistance. For analytical purposes, we've categorized them by individual and organizational sources. In the real world, the sources often overlap.

Individual Resistance

Individual sources of resistance to change reside in basic human characteristics such as perceptions, personalities, and needs. The following summarizes five reasons why individuals may resist change. (See Exhibit 17-5.)

HABIT Every time you go out to eat, do you try a different restaurant? Probably not. If you're like most people, you find a couple of places you like and return to them on a somewhat regular basis.

As human beings, we're creatures of habit. Life is complex enough; we don't need to consider the full range of options for the hundreds of decisions we have to make every day. To cope with this complexity, we all rely on habits or programmed responses. But when confronted with change, this tendency to respond in our accustomed ways becomes a source of resistance. So when your department is moved to a new office building across town, it means you're likely to have to change many habits: waking up 10 minutes earlier, taking a new set of streets to work, finding a new parking place, adjusting to a new office layout, developing a new lunchtime routine, and so on.

**Exhibit 17-5
Sources of Individual Resistance to Change**

SECURITY People with a high need for security are likely to resist change because it threatens their feelings of safety. For example, when CTV announces it is laying off thousands of people or Ford introduces new robotic equipment, many employees at these firms may fear that their jobs are in jeopardy.

ECONOMIC FACTORS Another source of individual resistance is concern that changes will lower one's income. Changes in job tasks or

established work routines also can arouse economic fears if people are concerned that they won't be able to perform the new tasks or routines to their previous standards, especially when pay is closely tied to productivity.

FEAR OF THE UNKNOWN   Changes substitute ambiguity and uncertainty for the known. The transition from high school to university is typically such an experience. By the time we've completed our high-school years, we understand how things work. You might not have liked high school, but at least you understood the system. Then you move on to college or university and face a whole new and uncertain system. You have traded the known for the unknown and the fear or insecurity that accompanies it.

Employees in organizations hold the same dislike for uncertainty. If, for example, the introduction of TQM means production workers will have to learn statistical process control techniques, some may fear they'll be unable to do so. They may, therefore, develop a negative attitude toward TQM or behave dysfunctionally if required to use statistical techniques.

SELECTIVE INFORMATION PROCESSING   As we learned in Chapter 3, individuals shape their world through their perceptions. Once they have created this world, it resists change. Individuals are guilty of selectively processing information in order to keep their perceptions intact. They hear what they want to hear. They ignore information that challenges the world they've created. To return to the production workers who are faced with the introduction of TQM, they may ignore the arguments their bosses make in explaining why a knowledge of statistics is necessary or the potential benefits that the change will provide them.

CYNICISM   In addition to simple resistance to change, employees often feel cynical about the change process, particularly if they have been through several rounds of change, and nothing appears (to them) to have changed. In a 1997 study, three researchers from Ohio State University identified sources of cynicism in the change process of a large unionized manufacturing plant.[18] The major elements contributing to the cynicism were:

- feeling uninformed about what was happening;
- lack of communication and respect from one's supervisor;
- lack of communication and respect from one's union representative;
- lack of opportunity for meaningful participation in decision-making.

They also found that employees with negative personalities were more likely to be cynical about change. While organizations might not be able to change an individual's personality, they certainly have the ability to provide greater communication and respect, as well as opportunities to participate in decision-making. The researchers found that cynicism about change led to such outcomes as lower commitment, less satisfaction, and reduced motivation to work hard. Exhibit 17-6 illustrates why some employees, particularly Dilbert, may have reason to feel cynical about organizational change. You can discover more about how comfortable you are with change by taking the "Managing-in-a-Turbulent-World Tolerance Test" in this chapter's Learning About Yourself Exercise.

Organizational Resistance

Organizations, by their very nature, are conservative.[19] They actively resist change. You don't have to look far to see evidence of this phenomenon.

Exhibit 17-6

Source: Dilbert by Scott Adams. August 3, 1996. DILBERT reprinted by permission of United Feature Syndicate, Inc.

Government agencies want to continue doing what they have been doing for years, whether the need for their service changes or remains the same. Organized religions are deeply entrenched in their history. Attempts to change church doctrine require great persistence and patience. (For instance, factions of Sikhs in British Columbia have been engaged in continuous controversy with each other throughout 1997 and 1998 over whether tables and chairs should be removed from the temples as decreed by Ranjit Singh, Sikhism's high priest in Amritsar, India.) Educational institutions, which exist to open minds and challenge established ways of thinking, are themselves extremely resistant to change. Most school systems are using essentially the same teaching technologies today as they were 50 years ago. Similarly, most business firms appear highly resistant to change.

Six major sources of organizational resistance have been identified.[20] They are shown in Exhibit 17-7.

STRUCTURAL INERTIA Organizations have built-in mechanisms to produce stability. For example, the selection process systematically selects certain people in and certain people out. Training and other socialization techniques reinforce specific role requirements and skills. Formalization provides job descriptions, rules, and procedures for employees to follow.

The people who are hired into an organization are chosen for fit; they are then shaped and directed to behave in certain ways. When an organization is confronted with change, this structural inertia acts as a counterbalance to sustain stability.

LIMITED FOCUS OF CHANGE Organizations are composed of a number of interdependent subsystems. You can't change one without affecting the others. For example, if management changes the technological processes without simultaneously modifying the organization's structure to match, the change in technology is unlikely to be accepted. So limited changes in subsystems tend to be nullified by the larger system.

GROUP INERTIA Even if individuals want to change their behaviour, group norms may act as a constraint. An individual union member, for instance, may be willing to accept changes in his or her job suggested by management. But if union norms dictate resisting any unilateral change made by management, he or she is likely to resist.

**Exhibit 17-7
Sources of Organizational Resistance to Change**

Threat to established resource allocations → Organizational Resistance ← Structural inertia

Threat to established power relationships → Organizational Resistance ← Limited focus of change

Threat to expertise ↗ Organizational Resistance ↖ Group inertia

THREAT TO EXPERTISE Changes in organizational patterns may threaten the expertise of specialized groups. The introduction of decentralized personal computers, which allow managers to gain access to information directly from a company's mainframe, is an example of a change that was strongly resisted by many information systems departments in the early 1980s. Why? Decentralized end-user computing posed a threat to the specialized skills held by those in the centralized information systems departments.

THREAT TO ESTABLISHED POWER RELATIONSHIPS Any redistribution of decision-making authority can threaten long-established power relationships within the organization. The introduction of participative decision-making or self-managed work teams is the kind of change that supervisors and middle managers often view as threatening.

THREAT TO ESTABLISHED RESOURCE ALLOCATIONS Those groups in the organization that control sizable resources often view change as a threat. They tend to be content with the status quo. Will the change, for instance, mean a reduction in their budgets or a cut in their staff size? Those that most benefit from the current allocation of resources often feel threatened by changes that may affect future allocations.

Overcoming Resistance to Change

Six tactics have been suggested for use by organizations dealing with resistance to change.[21] Let's review them briefly.

EDUCATION AND COMMUNICATION Resistance can be reduced through communicating with employees to help them see the logic of a change. This tactic basically assumes that the source of resistance lies in misinformation or poor communication; that is, if employees receive the full facts and any misunderstandings are cleared up, resistance will be decreased. Communication can be achieved through one-on-one discussions, memos, group presentations, or reports. Does this approach work? It does, provided that the source of resistance is inadequate communication and that management-employee relations are characterized by mutual trust and credibility. If these conditions don't exist, the change is unlikely to succeed. (For a detailed discussion of factors related to the effectiveness of employee communications during times of organizational change, see page 343 in Chapter 9.)

PARTICIPATION It's difficult for individuals to resist a change decision in which they participated. Prior to making a change, those opposed can be brought into the decision process. Assuming that the participants have the expertise to make a meaningful contribution, their involvement can reduce resistance, obtain commitment, and increase the quality of the change decision. However, against these advantages are the negatives: potential for a poor solution and great time consumption.

FACILITATION AND SUPPORT Organizations undergoing change can offer a range of supportive efforts to reduce resistance. When employee fear and anxiety are high, employee counselling and therapy, new-skills training, or a short paid leave of absence may facilitate adjustment. The drawback of this

Michael Ying, chairman of Esprit Asia Holdings, learned that communications can help overcome resistance to change. Ying, in trying to integrate Esprit's Asian and European operations, recognized major differences in the way they managed people and the business. The European operation was nationalistic, autocratic, and had rigid structures, whereas the Asian operation was more open-minded and willing to learn. During visits with the European managers, Ying communicated his common-sense approach to problem solving and listened to the Europeans' concerns. This communication helped the Europeans to become receptive to Ying's plan of merging the two operations.

tactic is that, as with the others, it is time-consuming. It is also expensive, and its implementation offers no assurance of success.

Esprit Asia Holdings
http://www.irasia.com/listco/
hk/esprit/index.htm

NEGOTIATION Another way for organizations to deal with potential resistance to change is to exchange something of value for a lessening of the resistance. For instance, if the resistance is centred in a few powerful individuals, a specific reward package can be negotiated that will meet their individual needs. Negotiation as a tactic may be necessary when resistance comes from a powerful source. Yet one cannot ignore its potentially high costs. Additionally, there is the risk that once senior management in an organization negotiates with one party to avoid resistance, he or she is open to the possibility of being beleaguered by other individuals in positions of power.

MANIPULATION AND COOPTATION Manipulation refers to covert influence attempts. Twisting and distorting facts to make them appear more attractive, withholding undesirable information, and creating false rumours to get employees to accept a change are all examples of manipulation. If corporate management threatens to close down a particular manufacturing plant if that plant's employees fail to accept an across-the-board pay cut, and if the threat is actually untrue, management is using manipulation. Cooptation, on the other hand, is a form of both manipulation and participation. It seeks to "buy off" the leaders of a resistance group by giving them a key role in the change decision. The leaders' advice is sought, not to seek a better decision, but to receive their endorsement. Both manipulation and cooptation are relatively inexpensive and easy ways to gain the support of adversaries, but the tactics can backfire if the targets become aware that they are being tricked or used. Once discovered, management's credibility may drop to zero.

COERCION Last on the list of tactics is coercion; that is, the application of direct threats or force upon the resisters. If the corporate management mentioned in the previous discussion is determined to close a manufacturing plant if employees don't acquiesce to a pay cut, then coercion would be the label attached to its change tactic. Other examples of coercion are threats of transfer, loss of promotions, negative performance evaluations, and a poor letter of recommendation. The advantages and drawbacks of coercion are approximately the same as those mentioned for manipulation and cooptation.

The Politics of Change

No discussion of resistance to change would be complete without a brief mention of the politics of change. Politics suggests that the impetus for change is more likely to come from employees who are new to the organization (and have less invested in the status quo) or managers who are slightly removed from the main power structure. Those managers who have spent their entire careers with a single organization and eventually achieve a senior position in the hierarchy are often major impediments to change. Change itself is a very real threat to their status and position. Yet they may be expected to implement changes to demonstrate that they're not merely caretakers. By trying to bring about change, they can symbolically convey to various constituencies—stockholders, suppliers, employees, customers—that they are on top of problems and adapting to a dynamic environment. Of course, as you might guess, when forced to introduce change, these long-time power holders tend to implement first-order changes. Radical change is too threatening. This, incidentally, explains why boards of directors that recognize the imperative for the rapid introduction of second-order change in their organizations frequently turn to outside candidates for new leadership.[22]

You may remember that we discussed politics in Chapter 12 and gave some suggestions for how to more effectively encourage people to go along with your ideas. That chapter also indicated how individuals acquire power, which provides further insight into the ability of some individuals to resist change.

Contemporary Issues in the Management of Change

Caveats on Undergoing Change

We have presented numerous examples of organizational change in this chapter and discussed how one goes about conducting effective organizational change. However, should all organizations set out to restructure? A consulting firm in Massachusetts studied several dozen *Fortune 500* companies to address this question. Their investigation suggests that continued bouts of reorganization were more likely to lead to poorer rather than improved performance. The study of 41 of these companies found that "90 percent of the companies whose financial performance had improved (during the 1980s) rarely embarked on major reorganization programs. By contrast, 90 percent of those that had lost market value had undergone frequent and difficult reorganization efforts."[23]

Why would change lead to poor results in so many cases? Sometimes reorganizing the structure of an organization seems easier than identifying the root problem of the organization. Hartmax Corporation, a U.S. apparel manufacturer, underwent several unsuccessful reorganizations in the 1980s. Finally, it realized that its problems were strategic, not structural. Sometimes the kinds of changes implemented may not be completely appropriate for the organization, as in this chapter's Case Incident, where measures more suitable to the private sector were applied in an effort to reduce costs and increase efficiency at a Toronto hospital. Another reason to carefully consider the decision to undergo change is that all reorganizations put the company into a form of shock, which can lead to lower efficiency, learning, and productivity.

Managing Change in a Unionized Environment

Canada's workplace is more likely to be unionized than it is in the United States, and this has led to some complications in accomplishing change in some organizations. In Chapter 16 we noted some of the difficulties that both MacMillan Bloedel and Canada Post had in dealing with a unionized environment, and in both Chapters 15 and 16 we discussed how the Vancouver Sun worked with its unions to change its printing process. In Chapter 15 we noted that some of the management of Bestar's Lac-Megantic plant did not want the union involved in quality programs if it meant that managers had to share their power. On the other hand, there are numerous examples of successful changes in a unionized environment. We discussed in Chapter 9 that part of the reason for New Brunswick-based Irving Paper's success with dealing with their union was the company's willingness to communicate openly with the members. We present two additional examples of working with unions, and then we discuss the factors that make it easier to manage change in a unionized environment.

Earlier in this chapter we discussed some of the changes that have occurred at Canadian National Railway under Paul Tellier. CN's employees are covered by the Brotherhood of Maintenance of Way Employees, the International Brotherhood of Electrical Workers, Rail Canada Traffic Controllers and the Canadian Autoworkers. Tellier brought to CN a philosophy about employees and change: "Managing change is first and foremost influencing mentalities: not the mentality of your customers so that they appreciate what you are trying to do, but the mentality of your employees so that they conform to the realities the customer must face."[24]

One of the mentalities Tellier had to change was the practice of "featherbedding."[25] Upon his arrival he discovered that because of union contracts, CN was paying 2000 employees whose jobs had been abolished, and therefore did not even report to work. Previous union contracts had guaranteed pay until age 65 for anyone who had worked at CN for eight years and whose job had disappeared. Union contracts also made it impossible to transfer employees against their will.

The result of this was that CN was hiring new workers in Edmonton even though there were employees who were not needed in Moncton but who refused to move. CN changed these rules after a 1995 strike. Under the new agreement, employees would receive 90 percent of their pay for six years, and workers who refused to be transferred would only receive 65 per cent of their pay for two years. Under the new contract, train conductors and engineers have to work longer shifts—up to 12 hours. This has reduced the number of shift changes required on routes like those from Sarnia, Ontario, to Halifax, Nova Scotia, from six to three.

Not all CN workers are happy, of course. Cliff Hamilton, a CN train engineer, says, "I think it's a crime what's going on. They're taking money out of the pockets of Canadian workers and putting it in the hands of American shareholders." And CN does not have a completely easy time with the unions. In 1995, CN faced strikes and lockouts for nine days before Ottawa legislated the unions back to work. However, in August 1998 contract negotiations ended successfully without any strikes. Nevertheless, as we noted earlier in this chapter, CN has managed a remarkable turnaround, while operating in a unionized environment.

In a similar case, when Hollis Harris took over at Air Canada in 1993, after the company had posted consecutive unprofitable quarters straight

Irving Paper
www.ifdn.com/paper/paper.htm

International Brotherhood of Electrical Workers
http://ibew.org/

back to 1989, one of his tasks was to get five unions to accept wage concessions and guarantee productivity improvements. In working through these concessions, the unions give Harris a lot of credit for his frank and open negotiating style. When he was in discussions with the Canadian Air Line Pilots Association (CALPA), Harris agreed to have Air Canada's financial books inspected by an outside consultant hired by CALPA. "When the consultants reported that the situation was indeed as desperate as Harris had been claiming, the pilots agreed to a five percent wage rollback."[26] Harris also earned the pilots' respect for this action.

Two consultants who have worked with a number of Canadian organizations in recent years note four essential elements for managing change in a unionized environment:[27]

- *An effective system for resolving day-to-day issues.* Employees should feel that they do not have to go through the formal grievance process in order to be heard. Instead, the workplace should be open to hearing workers' issues, as this will underscore a commitment to participation and empowerment.

- *A jointly administered business education process.* Union leaders and their members become uneasy about the future, particularly as Canadian organizations have gone through prolonged periods of downsizing. An education process that allows employees to understand the financial statements of the company and understand how their performance affects the bottom line helps them better understand the decisions the company makes.

- *A jointly developed strategic vision for the organization.* When union members are involved in setting the vision, they are more likely to focus on how change can be made, rather than whether it should be made. The vision "should describe performance expectations, work design, organizational structure, the supply chain, governance, pay and rewards, technology, education and training, operating processes, employee involvement, employment security, and union-management roles and relations."[28]

- *A non-traditional, problem-solving method of negotiating collective agreements.* It is important to promote an atmosphere of tolerance and willingness to listen, where issues are problems to be solved rather than victories to be claimed. It is also helpful to expand the traditional scope of bargaining to include complex issues such as strategic plans. Generally management does not want to bargain over these issues, but when they do, it signals further commitment to working jointly with unionized employees.

National Culture and Change

A number of change issues we've discussed are culture bound. To illustrate, let's briefly look at five questions: (1) Do people believe change is possible? (2) If it is possible, how long will it take to bring it about? (3) Is resistance to change greater in some cultures than in others? (4) Does culture influence how change efforts will be implemented? (5) Do successful idea champions do things differently in different cultures?

Do people believe change is possible? Remember that cultures vary in terms of beliefs about their ability to control their environment. In cultures where people believe that they can dominate their environment, individuals will take a proactive view of change. This would describe the United States

These Chinese couples prefer Western-style dancing over *t'ai chi,* the traditional meditative morning exercise. But in the workplace, Chinese workers are more resistant to change, holding fast to their past traditions. Significant cultural differences challenge foreign companies operating in China. They face China's rigid hierarchical structure, where the idea of younger managers telling older workers what to do is unheard of and employees work in state-controlled companies that provide no incentives for advancement.

and Canada. In many other countries, people see themselves as subjugated to their environment and thus will tend to take a passive approach toward change.

If change is possible, how long will it take to bring it about? A culture's time orientation can help us answer this question. Societies that focus on the long term, such as Japan, will demonstrate considerable patience while waiting for positive outcomes from change efforts. In societies with a short-term focus, such as the United States and Canada, people expect quick improvements and will seek change programs that promise fast results.

Is resistance to change greater in some cultures than in others? Resistance to change will be influenced by a society's reliance on tradition. Italians, as an example, focus on the past, while Americans emphasize the present. Italians, therefore, should generally be more resistant to change efforts than their American counterparts.

Does culture influence how change efforts will be implemented? Power distance can help with this issue. In high power distance cultures, such as the Philippines or Venezuela, change efforts will tend to be autocratically implemented by top management. In contrast, low power distance cultures value democratic methods. We'd predict, therefore, a greater use of participation in countries such as Denmark and Israel.

Finally, do successful idea champions do things differently in different cultures? The evidence indicates that the answer is "yes."[29] People in collectivist cultures, in contrast to individualistic cultures, prefer appeals for cross-functional support for innovation efforts. People in high power distance cultures prefer champions to work closely with those in authority to approve innovative activities before work is conducted on them; and the higher the uncertainty avoidance of a society, the more champions should work within the organization's rules and procedures to develop the innovation. These findings suggest that effective managers will alter their organization's championing strategies to reflect cultural values. So, for instance, while idea champions in the United States might succeed by ignoring budgetary limitations and working around confining procedures, champions in Venezuela, Greece, Italy, or other cultures high in uncertainty avoidance will be more effective by closely following budgets and procedures.

A 1997 study of the turnaround at Micron Corporation, one of the two largest semiconductor producers in Russia, provides first-hand evidence of

Micron Corporation
http://www.microncorp.com/

AT&T adapted to changes in the global economic and political arenas by reorganizing into three separate global companies, laying off 40 000 employees, and seizing the opportunities for growth in new markets. (For example, fibre optic cable exported from AT&T's Atlanta, Georgia-based plant competes with French and Swedish products.) With the passage of the North American Free Trade Agreement and entry into the Mexican market, AT&T has had to learn how to deal with culture changes in an international environment.

how the change process differs in North America compared to Russia. The researchers noted Russian culture differs in that the power to lay off employees and managers alike was considerably more restricted than in North American organizations. The researchers observed that Russian managers are less oriented towards the market, and more toward the collective good. Russian firms were also more likely to cut research and development spending in times of change. Micron did carry out a turnaround that has been somewhat successful, though less profitable than desired. The culture differences may be a partial explanation for Micron's outcome. Because of many years of communism and an emphasis on a collectivist society, it will take some time for Russian managers to adjust to a market orientation.

Work Stress and Its Management

Stress appears to be a major factor in the lives of many Canadians. In a survey conducted in late 1997, POLLARA found a great deal of stress among Canadians, with those from Quebec topping the list.[30] Almost two-thirds of Quebecers said they were as stressed as they can handle or were on their way to being completely overwhelmed. Atlantic Canadians came in second (41 percent), followed by Ontario (39 percent), Alberta (38 percent), British Columbia (37 percent), and the Prairies (32 percent). The survey also found that women were more stressed than men.

Among workers, stress is also a fact of life. An Angus Reid Group poll conducted in the fall of 1997 found that two-thirds of those surveyed said their job was either very or somewhat stressful.[31] Fifty-five percent of the workers said that their biggest problem was being asked to do too much in too little time. Juggling work and family demands created stress for 22 percent of those surveyed.

Front-line workers are not the only members of the organization who experience stress, however. In a 1997 study conducted by researchers Darren

Lancaster Labs, an analytical-testing laboratory, has expanded its day-care facility for children to include care for the elderly. Its on-site intergenerational family centre provides adult day care for up to 25 elderly or disabled relatives as well as day care for 151 children. Lancaster credits the child care centre with the company's 94 percent retention rate of working moms, up from about 50 percent before the centre was introduced. The family centre is one way organizations can provide resources to help employees reduce stress levels.

Larose and Bernadette Schell at Ontario's Laurentian University, 88 percent of the executives surveyed indicated elevated levels of stress and/or unhealthy personality traits.[32] They also had higher levels of predisposition to serious illnesses such as cancer and heart disease. See Exhibit 17-8 for a ranking of jobs based on stress scores.

Stress is not something that can be ignored in the workplace. It is likely responsible for the higher levels of absenteeism reported in 1997, compared to 1993. Statistics Canada reported that full-time workers took an average of 6.2 days off in 1997 for illness or disability.[33] This translates into the loss of an estimated 66 million workdays in 1997 alone. The report suggested that an aging workforce and increased workplace stress are responsible for the increase. "In the wake of years of fiscal downsizing, workers across all sectors are working harder and longer than ever while trying to balance family responsibilities," said Scott Morris, who heads the Calgary-based consulting firm Priority Management.[34]

Daniel Ondrack, of the University of Toronto's school of management, notes that "one of the major reasons for absenteeism is the logistical problems workers face in just getting to work, including transporting children to school and finding day care. Single parents, especially female, have to juggle all the day care and family responsibilities, and that makes it extremely difficult for people to keep up with work demands."[35]

In this section we'll look at the causes and consequences of stress. In the HR Implications feature at the end of the chapter, we address ways in which individuals and organizations can reduce stress.

What Is Stress?

stress
A dynamic condition in which an individual is confronted with an opportunity, constraint, or demand related to what he or she desires and for which the outcome is perceived to be both uncertain and important.

Stress is a dynamic condition in which an individual is confronted with an opportunity, constraint, or demand related to what he or she desires and for which the outcome is perceived to be both uncertain and important.[36] This is a complicated definition. Let's look at its components more closely.

Stress is not necessarily bad in and of itself. While stress is typically discussed in a negative context, it also has a positive value. It is an opportunity when it offers potential gain. Consider, for example, the superior performance that an athlete or stage performer gives in "clutch" situations. Such individuals often use stress positively to rise to the occasion and perform at or near their maximum.

Exhibit 17-8
The Most Stressful Jobs

How do jobs rate in terms of stress? The following shows how selected occupations ranked in an evaluation of 250 jobs. Among the criteria used in the rankings were: overtime, quotas, deadlines, competitiveness, physical demands, environmental conditions, hazards encountered, initiative required, stamina required, win-lose situations, and working in the public eye.

Rank Score	Stress Score	Rank Score	Stress Score
1. U.S. president	176.6	47. Auto salesperson	56.3
2. Firefighter	110.9	50. College professor	54.2
3. Senior executive	108.6	60. School principal	51.7
6. Surgeon	99.5	103. Market research	
10. Air traffic controller	83.1	analyst	42.1
12. Public relations		104. Personnel recruiter	41.8
executive	78.5	113. Hospital	
16. Advertising account		administrator	39.6
executive	74.6	119. Economist	38.7
17. Real estate agent	73.1	122. Mechanical engineer	38.3
20. Stockbroker	71.7	124. Chiropractor	37.9
22. Pilot	68.7	132. Technical writer	36.5
25. Architect	66.9	149. Retail salesperson	34.9
31. Lawyer	64.3	173. Accountant	31.1
33. General physician	64.0	193. Purchasing agent	28.9
35. Insurance agent	63.3	229. Broadcast technician	24.2
42. Advertising		245. Actuary	20.2
salesperson	59.9		

Source: Reprinted by permission of *The Wall Street Journal*, © 1996 Dow Jones & Company, Inc. All rights reserved worldwide.

constraints
Forces that prevent individuals from doing what they desire.

demands
The loss of something desired.

More typically, stress is associated with **constraints** and **demands**. The former prevent you from doing what you desire. The latter refer to the loss of something desired. So when you take a test at school or undergo your annual performance review at work, you feel stress because you confront opportunities, constraints, and demands. A good performance review may lead to a promotion, greater responsibilities, and a higher salary. But a poor review may prevent you from getting the promotion. An extremely poor review might even result in your being fired.

Two conditions are necessary for potential stress to become actual stress.[37] There must be uncertainty over the outcome, and the outcome must be important. Regardless of the conditions, it is only when there is doubt or uncertainty regarding whether the opportunity will be seized, the constraint removed, or the loss avoided that there is stress. That is, stress is highest for those individuals who perceive that they are uncertain as to whether they will win or lose and lowest for those individuals who think that winning or losing is a certainty. However, importance is also critical. If winning or losing is an unimportant outcome, there is no stress. If keeping your job or earning a promotion doesn't hold any importance to you, you have no reason to feel stress over having to undergo a performance review.

Understanding Stress: Causes and Consequences

What causes stress? What are its consequences for individual employees? Why is it that the same set of conditions that creates stress for one person seems to have little or no effect on another person? Exhibit 17-9 provides a model that can help to answer questions such as these.[38]

The model identifies three sets of factors—environmental, organizational, and individual—that act as *potential* sources of stress. Whether they become *actual* stress depends on individual differences such as job experience and personality. When an individual experiences stress, its symptoms can surface as physiological, psychological, and behavioural outcomes. Exhibit 17-9 provides a humorous example of some of the consequences of stress.

As the model in Exhibit 17-10 shows, there are three categories of potential stressors: environmental, organizational, and individual. Let's take a look at each.[39]

ENVIRONMENTAL FACTORS Just as environmental uncertainty influences the design of an organization's structure, it also influences stress levels among employees in that organization. Changes in the business cycle create *economic uncertainties*. When the economy is contracting, for example, people become increasingly anxious about their security. *Political uncertainties* don't tend to create stress among North Americans as they do for employees in countries such as Haiti or Iraq. The obvious reason is that Canada and the United States have stable political systems where change is typically implemented in an orderly manner. Yet political threats and changes, even in countries such as Canada and the United States, can be stress inducing. For instance, threats by Quebec to separate from Canada and become a distinct, French-speaking country increase stress among many Canadians. It is interesting to remember our earlier observation that Quebecers report much higher stress levels than the rest of the country. *Technological uncertainty* is a third type of environmental factor that can cause stress. Because new innovations can make an employee's skills and experience obsolete in a very short period, computers, robotics, automation, and similar forms of technological innovation are a threat to many people and cause them stress.

Exhibit 17-9

THE FAR SIDE By GARY LARSON

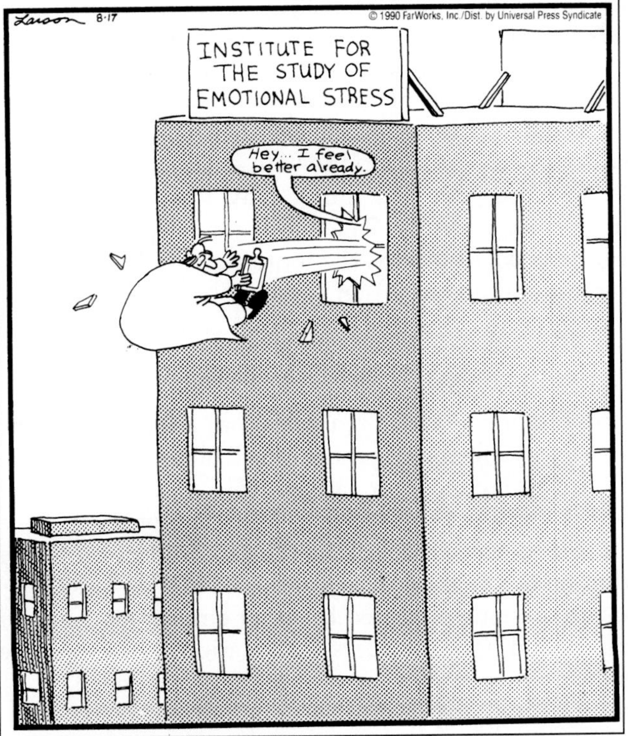

ORGANIZATIONAL FACTORS There is no shortage of factors within the organization that can cause stress. Pressures to avoid errors or complete tasks in a limited time period, work overload, a demanding and insensitive boss, and unpleasant co-workers are a few examples. (See Exhibit 17-11.) We've categorized these factors around task, role,

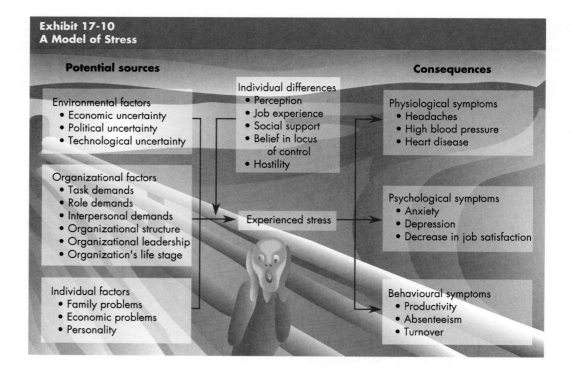

Exhibit 17-10
A Model of Stress

Potential sources

Environmental factors
- Economic uncertainty
- Political uncertainty
- Technological uncertainty

Organizational factors
- Task demands
- Role demands
- Interpersonal demands
- Organizational structure
- Organizational leadership
- Organization's life stage

Individual factors
- Family problems
- Economic problems
- Personality

Individual differences
- Perception
- Job experience
- Social support
- Belief in locus of control
- Hostility

Experienced stress

Consequences

Physiological symptoms
- Headaches
- High blood pressure
- Heart disease

Psychological symptoms
- Anxiety
- Depression
- Decrease in job satisfaction

Behavioural symptoms
- Productivity
- Absenteeism
- Turnover

and interpersonal demands; organizational structure; organizational leadership; and the organization's life stage.[40]

Task demands are factors related to a person's job. They include the design of the individual's job (autonomy, task variety, degree of automation), working conditions, and the physical work layout. Assembly lines can put pressure on people when the line speed is perceived as excessive. Data inputters who are electronically monitored for a certain number of keystrokes per minute, or telephone operators whose interactions with customers are monitored to ensure they don't exceed specified times, may feel harassed and stressed as a result of such close scrutiny. The more interdependence between a person's tasks and the tasks of others, the more potential stress there is. Autonomy, on the other hand, tends to lessen stress. Jobs where temperatures, noise, or other working conditions are dangerous or undesirable can increase anxiety. So, too, can working in an overcrowded room or in a visible location where interruptions are constant.

Role demands relate to pressures placed on a person as a function of the particular role that he or she plays in the organization. Role conflicts create expectations that may be hard to reconcile or satisfy. Role overload is experienced when the employee is expected to do more than time permits. Role ambiguity is created when role expectations are not clearly understood, and the employee is unsure what he or she is expected to do.

Interpersonal demands are pressures created by other employees. Lack of social support from colleagues and poor interpersonal relationships can cause considerable stress, especially among employees with a high social need.

Organizational structure defines the level of differentiation in the organization, the degree of rules and regulations, and where decisions are made. Excessive rules and lack of participation in decisions that affect an employee are examples of structural variables that might be potential sources of stress.

Organizational leadership represents the managerial style of the organization's senior executives. Some chief executive officers create a culture

Exhibit 17-11
Primary Causes of Stress at Work

What factors cause the most stress on the job? A *Wall Street Journal* survey reported:

Factor	Percentage Response*
Not doing the kind of work I want to	34
Coping with current job	30
Working too hard	28
Colleagues at work	21
A difficult boss	18

*Percentages exceed 100 as a result of some multiple responses.

Source: "Worries at Work," *The Wall Street Journal*, April 7, 1988, p. 27. Reprinted by permission of *The Wall Street Journal*, © 1988 Dow Jones & Company, Inc. All rights reserved worldwide.

characterized by tension, fear, and anxiety. They establish unrealistic pressures to perform in the short run, impose excessively tight controls, and routinely fire employees who don't "measure up."

Organizations go through a cycle. They're established, they grow, become mature, and eventually decline. An *organization's life stage*—that is, where it is in this four-stage cycle—creates different problems and pressures for employees. The establishment and decline stages are particularly stressful. The former is characterized by a great deal of excitement and uncertainty, while the latter typically requires cutbacks, layoffs, and a different set of uncertainties. Stress tends to be least in maturity, where uncertainties are at their lowest ebb.

INDIVIDUAL FACTORS In 1995, about half of Canadian employees worked about 35 to 40 hours a week. The experiences and problems that people encounter in those other 120-plus non-work hours each week can spill over to the job. Our final category, then, encompasses factors in the employee's personal life. Primarily, these factors are family issues, personal economic problems, and inherent personality characteristics.

National surveys consistently show that people hold *family* and personal relationships dear. Marital difficulties, the breaking off of a relationship, and discipline troubles with children are examples of relationship problems that create stress for employees that aren't left at the front door when they arrive at work.

Economic problems created by individuals overextending their financial resources is another set of personal troubles that can create stress for employees and distract their attention from their work. Regardless of income level—people who make $80 000 a year seem to have as much trouble handling their finances as those who earn $18 000—some people are poor money managers or have wants that always seem to exceed their earning capacity. Studies in three diverse organizations found that stress symptoms reported prior to beginning a job accounted for most of the variance in stress symptoms reported nine months later.[41] This led researchers to conclude that some people may have an inherent tendency to accentuate negative aspects of the world in general. If true, then a significant individual factor influencing stress is a person's basic dispositional nature. That is, stress symptoms expressed on the job may actually originate in the person's *personality*.

STRESSORS ARE ADDITIVE A fact that tends to be overlooked when stressors are reviewed individually is that stress is an additive phenomenon.[42] Stress builds up. Each new and persistent stressor adds to an individual's stress level. A single stressor may seem relatively unimportant in and of itself, but if it is added to an already high level of stress, it can be "the straw that breaks the camel's back." If we want to appraise the total amount of stress an individual is under, we must sum up his or her opportunity stresses, constraint stresses, and demand stresses.

Individual Differences in Experiencing Stress

Some people thrive on stressful situations, while others are overwhelmed by them. What is it that differentiates people in terms of their ability to handle stress? What individual difference variables moderate the relationship between *potential* stressors and *experienced* stress? At least five variables—perception, job experience, social support, belief in locus of control, and hostility—have been found to be relevant moderators.

PERCEPTION In Chapter 3, we demonstrated that employees react in response to their perception of reality rather than to reality itself. Perception, therefore, will moderate the relationship between a potential stress condition and an employee's reaction to it. One person's fear that he or she will lose his or her job because the company is laying off staff may be perceived by another as an opportunity to receive a large severance allowance and start a small business. Similarly, what one employee perceives as a challenging job may be viewed as threatening and demanding by others.[43] So the stress potential in environmental, organizational, and individual factors doesn't lie in their objective condition. Rather, it lies in an employee's interpretation of those factors.

JOB EXPERIENCE Experience is said to be a great teacher. It can also be a great stress reducer. Think back to your first date or your first few days in college or university. For most of us, the uncertainty and newness of these situations created stress. But as we gained experience, that stress disappeared or at least significantly decreased. The same phenomenon seems to apply to work situations. That is, experience on the job tends to be negatively related to work stress. Two explanations have been offered.[44] First is the idea of selective withdrawal. Voluntary turnover is more probable among people who experience more stress. Therefore, people who remain with the organization longer are those with more stress-resistant traits or those who are more resistant to the stress characteristics of their organization. Second, people eventually develop coping mechanisms to deal with stress. Because this takes time, senior members of the organization are more likely to be fully adapted and should experience less stress.

SOCIAL SUPPORT There is increasing evidence that social support—that is, collegial relationships with co-workers or supervisors—can buffer the impact of stress.[45] The logic underlying this moderating variable is that social support acts as a palliative, mitigating the negative effects of even high-strain jobs.

For individuals whose work associates are unhelpful or even actively hostile, social support may be found outside the job. Involvement with family, friends, and community can provide the support—especially for those with a high social need—that is missing at work, and this can make job stressors more tolerable.

BELIEF IN LOCUS OF CONTROL Locus of control was introduced in Chapter 3 as a personality attribute. Those with an internal locus of control believe they control their own destiny. Those with an external locus believe their lives are controlled by outside forces. Evidence indicates that internals perceive their jobs to be less stressful than do externals.[46]

When internals and externals confront a similar stressful situation, the internals are likely to believe that they can have a significant effect on the results. They, therefore, act to take control of events. Externals are more likely to be passive and defensive. Rather than do something to reduce the stress, they acquiesce. So externals, who are more likely to feel helpless in stressful situations, are also more likely to experience stress.

HOSTILITY For much of the 1970s and 1980s, a great deal of attention was directed at the Type A personality.[47] In fact, throughout the 1980s, it was undoubtedly the most frequently used moderating variable related to stress.

As noted in Chapter 3, the Type A personality is characterized by feeling a chronic sense of time urgency and by an *excessive* competitive drive. The Type A individual is "*aggressively* involved in a *chronic, incessant* struggle to achieve more and more in less and less time, and if required to do so, against the opposing efforts of other things or other persons."[48]

Until recently, researchers believed that Type A's were more likely to experience stress both on and off the job. More specifically, Type A's were widely believed to be at higher risk for heart disease. A closer analysis of the evidence, however, has produced new conclusions.[49] By looking at various components of Type A behaviour, it has been found that only the hostility and anger associated with Type A behaviour are actually related to heart disease. The chronically angry, suspicious, and mistrustful person is the one at risk.

The fact that a person is a workaholic, rushes around a lot, and is impatient or competitive does not mean that he or she is unduly susceptible to heart disease or the other negative effects of stress. Rather, it is the quickness to anger, the persistently hostile outlook, and the cynical mistrust of others that are harmful.

Consequences of Stress

Stress manifests itself in a number of ways. For instance, an individual who is experiencing a high level of stress may develop high blood pressure, ulcers, irritability, difficulty in making routine decisions, loss of appetite, accident proneness, and the like. These can be subsumed under three general categories: physiological, psychological, and behavioural symptoms.[50]

PHYSIOLOGICAL SYMPTOMS Most of the early concern with stress was directed at physiological symptoms. This was predominately due to the fact that the topic was researched by specialists in the health and medical sciences. This research led to the conclusion that stress could create changes in metabolism, increase heart and breathing rates, increase blood pressure, cause headaches, and induce heart attacks. The link between stress and particular physiological symptoms is not clear. There are few, if any, consistent relationships.[51] This is attributed to the complexity of the symptoms and the difficulty of objectively measuring them. One of the interesting features of illness in today's workplace is the considerable change in its manifestation. In the past, sick leave, workers' compensation, and short- and long-term disability were claimed by an organization's older employees—most often in

cases of catastrophic illness such as heart attacks, cancer, and major back surgeries. In recent years, however, it is not unusual for long-term disability programs to be filled with employees in their twenties, thirties, and forties. And they are claiming illness that is either psychiatric (such as depression) or more difficult to diagnose (such as chronic fatigue syndrome or fibromyalgia, a musculoskeletal discomfort). The authors report that the increase in disability claims may be the seemingly endless trend of downsizing taking its toll on the psyches of those in the workforce.[52]

PSYCHOLOGICAL SYMPTOMS Stress can cause dissatisfaction. Job-related stress can cause job-related dissatisfaction. Job dissatisfaction, in fact, is "the simplest and most obvious psychological effect" of stress.[53] However, stress also manifests itself in other psychological states—for instance, tension, anxiety, irritability, boredom, and procrastination.

The evidence indicates that when people are placed in jobs that make multiple and conflicting demands or in which there is a lack of clarity as to the incumbent's duties, authority, and responsibilities, both stress and dissatisfaction are increased.[54] Similarly, the less control that people have over the pace of their work, the greater the stress and dissatisfaction. While more research is needed to clarify the relationship, the evidence suggests that jobs that provide a low level of variety, significance, autonomy, feedback, and identity to incumbents create stress and reduce satisfaction and involvement in the job.[55]

BEHAVIOURAL SYMPTOMS Behaviourally related stress symptoms include changes in productivity, absence, and turnover, as well as changes in eating habits, increased smoking or consumption of alcohol, rapid speech, fidgeting, and sleep disorders.

There has been a significant amount of research investigating the stress–performance relationship. The most widely studied pattern in the stress–performance literature is the inverted-U relationship.[56] This is shown in Exhibit 17-12.

The logic underlying the inverted U is that low to moderate levels of stress stimulate the body and increase its ability to react. Individuals then often perform their tasks better, more intensely, or more rapidly. But too much stress places unattainable demands or constraints on a person, which result in lower performance. This inverted-U pattern may also describe the reaction to stress over time, as well as to changes in stress intensity. That is, even moderate levels of stress can have a negative influence on performance over the long term as the continued intensity of the stress wears down the individual and saps his or her energy resources. An athlete may be able to use the positive effects of stress to obtain a higher performance during every Saturday's game in the fall season, or a sales executive may be able to psych herself up for her presentation at the annual national meeting. But moderate levels of stress experienced continually over long periods of time, as typified by the emergency-department staff in a large urban hospital, can result in lower performance. This may explain why emergency-department staff members at such hospitals are frequently rotated and why it is unusual to find individuals who have spent the bulk of their career in such an environment. In effect, to do so would expose the individual to the

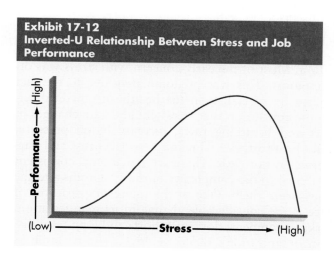

Exhibit 17-12
Inverted-U Relationship Between Stress and Job Performance

risk of "career burnout." In spite of the popularity and intuitive appeal of the inverted-U model, it doesn't yet receive much empirical support.[57] At this point in time, managers should be careful in assuming that this model accurately depicts the stress–performance relationship.

International Evidence of the Incidence of Work-Related Stress

Today's changing and competitive workplace is increasing the stress levels among workers and managers in countries other than Canada. For instance, a recent survey of U.S. workers found that 46 percent believed that their jobs were extremely stressful, and 34 percent had seriously considered quitting in the previous 12 months because of workplace stress.[58] In Asia, more and more managers are showing signs of chronic fatigue and burnout, and there is growing concern among senior executives in Asia that burned-out managers can mean a burned-out company.[59]

Hongkong Telecom
http://www.hkt.com/index.htm

Many executives thrive under pressure and enjoy the adrenaline rush that comes from competition and achievement, but human beings can burn out and that's apparently happening among a growing number of Asian managers. They're showing signs of chronic fatigue—moodiness, lethargy, erratic behaviour, physical ailments, and increased family problems. The chief executive of Hongkong Telecom believes that stressed-out managers are not good for their companies or shareholders. He says it leads "in most cases to greatly reduced efficiency in even the best of individuals and almost inevitably to decreased productivity."[60] Stress seems to be a problem regardless of whether the economy is strong or weak. In Thailand, for example, the economy is robust, but Thais working in highly competitive sectors such as advertising, securities, and consumer products are showing signs of stress and burnout. In contrast, the Japanese economy is stagnant. Yet managers there continue to work 80-plus hours per week and push themselves toward burnout. Japanese managers have long considered workaholism and evidence of work-related stress as a badge of honour. The Japanese even have a name for the "disease"—*karoshi* or death from overwork. Japanese managers prided themselves on having no social life and an inability to discuss any subject except business. Recent downsizing efforts by Japanese companies are only making matters worse. Lifetime employment with continuous advancement is being replaced by performance-related expectations. Merit pay plans are being installed. Non-contributors are getting coarse hints—such as hefty pay cuts—to shape up or ship out. Companies bulging at the seams with excess middle managers, now faced with more efficient foreign competitors, can no longer afford to keep unproductive people. And lower-level managers are finding their workloads increased. This downsizing climate is only heightening workplace stress. As discussed in Chapter 3, such a climate has resulted in a high rate of suicide among Japanese executives.

The Japanese government has begun to speak out against this culture of overwork, as the negative impact that stress is having on productivity can no longer be ignored. The government now wants Japan's workers and managers to get a life, enjoy their families, take vacations, produce less, and consume more. Not surprisingly, in a climate of cutbacks, few Japanese are listening. Apparently their peers in Thailand, Hong Kong, Malaysia, and other Asian economies aren't getting the message either. As these Canadian and international examples illustrate, stress can seriously inhibit effective organizational change. As employees and companies prepare for the workplace of the 21st century, coping with stress may prove one of their greatest challenges.

HR IMPLICATIONS

Helping Employees Manage Stress

Both the individual and the organization can take steps to help the individual manage stress. Below we discuss ways that individuals can manage stress, and then we examine programs that organizations are using to help employees manage stress.

Individual approaches An employee can take personal responsibility for reducing his or her stress level. Individual strategies that have proven effective include implementing time management techniques, increasing physical exercise, relaxation training, and expanding the social support network.

Many people manage their time poorly. The things they have to accomplish in any given day or week are not necessarily beyond completion if they manage their time properly. The well-organized employee, like the well-organized student, can often accomplish twice as much as the person who is poorly organized. So an understanding and utilization of basic *time management* principles can help individuals better cope with tensions created by job demands.[1] A few of the more well-known time management principles are: (1) making daily lists of activities to be accomplished; (2) prioritizing activities by importance and urgency; (3) scheduling activities according to the priorities set; and (4) knowing your daily cycle and handling the most demanding parts of your job during the high part of your cycle when you are most alert and productive.[2]

Non-competitive physical exercise such as aerobics, walking, jogging, swimming, and riding a bicycle have long been recommended by physicians as a way to deal with excessive stress levels. These forms of *physical exercise* increase heart capacity, lower at-rest heart rate, provide a mental diversion from work pressures, and offer a means to "let off steam."[3]

Individuals can teach themselves to reduce tension through *relaxation techniques* such as meditation, hypnosis, and biofeedback. The objective is to reach a state of deep relaxation, where one feels physically relaxed, somewhat detached from the immediate environment, and detached from body sensations.[4] Fifteen or 20 minutes a day of deep relaxation releases tension and provides a person with a pronounced sense of peacefulness. Importantly, significant changes in heart rate, blood pressure, and other physiological factors result from achieving the deep relaxation condition.

As we noted earlier in this chapter, having friends, family, or work colleagues to talk to provides an outlet when stress levels become excessive. Expanding your *social support network*, therefore, can be a means for tension reduction. It provides you with someone to hear your problems and to offer a more objective perspective on the situation. Research also demonstrates that social support moderates the stress–burnout relationship.[5] That is, high support reduces the likelihood that heavy work stress will result in job burnout.

Organizational approaches Several of the factors that cause stress—particularly task and role demands, and organizational structure—are controlled by management. As such, they can be modified or changed. Strategies that management might want to consider include improved personnel selection and job placement, use of realistic goal setting, redesigning of jobs, increased employee involvement, improved organizational communication, and establishment of corporate wellness programs.

While certain jobs are more stressful than others, we learned earlier in this chapter that individuals differ in their response to stress situations. We know, for example, that individuals with little experience or an external locus of control tend to be more prone to stress. *Selection and placement* decisions should take these facts into consideration. Obviously, while management shouldn't restrict hiring to only experienced individuals with an internal locus, such individuals may adapt better to high-stress jobs and perform those jobs more effectively.

We discussed *goal setting* in Chapter 6. Based on an extensive amount of research, we concluded that individuals perform better when they have specific and challenging goals and receive feedback on how well they are progressing toward these goals. The use of goals can reduce stress as well as provide motivation. Specific goals that are perceived as attainable clarify performance expectations. Additionally, goal feedback

reduces uncertainties as to actual job performance. The result is less employee frustration, role ambiguity, and stress.

Redesigning jobs to give employees more responsibility, more meaningful work, more autonomy, and increased feedback can reduce stress because these factors give the employee greater control over work activities and lessen dependence on others. But as we noted in our discussion of work design, not all employees want enriched jobs. The right redesign, then, for employees with a low need for growth might be less responsibility and increased specialization. If individuals prefer structure and routine, reducing skill variety should also reduce uncertainties and stress levels.

Role stress is detrimental to a large extent because employees feel uncertain about goals, expectations, how they'll be evaluated, and the like. By giving these employees a voice in those decisions that directly affect their job performances, management can increase employee control and reduce this role stress. So managers should consider *increasing employee involvement* in decision-making.[6]

Increasing formal *organizational communication* with employees reduces uncertainty by lessening role ambiguity and role conflict. Given the importance that perceptions play in moderating the stress–response relationship, management can also use effective communications as a means to shape employee perceptions. Remember that what employees categorize as demands, threats, or opportunities are merely an interpretation, and that interpretation can be affected by the symbols and actions communicated by management.

Our final suggestion is to offer organizationally supported wellness programs. These programs focus on the employee's total physical and mental condition.[7] For example, they typically provide workshops to help people quit smoking, control alcohol use, lose weight, eat better, and develop a regular exercise program. The assumption underlying most wellness programs is that employees need to take personal responsibility for their physical and mental health. The organization is merely a vehicle to facilitate this end.

Brampton, Ontario-based Nortel (Northern Telecom Limited) established Aralia Centre, a wellness centre, at its headquarters. Employees can enrol in a relaxation class, sign up for a social weekend, or take time out for a stretch break. These programs were specifically designed to help employees manage stress. Nortel's 3500 employees who work at corporate headquarters can choose from among 20 programs designed to improve and maintain their health. These programs include healthy eating, ulcer care, asthma management, motivation support, parenting classes and family social events. There's also a fitness centre complete with aerobic studios and a workout area for cardiovascular and weight training.[8]

Similarly, Bolton, Ontario-based Husky Injection Molding Systems has a fully equipped state-of-the-art wellness centre to meet the health needs of more than 1200 employees. It houses a day care centre, a fully equipped weight and training room, a library with health care books and videos, and offices for a variety of health care workers, practicing both regular and alternative medicine techniques.[9]

Organizations, of course, aren't altruistic. They expect a payoff from their investment in wellness programs. And most of those firms that have introduced wellness programs have found significant benefits. For instance, Johnson & Johnson calculated the following annual savings in insurance premiums when an employee exchanges bad habits for healthy ones: quitting smoking ($1550); starting to exercise ($360); lowering cholesterol from 240 to 190 milligrams ($1680); and slimming down from obese to normal weight ($248).[10] Husky does not fully measure the impact of its wellness program, but it has one of the best records on absenteeism in the industry. Its claims to the Workers' Compensation Board are also one of the lowest in the industry. Both of these are seen as related to the wellness program.[11]

Sources:

[1] T.H. Macan, "Time Management: Test of a Process Model," *Journal of Applied Psychology*, June 1994, pp. 381–91.

[2] See, for example, M.E. Haynes, *Practical Time Management: How to Make the Most of Your Most Perishable Resource* (Tulsa, OK: PennWell Books, 1985).

[3] J. Kiely and G. Hodgson, "Stress in the Prison Service: The Benefits of Exercise Programs," *Human Relations*, June 1990, pp. 551–72.

[4] E.J. Forbes and R.J. Pekala, "Psychophysiological Effects of Several Stress Management Techniques," *Psychological Reports*, February 1993, pp. 19–27; and G. Smith, "Meditation, the New Balm for Corporate Stress," *Business Week*, May 10, 1993, pp. 86–87.

[5] D. Etzion, "Moderating Effects of Social Support on the Stress-Burnout Relationship," *Journal of Applied Psychology*, November 1984, pp. 615–22; and S. Jackson, R. Schwab, and R. Schuler, "Toward an Understanding of the Burnout Phenomenon," *Journal of Applied Psychology* 71, no. 4 (November 1986), pp. 630–40.

[6] S.E. Jackson, "Participation in Decision Making as a Strategy for Reducing Job-Related Strain," *Journal of Applied Psychology*, February 1983, pp. 3–19; and P. Froiland, "What Cures Job Stress?", *Training*, December 1993, pp. 32–36.

[7] See, for instance, R.A. Wolfe, D.O. Ulrich, and D.F. Parker, "Employee Health Management Programs: Review, Critique, and Research Agenda," *Journal of Management*, Winter 1987, pp. 603–15; D.L. Gebhardt and C.E. Crump, "Employee Fitness and Wellness Programs in the Workplace," *American Psychologist*, February 1990, pp. 262–72; and C.E. Beadle, "And Let's Save 'Wellness.' It Works," *New York Times*, July 24, 1994, p. F9.

[8] R. Waymen, "Wellness Workout: For Northern Telecom, A Business Case was the Muscle Behind One of the Most Comprehensive Corporate Wellness Programs in Canada," *Benefits Canada*, January 1998, pp. 24–30.

[9] R. B. Mason, "Taking Health Care to Factory Floor Proves Smart Move for Growing Ontario Company," *Canadian Medical Association Journal*, November 15, 1997, pp. 1423–1424.

[10] S. Tully, "America's Healthiest Companies," *Fortune*, June 12, 1995, p. 104.

[11] Roger B. Mason, "Taking Health Care to Factory Floor Proves Smart Move for Growing Ontario Company."

Summary and Implications

For the Workplace

The need for change has been implied throughout this text. "A casual reflection on change should indicate that it encompasses almost all our concepts in the organizational behaviour literature. Think about leadership, motivation, organizational environment, and roles. It is impossible to think about these and other concepts without inquiring about change."[61]

If environments were perfectly static, if employees' skills and abilities were always up-to-date and incapable of deteriorating, and if tomorrow was always exactly the same as today, organizational change would have little or no relevance to managers. But the real world is turbulent, requiring organizations and their members to undergo dynamic change if they are to perform at competitive levels.

Managers are the primary introducers of change in most organizations. By the decisions they make and their role-modelling behaviours, they shape the organization's change culture. For instance, management decisions related to structural design, cultural factors, and human resource policies largely determine the level of innovation within the organization. Similarly, management decisions, policies, and practices will determine the degree to which the organization learns and adapts to changing environmental factors.

We found that the existence of work stress, in and of itself, need not imply lower performance. The evidence indicates that stress can be either a positive or negative influence on employee performance. For many people, low to moderate amounts of stress enable them to perform their jobs better, by increasing their work intensity, alertness, and ability to react. However, a high level of stress, or even a moderate amount sustained over a long period of time, eventually takes its toll and performance declines. The impact of stress on satisfaction is far more straightforward. Job-related tension tends to decrease general job satisfaction.[62] Even though low to moderate levels of stress may improve job performance, employees find stress dissatisfying.

For You as an Individual

Given the speed of change happening in today's world, it is unlikely that you will escape some type of organizational restructuring during your lifetime, and probably you will encounter this more than once. Many people are resistant to change, but one of the messages of this book is to encourage individuals to continue learning throughout their lifetime. By engaging in continuous learn-

ing, change does not have to be so upsetting, because you will have the skills you need to either work in the restructured organization or land yourself a new position. For example, you may want to view yourself as "self-employed" even when you are employed by an organization. This will encourage you to continue to upgrade your skills, giving you the opportunity to "sell" these skills to your existing employer or transfer these skills to a new employer elsewhere. We also noted that many people experience stress in their lives. Some of it is related to the workplace, although there are other sources of stress as well. The HR Implications at the end of the chapter offers suggestions for dealing with stress, from time management to meditation, to taking better care of your health.

ROADMAP REMINDER

With this chapter we conclude our discussion of organizational behaviour, but we do not believe you should end your study of organizational behaviour here. For all of your life you will be working with others in a variety of situations and the lessons of organizational behaviour will continue to apply.

For Review

1. What is meant by the phrase "we live in an age of discontinuity"?
2. "Resistance to change is an irrational response." Do you agree or disagree? Explain.
3. Why is participation considered such an effective technique for lessening resistance to change?
4. How does Lewin's three-step model of change deal with resistance to change?
5. How are opportunities, constraints, and demands related to stress? Give an example of each.
6. What can organizations do to reduce employee stress?

For Discussion

1. How have changes in the workforce during the past 20 years affected organizational policies?
2. "Managing today is easier than at the turn of the century because the years of real change took place between Confederation and World War I." Do you agree or disagree? Discuss.

LEARNING ABOUT YOURSELF EXERCISE

Managing-in-a-Turbulent-World Tolerance Test

Instructions

Listed below are some statements a 37-year-old manager made about his job at a large, successful corporation. If your job had these characteristics, how would you react to them? After each statement are five letters, A to E. Circle the letter that best describes how you think you would react according to the following scale:

A   *I would enjoy this very much: it's completely acceptable.*

B   *This would be enjoyable and acceptable most of the time.*

C   *I'd have no reaction to this feature one way or another, or it would be about equally enjoyable and unpleasant.*

D   *This feature would be somewhat unpleasant for me.*

E   *This feature would be very unpleasant for me.*

1. I regularly spend 30 to 40 percent of my time in meetings.   A B C D E

2. A year and a half ago, my job did not exist, and I have been essentially inventing it as I go along.   A B C D E

3. The responsibilities I either assume or am assigned consistently exceed the authority I have for discharging them.   A B C D E

4. At any given moment in my job, I have on the average about a dozen phone calls to be returned.   A B C D E

5. There seems to be very little relation in my job between the quality of my performance and my actual pay and fringe benefits.   A B C D E

6. About two weeks a year of formal management training is needed in my job just to stay current.   A B C D E

7. Because we have very effective equal employment opportunity in my company, and because it is thoroughly multinational, my job consistently brings me into close working contact at a professional level with people of many races, ethnic groups, and nationalities and of both sexes.   A B C D E

8. There is no objective way to measure my effectiveness.   A B C D E

9. I report to three different bosses for different aspects of my job, and each has an equal say in my performance appraisal.   A B C D E

10. On average, about a third of my time is spent dealing with unexpected emergencies that force all scheduled work to be postponed.   A B C D E

11. When I must have a meeting of the people who report to me, it takes my secretary most of a day to find a time when we are all available, and even then, I have yet to have a meeting where everyone is present for the entire meeting.   A B C D E

12. The university degree I earned in preparation for this type of work is now obsolete, and I probably should go back for another degree.

A B C D E

13. My job requires that I absorb 100 to 200 pages per week of technical materials.

A B C D E

14. I am out of town overnight at least one night per week.

A B C D E

15. My department is so interdependent with several other departments in the company that all distinctions about which departments are responsible for which tasks are quite arbitrary.

A B C D E

16. I will probably get a promotion in about a year to a job in another division that has most of these same characteristics.

A B C D E

17. During the period of my employment here, either the entire company or the division I worked in has been reorganized every year or so.

A B C D E

18. Although there are several possible promotions I can see ahead of me, I have no real career path in an objective sense.

A B C D E

19. Although there are several possible promotions I can see ahead of me, I think I have no realistic chance of reaching the top levels of the company.

A B C D E

20. Although I have many ideas about how to make things work better, I have no direct influence on either the business policies or the personnel policies that govern my division.

A B C D E

21. My company has recently put in an "assessment centre" where I and all other managers will be required to go through an extensive battery of psychological tests to assess our potential.

A B C D E

22. My company is a defendant in an antitrust suit, and if the case comes to trial, I will probably have to testify about some decisions that were made a few years ago.

A B C D E

23. Advanced computer and other electronic office technology is continually being introduced into my division, necessitating constant learning on my part.

A B C D E

24. The computer terminal and screen I have in my office can be monitored in my bosses' offices without my knowledge.

A B C D E

Turn to page 701 for scoring directions and key.

Source: From P.B. Vaill, *Managing as a Performing Art: New Ideas for a World of Chaotic Change* (San Francisco: Jossey-Bass, 1989), pp. 8–9. Reproduced with permission of the publisher. All rights reserved.

WORKING WITH OTHERS EXERCISE

The Beacon Aircraft Company

Objectives

1. To illustrate how forces for change and stability must be managed in organizational change programs.
2. To illustrate the effects of alternative change techniques on the relative strength of forces for change and forces for stability.

The Situation

The marketing division of the Beacon Aircraft Company has undergone two reorganizations in the past two years. Initially, its structure changed from a functional to a matrix form. But the matrix structure did not satisfy some functional managers. They complained that the structure confused the authority and responsibility relationships.

In reaction to these complaints, the marketing manager revised the structure to the functional form. This new structure maintained market and project groups, which were managed by project managers with a few general staff personnel, but no functional specialists were assigned to these groups.

After the change, some problems began to surface. Project managers complained that they could not obtain adequate assistance from functional staff members. It not only took more time to obtain necessary assistance, but it also created problems in establishing stable relationships with functional staff members. Since these problems affected their services to customers, project managers demanded a change in the organizational structure—probably again toward a matrix structure. Faced with these complaints and demands from project managers, the vice-president is pondering another reorganization. He has requested an outside consultant to help him in the reorganization plan.

The Procedure

1. Divide yourselves into groups of five to seven and take the role of consultants.
2. Each group identifies the driving and resisting forces found in the firm. List these forces in the spaces provided.

The Driving Forces	**The Resisting Forces**
_____	_____
_____	_____
_____	_____
_____	_____
_____	_____
_____	_____

3. Each group develops a set of strategies for increasing the driving forces and another set for reducing the resisting forces.
4. Each group prepares a list of changes it wants to introduce.
5. The class reassembles and hears each group's recommendations.

Source: Adapted from K. H. Chung and L. C. Megginson, *Organizational Behavior*, Copyright © 1981 by K. H. Chung and L. Megginson. Reprinted by permission of Harper Collins Publishers, Inc.

Organizational Change at St. Michael's Hospital

Dr. Philip Berger found out how tightly his new employer, St. Michael's Hospital in downtown Toronto, watches costs when he went to use the photocopy machine for the first time. He discovered that he was supposed to bring his own paper. Berger, chief of family and community medicine, says he now appreciates the policy because "it makes every employee individually responsible for how they spend the public's money."

For St. Michael's Hospital, after close to a decade of provincial funding cutbacks, plus the hospital's own financial problems, there have been other cutbacks as well. Volunteers bring supplies to the wards. On weekends, intensive care sometimes runs out of intravenous bags, bandages, and gauze.

In 1998, the hospital prepared for more problems as Ontario shut some of the other hospitals in the city. Many employees, including doctors and administrators, are wondering how much harder and faster they can work before they compromise health care. "Maybe we have to back up a bit on efficiency and spend more time per patient," admits Michael Heilbronn, chief financial officer at St. Michael's.

Due to a variety of causes, the hospital's debt reached $63 million in 1991, the largest total at any hospital in Canadian history. Jeff Lozon was recruited as president and, thanks to his cuts and to $15 million in loans forgiven by the Sisters of St. Joseph, who operate the hospital, and the government of Ontario, the debt was paid off. To do this, the hospital re-engineered—changing every job in the hospital, collapsing job classifications, and streamlining admissions.

The hospital uses a just-in-time delivery system for all of its medical supplies. As a result, inventory was slashed from $900 000 to about $200 000, but it doesn't always work. Steve Lobsinger, an intensive care nurse who heads the nurses' local bargaining unit, says, "The big joke at the hospital is that often just in time is a day late."

In six years at St. Michael's, Lozon has cut staff from 2900 to 2200 employees. At the same time, inpatient admissions have jumped to 19 000 from 18 000, and outpatient visits have increased to 290 000 from 200 000.

A study looking at the University of Toronto's 11 teaching hospitals has found cost per patient at St. Michael's to be the lowest. At the same time, St. Michael's trains more medical students per patient than the other hospitals and puts more of its nursing resources to direct patient care. This represents quite an accomplishment for the hospital.

However, another study of 12 Ontario hospitals, released in the fall of 1997 by the Richard Ivey School of Business at the University of Western Ontario, raises questions about how well St. Michael's is really performing. In 400 interviews, frontline workers, middle managers, senior executives, and board members pointed to declines in service, including "less nursing time per patient, less palatable food, lower levels of cleanliness in facilities, high employee stress, slow recording of patient data, and reduced patient supervision."

Even Heilbronn admits, "If you look at the numbers, we have probably taken it a little too lean and can back off a little bit," and agrees that there is a limit to applying private-sector efficiency to a hospital. "You've got to be sensitive that the core business is patient care. In the private sector, if you make a lousy product you get an unsatisfied customer. At a hospital, your patient is dead. So you've got to be sensitive and balance it out."

Questions

1. "Hospitals simply can't be run as business organizations." Do you agree with this statement?

2. Is Lozon trying to implement too much change too fast? Support your position.

3. Do you think the hospital can continue to run a just-in-time supply system with increased patient numbers? Explain your position.

Source: Based on Peter Kuitenbrouwer, "St. Efficiency's Caring Ways: Toronto's St Michael's Hospital is a Lean, Cost Efficient Machine. But staff is Harried and Administrators are Beginning to Wonder About Quality of Patient Care," *Financial Post*, February 7/9, 1998, pp. 8,9.

Do I Have to Move?

In 1996, CP Rail packed up its corporate offices and moved from Montreal to Calgary, accomplishing the largest corporate makeover in Canadian history. The task for the year was to downsize, change cities, and make the old company new again. At the same time, the company planned an internal restructure, cutting 1500 employees and saving $125 million by the year's end.

CP Rail's top management imposed the change on its employees, trying to convince employees that the company needed to re-establish a culture focusing on performance and personal accountability. Employees who were not downsized were told they had to move to Calgary, or accept buy-out packages. Tensions ran high as preparations for the move got under way.

In trying to bring the new order on management and employees, top management signalled that it was not interested in excuses to avoid moving towards new goals. As one senior executive instructed managers, "We don't want to hear why it didn't work (in the past). It's irrelevant." This was a clear signal that managers were not to focus on the past, but instead concentrate their energies on a radically new future.

Independent of workplace changes, the CP Rail move could be expected to be hard on the families of the 730 expected to be transferred to Calgary from Montreal, Vancouver, Toronto, Minneapolis, and Albany, N.Y. To make this adjustment easier, CP Rail arranged a two-day session to answer questions about Alberta, and real estate agents, counsellors for spouses, and other services were supplied to try to create an easier transition. Even the Alberta Francophone Society was brought in to help Quebecers who wanted to continue French-language instruction for their children, and maintain ties to the francophone community after their move.

Despite what appears to be a pretty gruelling move, CP Rail ended 1996 on a high note, producing a profit of $405 million, compared with a loss of $592 million in 1995.

Questions

1. To what extent does Lewin's "Unfreezing, Moving, and Refreezing" model apply to CP Rail's move?

2. Why might you expect CP Rail's mid-level managers to be resistant to the move to Calgary?

3. What suggestions might you make to a company planning a similar move in the future to make things easier on its employees?

Source: Based on "CP Move," *Venture* 586; aired April 14, 1996 and "Relocating Employees Involves Intensive Planning," *Financial Post*, February 10/12, 1996, p. 35.

POINT

Change Is an Episodic Activity

With very few exceptions, the study of planned organizational change has been viewed as an episodic activity. That is, it starts at some point, proceeds through a series of steps, and culminates in some outcome that those involved hope is an improvement over the starting point. When change is viewed as an episodic activity, it has a beginning, a middle, and an end.

Both Lewin's three-step model and action research follow this perspective. In the former, change is seen as a break in the organization's equilibrium. The status quo has been disturbed, and change is necessary to establish a new equilibrium state. The objective of refreezing is to stabilize the new situation by balancing the driving and restraining forces. Action research begins with a diagnostic assessment in which problems are identified. These problems are then analysed and shared with those who are affected, solutions are developed, and action plans are initiated. The process is brought to closure by an evaluation of the action plan's effectiveness. Even though supporters of action research recognize that the cycle may need to go through numerous iterations, the process is still seen as a cycle with a beginning and an end.

Some experts have argued that organizational change should be thought of as balancing a system made up of five interacting variables within the organization—people, tasks, technology, structure, and strategy. A change in any one variable has repercussions on one or more of the others. Again, this perspective is episodic in that it treats organizational change as essentially an effort to sustain an equilibrium. A change in one variable begins a chain of events that, if properly managed, requires adjustments in the other variables to achieve a new state of equilibrium.

Another way to conceptualize the episodic way of looking at change is to think of managing change as analogous to captaining a ship. The organization is like a large ship traveling across the calm Mediterranean Sea to a specific port. The ship's captain has made this exact trip hundreds of times before with the same crew. Every once in a while, however, a storm will appear, and the crew has to respond. The captain will make the appropriate adjustments—that is, implement changes—and, having maneuvered through the storm, will return to calm waters. Managing an organization should therefore be seen as a journey with a beginning and an end, and implementing change as a response to a break in the status quo, needed only in occasional situations. ■

counterPOINT

Change Is an Ongoing Activity

The episodic approach may be the dominant paradigm for handling planned organizational change, but it has become obsolete. It applies to a world of certainty and predictability. The episodic approach was developed in the 1950s and 1960s, and it reflects the environment of those times. It treats change as the occasional disturbance in an otherwise peaceful world. However, this paradigm has little resemblance to the 1990s environment of constant and chaotic change.

If you want to understand what it's like to manage change in today's organizations, think of it as equivalent to permanent white-water rafting. The organization is not a large ship, but more akin to a 40-foot raft. Rather than sailing a calm sea, this raft must traverse a raging river made up of an uninterrupted flow of permanent white-water rapids. To make things worse, the raft is manned by ten people who have never worked together or travelled the river before; much of the trip is in the dark; the river is dotted by unexpected turns and obstacles; the exact destination of the raft is not clear; and at irregular intervals the raft needs to pull to shore, where some new crew members are added and others leave. Change is a natural state, and managing change is a continual process. That is, managers never get the luxury of escaping the white-water rapids.

To get a feeling for what managers are facing, think of what it would be like to attend a college that had the following structure: Courses vary in length. When you sign up for a course, however, you don't know how long it will last. It might go for two weeks or thirty weeks. Furthermore, the instructor can end a course any time he or she wants, with no prior warning. If that isn't frustrating enough, the length of the class changes each time it meets—sometimes it lasts twenty minutes, while other times it runs for three hours—and determination of when the next class meeting will take place is set by the instructor during the previous class. And one more thing: The exams are all unannounced, so you have to be ready for a test at any time.

A growing number of managers are coming to accept that their jobs are much like what a student would face in such a university or college. The stability and predictability of the episodic perspective don't exist. Nor are disruptions in the status quo only occasional, temporary, and followed by a return to an equilibrium state. Managers today face constant change, bordering on chaos. They are being forced to play a game they've never played before, governed by rules that are created as the game progresses. To manage in this dynamic arena, they are moving toward creating learning organizations. ∎

Source: This perspective is based on P.B. Vaill, *Managing as a Performing Art: New Ideas for a World of Chaotic Change* (San Francisco: Jossey-Bass, 1989).

PROGRESSIVE CASE • PART 5

Lee Simpson: Managing Change

Maclean-Hunter has experienced a great deal of change during the 1990s. One of the bigger changes was to the organizational structure. Previously each of the magazines published by Maclean-Hunter operated completely separately, including competing against each other in the marketplace. In the early '90s this structure changed somewhat so that at the management level there is more cooperation and synergy across the magazines. Lee Simpson notes that while she really likes the new structure now, it was a bit of a struggle for her initially. She appreciated the individual autonomy of the previous structure and was uncertain about how a more team-oriented management style might work. However, as the structure changed, Simpson realized the positive benefits of the new system: "Under the previous structure, we were really ignoring tremendous synergies, resources, and friendship. The old structure set us at one another's throats. The new structure has much more team work at the senior management level while maintaining healthy competition for ad revenue."

The changes that occurred at Maclean-Hunter did not affect only those in management. In the late 1980s and early 1990s, before Maclean-Hunter was taken over by Rogers Communications [see Chapter 16's OB in the News feature for more discussion of this], there was significant downsizing, with 10 percent of the workforce laid off. Simpson notes that the downsizing was extremely well managed. Some publications were sold, some were consolidated, and the Business Publishing Division was restructured. But what were the effects of the downsizing? Simpson reflects that "All of this changed the working lives of most of us. I think it took us a while to recover. There were employees who volunteered to take early retirement and in some cases we lost people who brought teaching and training skills to the table, along with their regular job-related skills." Because downsizing involves eliminating positions rather than specific people, sometimes very good performers left, while some lower-performing employees survived the downsizing.

While employees in any organization that experiences downsizing and takeovers might exhibit stress, Simpson explains that the publishing industry is prone to stress anyway because of both the dependence on advertising dollars, and the difficulty of predicting and controlling that revenue. She believes that those on the sales side are probably drawn to stress much like moths to a flame. The editorial side of the business also presents a stressful environment for employees, as it is very deadline oriented.

Simpson notes that Maclean-Hunter offers a variety of programs to help its employees deal with both the physical responses to stress and the practical problems that cause stress. The organization offers a variety of programs, including a Monday yoga class, a weight watchers program, and speakers who come in to talk about stress management. In addition, the sales and editorial conferences usually include a segment on managing stress. The organization also provides child care and elder care services on call. For instance, if an employee discovers at 8:00 a.m. that childcare is not available for the day, a call to the service results in the name and phone number of a bonded childcare resource that can be counted on to care for an employee's child on a moment's notice.

What are Simpson's personal strategies for managing stress? She explains, "On an emotional level, I guess, I am one of life's optimists and I have an incredible fallback system in place." Simpson's mother lives with the family, and can be relied upon when either Simpson or her husband is called out of town. Simpson believes in exercising, getting enough sleep, and practising excellent nutrition. She also notes that she and her husband are passionately devoted to travel and take the vacations that are their due. "I am a great believer in not missing your vacation, particularly those with your family, and I think that these things are all part of your personal stress management program."

Maclean-Hunter offers more flexibility to its workers than it did before the Rogers takeover. Simpson notes that there are now permanent part-time employees, which would have been unthinkable several years ago. She says that her own attitude has changed. Previously she might have been less willing to retain someone who wanted to reduce their hours. However, she realizes now that losing an excellent employee to a competitor who is willing to be more flexible is not good business practice. She was quite

pleased to support an associate publisher who went to a three-day workweek after her third pregnancy leave.

Simpson offers another piece of advice for managing one's career: balance the competing demands of the workplace and the family. She notes the importance of a spiritual component to her own life. "I am very involved in my church and the peace that I obtain on a Sunday morning will lift me through a couple of days. I would like to think it would take me all the way through the week, but I'm not quite there yet." She is also quick to note that what works for her might not work for everyone else. Her closing advice? "Maybe somebody else hits their zone through marathons, maybe for another person it's the wonder of white-water rafting, but whatever it is, find something to give you peace, and pursue it."

Questions

1. In what ways is Simpson's response to organizational change at Maclean-Hunter typical of those experiencing organizational change?

2. To what extent would you expect Maclean-Hunter's stress reduction programs to have an impact on employee performance?

3. What impacts would you expect to have resulted at Maclean-Hunter after downsizing and then the takeover by Rogers?

4. Do you agree with Simpson that one can manage career and family issues? What concerns do you have in thinking about trying to do so?

SCORING KEYS FOR "LEARNING ABOUT YOURSELF" EXERCISES

Chapter 2: What's Your Learning Style?

This instrument measures cognitive, affective and motivational elements that affect learning. While all 13 items did not prove statistically meaningful, it is possible to identify your dominant or preferred learning style from this questionnaire.

Pragmatic learners prefer to learn applications first and then learn the theory underlying applications. Real-world problem-solving is your forte. To calculate your pragmatic score, add up your circled answers to questions 1 and 5, and reverse the number for question 11 (5 becomes 1, 4 becomes 2, etc.).

Discovery learners prefer instructors to allow them to discover the underlying principles rather than tell them the principles in a lecture. Question 9 taps this style.

Critical inquirers prefer to know the why behind the subject and go beyond the factual material. They want analysis, synthesis, and evaluation. They see learning as an intellectual pursuit. To calculate your critical inquiry score, add up your circled answers to questions 6 and 10, and reverse the number for question 13.

Lack of commitment refers to people who are unwilling to spend the time it takes to master a subject. To calculate your lack of commitment score, add up your circled answers to questions 7, 8, and 11.

Now place your scores below and compute the average:

Calculated score

Pragmatic learner	_____	divided by 3 =	_____
Discovery learner	_____	transfers to =	_____
Critical inquiry	_____	divided by 3 =	_____
Lack of commitment	_____	divided by 3 =	_____

On which learning style did you score *lowest?* That tells you your preferred learning style. Note, for instance, that a relatively high score on the pragmatic scale suggests you like abstract ideas and theory.

No one style is better than any other. The value of this exercise is to help you better understand yourself. You can then use this information to help guide you in selecting among learning techniques and methods.

Chapter 4: What Do You Value?

Transfer the numbers for each of the 16 items to the appropriate column; then add up the two numbers in each column.

	Professional	Financial	Family	Social
	1. _____	2. _____	3. _____	4. _____
	9. _____	10. _____	11. _____	12. _____
Totals	_____	_____	_____	_____
	Community	Spiritual	Physical	Intellectual
	5. _____	6. _____	7. _____	8. _____
	13. _____	14. _____	15. _____	16. _____
Totals	_____	_____	_____	_____

The higher the total in any value dimension, the higher the importance you place on that value set. The closer the numbers are in all eight dimensions, the more well rounded you are.

Chapter 5: What Motivates You?

To determine your dominant needs—and what motivates you—place the number 1 through 5 that represents your score for each statement next to the number for that statement.

Achievement	Power	Affiliation
1. _____	2. _____	3. _____
4. _____	5. _____	6. _____
7. _____	8. _____	9. _____
10. _____	11. _____	12. _____
13. _____	14. _____	15. _____
Totals: _____	_____	_____

Add up the total of each column. The sum of the numbers in each column will be between 5 and 25 points. The column with the highest score tells you your dominant need.

Chapter 6: How Equity Sensitive Are You?

Sum up the points you allocated to the following items: 1B; 2A; 3B; 4A; and 5B. Your total will be between zero and 50.

Researchers have identified three equity-sensitive groups. They are labeled and defined as follows:

◆ Benevolents—Individuals who prefer that their outcome/input ratios be less than the comparison others.

◆ Equity Sensitives—Individuals who prefer outcome/input ratios to be equal.

◆ Entitleds—Individuals who prefer that their outcome/input ratios exceed those of the comparison others.

Based on data from more than 3,500 respondents, the researchers have found that scores less than 29 are classified as Entitleds; those between 29 and 32 are Equity Sensitives; and those with scores above 32 are Benevolents.

What does all this mean? First, not all individuals are equity sensitive. Second, equity theory predictions are most accurate with individuals in the Equity Sensitives group. And third, Benevolents actually prefer lower outcome/input ratios and tend to provide higher levels of inputs than either Equity Sensitives or Entitleds.

Chapter 7: Are You Attracted to the Group?

Add up your scores for items 4, 6, 7, 8, 9, 10, 14, 17, 19, and 20. Obtain a corrected score by subtracting the score for each of the remaining questions from 10. For example, if you marked 3 for item 1, you would obtain a corrected score of 7 (10 2 3). Add the corrected scores together with the total obtained on the 10 items scored directly. The higher your score, the more positive are your feelings about the group.

Chapter 8: Do Others See Me as Trustworthy?

Add up your total score for the seven statements. The following provides general guidelines for interpreting your score.

57–70 points = You're seen as highly trustworthy.
21–56 points = You're seen as moderately trustworthy.
7–20 points = You're rated low on this characteristic.

Chapter 9: Listening Self-Inventory

The correct answers to the 15 questions, based on listening theory, are as follows: (1) No; (2) No; (3) No; (4) Yes; (5) No; (6) No; (7) No; (8) No; (9) No; (10) No; (11) No; (12) Yes; (13) Yes; (14) No; (15) Yes. To determine your score, add up the number of incorrect answers, multiply by 7, and subtract that total from 105. If you scored between 91 and 105, you have good listening habits. Scores of 77 to 90 suggest significant room for improvement. Scores below 76 indicate that you're a poor listener and need to work hard on improving this skill.

Chapter 10: Decision-Making Style Questionnaire

Mark each of your responses on the following scales. Then use the point value column to arrive at your score. For example, if you answered a to the first question, you would check 1a in the feeling column. This response receives zero points when you add up the point value column. Instructions for classifying your scores are indicated following the scales.

Sensation	Point Value	Intuition	Point Value	Thinking	Point Value	Feeling	Point Value
2b _____	1	2a _____	2	1b _____	1	1a _____	0
4a _____	1	4b _____	1	3b _____	2	3a _____	1
5a _____	1	5b _____	1	7b _____	1	7a _____	1
6b _____	1	6a _____	0	8a _____	0	8b _____	1
9b _____	2	9a _____	2	10b _____	2	10a _____	1

12a _____	1	12b _____	0	11a _____	2	11b _____	1
15a _____	1	15b _____	1	13b _____	1	13a _____	1
16b _____	2	16a _____	0	14b _____	0	14a _____	1
	___		___		___		___

Maximum
Point Value   (10)   (7)   (9)   (7)

Write *intuition* if your intuition score is equal to or greater than your sensation score. Write *sensation* if your sensation score is greater than your intuition score. Write *feeling* if your feeling score is greater than your thinking score. Write *thinking* if your thinking score is greater than your feeling score.

A high score on *intuition* indicates you see the world in holistic terms. You tend to be creative. A high score on *sensation* indicates that you are realistic and see the world in terms of facts. A high score on *feeling* means you make decisions based on gut feeling. A high score on *thinking* indicates a highly logical and analytical approach to decision making.

Chapter 11: Are You a Charismatic Leader?

The questionnaire measures each of the six basic behaviour leader patterns, as well as a set of emotional responses. Each question is stated as a measure of the extent to which you engage in the behaviour, or elicit the feelings. The higher your overall score, the more you demonstrate charismatic leader behaviours. The indices outline a variety of traits associated with charismatic behaviour. For each index, add up the scores you gave to the relevant questions. Your score on each index can range from 4 to 20.

Index 1: Management of Attention (1, 7, 13, 19). Your score _____. You pay especially close attention to people with whom you are communicating. You are also "focused in" on the key issues under discussion and help others to see clearly these key points. They have clear ideas about the relative importance or priorities of different issues under discussion.

Index 2: Management of Meaning (2, 8, 14, 20). Your score _____. This set of items centres on your communication skills, specifically your ability to get the meaning of a message across, even if this means devising some quite innovative approach.

Index 3: Management of Trust (3, 9, 15, 21). Your score _____. The key factor is your perceived trustworthiness as shown by your willingness to follow through on promises, avoidance of "flip-flop" shifts in position, and willingness to take a clear position.

Index 4: Management of Self (4, 10, 16, 22). Your score _____. This index concerns your general attitudes toward yourself and others' that is, your overall concern for others and their feelings, as well as for "taking care of" feelings about yourself in a positive sense (e.g., self-regard).

Index 5: Management of Risk (5, 11, 17, 23). Your score _____. Effective charismatic leaders are deeply involved in what they do, and do not spend excessive amounts of time or energy on plans to "protect" themselves against failure. These leaders are willing to take risks, not on a hit-or-miss basis, but after careful estimation of the odds of success or failure.

Index 6: Management of Feelings (6, 12, 18, 24). Your score _____. Charismatic leaders seem to consistently generate a set of feelings in others. Others feel that their work becomes more meaningful and that they are the "masters" of their own behaviour; that is, they feel competent. They feel a sense of community, a "we-ness" with their colleagues and their co-workers.

Chapter 12: How Political Are You?

According to the author of this instrument, a complete organizational politician will answer "true" to all ten questions. Organizational politicians with fundamental ethical standards will answer "false" to questions 5 and 6, which deal with deliberate lies and uncharitable behavior. Individuals who regard manipulation, incomplete disclosure, and self-serving behavior as unacceptable will answer "false" to all or almost all of the questions.

Chapter 13: What Is Your Primary Conflict-Handling Intention?

To determine your primary conflict-handling intention, place the number 1 through 5 that represents your score for each statement next to the number for that statement. Then total up the columns.

	Competing	Collaborating	Avoiding	Accommodating	Compromising
	1.__	4.__	6.__	3.__	2.__
	5.__	9.__	10.__	11.__	8.__
	7.__	12.__	15.__	14.__	13.__
Totals	__	__	__	__	__

Your primary conflict-handling intention is the category with the highest total. Your fall-back intention is the category with the second-highest total.

Chapter 14: Bureaucratic Orientation Test

Give yourself one point for each statement for which you responded in the bureaucratic direction:

1. Mostly agree		11. Mostly agree
2. Mostly agree		12. Mostly disagree
3. Mostly disagree		13. Mostly disagree
4. Mostly agree		14. Mostly agree
5. Mostly disagree		15. Mostly disagree
6. Mostly disagree		16. Mostly agree
7. Mostly agree		17. Mostly disagree
8. Mostly agree		18. Mostly agree
9. Mostly disagree		19. Mostly agree
10. Mostly agree		20. Mostly disagree

A very high score (15 or over) suggests that you would enjoy working in a bureaucracy. A very low score (5 or lower) suggests that you would be frustrated by working in a bureaucracy, especially a large one.

Chapter 15: Is an Enriched Job for You?

This questionnaire taps the degree to which you have a strong versus weak desire to obtain growth satisfaction from your work. Each item on the questionnaire yields a score from 1 to 7 (that is, "Strongly prefer A" is scored 1; "Neutral" is scored 4; and "Strongly prefer B" is scored 7). To obtain your individual growth need strength score, average the 12 items as follows:

Numbers 1, 2, 7, 8, 11, 12 (direct scoring)

Numbers 3, 4, 5, 6, 9, 10 (reverse scoring)

Average scores for typical respondents are close to the midpoint of 4.0. Research indicates that if you score high on this measure, you will respond positively to an enriched job. Conversely, if you score low, you will tend *not* to find enriched jobs satisfying or motivating.

You can use this questionnaire to identify areas where you can improve your interview skills. If you scored 3 or less on any statement, you should consider what you can do to improve that score.

Chapter 16: What Kind of Organizational Culture Fits You Best?

For items 5 and 6, score as follows:

$$
\begin{aligned}
\text{Strongly agree} &= +2 \\
\text{Agree} &= +1 \\
\text{Uncertain} &= 0 \\
\text{Disagree} &= -1 \\
\text{Strongly disagree} &= -2
\end{aligned}
$$

For items 1, 2, 3, 4, and 7, reverse the score (Strongly agree = −2, and so on). Add up your total. Your score will fall somewhere between +14 and −14.

What does your score mean? The higher your score (positive), the more comfortable you'll be in a formal, mechanistic, rule-oriented, and structured culture. This is often associated with large corporations and government agencies. Negative scores indicate a preference for informal, humanistic, flexible, and innovative cultures, which are more likely to be found in research units, advertising firms, high-tech companies, and small businesses.

Chapter 17: Managing-in-a-Turbulent-World Tolerance Test

Score 4 points for each A, 3 for each B, 2 for each C, 1 for each D, and 0 for each E. Compute the total, divide by 24, and round to one decimal place.

While the results are not intended to be more than suggestive, the higher your score, the more comfortable you seem to be with change. The test's author suggests analyzing scores as if they were grade-point averages. In this way, a 4.0 average is an A, a 2.0 is a C, and scores below 1.0 flunk.

Using replies from nearly 500 MBA students and young managers, the range of scores was found to be narrow—between 1.0 and 2.2. The average score was between 1.5 and 1.6—equivalent to a D+/C− grade! If these scores are generalizable to the work population, clearly people are not very tolerant of the kind of changes that come with a turbulent environment. However, this sample is now nearly a decade old. We should expect average scores today to be higher as people have become more accustomed to living in a dynamic environment.

PHOTO CREDITS

ENDNOTES

CHAPTER 1

1 Based on S. Silcoff, "The Sky's Your Limit," *Canadian Business*, 70 no. 4, (April 1997), pp. 58-66; "Clear Visions," *Financial Post Magazine*, April 1997, pp. 16-30; and B. Schecter, "Better Profit Heats Up Second Cup," *Financial Post Daily*, October 30, 1997, p. 20.

2 D. Milbank, "Managers Are Sent to 'Charm Schools' to Discover How to Polish Up Their Acts," *Wall Street Journal*, December 14, 1990, p. B1.

3 S. Sherman, "Are You As Good As the Best in the World?" *Fortune*, December 13, 1993, p. 96. This point is elaborated in J. Pfeffer, "Producing Sustainable Competitive Advantage through the Effective Management of People," *Academy of Management Executive*, February 1995, pp. 55-69.

4 M. Rothman, "Into the Black," *INC.*, January 1993, p. 59.

5 C. Hymowitz, "Five Main Reasons Why Managers Fail," *Wall Street Journal*, May 2, 1988, p. 25.

6 D. Milbank, "Managers Are Sent to 'Charm Schools' to Discover How to Polish Up Their Acts," *Wall Street Journal*, December 14, 1990, p. B1.

7 S.A. Waddock, "Educating Tomorrow's Managers," *Journal of Management Education*, February 1991, pp. 69-96; and K.F. Kane, "MBAs: A Recruiter's-Eye View," *Business Horizons*, January-February 1993, pp. 65-71.

8 See, for instance, J.E. Garcia and K.S. Keleman, "What Is Organizational Behavior Anyhow?" paper presented at the 16th Annual Organizational Behavior Teaching Conference, Columbia, MO, June 1989.

9 V. Smith, "Money Talks," *Report on Business Magazine*, April 1998, pp. 97-100.

10 J.D. Costa, "Getting It," *Report on Business Magazine*, April 1998, pp. 102-105. Other studies that also discuss the ill effects of downsizing include Tomasz Mroczkowski and Masao Hanaoka, "Effective Rightsizing Strategies in Japan and America: Is there a Convergence of Employment Practices?", *Academy of Management Executive*, 11 no. 2 (1997), pp. 57-67; and Stephen S. Roach, "The Hollow Ring of Productivity Revival," *Harvard Business Review*, November-December 1996, pp. 81-89.

11 J.D. Costa, "Getting It," *Report on Business Magazine*, April 1998, pp. 102-105.

12 "'Haves and Have-Nots' Canadians Look for Corporate Conscience," *Maclean's*, December 30, 1996, January 6, 1997, pp. 26, 37.

13 J.D. Costa, "Getting It," *Report on Business Magazine*, April 1998, pp. 102-105.

14 J.D. Costa, "Getting It," *Report on Business Magazine*, April 1998, pp. 102-105.

15 G. Crone, "Ontario Hydro Moves into Hiring Mode Again," *Financial Post*, April 11, 1998, p. 4.

16 "FP/COMPAS Poll: An Exclusive Survey of CEOs and Canadians at Large: This Week: New Burdens for Managers," *Financial Post*, November 22/24, 1997, p. 17.

17 "FP/COMPAS Poll: An Exclusive Survey of CEOs and Canadians at Large: This Week: New Burdens for Managers," *Financial Post*, November 22/24, 1997, p. 17.

18 Angus Reid Group, *Workplace 2000: Working Toward the Millennium*, Fall 1997.

19 C. Thompson, "State of the Union," *Report on Business Magazine*, April 1998, pp. 73-82.

20 C. Thompson, "State of the Union," *Report on Business Magazine*, April 1998, pp. 73-82.

21 B. Dumaine, "The New Non-Manager Managers," *Fortune*, February 22, 1993, pp. 80-84.

22 "Wanted: Teammates, Crew Members, and Cast Members: But No Employees," *Wall Street Journal*, April 30, 1996, p. A1.

23 M. Sashkin, "Participative Management Is an Ethical Imperative," *Organizational Dynamics*, Spring 1984, pp. 5-22.

24 See, "What Self-Managing Teams Manage," *Training*, October 1995, p. 72.

25 See, for instance, M. Sashkin and K.J. Kiser, *Putting Total Quality Management to Work* (San Francisco: Berrett-Koehler, 1993); and J.R. Hackman and R. Wageman, "Total Quality Management: Empirical, Conceptual, and Practical Issues," *Administrative Science Quarterly*, June 1995, pp. 309-42.

26 M. Hammer and J. Champy, *Reengineering the Corporation: A Manifesto for Business Revolution* (New York: HarperBusiness, 1993); and J. Champy, *Reengineering Management* (New York: HarperBusiness, 1995).

27 M. Kaeter, "The Age of the Specialized Generalist," *Training*, December 1993, pp. 48-53; and N. Templin, "Auto Plants, Hiring Again, Are Demanding Higher-Skilled Labor," *Wall Street Journal*, March 11, 1994, p. A1.

28 J. Lee, "Family Business Has Nerves of Steel," *Vancouver Sun*, December 22, 1997, pp. D1, D3.

29 J. H. Eggers, "The Dynamics of Asian Business, Culture," *The Globe and Mail*, March 13, 1998, p. C5.

30 See, for instance, R.R. Thomas Jr., "From Affirmative Action to Affirming Diversity," *Harvard Business Review*, March-April 1990, pp. 107-17; B. Mandrell and S. Kohler-Gray, "Management Development That Values Diversity," *Personnel*, March 1990, pp. 41-47; J. Dreyfuss, "Get Ready for the New Work Force," *Fortune*, April 23, 1990, pp. 165-81; and I. Wielawski, "Diversity Makes Both Dollars and Sense," *Los Angeles Times*, May 16, 1994, p. II-3.

31 See, for instance, P.L. McLeod and S.A. Lobel, "The Effects of Ethnic Diversity on Idea Generation in Small Groups," paper presented at the Annual Academy of Management Conference, Las Vegas, August 1992.

32 C. Thompson, "State of the Union," *Report on Business Magazine*, April 1998, pp. 73-82.

33 B. Livesey, "Making Nice," *Report on Business Magazine*, March 1998, pp. 96-104.

34 R. McQueen, "Companies that Raise the Bar—the Standards for Becoming One of the 50 Best Gets Higher Each Year," *Financial Post*, December 13/15, 1997, p. 11.

35 Lieber, "Why Employees Love These Companies," *Fortune*, January 12, 1998, pp. 72-74.

36 Fisher, "100 Best Companies to Work For in America," *Fortune*, January 12, 1998, pp. 68-70.

37 R. Weinberg and W. Nord, "Coping with 'It's All Common Sense'," *Exchange* 7, no. 2 (1982), pp. 29-33; R.P. Vecchio, "Some Popular (But Misguided) Criticisms of the Organizational Sciences," *Organizational Behavior Teaching Review* 10, no. 1 (1986-87), pp. 28-34; and M.L. Lynn, "Organizational Behavior and Common Sense: Philosophical Implications for Teaching and Thinking," paper presented at the 14th Annual Organizational Behavior Teaching Conference, Waltham, MA, May 1987.

38 See, for example, M.J. Driver, "Cognitive Psychology: An Interactionist View," R.H. Hall, "Organizational Behavior: A Sociological Perspective," and C. Hardy, "The Contribution of Political Science to Organizational Behavior," all in J.W. Lorsch (ed.), *Handbook of Organizational Behavior* (Englewood Cliffs, NJ: Prentice Hall, 1987), pp. 62–108.

39 D. Tjosvold, "Controversy for Learning Organizational Behavior," *Organizational Behavior Teaching Review*, 11, no. 3 (1986–87), pp. 51–59; and L.F. Moore, D.C. Limerick, and P.J. Frost, "Debating the Issue: Increasing Understanding of the 'Close Calls' in Organizational Decision Making," *Organizational Behavior Teaching Review* 14, no. 1 (1989–90), pp. 37–43.

40 S.R. Rhodes and R.M. Steers, *Managing Employee Absenteeism* (Reading, MA: Addison-Wesley, 1990).

41 Taken from "Controlling Sky-High Absenteeism," *Occupational Health & Safety*, January/February 1996, p. 54, and "Expensive Absenteeism," *Wall Street Journal*, July 29, 1986, p. 1.

42 M. Mercer, "Turnover: Reducing the Costs," *Personnel*, December 1988, pp. 36-42; and R. Darmon, "Identifying Sources of Turnover Cost," *Journal of Marketing*, April 1990, pp. 46-56.

43 See, for example, D.R. Dalton and W.D. Todor, "Functional Turnover: An Empirical Assessment," *Journal of Applied Psychology*, December 1981, pp. 716-21; and G.M. McEvoy and W.F. Cascio, "Do Good or Poor Performers Leave? A Meta-Analysis of the Relationship between Performance and Turnover," *Academy of Management Journal*, December 1987, pp. 744-62.

44 Cited in "You Often Lose the Ones You Love," *Industry Week*, November 21, 1988, p. 5.

45 H.J. Leavitt, *Managerial Psychology*, rev. ed. (Chicago: University of Chicago Press, 1964), p. 3.

46 Cited in "You Often Lose the Ones You Love," *Industry Week*, November 21, 1988, p. 5.

47 R.T. Mowday, L. W. Porter, and R.M. Steers, *Employee Organization Linkages: The Psychology of Commitment, Absenteeism, and Turnover* (New York: Academic Press, 1982).

48 Angus Reid Group, *Workplace 2000: Working Toward the Millennium*, Fall 1997.

49 Angus Reid Group, *Workplace 2000: Working Toward the Millennium*, Fall 1997.

50 Angus Reid Group, *Workplace 2000: Working Toward the Millennium*, Fall 1997.

51 J. H. Eggers, "The Dynamics of Asian Business, Culture," *The Globe and Mail*, Friday, March 13, 1998, p. C5.

CHAPTER 2

1 Based on D. Maley, "Canada's Top Women CEOs," *Maclean's*, October 20, 1997, pp. 52ff.

2 C. Harris, "Prime Numbers: A Statistical Look at the Trends and Issues That Will Dominate Our Future," *Financial Post*, 10, *no.* 46, November 15/17, 1997, p. P13.

3 StatsCan Daily, March 17, 1998.

4 Cameron and Quinn, *The Competing Values Framework*; Robert E. Quinn, Sue R. Faerman, Michael P. Thompson and Michael R. McGrath, *Becoming a Master Manager: A Competency Framework* (New York: John Wiley and Sons, 1990); Kim Cameron and Robert E. Quinn, *Diagnosing and Changing Organizational Culture* (Addison Wesley).

5 John McCallum, "New Managers, Same Old Skills," *Financial Post*, November 22/24, 1997, pp. P4-P6.

6 "People Power," *Canadian Business Review*, Spring 1996, p. 42.

7 C.R. Farquhar and J. A. Longair, "Creating High-Performance Organizations with People," Conference Board of Canada, 1996, Report #R164-96.

8 "People Power," *Canadian Business Review*, Spring 1996, p. 42.

9 R.E. Quinn, S. R. Faerman, M. P. Thompson and Michael R. McGrath, *Becoming a Master Manager: A Competency Framework* (New York: John Wiley and Sons, 1990).

10 D. Maley, "Canada's Top Women CEOs," *Maclean's*, October 20, 1997, pp. 52ff.

11 H. Mintzberg, *The Nature of Managerial Work* (New York: Harper & Row, 1973).

12 F. Luthans, "Successful vs. Effective Real Managers," *Academy of Management Executive*, May 1988, pp. 127-32; and F. Luthans, R.M. Hodgetts, and S.A. Rosenkrantz, *Real Managers* (Cambridge, MA: Ballinger, 1988).

13 "Mintzberg on Managers," *Harvard Business Review*, July-August 1996, pp. 65-66.

14 W. McGehee, "Are We Using What We Know about Training?: Learning Theory and Training," *Personnel Psychology*, Spring 1958, p. 2.

15 I.P. Pavlov, *The Work of the Digestive Glands*, trans. W.H. Thompson (London: Charles Griffin, 1902).

16 B.F. Skinner, *Contingencies of Reinforcement* (East Norwalk, CT: Appleton-Century-Crofts, 1971).

17 T.W. Costello and S.S. Zalkind, *Psychology in Administration* (Englewood Cliffs, NJ: Prentice Hall, 1963), p. 193.

18 F. Luthans and R. Kreitner, *Organizational Behavior Modification and Beyond*, 2nd ed. (Glenview, IL: Scott, Foresman, 1985).

19 A. Halcrow, "Incentive! How Three Companies Cut Costs," *Personnel Journal*, February 1986, p. 12.

20 D. Willings, "The Absentee Worker," *Personnel and Training Management*, December 1968, pp. 10-12.

21 B.H. Harvey, J.F. Rogers, and J.A. Schultz, "Sick Pay vs. Well Pay: An Analysis of the Impact of Rewarding Employees for Being on the Job," *Public Personnel Management Journal*, Summer 1983, pp. 218-24.

22 M.S. Forbes Jr., "There's a Better Way," *Forbes*, April 26, 1993, p. 23.

23 M.A. Glynn, T.K. Lant, and F.J. Milliken, "Mapping Learning Processes in Organizations: A Multi-level Framework Linking Learning and Organizing," *Advances in Managerial Cognition and Organizational Information Processing*, 5, pp. 43-84, 1994.

24 B. Levitt, and J.G. March, "Organizational Learning," *Annual Review of Sociology*, 14, 1988, pp. 319-340; J.G. March, "Footnotes to Organizational Change," *Administrative Science Quarterly*, 26, 1981, pp. 536-577; D. Levinthal and J.G. March, "A Model of Adaptive Organizational Search," Reprinted in J.G. March, *Decisions and Organizations*, (New York: Basil Blackwell, 1988), pp. 187-218; S. Herriot, D. Levinthal, and J.G. March, "Learning from Experience in Organizations," Reprinted in J.G. March, *Decisions and Organizations*, (New York: Basil Blackwell, 1988), pp. 219-227; T.K. Lant and S.J. Mezias, "Managing Discontinuous Change: A Simulation Study of Organizational Learning and Entrepreneurial Strategies," *Strategic Management Journal* 1, 1990, pp. 147-179.

25 R.B. Duncan and A. Weiss, "Organizational Learning: Implications for Organizational Design," in B.M. Staw (ed.) *Research in Organizational Behavior*, 1, 1979 pp. 75-123, (Greenwich, CT: JAI Press); R.H. Miles and W. Randolph, "Influence of Organizational Learning Styles on Early Development," in J.H. Kimberly and R.H. Miles (eds.), *The Organizational Life Cycle*, (San Francisco: Jossey-Bass. 1980); C. Argyris and D. Schon, *Organizational Learning* (Reading, MA: Addison-Wesley, 1978); M. Jelinek, *Institutionalizing Innovations: A Study of Organizational Learning Systems* (New York: Praeger, 1979); D. Epple, L. Argote and R. Devadas, "Organizational Learning Curves: A Method for Investigating Intra-plant Transfer of Knowledge Acquired Through Learning by Doing," *Organization Science*, 2, 1991, 58-70.

26 M.A. Glynn, Theresa K. Lant, and Frances J. Milliken, "Mapping Learning Processes in Organizations: A Multi-level Framework Linking Learning and Organizing," *Advances in Managerial Cognition and Organizational Information Processing*, 5, 1994 p. 46, 1994.

27 J.G. March, "Exploration and Exploitation in Organizational Learning," *Organization Science* 2, 1991, 80.

28 C. Argyris and D. Schon, *Organizational Learning* (Reading, MA: Addison-Wesley, 1978).

29 "Corporate Culture Club: Companies Are Focusing on Employee Morale and Training to Boost the Bottom Line," *Maclean's*, December 12, 1994, pp. 42-43.

30 "Corporate Culture Club: Companies Are Focusing on Employee Morale and Training to Boost the Bottom Line," *Maclean's*, December 12, 1994, pp. 42-43.

31 "Corporate Culture Club: Companies Are Focusing on Employee Morale and Training to Boost the Bottom Line," *Maclean's*, December 12, 1994, pp. 42-43.

32 H. Kluge, "Learning Leadership for a World of Change," *Canadian Speeches*, May 1993, pp. 48-52.

33 Based on Peter Senge, *The Fifth Discipline: The Art and Practice of the Learning Organization* (New York: Doubleday, 1990), pp. 18-25. Not all of his roadblocks are listed.

34 Cited in *Training*, October 1995, p. 38.

35 P. Kuitenbrouwer, "Firms Underinvesting in Staff Training," *Financial Post Daily*, 10, 147 (October 17, 1997), p.12.

36 See, for instance, C.C. Manz and H.P. Sims, "Self-Management as a Substitute for Leadership: A Social Learning Theory Perspective," *Academy of Management Review*, July 1980, pp. 361-67; and S.E. Markham and I.S. Markham, "Self-Management and Self-Leadership Reexamined: A Levels-of-Analysis Perspective," *Leadership Quarterly*, Fall 1995, pp. 343-60.

37 G.P. Latham and C.A. Frayne, "Self-Management Training for Increasing Job Attendance: A Follow-Up and a Replication," *Journal of Applied Psychology*, June 1989, pp. 411-16.

CHAPTER 3

1 Based on "Stronach's Pay Almost Matches Big 3 Combined," *Canadian Press Newswire*, October 31, 1997; B. Simon, "Work Ethic and the Magna Carta," *Financial Post Daily*, March 20, 1997, p. 14; "Magna in Overdrive: No Canadian Has Profited from Contracting Out as Much as Stronach," *Maclean's*, September 30, 1996, pp. 50-54; "Car and Striver (Will the World's Leading Auto-parts Supplier Become the Globe's Newest Automaker?)," *Canadian Business*, September 1996, pp. 92-94; "Magna-mania: Resurrecting His On-the-Brink Auto Parts Empire Didn't Satisfy Frank Stronach Who Plans Growth and Monuments with Equal Flair," *Financial Post*, August 12/14, 1995, pp. 12-13.

2 H.H. Kelley, "Attribution in Social Interaction," in E. Jones, et al. (eds.), *Attribution: Perceiving the Causes of Behavior* (Morristown, NJ: General Learning Press, 1972).

3 See L. Ross, "The Intuitive Psychologist and His Shortcomings," in L. Berkowitz (ed.), *Advances in Experimental Social Psychology* 10 (Orlando, FL: Academic Press, 1977), pp. 174-220; and A.G. Miller and T. Lawson, "The Effect of an Informational Option on the Fundamental Attribution Error," *Personality and Social Psychology Bulletin*, June 1989, pp. 194-204.

4 S. Nam, *Cultural and Managerial Attributions for Group Performance*, unpublished doctoral dissertation; University of Oregon. Cited in R.M. Steers, S.J. Bischoff, and L.H. Higgins, "Cross-Cultural Management Research," *Journal of Management Inquiry*, December 1992, pp. 325-26.

5 B. McKenna, "Modern Suicides Hold Little Glory," *The Globe and Mail*, June 2, 1998, p. A14.

6 D.C. Dearborn and H.A. Simon, "Selective Perception: A Note on the Departmental Identification of Executives," *Sociometry*, June 1958, pp. 140-44. Some of the conclusions in this classic study have recently been challenged in J.P. Walsh, "Selectivity and Selective Perception: An Investigation of Managers' Belief Structures and Information Processing," *Academy of Management Journal*, December 1988, pp. 873-96; M.J. Waller, G.P. Huber, and W.H. Glick, "Functional Background as a Determinant of Executives' Selective Perception," *Academy of Management Journal*, August 1995, pp. 943-74; and J.S. Bunderson, "Work History and Selective Perception: Fine-Tuning What We Know," in D.P. Moore (ed.), *Academy of Management Best Papers Proceedings* (Vancouver, BC, Academy of Management Conference, 1995), pp. 459-63.

7 S.E. Asch, "Forming Impressions of Personality," *Journal of Abnormal and Social Psychology*, July 1946, pp. 258-90.

8 J.S. Bruner and R. Tagiuri, "The Perception of People," in E. Lindzey (ed.), *Handbook of Social Psychology* (Reading, MA: Addison-Wesley, 1954), p. 641.

[9] See, for example, C.M. Judd and B. Park, "Definition and Assessment of Accuracy in Social Stereotypes," *Psychological Review*, January 1993, pp. 109-28.

[10] See, for example, S.T. Fiske, D.N. Beroff, E. Borgida, K. Deaux, and M.E. Heilman, "Use of Sex Stereotyping Research in Price Waterhouse vs. Hopkins," *American Psychologist*, 1991, pp. 1049-60; G.N. Powell, "The Good Manager: Business Students' Stereotypes of Japanese Managers versus Stereotypes of American Managers," *Group & Organizational Management*, 1992, pp. 44-56; and K.J. Gibson, W.J. Zerbe, and R.E. Franken, "Job Search Strategies for Older Job Hunters: Addressing Employers' Perceptions," *Canadian Journal of Counseling*, 1992, pp. 166-76.

[11] See, for example, E.C. Webster, *Decision Making in the Employment Interview* (Montreal: McGill University, Industrial Relations Center, 1964).

[12] See, for example, R.D. Bretz Jr., G.T. Milkovich, and W. Read, "The Current State of Performance Appraisal Research and Practice: Concerns, Directions, and Implications," *Journal of Management*, June 1992, pp. 323-24; and P.M. Swiercz, M.L. Icenogle, N.B. Bryan, and R.W. Renn, "Do Perceptions of Performance Appraisal Fairness Predict Employee Attitudes and Performance?" in D.P. Moore (ed.), *Proceedings of the Academy of Management* (Atlanta: Academy of Management, 1993), pp. 304-08.

[13] G.W. Allport, *Personality: A Psychological Interpretation* (New York: Holt, Rinehart & Winston, 1937), p. 48.

[14] Reported in R.L. Hotz, "Genetics, Not Parenting, Key to Temperament, Studies Say," *Los Angeles Times*, February 20, 1994, p. A1.

[15] See T.J. Bouchard Jr., D.T. Lykken, M. McGue, N.L. Segal, and A. Tellegen, "Sources of Human Psychological Differences: The Minnesota Study of Twins Reared Apart," *Science*, October 12, 1990, pp. 223-38; T.J. Bouchard Jr. and M. McGue, "Genetic and Rearing Environmental Influences on Adult Personality: An Analysis of Adopted Twins Raised Apart," *Journal of Personality* 58 (1990), pp. 263-92; D.T. Lykken, T.J. Bouchard Jr., M. McGue, and A. Tellegen, "Heritability of Interests: A Twin Study," *Journal of Applied Psychology*, August 1993, pp. 649-61; and R.D. Arvey and T.J. Bouchard Jr., "Genetics, Twins, and Organizational Behavior," in B.M. Staw and L.L. Cummings, *Research in Organizational Behavior*, 16 (Greenwich, CT: JAI Press, 1994), pp. 65-66.

[16] See B.M. Staw and J. Ross, "Stability in the Midst of Change: A Dispositional Approach to Job Attitudes," *Journal of Applied Psychology*, August 1985, pp. 469-80; and B.M. Staw, N.E. Bell, and J.A. Clausen, "The Dispositional Approach to Job Attitudes: A Lifetime Longitudinal Test," *Administrative Science Quarterly*, March 1986, pp. 56-77.

[17] R.C. Carson, "Personality," in M.R. Rosenzweig and L.W. Porter (eds.), *Annual Review of Psychology* 40 (Palo Alto, CA: Annual Reviews, 1989), pp. 228-29.

[18] L. Sechrest, "Personality," in M.R. Rosenzweig and L.W. Porter (eds.), *Annual Review of Psychology* 27 (Palo Alto, CA: Annual Reviews, 1976), p. 10.

[19] L. Sechrest, "Personality," in M.R. Rosenzweig and L.W. Porter (eds.), *Annual Review of Psychology* 27 (Palo Alto, CA: Annual Reviews, 1976), p. 10.

[20] See A.H. Buss, "Personality as Traits," *American Psychologist*, November 1989, pp. 1378-88.

[21] R.B. Catell, "Personality Pinned Down," *Psychology Today*, July 1973, pp. 40-46.

[22] See A.J. Vaccaro, "Personality Clash," *Personnel Administrator*, September 1988, pp. 88-92; and R.R. McCrae and P.T. Costa Jr., "Reinterpreting the Myers-Briggs Type Indicator from the Perspective of the Five Factor Model of Personality," *Journal of Personality*, March 1989, pp. 17-40.

[23] G.N. Landrum, *Profiles of Genius* (New York: Prometheus, 1993).

[24] See, for example, J.M. Digman, "Personality Structure: Emergence of the Five-Factor Model," in M.R. Rosenzweig and L.W. Porter (eds.), *Annual Review of Psychology* 41 (Palo Alto, CA: Annual Reviews, 1990), pp. 417-40; O.P. John, "The 'Big Five' Factor Taxonomy: Dimensions of Personality in the Natural Language and in Questionnaires," in L.A. Pervin (ed.), *Handbook of Personality Theory and Research* (New York: Guilford Press, 1990), pp. 66-100; M.K. Mount, M.R. Barrick, and J.P. Strauss, "Validity of Observer Ratings of the Big Five Personality Factors," *Journal of Applied Psychology*, April 1994, pp. 272-80; and P.J. Howard and J.M. Howard, "Buddy, Can You Paradigm?" *Training & Development Journal*, September 1995, pp. 28-34.

[25] M.R. Barrick and M.K. Mount, "The Big Five Personality Dimensions and Job Performance: A Meta-Analysis," *Personnel Psychology* 44 (1991), pp. 1-26; and M.R. Barrick and M.K. Mount, "Autonomy as a Moderator of the Relationships between the Big Five Personality Dimensions and Job Performance," *Journal of Applied Psychology*, February 1993, pp. 111-18.

[26] M.K. Mount, and Strauss, "Validity of Observer Ratings of the Big Five Personality Factors," *Journal of Applied Psychology*, April 1994, p. 272.

[27] J.F. Salgado, "The Five Factor Model of Personality and Job Performance in the European Community," *Journal of Applied Psychology*, 82, 1997, pp. 30-43.

[28] M.R. Barrick and M.K. Mount, "Autonomy as a Moderator of the Relationships Between the Big Five Personality Dimensions and Job Performance," *Journal of Applied Psychology*, 82, 1996, pp. 111-118.

[29] P. Thoms, "The Relationship Between Self-efficacy for Participating in Self-managed Work Groups and the Big Five Personality Dimensions," *Journal of Applied Psychology*, 82, 1996, pp. 474-482.

[30] B. Barry and G.L. Stewart, "Compositions, Process and Performance in Self-managed Groups: The Role of Personality," *Journal of Applied Psychology*, 82, 1997, pp. 62-78.

[31] J.B. Rotter, "Generalized Expectancies for Internal versus External Control of Reinforcement," *Psychological Monographs* 80, no. 609 (1966).

[32] See P.E. Spector, "Behavior in Organizations as a Function of Employee's Locus of Control," *Psychological Bulletin*, May 1982, pp. 482-97; and G.J. Blau, "Locus of Control as a Potential Moderator of the Turnover Process," *Journal of Occupational Psychology*, Fall 1987, pp. 21-29.

[33] R.T. Keller, "Predicting Absenteeism from Prior Absenteeism, Attitudinal Factors, and Nonattitudinal Factors, *Journal of Applied Psychology*, August 1983, pp. 536-40.

[34] P.E. Spector, "Behavior in Organizations as a Function of Employee's Locus of Control," *Psychological Bulletin*, May 1982, p. 493.

35 R.G. Vleeming, "Machiavellianism: A Preliminary Review," *Psychological Reports*, February 1979, pp. 295-310.

36 R. Christie and F.L. Geis, *Studies in Machiavellianism* (New York: Academic Press, 1970), p. 312; and N.V. Ramanaiah, A. Byravan, and F.R.J. Detwiler, "Revised Neo Personality Inventory Profiles of Machiavellian and Non-Machiavellian People," *Psychological Reports*, October 1994, pp. 937-38.

37 Christie and Geis, *Studies in Machiavellianism* (New York: Academic Press, 1970).

38 Based on J. Brockner, *Self-Esteem at Work* (Lexington, MA: Lexington Books, 1988), chapters 1-4.

39 See M. Snyder, *Public Appearances/Private Realities: The Psychology of Self-Monitoring* (New York: W.H. Freeman, 1987).

40 See M. Snyder, *Public Appearances/Private Realities: The Psychology of Self-Monitoring* (New York: W.H. Freeman, 1987).

41 M. Kilduff and D.V. Day, "Do Chameleons Get Ahead? The Effects of Self-Monitoring on Managerial Careers," *Academy of Management Journal*, August 1994, pp. 1047-60.

42 R.N. Taylor and M.D. Dunnette, "Influence of Dogmatism, Risk-Taking Propensity, and Intelligence on Decision-Making Strategies for a Sample of Industrial Managers," *Journal of Applied Psychology*, August 1974, pp. 420-23.

43 I.L. Janis and L. Mann, *Decision Making: A Psychological Analysis of Conflict, Choice, and Commitment* (New York: Free Press, 1977).

44 N. Kogan and M.A. Wallach, "Group Risk Taking as a Function of Members' Anxiety and Defensiveness," *Journal of Personality*, March 1967, pp. 50-63.

45 M. Friedman and R.H. Rosenman, *Type A Behavior and Your Heart* (New York: Alfred A. Knopf, 1974), p. 84 (emphasis in original).

46 M. Friedman and R.H. Rosenman, *Type A Behavior and Your Heart* (New York: Alfred A. Knopf, 1974), pp. 84-85.

47 M. Friedman and R.H. Rosenman, *Type A Behavior and Your Heart* (New York: Alfred A. Knopf, 1974), p. 86.

48 F. Kluckhohn and F.L. Strodtbeck, *Variations in Value Orientations* (Evanston, IL: Row Peterson, 1961).

49 M. Friedman and R.H. Rosenman, *Type A Behavior and Your Heart*, (New York: Alfred A. Knopf, 1974), p. 86.

50 J.L. Holland, *Making Vocational Choices: A Theory of Vocational Personalities and Work Environments*, 2nd ed. (Englewood Cliffs, NJ: Prentice Hall, 1985).

51 See, for example, A.R. Spokane, "A Review of Research on Person-Environment Congruence in Holland's Theory of Careers," *Journal of Vocational Behavior*, June 1985, pp. 306-43; D. Brown, "The Status of Holland's Theory of Career Choice," *Career Development Journal*, September 1987, pp. 13-23; J.L. Holland and G.D. Gottfredson, "Studies of the Hexagonal Model: An Evaluation (or, The Perils of Stalking the Perfect Hexagon)," *Journal of Vocational Behavior*, April 1992, pp. 158-70; and T.J. Tracey and J. Rounds, "Evaluating Holland's and Gati's Vocational-Interest Models: A Structural Meta-Analysis," *Psychological Bulletin*, March 1993, pp. 229-46.

CHAPTER 4

1 Taken from the web site of Procter & Gamble: www.pg.com.

2 M. Rokeach, *The Nature of Human Values* (New York: Free Press, 1973), p. 5.

3 See, for instance, P.E. Connor and B.W. Becker, "Personal Values and Management: What Do We Know and Why Don't We Know More?" *Journal of Management Inquiry*, March 1994, p. 68.

4 G. Hofstede, *Culture's Consequences: International Differences in Work Related Values* (Beverly Hills, CA: Sage, 1980); G. Hofstede, *Cultures and Organizations: Software of the Mind* (London: McGraw-Hill, 1991); and G. Hofstede, "Cultural Constraints in Management Theories," *Academy of Management Executive*, February 1993, pp. 81-94.

5 Hofstede called this dimension masculinity versus femininity, but we've changed his terms because of their strong sexist connotation.

6 The material presented in this section is based on the work of Michael Adams, *Sex in the Snow* (Toronto: Penguin Books, 1997).

7 G. Chiasson, "I Am Not a Seat Number, I Am a Person," *EnRoute*, March 1998, pp. 5-9.

8 R. McQueen, "Bad Boys Make Good," *The Financial Post*, April 4, 1998, p. 6.

9 R. A. Roe and P. Ester, "Values and Work: Empirical findings and Theoretical Perspective," *Applied Psychology: An International Review*, 47, 1998.

10 R. A. Roe and P. Ester, "Values and Work: Empirical findings and Theoretical Perspective," *Applied Psychology: An International Review*, 47, 1998.

11 R.M. Kanungo and J.K. Bhatnagar, "Achievement Orientation and Occupational Values: A Comparative Study of Young French and English Canadians," *Canadian Journal of Behavioural Science*, 12, (1978), pp. 384-92; M.W. McCarrey, S. Edwards, and R. Jones, "The Influence of Ethnolinguistic Group Membership, Sex and Position Level on Motivational Orientation of Canadian Anglophone and Francophone Employees," *Canadian Journal of Behavioural Science*, 9, (1977) pp. 274-282; M.W. McCarrey, S. Edwards, and R. Jones, "Personal Values of Canadian Anglophone and Francophone Employees and Ethnolinguistic Group Membership, Sex and Position Level," *Journal of Psychology*, 104, (1978) pp. 175-184; S. Richer and P. Laporte, "Culture, Cognition and English-French Competition," in D. Koulack and D. Perlman (eds.), *Readings in Social Psychology: Focus on Canada* (Toronto, ON: Wiley & Sons, 1973); L. Shapiro and D. Perlman, "Value Differences between English and French Canadian High School Students," *Canadian Ethnic Studies*, 8, (1976), pp. 50-55.

12 R.M. Kanungo and J.K. Bhatnagar, "Achievement Orientation and Occupational Values: A Comparative Study of Young French and English Canadians," *Canadian Journal of Behavioural Science*, 12, (1978) pp. 384-92.

13 R.M. Kanungo and J.K. Bhatnagar, "Achievement Orientation and Occupational Values: A Comparative Study of Young French and English Canadians," *Canadian Journal of Behavioural Science*, 12, (1978) pp. 384-92.

14 H.C. Jain, J. Normand, and R. N. Kanungo, "Job motivation of Canadian Anglophone and Francophone hospital employees," *Canadian Journal of Behavioural Science*, April 1979, pp. 160-163; R.N. Kanungo, G.J. Gorn, and H.J. Dauderis, "Motivational Orientation of Canadian Anglo-

phone and Francophone Managers," *Canadian Journal of Behavioural Science*, April 1976, pp. 107-121.

15 M. Major, M. McCarrey, P. Mercier and Y. Gasse, "Meanings of Work and Personal Values of Canadian Anglophone and Francophone Middle Managers," *Canadian Journal of Administrative Sciences*, 11, no. 3 pp. 251-263.

16 G.C. Anders and K. K. Anders, "Incompatible Goals in Unconventional Organizations: The Politics of Alaska Native Corporations," *Organization Studies*, 7, 1986, pp. 213-233; G. Dacks, "Worker-Controlled Native Enterprises," A vehicle for Community Development in Northern Canada?" *The Canadian Journal of Native Studies*, 3, 1983, p. 289-310; L. P. Dana, "Self-employment in the Canadian Sub-Arctic: An Exploratory Study," *Canadian Journal of Administrative Sciences*, 13, 1996, pp. 65-77.

17 L. Redpath, M. O. Nielsen, "A Comparison of Native Culture, Non-native Culture and New Management Ideology," *Canadian Journal of Administrative Sciences*, 14(3), 1997, p. 327.

18 R.B. Anderson, "The Business Economy of the First Nations in Saskatchewan: A Contingency Perspective," *Canadian Journal of Native Studies*, 2, 1995, pp. 309-345.

19 Discussion based on L. Redpath, M. O. Nielsen, "A Comparison of Native Culture, Non-native Culture and New Management Ideology," *Canadian Journal of Administrative Sciences*, 14(3), 1997, pp. 327-339.

20 Discussion based on L. Redpath, M. O. Nielsen, "A Comparison of Native Culture, Non-native Culture and New Management Ideology," *Canadian Journal of Administrative Sciences*, 14(3), 1997, pp. 327-339.

21 J. Paulson, "First Nations Bank Launches First Branch with Sweetgrass Ceremony," *Canadian Press Newswire*, September 23, 1997.

22 "Autowrecker Defies Stereotypes, Blazes Trail," *Windspeaker*, February 1997, p. 28.

23 See, for instance, D.A. Ralston, D.H. Holt, R.H. Terpstra, and Y. Kai-cheng, "The Impact of Culture and Ideology on Managerial Work Values: A Study of the United States, Russia, Japan, and China," in D.P. Moore (ed.), *Academy of Management Best Paper Proceedings* (Vancouver, BC: August 1995), pp. 187-91.

24 The material presented in this section is based on the work of M. Adams, *Sex in the Snow*. (Toronto: Penguin Books, 1997).

25 The material presented in this section is based on the work of M. Adams, *Sex in the Snow*. (Toronto: Penguin Books, 1997).

26 "Hands Across the Border," *Financial Post Magazine*, November 1996, pp. 6-7.

27 N.J. Adler, "Cross-Cultural Management Research: The Ostrich and the Trend," *Academy of Management Review*, April 1983, pp. 226-32; L. Godkin, C.E. Braye, and C.L. Caunch, "U.S.-Based Cross Cultural Management Research in the Eighties," *Journal of Business and Economic Perspectives*, 15, 1989, pp. 37-45; and T.K. Peng, M.F. Peterson, and Y.P. Shyi, "Quantitative Methods in Cross-National Management Research: Trends and Equivalence Issues," *Journal of Organizational Behavior*, vol. 12 (1991), pp. 87-107.

28 L. Godkin, C.E. Braye, and C.L. Caunch, "U.S.-Based Cross Cultural Management Research in the Eighties," *Journal of Business and Economic Perspectives*, 15, 1989, pp. 37-45; and T.K. Peng, M.F. Peterson, and Y.P. Shyi, "Quantitative Methods in Cross-National Management Research: Trends and Equivalence Issues," *Journal of Organizational Behavior*, vol. 12 (1991), pp. 87-107.

29 M. Erez and P.C. Earley, *Culture, Self-identity and Work* Oxford: Oxford University Press. 1993

30 See R.D. Arvey and T.J. Bouchard, Jr., "Genetics, Twins, and Organizational Behavior," in B.M. Staw and L.L. Cummings (eds.), *Research in Organizational Behavior*, vol. 16 (Greenwich, CT: JAI Press, 1994), pp. 66-68 for evidence demonstrating a genetic basis for attitude development and expression.

31 See, for example, S. Rabinowitz and D.T. Hall, "Organizational Research in Job Involvement," *Psychological Bulletin*, March 1977, pp. 265-88; G.J. Blau, "A Multiple Study Investigation of the Dimensionality of Job Involvement," *Journal of Vocational Behavior*, August 1985, pp. 19-36; and N.A. Jans, "Organizational Factors and Work Involvement," *Organizational Behavior and Human Decision Processes*, June 1985, pp. 382-96.

32 Based on G.J. Blau and K.R. Boal, "Conceptualizing How Job Involvement and Organizational Commitment Affect Turnover and Absenteeism," *Academy of Management Review*, April 1987, p. 290.

33 G.J. Blau, "Job Involvement and Organizational Commitment as Interactive Predictors of Tardiness and Absenteeism," *Journal of Management*, Winter 1986, pp. 577-84; and K. Boal and R. Cidambi, "Attitudinal Correlates of Turnover and Absenteeism: A Meta Analysis," paper presented at the meeting of the American Psychological Association, Toronto, Canada, 1984.

34 G. Farris, "A Predictive Study of Turnover," *Personnel Psychology*, Summer 1971, pp. 311-28.

35 G.J. Blau and K.R. Boal, "Conceptualizing How Job Involvement and Organizational Commitment Affect Turnover and Absenteeism," *Academy of Management Review*, April 1987, p. 290.

36 See, for instance, P.W. Hom, R. Katerberg, and C.L. Hulin, "Comparative Examination of Three Approaches to the Prediction of Turnover," *Journal of Applied Psychology*, June 1979, pp. 280-90; H. Angle and J. Perry, "Organizational Commitment: Individual and Organizational Influence," *Work and Occupations*, May 1983, pp. 123-46; and J.L. Pierce and R.B. Dunham, "Organizational Commitment: Pre-Employment Propensity and Initial Work Experiences," *Journal of Management*, Spring 1987, pp. 163-78.

37 Hom, Katerberg and Hulin, "Comparative Examination"; and R.T. Mowday, L.W. Porter, and R.M. Steers, *Employee Organization Linkages: The Psychology of Commitment, Absenteeism, and Turnover* (New York: Academic Press, 1982).

38 L.W. Porter, R.M. Steers, R.T. Mowday, and P.V. Boulian, "Organizational Commitment, Job Satisfaction, and Turnover Among Psychiatric Technicians," *Journal of Applied Psychology*, October 1974, pp. 603-09.

39 L. Festinger, *A Theory of Cognitive Dissonance* (Stanford, CA: Stanford University Press, 1957).

40 M. Crawford, "The New Office Etiquette," *Canadian Business*, May 1993, pp. 22-31.

41 M. Adams, *Sex in the Snow*. (Toronto: Penguin Books, 1997), p. 102.

42 M. Adams, *Sex in the Snow* (Toronto: Penguin Books, 1997), p. 98.

43 "Workplace 2000: Working Toward the Millennium," *Angus Reid Group*, Fall 1997.

44 For problems with the concept of job satisfaction, see R. Hodson, "Workplace Behaviors," *Work and Occupations*, August 1991, pp. 271-90; and H.M. Weiss and R. Cropanzano, "Affective Events Theory: A Theoretical Discussion of the Structure, Causes and Consequences of Affective Experiences at Work," in B.M. Staw and L.L. Cummings (eds), *Research in Organizational Behavior*, vol. 18 (Greenwich, CT: JAI Press, 1996), pp. 1-3.

45 The Wyatt Company's 1989 national WorkAmerica study identified 12 dimensions of satisfaction: work organization, working conditions, communications, job performance and performance review, co-workers, supervision, company management, pay, benefits, career development and training, job content and satisfaction, and company image and change.

46 See J.L. Price and C.W. Mueller, *Handbook of Organizational Measurement* (Marshfield, MA: Pitman Publishing, 1986), pp. 223-27.

47 V. Scarpello and J.P. Campbell, "Job Satisfaction: Are All the Parts There?" *Personnel Psychology*, Autumn 1983, pp. 577-600.

48 E.A. Locke, "The Nature and Causes of Job Satisfaction," in M.D. Dunnette (ed.), *Handbook of Industrial and Organizational Psychology* (Chicago: Rand McNally, 1976), pp. 1319-28.

49 R.A. Katzell, D.E. Thompson, and R.A. Guzzo, "How Job Satisfaction and Job Performance Are and Are Not Linked," in C.J. Cranny, P.C. Smith, and E.F. Stone (eds.), *Job Satisfaction* (New York: Lexington Books, 1992), pp. 195-217.

50 L.A. Witt and L.G. Nye, "Gender and the Relationship Between Perceived Fairness of Pay or Promotion and Job Satisfaction," *Journal of Applied Psychology*, December 1992, pp. 910-17.

51 See, for example, D.C. Feldman and H.J. Arnold, "Personality Types and Career Patterns: Some Empirical Evidence on Holland's Model," *Canadian Journal of Administrative Science*, June 1985, pp. 192-210.

52 For the data on this issue, see Staw, Bell, and Clausen, "The Dispositional Approach to Job Attitudes"; R.D. Arvey, T.J. Bouchard, Jr., N.L. Segal, and L.M. Abraham, "Job Satisfaction: Environmental and Genetic Components," *Journal of Applied Psychology*, April 1989, pp. 187-92; B. Gerhart, "How Important Are Dispositional Factors as Determinants of Job Satisfaction? Implications for Job Design and Other Personnel Programs," *Journal of Applied Psychology*, August 1987, pp. 366-73; R.D. Arvey, G.W. Carter, and D.K. Buerkley, "Job Satisfaction: Dispositional and Situational Influences," in C.L. Cooper and I.T. Robertson (eds.), *International Review of Industrial and Organizational Psychology*, vol. 6 (Chichester, England: John Wiley, 1991), pp. 359-83; T.J. Bouchard, Jr., R.D. Arvey, L.M. Keller, and N.L. Segal, "Genetic Influences on Job Satisfaction: A Reply to Cropanzano and James," *Journal of Applied Psychology*, February 1992, pp. 89-93; T.A. Judge, "Dispositional Perspective in Human Resources Research," in G.R. Ferris and K.M. Rowland (eds.), *Research in Personality and Human Resources Management*, vol. 10 (Greenwich, CT: JAI Press, 1992); R.D. Arvey and T.J. Bouchard, Jr., "Genetics, Twins, and Organizational Behavior," in B.M. Staw and L.L. Cummings (eds.), *Research in Organizational Behavior*; T.A. Judge and S. Watanabe, "Another Look at the Job Satisfaction-Life Satisfaction Relationship," *Journal of Applied Psychology*, December 1993, pp. 939-48; and R.D. Arvey, B.P. McCall, T.J. Bouchard, Jr., and P. Taubman, "Genetic Influences on Job Satisfaction and Work Values," *Personality and Individual Differences*, July 1994, pp. 21-33.

53 G. Bassett, "The Case Against Job Satisfaction," *Business Horizons*, May-June 1994, p. 65.

54 A.H. Brayfield and W.H. Crockett, "Employee Attitudes and Employee Performance," *Psychological Bulletin*, September 1955, pp. 396-428; F. Herzberg, B. Mausner, R.O. Peterson, and D.F. Capwell, Job Attitudes: *Review of Research and Opinion* (Pittsburgh: Psychological Service of Pittsburgh, 1957); V.H. Vroom, *Work and Motivation* (New York: John Wiley, 1964); G.P. Fournet, M.K. Distefano, Jr., and M.W. Pryer, "Job Satisfaction: Issues and Problems," *Personnel Psychology*, Summer 1966, pp. 165-83.

55 C.N. Greene, "The Satisfaction-Performance Controversy," *Business Horizons*, February 1972, pp. 31-41; E.E. Lawler III, *Motivation in Organizations* (Monterey, CA: Brooks/Cole, 1973); and Petty, McGee, and Cavender, "A Meta-Analysis of the Relationship Between Individual Job Satisfaction and Individual Performance."

56 C. Ostroff, "The Relationship Between Satisfaction, Attitudes, and Performance: An Organizational Level Analysis," *Journal of Applied Psychology*, December 1992, pp. 963-74.

57 L. Grant, "Happy Workers, High Returns," *Fortune*, January 12, 1998, p. 81.

58 L. Grant, "Happy Workers, High Returns," *Fortune*, January 12, 1998, p. 81.

59 Locke, "The Nature and Causes of Job Satisfaction," p. 1331; S.L. McShane, "Job Satisfaction and Absenteeism: A Meta-Analytic Re-Examination," *Canadian Journal of Administrative Science*, June 1984, pp. 61-77; R.D. Hackett and R.M. Guion, "A Reevaluation of the Absenteeism-Job Satisfaction Relationship," *Organizational Behavior and Human Decision Processes*, June 1985, pp. 340-81; K.D. Scott and G.S. Taylor, "An Examination of Conflicting Findings on the Relationship Between Job Satisfaction and Absenteeism: A Meta-Analysis," *Academy of Management Journal*, September 1985, pp. 599-612; R.D. Hackett, "Work Attitudes and Employee Absenteeism: A Synthesis of the Literature," paper presented at 1988 National Academy of Management Conference, Anaheim, CA, August 1988; and R.P. Steel and J.R. Rentsch, "Influence of Cumulation Strategies on the Long-Range Prediction of Absenteeism," *Academy of Management Journal*, December 1995, pp. 1616-34.

60 F.J. Smith, "Work Attitudes as Predictors of Attendance on a Specific Day," *Journal of Applied Psychology*, February 1977, pp. 16-19.

61 Brayfield and Crockett, "Employee Attitudes"; Vroom, *Work and Motivation*; J. Price, *The Study of Turnover* (Ames: Iowa State University Press, 1977); and W.H. Mobley, R.W. Griffeth, H.H. Hand, and B. M. Meglino, "Review and Conceptual Analysis of the Employee Turnover Process," *Psychological Bulletin*, May 1979, pp. 493-522.

62 See, for example, C.L. Hulin, M. Roznowski, and D. Hachiya, "Alternative Opportunities and Withdrawal Decisions: Empirical and Theoretical Discrepancies and an Integration," *Psychological Bulletin*, July 1985, pp. 233-50; and J.M. Carsten and P.E. Spector, "Unemployment, Job Satisfaction, and Employee Turnover: A Meta-Analytic Test of the Muchinsky Model," *Journal of Applied Psychology*, August 1987, pp. 374-81.

[63] D.G. Spencer and R.M. Steers, "Performance as a Moderator of the Job Satisfaction-Turnover Relationship," *Journal of Applied Psychology*, August 1981, pp. 511-14.

[64] T.A. Judge, "Does Affective Disposition Moderate the Relationship Between Job Satisfaction and Voluntary Turnover?" *Journal of Applied Psychology*, June 1993, pp. 395-401.

[65] S.M. Puffer, "Prosocial Behavior, Noncompliant Behavior, and Work Performance Among Commission Salespeople," *Journal of Applied Psychology*, November 1987, pp. 615-21; J. Hogan and R. Hogan, "How to Measure Employee Reliability," *Journal of Applied Psychology*, May 1989, pp. 273-79; and C.D. Fisher and E.A. Locke, "The New Look in Job Satisfaction Research and Theory," in C.J. Cranny, P.C. Smith, and E.F. Stone (eds.), *Job Satisfaction*, pp. 165-94.

[66] See D. Farrell, "Exit, Voice, Loyalty, and Neglect as Responses to Job Dissatisfaction: A Multidimensional Scaling Study," *Academy of Management Journal*, December 1983, pp. 596-606; C.E. Rusbult, D. Farrell, G. Rogers, and A.G. Mainous III, "Impact of Exchange Variables on Exit, Voice, Loyalty, and Neglect: An Integrative Model of Responses to Declining Job Satisfaction," *Academy of Management Journal*, September 1988, pp. 599-627; M.J. Withey and W.H. Cooper, "Predicting Exit, Voice, Loyalty, and Neglect," *Administrative Science Quarterly*, December 1989, pp. 521-39; and D. Farrell, C. Rusbult, Y-H Lin, and P. Bernthall, "Impact of Job Satisfaction, Investment Size, and Quality of Alternatives on Exit, Voice, Loyalty, and Neglect Responses to Job Dissatisfaction: A Cross-Legged Panel Study," in L.R. Jauch and J.L. Wall (eds.), *Proceedings of the 50th Annual Academy of Management Conference*, San Francisco, 1990, pp. 211-15.

[67] R.B. Freeman, "Job Satisfaction as an Economic Variable," *American Economic Review*, January 1978, pp. 135-41.

CHAPTER 5

[1] S. Desker-Shaw, "Revving Up Asia's Workers," *Asian Business*, February 1996, pp. 41-44.

[2] R. Katerberg and G.J. Blau, "An Examination of Level and Direction of Effort and Job Performance," *Academy of Management Journal*, June 1983, pp. 249-57.

[3] D. McGregor, *The Human Side of Enterprise* (New York: McGraw-Hill, 1960). For an updated analysis of Theory X and Theory Y constructs, see R.J. Summers and S.F. Cronshaw, "A Study of McGregor's Theory X, Theory Y and the Influence of Theory X, Theory Y Assumptions on Causal Attributions for Instances of Worker Poor Performance," in S.L. McShane (ed.), *Organizational Behavior*, ASAC 1988 Conference Proceedings, vol. 9, Part 5. Halifax, Nova Scotia, 1988, pp. 115-23.

[4] A. Maslow, *Motivation and Personality* (New York: Harper & Row, 1954).

[5] See, for example, E.E. Lawler III and J.L. Suttle, "A Causal Correlation Test of the Need Hierarchy Concept," *Organizational Behavior and Human Performance*, April 1972, pp. 265-87; D.T. Hall and K.E. Nougaim, "An Examination of Maslow's Need Hierarchy in an Organizational Setting," *Organizational Behavior and Human Performance*, February 1968, pp. 12-35; J. Rauschenberger, N. Schmitt, and J.E. Hunter, "A Test of the Need Hierarchy Concept by a Markov Model of Change in Need Strength," *Administrative Science Quarterly*, December 1980, pp. 654-70; A.K.

Korman, J.H. Greenhaus, and I.J. Badin, "Personnel Attitudes and Motivation," in M.R. Rosenzweig and L.W. Porter (eds.), *Annual Review of Psychology* (Palo Alto, CA: Annual Reviews, 1977), p. 178; and M.A. Wahba and L.G. Bridwell, "Maslow Reconsidered: A Review of Research on the Need Hierarchy Theory," *Organizational Behavior and Human Performance*, April 1976, pp. 212-40.

[6] F. Herzberg, B. Mausner, and B. Snyderman, *The Motivation to Work* (New York: John Wiley, 1959).

[7] R.J. House and L.A. Wigdor, "Herzberg's Dual-Factor Theory of Job Satisfaction and Motivations: A Review of the Evidence and Criticism," *Personnel Psychology*, Winter 1967, pp. 369-89; D.P. Schwab and L.L. Cummings, "Theories of Performance and Satisfaction: A Review," *Industrial Relations*, October 1970, pp. 403-30; and R.J. Caston and R. Braito, "A Specification Issue in Job Satisfaction Research," *Sociological Perspectives*, April 1985, pp. 175-97.

[8] D. Guest, "What's New in Motivation," *Personnel Management*, May 1984, pp. 20-23.

[9] C.P. Alderfer, "An Empirical Test of a New Theory of Human Needs," *Organizational Behavior and Human Performance*, May 1969, pp. 142-75.

[10] M. Haire, E.E. Ghiselli, and L.W. Porter, "Cultural Patterns in the Role of the Manager," *Industrial Relations*, February 1963, pp. 95-117.

[11] C.P. Schneider and C.P. Alderfer, "Three Studies of Measures of Need Satisfaction in Organizations," *Administrative Science Quarterly*, December 1973, pp. 489-505.

[12] J.P. Wanous and A. Zwany, "A Cross-Sectional Test of Need Hierarchy Theory," *Organizational Behavior and Human Performance*, May 1977, pp. 78-97.

[13] D.C. McClelland, *The Achieving Society* (New York: Van Nostrand Reinhold, 1961); J.W. Atkinson and J.O. Raynor, *Motivation and Achievement* (Washington, D.C.: Winston, 1974); D.C. McClelland, *Power: The Inner Experience* (New York: Irvington, 1975); and M.J. Stahl, *Managerial and Technical Motivation: Assessing Needs for Achievement, Power, and Affiliation* (New York: Praeger, 1986).

[14] D.C. McClelland, *The Achieving Society* (New York: Van Nostrand Reinhold, 1961).

[15] See, for example, A. Mehrabian, "Measures of Achieving Tendency," *Educational and Psychological Measurement*, Summer 1969, pp. 445-51; H.J.M. Hermans, "A Questionnaire Measure of Achievement Motivation," *Journal of Applied Psychology*, August 1970, pp. 353-63; and J.M. Smith, "A Quick Measure of Achievement Motivation," *British Journal of Social and Clinical Psychology*, June 1973, pp. 137-43.

[16] See W.D. Spangler, "Validity of Questionnaire and TAT Measures of Need for Achievement: Two Meta-Analyses," *Psychological Bulletin*, July 1992, pp. 140-54.

[17] D.C. McClelland and D.G. Winter, *Motivating Economic Achievement* (New York: Free Press, 1969).

[18] McClelland, *Power*; McClelland and D.H. Burnham, "Power Is the Great Motivator," *Harvard Business Review*, March-April 1976, pp. 100-10; and R.E. Boyatzis, "The Need for Close Relationships and the Manager's Job," in D.A. Kolb, I.M. Rubin, and J.M. McIntyre, *Organizational Psychology: Readings on Human Behavior in Organizations*, 4th ed. (Englewood Cliffs, NJ: Prentice Hall, 1984), pp. 81-86.

19 McClelland, *Power*; McClelland and D.H. Burnham, "Power Is the Great Motivator," *Harvard Business Review*, March-April 1976, pp. 100-10; and R.E. Boyatzis, "The Need for Close Relationships and the Manager's Job," in D.A. Kolb, I.M. Rubin, and J.M. McIntyre, *Organizational Psychology: Readings on Human Behavior in Organizations*, 4th ed. (Englewood Cliffs, NJ: Prentice Hall, 1984), pp. 81-86.

20 J.B. Miner, *Studies in Management Education* (New York: Springer, 1965).

21 D. Kipnis, "The Powerholder," in J.T. Tedeschi (ed.), *Perspectives in Social Power* (Chicago: Aldine, 1974), pp. 82-123.

22 D. McClelland, "Toward a Theory of Motive Acquisition," *American Psychologist*, May 1965, pp. 321-33; and D. Miron and D.C. McClelland, "The Impact of Achievement Motivation Training on Small Businesses," *California Management Review*, Summer 1979, pp. 13-28.

23 E.A. Locke, "Toward a Theory of Task Motivation and Incentives," *Organizational Behavior and Human Performance*, May 1968, pp. 157-89.

24 P.C. Earley, P. Wojnaroski, and W. Prest, "Task Planning and Energy Expended: Exploration of How Goals Influence Performance," *Journal of Applied Psychology*, February 1987, pp. 107-14.

25 G.P. Latham and G.A. Yukl, "A Review of Research on the Application of Goal Setting in Organizations," *Academy of Management Journal*, December 1975, pp. 824-45; E.A. Locke, K.N. Shaw, L.M. Saari, and G.P. Latham, "Goal Setting and Task Performance," *Psychological Bulletin*, January 1981, pp. 125-52; A.J. Mento, R.P. Steel, and R.J. Karren, "A Meta-Analytic Study of the Effects of Goal Setting on Task Performance: 1966-1984," *Organizational Behavior and Human Decision Processes*, February 1987, pp. 52-83; M.E. Tubbs "Goal Setting: A Meta-Analytic Examination of the Empirical Evidence," *Journal of Applied Psychology*, August 1986, pp. 474-83; P.C. Earley, G.B. Northcraft, C. Lee, and T.R. Lituchy, "Impact of Process and Outcome Feedback on the Relation of Goal Setting to Task Performance," *Academy of Management Journal*, March 1990, pp. 87-105; and E.A. Locke and G.P. Latham, *A Theory of Goal Setting and Task Performance* (Englewood Cliffs, NJ: Prentice Hall, 1990).

26 J.M. Ivancevich and J.T. McMahon, "The Effects of Goal Setting, External Feedback, and Self-Generated Feedback on Outcome Variables: A Field Experiment," *Academy of Management Journal*, June 1982, pp. 359-72.

27 See, for example, G.P. Latham, M. Erez, and E.A. Locke, "Resolving Scientific Disputes by the Joint Design of Crucial Experiments by the Antagonists: Application to the Erez-Latham Dispute Regarding Participation in Goal Setting," *Journal of Applied Psychology*, November 1988, pp. 753-72.

28 M. Erez, P.C. Earley, and C.L. Hulin, "The Impact of Participation on Goal Acceptance and Performance: A Two-Step Model," *Academy of Management Journal*, March 1985, pp. 50-66.

29 J.R. Hollenbeck, C.R. Williams, and H.J. Klein, "An Empirical Examination of the Antecedents of Commitment to Difficult Goals," *Journal of Applied Psychology*, February 1989, pp. 18-23. See also J.C. Wofford, V.L. Goodwin, and S. Premack, "Meta-Analysis of the Antecedents of Personal Goal Level and of the Antecedents and Consequences of Goal Commitment," *Journal of Management*, September 1992, pp. 595-615; and M.E. Tubbs, "Commitment as a Moderator of the Goal-Performance Relation: A Case for Clearer Construct Definition," *Journal of Applied Psychology*, February 1993, pp. 86-97.

30 A. Bandura, "Self-Efficacy: Toward a Unifying Theory of Behavioral Change," *Psychological Review*, May 1977, pp. 191-215; and M.E. Gist, "Self-Efficacy: Implications for Organizational Behavior and Human Resource Management," *Academy of Management Review*, July 1987, pp. 472-85.

31 E.A. Locke, E. Frederick, C. Lee, and P. Bobko, "Effect of Self-Efficacy, Goals, and Task Strategies on Task Performance," *Journal of Applied Psychology*, May 1984, pp. 241-51; and M.E. Gist and T.R. Mitchell, "Self-Efficacy: A Theoretical Analysis of Its Determinants and Malleability," *Academy of Management Review*, April 1992, pp. 183-211.

32 A. Bandura and D. Cervone, "Differential Engagement in Self-Reactive Influences in Cognitively Based Motivation," *Organizational Behavior and Human Decision Processes*, August 1986, pp. 92-113.

33 See J.C. Anderson and C.A. O'Reilly, "Effects of an Organizational Control System on Managerial Satisfaction and Performance," *Human Relations*, June 1981, pp. 491-501; and J.P. Meyer, B. Schacht-Cole, and I.R. Gellatly, "An Examination of the Cognitive Mechanisms by Which Assigned Goals Affect Task Performance and Reactions to Performance," *Journal of Applied Social Psychology*, 18, no. 5, (1988), pp. 390-408.

34 R.M. Steers and L.W. Porter, *Motivation and Work Behavior*, 2nd ed. (New York: McGraw-Hill, 1979), p. 13.

35 E.A. Locke, "Latham vs. Komaki: A Tale of Two Paradigms," *Journal of Applied Psychology*, February 1980, pp. 16-23.

36 V.H. Vroom, *Work and Motivation* (New York: John Wiley, 1964).

37 See, for example, H.G. Heneman III and D.P. Schwab, "Evaluation of Research on Expectancy Theory Prediction of Employee Performance," *Psychological Bulletin*, July 1972, pp. 1-9; T.R. Mitchell, "Expectancy Models of Job Satisfaction, Occupational Preference and Effort: A Theoretical, Methodological and Empirical Appraisal," *Psychological Bulletin*, November 1974, pp. 1053-77; and L. Reinharth and M.A. Wahba, "Expectancy Theory as a Predictor of Work Motivation, Effort Expenditure, and Job Performance," *Academy of Management Journal*, September 1975, pp. 502-37.

38 See, for example, L.W. Porter and E.E. Lawler III, *Managerial Attitudes and Performance* (Homewood, IL: Richard D. Irwin, 1968); D.F. Parker and L. Dyer, "Expectancy Theory as a Within-Person Behavioral Choice Model: An Empirical Test of Some Conceptual and Methodological Refinements," *Organizational Behavior and Human Performance*, October 1976, pp. 97-117; H.J. Arnold, "A Test of the Multiplicative Hypothesis of Expectancy-Valence Theories of Work Motivation," *Academy of Management Journal*, April 1981, pp. 128-41; and W. Van Eerde and H. Thierry, "Vroom's Expectancy Models and Work-Related Criteria: A Meta-Analysis," *Journal of Applied Psychology*, October 1996, pp. 575-86.

39 Vroom refers to these three variables as expectancy, instrumentality, and valence, respectively.

40 "Workplace 2000: Working Toward the Millennium," *Angus Reid Group*, Fall 1997, p. 14.

41 "Workplace 2000: Working Toward the Millennium," *Angus Reid Group*, Fall 1997, p. 14.

42 P.M. Muchinsky, "A Comparison of Within- and Across-Subjects Analyses of the Expectancy-Valence Model for Predicting Effort," *Academy of Management Journal*, March 1977, pp. 154-58.

43 R.J. House, H.J. Shapiro, and M.A. Wahba, "Expectancy Theory as a Predictor of Work Behavior and Attitudes: A Re-evaluation of Empirical Evidence," *Decision Sciences*, January 1974, pp. 481-506.

44 "Workplace 2000: Working Toward the Millennium," *Angus Reid Group*, Fall 1997, p. 14.

45 J.S. Adams, "Inequity in Social Exchanges," in L. Berkowitz (ed.), *Advances in Experimental Social Psychology* (New York: Academic Press, 1965), pp. 267-300.

46 P.S. Goodman, "An Examination of Referents Used in the Evaluation of Pay," *Organizational Behavior and Human Performance*, October 1974, pp. 170-95; S. Ronen, "Equity Perception in Multiple Comparisons: A Field Study," *Human Relations*, April 1986, pp. 333-46; R.W. Scholl, E.A. Cooper, and J.F. McKenna, "Referent Selection in Determining Equity Perception: Differential Effects on Behavioral and Attitudinal Outcomes," *Personnel Psychology*, Spring 1987, pp. 113-27; and T.P. Summers and A.S. DeNisi, "In Search of Adams' Other: Reexamination of Referents Used in the Evaluation of Pay," *Human Relations*, June 1990, pp. 497-511.

47 C.T. Kulik and M.L. Ambrose, "Personal and Situational Determinants of Referent Choice," *Academy of Management Review*, April 1992, pp. 212-37.

48 K. Torrance, "Robbing Peter to Pay Paula: Rising Female Wages Come Out of the Pockets of Men," *British Columbia Report*, April 13, 1998, p. 39.

49 See, for example, E. Walster, G.W. Walster, and W.G. Scott, Equity: *Theory and Research* (Boston: Allyn & Bacon, 1978); and J. Greenberg, "Cognitive Reevaluation of Outcomes in Response to Underpayment Inequity," *Academy of Management Journal*, March 1989, pp. 174-84.

50 P.S. Goodman and A. Friedman, "An Examination of Adams' Theory of Inequity," *Administrative Science Quarterly*, September 1971, pp. 271-88; R.P. Vecchio, "An Individual-Differences Interpretation of the Conflicting Predictions Generated by Equity Theory and Expectancy Theory," *Journal of Applied Psychology*, August 1981, pp. 470-81; J. Greenberg, "Approaching Equity and Avoiding Inequity in Groups and Organizations," in J. Greenberg and R.L. Cohen (eds.), *Equity and Justice in Social Behavior* (New York: Academic Press, 1982), pp. 389-435; R.T. Mowday, "Equity Theory Predictions of Behavior in Organizations," in R.M. Steers and L.W. Porter (eds.), *Motivation and Work Behavior*, 4th ed. (New York: McGraw-Hill, 1987), pp. 89-110; E.W. Miles, J.D. Hatfield, and R.C. Huseman, "The Equity Sensitive Construct: Potential Implications for Worker Performance," *Journal of Management*, December 1989, pp. 581-88; and R.T. Mowday, "Equity Theory Predictions of Behavior in Organizations," in R. Steers and L.W. Porter (eds.), *Motivation and Work Behavior*, 5th ed. (New York: McGraw-Hill, 1991), pp. 111-31.

51 J. Greenberg and S. Ornstein, "High Status Job Title as Compensation for Underpayment: A Test of Equity Theory," *Journal of Applied Psychology*, May 1983, pp. 285-97; and J. Greenberg, "Equity and Workplace Status: A Field Experiment," *Journal of Applied Psychology*, November 1988, pp. 606-13.

52 P.S. Goodman, "Social Comparison Process in Organizations," in B.M. Staw and G.R. Salancik (eds.), *New Directions in Organizational Behavior* (Chicago: St. Clair, 1977), pp. 97-132; and J. Greenberg, "A Taxonomy of Organizational Justice Theories," *Academy of Management Review*, January 1987, pp. 9-22.

53 See, for instance, B.H. Sheppard, R.J. Lewicki, and J.W. Minton, *Organizational Justice: The Search for Fairness in the Workplace* (New York: Lexington Books, 1992); and J. Greenberg, *The Quest for Justice on the Job* (Thousand Oaks, CA: Sage, 1996).

54 See, for example, R.C. Dailey and D.J. Kirk, "Distributive and Procedural Justice as Antecedents of Job Dissatisfaction and Intent to Turnover," *Human Relations*, March 1992, pp. 305-16; D.B. McFarlin and P.D. Sweeney, "Distributive and Procedural Justice as Predictors of Satisfaction With Personal and Organizational Outcomes," *Academy of Management Journal*, August 1992, pp. 626-37; and M.A. Korsgaard, D.M. Schweiger, and H.J. Sapienza, "Building Commitment, Attachment, and Trust in Strategic Decision-Making Teams: The Role of Procedural Justice," *Academy of Management Journal*, February 1995, pp. 60-84.

55 The remainder of this paragraph is based on W. Chan Kim and R. Mauborgne, "Fair Process: Managing in the Knowledge Economy," *Harvard Business Review*, July-August 1997, pp. 65-76.

56 A.S. Blinder, "Introduction" in *Paying for Productivity: A Look at the Evidence*, edited by Alan S. Blinder, (Washington, D.C.: Brookings Institution, 1990), p. 30.

57 This section is based on information from B. Nelson, L. Good and T. Hill, "Motivate Employees According to Temperament," *HR Magazine*, March 1997, pp. 51-56.

58 L.H. Peters, E.J. O'Connor, and C.J. Rudolf, "The Behavioral and Affective Consequences of Performance-Relevant Situational Variables," *Organizational Behavior and Human Performance*, February 1980, pp. 79-96; M. Blumberg and C.D. Pringle, "The Missing Opportunity in Organizational Research: Some Implications for a Theory of Work Performance," *Academy of Management Review*, October 1982, pp. 560-69; D.A. Waldman and W.D. Spangler, "Putting Together the Pieces: A Closer Look at the Determinants of Job Performance," *Human Performance*, 2, (1989), pp. 29-59; and J. Hall, "Americans Know How to Be Productive If Managers Will Let Them," *Organizational Dynamics*, Winter 1994, pp. 33-46.

59 For other examples of models that seek to integrate motivation theories, see H.J. Klein, "An Integrated Control Theory Model of Work Motivation," *Academy of Management Review*, April 1989, pp. 150-72; and E.A. Locke, "The Motivation Sequence, the Motivation Hub, and the Motivation Core," *Organizational Behavior and Human Decision Processes*, December 1991, pp. 288-99.

60 R. de Charms, *Personal Causation: The Internal Affective Determinants of Behavior* (New York: Academic Press, 1968).

61 E.L. Deci, *Intrinsic Motivation* (New York: Plenum, 1975); R.D. Pritchard, K.M. Campbell, and D.J. Campbell, "Effects of Extrinsic Financial Rewards on Intrinsic Motivation," *Journal of Applied Psychology*, February 1977, pp. 9-15; E.L. Deci, G. Betly, J. Kahle, L. Abrams, and J. Porac, "When Trying to Win: Competition and Intrinsic Motivation," *Personality and Social Psychology Bulletin*, March 1981, pp. 79-83; and P.C. Jordan, "Effects of an Extrinsic

Reward on Intrinsic Motivation: A Field Experiment," *Academy of Management Journal*, June 1986, pp. 405-12. See also J.M. Schrof, "Tarnished Trophies," *U.S. News & World Report*, October 25, 1993, pp. 52-59.

62 A. Kohn, *Punished by Rewards* (Boston: Houghton Mifflin Company, 1993).

63 J.B. Miner, *Theories of Organizational Behavior* (Hinsdale, IL: Dryden Press, 1980), p. 157.

64 A. Kohn, *Punished by Rewards* (Boston: Houghton Mifflin Company, 1993).

65 B. Nelson, "Dump the Cash, Load on the Praise," *Personnel Journal*, 75 (July 1996), pp. 65-66.

66 J. Pfeffer, *The Human Equation: Building Profits by Putting People First* (Boston, Massachusetts: Harvard Business School Press, 1998).

67 J. Pfeffer, *The Human Equation: Building Profits by Putting People First* (Boston, Massachusetts: Harvard Business School Press, 1998).

68 B.J. Calder and B.M. Staw, "Self-Perception of Intrinsic and Extrinsic Motivation," *Journal of Personality and Social Psychology*, April 1975, pp. 599-605; Jeffrey Pfeffer, *The Human Equation: Building Profits by Putting People First* (Boston, Massachusetts: Harvard Business School Press, 1998), p. 217.

69 B.M. Staw, "Motivation in Organizations: Toward Synthesis and Redirection," in B.M. Staw and G.R. Salancik (eds.), *New Directions in Organizational Behavior* (Chicago: St. Clair, 1977), p. 76.

70 N.J. Adler, *International Dimensions of Organizational Behavior*, 2nd ed. (Boston: PWS-Kent Publishing, 1991), p. 152.

71 A. Kohn, *Punished by Rewards* (Boston: Houghton Mifflin Company, 1993).

72 W. G. Ouchi, Theory Z, New York: Avon Books. 1982; "Bosses' Pay," *The Economist*, February 1, 1992, pp. 19-22; W. Edwards Deming, *Out of the Crisis,* (Cambridge: MIT Center for Advanced Engineering Study, 1986).

73 J. Pfeffer, *The Human Equation: Building Profits by Putting People First* (Boston, Massachusetts: Harvard Business School Press. 1998).

74 T. L. Besser, "Reward and Organizational Goal Achievement: A Case Study of Toyota Motor Manufacturing in Kentucky," *Journal of Management Studies* 32, 1995, p. 387.

75 G. Hofstede, "Motivation, Leadership, and Organization: Do American Theories Apply Abroad?," *Organizational Dynamics*, Summer 1980, p. 55.

76 G. Hofstede, "Motivation, Leadership, and Organization: Do American Theories Apply Abroad?," *Organizational Dynamics*, Summer 1980, p. 55.

77 I. Harpaz, "The Importance of Work Goals: An International Perspective," *Journal of International Business Studies*, First Quarter 1990, pp. 75-93.

78 G.E. Popp, H.J. Davis, and T.T. Herbert, "An International Study of Intrinsic Motivation Composition," *Management International Review*, January 1986, pp. 28-35.

79 This section is based on F.J. Landy and W.S. Becker, "Motivation Theory Reconsidered," in L.L. Cummings and B.M. Staw (eds.), *Research in Organizational Behavior*, vol. 9 (Greenwich, CT: JAI Press, 1987), pp. 24-35.

80 B. Ward, "Smiley Face Wins Tips for Waitresses," *Vancouver Sun*, April 25, 1998, p. B11.

CHAPTER 6

1 P. Simao, "Eureka!" *Canadian Business*, June 1996, pp. 66-69.

2 P.F. Drucker, *The Practice of Management* (New York: Harper & Row, 1954).

3 See, for instance, S.J. Carroll and H.L. Tosi, *Management by Objectives: Applications and Research* (New York, Macmillan, 1973); and R. Rodgers and J.E. Hunter, "Impact of Management by Objectives on Organizational Productivity," *Journal of Applied Psychology*, April 1991, pp. 322-36.

4 K.R. Thompson, W.A. Hochwarter, and N.J. Mathys, "Stretch Targets: What Makes Them Effective?", *Academy of Management Executive*, 11, no. 3, (1997), pp. 48-60; J. Hollenbeck and H. Klein, "Goal Commitment and the Goal-Setting Process: Problems, Prospects, and Proposals for Future Research," *Journal of Applied Psychology*, 72, no. 2 (1987), 212-220; G. Latham and E. Locke, "Self-Regulation Through Goal Setting," *Organizational Behavior and Human Decision Processes*, 50, no. 2 (1991), 212-247; E. Locke, K. Shaw, L. Saari and G. Latham, "Goal Setting and Task Performance: 1969-1980," *Psychological Bulletin*, 85, 1981, 125-152.

5 See, for instance, R.C. Ford, F.S. MacLaughlin, and J. Nixdorf, "Ten Questions About MBO," *California Management Review*, Winter 1980, p. 89; T.J. Collamore, "Making MBO Work in the Public Sector," *Bureaucrat*, Fall 1989, pp. 37-40; G. Dabbs, "Nonprofit Businesses in the 1990s: Models for Success," *Business Horizons*, September-October 1991, pp. 68-71; R. Rodgers and J.E. Hunter, "A Foundation of Good Management Practice in Government: Management by Objectives," *Public Administration Review*, January-February 1992, pp. 27-39; and T.H. Poister and G. Streib, "MBO in Municipal Government: Variations on a Traditional Management Tool," *Public Administration Review*, January/February 1995, pp. 48-56.

6 See, for instance, C.H. Ford, "MBO: An Idea Whose Time Has Gone?" *Business Horizons*, December 1979, p. 49; R. Rodgers and J.E. Hunter, "Impact of Management by Objectives on Organizational Productivity," *Journal of Applied Psychology*, April 1991, pp. 322-36; and R. Rodgers, J.E. Hunter, and D.L. Rogers, "Influence of Top Management Commitment on Management Program Success," *Journal of Applied Psychology*, February 1993, pp. 151-55.

7 "Look, Movie Tickets: With Budgets Tight, Alternatives to Pay Increases Emerge," *Wall Street Journal*, September 27, 1994, p. A1.

8 M. McNellis, "Celebrating Dalton and Other Luminaries," *The Financial Post*, February 28, 1998, p. 2.

9 W. Thorsell, "Globe Awards Reward the Seen and Unseen," *The Globe and Mail*, February 28, 1998, p. A2.

10 S. Navarette, "Multiple Forms of Employee Recognition," *At Work*, July/August 1993, pp. 9-10.

11 Cited in *Asian Business*, December 1994, p. 3.

12 "Clear Visions: The Top 40 under 40," *Financial Post Magazine*, April 1997, pp. 16-30.

13 S. Ross, "A Little Praise Goes a Long Way, Survey Tell Managers," *Vancouver Sun*, February 4, 1995, p. C8.

14 Cited in S. Caudron, "The Top 20 Ways to Motivate Employees," *Industry Week*, April 3, 1995, pp. 15-16. See also B. Nelson, "Try Praise," *INC.*, September 1996, p. 115.

15 "Praise Beats Raise as Best Motivator, Survey Shows," *Vancouver Sun*, September 10, 1994.

16 Based on S.E. Gross and J.P. Bacher, "The New Variable Pay Programs: How Some Succeed, Why Some Don't," *Compensation & Benefits Review*, January-February 1993, p. 51; and J.R. Schuster and P.K. Zingheim, "The New Variable Pay: Key Design Issues," *Compensation & Benefits Review*, March-April 1993, p. 28.

17 "Hope for Higher Pay: The Squeeze on Incomes is Gradually Easing Up," *Maclean's*, 109, no. 48 (November 25, 1996), pp. 100-101.

18 P. Booth, Challenge and Change: Embracing the Team Concept. Report 123-94, Conference Board of Canada, 1994, p. 18.

19 G. Steinmetz, "German Banks Note the Value of Bonuses," *Wall Street Journal*, May 9, 1995, p. A17.

20 J.A. Byrne, "That Eye-Popping Executive Pay," *Business Week*, April 25, 1994, p. 58.

21 J. O'C. Hamilton, "Levi's Pot O' Gold," *Business Week*, June 24, 1996, p. 44.

22 "Bonus Pay in Canada," *Manpower Argus*, September 1996, p. 5.

23 J. Pfeffer and N. Langton, "The Effects of Wage Dispersion on Satisfaction, Productivity, and Working Collaboratively: Evidence from College and University Faculty," *Administrative Science Quarterly*, 38, no. 3, (1983), pp. 382-407.

24 See, for instance, S.C. Hanlon, D.G. Meyer, and R.R. Taylor, "Consequences of Gainsharing," *Group & Organization Management*, March 1994, pp. 87-111; J.G. Belcher, Jr., "Gainsharing and Variable Pay: The State of the Art," *Compensation & Benefits Review*, May-June 1994, pp. 50-60; and T.M. Welbourne and L.R. Gomez Mejia, "Gainsharing: A Critical Review and a Future Research Agenda," *Journal of Management*, 21, no. 3, (1995), pp. 559-609.

25 P. Booth, "Challenge and Change: Embracing the Team Concept." Report 123-94, Conference Board of Canada, 1994, p. 19.

26 "Risk and Reward: More Canadian Companies Are Experimenting with Variable Pay," *Maclean's*, January 8, 1996, pp. 26-27.

27 D. Beck, "Implementing a Gainsharing Plan: What Companies Need to Know," *Compensation & Benefits Review*, January-February 1992, p. 23.

28 J. Fierman, "The Perilous New World of Fair Pay," *Fortune*, June 13, 1994, p. 63.

29 "Hope for Higher Pay: The Squeeze on Incomes Is Gradually Easing Up," *Maclean's*, 109, no. 48 (November 25, 1996), pp. 100-101.

30 D. Rumball, "Tycoon (Excerpt from Peter Munk: the Making of a Modern Tycoon,") *Financial Post Magazine*, October 1996, pp. 14-27.

31 See K.M. Young (ed.), *The Expanding Role of ESOPs in Public Companies* (New York: Quorum, 1990); J.L. Pierce and C.A. Furo, "Employee Ownership: Implications for Management," *Organizational Dynamics*, Winter 1990, pp. 32-43; J. Blasi and D.L. Druse, *The New Owners: The Mass Emergence of Employee Ownership in Public Companies and What It Means to American Business* (Champaign, IL: Harper Business, 1991); F.T. Adams and G.B. Hansen, *Putting Democracy to Work: A Practical Guide for Starting and Managing Worker-Owned Businesses* (San Francisco: Berrett-Koehler, 1993); and A.A. Buchko, "The Effects of Employee Ownership on Employee Attitudes: An Integrated Causal Model and Path Analysis," *Journal of Management Studies*, July 1993, pp. 633-56.

32 J.L. Pierce and C.A. Furo, "Employee Ownership" Employee Ownership: Implications for Management," *Organizational Dynamics*, Winter 1990, pp. 32-43"; C.H. Farnsworth, "One Employee Buyout That Actually Worked," *New York Times*, February 5, 1995, p. F4; A. Bernstein, "Should Avis Try Harder: For Its Employees?" *Business Week*, August 12, 1996, pp. 68-69.

33 "Tracking Success: Is Competency-based Human Resources Management an Effective Strategy or Simply the Flavor of the Month?" *Benefits Canada*, 20, no. 5 (May 1996), pp. 71-73.

34 A.A. Buchko, "The Effects of Employee Ownership on Employee Attitudes: An Integrated Causal Model and Path Analysis," *Journal of Management Studies*, July 1993, pp. 633-56.

35 C.M. Rosen and M. Quarrey, "How Well Is Employee Ownership Working?" *Harvard Business Review*, September-October 1987, pp. 126-32.

36 J.L. Pierce and C.A. Furo, "Employee Ownership Employee Ownership: Implications for Management," *Organizational Dynamics*, Winter 1990, pp. 32-43."

37 See data in D. Stamps, "A Piece of the Action," *Training*, March 1996, p. 66.

38 M. Fein, "Work Measurement and Wage Incentives," *Industrial Engineering*, September 1973, pp. 49-51.

39 See J.L. Cotton, *Employee Involvement*, pp. 89-113; and W. Imberman, "Boosting Plant Performance with Gainsharing," *Business Horizons*, November-December 1992, p. 79.

40 S. Yellin, "Top-to-Bottom Bonuses Wave of Incentive Future," *Vancouver Sun*, February 3, 1995.

41 Cited in "Pay for Performance," *Wall Street Journal*, February 20, 1990, p. 1.

42 J. Pfeffer and N. Langton, "The Effects of Wage Dispersion on Satisfaction, Productivity, and Working Collaboratively: Evidence from College and University Faculty," *Administrative Science Quarterly*, 38, no. 3 (1983), pp. 382-407.

43 "Risk and Reward: More Canadian Companies Are Experimenting with Variable Pay," *Maclean's*, January 8, 1996, pp. 26-27.

44 "Risk and Reward: More Canadian Companies Are Experimenting with Variable Pay," *Maclean's*, January 8, 1996, pp. 26-27.

45 These examples are cited in A. Gabor, "After the Pay Revolution, Job Titles Won't Matter," *New York Times*, May 17, 1992, p. F5; "Skilled-Based Pay Boosts Worker Productivity and Morale," *Wall Street Journal*, June 23, 1992, p. A1; L. Wiener, "No New Skills? No Raise," *U.S. News & World Report*, October 26, 1992, p. 78; and M.A. Verespej, "New Responsibilities? New Pay!" *Industry Week*, August 15, 1994, p. 14.

46 P. Booth, Challenge and Change: Embracing the Team Concept. Report 123-94, Conference Board of Canada, 1994, p. 14.

47 G.E. Ledford, Jr., "Paying for the Skills, Knowledge, and Competencies of Knowledge Workers," *Compensation & Benefits Review*, July-August 1995, pp. 55-62.

48 M. Rowland, "For Each New Skill, More Money," *New York Times*, June 13, 1993, p. F16.

49 E.E. Lawler III, G.E. Ledford, Jr., and L. Chang, "Who Uses Skill-Based Pay, and Why," *Compensation & Benefits Review*, March-April 1993, p. 22.

50 E.E. Lawler III, G.E. Ledford, Jr., and L. Chang, "Who Uses Skill-Based Pay, and Why," *Compensation & Benefits Review*, March-April 1993, p. 22.

51 M. Rowland, "It's What You Can Do That Counts," *New York Times*, June 6, 1993, p. F17.

52 Cited in E.E. Lawler III, S.A. Mohrman, and G.E. Ledford, Jr., *Creating High Performance Organizations: Practices and Results in the Fortune* 1000 (San Francisco: Jossey-Bass, 1995).

53 "Skill-Based Pay Boosts Worker Productivity and Morale, *Wall Street Journal*, June 23, 1992, p. A1.

54 "Skill-Based Pay Boosts Worker Productivity and Morale, *Wall Street Journal*, June 23, 1992, p. A1.

55 "Tensions of a New Pay Plan," *New York Times*, May 17, 1992, p. F5.

56 A. T. Mair, "Pixel Perfect," *Business in Vancouver*, March 17-23, 1998, p. 13-14.

57 A. T. Mair, "Pixel Perfect," *Business in Vancouver*, March 17-23, 1998, p. 14.

58 S. Sherman, "Stretch Goals: The Dark Side of Asking for Miracles," *Fortune*, 132, no. 10, (1995), pp. 231-232; A.V. Feigenbaum, "Quality Leadership in the Global Economy," *Journal of Quality and Participation*," 17, no. 2, (1994), pp. 36-41; S. Tully, "Why Go for Stretch Targets," *Fortune*, 130, no. 10, (1994), 145-158.

59 K.R. Thompson, W.A. Hochwarter, and N.J. Mathys, "Stretch Targets: What Makes Them Effective?", *Academy of Management Executive*, 11, no. 3, (1997), pp. 48-60. See also F. Hume, "Developing Technology to Increase Competitiveness," *Industry Week*, 241, no. 21, (1992), p. 35; A.V. Roth and C.A. Giffi, "Critical Factors for Achieving World Class Manufacturing: Benchmarking North American Manufacturing Strategies," *Operations Management Review*, 11, no. 2, (1995), 79-84.

60 K.R. Thompson, W.A. Hochwarter, and N.J. Mathys, "Stretch Targets: What Makes Them Effective?", *Academy of Management Executive*, 11, no. 3, (1997), pp. 48-60.

61 K.R. Thompson, W.A. Hochwarter, and N.J. Mathys, "Stretch Targets: What Makes Them Effective?", *Academy of Management Executive*, 11, no. 3, (1997), pp. 48-60.

62 L.E. Parker and R. H. Price, "Empowered Managers and Empowered Workers: The Effects of Managerial Support and Managerial Perceived Control on Workers' Sense of Control over Decision Making," *Human Relations*, 47, no. 8, (1994), pp. 911-928; S. Wernick, "Self-Directed Work Teams and Empowerment," *Journal of Quality and Participation*, 17, no. 4, (1994), 34-36, E.E. Lawlwer III, "Total Quality Management and Employee Involvement: Are They Compatible?", *Academy of Management Executive*, 8, no. 1, (1994), 68-76.

63 "Hope for Higher Pay: The Squeeze on Incomes is Gradually Easing Up," *Maclean's*, 109, no. 48, (November 25, 1996) pp. 100-101.

64 See, for instance, "When You Want to Contain Costs and Let Employees Pick Their Benefits: Cafeteria Plans," *INC.*, December 1989, p. 142; "More Benefits Bend with Workers' Needs," *Wall Street Journal*, January 9, 1990, p. B1; R. Thompson, "Switching to Flexible Benefits," *Nation's Business*, July 1991, pp. 16-23; and A.E. Barber, R.B. Dunham, and R.A. Formisano, "The Impact of Flexible Benefits on Employee Satisfaction: A Field Study," *Personnel Psychology*, Spring 1992, pp. 55-75.

65 H. Bernstein, "New Benefit Schemes Can Be Deceiving," *Los Angeles Times*, May 14, 1991, p. D3.

66 E.E. Lawler III, "Reward Systems," in Hackman and Suttle (eds.), *Improving Life at Work*, p. 182.

67 "One Smooth Operator: This Former Bell Canada Part-timer Has Come a Long Way," *Computing Canada*, January 23, 1997, p. 11.

68 See, for instance, M. Alpert, "The Care and Feeding of Engineers," *Fortune*, September 21, 1992, pp. 86-95; and G. Poole, "How to Manage Your Nerds," *Forbes ASAP*, December 1994, pp. 132-36.

69 See, for example, B. Geber, "The Flexible Work Force," *Training*, December 1993, pp. 23-30; M. Barrier, "Now You Hire Them, Now You Don't," *Nation's Business*, January 1994, pp. 30-31; J. Fierman, "The Contingency Work Force," *Fortune*, January 24, 1994, pp. 30-36; and D.C. Feldman, H.I. Doerpinghaus, and W.H. Turnley, "Managing Temporary Workers: A Permanent HRM Challenge," *Organizational Dynamics*, Autumn 1994, pp. 49-63.

70 "Temporary Jobs Replacing Careers, Study Finds Canadian Council for Social Development," *Canadian Press Newswire*, February 25, 1996.

71 G. Fuchsberg, "Parallel Lines," *Wall Street Journal*, April 21, 1993, p. R4; and A. Penzias, "New Paths to Success," *Fortune*, June 12, 1995, pp. 90-94.

72 K. Damsell, "Service With No Smile: Blame It on Looser Labor Laws and a Newly Cynical Young Workforce. From Waiters to Video Clerks, BC's Service Industry Employees Are Flocking to Unions," *Financial Post*, August 23/25 1997, p. 14.

73 D. Hage and J. Impoco, "Jawboning the Jobs," *U.S. News & World Report*, August 9, 1993, p. 53.

74 M.P. Cronin, "One Life to Live," *INC.*, July 1993, pp. 56-60.

75 W. Grossman and R. E. Hoskisson, "CEO Pay at the Crossroads of Wall Street and Main: Toward the Strategic Design of Executive Compensation," *Academy of Management Executive*, 12, no. 1, (1998), pp. 43. See also M.C. Jensen and K.J. Murphy, "Performance and Top Management Incentives," *Journal of Political Economy*, 98, (1990), pp. 225-264.

76 D. Berman, "Do They Deserve It?" *Canadian Business*, September 26, 1997, pp. 31-33.

77 A. Rappaport, "Execuive Incentives vs. Corporate Growth," *Harvard Business Review*, July-August 1978, pp. 81-88; C.W. L. Hill, M.A. Hitt, and R.E. Hoskisson, "Declining U.S. Competitiveness: Reflections on a Crisis," *Academy of Management Executive*, 2, pp. 151-160.

78 W. Grossman and R. E. Hoskisson, "CEO Pay at the Crossroads of Wall Street and Main: Toward the Strategic Design of Executive Compensation," *Academy of Management Executive*, 12, no. 1, (1998), pp. 43-57.

[79] L. Kroll, "Catching Up," *Forbes*, May 19, 1997.

[80] J. A. Ross, "Japan: Does Money Motivate?" *Harvard Business Review*, September-October 1997. See also R. Bruce Money and John L. Graham, "Salesperson Performance, Pay, and Job Satisfaction: Tests of a Model Using Data Collected in the U.S. and Japan," *Working Paper*, University of South Carolina, 1997.

[81] D.H.B. Welsh, F. Luthans, and S. M. Sommer, "Managing Russian Factory Workers: The Impact of U.S-Based Behavioral and Participative Techniques," *Academy of Management Journal*, 36, no. 1, (1993), pp. 58-79.

[82] S.K. Saha, "Managing Human Resources: China vs. The West," *Canadian Journal of Administrative Sciences*, 10(2), 1998, pp. 167-177; Chao C. Chen, "New Trends in Reward Allocation Preference: A Sino/U.S. Comparison. *Academy of Management Journal*, 38(2), 1995, pp. 408-492.

[83] M.E. de Forest, "Thinking of a Plant in Mexico?" *Academy of Management Executive*, 8, no. 1, (1994), pp. 33-40.

[84] "Risk and Reward: More Canadian Companies Are Experimenting with Variable Pay," *Maclean's*, January 8, 1996, pp. 26-27.

[85] S. Kerr, "On the Folly of Rewarding A, While Hoping for B," *Academy of Management Executive*, 9, no. 1, (1995), pp. 7-14.

[86] Story based on M. Gorelkin, "Sowing Seeds of Discontent Back in the U.S.S.R," *Vancouver Sun*, June 9, 1990, pp. D3-4.

[87] "More on the Folly," *Academy of Management Executive*, 9 no. 1, (1995), pp. 15-16.

[88] W. Grossman and R. E. Hoskisson, "CEO pay at the Crossroads of Wall Street and Main: Toward the Strategic Design of Executive Compensation," *Academy of Management Executive*, 12, no. 1, (1998), pp. 47.

[89] A. Rappaport, "Executive Incentives vs. Corporate Growth," *Harvard Business Review*, July-August 1978, pp. 81-88

[90] Y. Amihud and B. Lev, "Risk Reduction as a Managerial Motive for Conglomerate Mergers," *Bell Journal of Economics*, 12, pp. 605-617.

[91] The information for this story came from the website: http://www.bitslayer.com/Quigleys/97-11-01.html#Date: November 8, 1997.

[92] A. Kohn, *Punished by Rewards* (Boston: Houghton Mifflin Company, 1993), p. 181.

[93] A. Kohn, *Punished by Rewards* (Boston: Houghton Mifflin Company, 1993), p. 186, see also Peter R. Scholtes, "An Elaboration of Deming's Teachings on *Performance Appraisal*," in *Performance Appraisal: Perspectives on a Quality Management Approach*, edited by Gary N. McLean, Susan R. Damme, and Richard A. Swanson, Alexandria, VA: American Society for Training and Development, 1990; Meyer et al, 1965/1989; Halachmi and Holzer, 1987.

[94] A. S. Blinder, Introduction to *Paying for Productivity*: A Look at the *Evidence*, edited by Alan S. Blinder, (Washington, D.C.: Brookings Institution, 1990).

[95] A. Kohn, *Punished by Rewards* (Boston: Houghton Mifflin Company, 1993), p. 187.

[96] D. Tjosvold, *Working Together to Get Things Done: Managing for Organizational Productivity* (Lexington, MA: Lexington Books, 1986); P.R. Scholtes, *The Team Handbook: How to Use Teams to Improve Quality* (Madison, WI:

Joiner Associates, 1988), A. Kohn, *No Contest: The Case Against Competition*. rev. ed. (Boston: Houghton Mifflin, 1992).

[97] E. L. Deci, "Applications of Research on the Effects of Rewards," in *The Hidden Costs of Rewards: New Perspectives on the Psychology of Human Motivation*, edited by M.R. Lepper and D. Green, (Hillsdale, NJ: Erlbaum, 1978).

[98] S. E. Perry, *San Francisco Scavengers: Dirty Work and the Pride of Ownership* (Berkeley: University of California Press, 1978).

[99] A. Kohn, *Punished by Rewards* (Boston: Houghton Mifflin Company, 1993), p. 192.

[100] T. H. Naylor, "Redefining Corporate Motivation, Swedish Style," *Christian Century*, May 30-June 6 1990, pp. 566-570; Robert A. Karasek, Tores Thorell, Joseph E. Schwartz, Peter L. Schnall, Carl F. Pieper, and John L. Michela, "Job Characteristics in Relation to the Prevalence of Myocardial Infarction in the US Health Examiniation Survey (HES) and the Health and Nutrition Examination Survey (HANES)," *American Journal of Public Health*, 78, 1988, pp. 910-916; Doron P. Levin, "Toyota Plant in Kentucky is Font of Ideas for the U.S.," *New York Times*, May 5, 1992, A1, D8.

[101] M. Bosquet, "The Prison Factory," Reprinted from *Le Nouvel Observateur in Working Papers for a New Society*, Spring 1973, pp. 20-27; John Holusha, "Grace Pastiak's 'Web of Inclusion,'" *New York Times*, May 5, 1991, pp. F1, F6; John Simmons and William Mares, *Working Together: Employee Participation in Action*. New York: New York University Press, 1985; David I. Levine and Laura D'Andrea Tyson, "Participation, Productivity, and the Firms' Environment," in *Paying for Productivity: A Look at the Evidence*, edited by Alan S. Blinder. Washington, D.C.: Brookings Institution, 1990; William Foote Whyte, "Worker Participation: International and Historical Perspectives," *Journal of Applied Behavioral Science*, 19, 1983, pp. 395-407.

CHAPTER 7

[1] Based on K. Damsell, "MacBlo Cuts Bite Deep: Forestry Company Unveils Plans to Lay Off 20% of Its Workers in Bid to Cut Costs and Increase Efficiency," *Financial Post Daily*, 10(200) January 22, 1998, p. 1, S. Mertl, "MacBlo Restructuring Pleases Market, Worries Unions," *Canadian Press Newswire*, January 21, 1998, and M. Stevenson, "Be Nice for a Change," *Canadian Business*, November 1993, pp. 81-85.

[2] B.W. Tuckman, "Developmental Sequences in Small Groups," *Psychological Bulletin*, June 1965, pp. 384-99; B.W. Tuckman and M.C. Jensen, "Stages of Small-Group Development Revisited," *Group and Organizational Studies*, December 1977, pp. 419-27; and M.F. Maples, "Group Development: Extending Tuckman's Theory," *Journal for Specialists in Group Work*, Fall 1988, pp. 17-23.

[3] R.C. Ginnett, "The Airline Cockpit Crew," in J.R. Hackman (ed.), *Groups That Work (and Those That Don't)* (San Francisco: Jossey-Bass, 1990).

[4] C.J.G. Gersick, "Time and Transition in Work Teams: Toward a New Model of Group Development," *Academy of Management Journal*, March 1988, pp. 9-41; C.J.G. Gersick, "Marking Time: Predictable Transitions in Task Groups," *Academy of Management Journal*, June 1989, pp.

274-309; E. Romanelli and M.L. Tushman, "Organizational Transformation as Punctuated Equilibrium: An Empirical Test," *Academy of Management Journal*, October 1994, pp. 1141-66; and B.M. Lichtenstein, "Evolution or Transformation: A Critique and Alternative to Punctuated Equilibrium," in D.P. Moore (ed.), *Academy of Management Best Paper Proceedings* (National Academy of Management Conference; Vancouver, BC, 1995), pp. 291-95.

5 This model is based on the work of P.S. Goodman, E. Ravlin, and M. Schminke, "Understanding Groups in Organizations," in L.L. Cummings and B.M. Staw (eds.), *Research in Organizational Behavior*, 9 (Greenwich, CT: JAI Press, 1987), pp. 124-28; J.R. Hackman, "The Design of Work Teams," in J.W. Lorsch (ed.), *Handbook of Organizational Behavior* (Englewood Cliffs, NJ: Prentice Hall, 1987), pp. 315-42; G.R. Bushe and A.L. Johnson, "Contextual and Internal Variables Affecting Task Group Outcomes in Organizations," *Group and Organization Studies*, December 1989, pp. 462-82; and M.A. Campion, G.J. Medsker, and A.C. Higgs, "Relations Between Work Group Characteristics and Effectiveness: Implications for Designing Effective Work Groups," *Personnel Psychology*, Winter 1993, pp. 823-50.

6 F. Friedlander, "The Ecology of Work Groups," in J.W. Lorsch (ed.) *Handbook of Organizational Behavior*, pp. 301-14; P.B. Paulus and D. Nagar, "Environmental Influences on Groups," in P. Paulus (ed.), *Psychology of Group Influence*, 2nd ed. (Hillsdale, NJ: Erlbaum, 1989); and E. Sundstrom and I. Altman, "Physical Environments and Work-Group Effectiveness," in L.L. Cummings and B.M. Staw (eds.), *Research in Organizational Behavior*, 11 (Greenwich, CT: JAI Press, 1989), pp. 175-209.

7 See, for example, J. Krantz, "Group Processes Under Conditions of Organizational Decline," *The Journal of Applied Behavioral Science*, 21, no. 1, (1985), pp. 1-17.

8 J.R. Hackman, "The Design of Work Teams," in J.W. Lorsch (ed.), *Handbook of Organizational Behavior* (Englewood Cliffs, NJ: Prentice Hall, 1987), pp. 325-26.

9 Cited in A.D. Szilagyi, Jr., and M.J. Wallace, Jr., *Organizational Behavior and Performance*, 4th ed. (Glenview, IL: Scott, Foresman, 1987), p. 223.

10 See M. Hill, "Group Versus Individual Performance. Are N+1 Heads Better Than One?" *Psychological Reports*, April 1982, pp. 517-39; and A. Tziner and D. Eden, "Effects of Crew Composition on Crew Performance: Does the Whole Equal the Sum of Its Parts?" *Journal of Applied Psychology*, February 1985, pp. 85-93.

11 M.E. Shaw, *Contemporary Topics in Social Psychology* (Morristown, NJ: General Learning Press, 1976), pp. 350-51.

12 S. Lieberman, "The Effects of Changes in Roles on the Attitudes of Role Occupants," *Human Relations*, November 1956, pp. 385-402.

13 See S.L. Robinson, M.S. Kraatz, and D.M. Rousseau, "Changing Obligations and the Psychological Contract: A Longitudinal Study," *Academy of Management Journal*, February 1994, pp. 137-52.

14 E.H. Schein, *Organizational Psychology*, 3rd ed. (Englewood Cliffs, NJ: Prentice Hall, 1980), p. 24.

15 See M.F. Peterson, et al., "Role Conflict, Ambiguity, and Overload: A 21-Nation Study," *Academy of Management Journal*, April 1995, pp. 429-52.

16 For a recent review of the research on group norms, see J.R. Hackman, "Group Influences on Individuals in Organiza-

tions," in M.D. Dunnette and L.M. Hough (eds.), *Handbook of Industrial & Organizational Psychology*, 2nd edition, vol. 3 (Palo Alto, CA: Consulting Psychologists Press, 1992), pp. 235-50.

17 A. Harlan, J. Kerr, and S. Kerr, "Preference for Motivator and Hygiene Factors in a Hypothetical Interview Situation: Further Findings and Some Implications for the Employment Interview," *Personnel Psychology*, Winter 1977, pp. 557-66.

18 D.C. Feldman, "The Development and Enforcement of Group Norms," *Academy of Management Journal*, January 1984, pp. 47-53; and K.L. Bettenhausen and J.K. Murnighan, "The Development of an Intragroup Norm and the Effects of Interpersonal and Structural Challenges," *Administrative Science Quarterly*, March 1991, pp. 20-35.

19 C.A. Kiesler and S.B. Kiesler, *Conformity* (Reading, MA: Addison-Wesley, 1969).

20 C.A. Kiesler and S.B. Kiesler, *Conformity* (Reading, MA: Addison-Wesley, 1969). p. 27.

21 S.E. Asch, "Effects of Group Pressure upon the Modification and Distortion of Judgments," in H. Guetzkow (ed.), *Groups, Leadership and Men* (Pittsburgh: Carnegie Press, 1951), pp. 177-90.

22 R. Keyes, *Is There Life After High School?* (New York: Warner Books, 1976).

23 W.F. Whyte, "The Social Structure of the Restaurant," *American Journal of Sociology*, January 1954, pp. 302-08.

24 Cited in J.R. Hackman, "Group Influences on Individuals in Organizations," p. 236.

25 O.J. Harvey and C. Consalvi, "Status and Conformity to Pressures in Informal Groups," *Journal of Abnormal and Social Psychology*, Spring 1960, pp. 182-87.

26 J.A. Wiggins, F. Dill, and R.D. Schwartz, "On 'Status-Liability,'" *Sociometry*, April-May 1965, pp. 197-209.

27 J. Greenberg, "Equity and Workplace Status: A Field Experiment," *Journal of Applied Psychology*, November 1988, pp. 606-13.

28 E.J. Thomas and C.F. Fink, "Effects of Group Size," *Psychological Bulletin*, July 1963, pp. 371-84; A.P. Hare, *Handbook of Small Group Research* (New York: Free Press, 1976); and M.E. Shaw, *Group Dynamics: The Psychology of Small Group Behavior*, 3rd ed. (New York: McGraw-Hill, 1981).

29 See D.R. Comer, "A Model of Social Loafing in Real Work Groups," *Human Relations*, June 1995, pp. 647-67.

30 W. Moede, "Die Richtlinien der Leistungs-Psychologie," *Industrielle Psychotechnik*, 4 (1927), pp. 193-207. See also D.A. Kravitz and B. Martin, "Ringelmann Rediscovered: The Original Article," *Journal of Personality and Social Psychology*, May 1986, pp. 936-41.

31 See, for example, J.A. Shepperd, "Productivity Loss in Performance Groups: A Motivation Analysis," *Psychological Bulletin*, January 1993, pp. 67-81; and S.J. Karau and K.D. Williams, "Social Loafing: A Meta-Analytic Review and Theoretical Integration," *Journal of Personality and Social Psychology*, October 1993, pp. 681-706.

32 S.G. Harkins and K. Szymanski, "Social Loafing and Group Evaluation," *Journal of Personality and Social Psychology*, December 1989, pp. 934-41.

33 See P.C. Earley, "Social Loafing and Collectivism: A Comparison of the United States and the People's Republic of

China," *Administrative Science Quarterly*, December 1989, pp. 565-81; and P.C. Earley, "East Meets West Meets Mideast: Further Explorations of Collectivistic and Individualistic Work Groups," *Academy of Management Journal*, April 1993, pp. 319-48.

34 E.J. Thomas and C.F. Fink, "Effects of Group Size"; A.P. Hare, *Handbook*; M.E. Shaw, *Group Dynamics*; and P. Yetton and P. Bottger, "The Relationships Among Group Size, Member Ability, Social Decision Schemes, and Performance," *Organizational Behavior and Human Performance*, October 1983, pp. 145-59.

35 See, for example, P.S. Goodman, E.C. Ravlin, and L. Argote, "Current Thinking About Groups: Setting the Stage for New Ideas," in P.S. Goodman and Associates, *Designing Effective Work Groups* (San Francisco: Jossey-Bass, 1986), pp. 15-16; and R.A. Guzzo and G.P. Shea, "Group Performance and Intergroup Relations in Organizations," in M.D. Dunnette and L.M. Hough, eds., *Handbook of Industrial & Organizational Psychology*, 2nd edition, vol. 3 (Palo Alto, CA: Consulting Psychologists Press, 1992), pp. 288-90.

36 M.E. Shaw, *Contemporary Topics in Social Psychology* (Morristown, NJ: General Learning Press, 1976), p. 356.

37 W.E. Watson, K. Kumar, and L.K. Michaelsen, "Cultural Diversity's Impact on Interaction Process and Performance: Comparing Homogeneous and Diverse Task Groups," *Academy of Management Journal*, June 1993, pp. 590-602.

38 B.E. McCain, C.A. O'Reilly III, and J. Pfeffer, "The Effects of Departmental Demography on Turnover: The Case of a University," *Academy of Management Journal*, December 1983, pp. 626-41; W.G. Wagner, J. Pfeffer, and C.A. O'Reilly III, "Organizational Demography and Turnover in Top-Management Groups," *Administrative Science Quarterly*, March 1984, pp. 74-92; J. Pfeffer and C.A. O'Reilly III, "Hospital Demography and Turnover Among Nurses," *Industrial Relations*, Spring 1987, pp. 158-73; C.A. O'Reilly III, D.F. Caldwell, and W.P. Barnett, "Work Group Demography, Social Integration, and Turnover," *Administrative Science Quarterly*, March 1989, pp. 21-37; S.E. Jackson, J.F. Brett, V.I. Sessa, D.M. Cooper, J.A. Julin, and K. Peyronnin, "Some Differences Make a Difference: Individual Dissimilarity and Group Heterogeneity as Correlates of Recruitment, Promotions, and Turnover," *Journal of Applied Psychology*, August 1991, pp. 675-89; M.F. Wiersema and A. Bird, "Organizational Demography in Japanese Firms: Group Heterogeneity, Individual Dissimilarity, and Top Management Team Turnover," *Academy of Management Journal*, October 1993, pp. 996-1025; F.J. Milliken and L.L. Martins, "Searching for Common Threads: Understanding the Multiple Effects of Diversity in Organizational Groups," *Academy of Management Review*, April 1996, pp. 402-33.

39 For some of the controversy surrounding the definition of cohesion, see J. Keyton and J. Springston, "Redefining Cohesiveness in Groups," *Small Group Research*, May 1990, pp. 234-54.

40 I. Summers, T. Coffelt, and R.E. Horton, "Work-Group Cohesion," *Psychological Reports*, October 1988, pp. 627-36; and B. Mullen and C. Cooper, "The Relation Between Group Cohesiveness and Performance: An Integration," *Psychological Bulletin*, March 1994, pp. 210-27.

41 I.D. Steiner, *Group Process and Productivity* (New York: Academic Press, 1972).

42 R.B. Zajonc, "Social Facilitation," *Science*, March 1965, pp. 269-74.

43 C.F. Bond, Jr. and L.J. Titus, "Social Facilitation: A Meta-Analysis of 241 Studies," *Psychological Bulletin*, September 1983, pp. 265-92.

44 V.F. Nieva, E.A. Fleishman, and A. Rieck, "Team Dimensions: Their Identity, Their Measurement, and Their Relationships." Final Technical Report for Contract No. DAHC 19-C-0001, (Washington, DC: Advanced Research Resources Organizations, 1978).

45 See, for example, J.R. Hackman and C.G. Morris, "Group Tasks, Group Interaction Process and Group Performance Effectiveness: A Review and Proposed Integration," in L. Berkowitz (ed.), *Advances in Experimental Social Psychology* (New York: Academic Press, 1975), pp. 45-99; and R. Saavedra, P.C. Earley, and L. Van Dyne, "Complex Interdependence in Task-Performing Groups," *Journal of Applied Psychology*, February 1993, pp. 61-72.

46 J. Galbraith, *Organizational Design* (Reading, MA: Addison-Wesley, 1977).

47 Quoted from Richard Hackman, "The Design of Work Teams," in *Handbook of Organizational Behavior*, J.W. Lorsch, ed., Englewood Cliffs, NJ: Prentice-Hall, 1987, pp. 315-339.

48 While the specific subject points are taken from Richard Hackman, "The Design of Work Teams," in *Handbook of Organizational Behavior*, J.W. Lorsch, ed., (Englewood Cliffs, NJ: Prentice-Hall, 1987), pp. 315-339, the discussion of the individual items is developed separately.

49 G.M. Parker, *Team Player and Teamwork: The Competitive Business Strategy* (Jossey-Bass, San Francisco, 1990).

50 G.M. Parker, *Team Player and Teamwork: The Competitive Business Strategy* (Jossey-Bass, San Francisco, 1990), p. 44.

51 Stevens and Kristof, "Making the Right Impression: A Field Study of Applicant Impression Management During Job Interviews."

52 This section is based on B.E. Ashforth and R.T. Lee, "Defensive Behavior in Organizations: A Preliminary Model," *Human Relations*, July 1990, pp. 621-48.

53 This figure is based on G.F. Cavanagh, D.J. Moberg, and M. Valasquez, "The Ethics of Organizational Politics," *Academy of Management Journal*, June 1981, pp. 363-74.

54 R.M. Kanter, *Men and Women of the Corporation* (New York: Basic Books, 1977).

55 See, for instance, C.M. Falbe and G. Yukl, "Consequences for Managers of Using Single Influence Tactics and Combinations of Tactics," *Academy of Management Journal*, August 1992, pp. 638-52.

56 P.A. Wilson, "The Effects of Politics and Power on the Organizational Commitment of Federal Executives," *Journal of Management*, Spring 1995, pp. 101-18.

57 See, for example, M.A. Rahim, "Relationships of Leader Power to Compliance and Satisfaction with Supervision: Evidence from a National Sample of Managers," *Journal of Management*, December 1989, pp. 545-56.

58 T.P. Verney, "Role Perception Congruence, Performance, and Satisfaction," in D.J. Vredenburgh and R.S. Schuler (eds.), *Effective Management: Research and Application*, Proceedings of the 20th Annual Eastern Academy of Management, Pittsburgh, PA, May 1983, pp. 24-27.

59 T.P. Verney, "Role Perception Congruence, Performance, and Satisfaction," in D.J. Vredenburgh and R.S. Schuler

(eds.), *Effective Management: Research and Application*, Proceedings of the 20th Annual Eastern Academy of Management, Pittsburgh, PA, May 1983, pp. 24-27.

60 M. Van Sell, A.P. Brief, and R.S. Schuler, "Role Conflict and Role Ambiguity: Integration of the Literature and Directions for Future Research," *Human Relations*, January 1981, pp. 43-71; and A.G. Bedeian and A.A. Armenakis, "A Path-Analytic Study of the Consequences of Role Conflict and Ambiguity," *Academy of Management Journal*, June 1981, pp. 417-24.

61 Shaw, *Group Dynamics: The Psychology of Small Group Behavior*, 3rd ed. (New York: McGraw-Hill, 1981).

62 B. Mullen, C. Symons, L. Hu, and E. Salas, "Group Size, Leadership Behavior, and Subordinate Satisfaction," *Journal of General Psychology*, April 1989, pp. 155-70.

CHAPTER 8

1 Based on Iain MacIntyre, "Keenan is Getting Team's Mix Right," *Vancouver Sun*, March 25, 1998, p. F2.

2 Based on Iain MacIntyre, "Keenan is Getting Team's Mix Right," *Vancouver Sun*, March 25, 1998, p. F2.

3 This section is based on J.R. Katzenbach and D.K. Smith, *The Wisdom of Teams*, pp. 21, 45, and 85; and D.C. Kinlaw, *Developing Superior Work Teams* (Lexington, MA: Lexington Books, 1991), pp. 3-21.

4 P. Booth, *Challenge and Change: Embracing the Team Concept*. Report 123-94, Conference Board of Canada, 1994.

5 *Training Magazine*, October 1995, Lakewood Publications, Minneapolis, MN.

6 See, for example, D. Tjosvold, *Team Organization: An Enduring Competitive Advantage* (Chichester, England: Wiley, 1991); J. Lipnack and J. Stamps, *The TeamNet Factor* (Essex Junction, VT: Oliver Wight, 1993); J.R. Katzenbach and D.K. Smith, *The Wisdom of Teams* (Boston: Harvard Business School Press, 1993); and S.A. Mohrman, S.G. Cohen, and A.M. Mohrman, Jr., *Designing Team-Based Organizations* (San Francisco: Jossey-Bass, 1995).

7 "Working Smart: Management Strategies Smart BC Companies Are Using to Cope with the 1990s," *B.C. Business Magazine*, October 1993, pp. 35-41.

8 See, for example, the increasing body of literature on empowerment such as R.C. Ford and M.D. Fottler, "Empowerment: A Matter of Degree," *The Academy of Management Executive*, August 1995, pp. 21-31; and G.M. Spreitzer, "Psychological Empowerment in the Workplace: Dimensions, Measurement, and Validation," *Academy of Management Journal*, October 1995, pp. 1442-65.

9 M. Sashkin, "Participative Management Is an Ethical Imperative," *Organizational Dynamics*, Spring 1984, pp. 5-22.

10 R. Tannenbaum, I.R. Weschler, and F. Massarik, *Leadership and Organization, A Behavioral Science Approach* (New York: McGraw-Hill, 1961), pp. 88-100.

11 J.L. Cotton, *Employee Involvement* (Newbury Park, CA: Sage, 1993), p. 114.

12 See, for example, M. Poole, "Industrial Democracy: A Comparative Analysis," *Industrial Relations*, Fall 1979, pp. 262-72; IDE International Research Group, *European Industrial Relations* (Oxford, UK: Clarendon, 1981); E.M. Kassalow, "Employee Representation on U.S., German Boards," *Monthly Labor Review*, September 1989, pp. 39-42; T.H.

Hammer, S.C. Currall, and R.N. Stern, "Worker Representation on Boards of Directors: A Study of Competing Roles," *Industrial and Labor Relations Review*, Winter 1991, pp. 661-80; and P. Kunst and J. Soeters, "Works Council Membership and Career Opportunities," *Organization Studies*, 12, no. 1, (1991), pp. 75-93.

13 J. D. Kleyn and S. Perrick, "Netherlands," *International Financial Law Review*, February 1990, pp. 51-56.

14 J.L. Cotton, *Employee Involvement*, (Newbury Park, CA: Sage, 1993), pp. 129-30 and 139-40.

15 J.L. Cotton, *Employee Involvement*, (Newbury Park, CA: Sage, 1993), pp. 129-30 and 139-40.

16 A. Kohn, *Punished by Rewards* (Boston: Houghton Mifflin Company, 1993), p. 195; Michel Bosquet, "The Prison Factory," Reprinted from *Le Nouvel Observateur* in *Working Papers for a New Society*, Spring 1973, pp. 20-27; John Holusha, "Grace Pastiak's 'Web of Inclusion,'" *New York Times*, May 5, 1991, pp. F1, F6; John Simmons and William Mares, *Working Together: Employee Participation in Action* (New York: New York University Press, 1985); Alan S. Blinder, Introduction to *Paying for Productivity: A Look at the Evidence*, edited by Alan S. Blinder (Washington, D.C.: Brookings Institution, 1990).

17 A. Kohn, *Punished by Rewards* (Boston: Houghton Mifflin Company, 1993), p. 195, M. Bosquet, "The Prison Factory," reprinted from *Le Nouvel Observateur* in *Working Papers for a New Society*, Spring 1973, pp. 20-27; J. Holusha, "Grace Pastiak's 'Web of Inclusion,'" *New York Times*, May 5, 1991, pp. F1, F6; J. Simmons and W. Mares, *Working Together: Employee Participation in Action* (New York: New York University Press, 1985); A. S. Blinder, Introduction to *Paying for Productivity: A Look at the Evidence*, edited by A. S. Blinder. (Washington, D.C.: Brookings Institution, 1990).

18 A. Kohn, *Punished by Rewards* (Boston: Houghton Mifflin Company, 1993), p. 195, M. Bosquet, "The Prison Factory," reprinted from *Le Nouvel Observateur* in *Working Papers for a New Society*, Spring 1973, pp. 20-27; J. Holusha, "Grace Pastiak's 'Web of Inclusion,'" *New York Times*, May 5, 1991, pp. F1, F6; J. Simmons and W. Mares, *Working Together: Employee Participation in Action* (New York: New York University Press, 1985); K. I. Miller and P. R. Monge, "Participation, satisfaction, and productivity: A Meta-Analytic Review," *Academy of Management Journal* 29, 1986, pp. 727-753.

19 A. Kohn, *Punished by Rewards* (Boston: Houghton Mifflin Company, 1993), p. 195; Michel Bosquet, "The Prison Factory," reprinted from *Le Nouvel Observateur* in *Working Papers for a New Society*, Spring 1973, pp. 20-27; J. Holusha, "Grace Pastiak's 'Web of Inclusion,'" *New York Times*, May 5, 1991, pp. F1, F6; J. Simmons and W. Mares, *Working Together: Employee Participation in Action*. New York: New York University Press, 1985; A. J. Melcher, "Participation: A Critical Review of Research Findings," *Human Resource Management*, 15, 1976, 12-21; D. I. Levine and L. D'Andrea Tyson, "Participation, Productivity, and the Firms' Environment," in *Paying for Productivity: A Look at the Evidence*, edited by Alan S. Blinder (Washington, D.C.: Brookings Institution, 1990); E. L. Deci, "The History of Motivation in Psychology and Its Relevance for Management," in *Management and Motivation: Selected Readings*, edited by V. H. Vroom and E. L. Deci, 2nd ed. (London: Penguin, 1992); C. Pinder, "Concerning the Application of Human Motivation Theories in Organizational

Settings," *Academy of Management Review*, 2, 1977, 384-397.

20 A. Kohn, *Punished by Rewards* (Boston: Houghton Mifflin Company, 1993), p. 195; Michel Bosquet, "The Prison Factory," reprinted from *Le Nouvel Observateur in Working Papers for a New Society*, Spring 1973, pp. 20-27; John Holusha, "Grace Pastiak's 'Web of Inclusion,'" *New York Times*, May 5, 1991, pp. F1, F6; J. Simmons and W. Mares, *Working Together: Employee Participation in Action* (New York: New York University Press, 1985); C. O'Dell, *People, Performance, and Pay* (Houston: American Productivity Center, 1987); M. Loden, *Feminine Leadership: Or How to Succeed in Business Without Being One of the Boys* (New York: Times Books, 1985).

21 P. Booth, *Challenge and Change: Embracing the Team Concept*. Report 123-94, Conference Board of Canada, 1994.

22 A. Kohn, *Punished by Rewards* (Boston: Houghton Mifflin Company, 1993), p. 195, M. Bosquet, "The Prison Factory," reprinted from *Le Nouvel Observateur in Working Papers for a New Society*, Spring 1973, pp. 20-27; J. Holusha, "Grace Pastiak's 'Web of Inclusion,'" *New York Times*, May 5, 1991, pp. F1, F6; J. Simmons and W. Mares, *Working Together: Employee Participation in Action* (New York: New York University Press, 1985); C. O'Dell, *People, Performance, and Pay* (Houston: American Productivity Center, 1987); M. Loden, *Feminine Leadership: Or How to Succeed in Business Without Being One of the Boys* (New York: Times Books, 1985).

23 J.H. Shonk, *Team-Based Organizations* (Homewood, IL: Business One Irwin, 1992); and M.A. Verespej, "When Workers Get New Roles," *Industry Week*, February 3, 1992, p. 11.

24 M.L. Marks, P.H. Mirvis, E.J. Hackett, and J.F. Grady, Jr., "Employee Participation in a Quality Circle Program: Impact on Quality of Work Life, Productivity, and Absenteeism," *Journal of Applied Psychology*, February 1986, pp. 61-69; T.R. Miller, "The Quality Circle Phenomenon: A Review and Appraisal," *SAM Advanced Management Journal*, Winter 1989, pp. 4-7; and E.E. Adams, Jr., "Quality Circle Performance," *Journal of Management*, March 1991, pp. 25-39.

25 See, for example, G.W. Meyer and R.G. Stott, "Quality Circles: Panacea or Pandora's Box?" *Organizational Dynamics*, Spring 1985, pp. 34-50; M.L. Marks, P.H. Mirvis, E.J. Hackett, and J.F. Grady, Jr., "Employee Participation in a Quality Circle Program: Impact on Quality of Life, Productivity, and Absenteeism," *Journal of Applied Psychology*, February 1986, pp. 61-69; E.E. Lawler III and S.A. Mohrman, "Quality Circles: After the Honeymoon," *Organizational Dynamics*, Spring 1987, pp. 42-54; R.P. Steel and R.F. Lloyd, "Cognitive, Affective, and Behavioral Outcomes of Participation in Quality Circles: Conceptual and Empirical Findings," *Journal of Applied Behavioral Science*, 24, no. 1, (1988), pp. 1-17; T.R. Miller, "The Quality Circles Phenomenon: A Review and Appraisal," *SAM Advanced Management Journal*, Winter 1989, pp. 4-7; K. Buch and R. Spangler, "The Effects of Quality Circles on Performance and Promotions," *Human Relations*, June 1990, pp. 573-82; P.R. Liverpool, "Employee Participation in Decision-Making: An Analysis of the Perceptions of Members and Nonmembers of Quality Circles," *Journal of Business and Psychology*, Summer 1990, pp. 411-22, and E.E. Adams, Jr., "Quality Circle Performance," *Journal of Management*, March 1991, pp. 25-39.

26 J.L. Cotton, *Employee Involvement*, (Newbury Park, CA: Sage, 1993), p. 76.

27 "Corporate Culture Club: Companies Are Focusing on Employee Morale and Training to Boost the Bottom Line," *Maclean's*, December 12, 1994, pp. 42-43.

28 J.L. Cotton, *Employee Involvement*, (Newbury Park, CA: Sage, 1993), p. 76.

29 J.L. Cotton, *Employee Involvement*, (Newbury Park, CA: Sage, 1993), p. 76.

30 J.L. Cotton, *Employee Involvement*, (Newbury Park, CA: Sage, 1993), p. 3.

31 See, for example, C.C. Manz and H.P. Sims, Jr., *Business Without Bosses: How Self-Managing Teams Are Building High Performance Companies* (New York: Wiley, 1993); J.R. Barker, "Tightening the Iron Cage: Concertive Control in Self-Managing Teams," *Administrative Science Quarterly*, September 1993, pp. 408-37; and S.G. Cohen, G.E. Ledford, Jr., and G.M. Spreitzer, "A Predictive Model of Self-Managing Work Team Effectiveness," *Human Relations*, May 1996, pp. 643-76.

32 "Now Everyone Can be a Boss: Creating Self-directed Work Teams Means Giving Shop-floor Workers the Kind of Authority Once Reserved for Management," *Canadian Business*, May, 1994, p. 48.

33 P. Booth, *Challenge and Change: Embracing the Team Concept* (Report 123-94, Conference Board of Canada, 1994).

34 J. Hillkirk, "Self-Directed Work Teams."

35 "Through the Wringer: Squeezing Oil from Sand Created an Energy Boondoggle in Northern Alberta. Squeezing Costs from the Process is Finally Making Syncrude Viable," *Canadian Business*, 66, no. 8, (August 1993), pp. 32-35.

36 See, for instance, T.D. Wall, N.J. Kemp, P.R. Jackson, and C.W. Clegg, "Outcomes of Autonomous Workgroups: A Long-Term Field Experiment," *Academy of Management Journal*, June 1986, pp. 280-304; and J.L. Cordery, W.S. Mueller, and L.M. Smith, "Attitudinal and Behavioral Effects of Autonomous Group Working: A Longitudinal Field Study," *Academy of Management Journal*, June 1991, pp. 464-76.

37 R. Zemke, "Rethinking the Rush to Team Up," *Training*, November 1993, pp. 55-61.

38 See J. Lipnack and J. Stamps, *The TeamNet Factor*, pp. 14-17; G. Taninecz, "Team Players," *Industry Week*, July 15, 1996, pp. 28-32; and D.R. Denison, S.L. Hart, and J.A. Kahn, "From Chimneys to Cross-Functional Teams: Developing and Validating a Diagnostic Model," *Academy of Management Journal*, August 1996, pp. 1005-23.

39 T.B. Kinni, "Boundary-Busting Teamwork," *Industry Week*, March 21, 1994, pp. 72-78.

40 "Cross-Functional Obstacles," *Training*, May 1994, pp. 125-26.

41 For a more detailed breakdown on team skills, see M.J. Stevens and M.A. Campion, "The Knowledge, Skill, and Ability Requirements for Teamwork: Implications for Human Resource Management," *Journal of Management*, Summer 1994, pp. 503-30.

42 C. Margerison and D. McCann, *Team Management: Practical New Approaches* (London: Mercury Books, 1990).

43 See S.T. Johnson, "Work Teams: What's Ahead in Work Design and Rewards Management," *Compensation & Benefits Review*, March-April 1993, pp. 35-41; and A.M. Saunier and E.J. Hawk, "Realizing the Potential of Teams Through

Team-Based Rewards," *Compensation & Benefits Review*, July-August 1994, pp. 24-33.

44 P. Booth, *Challenge and Change: Embracing the Team Concept* (Report 123-94, Conference Board of Canada, 1994, pp. 14-15).

45 P. Booth, *Challenge and Change: Embracing the Team Concept* (Report 123-94, Conference Board of Canada, 1994, p. 14).

46 F. McGuire, "Empowering Employees," *Canadian Business Review*, Winter 1993, pp. 21-23.

47 F. McGuire, "Empowering Employees," Canadian *Business Review*, Winter 1993, pp. 21-23.

48 F.K. Sonnenberg, "Trust Me, Trust Me Not," *Industry Week*, August 16, 1993, pp. 22-28. For a more elaborate definition, see L.T. Hosmer, "Trust: The Connecting Link Between Organizational Theory and Philosophical Ethics," *Academy of Management Review*, April 1995, pp. 379-403.

49 P.L. Schindler and C.C. Thomas, "The Structure of Interpersonal Trust in the Workplace," *Psychological Reports*, October 1993, pp. 563-73. A similar, four-dimensional definition is offered in A.K. Mishra, "Organizational Responses to Crisis: The Centrality of Trust," in R.M. Kramer and T.R. Tyler, *Trust in Organizations* (Thousand Oaks, CA: Sage, 1996), pp. 264-70.

50 Schindler and Thomas, "The Structure of Interpersonal Trust in the Workplace," *Psychological Reports*, October 1993, pp. 563-73.

51 J.K. Butler and R.S. Cantrell, "A Behavioral Decision Theory Approach to Modeling Dyadic Trust in Superiors and Subordinates," *Psychological Reports*, August 1984, pp. 19-28.

52 See, for instance, M. Sashkin and K.J. Kiser, *Putting Total Quality Management to Work* (San Francisco: Berrett-Koehler, 1993); and J.R. Hackman and R. Wageman, "Total Quality Management: Empirical, Conceptual and Practical Issues," *Administrative Science Quarterly*, June 1995, pp. 309-42.

53 R.M. Stogdill, "Group Productivity, Drive, and Cohesiveness," *Organizational Behavior and Human Performance*, February 1972, pp. 36-43. See also M. Mayo, J.C. Pastor, and J.R. Meindl, "The Effects of Group Heterogeneity on the Self-Perceived Efficacy of Group Leaders," *Leadership Quarterly*, Summer 1996, pp. 265-84.

54 J.E. McGrath, *Groups: Interaction and Performance* (Englewood Cliffs, NJ: Prentice Hall, 1984).

55 This idea is proposed in S.E. Jackson, V.K. Stone, and E.B. Alvarez, "Socialization Amidst Diversity," p. 68.

56 "People Programs Pay Dividends," *Plant*, May 2, 1994, pp. 1, 5.

57 This section is based on M. Kaeter, "Repotting Mature Work Teams," *Training*, April 1994 (Supplement), pp. 4-6.

CHAPTER 9

1 This opening section is based on J. Ritter, "Poor Fluency in English Means Mixed Signals," *USA Today*, January 18, 1996, p. 1A; and "Miscommunication preceded Indonesian Air Crash," *The Associated Press Wire Service*, September 29, 1997. For an analysis of how communication problems cause aviation disasters, see also C. Linde, "The Quantita-tive Study of Communicative Success," *Language in Society*, Summer 1988, pp. 375-99.

2 See, for example, K.W. Thomas and W.H. Schmidt, "A Survey of Managerial Interests with Respect to Conflict," *Academy of Management Journal*, June 1976, p. 317.

3 Laura Ramsay, "Communication Key to Workplace Happiness," *Financial Post*, December 6/8, 1997, p. 58.

4 W.G. Scott and T.R. Mitchell, *Organization Theory: A Structural and Behavioral Analysis* (Homewood, IL: Richard D. Irwin, 1976).

5 D.K. Berlo, *The Process of Communication* (New York: Holt, Rinehart & Winston, 1960), pp. 30-32.

6 D.K. Berlo, *The Process of Communication* (New York: Holt, Rinehart & Winston, 1960), p. 54.

7 D.K. Berlo, *The Process of Communication* (New York: Holt, Rinehart & Winston, 1960), p. 103.

8 R.L. Simpson, "Vertical and Horizontal Communication in Formal Organizations," *Administrative Science Quarterly*, September 1959, pp. 188-96; and B. Harriman, "Up and Down the Communications Ladder," *Harvard Business Review*, September-October 1974, pp. 143-51.

9 P. Waal, "With a Vengeance," *Canadian Business*, April 10, 1998, pp. 34-42.

10 P. Booth, Challenge and Change: Embracing the Team Concept. Report 123-94, Conference Board of Canada, 1994, p. 9.

11 "The Document Executive: Profile of Diane McGarry," *Computing Canada*, September 13, 1995, p. 11.

12 D. M. Saunders and J. D. Leck, "Formal Upward Communication Procedures: Organizational and Employee Perspectives," *Canadian Journal of Administrative Sciences* 10, pp. 255-268.

13 See, for instance, J.W. Newstrom, R.E. Monczka, and W.E. Reif, "Perceptions of the Grapevine: Its Value and Influence," *Journal of Business Communication*, Spring 1974, pp. 12-20; and S.J. Modic, "Grapevine Rated Most Believable," *Industry Week*, May 15, 1989, p. 14.

14 K. Davis, "Management Communication and the Grapevine," *Harvard Business Review*, September-October 1953, pp. 43-49.

15 H. Sutton and L.W. Porter, "A Study of the Grapevine in a Governmental Organization," *Personnel Psychology*, Summer 1968, pp. 223-30.

16 K. Davis, cited in R. Rowan, "Where Did That Rumor Come From?" *Fortune*, August 13, 1979, p. 134.

17 L. Hirschhorn, "Managing Rumors," in L. Hirschhorn (ed.), *Cutting Back* (San Francisco: Jossey-Bass, 1983), pp. 49-52.

18 R.L. Rosnow and G.A. Fine, *Rumor and Gossip: The Social Psychology of Hearsay* (New York: Elsevier, 1976).

19 See, for instance, J.G. March and G. Sevon, "Gossip, Information and Decision Making" in J.G. March (ed.), *Decisions and Organizations* (Oxford: Blackwell, 1988), pp. 429-42; M. Noon and R. Delbridge, "News from Behind My Hand: Gossip in Organizations," *Organization Studies*, 14, no. 1, (1993), pp. 23-36; and N. DiFonzo, P. Bordia, and R.L. Rosnow, "Reining in Rumors," *Organizational Dynamics*, Summer 1994, pp. 47-62.

20 Jim Collins and Jerry Poras, Built to Last: *Successful Habits of Visionary Companies* (Harper Collins), 1994.

21 Material in this section is based, in part, on Jim Collins, "Forget Strategy, Build Mechanisms Instead," *Inc.*, October 1997, pp. 45-48.

22 R.L. Birdwhistell, *Introduction to Kinesics* (Louisville, KY: University of Louisville Press, 1952).

23 J. Fast, *Body Language* (Philadelphia: M. Evan, 1970), p. 7.

24 J.C. McCroskey, J.A. Daly, and G. Sorenson, "Personality Correlates of Communication Apprehension," *Human Communication Research*, Spring 1976, pp. 376-80.

25 See R.L. Daft and R.H. Lengel, "Information Richness: A New Approach to Managerial Behavior and Organization Design," in B.M. Staw and L.L. Cummings (eds.), *Research in Organizational Behavior*, vol. 6 (Greenwich, CT: JAI Press, 1984), pp. 191-233; R.E. Rice and D.E. Shook, "Relationships of Job Categories and Organizational Levels to Use of Communication Channels, Including Electronic Mail: A Meta-Analysis and Extension," *Journal of Management Studies*, March 1990, pp. 195-229; R.E. Rice, "Task Analyzability, Use of New Media, and Effectiveness," *Organization Science*, November 1992, pp. 475-500; S.G. Straus and J.E. McGrath, "Does the Medium Matter? The Interaction of Task Type and Technology on Group Performance and Member Reaction," *Journal of Applied Psychology*, February 1994, pp. 87-97; J. Webster and L.K. Trevino, "Rational and Social Theories as Complementary Explanations of Communication Media Choices: Two Policy-Capturing Studies," *Academy of Management Journal*, December 1995, pp. 1544-72.

26 R.L. Daft, R.H. Lengel, and L.K. Trevino, "Message Equivocality, Media Selection, and Manager Performance: Implications for Information Systems," *MIS Quarterly*, September 1987, pp. 355-68.

27 J. DeLorean, quoted in S.P. Robbins, *The Administrative Process* (Englewood Cliffs, NJ: Prentice Hall, 1976), p. 404.

28 S.I. Hayakawa, *Language in Thought and Action* (New York: Harcourt Brace Jovanovich, 1949), p. 292.

29 M. Young and J.E. Post, "Managing to Communicate, Communicating to Manage: How Leading Companies Communicate With Employees," *Organizational Dynamics*, Summer 1993, pp. 31-43.

30 L. Tabak, "Quality Controls," *Hemispheres*, September 1996, pp. 33-34.

31 L. Tabak, "Quality Controls," *Hemispheres*, September 1996, pp. 33-34

32 L. Tabak, "Quality Controls," *Hemispheres*, September 1996, pp. 33-34

33 L. Tabak, "Quality Controls," *Hemispheres*, September 1996, pp. 33-34

34 A. Van den Broek, "All's Quiet on the Eastern Front: Times Have Changed for the Better at Historically Turbulent Irving Paper Inc," *Plant*, 56, no. 17, (November 24, 1997), pp. 10-11.

35 "Common Characteristics of Successful Companies," *Manitoba Business*, May 1996, pp. 25-29.

36 See D. Tannen, *You Just Don't Understand: Women and Men in Conversation* (New York: Ballantine Books, 1991); and D. Tannen, *Talking from 9 to 5* (New York: William Morrow, 1995).

37 R.E. Axtell, *Gestures: The Do's and Taboos of Body Language Around the World* (New York: Wiley, 1991).

38 See M. Munter, "Cross-Cultural Communication for Managers," *Business Horizons*, May-June 1993, pp. 75-76.

39 N. Adler, *International Dimensions of Organizational Behavior*, 2nd ed. (Boston: PWS-Kent, 1991), pp. 83-84.

40 See, for instance, R. Hotch, "Communication Revolution," *Nation's Business*, May 1993, pp. 20-28; G. Brockhouse, "I Have Seen the Future," *Canadian Business*, August 1993, pp. 43-45; R. Hotch, "In Touch Through Technology," *Nation's Business*, January 1994, pp. 33-35; and P. LaBarre, "The Other Network," *Industry Week*, September 19, 1994, pp. 33-36.

41 A. LaPlante, "TeleConfrontationing," *Forbes ASAP*, September 13, 1993, p. 117.

42 Based on B. Crosariol, "E-mail Nightmares," *Report on Business Magazine*, March 1996, pp. 41-42.

43 E. Church, "Employers Read E-mail as Fair Game," *The Globe and Mail*, April 14, 1998, p. B16.

44 E. Church, "Employers Read E-mail as Fair Game," *The Globe and Mail*, April 14, 1998, p. B16.

45 See, for example, R.S. Schuler, "A Role Perception Transactional Process Model for Organizational Communication-Outcome Relationships," *Organizational Behavior and Human Performance*, April 1979, pp. 268-91.

46 J.P. Walsh, S.J. Ashford, and T.E. Hill, "Feedback Obstruction: The Influence of the Information Environment on Employee Turnover Intentions," *Human Relations*, January 1985, pp. 23-46.

47 S.A. Hellweg and S.L. Phillips, "Communication and Productivity in Organizations: A State-of-the-Art Review," in *Proceedings of the 40th Annual Academy of Management Conference*, Detroit, 1980, pp. 188-92.

48 R.R. Reilly, B. Brown, M.R. Blood, and C.Z. Malatesta, "The Effects of Realistic Previews: A Study and Discussion of the Literature," *Personnel Psychology*, Winter 1981, pp. 823-34.

CHAPTER 10

1 Information for this opening vignette based on R. Herbut, "Buy a Light Bulb, Kill a Job," *Alberta Report*, June 23, 1997, p. 25; M. Franssen, "Body Shop is Proud Canadian Franchise Re: Canadian Retailers Are Not Inferior to US Competitors," *Financial Post*, February 11/13, 1995, pp. 27, 28; and P. Mitchell, "Did You Say Makeover?" *Herizons*, Spring 1997, p. 8.

2 S. Cordon, "Some Corporations Say They Have Duty to Give," *Canadian Press Newswire*, October 19, 1997.

3 See H.A. Simon, "Rationality in Psychology and Economics," *The Journal of Business*, October 1986, pp. 209-24; and A. Langley, "In Search of Rationality: The Purposes Behind the Use of Formal Analysis in Organizations," *Administrative Science Quarterly*, December 1989, pp. 598-631.

4 For a review of the rational model, see E.F. Harrison, *The Managerial Decision-Making Process*, 4th ed. (Boston: Houghton Mifflin, 1995), pp. 75-85.

5 W. Pounds, "The Process of Problem Finding," *Industrial Management Review*, Fall 1969, pp. 1-19.

6 J.G. March, *A Primer on Decision Making* (New York: Free Press, 1994), pp. 2-7.

[7] D.L. Rados, "Selection and Evaluation of Alternatives in Repetitive Decision Making," *Administrative Science Quarterly*, June 1972, pp. 196-206.

[8] M. Bazerman, *Judgment in Managerial Decision Making*, 3rd ed. (New York: Wiley, 1994), p. 5.

[9] See H.A. Simon, *Administrative Behavior*, 3rd ed. (New York: Free Press, 1976); and J. Forester, "Bounded Rationality and the Politics of Muddling Through," *Public Administration Review*, January-February 1984, pp. 23-31.

[10] W.H. Agor, "The Logic of Intuition: How Top Executives Make Important Decisions," *Organizational Dynamics*, Winter 1986, p. 5; W.H. Agor (ed.), *Intuition in Organizations* (Newbury Park, CA: Sage Publications, 1989); O. Behling and N.L. Eckel, "Making Sense Out of Intuition," *Academy of Management Executive*, February 1991, pp. 46-47; and V. Johnson, "Intuition in Decision-Making," *Successful Meetings*, February 1993, pp. 148-51.

[11] O. Behling and N.L. Eckel, "Making Sense Out of Intuition," *Academy of Management Executive*, February 1991, pp. 46-54.

[12] As described in H.A. Simon, "Making Management Decisions: The Role of Intuition and Emotion," *Academy of Management Executive*, February 1987, pp. 59-60.

[13] W.H. Agor, "The Logic of Intuition: How Top Executives Make Important Decisions," *Organizational Dynamics*, Winter 1986," p. 9.

[14] W.H. Agor, "The Logic of Intuition: How Top Executives Make Important Decisions," *Organizational Dynamics*, Winter 1986," p. 15.

[15] See, for example, M.D. Cohen, J.G. March, and J.P. Olsen, "A Garbage Can Model of Organizational Choice," *Administrative Science Quarterly*, March 1972, pp 1-25.

[16] See J.G. Thompson, *Organizations in Action* (New York: McGraw-Hill, 1967), p. 123.

[17] C.E. Lindholm, "The Science of 'Muddling Through,'" *Public Administration Review*, Spring 1959, pp. 79-88.

[18] A. Tversky and K. Kahneman, "Judgment Under Uncertainty: Heuristics and Biases," *Science*, September 1974, pp. 1124-31.

[19] K. McKean, "Decisions, Decisions," *Discover*, June, 1985, pp. 22-31.

[21] See B.M. Staw, "The Escalation of Commitment to a Course of Action," *Academy of Management Review*, October 1981, pp. 577-87; and D.R. Bobocei and J.P. Meyer, "Escalating Commitment to a Failing Course of Action: Separating the Roles of Choice and Justification," *Journal of Applied Psychology*, June 1994, pp. 360-63.

[22] A.J. Rowe, J.D. Boulgarides, and M.R. McGrath, *Managerial Decision Making*, Modules in Management Series (Chicago: SRA, 1984), pp. 18-22.

[23] S.N. Chakravarty and A. Feldman, "The Road Not Taken," *Forbes*, August 30, 1993, pp. 40-41.

[24] A. Wildavsky, *The Politics of the Budgetary Process* (Boston: Little Brown & Co., 1964).

[25] N.J. Adler, *International Dimensions of Organizational Behavior*, 2nd ed. (Boston: Kent Publishing, 1991), pp. 160-68.

[26] See N.R.F. Maier, "Assets and Liabilities in Group Problem Solving: The Need for an Integrative Function," *Psychological Review*, April 1967, pp. 239-49; G.W. Hill, "Group versus Individual Performance: Are N+1 Heads Better Than One?" *Psychological Bulletin*, May 1982, pp. 517-39; and A.E. Schwartz and J. Levin, "Better Group Decision Making," *Supervisory Management*, June 1990, p. 4.

[27] See, for example, R.A. Cooke and J.A. Kernaghan, "Estimating the Difference Between Group versus Individual Performance on Problem-Solving Tasks," *Group & Organization Studies*, September 1987, pp. 319-42; and L.K. Michaelsen, W.E. Watson, and R.H. Black, "A Realistic Test of Individual versus Group Consensus Decision Making," *Journal of Applied Psychology*, October 1989, pp. 834-39.

[28] See, for example, W.C. Swap and Associates, *Group Decision Making* (Newbury Park, CA: Sage, 1984).

[29] I.L. Janis, *Groupthink* (Boston: Houghton Mifflin, 1982); and C.P. Neck and G. Moorhead, "Groupthink Remodeled: The Importance of Leadership, Time Pressure, and Methodical Decision-Making Procedures," *Human Relations*, May 1995, pp. 537-58.

[30] I.L. Janis, *Groupthink* (Boston: Houghton Mifflin, 1982).

[31] C.R. Leana, "A Partial Test of Janis' Groupthink Model: Effects of Group Cohesiveness and Leader Behavior on Defective Decision Making," *Journal of Management*, Spring 1985, pp. 5-17; and G. Moorhead and J.R. Montanari, "An Empirical Investigation of the Groupthink Phenomenon," *Human Relations*, May 1986, pp. 399-410.

[32] S. Silcoff, "The Sky's Your Limit," *Canadian Business*, 70, no. 4, (April 1997), pp. 58-66.

[33] See D.J. Isenberg, "Group Polarization: A Critical Review and Meta-Analysis," *Journal of Personality and Social Psychology*, December 1986, pp. 1141-51; J.L. Hale and F.J. Boster, "Comparing Effect Coded Models of Choice Shifts," *Communication Research Reports*, April 1988, pp. 180-86; and P.W. Paese, M. Bieser, and M.E. Tubbs, "Framing Effects and Choice Shifts in Group Decision Making," *Organizational Behavior and Human Decision Processes*, October 1993, pp. 149-65.

[34] See, for example, N. Kogan and M.A. Wallach, "Risk Taking as a Function of the Situation, the Person, and the Group," in *New Directions in Psychology* 3 (New York: Holt, Rinehart and Winston, 1967); and M.A. Wallach, N. Kogan, and D.J. Bem, "Group Influence on Individual Risk Taking," *Journal of Abnormal and Social Psychology* 65 (1962), pp. 75-86.

[35] R.D. Clark III, "Group-Induced Shift Toward Risk: A Critical Appraisal," *Psychological Bulletin*, October 1971, pp. 251-70.

[36] A.F. Osborn, *Applied Imagination: Principles and Procedures of Creative Thinking* (New York: Scribner's, 1941). See also P.B. Paulus, M.T. Dzindolet, G. Poletes, and L.M. Camacho, "Perception of Performance in Group Brainstorming: The Illusion of Group Productivity," *Personality and Social Psychology Bulletin*, February 1993, pp. 78-89.

[37] Based on information in Kevin Steel, "Wrapping the World in a Tortilla: The Successor to Bagel Barns and Sub Shops, Coming to a Strip Mall Near You," *Alberta Report*, January 12, 1998, p. 25.

[38] I. Edwards, "Office Intrigue: By Design, Consultants Have Workers Conspire to Create Business Environments Tailored to Getting the Job Done," *Financial Post Daily*, December 16, 1997, p. 25.

39 T. Graham, "The Keys to the Middle Kingdom: Experts Will Tell You It Takes Years of Patient Effort to Crack the Chinese Market, But That's Not Always the Case," *Profit: The Magazine for Canadian Entrepreneurs*, December 1997/January 1998, p. 29.

40 See A.L. Delbecq, A.H. Van deVen, and D.H. Gustafson, *Group Techniques for Program Planning: A Guide to Nominal and Delphi Processes* (Glenview, IL: Scott, Foresman, 1975); and W.M. Fox, "Anonymity and Other Keys to Successful Problem-Solving Meetings," *National Productivity Review*, Spring 1989, pp. 145-56.

41 See, for instance, A.R. Dennis and J.S. Valacich, "Computer Brainstorms: More Heads Are Better Than One," *Journal of Applied Psychology*, August 1993, pp. 531-37; R.B. Gallupe and W.H. Cooper, "Brainstorming Electronically," *Sloan Management Review*, Fall 1993, pp. 27-36; and R.B. Gallupe, W.H. Cooper, M-L. Grise, and L.M. Bastianutti, "Blocking Electronic Brainstorms," *Journal of Applied Psychology*, February 1994, pp. 77-86.

45 "Theatrics in the Boardroom: Acting Classes Are Not Widely Accepted as Management Tools," *Financial Post*, March 4/6, 1995, pp. 24-25.

46 K. Brooks and P. Thompson, "A Creative Approach to Strategic Planning," *CMA Management Accounting Magazine*, July/August 1997, pp. 20-22.

47 T.M. Amabile, "A Model of Creativity and Innovation in Organizations," in B.M. Staw, and L.L. Cummings (eds.) *Research in Organizational Behavior*, 10, 1988, p. 123-167. Greenwich, CT: JAI Press.

48 T.M. Amabile, *The Social Psychology of Creativity*, New York: Springer-Verlag,1983; T.M. Amabile, "A Model of Creativity and Innovation in Organizations," in B.M. Staw, and L.L. Cummings (eds.) *Research in Organizational Behavior*, 10, 1988, p. 123-167 (Greenwich, CT: JAI Press); C.E. Shalley, "Effects of Productivity Goals, Creativity Goals, and Personal Discretion on Individual Creativity," *Journal of Applied Psychology*, 76, 1991, pp. 179-185; R.W. Woodman, J.E. Sawyer, and R.W. Griffin, "Toward a Theory of Organizational Creativity," *Academy of Management Review*, 18, 1993, pp. 293-321; G. Zaltman, R. Duncan and J. Holbek, *Innovation and Organizations* (London: Wiley, 1973).

49 G.R. Oldham and A. Cummings, "Employee Creativity: Personal and Contextual Factors at Work," *Academy of Management Journal*, 39, 1996, pp. 607-634.

50 F.B. Barron and D.M. Harrington, "Creativity, Intelligence, and Personality," *Annual Review of Psychology*, 32, 1981, pp. 439-476; G.A. Davis, "Testing for Creative Potential," *Contemporary Educational Psychology*, 14, 1989, pp. 257-274; C. Martindale, "Personality, Situation, and Creativity," in J.A. Glover, R.R. Ronning, and C.R. Reynolds, eds., *Handbook of Creativity* (New York: Plenum, 1989), pp. 211-232.

51 G.R. Oldham and A. Cummings, "Employee Creativity: Personal and Contextual Factors at Work," *Academy of Management Journal*, 39, 1996, pp. 607-634; see also F.B. Barron and D.M. Harrington, "Creativity, Intelligence, and Personality," *Annual Review of Psychology*, 32, 1981, pp. 439-476; H.G. Gough, "A Creative Personality Scale for the Adjective Check List," *Journal of Personality and Social Psychology*, 37, 1979, pp. 1398-1405; C. Martindale, "Personality, Situation, and Creativity," in J.A. Glover, R.R. Ronning, and C.R. Reynolds, eds., *Handbook of Creativity* (New York: Plenum, 1989), pp. 211-232.

52 G. R. Oldham and A. Cummings, "Employee Creativity: Personal and Contextual Factors at Work," *Academy of Management Journal*, 39, 1996, pp. 607-634.

53 T.M. Amabile, "A Model of Creativity and Innovation in Organizations," in B.M. Staw and L.L. Cummings (eds.), *Research in Organizational Behavior*, vol. 10 (Greenwich, CT: JAI Press, 1988), p. 126.

54 Cited in C.G. Morris, *Psychology: An Introduction*, 9th ed. (Upper Saddle River, NJ: Prentice Hall, 1996), p. 344.

55 E. DeBono, *Six Thinking Hats* (Boston: Little, Brown & Company, 1985), and E. DeBono, *The Mechanism of Mind* (New York: Simon and Schuster, 1969).

56 K. Brooks and P. Thompson, "A Creative Approach to Strategic Planning," *CMA Management Accounting Magazine*, July/August 1997, pp. 20-22.

57 Adapted from E. DeBono, *Six Thinking Hats* (Boston: Little, Brown & Company, 1985).

58 K. Brooks and P. Thompson, "A Creative Approach to Strategic Planning," *CMA Management Accounting Magazine*, July/August 1997, pp. 20-22.

59 M.A. Colgrove, "Stimulating Creative Problem Solving: Innovative Set," *Psychological Reports* 22, 1968, pp. 1205-11.

60 See M. Stein, *Stimulating Creativity*, vol. 1 (New York: Academic Press, 1974).

61 E. DeBono, *Lateral Thinking: Creativity Step by Step* (New York: Harper & Row, 1971).

62 W.J.J. Gordon, *Synectics* (New York: Harper & Row, 1961).

63 Information in this section is based on T. Stevens, "Creativity Killers," *Industry Week*, January 23, 1995, p. 63.

64 G.F. Cavanagh, D.J. Moberg, and M. Valasquez, "The Ethics of Organizational Politics," *Academy of Management Journal*, June 1981, pp. 363-74.

65 See, for example, T. Machan, ed., *Commerce and Morality* (Totowa, NJ: Rowman and Littlefield, 1988).

66 L.K. Trevino, "Ethical Decision Making in Organizations: A Person-Situation Interactionist Model," *Academy of Management Review*, July 1986, pp. 601-17; and L.K. Trevino and S.A. Youngblood, "Bad Apples in Bad Barrels: A Causal Analysis of Ethical Decision-Making Behavior," *Journal of Applied Psychology*, August 1990, pp. 378-85.

67 See L. Kohlberg, *Essays in Moral Development: The Philosophy of Moral Development*, vol. 1 (New York: Harper & Row, 1981); L. Kohlberg, *Essays in Moral Development: The Psychology of Moral Development*, vol. 2 (New York: Harper & Row, 1984); and R.S. Snell, "Complementing Kohlberg: Mapping the Ethical Reasoning Used by Managers for Their Own Dilemma Cases," *Human Relations*, January 1996, pp. 23-50.

69 D. Todd, "Business Responds to Ethics Explosion," *Vancouver Sun*, April 27, 1998, pp. A1, A7.

70 D. Todd, "Business Responds to Ethics Explosion," *Vancouver Sun*, April 27, 1998, p. A7.

71 D. Flavelle, "Business Leaders Must Be 'Socially Responsible,'" *Vancouver Sun*, September 30, 1997, p. D4.

72 M. Friedman, *Capitalism and Freedom* (Chicago: University of Chicago Press, 1962).

73 R. Walker and S. Flanagan, "The Ethical Imperative: If You Don't Talk About a Wider Range of Values, You May Not Have a Bottom Line," *Financial Post 500*, 1997, pp. 28-36.

74 R. Walker and S. Flanagan, "The Ethical Imperative: If You Don't Talk About a Wider Range of Values, You May Not Have a Bottom Line," *Financial Post 500*, 1997, pp. 28-36.

75 R. Walker and S. Flanagan, "The Ethical Imperative: If You Don't Talk About a Wider Range of Values, You May Not Have a Bottom Line," *Financial Post 500*, 1997, pp. 28-36.

76 W. Chow Hou, "To Bribe or Not to Bribe?" *Asia, Inc.,* October 1996, p. 104.

77 T. Donaldson, "Values in Tension: Ethics Away From Home," *Harvard Business Review*, September-October 1996, pp. 48-62.

78 P. Digh, "Shades of Gray in the Global Marketplace," *HR Magazine*, April 1997, pp. 91-98.

79 A. Swift, "Executives Warned to Stay Clean: Bata Leaves Corrupt Nigeria," *Canadian Press Newswire*, October 7, 1997.

80 A. Gillis, "How Can You Do Business In A Country Where Crooked Cops Will Kill You For A Song?" *Report on Business Magazine*, March 1998, pp. 59-68.

81 A. Gillis, "How Can You Do Business In A Country Where Crooked Cops Will Kill You For A Song?" *Report on Business Magazine*, March 1998, p. 60.

82 A. Gillis, "How Can You Do Business In A Country Where Crooked Cops Will Kill You For A Song?" *Report on Business Magazine*, March 1998, p. 60.

83 A. Gillis, "How Can You Do Business In A Country Where Crooked Cops Will Kill You For A Song?" *Report on Business Magazine*, March 1998, p. 64.

84 A. Gillis, "How Can You Do Business In A Country Where Crooked Cops Will Kill You For A Song?" *Report on Business Magazine*, March 1998, p. 66.

85 A. Gillis, "How Can You Do Business In A Country Where Crooked Cops Will Kill You For A Song?" *Report on Business Magazine*, March 1998, p. 66.

CHAPTER 11

1 Based on "Jobs Does the Job on Apple," *Financial Post Daily*, March 12, 1998, p. 18; "Apple is Exciting Again, says Jobs," *Financial Post*, October 4/6, 1997, p. 14; "Amelio Resigns from Apple," *Financial Post Daily*, July 10, 1997, p. 5.

2 J. Carlton, *Apple: The Inside Story of Intrigue, Egomania & Business Blunders* (New York: Random House, 1998).

3 R.M. Stogdill, *Handbook of Leadership: A Survey of the Literature* (New York: Free Press, 1974), p. 259.

4 For a review of the controversies, see G. Yukl, "Managerial Leadership: A Review of Theory and Research," *Journal of Management*, June 1989, pp. 252-53.

5 A. Zaleznik, "Excerpts from 'Managers and Leaders: Are They Different'?" *Harvard Business Review*, May-June 1986, p. 54.

6 J.P. Kotter, "What Leaders Really Do," *Harvard Business Review*, May-June 1990, pp. 103-11; and J.P. Kotter, *A Force for Change: How Leadership Differs From Management* (New York: Free Press, 1990).

7 A. Bryman, "Leadership in Organizations," in *Handbook of Organization Studies,* edited by Stewart R. Clegg, Cynthia Hardy and W. R. Nord (London: Sage Publications, 1996), pp. 276-292.

8 See, for instance, R.G. Lord, C.L. DeVader and G.M. Alliger, "A Meta-analysis of the Relation Between Personality Traits and Leadership Perceptions: An Application of Validity Generalization Procedures," *Journal of Applied Psychology*, 71, pp. 402-410; R.G. Lord and K.J. Maher, *Leadership and Information Processing: Linking Perceptions and Performance* (Cambridge, MA: Unwin Hyman, 1991); E.A. Locke and Associates, *The Essence of Leadership: The Four Keys to Leading Successfully* (New York: Lexington, 1991); and R.J. House, W.D. Spangler and J. Woycke, "Personality and Charisma in the U.S. Presidency: A Psychological Theory of Leader Effectiveness," *Administrative Science Quarterly*, 36, 1991, pp. 364-396.

9 J.G. Geier, "A Trait Approach to the Study of Leadership in Small Groups," *Journal of Communication,* December 1967, pp. 316-23.

10 A. Bryman, "Leadership in Organizations," in *Handbook of Organization Studies,* edited by Stewart R. Clegg, Cynthia Hardy and W. R. Nord, (London: Sage Publications, 1996), pp. 277.

11 S.A. Kirkpatrick and E.A. Locke, "Leadership: Do Traits Matter?" *Academy of Management Executive,* May 1991, pp. 48-60.

12 G.H. Dobbins. W.S. Long, E.J. Dedrick, and T.C. Clemons, "The Role of Self-Monitoring and Gender on Leader Emergence: A Laboratory and Field Study," *Journal of Management,* September 1990, pp. 609-18; and S.J. Zaccaro, R.J. Foti, and D.A. Kenny, "Self-Monitoring and Trait-Based Variance in Leadership: An Investigation of Leader Flexibility Across Multiple Group Situations," *Journal of Applied Psychology,* April 1991, pp. 308-15.

13 G. Yukl and D.D. Van Fleet, "Theory and Research on Leadership in Organizations," in M.D. Dunnette and L.M. Hough (eds.), *Handbook of Industrial & Organizational Psychology,* 2nd ed., vol. 3 (Palo Alto, CA: Consulting Psychologists Press, 1992), p. 150.

14 A. Bryman, "Leadership in Organizations," in *Handbook of Organization Studies* edited by S. R. Clegg, C. Hardy and W. R. Nord, London: Sage Publications, 1996, pp. 277-278. For an example of this approach see R.G. Lord and K.J. Maher, *Leadership and Information Processing: Linking Perceptions and Performance* (Cambridge, MA: Unwin Hyman, 1991).

15 See, for instance, J.C. McElroy, "A Typology of Attribution Leadership Research," *Academy of Management Review,* July 1982, pp. 413-17; J.R. Meindl and S.B. Ehrlich, "The Romance of Leadership and the Evaluation of Organizational Performance," *Academy of Management Journal,* March 1987, pp. 91-109; J.C. McElroy and J.D. Hunger, "Leadership Theory as Causal Attribution of Performance," in J.G. Hunt, B.R. Baliga, H.P. Dachler, and C.A. Schriesheim (eds.), *Emerging Leadership Vistas* (Lexington, MA: Lexington Books, 1988); B. Shamir, "Attribution of Influence and Charisma to the Leader: The Romance of Leadership Revisited," *Journal of Applied Social Psychology,* March 1992, pp. 386-407; and J.R. Meindl, "The Romance of Leadership as a Follower-Centric Theory: A Social Constructionist Approach," *Leadership Quarterly,* Fall 1995, pp. 329-41.

16 R.G. Lord, C.L. DeVader, and G.M. Alliger, "A Meta-Analysis of the Relation Between Personality Traits and Leadership Perceptions: An Application of Validity Generalization Procedures," *Journal of Applied Psychology,* 71, pp. 402-410.

[17] J.R. Meindl, S.B. Ehrlich, and J.M. Dukerich, "The Romance of Leadership," *Administrative Science Quarterly,* March 1985, pp. 78-102.

[18] J. Pfeffer, *Managing With Power* (Boston: Harvard Business School Press, 1992), p. 194; and M. Loeb, "An Interview with Warren Bennis: Where Leaders Come From," *Fortune,* September 19, 1994, p. 241.

[19] R.M. Stogdill and A.E. Coons (eds.), *Leader Behavior: Its Description and Measurement,* Research Monograph No. 88 (Columbus: Ohio State University, Bureau of Business Research, 1951). This research is updated in S. Kerr, C.A. Schriesheim, C.J. Murphy, and R.M. Stogdill, "Toward a Contingency Theory of Leadership Based upon the Consideration and Initiating Structure Literature," *Organizational Behavior and Human Performance,* August 1974, pp. 62-82; and C.A. Schriesheim, C.C. Cogliser, and L.L. Neider, "Is It 'Trustworthy'? A Multiple-Levels-of-Analysis Reexamination of an Ohio State Leadership Study, with Implications for Future Research," *Leadership Quarterly,* Summer 1995, pp. 111-45.

[20] R. Kahn and D. Katz, "Leadership Practices in Relation to Productivity and Morale," D. Cartwright and A. Zander (eds.), *Group Dynamics: Research and Theory,* 2nd ed. (Elmsford, NY: Row, Paterson, 1960).

[21] R.R. Blake and J.S. Mouton, *The Managerial Grid* (Houston: Gulf, 1964).

[22] See, for example, R.R. Blake and J.S. Mouton, "A Comparative Analysis of Situationalism and 9,9 Management by Principle," *Organizational Dynamics,* Spring 1982, pp. 20-43.

[23] See, for example, L.L. Larson, J.G. Hunt, and R.N. Osborn, "The Great Hi-Hi Leader Behavior Myth: A Lesson from Occam's Razor," *Academy of Management Journal,* December 1976, pp. 628-41; and P.C. Nystrom, "Managers and the Hi-Hi Leader Myth," *Academy of Management Journal,* June 1978, pp. 325-31.

[24] See, for instance, P.M. Podsakoff, S.B. MacKenzie, M. Ahearne, and W.H. Bommer, "Searching for a Needle in a Haystack: Trying to Identify the Illusive Moderators of Leadership Behavior," *Journal of Management,* 1, no. 3, 1995, pp. 422-70.

[25] For controversy surrounding the Fiedler LPC scale see Alan Bryman, "Leadership in Organizations," in *Handbook of Organization Studies,* edited by S. R. Clegg, C. Hardy and W. R. Nord (London: Sage Publications, 1996), pp. 279-280; A. Bryman, *Leadership and Organizations* (London: Routledge & Kegan Paul, 1986); and T. Peters and N. Austin, *A Passion for Excellence* (New York: Random House, 1985). For supportive evidence on the Fiedler model, see L.H. Peters, D.D. Hartke, and J.T. Pohlmann, "Fiedler's Contingency Theory of Leadership: An Application of the Meta-Analysis Procedures of Schmidt and Hunter," *Psychological Bulletin,* March 1985, pp. 274-85; C.A. Schriesheim, B.J. Tepper, and L.A. Tetrault, "Least Preferred Co-Worker Score, Situational Control, and Leadership Effectiveness: A Meta-Analysis of Contingency Model Performance Predictions," *Journal of Applied Psychology,* August 1994, pp. 561-73; and R. Ayman, M.M. Chemers, and F. Fiedler, "The Contingency Model of Leadership Effectiveness: Its Levels of Analysis," *Leadership Quarterly,* Summer 1995, pp. 147-67; for evidence that LPC scores are not stable, see for instance, R.W. Rice, "Psychometric Properties of the Esteem for the Least Preferred Coworker (LPC) Scale," *Academy of*

Management Review, January 1978, pp. 106-18; C.A. Schriesheim, B.D. Bannister, and W.H. Money, "Psychometric Properties of the LPC Scale: An Extension of Rice's Review," *Academy of Management Review,* April 1979, pp. 287-90; and J.K. Kennedy, J.M. Houston, M.A. Korgaard, and D.D. Gallo, "Construct Space of the Least Preferred Co-Worker (LPC) Scale," *Educational & Psychological Measurement,* Fall 1987, pp. 807-14; for difficulty in applying Fiedler's model see E.H. Schein, *Organizational Psychology,* 3rd ed. (Englewood Cliffs, NJ: Prentice Hall, 1980), pp. 116-17; and B. Kabanoff, "A Critique of Leader Match and Its Implications for Leadership Research," *Personnel Psychology,* Winter 1981, pp. 749-64. For evidence that Hersey and Blanchard's model have received little attention from researchers, see R.K. Hambleton and R. Gumpert, "The Validity of Hersey and Blanchard's Theory of Leader Effectiveness," *Group & Organizational Studies,* June 1982, pp. 225-42; C.L. Graeff, "The Situational Leadership Theory: A Critical View," *Academy of Management Review,* April 1983, pp. 285-91; R.P. Vecchio, "Situational Leadership Theory: An Examination of a Prescriptive Theory," *Journal of Applied Psychology,* August 1987, pp. 444-51; J.R. Goodson, G.W. McGee, and J.F. Cashman, "Situational Leadership Theory: A Test of Leadership Prescriptions," *Group & Organization Studies,* December 1989, pp. 446-61; W. Blank, J.R. Weitzel, and S.G. Green, "A Test of the Situational Leadership Theory," *Personnel Psychology,* Autumn 1990, pp. 579-97; and W.R. Norris and R.P. Vecchio, "Situational Leadership Theory: A Replication," *Group & Organization Management,* September 1992, pp. 331-42; for evidence of partial support for the theory see R.P. Vecchio, "Situational Leadership Theory: An Examination of a Prescriptive Theory," *Journal of Applied Psychology,* August 1987, pp. 444-51; and W.R. Norris and R.P. Vecchio, "Situational Leadership Theory: A Replication," *Group & Organization Management,* September 1992, pp. 331-42; and for evidence of no support for Hersey and Blanchard see W. Blank, J.R. Weitzel, and S.G. Green, "A Test of the Situational Leadership Theory," *Personnel Psychology,* Autumn 1990, pp. 579-97. For support for the leader-member exchange theory, see, for example, G. Graen, M. Novak, and P. Sommerkamp, "The Effects of Leader-Member Exchange"; T. Scandura and G. Graen, "Moderating Effects of Initial Leader-Member Exchange Status on the Effects of a Leadership Intervention," *Journal of Applied Psychology,* August 1984, pp. 428-36; R.P. Vecchio and B.C. Gobdel, "The Vertical Dyad Linkage Model of Leadership: Problems and Prospects," *Organizational Behavior and Human Performance,* August 1984, pp. 5-20; T.M. Dockery and D.D. Steiner, "The Role of the Initial Interaction in Leader-Member Exchange," *Group and Organization Studies,* December 1990, pp. 395-413; G.B. Graen and M. Uhl-Bien, "Relationship-Based Approach to Leadership: Development of Leader-Member Exchange (LMX) Theory of Leadership Over 25 Years: Applying a Multi-Level Multi-Domain Perspective," *Leadership Quarterly,* Summer 1995, pp. 219-47; and R.P. Settoon, N. Bennett, R.C. Liden, "Social Exchange in Organizations: Perceived Organizational Support, Leader-Member Exchange, and Employee Reciprocity," *Journal of Applied Psychology,* June 1996, pp. 219-27; and A. Jago, "Leadership: Perspectives in Theory and Research," *Management Science,* March 1982, p. 331.

[26] R.J. House, "A Path-Goal Theory of Leader Effectiveness," *Administrative Science Quarterly,* September 1971, pp. 321-38; R.J. House and T.R. Mitchell, "Path-Goal Theory of Leadership," *Journal of Contemporary Business,* Autumn

1974, p. 86; and R.J. House, "Retrospective Comment," in L.E. Boone and D.D. Bowen (eds.), *The Great Writings in Management and Organizational Behavior,* 2nd ed. (New York: Random House, 1987), pp. 354-64.

27 See J. Indik, "Path-Goal Theory of Leadership: A Meta-Analysis," paper presented at the National Academy of Management Conference, Chicago, August 1986; R.T. Keller, "A Test of the Path-Goal Theory of Leadership with Need for Clarity as a Moderator in Research and Development Organizations," *Journal of Applied Psychology,* April 1989, pp. 208-12; and J.C. Wofford and L.Z. Liska, "Path-Goal Theories of Leadership: A Meta-Analysis," *Journal of Management,* Winter 1993, pp. 857-76.

28 See M.G. Evans, "R.J. House's 'A Path-Goal Theory of Leader Effectiveness,'" *Leadership Quarterly,* Fall 1996, pp. 305-09; and C.A. Schriesheim and L.L. Neider, "Path-Goal Leadership Theory: The Long and Winding Road," *Leadership Quarterly,* Fall 1996, pp. 317-21.

29 G.H. Dobbins. W.S. Long, E.J. Dedrick, and T.C. Clemons, "The Role of Self-Monitoring and Gender on Leader Emergence: A Laboratory and Field Study," *Journal of Management,* September 1990, pp. 609-18; and S.J. Zaccaro, R.J. Foti, and D.A. Kenny, "Self-Monitoring and Trait-Based Variance in Leadership: An Investigation of Leader Flexibility Across Multiple Group Situations," *Journal of Applied Psychology,* April 1991, pp. 308-15.

30 Information about Fleming and the TSE based on Karen Howlett, "Tense Times at TSE as Leadership Questioned," *The Globe and Mail,* May 2, 1998, pp. B1, B4.

31 S. Gordon, "Trading Places, *The Financial Post Magazine,* October 1997, pp. 42-49.

32 S. Kerr and J.M. Jermier, "Substitutes for Leadership: Their Meaning and Measurement," *Organizational Behavior and Human Performance,* December 1978, pp. 375-403; J.P. Howell and P.W. Dorfman, "Substitutes for Leadership: Test of a Construct," *Academy of Management Journal,* December 1981, pp. 714-28; J.P. Howell, P.W. Dorfman, and S. Kerr, "Leadership and Substitutes for Leadership," *Journal of Applied Behavioral Science,* 22, no. 1, (1986), pp. 29-46; J.P. Howell, D.E. Bowen, P.W. Dorfman, S. Kerr, and P.M. Podsakoff, "Substitutes for Leadership: Effective Alternatives to Ineffective Leadership," *Organizational Dynamics,* Summer 1990, pp. 21-38; P.M. Podsakoff, B.P. Niehoff, S.B. MacKenzie, and M.L. Williams, "Do Substitutes for Leadership Really Substitute for Leadership? An Empirical Examination of Kerr and Jermier's Situational Leadership Model," *Organizational Behavior and Human Decision Processes,* February 1993, pp. 1-44; P.M. Podsakoff and S.B. MacKenzie, "An Examination of Substitutes for Leadership Within a Levels-of-Analysis Framework," *Leadership Quarterly,* Fall 1995, pp. 289-328; P.M. Podsakoff, S.B. MacKenzie, and W.H. Bommer, "Transformational Leader Behaviors and Substitutes for Leadership as Determinants of Employee Satisfaction, Commitment, Trust, and Organizational Citizenship Behaviors," *Journal of Management,* 22, no. 2, (1996), pp. 259-98; and P.M. Podsakoff, S.B. MacKenzie, and W.H. Bommer, "Meta-Analysis of the Relationships Between Kerr and Jermier's Substitutes for Leadership and Employee Attitudes, Role Perceptions, and Performance," *Journal of Applied Psychology,* August 1996, pp. 380-99.

33 B. Karmel, "Leadership: A Challenge to Traditional Research Methods and Assumptions," *Academy of Management Review,* July 1978, pp. 477-79.

34 See L.R. Anderson, "Toward a Two-Track Model of Leadership Training: Suggestions from Self-Monitoring Theory," *Small Group Research,* May 1990, pp. 147-67.

35 A. Bryman, "Leadership in Organizations," in *Handbook of Organization Studies* edited by Stewart R. Clegg, Cynthia Hardy and Walter R. Nord (London: Sage Publications, 1996), pp. 276-292.

36 J.A. Conger and R.N. Kanungo, "Behavioral Dimensions of Charismatic Leadership," in J.A. Conger, R.N. Kanungo and Associates, *Charismatic Leadership* (San Francisco: Jossey-Bass, 1988), p. 79.

37 J. M. Howell and P. J. Frost, "A Laboratory Study of Charismatic Leadership," *Organizational Behavior & Human Decision Processes,* 43, no. 2, (April 1989), pp. 243-269.

38 "Building a Better Boss," *Maclean's,* September 30, 1996, p. 41.

39 R.J. House, "A 1976 Theory of Charismatic Leadership," in J.G. Hunt and L.L. Larson (eds.), *Leadership: The Cutting Edge* (Carbondale: Southern Illinois University Press, 1977), pp. 189-207.

40 "Building a Better Boss," *Maclean's,* September 30, 1996, p. 41.

41 W. Bennis, "The Four Competencies of Leadership," *Training and Development Journal,* August 1984, pp. 15-19.

42 J.A. Conger and R.N. Kanungo, "Behavioral Dimensions of Charismatic Leadership," in J.A. Conger, R.N. Kanungo and Associates, *Charismatic Leadership* (San Francisco: Jossey-Bass, 1988), pp. 78-97. See also J.A. Conger and R.N. Kanungo, "Perceived Benavioral Attributes of Charismatic Leadership," *Canadian Journal of Behavioural Science,* 24, 1992, pp. 86-102, J.A. Conger and R.N. Kanungo, "Charismatic Leadership in Organizations: Perceived Behavioral Attributes and Their Measurement," *Journal of Organizational Behavior,* 15, 1994, pp. 439-452, and J.A. Conger, R.N. Kanungo, S.T. Menon, and P. Mathur, "Measuring Charisma: Dimensionality and Validity of the Conger-Kanungo Scale of Charismatic Leadership," *Canadian Journal of Administrative Sciences,* 14, 1997, pp. 290-302.

43 B. Shamir, R.J. House, and M.B. Arthur, "The Motivational Effects of Charismatic Leadership: A Self-Concept Theory," *Organization Science,* November 1993, pp. 577-94.

44 R.J. House, J. Woycke, and E.M. Fodor, "Charismatic and Noncharismatic Leaders: Differences in Behavior and Effectiveness," in Conger and Kanungo, *Charismatic Leadership,* pp. 103-04; D.A. Waldman, B.M. Bass, and F.J. Yammarino, "Adding to Contingent-Reward Behavior: The Augmenting Effect of Charismatic Leadership," *Group & Organization Studies,* December 1990, pp. 381-94; and S.A. Kirkpatrick and E.A. Locke, "Direct and Indirect Effects of Three Core Charismatic Leadership Components on Performance and Attitudes," *Journal of Applied Psychology,* February 1996, pp. 36-51.

45 "Building a Better Boss," *Maclean's,* September 30, 1996, p. 41.

46 J.A. Conger and R.N. Kanungo, "Training Charismatic Leadership: A Risky and Critical Task," in Conger and Kanungo, *Charismatic Leadership,* pp. 309-23.

47 R.J. Richardson and S.K. Thayer, *The Charisma Factor: How to Develop Your Natural Leadership Ability* (Englewood Cliffs, NJ: Prentice Hall, 1993).

[48] J.M. Howell and P.J. Frost, "A Laboratory Study of Charismatic Leadership," *Organizational Behavior and Human Decision Processes,* April 1989, pp. 243-69.

[49] R.J. House, "A 1976 Theory of Charismatic Leadership," in J.G. Hunt and L.L. Larson (eds.), *Leadership: The Cutting Edge* (Carbondale: Southern Illinois University Press, 1977), pp. 189-207.

[50] "Corporate Cults," *Financial Post Magazine,* November, 1993, pp. 118-123.

[51] "Corporate Cults," *Financial Post Magazine,* November 1993, pp. 118-123.

[52] "Corporate Cults," *Financial Post Magazine,* November 1993, pp. 118-123.

[53] J.A. Conger, *The Charismatic Leader: Behind the Mystique of Exceptional Leadership* (San Francisco: Jossey-Bass, 1989); R. Hogan, R. Raskin, and D. Fazzini, "The Dark Side of Charisma" in K.E. Clark and M.B. Clark (eds.), *Measures of Leadership* (West Orange, NJ: Leadership Library of America, 1990); D. Sankowsky, "The Charismatic Leader as Narcissist: Understanding the Abuse of Power," *Organizational Dynamics,* Spring 1995, pp. 57-71; and J. O'Connor, M.D. Mumford, T.C. Clifton, T.L. Gessner, and M.S. Connelly, "Charismatic Leaders and Destructiveness: An Historiometric Study," *Leadership Quarterly,* Winter 1995, pp. 529-55.

[54] See, for instance, J.M. Burns, *Leadership* (New York: Harper & Row, 1978); B.M. Bass, *Leadership and Performance Beyond Expectations* (New York: Free Press, 1985); B.M. Bass, "From Transactional to Transformational Leadership: Learning to Share the Vision," *Organizational Dynamics,* Winter 1990, pp. 19-31; F.J. Yammarino, W.D. Spangler, and B.M. Bass, "Transformational Leadership and Performance: A Longitudinal Investigation," *Leadership Quarterly,* Spring 1993, pp. 81-102; J.M. Howell and B.J. Avolio, "Transformational Leadership, Transactional Leadership, Locus of Control, and Support for Innovation: Key Predictors of Consolidated-Business-Unit Performance," *Journal of Applied Psychology,* December 1993, pp. 891-902 and J.M. Howell and B.J. Avolio, "The Leverage of Leadership," in Leadership: Achieving Exceptional Performance, A Special Supplement Prepared by the Richard Ivey School of Business, *The Globe and Mail,* May 15, 1998, pp. C1, C2.

[55] J.M. Howell and B.J. Avolio, "The Leverage of Leadership," in Leadership: Achieving Exceptional Performance, A Special Supplement Prepared by the Richard Ivey School of Business, *The Globe and Mail,* May 15, 1998, pp. C1, C2.

[56] J.M. Howell and B.J. Avolio, "The Leverage of Leadership," in Leadership: Achieving Exceptional Performance, A Special Supplement Prepared by the Richard Ivey School of Business, *The Globe and Mail,* May 15, 1998, pp. C1.

[57] J. Howell, B. Avolio and J. Sosik, "A Funny Thing Happened on the Way to the Bottom Line," in Leadership: Achieving Exceptional Performance, A Special Supplement Prepared by the Richard Ivey School of Business, *The Globe and Mail,* May 15, 1998, pp. C1, C2.

[58] B.M. Bass, "Leadership: Good, Better, Best," *Organizational Dynamics,* Winter 1985, pp. 26-40; and J. Seltzer and B.M. Bass, "Transformational Leadership: Beyond Initiation and Consideration," *Journal of Management,* December 1990, pp. 693-703.

[59] B.J. Avolio and B.M. Bass, "Transformational Leadership, Charisma and Beyond," working paper, School of Management, State University of New York, Binghamton, 1985, p. 14.

[60] Cited in B.M. Bass and B.J. Avolio, "Developing Transformational Leadership: 1992 and Beyond," *Journal of European Industrial Training,* January 1990, p. 23.

[61] J.J. Hater and B.M. Bass, "Supervisors' Evaluation and Subordinates' Perceptions of Transformational and Transactional Leadership," *Journal of Applied Psychology,* November 1988, pp. 695-702.

[62] J.M. Howell and B.J. Avolio, "The Leverage of Leadership," in *Leadership: Achieving Exceptional Performance,* A Special Supplement Prepared by the Richard Ivey School of Business, *The Globe and Mail,* May 15, 1998, pp. C2.

[63] B.M. Bass and B.J. Avolio, "Developing Transformational Leadership: 1992 and Beyond," *Journal of European Industrial Training,* January 1990, p. 23; and J.M. Howell and B.J. Avolio, "The Leverage of Leadership," in *Leadership: Achieving Exceptional Performance,* A Special Supplement Prepared by the Richard Ivey School of Business, *The Globe and Mail,* May 15, 1998, pp. C1, C2.

[64] J.M. Howell and B.J. Avolio, "The Leverage of Leadership," in *Leadership: Achieving Exceptional Performance,* A Special Supplement Prepared by the Richard Ivey School of Business, *The Globe and Mail,* May 15, 1998, p. C2.

[65] This definition is based on M. Sashkin, "The Visionary Leader," in J.A. Conger and R.N. Kanungo (eds.), *Charismatic Leadership,* pp. 124-25; B. Nanus, *Visionary Leadership* (New York: Free Press, 1992), p. 8; and N.H. Snyder and M. Graves, "Leadership and Vision," *Business Horizons,* January-February 1994, p. 1.

[66] B. Nanus, *Visionary Leadership* (New York: Free Press, 1992), p. 8.

[67] P.C. Nutt and R.W. Backoff, "Crafting Vision." A working paper. College of Business; Ohio State University; July 1995, p. 4.

[68] B. Nanus, *Visionary Leadership* (New York: Free Press, 1992), pp. 178-79.

[69] N.H. Snyder and M. Graves, "Leadership and Vision," *Business Horizons,* January-February 1994, p. 2.

[70] Cited in L.B. Korn, "How the Next CEO Will Be Different," *Fortune,* May 22, 1989, p. 157.

[71] J.C. Collins and J.I. Porras, *Built to Last: Successful Habits of Visionary Companies* (New York: HarperBusiness, 1994).

[72] P.C. Nutt and R.W. Backoff, "Crafting Vision," A working paper. College of Business; Ohio State University; July 1995, pp. 5-7.

[73] S. Van Houten, "Competing to Win: Canadian Companies Share Their Experiences Using the Alliance's Successful Compete to Win System," *Plant,* 56, no. 12, (September 1, 1997), p. 38.

[74] J. F. Shepard, "Renewing the Corporation," *Canadian Business Review* 23 no. 3, (1996), pp. 25-26.

[75] Cited in B. Nanus, *Visionary Leadership* (New York: Free Press, 1992), pp. 141, 173, 178; and P.C. Nutt and R.W. Backoff, "Crafting Vision," A working paper. College of Business; Ohio State University; July 1995, pp. 1 and 3.

[76] Based on M. Sashkin, "The Visionary Leader," in J.A. Conger and R.N. Kanungo (eds.), *Charismatic Leadership,* pp. 124-25 (New York: Free Press, 1992) pp. 128-30.

77 A. Bryman, "Leadership in Organizations," in *Handbook of Organization Studies* edited by S. R. Clegg, Cynthia Hardy and Walter R. Nord (London: Sage Publications, 1996), p. 283.

78 J.M. Kouzes and B.Z. Posner, *Credibility: How Leaders Gain and Lose It, Why People Demand It* (San Francisco: Jossey-Bass, 1993); C.C. Manz and H.P. Sims, "SuperLeadership: Beyond the Myth of Heroic Leadership," *Organizational Dynamics*, 19, 1991, pp. 18-35; and H.P. Sims and P. Lorenzi, *The New Leadership Paradigm* (Newbury Park: Sage, 1992).

79 C.C. Manz and H.P. Sims, "SuperLeadership: Beyond the Myth of Heroic Leadership," *Organizational Dynamics*, 19, 1991, pp. 18-35; H.P. Sims and P. Lorenzi, *The New Leadership Paradigm* (Newbury Park: Sage, 1992).

80 H.P. Sims and P. Lorenzi, *The New Leadership Paradigm*, (Newbury Park: Sage, 1992), p. 295.

81 See, for instance, M. Frohman, "Nothing Kills Teams Like Ill-Prepared Leaders," *Industry Week,* October 2, 1995, pp. 72-76.

82 See, for instance, M. Frohman, "Nothing Kills Teams Like Ill-Prepared Leaders," *Industry Week,* October 2, 1995, p. 93.

83 See, for instance, M. Frohman, "Nothing Kills Teams Like Ill-Prepared Leaders," *Industry Week,* October 2, 1995, p. 100.

84 J.R. Katzenbach, and D.K. Smith, *The Wisdom of Teams: Creating the High-Performance Organization* (Boston, MA: Harvard Business School, 1993).

85 N. Steckler and N. Fondas, "Building Team Leader Effectiveness: A Diagnostic Tool," *Organizational Dynamics,* Winter 1995, p. 20.

86 R.S. Wellins, W.C. Byham, and G.R. Dixon, *Inside Teams* (San Francisco: Jossey-Bass, 1994), p. 318.

87 N. Steckler and N. Fondas, "Building Team Leader Effectiveness: A Diagnostic Tool," *Organizational Dynamics,* Winter 1995, p. 21.

88 See W.W. Burke, "Leadership as Empowering Others," in S. Srivastva and Associates, *Executive Power* (San Francisco: Jossey-Bass, 1986); J.A. Conger and R.N. Kanungo, "The Empowerment Process: Integrating Theory and Practice," *Academy of Management Review,* July 1988, pp. 471-82; J. Greenwald, "Is Mr. Nice Guy Back?" *Time,* January 27, 1992, pp. 42-44; J. Weber, "Letting Go Is Hard to Do," *Business Week,* November 1, 1993, pp. 218-19; and L. Holpp, "Applied Empowerment," *Training,* February 1994, pp. 39-44.

89 See, for instance, D.A. Waldman, "A Theoretical Consideration of Leadership and Total Quality Management," *Leadership Quarterly,* Spring 1993, pp. 65-79.

90 For problems with empowerment, see J.A. Belasco and R.C. Stayer, "Why Empowerment Doesn't Empower: The Bankruptcy of Current Paradigms," *Business Horizons,* March-April 1994, pp. 29-40; L. Holpp, "If Empowerment Is So Good, Why Does It Hurt?" *Training,* March 1995, pp. 52-57; and M.M. Broadwell, "Why Command and Control Won't Go Away," *Training,* September 1995, pp. 63-68.

91 Information in this paragraph based on Jennifer Wells, "Stuck on the Ladder: Not Only is the Glass Ceiling Still in Place, But Men and Women Have Very Different Views of the Problem," *Maclean's,* October 20, 1997, p. 60.

92 J. Wells, "Stuck on the Ladder: Not Only is the Glass Ceiling Still in Place, But Men and Women Have Very Different Views of the Problem," *Maclean's,* October 20, 1997, p. 60.

93 J. Wells, "Stuck on the Ladder: Not Only is the Glass Ceiling Still in Place, But Men and Women Have Very Different Views of the Problem," *Maclean's,* October 20, 1997, p. 60.

94 Information in this paragraph based on Michelle Martinez, "Prepared for the Future: Training Women for Corporate Leadership," *HRM Magazine,* April 1997, pp. 80-87.

95 J. Wells, "Stuck on the Ladder: Not Only is the Glass Ceiling Still in Place, But Men and Women Have Very Different Views of the Problem," *Maclean's,* October 20, 1997, p. 60.

96 J. Wells, "Stuck on the Ladder: Not Only is the Glass Ceiling Still in Place, But Men and Women Have Very Different Views of the Problem," *Maclean's,* October 20, 1997, p. 60.

97 D. Maley, "Canada's Top Women CEOs," *Maclean's,* October 20, 1997.

98 D. Maley, "Canada's Top Women CEOs," *Maclean's,* October 20, 1997.

99 The material in this section is based on J. Grant, "Women as Managers: What They Can Offer to Organizations," *Organizational Dynamics,* Winter 1988, pp. 56-63; S. Helgesen, *The Female Advantage: Women's Ways of Leadership* (New York: Doubleday, 1990); A.H. Eagly and B.T. Johnson, "Gender and Leadership Style: A Meta-Analysis," *Psychological Bulletin,* September 1990, pp. 233-56; A.H. Eagly and S.J. Karau, "Gender and the Emergence of Leaders: A Meta-Analysis," *Journal of Personality and Social Psychology,* May 1991, pp. 685-710; J.B. Rosener, "Ways Women Lead," *Harvard Business Review,* November-December 1990, pp. 119-25; "Debate: Ways Men and Women Lead," *Harvard Business Review,* January-February 1991, pp. 150-60; A.H. Eagly, M.G. Makhijani, and B.G. Klonsky, "Gender and the Evaluation of Leaders: A Meta-Analysis," *Psychological Bulletin,* January 1992, pp. 3-22; A.H. Eagly, S.J. Karau, and B.T. Johnson, "Gender and Leadership Style Among School Principals: A Meta-Analysis," *Educational Administration Quarterly,* February 1992, pp. 76-102; L.R. Offermann and C. Beil, "Achievement Styles of Women Leaders and Their Peers," *Psychology of Women Quarterly,* March 1992, pp. 37-56; T. Melamed and N. Bozionelos, "Gender Differences in the Personality Features of British Managers," *Psychological Reports,* December 1992, pp. 979-986; G.N. Powell, *Women & Men in Management,* 2nd ed. (Thousand Oaks, CA: Sage, 1993); R.L. Kent and S.E. Moss, "Effects of Size and Gender Role on Leader Emergence," *Academy of Management Journal,* October 1994, pp. 1335-46; C. Lee, "The Feminization of Management," *Training,* November 1994, pp. 25-31; H. Collingwood, "Women as Managers: Not Just Different: Better," *Working Woman,* November 1995, p. 14; and J.B. Rosener, *America's Competitive Secret: Women Managers* (New York: Oxford University Press, 1995).

100 J. Howell and K. Hall-Merenda, "Leading From a Distance," in Leadership: Achieving Exceptional Performance, A Special Supplement Prepared by the Richard Ivey School of Business, *The Globe and Mail,* May 15, 1998, pp. C1, C2.

101 R.E. Kelley, "In Praise of Followers," *Harvard Business Review,* November-December 1988, pp. 142-48; E.P. Hollander, "Leadership, Followership, Self, and Others," *Leadership Quarterly,* Spring 1992, pp. 43-54; and I. Challeff, *The Courageous Follower: Standing Up To and For Our Leaders* (San Francisco: Berrett-Koehler, 1995).

102 Kelley, "In Praise of Followers," *Harvard Business Review,* November-December 1988, pp. 142-48.

103 For a review of the cross-cultural applicability of the leadership literature, see R.S. Bhagat, B.L. Kedia, S.E. Crawford, and M.R. Kaplan, "Cross-Cultural Issues in Organizational Psychology: Emergent Trends and Directions for Research in the 1990s," in C.L. Cooper and I.T. Robertson (eds.), *International Review of Industrial and Organizational Psychology,* 5 (Chichester, England: John Wiley & Sons, 1990), pp. 79-89.

104 "Military-Style Management in China," *Asia Inc.,* March 1995, p. 70.

105 Information in this paragraph based on Karen Boehnke, Andrea C. Di Stefano, Joseph J. DiStefano, and Nick Bontis, "Leadership for Extraordinary Performance," *Business Quarterly,* Summer 1997, pp. 57-63.

106 This section is based on R.B. Morgan, "Self- and Co-Worker Perceptions of Ethics and Their Relationships to Leadership and Salary," *Academy of Management Journal,* February 1993, pp. 200-14; J.B. Ciulla, "Leadership Ethics: Mapping the Territory," *Business Ethics Quarterly,* January 1995, pp. 5-28; E.P. Hollander, "Ethical Challenges in the Leader-Follower Relationship," *Business Ethics Quarterly,* January 1995, pp. 55-65; J.C. Rost, "Leadership: A Discussion About Ethics," *Business Ethics Quarterly,* January 1995, pp. 129-42; and R.N. Kanungo and M. Mendonca, *Ethical Dimensions of Leadership* (Thousand Oaks, CA: Sage Publications, 1996).

107 J.M. Burns, *Leadership* (New York: Harper & Row, 1978).

108 J.M. Howell and B.J. Avolio, "The Ethics of Charismatic Leadership: Submission or Liberation?" *Academy of Management Executive,* May 1992, pp. 43-55.

CHAPTER 12

1 B. Came, "Counting the Costs: Ottawa Legislates an End to the Postal Strike," *Maclean's,* December 15, 1997, p. 12.

2 R.M. Kanter, "Power Failure in Management Circuits," *Harvard Business Review,* July-August 1979, p. 65.

3 J. Pfeffer, "Understanding Power in Organizations," *California Management Review,* Winter 1992, p. 35.

4 Based on B.M. Bass, *Bass & Stogdill's Handbook of Leadership,* 3rd ed. (New York: Free Press, 1990).

5 J.R.P. French, Jr., and B. Raven, "The Bases of Social Power," in D. Cartwright (ed.), *Studies in Social Power* (Ann Arbor: University of Michigan, Institute for Social Research, 1959), pp. 150-67. For an update on French and Raven's work, see D.E. Frost and A.J. Stahelski, "The Systematic Measurement of French and Raven's Bases of Social Power in Workgroups," *Journal of Applied Social Psychology,* April 1988, pp. 375-89; T.R. Hinkin and C.A. Schriesheim, "Development and Application of New Scales to Measure the French and Raven (1959) Bases of Social Power," *Journal of Applied Psychology,* August 1989, pp. 561-67; and G.E. Littlepage, J.L. Van Hein, K.M. Cohen, and L.L. Janiec, "Evaluation and Comparison of Three Instruments Designed to Measure Organizational Power and Influence Tactics," *Journal of Applied Social Psychology,* January 16-31, 1993, pp. 107-25.

6 D. Kipnis, *The Powerholders* (Chicago: University of Chicago Press, 1976), pp. 77-78.

7 R.E. Emerson, "Power-Dependence Relations," *American Sociological Review,* 27 (1962), pp. 31-41.

8 H. Mintzberg, *Power In and Around Organizations* (Englewood Cliffs, NJ: Prentice Hall, 1983), p. 24.

9 R.M. Cyert and J.G. March, *A Behavioral Theory of the Firm* (Englewood Cliffs, NJ: Prentice Hall, 1963).

10 C. Perrow, "Departmental Power and Perspective in Industrial Firms," in M.N. Zald (ed.), *Power in Organizations* (Nashville, TN: Vanderbilt University Press, 1970).

11 Adapted from J. Pfeffer, *Managing With Power* (Boston: Harvard Business School Press, 1992), pp. 63-64.

12 Adapted from R.M. Kanter, "Power Failure in Management Circuits," *Harvard Business Review,* July-August 1979, p. 67.

13 See, for example, D. Kipnis, S.M. Schmidt, C. Swaffin-Smith, and I. Wilkinson, "Patterns of Managerial Influence: Shotgun Managers, Tacticians, and Bystanders," *Organizational Dynamics,* Winter 1984, pp. 58-67; T. Case, L. Dosier, G. Murkison, and B. Keys, "How Managers Influence Superiors: A Study of Upward Influence Tactics," *Leadership and Organization Development Journal,* vol. 9, no. 4, 1988, pp. 25-31; D. Kipnis and S.M. Schmidt, "Upward-Influence Styles: Relationship with Performance Evaluations, Salary, and Stress," *Administrative Science Quarterly,* December 1988, pp. 528-42; G. Yukl and C.M. Falbe, "Influence Tactics and Objectives in Upward, Downward, and Lateral Influence Attempts," *Journal of Applied Psychology,* April 1990, pp. 132-40; B. Keys and T. Case, "How to Become an Influential Manager," *Academy of Management Executive,* November 1990, pp. 38-51; D.A. Ralston, D.J. Gustafson, L. Mainiero, and D. Umstot, "Strategies of Upward Influence: A Cross-National Comparison of Hong Kong and American Managers," *Asia Pacific Journal of Management,* October 1993, pp. 157-75; G. Yukl, H. Kim, and C.M. Falbe, "Antecedents of Influence Outcomes," *Journal of Applied Psychology,* June 1996, pp. 309-17; K.E. Lauterbach and B.J. Weiner, "Dynamics of Upward Influence: How Male and Female Managers Get Their Way," *Leadership Quarterly,* Spring 1996, pp. 87-107; and K.R. Xin and A.S. Tsui, "Different Strokes for Different Folks? Influence Tactics by Asian-American and Caucasian-American Managers," *Leadership Quarterly,* Spring 1996, pp. 109-32.

14 This section is adapted from D. Kipnis, S.M. Schmidt, C. Swaffin-Smith, and I. Wilkinson, "Patterns of Managerial Influence: Shotgun Managers, Tacticians, and Bystanders," *Organizational Dynamics,* Winter 1984, pp. 58-67.

15 R. C. Ford and M. D. Fottler, "Empowerment: A Matter of Degree," *Academy of Management Executive,* 9, 1995, pp. 21-31.

16 Points are summarized from Robert C. Ford and Myron D. Fottler, "Empowerment: A Matter of Degree," *Academy of Management Executive,* 9, 1995, pp. 23-25.

17 T.D. Wall, N.J. Kemp, P.R. Jackson, and W.W. Clegg, "Outcomes of Autonomous Work Groups: A Long-term Field Experiment," *Academy of Management Journal,* 29, 1986, pp. 280-304.

18 M. Kane, "Quality Control Can Save Firms Millions, New Data Suggests," *Vancouver Sun*, May 29, 1998, pp. H1, H6.

19 P.P. Poole, "Coalitions: The Web of Power," in *Research and Application, Proceedings of the 20th Annual Eastern Academy Conference.* D.J. Vredenburgh and R.S. Schuler (eds.), *Effective Management: Academy of Management,* Pittsburgh, May 1983, pp. 79-82.

20 J. Pfeffer, *Power in Organizations*, Marshfield, MA: Pittman, 1981.

221 The following section is based on J.N. Cleveland and M.E. Kerst, "Sexual Harassment and Perceptions of Power: An Under-Articulated Relationship," *Journal of Vocational Behavior,* February 1993, pp. 49-67.

22 J. Goddu, "Sexual Harassment Complaints Rise Dramatically," *Canadian Press Newswire*, March 6, 1998.

23 G. Keenan and J. McFarland, "Auto Industry a Bastion of Macho Behavior," *Canadian Press Newswire*, October 1, 1997.

24 "Harassment Barely Recognized in Japan," *Financial Post Daily*, May 15, 1996, p. 8.

25 Information in this paragraph based on "Mitsubishi Motor is Hit with Major Sexual Harassment Suit," *Financial Post Daily*, April 10, 1996, p. 13.

26 "Harassment Barely Recognized in Japan," *Financial Post Daily*, May 15, 1996, p. 8.

27 "Energy Roughneck," *Canadian Business*, August 1996, pp. 20-25.

28 "Energy Roughneck," *Canadian Business*, August 1996, pp. 20-25.

29 S.A. Culbert and J.J. McDonough, *The Invisible War: Pursuing Self-Interest at Work* (New York: John Wiley, 1980), p. 6.

30 Mintzberg, *Power In and Around Organizations* (Englewood Cliffs, NJ: Prentice Hall, 1983), p. 26.

31 D.J. Vredenburgh and J.G. Maurer, "A Process Framework of Organizational Politics," *Human Relations,* January 1984, pp. 47-66.

32 D. Farrell and J.C. Petersen, "Patterns of Political Behavior in Organizations," *Academy of Management Review,* July 1982, p. 405. For a thoughtful analysis of the academic controversies underlying any definition of organizational politics, see A. Drory and T. Romm, "The Definition of Organizational Politics: A Review," *Human Relations,* November 1990, pp. 1133-54.

33 D. Farrell and J.C. Petersen, "Patterns of Political Behavior in Organizations," *Academy of Management Review,* July 1982," pp. 406-07; and A. Drory, "Politics in Organization and Its Perception Within the Organization," *Organization Studies,* 9, no. 2, (1988), pp. 165-79.

34 J. Pfeffer, *Power in Organizations*, Marshfield, MA: Pittman, 1981.

35 K.K. Eastman, "In the Eyes of the Beholder: An Attributional Approach to Ingratiation and Organizational Citizenship Behavior," *Academy of Management Journal,* October 1994, pp. 1379-91.

36 See, for example, G. Biberman, "Personality and Characteristic Work Attitudes of Persons with High, Moderate, and Low Political Tendencies," *Psychological Reports,* October 1985, pp. 1303-10; and G.R. Ferris, G.S. Russ, and P.M. Fandt, "Politics in Organizations," in R.A. Giacalone and P.

Rosenfeld (eds.), *Impression Management in the Organization* (Hillsdale, NJ: Lawrence Erlbaum Associates, 1989), pp. 155-56.

37 D. Farrell and J.C. Petersen, "Patterns of Political Behavior, in Organizations," *Academy of Management Review,* July 1982, p. 408.

38 S. C. Goh and A.R. Doucet, "Antecedent Situational Conditions of Organizational Politics: An Empirical Investigation," paper presented at the Annual Administrative Sciences Association of Canada Conference, Whistler, B.C., May 1986; C. Hardy, "The Contribution of Political Science to Organizational Behavior," in J.W. Lorsch (ed.), *Handbook of Organizational Behavior* (Englewood Cliffs, NJ: Prentice Hall, 1987), p. 103; and G.R. Ferris and K.M. Kacmar, "Perceptions of Organizational Politics," *Journal of Management,* March 1992, pp. 93-116.

39 See, for example, D. Farrell and J.C. Petersen, "Patterns of Political Behavior, in Organizations," *Academy of Management Review,* July 1982, p. 409; P.M. Fandt and G.R. Ferris, "The Management of Information and Impressions: When Employees Behave Opportunistically," *Organizational Behavior and Human Decision Processes,* February 1990, pp. 140-58; and G.R. Ferris, G.S. Russ, and P.M. Fandt, "Politics in Organizations," in R.A. Giacalone and P. Rosenfeld (eds.), *Impression Management in the Organization* (Hillsdale, NJ: Lawrence Erlbaum Associates, 1989), p. 147.

40 Robert C. Ford and Myron D. Fottler, "Empowerment: A Matter of Degree," *Academy of Management Executive,* 9, 1995, pp. 21-31.

41 M.R. Leary and R.M. Kowalski, "Impression Management: A Literature Review and Two-Component Model," *Psychological Bulletin,* January 1990, pp. 34-47.

42 S.P. Robbins and P.L. Hunsaker, *Training in InterPersonal Skills: TIPS for Managing People at Work,* 2nd ed. (Upper Saddle River, NJ: Prentice Hall, 1996), pp. 131-34.

43 See, for instance, B.R. Schlenker, *Impression Management: The Self-Concept, Social Identity, and Interpersonal Relations* (Monterey, CA: Brooks/Cole, 1980); W.L. Gardner and M.J. Martinko, "Impression Management in Organizations," *Journal of Management,* June 1988, pp. 321-38; D.C. Gilmore and G.R. Ferris, "The Effects of Applicant Impression Management Tactics on Interviewer Judgments," *Journal of Management,* December 1989, pp. 557-64; Leary and Kowalski, "Impression Management: A Literature Review and Two-Component Model," pp. 34-47; S.J. Wayne and K.M. Kacmar, "The Effects of Impression Management on the Performance Appraisal Process," *Organizational Behavior and Human Decision Processes,* February 1991, pp. 70-88; E.W. Morrison and R.J. Bies, "Impression Management in the Feedback-Seeking Process: A Literature Review and Research Agenda," *Academy of Management Review,* July 1991, pp. 522-41; S.J. Wayne and R.C. Liden, "Effects of Impression Management on Performance Ratings: A Longitudinal Study," *Academy of Management Journal,* February 1995, pp. 232-60; and C.K. Stevens and A.L. Kristof, "Making the Right Impression: A Field Study of Applicant Impression Management During Job Interviews," *Journal of Applied Psychology,* October 1995, pp. 587-606.

44 M. Snyder and J. Copeland, "Self-Monitoring Processes in Organizational Settings," in Giacalone and Rosenfeld, *Impression Management in the Organization,* p. 11; and E.D. Long and G.H. Dobbins, "Self-Monitoring, Impression Management, and Interview Ratings: A Field and Labora-

tory Study," in J.L. Wall and L.R. Jauch, eds., *Proceedings of the 52nd Annual Academy of Management Conference*; Las Vegas, August 1992, pp. 274-78.

45 M.R. Leary and R.M. Kowalski, "Impression Management: A Literature Review and Two-Component Model," *Psychological Bulletin*, January 1990, p. 40.

46 W.L. Gardner and M.J. Martinko, "Impression Management in Organizations," *Journal of Management*, June 1988, p. 333.

47 R.A. Baron, "Impression Management by Applicants During Employment Interviews: The 'Too Much of a Good Thing' Effect," in R.W. Eder and G.R. Ferris (eds.), *The Employment Interview: Theory, Research, and Practice* (Newbury Park, CA: Sage Publishers, 1989), pp. 204-15.

48 G.R. Ferris, G.S. Russ, and P.M. Fandt, "Politics in Organizations," in R.A. Giacalone and P. Rosenfeld (eds.), *Impression Management in the Organization* (Hillsdale, NJ: Lawrence Erlbaum Associates, 1989), pp. 155-56.

49 R.A. Baron, "Impression Management by Applicants During Employment Interviews: The 'Too Much of a Good Thing' Effect," in R.W. Eder and G.R. Ferris (eds.), *The Employment Interview: Theory, Research, and Practice* (Newbury Park, CA: Sage Publishers, 1989), pp. 204-15; D.C. Gilmore and G.R. Ferris, "The Effects of Applicant Impression Management Tactics on Interviewer Judgments," *Journal of Management* , December 1989, pp. 557-64; and C.K. Stevens and A.L. Kristof, "Making the Right Impression: A Field Study of Applicant Impression Management During Job Interviews," *Journal of Applied Psychology*, October 1995, pp. 587-606.

50 D.C. Gilmore and G.R. Ferris, "The Effects of Applicant Impression Management Tactics on Interviewer Judgments," *Journal of Management*, December 1989, pp. 557-64.

51 K.M. Kacmar, J.E. Kelery, and G.R. Ferris, "Differential Effectiveness of Applicant IM Tactics on Employment Interview Decisions," *Journal of Applied Social Psychology*, August 16-31, 1992, pp. 1250-72.

52 C.K. Stevens and A.L. Kristof, "Making the Right Impression: A Field Study of Applicant Impression Management During Job Interviews," *Journal of Applied Psychology*, October 1995, pp. 587-606.

53 This section is based on B.E. Ashforth and R.T. Lee, "Defensive Behavior in Organizations: A Preliminary Model," *Human Relations*, July 1990, pp. 621-48.

54 This figure is based on G.F. Cavanagh, D.J. Moberg, and M. Valasquez, "The Ethics of Organizational Politics," *Academy of Management Journal*, June 1981, pp. 363-74.

55 R.M. Kanter, *Men and Women of the Corporation* (New York: Basic Books, 1977).

56 See, for instance, C.M. Falbe and G. Yukl, "Consequences for Managers of Using Single Influence Tactics and Combinations of Tactics," *Academy of Management Journal*, August 1992, pp. 638-52.

57 P.A. Wilson, "The Effects of Politics and Power on the Organizational Commitment of Federal Executives," *Journal of Management*, Spring 1995, pp. 101-18.

58 See, for example, M.A. Rahim, "Relationships of Leader Power to Compliance and Satisfaction with Supervision: Evidence from a National Sample of Managers," *Journal of Management*, December 1989, pp. 545-56.

59 J.G. Bachman, D.G. Bowers, and P.M. Marcus, "Bases of Supervisory Power: A Comparative Study in Five Organizational Settings," in A.S. Tannenbaum (ed.), *Control in Organizations* (New York: McGraw-Hill, 1968), p. 236.

60 J. Pfeffer, *Managing With Power* (Boston: Harvard Business School Press, 1992), p. 137.

61 G.R. Ferris and K.M. Kacmar, "Perceptions of Organizational Politics," *Journal of Management*, March 1992, pp. 93-116.

62 A. Drory, "Perceived Political Climate and Job Attitudes," *Organization Studies*, vol. 14, no. 1, 1993, pp. 59-71.

CHAPTER 13

1 Based on P. Kuitenbrouwer, "Simmer...Then Raise to a Boil: A Family Stew Over Succession at the McCain Foods Empire Spills into the Courts [1993 review]," *Financial Post Daily*, v.10(205A) F 2'98 Anniversary edition, p. 22; and Peter Newman, "Tales from a Mellower Harrison McCain: Four Years After Winning a Bitter Feud with his Brother, Harrison Acknowledges that "Strained" Family Relations Still Exist," *Maclean's*, 111, no. 3, (January 19, 1998), p. 50.

2 See, for instance, C.F. Fink, "Some Conceptual Difficulties in the Theory of Social Conflict," *Journal of Conflict Resolution*, December 1968, pp. 412-60. For an updated review of the conflict literature, see J.A. Wall, Jr. and R.R. Callister, "Conflict and Its Management," *Journal of Management*, 21, no. 3 (1995), pp. 515-58.

3 L.L. Putnam and M.S. Poole, "Conflict and Negotiation," in F.M. Jablin, L.L. Putnam, K.H. Roberts, and L.W. Porter (eds.), *Handbook of Organizational Communication: An Interdisciplinary Perspective* (Newbury Park, CA: Sage, 1987), pp. 549-99.

4 K.W. Thomas, "Conflict and Negotiation Processes in Organizations," in M.D. Dunnette and L.M. Hough (eds.), *Handbook of Industrial and Organizational Psychology*, 2nd ed., vol. 3 (Palo Alto, CA: Consulting Psychologists Press, 1992), pp. 651-717.

5 G. Smith, "How to Lose Friends and Influence No One," *Business Week*, January 25, 1993, pp. 42-43.

6 See A.C. Amason, "Distinguishing the Effects of Functional and Dysfunctional Conflict on Strategic Decision Making: Resolving a Paradox for Top Management Teams," *Academy of Management Journal*, February 1996, pp. 123-48.

7 This section is based on S.P. Robbins, *Managing Organizational Conflict: A Nontraditional Approach* (Englewood Cliffs, NJ: Prentice Hall, 1974), pp. 31-55.

8 L.R. Pondy, "Organizational Conflict: Concepts and Models," *Administrative Science Quarterly*, September 1967, p. 302.

9 See, for instance, R.L. Pinkley, "Dimensions of Conflict Frame: Disputant Interpretations of Conflict," *Journal of Applied Psychology*, April 1990, pp. 117-26; and R.L. Pinkley and G.B. Northcraft, "Conflict Frames of Reference: Implications for Dispute Processes and Outcomes," *Academy of Management Journal*, February 1994, pp. 193-205.

10 R. Kumar, "Affect, Cognition and Decision Making in Negotiations: A Conceptual Integration," in M.A. Rahim (ed.), *Managing Conflict: An Integrative Approach* (New York: Praeger, 1989), pp. 185-94.

11 R. Kumar, "Affect, Cognition and Decision Making in Negotiations: A Conceptual Integration," in M.A. Rahim (ed.), *Managing Conflict: An Integrative Approach* (New York: Praeger, 1989), pp. 185-94.

12 P.J.D. Carnevale and A.M. Isen, "The Influence of Positive Affect and Visual Access on the Discovery of Integrative Solutions in Bilateral Negotiations," *Organizational Behavior and Human Decision Processes,* February 1986, pp. 1-13.

13 K.W. Thomas, "Conflict and Negotiation Processes in Organizations," in M.D. Dunnette and L.M. Hough (eds.), *Handbook of Industrial and Organizational Psychology,* 2nd ed., vol. 3 (Palo Alto, CA: Consulting Psychologists Press, 1992), pp. 651-717.

14 K.W. Thomas, "Conflict and Negotiation Processes in Organizations," in M.D. Dunnette and L.M. Hough (eds.), *Handbook of Industrial and Organizational Psychology,* 2nd ed., vol. 3 (Palo Alto, CA: Consulting Psychologists Press, 1992), pp. 651-717.

15 "In the Name of the Father and of the Son," *Financial Post,* September 30/October 2, 1995, p. 14-15.

16 See R.J. Sternberg and L.J. Soriano, "Styles of Conflict Resolution," *Journal of Personality and Social Psychology,* July 1984, pp. 115-26; R.A. Baron, "Personality and Organizational Conflict: Effects of the Type A Behavior Pattern and Self-Monitoring," *Organizational Behavior and Human Decision Processes,* October 1989, pp. 281-96; and R.J. Volkema and T.J. Bergmann, "Conflict Styles as Indicators of Behavioral Patterns in Interpersonal Conflicts," *Journal of Social Psychology,* February 1995, pp. 5-15.

17 K.W. Thomas, "Conflict and Negotiation Processes in Organizations," in M.D. Dunnette and L.M. Hough (eds.), *Handbook of Industrial and Organizational Psychology,* 2nd ed., vol. 3 (Palo Alto, CA: Consulting Psychologists Press, 1992), pp. 651-717.

18 See, for instance, R.A. Cosier and C.R. Schwenk, "Agreement and Thinking Alike: Ingredients for Poor Decisions," *Academy of Management Executive,* February 1990, pp. 69-74; K.A. Jehn, "Enhancing Effectiveness: An Investigation of Advantages and Disadvantages of Value-Based Intragroup Conflict," *International Journal of Conflict Management,* July 1994, pp. 223-38; and R.L. Priem, D.A. Harrison, and N.K. Muir, "Structured Conflict and Consensus Outcomes in Group Decision Making," *Journal of Management,* 21, no. 4 (1995), pp. 691-710.

19 J. Heinzl and P. Waldie, "Eaton's Drowning in Red Ink", *Globe and Mail,* February 28, 1997, p. B1; and John Heinz, Carolyn Leitch, John Saunders, Marina Strauss, and Paul Waldie, "Inside the Debacle at Eaton's," *Globe and Mail,* March 1, 1997, pp. B1, B4.

20 J. Hall and M.S. Williams, "A Comparison of Decision-Making Performances in Established and Ad-Hoc Groups," *Journal of Personality and Social Psychology,* February 1966, p. 217.

21 R.L. Hoffman, "Homogeneity of Member Personality and Its Effect on Group Problem-Solving," *Journal of Abnormal and Social Psychology,* January 1959, pp. 27-32; and R.L. Hoffman and N.R.F. Maier, "Quality and Acceptance of Problem Solutions by Members of Homogeneous and Heterogeneous Groups," *Journal of Abnormal and Social Psychology,* March 1961, pp. 401-07.

22 See T.H. Cox and S. Blake, "Managing Cultural Diversity: Implications for Organizational Competitiveness," *Academy of Management Executive,* August 1991, pp. 45-56; T.H. Cox, S.A. Lobel, and P.L. McLeod, "Effects of Ethnic Group Cultural Differences on Cooperative Behavior on a Group Task," *Academy of Management Journal,* December 1991, pp. 827-47; P.L. McLeod and S.A. Lobel, "The Effects of Ethnic Diversity on Idea Generation in Small Groups," paper presented at the Annual Academy of Management Conference, Las Vegas, August 1992; and C. Kirchmeyer and A. Cohen, "Multicultural Groups: Their Performance and Reactions with Constructive Conflict," *Group & Organization Management,* June 1992, pp. 153-70.

23 R.E. Hill, "Interpersonal Compatibility and Work Group Performance Among Systems Analysts: An Empirical Study," *Proceedings of the Seventeenth Annual Midwest Academy of Management Conference,* Kent, OH, April 1974, pp. 97-110.

24 D.C. Pelz and F. Andrews, *Scientists in Organizations* (New York: John Wiley, 1966).

25 For studies that focus on the dysfunctional consequences of conflict, see the *Journal of Conflict Resolution* and the *International Journal of Conflict Management.*

26 P. Kuitenbrouwer, "The Mail Must Go Through: Canada Post is Trying Hard to Get Better by Improving Its Services and Changing its Relationship with Employees," *Financial Post,* 91, no. 9 (February 28/March 2, 1998), pp. 8-9.

27 K. Jehn, "A Multimethod Examination of the Benefits and Detriments of Intragroup Conflict," *Administrative Science Quarterly,* June 1995, pp. 256-82.

28 A. C. Amason, "Distinguishing the Effects of Functional and Dysfunctional Conflict on Strategic Decision Making: Resolving a Paradox for Top Management Teams,: *Academy of Management Journal,* 39(1), pp. 123-148.

29 This section is based on F. Sommerfield, "Paying the Troops to Buck the System," *Business Month,* May 1990, pp. 77-79; W. Kiechel III, "How to Escape the Echo Chamber," *Fortune,* June 18, 1990, pp. 129-30; and B. Angelo, "Musical Chairs in Maryland," *Time,* August 26, 1991, p. 21. See also E. van de Vliert and C.K.W. de Dreu, "Optimizing Performance by Conflict Stimulation," *International Journal of Conflict Management,* July 1994, pp. 211-22.

30 K. M. Eisenhardt, J. L. Kahwajy, and L.J. Bourgeois III, "How Management Teams Can Have a Good Fight," *Harvard Business Review,* July-August 1997, p. 78.

31 R.E. Walton and R.B. McKersie, *A Behavioral Theory of Labor Negotiations: An Analysis of a Social Interaction System* (New York: McGraw-Hill, 1965).

32 J.A. Wall, Jr., *Negotiation: Theory and Practice* (Glenview, IL: Scott, Foresman, 1985).

33 This model is based on R.J. Lewicki, "Bargaining and Negotiation," *Exchange: The Organizational Behavior Teaching Journal,* vol. 6, no. 2, 1981, pp. 39-40; and B.S. Moskal, "The Art of the Deal," *Industry Week,* January 18, 1993, p. 23.

34 M.H. Bazerman and M.A. Neale, *Negotiating Rationally* (New York: Free Press, 1992), pp. 67-68.

35 These suggestions are based on J.A. Wall, Jr. and M.W. Blum, "Negotiations," *Journal of Management,* June 1991, pp. 278-82.

36 M.H. Bazerman and M.A. Neale, *Negotiating Rationally* (New York: Free Press, 1992), pp. 67-68.

[37] For a negative answer to this question, see C. Watson and L.R. Hoffman, "Managers as Negotiators: A Test of Power versus Gender as Predictors of Feelings, Behavior, and Outcomes," *Leadership Quarterly,* Spring 1996, pp. 63-85.

[38] See N.J. Adler, *International Dimensions of Organizational Behavior,* 2nd ed. (Boston: PWS-Kent, 1991), pp. 179-217.

[39] D. M. Kolb and G. G. Coolidge, "Her Place At the Table," *Journal of State Government,* 64, no. 2 (Apr-Jun 1991), 68-71.

[40] "Women Must Be Ready to Negotiate for Equal Pay," *Financial Post,* October 5/7, 1996, p. 41.

[41] "Women Must Be Ready to Negotiate for Equal Pay," *Financial Post,* October 5/7, 1996, p. 41.

[42] "Women Must Be Ready to Negotiate for Equal Pay," *Financial Post,* October 5/7, 1996, p. 41.

[43] "The Battle of the Sexes: Do Men and Women Really Have Different Negotiating Styles?" *CMA Management Accounting Magazine,* 71, no. 1 (February 1997), p. 8.

[44] I. Ayres, "Further Evidence of Discrimination in New Car Negotiations and Estimates of Its Cause," *Michigan Law Review,* 94, no. 1 (October 1995), pp. 109-147.

[45] B. Gerhart and S. Rynes, "Determinants and Consequences of Salary Negotiations by Male and Female MBA Graduates," *Journal of Applied Psychology,* 76, no. 2 (April 1991), pp. 256-262

[46] J.D. Thompson, *Organizations in Action* (New York: McGraw-Hill, 1967), pp. 54-55.

[47] C. Perrow, "A Framework for the Comparative Analysis of Organizations," *American Sociological Review,* April 1967, pp. 194-208.

[48] P.R. Lawrence and J.W. Lorsch, *Organization and Environment* (Homewood, IL: R.D. Irwin, 1969), pp. 34-39.

[49] A. T. Mair, "Pixel Perfect," *Business in Vancouver,* March 17-23, 1998, pp. 13-14.

[50] J.M. Brett and J.K. Rognes, "Intergroup Relations in Organizations," in P.S. Goodman and Associates (eds.), *Designing Effective Work Groups* (San Francisco: Jossey-Bass, 1986), p. 212.

[51] K.W. Thomas, "Toward Multidimensional Values in Teaching: The Example of Conflict Behaviors," *Academy of Management Review,* July 1977, p. 487.

[53] T. Tillson, "Common Sense Resolution," *Canadian Business,* March 1997.

[54] K.W. Thomas, "Toward Multidimensional Values in Teaching: The Example of Conflict Behaviors," *Academy of Management Review,* July 1977, p. 487.

CHAPTER 14

[1] G. Mallet, "Spotlight on Success: The Canadian Woman Entrepreneur of the Year Awards," *Financial Post Magazine,* December 1997, pp. 82-91.

2 See, for instance, R.L. Daft, *Organization Theory and Design,* 5th ed. (St. Paul, MN: West Publishing, 1995).

[3] J.H. Sheridan, "Sizing Up Corporate Staffs," *Industry Week,* November 21, 1988, p. 47.

[4] J.B. Treece, "Breaking the Chains of Command," *Business Week/The Information Revolution* 1994, p. 112.

[5] See, for instance, L. Urwick, *The Elements of Administration* (New York: Harper & Row, 1944), pp. 52-53.

[6] R. Hayter. "High-Performance Organizations and Employment Flexibility: A Case Study of In Situ Change at the Powell River Paper Mill, 1980-1994," *Canadian Geographer,* 41(1), Spr'97, pg 26-40.

[7] J.S. McClenahen, "Managing More People in the '90s," *Industry Week,* March 20, 1989, p. 30.

[8] L. Surtees, "Cantel's New CEO Ringing in Change," *The Globe and Mail,* June 10, 1998, p. B1.

[9] D.B. Harrison, "Shaping the Organization of the Future," *Canadian Business Review,* Winter, 1995, pp. 13-16.

[10] A. Ross, "BMO's Big Bang," *Canadian Business,* January 1994, pp. 58-63.

[11] J.B. Levine, "For IBM Europe, 'This Is the Year of Truth,'" *Business Week,* April 19, 1993, p. 45.

[12] G. Morgan, *Images of Organization* (Newbury Park, CA: Sage Publications, 1986), p. 21.

[13] T. Burns and G.M. Stalker, *The Management of Innovation* (London: Tavistock, 1961); and J.A. Courtright, G.T. Fairhurst, and L.E. Rogers, "Interaction Patterns in Organic and Mechanistic Stystems," *Academy of Management Journal,* December 1989, pp. 773-802.

[14] H. Mintzberg, *Structure in Fives: Designing Effective Organizations* (Englewood Cliffs, NJ: Prentice Hall, 1983), p. 157.

[15] J. Lee, "Sepp's Steps Up With Niche Foods and Acquisitions," *Vancouver Sun,* May 11, 1998, pp. C1, C3.

[16] S. Baker, "Can Nucor Forge Ahead: And Keep Its Edge?" *Business Week,* April 4, 1994, p. 108.

[17] See, for instance, the interview with Edward Lawler in "Bureaucracy Busting," *Across the Board,* March 1993, pp. 23-27.

[18] W.E. Halal, "From Hierarchy to Enterprise: Internal Markets Are the New Foundation of Management," *The Executive,* November 1994, pp. 69-83.

[19] Cited in *At Work,* May-June 1993, p. 3.

[20] K. Knight, "Matrix Organization: A Review," *Journal of Management Studies,* May 1976, pp. 111-30; and L.R. Burns and D.R. Wholey, "Adoption and Abandonment of Matrix Management Programs: Effects of Organizational Characteristics and Interorganizational Networks," *Academy of Management Journal,* February 1993, pp. 106-38.

[21] See, for instance, S.M. Davis and P.R. Lawrence, "Problems of Matrix Organization," *Harvard Business Review,* May-June 1978, pp. 131-42.

[22] "Initiating and Managing Change in your Organization Using a Form of Organizational Structuring Called the Soft Matrix," *CMA Management Accounting Magazine,* 69, no. 7 (September 1995), pp. 28-31.

[23] G.G. Dess, A.M.A. Rasheed, K.J. McLaughlin, and R. Priem, "The New Corporate Architecture", *Academy of Management Executive,* August 1995, pp. 7-18; C. Y. Baldwin and K. B. Clark, "Managing in an Age of Modularity," *Harvard Business Review,* September-October 1997, pp. 84-93.

[24] P. Booth, "Embracing the Team Concept," *Canadian Business Review,* 21, no. 3 (1994), pp. 10-13.

25 M. Kaeter, "The Age of the Specialized Generalist," *Training*, December 1993, pp. 48-53.

26 L. Brokaw, "Thinking Flat," *INC.*, October 1993, p. 88.

27 P. Jarvis, "Palmer Jarvis: Celebrating 25 Years Promotion supplement," *B.C. Business Magazine*, June, 1994, pp. Insert 1-30.

28 "Developing International Competitiveness: The Five Partners Model," *Business Quarterly*, Winter 1993, pp. 60-72.

29 S. McKay, "Marriages of Convenience: Have You Noticed How Many Eligible Canadian Firms Have Been Wooed by Big Foreign Competitors Lately?," *Financial Post Magazine*, June 1997, pp. 26-36.

30 G.G. Dess, A.M.A. Rasheed, K.J. McLaughlin, and R. Priem, "The New Corporate Architecture," *Academy of Management Executive*, August 1995, pp. 7-18.

31 Why Do Canadian Companies Opt for Cooperative Ventures?", *Micro: the Micro-Economic Research Bulletin*, 4, no. 2 (Summer 1997) pp 3-5.

32 G.G. Dess, A.M.A. Rasheed, K.J. McLaughlin, and R. Priem, "The New Corporate Architecture," *Academy of Management Executive*, August 1995, 13. See also P. Lorange and J. Roos, "Why Some Strategic Alliances Succeed and Why Others Fail," *Journal of Business Strategy*, January/February 1991, 25-30; and G. Slowinski, "The Human Touch in Strategic Alliances," *Mergers and Acquisitions*, July/August 1992, pp. 44-47.

33 "GE: Just Your Average Everyday $60 Billion Family Grocery Store," *Industry Week*, May 2, 1994, pp. 13-18.

34 This section is based on P. LaBarre, "The Seamless Enterprise," *Industry Week*, June 19, 1995, pp. 22-34; and R. Ashkenas, D. Ulrich, T. Jick, and S. Kerr, *The Boundaryless Organization: Breaking the Chains of Organizational Structure* (San Francisco: Jossey-Bass, 1995).

35 D. Woodruff and K.L. Miller, "Chrysler's Neon: Is this the Small Car Detroit Couldn't Build?" *Business Week*, May 3, 1993, 116-126.

36 See J. Lipnack and J. Stamps, *The TeamNet Factor* (Essex Junction, VT: Oliver Wight Publications, 1993); J.R. Wilke, "Computer Links Erode Hierarchical Nature of Workplace Culture," *The Wall Street Journal*, December 9, 1993, p. A1; and T.A. Stewart, "Managing in a Wired Company," *Fortune*, July 11, 1994, pp. 44-56.

37 This analysis is referred to as a contingency approach to organization design. See, for instance, J.M. Pennings, "Structural Contingency Theory: A Reappraisal," in B.M. Staw and L.L. Cummings (eds.), *Research in Organizational Behavior*, 14 (Greenwich, CT: JAI Press, 1992), pp. 267-309.

38 The strategy-structure thesis was originally proposed in A.D. Chandler, Jr., Strategy and Structure: Chapters in the History of the Industrial Enterprise (Cambridge, MA: MIT Press, 1962). For an updated analysis, see T.L. Amburgey and T. Dacin, "As the Left Foot Follows the Right? The Dynamics of Strategic and Structural Change," *Academy of Management Journal*, December 1994, pp. 1427-52.

39 See R.E. Miles and C.C. Snow, Organizational Strategy, Structure, and Process (New York: McGraw-Hill, 1978); D. Miller, "The Structural and Environmental Correlates of Business Strategy," *Strategic Management Journal*, January-February 1987, pp. 55-76; and D.C. Galunic and K.M. Eisenhardt, "Renewing the Strategy-Structure-Performance

Paradigm," in B.M. Staw and L.L. Cummings (eds.), *Research in Organizational Behavior*, 16 (Greenwich, CT: JAI Press, 1994), pp. 215-55.

40 See, for instance, P.M. Blau and R.A. Schoenherr, *The Structure of Organizations* (New York: Basic Books, 1971); D.S. Pugh, "The Aston Program of Research: Retrospect and Prospect," in A.H. Van de Ven and W.F. Joyce (eds.), *Perspectives on Organization Design and Behavior* (New York: John Wiley, 1981), pp. 135-66; R.Z. Gooding and J.A. Wagner III, "A Meta-Analytic Review of the Relationship Between Size and Performance: The Productivity and Efficiency of Organizations and Their Subunits," *Administrative Science Quarterly*, December 1985, pp. 462-81; and A.C. Bluedorn, "Pilgrim's Progress: Trends and Convergence in Research on Organizational Size and Environments," *Journal of Management*, Summer 1993, pp. 163-92.

41 See J. Woodward, Industrial Organization: Theory and Practice (London: Oxford University Press, 1965); C. Perrow, "A Framework for the Comparative Analysis of Organizations," *American Sociological Review*, April 1967, pp. 194-208; J.D. Thompson, Organizations in Action (New York: McGraw-Hill, 1967); J. Hage and M. Aiken, "Routine Technology, Social Structure, and Organizational Goals," *Administrative Science Quarterly*, September 1969, pp. 366-77; and C.C. Miller, W.H. Glick, Y. Wang, and G.P. Huber, "Understanding Technology-Structure Relationships: Theory Development and Meta-Analytic Theory Testing," *Academy of Management Journal*, June 1991, pp. 370-99.

42 See F.E. Emery and E. Trist, "The Causal Texture of Organizational Environments," *Human Relations*, February 1965, pp. 21-32; P. Lawrence and J.W. Lorsch, *Organization and Environment: Managing Differentiation and Integration* (Boston: Harvard Business School, Division of Research, 1967); M. Yasai-Ardekani, "Structural Adaptations to Environments," *Academy of Management Review*, January 1986, pp. 9-21; and A.C. Bluedorn, "Pilgrim's Progress."

43 G.G. Dess and D.W. Beard, "Dimensions of Organizational Task Environments," *Administrative Science Quarterly*, March 1984, pp. 52-73; E.A. Gerloff, N.K. Muir, and W.D. Bodensteiner, "Three Components of Perceived Environmental Uncertainty: An Exploratory Analysis of the Effects of Aggregation," *Journal of Management*, December 1991, pp. 749-68; and O. Shenkar, N. Aranya, and T. Almor, "Construct Dimensions in the Contingency Model: An Analysis Comparing Metric and Non-Metric Multivariate Instruments," *Human Relations*, May 1995, pp. 559-80.

44 T. Fennell, "Paying the Price: How Asia's Financial Crisis Hurts Canadians," *Maclean's*, 110, no. 49 (December 8, 1997), p. 44.

45 T. Fennell, "Paying the Price: How Asia's Financial Crisis Hurts Canadians," *Maclean's*, 110, no. 49 (December 8, 1997), p. 44.

CHAPTER 15

1 Based on J. Wells, "Winning Colours," *Report on Business*, July 1992, pp. 26-35.

2 R.M. Steers and R.T. Mowday, "The Motivational Properties of Tasks," *Academy of Management Review*, October 1977, pp. 645-58.

3 A.N. Turner and P.R. Lawrence, *Industrial Jobs and the Worker* (Boston: Harvard University Press, 1965).

4 J.R. Hackman and G.R. Oldham, "Motivation Through the Design of Work: Test of a Theory," *Organizational Behavior and Human Performance,* August 1976, pp. 250-79.

5 J.R. Hackman, "Work Design," in J.R. Hackman and J.L. Suttle (eds.), *Improving Life at Work* (Santa Monica, CA: Goodyear, 1977), p. 129.

6 See "Job Characteristics Theory of Work Redesign," in J.B. Miner, *Theories of Organizational Behavior* (Hinsdale, IL: Dryden Press, 1980), pp. 231-66; B.T. Loher, R.A. Noe, N.L. Moeller, and M.P. Fitzgerald, "A Meta-Analysis of the Relation of Job Characteristics to Job Satisfaction," *Journal of Applied Psychology,* May 1985, pp. 280-89; W.H. Glick, G.D. Jenkins, Jr., and N. Gupta, "Method versus Substance: How Strong Are Underlying Relationships Between Job Characteristics and Attitudinal Outcomes?" *Academy of Management Journal,* September 1986, pp. 441-64; Y. Fried and G.R. Ferris, "The Validity of the Job Characteristics Model: A Review and Meta-Analysis," *Personnel Psychology,* Summer 1987, pp. 287-322; S.J. Zaccaro and E.F. Stone, "Incremental Validity of an Empirically Based Measure of Job Characteristics," *Journal of Applied Psychology,* May 1988, pp. 245-52; and R.W. Renn and R.J. Vandenberg, "The Critical Psychological States: An Underrepresented Component in Job Characteristics Model Research," *Journal of Management,* 21, no. 2, (1995), pp. 279-303.

7 See R.B. Dunham, "Measurement and Dimensionality of Job Characteristics," *Journal of Applied Psychology,* August 1976, pp. 404-09; J.L. Pierce and R.B. Dunham, "Task Design: A Literature Review," *Academy of Management Review,* January 1976, pp. 83-97; D.M. Rousseau, "Technological Differences in Job Characteristics, Employee Satisfaction, and Motivation: A Synthesis of Job Design Research and Sociotechnical Systems Theory," *Organizational Behavior and Human Performance,* October 1977, pp. 18-42; and Y. Fried and G.R. Ferris, "The Dimensionality of Job Characteristics: Some Neglected Issues," *Journal of Applied Psychology,* August 1986, pp. 419-26.

8 Y. Fried and G.R. Ferris, "The Dimensionality of Job Characteristics: Some Neglected Issues," *Journal of Applied Psychology,* August 1986, pp. 419-26.

9 See, for instance, Y. Fried and G.R. Ferris, "The Dimensionality of Job Characteristics: Some Neglected Issues," *Journal of Applied Psychology,* August 1986, pp. 419-26; and M.G. Evans and D.A. Ondrack, "The Motivational Potential of Jobs: Is a Multiplicative Model Really Necessary?" in S.L. McShane (ed.), *Organizational Behavior,* ASAC Conference Proceedings, vol. 9, Part 5, Halifax, Nova Scotia, 1988, pp. 31-39.

10 R.B. Tiegs, L.E. Tetrick, and Y. Fried, "Growth Need Strength and Context Satisfactions as Moderators of the Relations of the Job Characteristics Model," *Journal of Management,* September 1992, pp. 575-93.

11 C.A. O'Reilly and D.F. Caldwell, "Informational Influence as a Determinant of Perceived Task Characteristics and Job Satisfaction," *Journal of Applied Psychology,* April 1979, pp. 157-65; R. V. Montagno, "The Effects of Comparison Others and Prior Experience on Responses to Task Design," *Academy of Management Journal,* June 1985, pp. 491-98; and P.C. Bottger and I. K-H. Chew, "The Job Characteristics Model and Growth Satisfaction: Main Effects of Assimilation of Work Experience and Context Satisfaction," *Human Relations,* June 1986, pp. 575-94.

12 J.R. Hackman, "Work Design," in J.R. Hackman and J.L. Suttle (eds.), *Improving Life at Work* (Santa Monica, CA: Goodyear, 1977), pp. 132-33.

13 G.R. Salancik and J. Pfeffer, "A Social Information Processing Approach to Job Attitudes and Task Design," *Administrative Science Quarterly,* June 1978, pp. 224-53; J.G. Thomas and R.W. Griffin, "The Power of Social Information in the Workplace," *Organizational Dynamics,* Autumn 1989, pp. 63-75; and M.D. Zalesny and J.K. Ford, "Extending the Social Information Processing Perspective: New Links to Attitudes, Behaviors, and Perceptions," *Organizational Behavior and Human Decision Processes,* December 1990, pp. 205-46.

14 See, for instance, J. Thomas and R.W. Griffin, "The Social Information Processing Model of Task Design: A Review of the Literature," *Academy of Management Journal,* October 1983, pp. 672-82; M.D. Zalesny and J.K. Ford, "Extending the Social Information Processing Perspective: New Links to Attitudes, Behaviors, and Perceptions," *Organizational Behavior and Human Decision Processes,* December 1990, pp. 205-46; and G.W. Meyer, "Social Information Processing and Social Networks: A Test of Social Influence Mechanisms," *Human Relations,* September 1994, pp. 1013-45.

15 "Born-again Basket Case: Imperial Oil's Refinery in Dartmouth, NS, Used to Be One of the Least Efficient in North America. Now It's an Industry Leader, Using 46% Less Human Effort and Far More Flexible Work Rules," *Canadian Business,* 66, no. 5 (May 1993) pp. 38-44.

16 See, for example, P. Kuitenbrouwer, "The Mail Must Go Through," *The Financial Post,* February 28, 1998, pp. 8-9.

17 J.E. Rigdon, "Using Lateral Moves to Spur Employees," *Wall Street Journal,* May 26, 1992, p. B1.

18 B.G. Posner, "Role Changes," *INC.,* February 1990, pp. 95-98.

19 C. Garfield, "Creating Successful Partnerships with Employees," *At Work,* May/June 1992, p. 8.

20 See, for instance, data on job enlargement described in M.A. Campion and C.L. McClelland, "Follow-Up and Extension of the Interdisciplinary Costs and Benefits of Enlarged Jobs," *Journal of Applied Psychology,* June 1993, pp. 339-51.

21 B. Livesey, "Glitch Doctor," *Report on Business Magazine,* November 1997, pp. 97-102.

22 W. Karl, "Bombardier Reaches Lofty Heights: The Challenge Now is Maintaining Cruise Altitude," *Plant,* August 11, 1997, p. 1, 12+.

23 J.R. Hackman and G.R. Oldham, *Work Redesign* (Reading, MA: Addison Wesley, 1980).

24 Cited in *U.S. News & World Report,* May 31, 1993, p. 63.

25 See, for example, J.R. Hackman and G.R. Oldham, *Work Redesign* (Reading, MA: Addison Wesley, 1980); J.B. Miner, *Theories of Organizational Behavior* (Hinsdale, IL: Dryden Press, 1980), pp. 231-66; R.W. Griffin, "Effects of Work Redesign on Employee Perceptions, Attitudes, and Behaviors: A Long-Term Investigation," *Academy of Management Journal,* June 1991, pp. 425-35; and J.L. Cotton, *Employee Involvement* (Newbury Park, CA: Sage, 1993), pp. 141-72.

26 R.W. Griffin and G.C. McMahan, "Motivation Through Job Design," in J. Greenberg, ed. *Organizational Behavior: The State of the Science* (Hillsdale, NJ: Lawrence Erlbaum Associates, 1994), pp. 36-38.

27 J.R. Hackman, "The Design of Work Teams," in J.W. Lorsch, ed., *Handbook of Organizational Behavior* (Englewood Cliffs, NJ: Prentice Hall, 1987), pp. 324-27.

28 See, for instance, M. Sashkin and K.J. Kiser, *Putting Total Quality Management to Work* (San Francisco: Berrett-Koehler, 1993); and J.R. Hackman and R. Wageman, "Total Quality Management: Empirical, Conceptual, and Practical Issues," *Administrative Science Quarterly*, June 1995, pp. 309-42.

29 See, for example, P. Kuitenbrouwer, "The Mail Must Go Through," *The Financial Post*, February 28, 1998, pp. 8-9; T.H. Berry, *Managing the Total Quality Transition* (New York: McGraw Hill, 1991); D. Ciampa, *Total Quality* (Reading, MA: Addison-Wesley, 1992); W.H. Schmidt and J.P. Finnegan, *The Race Without a Finish Line* (San Francisco: Jossey-Bass, 1992); and T.B. Kinni, "Process Improvement," *Industry Week*, January 23, 1995, pp. 52-58.

30 M. Sashkin and K.J. Kiser, *Putting Total Quality Management to Work* (San Francisco: Berrett-Koehler, 1993), p. 44.

31 Gordon Arnaut, "The Taxpayer as Customer," *in The Total Quality Imperative*, an insert to *Report on Business*, January 1995.

32 S. Becker, "TQM Does Work:: Ten Reasons Why Misguided Efforts Fail," *Management Review*, 82, 1993, pp. 30-34.

33 K. Doyle, "Who's Killing Total Quality?" *Incentive*, 16, 1992, pp. 12-19.

34 K. Doyle, "Who's Killing Total Quality?" *Incentive*, 16, 1992, pp. 12-19.

35 R.E. Numeroff, "How to Avoid Failure When Implementing a Quality Effort," *Tapping the Network Journal*, 3, 1992, pp. 1-14; R.E. Numeroff, "How to Prevent the Coming Failure of Quality," *Quality Progress*, 27, 1994, pp. 93-97.

36 Thomas Y. Choi and Orlando C. Behling, "Top Managers and TQM Success: One More Look After All These Years," *Academy of Management Executive*, 11, 1997, pp. 37-47.

37 Thomas Y. Choi and Orlando C. Behling, "Top Managers and TQM Success: One More Look After All These Years," *Academy of Management Executive*, 11, 1997, pp. 46.

38 D.C. Kinlaw, *Developing Superior Work Teams*, (Lexington, MA: Lexington Books, 1991), p. 43.

39 B. Krone, "Total Quality Management:: An American Odyssey," *The Bureaucrat*, Fall 1990, p. 37.

40 *Profiles in Quality: Blueprints for Action from 50 Leading Companies* (Boston: Allyn & Bacon, 1991), pp. 71-72 and 76-77.

41 C. Bak, "Lessons from the Veterans of TQM", *Canadian Business Review*, Winter 1992, pp. 16-19.

42 M. Hammer and J. Champy, *Reengineering the Corporation: A Manifesto for Business Revolution* (New York: HarperBusiness, 1993). See also J. Champy, *Reengineering Management: The Mandate for New Leadership* (New York: HarperBusiness, 1995); and M. Hammer and S.A. Stanton, *The Reengineering Revolution* (New York: HarperBusiness, 1995).

43 M. Hammer and J. Champy, *Reengineering the Corporation: A Manifesto for Business Revolution* (New York: HarperBusiness, 1993). See also J. Champy, *Reengineering Management: The Mandate for New Leadership* (New York: HarperBusiness, 1995); and M. Hammer and S.A.

Stanton, *The Reengineering Revolution* (New York: HarperBusiness, 1995).

44 R. Karlgaard, "ASAP Interview: Mike Hammer," *Forbes ASAP*, September 13, 1993, p. 70.

45 R. Karlgaard, "ASAP Interview: Mike Hammer," *Forbes ASAP*, September 13, 1993, p. 70.

46 "Born-again Basket Case: Imperial Oil's Refinery in Dartmouth, NS, Used to Be One of the Least Efficient in North America. Now It's an Industry Leader, Using 46% Less Human Effort and Far More Flexible Work Rules," *Canadian Business*, 66, no. 5 (May 1993) pp. 38-44.

47 "The Age of Reengineering," *Across the Board*, June 1993, pp. 26-33.

48 "The Age of Reengineering," *Across the Board*, June 1993, pp. 26-33.

49 N. D. Chander and Howard Armitage, "An Assessment of Business Process Reengineering Among Canadian Organizations." Working Paper: University of Waterloo.

50 N. D. Chander and Howard Armitage, "An Assessment of Business Process Reengineering Among Canadian Organizations." Working Paper: University of Waterloo.

51 N. D. Chander and Howard Armitage, "An Assessment of Business Process Reengineering Among Canadian Organizations." Working Paper: University of Waterloo.

52 "SaskTel Dials the Wrong Number; Employees Rebel at Being 'Re-engineered' by a Psychobabbling Yankee Consultant", *Western Report*, February 26, 1996, pp. 14-17; "The Ghost in the Machine (Re-engineering)", *Financial Post 500*, 1996, pp. 8, 16.

53 Cited in "The Bigger Picture: Reorganizing Work," *Industry Week*, August 2, 1993, p. 24.

54 "Reengineering Revisited: Survey of Top Financial Officers," *B.C. Business Magazine*, 23, no. 9 (September 1995) p. 9

55 A. Ehrbar, "'Reengineering' Gives Firms New Efficiency, Workers the Pink Slip," *Wall Street Journal*, March 16, 1993, p. A1.

56 A. Ehrbar, "'Reengineering' Gives Firms New Efficiency, Workers the Pink Slip," *Wall Street Journal*, March 16, 1993, p. A1.

57 Based on J. Wells, "Winning Colours," *Report on Business*, July 1992, pp. 26-35; "Canadian Jobs Lost in Plant Move (From Lindsay, Ontario to Pennsylvania)," *Plant*, February 10, 1997, p. 5; and "Top of the Class," *Canadian Packaging*, February, 1994, p. 26.

58 John Heinzl, "Crayon Maker Draws in an Older Kid," *The Globe and Mail*, March 5, 1998, p. B13.

59 See, for instance, O. Port, "Moving Past the Assembly Line," *Business Week/Reinventing America Special Issue*, November 1992, pp. 177-80; D.M. Upton, "The Management of Manufacturing Flexibility," *California Management Review*, Winter 1994, pp. 72-89; G. Bylinksy, "The Digital Factory," *Fortune*, November 14, 1994, pp. 96-100; and P. Coy, "The Technology Paradox," *Business Week*, March 6, 1995, pp. 76-84.

60 "The Right Stuff: Pratt & Whitney Canada Inc Uses Automated Technology and Modern Management Techniques to Build a Uutopian' Manufacturing Operation in Halifax," *Plant*, 55, no. 18 (December 16, 1996) pp 18-19.

61 S. Moffat, "Japan's New Personalized Production," *Fortune,* October 22, 1990, p. 44.

62 See E. Norton, "Small, Flexible Plants May Play Crucial Role in U.S. Manufacturing," *Wall Street Journal,* January 13, 1993, p. A1.

63 F. Pomeroy, "Workplace Change: A Union Perspective," *Canadian Business Review*, 22, no. 2 (Summer 1995), pp. 17-19.

64 Information about Bestar was obtained from "Quality Comes out of Hiding," in *Labour-Management Innovation in Canada*, Ottawa: Minister of Supply and Services, 1994, pp. 26-29; "Bestar Embarks on $10m Expansion," *Financial Post Daily*, December 4, 1997, p. 19; and "Bestar Hammers Out Record Profit, Sales," *Montreal Gazette*, April 22, 1998, p. E3.

65 "Fewer Workers Had Jobs in June But They Made Slightly More Money," *Canadian Press Newswire*, August 29, 1996.

66 M. Kane, "Flexwork Finds More Favour," *Vancouver Sun,* 15 May 1998, p. F1, F2.

67 "Happy Workers Get Support," *Vancouver Sun*, April 23, 1998, p. D13.

68 M. Kane, "Flexwork Finds More Favour," *Vancouver Sun,* 15 May 1998, p. F1, F2; Margot Gibb-Clark, "Royal Bank Scores with Flexible Work Programs," *The Globe and Mail*, 15 May 1998, P. B23.

69 E.J. Calvasina and W.R. Boxx, "Efficiency of Workers on the Four-Day Workweek," *Academy of Management Journal,* September 1975, pp. 604-10.

70 See, for example, J.C. Latack and L.W. Foster, "Implementation of Compressed Work Schedules: Participation and Job Redesign as Critical Factors for Employee Acceptance," *Personnel Psychology,* Spring 1985, pp. 75-92; and J.W. Seybolt and J.W. Waddoups, "The Impact of Alternative Work Schedules on Employee Attitudes: A Field Experiment," paper presented at the Western Academy of Management Meeting, Hollywood, CA, April 1987.

71 C. Goodale and A.K. Aagaard, "Factors Relating to Varying Reactions to the 4-Day Work Week," *Journal of Applied Psychology,* February 1975, pp. 33-38.

72 "Compressed Work Week Stressful for Women, says Stats Can," *Canadian Press Newswire*, January 7, 1997.

73 This section is based on T. Roth, "Europe Ponders the Shorter Workweek," *Wall Street Journal,* November 12, 1993, p. A11.

74 "France to Cut Work Week to 35 Hours," *Financial Post*, October 11/13, 1997, pg 21

75 M. Kane, "Flexwork Finds More Favour," *Vancouver Sun,* May 15, 1998, pp. F1, F2.

76 Cited in C.M. Solomon, "Job Sharing: One Job, Double Headache?" *Personnel Journal,* September 1994, p. 90.

77 D.R. Dalton and D.J. Mesch, "The Impact of Flexible Scheduling on Employee Attendance and Turnover," *Administrative Science Quarterly,* June 1990, pp. 370-87; and K.S. Kush and L.K. Stroh, "Flextime: Myth or Reality," *Business Horizons,* September-October 1994, p. 53.

78 See, for example, D.A. Ralston and M.F. Flanagan, "The Effect of Flextime on Absenteeism and Turnover for Male and Female Employees," *Journal of Vocational Behavior,* April 1985, pp. 206-17; D.A. Ralston, W.P. Anthony, and D.J.

Gustafson, "Employees May Love Flextime, But What Does It Do to the Organization's Productivity?" *Journal of Applied Psychology,* May 1985, pp. 272-79; J.B. McGuire and J.R. Liro, "Flexible Work Schedules, Work Attitudes, and Perceptions of Productivity," *Public Personnel Management,* Spring 1986, pp. 65-73; P. Bernstein, "The Ultimate in Flextime: From Sweden, by Way of Volvo," *Personnel,* June 1988, pp. 70-74; and D.R. Dalton and D.J. Mesch, "The Impact of Flexible Scheduling on Employee Attendance and Turnover," *Administrative Science Quarterly,* June 1990, pp. 370-87.

79 "Job Sharing, 1995," *The Daily Statistics Canada*, June 9, 1997.

80 Cited in C.M. Solomon, "Job Sharing: One Job, Double Headache?" *Personnel Journal,* September 1994, p. 90.

81 M. Gibb-Clark, "Royal Bank Scores with Flexible Work Programs," *The Globe and Mail*, 15 May 1998, p. B23.

82 S. Shellenbarger, "Two People, One Job: It Can Really Work," *Wall Street Journal,* December 7, 1994, p. B1.

83 See, for example, R. Maynard, "The Growing Appeal of Telecommuting," *Nation's Business,* August 1994, pp. 61-62; F.A.E. McQuarrie, "Telecommuting: Who Really Benefits?" *Business Horizons,* November-December 1994, pp. 79-83; and M. Hequet, "Virtually Working," *Training,* August 1996, pp. 29-35.

84 "More Canadians Tailor Work to Suit Lifestyles," *Daily Commercial News*, December 23, 1996, pg A7.

85 J. Cote-O'Hara, "Sending Them Home to Work: Telecommuting," *Business Quarterly*, Spring 1993 pp. 104-109.

86 M. Hequet, "Virtually Working," *Training,* August 1996, p. 30.

87 H. Scoffield, "Nortel Leaves Employees at Home," *The Globe and Mail*, May 27, 1998, p. B24.

88 J. Cote-O'Hara, "Sending Them Home to Work: Telecommuting," *Business Quarterly*, Spring, 1993 pp. 104-109.

89 J. Cote-O'Hara, "Sending Them Home to Work: Telecommuting," *Business Quarterly*, Spring, 1993 pp. 104-109.

90 "American Express: Telecommuting," *Fortune,* Autumn 1993, pp. 24-28.

91 S. Silverstein, "Telecommuting Boomlet Has Few Follow-Up Calls," *Los Angeles Times,* May 16, 1994, p. A1.

92 Information in this section based on Paul Weinberg, "The Space Race," *Report on Business Magazine*, November 1997, pp. 134-138.

CHAPTER 16

1 S. Sugawara, "A Stranger in a Strange Land? Making Changes at Mazda," *International Herald Tribune,* October 11, 1996, p. 1.

2 P. Selznick, "Foundations of the Theory of Organizations," *American Sociological Review,* February 1948, pp. 25-35.

3 See L.G. Zucker, "Organizations as Institutions," in S.B. Bacharach (ed.), *Research in the Sociology of Organizations* (Greenwich, CT: JAI Press, 1983), pp. 1-47; A.J. Richardson, "The Production of Institutional Behaviour: A Constructive Comment on the Use of Institutionalization Theory in Organizational Analysis," *Canadian Journal of Administrative Sciences*, December 1986, pp. 304-16; L.G. Zucker,

Institutional Patterns and Organizations: Culture and Environment (Cambridge, MA: Ballinger, 1988); and R.L. Jepperson, "Institutions, Institutional Effects, and Institutionalism," in W.W. Powell and P.J. DiMaggio (eds.), *The New Institutionalism in Organizational Analysis* (Chicago: University of Chicago Press, 1991), pp. 143-63.

4 "Organization Man: Henry Mintzberg Has Some Common Sense Observations About the Ways We Run Companies," *Financial Post*, November 22/24, 1997, pp. 14-16.

5 See, for example, H.S. Becker, "Culture: A Sociological View," *Yale Review*, Summer 1982, pp. 513-27; and E.H. Schein, *Organizational Culture and Leadership* (San Francisco: Jossey-Bass, 1985), p. 168.

6 This seven-item description is based on C.A. O'Reilly III, J. Chatman, and D.F. Caldwell, "People and Organizational Culture: A Profile Comparison Approach to Assessing Person-Organization Fit," *Academy of Management Journal*, September 1991, pp. 487-516; and J.A. Chatman and K.A. Jehn, "Assessing the Relationship Between Industry Characteristics and Organizational Culture: How Different Can You Be?" *Academy of Management Journal*, June 1994, pp. 522-53. For a description of other popular measures, see A. Xenikou and A. Furnham, "A Correlational and Factor Analytic Study of Four Questionnaire Measures of Organizational Culture," *Human Relations*, March 1996, pp. 349-71.

7 The view that there will be consistency among perceptions of organizational culture has been called the "integration" perspective. For a review of this perspective and conflicting approaches, see D. Meyerson and J. Martin, "Cultural Change: An Integration of Three Different Views," *Journal of Management Studies*, November 1987, pp. 623-47; and P.J. Frost, L.F. Moore, M.R. Louis, C.C. Lundberg, and J. Martin (eds.), *Reframing Organizational Culture* (Newbury Park, CA: Sage Publications, 1991).

8 See J.M. Jermier, J.W. Slocum, Jr., L.W. Fry, and J. Gaines, "Organizational Subcultures in a Soft Bureaucracy: Resistance Behind the Myth and Facade of an Official Culture," *Organization Science*, May 1991, pp. 170-94; S.A. Sackmann, "Culture and Subcultures: An Analysis of Organizational Knowledge," *Administrative Science Quarterly*, March 1992, pp. 140-61; and R.F. Zammuto, "Mapping Organizational Cultures and Subcultures: Looking Inside and Across Hospitals," paper presented at the 1995 National Academy of Management Conference, Vancouver, BC, August 1995.

9 T.A. Timmerman, "Do Organizations Have Personalities?" paper presented at the 1996 National Academy of Management Conference; Cincinnati, OH, August 1996.

10 See, for example, G.G. Gordon and N. DiTomaso, "Predicting Corporate Performance From Organizational Culture," *Journal of Management Studies*, November 1992, pp. 793-98.

11 Y. Wiener, "Forms of Value Systems: A Focus on Organizational Effectiveness and Cultural Change and Maintenance," *Academy of Management Review*, October 1988, p. 536.

12 V. Hempsall, "Family Matters: Unique Culture and Strategic Acquisitions Key to St. Joseph Corp's Financial Success," *Canadian Printer*, June 1997, pp. 24-27.

13 R.T. Mowday, L.W. Porter, and R.M. Steers, *Employee-Organization Linkages: The Psychology of Commitment, Absenteeism, and Turnover* (New York: Academic Press, 1982).

14 A. Rose, "A Cut Above: Kitchener, Ontario Based MGI has Carved Out a Market Selling Halal Beef to the Muslim World," *Report on Business Magazine*, May 1997, p. 78-82.

15 Ideas in this box were influenced by A.L. Wilkins, "The Culture Audit: A Tool for Understanding Organizations," *Organizational Dynamics*, Autumn 1983, pp. 24-38; and H.M. Trice and J.M. Beyer, *The Cultures of Work Organizations* (Englewood Cliffs, NJ: Prentice Hall, 1993), pp. 358-62.

16 S.C. Schneider, "National vs. Corporate Culture: Implications for Human Resource Management," *Human Resource Management*, Summer 1988, p. 239.

17 S.C. Schneider, "National vs. Corporate Culture: Implications for Human Resource Management," *Human Resource Management*, Summer 1988, p. 239.

18 James Harding, "Rising Star in China's Infant Corporate Culture: The Boss at State-owned White Goods Maker Haier, Is Known for Smashing Fridges as a Lesson in Quality Control," *Financial Post Daily*, November 21, 1997, p. 69.

19 See C.A. O'Reilly and J.A. Chatman, "Culture as Social Control: Corporations, Cultrs, and Commitment," in B.M. Staw and L.L. Cummings (eds.), *Research in Organizational Behavior*, 18 (Greenwich, CT: JAI Press, 1996), pp. 157-200.

20 T.E. Deal and A.A. Kennedy, "Culture: A New Look Through Old Lenses," *Journal of Applied Behavioral Science*, November 1983, p. 501.

21 J. Case, "Corporate Culture," *INC.*, November 1996, pp. 42-53.

22 T. Cole, "How to Stay Hired," *Report on Business Magazine*, March 1995, pp. 46-48.

23 R. McQueen, "Bad Boys Make Good," *Financial Post*, April 4, 1998, p.6

24 See, for instance, D. Miller, "What Happens After Success: The Perils of Excellence," *Journal of Management Studies*, May 1994, pp. 11-38.

25 This paragraph is based on information in "Nuclear Workers Thought They Were Best, Says ex-Hydro Boss," *Canadian Press Newswire*, August 24, 1997.

26 This paragraph is based on information in Peter Waal, "With a Vengeance," *Canadian Business*, April 10, 1998, pp. 34-42.

27 See C. Lindsay, "Paradoxes of Organizational Diversity: Living Within the Paradoxes," in L.R. Jauch and J.L. Wall (eds.), *Proceedings of the 50th Academy of Management Conference* (San Francisco, 1990), pp. 374-78; and T. Cox, Jr., *Cultural Diversity in Organizations: Theory, Research & Practice* (San Francisco: Berrett-Koehler, 1993), pp. 162-70.

28 See C. Lindsay, "Paradoxes of Organizational Diversity: Living Within the Paradoxes," in L.R. Jauch and J.L. Wall (eds.), *Proceedings of the 50th Academy of Management Conference* (San Francisco, 1990), pp. 374-78; and T. Cox, Jr., *Cultural Diversity in Organizations: Theory, Research and Practice* (San Francisco: Berrett-Koehler, 1993), pp. 162-70.

29 A.F. Buono and J.L. Bowditch, *The Human Side of Mergers and Acquisitions: Managing Collisions Between People, Cultures, and Organizations* (San Francisco: Jossey-Bass, 1989); Y. Weber and D.M. Schweiger, "Top Management Culture Conflict in Mergers and Acquisitions: A Lesson

From Anthropology," *The International Journal of Conflict Management,* January 1992, pp. 1-17; and S. Cartwright and C.L. Cooper, "The Role of Culture Compatibility in Successful Organizational Marriages," *Academy of Management Executive,* May 1993, pp. 57-70.

30 P.L. Zweig, "The Case Against Mergers," *Business Week,* October 30, 1995, pp. 122-30.

31 R. McQueen, "It All Comes Down to Chemistry," *The Financial Post,* January 24, 1998, p. 9.

32 E.H. Schein, "The Role of the Founder in Creating Organizational Culture," *Organizational Dynamics,* Summer 1983, pp. 13-28.

33 See, for example, J.R. Harrison and G.R. Carroll, "Keeping the Faith: A Model of Cultural Transmission in Formal Organizations," *Administrative Science Quarterly,* December 1991, pp. 552-82.

34 See B. Schneider, "The People Make the Place," *Personnel Psychology,* Autumn 1987, pp. 437-53; J.A. Chatman, "Matching People and Organizations: Selection and Socialization in Public Accounting Firms," *Administrative Science Quarterly,* September 1991, pp. 459-84; D.E. Bowen, G.E. Ledford, Jr., and B.R. Nathan, "Hiring for the Organization, Not the Job," *Academy of Management Executive,* November 1991, pp. 35-51; B. Schneider, H.W. Goldstein, and D.B. Smith, "The ASA Framework: An Update," *Personnel Psychology,* Winter 1995, pp. 747-73; and A.L. Kristof, "Person-Organization Fit: An Integrative Review of Its Conceptualizations, Measurement, and Implications," *Personnel Psychology,* Spring 1996, pp. 1-49.

35 R. Pascale, "The Paradox of 'Corporate Culture': Reconciling Ourselves to Socialization," *California Management Review,* Winter 1985, pp. 26-27.

36 "Who's Afraid of IBM?" *Business Week,* June 29, 1987, p. 72.

37 "Who's Afraid of IBM?" *Business Week,* June 29, 1987, p. 72.

38 D.C. Hambrick and P.A. Mason, "Upper Echelons: The Organization as a Reflection of Its Top Managers," *Academy of Management Review,* April 1984, pp. 193-206; B.P. Niehoff, C.A. Enz, and R.A. Grover, "The Impact of Top-Management Actions on Employee Attitudes and Perceptions," *Group and Organization Studies,* September 1990, pp. 337-52; and H.M. Trice and J.M. Beyer, "Cultural Leadership in Organizations," *Organization Science,* May 1991, pp. 149-69.

39 "The Cruickshank Redemption: Can the New Editor-in-chief of the *Vancouver Sun* Save the Paper from Hopeless Mediocrity?" *B.C. Business Magazine,* 23, no. 12 (December 1995), pp. 28-35.

40 "Newspaper Sales Stabilizing," *Canadian Press Newswire,* January 16, 1998.

41 See, for instance, N.J. Allen and J.P. Meyer, "Organizational Socialization Tactics: A Longitudinal Analysis of Links to Newcomers' Commitment and Role Orientation," *Academy of Management Journal,* December 1990, pp. 847-58; J.P. Wanous, *Organizational Entry,* 2nd ed. (New York: Addison-Wesley, 1992); G.T. Chao, A.M. O'Leary-Kelly, S. Wolf, H.J. Klein, and P.D. Gardner, "Organizational Socialization: Its Content and Consequences," *Journal of Applied Psychology,* October 1994, pp. 730-43; and J.S. Black and S.J. Ashford, "Fitting In or Making Jobs Fit: Factors Affecting

Mode of Adjustment for New Hires," *Human Relations,* April 1995, pp. 421-37.

42 "McGarry Queen of the Xeroids Document Co CEO," *Financial Post Magazine,* June, 1995 , pp. 14,16+.

43 J. Impoco, "Basic Training, Sanyo Style," *U.S. News & World Report,* July 13, 1992, pp. 46-48.

44 B. Filipczak, "Trained by Starbucks," *Training,* June 1995, pp. 73-79.

45 J. Van Maanen and E.H. Schein, "Career Development," in J.R. Hackman and J.L. Suttle (eds.), *Improving Life at Work* (Santa Monica, CA: Goodyear, 1977) pp. 58-62.

46 D.C. Feldman, "The Multiple Socialization of Organization Members," *Academy of Management Review,* April 1981, p. 310.

47 J. Van Maanen and E.H. Schein, "Career Development," in J.R. Hackman and J.L. Suttle (eds.), *Improving Life at Work* (Santa Monica, CA: Goodyear, 1977) p. 59.

48 T. Cole, "How to Stay Hired," *Report on Business Magazine,* March 1995, pp. 46-48.

49 Information on Husky based on Bruce Livesey, "Provide and Conquer," *Report on Business Magazine,* March 1997, pp. 34-44.

50 J. Greenwood, "Job One: When Bobbie Gaunt Became Ford of Canada President Earlier This Year, the Appointment Put a Spotlight on the New Rules of the Auto Industry: It's Less About Manufacturing These Days Than About Marketing and Sales," *Financial Post Magazine,* June 1997, pp. 18-22.

51 D.M. Boje, "The Storytelling Organization: A Study of Story Performance in an Office-Supply Firm," *Administrative Science Quarterly,* March 1991, pp. 106-26; and C.H. Deutsch, "The Parables of Corporate Culture," *The New York Times,* October 13, 1991, p. F25.

52 A.M. Pettigrew, "On Studying Organizational Cultures," *Administrative Science Quarterly,* December 1979, p. 576.

53 A.M. Pettigrew, "On Studying Organizational Cultures," *Administrative Science Quarterly,* December 1979, p. 576. See also K. Kamoche, "Rhetoric, Ritualism, and Totemism in Human Resource Management," *Human Relations,* April 1995, pp. 367-85.

54 Cited in J.M. Beyer and H.M. Trice, "How an Organization's Rites Reveal Its Culture," *Organizational Dynamics,* Spring 1987, p. 15.

55 A. Rafaeli and M.G. Pratt, "Tailored Meanings: On the Meaning and Impact of Organizational Dress," *Academy of Management Review,* January 1993, pp. 32-55.

56 "Clear Visions: The Top 40 under 40," *Financial Post Magazine,* April 1997, pp. 16-30.

57 M. Posner, "The 28 Billion Dollar Woman." *Chatelaine,* 70, no. 12, (December 1997), pp. 70-75.

58 J. Greenwood, "Job One: When Bobbie Gaunt Became Ford of Canada President Earlier This Year, the Appointment Put a Spotlight on the New Rules of the Auto Industry: It's Less About Manufacturing These Days Than About Marketing and Sales," *Financial Post Magazine,* June 1997, pp. 18-22.

59 V. Hempsall, "Family Matters: Unique Culture and Strategic Acquisitions Key to St. Joseph Corp's Financial Success," *Canadian Printer,* June 1997, pp. 24-27.

60 J. Harris, "Talk About a Revolution," *Canadian Business,* November 28, 1977.

61 V. Hempsall, "Family Matters: Unique Culture and Strategic Acquisitions Key to St. Joseph Corp's Financial Success," *Canadian Printer*, June 1997, pp. 24-27.

62 "LOB, Anyone?" *Business Week*, October 4, 1993, p. 94.

63 J.A. Chatman, "Matching People and Organizations: Selection and Socialization in Public Accounting Firms," pp. 459-84; and B.Z. Posner, "Person-Organization Values Congruence: No Support for Individual Differences as a Moderating Influence," *Human Relations*, April 1992, pp. 351-61.

64 J.E. Sheridan, "Organizational Culture and Employee Retention," *Academy of Management Journal*, December 1992, pp. 1036-56.

CHAPTER 17

1 Based on information in Gaye Emery, "Overcoming Success at IBM: When the Wheels Fall Off, Change is Easier," *Business Quarterly*, Winter 1994, pp. 39-44 and Paul Barker, "Dissecting the New IBM: The President and CEO of the Canadian Subsidiary Talks of the Company's Rise from 'Near Death,'" *Computing Canada*, May 26, 1997, p. 11.

2 A. Levy, "Second-Order Planned Change: Definition and Conceptualization," *Organizational Dynamics*, Summer 1986, pp. 4-20.

3 K.L. Miller, "The Factory Guru Tinkering With Toyota," *Business Week*, May 17, 1993, pp. 95-97.

4 J.S. McClenahen, "Condit Takes a Hike," *Industry Week*, December 2, 1996, pp. 12-16.

5 Based on H.J. Leavitt, "Applied Organization Change in Industry," in W. Cooper, H. Leavitt, and M. Shelly (eds.), *New Perspectives on Organization Research* (New York: John Wiley, 1964); and P.J. Robertson, D.R. Roberts, and J.I. Porras, "Dynamics of Planned Organizational Change: Assessing Empirical Support for a Theoretical Model," *Academy of Management Journal*, June 1993, pp. 619-34.

6 P. Tellier, "Turning CN Around," *Canadian Business Review*, Spring 1995, pp. 31-32+.

7 P. Fitzpatrick, "CN's Tellier Took Home $1.3m," *Financial Post Daily*, March 26, 1998, p. 6.

8 J. Powell, "Under Pressure: Take Two Former Natural Gas Monopolies. Make Them One. Tall Order," *Financial Post*, April 19/21, 1997, p. 35, 36.

9 J. Powell, "Under Pressure: Take Two Former Natural Gas Monopolies. Make Them One. Tall Order," *Financial Post*, April 19/21, 1997, p. 35, 36.

10 J. Powell, "Under Pressure: Take Two Former Natural Gas Monopolies. Make Them One. Tall Order," *Financial Post*, April 19/21, 1997, p. 35, 36.

11 J. Powell, "Under Pressure: Take Two Former Natural Gas Monopolies. Make Them One. Tall Order," *Financial Post*, April 19/21, 1997, p. 35, 36.

12 Information on Rusco based on "Reorganizing to Save the Company: Improving the Production Flow Became a Life and Death Situation for Rusco Canada Ltd.," *Plant*, February 10, 1997, p. 14.

13 Information on IMMI based on "Turnarounds of the Year," *Profit: The Magazine for Canadian Entrepreneurs*, December 1996/January 1997, pp. 64-71.

14 Information on Sutherland Schultz Inc. based on George Koch, Micehla Pasquali, and Donna Green, "A Change for the Bettor," *Profit: The Magazine for Canadian Entrepreneurs*, December 1997/January 1998, pp. 58-61+.

15 Information on Suncor based on Peter Spelliscy, "Changing the Corporate Culture from Downsizing to Growth (Speech)," *Canadian Speeches*, June, 1996, pp. 45-50.

16 K. Lewin, *Field Theory in Social Science* (New York: Harper & Row, 1951).

17 The actual names of the points based on the After Action Review are taken from R. Pascale, M. Millemann, and L. Gioja, "Changing the Way We Change," *Harvard Business Review*, November-December 1997, pp. 127-139, although the summaries are provided by the authors of this textbook.

18 A. E. Reichers, J. P. Wanous, and James T. Austin, "Understanding and Managing Cynicism about Organizational Change," *Academy of Management Executive*, 11, 1997, pp. 48-59.

19 R.H. Hall, *Organizations: Structures, Processes, and Outcomes*, 4th ed. (Englewood Cliffs, NJ: Prentice Hall, 1987), p. 29.

20 D. Katz and R.L. Kahn, *The Social Psychology of Organizations*, 2nd ed. (New York: John Wiley & Sons, 1978), pp. 714-15.

21 J.P. Kotter and L.A. Schlesinger, "Choosing Strategies for Change," *Harvard Business Review*, March-April 1979, pp. 106-14.

22 See, for instance, W. Ocasio, "Political Dynamics and the Circulation of Power: CEO Succession in U.S. Industrial Corporations, 1960-1990," *Administrative Science Quarterly*, June 1994, pp. 285-312.

23 J. A. Ross, "Does Shuffling the Deck Work?" *Harvard Business Review*, November-December, 1997, p. 17.

24 P. Tellier, "Turning CN Around," *Canadian Business Review*, Spring 1995, pp. 31-32+.

25 Featherbedding discussion based on "Back on the Rails: Years of Cutting Have Produced a Leaner and Meaner CN," *Maclean's*, January 13, 1997, pp. 36-38.

26 "Tough Guys Don't Cuss. Air Canada's Employees Didn't Quite Know What to Make of Hollis Harris," *Canadian Business*, February 1995, pp. 22-28.

27 J. R. Stepp and T. J. Schneider, "Fostering Change in a Unionized Environment," *Canadian Business Review*, Summer 1995, pp. 13-16.

28 J. R. Stepp and T.J. Schneider, "Fostering Change in a Unionized Environment," *Canadian Business Review*, Summer 1995, pp. 13-16.

29 See S. Shane, S. Venkataraman, and I. MacMillan, "Cultural Differences in Innovation Championing Strategies," *Journal of Management*, 21, no. 5 (1995), pp. 931-52.

30 "Stress is Everywhere and Getting Worse, Survey Says," *Canadian Press Newswire*, December 17, 1997

31 S. Cordon, "Workers Underpaid, Overworked, Stressed: But Still Satisfied," *Canadian Press Newswire*, October 7, 1997.

32 R. B. Mason, "Taking Health Care to Factory Floor Proves Smart Move for Growing Ontario Company," *Canadian Medical Association Journal*, November 15, 1997, pp. 1423-1424.

33 N. Ayed, "Absenteesim Up Since 1993," *Canadian Press Newswire*, March 25, 1998.

[34] N. Ayed, "Absenteesim Up Since 1993," *Canadian Press Newswire*, March 25, 1998.

[35] N. Ayed, "Absenteesim Up Since 1993," *Canadian Press Newswire*, March 25, 1998.

[36] Adapted from R.S. Schuler, "Definition and Conceptualization of Stress in Organizations," *Organizational Behavior and Human Performance*, April 1980, p. 189. For an updated review of definitions, see R.L. Kahn and P. Byosiere, "Stress in Organizations," in M.D. Dunnette and L.M. Hough, *Handbook of Industrial and Organizational Psychology*, 2nd ed., vol. 3 (Palo Alto, CA: Consulting Psychologists Press, 1992), pp. 573-80.

[37] Adapted from R.S. Schuler, "Definition and Conceptualization of Stress in Organizations," *Organizational Behavior and Human Performance*, April 1980, p. 191.

[38] This model is based on D.F. Parker and T.A. DeCotiis, "Organizational Determinants of Job Stress," *Organizational Behavior and Human Performance*, October 1983, p. 166, S. Parasuraman and J.A. Alutto, "Sources and Outcomes of Stress in Organizational Settings: Toward the Development of a Structural Model," *Academy of Management Journal*, June 1984, p. 333; and R.L. Kahn and P. Byosiere, "Stress in Organizations," in M.D. Dunnette and L.M. Hough, *Handbook of Industrial and Organizational Psychology*, 2nd ed., vol. 3 (Palo Alto, CA: Consulting Psychologists Press, 1992), p. 592.

[39] This section is adapted from C.L. Cooper and R. Payne, *Stress at Work* (London: John Wiley, 1978); and Parasuraman and Alutto, "Sources and Outcomes of Stress in Organizational Settings: Toward the Development of a Structural Model," *Academy of Management Journal*, June 1984, pp. 330-50.

[40] See, for example, D.R. Frew and N.S. Bruning, "Perceived Organizational Characteristics and Personality Measures as Predictors of Stress/Strain in the Work Place," *Journal of Management*, Winter 1987, pp. 633-46; and M.L. Fox, D.J. Dwyer, and D.C. Ganster, "Effects of Stressful Job Demands and Control of Physiological and Attitudinal Outcomes in a Hospital Setting," *Academy of Management Journal*, April 1993, pp. 289-318.

[41] D.L. Nelson and C. Sutton, "Chronic Work Stress and Coping: A Longitudinal Study and Suggested New Directions," *Academy of Management Journal*, December 1990, pp. 859-69.

[42] H. Selye, *The Stress of Life*, rev. ed. (New York: McGraw-Hill, 1956).

[43] J.L. Xie and G. Johns, "Job Scope and Stress: Can Job Scope Be Too High?" *Academy of Management Journal*, October 1995, pp. 1288-1309.

[44] S.J. Motowidlo, J.S. Packard, and M.R. Manning, "Occupational Stress: Its Causes and Consequences for Job Performance," *Journal of Applied Psychology*, November 1987, pp. 619-20.

[45] See, for instance, J.J. House, *Work Stress and Social Support* (Reading, MA: Addison Wesley, 1981); S. Jayaratne, D. Himle, and W.A. Chess, "Dealing with Work Stress and Strain: Is the Perception of Support More Important Than Its Use?" *The Journal of Applied Behavioral Science*, 24, no. 2 (1988), pp. 191-202; R.C. Cummings, "Job Stress and the Buffering Effect of Supervisory Support," *Group & Organization Studies*, March 1990, pp. 92-104; C.L. Scheck, A.J. Kinicki, and J.A. Davy, "A Longitudinal Study of a Multivariate Model of the Stress Process Using Structural Equa-

tions Modeling," *Human Relations*, December 1995, pp. 1481-1510; and M.R. Manning, C.N. Jackson, and M.R. Fusilier, "Occupational Stress, Social Support, and the Cost of Health Care," *Academy of Management Journal*, June 1996, pp. 738-50.

[46] See L.R. Murphy, "A Review of Organizational Stress Management Research," *Journal of Organizational Behavior Management*, Fall-Winter 1986, pp. 215-27.

[47] M. Friedman and R.H. Rosenman, *Type A Behavior and Your Heart* (New York: Alfred A. Knopf, 1974).

[48] M. Friedman and R.H. Rosenman, *Type A Behavior and Your Heart* (New York: Alfred A. Knopf, 1974).

[49] R. Williams, *The Trusting Heart: Great News About Type A Behavior* (New York: Times Books, 1989).

[50] R.S. Schuler, "Definition and Conceptualization of Stress in Organizations," *Organizational Behavior and Human Performance*, April 1980, p. 191; and R.L. Kahn and P. Byosiere, "Stress in Organizations," in Organizations," *Organizational Behavior and Human Performance*, April 1980, pp. 604-10.

[51] See T.A. Beehr and J.E. Newman, "Job Stress, Employee Health, and Organizational Effectiveness: A Facet Analysis, Model, and Literature Review," *Personnel Psychology*, Winter 1978, pp. 665-99; and B.D. Steffy and J.W. Jones, "Workplace Stress and Indicators of Coronary-Disease Risk," *Academy of Management Journal*, September 1988, pp. 686-98.

[52] KPMG Canada, *Compensation Letter*, July 1998.

[53] B.D. Steffy and J.W. Jones, "Workplace Stress and Indicators of Coronary-Disease Risk," p. 687.

[54] C.L. Cooper and J. Marshall, "Occupational Sources of Stress: A Review of the Literature Relating to Coronary Heart Disease and Mental Ill Health," *Journal of Occupational Psychology*, 49, no. 1 (1976), pp. 11-28.

[55] J.R. Hackman and G.R. Oldham, "Development of the Job Diagnostic Survey," *Journal of Applied Psychology*, April 1975, pp. 159-70.

[56] See, for instance, J.M. Ivancevich and M.T. Matteson, *Stress and Work* (Glenview, IL: Scott, Foresman, 1981); and R.D. Allen, M.A. Hitt, and C.R. Greer, "Occupational Stress and Perceived Organizational Effectiveness in Formal Groups: An Examination of Stress Level and Stress Type," *Personnel Psychology*, Summer 1982, pp. 359-70.

[57] S.E. Sullivan and R.S. Bhagat, "Organizational Stress, Job Satisfaction and Job Performance: Where Do We Go From Here?" *Journal of Management*, June 1992, pp. 361-64.

[58] T.H. Macan, "Time Management: Test of a Process Model," *Journal of Applied Psychology*, June 1994, pp. 381-91.

[59] Reported in T.D. Schellhardt, "The Pressure's On," *Wall Street Journal*, February 26, 1996, p. R4.

[60] The information on stress in Asian organizations is based on Z. Abdoolcarim, "Executive Stress a Company Killer," *Asian Business*, August 1995, pp. 22-26.

[61] P.S. Goodman and L.B. Kurke, "Studies of Change in Organizations: A Status Report," in P.S. Goodman (ed.), *Change in Organizations* (San Francisco: Jossey-Bass, 1982), pp. 1-2.

[62] R.L. Kahn and P. Byosiere, "Stress in Organizations," in M.D. Dunnette and L.M. Hough, *Handbook of Industrial and Organizational Psychology*, 2nd ed., vol. 3 (Palo Alto, CA: Consulting Psychologists Press, 1992), pp. 605-08.

GLOSSARY/SUBJECT INDEX

The page on which the keyterm is defined is printed in boldface.

NAME AND ORGANIZATION INDEX

The page on which a weblink appears is printed in boldface.